BYU-NW

THE RELATIONSHIP AMONG THE MIXE-ZOQUEAN LANGUAGES OF MEXICO

The Relationship among the Mixe-Zoquean Languages of Mexico

Søren Wichmann

University of Utah Press

Salt Lake City

1995

Library of Congress Cataloging-in-Publication Data

Wichmann, Søren, 1964–
    The relationship among the Mixe-Zoquean languages of
Mexico / Søren Wichmann.
        p.   cm.   — (Studies in indigenous languages of the
Americas)
    Includes bibliographic references and indexes.
    ISBN 0-87480-487-6 (alk. paper)
    1. Mixe language—Phonology. 2. Mixe language—
Comparison. 3. Mixe language—Cognate words. 4. Zoque
language—Phonology. 5. Zoque language—Comparison.
6. Zoque language—Cognate words.
I. Title. II. Series.
PM4011.Z77W53   1995
497'.41—dc20   95-20063

Contents

Part Two. Cognate Sets

Preface and Acknowledgments

The present work came about as a master's thesis written in response to a prize topic posted in the fall of 1989 by The Institute of History of Religions with American Indian Languages and Cultures of the University of Copenhagen. The announcement called for a work which deals with "slægtskabsforholdet mellem mixe-zoque sprogene i Mexico," or the "(genetic) relationship among the Mixe-Zoquean languages of Mexico." The minimal requirement in treating this subject was obviously a discussion of the classification of those languages. Other than that, the formulation left many options open. The preference was eventually given to comparative phonology and lexicography for two reasons. First, the descriptive materials available had reached a point of particular ripeness in these respects. Second, so many new lexical data were handed over to me by Norman Nordell in the summer of 1990 that my work then in progress on the morphology and morphosyntax had to be put aside. Instead, I concentrated on analyzing his data and on incorporating it into the existing database.

I handed in the work in the early spring of 1991 and earned the "gold medal" prize. The years since then I have devoted much time to other things, especially descriptive work on Azoyú Tlapanec, but have pursued further studies in the Mixe-Zoquean languages as well. Two works (Wichmann 1993c, 1993d) are complementary diachronic morphological studies, the latter of which has been incorporated into this book, where it has been divided into section 4.3 and the section "Derivational Morphology" in Part Two. Another study (Wichmann fc.-c) gives an overview of research on Mixe-Zoquean languages which, as a potentially useful supplement to the present work, includes a very extensive bibliography. I have also conducted fieldwork on the Southern dialect of Chiapas Zoque, Ayapa Zoque, Soteapan Zoque, and Texistepec Zoque (Popoluca). My encounter with Texistepec Zoque has so far led to the production of a dictionary (Wichmann fc.-b), a phonological study (Wichmann 1994), and a text collection (Wichmann, in prep.). The fieldwork has allowed me to revise my view on the internal classification of the Gulf Zoquean branch of Zoquean and to add some new cognate sets. These improvements on the original work are included in the present edition. Other improvements are the incorporation of more data from colonial Chiapas Zoque and Lowland Mixe, the pruning of many cognate sets of shallower time depth than originally postulated or building on unacceptable semantic matchings, the addition of a large number of annotations including reconstructions of intermediate steps in the development of lexemes and the revision of style and presentation.

As this book goes to press, Terry Kaufman is working with a group of linguists on gathering and analyzing data from nearly the whole range of the Mixe-Zoquean languages. The project is conceived of as a part of Justeson and Kaufman's study of the so-called Epi-Olmec writing system (cf. Justeson and Kaufman 1993). I deeply hope that this project may lead to an increase in published, descriptive sources for the Mixe-Zoquean languages and a wider recognition of the importance of these languages.

Quite a number of people helped in the production of this study. I shall first list the people that I have principally worked with in the field and indicate how much time I spent with them. From my oral expressions of thanks I hope that they all know how sincerely I appreciate their help.

E. Juarez and others (Oxolotán and Amatán; seven weeks; 1988)
A. Lopez (Tamazulapan; two weeks; 1990)
E. Galbán (Ayutla; two days; 1990)
E. and M. Segovia, I. Vásquez (Ayapa; eleven days; 1993)
S. Gutiérrez (Amamaloya, Soteapan; one week; 1993)
C. Román and T. Lopez (Texistepec; three months; 1993-94).

Items obtained in the field are included on a selective basis and in numbers that are roughly proportionate to the time I spent on the individual dialect or language.

About half of the data on which the study is based was obtained in the form of unpublished manuscripts and field notes. In 1988 Terry Kaufman kindly let me have a copy of his *Mixe-Zoque Diachronic Studies*. In 1990 I received permission to xerox various manuscripts prepared by native fieldworkers and gathered in the archives of the Centro de Investigación Ayuuk Juhkytïn Jinma'ny A.C. in Ayutla.

A warm thanks goes to Doris Bartholomew, Linguistic Director of the SIL Mexico Branch, whose introductory letter facilitated my getting in touch with members of her institution. One of them was Norman

Nordell, whom I had the luck to be able to talk to in Matías Romero, Oaxaca, just before his unexpected death. Nordell discussed his opinions on the classification of Mixe-Zoquean with me and added data from the Guichicovi Mixe dialect to a list of 1,373 MZ etyma that I had brought. His ideas and information are credited with a (Nordell p.c.) wherever they reappear in this study. He also lent me Xeroxed field notes and manuscripts by himself, Lyle Knudson, and others. These works provided me with many new and unexpected possibilities of contributing to our knowledge of Mixe-Zoquean diachrony. I am of course solely responsible for the interpretations of these various manuscripts.

Lyle Campbell and a scholar who has chosen to be anonymous served as readers for the University of Utah Press. I am grateful for the many valuable suggestions they made, and have tried to do my very best to follow or at least respond to every single one of them. Needless to say, no one but myself is to blame for the result. I am also grateful to the late Wick Miller who, in his function as an advisor to the press, supported the publication and contributed with some minor suggestions. Financial support from the Faculty of Humanities at the University of Copenhagen made it possible to have professional assistance in the weeding of my English. David Robert Lipscomb, who undertook this job, actually took it much further and provided some very interesting comments on phonological matters. Finally, I am indebted to the ethnobotanist Gary Martin for discussing plant names with me. His comments are credited individually as they are quoted in the cognate collection.

The field travels were supported by Københavns Universitets Individuelle Rejsestipendium (1988), Stud Mag. Peter Slomanns Legat for Udøvere af Sammenlignende Sprogvidenskab ved Københavns Universitet (1990), and Professor Ludvig Wimmer og Hustrus Legat (1991, 1992).

In recognition of his many contributions to what we today know about Mixe-Zoquean languages and in appreciation of his extraordinary kindness and generosity I should like to dedicate this study to the memory of Norman Nordell.

Purpose and Organization of the Book

The primary purpose of this book is to describe the phonological development of the Mixe-Zoquean languages. The phonology serves, among other things, to verify and substantiate a new classification of the languages. Secondly, a morphology is reconstructed for the MZ proto-language. One of the purposes of this is to provide a tool for understanding aspects of the modern grammatical systems. Thirdly, a reconstructed lexicon is presented which will be an aid to decipherers of Epi-Olmec writing, students of Mesoamerican prehistory, and people interested in long-distance relationships.

Part One: Comparative Phonology

Chapter 1 contains an informal outline of my internal classification of Mixe-Zoquean and a brief discussion of other work in this area.

Chapter 2 is an overview of the phonology of Mixean languages. I restrict this overview to Mixean since (1) it is phonologically more conservative than Zoquean; (2) the data from most OM dialects date back no further than to the summer of 1990 and the phonology of these dialects has never been treated before; (3) Zoquean phonology is reasonably well known.[1] The reader may wish to focus on section 2.4 and skip the remaining sections on the first reading.

---

[1] The phonology of the central dialect of Chiapas Zoque, represented by the location of Copainalá, for instance, has already been delivered in two versions by Wonderly (1946, 1951-52) and restated by Kaufman (1963), Garvin (1974), and Harrison et al. (1981). Engel and Engel's dictionary of 1987 includes morphophonemic rules for the northern dialect as spoken in Francisco León. Santa María Chimalapa Zoque is treated extensively in a natural phonology framework by Knudson (1975). Elson treated Soteapan Zoque syllable structure in 1947, the intonation in 1954 and 1965, and the morphophonemics in 1960. Foster and Foster (1948) is an additional, though less authoritative (cf. reviews by Voegelin 1950, Trager 1950, and Elson 1951) source for SoZ data. Kaufman (1963) includes a restatement of SoZ phonemics, and yet another restatement is found in Hockett (1947). I treated the fundamentals of Texistepec Zoque phonology in a 1994 work.

Chapter 3 is a summary of my view on proto-Mixe-Zoquean (pMZ) phonology with indications of how this view differs from that of Kaufman (1963). I discuss some major sound laws and give examples of main division correspondences. The chapter also contains a reconstruction of the entire pMZ inflectional system and a section on the numerals.

Chapter 4 is an overview of Mixean diachronic phonology; charts are provided that display correspondences, and solutions are suggested for the various problems identified.

Chapter 5, which is concerned with Oaxaca Mixean only, attempts to describe language change not only in terms of shared innovations (5.1) but also in terms of innovative trends. It is often recognized empirically that closely related languages may undergo similar changes seemingly independently. In OM this happens too. To resolve mysticism and to give a future OM dialectology something to go by, an attempt is made at explaining these phonological trends. The trend having to do with the umlaut is explained by shared blocking conditions (5.2), and the trend related to syllable quantity is explained by shared promoting conditions (5.3).

Chapter 6 discusses Chiapas Zoque dialectology and the languages spoken in San Miguel and Santa María Chimalapa. It points out important gaps in our knowledge of Zoquean languages.

Chapters 7 and 8 summarize all the sound laws that have been touched upon in preceding chapters and include a host of other sound laws characterizing the language family and its branches all the way to the dialect level. They constitute the formal statement of the classification which is informally stated in chapter 1.

Chapter 9 presents evidence for language contact cutting across established subgroups and dialect areas. I consider these phenomena just as important as the genetic classification for the understanding of the internal relationships among the Mixe-Zoquean languages. Language contact is exemplified in 9.1 at the dialect level, in 9.2 at the language level, and in 9.3 at the protolanguage level.

Part Two: Cognate Sets

The second part of the book consists of 2,218 cognate sets, 2,207 of which are headed by reconstructed forms. They are introduced by a guide and followed by indices.

Orthography, Abbreviations, Conventions

ORTHOGRAPHY

Feature Symbols

:   vowel length when only a two-way contrast is present; where there is a three-way contrast, this symbol symbolizes "extra-long"

·   middle length when there is a three-way contrast

‾   fortis (relevant for Midland and Lowland Oaxaca Mixe)

~   nasalization

.   retroflexion

(Only in the case of Ayapa Zoque is retroflexion indicated. Retroflexion of /š/ is widespread in Mixean, but is never phonemic.)

Segment Symbols

'   after a vowel marks glottalization wherever this is predictable and the phonemic status is controversial; this is the case in polysyllabic forms in OIP, the last closed syllables of which seem to be glottalized in the citation forms only. I disagree with the way that Clark (1981) writes these.

"   glottal stop plus vowel rearticulation

?   glottal stop not followed by vowel rearticulation

!   a weak glottal check causing partial rearticulation of the vowel (stands for a symbol invented by Nordell composed of v and a raised glottal stop symbol)

rr as in Spanish orthography (vibrant r)

ï   a central vowel higher than and contrasting with /ɨ/

E   IPA "e"

æ an extra-low front to mid vowel

    a   a low to extra-low central to back vowel
    A   an extra-low central unrounded vowel when /æ a A/ are or seem
        to be in contrast

The vowel symbols "ï, U, E, A" fulfill the needs in describing vowel-innovative Mixe dialects and are devised to make the phonologies of these languages stand out clearly. Those interested in the phonetic realizations of the vowels in the various languages are referred to the sources.

Other Symbols

    *   introduces externally and internally reconstructed forms
    < > 1. orthography of the source is fully (older sources) or partly (modern sources) left as it is
          2. the enclosed form(s) is/are verb word(s), and not, as is the usual practice with verbs, a root. Only relevant for Part Two.
    $ syllable boundary
    +   morpheme boundary
    #   word boundary
    ≠   except
    C   any consonant
    V   any vowel
    ^   glottal stop and/or length disregarded in the rendering of a canonical shape
    ▸   introduces irregular forms
    ← introduces an analysis of morphemes or an otherwise underlying form; general meaning: "derived from"
    → introduces an unanalyzed or otherwise surface form, general meaning: "becomes"

SOURCES, DIALECT, AND LANGUAGE ABBREVIATIONS

I have chosen the term "default" to describe a practical means of supplying information (reference sources and language and dialect locations) for repetitive material. Supplying this information each time it would be required would result in a highly unwieldy presentation of the data. I have, therefore, provided keys for this information. The following is a listing of default sources and locations which the reader can refer to when needed.

Default Sources

Whenever language data are given throughout this work (this also means for Part Two), they are attributed to either a default source or a specified source. Default sources below are listed in the right-hand column. When a source for data is specified, it will typically be a comparative work, an older source giving only scattered lexical information, or a work treating grammar and/or phonology.

OAXACA MIXEAN (OM)
North Highland Mixe (NHM)
To Totontepec   Schoenhals and Schoenhals (1965)
Hu Huitepec   (specified source given)
South Highland Mixe (SHM)
Tl Tlahuitoltepec   Lyon (1980)
Ay Ayutla   Wichmann (1990)
Tm Tamazulapan   Wichmann (1990)
Tu Tepuxtepec   Nordell (1990)
Tp Tepantlali   Nordell (1990)
Mi Mixistlan   Nordell (1990)
Midland Mixe (MM)
Ju Juquila   Nordell (1990)
Cc Cacalotepec   Nordell (1990)
Ja Jaltepec   Nordell (1990)
Pu Puxmecatán   Nordell (1990)
At Atitlan   Nordell (1990)
Ct Cotzocón   Nordell (1990)
Ma Matamoros (El Chisme)   Nordell (1990)
Lowland Mixe (LM)
Mz Mazatlán   Nordell (1990)
Ml Malacatepec   Hoogshagen and Hoogshagen (1993)
Ix Ixcuintepec   Hoogshagen and Hoogshagen (1993)
SJ San José El Paraíso   Van Haitsma and Van Haitsma (1976)
Cn Coatlán   Hoogshagen and Hoogshagen (1993)
Ca Camotlán   Nordell (1990)
Gu Guichicovi   Nordell (1990)

Tapachultec
TaM Tapachultec	Lehmann (1920)

Oluta Popoluca
OlP Oluta Popoluca	Clark (1981)

Sayula Popoluca

SaP Sayula Popoluca
(nonverbs)	Clark and Clark (1960)
(verbs)	Appendixes to Clark (1981)

GULF ZOQUEAN (GZ)
SoZ Sierra Popoluca	Gutiérrez Morales (1993)
TxZ Texistepec Popoluca	Wichmann (fc.-b)
AyZ Ayapa Zoque	Wichmann (1993a)

Chiapas Zoque (ChisZ)

Divides into C(entral), N(orthern), N(orth)E(astern) and S(outhern) dialects
C [Co] Copainalá	Harrison et al. (1981)
C [Te] Tecpatán	González (1672)
N [Ma] Magdalena	Wonderly (1949)
N [FL] Francisco León	Engel and Engel (1987)
NE [Ox] Oxolotán	Wichmann (1988)
NE [Ra] Rayón	Harrison and Harrison (1984)
S [Tu] Tuxtla Gutiérrez	(specified source given)
S [Cp] Copoya	Wichmann (1993b)

Chimalapa Zoque (ChZ)
StaMaCh Santa María Chimalapa	
	Knudson (1980)
SnMiCh San Miguél Chimalapa	
	Cruz Lorenzo (1987)

Default Locations

Data are often cited introduced by a language or dialect abbreviation without any notice about where the data come from. This will either be because the language does not have dialects or because a default convention is at work. "→" means "has the following default dialect/location":

NHM	→	To (Totontepec)
ChisZ: C	→	Co (Copainalá)

ChisZ: N	→ FL (Franscisco León)
ChisZ: NE	→ Ra (Rayón)
ChisZ: S	→ Cp (Copoya)
ChZ	→ StaMaCh (Santa María Chimalapa)

The sources will be the default ones given above. FL is the default location representing ChisZ-N, but note that Ma is in fact both the same dialect and the same village. The village changed its name sometime between 1949 and 1987. Writing Ma and FL, then, are just indirect ways of distinguishing between the data of Wonderly (1949) and those of Engel and Engel (1987).

Other Abbreviations

UR   Underlying Representation
SR   Surface Representation

CONVENTIONS USED IN WRITING PHONOLOGICAL RULES

Whenever distinctive features are used in writing phonological rules, the conventions are those of Halle and Clements (1983) with the addition of the feature [pal]. This feature does not have the values specified in Chomsky and Halle (1968), which does not allow for palatal consonants articulated with the body of the tongue. It is sometimes used for the description of Oaxaca Mixean dialects, where all consonants except /ʔ/ may undergo palatalization, to distinguish these palatalized consonants from their nonpalatalized counterparts.

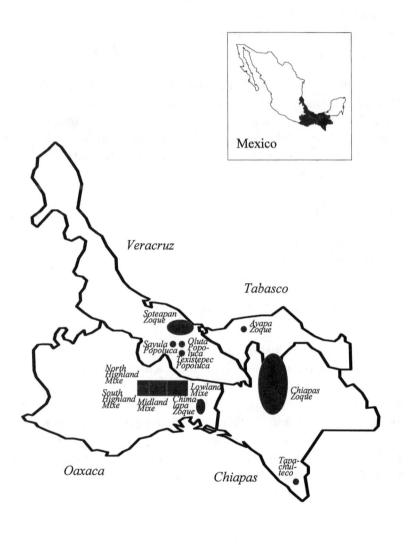

MAP 1. LOCATION OF THE MIXE-ZOQUEAN LANGUAGES

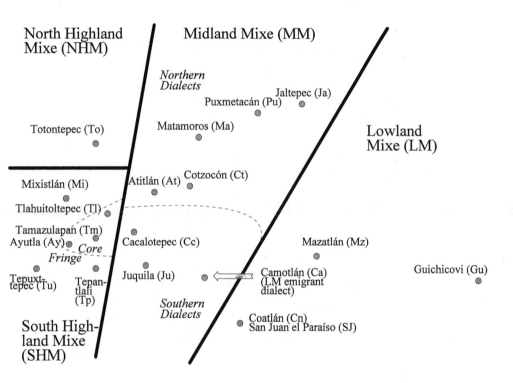

MAP 2. OAXACA MIXEAN LANGUAGES AND DIALECTS

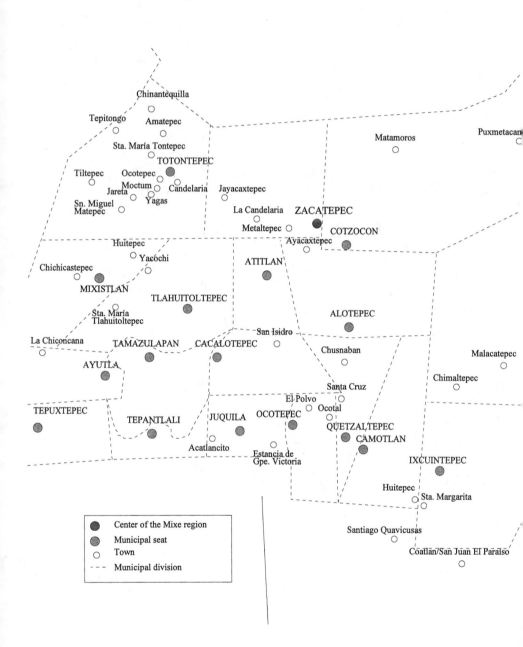

MAP 3. LOCATIONS WHERE OAXACA MIXEAN IS SPOKEN

(This map is based on Nahmad 1965)

PART ONE

Comparative Phonology

CHAPTER 1

Outline of the Classification of the MZ Languages

1.0. INTRODUCTION

The order in which the MZ languages were mentioned in the section "Orthography, Abbreviations, Conventions" is a precursor of my classification of the Mixe-Zoquean languages, which is to be substantiated in the following pages. The suffix -an is a device for setting groups of languages off from single languages. Designation by location occurs in some of the classificatory language designations, in which case the village or town will also be the municipal center.

The language designations have been picked from the existing stock or created in such a manner that they should be acceptable to both linguists and the speakers themselves. Names of Oaxaca Mixean dialects are my own adaptations of the less differentiated local usage (mixe alta, mixe media, mixe baja), Chiapas Zoquean dialects were named by William Wonderly (1949), and Norman Nordell (p.c.) coined the language group designation "Gulf Zoque." "Soteapan Zoque" was occasionally used by Terrence Kaufman (1963) instead of "Sierra Popoluca" which has been a source of confusion even among linguists. Although "Soteapan Zoque" is a designation which has no chance of gaining general acceptance, I will be using it for practical and technical reasons. Texistepec Popoluca has been renamed Texistepec Zoque since, in the present context, it is important to keep in mind that it belongs to the Zoquean main division. Sayula Popoluca and Oluta Popoluca, however, have not been renamed although they could more properly have been termed Mixe. Spanish- or Nahuatl-based designations of those MZ languages which are still thriving and have not yet become mere deposits in the philological archive everywhere replace autodesignations. Only "Ayuujk" for Mixe (in the government-accepted orthography) seems to be gaining ground, although so far only among the Mixes themselves.

The etymology of "Mixe" seems to be a Nahuatl word for 'cloud', that of "Popoluca" another Nahuatl word for 'to babble'. The comparatively larger stock of loan-words in those languages labeled "popoluca" by the Aztecs indicates a particularly strong influence from that group. "Zoque" may or may not stem from a greeting in one of the Chiapas Zoquean languages as I propose in Part Two, SO#013, under the etyma *sokeCV*.

An ethnographic and historical introduction to the speakers of MZ languages is not given in this study. Foster (1969) is a short introduction to the present and historical extension of MZ speakers and to their ethnography; Thomas (1974) is a guide to MZ speakers with particular reference to the Zoques; Nahmad (1965) is the classic work on the ethnography of the Mixes of Oaxaca; my forthcoming work (fc.-c) is the most up-to-date guide to the numbers of speakers of the various extant languages.

1.1. HISTORY OF THE CLASSIFICATION

Before presenting a new classification of Mixe-Zoquean, I shall outline how the classification developed during the past thirty years. Histories of the classification prior to Nordell (1962), including resumés of proposals about external affinities, are given in Thomas (1974) and by me (Wichmann fc.-c). In 6.1 I discuss the 1949 contribution of Wonderly, which is the first modern attempt at a classification of MZ. That section is mainly concerned with the methodology of historical linguistics and with pointing out some gaps in Zoquean research.

The main division Mixe-Zoque emerged as a result of partly independent endeavours of Norman Nordell and Terrence Kaufman in the beginning of the sixties. Nordell's 1962 article presents both evidence and arguments for a classification of some of the MZ languages. It can be set up as follows:

Mixe

1. San Juan Guichicovi Mixe
2. Sayula Popoluca
3. Oluta Popoluca

Zoque

1. Sierra Popoluca
2. Copainalá Zoque
3. Chimalapa Zoque

In the early sixties nothing new was available on what Wonderly (1949) had called North Zoque, Northeast Zoque, and South Zoque. The closer similarity between these dialects and Copainalá Zoque than exists between them and Chimalapa Zoque was apparent from Wonderly's isoglosses. The characteristic Sierra Popoluca innovations were described in Nordell (1962) and further treated in Kaufman (1963). Kaufman (1964) showed that a number of lexical isoglosses unite Tapachulteco with "Mixe." This, together with the statement of Belmar (1902) that some Oaxaca Mixe dialects are vowel-innovative while others are not, and speculations on the positions of then largely unknown Texistepec Zoque (Popoluca) and the completely unknown Tabasco (Ayapa) Zoque, adds up to Kaufman's 1963 classification. In the original study the MZ languages are referred to as "Mixe" and "Zoque" "main type dialects" (numbers 1-7) some of which have "subtypes" (lettered).

Zoque

1. Chiapas Zoque
   a. Central b. Northern c. Northeastern d. Southern
2. Oaxaca Zoque
   San Miguel Chimalapa and Santa María Chimalapa
3. Veracruz Zoque
   a. Sierra Popoluca b. Texistepec
4. Tabasco Zoque

Mixe

5. Veracruz Mixe
   a. Sayula Popoluca   b. Oluta Popoluca
6. Oaxaca Mixe
   a. with conservative vocalism (districts of Yautepec,
      Tehuantepec, and Juchitan, including such towns as
      Juquila, Camotlán, Coatlán, and San Juan Guichicovi)
   b. with innovative vocalism (districts of Villalta and
      Choapam, including such towns as Totontepec and Ayutla)
7. Chiapas Mixe: Tapachulteco.

Because of a lack of descriptive materials, developments of phonology
and morphology are traced into only five of the alleged thirteen "main
type dialects," namely Central Zoque, Sierra Popoluca, Sayula Popoluca, Oaxaca Mixe, and Tapachulteco. The morphological reconstructions rest almost entirely upon the first three of these languages.
There are thus quite a few gaps in the validation of Kaufman's
classification.

   Elson (1992), although a recent contribution, takes as its point of departure Nordell (1962) and ignores all later discussions of comparative
Mixe-Zoquean, published or unpublished. He includes Tapachultec with
Zoquean, arguing that "[f]rom the evidence I have seen, it has fewer
cognates with Mixe than with Zoque" (Elson 1992: 578). Note that
Kaufman (1964) already had made a rather solid case for the exact
opposite point. A single, relatively insignificant innovation in Oluta
Popoluca, namely the development of a final schwa in stressed monosyllables, leads Elson to consider the hypothesis that "Oluta Popoluca
broke away from PMZ before Mixe and Zoque split off from each
other" (Elson 1992: 590). A configuration where Oluta Popoluca stands
off from the rest of the MZ languages would imply that these other
languages have some shared innovation. Elson does not discuss the
possibility of such a shared innovation and thus seems to have mis-
understood the standard methodology of comparative linguistics. Concerning phonological reconstruction, the article is not very helpful
either. For pMZ both *η and *w are reconstructed, although *η is
absent in Mixean and *η and *w are complementarily distributed in
Zoquean. Finally, an /h/, which is predictable in the position before
word-final obstruents in the NE dialect of Chiapas Zoque (data from the

Rayón location), is projected all the way back to pMZ. These are but some points about which I am in disagreement with Elson (1992).

The following classification is the joint effort of Norman Nordell[1] and me. In addition to the above-mentioned scheme, Nordell contributed to the classification of MZ languages by establishing a Gulf Zoquean subgroup (p.c.) and by gathering data for the setting up of an internal classification of the Mixean languages of Oaxaca. As a help in the interpretation of his OM word files (Nordell 1990), Nordell told me how the dialects from which data are found in those files were arranged in his view.

Eastern dialects: Guichicovi, Mazatlán, Camotlán, Coatlán.
Central dialects: Juquila, Cacalotepec, Jaltepec, Puxmetacán, Matamoros, Cotzocón.
Southwestern dialects: Tepuxtepec, Tepantlali, Mixistlán.

At the time of his communication to me, April 1990, I had worked out the differences between Totontepec, Tlahuitoltepec, and San Juan el Paraíso/Coatlán. I assumed, then, that there were three OM languages corresponding to the three locations and the surrounding areas and had foreseen the possible existence of a fourth one spoken in what corresponds to Nordell's Central area, an area from which no published descriptive materials are available. Nordell left it to me to work out the phonological arguments that would support his dialect configuration. These arguments are laid down in this work. The analyses have yielded the following results: Totontepec belongs to a separate language, NHM. Tlahuitoltepec together with Nordell's "Southwestern" dialect group make up South Highland Mixe. The vocalism of Tlahuitoltepec, however, sets this dialect somewhat apart from the others. This relationship is captured by drawing a "Core" vs. "Fringe" frontier. The dialects of Ayutla and Tamazulapan can, on the basis of data collected by me in April 1990, be added to SHM (Core). Nordell's Central dialects form

---

[1] Nordell is the only person to have been personally confronted with the entire range of extant MZ languages. As a student he visited Guichicovi. From then on he devoted himself mainly to Mixe-Zoquean as an associate of the SIL. He visited the whole of the Mixe area of Oaxaca and spoke at least two dialects fluently. He at one time learned to speak Sayula Popoluca, collaborated with Clark on Oluta Popoluca (Clark 1981), did fieldwork on Texistepec and Ayapa Zoque, and participated in Chiapas Zoque dialect surveys.

a separate language, Midland Mixe. In certain respects the Juquila and Cacalotepec varieties to the south differ from the northern dialects, so Midland Mixe can be divided into two dialect areas. Nordell's Eastern Dialects, including San Juan El Paraíso and Coatlán, make up Lowland Mixe. It turned out that Camotlán is a borderline case. In the definitional features I set up, it belongs with Lowland Mixe, but the dialect has borrowed heavily from MM.

As for Zoquean, a new location can be added to Wonderly's "Northeast Zoque" on the basis of data collected by me in 1988, namely Oxolotán (Tabasco). Amatán and Tapijulapa (also Tabasco) probably belong with Oxolotán, but positive evidence is lacking.

Descriptive materials, mostly of a lexicographical nature, collected by workers of the Summer Institute of Linguistics during the past three decades have facilitated the substantiation of MZ internal relations. These materials form the core of the cognate collection in Part Two.

1.2. INFORMAL OUTLINE OF A NEW CLASSIFICATION

In this section two graphically alternative ways of presenting my classification of the Mixe-Zoquean languages are offered. The first (fig. 1.1) employs letters and indentation as its only iconic devices. While practical for the purpose of listing locations at which the various dialects are spoken, this way of presenting the evolutionary scheme is not satisfactory on the whole. For the sake of economy, the principle of subgrouping is employed in a simplistic way, which leaves out the possibility of indicating relative closeness between languages within a subgroup. It also implies the purposefulness of reconstructing every single subgroup. As an alternative, a family tree (fig. 1.2) is offered.

Figure 1.1. A new classification of the Mixe-Zoquean languages.[2]

MIXEAN OAXACA MIXEAN
   North Highland Mixe
   (Totontepec)
   South Highland Mixe
   Core (Tlahuitoltepec, Ayutla, Tamazulapan)
   Fringe (Tepuxtepec, Tepantlali, Mixistlán)
   Midland Mixe
   North Midland Mixe (Jaltepec, Puxmetacan,
   Matamoros, Cotzocón)
   South Midland Mixe (Juquila, Cacalotepec)
   Lowland Mixe (Camotlán, San José El Paraíso
   /Coatlán, Mazatlán, Guichicovi)
   Tapachulteco
   Sayula Popoluca
   Oluta Popoluca
ZOQUEAN GULF ZOQUEAN
   Soteapan Zoque (Sierra Popoluca)
   Texistepec Zoque (Texistepec Popoluca)
   Ayapa Zoque
   Chimalapa (Oaxaca) Zoque
   Santa María Chimalapa
   San Miguel Chimalapa
   Chiapas Zoque
   North (Magdalena = Francisco León)
   Northeast[3]
   A. (Tapalapa, Ocotepec, Pantepec, Rayón)
   B. (Chapultenango, Oxolotán)
   Central (Copainalá, Tecpatán, Ostuacán)
   South (Tuxtla Gutiérrez, Ocozocuautla)

---

[2] Legend: **MAIN DIVISION**; SUBGROUP; **Language**; Dialect area; (Dialect).

[3] San Bartolomé belongs with the NE dialect, but it is not possible to place it in one of the dialect areas on the basis of the information given in Wonderly (1949).

A family tree such as figure 1.2 is in some respects more informative than the classificatory scheme of figure 1.1. Only the nodes that have one of the labels proto-Mixe-Zoquean, proto-Mixean, proto-Oaxaca-Mixean, proto-Zoquean, or proto-Gulf Zoquean are being reconstructed (i.e., formally recognized as subgroups) in this study. There are, however, more nodes than just these five. What is the information contained in these nodes?

Figure 1.2. The evolution of the Mixe-Zoquean languages.

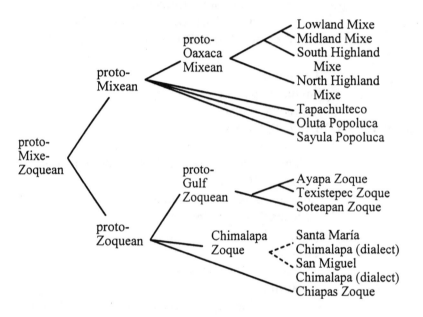

At the top of figure 1.2, we encounter first the Oaxaca Mixean languages. The model says that if LM and SHM are compared, a proto-language can be reconstructed which can be taken as the basis from which MM evolved. However, it excludes the possibility of comparing MM and LM with the aim of reconstructing the evolutionary basis of NHM. It also tells us that LM is closer to MM than to SHM. An example of the phonological evidence for this is that LM and MM have a quantity distinction both in consonants and vowels, whereas SHM and NHM only have distinctive length in the vowels; LM and MM further agree on basing one subclass of verbs analogically on another verb class; SHM and MM also share certain innovations, mostly in what concerns the vocalism. Finally, NHM is set off from SHM, MM, and LM by innovations concerning the umlaut, stress, syncope, and anaptyxis, as well as by retentions. NHM retention corresponding to various types of innovations in non-NHM OM languages is particularly conspicuous in the alternation of the verb. The three successive nodes summarize these relations, which must remain hidden when just one single node is employed.

Tapachultec Mixe is directly dominated by the pM node. It is just as impossible to set up rules for innovations which TaM shared with (an)other Mixean language(s) as it is to account for the ill-transmitted data by way of regular, uncontradicted sound laws.

The Mixean languages of Veracruz, Sayula Popoluca and Oluta Popoluca, are characterized by common retention rather than by shared innovations. It has not been possible to confirm that they form a true subgroup as is assumed in Kaufman's classification. The situation is probably that OlP and SaP have been different dialects ever since Common Mixean times. Common retention and probably some conversion, however, have made them so much alike that they share a host of features not found anywhere else. Among these there is a number of lexemes. These appear in Part Two headed by a reconstructed phonological form which is introduced by "pM" and a star. Although as such they are formally recognized as proto-Mixean, it is deemed necessary to indicate that reflexes are only attested in Sayula Popoluca and Oluta Popoluca. This is done by adding a bracket: "[Veracruz]."

AyZ, TxZ, and SoZ share the palatalizing effect of front vowels and the redevelopment of phonemic vowel length. They also have some retention in common. This accounts for the node leading to these languages. The Gulf Zoquean languages also have some internal configuration. Immediately prior to the splitting up of Texistepec Zoque and Azapa Zoque, syllable-initial nasals developed in their corresponding prenasalized stops, /t/ and /c/ merged before and after /i/, and there was a tendency to devoice final, open syllables.

The Chiapas Zoque dialects are rather close. A good characterization in terms of phonological isoglosses still needs to be made. The only attempt to provide this to date has been Wonderly (1949). But this study missed its aim because the isoglosses set up were prestructural and lacked the potential of characterizing more than one dialect at a time. Future attempts may prove that a focus on grammatical differences may yield more insights concerning the dialectology than phonological differences. Naturally a testing of mutual intelligibility would also be helpful in studying the relationship among the dialects. The classificatory indeterminacy is symbolized by the triangle, which expresses that there are internal structures still awaiting to be disclosed. For the historical setting I imagine a dialect area which saw both expansion, differentiation, and conversion during different historical periods. As a whole, ChisZ is characterized by the insertion of /h/ into verb roots before final obstruents.

Oaxaca Zoquean has its own marked characteristics due, almost exclusively, to morphological innovations. Santa María Chimalapa and San Miguel Chimalapa Zoque differ from each other quite a lot. They are, however, set up as forming a single language since they share morphological and lexical isoglosses that unite them against ChisZ. For StaMaCh there is phonological evidence that this dialect is neither Chiapas nor Gulf Zoquean, but SnMiCh data are not sufficiently reliable to set up shared phonological innovations for the two Chimalapas. An important feature shared with Chiapas Zoque is the development of ergative case marking on nouns. The ergative morpheme -*?is* also took the function of marking the genitive in ChisZ (NE/N). Although I consider it very likely that ChisZ and ChZ form a subgroup, my final judgment on this matter must be postponed until better descriptions become available for ChZ.

CHAPTER 2

Phonologies of Mixean Languages

2.1. A REPORT ON THE DATA

Except for NHM, SHM (Tl,Ay,Tm), and LM (Cn,SJ) all OM languages and dialects are treated with reference to Nordell (1990). The preliminary investigations into this manuscript had the following phases: a recomputerization of the data, proofreading, count of graphics used, distributional analyses, and rearrangement into cognate sets. The main problems with Nordell's manuscript were its prephonemic character, inconsistencies, and a few typos. The changes I have made in the representations are (1) cosmetic; that is, conversion to my own grapheme conventions, (2) phonologically motivated, and (3) philologically motivated; that is, aimed at eliminating typos and inconsistencies on internal grounds. (1) and (2) are intertwined in the sense that my notational system only works if it is interpreted phonemically.

A number of word forms have had their vowel graphics converted into one of the following graphemes: "i, e, æ, ï, i, a, u, o." In addition, "A" is used in Cc forms. The symbols that I have converted for phonological reasons occur with a frequency of 1 percent or less of the total number of vowel symbols in the data from the dialect concerned (with the one exception, Ja "iota" → "i"). Apart from the unlikelihood of such a rare occurrence of a systematic phoneme, I have found my reasons either in the distributional analysis of the phones (graphics) or in the comparison of "same" words found under different headings in Nordell's manuscript. There is perhaps a 15 percent redundancy in his material because of the glossing arrangement. For instance, a form meaning 'sun', 'day', 'name', and 'fiesta' will appear under these four headings. Quite often the forms cited will then vary, especially in what concerns diacritic features of consonants and qualities of vowel allophones. This is safe evidence for inconsistency, and is in itself a good reason for carrying out a phonemicization. This notational variation, had I cited it, would have called for a [sic!]. As it is, only graphic variation which cannot be leveled out is marked [sic!] (e.g., "a" ~ "æ" in the At causative prefix).

The diacritic indicating fronting of /š t c/ is removed, and likewise the one showing postaspiration of final stops or clusters thereof. Such phenomena are noted once only in the statements of allophones in sections 2.3 and 2.5. Untouched are " · ", "!", and the fortis diacritic, although with these graphics the same procedure toward phonemicization suggests itself for some dialects. My reason for leaving these symbols untouched is the greater (but certainly not perfect) consistency in Nordell's notation of the sounds involved and the rather intricate morphophonemics in which they participate.

Consistent phonetic variation is noted in rule statements for the individual dialects. Some details about the pronunciation of some forms have been lost, but these details are obscured by the Nordell's inconsistencies anyway. The gain is a much clearer perception of structural similarities and differences among the individual dialects.

2.2. NORTH HIGHLAND MIXE

Totontepec Dialect

Phoneme inventory (based on Crawford (1963):

Consonants:					*Vowels:*		
p	t		k	?	i	ï	u
	d		g		E	ɨ	ʋ
	c				e	a	o
v	s	š		h			
		ž				V:	
m	n						
		y					

Syllable nuclei (as they occur in Schoenhals and Schoenhals 1965):
-V-, -Vh-, -V:-, -V:h-, -V?-, -V:?-, -V"-, -V"h-

I interpret -V?- and -V?V- as two different degrees (fortis/lenis) of glottalization in agreement with the view of Van Haitsma and Van Haitsma (1976) on LM (SJ) phonology. -V?V- is thus written V".

Allophones (based on Crawford 1963):
　/p c/ → [b z̦]/N$__　　　　　(N = nasal, $ = syllable border)
　/t k š/ → [d g ž]/V$__V
　/p t k š/ → [b d g ž]/N__V
　/p t c k n/ → [pʸ tʸ č kʸ ñ]/$__y

"As simple termini of syllables, /p, t, k/ are manifested by allophones which are either aspirated or not perceptibly released—that is, either unreleased or released imperceptibly into a following phoneme. . . . As members of complex termini, /p, t, k/ are also manifested by aspirated and unreleased allophones" (Crawford 1963: 42). "For the phoneme /š/ there are two major allophones. One is a voiceless retroflexed alveopalatal grooved fricative, the other is a somewhat fronted and not retroflexed variant. The fronted variant occurs as a manifestation of the sequence /šy/" (Crawford 1963: 42).

　/v/　→ [w]/V__V (in the extreme case—degree of lenition varies)
　　　→ [w]/n$__ , /a__#
　　　→ [f]/{V,V?}__ , where V is ≠ /a/, and __C(C)#
　　　→ [v]/ elsewhere
　/n/　→ [m]/__p ,[ñ]/__y ,[ŋ]/__k
　/N/　→ [N̦]/$__CV
　/hN/　→ [N̦]/__#

Distributional constraints within syllables (based on Crawford 1963):
　/i/ and /ï/ do not occur following /y/
　/ï/ rarely occurs following /š/ (according to Crawford, but there are
　　　at least three examples in Schoenhals and Schoenhals 1965)
　/i,u/ do not occur preceding /y/
　/e/ rarely occurs preceding /y/ (> six examples in Schoenhals and
　　　Schoenhals 1965)
　/u/ does not occur preceding /v/
　/s/ occurs only:　1) intervocalically (probably rarely)
　　　　　　　　　2) before stops where it is a dissimilation product
　　　　　　　　　　　of /c/

The following are my own additions to Crawford's analysis.

The NHM umlaut system is not easily discernible from either Crawford's work or from the dictionary of Schoenhals and Schoenhals (1965). The latter source includes a grammatical appendix. The sample paradigms in this appendix seem to have been chosen so as to obscure the phenomenon of the umlaut. Two of the inflected roots contain either /a/ or /i/, which are the only vowels that do not umlaut, and the third inflected root has /y/ as its final consonant. The only root-final consonant to hinder umlauting is precisely /y/. Otherwise, the system is quite regular: /ï, u, E, ɨ/ are the umlauted products of /i, ʋ, e, o/. Since the umlaut product of /o/ apparently cannot be distinguished from /ɨ/, the system arrives at nine vowels rather than ten. The suffix -y, which causes this umlaut, is an inflectional morpheme that is only overtly present when the root contains an /a/. One of its functions is to mark the "dependent"[1] inflection of the nonfuture aspects. It can certainly be posited in the underlying forms of the inflected verb. Whether it is possible to posit an underlying /y/ for nonverbs is, however, more debatable.

Besides the qualitative alternation, the NHM verbs alternate quantitatively. Quantitative alternation (ablaut[2]) is found in all OM dialects as well as in one of the verb classes of the Mixean languages of Veracruz. I now, for the rest of this work, introduce the convention that the BASIC (BAS) root is the one which appears in the completive and the

---

[1] This characteristic Mixean grammatical category is discussed in my fc.-a.

[2] "Ablaut, as first defined in the study of Indo-European languages, is a morphological process of root mutation, most often involving changes in the length and/or quality of vowels in a verb (or noun) root, whereby a number of formally distinct stems are created. Ablaut differs from various types of reduplication and/or affixation, as well as from *umlaut*, which usually refers to more or less automatic phonological adjustments of a root conditioned by the phonetics of an affix. . . . By contrast, *ablaut* in general refers to phonologically arbitrary root mutations (shortening, lengthening, zeroing, epenthesis, qualitative shifts, etc.) which are *morphologically* conditioned" (Whistler 1981: 42-43). Ablaut and umlaut are quite distinct phenomena. This fact, as well as their respective definitions, are emphasized at this point because reference to the two phenomena will be found throughout the present work. It should be borne in mind that today's ablaut may be the result of yesterday's morphophonological processes. This is true of Mixean languages. All have ablauting verb roots. The alternations, however, originally arose under specific phonological conditions. The discussion of these matters will be taken up again in chapters 3, 4, 5, and 7.

incompletive independent inflections, whereas the ALTERNATE (ALT) root is the one used in the incompletive dependent and the future inflections as well as in the imperative. BAS and ALT are completely arbitrary labels. Whenever an alternating verb root is cited in this work, both alternants will be cited, that is, *BAS ~ ALT*.

An investigation has been made of quantitative alternation in the total assembly of monosyllabic verbs. Something similar may perhaps be found in Schoenhals (1962), but that work is not at my disposal. The classificatory system in Schoenhals and Schoenhals (1965), which is by all likelihood based on Schoenhals (1962), shows, however, that he looked only at the syllabic nucleus and disregarded the final consonant(s). Thus, the CVhCC type is classified like the CVhC ~ CVC type but differently from the CV:C ~ CVC type, although it is evident from the complementary distribution of the final root consonants that the last two essentially belong to the same class. According to my internal reconstruction there are four types of nuclei in monosyllabic verbs (and not ten as Schoenhals's analysis would have it): V, V:?, V?, V: ~ V". In Table 2.1 it is indicated in which syllable structures these nuclei occur.

Table 2.1. Verb Root Shapes Ordered According to Basic Nucleus Type

V	V:?
CVC C_2 = š h ") CVhC ~ CVC (C_2 = p t c k š) CV:C ~ CVC (C_2 = m n v y) CVhCC (C_2 = pš kš)	CV:h (C_2 = h) CV:?C (C_2 = p t c k š m n v y) CV:?CC (C_2 = pš kš)
V?	V: ~ V?
CV?C ~ CV"C (C_2 = p t c š n y) CV?CC (C_2 = pš kš)	CV:C ~ CV:?C (C_2 = k t) CV:C ~ CV"C $\qquad\qquad$ (C_2 = p t c k š m v) CV:C ~ CV" (C_2 = h y) CV: ~ CV"

A further distributional analysis comprising the total lexical inventory yields the results shown in Table 2.2.

Table 2.2. The Distribution of Types of Syllable Nuclei

(Percentages, where numbers greater than five are rounded off to multiples of 5, indicate the relative frequency of the occurrence of a given nucleus type in a given environment; e.g., 10% of the occurrences of V is before /p/).

	-pš	-kš	-p	-t	-c	-k	-š	-v	-y	-m	-n	-g
V	0	0	10	3	10	10	25	10	3	10	6	0
Vh	4	10	10	15	20	5	10	1	0	2	3	0
V:h	0	0	0	0	0	10	0	0	25	10	55	0
V:	0	0	5	10	15	15	10	10	5	5	10	1
V?	2	10	3	5	10	10	10	5	10	10	3	0
V:?	3	4	10	10	15	15	4	2	5	2	5	0
V"	0	0	5	10	15	15	20	5	10	20	10	5
V"h	0	0	0	5	30	40	0	0	0	0	5	0

The V"h type has a very limited distribution. In fact it is only found in the following forms, which are all nonverbs:

ʔɨšyo"htɨk 'restless person' [root: *yoʔy ~ yo"y* 'to walk']
ʔama"htɨkʔa:k 'open spot in cranium of babies' [root: *maʔt ~ ma"t* 'to get out of joint (bone)']
pʋ"hc 'pock' [root: *pʋ:c ~ pʋ"c* 'to rot']
tɨ"hc 'dry' [root: *tɨ:c ~ tɨ"c* 'to dry']
va"hc 'clean, clear' [root: *va:c ~ va"c* 'to clean']
ku"hkɨmpahk 'laurel'
kušo"hk 'common bobwhite'
kɨ"hk 'sandal'
mʋ"hk 'bitter'
pa"hk 'sweet, unrefined sugar'

šo"hk 'soaked' [root: *šo:?k* 'to soak']
šʋ"hk 'savory' [← *šʋ:?k* 'to smell']
natyukna:hkšɨ"hkihi ~ *natyukna:hkšɨ"hkaha* 'to hurt, be hurt with'
nʋ"hntk 'string bean'
pɨ"hn 'beech'

Although restricted in its distribution, this nucleus type does not seem
to be involved in a complementary distribution.

Other noteworthy distributional characteristics are that

V: is largely limited to syllables ending in   p, t, c, k, š, v
V:?   "   p, t, c, k
V:h   "   y, n
V:h is in near-complementary distribution with Vh

Syllable nuclei thus behave differently in verbs and nonverbs:
(SYN = synchronically operative; REC = internally reconstructed)

Verbs: SYN (See Table 2.1)
            REC V V: V?   V:~V?
Nonverbs: SYN V Vh   V:h   V: V?   V:?   V"   V"h
            REC V Vh   V: V?   V:?   V"   V"h

A characteristic shared by nonverb V:, V:?, and V"h syllable nuclei is
their (almost exclusive) nonoccurrence before sonorants.

2.3. SOUTH HIGHLAND MIXE

South Highland Mixe (SHM) has the dialects of Tlahuitoltepec (Tl),
Ayutla (Ay), Tamazulapan (Tm), Tepuxtepec (Tu), Mixistlán (Mi), and
Tepantlali (Tp). All phonological statements in this section are based on
my analyses of data in Lyon (1980) (for Tl), the word lists of Nordell
(1990) (for Tu, Mi, Tp), and on my own field data (for Ay and Tm).[3]

---

[3] The analyses can only be considered very preliminary. Lyon (1980) is useful
but not exactly ample. Nordell (1990) has only a limited number of words from
each of the SHM dialects he recorded (Tu: 407, Tp: 450, Mi: 209). Finally, my
own data from Tm and Ay are even more scanty.

Some diagnostic features unite Tu and Tp as against Mi and Tl:

	Tu,Tp	Tl,Mi
Shape of causative prefix	*yahk-*	*yik-*
Nucleus type -V·?-	absent	present
/w/ has an allophone [ß]	yes	no

However, Mi and Tl disagree on the rule of loss of /y/ before /p/ which is present in Mi (as well as in Tp) but absent from Tl, as the form '3p burns INCOMPL INDEP' shows:

Tl /tʋːpʸ/   Tp /toːpʸ/   Mi /to·ypʸ/

Apart from these minor isoglosses, there is a more significant isogloss which sets the Tl dialect off from Tu, Tp, and Mi, namely the Tl vowel shift. This is shown in Figure 2.1.

Figure 2.1. Main Tl allophones (to the right and the left).

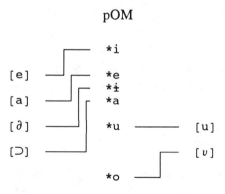

Generally speaking, the vowel shift consists of a lowering of front and central vowels and a raising of back vowels. The lowering of *e* and *a* is typical of SHM and MM dialects, the raising of *o* is atypical, and the lowering of *i* a real rupture. The replacement of *i* with [e] before nonpalatalized consonants is thus indicative of the special position of Tl among the other SHM dialects. This is an isogloss affecting the whole system, which is why it may be said to override the minor isoglosses already mentioned. Tl is not alone in having this lowering of *i*. As Table 2.3 shows, it is shared with Ay and Tm.

Table 2.3. Evidence for the Lowering of *i* in Tl, Ay, and Tm

	Tl	Ay	Tm	Tu	Mi	Tp	
1.	*ce?ck*	*ce?ck*	-	-	-	-	'female breast'
2.	-	*ce"*	-	*ci"*	*ci?ι*	*ci"*	'gourd'
3.	*šehc*	-	-	*šihc*	*šihc*	*šihc*	'a kind of tree'
4.	*wet*	*wet*	-	-	-	-	'clothing'
5.	*cem*	*cem*	*cem*	-	-	-	'small gourd bowl'
6.	*?e:?pš*	*?e?pš*	*?e?pš*	-	-	-	'twenty'
7.	-	*šem*	-	*šim*	-	*šim*	'there'

The raising of *o* is not found in Ay and Tm; this development is explained as part of the overall vowel adjustment in Tl. The lowering of *i*, however, is sufficient evidence for positing a dialect area comprising Ay, Tm, and Tl to the exclusion of Tu, Tp, and Mi. I name this dialect area the "Core Area" as opposed to the "Fringe Area."

In other respects, the SHM dialects are close enough to be treated collectively.

SHM consonants:

p	t	c		k	?
	s		š		h
	r				
	l				
m		n			
w			y		

All consonants except /? s r l/ have palatalized counterparts. /y/ should perhaps be admitted. This sound always occurs word-finally but not in complementary distribution with /y/. With more data at hand an underlying /h/ could probably be inserted before devoiced /y̥/, but such an analysis is not achievable at present. /r l/ are marginal. /s/ is restricted to Spanish loans.

SHM vowels:

The symbols used are those of the representations in Part Two:

Tl			Tp			Mi			Tu		
i	ɨ	u	i	ɨ	u	i	ɨ	u	i	ɨ	u
e	ʋ		e		o	e		o	æ ~ e		o
a		o	æ		a	æ	a(?)	A	(?)		a

There are everywhere two degrees of vowel length.

SHM Syllable nuclei:

V Vh V:h V? V: V:? V" V?h (V:? not in Tu and Tp)

The umlaut is not as pervasive and systematic as in NHM. As shown in Table 2.4, its effects vary from location to location.

Table 2.4. Vowel Alternation Conditioned by Following Palatalized
Consonants

Tl,Tp,Tu	/i/ ~ /i/	Mi ?		
Tl,Tp,Tu	/æ/ ~ /e/	Mi ?		
Tl,Tp,Tu	/ɨ/ ~ /i/	Mi /ɨ/ ~ /e/		
		(Tl: only in unstressed syllables)		
Tl,Tu	/a/ ~ /a/	Tp /a/ ~ /æ/	Mi ?	
Tp,Tl	/u/ ~ /u/	Tu /u/ ~ /ui~i/	Mi ?	
Tu	/o/ ~ [oe~e]	Tp /o/ ~ /o/	Tl /ʋ/ ~ /ɨ/	Mi?

The following umlaut blocking conditions are valid in Tu: the back vowels /ɨ u o/ resist umlauting before the coronal obstruents /t c š/. In Tp the only vowels which undergo umlauting are /æ/ ~ /e/ and /ɨ/ ~ /e/. The umlaut processes in Tp have no blocking conditions. /a/ is in partly free, partly conditioned variation. Compare:

[mac] 'grab it!'   [mʸAhc] '3p grabs it'
[mʸæhcʸpʸ] '3p grabbed it'   [mʸAcǽmpʸ] '3p will grab it'
[ʔAβÁcp] 'it opens'   [yʔAβÁ"č] '3p opens it'

[ca"y ~ cA"y] 'roast it!'   [čA.y] '3p roasted it'
[čæ:pʸ] '3p roasts it'   [čA"yǽmpʸ] '3p will roast it'

Many different interpretations seem possible, and not one of them is safe on the basis of the scarce and inconsistently recorded examples. Only the hypothesis that there is umlauting of [A ~ a] to [æ], which is blocked before coronal obstruents except when the preceding consonant is also palatalized, is to some degree justified. The umlaut is probably not blocked in Mi; in the one case where umlauting is attested, this happens before /šʸ/.

Syllable nuclei for Mi, Tu, and Tp are treated collectively. Nuclei with nonrestricted distribution are V V? V: V" (although V" seems to be preferably followed by /c k/ in Mi). Table 2.5 gives an overview of nuclei with restricted distribution in Mi, Tu, and Tp.

Table 2.5. Nuclei with Restricted Distribution

	Mi	Tu	Tp
Vh_	voiceless Cs	p t c k š n̥ ß pš kš	nonglides
V·_	g # (loans) r w y	sporadic	y ʸ y ž
V?h	k	p t c	c
V·h_	p t k š	p t c k š	p t c k š
V·?_	pš kš n t	nonoccurring	nonocc.

The limited distribution of V· renders this a variant of the plain short syllable nucleus V. Tl has the nucleus types V, Vh, V:h, V?, V:, V:?, V", V?h (V· does not occur); Lyon (1980) has no information on their distribution.

Restricted sets of nucleus types appear before /pš/ and /kš/:

	Before /pš/	Before /kš/
Mi:	V·?, V?	V, Vh, V·?
Tu:	Vh, V?	V, Vh, V?
Tp:	Vh, V?	V, Vh, V?

In Table 2.6 all the morphophonemic and allophonic rules that can be set up for the four recorded dialects are shown. In addition to the rules in Table 2.6 there are some allophonic rules concerning /w/ that are only valid for Tp and Tu:

/w/ → [Ø]/V:__{#,p}

→ [w]/__$ (syllable-finally)

→ [ß]/$__   (syllable-initially)

The only exceptions are Tp *tʌtwel* 'grandfather (abuelo)' and *nʌnwel* 'grandmother (abuela)'; they both contain the suffix *-wel*, approximately 'grand-', which is a reanalysis of Sp. *abuelo/a*.

Table 2.6. A Comparative Chart of Morphophonemic and Allophonic Rules in SHM Dialects

	Tl	Mi	Tu	Tp
/p t k/ → [pʰ, tʰ, kʰ]/(P)__# ,where P = a stop; may extend to clusters of stops	yes	no	no	no
/p t c š k/ → [b d ẓ ž g]/N__V	yes	?	yes	yes
/p t c š k/ → [b d ẓ ž g]/V(")__V	yes	yes	yes	yes
/p/ → [b]/V__V (V unstressed)	?	yes	?	yes
/p/ → [b]/V:__$	yes	no	no	no
/p/ → [b]/V:__y	?	yes	no	no
/p/ → [b]/N__V	?	yes	yes	yes
/t/ → [d]/V(")__(?)V	-	yes	yes	yes
/t/ → [d]/V:__V (V unstressed)	?	yes	yes	yes
/c/ → [ẓ]/V__V	-	yes	yes	yes
/c/ → [ẓ]/V__w	?	yes	?	?
/c/ → [ẓ]/N__V	?	yes	yes	yes
/k/ → [g]/V__V	-	yes	yes	yes
/k/ → [g]/N__V	?	yes	yes	yes
/N/ → [Ṇ]/h__C	yes	?	?	yes
/N/ → [Ṇ]/#__h	yes	?	?	?
/N/ → [Ṇ]/C(ʾ)__(ʾ)#	no	yes	yes	yes
/n/ → [ŋ]/__k	yes	yes	yes	yes
/n/ → [m]/__p	yes	yes	yes	yes
yCV → CʸV (metathesis)	?	yes	yes	yes
V → V:/__wp, w -> Ø/__p	?	yes	yes	yes
V → V:/__yp, y -> Ø/__p	?	no	no	yes

Exceptions to rules stated for **Tepantlali***:*
Voicing of stops is resisted before the suffix *-Am* 'future', after the prefix *ku-* 'pertaining to the head', and in *seripÁ"k* 'honey'. The voiced allophone of /t/ is optionally either [d] or [ð].

Exceptions and notes to rules stated for **Tepuxtepec***:*
t → [ð]/V(")__V except under certain conditions which cannot be determined at present.

Exceptions and notes to rules stated for **Tlahuitoltepec***:*
Lyon (1980: 25) has an example /ce·hpɨ/ [tsé·bɨ].

Exceptions and notes to rules stated for **Mixistlán***:*
(1) Voicing of stops is not always predictable: [kAmbÁnA] BUT [kampo]. Compare also [mAtów], [pudúnes], and [kupo"kÁ:]. There is one example of the voicing of /k/ intervocalically, but also counter-examples: [yɨk?AwÁ"c], [kukuyɨ·?nʸ], [?Akɨyɨ], [se·rɨkohpǽht], [pi?k?unA?hk?ú?ŋk], [kupo"kÁ:], [kakÁ:wa], [čikɨ·wɨ], [yik?oyⁱé:pʸ] [hʸɨpa].
(2) /c/ → [ẓ]/V__V except after the prefixes *ni"-*, and *ko-*
(3) /c/ → [ẓ]/V__w

Stress:
Don Lyon (1980: 33) thinks that the Tl accent is phonemic insofar as it is unpredictable except under the following three conditions: (1) when the last heavy syllable carries the primary accent, (2) when there are no heavy syllables, in which case the accent falls on the ultimate, (3) when neither condition (1) nor (2) is fulfilled, in which case the accent is on the penultimate. These rules may tentatively be carried over to the other dialects.

2.4. INTERLUDE: ON THE ALLEGED THREE CONTRASTIVE VOWEL LENGTHS IN MIXE (I.E., MM AND LM)

Before his passing, Nordell told me that his orthography, which was devised for the recording of Oaxaca Mixean dialects, both served the precise and detailed notation of phonetic features in Mixean languages as well as a phonological analysis, which he had still to develop. The phonological analysis would deviate from the standard one practiced by other Mixe specialists. His orthography (which in these respects is carried over in all citations from his data in this work) operates with a fortis/lenis opposition on all consonants[4] as well as with three degrees of_vowel_length. This makes possible the sequences VC, V·C, V:C, VC, V·C, V:C. But not all six sequences actually occur in the data—as little as do the twelve possible sequences resulting from the insertion of a laryngeal /ʔ/ into these possible sequences. In terms of traditional phonemics, V, V·, and V: suffice to uphold the distinctions, and the fortis marking on consonants can be done away with. This, however, also means doing away with the possibilities of a sophisticated analysis. Before going into the more theoretical considerations, I will compare three competing analyses, namely that of Hoogshagen (1959) (SH), Nordell (NN) (p.c.), and mine (SW) using what would be standard examples of minimal pairs involving syllable quantity. These are given in Table 2.7. SH's examples are from Coatlán, NN's and SW's examples are broadly attested and found in Nordell (1990). The three items assume the cited shapes in, respectively, MM [Ma,At,Ct], LM [Gu] ('coati'), MM [Ct,At,Pu,Ma] ('grasshopper'), and MM [Ct,Pu,At,Ja,Ma] ('punch!'). These minimal pairs as well as quite a few others can be pieced together from data gathered in Part Two.

Table 2.7. Examples of LM and MM Minimal Pairs Involving Quantity

SH	[poš]	/poš/		'guava'
	[po·š]	/po·š/		'spider'
	[po̠:š]	/po̠·hš/		'knot'
NN	[cikˡ]	/cikˡ/		'coati'
	[ci·k]	/ci:k/		'grasshopper'
	[ci̠:k]	/ci̠:k/		'punch!'
SW	[cikˡ]	/cikˡ/	//cik//	
	[ci·k]	/ci·k/	//ci·hk//	
	[ci:k]	/ci·k/	//ci·k//	

SH's analysis, as indicated in Table 2.7, is a traditional one. An underlying /h/ is posited for [po:š]. This analysis is reiterated in Hoogshagen (1984). The argument, as given in the 1959 article, is one

---

[4] Nordell used a subscript quotation mark to indicate "fortis." "Lenis" is symbolized by the absence of a subscript quotation mark; subscript quotation marks have been converted into superscript bars throughout the present work.

of distribution: V may occur single or followed by /h/. The same distribution would hold for V·, if V: was substituted for V·h, as SH suggests. A supporting argument is that [h] is a vocoid and only differs from vowel length in its lack of voicing. My counterarguments would be the following three: (1) It is not a phonological imperative that things should be arranged so that phonemes are distributed evenly. (2) Underlying forms should be motivated by the need for an adequate phonological description of phonetic processes; in the San Juan el Paraíso dialect, which is virtually identical with Coatlán Mixe, stops and, usually, affricates and fricatives, are voiced following V: (cf. Van Haitsma and Van Haitsma 1976: 6). Following an /h/, as in V·h, this would hardly be expected. Even if voicing or some sort of lenition is absent from Cn (this is highly improbable), there are no motivating factors. (3) If /h/ can be substituted for vowel length as a matter of course, what is then the difference, phonologically speaking, between V· and Vh in SH's final analysis?[5]

---

[5] Hoogshagen (p.c., 1990) admits that his analysis of Coatlán Mixe phonology may be incomplete since it does not take the consonantal tenseness opposition into account. Nevertheless, the choice in Hoogshagen and Hoogshagen (1993) was to operate with three degrees of vowel length. While this is perhaps a legitimate choice, the Hoogshagens have unfortunately not even been consistent in marking their alleged three degrees of vowel length—they are marked for verb roots only (in special bracketed forms provided for the use of linguists). Their arguments for this choice of underdifferentiation are that (1) "el grupo de tres vocales parece excesivo"; (2) "la distinción entre medio largo y largo no juega un papel muy importante en la distinción de las palabras"; and (3) "los mixes, al escribir su lengua experimentan dificultades en la percepción de la duración vocálica, posiblemente porque aprendieron a leer en el español, en el que la diferencia de duración nunca tiene una función fonológica." We are informed, however, that "[l]os escritores mixes reflejan cierto conocimiento de los núcleos largos al escribir las oclusivas sonoras en vez de las oclusivos sordas al final de la sílaba, después de un núcleo largo: *Peed* 'Pedro'. Así, en la escritura, una oclusiva sonora después de dos vocales al final de la palabra indica que la vocal es de máxima duración" (all quotations from Hoogshagen and Hoogshagen 1993: 338). The third argument is the most interesting one. The native speakers' experiences must of course be decisive for one's choice of a practical orthography. Now, when speakers write < Peed > for /pe:t/ it clearly indicates a recognition of a fortis-lenis contrast in the stops, and this way of writing the word is fully adequate. In contrast, < Peeed > would be an unnecessarily overdifferentiated representation. There does not seem to be any reason why speakers would not also recognize a fortis-lenis opposition in consonants other than oral stops. The only question is how to represent the opposition in a practical orthography. I would suggest using double letters to represent the fortis sonorants and glides (e.g., < mm >) or, alternatively, using

The underlying forms posited by NN (p.c.) correspond to the forms posited by SW at the level of intermediate abstraction except on one point, which is the relative degrees of vowel length between the SRs and the URs. Deriving [ci·k] from /ci:k/, as in NN's analysis, requires a redundancy rule affecting the whole lexicon whereby long vowels are shortened by one mora before fortis consonants. The corresponding rule in SW's analysis lengthens *all* vowels by a mora before lenis consonants. This little incongruence between NN and SW is not arbitrary. The redundancy rule of SW is more general than it is possible for NN's rule to be. If NN's rule were extended to shortening *all* vowels before fortis consonants, the short vowel of 'coati' would disappear completely. The result, of course, does not turn out better if we operate with half moras, since then the long vowel of 'punch!' would turn out four times as long as the short vowel of 'grasshopper'. The lengthening rule is thus a true redundancy rule, whereas it is not certain what sort of status a shortening rule would have in the overall system. Note that the difference between the opinions of SW and NN concerns only the interface between surface forms and underlying representations. These underlying forms are, other things being equal, identical.

The forms surrounded by double obliques represent SW's attempt at going one step further in the analysis. At this deeper level of abstraction, the consonantal tenseness opposition is done away with, and, as on the intermediate level, only two degrees of vowel length are needed. This analysis is thus motivated by simplicity. An /h/ is inserted to yield //ci·hk//. As in SH's analysis an even distribution of the nuclear components is arrived at, though SH and SW insert the /h/ in two different places. In SH's analysis, even distribution is the goal; SW, however, arrives at this distribution as a pure side effect. Thus, my counterarguments (1 and 3) to SH do not apply to my own analysis. The phonetic motivation, which is opted for as a principle in counterargument (2), is that there are cases in some MM and LM dialects of the devoicing of glides following V·. Unfortunately there is too much inconsistency in the source to argue convincingly for an underlying /h/ as the causee.[6] A final feature of SW's analysis is that the input (e.g., //ci·hk//) corresponds to what is found in the more conservative SHM

---

combinations with <h>, a letter which is not used for other purposes (e.g., <hm> or <mh>).

[6] The place to look for devoiced glides is in the completive independent inflection of the verb, and this is only scantily recorded in Nordell (1990).

dialects. This concordance with the diachronic facts did not in itself motivate the analysis, but, as everyone would agree, it certainly makes life easier. The phonological rules required to derive the SRs from the URs suggested by my analysis are presented in sections 2.5 and .6.

Here follows a brief summary and an elaboration of the implications of the rule whereby vowels are lengthened before lenis consonants.

The liberal use of diacritics in Nordell (1990) can only be understood when his representations are translated back into feature representations. The different types of syllable codas can be described in terms of the distinctive features [syl] ("syllabic") and [tns] ("tense"). In Table 2.8 the calculus of possible feature matrices, in Column A, are followed by phonemic representations corresponding to these matrices, in Column B. Column C presupposes a rule, Rule P,[7] operating on the entire lexicon whereby all stressed vowels acquire an extra mora before lenis consonants. In Column D, the sequences of Column E have been cosmetically converted into the symbols actually used by Nordell (read subscript quotation mark for superscript bar). Barred means "fortis" (tense) and the absence of a bar, "lenis" (lax).

Table 2.8. A Calculus of MM and LM Feature Matrices

A		B	C	D
$\begin{bmatrix} +syl \\ +tns \end{bmatrix}$	$\begin{bmatrix} -syl \\ -tns \end{bmatrix}$	V:C	V::C	V:C
$\begin{bmatrix} +syl \\ -tns \end{bmatrix}$	$\begin{bmatrix} -syl \\ -tns \end{bmatrix}$	VC	V:C	V·C
$\begin{bmatrix} +syl \\ +tns \end{bmatrix}$	$\begin{bmatrix} -syl \\ +tns \end{bmatrix}$	V:C̄	V:C̄	V·C̄
$\begin{bmatrix} +syl \\ -tns \end{bmatrix}$	$\begin{bmatrix} -syl \\ +tns \end{bmatrix}$	VC̄	VC̄	VC̄

---

[7] "P" stands for "Perception" or "Phonetic Cue." Why this is so will follow from the ensuing discussion.

This, then, would be the simple rationale of Nordell's orthography. In order to test the synchronic validity of our system, we need to look at a specific dialect. For this purpose the Cotzocón dialect of MM has been chosen. The choice was made on the basis of a machine count of the frequency of the diacritic subscript quotation mark in Nordell's data from MM and LM dialects. The count showed that fortis marking was most frequent in the Ct material, indicating that the author in his recording of this dialect could have been particularly meticulous. The calculus predicts that there are four possible sequences: V:C, V·C, V·C, VC. In the Ct data of Nordell (1990), V:C is found 822 times; V·C is found 153 times; V· is found 198 times; V is found 1035 times. Sequences disallowed by the calculus are V:C, VC. The sequence V: is not found; VC is found in unstressed syllables only. The qualification contained in this last piece of information reveals the important fact that the interplay of vocalic and consonantal quantity is a property of the stressed syllable only.

I have hitherto postponed the description of how fortis consonants are actually pronounced for the simple reason that I am uncertain about this. A very short *postfestum* conference with a principal informant of Nordell's, Luís Vasquez of Atitlán, gives me reason to believe that prolonged articulation may be the defining phonetic property of fortis consonants. Whatever the actual properties may be, the feature [tns] is certainly appropriate and the phonological calculus would turn out the same.[8]

According to Ilse Lehiste (1970: 42), in languages such as Icelandic, Norwegian, and Swedish, "there exists an inverse relationship between the quantity of a vowel and that of the following consonant, so that a

---

[8] After having completed the present study I became aware of Bickford's 1985 paper which reports on a pilot study of the acoustic properties of fortis and lenis versions of the consonants *p*, *h*, *n*, *y*, and *t* in the Guichicovi dialect. Both in intervocalic and final position the most consistent difference between fortis and lenis consonants actually turned out to be one of duration, fortis consonants being longer than lenis ones. A tendency was also found for duration to be distributed over whole syllables. Both phonemically long vowels and phonemically short ones were relatively shorter before fortis than before lenis consonants. This leads Bickford to suggest that phonetic vowel length may serve as a cue for the contrast in consonant length. The interesting results of this acoustic investigation, which was carried out in collaboration with N. Nordell, call for further, more extensive instrumental studies (see Bickford 1985: 204-205 for some directions for further research).

short vowel is followed by a long consonant, and a long vowel by a short consonant." Thorough acoustical measurements of Swedish quantity is found in Elert (1964), and Icelandic quantity is discussed in relation to the phonological makeup as a whole of that language, its diachrony, and general phonology in Árnason (1980). Icelandic provides a particularly interesting parallel to Midland and Lowland Mixe, since it also has preaspiration (as well as devoiced sonorants). Árnason, who does not operate with distinctive features, is forced to make decisions about whether to make length phonemically relevant for consonants or for vowels. Making length relevant for both is deemed uneconomical. According to my view, this decision hinges upon orthography rather than phonology. If distinctive features are employed, the highest economy is reached when length is posited as being relevant for both consonants and vowels.

Árnason (1980: 23-26) also discusses preaspiration. Among the various possible interpretations of this typologically rare phenomenon, the one of Pétursson (1974) is the closest parallel to the one that I opt for in the Mixe case. It concludes (according to Árnason 1980: 24) that "preaspiration is an instance of the phoneme /h/ which also occurs in initial position in forms like *hús* and *hestur*, and has the same or similar phonetic characteristics as the preaspiration: voicelessness ('spread glottis') and a vocal tract configuration appropriate to the adjacent vowel."

Finally, the Icelandic case provides a highly interesting clue to the theoretical status of Rule P formulated above. Initially I fathomed that it was some sort of redundancy rule or phonotactic constraint (and called it Rule L for lengthening). This may be adequate as long as the rule is considered just a piece of phonological machinery. However, from a viewpoint which is external to the particular phonological framework, it becomes unclear what the ramifications are.

Árnason, in his discussion of whether length should be made phonemically relevant for vowels alone or consonants alone, reports one view according to which the vowels should carry this function. Garnes (1974), who is the one opting for this view, was led to her conclusion by an experiment.

> The experiment tested the responses of native Icelandic speakers to synthetic tokens made out of e.g. the sounds corresponding to Icelandic *t* [i] and *s* [s]. The length of the segments was varied systematically, and

the subjects were told to identify the sound sequences as either *ís* 'ice' (nom.) or *íss* 'ice' (gen.). The result of this experiment was that the judgements of the speakers were almost solely based on the length of the vowel. . . . . The argument is, then, that since speakers use the duration of vowels to distinguish between the stimuli, vowel length must be 'distinctive' and pairs like *ís-íss*; *man-mann* are to be analyzed phonologically as /i:s/ vs /is/ and /ma:n/ vs /man/ respectively.

(Árnason 1980: 17)

Garnes's phonemization corresponds to the insertion of my Rule P. In a calculus of possible VC sequences for Icelandic, the output is V:C:, VC:, V:C, VC. As a result of historical processes,[9] the first and the last are deleted. The remaining two can be rewritten VC and V:C. Rule P for Mixe made it possible to distinguish orthographically between three vowel lengths without changing the (now phonemically super-fluous) notation of consonantal tenseness. Likewise, Garnes's decision puts the burden of the phonological representation on the vowels, thus rendering the notation of consonantal quantity superfluous. She then omits it. Nordell retains consonantal diacritics, leaving open the possibility of different interpretations.

Garnes's argument and the Rule P touch upon a possible truth about phonemic orthographies, namely that they reflect properties of speech perception rather than properties of speech production. In sequences -VC-, the quantity of the vowel appears to be perceptually more salient than that of the consonant (which may perhaps be due to their temporal ordering and the way that the brain stores information). The function of devices such as Rule P would then be to provide an interface between the description of Production and Perception of speech. This whole line of reasoning, of course, needs to be thoroughly tried both empirically and theoretically.

The topic remaining is to decide how to handle syllable nuclei containing a glottal component. There are three such nucleus types across the OM dialects: V? V·? V?V. The last is written V" by Van Haitsma and Van Haitsma (1976), a convention carried over into this work for

---

[9] The parallel between Mixean and Germanic languages is hinted at again in 5.3, n. 1, from the diachronic point of view; for the present purposes the diachrony is irrelevant.

practical reasons.[10] I would not, however, set up /ʔ/ and /"/ as two different phonemes. This would obscure the fact that the difference between the two nucleus types has to do with vowel length. The alternation V? ~ V" of one of the verb classes is one of quantity, not of, say, the quality of the glottal stop. V? and V" are mutually interrelated, whereas V·? generally does not interact with any of those two nucleus types. According to Crawford's phonetic description of these nucleus types as he recorded them in Totontepec, the /ʔ/ of V? "is manifested as a relatively discrete stop allophone" (1963: 45). Crawford states about the other two that "[i]n the form V?V the greatest laryngealization occurs towards the central part of the duration of the vocoid, whereas in V·? it occurs towards the end of that span" (1963: 45). Nordell (1990) operates with yet another type. For this a special symbol was devised, which can be described as a raised glottal stop symbol inserted into the letter "v". This symbol is, in the present work, rendered by means of an exclamation mark. Again, a problem is that it is not certain how this glottal stop is actually pronounced. The problem diminishes, however, whenever it can be determined what the conditions are for its occurrence. In the following two sections, these conditions are worked out. One rule in particular is revealing. This is the Gu rule that V! is a product of the neutralization of the opposition between V·? and V?. A realistic conjecture would be that [!] represents a laryngealization occurring toward the center of the vocoid span without full rearticulation of the vowel.

How are these nucleus types to be handled phonologically? It has not proven to be rewarding to set up a calculus for them corresponding to the one above for plain vowel + consonant sequences, since V?, which contains a short vowel, according to the principles of the calculus would have to be invariably followed by a fortis consonant. This is not in accordance with the empirical facts. It seems wisest, then, to analyze the /ʔ/ of V? as belonging to the syllable coda on a par with preconsonantal /h/. By that token, V", more properly written V?V, would consist of two syllables interrupted by an ambisyllabic /ʔ/. V·?, finally, could be said to consist of a long vowel + consonantal /ʔ/. There is at least one problem with this analysis, however: if V?V does indeed

---

[10] In this way the distributional analysis of V? as against V?V is facilitated technically. It is much easier for a computer to search for occurrences of the symbol < " > than for different kinds of V?V combinations.

consist of two syllables, the description of Mixean morpheme canons is complicated as are the rules involving morphological alternation of V? and V". Another problem is that V" hardly ever occurs before fortis consonants. This confirms the phonological calculus and gives us a good reason for treating V" as a combination of a long vowel and a glottal component. But if this analysis is chosen, how may we now distinguish in phonological terms between V" and V·?, which is also a combination of a long vowel and a glottal component? Even if this analysis, according to which V" contains two syllables, would probably still be preferable, the notion of complex nuclei whereby V, Vh, V, V·, V:, V?, V·?, and V" may be treated on a par is often invoked in this work for reasons of indeterminacy, convenience, and because this seems to be the view held by all the workers who have provided the descriptive materials.

2.5. MIDLAND MIXE

Midland Mixe is spoken in Jaltepec (Ja), Puxmetacán (Pu), Matamoros (Ma), Cotzocón (Ct), Atitlán (At), Cacalotepec (Cc), Juquila (Ju).

The general system of consonants is displayed below. The statuses of /w̥/ and /y/ have not been fully worked out. Certainly, in Ju /y/ is not predictable. Ju and Cc lack the series of fortis consonants. The major Ma allophones of /w/ are [β φ w̥ f]. They are in free variation (Nordell, p.c.). The allophone [β ~ φ ~ w̥ ~ f] of /w/ is symbolized "w̌" in the source; this symbol has been converted to capital "W" throughout the present work. /s/, though marginal, should probably be added for all dialects; it is found in Spanish loans and in a few native words. /ř, r̃/ likewise probably occupy marginal positions in the inventory for most dialects, as does /l/. For all dialects /l/ is attested in one or two native words (cf. Part Two, LV#001) and in borrowings of Spanish items such as *escuela, color, clavos, libro* or Nahuatl-derived words such as *zopilote* (Ja,Ma *lut*, probably directly from Nahuatl) and *hule* (Ju *?úlɨ*, probably via Spanish).

General system of consonants:[11]

[-vc,-pal,-tns]	p̱	ṯ	š̱	c̱	ḵ		y	w̥	ẖ	?
[-vc,-pal,+tns]	p	t	š̄	c̄	k				h	
[-vc,+pal,-tns]	p̱ʸ	ṯʸ	š̱ʸ	č̱	ḵʸ				ẖʸ	
[-vc,+pal,+tns]	p̄ʸ	t̄ʸ	š̄ʸ	c̄ʸ	k̄ʸ				hʸ	
[+vc,-pal,-tns]	b	d	ž	z̧	g	m	n	y	w	
[+vc,+pal,-tns]	bʸ	dʸ	žʸ	j	gʸ	mʸ	nʸ	yʸ	wʸ	
[son]	−	−	−	−	−	+	+	+	+	
[nas]	−	−	−	−	−	+	+	−	−	
[cont]	−	−	+	−	−	−	−	+	+	
[cor]	−	+	+	+	−	−	+	+	−	

General vowel system:

	/i	e	æ	ɨ	u	o	a/
high	+	−	−	−	+	−	−
low	−	−	+	−	−	−	+
back	−	−	−	+	+	+	+
round	−	−	−	−	+	+	−

The 463 Cc items in Nordell (1990) do not allow for a straightforward phonemic analysis. Eight symbols, "i e æ ɨ a A u o" are used when Nordell's data are cited here (including Part Two). Whether "a" and "A" represent variants of a single phoneme /a/ must be left un-determined.[12]

---

[11] The purpose of the feature specifications is not to provide an exhaustive dif-ferentiation of the entire inventory. They only serve to mark off the major natural classes to which the phonological rules (see below) make reference. In these rules I shall sometimes use the expression "palatalized consonant" and the informal symbol Cʸ. By these means, reference is made to the consonants specified here as being [+pal]. In the same informal vein I shall be referring to [-cont(inuant)] consonants as "stops", [-nas(al), +son(orant)] consonants as "glides," and [-son] consonants as "obstruents." I have consciously avoided overformalization in order to make the statements more easily digestible. These remarks also apply to the analysis of the Guichicovi dialect presented in the following section.

[12] There seems to be little doubt about the vowel system of the Ju dialect, a dia-lect which in many respects resembles Cc. The SIL New Testament translation (*Ja oibyu tui'yajtun mudu Hesukristu kujxm* . . . 1980), however, operates with eight vowels. The additional vowel of this source may either be a reduced vowel or have to do with an umlaut, a phenomenon which cannot be described for Ju on the basis of Nordell's data. A seven-vowel system is supported, albeit not proved, by the

Major allophones:

	/i	e	æ	ɨ	u	o	a/
Ju	[i	e	a	ɨ	u	o	a]
Cc	[i	e	ä	ɨ	u	o	a,a(?)]
Ma	[ɪ	e	a	ï	u	o	a]
Ja	[i	e	æ	ɨ	u	o	a]
Pu	[i	e	æ	ɨ	u	o	a]
At	[i	e	æ	ɨ	u	o	a]
Ct	[i	e	ä	ɨ	u	o	a]

The phonemic symbols (emphasized) are used in all citations from Nordell's data. The "major allophones" are represented with the symbols actually used by him.

In his notation [i ɪ e ɛ æ a ä] have increasingly lower values (p.c.). [ü] and [ö] would be centered versions of [u] and [o]; whether [ï] is higher and more fronted or lower and more centered than [ɨ] has not been communicated to me. I assume that it is slightly lower since this would correspond with the lowering of the high front vowel in the Ma dialect.

Overview of umlaut systems:

/i/ no umlaut   BUT   Ma /i/ → [ɪ]/__nonpalatized C's
/æ/ ~ /e/
/ɨ/ ~ /e/   BUT   no data from Ju. Cc probably no umlaut
/a/ ~ /æ/   BUT   Ja /a/ → [a]/__{š,y,Cʸ}
/u/ ~ /i/   BUT   At /u/ ~ [uü]. Cc no umlaut
/o/ ~ /e/   BUT   At /o/ ~ [oö]. Cc no umlaut. Ct /o/ ~ /ɨ/

To clarify: /a/ ~ /æ/ is to be read "/a/ has the same realization as /æ/ before a palatalized consonant." Obliques around an umlauted vowel signal that this element is not a mere variant, but plays a distinctive role within the system since overlapping is involved. In Praguean terms: the

---

following minimal pairs:

		/ʔɨy/	/ʔæy/			/ʔoy/
	/ney/	/hɨy/	/wæy/		/huy/	/hoy/
				/ca"y/	/ku"y/	/ho"y/
/ni:y/				/ʔa:y/		/co:y/

The NT translation also operates with three degrees of vowel length. But middle length has a very limited distribution in Ju and may not be phonemic.

archiphoneme /Æ/ will be represented by one of the members of the opposition. To avoid complicating the notational system, archiphoneme symbols are not employed. See, however, 5.2 for a suggestion as to how this could be done.

Where no special remarks are made about individual dialects, these synchronic statements of the MM umlaut apply to all dialects.[13]

Underlying nucleus types of alternating verb roots are

NUCLEUS	CODA
Vh ~ V	obstruents
V: ~ V"	obstruents
Vh ~ V"	sonorants
V: ~ V:	t, k
V? ~ V:	any consonant
V? ~ V"	obstruents and /y/

These underlying nucleus types (based on Pu and Ma data) form the input to the phonological rules for the verb. The environments to which they are restricted are also indicated. Pu in addition has Vh ~ V! before /t/ in two cases.

[13] There is, however, an exeption to the first rule stating that /i/ does not suffer umlauting. According to Nordell's manuscript, /i/ usually goes to [ι] before nonpalatalized consonants in the Ma dialect. He is rather inconsistent on this point as the following examples of the same words found under different headings illustrate (the use of symbols is as in Nordell, only read "glottal stop symbol" for "?" and "subscript quotation mark" for "superscript bar"); the reader will notice a few other inconsistencies as well:

[?az̨ί?ιt] vs. [?az̨i?it]; [?ihštan] vs. [?ιhštan̄]; [cιp̄] vs. [cip̄]; [ci·š̄p],[ci?iža·m̄p] vs. [cι·š̄p],[cι?ιšam̄p]; [hι?cp] vs. [hi?cp^{h}]; [tίhpï] vs. [tíhpï]; [tι?pšn̥] vs. [ti?pšn̥]

The conversion of "iota" to "i" is the only conversion which is not just cosmetic and which affects a symbol occurring with a frequency higher than 1% in the data from the given dialect.

Underlying nucleus types of nonalternating verb roots (based on Pu,Ma) are

NUCLEUS	CODA
V	laryngeals
V:	t, k (based on Pu)
Vh	pš, kš
V?	pš, kš

> The *distribution of nucleus types* in the surface representations of the source has been examined for the total recorded lexical inventory across the dialects. This examination has not been fully completed, but it has been completed to such a degree as to give an impression of the intimate relation between nucleus and coda in the MM syllable.

The plain, short vowel V has an unlimited distribution in all dialects. Other nuclei, however, have restricted distributions, the main restrictor being the fortis quality of the following consonants:[14]

Nucleus	Only before	Dialects	BUT
Vh_	lenis C's	Ct, At, Cc, Pu	Ct also / __$\bar{\text{š}}$
			Only in Ju, Ja / __m̥, n̥
V?_	lenis C's	Ct, At, Cc, Pu	C t , P u a l s o
			/ __+tns,+voiced C's
			Ju not before glides
V"	lenis C's,/ȳ/	Ct, At, Pu, Ja	
V:	lenis C's	Ju, Pu, Ct, Cc, Ja	At only / __lenis obstruents
V·	fortis C's	At, Ct, Pu	Ct, Pu also / __-tns,+voiced C's
			Cc only / __voiced stops
			Ju only / __sonorants and in unstressed prefixes
			Ja no restrictions

Nuclei that do not occur in any of the eight dialects are
V?h   V·? (BUT one case in Ct)   V:h (BUT one case in At)

---

[14] [!] represents an allophone of /?/. The rules of its occurrence have, to every degree possible, been given in the phonological rules below.

By *other distributional constraints*, the sequences /iy/, /i·y/, /i:y/, /yi/, /yi·/, /y:/, /uw/, /u·w/, /u:w/, /wu/, /wu·/, /wu:/ are generally disallowed (fortis-marking is irrelevant here). /iy/ is found once in Cc, /i·y/ once in Ct, and /i:y/ one to three times in all dialects. These sequences are historically the result of final */w^y/ becoming /y/. /uw/ and /u:w/ are never found, whereas /u·w/ is attested to once in Ja and Ma in the verb 'to rain', the original final /h/ of which in pre-MM times was analogically replaced with /w/. The sequence of /y/ and a high, front vowel is found a few times in all dialects; the high front vowel will then usually, but not always, represent an umlauted vowel. The sequence of /w/ and a high, back, rounded vowel is only found in Ja—in one item.

Phonological rules:

The following rules have been adjusted so that they provide an interpretive framework for all the MM dialects described in Nordell (1990). By calling them an "interpretive framework" I mean to avoid postulating that they amount to a full and adequate description. What I have done is to take the forms given in Nordell's lists and tried to posit underlying forms that would apply across the various dialects. In this way the rules posited in order to derive individual dialectal forms become indicatory of dialect differences. The rules, then, may be seen both as a preparatory study toward a synchronic description of any one of the individual dialects as well as a preparatory study toward a dialectology. The primary purpose in presenting them, however, is a third one. In the present work their function is to serve as a reference for the study of Part Two. If the reader encounters a MM form in Part Two and is curious about it, he or she may run it through the rules in their reverse order and construct an underlying form. The reader may now take the underlying form and then run it through the diachronic rules in chapter 7—again in their reverse order—in order to finally arrive at a protoform. This should be identical to a form in Part Two. By this means the reader is able to check through all my protoforms. The rules cannot be dispensed with since they serve to make my assumptions explicit. I have consciously avoided providing extensive exemplification. Such "examples" would only bring about the illusion that I have been able to pick from a full resource. A cited form could not be called an example proper—it would simply be one of anything from one to a few hundred words in the data-set that happen to allow for setting up the particular rule. Following the rules I have, however, provided some sample derivations that show how the system as a whole works.[15]

The Southern dialects, Ju and Cc, require some special remarks. In order to understand these dialects in terms of the rule set, Rule Section I must be interpreted diachronically (which is also possible, but not necessary, for the other dialects). This is because the essential fortis/lenis opposition has been lost in Ju and Cc. If Rule Section I is interpreted diachronically, two rules can then be inserted at the end of the section. Rule A shortens long vowels before fortis consonants. This could be explained as the resolution of overcharacterized (four morae-) syllable rhymes (see discussion in 5.3). Rule B eliminates the consonantal fortis/lenis opposition. Rule Sections II and III can then be interpreted synchronically for Ju and Cc also. I chose this conflation of the viewpoints rather than write an entirely different (and less illuminating) set of rules for Cc and Ju.

Rule Section I derives forms in which only two vowel quantities and the consonantal tenseness opposition is relevant from rather abstract representations that do not operate with a consonantal tenseness opposition. Rule Section II deals with deletion of segments, palatalization, and adjustments of the syllable nucleus. Rule Section III treats umlaut conditions, that is, the conditions under which a palatalized consonant may influence the quality of the preceding vowel. Rule Section IV contains the final steps needed to arrive at the Surface Representation, that is, the form as it appears in the source.

Rule Section I

(2.5.1) $V \rightarrow V:/\_hC_{[+son]}T$
"Vowels are lengthened before the sequence of /h/+sonorant+stop."
Verb roots affected by this rule when inflected in the independent, incompletive are, by analogy, carried over to the completive inflection (see sections 4.3 and 5.3).

---

[15] These remarks also apply to the section on the LM Guichicovi dialect below.

(2.5.2) $Vh \rightarrow V{:}/\_C_{[+son]}\$$

"/h/ following short vowels is replaced with vowel length before single sonorants." Future investigations will have to show whether a rule which devoices glides /w y/ following /h/ should be ordered before this rule. I argue that this is a possibility in the Gu case (cf. in section 2.6).

(2.5.3) $\acute{V}{:}hC \rightarrow \acute{V}{:}\overline{C}$

"Consonants become fortis following the sequence of a long, stressed vowel and /h/, and /h/ is subsequently deleted." If devoicing of fortis sonorants is involved in any one dialect, this should be noted prior to the rule.

(2.5.4) $\acute{V}C \rightarrow \acute{V}\overline{C}/\_(y)\#$

"Consonants become fortis following short, stressed vowels and preceding a word boundary or a sequence of a palatal glide and a word boundary."

$\Longrightarrow$ [JU AND CC DIACHRONIC RULES A-B]

Rule Section II

(2.5.5) $V? \rightarrow V!/\_\{\overline{C}_{[+son]}, \overline{š}\}$

"V? goes to V! before fortis sonorants and the fortis sibilant."
Only applies to Ja and Pu.

(2.5.6) $V? \rightarrow V!/\_Y$

"V? goes to V! before glides." Applies to Pu,At,Ct,Cc,Ja. In Ma V? goes to V" in this environment. For Ju, data is missing.

(2.5.7) $C\ (\neq?) \rightarrow [+pal]/y\_$

"Any consonant other than /?/ is palatalized following /y/."

(2.5.8) $y \rightarrow \emptyset/\_C^y$

"/y/ is deleted before a palatalized consonant." Applies to all dialects except Cc where the rule is restricted to stating that "word-initial /y/ is deleted before a palatalized consonant."

(2.5.9)   Y → Ø_p$^{(y)}$
"Glides (fortis as well as lenis) are deleted before /p p^y/." All dialects
except Cc.

(2.5.10)   w → Ø/V"__#
At,Pu,Cc,Ju. In Ct,Ja,Ma /w/ is not deleted in this position. The rule
applies to verbs that have an alternating nucleus V?~V" or V:~V".

(2.5.11)   y → w/V"__# (Ct,Ja)
(2.5.12)   y → Ø/V"__# (At,Cc,Pu)
(2.5.13)   y → y/V"__#   (Ju)
Apply to verbs that have an alternating nucleus V?~V", *not* to verbs
alternating V:~V". (The historical reason is that the latter kind of
verbs contained a postconsonantal /?/. This metathesized with the glide
to give rise to *V? > V", during which process the glide was
deleted. What we see in 2.5.11-13 as in the rules below concerning /w/
are various restoration strategies).

(2.5.14)   w → Ø/V"__V́
At and Cc. Applies to verbs that have an alternating nucleus V?~V"
or V:~V".

(2.5.15)   y → Ø/V"__V́
At and Ct. Applies to verbs that have an alternating nucleus V:~V".
Verbs alternating V?~V" do not delete /y/ in this position.

(2.5.16)   Ø → h/V"__V́
"Insertion of a transitional /h/ in the place where glides have been deleted." At and Cc.

(2.5.17)   w → y/V"__V́
Ma. Applies to verbs that have alternating nucleus V:~V".

(2.5.18)   y → w/V"__V́
Ma and Pu. Applies to verbs that have an alternating nucleus V:~V".

(2.5.19)   T$_i$ → h/__T$_i$, T = {p t k}   (tentative rule)
"Any oral stop, but /c/ is reduced to /h/ before a like stop." Ja is the
dialect most closely examined concerning this rule, which for this

dialect is positively confirmed for /p t k/. The rule may also apply to /c/, but we lack evidence for this. Even for Ja the rule is not without exceptions, so a closer examination is needed. For all other dialects than Ja it can, at the present moment, only be confirmed that sequences of like stops do occur. The causative prefix pOM *yak-* assumes the shape *yahk-* in Ma,Ct,Cc,At (quality of vowel may vary), and *yæh-* in Ja,Pu,Ju. We might, then, first want to turn to Ja,Pu,Ju when looking for the workings of a rule such as (2.5.19). Ja,Pu,Ma probably had /k/ + /k/ → /hk/ at some point, which resulted in a reanalysis of the /k/ of the causative prefix when it occurred with roots in *k-* and subsequently full reanalysis.

(2.5.20) $C (\neq ?) \rightarrow C^y/\_\_y$
"Consonants other than /?/ are palatalized preceding /y/."

(2.5.21) $C_{[-son]} \rightarrow [+pal]/\_\_C^y$
"Palatalization of a consonant extends to a preceding obstruent."

(2.5.22) $y \rightarrow \emptyset/C^y\_\_$
"/y/ is deleted following a palatalized consonant."

(2.5.23) $V? \rightarrow V! /\_\_T_{[-cont,-nas,-tns]}C_0\$$
"V? goes to V! before lenis oral stops within the same syllable." Only applies to Pu. The rule is violated in forty-four cases. Some of these cases are demonstrably due to inconsistency in the source, others may have to do with the rule being too broadly formulated. Stress is perhaps an accompanying factor.

(2.5.24a-b)   a. $V? \rightarrow V!/\_\_š$
                b. $š \rightarrow [+tns]/V!\_\_$
"Readjustment of the sequence -V?š- to -V!s̄-." This rule is valid for at least Pu. For Ja,Ma,At,Ct, there are inconsistencies in the source. See data under pM *ha?š* (HA#023) and pM *ke?š* (KE#024) in Part Two.

(2.5.25) $kš \rightarrow š / VH\_\_$, where H = {h,h̄,h^y,h̄^y,?,!}
"The cluster -kš- is reduced to -š- following nuclei composed of a short vowel and a laryngeal." This rule, which is perhaps more of a dia-chronic than a synchronic rule, only applies to Ja,Ma,Ju. In Nordell

(1990) a variation /kš/ ~ /š/ is noted in some of the forms that would be affected by this rule. Nordell personally informed me that he thinks that the change occurred as late as about twenty-five years ago in Ja and a few years later in Ma, where there is still variation in the speech of younger people. A note from my conversations with Nordell states that the change is supposed to have occurred about fifty years ago in Juquila. The Ju data, however, more consistently show retention of -kš- than do the Ja and Ma data: there are in the Ju data at least ten cases of retention, at least two cases of loss, and at least one case of variation. The clarification of these matters will have to await future investigations.

Rule Section III

In order to be able to generalize about the conditions that block or promote umlauting in the various dialects, I shall use the convention that [+U] stands for any set of features acquired or lost in the umlauting process, whereas [-U] stands for an absence of umlauting. The overview of these umlaut systems specifies how umlauted vowels are realized in the various dialects. Another convention is the ad hoc notation (X) which signals that a laryngeal /? ! h/ may partake in the syllable nucleus without this having consequences for the workings of the umlaut. The lexicalized umlaut, as in nonverbs, falls outside the scope of these synchronic statements.

(2.5.26) $V (\neq i) \rightarrow [+U]/\_(X)C^y_{[-cor]}$
"Any vowel other than /i: i· i/ umlauts before a palatalized noncoronal consonant." Ja in addition umlauts /ɩ/ to /i/ before any palatalized consonant. That same dialect is beginning to lose the umlaut of /ɨ: ɨ· ɨ/ before palatalized glides; optional absence/presence is attested to for one verb; other verbs disagree on umlauting in identical contexts. In Pu umlauting of /ɨ/ before palatalized glides has completely ceased. Otherwise valid for all dialects.

(2.5.27) $æ:, æ·, æ \rightarrow [+U]/\_(X)C^y_{[+cor]}\$$
"/æ: æ· æ/ umlaut before a palatalized coronal consonant." All dialects.

(2.5.28) $ɨ:, ɨ·, ɨ → [-U]\_\_(X)C^y_{[+cor, -son]}$
"/ɨ: ɨ· ɨ/ do not umlaut before a palatalized coronal obstruent." This
rule applies to all dialects except At, from which there is one example
of umlauting /ɨ/ in this environment and one example of the opposite.

(2.5.29) $a:, a·, a → [+U]\_\_(X)C^y_{[+cor]}$
"/a: a· a/ umlaut before a palatalized coronal consonant." The rule is
exceptionless for At only.

(2.5.30) $a:, a·, a → [-U]\_\_(X)C^y_{[+cor, -son]}$
"/a: a· a/ do not umlaut before a palatalized coronal obstruent." The
rule is exceptionless for Ja and Pu. For Cc and Ju there are no counter-
examples, but only very little positive evidence. In Ma and Ct some
verbs in /a/ + palatalized coronal obstruent defer umlauting. For other
verbs there is a tendency in both dialects for the /a/ to be affected such
that it gains a quality intermediate between nonumlauted and umlauted
/a/. These verbs are not necessarily the same for both dialects.

(2.5.31) $V_{[+round]} → [-U]/\_\_(X)C^y_{[+cor]}$
"Rounded vowels do not umlaut before palatalized coronal consonants."
All dialects.

Comment to the umlaut rules: the general statement is that back
vowels cannot be fronted (umlauted) before the front coronal obstruents
/t c š/. The source records that /t š/ are fronted when palatalized. So
the special conditions for umlaut blocking may be described as the
struggle of two assimilatory processes competing for the same point of
articulation, a struggle won out by the terminal articulatory movements.
The At dialect is more liberal than the others in that it allows /ɨ a/ to
umlaut in this position; the dialect of Pu and, more recently, the Ja
dialect are less liberal since /ɨ/ is fully (Pu) or in part (Ja) blocked from
umlauting before the glides /w y/. It seems that for all dialects there is
a further restriction on /o u/ for which the umlaut blocking environment
is extended to include the coronal sonorant /n/, but this rule can only
be set up tentatively since examples are few and not found across the
board.

The summary above of the MM umlaut systems shows that no two
dialects behave exactly alike. For instance, the umlaut products of /o/

will vary a great deal phonetically and the vowel systems (though not the inventory of vowel phonemes) as a whole will also turn out differently. Nevertheless it does make sense to treat the umlaut as a cross-dialectal phenomenon since there is both systematic agreement and disagreement about the blocking factors. These factors or conditions, rather than the individual systems they yield, are likely to be useful as tools for characterizing MM and its dialect areas.

Rule Section IV

(2.5.32) $C_{[-son]} \rightarrow C_{[+vc]}/V(")\_(?)V$ and $/C_{[+nas]}\_(?)V$

"Intervocalic and post-nasal voicing of obstruents." All dialects. Exceptions to the general rule: in Pu,Ct,At, /š/ resists voicing when /ʔ/ follows or precedes. In Cc all obstruents seem to resist voicing when /ʔ/ follows. /c/ resists voicing when preceded by an underlying /h/ in Ju and Cc. /k/ resists voicing between a short vowel and /ʔ/ in Ja and Ju. When either one of the affixes *ni-*, *ku-*, and *-á:m* is involved in the environment of obstruent voicing this may cause blocking in at least one dialect (e.g., Ja).

(2.5.33) $k \rightarrow g/V(X)\_w$

"Cases of voicing of /k/ between a syllable nucleus other than -Vh- and /w/." This is a tentative rule. Examples are found in all dialects but Ju and Cc.

(2.5.34)   Place assimilation of /n/

"/n/ assimilates to the point of articulation of a following oral stop." All dialects.

(2.5.35) $m \rightarrow n/\_t$

"/m/ is homorganic with a following /t/." All dialects except Ma and At.

(2.5.36) $V? \rightarrow V!/\_\{pš, kš\}$

"V? has the allophone V! before clusters pš,kš." Pu only.

(2.5.37) $C_{[+nas]} \rightarrow [-vc]/C\_\$$, where $C \neq /?/$

"Nasals are devoiced between any consonant but /ʔ/ and a syllable border." All dialects.

(2.5.38)   T → Tʰ/__#, where T = C$_{[-cont,-nas]}$
"Oral stops are aspirated word finally." The aspiration may extend to whole clusters of stops. Present in Pu,Ma,Ct; absent in Ja,At,Ju.

(2.5.39)   šʸ, tʸ → [+dental]
"/š/ and /t/ become fronted when palatalized." All dialects.

(2.5.40)   V́(:) → V́(:):/__C$_{[-tns]}$$
"Any stressed vowel acquires an extra mora before a syllable-final lenis consonant." This is Rule P. The rule exempts Ju and Cc, which do not have the fortis-lenis opposition. After the operation of this rule the representations operate with three degrees of vowel length, symbolized "V", "V:", and "V::." These should be converted orthographically to "V", "V·", and "V:," respectively. The stressed vowels of Spanish loans have the duration of V· (middle length).

Stress:

In Ja, stress is on the ultimate syllable except when this syllable is open and contains a short vowel or is constituted by the suffixes or enclitics -*ip*, -*ipʸ*, -*itʸ*, -*in*, -*inʸ*, -*nim*, -*ic*. Spanish loans retain their original stress pattern when not incorporated into the Mixe word. These stress rules appear to be similar in the other dialects.

Some examples of derivations:

Except in the following cases, the URs are identical with the forms reconstructed for pOM: (8) /næ:hš/ < pOM **na:hš*, (9) /pohm/ < pOM **po:m*, (10-11) /ca:nc/, /ca:hnc/ < pOM **ca:hncn*, (12) /nihy/ < pOM **ni:wy*, (14) /ʔuhm/ < pOM **ʔu:m*, (15) /neky/ < pOM *noky; (17) /šušp/ < pOM **šu:hšp*; note that there are cases where locations differ as to whether or not the UR is identical to its ancestral pOM form.

For the glosses see footnote.[16] The right-hand column refers the reader to the rules involved in the derivation.

---

[16] Glosses: 1. 'soak maize' (2p transitive, incompletive, independent); 2. 'walk' (3p intransitive, incompletive, independent); 3-4. 'who, somebody'; 5. 'bone'; 6. 'bird'; 7-8. 'earth, etc.'; 9. 'copal'; 10-11. 'bad smell'; 12-13. 'chili pepper'; 14. 'dumb'; 15. 'paper'; 16-17. 'play flute, etc.' (3p intransitive, incompletive, independent).

	UR	SR	Dialect(s)	By (2.5.__)
1.	/m+šu?c+py/	mžu!čpʸ	Pu	20,22,23,31,32
2.	/Ø+yo?y+p/	yoö!pʸ	At	6,7,8,26
3.	/pɨn/	pɨn̄	Ma,Ja,At,Ct	4
4.	=	pɨn	Ju	4,B
5.	/pahk/	pahk	Ju,Ma,Ja,Pu,At,Ct	
6.	/hohn/	ho:n	Ju,Ma,Ja,Pu,At,Ct	2
7.	/na:hš/	na·s̄	Ma,Ja,At,Ct	3
8.	/næ:hš/	næš	Ju	3,A,B
9.	/pohm/	po:m	Ju,Cc,Ja,Pu,At	2,40
10.	/ca:nc/	ca:nc	Pu,At	40
11.	/ca:hnc/	ca·n̄c	Ja,Ct	3
12.	/nihy/	ni:y	Ja,At,Ct	2,40
13.	/nihy/	ni:y	Ju,Ma,Pu	2
14.	/?uhm/	?u͟:m	Ju,Ma,Ja,Pu,At,Ct	2,40
15.	/neky/	nekʸ	Ma,Ja,Pu,At,Ct	20,22
16.	/šu:hšp/	šu·s̄p	Pu,At,Ct,Ma,Ja	3
17.	/šušp/	šušp	Ju	3,A,B

2.6. LOWLAND MIXE

San Juan el Paraíso and Coatlán

These two dialects are virtually identical and their phonologies are here treated as one. Van Haitsma and Van Haitsma (1976) is the source for SJ; Hoogshagen (1984), for Cn. This summary will follow the Van Haitsmas' presentation, although no information is left out for any of the two dialects. The question of a possible fortis-lenis opposition in the consonants cannot be dealt with since the analyses in the two sources never touch upon it and take three vowel lengths as their only measure of quantity.

In the following chart of phonemes, "( )" indicates a marginal phoneme occurring mostly in Spanish loans.

The voiced obstruents are secondary phonemes with a limited occurrence as parts of Spanish loanwords or as predictable allophones of the voiced obstruents. They also occur in a few shortened forms, such as *du?n* 'thus' < *hadu?n*.

All phonemes except the marginal ones /ř, ī, f/ have palatalized counterparts (though /yʸ/ occurs only word initially). Since the palatalized consonants /nʸ mʸ/ are phonetically distinct from /ny my/, and for reasons of simplicity, the authors choose to deal with palatalization as a suprasegmental phoneme.

SJ/Cn *phoneme inventory*

Consonants:

p,b	t,d		k,g	?
	c,ʐ			
(f)	(s,z)	š,ž		h
m	n		ŋ	
	(l)			
	(ř),(ī)			
w		y		

Vowels:

i	ɨ	u
e		o
	a	

V·, V:

SJ/Cn *syllable nuclei:*
-V-, -V?-, -Vh-, -V·-, -V:-, -V"-

Morphophonemics (unordered rules)

(2.6.1.1)   p → Ø/m__#   (Cn)

(2.6.1.2)   p t k → b d g /N__ , N = a nasal   (Cn)
                                /V__V except following verb
                                prefixes *ha·-* and *ka·-*)
            p t c k → b d ʐ g   /{y, N}__   (SJ)
                                /{V, V·, V:, V"}__V
                                /{V:, V"}__ (after V" optionally)
            p(ʸ) → b(ʸ)/V·__
            p → b/W__, where W = a /w/ deleted by (2.6.1.7)

(2.6.1.3)   c → s/k__$ (Cn)
SJ: "The marginal phoneme /s/ occurs in words of Mixe origin, principally in cluster with /m/, /p/, or /k/, and as such could be considered an allophone of /c/, which does not occur in this position. The /c/ occurs in cluster with /n/ in words which have probably lost a final

syllable, but /s/ does not occur there" (Van Haitsma and Van Haitsma 1976: 8).

(2.6.1.4)   n   →   m/X__{p,b},   where X =   "non-initial environment"   (Cn,SJ)

(2.6.1.5)   n → ŋ/X__{k,g}   (Cn,SJ)
The restriction to noninitial position for this rule is not explicitly stated for Cn.

(2.6.1.6)   k → Ø/n__#   (Cn,SJ)
Rules (2.6.1.5-6) may work simultaneously causing the cluster *nk* to become ŋ.

(2.6.1.7)   w → Ø/__+C   (Cn,SJ)
"/w/ is deleted morpheme finally when followed by a suffix beginning with a consonant." Add to SJ: when this consonant is not /ʔ/.

(2.6.1.8) $C_i + C_i$ → C_i (SJ)
"Contiguous identical consonants are reduced."

(2.6.1.9)   Underlying geminates C_iC_i resist voicing medially
                                                                    (Cn,SJ)

(2.6.1.10)   C → C^y/Xy(C^y)__X   (Cn)
"Word medial palatalization with occasional loss of /y/." The rule excludes /f, s, l, r/ and does not work when /y/ is the last member of a nonword-final cluster (SJ).

(2.6.1.11)   Ø → h/X+__V   (SJ)
"A transitional /h/ occurs between stems ending in a syllable nucleus and suffixes beginning with a vowel. This /h/ also occurs between two suffixes, the first ending in a syllable nucleus and the second beginning with a vowel. In the case of the two suffixes, many speakers have dropped the transitional *h*" (Van Haitsma and Van Haitsma 1976: 34). "Some speakers use an *h* as a transition consonant between a morpheme ending in a vowel and the postclitics. . . . The younger people use it less than the older people, reflecting the tendency to use shortened forms" (Van Haitsma and Van Haitsma 1976: 43).

Allophones:

/p t k/ → [pʰ tʰ kʰ]/V́__#   (SJ)
    (the aspiration may extend to whole clusters)
/p t k/ → [pʰ tʰ kʰ]/X__#, where X = any nucleus ≠ Vh
                                                (Cn)
/c/ → [ẓ]   /V__V
           /N__   (Cn)
/š/ → [ž]   /V__V   (Cn)
   → [ž]   /{n,m,ŋ}__   (Cn)

Distributional constraints:
    /ŋ/ does not occur syllable initially   (SJ/Cn)
    /b d g/ do not occur word initially except in shortened forms
                                                    (SJ/Cn)
Phonetic stress (Cn):
    "Stress occurs on the last syllable of an uninflected word that ends in a consonant or a long vowel and on the next to the last syllable of an uninflected word that ends in a short vowel. Stress occurs on the last syllable of the stem of an inflected word unless a stress-carrying suffix is present, in which case the suffix will carry the stress. The stress-carrying suffixes are -*yi*·- (object person focus), -*i*· (nominalizer), and -*o?k* (repetitive action)" (Hoogshagen 1984: 5). "Under certain as yet undefined conditions -*ip*ʸ (future tense) may also carry stress" (Hoogshagen 1984: 18, note 8).

    "The accented syllable nucleus is of longer duration than its unaccented counterpart (an accented V may well be longer in duration than an unaccented V:); and it is pronounced with greater intensity" (SJ; Van Haitsma and Van Haitsma 1976: 79).

    Word stress, the presence of which depends on the general phrasal pattern (see Van Haitsma and Van Haitsma 1976 for more detail), generally falls on the last syllable. Exceptions are when the last syllable has the nucleus -V- or the last or two last syllables belong to the set of verbal suffixes -*ip*, -*im*, -*ik*, -*kiš*, the nominalizer -*in*, the stative clause nucleus marker -*it*ʸ and its alternate forms -*id*ʸ*i* and -*igi*, and the postclitics *ič* and *ik*, in which cases the stress immediately precedes the one or two final light syllables. Spanish loans which are not incorporated grammatically, follow their Spanish pattern, while affixed or incorporated loans follow the Mixe pattern.

Concerning orthography (SJ/Cn):
V?V is written V" in Van Haitsma and Van Haitsma (1976); this convention is carried over into this work, where it is used for citing any OM dialect.

Concerning orthography (SJ):
The Van Haitsmas view the preaspiration of consonants as a glottalization of the syllable nucleus and write it "H." This has been converted to "h."

Additional information about SJ:
"Stems which have the final syllable ending in /w/ or /y/ in the non-conjunct past form of the clause nucleus (which is the basic form of the stem), but do not have /w/ or /y/ in the 2nd person imperative clause nucleus (which is the alternate form of the stem), have an unstable terminus /w/ or /y/. The stable terminus /w/ or /y/ occurs both in the non-conjunct past and in the 2nd person imperative. . . . Unstable syllable termini are those that drop final /w/ or /y/ in the alternate form of the stem (such as the 2nd person imperative). Note that not all roots in -/y/ and -/w/ have unstable termini. . . . Unstable /y/ changes to /w/ before the suffixes *-a·n, -ip, -ɨp*" (Van Haitsma and Van Haitsma 1976: 22).

"In subclass V'/V" they may be either stable or unstable and must be further subclassified in this respect. The class has relatively few stems ending in /w/ or /y/. Only two stems end in *y*, and both are stable. Five stems end in /w/; one is stable and four are unstable. . . . In subclasses V·/V and V·/V: terminus /w/ or /y/ is always stable. In subclass V·/V" terminus /w/ or /y/ is always unstable" (Van Haitsma and Van Haitsma 1976: 23).

Roots in final /w/ of subclass V'/V" are *ha?w~ha", ka?w~ka", pa?w~pa", pu?w~pu", ši?w~ši"*. The authors do not tell us which of these roots has the stable /w/, and the diachronic evidence is not sufficiently clear to point out the item in question.

Guichicovi

Introductory remarks:

The Gu dialect of LM is probably the Oaxaca Mixean dialect, which is most difficult to use in the reconstruction of pM phonology. The analysis that follows is a kind of experiment in the use of formal means of arriving at structures that are not apparent to the immediate perception. These underlying structures or internal reconstructions have, in spite of the many innovations of Gu, the property of providing clues to the development of MM and LM and even some features of pM phonology.

Vocalism:

Concerning the six symbols "e," "ɛ," "ï," "ɨ," "a," and "*a*" used for low front and high-to-low central vowel qualities in the source it may be observed that

(1) There are 28 times more occurrences of "a" than "*a*."

(2) Such pairs as

    <pa"k> 'sweet' vs. <p*a*"k> 'unrefined sugar'

    <?akš> 'skinned and salted fish' vs. <?*a*kš> 'fish'

occur under different headings; they must be typographical errors.

(3) Among the few cases where different verbal inflections are given for a verb, there are two examples of the alternation of [a] and [*a*].

Numbers 1 to 3 lead to the conclusion that the two symbols "a" and "*a*" stand for a single phoneme which undergoes some insignificant variation the conditions of which are blurred by typographical errors.

(4) /ɨ/ never occurs in a stressed syllable and is always short.

(5) Short vowels other than /ɨ/ never occur word-finally. The few exceptions are particles (*ni, ne, ha, ma*). Particles, then, appear to be subjected to a special phonotactic rule that permits short, word-final vowels other than /ɨ/. The only other forms that have full vowels word-finally are [mɨgʸépɛ] 'greeting' and [mogo] 'clear (weather)'.

(6) [ï] occasionally occurs outside stressed syllables.

(4 to 6) lead to interpreting [ɨ] as a reduced vowel. In most cases it would be a variant of /ï/; in other cases it would reflect some other vowel that has lost its distinctive quality.

(7) [e] is a positional variant of [ɛ]; as such it occurs before an overt or underlying /y/ and before palatalized consonants. It is found elsewhere only in Spanish loans and in the particle *ne*. [e] and [ɛ] are thus variants of a single phoneme, /e/.

The vowels can be set up as follows:

i	ï	u		i·	ï·	u·		i:	ï:	u:
e	ɨ	o		e·		o·		e:		o:
	a				a·				a:	

(These are the symbols used in the representations in Part Two)

Syllable nuclei:
-V-, -V·-, -V:-, -V?-, -V·?-, -V!-, -V?V-, -Vh-

These are the nuclei as represented in the source. -V?V- is for practical reasons rendered -V"- in this work. The morphophonemic rules below demonstrate that -V·- is not needed on the levels of intermediate and high abstraction. The remaining nuclei in their original representation sometimes figure as input to these rules, but in an alternative interpretation, the nuclei could be represented as in Table 2.9.

The analysis suggested in Table 2.9 would make some of the rules simpler or more adequate and cast new light on the statement of quantitative ablaut. This analysis is not carried through for practical reasons: the same sort of analysis would be needed for all Mixean languages before comparative statements could be made and such a goal is not obtainable at present.

Table 2.9. An Analysis of Gu Syllable Nuclei

Part of Peak	Peak	Edge of Peak	Analyzed as
	V	< =	-V-
	V	h < =	-Vh-
	VV	< =	-V:-
	V	? < =	-V?-
	VV	? < =	-V·?-
?	VV	< =	-V"-

The source operates with yet another glottal element for which a nonstandard symbol was devised; this symbol is here given as "!." I am not in any position to give an articulatory description, since such a description was not communicated to me. After the discovery that -V!- represents the neutralization of -V?- and -V·?- in a specific environment, however, the phonologic status has been clarified and phonetic comments made insignificant.

Classes of ablauting syllable nuclei:

There are four classes of verbs having nuclei which alternate morphologically. Although numbered according to historical principles they are set up on synchronic grounds alone. These nuclei form input to the morphophonemic rules below.

	BASIC	ALTERNATE
1.	-V·?	-V:-
2.	-V:h-	-V"-
3-4.	-V?-	-V"-
5.	-Vh-	-V-

Consonants:

For all consonants there are tokens which exhibit a fortis-lenis opposition. This opposition is, however, only relevant to the rhymes of stressed syllables, so fortis consonants only appear following the stressed syllable nuclei V· and V.

Classes of consonants that behave distinctly in phonological rules are stops, the sibilant, nasals, glides /w,y/, the glottal stop, and /h/. Palatalization neither feeds nor bleeds any rules but those which have to do with palatalization.

[-vc, -pal, -tns]	p̲	t	š̲	c	k̲				h̲	?
[-vc, -pal, +tns]	p̄	t	š̄	c̄	k			y̱	w̥	h
[-vc, +pal, -tns]	pʸ	t̲ʸ	šʸ	č	kʸ				h̲ʸ	
[-vc, +pal, +tns]	p̄ʸ	t̄ʸ	š̄ʸ	č̄	kʸ				hʸ	
[+vc, -pal, -tns]	b	d	ž	z̩	g	m	n	y	w	
[+vc, +pal, -tns]	bʸ	dʸ	žʸ	j	gʸ	mʸ	nʸ	yʸ	wʸ	

Add to these the phonemes /l, r, rr/ (alveolar approximant, alveolar tap, alveolar trill). These approximants occur in Spanish loans and in a few native words. /l r/ may follow /k/ in initial clusters.

/ẙ w̥/ have been characterized as unvoiced rather than by assigning the feature [+spread] to them, since this would inexpediently associate them more closely with /h/ than with /w y/ with which they are identical on the more abstract level.

It will be shown that an abstract analysis can be made whereby voiceless glides and the features [pal] and [tns] are done away with so that the inventory of consonants is reduced to /p b t d š ž c ʐ k g m n l r rr y w h ʔ/. The voicing of stops is usually predictable, but it is expected that there may a few examples of CVTVC roots where this is not so (T=any oral stop).

Vowels:	i	i·	i:	e	e·	e:	ɨ	ï	ï·	ï:	a	a·	a:	u	u·	u:	o	o·	o:
high	+	+	+	−	−	−	−	+	+	+	−	−	−	+	+	+	−	−	−
low	−	−	−	−	−	−	−	−	−	−	+	+	+	−	−	−	+	+	+
back	−	−	−	−	−	−	+	+	+	+	+	+	+	+	+	+	+	+	+
round	−	−	−	−	−	−	−	−	−	−	−	−	−	+	+	+	+	+	+
1 tns	−	+	−	−	+	−	−	−	+	−	−	+	−	−	+	−	−	+	−
2 tns	−	−	+	−	−	+	−	−	−	+	−	−	+	−	−	+	−	−	+

It will be shown that the inventory of vowels can be reduced to
/i i: e e: ï ï: ɨ a a: u u: o o:/

Ordered morphophonemic rules

(2.6.2.1)   w → w̥/h__{V, #}
"/w/ is devoiced between /h/ and a short vowel or word boundary."

(2.6.2.2)   V → V:/__hC$_{[+son]}$T
"Vowels are lengthened before the sequence of /h/+sonorant+stop." Verb roots affected by this rule when inflected in the independent incompletive are, by analogy, carried over to the completive inflection.

(2.6.2.3)   Vh → V:/__C$_{[+son]}$$
"/h/ following short vowels is replaced with vowel length before single sonorants."

(2.6.2.4)   V́:hC → V́:C̄
"Consonants become fortis following the sequence of a long, stressed vowel and /h/, and /h/ is subsequently deleted."

(2.6.2.5) $\acute{V}C \sim \acute{V}\bar{C}/\_\#$
"Consonants become fortis word-finally following short, stressed vowels."

(2.6.2.6) $h \rightarrow \emptyset/\_Y+$
"/h/ is deleted before the sequence of a glide and a morpheme boundary."

(2.6.2.7) $\{V\cdot?, V?\} \rightarrow V!/\_\{š, m, n, w, y\}$
"Before /š m n w y/, the opposition between -V·?- and -V?- is neutralized." Before lenis obstruents, V? and V·? do not change. These nuclei are not found before fortis stops since only the nuclei -V- and -V·- may appear in this environment.

(2.6.2.8) $C (\neq?) \rightarrow C^y/y\_$
"Any consonant other than /?/ is palatalized following /y/."

(2.6.2.9) $y \rightarrow \emptyset/\_C^y$
"/y/ is deleted before a palatalized consonant."

(2.6.2.10) $Y \rightarrow \emptyset/\_+p$
"Voiced glides (fortis as well as lenis) are deleted before the morpheme -*p*."

(2.6.2.11) $š, š^y, m, m^y, n, n^y, w, w^y, y \rightarrow [+tns]/V!\_$
"/š m n w y/ and their palatalized counterparts become tense following -V!-."

(2.6.2.12) $p, k \rightarrow \emptyset/V(\cdot)?\_š$
"/p k/ are deleted between a glottal stop and /š/." This rule must not feed (2.6.2.7), which is why is it ordered later. The only way of knowing that /p k/ are the consonants forming the input to (2.6.2.12) is by inference from phonotactics: /p k/ are the only consonants to precede /š/ morpheme-finally.

(2.6.2.13) $w \rightarrow y/V"\_\#$
Condition: Class [3/4] verbs only.

(2.6.2.14) $T_i \rightarrow \emptyset /\_\_T_i$
"Like stops are degeminated."

(2.6.2.15) $t, k \rightarrow \emptyset /\{?, h\}\_\_p$
"/t k/ are deleted between /?/ or /h/ and /p/."

(2.6.2.16) $C (\neq ?) \rightarrow C^y\_\_y$
"Consonants other than /?/ are palatalized preceding /y/."

(2.6.2.17) $y \rightarrow \emptyset /\{C^y, y\}\_\_$
"/y/ is deleted following a palatalized consonant or /y/."

(2.6.2.18)   Place assimilation of /n/
"/n/ assimilates to the point of articulation of a following oral stop."

(2.6.2.19) $C_{[-son]} \rightarrow [+vc] \quad /N\_\_V$
$$/ V(")\_\_(?)V$$
"Obstruents are voiced following nasals and intervocalically."

(2.6.2.20) $hc \rightarrow s/\_\_p$
Optional (e.g., [nahcpa:dǐ"w] ~ [naspa:dǐ"w])

(2.6.2.21) $C \rightarrow C^y /\_\_+p^y$
"Any consonant is palatalized before *-p^y* (which is a morpheme of the verbal inflection)."

(2.6.2.22) $p^y \rightarrow p/C^y_{[-son]}+\_\_$
"/p^y/ loses its palatalization following obstruents palatalized according to the preceding rule (it is retained following /m^y n^y/)."

(2.6.2.23) $t^y, š^y \rightarrow [+dental]$
"/š/ (obligatorily) and /t/ (optionally) are dentalized when palatalized."
The feature [+dental] is devised ad hoc to describe this process which operates on the SRs (i.e., it is just an indication of pronunciation).

(2.6.2.24) $\acute{V}(:) \rightarrow \acute{V}(:):/\_\_C_{[-tns]}\$$
"Any stressed vowel acquires an extra mora before a syllable-final lenis consonant." (Rule P) Convert "V," "V:," and "V::" to, respectively,

"V," "V·," and "V:" after applying this rule. The stressed vowels of Spanish loans also have the duration of V· (middle length).

Discussion:

The analysis given has the advantage of reducing the phonemic inventory drastically. The consonantal tense opposition and the feature [pal] as well as devoiced glides are done away with on the most abstract level by simple rules, and the only addition is the insertion of an underlying /h/ in certain positions. On the intermediate level there are only two degrees of vowel length, since the "middle length" of the SRs here is a function of the combination of a long vowel and a tense consonant. On the level that matches the forms cited in the source, middle length is installed (without removing the fortis quality from the representations) and voicing and dentalization enter into the SRs.

The motivation for these rules is purely synchronic and it only so happens that the twenty-odd ordered rules map the way that the phonology of the dialect in all recoverable aspects is derived historically. In some respects the input closely resembles pM, in other respects the underlying representations are more like the more immediate ancestor, pOM, and in still other respects it takes us no further back than LM. The equivalent of 2.6.2.24 was suggested by Nordell (p.c.) for those MM and LM dialects that have three vowel lengths; this suggestion initially inspired the present analysis.

Some examples of derivations:

The devoicing of /w/ in the SRs of /ʔïhw/ and /ma:hw/ is the main reason why it is true to say that the derivation in its entirety is synchronically motivated. The other forms are chosen so as to provide examples of crucial aspects of the rule system.

	UR	SR	By rule (2.6.__)
1.	/ʔïhw/	ʔïẉ[17]	1, 4
2.	/y+to·ʔk+py/	tʸo·ʔpʸ	8, 9, 15, 16, 17
3.	/y+hɨ·ʔn+py/	hʸɨ!m̄pʸ	7, 8, 9, 11
4.	/yoʔy+p/	yo!pʸ	7, 8, 9, 10
5.	/yuhw+p/	yu:p	2, 6, 10
6.	/yuhw/	yu·ẉ[15]	1, 3
7.	/mahw+p/	ma:p	2, 6, 10
8.	/mahw/	ma·w̄[15]	1, 3
9.	/y+yehm+py/	ye·m̄pʸ	2, 4, 16, 17

For glosses see footnote.[18]

Stress:

Word stress in URs is assigned to the rightmost heavy syllable. A heavy syllable is defined as any syllable containing -V·ʔ-, -Vʔ-, -Vh-, or -V:-. This stress remains fixed throughout the derivation of the SRs. Word stress in the SRs, then, is assigned to the rightmost heavy syllable. A heavy syllable is now defined as any syllable which does not end in a plain short vowel or in a plain short vowel plus a lenis consonant. The first person pronominal enclitic is not stressed.

Borrowings from Spanish retain the stress pattern of the donor language when they are not incorporated into the word.

Sentence stress may probably override word stress in the sense that some words do not receive stress. A case in point would be /pïn/ [pīn] 'who,' which must not receive stress since the SR would otherwise turn out as *pï·n̄*.

---

[17] Nordell (1990) either only notes that /w/ is fortis or only notes that it is devoiced, when in fact it is in all likelihood both fortis and devoiced. Presumably this is so because it was not technically possible to combine a subscript circle with a subscript quotation mark, the symbols for, respectively, "devoiced" and "fortis." All consonants (including /y/) in the same position in this class of verbs turn out [+tns], so we expect the final consonant in the forms to which this note is attached to also be [+tns].

[18] Glosses: 2. '3p sells it (TR, INDEP)'; 3. '3p swallows (TR, INDEP)'; 4. '3p walks (INTR, INDEP)'; 5. '3p clears land (INTR, INDEP)'; 6. '3p cleared land (INTR, DEP)'; 7. '3p sleeps (INTR, INDEP)'; 8. '3p slept (INTR, DEP)'; 9. '3p fans (TR, INDEP)'.

2.7. OLUTA POPOLUCA

Consonants: *Vowels:*

p	t	c	č	k	ʔ		i	ɨ	u
v	s		š		h		e	a	o
m	n								
	rr,r							V:	
	l								
w			y						

Syllable nuclei:
-V-, -Vh-, -Vʔ-, V:

Additional phonemes that only occur in loans from Spanish:
/b, d, g, f, w, r, rr/, where /d/ is lenis.

Distributional constraints:
/l/ is rare in native words and occurs mostly in onomatopoiec words.
/w/ only occurs intervocalically or after an unvoiced consonant.

Morphophonemics (after Clark 1981: 112-115)

(2.7.1)   (h)ɨ → Ø/__+C
"Final /ɨ/ or /hɨ/ in nouns goes to zero under compounding with a consonant-initial noun." This rule is not without exceptions, since it only affects original monosyllabic lexemes that have added /ɨ/ as a late innovation.

(2.7.2)   -ta → Ø/__+C
"Final -*ta* goes to zero under compounding with a consonant-initial noun." For example, *kɨʔšta* 'foot' + *hipɨ* 'nose' → *kɨʔšhipɨ* 'toe'; *tuʔsta* 'tail' + *pakɨ* 'bone' → *tuʔspakɨ* 'young of the fer-de-lance snake'.

(2.7.3)   V: → V/__+ʔ
"A long vowel is shortened before a glottal-initial morpheme."

(2.7.4)   V́' → V́'/__C+$

"When polysyllabic nonverbs, in which there is an automatic check in the last syllable, are followed by another morpheme (i.e., a syllable), the glottal check is lost."

(2.7.5)   CV?V'C → CV?C/__+$
"CV?V'C structures likewise lose the glottal check under composition and are shortened."

(2.7.6)   CV?Vh → CVh   (optional)
"Optional reduction of CV?Vh structures during normal speech."

(2.7.7)   Vw → V:/__+p
"Loss of /w/ with compensatory lengthening before a morpheme with initial /p/."

(2.7.8)   w → m/__+n
"/w/ goes to /m/ under composition with a morpheme with initial /n/."

(2.7.9)   n → Ø/__{v,y}

(2.7.10) C_1 → Ø/__C_1 , C_1 = {p t k n h ?}

(2.7.11)   n → m/__p

(2.7.12)   m → n/__k   (especially in fast speech)

(2.7.13) V_1V_1 → V:

(2.7.14) V_1 → Ø/__V_1?

(2.7.15) V_2(:) → V_1/V_1C_0__{n,m}
             V_2(:) → V_1/V_1C_0{n,m}__
"An affix containing a nasal assumes the quality of the preceding vowel; if the vowel undergoing this harmony was long, it is shortened" (See Clark 1981: 115 for examples.)

(2.7.16)   c → s/__{C,#}
Condition: native words only

(2.7.17)   Addition of -*k*/-*ak*
"-*k*/-*ak* are sometimes added to 'some words,' -*k* following vowels, -*ak* following consonants." This affix, the function of which is left unexplained, does not cause a change in the accent.

Notes to Clark's presentation:
   It is sometimes difficult to know if the affix -*ak*/-*k* is lexicalized or just appears to be so from Clark's vocabulary. A case in point would be *ma:ca?a'k* 'star' (< pMZ *ma:ca?((a)k)*), which does not have a /k/ in any other MZ language. Cases such as these can only be treated diachronically.

2.8. SAYULA POPOLUCA

Consonants:						*Vowels:*		
p	t	c	č	k	?	i	i	u
b	d			g		e	a	o
		s	š		h			
m	n					V:		
	r					V́		
w			y					

Additional phonemes that only occur in loans from Spanish:
/f, v, d, rr/, where /v/ and /d/ are lenis and /rr/ a vibrant.

Distributional constraints: /s/ is rare; /b, d, g/ occur only intervocalically in native words.

Free alternation: /d/ and /r/ alternate freely (?) intervocalically.

Morphophonemics (following Kaufman 1963: 21, a restatement of Clark 1961)

In rules 2.8.6, 2.8.10, 2.8.11 I have made additions; rules are not ordered.

(2.8.1)   h → Ø/{š,CC}__

(2.8.2)   VCh → VhC (metathesis; C ≠ /š/)

(2.8.3)   CVhC → CVC in bound constructions (with exceptions)

(2.8.4) C_i → h/__C_i when C_i = /p t c k/
            → Ø/__C_i when C1 = /? š h m n w/ (but see 2.8.5)

(2.8.5)   n → y/n__ when /n/ is the final segment of a person marker

(2.8.6)   c → č/{i,e}(n)__, __{i,e}

(2.8.7)   p, t, k → [+voiced]/{m,n,w,y}__ (a generalization, not a rule)

(2.8.8)   k → g/V__V

(2.8.9)   /m n/ are homorganic with following consonants

(2.8.10)   a. V → V:/w{p, m}
            b. w → Ø/__{p, m}

(2.8.11)   a → Ø/{a, u, i}__
            → ɨ/__C(C)ɨ

Some verb roots alternate CVN~CV?N or CV:T~CV?T (N = a sonorant or zero, T = an obstruent). This is a morphologically conditioned alternation (ablaut).

2.9. TAPACHULTECO

According to Kaufman (1963: 24), "Tapachulteco probably had the following phonetic segments:"

Consonants:						Vowels:		
p	t	ts	tš	k	?	i	ɨ	u
b	d			g		e	a	o
		s	š		h			
m	n					V́		
w			y					

"[p] and [b], [t] and [d], [k] and [g], [s] and [š] were probably in free variation, and [ts] and [tš] probably in conditioned variation. No inferences can be made about vowel length. No morphophonemic statements can be attempted. [b], [d], [g] may be merely the sporadic Teutonic rendering of voiceless unaspirated stops, and voiced stops may therefore not even have been present" (Kaufman 1963: 24).

CHAPTER 3

Proto-Mixe-Zoquean

3.1. PMZ PHONOLOGICAL SYSTEM

Consonants: *Vowels:*

*p	*t	*c	*k	*?		*i	*ɨ	*u
	*s						*e	*o
*m	*n						*a	
*w	*y			*h	*V:			

1. */p t k/ have nonpredictable voiced allophones intervocalically in some CVCVC roots in Mixean languages. In no cases do the languages agree as to which roots are involved, however. Neither is it possible to find minimal pairs. Therefore no systematic voiced stop phonemes are set up.

2. A marginal phoneme /l/ occurs in probably all MZ languages. One item containing /l/ appears in pOM and another one in pMZ, but these may be onomatopoeic.

Syllable nuclei: V, Vh, V?, V:, V:?, V?V

The notion of complex nuclei is useful in treating the daughter languages and their most immediate ancestors; for earlier stages of pMZ, however, the elements *h and *? can be treated as parts of the onset and/or coda. The vowels of the sequence -V?V- would in this interpretation belong to two different syllables.

The following morpheme-final *clusters* are allowed: *ps, *ks, *p?, *t?, *c?, *k?, *s?, *h?, *m?, *n?, *w?, *y?.

Only following long vowels are all the sequences found. *s?, *h?, and *y? are not found following short vowels.

Primary Stress (PS):

Assign PS to the rightmost heavy syllable in the word string if any such syllables are present. (A heavy syllable contains V:, V:?, V?, or Vh as its nucleus.) Or else assign PS to the rightmost root. If that root is a polysyllabic nonverb, it receives stress on its penultimate syllable; if it is a polysyllabic verb it receives stress on its last syllable.

There may be a few inherently stressed suffixes that override this pattern because they have been recently grammaticalized.

3.2. VERB PHONOLOGY

Table 3.1. displays the regular correspondences of verb root canonical forms. The numbers correspond to Table 4.1 in the next chapter, where descendant Mixean canons are specified.

The CC cluster in [6] to [8] consists of either one of the noncoronal obstruents /p k/ plus the coronal obstruent /s/. Only in [5] does /?/ occur in the second C-slot. /h/ may take that position in [2a] and [5]. N = sonorant, T = nonsonorant.

Table 3.1

	pZ		pMZ		pM
[1]	*CV?C	<	*CV:?C	>	*CV:?C
[2a]	*CVT	<	*CV:T?	>	*CV:C~CV?C
[2b]	*CVN	<	*CV:N?	>	*CVN~CV?N
[3]	*CV?C	<	*CV?C	>	*CV?C
[4]	*CVC	<	*CVC?	>	*CV?C
[5]	*CVC	<	*CVC	>	*CVC
[6]	*CV?CC	<	*CV:?CC	>	*CV:?CC
[7]	*CV?CC	<	*CV?CC	>	*CV?CC
[8]	*CVCC	<	*CVCC	>	*CVCC
[9]	*CVCVC	<	*CVCVC	>	*CVCVC

Algebraically speaking, -V:?- has the value of -V:-, since these two nucleus types are in complementary distribution. We may surmise that preproto-MZ -V:- developed a glottal check when it occurred in the verb root. By dissimilation this was hindered before C?.

In common MZ times, this allophonic rule became phonologized, since postconsonantal /ʔ/ was dropped except word-finally and before vowel-initial suffixes, in which positions it metathesized into preconsonantal position. At the time when two daughter languages emerged distinctly, one, pZ, had lost all traces of postconsonantal /ʔ/, whereas the other, pM, had the following reflexes:

Table 3.2

	pM		pMZ
[2a]	*CV:T ~ CVʔT	<	*CV:Tʔ
[2b]	*CVN ~ CVʔN	<	*CV:Nʔ
[4]	*CVʔC	<	*CVCʔ

The pM reflex of [4] does not alternate CVC ~ CVʔC, since metathesized /ʔ/ of these roots containing short vowels spread throughout the paradigm, with the effect that CVʔC everywhere analogically replaced CVC. [2], however, retained the alternation. This is the origin of the first ablaut in Mixean (later ablauts will be treated in the next chapter and in 5.3). Table 3.2 postulates that vowels were shortened before sonorants in pM. Their length in pM can be determined from OM evidence. Their length in pMZ is determined on the evidence of such forms as pMZ *sowʔ 'to peck, punch' vs. pMZ *ci:wʔ 'to bathe'. These forms have different types of reflexes and should correspondingly represent different canons.

Since /ʔ/ can follow any consonant except /ʔ/, it is analyzed as a separate phoneme. Choosing the option within this framework of posing a whole set of glottalized consonants is both unnecesary and typologically untenable.

An alternative overall view would be to posit a series of glottalized consonants and the canons [1] CV:ʔC, [2] CV:C, [3] CVʔC, [4] CVC' (the rest as above). The theory of pre-pMZ **V: > pMZ *V:ʔ would have to be dismissed, as would the symmetry of the system since there would be no cases of CV:C'. This alternative view may be more realistic, but it is neither simpler nor any more structurally adequate. In fact we would have to commit ourselves to an incomplete set of glottalized consonants /p' t' c' k' m' n' y' w'/ (/m'/ and /y'/ are added on the evidence from nonverbs). Further, a series of glottalized stop phonemes would be expected to be distributed evenly just as any other phoneme class, and at present no evidence can be given for any occurrence outside of the environment discussed here.

To substantiate the points made above, all pMZ representatives of the crucial types [1] to [4] are now specified. Stars are omitted.

[1]   *CV:?C*
he:?p, ?i:?p, ti:?p, hu:?t, pi:?t, yo:?t, ki:?t, mo:?t, wi:?t, po:?t, ?i:?c, ?o:?c, so:?c, ke:?c, ko:?c, me:?c, mu:?c, ?e:?k, ce:?k, mu:?k, su:?k, wo:?k, pi:?k, yu:?k, ci:?, hu:?m, yu:?m, ho:?m, pi:?n, ce:?n, te:?n, hi:?n, hu:?n, co:?n, ho:?s, wo:?s, ki:?s, si:?w, he:?y

[2]   *CV:C?*
ni:p?, pe:t?, pu:c?, ti:c?, si:k?, (yak-)co:k?, ta:k?, ke:k?, mi:k?, ma:k?, ca:m?, ti:n?, ci:s?, ce:s?, me:s?, ha:s?, ku:s?, su:s?, so:s?, me:h?, ma:h?, pa:h?, mu:h?, su:h?, yu:h?, ci:w?, ke:w?, ki:w?, hi:y?, ki:y?, ca:y?, ha:y?, po:y?

[3]   *CV?C*
ye?p, mu?t, ho?t, pi?c, cu?c, ka?c, ma?c, mo?c, ta?c, me?k, ho?k, to?k, ka?k, ne?m, pa?m, so?m, pe?n, ta?n, ho?n, hu?s, ni?s, nu?s, ne?w, si?w, pu?w, yo?y

[4]   *CVC?*
hup?, cat?, kic?, woc?, huk?, nek?, mon?, sow?

Semantic Correlates to *CV^CC Canons

Roots of the structure CV^CC are the only ones for which a correlate between expression and content can be established. The *CV:?CC class roughly correlates with the meaning 'breaking and penetration of a surface'; the *CVCC class, with 'pointed intrusion upon an object'; and the *CV?CC class, with 'the meeting of two uniform objects'. This should be borne in mind when external relationships are tested.

A Scenario for the Rise of -p/ks

Speculating on why precisely *-ps-* and *-ks-* should be the only permitted clusters in pMZ morphemes is bound to be indecisive. I will mention just one hypothesis. *-ps* and *-ks* could have arisen from the same sequence, namely -kʷVs-. The roundedness of V would determine whether the labiovelar fell out as *p* or *k*. This implies either various roots with different vowels or, more interestingly, a suffix containing a vowel harmonizing with the backness of the preceding vowel. If this is so, there ought to be a significant pattern in the statistical frequence of each of the six vowels found before *-ps* and *-ks*. This is not so. It can be attributed to developments in the vowel system or to the continuous productivity of CV^CC roots. In any case, internal reconstruction must end here. Looking around for external relations is the only way to proceed with the matter. Even here I have had only limited success. There is, however, an interesting possible cognate to pM **hiʔkš* 'to suffocate' (HI#007) in the proto-Uto-Aztecan form **hikʷi(si)* 'to breathe' as reconstructed by Voegelin, Voegelin, and Hale (1962). Now, a relationship between Mixe-Zoquean and Uto-Aztecan is not generally accepted or even generally thought of. The way to go about establishing such a relationship would be to reconsider the Macro-Penutian phylum (the relatedness of Penutian, Sahaptian, Aztec-Tanoan, Zuni, Kiowa, Mayan, and Totonac) proposed by Whorf in 1935 and include Mixe-Zoquean in that phylum. I have made a small beginning (fc-d).

A Note on the Disyllables

*CVCVC is the only pMZ disyllabic canon for which there is more than one representative. The three representatives are **picɨm* 'to go out', **tinin* 'to crackle', and **tokoy* 'to lose'. There is, however, in-dications that more canons were in fact represented. pMZ **cɨ:nay* 'to sit down' contains a long vowel; but it is the only item of its sort, and it looks derived insofar as it does not contain at least two identical seg-ments as underived disyllables usually do. In Mixean there are the items pM **ʔama:ʔy* 'to look after' and pOM **wanahn ~ wana"n* 'to say', which point to the possibility that the protolanguage had different types, the last syllable of which would be identical in structure to one of the Class [1] to [5] roots, so that these types could accordingly be grouped into five different classes. *CVCVC is, however, positively the best established canon and continues to be the one most frequently represented in Mixean (cf. pOM *mopohp ~ mopop* 'to flap', pOM *šukuhk ~ šukuk* 'to make tortillas', pM *timam* 'to swell').

Progress Made in the Understanding of pMZ Verb Roots

A comparison between Kaufman's (1963: 36-36, 2253) and my own reconstructions yields the following:

Class	TK	SW
[1]	(not reconstructed)	*CV:?C
[2]	*CV:C	*CV:C?
[3]	*CV?C	*CV?C
[4]	(not reconstructed)	*CVC?
[5]	*CVC (and *CVh)	*CVC
[6]	(not reconstructed)	*CV:?CC
[7]	*CV?C(s)	*CV?CC
[8]	*CVCs	*CVCC
[9]	*CVCVC	*CVCVC

Kaufman has two examples which he reconstructs CV·?C. One is *pa·?t,* which is based on irregular correspondences with some adherence to my *CV:?C pattern (see Part Two, PA#055 pMZ *pa:?t* [?] (vt) 'to find'), another is *me·?s* which patterns not as a Class [2] but as a Class [1] root (see Part Two, ME#016 pMZ *me:s?* (vi, vt) 'to apply to a surface (e.g., clothes, cloth, mud)'. Kaufman's *CV?C(s) is set up on two false correspondences: pZ *mɨ?k* 'to extract' is not related to pMZ *mɨ?ks* 'to squeeze, extract', although they are close in meaning and form, and *he?k(s)* is probably made out of a pZ and a pM set which has incompatible meanings (cf. Part Two, HE#009, HE#011) (Kaufman does not provide the data on which his canons are based). Thus, two of Kaufman's canons are rather ill-founded; further, Kaufman has nothing corresponding to class [4] and [6] roots. Finally, Kaufman does not deal with the origin of alternation in the Mixean verb.

3.3. pMZ NONVERB CANONS

Special symbols:
N = a nasal; T = an obstruent; E = a front vowel; A = a back vowel

Major Canons

The following table displays canons of underived nonverbs for which
there is more than one example. They are ordered according to frequency. There are forty examples of CVCV and two of each of the
canons CVhCV, CVC?, CV:CCVC, and CV:CVCVC. CV^CV(k) is
a disyllable containing a final k-mobile. *(k), or k-mobile, occurs
mostly in OIP forms, where it may be a remnant of some suffix
(suffixes in -*Vk* abound in OIP), for instance a directional suffix.
k-mobile also occurs in a few nouns in some OM dialects, seemingly
without motivation.

CVCV	CV:CVC	CV?CV	CVhCV
CVC	CV^CV(k)	CV	CVC?
CVCVC	CV?C	CVCVCV	CV:CCVC
CV:CV	CVCCVC	CV?CVC	CV:CVCVC
CV:C	CVC?V	CV?CCVC	

Representatives

CVCV (C₂ = /p t c k m n s h w y/)   (40 examples)

CVCV (C_2 = /p t c k m n s h w y/)   (40 examples)
*hɨp(ɨ) (n) 'nose'; **kɨpi* (n) 'tree, wood'; **kape* (n) 'type of bamboo';
*?apu (n) 'grandfather'; **tata* (n) 'father'; **mici* (pron) 'you' (sg);
*paci (n) 'lizard'; **?oko* (n) 'grandmother'; **?uku* (n) 'agouti'; **taka*
(n) 'dog'; **ciku* (n) 'coati'; **hoko* (n) 'smoke'; **pakV* (adj) 'old
(thing)'; **noki* (n) 'paper'; **tuka* (n) 'tortoise'; **tuku* (adj) 'old (thing)';
*cima (n) 'bowl made out of a gourd'; **kuma* (n) 'type of palm';
*kumu (n) 'worm'; **mumu* (adj) 'everything'; **namV* (adj) 'new';
*home (adj) 'new'; **kama* (n) 'cornfield'; **kunu* (n) 'Montezuma
oropendola'; **mɨn(i)* (n) 'sweet potato'; **nana* (n) 'mother'; **sis(i)* (n)
'meat'; **pisi* (n) 'yucca'; **cas(i)* (n) 'crayfish'; **kahi* (adj) 'narrow,
square'; **mɨha* (adj) 'greater, big'; **soho* (n) 'oak'; **?aha* (n) 'canoe';

*?aha (n) 'cedar'; **cehe* (n) 'carpenter'; **pɨhi* (adj) 'long'; **kowa* (n) 'drum'; **koya* (n) 'rabbit'; **?oyV* (adj, adv) 'good, well'; **meya* (n) 'sea'

CVC (C₂ = /t k ? m n s h w y/)   (34 examples)
*?it (n) 'place'; **sak-...* (n) 'armpit'; **pɨk* (n) 'skin, feather'; **tɨk* (n) 'house'; **?ak* (n) 'bark, skin'; **?ok* (n) 'molar tooth'; **pak* (n) 'bone'; **kuk* (n?) 'middle'; **sɨk* (n) 'bean'; **yɨ?* (dem pron) 'this'; **kɨ?* (n) 'hand, arm'; **tɨm* (n) 'fruit'; **ham* (n) 'lime'; **hem* (loc adv) 'there'; **pɨn* (n) 'man'; **cin* (n) 'pitchpine'; **hon* (n) 'bird'; **can-can* (adj) 'to have a bad smell of fish'; **tin* (n) 'excrement'; **win* (n) 'eye'; **?us* (n) 'tremor'; **kɨs* (n) 'body'; **cus* (adj) 'green (unripe)'; **sah* (n) 'armful'; **kɨh* (n) 'peal'; **puh* (n) 'seed'; **?aw* (n) 'mouth'; **sɨw* (n) 'fiesta, name, sun'; **may* (adj, adv) 'much'; **?ay* (n) 'leaf'; **coy* (n) 'remedy, medicine'; **puy* (n) 'thigh'; **kuy* (n) 'tree, wood'; **cay* (n) 'rope'

CVCVC (C₂ = /p c k ? m n s h w y/)   (33 examples)
*capac (adj) 'red'; **cipin* (n) 'wart'; **?apit* (n) 'thorn'; **hepey* (n) 'species of plant or tree'; **kapay* (n) 'sister-in-law of man, brother-in-law of woman'; **mucVC* (adj) 'little'; **wece(w)* (n) 'termite'; **kacu(c)* (adj) 'bitter'; **pakVk* (n) 'cold'; **pokok* (n) 'cotton tree'; **tak(us)* (n) 'walking stick'; **cikin* (adj) 'spotted'; **hokos* (adj) 'tepid'; **yɨk(ɨk)* (adj) 'black'; **pok(ok)* (n) 'gourd'; **nak(Vk)* (n) 'frog, toad'; **sake(s)* (n) 'mother-, daughter-in-law of woman'; **mɨ?ut* (n) 'son-in-law'; **hemec* (adj) 'heavy'; **camam* (n) 'a kind of edible green'; **kom(om)* (n) 'house pole'; **wonon* (n) 'partridge'; **panac* (adj) 'slippery'; **manik* (n) 'night humidity'; **manɨk* (n) 'son'; **?oso(s)* (n) 'sweat'; **pos ∼ posos ∼ pohos* (n) 'guava'; **maháw* (n) 'strength'; **waha(w)* (n) 'horn'; **pahak* (n, adj) 'sweet'; **?awin* (n) 'elder brother of woman'; **nawin* (n) 'agave fiber'; **hayáw* (n) 'man'

CV:CV (C₂ = /p t c k m n s h w y/)   (22 examples)
*muːtu (n) 'squirrel'; **puːci* (n) 'waste'; **?uːci* (n) 'younger brother or sister'; **?aːka* (n) 'cheek, edge'; **?ɨːki* (n) 'pricklenut tree'; **saːka* (n) 'shell'; **naːka* (n) 'various'; **toːki* (n) 'iguana'; **?uːma* (n) 'dumb'; **?aːme* (n) 'year'; **poːm(o)* (n) 'incense'; **caːne* (n) 'descendants'; **ciːnu* (n) 'honey'; **tuːni* (n) 'type of fruit resembling the plum'; **kaːna* (n) 'salt'; **?eːsi* (n) 'crab'; **tɨːsi* (n) 'bat'; **heːhe* (n)

'mosquito'; *ca:wi* (n) 'monkey'; *ya(:)wa* (adj) 'tender'; *ni:wi* (n) 'chili pepper'; *wɨ:yi* (n) 'mange'

CV:C (C$_2$ = /c k ? s h/) (15 examples)

pa:c (n) 'skunk'; *ni:c* (n) 'armadillo'; *to:c* (n) 'tongue'; *tɨ:c* (n) 'tooth'; *cu:k* (n) 'rat, mouse'; *?o:k* (n) 'bottom'; *mo:k* (n) 'corn'; *mo:k* (n) 'pimple'; *yu:?* (n) 'hunger'; *hɨ:?* (part) 'yes'; *ca:?* (n) 'stone'; *cu:?* (n) 'night'; *nɨ:?* (n) 'water'; *na:s* (n) 'earth'; *tu:h* (n) 'rain'

CV:CVC (C$_2$ = /p c k s h w y/) (9 examples)

hɨ:pak (n) 'corncob'; *ta:cɨk* (n) 'ear'; *tɨ:cɨC* (n) 'iguana'; *co:koy* (n) 'heart'; *ma:san* (n) 'mana'; *?u:suk* (n) 'mosquito'; *ká:haw* (n) 'wild feline'; *?a:wat* (n) 'louse'; *?o:yo(?)* (n) 'shrimp'

CV^CV(k) (C$_2$ = /m n s h/) (8 examples)

tome(k) (adv) 'close'; *kono(k)* (adj) 'short'; *?unV(k)* (n) 'child'; *we:?nV(k)* (n) 'wasp'; *cisi(k)* (n) 'bedbug'; *koso(k)* (n) 'knee'; *cusu(k)* (adj) 'green'; *pɨhi(k)* (n) 'flower'

CV?C (C$_2$ = /c k s w y/) (6 examples)

tu?c(ta) (n) 'tail'; *tɨ?c* (adj) 'dry, thin'; *yo?k(-tu)* (n) 'neck'; *ce?s* (n) 'corn granary'; *ke?w* (n) 'spurge nettle'; *wa(?)y* (n) 'hair'

CVCCVC (6 examples)

?uspin (n) 'alligator'; *?ohyah* (n) 'woman's sister-in-law'; *pistɨk* (n) 'flea'; *pistin* (n) 'ceiba, kapok tree'; *cikwiC* (n) 'bromeliad'; *liklik* (n) 'American kestrel'

CVC?V (C$_2$ = /p k y/) (5 examples)

cɨp?V (n) 'edible green'; *cok?a* (n) 'shaman'; *kok?e* (n) 'fish'; *pok?i* (n) 'heel'; *poy?a* (n) 'moon; month'

CV?CV (C$_2$ = /p c m y/) (5 examples)

pu?pu (n) 'intestines'; *nu?pu* (n) 'buzzard'; *pu?c(V)* (adj) 'yellow'; *kɨ?mɨ* (adv) 'down'; *hu?yi* (n) 'coal'

CV (3 examples)

hu (part) 'question marker'; *ni* (part) 'negation'; *ti* (part) 'what?'

CVCVCV (C$_2$ = /k/)   (3 examples)
sokeCV (interj) 'greeting'; *kakawa* (n) 'cacao'; *makoko* (n) 'cockroach'

CV?CVC   (3 examples)
pu?si(s) (n) 'pieces'; *ni?pin* (n) 'blood'; *(h)a(?)y(aw)* (n) 'snook'

CV?CCVC   (3 examples)
ti(?m)pic (n) 'gopher'; *ta?c(k)V(k)* (n) 'jinicuil, inga'; *su?ksuk* (n) 'hummingbird'

CVhCV (C$_2$ = /c s/)   (2 examples)
?ihsi (n) 'trunk'; *?a(h)ci* (n) 'elder brother'

CVC? (C$_2$ = /k m/)   (2 examples)
mik? (n) 'dew'; *tam?* (adj) 'bitter'

CV:CCVC   (2 examples)
?o:kwin (n) 'reed'; *?u:syan* (adj, adv) 'a little'

CV:CVCVC   (2 examples)
si:kitiw (n) 'cicada'; *ce:wE(kV?)* (n) 'chicken, hen'

OTHERS

One syllable: *kacc* [?] (adj) 'variegated'; *he ~ he?* (pron) 'he, her'; *his...* (n) 'back'

Two syllables: *?akwa?n* (n) 'hearth'; *wi(?)yuk(s)* (n) 'kinkajou'; *?i:ci ~ ?ic* (pron) 'I'; *po:p?o?* (adj) 'white'; *cap(-hi)* (n) 'sky'; *ki(c)cu(?k)s* (n) 'fingernail'; *?aksa* (n) 'fish'; *?o:k?o:?k* (n) 'squirrel cuckoo'; *?a:?ksyi* (n) 'grackle'; *?i:?(n)ki* (n) 'jinicuil'

Three syllables: *pu?huyu* (n) 'roadrunner'; *ma:stiki* (n) 'the day before yesterday'; *suse:pe* (n) 'butterfly'; *ma:ca?((a)k)* (n) 'star'; *nuku(N(ik))* (n) 'leaf-cutter ant'; *pi:?sisi* (n) 'black-bellied tree-duck'; *tihik(ay)* (adv) 'yesterday'

Some Main Division Correspondences

pM		pMZ		pZ	Number of syllables
*CV	<	*CV	>	*CV	1
*CVN	<	*CVN	>	*CVN	
*CVhC	<	*CVC	>	*CVC	
*CV:hT	<	*CV:T	>	*CVT	
*CV?C	<	*CV?C	>	*CV?C	
*CV?CV	<	*CV?CV	>	*CV?CV	2
*CV:CV	<	*CV:CV	>	*CVCV	
*CVCV	<	*CVCV	>	*CVCV	
*CVhCV	<	*CVhCV	>	*CVCV	
*CVCVC	<	*CVCVC	>	*CVCVC	
*CV:CVC	<	*CV:CVC	>	*CVCVC	
*CVCCVC	<	*CVCCVC	>	*CVCCVC	
*CV:CVCVC	<	*CV:CVCVC	>	*CVCVCVC	3

Length is lost in pZ. pM inserts /h/ into CVC and CV:T shapes (CV:N is conspicuously absent). Zoquean loses the /h/ of CVhCV shapes.

pMZ *CV is represented by items belonging to a word class which we may call particles. The best example is pMZ *ti 'what?'. A few more examples could perhaps be found among morphological elements that have become cliticized. Another example from a lower-level node in the family tree is pM *ni 'negation'. If pOM *hɨ-m 'there' and pM *ya-m 'here' are analyzed as indicated (containing a locational suffix = pZ *-mɨ), they would belong here too. pOM *ma: 'where', pOM *ya: 'here', and pOM *ši: 'there' have long vowels, but a canon CV: is not represented in pMZ.

pM *CVN is set up to account for pM *pɨn 'who, who?' = pZ *pɨn 'man, person'. It is, however, included under the more general pMZ *CVC canon since we can account for the lack of lengthening in pOM and the absence of the expected reflexes OIP pini* and SaP pɨhn* of *pɨn by assuming that this word, functioning as a relative pronoun immediately preceding a stressed verb, did not receive sentence stress (my suggestion). Or, we can append a dummy protovowel (Kaufman 1963: 29, 2245), but we cannot deny that pOM *pɨn actually exists. Comparable cases are pOM *hɨm 'there' and pM [Veracruz] *yam 'here', which, if dating to pMZ, would have assumed the shape *CVN. The rule of /h/-insertion in pM should thus be confined to stressed monosyllables.

Examples of correspondences

pM	< pMZ		>	pZ
*pɨn	*pɨn	'who'		*pɨn (irreg. in GZ)
*ʔuhš	*ʔus	'tremor'		*ʔus (only ChZ)
*pɨhk	*pɨk	'skin, etc.'		*pɨk
*pahk	*pak	'bone'		*pak
*tɨhk	*tɨk	'house'		*tɨk
*šihk	*sɨk	'bean'		*sɨk
*cihn	*cin	'pine'		*cin
*hohn	*hon	'bird'		*hon
*hahm	*ham	'lime'		*ham
*wihn	*win	'eye'		*win 'body'
*tɨhm	*tɨm	'fruit'		*tɨm
*ʔahw	*ʔaw	'mouth'		*ʔaŋ-
*šihw	*sɨw	'fiesta, etc.'		*sɨŋ
*ʔahy	*ʔay	'leaf'		*ʔay
*cohy	*coy	'remedy, medicine'		*coy
*puhy	*puy	'thigh'		*puy
*wahy	*way	'hair'		*way
*paːhc	*paːc	'skunk'		*pac
*tɨːhc	*tɨːc	'tooth'		*tɨc
*toːhc	*toːc	'tongue'		*toc
*nɨːhc	*nɨːc	'armadillo'		*nɨc
*naːhš	*naːs	'earth'		*nas
*ceʔš	*ceʔs	'corn granary'		*ceʔs 'bed'
*cuʔci	*cuʔci	'breast of woman'		*cuʔci
*nuʔpu	*nuʔpu	'buzzard'		*nuʔpu
*ʔeːši	*ʔeːsi	'crab'		*ʔesi
*tɨːši	*tɨːsi	'bat'		*ʔtɨsi
*caːwi	*caːwi	'monkey'		*cawi
*niːwi	*niːwi	'chile'		*niwi
*ʔuːma	*ʔuːma	'dumb'		*ʔuma
*kaːna	*kaːna	'salt'		*kana

*kape	*kape	'type of bamboo'	*kape
*ʔaha	*ʔaha	'canoe'	*ʔaha
*pici	*pici	'leached corn meal'	*pici
*ʔece	*ʔece	'dance'	*ʔece
*šiši	*sis(i)	'meat'	*sis
*noki	*noki	'paper'	*noki
*tuka	*tuka	'tortoise'	*tuka
*hoko	*hoko	'smoke'	*hoko
*kama	*kama	'cornfield'	*kama
*kuma	*kuma	'type of palm'	*kuma
*kunu	*kunu	'Montezuma oropendola'	*kunu
*ʔoya	*ʔoyV	'good'	*ʔoye
*ʔohya	*ʔohya	'sister-in-law'	*ʔohya
*pahak	*pahak	'sweet'	*pahak
*hokoš	*hokos	'tepid'	*hokos
*kapay	*kapay	'sister-in-law'	*kapay
*hɨ:pak	*hɨ:pak	'corncob'	*hɨpak
*nɨʔpin	*nɨʔpin	'blood'	*nɨʔpin
*pištin	*pistin	'ceibe, kapok tree'	*pistin
*ši:kitiw	*si:kitiw	'cicada'	*sikitiŋ

Evidence for a Postconsonantal Glottal Stop

For nine nonverbal roots a postconsonantal glottal stop is reconstructed; these are *cɨpʔV (n) 'edible green', *cokʔa (n) 'shaman', *kokʔe (n) 'fish', *mɨkʔ (n) 'dew', *monʔi (num) 'measure of 400 (Sp. *zontle*)', *pokʔi (n) 'heel', *po:pʔoʔ (adj) 'white', *poʔya (n) 'moon, month', and *tamʔ (adj) 'bitter'. This postconsonantal glottal equals that of Class [2] and [4] verbs. In both contexts the postconsonantal glottal accounts for forms where a glottalized syllable nucleus in Mixean corresponds to a plain nucleus in Zoquean (for data see Part Two, Cɨ#025, CO#008, KO#013, Mɨ#016, PO#020, PO#032, PO#055, TA#023, NS#060). The glottal in Mixean reflexes of *cɨpʔV, *kokʔe, *mɨkʔ, *monʔi, *pokʔi, *po:pʔoʔ, and *poyʔa cannot be the product of morphophonemic processes since these forms are underived. This is a good argument for positing a special element to account for these reflexes. Notice that this element combines with oral stops in six out of eight cases. In Class [4] verbs, six out of the eight roots contain oral stops as the second consonant.

Evidence for Reduplication

There are a few pMZ cases where the last vowel + consonant is copied onto the right side of the root (e.g., *yɨk(ɨk)* 'black', *pos ~posos~pohos* 'guava', *pok(ok)* 'gourd').

Irregular Correspondences

Some forms must be listed as irregular.

Mixean seems to have lost a final segment:

'nose'	pM *hɨhp	pZ *hɨp(ɨ)
'incense'	pM *po:m	pZ *pomo
'termite'	pM *wece	pZ *wece(ŋ)
		(ChisZ *weceŋ*,
		TxZ lost /ŋ/)

Zoquean seems to have lost a final segment:

'sweet potato'	pM *mɨni	pZ *mɨn
'important man'	pM *hayáw	pZ *haya

Other disagreements:

'butterfly'	pM *tótok	ChisZ-C *to?titandan*
'totomostle'	pM *kohk	pZ *tokok [?]
		(ChisZ C *tokok*,
		NE *tohok*)

In the cases where a final segment is lost in one of the main divisions, this segment will be included in parentheses in the protoforms suggested in Part Two. 'Totomostle' and 'butterfly' are reconstructed only for pM, but Zoquean data, followed by question marks, is included in the sets in Part Two together with the Mixean data.

Finally, three different forms are reconstructed which could be united in one set if the irregularities they involve were resolved: pOM *cukn* 'ant', pZ *cu?kin* 'worm', pM [Veracruz] *cukut(ik)* 'ant'.

3.4. ARGUMENTS CONCERNING pMZ STRESS

Although both SaP and OlP verge toward having phonemic stress, stress assignment rules in both languages can be shown to directly reflect pM stress rules which were automatic.

Sayula Popoluca Primary Stress

The representation of SaP forms in Clark (1961) admits of an analysis of primary stress assignment. It is implied in Clark's works that stress is phonemic. Kaufman (1963), however, views stress as phonemic but morphophonemically predictable. The phonemicity, in my view, is due to the lexicalization of formerly derivational processes and to the historical merging of compounds into unanalyzable simplex forms. The rules of stress assignment still easily discernible from the data are as follows:

(Sa/1a). Assign primary stress to the rightmost heavy syllable in the word string if any such syllable is present. (A heavy syllable contains V:, V?, or Vh as its nucleus). (Sa/1b). Or else assign primary stress to the leftmost syllable in the rightmost root.

(Sa/2). Certain suffixes may override this pattern: inflectional suffixes -*wáy* 'diminutive', -*kíš* 'pl. descending', -*áh* ~ -*ám* 'future'; derivational suffixes -*húgum* 'inside', -*húk* 'extensive', -*ít* 'condition'. (Some of these suffixes are former or coexisting roots that have been incorporated into the morphology.)

(Sa/3). Apply stress-rules from the Spanish donor language to loans into SaP. Such loans are not affected by (Sa/1).

This view is directly opposed to that of Kaufman (1963: 41, 2264): "In Sayula stress is generally on the first syllable of the stem unless a suffix with morphophonemic primary stress occurs in the form: the suffix stress overrides the stem stress unless there is one or more intervening unstressed syllables, in which case stress is retained both on the stem and the suffix. Prefixes are never stressed."

(Sa/1b) more or less subsumes Kaufman's view on primary stress in SaP. Since he does not operate with heavy syllables he must account for many more special cases of suffixes with "morphophonemic stress" than the six mentioned in (Sa/2) (the extra ones containing heavy syllables) and no hypothesis is formed concerning the history of these suffixes; a special rule concerning prefixes is needed; but the fact is simply that no SaP prefixes contain heavy syllables; all examples of the main rule (1a) come to appear as exceptions (viz., *kayčé?n* 'hunt for food', *kuypíš* 'yucca', *hapú:t* 'the rest, more', *hatú?k* 'another', *mo:kwíhn* 'shelled corn', *šandá?k* 'muddy', etc.).

The strict overall application of (Sa/1) means that a number of forms have an analysis which is different from the distributional synchronic morpheme analysis. For these forms I tentatively posit the following classes:

A Roots that have become bound to other composite members
B Unproductive derivational prefixes
C Unproductive derivational suffixes

Admittedly there are also:

D Analyzable violations of (Sa/1) (one case)
E Violations of (Sa/2) (two cases)

The nonverbs that belong to A to E are listed below. The symbol = > means "must be analyzed as." Underlined members are bound forms.

kutpóh 'type of twiner'	= >	<u>kut</u> + *poh* 'twiner'	A
čitimít 'dark'	= >	<u>čitim</u> + *?it* '(where) there is'	A
?awék 'branch'	= >	*?ahw* 'mouth' + <u>wek</u>	A
kukék 'agouti'	= >	<u>ku</u> + <u>kek</u>	A
šagapúč 'type of crab'	= >	<u>šaga</u> + <u>puč</u>	A
šagaláy 'shell-carrying'	= >	<u>šaga</u> + <u>lay</u>	A
wehnú?payná? 'municipal head'	= >	*wehnu?* 'to advance' + *p* 'incompletive' + *ay* 'participial' + <u>na?</u>	A
yú:gipayná? 'female healer'	= >	*yú:gi* 'to heal' + *p* + *ay* + <u>na?</u>	A
nu?payná? 'tailor'	= >	*nu?* 'to sew' + *p* + *ay* + <u>na?</u>	A
mí?tná? 'father-in-law of man'	= >	*mí?t* 'son-in-law' + <u>na?</u>	A
pu:tpík 'one half'	= >	<u>pu:t</u> + <u>pik</u>	A

wimpík
  'evil eye' (Sp. mal de ojo)   =>   *wihn* 'eye' + <u>pik</u>[1]   A

windugít 'face'   =>   *wihn* 'eye' + <u>tugit</u>   A

we:tkóč 'to joke'   =>   *we:t* 'to lie' + <u>koč</u>   A

ho:tóy 'slowly'   =>   <u>ho:t</u> + <u>oy</u>   A

hím inyíš 'where are you going?'   =>   *hím* 'where' *in* '2p' + <u>yiš</u>   A

čingunánk 'fig tree'   =>   <u>čingu</u> + <u>nank</u>   A

na:šnánk 'talaje '   =>   *na:š* 'earth' + <u>nank</u>   A

patám 'down'   =>   <u>pat</u> + <u>ʔam</u>   A

ʔayé 'this'   =>   <u>ʔa-</u> + <u>ye</u>   B

hutím 'when?'   =>   <u>hu-</u> + <u>tim</u>   B

pa:mín 'a kind of sweet
  potato' (Sp. camotillo)   =>   <u>pa:-</u> + *mín* 'sweet potato' B

kúkwin 'breast meat of fowl'   =>   <u>kuk</u> + <u>-win</u>   C

kúywin 'attic'   =>   *kuy* 'tree' + <u>-win</u>   C

ʔígi:k 'pricklenut tree'   =>   <u>ik</u> + <u>-i:k</u>   C

ʔištik 'mirror, glass'   =>   *ʔiš* 'to see' + <u>-tik</u>   C

húštikm 'the day after tomorrow'   =>   <u>huš</u> + <u>-tikm</u>   C

máktašp 'four'   =>   <u>mak</u> + <u>-tašp</u>   C

kówči:n 'type of insect'   =>   *kow* 'tortoise'
                                   + *či:n* 'bee honey'   D

ʔaníma:t 'animal'   E

pírto:n 'walking stick'   E

The internally reconstructed morphemes underlined above which can tentatively be assigned an individual meaning are listed below.

    ʔa- 'deictic specification'

    -am 'location'

    -tikm 'time word suffix'

    -tašp 'count word suffix'

    -tik 'instrument'. There is a suffix, *-tik,* in Zoquean which is very common. OlP has *ʔišti'k* and pOM *ʔiš-an* for 'mirror'. The vowel of the suffix has been leveled out in SaP. Otherwise, this happens only in roots. Presumably it was analyzed as a suffix when the word was formed and later analyzed as part of the root. The word may be from Zoquean or the suffix may be an archaism.

    -win (two examples)   'long, flat entity'. Cognate with *-wi:n* 'surface' in OM.

---

[1] *Pik* is perhaps just a derivative of the verb *pik* 'to hurt'. But a zero derivational morpheme is not to be found in the morphology.

ʔɨk + ɨːk 'having to do with pricklenut trees'. A pMZ verbal root meaning 'incline' would, if attested, have the shape *ʔɨːk* in SaP. Perhaps this root recurs here. We may speculate further that it is a reduplicated form.

čitim 'darkness'. Another SaP form *čiʔč* means 'black'. A pOM form *cišy* means 'dark'. The relationship is not clear.

hoː/hoːt 'slowness'
hu- 'question marker'
huš 'specified future'
koč 'to speak (feigned)'
kuk 'middle'
mak 'number'
naʔ (four examples) 'professional or kin m/f authority'
pɨk (two examples) 'motion from/to a specified point'
paː- 'uncultivated'
pat 'down'
puːt 'middle'
puč 'quality that a crest or shell can have'
šaga (two examples) 'crest'
tim 'when'
tugɨt 'place of (eye)'
yɨš 'go, walk'
ye 'demonstrative root'

Every synchronic analysis sets up rules and lists the exceptions. The list above is not longer than what is to be expected. More important, the exceptions are not arbitrary, as are the (far more numerous) exceptions to Kaufman's rules. They generate specific hypotheses about the history of Sayula Popoluca.

Secondary stress seems to be assigned cyclically according to the same rules as primary stress, provided that there are at least two syllables between the syllable carrying primary stress and the one receiving secondary stress. Such a possibility arises only in tri- and tetra-syllabic stems. Since examples are scanty, this rule must be tentative.

Oluta Popoluca Stress

The statement of Clark (1981: 110-111) concerning OlP stress is

> [L]as palabras terminadas en vocal llevan el acento prosódico en la penúltima sílaba y las palabras terminadas en consonante, en vocal con saltillo o en vocal con jota, llevan el acento prosódico en la última sílaba. . . . Las palabras que no siguen esta regla llevan acento escrito. . . . En el tiempo futuro el acento prosódico recae en el sufijo. . . .

This statement appears to be synchronically adequate. In fact, an accent diacritic is *only* written in the future. For our purposes, however, it is insufficient. It is stated as a general rule that any word ending in a consonant takes final accent. That nearly all stems ending in a consonant have a final glottalized syllable is not mentioned. If this fact is taken into account, the stress system begins to look more like that of SaP. The glottal check, we may assume, developed while the rule of stressing heavy syllables was still active, thus attracting stress to the final closed syllables affected by the glottalization. Sometime later, the final stress placement described by Clark was generalized. To the confusion of those primarily interested in OlP diachrony, Clark gives as one of his examples of final stress in consonant-final words the item *maháw* 'woman', which is cognate with NHM *máhu* 'strength' (< pre-NHM *mahw*). This is one of fewer than five examples of the absence of a glottal check in a final closed syllable. I propose the analysis *mah* 'strength' + *?aw* 'mouth' (see Part Two, MA#013 for data), whereby the item turns out to be an example of the pM rule that the rightmost member of composites receives primary stress.

NHM Stress

The statements of Schoenhals and Schoenhals (1965: 302) are

(Sch/1). The rightmost heavy syllable (a heavy syllable contains V:, V:?, V", V?, or Vh as its nucleus) of the word carries primary stress (this will usually coincide with root stress).

(Sch/2). In the absence of heavy syllables, final closed syllables take the accent.

(Sch/3). In the absence of heavy syllables and final closed syllables, the word is stressed on the penultimate.

(Sch/4). When a word does not conform to these rules, write the accent.

Stress rules yielding identical outputs can be stated in different ways. Since we are interested in a statement that makes Mixean languages more comparable, we should like to reformulate (Sch/2) so that it becomes identical to the SaP stress rule (Sa/1b) above. For example, we would like to interpret the minimal pair given by the Schoenhalses

ʔapít 'to roll up' vs. *ʔápit* 'thorn'

differently. They write the accent in 'thorn' and take 'to roll up' to be in conformity with the more general pattern. The result is pure arbitrariness. The SaP stress rule (1b), however, correctly predicts the prosodic outputs of

ʔa-pít vs. *ʔápit*

Likewise, it accounts for such entry forms as *ʔiš-kúhip / ʔiš-kúha* 'to flatten by pounding' (Schoenhals and Schoenhals 1965: 14). Rule (Sch/2) predicts that the derived verb -*ʔiš-kuh*- moves its stress to the right side of the root -*kuh*- when inflected with -*ip*. Thus, the Schoenhalses write the stress in *ʔiškúhip*, but leave it out in *ʔiškuha*. Clearly their rules (Sch/2) and (/3) are intended as orthographical rules, not phonological ones.

pM Stress

As we have seen, SaP and NHM agree on a first priority rule of stressing the rightmost heavy syllable of the word. That this rule was once present in OIP explains the stress shift in this language. OIP developed glottalization in the last syllable of nearly all polysyllabic stems closed by a consonant. These new heavy syllables attracted the accent toward the right of the word where it came to be fixed before the last consonant of the word. pM stress rules, then, must include (Sa/1a) and (Sa/2) stated for SaP above. They concern the heavy syllable stress and the future suffixes which are stressed in all the Mixean sister languages. The only remaining question is to decide on what happens in pM polysyllabic stems that do not contain a heavy syllable. Zoquean lost length. We cannot but assume that pMZ stress was also determined by the weight of the syllable. Since Zoquean was innovative in the loss of length it must have shown innovation with regard to the overall stress pattern as well. Two possible assumptions about pZ stress are that it (1) generalized root stress (which in Mixean often coincides with heavy syllable stress) and (2) generalized the pattern of polysyllables that do not contain heavy syllables. Whether these two tendencies conflict or converge in pZ will emerge from the discussion of Zoquean stress. First, we shall take a look at Mixean polysyllables. The languages where stress is fixed are NHM, OlP, and SaP. In NHM and SaP stress in polysyllables always moved to the first syllable, and in OlP it became fixed on the last syllable. None of these languages provide evidence for stress placement that need not have been fixed. We are thus left with non-NHM OM languages for the determining evidence. Whether or not the decomposition of *maháw* is correct, we know that this item had last syllable stress from the LM evidence. Clearly NHM shifted the pOM stress and later underwent syncope. The same holds for *motów*. The reflexes of pM *péhay* and *hókoš*, however, syncopated already in Common OM, as the LM evidence shows. The same sort of reasoning holds for the rest of the examples.

| NHM máhu | OlP maháw | pM *maháw | (n) 'strong mouth' |
| LM mɨhá: | SaP - | | |

| NHM mótu | OlP motóv | pM *matów | (vt) 'to hear' |
| LM mɨdó·w ~ mɨdów | SaP márau | | |

| NHM pÉ̱hi | OlP - | pM *péhay | (adj) 'thin' |
| LM peh̯ʸ | SaP péhay | | |

| NHM hokš | OlP hokó'š | pM *hókoš | (adj) 'tepid' |
| LM hokš | SaP hógoš | | |

| NHM nay-hɨp | OlP hopóy | pM *hópoy | (n) 'morning' |
| LM hop̄ʸ | SaP hópoy | | |

| NHM káku | OlP kaká'u | pM *kakáwa | (n) 'cacao' |
| LM kɨgá: | SaP kágau | | |

| NHM pícɨm | OlP picɨ́m | pM *picɨ́m | (vi) 'to go out' |
| LM pɨẕɨ́m | SaP píčin | | |

| | OlP *šoko't* | pM **sokót* | (n) 'grass' |
| LM *šĭgóŕ* | | SaP *šógot* | |

| NHM *tikc ~ tíkïc* | | pM **tikác* | (vi) 'to change' |
| LM *tĭgáhc ~ tĭgác* | SaP *tigac* | | |

I mention once more the possibility of **maháw* not being an original simplex. **sokót* is dubious since the final palatalization in LM is unaccounted for and since early import from a Uto-Aztecan language may be involved (cf. Classical Nahuatl *sakaλ* 'grass, hay'). The final vowel of pM **kakawa* is reconstructed on additional evidence from SHM [Mi] *kaká:wa*. **hópoy* is used as an attributive in OM and as a noun in SaP and OlP. In general, attributives and nouns share many morphological features. So it is natural that noun stress and attributive stress should be identifiable. We are now able to fill in the last details of the pM stress rules:

pM primary stress (PS):

(pM/1a). Assign PS to the rightmost heavy syllable in the word string if any such syllables are present. (A heavy syllable contains V:, V:?, V?, or Vh as its nucleus.) (pM/1b). Or else assign PS to the rightmost root. If that root is a polysyllabic nonverb, it receives stress on its penultimate syllable; if it is a polysyllabic verb it receives stress on its last syllable.

(pM/2). A few suffixes may override this pattern, including the recently grammaticalized future-tense marker.

pZ Stress

Kaufman uses a formal approach in setting up the pMZ (read: pZ) stress system in that he operates with "junctures." For example, **kuytim* 'avocado' is written **+kuytim+* with external open junctures in the beginning and in the end of the stem and rewritten */kúytim/* since the morphophonemic stress rules predict that polysyllables in between + . . . + are stressed on the first syllable. The fact that the decomposition into *kuy* 'tree' + *tim* 'fruit' is correct makes it necessary to specify that *tim* does not involve internal open juncture when occurring in */kúytim/*. According to the rules, *+kuy-tim+* should yield */kuytím/*. Specifying the junctures for all such items amounts to placing a stress mark when they are cited. Since no simplicity is gained, I shall not adopt this kind of formalism.

The pMZ stress system based on SoZ and ChisZ-C data set up by Kaufman resembles that of TxZ, as I have stated (1994: 469), except in what concerns polysyllabic verb roots. Disyllabic TxZ roots (there are no trisyllabic ones) are stressed on the first syllable. Assuming that this is an innovation, Kaufman's rules for pMZ stress can be equated with the rules for pZ. His rules (1963: 39-40, 2260-2263), are now restated in an informal way.

(pZ/1). pZ has root stress.

(pZ/1a). Simplex stems: monosyllabic roots receive primary stress; disyllabic nonverb roots are stressed on the first syllable; disyllabic verb roots are stressed on the last syllable.

(pZ/1b). Compound stems: the second member receives primary stress in the same manner as simplex stems (a few compound nouns behave exceptionally and must be specified). If the stem consists of three or more syllables, secondary stress is assigned in a cyclical way to the first member of the compound.

(pZ/2). At least six suffixes form an exception to (pZ/1), since they are stressed. These must be specified. No prefixes form exceptions.

Conclusion: pMZ Stress

Only primary stress is reconstructed. It is assumed that secondary stress is assigned in a cyclical manner to stems involving compounds roots which together have three or more syllables. Such compounds would not be infrequent, but none can actually be reconstructed. The rules (pZ/1a) and (pM/1b) concerning polysyllables are in agreement. pMZ stress rules can then be straightforwardly equated with the pM rules. Reservations must be made about rule (pM/2) concerning stressed suffixes. It is expected, however, that suffixes that had arisen from grammaticalization received stress. The equation (pM/2 = pMZ/2) is tentative; the equation (pM/1 = pMZ/1), final.

3.5. pMZ INFLECTIONAL MORPHOLOGY

In this particular section, where the concern is morphology, my sources are LM: Van Haitsma and Van Haitsma (1976), MM: Nordell (1990), NHM:

Schoenhals and Schoenhals (1965), TaM: Lehmann (1920), OlP: Clark
(1981), SaP: Clark (1961), TxZ: Clark (no date), SoZ: Elson (1960),
StaMaCh: Knudson (1980), ChisZ-N: Engel and Engel (1987), ChisZ-NE:
Harrison and Harrison (1984), ChisZ-C: Wonderly (1951-52).

Person Prefixes

To the far left in the verbal layout are found the person markers. There are
so many changes and complications here that we must carefully reconstruct
step by step, that is, by starting with the subgroups. The system appears to
be more fully preserved in the Mixean subgroup than in the Zoquean one. In
the former the person markers divide into those used with transitive and
intransitive verbs. The transitive ones further distinguish between "direct" and
"inverse." "Direct" person markers are used when first, second, or third
person is acting on an entity lower in the following person hierarchy:

$$1 \ > 2 \ > 3 \ > 4.$$

The inverse marking set is used in the opposite situation. "Fourth person" is
a third-person participant who ranks lower in the hierarchy than some other
third-person participant in the action described by the verb.

For each of the resulting three person paradigms (transitive direct, transitive inverse, intransitive) there is a distinction between "dependent" and
"independent" paradigms. These neutral terms were invented by Larry Clark.
They refer to the fact that the "dependent" paradigm usually occurs with
verbs that are in one way or another subordinate. Typically, "dependent"
verbs are preceded by an expression of time, place, manner, etc. I suggest
(in fc.-a) that the distinction is discourse-motivated in the sense that the
"dependent" paradigms mark background and the independent paradigm
foreground in the discourse. For the present, we shall be content with Clark's
terminology. To summarize: ideally speaking, the Mixean person markers
come in six paradigms as sketched in Figure 3.1.

When we examine each of the six paradigms in detail it will be seen that
this is an idealization since each of the languages makes neutralizations
corresponding to different nodes in the tree of Figure 3.1. Refer to Table 3.1
for paradigms for the individual languages.

Figure 1.3. Categories expressed by pM person markers.

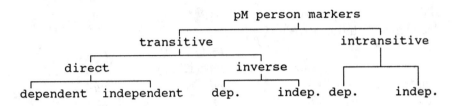

Reconstructing the parent morphemes is a puzzle open to many solutions. As a methodological guideline I have chosen to reconstruct morphemes only when there is actual agreement between two languages concerning the shape of the morpheme in question. This brings the number of solutions down considerably. The principle dictates (in outline) that NHM and SaP be compared with respect to morphemes involving first person, while NHM and OIP be compared with respect to morphemes involving nonfirst person. This is departed from in only three cases. These are shown in Table 3.2.

NHM reduces the morphemes quite drastically by the general developments (a) $CV > C$ and (b) $C_i VC_j > C_j$. We would expect *min- > n- but instead find m-. This is due to an analogy with the 'indep., intr./inv.' marker which serves the purpose of avoiding morphemes of the identical shape n- within one and the same paradigm. The prefix *ti- '1,excl.' presumably went to t- by (a), and was then further reduced because the t would not fare well with the verb roots, which are exclusively consonant-initial. Otherwise sound changes as such have little import in the development of person prefixes in Mixean.

It is assumed that SaP borrowed na- and, with that, the distinction between exclusive and inclusive from Zoquean. It is curious that this form means 'incl.', while the most likely donor form attested, SoZ an-, means 'excl.'. The prefix igi- (where g, according to Larry Clark, p.c., is realized almost as a fricative and tends to be lost in rapid speech) is apparently an innovation.

The overall changes in the individual systems served, in different ways, the purpose of bringing more balance into the system. OIP made systematic replacements in the morphemes involving first person in order to achieve an identification of the intransitive and the inverse in an ergative-type system (a direction of drift, which is repeated in

Table 3.1. Person Markers of the Mixean Verb

pM		NHM	SaP	OIP
Independent, Intransitive				
*ti-	1	Ø-	ti- (1,excl)	ti-
			na- (1,incl)	
*mi-	2	m-	mi-	mi-
*Ø-	3	Ø-	Ø-	Ø-
Independent, Inverse				
*ti-iš-	3-1	š- (-1)	tiš- (3-1excl)	ti-
			naš- (3-1incl)	
*mi-	3-2	m- -hï (-2)	iš- (3-2,2-1)	mi- (3-2)
*Ø-	4-3	Ø- -hï (-3)	igi-	Ø-
Dependent, Intransitive				
*tin-	1	n-	ti- (1,excl)	tin-
			na- (1,incl)	
*min-	2	m-	in-	min-
*i-	3	y-	i-	i-
Dependent, Inverse				
*ti-iš-	3-1	š- (-1)	tiš- (3-1excl)	tin-
			naš- (3-1incl)	
*min-	3-2	m- -hï (-2)	iš- (3-2,2-1)	min- (3-2)
*i-	4-3	y- -hï (-3)	igi-	i-
Independent, Direct				
			ti- (1excl-2)	tiš- (1-2,2-1)
			na- (1incl-3)	
*tin-	1-3	n- (1-)	tin- (1excl-3)	tin-
*min-	2-3	m- (2-)	in- (2-3)	min-
*i-	3-4	y- (3-)	i- (3-4)	i-
Dependent, Direct				
			ti- (1excl-2)	
			naš- (1incl-3)	
*ti-iš-	1-3	n- (1-)	tiš- (1excl-3)	tiš- (1-2,1-3,2-1)
*mi-iš-	2-3	š- (2-)	iš-	miš-
*ti-	3-4	tï- (3-)	igi-	ti-

Table 3.2

pM Morpheme		Based on
*ti-	1, excl, indep, intr	NHM and OIP
*tin-	1, excl, dep, intr	NHM and OIP
*ti-iš-	1-3, dep	SaP and OIP

Zoquean), while keeping up the distinction between dependent and in-dependent. Sayula Popoluca, however, made replacements in mor-phemes involving non-first person in order to reduce the number of dif-ferent paradigms. This reduction resulted in the complete identification of indep. and dep. in the inverse and a neutralization of the inverse/direct opposition in the person marking of dependent verbs. NHM on the whole still reflects the imbalance of the parent system.

A special feature of my reconstructions is the morpheme -iš '3', which only surfaces in combinations with other morphemes. The reason I have chosen a hypothesis involving morpheme combination here is twofold. First, the hypothesis that combinations involving -iš were novel in Mixean fits the Zoquean data in a nice way: by stripping off -iš we are left with a set of prefixes which all have direct reflexes in Zoquean; this makes the account of the development from pMZ to pZ much less problematic. Second, -iš seems to have a direct reflex in Zoquean. This is the third-person ergative nominal case marker -ʔiš found in Chiapas Zoque and Sta. María Chimalapa Zoque. The exact function of this morpheme in pMZ, except for the content 'third person', is a little unclear, but a protoform *is does tie quite a lot of facts together. We must assume that this was a clitic which floated around between the subject noun phrase and the predicate in pMZ and then attached to the word on its right in pM and to that on its left in pZ. Perhaps the most important implication of this is that pMZ must have had the word order SV with the O in one of the peripheral positions. OSV is unlikely for at least two reasons: first, objects rarely precede subjects typologically; secondly, there are no synchronic indications that Mixe-Zoquean were verb-final. So a likely word order for pMZ would be *SVO.[2]

---

[2] Campbell et al. (1986: 547-548) present arguments to the effect that pMZ was not verb-final. *VOS or *VSO are possibilities that emerge from their discussion, but they do not make positive claims as to what the actual word order was. The

When we strip off -*iš* '3' we find that there are two basic paradigms and a single morpheme. The resulting system, which we identify with pMZ, configures as shown in Table 3.3.

Table 3.3. Proto-Mixe-Zoquean Person Prefixes

pMZ

A	*tin-	'1, dep, intr', '1, indep, direct'
	*min-	'2, dep, intr', '2, dep, direct', '3-2, dep, inverse'
	*iy- > *i-	'3, dep, intr/inverse', '3 indep, direct'
B	*ti-	'1, indep, intr/inverse', '1, dep, direct/inverse'
	*mi-	'2, indep, intr/inverse', '2, dep, direct'
	*ø-	'3, indep, intr/inverse'
C	*ti-	'3, dep, direct'

Although I have labeled the paradigms "A" and "B"—as originally introduced by Kaufman (1963)—it does not mean that our approaches agree. The whole argumentation just given is different from Kaufman's. He lacked OlP and NHM data, and he approached the remaining data in a fundamentally different way.[3] While our reconstructions are quite

---

whole issue is dependent upon textual material from Oluta Popoluca, Gulf Zoquean, and Chimalapa Zoquean.

[3] Even though Kaufman (1963: 90-99) lacked OlP and NHM to base his reconstructions on, it is worth briefly discussing the basic principles of his thinking. It is quite ingenious, but not without flaws. Kaufman wants to derive all the transitive person markers from combinations of morphemes. In his pMZ reconstructions there are two sets, called A and B. Below I reproduce his protoforms and their Sayula Popoluca reflexes:

	A (DEP,INTR)		B (INDEP,INTR)	
	pMZ	SaP	pMZ	SaP
excl	*na	> ti-	*i-	> ti-
incl	*tin	> na-	*ti-	> na-
2	*in	> in-	*mi-	> mi-
3	*i	> i-	*ø-	> ø-

It is crucial to the enterprise of deriving the transitive markers from combinations of morphemes that this must work at least for the only fully described Mixean language at hand if it is to make sense at all. Kaufman goes a long way to make things work for Sayula Popoluca. The steps are as follows:

(1) Exclusive/inclusive markers were reversed in SaP.

(2) *i > $\check{s}$ when *i is the phonological manifestation of a person marker following another person marker.

(3) In the indep. paradigm Mixean person markers combine in the order object-subject, while in the dep. paradigm they combine in the order subject-object.

(4) Both indep. and dep. transitive paradigms are made up of combinations of set A morphemes.

Step (1) does indeed suggest itself. I shall accept this step for the sake of the argument, although, in fact, I think SaP borrowed the incl./excl. distinction.

Step (2) is not very plausible, especially since no parallel has been uncovered for other parts of SaP phonology.

If, for the sake of the argument, we accept all these premises, the least that we may expect is that they work. Let us see how the transitive paradigms are now derived:

INDEP, TR (object-subject order)

'excl-3'	ti- + na-		>	tin-
'incl-3'	i- + na-		>	na-
'2-3'	i- + in-		>	in-
'3-3'	i- + i-		>	i- (should we expect $i\check{s}$- ?)
'3-excl'	ti- + i-		>	$ti\check{s}$-
'3-incl'	na- + i-		>	$na\check{s}$-
'3-2'	in- + i-	> $-in\check{s}$	>	$i\check{s}$-

DEP, TR (subject-object order)

'excl-3'	ti- + i-		>	$ti\check{s}$-
'incl-3'	na- + i-		>	$na\check{s}$-
'2 + 3'	in- + i-	> $-in\check{s}$	>	$i\check{s}$-

Two suggestions:

| | 'excl-2' | in- + ti- (?) |
| and | '2-excl' | ti- + in- (?) |

are listed (Kaufman 1963: 98), presumably as predictions about the shape the morphemes 'excl.-2' and '2-excl.' would have had if they were found in the language. Now, while '2-excl.' indeed cannot be expressed by means of inflectional morphemes, 'excl.-2' can. Kaufman seems simply to have overlooked the morpheme ti- 'excl.-2'. Had he not overlooked (ignored?) this, he would be obliged to makes changes in the reconstructions, because the shape of the morpheme cannot even be accounted for by analogy, and it certainly doesn't follow from his rules of combinations. The same holds for two additional morphemes, which (as he himself admits) are left unaccounted for in this framework. To the left I cite the two morphemes, and to the right I give the predictions about their derivation according

different with respect to the meaning of the morphemes, their shapes
are alike, since, by happenstance, Zoquean preserves the two paradigms
well. The single morpheme labeled "C" is not reconstructed in
Kaufman, though.

Table 3.4. Zoquean Person-Marker Reflexes and Their Ancestral Forms

	pMZ	pM	pZ		SoZ	ChisZ-N	StaMaChZ
A	-	-	*in-	excl	an-	(i) N-	?in-
	*tin-	*tin-	*tin-	incl	tan-	ndi-	-
	*min-	*min-	*min-	2	in-	(mi) N-	min-
	*iy-	*i-	*iy-	3	i-	y-	?iy-
B	-	-	*i-	excl	a-	Ø-	-
	*ti-	*ti-	*ti-	incl	ta-	ti-	-
	*mi-	*mi-	*mi-	2	mi-	Ny-	-
	*Ø-	*Ø-	*Ø-	3	Ø-	Ø-	-
C	*ti-	*ti-	*ti-	3, dep	-	-	-ti

In the Zoquean languages the meanings of the various person prefixes were reduced. The dependent/independent opposition was sacri-
ficed for transitive predicates to the benefit of a much more balanced

---

to Kaufman's theory:

  igi- '4-3' (indep./dep.) <? *i-* + *i-*
  iš- '2-excl' <? *ti-* + *in-* (indep.), *in-* + *ti-* (dep.)
              (the theory predicts the existence of two morphemes both of
              which are different in shape from the morpheme the language
              actually has, namely *iš-*)

It turns out that the proposed framework, even with the extravagant sound laws it
employs, applies only to transitive morphemes involving third person. If Kaufman
cannot make his own theory about the combinative character of the transitive
morphemes work, I doubt that it is possible at all. My own failures in similar
attempts repeated several times over the last three years suggests to *my* mind the
unviability of this procedure. I shall make no judgment about the possibility of the
procedure being applicable in some preproto-Mixe-Zoquean stage.

system. The pZ shapes of the set A-B-C prefixes are almost identical to their pMZ shapes, but the paradigms have in Zoquean been enriched with prefixes meaning 'exclusive' and their content (to which I shall return) simplified. See Table 3.4.

SoZ has a regular development *ɨ > a*, drops the *m* of **min* and, like ChisZ-N, the *i* of **iy*. The A paradigm is, among other things, used to express direct transitive action involving third person, while paradigm B expresses inverse transitive action involving third person. A need arose for expressing transitive action involving only nonthird persons. So appropriate prefixes were combined in the following ways:[4]

SoZ *mi-* '2' (set B) + *an-* 'excl' (set A) → *man-* '1-2'
      a- 'excl' (set B) + *in-* '2' (set A) → *an-* '2-1'

The northern (Francisco León) dialect of ChisZ has still ongoing general syncopation of initial vowels and a metathesis such that **tɨn > ndɨ*. Nasals are realized homorganically with the following root-initial consonant. According to the analysis of Engel and Engel (1987: 343), possessive forms have been reanalyzed into two parts, one of which is a "pronominal" one, which has come to look like a shortened form of the personal pronouns (i.e., *i* ← *ɨhci* 'I' and *mi* ← *mihci* 'you'). In a diachronic light, however, the 'excl' is not *i N-*, but simply *iN-*, and '2' is not *mi N-*, but *miN-*. In this light, it would be more appropriate to analyze the occurrence of *N-* (without *i*) as a short form of *iN* and *N-* as a short form of *miN-*.

---

[4] Kaufman (1963: 96) derives these prefixes in the same way. But our views differ in two respects: (1) Kaufman projects the prefix combinations back to a stage earlier than the formation of Soteapan Zoque, while I consider them to be recent; (2) he also thinks that *a-* 'excl' in the function '3-excl' and *ta-* 'incl' in the function '3-incl' should be derived by combinations, namely by *a-* 'excl' + *i-* '3' > *a-* '3-excl' and *ta-* 'incl' + *i-* '3' > *ta-* '3-incl'. He does not attempt to derive the expression of other person combinations involving third person in this way —perhaps because it would be too implausible phonologically. Since *a-* already in itself means both 'excl' *and* '3-incl', just as *ta-* in itself means both 'incl' and '3-incl', Kaufman creates unnecessary problems. The elegant and economical way in which SoZ expresses both direct/inverse, dependent/independent (with intransitives), as well as all possible person combinations by means of just two paradigms (plus two morphemes created from existing material), is not brought to light in his account.

Also ChisZ-N had the need for expressing '1-2' and '2-1'. The two expressions, which were created independently from those of SoZ, are

ChisZ-N   2-1   *ndɨ-*
                 1-2   *N-*

N- is homophonous with the 'excl.' marker of the A paradigm. It can be seen as a simple extension of the meaning 'excl., direct, involving third person' (i.e., 1-3) to 'excl., direct, involving third *and* second person'. The '2-1' marker is homophonous with 'incl.' of the A paradigm. The latter must have assumed the additional function of the former, although the exact circumstances under which this took place escape us.

StaMaCh, while having completely lost set B, preserves set A remarkably well. The prefixes cited in Table 3.3 above indicate 1sg, 2sg, and 3sg, and they combine with the root *-he?* to yield the expression *?ɨn-he?* 'mine', *min-he?* 'yours', *?ɨy-he?* 'his/her'. The possessive markers *newin-* 1,pl.,incl. and *tɨwan-* 1,pl.,excl. could well have been borrowed from Nahua; thus, for *newin-* compare Classical Nahuatl *newaːn(-tin)* 'both together' and for *tɨwan-* compare Cl. Nahuatl *te?waːn(-tin)* 'we'.[5] The 2,pl. form is *miyan-*; and the 3,pl. form, *te?pɨ-tɨk*. These latter are native and also have a pronominal character. Series A prefixes have additional reflexes in StaMaCh. First, there is a set of suffixes found on auxiliaries and the lexical expression of negation. These I take to be original head-verb "dependent" proclitics which jumped to the left to become enclitics and were somewhat reduced in the process. Thus, they took the shapes *-n, -m, -y*. Second, there is a cognate series combining with pronominal forms to express the subject participants of a transitive action. In these combined forms,

---

[5] The apparent absence of the plural suffix *-tin* from the donor forms may be a clue to which dialect these forms might have been borrowed from. The complete absence of *-tin* is, indeed, characteristic of some of those Nahua dialect areas that are closest to the Chimalapas of Oaxaca, namely the Eastern dialects (Sierra de Puebla, Isthmus, Pipil) (Canger 1980: 94-98). However, these dialects (except the remote one of Sierra de Puebla) have another suffix, *-meh*, in place of (replacing?) *-tin*. Geographically closest of all Nahua dialects, of course, is the aberrant, now extinct dialect of Pochutla, Oaxaca. This cannot, however, be the donor since the form for 'we' is *tue'n* (Boas 1917: 33). On the whole, the question concerning which Nahua dialect donated *newin-* and *tɨwan-* is unresolved.

the object pronoun precedes the subject suffix. Their shapes (according to information pieced together from Knudson 1980: 61-63, 95-100) are as follows:

	Obj	Subj
1sg	*ʔɨc-*	*-ʔɨn*
2sg	*mic-*	*-ʔɨm ~ -min*
3sg	*teʔp-*	*-ʔɨy*
1excl	*tɨwan-*	*-tɨn*
1incl	*newin- ~ nen-*	*-ney*
2pl	*miyan-*	*-ʔɨm ~ -min*
3pl	*teʔpɨtɨk-*	*-ʔɨy*

The source for the sg/pl distinction in the pronominal series is, as mentioned, some Nahua dialect. The subject suffixes are mostly identical with the possessor prefixes discussed above: *-ʔɨm* is a recently analogically leveled variant of *-min*. *-tɨn* 'pl. excl.' and *-ney* 'pl. incl.' need more explanation. They are somewhat reminiscent of SaP *-tɨ* 'excl.' and *na-* 'incl.' while being at odds with the putative pZ forms **ɨn-* 'excl.' and **tɨn-* 'incl.'. I do not think, however, that either the pZ or the SaP forms have anything to do with *-tɨn* and *-ney*. It seems, rather, that they are shortened forms of the imported pronouns *tɨwan* and *newin*, these pronouns having been transferred to the Subj. paradigm to make up for the lost exclusive/inclusive distinction.

To sum up: The B paradigm was lost in StaMaCh and replaced by free pronouns. The A paradigm became used in different morphological environments such that three different paradigms arose: one (1) used with *-heʔ* to express possession, another (2) occurred on auxiliaries, and a third (3) suffixed to pronouns to express the subject in transitive actions:

pZ		Santa María Chimalapa Zoque		
		(1)	(2)	(3)
*ɨn-	>	*ʔɨn-*	*-n*	*-ʔɨn*
*min-	>	*min-*	*-m*	*-ʔɨm ~ -min*
*ɨy-	>	*ʔɨy-*	*-y*	*-ʔɨy*

StaMaCh is the only language for which a reflex of pMZ **tɨ-* '3,dep., direct' is attested. The morpheme that I identify as a reflex of this means '3,dep.,intr' and surfaces only on the negative incomplete proclitic *wa* (cf. expressions such as *wa-t min-i* 'she/he is not coming'; Knudson 1980: 63).

This ends the summary account of the development of the expression of the person category in Mixe-Zoquean. The procedure followed is different from that of Kaufman (1963: 90-99), who operates with two sets of prefixes from which he derives the various person markers. His theory ran into problems (cf. my footnotes) even with the few languages (Sayula Popoluca, Midland Mixe, Chiapas Zoque, Soteapan Zoque) from which data were available at Kaufman's time of writing, and the data which have become available since then does not offer any particular support.

The various functions of the two paradigms in MZ languages have hitherto only been alluded to. In Table 3.5 the functions of the reflexes of the paradigms are tabulated for each of the languages as they are described in the sources. Shared functions are reconstructed for pZ and pMZ.

Table 3.5. Functions of the A and B Paradigms throughout Mixe-Zoquean

	pMZ	pM	NHM	O1P	SaP	pZ	SoZ	N[6]	ChZ
dep, intr	*A	*A	A	A	A	*A	A	A	A
dep, inv		*A	A	A					
indep, dir		*A	A	A	A				
dir (3p obj)	*A	*A				*A	A	A	
possession	*A	*A		A	A	*A	A	A	A
subj (pron-__)									A
indep, intr	*B	*B	B	B	B	*B	B	B	
indep, inv		*B	B	B					
inv (3p subj)	*B	*B				*B	B	B	
pass/imp	*B	*B	B				A,B	B	
recipr/refl	*B	*B	B			*B	B	B	
nonvrb pred	*B	*B	B	B		*B	B	B	

As indicated by the placement of capital letters A and B, introduced by stars, I reconstruct the direct and inverse functions for A and B in pMZ. Zoquean does not have an indep./dep. distinction with transitive predicates, while Mixean does. If, as I believe, the Mixean system can be projected back to pMZ, we should more precisely reconstruct the meanings given for the reconstructed morphemes in Table 3.2 above.

---

[6] "N" and "ChZ", respectively, abbreviate Chiapas Zoque, northern dialect (location of Francisco León) and Sta. María Chimalapa Zoque.

The expressions of passive/impersonal and reciprocal/reflexive require morphemes in addition to the B paradigm. These vary from language to language as do the exact nature of the categories. pMZ nonverbal predications include at least nominal predication. Thus, there are a number of precisions to make concerning the three bottom rows in Table 3.5. Such would require better data across the board.

Other Inflectional Verb Prefixes

Between the person-marking prefixes and the (derived) stem there were in pMZ perhaps two inflectional morphemes which I cite below along with their reflexes:

p(M)Z	*ni-*	'negative incompletive'
SaP	*ni-*	'negative incompletive (not yet)'
ChisZ-C	*ni-*	'incompletive (?)'

p(M)Z	*ha(y)-*	'negative completive'
SaP	*ha-*	'negative completive (not any more)'
ChisZ-C	*hay-*	'negative completive'

While Kaufman (1963: 100) projected both of these morphemes back to pMZ, I would do so only with doubt. In 9.2 I follow the hypothesis that any lexical item or phonological phenomenon shared between SaP and at least one of the Zoquean languages, but with none of the Mixean ones other than SaP itself, may be isolated as a case of internal borrowing from Gulf Zoquean. While the morphemes in question have not been found for any of these languages, the distribution is still too limited for a time depth corresponding to pMZ to be certain.

Tense-Aspect Suffixes

The data and reconstructions of Mixean aspectual verb suffixes are given in Table 3.6. Mixean *-hi-* marks 'inverse'. To determine its presence or absence in pMZ is just as difficult as it is to make decisions about the prehistory of the dep/indep distinction in the person prefixes. I believe, however, that it can be projected backwards to pMZ. The paradigms of the individual languages can mostly be derived by regular sound laws. One thing not apparent in Table 3.6 is that the reconstructed *-pe* is supported not only by OIP but also by LM, which has the form *-py*.

Table 3.6. Mixean Aspectual Verb Suffixes

pM		NHM	OIP	SaP
-pa	intr, indep, incompl	-p	-pa	-p
-pe	dir, indep, incompl	-p	-pe	-p
-hi-pe	inv, indep, incompl	-hï-p	-ɨ-p	-p
-u	intr/dir, indep, compl	-Ø	-u	-w,-u,-wu
-hi-u	inv, indep, compl	-hï-Ø	-ɨ-w	-w,-u,-wu
-i/e	intr/dir, dep, incompl	-y	-i/e	-Ø
-hi-i/e-	inv, dep, incompl	-hï-y	-ih/eh	-p
-hi	intr/dir, dep, compl	-y	-i	-h
-hi-hi	inv, dep, compl	-hï-y	-iy	-w,-u,-wu

The shape *-hï* of the inverse-marking suffix in NHM is potentially misleading. One might think that /ï/ (a high, central vowel) < *i*, but the development is a little more complicated than that: the sequences *-hi-p* and *-hi-y* went to *-hp* and *-hy* in pre-NHM and then regained a vowel *ï* by epenthesis. *-hï-Ø* is from *-h* with an analogical spread of *ï* such that we can now identify a morpheme *-hï* 'inverse'. This scenario is in accordance with phonological sounds laws that operate on the lexicon in NHM (see 7.2).

All Mixe-Zoquean verb roots are consonant-final, which explains why *h* of *-hi-* got suppressed in OIP. It did however survive in the vowel-harmonic suffix *-ih/-eh*, where its segments are metathesized.

In SaP some great structural changes came about because of the general dropping of final, unprotected vowels in this language and because of analogy. By the latter process, the 'indep., intr./dir., incompl.' suffix (topmost in Table 3.6) replaced the 'indep., inv., incompl.' and 'dep., inv., incompl.' suffixes, and the 'indep., inv., compl.' suffix replaced the 'dep., inv., compl.' suffix.

We are now ready to compare the suffixes to those found in Zoquean. In Zoquean there is, as already indicated, no inverse marker, so things look somewhat simpler in this system (Table 3.7).

StaMaCh (abbreviated ChZ in Table 3.7) -*wɨ* provides definite proof of the shape pZ *-*wɨ*. Even without having the StaMaCh data, Kaufman (1963) made the right reconstruction. He based it on SoZ internal reconstruction. Besides -*u*, there are the suffixes -*wɨ:m* 'completive subordinate' and -*wɨ?:p* 'completive of participial'. Both contain -*wɨ*. This reconstruction of Kaufman's is further based on a comparison with a Midland Mixe (Juquila) suffix -*ɨ* extracted from somewhere in the data of Belmar (1902) (and not discussed any further). It could be a cognate by *-*wɨ* > *-*w* > *-*u* > -*ɨ*, but not if the ancestral form were *-*u*. It seems that Mixean too may have had an alternation *-*wɨ* ~ *-*u*.

Table 3.7. Zoquean Aspectual Verb Suffixes and Their Ancestral Shapes

pMZ		pM	pZ	SoZ	ChisZ	ChZ
*-*pa*	indep, incompl, intr	*-*pa*	*-*pa*	-*pa*	-*pa*	-*pa*
*-*pe*	indep, incompl, tr	*-*pe*				
*-*wɨ* ~ -*u*	indep, compl	*-*u*	*-*wɨ* ~ -*u*	-*u*	-*u*	-*wɨ*
*-*i/e*	dep, incompl	*-*i/e*	*-*i/e*	-*i*; -*Ø*	-*i/e*	-*ɨ/a*
				(dep,intr ; dep,tr)		
*-*hi*	dep, compl	*-*hi*				

The dep., incompl. marker is reconstructed as such on the assumption that SoZ regularized the vowel-harmony and ChZ changed it. The Mixean match has of course guided these assumptions.

The reconstructed dep., compl. marker does not reflect the SoZ zero morpheme. But notice that the two SoZ morphemes mark another distinction, that of intransitive vs. transitive. How this distinction came about is not explained.

Future Markers in Mixean

The subject matter to be discussed in this section may not bear directly on pMZ since it is only in Mixean that the future is marked by morphological means. But it is, as we shall soon see, closely intertwined with our view of other developments in Mixean. The subsystem of future marking probably developed as suggested in Table 3.8.

Table 3.8. The Development of Future Marking in Mixean

pM		LM	OlP	SaP
*-wán?-p	indep, dir/intr	-	-ám	-ám ~ áh
*-wán?-hi-p	indep, inv	-	-anip	-ám ~ áh
*-wán?	dep, inv/intr	-a·n ~ -a"n (fut)	-a?n	-wá?n
*-wán?-hi	dep, dir	-	-a?neh	-ám ~ áh

The *p* reconstructed in the indep. may ultimately be related to **-pa* (incompl., indep.). If so, we might also expect *-i/e* to have followed the fut., dep. markers. In this line of thinking, pre-pM **-pa* > pM **-p* and pre-pM **-i/e* > **-Ø*. So the theory actually predicts that there will be no trace left of **-i/e* in pM. While the loss of *-p* is troublesome because it has no precedents, the segment did leave clear traces in both OlP and SaP in the shape of a *p* in the indep., dir./intr. and as a source of regressive assimilation of the nasal in the indep.,inv.

The postconsonantal glottal stop is a phonological phenomenon not found in any of the modern languages. In 3.2 and .3 I posited glottal stops in this position in order to account for certain lexical correspondences. A simple rule established there is that when another consonant follows the sequence -C?-, the glottal stop is suppressed; when a vowel or zero follows, the glottal stop undergoes metathesis with C. This rule is the origin of the kind of alternation we see in LM and it works well for all four of the OlP suffixes. The last of these, *-a?neh*, came about by **-án?-hi* > *-an?ih* > *-a?nih* > *-a?neh*. The metathesis *hi > ih* has a sort of parallel in **-hi-i/e* 'dep., inv., incompl.' > *-ih/eh* (cf. above). The plausibility of the last development, **i > e*, is strengthened by the existence of the high-low vowel-harmonic suffixes *-ih/eh* and *-i/e*.

In LM distinctions involving direct/inverse and dep./indep. became expatriated from the domain of the fut. suffix. The former 'fut., dep., inv./intr.' marker spread and replaced the whole paradigm.

SaP also suffered from analogy: the 'indep., inv.' suffixes replaced the 'indep., dir./intr.' and 'dep., dir.' suffixes. SaP is the only one of the languages cited here which has retained the *w* of **wán?* (in

-*ám* ~ *áh* it was lost because of the presence of another bilabial, *m*, in the syllable). This piece of data makes it clear that the future-marking suffix must be identical with pM **wan* ~ *wa?n* 'to want'. This verb was grammaticalized already in pre-pM times when it had the shape **wan?*. The future marker's origin in a former independent verb explains why it carries stress (cf. my hypothesis in 3.4 that only lexical roots were stressed) and, reversely, the fact of its carrying stress requires that its origin be lexical.

To sum up: The future paradigm provides further support for the "laryngeal theory" of postconsonantal glottal stops. It also, independently, supports the reconstruction of the very key to our understanding the development of the tense-aspect system, namely **-hi-* 'inverse'.

Imperative and Direction

The imperative was expressed by means of a zero prefix and a suffix whose ancestral form and reflexes look as follows:

pMZ	**-i/a* 'imperative'
LM	-*i*-*k*/-*k* 'directional, 1p object'
SaP	-*a*-*k* 'directional (3-1, 2-1, 3-2, 4-3)'
OlP	-*i*/-*e*/-*i*/-*a* 'imperative'
	(-*i* when preceded by *i*, -*a* when preceded by *a* or *o* + internal juncture, -*e* when preceded by *a*, -*i* when preceded by *a* or *u*)
SoZ	-*i* 'imperative'
ChisZ-N	-*i*/-*a* 'imperative; negative'
	(-*i* when preceded by *i*, *i*, *u*, or *a*; -*a* when preceded by *e* or *o*)
StaMaCh	-*i?*/-*a?* 'imperative'
	(-*i* when preceded by *i*, *i*, *u*, or *a*; -*a* when preceded by *e* or *o*)

The vowel-harmonic rules for pMZ **-i/a* were probably as in ChisZ and StaMaCh, but Mixean reflexes of these rules are not easy to unravel since (1) the OlP data are not very clear, (2) SaP imposed a uniform vowel quality, and (3) LM reduces the quality of unstressed vowels to schwa.

I have hyphenated the LM and SaP suffixes because they contain the morpheme pMZ *-k* 'transitive direction away from nonfirst person toward first person'. This phenomenon is reminiscent of the quasi-grammaticalized status of *her* 'here' in the Modern German expression *gib's her* 'give it to me' (Balthazar Bickel, p.c.). The directional element itself is found as a free morpheme *-k* in ChisZ-C, where it occurs on demonstratives and nouns with the meaning 'motion from' (e.g., *kumguy-ʔohmo-k* (town-in-from) 'from town', *yɨmɨ-k* 'from here', *ʔɨmɨ-k* 'from there').

"Applicative"

The functions of the "applicative" (as it is widely labeled in traditional grammar) are to signal the presence in the predication of a Benefactive or Recipient. It was also recognized as a pMZ morpheme by Kaufman, who called it "benefactive/indirective." It occurred in the slot between the derived stem and the other inflectional suffixes. Its ancestral shape and reflexes are:

pMZ *-hay* 'applicative'
> OlP *-ay*, SaP *-ha*, SoZ *-aʔy*, ChisZ *-hay*, StaMaCh *-hay(-)*

Conclusion

In Tables 3.9 to 3.13 all the morphemes reconstructed for pMZ on the previous pages as well as those reconstructed in the section on derivational morphology in Part Two are reproduced and placed in a hypothetical overall morphological structure. The distinction between inflectional and derivational affixes has become standard in Mixe-Zoquean linguistics. In footnotes for each table the morphemes are repeated with their meanings. When a reconstructed form may not be as old as the MZ ancestor or if it is otherwise particularly problematic, it is parenthesized.

Table 3.9. Proto-Mixe-Zoquean Verb Word-Formation (Stem + Inflection)[7]

(*iš)	*tɨn	(*ni)	STEM	*ɨ/a	(*hi)	*pa
	*min	(*ha(y))				*pe
	*ɨy					*wɨ ~ -u
	*tɨ					*i/e
	*mi					*hi
	*Ø					
	*tɨ					

Table 3.10. Proto-Mixe-Zoquean Verb Stem-Formation (Root + Inflection)[8]

*yak	(*mu:)	*hɨ(s)	ROOT	*ʔoy	*ɨːyʔ
*nay	*ko:	*ʔaw		*ay	(*piʔ)
	*ni	*ni:		*ɨy	(*ɨtah)
		*ku		(*nay)	
		(*nah)			

---

[7] Glosses: *iš- '3 agent' (clitic?), *tɨn- '1, dep(, intr', '1, indep, direct'), *min- '2, dep(, intr/direct', '3-2, dep)', *ɨy '3, dep(, intr/inverse', '3 indep, direct)', *tɨ- '1, indep(, intr/inverse', '1, dep, direct/inverse'), *mi- '2, indep(, intr/inverse', '2, dep, direct'), Ø- '3, indep(, intr/inverse'), *tɨ- '3, dep(, direct)', *ni- 'negative, incompletive', *ha(y)- 'negative completive', *-ɨ/a 'imperative', *-hi 'inverse', *-pa 'indep, incompl, intr', *-pe 'indep, incompl, tr', *wɨ ~ -u 'indep, compl', *-i/e 'dep, incompl', *-hi 'dep, compl'.

[8] Glosses: yak- 'causative', nay- 'reciprocal/reflexive', *mu:- 'comitative', *ko:- 'benefactive', *ni- 'associative', *hɨ(s)- 'back', *ʔaw- 'pertaining to one's mouth or other opening', *ni:- 'to surface, corporeal', *ku- 'from surface', *nah- 'circumvention', *ʔoy 'antipassive', *-ʔay 'applicative', *-ɨy 'inchoative, etc.', *-nay 'aimless, corporeal, reduplication', *ɨːyʔ 'directional', *-piʔ 'all, distributive', *-ɨtah 'reciprocal'.

Table 3.11. Proto-Mixe-Zoquean Noun Formation (Derivation and Inflection)[9]

(*ko:)	ROOT	*Ø	*tɨk(ay)	*taka
*?aw	(+ *ko	*ɨ/a		*kuk
*ko~ko?+	ROOT)	*i/e		*kɨs
*ma		*ik		*i
*ni:		*pɨ?		
		*kuy		
		*tɨk		
		*tɨk		

Table 3.12. Proto-Mixe-Zoquean Attributive Stem Formation (All Derivational)[10]

*ni(?)	*ni:	ROOT	*in
			*hi
			*ɨ/a
			*i/e
			*ik

---

[9] Glosses: *ko:- 'ownership, step-, half-', *?aw- 'perception, pertaining to the mouth', *ko-~ko?- 'head, reach', *ma- 'days hence', *ni:- 'to surface, corporeal', *-ko- 'ligature in nominal compounds', *-Ø 'deverbalizer', *-ɨ/-a 'deverbalizer', *-i/-e 'deverbalizer', *-ik 'deverbalizer', *-pɨ? 'participial', *-kuy 'instrument', *-tɨk 'instrument', *-tɨk 'place', *-tɨk(ay) 'plural, *-taka 'without', *-kuk 'in the middle of', *-kɨs 'on', *-i 'locative'.

[10] Glosses: *ni(?)- 'like, very', *ni:- 'to surface, corporeal', *-in 'position (time or space)', *-hi 'before (time or space)', *ɨ/a 'deverbalizer', *-i/-e 'deverbalizer', *-ik 'deverbalizer'.

Table 3.13. Question Marker and Omnipresent Suffixes/Enclitics[11]

*hu   PARTICLE
       STEM/WORD **ti*
                 *nam
                 *ʔamV?
                 *ay

3.6. pMZ NUMERALS

Kaufman (1963: 82-86, 3180-3187, henceforth TK), provided a good starting point for understanding the numerals; my own understanding has come about chiefly by a critical examination of his suggestions. I agree in the general procedure whereby suffixes are stripped from the roots even if the content of these suffixes cannot always be identified. The suffixes are different from language to language and do not recur consistently throughout the individual numeral systems, which indicates that they are relics of some lost accompanying system. These suffixes and the languages and stems in which they occur are

-k	All of OM (all numerals; from either **-k* or **-ko*, cf. OIP)
-ko	OIP ('2', all above '3')
-k	SaP ('1', '2'; respectively < **-k* and < **-ko*)
	OIP ('1', '3')
-p	SaP (all above '2')
-na?	TxZ (all above '1'; note the gloss 'cinco (contar)' introducing *Bosna?* in Clark n.d.), SoZ (mostly found when the numeral is attributive)
-tén	SoZ (obligatory with '2' through '5' and with 'how many')
-te:ñe?	TxZ (attested with '2', '3', '5' in Clark n.d.; note the gloss 'cinco [personas]' introducing *Boste:ñe?*)
-a?y	ChisZ-C ('2', '15' and all in between '4' and '14' as well as compounds with '1', '2', '3', '6', '7', '8', '9'). A cognate morpheme in other ChisZ dialects.

---

[11] Glosses: **hu* 'question marker', **ti* 'emphatic', **nam* 'still', **ʔamV?* 'just, now, already', **ay* 'perfective'.

-*ⁱ*/*ₐ*　　ChisZ-C (I have one vowel-harmonic suffix; TK has two different suffixes: -*ɨ* found with 'one', -*a* with 'two')

-*ku?y*　　ChisZ-C ('4'; TK analyzes this into *ku-?y*, presumably because -*?y* could then be identified with *a?y*; but how does TK account for -*ku* ?. I take -*ku?y* to be one morpheme, perhaps a former classifier for something that often comes in fours. If this putative classifier is related to pZ *-*kuy* 'tree', *?* would be an addition explained as accompanying the functional shift. As Lee (1987: 404) observes, "shape-based classifiers . . . derive with fair regularity from plant terms." See also Adams and Conklin (1973).

-*aŋ*　　ChZ (found with all attested numerals except '1' and compounds that include '1', that is, in '2', '3', '4', '5', '6', '7', '8', '9', '10', '20', '60', '100')

　　I suggest that these suffixes may all be relics of an elaborate system of classifiers. -*na?* and -*tén*/-*te:ñe* are the best evidence. They are both found in the Gulf Zoquean languages SoZ and TxZ. In TxZ -*te:ñe* is used specifically for counting humans. This would then be one of the last languages to have given up numeral classifiers.

　　What remains of the stems can be analyzed as either simplex or complex numerals. In what concerns the complex numerals '6' through '9', I (SW) have departed from TK:

'5'	**m(ok)os*		(TK)
	*m(ok)os		(SW)
'6'	**tuh-tu*	= '1+5'	(TK)
	*tuhtu	= 'one more (than five)'	(SW)
'7'	**wɨs-tu*	= '2+5'	(TK)
	*huwɨs-tuhtu	= 'two of one more (than five)'	(SW)
'8'	**tukʷ/ᵢ-tu*	= '3+5'	(TK)
	*tukʷ/ᵢ-tuhtu	= 'three of one more (than five)'	(SW)
'9'	**(mak)tas-tu*	= '4+5'	(TK)
	*maktas-tuhtu	= 'four of one more (than five)'	(SW)

The difference can be illustrated by an example of a descendant form, for which TK fails to account:

ChisZ-C *tuh-t-a?y* '6'   <   pMZ (TK) **tuh-tu-*
ChisZ-C *tuk-tuh-t-a?y* '8' <   pMZ (TK) **tuk^u/$_i$-tu-*

If the developments in Kaufman's system are to be regular, the emphasized part of the ChisZ-C word for '8' must first be erased. His reductionism becomes even more critical when we turn to some of the data which was not available in 1963. For example:

OIP *huštukuhtuhko* '7'   <?   pMZ (TK) **wɨs-tu*

The fallacy of his position consists in the imposition of a wrong system on the numerals. He identifies a morpheme *-tu* and assigns the meaning '5' to it, whereby it must be set up as an allomorph of **m(ok)os*, which in itself is strange. Once '6' is said to be '5 + 1' the count runs out of control. In a straightforward arithmetic the ChisZ-C stem *tuht-t-* '6 = 5+1' would necessitate that ChisZ-C *tuk-tuh-t* be interpreted as '4+5' and not as '8', which is the actual meaning. As is clear from Table 3.14, ChisZ-C did not remodel the system. In fact, it faithfully reflects it. *tuhtu* is a whole morpheme meaning 'one in addition to', and may or may not be an ancient reduplication of yet another allomorph, *tuh*, of *tum ~ tu ~ tu?* '1'. In any case, one only has to read "one in addition (to five)" or "one more than (five)" into *tuhtu* and continue $(2 \times 1) + 5$, $(3 \times 1) + 5$, $(4 \times 1) + 5$ to make sense of this system. It looks a bit complicated, but then again, running out of fingers can be complicated. As can adhering to given phonological facts.

The simplex numerals are '1', '2', '3', '4', '5', '10', '15', '20'. In addition, there is **mon?e* '400', which is a standard measure as well as a numeral. The Nahuatl-derived equivalent term is "un zontle." This term is still used by present-day Indians as a measure of 400 ears of corn (my observations among Zoques of Oxolotán, Tabasco). **mon?e* does combines with other numeral roots in ChisZ. Some MZ languages, however, prefer expressing '400' by '4 × 100'. It is assumed that **mon?e* was more of a standard measure and '4 × 100' the true numeral.

Table 3.14. Comparative chart of some MZ numerals[12]

	NHM	LM Gu	OlP	SaP
'1'	tʋ?-k	tu"-k	tu?-k	tu?-k
'2'	mehc-k	mec-k	mec-ko	mec-k
'3'	tʋ:h-k	tɨgĭ:-k	tuvɨ'-k	tú:gu-p
'4'	mak-ta:š-k	-	maktas-ko	máktaš-p
'5'	mugo:š-k	mɨgó:š̄-k	mokoš-ko	mógoš-p
'6'	tʋht-ïk	tɨdúhk	tuhtuh-ko	túhtu-p
'7'	vuštʋht-ïk	huštúh-k	huš-tukuhtuh-ko	huš-tuhtu-p
'8'	tʋdʋht-ïk	tuktúhk	tukutuh-ko	tugu-tuhtu-p
'9'	tás-tʋht-ïk	ta·š̄-tuh-k	ta:s-tuhtuh-ko	taš-tuhtu-p
'10'	mahk	mahk	maku	mak
'11'	mak-tʋ?k	mah-tú"k	-	mak-pimuh-tu-p
'15'	-	-	-	-
'20'	?i:?pš	?i·?š	?i:pšɨ	?i?pš

	TxZ	ChisZ	pMZ
'1'	tum	tum-ɨ	*tu?, *tum
'2'	be:c	mec-k	*mec
'3'	túk-na?	tuk-a?y	*tu:ku
'4'	báks-na?	makšku?y	*maktas
'5'	bós-na?	mohs-a?y	*m(ok)os
'6'	túh-na?	tuht-a?y	*tuhtu
'7'	wɨstúh-na?	ku?y-a?y	*huwɨs-tuhtu
'8'	tuktúh-na?	tukutuht-a?y	*tuku-tuhtu
'9'	baks-túh-na?	maks-tuht-a?y	*maktas-tuhtu
'10'	bák-na?	mahk-a?y	*mak(u)
'11'	baktúm-na?	mak-tum-a?y	*mak-tum-
'15'	-	yɨht-a?y	-
'20'	?é?pš-ña?	?ips	*?i:?ps

Now, in this system the numbers 6 to 9, as well as any numbers above 5, which are not twenties, would belong to a secondary sub-system and are probably indicative of a later step in the evolution of the system. TK's inference that "[t]he expression 'forty', 'sixty', 'eighty', and so on by twenties up to '380' are multiplicative compounds"

---

[12] For the complete data see Part Two, section on numerals.

(§3180) is wrong. The data show that *only simplex numerals can be multiplied by twenty*. The resulting expressions are '40', '60', '80', '100', '200', '300'. The numeral '120', for instance, is not expressed '6 x 20', but '100 + 20':

SHM	(Ayutla)	< *tukmugépsh kaépsh* >	(Beals 1945)
	(Tamazulapan)	*mǐge ʔpš ʔe ʔpš*	(Wichmann 1990)
ChisZ	(Copainalá)	*mohsi ʔs-ko-ips*	(Harrison et al. 1981)

The morpheme *-ko-* 'and' or 'plus' is only attested in SHM [Ay] (in the crude notation of the ethnographer Beals) and in ChisZ-C. This, however, is sufficient evidence for positing the morpheme for the proto-language. Since it is absent from the daughter languages more often than not, it must have been optional or restricted to more special (high numbers) or emphatic (making things clear) use. With or without the use of this morpheme, additive numbers could be conflated with the basic system to make it possible to count all numbers from 1 to 8,000. In principle, the count could probably continue indefinitely, although numerals higher than 8,000 (ChisZ-C: *ʔips mone ʔ*) are not attested.

CHAPTER 4

Mixean Diachronic Phonology

The pMZ phoneme inventory is retained in pM. Zoquean [s] corresponds to Mixean [š]. The way pMZ forms are written it is implied that Mixean innovated the quality of */s/. The choice between */š/ and */s/ is, however, arbitrary. Reflexes of the bilabial glide may in some languages and dialects acquire some friction, thus becoming /v/ in OlP and NHM and having bilabial to labial voiceless fricative allophones in some dialects of SHM. The phonological system is extended in OM because of factors such as palatalization and strengthening of consonants and lowering and umlauting of vowels. But since, as can be seen from the individual phonologies, the historical core is still perceptible in the modern languages, there is no point in offering a comprehensive chart of phoneme correspondences. Offering correspondences of canonical forms, however, is unusually well motivated in the Mixean case because most changes involve whole syllables, if not whole roots, rather than single segments.

4.1. VERB CANONS

Table 4.1 displays the reflexes of all types of pOM monosyllabic verb canons in the OM languages and dialect areas. The data on which the chart is based occupy a large portion of Part Two. Class [3/4] is so named because it corresponds to two different classes in Zoquean.

The quantitative ablaut developed in three successive steps. The oldest alternation goes back to the time when pM was formed. This is the alternation in Class [2] verbs, which was discussed in 3.2. This is also the only alternation found in the Veracruz Mixean languages. The reflexes of the nucleus *V:? of Classes [1] and [6] roots in these languages are OlP V: and SaP V?. In all other respects the pM pattern

Table 4.1. Reflexes of pM Monosyllabic Verb Canons
(T = an obstruent, N = a sonorant)

	pM	pOM	NHM	SHM [Tu,Tp]
[1]	*CV:?C	*CV:?C	CV:?C	CV?C~CV:C
[2a]	*CV:T~CV?T	*CV:hT~CV"T	CV:T~CV"T	CV:hT~CV"T
[2b,c]	*CVN~CV?N	*CVhN~CV"N	CV:N~CV"N	CVN~CV"N
[3/4]	*CV?C	*CV?C~CV"C	CV?C~CV"C	CV?C~CV"C
[5a]	*CVT	*CVhT~CVT	CVhT~CVT	CVhT~CVT
[5b,c]	*CVN	*CVhN~CVN	CV:N~CVN	CVN
[5d]	*CVh	*CVh	CVh	CVh
[6]	*CV:?CC	*CV:?CC	CV:?CC	CV?CC
[7]	*CV?CC	*CV?CC	CV?CC	CV?CC
[8]	*CVCC	*CVhCC	CVhCC	CVhCC

resembles what is found in Veracruz.

The insertion of /h/ into the BAS root of Class [5] verbs (as well as into the stressed syllable of Class [9] verbs)[1] and into Class [8] only affects OM languages and is the next ablaut-causing change.

Finally, Classes [3/4] and [1] are restructured in OM languages as a response to individual sound laws most of which can be explained in terms of the tendency toward syllable quantity resolution. This tendency also affected the ALT root of Class [5] verbs in NMM and LM [Gu]. Quantity resolution is discussed in 5.3. The phonological environments that characterize BAS/ALT roots are also discussed in that section. It will be argued that the difference in the environments is primarily that BAS roots were shaped in syllables containing a final cluster, whereas ALT roots were shaped in syllables having a single consonant as coda. This explains why there is no alternation in Root Classes [6] to [8].

Below, the pM forms (omitting the stars) that pertain to each of the canons [1], [2], [3/4], [6], [7], [8] are listed. They provide an overview

---

[1] Class [9] verbs are only scantily represented. Only forms where the two final consonants are stops are broadly attested. They reconstruct as pM *CVTVT > pOM *CVTVhT~CVTVT. NHM has the reflex CVTT~CV́TVT and everywhere else the reflex is CVTV́hT~CVTV́T.

NMM	SMM	LM [SJ]	LM [Gu]
CV?C ~ CV:C	CV?C ~ CV:C	CV·C ~ CV:C	CV·?C ~ CV:C
CV·T ~ CV"T	CVT ~ CV"T	CV·C ~ CV"C	CV·C ~ CV"C
CV·N ~ CV"N	CVN ~ CV"N	CV·N ~ CV"N	CV·N ~ CV"N
CV?C ~ CV"C	CV?C ~ CV"C	CV?C ~ CV"C	CV?C ~ CV"C
CVhT ~ CVT	CVhT ~ CVT	CVhT ~ CVT	CVhT ~ CVT
CV·N ~ CVN	CV:N ~ CVN	CV·N ~ CVN	CV·N ~ CVN
CVh ~ CVh	CVh	CVh	CVh ~ CVh
CV?CC	CV?CC	CV·CC	CV·?C
CV?CC	CV?CC	CV?CC	CV?C
CVhCC	CVhCC	CVCC	CVCC

of their relative number of occurrence and the fillers of the Cs and the V in the CV^(C)C grid. Since any consonant may fill the last slot of Class [5], and because this class is so abounding, representatives of Class [5] are not specified. I only specify representatives whose time depth reach back no further than to pM. In addition to these there are a host of forms going back to pMZ. These have been specified in 3.2.

[1] *CV:?C
ku:?p, ?o:?p, hɨ:?t, wɨ:?t, we:?c, kɨ:?c, ?a:?c, no:?c, ci:?k, ye:?k, šo:?k, to:?k, wɨ:?š, po:?š, ?e:?m, še:?m, wɨ:?n, wo:?n, še:?w, tɨ:?y, ?u:?y, ?o:?y,

[2a] *CV:C ~ CV?C
ši:p ~ ši?p, tu:t ~ tu?t, ša:c ~ ša?c, wa:c ~ wa?c, ta:c ~ ta?c, wi:k ~ wi?k, pu:k ~ pu?k, ya:š ~ ya?š

[2b,c] *CVN ~ CV?N
yak-kɨw ~ yak-kɨ?w, wan ~ wa?n

[3/4] *CV?C
ci?t, me?t, ci?c, he?c, ni?c, na?c, wa?k, no?k, hi?k, ke?š, ha?š, na?n, ka?w, ho?y, pu?y

[6] *CV:?CC
ke:?pš, šu:?pš, ni:?kš, ma:?kš, cu:?kš

[7] *CV?CC
hi?kš, ti?kš, ti?kš, ci?kš, pi?kš

[8] *CVCC
kapš, wipš, tipš, yakš

[9] CVCVC
witit, tikac, cukut, timam

MM and LM Reflexes of Class [2d]

Class [2d] roots are descendants of the pMZ canon *CV:h?. A comparison of reflexes of Class [2d] and [2c] roots in a final /w/ clearly shows that analogy is at work in at least one dialect of LM. Consider the forms in Table 4.2.

Table 4.2

	NHM	LM [SJ]	OlP	SaP	pZ
[2d]	*me:~me"*	*me·w~me"*	*me:h~me?h*	*me:~me?*	**meh*
[2c]	*ci:w~ci"w*	*ci·w~ci"*	*čiv~či?v*	*čiw~či?w*	**ciŋ*
	ca:y~ca"	*ca·y~ca"*	*cay~ca?*	*cay~ca?*	**cay*

A review of the data in Nordell (1990) shows that all LM and MM dialects base Class [2d] roots analogically on Class [2c] in /w/, whereas at least the Tepantlali dialect of SHM upholds the distinction. There is not sufficient data from the other dialects of SHM to prove that this is a general SHM feature, but it is plausible that it should be so. NHM, as we saw, also retains the distinction. This feature thus unites the two Highlands against Midland and Lowland Mixe. All the data are gathered in Part Two under the pMZ headings *me:h?*, ME#006; *ma:h?*, MA#015; *pa:h?*, PA#010; *mu:h?*, MU#007; *su:h?*, SU#006; *yu:h?*, YU#008; *ci:w?*, CI#050; *ke:w?*, KE#028; *ki:w?*, Ki#030; *hi:y?*, Hi#029; *ki:y?*, Ki#034; *ca:y?*, CA#044; *ha:y?*, HA#033; *po:y?*, PO#052, and under the pM heading *yak-kiw ~ yak-ki?w*, Ki#031.

Table 4.3. Developments of the Final Consonant of Class [2c-d] Roots in SHM, MM, and LM

Mode/Aspect		IMP	FUT	INCOM INDEP	COMP INDEP	
Environment		V"__#	V"__V́	V́·__p	V́·__Ø	
SHM	(UR)	h/w/y	h/w/y	h/w/y	h/w/y	
Tu	(SR)	Ø/Ø/y	*/Ø/*	Ø/Ø/y	*/*/*	SHM
Tp	(SR)	Ø/Ø/y	w/w/y	Ø/Ø/Ø	h/Ø/y	
M/LM	(UR)	w /y	w /y	w /y	w /y	
At	(SR)	Ø,*/Ø	h,h/h	Ø,Ø/Ø	*,*/*	MM
Cc	(SR)	Ø,Ø/Ø	*,h/h	Ø,Ø/y	*,y/y	
Ct	(SR)	w,w/w	w,*/w	Ø,Ø/Ø	w,*/*	
Ja	(SR)	w,w/w	w,*/*	Ø,Ø/Ø	w,w/y	
Ma	(SR)	w,w/w	y,*/w	Ø,Ø/Ø	w,*/*	
Pu	(SR)	Ø,Ø/Ø	w,*/w	Ø,Ø/Ø	*,w/*	
Ju	(SR)	Ø,Ø/y	*,*/*	Ø,*/Ø	*,*/*	
Gu	(SR)	w,w/w	w,w/w	Ø,Ø/Ø	w,w/y	LM
Ca	(SR)	Ø,Ø/Ø	*,*/*	*,*/*	*,*/*	

A quick, cross-dialectal overview of the data cannot be given without the introduction of some conventions. Table 4.3 displays the fillers of the G-slot in CV:G ~ CV"G shapes where G=/h w y/. Four morphological environments are chosen: the imperative, future, incompletive (independent clauses), and completive (independent clauses).

These are the only morphological environments to be well attested. Their corresponding phonological environments head each column.

The inputs (URs) to the phonological rules that would specify these environments and derive the outputs for the individual dialects are emphasized. In some cases, two rules would have to be set up to account for a particular "filler." For example, in At, /h/s appear in the final root consonant slot in the FUT replacing both /w/ and /y/. A first rule would have to be set up whereby /w y/ go to zero in this environment and then a second rule whereby a transitional /h/ is derived from zero.

It should be kept in mind that even if both /w/ and /y/ are deleted in the INCOM INDEP (any dialect), as is the case everywhere but in Cc and Tu, a previous palatalization of the inflectional morpheme -*p* caused by /y/ will make it possible to posit this segment for the underlying root. This means that even if the products of /y w/ everywhere turn out the same, as is the case in Tp, At, Ct, Cc, Pu, Ca (to judge from the insufficient data), a distinction will nevertheless be upheld in the INCOM INDEP which will make it possible to set up underlying roots containing /w/ or /y/. A star, *, symbolizes lack of data. Underscoring indicates that a full distinction is made in the opposition. The opposition is three-way in SHM-Tp, and two-way in M/LM, where /h/ is everywhere analogically replaced with a /w/, which may later undergo various mutations. These mutations, deletions, and the insertion of a transitional /h/, which is *not* identical with original */h/ of Class [2d] verbs, conspire with the shortage of data to make for a tricky problem. Table 4.3, however, clears things up.

In NHM, a transitional /h/ is inserted between a verbal root consisting of an open syllable and a following vowel-initial inflectional morpheme (cf. Schoenhals and Schoenhals 1965: 314). It is possible that this is also the case in LM-SJ (cf. Van Haitsma and Van Haitsma 1976: 43). If the LM-SJ roots *me·w ~ me"* and *ci·w ~ ci"* differ such that one of them contains the transitional /h/, whereas the other does not, the distinction between [2d] and [2c] roots may be upheld on synchronic grounds. The information given does not betray any difference, however, so the analogy seems to be complete. Moving to Table 4.3, the rest of OM, we discover that all LM and MM dialects conflate the two verb classes (i.e., reanalyze [2d] verbs as being [2c]). For SHM we have rather little data to go by. Among the forms cited under the heading "afilar" in Nordell (1990) there are the Tp forms *mʸæ:h* (TR,

3p, COMPL, INDEP) and *mæ"ßámp* (3p, FUT) and the Mi form *mæ?h cuhš?ú?ŋk*. They show that analogical change is in process in Tp: the FUT introduces /w/, the COMPL INDEP does not. We may surmise that MM traversed this intermediate station on its way to full analogous replacement. In Mi, /h/ is retained (in the one form we have where it is expected). The At and Cc dialects of MM have a transitional /h/ in the FUT of both Class [2c] and [2d] roots replacing /w y h/. /h/ compensates for the loss of /w y h/ in this environment. Ma curiously has a mirror rule whereby /w/ goes to /y/ and /y/ goes to /w/ in the phonological environment of the FUT, and so on. The data do not allow for a full treatment of the morphophonemics of any one dialect. Approximations can and have been made by involving other root classes (see 2.5 and 2.6), so we need not repeat this treatment.

Albeit scanty, the data do suggest an overall conclusion, namely that the /h/ of Class [2d] verbs, due to actual or potential loss, was analogically replaced by the /w/ of Class [2c] verb roots in /w/. This analogical replacement probably started in the FUT and subsequently spread throughout the paradigm.

Irregular Reflexes

There are six roots the reflexes of which do not conform to any of the patterns [1] to [9]. Rather than setting up uncertain new types of proto-forms for these singular cases, I propose to understand them as deviations from given patterns. As a matter of fact they can all be described as deviations from a single pattern, namely [1]. Items that behave irregularly in terms of pattern [1] are introduced with the symbol ▸. These data are given in Table 4.4.

Clearly the columns in Table 4.4 headed by 'to skin, peel off', 'to drink', and 'to find' resemble each other more than any of them resembles Class [1]. But even between these three columns, which all contain the same NHM ablaut type—the rare type called IIA3 by Schoenhals and Schoenhals (1965)—there is internal deviation. There is external deviation as well, since pOM *?e:?k* [?] corresponds to a ChisZ-C form *?e?k* and pM *pa:?t* [?] to pZ *pa?t*, whereas pM *?u:?k* [?] corresponds to pZ *?uk* (without the glottal). The cognate sets in question are in Part Two furnished with a tentative reconstruction of the shape *CV:?C* followed by a [?] indicating that no real solution is at hand.

Table 4.4

	'to die'	*'to flame'*	*'to comb'*
NHM	ʔo:ʔk	ye:ʔn	ka:ʔš
SHM	-	-	-
MM	ʔoʔk ~ ʔo:k	-	kaʔš ~ ka:š
LM [SJ]	▸ʔoʔk ~ ʔo:k	▸ye?n ~ ye"n	▸ka·š ~ kaš
[Gu]	▸ʔoʔk ~ ʔo:k	-	ka!š ~ ka:š
OlP	ʔo:k	-	ka:š
SaP	ʔoʔk	-	▸ka:š ~ kaʔš

	'to skin, peel off'	*'to drink'*	*'to find'*
NHM	▸ʔe:k ~ ʔe:ʔk	▸ʔʋ:k ~ ʔʋ:ʔk	▸pa:t ~ pa:ʔt
SHM	-	▸ʔu:k̲ ~ ʔu·hk ~ ʔuk	▸pat̲ ~ pa:t
MM	▸ʔe·k̄ ~ ʔe:k	▸ʔu·k ~ ʔuʔk ~ ʔu:k	▸pa·t ~ pa:t
LM [SJ]	▸ʔe·k̲ ~ ʔe"k	▸ʔu·k̲ ~ ʔu"k	pa·t ~̲ pa:t
[Gu]	▸ʔe·k ~ ʔe"k	▸ʔu·k ~ ʔu·k ~ ʔu"k	▸pa·t ~ pa:t
OlP	-	ʔu:k	pa:t
SaP	-	▸ʔu:k ~ ʔuʔk	▸pa:t ~ paʔt

4.2. MAJOR MIXEAN NONVERB CANONS

Special symbols:
^ = glottal stop and/or length disregarded in the summary of related types of canonical shapes
▸ = introduces irregular forms
T = obstruent
N = sonorant
E = unspecified front vowel
A = unspecified back vowel

SHM data are usually from the Tl dialect, MM data usually from one of the NMM dialects, and LM data from Gu. Refer to Part Two for more extensive documentation.

CV^C

[2] *pM *CVN*

pOM *CVN

pM	OIP	SaP	NHM	SHM	MM	LM
1. *pɨn	pɨn	pɨn	pɨn	pɨn	pɨn̄	pɨn̄
2. *hem	hem	hem	-	hæm	hæm	-
3. *hɨm	-	hɨm	-	-	-	hɨm

[3] *pM *CVhC*

pOM *CVhC

pM	OIP	SaP	NHM	SHM	MM	LM
4. *ʔuhš	ʔuši	►ʔuš	ʔuhš	ʔuhš	ʔuhš	ʔuhš
5. *hɨhp	hɨpɨ	hɨhp	hɨhp	►hɨːhp	hɨhp	hɨhp
6. *pɨhk	pɨkɨ	pɨhk	pɨhk	pɨhk	-	-
7. *pahk	pakɨ	pahk	pahk	pohk	pahk	pahk
8. *tɨhk	tɨkɨ	tɨhk	tɨhk	tɨhk	tɨhk	tɨhk
9. *šɨhk	šɨkɨ	šɨhk	šɨhk	šɨhk	šɨhk	šɨhk
10. *kohk	kokɨ	►kok	kohk	kʋhk	-	-
11. *cihn	činɨ-	čihn-	ciːhn	ceːn	ciːn	ciːn
12. *hohn	-	hohn	hoːhn	hʋːn	hoːn	hoːn
13. *hahm	hamɨ	hahm	haːhm	hoːm	haːm	haːm
14. *wihn	vinɨ	wihn	wiːhn	weːn	wiːn	wiːn
15. *tɨhm	tɨmɨ	tɨhm	-	-	tɨːm	-
16. *hɨhn	hɨnɨ	hɨhn	hɨːhn	hɨːn	hɨːn	hɨːn
17. *ʔahw	ʔavɨ	ʔahw	ʔaːh	ʔaːw	ʔaː	ʔaːw
18. *šɨhw	šɨvɨ	šɨhw	šɨː	šɨːw	šɨːw	šɨː
19. *ʔahy	ʔayɨ	ʔahy	ʔaːhy	ʔaːy	ʔaːy	ʔaːy
20. *cohy	coyɨ	-	coːhy	-	coːy	coːy
21. *puhy	puyɨ	puhy	pʋːhy	puːy	-	-
22. *wahy	vayɨ	kwahy	waːhy	waːy	waːy	waːy

---

[2] 1. 'who, who?' 2. 'there' 3. 'there'

[3] 4. 'tremor' 5. 'nose, point' 6. 'skin, feather' 7. 'bone' 8. 'house' 9. 'bean' 10. 'ear of corn' 11. 'pitchpine' 12. 'bird' 13. 'lime' 14. 'eye' 15. 'fruit' 16. 'fire, light' 17. 'mouth' 18. 'day, fiesta, name, sun' 19. 'leaf' 20. 'remedy, medicine' 21. 'thigh' 22. 'hair'

OM develops length before sonorants in monosyllabic nonverbs just as it develops a new subclass of alternating V: ~ V syllable-nuclei in CVC verb roots, where the final C is a sonorant. Lengthening in OM is phonetically explained by the voiceless off-glide of the syllabic nucleus becoming voiced. The differences in the OM reflexes of *?ahw and *šɨhw are not explained.

[4] *pM *CV:hT*   *pOM *CV:hT*

	pM	OlP	SaP	NHM	SHM	MM	LM
23.	*ho:ht	►hotɨ	ho:ht	ho:t	hʊ:ht	ho·t	ho·t
24.	*pa:hc	-	pa:hc	pa:c	po:hc	pa·c̄	pa·c̄
25.	*tɨ:hc	tɨ:cɨ	tɨ:hc	tɨ:c	tɨ:hc	tɨ·c̄	tï·c̄
26.	*to:hc	to:cɨ	to:hc	to:c	tʊ:hc	to·c̄	to·c̄
27.	*nɨ:hc	►nɨ:cu	nɨ:hc	nɨ:c	►nic	nɨ·c̄	►nïːc̄
28.	*kɨ:hk	kɨ:kɨ	-	kɨ:k	kink	kɨ·k	kï·k
29.	*na:hš	na:šɨ	►na:š	na:š	na:hš	na·š̄	na·š̄

[5] *pM *CV:C*   *pOM *CV:C*

30.	*pu:p	pu:pɨ	pu:p	-	-	pu:p	pu:p
31.	*po:m	po:mɨ	po:m	po:m	pʊ:m	po:m	po:m

[6] *pM *CVhN-*   *pOM *CV:N-*

32.	*cahn-can	canca'n	-	ca:ncïn	-	ca:nc	ca:nc
33.	*wihnc	-	winč	vi:nc	winc	wi:nc	wi:nc
34.	*tihn-cay	tinca'y	tinčay	ti:nc	ti:nč	ti:nč	ti:nč

[7] *pM *CV?T*   *pOM *CV?T*

35.	*ce?š	-	če?š	ce?š	-	cæ?š̄	ce?š̄

---

[4] 23. 'liver, heart' 24. 'skunk' 25. 'tooth' 26. 'tongue' 27. 'armadillo' 28. 'bottom, well' 29. 'earth'

[5] 30. 'a kind of fish' 31. 'incense'

[6] 32. 'bad smell' 33. 'blind' 34. 'intestines'

[7] 35. 'corn granary'

CV^CV

[8] *pM *CVhTE*   *pOM *CVhTy*

pM	OIP	SaP	NHM	SHM	MM	LM
36. **ʔahci	ʔahči	ʔahč	ʔahč	ʔohč	ʔahč	ʔahč

[9] *pM *CVʔCE*   *pOM *CV"Cy*

37. **cuʔci	cuʔči	-	cu"c	cu"č	cu"č	cu"č
38. **toʔki	toʔki	toʔk	tɨ"k	tʋ"kʸ	te"kʸ	to"kʸ
39. **huʔki	-	-	hu"k	hu"kʸ	hi"kʸ	hu"kʸ
40. **tɨʔni	tɨʔni	tɨʔn	tɨ"n	tɨ"nʸ	tɨ"nʸ	tɨ"nʸ

[10] *pM *CVʔTA*   *pOM *CV"T*

41. **nuʔpu	nuʔpu	nuʔp	nʋ"p	-	nu"p	nu"p
42. **coʔka	coʔka	coʔk	co"k	-	co"k	co"k

[11] *pM *CV:CE*   *pOM *CV:Cy*

43. **šo:ki	šo:ki	▶šo:hk	šɨ:ʔk	šʋ:kʸ	še:kʸ	šo:kʸ
44. **te:tE	-	te:t	▶tE:ʔ	te:tʸ	te:tʸ	te:tʸ
45. **ʔe:ši	ʔe:ši	ʔe:š	ʔE:š	ʔe:šʸ	ʔe:šʸ	ʔe:šʸ
46. **tɨ:ši	tɨ:ši	tɨ:š	tɨ:š	tɨ:šʸ	tɨ:šʸ	tɨ:šʸ
47. **hu:ni	hu:ni	-	▶hʋ?n	-	▶hu:n	hu:nʸ
48. **še:ne	še:ne	-	šE:n	-	še:nʸ	-
49. **ca:wi	ca:wi	-	ca:ʔy	-	-	-
50. **ni:wi	ni:vi	ni:w	ni:v	ni:y	ni:y	ni:y
51. **ce:wE	-	-	cE:v	-	ce:y	ce:y

Concerning the NHM forms: *ca:ʔy* is from pOM **ca:wy*, *cE:v* from pOM **ce:wy*. According to the NHM umlaut rules, the sequences -VCy only retain /y/ when V = /a/. -iCy, -eCy, etc., lose /y/ and have umlauted vowels instead. NHM /wʸ/ in final position goes to /y/. Thus,

---

[8] 36. 'elder brother'

[9] 37. 'meat' 38. 'mat' 39. 'cigarette' 40. 'excrement'

[10] 41. 'buzzard' 42. 'shaman'

[11] 43. 'nail' 44. 'father' 45. 'crab' 46. 'bat' 47. 'hard tree' 48. 'twin' 49. 'monkey' 50. 'chili pepper' 51. 'chicken, hen'

the process */wy/ > NHM /w/ must have occurred after the umlaut rules were regularized. If it happened before the umlaut, pOM *ce:wy would have yielded NHM *ce:y*. Thus, */wy/ > /y/ happened quite late in NHM and independently from the similar development in the other OM languages.

[12] pM *CV:(?)CA   pOM *CV:C

pM	OlP	SaP	NHM	SHM	MM	LM
52. *po:?po?	po:po?	po?p	po:?p	pʋ:p	po:p	po:p
53. *?a:?ca	?a:ca	-	?a:?c	?o:c	?a:c	?a:c
54. *ko:?co	ko:co	-	ko:?c	kʋ:c	-	-
55. *?o:yo	?o:yo	?o:y	-	-	-	-
56. *?u:ma	?u:ma	?u:m	?u:m	?u:m	?u:m	?u:m
57. *ka:na	ka:na	ka:n	ka:n	ko:n	ka:n	ka:n

[13] pM *CVCI   pOM *CVCy

58. -	-	-	?apïk	?aßikʸ	?abekʸ	-
59. *kape	kape	kap	kapy	kapʸ	kæpʸ	-
60. *hɨci	hiči	-	hïc	hič	hɨč̄	hɨč
61. *pici	piči	-	pic	pič	pič̄	-
62. *?ece	-	?eč	-	?eč	?eč̄	-
63. *wece	vece	weč	▸vec	ßeč	Weč̄	weč
64. *šiši	-	šiš	šiš	šišʸ	šiš̄ʸ	šiš̄ʸ
65. *noki	noki	nok	nɨk	nʋkʸ	nekʸ	nokʸ
66. *mɨni	mɨni	mɨn	mïn	munʸ	mɨn̄ʸ	munʸ
67. *hɨyi	hɨyi	hiy	hɨy	hiy	hɨȳ	hïȳ
68. *?ɨwi	?ɨvi	-	?ïv	?ɨy	?ɨȳ	?ïȳ
69. -	-	-	tïv	-	tɨȳ	tɨȳ

Prior to the diversification of the Mixean subgroup, common Mixean in one case lost a medial glide: pMZ *poy?a 'moon' went to pM *po?a, with subsequent truncation in SaP and OM. The canon $CV_1?V_2$ is not otherwise represented in Mixean, the uniqueness of 'moon' having to do with the original rare combination of a glide + postconsonan-

---

[12] 52. 'white' 53. 'vine' 54. 'dark' 55. 'shrimp' 56. 'dumb' 57. 'salt'

[13] 58. 'aside' 59. 'type of bamboo' 60. 'dough' 61. 'leached cornmeal' 62. 'dance' 63. 'termite' 64. 'meat' 65. 'paper' 66. 'sweet potato' 67. 'brother-in-law of man' 68. 'song' 69. 'certain'

nantal glottal stop. pM *po?a*, then, was subjected to the pre-pM phonological rule by which a glide is lost when undergoing metathesis with /?/.

[14] pM *CVCA   pOM *CVC

pM	OlP	SaP	NHM	SHM	MM	LM
70. *yɨmA	-	yɨm	yɨm	-	yi̅m	yïm
71. *šico	šico	-	šic	šic	ši̅c	-
72. *witɨ(?)	vitɨ?	-	vit	wet	wit	wit̲
73. *?akɨ	?akɨ	?ak	?ak	?ok	▸?ak	?ak
74. *wɨkɨ	vɨkɨ	-	vɨk	-	-	-̲
75. *ciku	-	čik	cik	cek	ci̅k	cik̲
76. *tuka	tuka	-	-	-	tuk̲	tuk̲
77. *hoko	hoko	hok	hok	hʋk	hok	hok
78. *košo(k)	košo	košk	koš	kʋš	-	-
79. *kama	kama	kam	kam	kom	ka̅m	ka̅m
80. *kuma	kuma	kum	kʋm	-	ku̅m	ku̅m
81. *kunu	kunukunu	-	-	kun̅	kun̅	-
82. *?oya	?oya	?oy	?oy	?oy	?oy̅	?oy̅

[15] pM *Ca?ka   pOM *Cak

pM	OlP	SaP	NHM	SHM	MM	LM
83. *ka?ka	ka?ka ka?k	-		kAk	kak	-
84. *na?ka	na?ka	-	-	-	-	nak

[16] pM *CV?VT   pOM *CV"hT

85. *šo?ok	šo?o'k	-	šo"hk	-	šo"k	▸šo:k
86. *pa?ak	pa?a'k	pa?k	pa"hk	po"k	pa"k	pa"k
87. *pu?uc	pu?u's	pu?c	pʋ"hc	pu"c	pu"c	pu"c
88. *tɨ?ic	tɨ?ɨ's	tɨ?c	tɨ"hc	-	tɨ"c	tï"c
89. *wa?ac	va?a's	-	va"hc	wo"c	wa"c	wa"c

---

[14] 70. 'bird louse' 71. 'a kind of insect' 72. 'clothes, cloth' 73. 'bark, skin' 74. 'a type of wasp' 75. 'coati' 76. 'tortoise' 77. 'smoke' 78. 'knee' 79. 'cornfield' 80. 'type of palm' 81. 'Montezuma oropendola' 82. 'good'

[15] 83. 'basket' 84. 'flat object'

[16] 85. 'wet' 86. 'bone' 87. 'pimple' 88. 'dry, thin' 89. 'clean'

CV^CCV

[17] *pM *CVTTV(h)*　　　　　　*pOM *CVhTT(Vh)*

pM	OIP	SaP	NHM	SHM	MM	LM
90. -	ʔespaʔ	-	ʔehcpa	-	ʔæhcpɨ	ʔehcpɨ
91. *ʔakša	ʔakša	ʔakš	ʔahkš	ʔohkš	ʔahkš	ʔakš _
92. *ʔekšah	ʔekša	▸ʔekšna	ʔehkš	ʔokšoh	ʔækšah	ʔakšah
93. -	-	-	▸cišk	▸cešk	cihtk	cišk

[18] *pM *CVhyV*　　　　　　*pOM *CVhy*

94. *ʔohya	ʔohya	ʔohy	ʔɨh	ʔuhʸ	ʔohʸ	ʔohʸ
95. *mehya	-	-	mEh	mehʸ	mehʸ	mehʸ

NHM *ʔɨh* has been subjected to the mutually dependent rules of umlauting and dropping of final /y/. The pOM form was **ʔohy*. NHM *haːč* is nice evidence for an intermediate stage -VyCy in the general umlaut development. Pre-NHM **haːycy* was treated just like this intermediate stage was treated, although preconsonantal /y/ is original and not an assimilatory diphthongization. The vowel /u/ in NHM *kúːydum* and *ʔáːydum* is probably a rounded version of the anaptyctic schwa.

CV^CV^C

[19] *pM *CVTVC*　　　　　　*pOM *CVTC*

pM	OIP	SaP	NHM	SHM	MM	LM
96. *cípin	čipiʼn	čípin	cípïn	-	cipʸnʸ	cipʸtʸ
97. *cúkut(ik)	cukutiʼk	cugut	-	-	-	-
98. *cúkAn	-	-	cʋkïn	-	cukn̥	cukt
99. *yɨ́kɨk	yɨkɨʼk	yɨ́gɨk	yɨk	-	yɨk	-
100. *túhan	tuhaʼn	tuhan	tʋhïn	tuhn̥	tuhn̥	cuht

---

[17] 90. 'dancer' 91. 'fish 92. 'vegetable pear' 93. 'sweathouse'

[18] 94. 'woman's sister-in-law' 95. 'sea'

[19] 96. 'wart' 97. 'ant' 98. 'ant' 99. 'black' 100. 'shooting weapon' 101. 'thin' 102. 'guava' 103. 'copal tree' 104. 'a kind of gourd bottle (Sp. tecomate)' 105. 'tepid' 106. 'slippery' 107. 'butterfly' 108. 'morning' 109. 'sister-in-law of man, brother-in-law of woman' 110. 'lime' 111. 'food'

pM	OlP	SaP	NHM	SHM	MM	LM
101. *péhay	-	péhay	pÉhi	-	peh^y	-
102. *póšoš	pošo'š	póšoš	poš	pυš	po̱š	poš
103. *cíkɨk	?cɨkɨ'k	►cígɨ:k	-	-	cɨk̲	►cɨ:k^y
104. *pókok	poko'k	pogok	pok	pohk	pok	pok
105. *hókoš	hoko'š	hogoš	hokš	hokš	hokš	hokš
106. *nókoc	-	nogoc	nokïc	-	nokc	nokc
107. *tótok	-	totok	totïk	tυtk	to·tk	-
108. *hópoy	hopoy	hópoy	nayhop	hop^y	hep̄^{y}	hop̄^{y}
109. *kápay	kapa'y	kápay	kap	►kop	kæp̄^{y}	kap̄^{y}
110. *?ákaš	?aká'š	-	?akš	-	-	-
111. *káyan	kaya'n	káyan	-	-	-	ka·yɨn

^{20} *pM *CVCÝC*   *pOM *CVCÝC*

| 112. *hapóm | - | hóbom | - | hapυm | habom | habo:m |
| 113. *maháw | maháw | - | máhu | - | mɨhá: | mɨhá: |

^{21} *pM *CV(:?NVC*   *pOM *CV:?Ny*

| 114. *canay | cana'y | canay | ca:?n | co:?n^y | ca?n^y | ca?n^y |

^{22} *pM *CV:NVC*   *pOM *CV"N*

| 115. *ta:mac | ta:ma's | ta:mac | ta"m | to"m | ta"m | ta"m |

^{23} *pM *CVN-?VC*   *pOM *CVy-?VC*

| 116. *hayaw | ha?yu | hayau | hayu | ho:?y | ha"y | hɨya"y |

^{24} *pM *CVNVC*   *pOM *CV:C*

| 117. *pawan | pa?a'n | pa:wan | pa:n | po:n | pa:n | pa:n |
| 118. - | ho?ya'n | - | ho:ydum | - | - | - |

---

^{20} 112. 'tomorrow' 113. 'woman'

^{21} 114. 'snake'

^{22} 115. 'bitter'

^{23} 116. 'man'

^{24} 117. 'grinding stone' 118. 'honeycomb'

[25] pM *CV:CVC   pOM *CV:CC

pM	OlP	SaP	NHM	SHM	MM	LM
119. *wa:šuk	wa:šu'k	wa:šuk	va:šk	wošk	▸wa·s̄k	wa·s̠k
120. *ʔa:šik	▸ʔaši'k	ʔa:šik	ʔa:šk	ʔošk	ʔa·šk	▸ʔa!šk
121. *tu:tuk	tu:tu'k	-	tʋ:tk	tutk	tu·tk	tu·t
122. *pu:cik	pu:ci'k	pu:cik	pʋ:ck	puck	▸pu·c̄k	pu·c̠k
123. *hɨ:pak	hɨ:pa'k	hɨ:pak	▸hɨpk	hɨpk	▸hɨp̄k	hɨ·p̠k
124. *pe:tan	pe:ta'n	pe:tan	pe:tïn	pa:ht	pæ·tn̥	pe·tk
125. *po:tan	po:ta'n	-	po:dïn	-	po:tn̥/m̥	po:tp
126. *šu:šan	šu:ša'n	šu:šan	šʋ:šïn	-	šu·s̄n̥	šu·št

[26] pM *CV:wVC   pOM *CV:C

127. *ma:wac	ma:wa's	mawac	-	-	ma:c	ma:c

[27] pM *CV-CVC   pOM *CV-CVhC

128. *kopák	koʔpa'k	kópak	kupahk	kupohk	kupahk	kwahk

[28] pM *CV:ʔCVC   pOM *CV:ʔCC

129. *hé:ʔpVn	-	-	he:ʔpïn	-	hæʔpn̥	he·ʔpt

[29] pM *CVʔCVC   pOM *CVʔCC

130. *cɨʔm-an	-	-	cɨʔmïn	cɨ:ʔm	cɨʔmn	cɨ"mt
131. *kaʔwak	kava'k	kaʔwak	kaʔahk	ko:ʔk	ka!wk	ka"k

[30] pM *CVʔhCVC   pOM *CVʔhCC

132. *nɨʔhpin	nɨʔpi'n	nipin	nï:ʔpïn	nɨʔhpy	neʔpʸn̥ʸ	nïʔtʸ

---

[25] 119. 'sugar cane' 120. 'nit' 121. 'turkey' 122. 'navel' 123. 'corncob'
124. 'broom' 125. 'spell of rainy weather' 126. 'flute, horn'

[26] 127. 'placenta'

[27] 128. 'head'

[28] 129. 'gourd'

[29] 130. 'tumpline' 131. 'marmalade fruit'

[30] 132. 'blood'

[31] *pM *CVCV?C*   *pOM *CVCV?C*

pM	OIP	SaP	NHM	SHM	MM	LM
133. *hatú?k	hatu?k	hatu?k	hadʋ?k	hatu"k	hadu"k	hatu"k

CV^CCV^C

[32] *pM *CÝTCVC*   *pOM *CVTCC*

134. *píštin	pišti'n	pištin	pišïn	pišʸ	pišʸn̥ʸ	pišʸ

[33] *pM *CÝyCVC*   *pOM *CV:CC*

135. *haycu?	haycú?	háyču	ha:č	hacyu?	haǰu"	-
136. *kuytɨm	kuytɨ'm	kúytɨm	kʋ:ydum	kutʸpʸ	ku·tʸm̥ʸ	kʋ·ɨ̆p
137. -	-	-	?á:ydum	?atʸpʸ	?a·tʸm̥ʸ	-

Others[34]

pM	OIP	SaP	NHM	SHM	MM	LM
138. *?i:cɨm	?i:cɨmɨ	?i:čim	?i:cïm	-	?azɨm	?ɨdcïm
139. *ši:škitiw	si:škiti	ši:git	šikïtiv	-	šigɨdiw	šigɨdiw
140. *šɨhk-kama	-	šɨhkam	šɨkam	-	-	šïhkám
141. *yo?ktu	yo?ktu	yo?kt	yo?kt	yʋ?kt	yo?kn̥	yo?t

The reflexes of pM *?akša show that pOM inserts an /h/ before the cluster. This /h/ is at a late stage lost again in LM.

4.3. AN INTEGRATED VIEW OF MIXEAN DIACHRONIC PHONOLOGY

An integration of verbs and nonverbs can be arrived at by relatively simple measures as long as it is recognized that

---

[31] 133. 'another'

[32] 134. 'cotton'

[33] 135. 'boa constrictor' 136. 'avocado' 137. 'sweet apple'

[34] 138. 'wild pig' 139. 'cicada' 140. 'bean plantation' 141. 'neck'

(1) The shape of the BAS root is at all historical stages determined by the presence of the suffixes pM *-pa, *-pe > pOM *-p, *-p[y]. The BAS root is then carried over to other morphological and phonological environments by analogy.

(2) A prior condition for OM quantitative verb alternation was the deletion of final, unstressed syllables.

(3) When *-pa, *-pe go to *-p, *-py a new situation arises whereby the final consonant of the verb root will either participate in a cluster or not participate in a cluster.

The examples in Table 4.5 have been carefully chosen so as to highlight the intricate interdependency of Mixean diachronic phonology (read: quantity). SaP or OlP examples have not been provided since they differ little from the pM forms, and they can be

Table 4.5

	pM	pOM	NHM
142.	*cihn	*cihn	ci:hn
143.	*po:m	*po:m	po:m
144.	*pɨn	*pɨn	pɨn
145.	*wo:?n-a [1/ALT]	*wo:?n-Ø	vo:?n-Ø
146.	*i-wo:?n-p [1/BAS]	*y-wo:?n-p	vyo:?n-p
147.	*tɨn-p	*tɨhn-p	tɨ:n-p
148.	*?an-ɨ [5/ALT]	*?an-Ø	?an-Ø
149.	*?an-pa	*?ahn-p	?a:n-p
150.	*?an-hi	*?ahn-y	?a:hn-y
151.	*ho:ht	*ho:ht	ho:t
152.	*witɨ?	*wit	vit
153.	*i-šu:?k-i [1/ALT]	*y-šu:?k-i	šyu:?k-y
154.	*šu:?k-p [1/BAS]	*šu:?k-p	šu:?k-p
155.	*pe:t-p [2/BAS]	*pe:ht-p	pe:t-p
156.	*pe:t-u [2/BAS]	*pe:ht-Ø	pe:t-Ø
156.	*?ec-a [5/ALT]	*?ec-Ø	?ec-Ø
157.	*?ec-p [5/BAS]	*?ehc-p	?ehc-p
158.	*cekš-a [8]	*cehkš-Ø	cehkš-Ø

looked up in Part Two. What matters in the examples are not so much
the individual forms as the canons they represent. In pM there is, for
unknown reasons, no distinction in vowel length before sonorants in
monosyllabic roots. If other things were equal, the comparativist would
be brought to the unpleasant situation of having to make an arbitrary
choice between reconstructing short and long vowels. It is, however,
a feature of the integrated view of OM diachrony that the developments
only receive natural and simple explanations when short vowels are the
point of departure. Short vowels are also what we find in SaP and OlP.
If we can successfully posit short vowels before sonorants in
monosyllabic pM roots, we shall also be able to defend our view that
OlP and SaP do not form a subgroup (i.e., that they did not share
innovations).

SHM	NMM	
ce:n	ci:n	'pine'
po:m	po:m	'incense'
pɨn	pɨn̄	'who'
-	wo:n-Ø	'pull!'
-	wʸo?n-p	'3p pulls (INDEP)'
-	tɨ·n̄-p	'3p defecates (INDEP)'
?An-Ø (Tp)	?an̄	'burn!'
?Am-p (Tp)	?a·m̄-p	'3p burns (INDEP)'
-	-	'3p burned (DEP)'
ho·ht (Tp)	ho·t	'stomach'
wet (Tl)	wit	'clothes'
šʸu:k-ʸ (Tp)	šu:k-Ø	'3p kisses (DEP)'
šu?k-p (Tp)	šu?k-p	'3p kisses (INDEP)'
pʸetʸpʸ (Tp)	pæ·t-p	'3p sweeps (INDEP,INTR/Tp: TR)'
pæ·ht-Ø (Tp)	tu·t-Ø (Ja)	'3p swept/Ja: lays eggs/(INDEP)'
?æc-Ø (Tp)	?æc-Ø	'dance!'
?æhc-p (Tp)	?æhc-p	'3p dances'
cehkš-Ø (Tp)	cæhkš	'scratch!'

pOM inserts an /h/ between stressed vowels and *clusters*. This is the very key to understanding subsequent developments. There can be no doubt about the rule of h-insertion before clusters, since this is seen in roots of the canonical shape [8] (cf. pOM *cehkš-Ø*). When the root does not itself contain a cluster, h-insertion must have taken place when a consonant follows the root. This happens in the incompletive, independent inflection, which is marked by a pOM suffix *-p* (cf. pOM *tɨhn-p*, *?ahn-p*, *pe:ht-p*, *?ehc-p*). Having identified the phonological environment to which h-insertion was initially confined, we can go on to identify the morphological environment to which h-insertion was analogically carried over. From the incompletive, independent h-insertion was analogically carried over to the completive, independent (e.g., as in pOM *pe:ht-Ø*). We also find an *h* in the completive, dependent (e.g., as in pOM *?ahn-y*), but this is from the suffix reconstructed as pM *-hi* (see Table 3.6).

Subsequently, the following developments took place. NHM lengthened short vowels before the sequence of /h/ and a sonorant + #, and then dropped /h/ between a long vowel and an obstruent or a sonorant + obstruent sequence. NHM has an additional alternant of Class [5] roots in sonorants. To judge from Van Haitsma and Van Haitsma (1976) LM [SJ] does not have this alternant. Nordell (1990) does not contain the kind of data that would allow us to judge about other OM dialects. But we do not expect an extra alternant in non-NHM OM dialects. This is because the canon represented by NHM *ci:hn* is unique to NHM—*ci:hn* and *?a:hny* are parallel, purely phonetic developments.

SHM (a) loses /h/ before sonorants with compensatory lengthening of the vowel and (b) shortens V: and V:h to V before *clusters*. These two rules are ordered. *?ahnp* underwent (a) to yield *?a:np* (vocalism and nasal assimilation irrelevant), which, according to (b) was shortened to *?anp*. A parallel loss of /h/ is *cihn* > *ci:n* (or *ce:n* in the Core area). Parallel shortenings are *šu:?kp* > *šu?kp*, *pʸe·htʸpʸ* > *pʸetʸpʸ*.

NMM developments are described in the simplest fashion by holding on to the rules that *V́:hC* > *V́:C* and *V́C* > *V́C*. In order to avoid the merging of the canons represented by *cihn* and *tɨhn-p*, I need to state that, first, /h/ is lost before *single sonorants* with compensatory lengthening and V:? is reduced to V? before *clusters*. Next, at a later stage, vowels are lengthened before the sequence of /h/ + sonorant + stop. At this stage we have the parallel forms *tɨ:hn-p*,

*?a:hn-p, **ho:ht*, **pe:ht-p*, which are inputs to the rule **V́:hC > V́:C̄.*
Then, **V́C > V́C* and Rule P (cf. 2.4) take care of the rest.

CHAPTER 5

Main Variables in Oaxaca Mixean Dialectology

5.1. COMMON OAXACA MIXE ISOGLOSSES

This section is concerned with phonological features that characterize more than one of the four OM languages and their main dialect areas at a time, features which cut across the established linguistic borders and are reminiscent of an earlier stage of less differentiation. This earlier dialect continuum is labeled Common Oaxaca Mixe. It is the realistic counterpart to the ideal notion of pOM. In its maximal differentiation, OM consists of North Highland Mixe (NHM), South Highland Mixe (SHM: Tl,Tu,Tp,Mi), South Midland Mixe (SMM: Ju,Cc), North Midland Mixe (NMM: Ja,Pu,Ma,Ct,At), Camotlán Mixe (LM: Ca), and Non-Camotlán Lowland Mixe (LM: Gu,SJ,Cn). Tables 5.1 to 5.6 provide examples of six different isoglosses.

Table 5.1. Loss of pOM *V:h

NHM	SHM	SMM	NMM	Ca	LM	
ʔoːk	ʔoːhk	ʔok	ʔo·k̲	ʔo·k	ʔo·k̲	'bottom'
hoːt	hoːht	hot	ho·t̲	-	ho·t	'stomach'
paːc	paːhc	pæc	pa·c̲	pa·c	pa·c̲	'skunk'
maːš	naːhš	næš	na·š̲	na·š	na·š̲	'earth'
peːtᵃ	pæ·htᵇ	šipᶜ	co·k̲ᵈ	-	co·k̲ᵉ	'to lay eggs'ᶠ
tʋːtp	-	tutp	tu·tp	tu·tp	tu·tp	'to lay eggs'ᶠ

ᵃ '3p swept (INDEP)'; ᵇ SHM form from Tp, meaning as in NHM; ᶜ '3p itched (INDEP)' (from Ju); ᵈ '3p healed (INDEP, INTR)' (from Ja); ᵉ same meaning as in MM (from Gu) ᶠ '3p INCOMPL, INDEP'

Table 5.2. Shortening

NHM	SHM	SMM	NMM	Ca	LM	
va:šk	wašk	wæšk	wa·s̄k	wa·šk	wa·s̄k	'sugarcane'
ʔa:šk	ʔašk	ʔæšk	ʔa·s̄k	ʔa·šk	ʔa!s̄k	'nit'
pʋ:ck	puck	puck	pu·c̄k	pu·ck	pu·c̄k	'navel'

Table 5.3. Loss of /h/ before Clusters of Obstruents

NHM	SHM	SMM	NMM	Ca	LM	
-	wekšʸ	wehkš	wehkš	wekšʸ	wekšʸ	'griddle'
-	šutʸkʸ	šuhtʸkʸ	šuhtʸkʸ	šuhtʸ	šuhtʸkʸ	'snail'

Table 5.4. Development of Consonantal Tenseness

NHM	SHM	SMM	NMM	Ca	LM	
vit	wit	wit	wit̲	wit	wit̲	'cloth'
nɨk	nʋkʸ	nekʸ	nekʸ	noʸkʸ	nokʸ	'paper'
taš	taš	tæš	tas̄	taš	tas̄	'cascade'

Table 5.5. m(ʸ) > m̥(ʸ) > p(ʸ) in Final Position after Consonants

NHM	SHM	SMM	NMM	Ca	LM	
kʋ:ydum	kutʸpʸ	kutʸm̥ʸ	ku·tʸm̥ʸ	-	ku·tʸp	'avocado'

Table 5.6. Lexicalized Umlaut of /ɨ/

NHM	SHM	SMM	NMM	Ca	LM	
kïp	kipʸ (Mi kepʸ)	kepʸ	kep̄ʸ	kep̄ʸ	-	'tree'
mïn	munʸ	munʸ	mɨn̄ʸ	-	mïnʸtʸ	'sweet potato'

It appears that Ju and Cc do not have middle length, but this is partly predictable. Ju has middle length in
   (a) stressed syllables before sonorants;
   (b) in the prefixes *ʔa·-, hɨ·-, ha·-, kɨ·-, mɨ·-, ni·-, pa·-, ku·-*;

(c) in certain other positions before voiced consonants (eight examples).

To judge from the scanty data, Cc has middle length in the same positions.

The traditional way of proving the presence of phonological oppositions in a language is by presenting minimal pairs. With only a limited corpus such as Nordell (1990), this is not always possible. The closest we can come to presenting minimal pairs is by simulating one of a set of phonological forms belonging to the same word class and differing as little as possible. Now we know that OM last syllable deletion was the first step toward the development of three vowel lengths in some dialects. If we isolate the canonical forms that turned out to be monosyllabic and further narrow our attention to such roots ending in an obstruent (symbolized as T), our data give us the scenario indicated in Table 5.7.

Table 5.7	pM		NMM
	*CV:TV	>	CV:T̲
	*CV:hT	>	CV̲·t
	*CVTV(C)	>	CVt
	*CVT	>	CVhT

In fact, monosyllables in final obstruents are the only forms suited to our purposes. Middle length is not systematically developed before sonorants or laryngeals in monosyllabic nonverbs in NMM. The verbs do not produce minimal pairs that can be taken as evidence for three degrees of length, because only one verb class (Class [2]) has members with middle length. Finally, disyllabic nonverbs are too scanty. It turns out, then, that if middle length is to have any functional load in a dialect that in other respects resembles NMM, the development

$$\text{pM *CV:hT} \quad > \quad \text{pOM **CV:hT} \quad > \quad \text{CV·}\overline{\text{t}}$$

has to have taken place. Now, this is exactly what did not happen in Juquila and Cacalotepec. Instead, we get the development

$$\text{pM *CV:T} \quad > \quad \text{pOM **CV:hT} \quad > \quad \text{CVT}$$

We must conclude, then, that Juquila and Cacalotepec do not have
middle length (i.e., a distinctive fortis-lenis opposition in the consonants), which thus sets these dialects structurally off from NMM.

5.2. VOCALISM

Primary Vowels

The NHM vowel system consists of six underlying vowels and four
phonologized umlaut vowels of which one overlaps with one of the
primary vowels resulting in a perfectly symmetrical nine-vowel system.
The phonologization of /e/ is carried through in all non-LM dialects as
a result of a lexicalized umlaut. For a simple statement of the typical
non-LM OM vowel system, we may, with certain reservations concerning Mi and Cc, postulate three front vowels /i e æ/, symmetrically
opposed to the three back vowels /u o a/. The horizontal middle of this
system is occupied by a high central vowel, /ɨ/. A comparison of
primary vowels across the OM languages and dialects is given in Table
5.8.

Table 5.8. Primary Vowels

pOM	NHM	SHM			
	To	Tl	Tp	Tu	Mi
*i	/i/	/i/	/i/	/i/	/i/
*e	/e/	/a/	/æ/	/æ/	/æ/
*ɨ	/ɨ/	/ɨ/	/ɨ/	/ɨ/	/ɨ/
*a	/a/	/o/	/a/	/a/	/a,A/
*u	/ʋ/	/u/	/u/	/u/	/u/
*o	/o/	/ʋ/	/o/	/o/	/o/

Secondary Vowels

A comparison of the secondary (umlauted) vowels in those OM languages that have the umlaut is given in Table 5.9. As far as the data informs us, Cm does not have a morphological umlaut and is therefore not represented. Symbols used in Table 5.9 are "=": the reflex of the protovowel does not undergo umlauting; "[ ]": pure allophonic realization; "[ ]$_o$": allophonic realization which overlaps with another vowel in the system; "$< >_A$": archiphoneme represented by one of the members of the opposition; "$< >_B$": archiphoneme represented by neither a member of the opposition nor any other vowel appearing outside of the umlaut-conditioning environment; "//": phonologized umlauted vowel; "//$_o$": phonologized umlauted vowel which overlaps with another vowel. If the secondary vowel is the same as the protovowel, but is nevertheless represented in "$< >_B$", it means that the protovowel has earlier undergone a change. This change is invariably a lowering. If the vocalisms are seen in isolation, the system of secondary vowels can thus be seen as pattern pressure, presupposing the lowering of /u/ to [ʊ] in NHM, the lowering of /e/ to [æ] in SHM and MM, the lowering of /i/ to [I] in the [Ma] dialect of MM, etc.

The desyllabification of front vowels to /y/ took place in Common Oaxaca Mixean times *after* the separation from the other Mixean languages and *before* the breakup into individual languages. At that time,

MM

Ju	Cc	Ma	Ja	Pu	At	Ct
/i/	/i/	/ɪ/	/i/	/i/	/i/	/i/
/æ/	/æ/	/æ/	/æ/	/æ/	/æ/	/æ/
/ɨ/	/ɨ/	/ɨ/	/ɨ/	/ɨ/	/ɨ/	/ɨ/
/a/	/a,A/	/a/	/a/	/a/	/a/	/a/
/u/	/u/	/u/	/u/	/u/	/u/	/u/
/o/	/o/	/o/	/o/	/o/	/o/	/o/

Table 5.9 Secondary Vowels

pOM	NHM	SHM			
	To	Tl	Tp	Tu	Mi
*i	=	<i>$_A$	<i>$_A$	<i>$_A$	=
*e	/E/	[e]	[e]	[e]	<e>$_B$
*ɨ	/i/	<i>$_A$	<i>$_A$	<i>$_A$	<e>$_B$
*a	=	=	[æ]$_O$	=	?
*u	/u/	=	=	[ui~i]	?
*o	/ɨ/$_A$	[ɨ]$_O$	=	[oe~e]	?

an allophonic rule /ɛ/ → [e]/__Cy developed. Such a rule is still present in Lowland Mixe today. We may imagine that the dialects then split off by migration. Some of the speakers of Common OM went off to the Northern Highlands of Oaxaca and formed an umlaut system on their own. The development of NHM vocalism is described in detail in 7.2. SHM and MM were probably adjacent dialects all the time. The best evidence from the vocalism for a basic split is not very grand. This evidence is the umlauted products of /ɨ/, which in MM is /e/ and in SHM is /i/ with Mi later converging toward the MM pattern (the geographical proximity of Mi to the Midlands heightens the probability of this).

   When umlaut-blocking conditions are considered, this putative basic split comes to look like a more recent phenomenon. In MM, the umlauting of /u o/ is always and the umlauting of /ɨ a/ is sometimes blocked before coronal obstruents; the more limited SHM data show that in Tu the back vowels /ɨ u o/ resist umlauting before coronal obstruents and that in Tp and Mi there is no manifest blocking since there is no umlauting of the rounded vowels which would invariably provoke it. Since MM and NHM dialects share in essentially the same conditions for umlauting, what we have is a group of both gradually diverging and converging dialects that were never very different. That there are no traces of the SHM and MM umlaut-blocking conditions in NHM is a good argument for the claimed independence of the development of the vocalism of this language. We may further note that

MM

Ju	Cc	Ma	Ja	Pu	At	Ct
$<$i$>_A$	=	$<$i$>_B$	$<$i$>_A$	$<$i$>_A$	=	$<$i$>_A$
$<$e$>_B$	[e]	$<$e$>_B$	$<$e$>_B$	$<$e$>_B$	$<$e$>_B$	$<$e$>_B$
?	?	$<$e$>_B$	$<$e$>_B$	$<$e$>_B$	$<$e$>_B$	$<$e$>_B$
[æ]$_O$	[æ]$_O$	[æ]$_O$	[a]$_O$	[æ]$_O$	[æ]$_O$	[æ]$_O$
$<$i$>_A$	=	$<$i$>_B$	$<$i$>_A$	$<$i$>_A$	[uü]	$<$i$>_A$
$<$e$>_B$	=	$<$e$>_B$	$<$e$>_B$	$<$e$>_B$	[oö]	[ɨ]$_O$

only in NHM have the secondary or umlauting vowels become phonologized (i.e., the environment that conditioned umlauting has been lost).

Diachronically we cannot get much further with the SHM and MM vocalism. The rest belongs to the description of the individual dialects (see the synchronic sketches in chapter 2).

Finally, those speakers of Common OM who settled in the Lowlands retained the old Common OM vocalism.

5.3. QUANTITY

Table 4.1 displays the various alternating and nonalternating OM verb root classes headed by their reconstructed pM ancestors. While the reconstructions involve hypothesis-making, the matchings of roots found within OM are quite straightforward. Only when explanations are sought for why each root class should develop the way it does in individual OM languages and dialects is some real thinking required. An attempt to find such an explanation will be made in this section. It is a continuation of the statements made in 4.3 and seeks to cover some further aspects of the evolution of quantitative alternation in OM verbs.

Of the eight pMZ monosyllabic root classes [1] *CV:?C, [2] *CV:C?, [3] *CV?C, [4] *CVC?, [5] *CVC, [6] *CV:?CC, [7]

*CV?CC, [8] *CVCC, only one, namely [2], had already given rise to alternation in pM times; [3] and [4] had merged. A BAS alternant of Class [5] verbs was created by the insertion of /h/ in pOM after the final syllable deletion took place (see 4.3). This h-insertion spread analogically to the BAS alternant of Class [2] (see, again, 4.3). The nucleus type V" of the ALT root CV"C, which is used in the completive, dependent inflection of Class [2] and [3/4] verbs, became phonologized after the final syllable deletion took place. [6] to [8] are the only root classes that do not alternate in any OM language.

I hypothesize that alternation in root classes other than what has just been mentioned came about later and may be viewed as developments characterizing the individual OM languages and dialects rather than OM as a whole. Although the developments are dissimilar and independent, it nevertheless seems that they can generally be understood with reference to a shared phonetic motivation or direction. This motivation has to do with the structure of the syllable.

In current phonological literature it has become widely acknowledged that the syllable is central to the phonological description of languages and that syllabic structures are best stated in terms of hierarchies. Clements and Keyser (1983) is one of the pioneering works in this area. Lass (1983) is a study with a more direct affinity to the present discussion since it employs the concept of the hierarchically structured syllable in the explanation of language change.

In the terminology followed by Lass (1983), a syllable (σ) is composed of an optional onset (O), a peak (P) and an optional coda (Co). The peak and the coda together make up the rhyme (R). We have hitherto for practical reasons used the term "nucleus" for sequences such as V:?, V?, Vh, etc. Such complex nuclei are rarely the subject of theoretical debate, which means that there is little advice about how to deal with them. Clements and Keyser (1983: 79-84) suggest that the Danish *stød* be handled with a separate laryngeal tier. It seems that such a separate tier is also needed in the Mixean case to extract the [+syl] material from the -V:?- nucleus class, which makes it possible to deal with the long vowel on a separate level as a V-V branching of the Peak. A similar approach would be useful concerning -V·?-, -V?-, and -V?V- (or -V"- in our practical notation). However, /h/ of the nucleus -Vh- is better treated with the C's (i.e., as part of the coda on the segmental level).

The only verb root classes that do not alternate have final clusters. While all root classes are inflected in the same way (they are only phonotactic classes, not morphological ones), only roots that contain a single C root-finally turn out to alternate in Oaxaca Mixean. Why is this so? An obvious answer is that the alternation initially was a reaction to differences in the quantity of the rhyme caused by the different shapes of affixes. No such reaction is found in verb root classes in final clusters because an additional consonant would not matter here, it would simply count as an appendix. What are the suffixes involved, then? The sources for OM dialects do not allow us to reconstruct the full array of suffixes with certainty. Only grounding/aspectual suffixes occurring on intransitive verbs can safely be reconstructed (Table 5.10). The pM paradigm was reconstructed in 3.5. In 4.3 I argued that h-insertion, which defines the BAS root of Class [5] verbs, was carried over analogically from the incompletive, independent to the completive, independent. I can add here that for roots of all shapes the completive, independent is in fact identical with the incompletive, independent, the former having been completely modeled on the latter. NHM and LM descendant paradigms are identical with the pOM paradigm.

Table 5.10. Aspect/Grounding Suffixes of Intransitive Verbs in pOM

pM			pre-pOM		pOM
-hi	'dependent, completive'	>	*ROOT-*hy*	>	*BAS-*y*
-y	'dependent, incompletive'	>	*ROOT-*y*	>	*ALT-*y*
-u	'independent, completive'	>	*ROOT-Ø	>	*BAS-Ø
-pa	'independent, incompletive'	>	*ROOT-*p*	>	*BAS-*p*

By the aforementioned analogy and the submerging of *h* of *-hy* in the root, the pOM root shapes were dissociated from their conditioning phonological environment and became ablaut roots. It seems, however, that when BAS roots become further modified in individual OM languages and dialects, these modifications are best understood as resulting from the presence vs. absence of a consonantal suffix. In other words, there continue to be regular phonological changes carried over along the original paths of analogy. To show that this must be the case I shall list the rhyme structures of the various classes of roots under inflection as if BAS roots always carried the suffix *-p*—which means adding a C to the root—and as if ALT roots always were merely palatalized—which means not adding a C to the root. If the presence vs. absence of a consonant is really what triggers the changes, we may begin to understand the developments in individual OM languages and dialects in terms of quantity resolution strategies.

The rhyme structures of the various classes of roots with and without an inflectional C are listed in Table 5.11. Ċ is a fortis conso-nant, C means any consonant, and CC means a sequence of two *or more* consonants. If a syllable contains more than two C's, then the number of the rest of the C's is irrelevant since these extra C's would only count as an appendix. Since a C in the coda probably counts as a branching of the coda into CC, any additional C in the string is ir-relevant.

Table 5.11. Alternating Syllable Rhymes in OM Verbs

(The pOM pattern is everywhere equal to that of NHM.)

CLASS		NHM	SHM	NMM	LM [SJ]	LM [Gu]
[1]	BAS	V:ʔCC	VʔCC	VʔCC	V·CC	V·ʔCC
	ALT	V:ʔC	V:C	V:C	V:C	V:C
[2]	BAS	V:CC	VCC	V·CC	V·CC	V·CC
	ALT	VʔVC	VʔVC	VʔVC	VʔVC	VʔVC
[3/4]	BAS	VʔCC	VʔCC	VʔCC	VʔCC	VʔCC
	ALT	VʔVC	VʔVC	VʔVC	VʔVC	VʔVC
[5a]	BAS	VhCC	VhCC	VhCC	VhCC	VhCC
	ALT	VC	VC	VC	VC	VC
[5b/c]	BAS	V:CC	VCC	V·CC	V·CC	V·CC
	ALT	VC	VC	VC	VC	VC
[5d]	BAS	VhC	VhC	VhC	VhC	VhC
	ALT	VC	VC	Vh	VC	Vh
[6]		VhCC	VhCC	VhCC	VCC	VCC
[7]		VʔCC	VʔCC	VʔCC	VʔCC	VʔCC
[8]		V:ʔCC	VʔCC	VʔCC	V·CC	V·ʔCC

In pOM, root Class [1] has no alternation. NHM directly reflects the pOM state of affairs. The least conservative dialect with respect to Class [1] roots is LM-SJ. Glottalization has disappeared everywhere and the remaining plain long vowel has in the BAS alternant of the root been adjusted so as to conform with the tendency to level the quantity of the rhymes. The rhymes V·CC and V:C count as 3½ and 3 moras respectively (see Table 5.12). A constant of 3 or 3½ moras rhyme quantity is achieved by the LM-SJ dialect under the inflection of all root classes except [5]. Class [1] verbs have this kind of adjustment in all non-NHM languages. Whether the /ʔ/ of [1/BAS] in SHM, NMM, LM-Gu is relegated to a separate laryngeal tier or whether it is put on a par with the C's does not have consequences for the mora count as long as -VʔC- does not occur—in which case it would have to be decided whether this sequence is to be interpreted as -VCC- or as -VC- with /ʔ/ on a separate tier. In SHM Class [2/BAS] roots the over-characterized pOM sequence *V:CC is reduced to *VCC in SHM in accordance with the rule of this language by which rhymes other than those resulting from the use of Class [5] verbs may occupy only precisely three moras. A similar shortening is found in the Juquila and Cacalotepec dialects of SMM. This has not taken place in the NMM dialects, and LM [2/BAS] is still overcharacterized. In Class [3/4] the quantity is already leveled in pOM. VʔV is to be interpreted as a long (in NMM and LM overlong) vowel plus /ʔ/ and Vʔ as a short vowel plus /ʔ/. -VʔVCC# is disallowed because this would mean overcharac-terization. In [5], -VC# is a disallowed rhyme. The resistance against such an "undercharacterized" rhyme manifests itself in NMM and LM-Gu as a stronger articulation of C. If C is interpreted as a branching into CC, the development of a fortis-lenis contrast on the consonants in MM and LM has found a tidy explanation in the rhyme quantity resolution hypothesis. Other than that, we observe the vowel shortening in SHM *V:CC > VCC as in (2/BAS). In [8] SHM is likewise in conformity with the threemoras-only rule of this language, as is NMM. The overall tendency is thus to avoid under- and overcharacterized rhymes, and the measures taken are either coda-branching following short vowels or shortening of long vowels before CC codas as illustrated in Figures 5.1 and 5.2.[1]

---

[1] The two different strategies of quantity resolution followed by SHM and MM (Figs. 5.1 and 5.2) correspond to phenomena in, respectively, northern and southern Swedish dialects (Lass 1983; Árnason 1980). For other parallels with the Germanic languages that have to do with quantity, see the discussion in 2.4.

Figure 5.1. SHM quantity resolution.

Figure 5.2. MM and LM quantity resolution.

$$
\begin{array}{ccc}
P & \to & P \ / \ \underline{\quad} \ Co \\
/\ \backslash & & | \qquad /\ \backslash \\
V \quad V & & V \qquad C \quad C
\end{array}
\qquad
\begin{array}{ccc}
Co & \to & Co \ / \ P \underline{\quad} \\
| & & /\ \backslash \qquad | \\
C & & C \quad C \quad V
\end{array}
$$

/h/ is interpreted as a C on the CV tier, C̄ counts as two C's on the CV tier, /ʔ/ is relegated to a separate tier, and the mora count is 1 for V, 1½ for V·, and 2 for V:. An argument for this quantification is that compensatory lengthening in place of a deleted glide results in V → V: rather than in V → V·. If Vw or Vy counts as two moras, V: should equally count as two moras. The quantity of rhymes of all classes of inflected monosyllabic verbs is generally fixed to 3 to 3½ in non-NHM languages, as shown in Table 5.12. Note that Table 5.12 is not arranged according to historical principles. The verb rhyme types listed for each language are simply those that occur in the given language. Vertically the only ordering principle is that like types appear below each other. The table illustrates the imbalance in the NHM rhyme quantities contrasted with the greater balance in SHM, NMM, and LM, which is achieved by means of quantity resolution and which leaves nonaccidental gaps in the realization of some combinatory possibilities.

Table 5.12. Mora Count of Verb Rhyme Types

NHM	VC	V:C	VCC	V:CC		V?CC	V?VC
	2	3	3	4		3	3
SHM	VC	V:C	VCC			V?CC	V?VC
	2	3	3			3	3
NMM	V:C	VCC	V·CC			V?CC	V?VC
	3	3	3½			3	3
LM [SJ]	VC	V:C	VCC	V·CC		V?CC	V?VC
	2	3	3	3½		3	3
LM [Gu]	V:C	VCC	V·CC	V?CC	V?VC	V·?CC
	3	3	3½	3	3	3½

A simple explanation that attempts to cover a large set of phenomena in a wide array of dialects must allow for deviations. A fact that favors the explanation depicted in Figures 5.1 and 5.2 is that deviations from the explanatory pattern are always linked up with retention and that, conversely, cases of innovation fit the pattern. In fact, the more innovative a certain dialect has become, the greater the conformity with the overall tendency.

CHAPTER 6

Zoquean Issues

6.1. ON WONDERLY (1949)

Wonderly (1949) is the first modern attempt at a classification of MZ languages. The first part of the article is a statement of pMZ phoneme inventory and of consonant correspondences in lexemes from the languages corresponding to my ChisZ-C,N,NE,S, ChZ, SoZ, TaM, and LM-Ca. The second part discusses five morphophonemic isoglosses across these languages:

(1) Voicing of stops after nasals
(2) Metathesis of *$*y$ with a following consonant
(3) Loss of *$*h$ in word-final clusters of *$*-hC$
(4) Palatalization of *$*c$ to *$*č$ before i
(5) Reflexes of *$*W$

This article provides an occasion to put forward some remarks on the methodology of historical linguistics.

Wonderly (1949; henceforth WW) commits an error in applying the methods of dialectology to the family as a whole without first having applied the Stammbaum model. The Stammbaum model classifies a language family into ever-finer units by setting up shared innovations for subgroups at various levels of the family. Only when this has been done can diffusion between languages or dialects at various points along the route of historical separation be disclosed and the methods of dialectology be employed. Neglecting the Stammbaum means neglecting the temporal perspective. If geographical isoglosses are applied to the whole of a fully diversified language family, the result is an anachronistic picture of crisscrossing lines and intersecting circles. This is neatly, though unwillingly, demonstrated by Longacre (1967), who, in an attempt to make a systemic restatement of WW, only succeeds in carrying WW's approach systematically *ad absurdum*.

In discussing the five isoglosses of WW I show that none of them —at least not as they are formulated in WW—can be used for broad classificatory purposes.

Isogloss (1): "Voicing of Stops after Nasals"

The voicing influence of nasals is both nonstructural and natural. Further, it may be expected that voicing occurs in some environments rather than others, but not that "stops are voiced after nasals in some words and voiceless in others" as assumed by WW (p. 6) for TaM and ChisZ-S. Voicing of stops is phonemic (not predictable) intervocalically in disyllabic roots at most; there are no minimal pairs involving voicing of stops for any MZ language, however. Wonderly (1946) shows that voicing of stops is relevant to an analysis of ChisZ of today which has been phonologically acculturated to Spanish. But historically speaking, voicing of stops after nasals would be purely allophonic and irrelevant to the overall characterization of MZ languages.

Isogloss (2): "Metathesis of *y with a Following Consonant"

This change does not affect all ChisZ dialects to the same degree. It is an ongoing shared innovation rather than a shared innovation in the usual sense. WW (p. 7) writes: "Historical note: For C[entral] Z[oque] materials, the data from González of 1672, and manuscripts shown by Cordry [Cordry and Cordry 1941] dating from the middle of the 18th century, both show the absence of this type of metathesis in sequences where it occurs today. We therefore conclude that it is a late innovation at least in so far as CZ is concerned." The feature is absent from non-ChisZ Zoquean languages. Within ChisZ it is absent from the southern dialect. In the northern, northeastern, and central dialects it affects all consonants except /t/ and /h/, where metathesis has not completely been carried out in medial sequences *-yC-. The product varies geographically as follows:

	-yt-	*-yh-*
N	-*tʸ*-	-*hʸ*-
NE	-*ytʸ*-	-*yhʸ*-
C	-*ytʸ*-	-*yh*-
S	-*yt*-	-*yh*-

The suppletion of WW's data, which yields the above distribution, makes it possible to improve on his historical note. Clearly the extended effect of palatalization to complete metathesis C^y (or Cy) < $*yC^y$ < $*yC$ spread north-by-south. Starting in the north it probably first affected /n/, then the other sonorants and progressively all other consonants. /t/ and then /h/ must have been the last consonants to yield to the full metathesis since -*yhʸ*- and -*ytʸ*- are still found in the northeast area. When palatalization of /t/ but not the somewhat later palatalization of /h/ had reached the central area, the south was unaffected. This whole process must have started not much earlier than the beginning of the eighteenth century, and is likely to continue in the future for as long as ChisZ is spoken. The not too hypothetical situation of a wave process like this finally resulting in a simple rule of metathesis of all C's with /y/ and characterizing all dialects would be a situation usually characterized as "shared innovation" and described as a "sound law." Whenever I deal with "shared innovations" and "sound laws" in this study, these concepts will be cover terms for such waves that have reached their destination. These cover terms are practical and easy to deal with. "Waves" are more difficult to deal with, one reason being that it is never possible on internal evidence alone to establish the direction of the waves once they have "flooded" an area completely. Some historical linguists are lured by their own projections into thinking that the contours of a dialect area provide evidence for the direction of waves within that area. The ChisZ area almost forms a perfect circle with Copainalá close to the middle. But this does not mean that innovation must necessarily radiate from Copainalá. The innovation just discussed in all likelihood started on the periphery of the circle.

The use of metathesis of /y/ as an isogloss characterizing the whole MZ language family is clearly off the mark. As shown, it is in ChisZ associated with local "waves." Something similar holds for Oaxaca Mixean. Here, it is absent in NHM but present in different degrees in

SHM, MM, and LM. Only after the application of the Stammbaum model may this feature be used for local characterization.

Isogloss (3): "Loss of *h*"

The monosyllabic nonverb cognates I have compiled offer us a clear pattern:

pMZ	pM	pZ	GZ	ChZ	ChisZ	
					NE dialect	other
*CVT	*CVhT	*CVT	CVT	CVT	CVhT	CVT
*CV:T	*CV:hT	*CVT	CVT	CVT	CVhT	CVT

T = obstruent

/h/ is inserted before obstruents word-finally in these monosyllabic nonverb roots in pM. The shape CVT exists alongside CVhT in SaP, NHM, SHM, MM, and LM. But this is only so because of final syllable deletion in these languages.

The Mixean reflexes of the /h/ inserted in pM have already been discussed in preceding chapters. In ChisZ-NE a like element occurs before final obstruents in stressed syllables, the reason being that here a phonological rule operates whereby [+nas] → [-nas]/__#. Thus, we find a form like *sɨk* [sɨk] 'day, etc.' (from pZ *sɨŋ < pMZ *sɨw) nearly merging with *sɨk* [sɨhk] 'bean'. Perhaps there was a tendency to slightly lengthen the vowels of the obligatorily stressed monosyllables in pMZ. This lengthening would manifest itself as preaspiration of obstruents. This preaspiration became phonemic in ChisZ-NE because of the denasalization rule.

Thus /h/ was never really there in pZ except perhaps allophonically. It is wrong, then, when WW speaks of "loss of /h/." Speaking of "gain" would apply to Mixean but not to ChisZ-NE, where the gain is purely compensatory. The question is: can secondary compensatory phenomena be put to use as isoglosses? I think not. The developments underlying these phenomena ought to be of greater interest. This does away with isogloss (3).

Isogloss (4): "Palatalization of *c to *$\check{c}$ before i"

SaP palatalizes /c/ before and after /i/ and /e/, OIP only before i. In OM all consonants except /ʔ/ palatalize before desyllabified /i/ and /e/, but this is a late, different, and independent process. In TaM /c/ is palatalized before the front vowels /i/ and /e/ (the latter from pMZ *a); compare such forms as <chei> 'vine', <ché> 'stone', <tèchíc> 'ear', <chichú> 'dog', <chí> 'knee' (Lehmann 1920: 781-786). In pGZ the coronals */t c s n/ are palatalized to [t^y c^y s^y ñ]. The palatalization products which may, at an early stage, have been allophonic, become phonemic in at least TxZ (where /t^y/ and /c^y/ further merge to /č/). No Zoquean languages other than TxZ, AyZ, and SoZ have palatalization caused by front vowels. From this overview of the extent and character of palatalization in MZ languages, it appears that WW's isogloss is too narrowly formulated. More important, palatalization of stops is a feature which is involved in either diffusion or shared innovation depending on the geographical space and the linguistic time horizon. At an early level of common Gulf Zoquean (cGZ), the palatalization of /t c n s/ spread wavelike to all the cGZ dialects and came to appear historically as a shared innovation, which along with other such shared innovations permits us to connect the GZ languages to a separate node in the family tree. During that time or later, perhaps as a result of diffusion, SaP developed palatalization of /c/ in the environment of both of the front vowels and OIP began to palatalize /c/ before /i/. The extent of palatalization is not the same in GZ nor in SaP and OIP; further, GZ palatalization may be used for classificatory purposes, whereas palatalization in the Mixean languages of Veracruz may be treated as a phenomenon characterizing the two languages individually or as a feature that diffused from GZ sometime between cGZ times and today. GZ palatalization is fixed to a point in the relative linguistic horizon, whereas OIP and SaP palatalization "floats" in time. When the 'isogloss' $c \rightarrow c^y/\_\_i$ is set up and used as in WW, the result is an anachronistic picture which obscures rather than reveals facts about the history of MZ.

Isogloss (5): "Reflexes of *W*"

The morphophoneme *W is set up by WW to account for the correspondence Mixe -w# = Zoque -ŋ# as well as for a ChisZ-C morphophonemic process whereby /h/ goes to /y/ between nonlabial vowels
and the vowel-harmonic suffixes -i/e and -ɨ/a, and goes to /w/ between
rounded vowels and -i/e, -ɨ/a (with the exception that it goes to /y/
when preceded by /o/ in certain roots; cf. Harrison et al. (1981: 465).
The correspondence, which today we would formulate as two different
reflexes of pMZ final *w in Mixean and Zoquean and use as part of the
definition of the main MZ division, is not related to the morphophonemic processes involving /h/ in ChisZ-C. If there is any relationship
between these morphophonemic processes and the reflex of *w, it
would be one of analogy. The morphophonemic processes involving /h/
are, incidentally, restricted to ChisZ-C. Protoelements should first be
related to the particular family tree which is set up to describe the main
historical developments within that family. When this is done, their
reflexes within the individual dialects may be studied. Thus, we set up
*w and the rule that pMZ *w > pZ *ŋ/__$. Descending from the pZ
node, we discover that pZ *ŋ is involved in morphophonemic processes
which differ from one Zoquean language to another. As Kaufman
(1963: 46, 2310-11) argues, /w/ was in complementary distribution
with [ŋ] in common Zoque, but was later phonemicized. In SoZ and
TxZ, [ŋ] analogically replaced /w/ wherever /w/ alternated with [ŋ], so
that [ŋ] became a separate phoneme, /ŋ/. This analogical replacement
is one of the features defining the GZ subgroup. In both ChisZ and
ChZ, /ŋ/ retains an alternation with /w/ in certain phonological environments. Generally speaking, *w is retained before nonlabial vowels. It
is possible, however, that there are some ChisZ dialects where the more
cautious term "certain morphological environments" would be more
appropriate. At the level of ChisZ dialectology, "reflexes of *w" may
thus be tried as a geographical isogloss; at the more general level of
internal MZ classification, however, "reflexes of *w" is best understood
in terms of the Stammbaum model.

Conclusion

The above discussion leads to a theoretical conclusion and an empirical one.

The theoretical conclusion is a confirmation of the validity of the Stammbaum model of historical, linguistic divergence. This model and its implications are well known, so the discussion need not be taken any further.

The empirical conclusion is that none of WW's isoglosses, as originally formulated and implemented, are useful for broader classificatory purposes. For our view on the relationship among SaP, OlP, and the OM, GZ, and ChZ languages within the MZ family, this has no consequences since WW in these respects has been superseded by later studies, including this one. There remains, however, a "blind spot": Chiapas Zoque. The four ChisZ dialects have been internally classified as in WW ever since the publication of that article. This internal classification must now be questioned. Apart from the intuitions WW may have had about the differences among ChisZ-N,NE,C,S, no basis remains for setting up these four units. In this study it is surmised that they are a single unit comprising complex dialect configurations characterized by various conflicting directions of diffusion. To confirm this it is necessary to (1) set up the evolutionary basis for the formation of ChisZ, (2) map all internal variation geographically—be it phonological, grammatical, or lexical variation—something which requires that (3) a grammatical description of the NE dialect and that (4) a full description of the S dialect is made in order to fill out the present gaps in our knowledge and that (5) a comprehensive set of potential structural isoglosses is produced which may be (6) employed in a thorough survey of Zoque villages in the area within and bordering on Chiapas. Such a study is urgent since the S dialect is on the verge of extinction and the C, N, and NE dialects are being affected by population movements.

Such a detailed and time-consuming enterprise cannot be undertaken here. The description of major MZ phonological developments is, however, a contribution to (1), and the rule statements in chapter 8 are a contribution to (2). Further, (3) may be partly achieved in the future when my 1988 text-corpus from Oxolotán (NE dialect) and my 1993 lexical files from Copoya (S dialect) have been completely processed. A preliminary orientation gives me reasons to believe that interesting results could be achieved by correlating such a dialectological study with postconquest Zoque ethnohistory. A good starting point would be the works of Navarrete (1970) and Villa Rojas et al. (1975).

Until further investigations are made that would change the picture, the one possible course is to adhere to the heuristic view that there are four Chiapas Zoque dialects and to make the most of the differences among them, as done for the phonology in the shape of rule statements in chapter 8.

6.2. THE TWO CHIMALAPAS

Since nothing has hitherto been published concerning the relationship between the two dialects of Chimalapa Zoque, Santa María (StaMa) Chimalapa and San Miguel (SnMi) Chimalapa, I shall here briefly give an overview of the differences that set these two dialects apart and of some features wherein they share a common contrast with the Zoquean languages as a whole. StaMa data are from Knudson (1975; 1980; n.d.). SnMi data are from the less reliable but still useful Cruz Lorenzo (1987).

Chimalapa Zoque Internal Isoglosses

Phonological isoglosses

(1) The two dialects often differ concerning retention and dropping of a final glottal stop in pZ nonverbs of the structure CVCV(?). For example:

StaMa	SnMi		StaMa	SnMi	
kacu?	*kacu*	'bitter'	*sepe?*	sepe	'moon, month'
yati?	*yati*	'sweet apple'	hepe?	hepe	'century plant'
?ahu?	*?ahu*	'grasshopper'	suyu?	*suyu*	'pot'
opsa?	?opsa	'foam'	*toto?*	toto	'paper'
hiyɨ?	*hiyɨ*	'flower'	coko?	*coko*	'mud'
hate?	hate	'man'	wiki	wiki?	'finger'
nuku?	nuku	'ant'	*kɨkuma*	kɨ?kuma?	'ring'
cihi?	cihi	'Mexican opossum'			

The underlined forms are those that are conservative with respect to the final /?/. 'Foam', 'century plant', 'man', and 'finger' are restricted to the Chimalapas.

(2) The StaMa dialect usually inserts /?/ before final /y/. This feature is not found in SnMi. For example:

StaMa	SnMi		StaMa	SnMi	
petku?y	petkuy	'broom'	kumgu?y	kumkuy	'village'
waya?y	wayay	'cold'	wa?y	way	'hair'
maŋku?y	maŋkuy	'foot'			

(3) StaMa ...*e?#* = SnMi ...*ɨ#*. For example:

StaMa	mokoye?	SnMi	mokoyɨ	'drunk'
	mowe?		mowɨ	'sleep'

(4) Medial glides are replaced with /?/ in StaMa. For example:

StaMa	pu?ɨ?	SnMi	puwɨ	'pus'
	ti?e		tiyɨ	'why?'
BUT	meya		me?a	'sea'

(5) StaMa CV?C(C)V(?) = SnMi CVC(C)V. For example:

StaMa	SnMi		StaMa	SnMi	
si?ci	sici	'reed'	?i?nɨ?	inɨ?	'cloud'
kɨ?si	kɨsi	'food'	nu?mpa	numba	'clothes'
ma?ne?	mane	'male turkey'	ko?ma?	koma?	'knee'
?o?ma?	?oma	'smoke'	?a?ksi?	?akši	'grackle'
ya?hi	yahe	'far'	hi?ya?	hiya	'sapote'
ka?hpa	kaba	'dies'	wi?si?	wiši	'buzzard'
cu?hi	cuhi?	'night'			

StaMa is everywhere conservative. 'Male turkey', 'knee', and 'buzzard' are restricted to the Chimalapas. /?/ has a high functional load in this position. If the SnMi data are correct, we have a very significant innovation.

(6) SnMi develops "tone." The status of this phenomenon is doubtful. According to Cruz Lorenzo (1987: 41) "tone" (the properties of which he does not describe any further) is involved in the following minimal pairs:

(a)	*ʔaša* 'raccoon'	:	*âša?* 'native blouse'
(b)	*aci* 'uncle'	:	*áci* 'elder'
(c)	*pâta* 'mat'	:	*pataha* 'guava'
(d)	*hâya* 'husband'	:	*haya?* 'male'
(e)	*de?* 'he'	:	*dê?* 'this'
(f)	*hate* 'fat'	:	*hâte* 'man'
(g)	*hûkpa* 'swallows'	:	*hukpa* 'smokes'

(b, d, e) are almost certainly polysemous words that Cruz Lorenzo by a sort of scientific hypercorrection wants to set apart. In (g), *-hûk-* corresponds to a pZ root **-hu?k-* and *-huk-* to pZ **-huk-*. So here some such phenomenon as tone may be at work. The unlikely dropping of *?* in CV?C(C)V structures exemplified in (5) may really be the replacement of *?* with tone. But Cruz Lorenzo does not note tone in the cases where we would have expected it to be. In fact just a handful of words are supposed to have tone, and *hûkpa* is the only example that we can make some sense of.

(7) StaMa $V_i?V_i$ corresponds to SnMi V_ihV_i. For example:

StaMa	*pa?ak*	SnMi	*pahak*	'sweet'
	po?ok		*pohok*	'egg'

If SnMi *pahak* represents a retention, we may reconstruct pMZ **pahak*. It should be noted that *all* other MZ languages, however, have *pa?ak* (or *pa?ahk*).

(8) StaMa CVC corresponds to SnMi CV_ihV_iC. For example:

StaMa	*nak*	SnMi	*nahak*	'frog'
	kaŋ		*kahaŋ*	'feline'

'Frog' corresponds to ChisZ and GZ *nak* and pOM *nakk*. The SnMi form must be an archaism, and on this evidence I reconstruct pMZ **nakak* > pZ **nahak*. SnMi *kahaŋ* is certainly an archaism since the

pMZ form is *kahaw. All other Zoquean languages have reduced *-aha*-
to *-a*-.

(9) StaMa *-uyi-* corresponds to SnMi *-uwi-*, for example as in 'net':
StaMa *suyi* vs. SnMi *suwi*. Here, SnMi is conservative.

(10) Sometimes a final stop is preserved in StaMa and dropped in SnMi
(e.g., StaMa *?apit* vs. SnMi *?api* 'chayote'). More often, however, the
reverse holds. For example:

StaMa	*hukutɨ*	SnMi	*hukutɨk* 'fire'
	pu?hu?		*puhuk* 'intestine'
	cuhi?		*cuhit* 'spit'

(11) SnMi has an alveopalatal /š/ corresponding to StaMa /s/ [s].

Lexical isoglosses

StaMa	SnMi		StaMa	SnMi	
ma?si?	*pašte*	'thorn'	<u>*pasoŋ*</u>	*?ukum*	'pumpkin'
yenku?y	<u>*toc*</u>	'tongue'	*tɨwan ~ tɨn*	*dɨšha?*	'we (excl)'
?o?se?	*honen*	'nest'	*haŋko*	<u>*šah*</u>	'arm'
<u>*?usi?iŋ*</u>	*?omen*	'little'	<u>*?ɨcci?, ?ɨc*</u>	*dɨš*	'I'
<u>*sawa*</u>	<u>*he?*</u>	'air, wind'	*newin ~ nen*	*nenha?*	'we (incl)'
<u>*coko?y*</u>	*pat*	'liver'	*hɨbɨy naka*	*šeta*	'lips'
<u>*kuy*</u>	*?okoš*	'tree'	*moce mok*	<u>*yaumok*</u>	'ear of corn'
<u>*po?s*</u>	*pataha?*	'guava'			
sa?ak	*heta*	'sowing stick'			
<u>*weki?*</u>	<u>*pekpek*</u>	'shoulder'			
pɨ?i	<u>*pici*</u>	'leached corn meal'			

These lexical isoglosses were found by comparing the word list of
Knudson (1980; ca. 640 items) with that of Cruz Lorenzo (1987; ca.
400 items). From the distribution of the underlined forms, that is,
forms that have Zoquean cognates (semantic shifts may be involved),
it appears that the two dialects are about equally innovative in their
vocabulary. The internal differences are greater than the differences
between the dialects of Chiapas Zoque that agree on almost all of the
corresponding ChisZ forms of the eighteen items in the sample.

Grammatical isoglosses

Cruz Lorenzo (1987) cites only about half of the grammatical morphemes expected to be found in SnMi; and Knudson (1980), though
more ample, is by no means a full grammar. Thus, only a superficial
impression of some differences between the dialects can be given.

	Personal pronouns:		*Possessive person markers:*	
	StaMa	SnMi	StaMa	SnMi
1.	ʔɨc	dɨš	ʔɨn	bin
2.	mic	miš	min	dɨm
3.	teʔp	deʔ	ɨy	biy
1excl.	tɨwan ~ tɨn	dɨš-haʔ	tɨwan ~ tɨn	???
1incl.	newin ~ nen	nen-haʔ	newin ~ nen	???
2.	miyan	miš-haʔ	miyan	bim
3.	teʔpɨtɨgay	deʔ-dɨkay	kaʔpɨtɨgay	dey

From the comparison of these functionally equivalent paradigms it appears that grammatical differences between the two dialects are rather
great.

Concluding remarks on internal isoglosses

The phonological isoglosses show that when the two Chimalapas differ
it is usually because the Santa María dialect has innovated. In a few
cases differences are due to the archaicisms of the San Miguel dialect,
which sometimes preserves an intervocalic /h/ that has been lost in all
other Zoquean languages. Differences in vocabulary are rather noticeable and the category of person expressed in very different ways. We
conclude that SnMi is a divergent dialect the investigation of which will
be of decisive importance to comparative Mixe-Zoquean studies.

CHAPTER 7

Developments in Mixean Languages

Conventions used in chapters 7 and 8

≈   In the languages and dialects lined up after this symbol there are examples similar to the example preceding the symbol of a particular sound law. The law need not, however, be formulated identically for the languages and dialects following and preceding the symbol.

= Developments are always traced from the most immediate ancestor to the dialect, language, or protolanguage that is treated. When the distributional criteria for establishing an etymon (see Guide to the Cognate Sets in Part Two) are not met, but examples that presuppose such an etymon are nevertheless given, " < " + a protoform have been substituted for " = " + attestations from related languages or dialects.

Developments in this chapter are traced from pMZ to pM, from pM to pOM, from pOM to individual OM dialects and from pM to SaP and OIP.

7.0. MIXEAN SHARED INNOVATIONS

(7.0.1)   Shortening of vowels in Class [2] verbs in sonorants

(7.0.2)   a. $*C? > ?C/\_\{V,\#\}$
               b. $*C? > C/\_C$

For discussion and examples of (7.0.1) and (7.0.2) see sections 3.2 and 3.3.

(7.0.3)   *Ø > h/V́(:)__C#

"Insertion of /h/ before final consonants in stressed syllables." See discussion and examples in 3.3.

7.1. OAXACA MIXEAN SHARED INNOVATIONS

(7.1.1)   *V́? → *V́"/C__CV#

The feature of length which V? acquires in this environment becomes phonemic when (7.1.2) has been carried through. The allophonic rule itself is pre-pOM and CV?CV shapes are not reconstructed for pOM as such. Examples are given in section 4.2. Compare pOM *ce?š < pM *ce?š and *hatu?k 'other' < pM *hatu?k, which do not have *V? > V". The completive dependent inflection of Classes [2] and [3/4] verbs, which at this stage is characterized by a suffix -i/e, is also affected by the allophonic rule.

(7.1.2a) $V_{[+back, -stressed, -long]}$ > Ø/__(C)#
(7.2.2b) $V_{[-back, -stressed, -long]}$ > y/C__(C)#
"Final syllable deletion." Examples are given in section 4.2.[1]

(7.1.3)   *Ø > h/V́__C_2
"/h/ inserted between stressed vowels and clusters."

E.g., CVhCC < *CVCC Class [8] verbs
       CVhC < *CVC Class [5/BAS] verbs (starting in the
                                  incompletive independent)
See discussion and examples in section 4.3.

(7.1.4)   *V > V:/#C__#

E.g., ti: 'what?' < pM *ti

---

[1] pM *hemec 'heavy', a difficult item, follows the rules, but since there is a cluster constraint on -myc-, the reflexes of pOM *hemyc are hemč, he?mč, or he"mč in the various dialects with an occasional compensatory glottal stop (HE#015); in LM-SJ /p/ is inserted to yield hempyč > hempʸš, a way of protecting /y/.

This is the only cognate CV item attested in OIP and SaP. Presumably pOM *ya:* 'here' and *ši:* 'there' took the same course.

(7.1.5) $*e \rightarrow [\epsilon]$ or $[æ]/\_\_...C, C \neq y$

"Lowering of */e/ in an environment excluding /y/." A widespread allophonic rule in common OM. Although a six-vowel system is reconstructed for OM, the system must early have been out of balance in most areas of the cOM dialect continuum.

7.2. NORTH HIGHLAND MIXE

Syllabification of glides:
Schoenhals and Schoenhals (1965: 314) note three subclasses of verb roots "que presentan variación en el núcleo silábico y extensión a/i." Since the examples given of each of the three subclasses happen to have cognates nearly across the board, I will let them be my point of reference:[2]

A. CVhC-i ~ CVC-a
   ti: tyika 'ya entró (root I, indeterminative conjunctive)'
   tihkip he" 'está entrando (root II, indeterminative disjunctive)'
   van?ic he" tyihki 'y luego entró (root II, past conjunctive)'
B. CV?C-i ~ CVC-a
   ti: dïcoya 'ya lo curó (root I, indeterminative conjunctive)'
   čo?yip he" 'lo está curando (root II, indeterminative disjunctive)'
   van?ic tïco?yi 'y luego lo curó (root II, past conjunctive)'
C. CV?C-i ~ CV"C-a
   ka" čï"ga 'no tiene miedo (root I, indeterminative conjunctive)'
   cï?kip he" 'tiene miedo (root II, indeterminative disjunctive)'
   van?ic čï?ki 'y luego tuvo miedo (root II, past conjunctive)'

---

[2] I have retained the Spanish glosses because an English translation would blur the aspectual distinctions which the Schoenhalses are trying to render by means of Spanish equivalents. In the grammatical glossing '(con/dis)junctive' = (In)dependent'; 'Indeterminative = incompletive'; 'past' = 'completive'. The examples in A may roughly be translated 'he has already entered', 'he is entering', and 'and he entered right away'. The examples in B and C may be similarly translated (*curar* = 'to heal', *tener miedo* = 'to fear').

In all three cases a pre-NHM suffix -*ʔɨy* seems to have given rise to the "extension" -*i*/-*a*. Adding *-*ɨy* to the etymological basis of the types of monosyllabic verbs in question (see Table 4.1) gives us forms that are more easily compared with the MZ cognates, for example:

1.	**y-tɨk-ʔɨy-y*	>	**y-tɨk-ʔyy*	?>	*y-tɨk-a*	
2.	**Ø-tɨk-ʔɨy-p*	>	**Ø-tɨhk-ʔy-p*	>	*Ø-tɨhk-i-p*	
3.	**y-tɨk-ʔɨy-hy*	>	**y-tɨk-ʔyhy*	>	*y-tɨhk-i*	

The development left unexplained has been indicated by "?." However flawed the scenario looks, it seems impossible to find an alternative to the explanation of the rise of /i/ from a syllabified /y/ with previous syncope. More comparative data are found in those sets of Part Two that include the following NHM verbs: *ʔoʔyi ~ ʔoya* (ʔO#046), *cɨʔki ~ cɨ"ga* (Cɨ#008), *coʔyi ~ coya* (CO#027), *nɨhaʔvi ~ nɨhava* (HA#031), *maʔyi ~ maya* (MA#063), *tɨhki ~ tɨka* (Tɨ#019), *taʔni ~ tana* (TA#027). Hopefully, this collection of data will speed the solution to problems involved in the reconstruction of stems of this type.

In nonverbs, the workings of the syllabification rule is more transparent:

(7.2.1)   **y* > i/C__{C,#},   C = /h/

                                (and possibly others, but not /p/)
"/y/ entering into syllabic position by previous syncope is syllabified."

E.g., *pEhi* 'thin' < pOM **pehy* < pM **pehay*
      pEʔtpit 'agile, etc.' < pOM **peʔtypyt*
BUT, *kap* 'in-law of the opposite sex' < pOM **kapy* < pM
      *kapay (≈ SHM)

(7.2.2)   **w* > u/C__#
"/w/ entering into syllabic position by previous syncope is syllabified."
Note that /u/, not /ʋ/, is the resulting vowel, for example:

kaku 'cacao'	< pre-NHM **kakw*	< pM **kakawa*	
mahu 'strength'	< pre-NHM **mahw*	< pM **mahaw* 'woman'	
motu 'to hear'	< pre-NHM **matw*	< pM **matow*	
ʔanyu 'thunder'	< pre-NHM **ʔanyw*	< pM **ʔán-i-way*	

Umlaut:

As mentioned in 5.2, NHM developed an umlaut system of its own. The *typical* SHM and MM umlaut vowels (a) have qualities different from those in NHM, (b) they are sometimes blocked—which never happens in NHM—(c) they are not phonologized, as are the NHM umlaut vowels. Both NHM and SHM/MM umlauts presuppose the development VCE > V^{y}Cy, where "E" is a front vowel, but the comparison cannot be taken further.

The NHM umlaut, then, developed in sequences of a vowel and one or more consonants followed by /y/. /i/ and /a/ both retained their distinctive qualities, but only in the case of the latter do(es) the consonant(s) remain palatalized. C here stands for one or two consonants; the vowel symbols stand for any quantity:

	pM		pOM		pre-NHM		NHM [To]
(7.2.3)	*-iCE#	>	*-iCy#	>	*-i^{y}Cy#	>	-iC#
(7.2.4)	*-eCE#	>	*-eCy#	>	*-e^{y}Cy#	>	-EC#
(7.2.5)	*-ɨCE#	>	*-ɨCy#	>	*-ɨ^{y}Cy#	>	-ɨC#
(7.2.6)	*-aCE#	>	*-aCy#	>	*-a^{y}Cy#	>	-aCy#
(7.2.7)	*-uCE#	>	*-uCy#	>	*-ʋ^{y}Cy#	>	-uC#
(7.2.8)	*-oCE#	>	*-oCy#	>	*-o^{y}Cy#	>	-ɨC#

Notice that NHM is in this work used synonymously with the Totontepec dialect. Other NHM dialects may have developed the pre-NHM pattern a little differently. Up to twelve vowels is a theoretically possible output, and ten or eleven vowels a likely output if the phonologization of pre-NHM *a^y is carried through and/or if the quality of umlauted /o/ does not overlap with /ɨ/. The representations of the NHM-To output is in agreement with the phonological analysis of Schoenhals and Schoenhals (1965). The phonetic facts probably also allow for the analysis of umlauted vowels as diphthongs and of the sequence Cy as one palatalized consonant, but this is of secondary importance.

The NHM umlaut system is synchronically perceptible in the verbal qualitative ablaut. Whether on the basis of synchronic data alone a system of six underlying vowels can be posited for the language as a whole remains an open question. That Crawford (1963) does not attempt it testifies to the difficulties inherent in such an enterprise. One of the reason would be that /u/, as we saw, not only is a product of umlaut but also is the product of syllabified /w/. Another reason is that /ï/ develops not only from an umlaut vowel but also from an anaptyctic schwah.

Epenthesis:

   In a number of instances, NHM apparently fails to syncopate along with the other OM languages. Some of the cases have already been cited in section 4.2:

pM	OlP	SaP	NHM	SHM	MM	LM
*nokoc	-	nogoc	nokïc	-	nokc	nokc
*totok	-	totok	totïk	tʋtk	to·tk	-
*pe:tan	pe:ta'n	pe:tan	pe:tïn	pa:ht	pœ·tn̥	pe·tk
*po:tan	po:ta'n	-	po:dïn	-	po:tn̥/m	po:tp
*šu:šan	šu:ša'n	šu:šan	šʋ:šïn	šu·s̄n̥	šu·s̄n̥	šu·št

If a rule such as $V_{[-stress]}$ > /ï/ had been pervasive, it would have been wrong to prefer epenthesis to avoiding syncope in explaining these cases. But such a rule is (in contrast to LM and some MM dialects) not pervasive in NHM. Now, to support the epenthesis hypothesis, it must be shown that /ï/ appears between consonants that do not, according to some certain phonotactic pattern, combine. Preliminarily I present a list of all items containing an /ï/ that is not the umlaut product of /i/ which have transparent MZ cognates.

ʔi:cïm 'wild pig'	< pOM *ʔi:cɨm
ʔíšïn 'mirror, etc.'	< pOM *ʔiš-n
ʔaʔvït 'louse'	< pMZ *ʔa:wat
ʔʋnïk 'child, etc.'	< pOM *ʔunk
hEmïc 'heavy'	< pOM *hemyc
hʋʔpšïn 'whip'	< pOM *huʔpš-n
kihpšïn 'a kind of measure'	< pOM *kihpš-n
ké:kïn 'wing'	< pOM *ke:k-n
kahpïn 'village'	< pOM *kahp-n
ka:ʔšïn 'brush'	< pOM *ka:ʔš-n
meʔpšïn 'scissors'	< pOM *meʔpš-n
ʔama:šïn 'Spanish'	< pOM *ʔa-ma:š-an
ni:pïn 'sowing stick'	< pM *ni:p-an
nókïc 'slippery'	< pOM *nokc < pM *nokoc

pícïm 'to go out'	< pOM **picím*	
píhïn 'bag'	< pOM **pih-n*	
pištïn 'cotton'	< pM **pištin*	
pe:tïn 'broom'	< pM **pe:t-an*	
po:dïn 'rainy season, etc.'	< pM **po:t-an*	
tikc ~ tíkïc[3] 'to change, etc.'	< pOM **tikáhc ~ tikác*	
tinn ~ tínïn 'to make noise'	< pM **tinin*	
tïpïc 'gopher'	< pM **tïpic*	
ta?mïc 'salty'	< pOM **ta?mc*	
tvhïn 'shotgun'	< pOM **tuh-n*	< pM **tuh-an*
tótïk 'butterfly, etc.'	< pM **totVk*	
vit ~ vídït 'to go about visiting, etc.'	< pM **witit*	

Diachronic rules can do nothing more than describe the empirical facts. Since these are limited, the rules of anaptyxis turn out not to be very general. But they are not contradicted:

(7.2.9) $*\emptyset$ > ï   /{t,v}__t
                    /{p,k,m}__c
                    /{n,t}__k
                    /C__n
                    /c__m
          u   /{t,k}__m
          i/t__c

These rules cannot simply be equated with the phonotactics of the present-day language, as is apparent from a comparison with Crawford's 1963 treatment of cluster constraints.

---

[3] This and the two other disyllabic verb roots listed suffered a stress displacement and developed as follows:

tikc ~ tíkïc	<	**tikhc ~ tikc*	<	**tikáhc ~ tikác*
tinn ~ tínïn	<	**tinhn ~ tinn*	<	**tiníhn ~ tinín*
vit ~ vídït	<	**vitht ~ vitt*	<	**vitíht ~ vitít*

It would have been gratifying to be able to offer typological evidence for the syllabification of a laryngeal since this is a desideratum of comparative Indoeuropean. Rather, the opposite is offered.

Examples of the last parts of rule (7.2.9) are

hEkum 'far way'	< pre-NHM **hÉkm*	< pOM **hekém*
?a:ydum 'sweet apple'	< pre-NHM **?a:ytm*	< pOM **?a:ytm*
na:ydum 'alone, bachelor'	< pre-NHM **na:ytm*	< pMZ **na:y-tum*
?ahktic 'totomostle'	< pOM **?ahktc*	

Among the examples of (7.2.9) there were some especially revealing cases, namely *hEmïc* 'pesado' (< pOM **hemec*) and *tïpïc* 'tuza' (< pOM **tïpic*). They contain umlauted vowels, which means that a relative chronology can be posited:

pM **tïpic*　> pOM **tïpyc* > pre-NHM **tïᵞpyc*
　　　　　　　　　　　　　　> **tïpc*　　> NHM *tïpïc*
pM **hemec* > pOM **hemyc*　> pre-NHM **heᵞmyc*
　　　　　　　　　　　　　　　> **hEmc*　> NHM *hEmïc*
pM **nokoc* > pOM **nokc*　　　　　　　　　　> NHM *nokïc*

The control case pM **nokoc* 'slippery' is supplied to show that syllabified /i/ has nothing to do with the anaptyctic vowel. The forms reconstructed for pOM bear out on a comparison with other OM languages. Adding yet a detail to the history of NHM, I repeat the rule touched upon in 4.2, according to which

(7.2.10)　　　　wʸ > y/__#

As was mentioned, this happened after the umlaut rules were regularized. We are now in the position to establish a rather detailed relative chronology:

(7.2.11)　　　I.　　Syllable deletion (Common OM)
　　　　　　　II.　Umlaut
　　　　　　　III.　*wʸ > y
　　　　　　　IV.　Anaptyxis

Notice that epenthesis is productive in word formation as these nominal compounds suggest:

ʔa:ʔš-ï-kák 'plain chachalaca' [a kind of bird]
kïp-ï-ka ʔahk 'marmalade fruit'
šahk-ï-pa ʔtk 'armpit'
vin ʔak-ï-ni ʔkš 'eyelid'

Other rules:

(7.2.12)   *V > V́:/__hN   , N = a sonorant

(7.2.13)   *h > Ø/V́:__(N)T , T = an obstruent

See section 4.2.

(7.2.14)   *y > Ø/V"__#

E.g., *hu"* 'carbón' < pOM **hu"y*
      ku" 'ardilla' < pOM **ku"y*

A peculiar problem is the occurrence in NHM of a cluster -st- in a very limited part of the vocabulary. For four of the six items in question we fortunately have some possibly cognate material:

OlP	SaP	NHM	SHM	MM	LM	
-	*káhcay*	*kahst*	-	-	-	'hammock'
-	-	*cEhst*	-	*cehč*	*cehčk*	'drum'
-	-	*kast*	*kahc*	*kac̄*	*kac̄*	'painted'
-	-	*cu:hst*	-	*cuc*	*cu·c̄*	'moss'

Both *kahst and *kast may involve earlier geminates -cc- and -hcc-. A more immediate solution suggests itself for *cEhst* 'woven container for tortillas' and *cu:hst*: dissimilation of /c/ caused by the preceding identical consonant. Both *cEhst* and *cu:hst* contain vowels usually associated with an umlaut. In these particular cases the raising would have come about as an assimilation to /s/. Thus, the following rule may be set up:

(7.2.15)   *c > st/c...__#, whereby V → [+high]

(7.2.16)   *V: > V/#C__#

E.g., *ši* 'there' < pOM **ši:*
    ti 'which, what' < pOM **ti:*   (≈ SHM: Tl)
    ya 'here' < pOM **ya:*   (≈ SHM: Tl, LM: Cn)

(7.2.17)   **Ø > t/hn__k*

E.g., *mahntk* 'son'   < pOM **mahnk*
    pɨ"hntk 'soft, etc.'   < pOM **pɨ?hnky*
A possibly related example of t-insertion:
ki"štk 'muddy, etc.'   < pOM **ki?šk*

7.3. NON-NHM OM SHARED INNOVATIONS

(7.3.1)   **V:? > V:/__C{V,#}*

E.g., *?ɨ:č* 'vomit'   (MM: Ju,Ma,Ja,Pu,At; LM: Gu)
      < pOM **?ɨ:?c-y*
   ?a:c 'twiner'   (SHM: Tl,Tu,Tp,Mi,
                   MM: Ju,Cc,Ma,Ja,At,Ct; LM: Ca,Gu)
      < pOM **?a:?c*   (≈ OlP)
   wi:tʸ 'twisted'   (MM: Ja,At; LM: Gu)
      < pOM **wi:?t-y*
   te:nʸ 'ladder'   (MM: Ju,Ma,Ja,Pu,At,Ct; LM: Gu,Ca)
      < pOM **te:?ny*   (≈ OlP)
   te:kʸ 'goods'   (MM: Ma,Ja,Pu,Ct)
      < pOM *to:?k-y*
   po:p 'white'   (SHM: Tu,Tp,Ay;
                      MM: Ju,Cc,Ma,Ja,Pu,At,Ct;
                      LM: Ca,Gu,Cn)
      < pOM **po:?p*   (≈ OlP)
   CV:C < pOM **CV:?C*   (The ALT root of Class [1] verbs)
                                         (≈ OlP)

The allophonic rule set which concerns the homorganicity of nasals with following stops is widespread in non-NHM OM dialects. The rule set includes m → n/__c. In just one non-NHM dialect do we find violations of this rule (e.g., Gu *nam̄zɨ̄m* 'necklace'; compare other OM forms in Cɨ#019). This, however, is enough to disqualify this rule as a strictly classificatory feature. It properly belongs with the synchronic descriptions.

(7.3.2)   *n, *m > [-voiced]/C__#

This development is generally taken one step further in LM and, less pervasively, in SHM, such that */n̥/ > /t/ and */m̥/ > /p/ in the same environment.

7.4. SOUTH HIGHLAND MIXE

(7.4.1)   *ʔ > h/V:__#

E.g., Tp *niːh* < pOM *niː?* (/h/ later lost in Tl *niː*)   (≈OIP)
      Ay *caːh* < pOM *caːʔ* (Tl *coː*)   (≈OIP)

(7.4.2)   V: > V/__C₂ , C ≠ /h/
"Shortening of vowels before clusters of at least two consonants other than /h/."

E.g., CVC < *CV:C The BAS root of Class [2] and [5b] verbs
      ʔošk 'nit' (Tl)   < pOM *ʔaːšk*   (≈Ju)
      hišk 'back' (Tl)   < pOM *hiːšk*   (≈Ju)

(7.4.3)   *ɨ > i/__Cʸ
"Lexicalized umlaut of short /ɨ/ to /i/."

E.g., *hič* 'masa' < pOM *hɨcy*
      kipʸ 'árbol' < pOM *kɨpʸ*

Tlahuitoltepec

Vowel shift:
(7.4.3.1)   *í, *íː > é, éː / __C₍₋ₚₐₗ₎
"Lowering of */i iː/ outside of the environment of palatalized conso-nants." The rule is also found in Tm and Ay and characterizes the core

area. Examples are given in Table 2.3. Further examples are found throughout Part Two under ?I, CI, HI, KI, MI, etc.

(7.4.3.2)   *é, *é: > á, á:
"Lowering and backing of */e e:/."

(7.4.3.3)   *á, *á: > ó, ó:
"Lowering and backing of */a/." The resulting vowel is perhaps rather an extra-low back unrounded vowel, although according to Lyon (1980) this is a low back rounded vowel.

(7.4.3.4)   *ó, *ó: > ú, ú:
"Raising of */o/."

The vowel shift is systematic and uncontradicted in the stressed syllable only as is seen from pOM *yak-?iš-pɨk* (vt) 'to show, teach (CAUS-see-meet)' > *yik?išpɨk* where */a/ and */i/ have a unique kind of development. The vocalism of the Tl word periphery has not been worked out completely. But as a rule of thumb it may be noted that 'to show, teach' is unusual and that the vowel shift is generally all-pervasive. Notice also cases of a lexicalized umlaut as in *tehpš* 'string, rope' < pOM *tɨhpš* and *?ɨ·?pkʸ* 'foam' < pOM *?o:?pyk*.

Other rules:
(7.4.3.5)   *∅(h) > n/k...__k(C)#
"Insertion of a /n/ into original monosyllables beginning and ending in /k/." Shortening as described in (7.4.2) must still be an active rule, since the resulting clusters in *kɨ:nk* and *ke:nk(n)* are responsible for the shortening to *kɨnk*. However, (7.4.2) must be ordered earlier than (7.4.3.5) since the latter is restricted to the Tl dialect.

E.g., *kank* 'wing'   < pOM *ke:kn*
      kenkʸ 'shoulder'   < pOM *kehky*
      kɨnk 'deep'   < pOM *kɨ:k*
BUT, *ko:?k* 'marmalade fruit' < pOM *ka?wk*   [/w/ retained in
                                                  MM: At,Ct]

(7.4.3.6)   *n̥ > ∅/C__# , where C = {k, š} and possibly others

E.g., *puhš* 'iron, metal' < pOM **puhš-n*
    kank 'wing'   < pOM **ke:k-n* (≈ Tu *kœ·hk* 'fin')
    ʔeš 'mirror'   < pOM **ʔihš-n*

(7.4.3.7)   *h > Ø/V:__#

E.g., *ni:* 'water' < **ni:h*
    co: 'stone' < **ca:h*

Tepuxtepec

Lenition:
(7.4.4.1)   *[b] > β

E.g., *ʔi:βÁ* 'singer' < pOM **ʔi:w-pa*

(7.4.4.2)   *[d] > δ

E.g., *puδihk ~ puδik* 'to help'   < pOM **pudik*
    šíʺδi 'that'   = MM *šíʺti*

Other rules:
(7.4.4.3)   *o > u/{Cʸ,y}__

E.g., *yuʔkpáhk* 'collarbone'   < pOM **yoʔkpahk*
    komʸúʺ 'a type of bumblebee' < pOM **kumyoʺ* (≈ Tp)

For Tepantlali and Mixistlán no rules can be established for each of which more than one example is found.

7.5. SOUTH HIGHLAND MIXE AND MIDLAND MIXE SHARED INNOVATIONS

(7.5.1) $*V{:}? > V?\_\_C_2$

E.g., *pi?tn̥* 'spindle' (MM: Ma,At,Ct)   < pOM *pi:?t-n*
   CV?C   < CV:?C   The BAS root of Class [1] verbs starting
                       in the incompletive independent
   CV?CC   < *CV:?CC   Class [6] verbs

7.6. MIDLAND MIXE AND LOWLAND MIXE SHARED INNOVATIONS

The abstract analyses offered in 2.5 and 2.6 give us some clues to the histories of MM and LM, but cannot simply be converted into diachronic rules. To give but one example: *po:m* 'copal' could, according to the rules, be posited as underlyingly /pohm/, although the pOM form is in fact *po:m*. If one were to posit a set of axioms concerning the interface between synchronic and diachronic rules, one of them would state that "mergers block the transposition of synchronic into diachronic rules" (suchs axioms would, incidentally, form part of a more general theory of translation.) For these reasons, Rule Section I of 2.5 and 2.6 must be restated here. The other rule sections need not, however, be restated since they do not involve mergers.

(7.6.1a) $*\acute{V}{:}hC > \acute{V}{:}\bar{C}$
(7.6.1b) $*\acute{V}C > \acute{V}\bar{C}$
"Development of consonantal fortis-lenis opposition."

(7.6.2)   CV:w ~ CV"w < *CV:h ~ CV"h of Class [2] verbs
"Class [2d] verbs in (final /h/) are analogically replaced with Class [2c] verbs in final /w/." See "MM and LM Reflexes of Class [2d]" in section 4.1.

7.7. MIDLAND MIXE

The umlaut and other synchronic phenomena are not described here. All major defining features of the less innovative Northern dialects (NMM) are shared with either SHM, to the one side, or LM, to the other. The more innovative Southern dialects (SMM) *must*, according to the conventions of the family tree, have split off from a line coming down from a node that is separately attached to the OM line of descent between the SHM and LM nodes. This necessitates that MM be defined as a separate language although its more conservative dialects at first glance look like amalgamations of SHM and LM:

<u>Figure 7.1.</u>

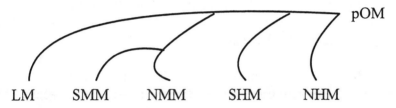

The one innovation which characterizes MM to the exclusion of SHM and LM is not large. This is the lexicalized umlaut of the item 'tree, wood': *kep̄ʸ*, SMM *kepʸ* < pOM **kɨpy*. Even this is not wholly exclusive since it is found in Mi, one of the SHM dialects. Presumably Mi, which is situated adjacent to the midlands, borrowed the item.

Sporadic changes affecting individual dialects

Many of the phonological changes characterizing MM dialects are of a spontaneous nature and affect both MM dialects and non-MM OM dialects individually. Some of these changes are ('+' = 'attested change'; '÷' = 'counterexample(s) have been found'; '±' 'attestations of the change and counterexamples within a single dialect').

Loss of a segment:
- Morpheme initial **h* is lost when a stop comes to precede it
  under composition   (+At, +Tu, +Ct, ÷Ja)
- **p* > Ø/h__k   (+Ju, +Ja, +At)
- **k* > Ø/Vh__?V   (+Ju, ÷At, ÷Ct)

- Reduction of the cluster *kš*. See 2.5, Rule Section II.
- Loss of final **w* following a long vowel

(+Tu, +Tp, +Ja, +Ca, +Pu, +Tl, +Ju, +Ca, +Gu, ÷Ma, ÷At)
- Degemination of like stops

(+Ct, +Ja, ±Gu, ±Ma, ÷Ja, +Pu, ÷At)
- **t* > Ø/?__n   (+Ct, +Ja, ÷Ma)

Vowel quantity in the word periphery:
- Shortening **V:* > V·, e.g. **pa:-* 'uncultivated' (+At, +Cc)
- Unstressed short vowels in initial syllables are lengthened half a
  mora   (+Ma, +Pu, +Ct, +Gu, ÷Ja, ÷At)

Vowel quality in the word periphery:
- Unstressed **i* of initial syllables frequently goes to *ɨ*

(+At, ÷Ju, ÷Tu, +Ct, +Ma, ±Pu)
- Unstressed **a* of initial syllables sometimes goes to *ɨ*

(+Ct, +Ma, +Pu ±Ja, ±Ju, ±At, ±Gu)
- Unstressed **u* of initial syllables frequently goes to *ɨ*

(±At, ÷Ca, +Ct, +Ma, +Gu, ±Ju, ÷Ja, +Pu, ÷Mi)
- Unstressed short vowels in initial syllables frequently go to *a*

(+Ja, ÷Ct, ÷Ma, ÷At, ÷Gu)

Other:
- *n̥* > p/C__#   (+Ja, ÷Ma, ÷Ct)
- *ku-* 'pertaining to the head' > *ku"-* (+Ja, +Gu, +Cc, -Ju)
- *m̥* > p/?š__#   (+Ct, +Ja, +Ca)

In the Ja dialect of NMM *t* is inserted in two cases, that is, *ka?tʸm̥ʸ* 'scorpion' < MM *kæ?pʸn̥ʸ* and *kɨ"tgá:* 'thumb' < pOM *kɨ"-ka:*.

This gives an impression of some of the changes that take place in MM dialects—some rules of thumb, as it were. We now turn our attention to some more pervasive and regular changes found in the southern dialects.

SMM sound laws

Quantity:
(7.7.2.1)   **V:* > V/__C$_{[+tns]}$

"Vowels are shortened before fortis consonants." Shared with Cc and a defining feature of SMM. The change is explained as a case of syllable quantity resolution of the type depicted in Figure 5.1. Diffusion from SHM may be a factor.

(7.7.2.2) $*[\pm\text{tns}] \; > \; \left[\dfrac{\varnothing}{[-\text{syl}]} \right]$

"The consonantal fortis-lenis opposition is lost." This rule is ordered later than (7.7.2.1) and is shared with Cc. One of the examples, *šipp*, is attested and can be formulated identically for Cc. The other examples are from the more ample Ju data.

E.g.,

šipp 'to itch (intr. incom. indep.)' < **ši:p̄p* < pOM **ši:hp-p*
hot 'stomach, etc.' < **ho:t* < pOM **ho:ht̄*
tutp 'to lay eggs (3p intr. incom. indep.)' < **tu:t̄p* < pOM **tu:ht-p*
pæc 'skunk' < **pa:c̄* < pOM **pa:hc*
puck 'navel' **pu:c̄k* < pOM **pu:hck*
kɨk 'bottom, well, etc.' < *kɨ:k* < pOM **kɨ:hk*
šušp 'to whistle, play a flute or horn' < **šu:šp̄* < pOM **šu:hš-p*
wæšk 'sugarcane' < **wa:s̄k* < pOM **wa:šk*

Vocalism:
    A development peculiar to the Ju dialect is the fronting of pOM **a* to /æ/, causing merging with the reflex of pOM **e* in nonpalatal environments.

(7.7.2.3)   **a > æ/__C₀$*, where C ≠ /h ʔ/
"Short /a/ is fronted to /æ/ in closed syllables; preconsonantal or syllable-final /h ʔ/ blocks the fronting." An example of blocking would be *cahp* 'sky'. This rule is ordered later than the two preceding ones, since vowels shortened according to (7.7.2.1) are also affected. A secondarily developed /h/ as in the causative prefix does not block the development.

E.g.,   *wæš* 'skunk'   < pOM **wa:hs*
        cæc 'aloe'   < pOM **ca:hc*
        tæš 'cascada'   < pOM **taš*
        ʔæy 'elder brother of woman'   < pOM **ʔay*
        næt 'deaf'   < pOM **nat*
        ʔæyúk 'language'   < pOM **ʔayu:hk*

?æwá:y̥ 'large mustache'	< pOM *_?awáhy_
?æmá:y 'delicate'	< pOM *_?amahy_
?ænáhn̥^{y} 'left'	< pOM *_?anahyn_
?æyó:p 'poverty'	< pOM _?ayohwp_
yæh- 'causative'	< pOM *_yak-_
?æz̬íhp 'obstructs (indep.)'	< pOM *_?a-cih-p_
hætú"k 'other'	< pOM *_hatu?k_
mæník 'night humidity'	< pOM *_maník_
?æmɨžǽn 'Spanish (language)'	< pOM *_?ama:sán_
?æmú:m 'whole'	< *_?amu:m_
pænɨ́hš 'to follow'	< pOM *_pa-nɨhkš_

Others:

(7.7.2.4) *V? > V/__C_0+C_0V́

"An unaccentuated nucleus V? is reduced to V under composition." Ju. This synchronic rule is found in SHM, but not in the other MM dialects as far as the data show.

E.g., _kɨhí:c_ /kɨ"+hi:c/ 'ring'
tukpáhk /tu"k+pahk/ 'unique'
kɨhót /kɨ"+hot/ 'palm of the hand'

(7.7.2.5a) *_pš_ > _pš~š_
(7.7.2.5b) *_kš_ > _kš~š_

"Optional reduction of the clusters /pš/ and /kš/." Ju. Apart from the reduction of /kš/, which has already been mentioned under the synchronic rule (2.5.25), Ju reduces /pš/ in the following cases:

kihpš^{y}~_kihš_^{y} 'equal'	< pOM *_kihpš_^{y}
kæhpš^{y}~_kæhš_^{y} 'word'	< pOM *_kahpš_

There are more examples of the reduction of _kš_; they contribute to a closer definition of the environment involved in (7.7.2.5b) such that it can be restricted to:

*k > Ø/h__{p,t,š,m}

E.g., _cohmá:ŋk_ 'nephew' < *_cohkma:nk_
pɨhtá"k 'to arrange many things (imperative)' < *_pɨhkta"k_

yæhšón 'beautiful'   < **yahkšon*
kuhm̦ 'middle'   < pOM **kuhk-m*

(7.7.2.6)   **y > y̦/__#*
Ju. An example such as *hoy̦* 'plain' < pOM **hoy* is also found in
Ma. But only in Ju does devoicing of word-final /y/ seem to be com-
pletely generalized.

E.g., *wa꞉y̦* 'hair'   < pOM **wahy*
    pu꞉y̦ 'thigh'   < pOM **puhy*
    co꞉y̦ 'remedy, medicine'   < pOM **cohy*
    mɨ꞉y̦ 'grass'   < pOM **mɨhy*
    ni꞉y̦ 'chili pepper'   < pOM **nihw*
    ʔɨy̦ 'song'   < **ʔɨy*   < pOM **ʔɨwy*
    hɨy̦ 'brother-in-law of man'   < pOM **hɨy*
    huy̦ 'buy!'   < pOM **huy*
    kæy̦ 'eat! (tortillas, bread)' < pOM **kay*
    pu"y̦ 'board, etc.'   < pOM **pu"y*
    ho"y̦ 'to beat liquid'   < pOM **ho"y*
    ku"y̦ 'squirrel (big and red)' < pOM **ku"y*
BUT, *hu"y* 'coal'   < pOM **hu"y*

(7.7.2.7)   **y → y/__C*
Preconsonantal /y/ is not deleted or merged into the quality of the
vowel in this dialect. Although not an innovation, the fact is noted here
since it is a distinguishing characteristic of Ju. An example, which is
by no means singular, would be *kuʸhʸá꞉m* 'ashes'.

7.8. LOWLAND MIXE

(7.8.1)   **n̦ > t/{p, t, c, k, š, h}__#*

E.g., Ca *hæ·pt* Gu *he· ʔpt* 'gourd'   < pOM **he꞉ʔpn*
    Ca *hoʔkt* Gu *hoʔt* 'hook'   < pOM **hoʔkn*
    Ca,Gu *kahpt* 'village'   = MM **kahpn̦*
    Ca *ka·št* Gu *kaʃšt̲* 'comb'   < pOM **ka꞉ʔšn*
    Ca *kæ·kt* Gu *ke·kt* 'wing'   < pOM **ke꞉kn*
    Ca,Gu *kipšt* 'measure'   < pOM **kihpšn*

Gu *ma:béht* Ca *ma:bǽht* 'bed'　　　　< pOM **ma:hpehn*
Ca,Gu *piht*ᵞ 'bag'　　　　　　　　< pOM *pihn
Ca,Gu *puhšt* 'metal, etc.'　　　　　< pOM *puhšn
Ca *šu·št* Gu *šu·s̄t* 'flute, horn'　　< pOM **šu:hšn*
Ca,Gu *cukt* 'ant'　　　　　　　　< pOM *cukn

(7.8.2)　　m̥ > p/C_#

E.g., Ca *wištɨkp* 'the day after tomorrow'　< pOM *hwɨštɨhkm
　　　Ca *pu"šp* 'waste'　　　　< pOM **pu?c-m* Shared with Ma,Ct
　　　Gu *kupk* 'middle'　　　　< pOM *kuhkm (see 7.8.3)
　　　Gu *nʸɨ"gɨ̌šp* 'over'　　　　= pre-MM *nikɨhšm

(7.8.3)　　1 2 > 2 1 /_#
　　　　　k p　　p k

E.g., Gu *huštɨ̌pk* 'the day after tomorrow'　< pOM *hwɨštɨhkm
　　　Ca *kupk* Gu *kupk* 'middle'　　　　< pOM *kuhkm

(7.8.4)　　*h > Ø/__CC

E.g., Class [8] verbs. All dialects.
　　　Gu *?akš* 'fish, etc.'　　　　　　< pOM **?ahkš*
　　　Ca,SJ *?aks* Gu *?akc* 'husk of corn'　< pOM **?ahkc*
　　　Gu,Ca *kipšt* 'measure'　　　　　< pOM *kihpšn

San Juan El Paraíso

(7.8.1.1)　　*V:? > V:
SJ. This change affects Class [1/BAS] and Class [6] verb roots alike.

Guichicovi

(7.8.2.1)　　*T > Ø/__T　　, T = a stop

E.g., *hɨhpů̄š* 'annoyance'　　= Ju *hɨhppů̄š*
　　　pa:mbó?t 'shotgun'　　= Ma *pa:mbó?tn̥* (Presupposes n̥ > t)
　　　wi·?t 'drill, gimlet'　　< pOM **wi:?t-n*
　　　ta"kám̄ 'a type of sown field (Sp. tonamil)'　= At *ta"kkám̄*

(7.8.2.2)   *p, t, k > Ø/{?, h}__{p, m, s}

See further the synchronic phonological rules of the verb (2.6.2.12).
Some examples of nonverbs that extend the rule are:

kïʾ?í·?š 'centipede'	< pOM **?i:?pš-kï* "
yo?páhk _'collarbone'	< pOM **yo?kpahk*
?ame?múk 'pinch!'	< pOM **?a-ma?t-muk* 'tighten it!'
ho?t 'hook'	= Ca *ho?kt*, other MM *ho?kn̥*
pidá"k 'arrange!'	= Ma,Pu,Ct,Ca *pihktá"k*

(7.8.2.3)   Ø > t/n__#   Nonpervasive

"Postthetic /t/." (*?adé:m̄t* 'labio' < pOM **?a-te:m* is an example of
a similar rule conditioned by final /m/. But there are at least fourteen
counterexamples to this one example).

E.g.,

pamĭnʸtʸ 'a type of sweet potato'	< pOM **pa:miny*
mĭnʸtʸ 'sweet potato'	< pOM **miny*
šu!nʸdʸ 'hook'	< pOM **šu?ny*
hu!n̄ʸtʸ 'coal'	= Ca *hu"nʸ*. Both from pOM **hu?y*
pa!nt 'wide chisel'	< pM **pa?han*
ciwá!nt 'mark'	= Ju,Ct *cibá?n̄*
ca!n̄ʸtʸ 'snake'	< pOM **ca?nʸ*

(In the composite 'garter snake'—but not in the simplex 'snake'—Ja has
ni:z̧á!nn̄ʸtʸ)

The rule is not pervasive and the environment cannot be specified
further; examples are less frequent than counterexamples, for example:

hï:n 'fire', *ho:n* 'bird', *wi:n* 'eye'
ša:nʸ 'praying mantis', *te:nʸ* 'ladder', *tu:nʸ* 'plum'
hadú!n̄ 'like this', *wi:nmá!nʸ* 'thought'
nun̄ 'type of palm', *šun̄* 'bitter'
na"nʸ 'type of corn drink', *tï"nʸ* 'excrement'

Camotlán

See Section 9.1.

7.9. OLUTA POPOLUCA

(7.9.1)   *V:? > V:/__

E.g., CV:C < CV:?C Class [1] verbs   ($\approx$ SHM,MM,LM)
       CV:CC < CV:?CC Class [6] verbs

(7.9.2)   *? > h/V:__#

E.g., *ni:hɨ* 'water'   < pM *ni:?*   ($\approx$ SHM)
       ca:hɨ 'stone'   < pM *ca:?*   ($\approx$ SHM)
       cu:hɨ 'dark'   < pM *cu:?* 'night'   ($\approx$ SHM)

(7.9.3)   *c > s/__#

E.g., *ma:va's* 'afterbirth'   < pM *ma:vac*
       mi:s 'you'   < pM *mi:c*
       kácu's 'bitter'   = SaP *káduc* = pZ *kacu*
       pana's 'corkwood tree'   < pM [Veracruz] *panac*
       pu?u's 'rotten'   < pM *pu?uc*
       pu?spu's 'yellow'   < pM *pu?cpuc* (only in Veracruz)

(7.9.4)   *n > m/m...__
"Sporadic progressive nasal assimilation."

E.g., *ma:mɨ'k* 'night humidity'   < pM *má:nik*

(7.9.5)   *c > č/__i
"c palatalizes before a high front vowel."

E.g., *?ahči* 'elder sibling'   < pM *?ahci*
       piči 'leached corn meal'   < pM *pici*
       pači 'a type of crested lizard' < pMZ *paci*

(7.9.6)   *CV^CVC > CV^CV'C
"The last syllable of polysyllabic consonant-final stems is checked."
This innovation conditions the OIP stress shift.

E.g., *hu?pa'k* 'legs'   = SaP *hú?pak*

kácu's	'bitter'	= SaP *káduc* = pZ **kacu*
kopa'k	'mountain'	< pM **kopak*
pa?a'k	'sweet'	< pMZ **pa?ak*
paka'u	'straight'	= SaP **pahku*
pa?a'n	'grinding stone'	< pM [Veracruz] **pa:wan*
pa?a'u	'shore'	< pM **pa?aw*
pu?hɨ'k	'wax'	< pM **pu?hɨk*
pumpu'm	'a kind of flower (Sp. sulisuchi)'	
		< pM [Veracruz] **pumpum*

(7.9.7)   **CVhC# > CVCɨ#*
"Epenthesis." This change is pervasive and was already noted in Nordell (1962).

E.g.,
pɨkɨ	'body hair, feather'	< pM **pɨhk*
pakɨ	'bone, etc.'	< pM **pahk*
yu:hɨ	'hunger'	< pM **yu:h*
?akɨ	'skin, peel; rope'	< pM **?ahk*

The element set up as pMZ **(-k)*, k-mobile, is frequently motivated by OIP reflexes. It may be a sandhi phenomenon or the relic of some suffix. But these are only guesses.

E.g.,
?u:pi'k	'sauce'	< pM **?u:pi(k)*
?u:šu'k	'gnat'	< pMZ **?u:su(k)* (n) 'mosquito'
?ay ša:ce'k	'roll of tobacco leaf'	< pM **ša:?c-e(k)*
komi'k	'pus'	< pM **komi(k)*

In the neighbouring village Sayula, we also find an example of k-mobile: *košk* 'knee' < pMZ **košo(k)*. K-mobile is also found in a couple of OM items. But nowhere is it as frequent as in OIP, where more than five examples are found.

7.10. SAYULA POPOLUCA

(7.10.1)   **c > č/{__i,i__}*
"/c/ is palatalized in the environment of a high front vowel." The /i/ may subsequently be deleted by a more general rule of truncation.

E.g.,   *ʔahč* 'elder brother, uncle'   < pM **ʔahci*
        ʔakóči 'to give advice'   < pM **ʔaw-koc-ɨy*
        pičin 'go out, come out'   < pM **picɨm*
        piʔč 'extinguish, etc.'   < pM **piʔc*
        pač 'lizard'   < pM **paci*

(7.10.2)   *V > Ø/CV^C__#
"Final vowel truncation."

E.g.,   *ʔah* 'canoe'   < pMZ **ʔaha*
        ʔaːhk 'cheek'   < pMZ **ʔaːka*
        ʔakš 'fish'   < pMZ **ʔaksa*
        kam 'milpa'   < pMZ **kama*
        kandɨʔn 'lazy'   < pMZ **kantVnʔi*
        kuʔk 'person interested in indigenous customs and in the community (Sp. indigenista)'   < pM [Veracruz] *kuʔku* 'relative'
        kum 'type of palm'   < pM **kuma*
        pon 'knot of tree'   < pM [Veracruz] **poni*
        pač 'lizard'   < pM **paci*
        paːmɨn 'a kind of sweet potato'   < pM **paːmɨni*
        šíːgit 'cicada' = OIP *šiːškiti*   < pMZ **siːkitiw*
        šoh 'oak'   < pMZ **soho*
        tukš 'cotton trousers'   < pM [Veracruz] **tukši*
        wɨːy 'mange'   < pMZ **wɨːyi*

(7.10.3)   Vowel-leveling   (Sporadic)

E.g.,   *hóbom* 'tomorrow'   < pM **hapom*
        píštik 'flea'   < pMZ **pistɨk*

(7.10.4)   *c > d/__...c   (Sporadic)
              *š > h/__...š
"Regressive obstruent dissimilation."

E.g.,   *káduc* 'bitter'   < pMZ **kacu(c)*
        páyik 'cold'   < pM **pakik*

(7.10.5)   *m > n/p...__   (Sporadic)
"Progressive nasal stop dissimilation."

E.g., *pičin* 'go out, come out' < pM **picɨm*

(7.10.6)   **V:? > V?*

E.g., *nɨ?* 'water' < pM **nɨ:?*
    ca? 'stone' < pM **ca:?*
    cu? 'night' < pM **cu:?*
    CV?C   < CV:?C   Class [1] verbs   (≈ SHM,MM)
    CV?CC   < CV:?CC Class [6] verbs   (≈ SHM,MM)

Rules (7.10.1) to (7.10.4) were recognized by Kaufman (1963: 58-63, 2350). A major disagreement concerns the level of diversification at which h-insertion took place. Kaufman recognizes that /h/ is inserted into pM monosyllabic nonverbs containing short vowels, but thinks that /h/ was only inserted into monosyllables containing long vowels in SaP, whereas I hold the view that /h/ was already inserted into both types of monosyllables in pM. OM data prove this.

7.11. A NOTE ON TAPACHULTECO

A noticeable difference between Kaufman's 1964 Americanist Congress article on Tapachulteco and his large MZ diachronic study from 1963 is the inventory of vowels reconstructed for pMZ in the two works. In Kaufman (1964) eight vowels are reconstructed. Two of these are set up solely in order to account for the correspondences TaM /e/ = other MZ /a/ and TaM /a/ = other MZ /o/. In Kaufman (1963), actually the later statement, these correspondences are implicitly taken to represent secondary developments; the author now sets up six pMZ vowels. I agree with the later statement since (1) the correspondence TaM /e/ = other MZ /a/ can easily be accepted as a lowering that came about independently; a similar, though lesser, lowering is found in SHM and MM dialects (unconnected to the TaM development); (2) no evidence for the two extra vowels is found in any of the other MZ languages; (3) the TaM data are dubious. Admittedly, the six items cited in Kaufman (1964: 409) that have /a/ corresponding to other MZ /o/ remain problematic. That the lowering /a/ > /e/ did in fact take place is perhaps attested to by the form *?eke?n* 'griddle' in StaMaCh (Knudson 1980). This is identical with pZ **?aka?ŋ*, but the vowels do not correspond (as little as do ChZ /e/ with pZ *a in any other items). This could be a borrowing from TaM.

CHAPTER 8

Developments in Zoquean Languages

8.0. ZOQUEAN SHARED INNOVATIONS

(8.0.1) $*V:(?) > V(?)$
"Loss of phonemic vowel length."

(8.0.2) $*? > \emptyset/C\_\_+$
"In sequences of a consonant and /?/ within the same morpheme /?/ is lost."

(8.0.3)   Primary word stress is shifted from being determined primarily by syllable weight to being fixed on the rightmost lexical morpheme of the word string. Polysyllables generalize the stress pattern of those pMZ polysyllables that do not contain heavy syllables, with the effect that verbs are stressed on the ultimate and nonverbs on the penultimate syllable of the root.

(8.0.4) $*h > \emptyset/\#CV\_\_CV\#$
"Loss of /h/ from nonverbs of the structure CVhCV."

(8.0.5) $*w > \eta/\_\_\$$

(8.0.1) and (8.0.5) were first described in Nordell (1962). The other major developments have not been described before.

8.1. GULF ZOQUEAN SHARED INNOVATIONS

(8.1.1) $\acute{V}$ > $\acute{V}$:/C__$C_{[\neq ?]}V(C)$#

"Vowel length developed in the first, stressed syllable of disyllables where the medial consonant is different from /?/." For example:

TxZ		SoZ	pZ	
?a:?pe?č		*?a:pitʸ*	< **?apit*	'thorn'
pá:ta?		*pa:ta?*	< **pata*	'mat'
ta:cɨk		*tá:cɨk*	< **tacɨk*	'ear'
čê:ku?		*či:ku?*	< **ciku*	'coati'
po:m		*po:ma?*	< **pomo*	'incense'
?a:n		*?á:ñi?*	< **?ane*	'tortilla'
pa:suŋ	'vagina'	*pá:suŋ*	< **pasuŋ*	'squash'
hɨ:h		*hɨ:hɨ?*	< **hɨhɨ*	'fly'
ďê:w		*ñí:wi?*	< **niwi*	'chili pepper'
wa:y		*wa:yi?*	< **waye*	'corn drink'

Exceptions (TxZ examples):
TxZ *popo?* SoZ *po:po* < pZ **popo?* 'white'
TxZ *bey* < pZ **mey* 'sea'

Exceptions (SoZ examples):
AyZ *[mbɨ:h]* SoZ *mɨh* < pZ **mɨha* 'big'
SoZ *peka* < pZ **peka* 'old'
SoZ *?asa* < pZ **?asa* 'blouse'

The SoZ exceptions 'old' and 'blouse' may be attributed to the unreliability of the source, which in both cases is Foster and Foster (1948). In a large number of cases this source has short vowels where other sources have long vowels in the expected places. 'Big' may perhaps be construed as a borrowing from SaP.

(8.1.2) $*CV_iC_{\{k/h\}}VC > CV_i:C$ (nonpervasive?)
"Long monosyllables acquired by the loss of a medial consonantal segment /h/ or /k/ in a disyllable." While it is difficult to make judgments about how pervasive this rule is, a deletion of medial material certainly took place in at least a few cases. These are very important because they serve to phonologize vowel length in pGZ. Only

when these medial deletions have taken place does rule (8.1.1) cease to be an allophonic rule and become a phonological one. The following examples have been identified:

TxZ	SoZ		pGZ		pZ	
po:k-kê?m		<	**po:k*	<	**pokok*	'cotton tree'
hu:k		<	**hu:k*	<	**hukuk*	'to smell bad'
ca:ñ	*ca:ñ*	<	**ca:ñ*	<	**cahin*	'snake'
pu:y		<	**pu:y*	<	**pu?huyu*	'roadrunner'
wɨ:	*wɨ:*	<	**wɨhɨ*	<	**wɨhɨ*	'good'

(8.1.3) $*C_{[+cor]} > [+pal]/\_\_i, i\_\_$, where $C_{[cor]} = $ /t c n s/
"Coronal stops /t c n s/ become palatalized to /tʸ č ñ š/ in the vicinity of /i/." For example:

TxZ	AyZ	SoZ		pGZ		pZ	
		ya:tʸi	<	**ya:tʸi*	<	**yati*	'sweet apple'
če?			<	**tʸi*	<	**ti*	'what?'
čê:?he?	*[ci?i]*	*či:hi?*	<	**či:hi*	<	**cihi?*	'opossum'
hu:ñ		*hu:ñi?*	<	**hu:ñi*	<	**huni*	'type of tree'
?e:še?	*[e:si]*	*?e:ši?*	<	**?e:ši*	<	**?esi*	'crab'
šêš	*[sis]*	*šiš*	<	**šiš*	<	**sis*	'meat'
čêñ		*tʸiñ*	<	**tʸiñ*	<	**tin*	'excrement'

For the developments in AyZ see section 8.4 below.

8.2. SOTEAPAN ZOQUE (SIERRA POPOLUCA)

(8.2.1)   Unexpected sporadic cases of palatalization.

E.g., *sʸó:ki* < pGZ **so:ki* < pZ **soki* 'snail'
  tʸú:ki < pGZ **tu:ka* < pZ **tuka* 'tortoise'

(8.2.3) $*V_{[-high]} > i/CV^C\_\_\#$
"Raising of final vowel."

E.g., *kí:ñi* 'nose'   < pZ **kinɨ*
  po?tʸi 'pinol'   < pZ **po?te*

tó:mi 'close'	<	pZ **tome*
ʔá:ñi 'tortilla'	<	pZ *ʔane
tʸú:ki 'tortoise'	<	pZ **tuka*
sá:ki 'mother-in-law'	<	pZ **sake*
wáyi 'corn drink (Sp. pozole)'	<	pZ **waye*

Note that palatalization, as described in (8.1.3), continues to operate after final vowel raising.

8.3. AyZ AND TxZ SHARED INNOVATIONS

(8.3.1)   *m > ᵐb'/\$__
          *n > ⁿd'/\$__

"Syllable-initial nasals become their prenasalized implosive counterparts."

Two additional rules may perhaps be posited as a result of future research: (1) AyZ has a tendency to devoice final vowels and TxZ a tendency to delete final vowels. It is likely that TxZ vowel dropping was preceded by devoicing. In order to show that there is a connection between the two phenomena, more extensive data from AyZ are needed. (2) A rule describing the merging of the reflexes of pZ *t and *c as conditioned by a preceding or following /i/ (i.e., pGZ *tʸ, *č > č) may perhaps be posited, provided that pGZ *tʸ and *č did indeed fall together in AyZ. This is not clear at present.[1] In addition to (1) and (2) there are certain shared grammatical innovations the description of

---

[1] On a separate sheet in Nordell (1967/69/70), a chart is found which compares coronal stops and the products of these stops under palatalization across the three GZ languages. According to the chart, the unconditioned AyZ reflex of pZ *c is /c/, whereas the palatalized product is /tⁱi/. It is not clear which phonetic difference Nordell intended to signal by means of these two symbols. I did not hear any difference, but I cannot exclude that, under a more careful analysis, there may in fact be one. Nordell lists /š/ as both the unconditioned and the palatalized reflexes of pZ *s as /š/. In this case Nordell apparently did not hear any difference, whereas I did. I heard the unconditioned reflex as a fronted /s/ and the palatalized reflex as more backed, retroflex /s/. It is likely that both of the two pairs that reflect pGZ *s : *š and pGZ *c : *č are in fact distinguished in AyZ by a feature of relative frontedness.

which I choose to postpone until I am able to present morphological and morphosyntactic descriptions for both languages.

8.4. AYAPA ZOQUE

The realizations of several sounds are different from what they are in other Mixe-Zoquean languages. The realization of the reflex of pZ *a approaches the quality of the fifth cardinal vowel; /i/, when unstressed, is realized as a rather low front vowel, approximately on the scale between [I] and [e]; final vowels or even final sequences of sonorants and vowels tend to devoice; the reflex of pZ *w is usually realized [gʷ]; the reflex of pGZ *s is mainly realized as a retroflex sound [ʂ] whereas pGZ *$š$ becomes /s/; pZ *p becomes [ƀ] intervocalically; initial /ʔ/ is not heard and is apparently dropped; long vowels often become glottalized, especially before sonorants. Since a full phonemization for the language has not been carried out, I cannot state the structural consequences of these changes. I prefer to reserve the more formal rule format for the kinds of changes that have to do with the deletion, replacement, or addition of a segment.

(8.4.1)   *(C)V(C)CVN > (C)V(C)CV,   where N = a nasal
"Final nasals dropped in polysyllables."

E.g., | *[aːʔga]* | < | pGZ *$ʔakaŋ$ 'griddle' |
|---|---|---|
| *[uspi]* | < | pZ *$ʔuspin$ 'alligator' |
| *[cuːhe]* | < | pZ *$cuhi(n)$ 'spit' |
| *[cuːʔgi ~ cuːʔge]* | < | pZ *$cuʔkin$ 'worm' |
| *[pɨːsi]* | < | pGZ *$pɨːšiñ$ 'man' |
| *[paːsu]* | < | pZ *$pasoŋ$ 'squash' |

(8.4.2)   *h > ʔ/V$_i$_V$_i$
"*h is replaced by /ʔ/ between like vowels." A similar but unrelated development occurs in the central dialect of Chiapas Zoque.

E.g., | *[uʔu]* | < | pGZ *$ʔuhu$ 'pineapple' |
|---|---|---|
| *[aʔa]* | < | pZ *$ʔaha$ 'canoe' |
| *[ciʔi]* | < | pZ *$cihi$ 'Mexican opossum' |

(8.4.3)   Ø > ?/a__y   Condition: nouns only.

E.g., *[a?y]*   <   pZ *?ay* 'leaf'
      [ca?y]   <   pZ *cay* 'rope, etc.'

8.5. TEXISTEPEC ZOQUE

(8.5.1)   *i > ê/inflectional environments
            > e/elsewhere

"*i* is lowered to [e] (thus merging with the reflex of *e*). In inflectional environments the difference between the reflexes of *i* and *e* is recoverable since their morphophonological properties here are different." Since *i* caused palatalization in pGZ the reflexes of *i* and *e* may also be distinguished whenever an adjacent coronal stop is present. This is a diachronically biased analysis, however. I distinguish (fc.-b) between /e/ and /ê/ in inflectional environments and adjacent to coronal stops and write "E" for the complete merger of *i* and *e* outside of this environment. However, I show (1994) that a strict synchronic analysis should only distinguish between /e/ and /ê/, where the latter is an abstract element that occurs in inflectional environments only (and further propose that /ê/ may be analyzed as an empty vowel slot). My 1994 article has directed the way I cite TxZ forms in this work although a forthcoming work (fc.-b) is given as the source.

(8.5.2)   *V$_{[-long]}$ > Ø/C__#

"Short vowels delete word-finally." Examples of this rule are numerous and may be found throughout Part Two. The interesting cases are those where TxZ has a vowel + /?/ sequence word-finally (i.e., a retention of the pZ vowel). I have explained these cases in an ad hoc manner by positing a final glottal stop for pGZ. pGZ now becomes the target of explanation, but the problem remains. The truth is that I have no real solution. SoZ provides no help since in this language all short, word-final vowels are glottalized. The AyZ data are not extensive enough to be of help. The record for final vowels in the Chimalapa Zoque dialects is confusing and possibly erroneous. Finally, Mixean languages do not have final glottal stops in polysyllables. We would like to be able to posit final glottal stops in pZ reconstructed forms on the basis of at least two languages. Until more adequate data become available we may only speculate that the final glottal stops posited here for pGZ are in fact present in pZ.

TxZ	SoZ	pGZ	pZ	
yo:ma? ~ yo:mɨ?	yo:mo?	*yo:mo?		'woman'
?u:cu?	?u:cu?	*?u:cu?		'monkey'
?u:?hu?	?uhu?	*?uhu?		'pineapple'
?u:nu?	?u:nu?	*?u:nu?		'corn drink'
čê:ku? ~ čê:ko?	či:ku?	*či:ku?	*ciku	'coati'
to:to?	to:to?	*to:to?	*toto	'paper'
to:ye?	to:ya?	*to:ya?	*toya	'pain'
ko:so?	ko:so?	*ko:so?	*koso	'knee'
ko:ya?		*ko:ya?	*koya	'rabbit'
bo:ncɨ:pɨ?	cɨ:pɨ?	*cɨ:pɨ?	*cɨpɨ	'edible green'
cu:tu?		*cu:tu?	*cutu	'ear of corn'
hê:?ya?		*hi?iya?	*hi?ya	'chewing-gum tree'
ka:mu?	ka:ma?	*ka:ma?	*kama	'cornfield'
ku:ma?	ku:ma?	*ku:ma?	*kuma	'type of palm'
bu:tu?		*mu:tu?	*mutu	'squirrel'
bo:ya?	mo:ya?	*mo:ya?		'flower'
pa:ta?	pa:ta?	*pa:ta?	*pata	'mat'
do:ke?	no:ki?	*no:ki?	*noki	'type of seed, etc.'
tu:nu?	tu:nu	*tu:nu?	*tunu	'navel'
yu:?če?	yu:či	*yu:či?		'army ant'
sa:ka?	sa:ki [Foster 1949]		*sa:ke?	'female in-law of woman'
ba:ca?	ma:ca?	*ma:ca?	*maca?	'star'
popo?	po:po?	*po:po?	*popo?	'white'
we:ke?		*we:ki?	*weki?	'shoulder'

The six last examples exhibit special cases. In the first three of this group the SoZ forms lack a final glottal stop. As with all the forms from SoZ my source is Gutiérrez M. (1993), which represents the speech of a person who does not currently live in Veracruz. Thus, the lack of a glottal stop in *tu:nu* and *yu:či* is not necessarily representative. The form *sa:ki* was recorded by the anthropologist George Foster, who does not generally have a good ear for glottal stops. The last four examples are special because a final glottal stop is posited for pZ. This is done on non-GZ evidence. See Part Two for the data.

(8.5.3) $*^{m}b' > b' \sim b$
         $*^{n}d' > d' \sim d$

"The prenasalized implosives (developed together with AyZ) lose their nasalization and become plain, voiced stops; plosive and implosive realizations are in free variation."

(8.5.4) $*t^{y}, č > č$

"$*t^{y}$ and *č* merge."

8.6. SANTA MARÍA CHIMALAPA ZOQUE

(8.6.1)   Ø > ?/V__#   Irregular

"Sporadic word-final insertion of a glottal stop." As the counter-examples show, the environment specified in this rule is too general. There seems to be no regularity that would allow us to posit a sound law as such.

E.g., *hiyɨ?* 'flower'   < pZ *hiyɨ*
      kɨnɨ? 'voice'   < pZ *kɨnɨ* 'throat' (TxZ,
                                      SoZ: *kɨnkɨ?*)

      kacu? 'bitter'   < pZ *kacu* (M *kacus*)
      kɨ?kuma? 'ring'   < pZ *kɨ?kuma* (M *kɨ?kuma*)
      kono? 'short'   < pZ *kono* (OIP *kono'k*)
      koya? 'hare'   < pZ *koya* 'conejo' (OM *koy*)
      paki? 'hard'   < pZ *paki* (OIP *pakpa'k*)
      pata? 'mat'   < pZ *pata* (Zoquean only)
      pu?hu? 'intestine'   < pZ *pu?hu* (OIP *pu?pu*
                                      'belly')

      pu?ci? 'yellow'   < pZ *pu?ci* (OM *pu?c*)
      tunu? 'navel'   < pZ *tunu* (Zoquean only)
      suyu? 'pot'   < pZ *suyu* (TxZ *su?uŋ* [?]
                                      SoZ *su?ŋ*)

      tuni? 'plum'   < pZ *tuni*
      tome? 'close'   < pZ *tome* (OIP *tome'k*)

toya? 'wound'	< pZ **toya* (NHM *to:?y* 'burn')
hi?ya? 'chewing-gum tree'	< pZ **hi?ya* (Zoquean only)
yomɨ? 'woman'	< pZ **yomo* (TxZ *yo:ma?*)

BUT,

?ane 'tortilla'	< pZ **?ane*
?apu	< pZ **?apu* 'grandfather'
haya 'husband'	< pZ **hayah*
?oko 'female'	< pZ **?oko*
?oya 'sister-in-law'	< pZ **?ohya*
ciku 'coati'	< pZ **ciku*
came 'word'	< pZ **came*
hɨhɨ 'fly'	< pZ **hɨhɨ*
hama 'day, sun'	< pZ **hama*
huki 'cigarette'	< pZ **huki*
kinɨ 'nose'	< pZ **kinɨ*
kana 'salt'	< pZ **kana*
koha 'sin, transgression'	< pZ **koha*
koke 'fish'	< pZ **koke*
meya 'sea'	< pZ **meya*
mama 'mother'	< pZ **mama*
naka 'bark, etc.'	< pZ **naka*
pini 'br-in-law of man'	< pZ **pini*
peka 'old'	< pZ **peka*
pɨmi 'strong'	< pZ **pɨmi*
paci 'shirt'	< pZ **paci*
puci 'pimple'	< pZ **puco*
sawa 'wind'	< pZ **sawa*
waye 'dough'	< pZ **waye*
yoya 'pig'	< pZ **yoya*

(8.6.2)   Ø > ?/CVCV_N, where N = a sonorant

E.g., *kama?m* 'hard'	< pZ **kamam*
pono?n 'weak'	< pZ **ponon* 'soft'
petku?y 'broom'	< pZ **petkuy*
wa?y 'hair'	< pZ **way*
?aŋwa?y 'moustache'	< pZ **?aŋway*
ca?y 'rope, etc.'	< pZ **cay*

> *coko?y* 'liver'   < pZ **cokoy*
> *kumku?y* 'village'   < pZ **kumkuy*
> *pu?huyu?* 'roadrunner'   < pZ **pu?huyuy* (subsequent loss of /y/)

BUT, *kapay* 'sister-in-law of man'   < pZ **kapay*

In some cases a ChZ sequence /hi/ corresponds to /yi/ in other Zoquean languages, for example: *nɨhi* 'name' < pZ **nɨyi*, *yɨhi* 'here' < pZ **yɨy*, *ya?hi* 'far' < pZ **ya?y*. We only reconstruct **hi* for pZ in cases where there is support found outside of Oaxaca, as in *me?y* 'sharpened' < *meh+?i*, *ponhi* 'soft, etc.' < pZ *ponhi*, *yuhi* < pZ **yuhi*.

8.7. CHIAPAS ZOQUE

(8.7.0) $*Ø > h/\_T + V$

Condition: verb roots only. T = oral stop.

In the entries of Part Two, verbal roots of the type CVT in ChisZ are given as CVhT in order to point to the difference between ChisZ and the two other Zoquean subgroups with respect to the morphophonemic rule (8.7.0) which is only present in ChisZ. The rule has no exceptions and there are hundreds of examples. Just one needs to be given: *-kahk-* 'to borrow' *-kak-pɨ?-* 'to change' *kyahk-u* '3p borrows it' (widely attested).

No other pervasive phonological rules are found that support a ChisZ entity, only minor phenomena such as dissimilation of nasals in ChisZ: C,N,NE *yaŋbak* = ChZ *yaŋmak* and dissimilation of /c/ to /s/ in ChisZ: C,N,NE *capas* = SoZ *capac*, ChZ *capac*.

North Dialect (N)

(8.7.1) $*h > Ø/V\_#$
"h is lost word-finally."

E.g., *?aksa* 'sugarcane'   < pChisZ **?aksah*
     kaci 'toucan, etc.'   < pChisZ **kacih*
     po?a 'majagua bush'   < pChisZ **po?ah*
     mihapuci 'smallpox'   = C *mihapucih*
BUT, *puci* 'pimple, etc.'   = C *puci* < pMZ **puci*

(8.7.2)   *? > Ø/__#
"Loss of a word-final glottal stop."

E.g., *kohe* 'fleur-de-lance (snake)'   < pChisZ **kohe?*
     peya 'a type of bird (Sp. pea)'   < pChisZ **peya?*
     punu 'small fish, etc.'   < pZ **punu?*
     sihki 'smile, etc.'   = NE *siki?*
     siwi 'sore'   = C *siwi?*
     singi 'swelling'   = C *singi?*
     sepe 'female master, owner'   < pChisZ **sepe?*

(8.7.3)   n > ñ/[+nasal] ___
"n is palatalized when following another nasal."

E.g., *konña* 'whole' < pChisZ **konna*
     pu?mña 'hill' < pChisZ **pu?mna*

NorthEast Dialect (NE)

(8.7.4)   *y > ?/__ +   Nonpervasive
"y is replaced with ? morpheme-finally."

E.g., *-ku?* deverbalizing suffix: 'instrument'   < pZ **-kuy*
     -tʸo?- verb suffix: 'desiderative'   = C *-tyo?y-*

(8.7.5) $*C_{[+nas]}$ > [-nas]/__#
"Nasal stops become their corresponding oral stops word-finally."

E.g., *kop* 'house pole'   < pZ **kom*
     ponot, pononbi 'soft, etc.'   < pZ **ponon*
     pit 'man'   < pZ **pin*
     pinbit 'insect'   < pChisZ **pinpin*

kɨmuk 'shadow'   < pChisZ *kɨmuŋ
kak 'jaguar'   < pZ *kaŋ
koyok 'chinini, etc.'   = N *koyoŋ

(8.7.6)   *T → [+vc]/V__V, where T = C$_{[-cont, -nas]}$
"Intervocalic voicing of stops." (Also a synchronic rule.)

E.g., hɨbak 'corncob'   < pZ *hɨpak
pokabuʔcbuʔc 'egg yolk'   = C pokapuʔcpuʔc
kede? (vt) 'to roll up'   < pChisZ *kete?
kuʔdis (vt) 'to savor, etc.'   < pChisZ *kuʔt-is
poʔde 'pinole made of chocolate'   < pZ *poʔte
ʔaŋbaʔde (adj) 'much, many'   < pZ *ʔaŋpaʔte

(8.7.7)   t > r/V__V
Chapultenango [Chap] and Oxolotán [Ox] dialects. The rule requires
that /t/ is voiced by a previous rule shared by all NE dialects. Still
productive as can be seen from the alternation in the plural suffix
-ta~-ra. I recorded [hata?] 'father' in Oxolotán, a form in which [r] is
expected. The nonpredictability of the treatment of intervocalic /t/ requires that /r/ be set up as a separate phoneme for that dialect.

E.g., para 'mat' [Chap] = NE pada < pZ *pata
                                        (from Wonderly 1949)

(8.7.8)   *y > w/u__i

E.g., tuwi 'dog' < pZ *tuyi Shared with C and S.

(8.7.9)   *Ø > h/V́__{p, t, k}#
The insertion of /h/ is the phonologization of an allophonic rule whereby final stops following stressed vowels and preceding word-boundary
become preaspirated. This rule serves to maintain the distinction
between original */p t k/ in this position and /p t k/ from the source
described in Rule (8.7.5).

Central Dialect (C)

This section neither includes changes that could just as well be described in terms of synchronic morphophonemic rules nor the post-Conquest change whereby voicing of stops becomes phonemic. See Wonderly (1951: §§ 3.1-18) and Kaufman (1963: 48-49, 2323-24).

(8.7.10a) $*h > ?/V_i\_V_i$
(8.7.10b) $*V_i?V_i > V_i?\#$

"Between two identical vowels, /h/ becomes a glottal stop and the last of the vowels, when the sequence is word-final, is subsequently deleted." The workings of (8.7.10a) with open syllables is restricted to ChisZ-C. With closed syllables, as in pZ *pohos* 'guava' and *pahak* 'sweet', all Zoquean languages except San Miguel Chimalapa are affected. Kaufman (1963: 47, 2323(5c)) sets up a separate pMZ element, *[h], in the place of */h/, which complicates the diachronic description unnecessarily. In a derivation, the final output of the two rules is further reduced to just V_i (cf. *?akuy* 'cedar' from pZ * *?aha-kuy*).

E.g.,				
?a?	'big canoe'	<	pZ * *?aha*
he?	'mosquito'	<	pZ *hehe*
hɨ?	'fly'	<	pZ *hɨhɨ*
?o?	'century plant'	<	pZ * *?oho*
ci?	'Mexican opossum'	<	pZ *cihi*
ce?	'carpenter'	<	pZ *cehe*
po?os	'guaba'	<	pZ *pohos*
pa?ak	'sweet'	<	pZ *pahak*

(8.7.11) $*\emptyset > h/V\_\#$

"Final /h/ is sometimes inserted word-finally in disyllabic nonverbs." It was assumed in Kaufman (1963: 49, 2325) that this is secondary, but it was not unaccounted for. Even with the additional Zoquean data, no regularity can be disclosed.

E.g., | | | |
|---|---|---|
| *?aksʸih* | 'great-tailed grackle' | < pZ * *?a?ksyi* |
| *pacih* | 'lizard' | < pZ *paci* |
| *?i?kih* | 'jinicuil' | < pZ * *?i?(n)ki* |
| *hinih* | 'thick, muddy' | < pZ *hini* |
| *manih* | 'type of squash (Sp. chilacayote)' | < pChisZ *mani* |

mokih	'black pepper'	< pChisZ	**moki*
hipɨh	'chin'	< pZ	**hɨp(ɨ)* 'mouth'
hokoh	'smoke'	< pZ	**hoko*
pomoh	'incense'	< pZ	**pomo*
kowah	'drum'	< pZ	**kowa*
polah-	'without edge or point'	< pChisZ	**pola*
poyah	'moon, month'	< pZ	**poya*
ʔapah	'grandmother'	< pZ	**ʔapa*
nanah	'mother'	< pMZ	**nana*

BUT,

ʔaci	'elder brother'	< pZ	**ʔaci*
ʔoci	'tobacco'	< pZ	**ʔoci*
cine	'annatto (Sp. achiote)'	< pChisZ	**cine*
ceke	'tortoise'	< pZ	**ceke*
cɨpɨ	'edible green (Sp. quelite)'	< pZ	**cɨpɨ*
hiyɨ	'flower'	< pZ	**hiyɨ*
kɨnɨ	'neck'	< pZ	**kɨnɨ*
kɨpi	'firewood'	< pZ	**kɨpi*
kahsʸi	'hen'	< pChisZ	**kahsyi*
koya	'rabbit'	< pZ	**koya*
meya	'sea'	< pZ	**meya*
mɨki	'honeycomb'	< pZ	**mɨki*
muki	'measure'	< pChisZ	**muki*
pici	'leached corn meal'	< pZ	**pici*
... etc.			

(8.7.12a) $*y > w/V_{[+high]}\_\_V_{[+high, -back]}$

"**y* goes to /w/ between a high vowel and /i/ by dissimilation." C here adheres to an inherited pMZ pattern by which /y/ is excluded before /i/. Shared with NE and S.

E.g., *kɨwin* 'chore, etc.'   =   N *kɨyin*
     tuwi 'dog'   <   pChisZ **tuyi*
     ʔiwɨ (rel pron) 'who, etc.'   <   pZ **ʔiyɨ*

(8.7.12b) $*i > \emptyset/V_{[+back]}y\_\_\#$

"**i* is lost between a back vowel + /y/ and a word boundary." Also a reaction to the tendency to avoid contiguous /i/ and /y/.

E.g., *kay* 'narrow, etc.'   < **kayi* < pZ **kahi*
     pɨy 'long'   < **pɨyi* < pZ **pɨhi*

(8.7.13)   **h* > w/V$_{[+rnd]}$___V$_{[-rnd]}$
          *h > y/V$_{[-rnd]}$___V$_{[-rnd]}$
"**h* goes to /w/ between a rounded and an unrounded vowel; between an unrounded and a rounded vowel it goes to /y/." This rule is reflected in ongoing morphophonemic processes; see Wonderly (1951: §3.13). Shared with S.

E.g., *kowa* 'sin, transgression'   < pZ **koha*
     kowi 'hearing'   < pChisZ **kohi*
     koyowa 'price'   < pChisZ **koyoha* (derived
                                  from -*yoh*-)
     cuwin 'spit'   < pZ **cuhi(n)*
     kay 'narrow'   < pZ **kahi*
BUT,
     kohe? 'fleur-de-lance (snake)' < pChisZ **kohe?*

(8.7.14a)   **c* > č/C$_{[+cor, -son]}$___
(8.7.14b)   **n* > ñ/___č
"**c* palatalizes to /č/ following a coronal obstruent. Subsequently **n* is palatalized before /č/." No examples of /t/ are attested, so the rule may be a little too broadly formulated.

E.g., *pokscɨ?y ~ poksčɨ?y* (vi) 'to remain seated' < *poks + cɨ?y*
     pe?ñču 'duck'   < pChisZ **pe?ncu*
     piñčɨki 'figure, etc.'   = NE *pindzɨki*
     ha?cči? 'give credit'   < pZ **ha?c-ci?*
     kɨ?čus 'nail, claw'   < pZ **kɨ(c)cu?ks* (the /?/ is from con-
                                  tamination with *kɨ?* 'hand')
     ka?ñči 'turkey'   < pChisZ **ka?nci*

(8.7.15)   Ø > h/V́___sV
"/h/ is inserted before /s/ into the stressed syllable of polysyllabic words." This rule is also found in ChisZ-N. Kaufman (1963: 47, 2322 and 50-51, 2328) described this rule for ChisZ-C. The rule is universal: it affects both verbs and nonverbs. In verbs the rule becomes part of the morphophonemic description since /h/ is conditioned by the

morpheme that follows. When ChisZ-C and ChisZ-N roots are cited in Part Two, the /h/ will, by convention, be posited as part of the root or underlying form. This is reiterated in the examples of verb roots below. The three counterexamples remain to be explained.

E.g., *ʔehsi* 'crab'   < pZ **ʔesi*
       ʔahsa 'native blouse (Sp. huipil)'   < pZ **ʔasa*
       ʔuhsu 'mosquito, etc.'   < pZ **ʔusu(k)*
       hawahs (vi) 'to yawn'   < pChisZ **hawas*
       hahs (vt) 'to anoint'   < pZ **has*
       kehsi 'slab'   < pChisZ **kesi*
       mehs (vt) 'to wear (for the first time)'   < pZ **mes*
       mɨhs (vt) 'to disgust'   < pZ **mɨs*
       muhs (vi) 'to know, be able'   < pZ **mus*
       pɨhs 'to sweat'   < pZ **pɨs*
       pahsun 'squash, gourd'   < pZ **pasoŋ*
       suhs (vi) 'to whistle'   < pZ **sus*
       sohs (vi, vt) 'to cook'   < pZ **sos*
       tɨhsi 'bat, etc.'   < **tɨsi*
       tahs (vi) 'to become full'   < pZ **tas* Shared with NE
       wihs (vt) 'to uproot, etc.'   < pZ **wis* Shared with NE
       wahs (vt) 'to chew'   < pZ **was* Shared with NE
       yohs (vi) 'to work'   < pZ **yos* Shared with NE
BUT,
         cisiʔ 'bedbug'   < pZ **cisi*   < pMZ **cisi(k)*
         kose 'elder sister' < pChisZ **ko-se*
         pisi 'yucca'   < pZ **pisi*

(8.7.16)   Sporadically occurring cases where **k* becomes /h/ morpheme-finally have been observed.

E.g., *yah-* (verb prefix) 'causative'   < pZ **yak*
       ʔaŋwah (vs) 'to open, be open'   < pZ **ʔaŋwak*
       wiloh 'kinkajou (Sp. mico de noche)'   < pZ **wi(ʔ)yuk*

The last example also has a change of **y* to /l/ and **u* to /o/, which is unique to this item.

South Dialect (S)

This dialect shares (8.7.8) and (8.7.12a) with C and NE and also shares (8.7.13) with C. The most conspicuous change, however, is the following:

(8.7.17a)   *...CÝ(?)CV# > ...CV(?)CÝ?#
(8.7.17b)   *...CÝ(C)CVC# > ...CV(C)CÝC#
"Plurisyllables shift the stress to the last syllable and, if they end in a vowel, insert a glottal stop in final position."

E.g., *[ko·ké?]*   <   pZ *koke 'fish'
     [cu?gín]   <   pZ **cu?kin* 'worm'
     [puhtú?]   <   pZ *puhtu 's/he/it came out'

The stress shift is nearly all-pervasive and even affects Spanish loan-words such as *[?ašnú?]* 'donkey' (Sp. *asno*). A few items do, however, seem to behave differently, for example: *[čináko]* 'bat' and *[púmpo]* 'gourd' (two words of unknown provenience). I have not studied the dialect to such a degree that I am able to determine the structural status of stress, but I doubt that it is phonemic.

CHAPTER 9

Language Contact

9.1. TRACING THE HISTORY OF CAMOTLAN SPEECH

The *Mixes* region of Oaxaca divides into three regions in terms of altitudes: the Highlands, Midlands, and Lowlands. Linguistically the Highlands correspond to two fundamentally different areas: the Northern and
the Southern Highlands. The Midlands and Lowlands, however, each
has a one-to-one correspondence to a linguistically defined area. As a
surprising outcome of this study we may roughly state that in villages
situated lower than 1,300 m (in a hot climate[1]) one language is spoken,
in villages situated between 1,300 and 1,800 m (temperate climate)
another is spoken, and in villages situated higher than 1,800 m (cold
climate) a third and a fourth are spoken. The geographic facts are
displayed in Table 9.1.

Needless to say, the correlation is neither a matter of direct causa-
tion nor can it be quite arbitrary. The Highlands, Midlands, and Lowlands are both vertically and horizontally defined. Dialectologists are
used to mapping space at the horizontal level. In the case of Oaxaca
Mixean there is a choice between horizontal and vertical demarcation.
This may be a consequence of people's preference for a particular climate or, rather, the particular patterns of farming and other living conditions associated with that climate. It may also have to do with routes
of communication. Whatever the reason, there is an observable correlation between linguistic and vertical geographical space. The correlation
breaks down in just three cases: the villages of Camotlán, Cacalotepec,
and Puxmetacán. Camotlán is linguistically Lowland and geographically
Midland, situated at a 1,440 m altitude. It is the westernmost Lowland
Mixe dialect located right on the border between

---

[1] The geographic data are from Nahmad (1965: 16-17).

Comparative Phonology

Table 9.1. OM Languages and Their Geographic Correlates

Village	Altitude (m)	Climate	Language
Totontepec	1,900	cold	NHM
Ayutla	2,060	cold	SHM
Mixistlán	1,800	cold	SHM
Tamazulapan	1,800	cold	SHM
Tepantlali	2,050	cold	SHM
Tepuxtepec	2,000	cold	SHM
Tlahuitoltepec	2,200	cold	SHM
Atitlán	1,600	temperate	MM
Cacalotepec	2,050	cold	MM
Cotzocón	1,380	temperate	MM
Jaltepec	?	?	MM
Juquila	1,500	temperate	MM
Matamoros	?	?	MM
Puxmetacan	440	hot	MM
Zacatepec	1,400	temperate	MM (?)
Camotlán	1,440	temperate	LM
Coatlán	?	?	LM
Guichicovi	297	hot	LM
Mazatlán	720	hot	LM

the Midlands and Lowlands at an equal distance from Coatlán (LM) and Juquila (MM). Although Cacalotepec and Puxmetacan are respectively situated in the Highlands and Lowlands (in terms of altitudes), both are linguistically Midland. We would certainly not on these grounds alone expect these dialects to be peculiar in any way. As a matter of fact, however, one of them, namely Camotlán, is peculiar.

This suffices as an introduction to the presentation of the purely linguistic facts that lead me to formulate the hypothesis that Camotlán speech is a product of the confrontation between Lowland and Midland

Mixe, which came about by an east-west migration. The hypothesis[2] should be judged on these data first, only secondarily may the geographical facts be called upon for support. The linguistic arguments build on (1) phonological, (2) lexical, and (3) morphological evidence, and will be presented in that order. The scanty data will be exploited to the fullest possible degree. Even if the case should turn out unconvincing, it is hoped that by attracting the attention of other researchers it may eventually be satisfactorily strengthened.

Phonology

Agreements with MM:
(1) Ca has no consonantal fortis/lenis opposition. Neither does Ju. This is an areal characteristic which, to judge from the data available, applies to Cc, Ju, and Ca only.
(2) Ca follows the MM pattern of quantitative ablaut in Class [1] verbs (e.g., *Ø-ʔɨʔc-p* 'it boils'). Gu has *Ø-ʔïˑ ʔc-p*, and SJ *Ø-ʔɨˑc-p*, whereas all MM dialects would have a form similar to the Ca form.
(3) As in the MM dialects, Ca has a three-way front vowel opposition /i e æ/, whereas LM only distinguishes between two front vowels /i e/. The added vowel in Ca came about through borrowing of such items as *kæč* 'basket', *kæpʸ* 'sister-in-law of man, brother-in-law of woman', *kæʔpʸ* 'scorpion', *neʔpʸtʸ* 'blood', and *maštéhkʸ* 'the day before yesterday' that have the lexicalized umlaut of /a/, which is typical of MM but absent from LM.

---

[2] According to a note taken during one of my brief conferences with Nordell, he mentioned that "Camotlán is Eastern, but close to Quetzaltepec." During the analysis of Nordell's data I first placed Camotlán with Midland Mixe (Nordell's "Central" dialects). After finally having set up the defining features of Lowland ("Eastern") Mixe, I had to move the descriptions of the Camotlán dialect over to LM. It was this change of opinion together with Nordell's remark that induced me to take a closer look at Camotlán and to pay full attention to the possibility of linguistic interference. Since there are no Queltzaltepec data in Nordell (1990) it cannot presently be verified that the Quetzaltepec dialect is the source of MM interference in Camotlán. We are forced to operate with a missing link which may only be identified with Quetzaltepec by way of hypothesis. Quetzaltepec is situated right next to Camotlán.

Agreements with LM:

(4) Important LM features are the diachronic rules *$\underset{\circ}{n}$ > t/C__# and *$\underset{\circ}{m}$ > p/C__#. These are also found in Ca.

(5) The most important and defining feature of LM, however, is the diachronic rule that /h/ is lost before clusters. This is also found in Ca.

(6) At some point Ca must have participated in the appending of /t/ to some words in word-final /n/ (e.g., *midó"nt* 'hearing') along with Gu.

(7) Ca follows the LM pattern of quantitative ablaut in the deviant Class [1] verb 'to drink': Ca *?u?k* 'drink!' = Gu,SJ *?u"k* vs. MM *?u:k*.

(8) Along with SJ, Ca lost the glottal of Class [6] verbs: *CV:?CC > CV·CC (e.g., *po·kš* 'to rest', *šæ·kš* 'to drip'). More important: Ca did not participate in the development *V:? > V? that is typical of MM with this class of verbs. That development is one of the principal defining features of MM.

Lexicon

Agreements with MM:

(9) Ca *cahpóš* 'lemon' is phonologically identical with the correspon-ding Ma, Ja, Pu, and Ct forms, whereas Gu has *cɨbóš*. 'Lemon' is one of thirty-eight forms in which Nordell recorded a fortis consonant. The status of the diacritic in this particular item is not of relevance to the argument.

(10) Ca *cehč* 'drum' is identical with the Ju, Ma, Ja, Pu, At, and Ct word for 'drum', whereas Gu has *cehčk*.

(11) Presence/absence of /k/ is likewise conspicuous in Ca *cu:č* 'horse-fly' (cf. Ja *cu:č*, but Gu *cu·?čk*).

(12) This recurs in Ca *me?tʸ* 'hawk' = Ju and At forms vs. Gu *me?k*

(13) Ca *na:ncɨm̄* 'necklace' has a homorganic nasal as does all of MM, whereas Gu *nam̄dzɨm̄* does not.

(14) Ca *cahp* 'sky' is identical with MM forms and different from Gu *caht*.

(15) A form similar to Ca *tá·ta* 'father' is attested in MM, but not in Gu.

(16) Ca *ta:k* 'mother' is identical with MM forms, whereas SJ and Gu, respectively, have *tah* and *tah*.

(17) Ca *?apté:tʸ* 'grandfather' has the same order of the compound members as MM; Gu reverses the order: *te:dʸ?áp*.

Agreement with LM:

(18) 'Louse' is a word which is to an unusual degree diagnostic of Mixean diversification: pM *?á:wat* > OIP *?a:vá't*, SaP *?á:wat*, NHM *?á?vït*, MM *?a?t*, LM *?a:t*. There is no internal disagreement between MM and LM dialects on this item. Ca has *?a:t*.

(19) Ca *?i:č* 'I' is identical with forms found in LM, whereas MM has forms like *?i̅c* or *?ihc*. Alternation in the first person pronoun goes all the way back to pMZ for which *?i:ci ~ ?ic* is reconstructed. MM and LM parted on the choice of the two descendant Common Oaxaca Mixean forms and Ca retains the alternative chosen by LM in spite of the MM interference into other parts of the pronominal system, which is treated in the next section.

Grammar

The pronominal system is notoriously difficult in MZ historical reconstruction. Making a survey of OM person markers was therefore a high priority of my 1990 trip to Oaxaca. My meeting with Nordell eased the task considerably since he was able to tell me how the prefixed person markers pattern across the OM dialects. The configuration that I "elicited" shows that Ca disagrees with LM whenever there are discrepancies concerning these person markers across OM. 2p acting on 3p (dependent clauses) is expressed by *šʸ*- or *š*- in non-LM plus Ca, whereas LM-Ca has *m-*. 3p acting on 4p (dep. clauses) is expressed by the morphemes *t(i)*- (non-LM), *Ø*- (LM minus Gu), or *y*- (Gu). 3p acting on 2p (independent clauses) is either expressed *š*- (LM minus Ca) or *m*- (non-LM plus Ca). There is no variation in the intransitive paradigm.

Since the emphasis here is on comparative phonology, I hesitate to delve more deeply into these matters. Suffice it to state that Ca has remodeled its system of person markers in a departure from other LM dialects such that the system has become nearly identical with the MM (and non-LM in general) system. Contrary to what one might expect from a background of Indo-European comparative linguistics, pronominal systems can be rather unruly and unsuitable for classificatory purposes. They can be borrowed, as the Ca case clearly shows.

For lack of data, no other grammatical features are discussed. It is expected that Ca agrees with MM in the parts of grammar most frequently employed, whereas it would probably reveal its LM point of departure in less productive aspects of the grammar, such as parts of the derivational morphology.

Conclusion

As the geographical correlate to OM linguistic diversification shows, there has been a tendency for speakers to remain in the same type of habitat over generations. Some major phonological and grammatical features have diffused only within certain boundaries which can be described in terms of horizontal and vertical space. Such multiple diffused features allow us to set up entities such as a "language" or a "dialect area," which we set off from other "languages" or "dialect areas" by means of definitional sound laws. These sound laws, in turn, form the background on which we are able to discern contact phenomena. More than just forming a rather insignificant ethnohistorical hypothesis concerning the migration of a few speakers from one little village to another, we have been testing the framework of OM linguistic diversification. If the migration hypothesis could somehow be verified, this would mean a confirmation not only of the validity of this framework but also of the method employed. Language contact, which is perhaps sometimes thought to be an argument against the comparative method, seems in fact to be the one and only way of verifying this method empirically.

More specifically, it has been pointed out that Ca has undergone a rather heavy borrowing from MM. Some superficial MM phonological traits were shown to have entered Ca via lexical borrowing. More pervasive phonological characteristics affecting specific lexical subsystems, however, are retained. These betray the LM point of departure of Ca. The loss of the consonantal fortis-lenis opposition which affects the system as a whole is also supposed to have diffused into Ca. This suggests that in situations such as these, it is possible that both overall features and superficial features (e.g., the lexicalized umlaut) is borrowed, while features of intermediate generality (e.g., the structure of a certain class of verbs) are left intact. It is hard to single out what is borrowed in the lexicon because of the closeness between MM and LM, but when there are discrepancies, these more often than not give clues to borrowings. The same holds for the one little portion of grammar that is at hand.

9.2. ZOQUEAN INTERFERENCE IN SAYULA POPOLUCA

The attestations given in a collection of cognate sets of an etymon in the various languages will rarely be evenly distributed. A certain emphasis on one or more languages is to be expected as a result of the quantity of data available from the different languages. This is true for Part Two as well. A skewed distribution may, however, also have a correlate among the languages themselves since it may be a result of language contact. A case in point is that there are over sixty items which are recorded for one or more Zoquean languages, but only for one of the Mixean languages: Sayula Popoluca. Since the phonologies of the MZ languages are very similar, borrowings cannot immediately be detected on phonological grounds. This makes an uneven distribution of lexical attestations an almost unique indicator of language contact. The sixty odd cases of possible loans from Zoquean into SaP is all the more conspicuous since Oluta Popoluca is not involved. Cases where OlP could be or is involved are kept strictly isolated. In twenty-five cases evidence for a pMZ etymon is found only in Zoquean, SaP, and OlP. In all these cases, the reconstructed form is labeled pMZ, whereas in the cases where only SaP is involved the label pZ is used. In other words, I do not consider the restricted distribution of an item to OlP, SaP, and Zoquean to be indicatory of diffusion in itself. After all, the number of instances is quite small and the distribution is only slightly skewed, OM being the only subgroup for which the item is not attested.

pMZ etyma that involve just OlP, SaP, and Zoquean are listed here without further commentary:

?aha (n) 'canoe'; *?uyuk* (adj) 'crooked'; *cik-wiC* (n) 'bromeliad'; *ce:?k* (vt) 'to growl'; *cak* (vt) 'to leave'; *capac-kuy* (n) 'buckthorn'; *he:he* (n) 'mosquito'; *hitic* (vt) 'to rub'; *hamay-kuy* (n) 'hog plum tree'; *(h)a(?)y(aw)* (n) 'snook'; *hoks* (vt) 'to weed' *kacu(c)* (adj) 'bitter'; *ki?-kuma* (n) 'ring'; *kumu* (n) 'worm';

ma:san-kuy (n) 'cedar'; *mu:tu* (n) 'squirrel'; *mot* (vt) 'mix'; *nawin* (n) 'agave fiber'; *pu?ks* (vi) 'to color, ripen'; *pot?ot* (n) 'slab'; *kuy-sɨk* (n) 'string bean'; *sɨk-nɨ:?* (n) 'bean soup'; *tɨhɨk(ay)* (adv) 'yesterday'; *tome(k)* (adj) 'close'; *win-pak* (n) 'forehead, tumpline'; *wi(?)yuk(s)* (n) 'kinkajou'.

In dealing now with the items that are restricted to Zoquean (Zo) and SaP I follow the principle that all these items, contrary to the ones just cited, are considered loans until this be disproved. The methodological strictness is aimed at rendering the postulates falsifiable following the well-known epistemological principle of K. Popper. The way to falsify the postulates is by pointing to the existence in Mixean languages other than SaP of the items in question. It may be surmised that there are loans from Zo into SaP which were reintroduced, but the methodology chosen does not allow for specific postulates (except when a semantic or phonological intermediate change is involved) since these postulates would not be falsifiable. The distributional criterion has the highest priority. After this criterion has been satisfied, matters such as phonological adaptation and semantics may be introduced into the discussion in order to characterize the individual loans and the contact situation as a whole.[3] In the item-by-item discussion that now follows, such matters will be given full attention. Following this discussion the focus of the searchlight will be widened to include phonological interference, and finally an attempt to characterize the sociolinguistic setting as a whole will be made.

(1) *?i?k?ik* 'species of hawk'. Only Zo attestation is TxZ *?e?k?e?k* 'hawk (brown)'.
(2) *mo:k?áhy* 'corn leaf'. ChisZ-C,N *mohko?ay* has same meaning.
(3) *?u?c* (vi) 'to be heavy'. Zo: a basically intransitive verb, *?u?c* 'bent over', is attested in ChisZ-N,C,NE.

---

[3] The lines of refutation recommended were followed by L. Clark (p.c., December 1990) concerning two items that were included in an earlier version of this section. These two items have now been removed from the list. Concerning the general conclusions, Clark was somewhat in agreement although he was not in any position to confirm these conclusions positively. His comments are gratefully acknowledged.

(4) *?o?m* (vi) 'to be delicious'. This could be from Zo: *?o?m* (vt) 'to roast, fumigate', which is attested in TxZ, ChisZ-C,N. The semantic gap could be due to the SaP form being intransitive and the Zo ones everywhere transitive. Since not all would agree that the semantic gap can be bridged, however, the item has been excluded from Part Two.

(5) *?o:t-ot* 'roadrunner'. Zo: Only TxZ has a cognate, namely *?o:t?o:t* 'species of bird (white beak, black feathers)'.

(6) *če?š* 'bed'. This depends on whether one prefers to reconstruct the meaning 'corn granary' or 'bed' for pMZ *ce?s*. If *'corn granary' is preferred, SaP 'bed' must have been reintroduced from Zoquean (attested in ChisZ-N and SoZ); if *'bed' is preferred, OM must have made a semantic innovation and SaP is simply a direct reflex of the proto-word. I choose 'granary' and must consequently postulate a reintroduction here.

(7) *cik* (vi, vt) 'to touch'. The corresponding Zo forms have the meaning 'to touch' in Gulf Zoquean (TxZ and SoZ), but 'to do (in general)' in ChisZ-C,NE and ChZ. These facts indicate that Gulf Zoquean is the donor.

(8) *cimiš* 'rope'. Zo: Only cognates are SoZ *cí:miš* and TxZ *ťi:meš* 'tumpline'.

(9) *kuciy* 'to carry on head'. Zo: attested only in the Gulf Zoquean languages TxZ and SoZ *ciy* with same meaning.

(10) *ca?tú:* 'hail'. Zo: ChisZ-N *catuh*, -NE *caduh*, -C *ca?tuh*.

(11) *caw* (vi, vt) 'to make tortillas'. Zo: *caŋ* 'to slap, pat' (ChisZ-C,N,NE). For a transferral to be possible, /ŋ/ must have alternated morphophonemically with /w/ in the donor language.

(12) *ca:u* 'fresh-water fish' (Sp. 'juil(e)'). AyZ, TxZ, and ChisZ have rather similar phonological forms. The exact species of the fishes in question cannot be determined on the basis of the various Spanish glosses. 'Juile', 'bagre', and 'bobo' all signify a variety of small, scaleless fishes, and it is probably not significant that the gloss for the TxZ word seems to agree better with SaP than the ChisZ one. The Zoquean items are AyZ: *[ca:?gʷa]* 'juile', TxZ: *ca:wɨ? ~ ca:wa?* 'juile'; ChisZ-N: *cawa* 'bobo liso, bagre'.

(13) *cu?c* (vi) 'to nurse, suck'. Attested across the board. But neither OIP nor any other Mixean language has 'to suckle', which is the only meaning in Zoquean (SoZ, AyZ, TxZ, ChZ, ChisZ-NE). Mixean has 'to gnaw, bite'. Thus the semantics of the SaP form was tainted with a Zoquean substrate.

(14) *čú?nčun* 'cricket'. Not so convincing since the corresponding Zoquean forms are not reduplicated: *cú?uñi* (SoZ), *cu:?ñe?* (TxZ), *cu?ni* (ChisZ-C,N).

(15) *cut* (vi) 'to jump'. Zoquean attestations are SoZ *cut* 'to fall', TxZ *cutde?* 'to squat', and ChisZ-C [Te] <*tzutnaypa*> 'asentarse en cuchillas/sentarse en cuchillas'.

(16) *pɨkcow* 'to receive'. Cf. ChisZ-NE *pɨkčoŋ* (vt) 'to receive, accept'. MZ languages generally do not agree on how they form composites nor on which ones they have. pZ **pɨk* means 'to take, get'; this meaning is also found in Mixean, but is extended to mean 'marry'. Reflexes of pMZ **cow* everywhere mean 'to join'.

(17) *háhcuk* 'ant'. Among the modern Zoquean languages, ChZ is the only one to provide a phonological fit: TxZ *hasuk ~ hassuk ~ ha:suk ~ ha:ssuk*; ChisZ-C *huhčuku*, -N *nahčuku*, -NE *hahčuku*, -S *[hasčúk]*; ChZ *hahcuku*. A difficult item, since none of the Zoquean forms have satisfactory explanations.

(18) *ha?p* (vi, vt) 'to grind cooked corn'. Zo: 'to grind in metate' in TxZ and 'to crush' in ChZ.

(19) *ha?p* 'uneven (Sp. áspero)'. This attributive derivation of the verb root *ha?p* is matched by ChisZ-N *ha?pe* and TxZ *ha:?p* in that both refer to a rough dough.

(20) *ke?w* (vi, vt) 'to scrape (cactus)' (cactus being the subject). ChisZ-C *ke?ŋ* is the only Zoquean attestation; it refers to something very similar, namely the stinging of certain plants.

(21) *kɨ?t* 'pozol, dough'. Cf. ChisZ-N *kɨ?ti* 'that which is well ground' and TxZ *kɨ:?č* (adj) 'well ground, fine (dough, coffee)'. The ChisZ form provides the best match phonologically.

(22) *káhcay* 'hammock'. The exact same form in ChisZ.

(23) *ka:mpá?k* 'salty'. A parallel composite (salt+sweet) in ChisZ-NE, C *kana pa?ak*. Only the construction as such, not the individual members, were borrowed.

(24) *kumí?n* 'to come, make an approach'. Cf. ChisZ-C,N *kɨ?min.* (vt) 'to come to somebody or something, to approach'.

(25) *mahk* 'pitcher'. SaP: replaced pM **mah-an* with the equivalent Zoquean form *mah-kuy* before truncation set in. Cf. TxZ *bahku? ~ bahko?*; ChisZ-C,N *mahkuy*; ChZ *mahku?y*. TxZ is unlikely to be donor.

(26) *ma?k* (vi, vt) 'to load a gun, set a trap'. Attested in ChisZ-C,N and in ChZ, but only as a free form in ChZ.

(27) *ma:m* 'mother'. Zo: ChisZ-N,NE, ChZ *mama*. Also in LM-SJ, but probably by introduction from Spanish, since no other OM dialects have it. The SaP and Zo forms may of course also be from Spanish, but then stress on the second syllable would be expected, and this is not found.

(28) *ko:má:m* 'stepmother'. Cf. ChisZ-N,NE *komama*.

(29) *yaumó:hk* 'soft corn' = *yau* 'tender, soft' + *mo:hk* 'corn'. Cf. ChisZ-N *yamok*, -NE *yawamohk*. Construction alone borrowed.

(30) *tu:hni?* 'rainwater'. Cf. TxZ *tuh-di?*, ChisZ-C *tuhkini?*. Construction alone borrowed.

(31) *ni?hy* 'name'. Cf. TxZ *diy* 'name'; SoZ *niyi*; ChisZ-C *niy*, -N,NE *niyi*; ChZ *nihi*. ChZ is the most conservative language with regard to the sequence *-hi-*. The /h/ in *ni?hy* points toward this language or a Zoquean language old enough to have conserved something similar.

(32) *na?h* 'gum tree'. Cf. TxZ *da?* and AyZ *[nda?]* 'gum'. Probably borrowed from SoZ or early Gulf Zoquean where initial /n/ did not go to /ⁿd/ or /d/.

(33) *nu?m* (vi, vt) 'to steal, rob'. Exact parallels in SoZ, TxZ, and ChisZ.

(34) *pac* (vi, vt) 'to clap hands' (vt) 'to fill up (containers)'. Zo attestations in TxZ; SoZ; ChisZ-C,N,NE; ChZ. The ChisZ dialects provide the closest matches semantically.

(35) *kuyá:mak* 'orphan'. ChisZ-C,N,NE have *yaŋbak*; ChZ *yaŋmak*. pZ **ko-*/pM **ku-* is a prefix meaning 'step-' which could easily have been added later. But to which base? It must have looked much like the present-day ChZ forms. We must accept that speakers of SaP performed a heavy phonetic adaptation, because the change **/w/ > /ŋ/* forms part of our definition of Zoquean.

(36) *pu:h* 'seed'. Zo: TxZ, ChisZ-C,N,NE; ChZ *puh*.

(37) *poh* 'vein, vine'. Zo: a possible cognate forms part of TxZ *poh-?ohwe?ñ* 'species of hollow cane', but ChZ *poh* 'vine' is a better candidate.

(38) *kuypuhkuhy* 'annatto'. Zo: only TxZ *ku:?ypok*.

(39) *pú:nik* 'pus'. Of the Zoquean forms, TxZ *pu:?nu?k* is the only one to make for a phonological fit.

(40) *pi:u* 'pale'. Zo: ChisZ-C,N *puwa*.

(41) *po?t* 'pinol'. Zo: *po?te* in ChisZ-C,N,NE; ChZ. SoZ *po?tyi* deviant.

(42) *pow* 'to cook in steam'. An exact semantic parallel in TxZ *poŋ*. Similar forms in ChisZ-C,N,NE.

(43) *šikš* (vi, vt) 'to sift, strain, shake'. Zo: only TxZ *ši?kš* 'to shake', with a semantic fit but a troublesome glottal stop.

(44) *ši?n* (vi) 'to unravel (thread)'. Cf. ChisZ-C,N,NE *si?n* 'to tie rope'. The meanings are different, but not incompatible.

(45) *?au-šíš* 'lip'. Cf. ChisZ-C,N,NE *?aŋsis*. Again heavy adaptation.

(46) *šuy* 'pot'. As in (17), (32), (35) we have to look to ChZ for a phonological fit. ChZ has *suyu?*, whereas TxZ *su:?ŋ* and SoZ *su?ŋ* deviate (just as they deviate within the internal Zoquean history).

(47) *tikin* (vi, vt) 'to tickle someone'. Cf. ChisZ-C *tiknikɨtɨhk* (vt) 'to touch in passing'. Dubious.

(48) *méštek* 'skirt'. Cf. SoZ, ChisZ-C,N *teksi*. Dubious; *més-* may be from Spanish *camisa* and *tek* is far different from *teksi*.

(49) *tet* (vi, vt) 'to tear (paper, cloth)'. ChisZ-C,N *teht* 'to tear, open'. TxZ *tet* 'to smash (tomato, grape)' has a poorer semantic fit.

(50) *tahp* 'hawk'. Cf. SoZ, AyZ, ChisZ-C,N,NE *tahpi*. TxZ *tahpe?ñ* an unlikely source.

(51) *tu?n* (vi, vt) 'to hurt (emotions)'. Cf. ChisZ-N,C *tu?n* 'to read, spy on, visit, look over'. The Zoquean semantics is in itself not much more transparent than is the one received by the target language.

(52) *tú?nuk* 'turkey'. Cf. TxZ *tu:?n*; SoZ, ChisZ-N *tú?nuk* 'turkey'; ChZ *tunuk*; ChisZ-C *tu?kune*. Both SoZ and ChisZ-N and ChZ match.

(53) *tu?y* (vi, vt) 'to pat out tortillas'. *Tu?y* is found in TxZ; ChisZ-C,N,NE; and ChZ. Only by the ChZ and TxZ evidence, however, does the relationship become clear. Here we have the meaning 'to stretch out (oneself)'. ChisZ dialects extend the semantics considerably.

(54) *toc* (vi) 'to break (hard things)'. Cf. ChisZ-C,N and ChZ *tohc* 'to puncture, nail, etc.', TxZ *toc* 'to pick fruit with stick'.

(55) *?aktógoy* (vt) 'to loose'. This causative derivation would be grammatical in any MZ language, but it so happens that it is only attested in ChisZ-C,N *yahtokoy*.

(56) *to?kš* (vi) 'to hatch (eggs)'. Parallel phonologically in ChisZ-C,N *to?ks* and in TxZ *to?ks*. The semantic congruence especially fine in ChisZ-C.

(57) *wik* (vi, vt) 'to beat (eggs, syrup)'. The only Zoquean attestation is ChisZ-N *wihk* (vt) 'to sprinkle, scatter'.

(58) *wígi / wiguy* 'to move back and forth'. Cf ChisZ-N *wi?yu?* (vi) 'to become twisted, turn' (vt) 'to turn'. Dubious.

(59) *we ʔk* 'to split (logs)'. Exact parallels in TxZ and SoZ.

(60) *wɨʔkš* (vi) 'to limp'. ChisZ-C,N *wɨʔks* means 'to hook', but the difference is only the transitivity if 'to hook' = 'to make limp'.

(61) *niʔktíyuːš* 'thanks'. The element *-yuːš* parallelled by *yus-* of ChisZ-N,NE *yus-ciʔ* 'to greet'. But the element may very well be Spanish *Dios*. Thus, dubious.

(62) *woʔc* (vi, vt) 'to scratch, play a quitar'. Cf. ChisZ-C *wohc* (vt) 'to stake', -N *wohc* (vt) 'to prick, puncture'.

(63) *woy* (vi) 'to go in a circle, revolve'. Only in TxZ is the verb used to describe humans in motion. Here *woy* has the intransitive meaning of 'to parade' and the transitive meaning 'to roll up (thread)'. The latter meaning only is found in ChisZ-C,N,NE *woy*.

Lexical Interference

As a means of distinguishing between loanwords indicative of a certain sociolinguistic setting and loanwords that do not point to any specific setting I have opted (1991: 220) for the terms "domain-centered" vs. "domain-neutral" vocabulary transfer. The terms were meant to replace "basic" vs. "nonbasic" vocabulary. The borrowing of "basic" vocabulary in the traditional terminology is usually taken to imply a more intimate interference. Pointing to examples of this amounts to focusing on the extent of the interference and not specifying the kind of interference. The historical linguist will, however, primarily want to know the history of the interference, and this usually becomes perceptible from the kinds of semantic domains that are involved. But within any semantic domain there is sure to be a great variability of basicness. So the term "basic," which is ill defined anyway, loses its functionality here. Applying my terminology to the SaP case, I may now say that the vocabulary transfer is domain-centered (i.e., indicative of a specific social setting). It centers on two domains that have an obvious mutual relation. There is also a residue of words that do not lend themselves to any meaningful subgrouping. The referents of the above forms (omitting only the dubious cases) can be grouped as follows:

Food preparation, etc.:
'to make tortillas', 'to pat out tortillas', 'to clap hands', 'grind cooked corn', 'uneven', 'corn drink (Sp. pozole), dough', 'soft corn', 'corn drink (Sp. pinol)', 'corn leaf', 'to be delicious', 'salty', 'pitcher', 'seed', 'to cook in steam', 'to sift, strain, shake', 'pot', 'hatch (eggs)', 'to beat (eggs, syrup)', 'to split (logs)', 'to carry on the head'

Family and upbringing of children:
'to nurse, suck', 'name', 'mother', 'stepmother', 'orphan'

Other:
'to loose', 'to be heavy', 'to touch', 'to scratch, play a guitar', 'to go in a circle, revolve', 'to jump', 'to compare', 'to scrape cactus', 'to come making an approach', 'to load a gun, set a trap', 'to steal, rob', 'pale', 'to unravel (thread)', 'to tear (paper, cloth)', 'to hurt (emotions)', 'to break (hard things)', 'to limp', 'to receive', 'bed', 'hammock', 'hail', 'rainwater', 'annatto', 'pus', 'lip', 'ant', 'hawk' (two different species), 'roadrunner', 'turkey', 'fresh-water fish'

The two central domains of food preparation and family point toward the hypothesis that the Zoquean speakers who brought their language (the donor) into contact with SaP were predominately women. Such a situation could have come about if for an extended period of time young men from Sayula picked their wives from the same neighboring Zoquean village(s) adhering to a patrilocal exogamous pattern. The immediate questions that arise are: from which Zoquean village(s) and during which period? To answer these questions, we must try and see what Zoquean languages provide the best semantic and phonological fits. We must also ask in what languages the words are actually attested, or, "when an item is attested in only one out the three Zoquean language groups, Chiapas, Gulf, and Chimalapa, which group is it then?" This is the distributional question. Here are the answers:
Semantics. (7), (42), (63) favor Gulf Zoquean; (34), (56) ChisZ.
Phonology. (17), (32), (35), (46) favor ChZ; (25), (32) disfavor TxZ; (39) favors TxZ.
Distribution. Eight items favor Gulf Zoquean, twenty-five items favor ChisZ. The distribution points to ChisZ. This cannot just be an artifact of the cognate collection, although this has a slight ChisZ bias. The phonol-ogy, however, favors ChZ. Finally, Gulf Zoquean is the

best candidate with respect to the semantics. All Zoquean languages, then, seem to be possible candidates for the position as major donor. Alternatively, some earlier stage of Zoquean may be involved. To narrow down the case, we need to look more closely at the phonology.

Phonological Interference

There are two phonological traits that unite SaP with TxZ, that is, traits that are not found in OIP and Zoquean languages other than TxZ [(a) is found in other GZ languages too, though]. These are (a) palatalization of /c/ to /č/ by a *preceding* /i/ (synchronically operative) and (b) final vowel truncation (diachronic rule).

(a) is still operative in both languages; many examples are not necessary. I will just cite SaP *mi:č* and TxZ *bič*, both 'you (sg)', which happen to be etymologically identical.

(b) is a drastic phenomenon and the phenomenon most evidently pointing to TxZ as the source of Zoquean interference. Examples are given for each of the two languages elsewhere. Here I shall give just a single example for each language of what happens to be related words: SaP *pač* 'lizard' and TxZ *pa:č* 'iguana'.

Among the loanwords there were four that favored ChZ and one that favored TxZ phonologically. Further, the phonological rules concerning implosives in TxZ seem to disfavor TxZ. But this rule can very well have been lost by the speakers who (fully or partly) shifted to SaP. If ChZ was indeed a donor it must have been at an early stage since no two MZ languages are further removed from each other geographically than SaP and ChZ are. In contrast, Texistepec and Sayula are neighboring towns.

Conclusion

I tentatively posit an early stage where Sayula borrowed a few words such as 'ant', 'name', 'orphan', 'pot' from ChZ or from a Zoque dialect back in Common Zoquean times, and a late(r) stage where marriages would motivate bringing women from Texistepec to Sayula. These women would shift to Sayula Popoluca, but retain their own technical vocabulary for food preparation, etc. Apart from this domain-centered vocabulary transfer, lexical interference is slight, as would be expected in shift situations. Thomason and Kaufman (1988) make the point that interference through language shift often results in phonological and grammatical interference rather than lexical interference. The prediction is borne out in the TxZ-SaP case. The shifting speakers would drop their final vowels and retain various TxZ phonological rules. The vowel dropping and the special palatalization rule was adopted by people in the community (some of which would be the sons and daughters of Texistepec women) over the years.

9.3. ANACHRONISMS IN THE OLMEC-MZ HYPOTHESIS

In Campbell and Kaufman (1976) (henceforth C&K—this abbreviation also introduces reconstructions presented in the 1976 article), the hypothesis is advanced that the Olmecs, at least in part, spoke Mixe-Zoquean language(s). Loanwords from MZ into other Mesoamerican languages are examined and an overview given of some features of Olmec civilization that are attested to in the shape of pMZ lexical items. I see my own studies partly as a contribution to the research area that C&K opened in 1976. Having come full circle now, I have reexamined all the proposals as to MZ loanwords from the point of view of the donor language and have encountered so many deviations from my own findings that I feel a brief critique should be offered. I would like to avoid the assumption that the protolexicon in Part Two be considered 100 percent Olmecoid and recommend that it be used with the same kind of care that I demonstrate in the following. The numbering of the comments follows the organization of C&K. No comment means agreement on essential points.

The following are items with a smaller time span or otherwise differing from the suggestions in C&K:

(5) C&K *koya* 'tomato' is not pMZ, only pZ. Unless = NHM. [To] koy 'painted'—but even then the meaning 'tomato', referring to a specific cultivated item, would not be pM.

(9) C&K pMZ *sapani* is only pZ. The protomeaning was 'zapote', not 'plantain'. There is ChZ evidence for this. Cf. also pZ *taki-sapane* 'zapote colorado (mamey)'.

(11) Partial agreement on 'papaya': *ʔoco* is found in ChisZ-C,N, but is apparently not pZ.

(12) C&K *kaʔwak* 'zapote' is not pMZ, only pM.

(14) Agree on C&K pMZ *way* 'to grind corn', except the generic 'to grind' would be more appropriate; C&K pMZ *waye* 'pozole' is more precisely 'dough'.

(16) C&K pMZ *poʔt* 'to grind corn' is pZ only. The Mixean cognate (if a cognate) means 'cut with machete'. C&K pMZ *poʔte* 'pinole' is also only pZ, since SaP *poʔt* 'pinol' is most probably a Zoquean loan.

(17) C&K pMZ *hɨc* 'to grind' is not pMZ, only pM.

(21) C&K misinterpret NHM phonology and overlook ChisZ-C *ʔukuhyoyah* 'peccary'; cf. also ChisZ-N *ʔuku* 'agouti'. I reconstruct pMZ *ʔuku* 'agouti' > pM *ʔuk* 'dog'.

(22) *pus* and *pusan*—the former referring to the act of cutting and the latter to a cutting instrument—are both only pM, not pMZ as C&K claim. We may add, for the sake of interest, that MM and LM coin forms such as *ʔanæ:búhšn* 'obsidian' (Cotzocón location).

(23) Agree on C&K pM *naʔwa(y)*, although the phonological form can be improved; notice that 'witch, nagual' is designated by a separate term, pM *coʔka*, so it is unlikely that *naʔwa(y)* would mean anything but 'old man' or 'husband'.

(24) C&K pMZ *pata* 'petate' is only pZ.

(26) Agree with C&K pZ *tuʔnuk* 'turkey'. Notice that this was also borrowed into Sayula Popoluca.

(27) C&K pMZ *ʔa·kaw* 'bee, etc.' is not in my files.

(29) C&K *oH* 'pulque, maguey' vs. my *ʔoho* 'maguey'.

(36) An original meaning 'good' is not contained in pMZ *ca:mʔ* (C&K pMZ *ca:m*) 'to ripen'.

(37) C&K pM *wa:š* 'fox' is not pM, it is only pOM.

(38) C&K pZ *we·tu* 'fox' is not in my files. Does pZ have length?

(39) C&K pZ *nas-oʔna* 'fog' is not pZ; even *ʔoʔna* 'cloud' may not be pZ since its reflexes are highly irregular.

(46) C&K pZ *ci(?)* 'opossum' vs. my pZ *cihi*; notice that C&K adjust the protoform to the shape it assumes in the borrowing language.

ciH should be C&K's reconstruction since 'opossum' is of the exact same canonical shape as C&K *?oH* in (29) above.

(47) C&K pMZ *pa:hu?* 'coyote' rests on shallow evidence. The reconstruction is supported by SaP and ChisZ-C evidence alone—other languages have various deviating forms.

Other items (C&K, pp. 87-88):

C&K *nuhpe(n)* 'chokeberry' not in my files. Must be restricted to Veracruz (SaP and SoZ?).

C&K pMZ *?owi?* 'avocado' only ChisZ *?owi* (i.e., not even pZ).

C&K pMZ *ka?wak* 'zapote' vs. my pM *ka?wak* 'marmalade fruit'.

C&K pMZ *mɨ?a* 'deer' vs. my pZ *mɨ?ah*.

C&K pMZ *cak* 'fish' vs. my pM *?akša* (nothing remotely like *cak* is in my files).

C&K pMZ *ma:k* 'to fish'; the meaning 'to fish' only occurs in Veracruz.

C&K pMZ *kahcay* 'hammock' only perhaps pMZ, borrowed into SaP later and weak chance of an OM cognate.

C&K pMZ *?ame* 'year'—at least in the broad meaning 'long time span' is pZ with possible OM cognates (which C&K did not have access to in 1976).

C&K pMZ *cɨwi* 'tobacco' is pZ only.

C&K pMZ *cow* 'to cost, be worth' nonexistent. Existent is pM *cowa* 'expensive' and perhaps a pMZ root *cow-*, which is only attested as a bound form; it has to do with engaging in contract relations.

C&K pMZ *te?n* 'ladder' vs. my pM *te:?ni(k)* 'ladder made of one piece of wood'.

C&K pMZ *me?esi* 'adobe wall' vs. my pM [Veracruz] *me:?š-i* 'wall'. The pM status not certain. May be a SaP innovation.

C&K pMZ *na?a* 'rubber, chicle' restricted to Veracruz.

C&K pMZ *ce?s* means 'corn granary' in Oaxaca Mixean, not 'bed', which is restricted to Zoquean and SaP. Why would the Highlanders in Oaxaca forget their word for bed? But 'corn granary' is still a nice alternative Olmecoid item.

"Not in my files" means not found among some 5,500 comparative sets that minimally contain two cognates (all the way from pMZ down to the dialect level). I may have overlooked a few things, but hardly pMZ items reconstructible from data available in 1976—data which were already published by then are at the core of my cognate collection.

Items with a greater time span than suggested in C&K (strengthening their case) are

(4) "Oaxaca Zoque *?awa*" 'squash, gourd' appears to be pZ.

(25) C&K pM **nokE* 'paper' is in fact pMZ **noki*.

(32) SaP *šuy* and ChimZ *suyu?* perhaps add up to pMZ **suyu* 'pot'. TxZ *su?uŋ* and SoZ *su?ŋ*, both 'pot', deviate from the expected phonological pattern; these, then, remain to be accounted for.

The authors count on a MZ time depth of 3,500 years, which is said to correlate with "the first glimmerings of Olmec civilization" (p. 80). To reach this sort of time depth a lexeme must appear in both the Mixean and the Zoquean branches. It is admitted that "items we list as Proto-Mixean (PMi) which are based on the Mixean languages may actually reflect PMZ items for which we as yet lack Zoquean information" (p. 82). But the problem is usually that the authors fail to have Mixean evidence for putative pMZ items which are only pZ. If an item is not attested in both branches, anything goes. The Olmecs can be made to do almost anything that a modern MZ speaker does. There would even be evidence for Olmecs wearing glasses and going to Catholic churches. To sum up, there are many important items that cannot *positively, on the basis of the C&K's protoforms* be traced as far back as the authors would want. The history of the words in question both within MZ and in other Mesoamerican languages must therefore be reconsidered. The referents are the following:

plantain; zapote; pinole; dog; axe; woven mat; bee, wasp, wasp's nest; fox; fog; coyote; chokeberry; avocado; zapote colorado; deer; fish; to fish; hammock; year; tobacco; ladder; adobe wall; rubber, chicle; bed.

Still, many items cited by C&K are indeed pMZ, including

milpa; to clear land; to sow (plant); seed; to harvest, etc.; chile; beans; honey; to spin thread; to twist rope, etc.; Holy; to write; to count/ divine; drum; complex numeral system, zontle; cigar; to cost; remedy; house pole; sandals.

Further, some of the reductions in C&K's Olmec inventory are compensated for by other protoforms.

If C&K postulate some unlikely pMZ roots, these will in some cases only represent the square roots of Brown and Witkowski's reveries. Commenting on the C&K article, these authors declare that "[s]everal of the lexical items listed by them as Zoquean loanwords in Mayan languages may as plausibly be construed as Mayan cognates of Zoquean words traced to Proto-Mayan-Zoquean. Similarly, other proposed Zoquean loans in other Mesoamerican languages may in fact be linked to common parent words of a Proto-Mesoamerican lexicon" (Witkowski and Brown 1978: 943).

Having reached the natural confines of this study, I invite the reader to explore Part Two for additional pMZ lexemes bearing on the prehistory of the MZ peoples and Mesoamerican civilization and on external affinities. *Suche keine Etymologien, finde sie!*

PART TWO

Cognate Sets

Guide to the Cognate Sets

The collection comprises 2,218 **entries**. Each entry is, except in eleven cases,[1] headed by a form reconstructed for the protolanguage or one of the subgroups according to the following criteria:

Phonological criteria. Whereas the semantic criteria must to some degree remain subjective, phonological criteria can be objective. If an item does not follow the sound laws established in Part One, it is excluded. Only in strikingly close cases, both phonologically and semantically, will an item be included under a heading. But it will then be furnished with a [?], indicating that this item is problematic and that it is consequently disregarded in the establishment of the etymon. When the whole set as such is dubious, the protoform itself is marked by a [?]. Such problematic sets are left in in the hope that the solution to some of the problems they pose may be more easily found.

Semantic criteria. Verbs will typically vary in the action they describe, but not in the implied shape of objects participating in this action (metaphorical extension). Nominal meaning tends to vary metonymically. Relatively large variation is accepted, but only if it moves along these lines or is in some way culturally determined.

Distributional criteria. A protolanguage pMZ and four subgroups, pM, pOM[2], pZ, and pGZ, are reconstructed. When a pM item is

---

[1] Sets which are not headed by reconstructed forms contain material which is interesting in itself, for instance, for understanding the numeral system.

[2] OM data from the files of Nordell (1990) were added during the autumn of 1990. By the addition of this data, the cognate collection became about twice as large although the actual amount of forms that could be reconstructed for pMZ increased surprisingly little. Verbs contained in Nordell's OM files are in the source always cited as one or more fully inflected forms headed by a Spanish gloss in the infinitive. Having to choose from (1) extracting the bare roots with the danger of omitting important phonological information, (2) citing the forms inflected as in the source but with the addition of some system of grammatical codes, or (3) citing the inflected forms without such a reference system, I chose option (3). Pointed brackets surrounding the forms from Nordell (1990) indicate that the material they contain is not roots but inflected forms. By combining the information given in the comparative chart of verb roots in Part One, Table 4.1, with the verb paradigms on pp. 60-61 of Van Haitsma and Van Haitsma (1976) anyone should be able to

restricted in distribution to Sayula Popoluca and Oluta Popoluca, this
is indicated by placing the information "pM [Veracruz]" before the
protoform. Being attested in two out of three branches, such items formally meet the criterion for pM-hood, but their restricted occurrence
in two geographically close languages suggests that their origin is more
recent. A pMZ item must have at least one reflex in each of the two
major divisions. A pOM item must have reflexes in at least three of the
four OM languages, and a pZ item must be present in at least two of
the three areas: Gulf, Oaxaca, or Chiapas.

The **number of reconstructions at the various levels** is as follows:
pMZ 699, pM 451, pOM 627, pZ 382, pGZ 48.

Each cognate set is assigned a **cognate number** consisting of the reconstruction of the two initial segments plus a three-digit number.

Derived forms appear beneath the root from which they are derived,
just as compounds follow the last member (head) of the compound. An
analysis into morphemes is provided which clarifies the derivational
relationships. For practical reasons no distinction is made between the
way that simplex and complex forms are numbered. For example, pM
won-i 'snail' follows pMZ *won* 'to pull, carry' since *won-i*, although this cannot be detected synchronically, is originally derived
from the pMZ root.

All sets have a **heading** giving, along with a cognate number and a
protoform, one or more Spanish **glosses**. The glosses represent my suggestions as to the **reconstructed meaning** of the item that they accompany. The English gloss both translates and complements the Spanish
gloss. In cases where a Spanish gloss is either a polysemous lexeme or
a Mexicanism, the English gloss serves to clarify. Schoenhals (1988)
has frequently been consulted for English flora and fauna terminology
corresponding to the popular Spanish terms. For scientific Latin terms,
that work can be referred to as a supplement to the glosses or
reconstructed meanings of MZ protoforms. The glosses also have the
function of assigning a **default meaning** to the various forms within the
entry. Typically, a root will not vary considerably semantically across
the family. If the cognate forms simply have the same meanings
everywhere, the default gloss will give the meaning. Individual items
to which the default meaning does not apply will have a specified

---

interpret most of the OM verbs from Nordell (1990) that are cited in the cognate
collection.

meaning following each phonological form or there will be a default meaning for a group of languages or dialects immediately following the designation of that group of languages or dialects. Please note that by using the reconstructed meaning as the default gloss I do not wish to imply that the most widespread meaning is always or even in most cases the original one. The reader will find many cases where the default meaning only applies to a minority of the forms cited for individual languages. See the description in "Orthography, Abbreviations, Conventions" on the use of the term "default."

Grammatical information for the daughter languages cited within the entries is limited (usually absent) when the set contains nonverbs. Verbs, however, are specified with respect to transitivity whenever the source gives that kind of information. Given the nature of the sources it has not been possible to impose a uniform system of grammatically annotating forms cited for the daughter languages. The following abbreviations are used:

adj	adjective
adv	adverb
dem	demonstrative
interj	interjection
loc	locative
n	noun
part	particle
pos	possessed (always)
pron	pronoun
v-attr	attributive verb
v-aux	auxiliary verb
v-imp	imperative verb
vditr	ditransitive
vi	intransitive verb
vi-a	agent-oriented intransitive verb
vi-p	patient-oriented intransitive verb
vi-pl	intransitive verb taking a plural agent only
vi-s	stative verb
vr	reflexive verb
vt	transitive verb

vt-ap	applicative verb (cross-references a benefactive, recipient, or possessor)
vt-caus	causative verb
vt-d	dative verb

For the protoforms a grammatical classification is always supplied. The reconstruction of transitivity is usually to be taken with a grain of salt, since the individual languages may sometimes vary a good deal in this respect.

Internally reconstructed forms are introduced by a star, and the forms in which they have become bound follow in square brackets.

For certain languages and dialects special measures are taken to indicate the **character of the data**. While, as a rule, the forms cited are phonological, some sources overdifferentiate and other sources underdifferentiate.

The default source for ChisZ-C [Te], a seventeenth-century manuscript, does not show glottal stops and is not in all respects dependable. Thus, forms cited from this source are given in pointed brackets.

This convention is also used for OM verbs cited from Nordell (1990). In this case, however, the pointed brackets indicate that the forms are inflected and that roots are not isolated. Pointed brackets are also used for citing LM-Cn forms from Hoogshagen and Hoogshagen (1993). Here they indicate both over- and underdifferentiation. The authors are of the opinion that there are three contrastive vowel lengths and further argue that it is not manageable for native speakers to distinguish between long and extra-long vowels in writing. Thus the Hoogshagens choose not to indicate this distinction. A complicated situation arises since both the analysis and the argument concerning choice of orthography are questionable. Concerning the analysis it is possible to argue (see my section 2.4) that the putative three vowel lengths may be reduced to two degrees of vowel length plus a tense-lax opposition in the consonants. In the Hoogshagens' data, a tense-lax opposition is indeed indicated—but only for stops. The reason for this is that they include voiced stops as part of their orthography (presumably because these occur in the Spanish orthography) and represent lax consonants as voiced. For verb roots the Hoogshagens make an exception and indicate three vowel lengths. This subclass of the lexicon, then, may be phonologized, but for nonverbs it is only possible to arrive at a proper phonological interpretation of a given form if they happen to contain stops in all syllable-final positions. So my choice has been to include the data as given in the source.[3] A full phonological conversion in conformity with my own analysis is often possible, but would sometimes involve a risk of creating distortions. The LM-Cn data are in any case usually matched by phonological forms from other OM languages and dialects. For comparative purposes these data are mainly of importance for the relatively extensive grammatical information and the Spanish glosses that accompany the Mixe forms.

When citing data from AyZ and ChisZ-S [Cp] I employ square brackets to indicate that the forms are given as I heard them. Features whose phonological status have not yet been fully worked out for ChisZ-S are voicedness in stops, stress, length, and initial glottal stops. All these may turn out to be nondistinctive. For AyZ, prenasalization, length, and nasalization are all features of the phonology, while it is less certain what statuses may be assigned to voicedness in vowels and to stress. In contrast, the data for TxZ, which I also collected, are fully phonologized. A special symbol "ê" is employed to indicate an [e] which behaves like an underlying /i/ under inflection (see my 1994 article for an alternative analysis).

In general, **comments** of all sorts are included in square brackets. Square brackets are also used for including scientific classification of flora and fauna whenever the source has that information.

For purposes of **alphabetization** the following conflation of ascii and phonetically motivated order conventions is followed: initial ?, i, e, i̵, a, u, o, c, h, k, l, m, n, p, s, t, w/ŋ, y. The reason why "ŋ" and "w" have the same alphabetical status is their mutual origin in pMZ *w. Laryngeals /", ?, !, h/ have no alphabetical status when following vowels. Numerals and derivational morphemes are presented separately as the last sections of the Cognate Sets.

Please refer to the section "Orthography, Abbreviations, Conventions" for a list of **Sources, Dialect, and Language Abbreviations** and further information on **orthography**.

Following the Cognate Sets the reader will find a Spanish-MZ index and a English-Spanish one. In the former are found all reconstructed

---

[3] As in all citations from Summer Institute of Linguistics dictionaries, characters in the Spanish-based orthography have been converted (in this case c, ch, hu, j, ', ng, qu, tz, x have been changed to k, č, w, h, ?, ŋ, k, c, š), but this is of no consequence for the phonological interpretation.

forms appearing in the Cognate Sets except the derivational morphemes and the numerals.

COGNATE SETS IN ALPHA-BETICAL ORDER

?I-?O

?I#001 pM *?i:cɨmɨ (n) 'jabalí/wild pig' [pOM *?i:cɨm; all languages develop an epenthetic vowel between *c* and *m*; in MM and LM the stress is subsequently shifted to the last syllable, whereby the first syllable is shortened] NHM: *?i:cɨm* 'cerdo montés, jabalí, cochino de monte, pécari' MM: 'cohino' Ju *?ɨzɨ́m* Ja *?azɨ́m* '=puerco' Pu *?ɨzɨ́m* Ma,At *?ɨzɨ́m* 'jabalí' Ct *?a·zɨ́m* 'puerco', *?azɨm* 'cochino' [sic!] LM: Cn <*ɨdzɨm*> 'marrano' Ca *?ɨzɨ́m* 'cochino' Gu *?ɨzɨ́m* '=puerco' SJ *?ɨzɨm* Cn *?icɨm* 'puerco' [Hoogshagen 1984] OlP: *?i:cɨmɨ* 'cochino, puerco' SaP: *?í:čim* 'cochino'

?I#002 pZ *?i?k?i?k (n) 'especie de gavilán/species of hawk' SaP: *?í?k?ik* 'clase de gavilán' [Zo loan] TxZ: *?e?k?e?k* 'gavilán (color café abado)'

?I#003 pM *?i:k-an (n) 'juguete/toy' LM: Cn <*i:g*> [from pOM *?i:kn with unexplained loss of final *n*] SaP: *?í:gan*

?I#004 pMZ *?in (vi) 'tener rabia/to rage' MM: 'rabioso, tiene rabia' Ju <*?in*> Ma <*?i·m̄p*> At <*?īn, ?uk?ín*> Ct <*?í·nɨp*> 'chistoso', <*?i·m̄p*> LM: Ca <*?imp*> Gu <*?īn*> 'chistoso' <*?in, ?i·m̄p*> 'enloquecerse' [Nordell, p.c.] ChisZ: C *?in* (vi) 'aburrirse; fastidiarse' (vt) 'empalagarle' N *?i?n* (vi) 'aburrirse' [?] NE *?in* (vi) 'fastidiarse'

?I#005 pM *?i(:?)nciC... (n) 'arco iris/rainbow' [pOM *?i:?(n)cc] NHM: *?i:?cic* SHM: Tl,Tu,Tp *?i?hč* MM: Ju,Cc,Ma,At *?i?č* Ja *?i!n̄ʸč* Pu *?ič* [?] LM: Gu *?i!n̄ʸč* OlP: *?inči?tona*

?I#006 pMZ ***?i:?(n)ki** *(n)* *'cuajinicuil/jinicuil'* [pM **?i:?(n)ki* > pOM **?i:?(n)ky*; pZ **?i?(n)ki*] NHM: *?i:?k* 'yatolito, palo atolito, palo de campeche' [types of Ingas other than Inga paterna and Inga jinicuil (G. Martin, p.c.)] MM: Ju,Ja,At *?i?kʸ* 'guajinicuil, guajinicuilillo, acotope, cuajinicuillo, guasamandillo' Pu *?i!kʸ* 'cuajinicuillo, guajinicuil, guajinicuilillo, acotope, guasamandillo' Ct *?i?ŋʸkʸ* 'guajinicuil, guajinicuilillo, acotope', *?i?kʸpʸohká:* 'cuajinicuillo, guasamandillo' LM: Cn <*i?ky*> 'cuajinicuil, jinicuil [Inga sp.]' OlP: *?i:kita?skɨ'k* 'acotope (árbol)' SoZ: *?i?ŋki?* 'acotope' TxZ: *?e:?ŋkuy* 'acotope' ChisZ: C *?i?kih* 'guajinicuil' N *?i?ki* 'chelele [Inga fissicalyx]'

?I#007 pMZ ***?is** *(vi, vt)* *'ver/to see'* NHM: *?iš* 'ver (p.ej., un libro), cuidar' SHM: Tl *?eš* Ay <*?ešp*> 'mirar' MM: Ju <*?iš*> Ma <*?i͞š, y?ihsᵒpʸ, m?ihsᵒpʸ*> '=mirar, revisar' <*?i͞š*> 'visitar' Ja <*?i͞š, y?ihš, y?ihšᵒpʸ*> '=mirar' Pu <*?i͞š, m?ihšᵒpʸ, y?ihšᵒpʸ*> '=mirar' At <*?i͞š, ?ihšp*> '=revisar', <*?i͞š, ?ihšᵒpʸ*> '=mirar' [sic!] Ct <*?i͞š, y?ihšᵒpʸ*> LM: SJ *?ihš* Gu <*?i͞š, ?ihšp, y?ihšᵒp*> Cn <*ihš~iš*> (vt) 'ver, mirar; fijar; mantener' SaP: *?iš* (vi, vt) 'have looked at, have seen' TxZ: *êš* '=saber' ChisZ: C *?is* (vt) N *?is* (vt) 'verlo; destar; dar a luz' NE *?is* (vt) [in the phrase *?yisu toya* 'sufrirlo, padecerlo']

?I#008 pM ***?aw-?iš** *(vi)* *'esperar/to wait'* NHM: *?a?iš?iht ~ ?a?iš?it* MM: Ju <*?æwíš*> Ma <*?awɨžít, ?awɨžíht*> Ja <*?a·wí͞š, y?a·wíhsᵒpʸ*> Pu <*?a·wí͞š, m?a·wíhsᵒpʸ*> LM: Ca <*?æwíš*> Gu <*?a?í͞š, ?a?ihšp, y?a?íhšᵒp*> [Nordell 1990 and p.c.] OlP: *?aviš* (vi, vt)

?I#009 pOM ***ku-?ihš ~ ku-?iš** *(vt)* *'visitar/to visit'* NHM: *ku?iš* MM: Ju,Ja <*ku?í͞š*> Ma <*kɨ?í͞š*> Pu <*kɨ?í͞š, tæm tk?í͞šᵛ*> Ct <*kɨ?í͞šɨ*> LM: Gu <*ku?í͞š*>

?I#010 pOM ***nɨ-?ihš ~ nɨ-?iš** *(vt)* *'divisar/to distinguish'* NHM: *nɨ?iš* 'escoger o elegir un joven para casarse, ver para sí algo con deseo' MM: Ju <*ni?í͞š*> 'examinar' Ma <*nɨ?í͞šɨ, nʸi?íh͞š?ɨpʸ*> Ct <*nɨ?í͞šɨ, nʸi?í͞š?ɨpʸ*> LM: Gu <*nɨ?ižⁿ"w*>

?I#011 pOM ***tuk-?ihš ~ tuk-?iš** *(vt)* *'enseñar, mostrar/to show'* NHM: *tuk?iš* MM: Ju <*tuk?íš*> Ja <*tuk?í͞š*> Ma,Pu,At,Ct *tɨg?í͞š*>

?I#012 pOM ***win-?ihš ~ win-?iš** *(vt)* *'escoger/to choose'* NHM: *vin?iš* 'escoger (p.ej., ropa), ver (p.ej., la cara de alguien, mirar) MM: Ju <*win?íš*> Ja <*win?í͞š*> At <*hɨn?í͞š*> LM: Ca <*win?íš*>

?I#013 pOM ***win-?ihš-n** *(n) 'anteojos/glasses'* [Whereas the OM forms may be true cognates—something which would require a late, post-Conquest date for OM diversification—the following forms from the Veracruz area cannot be true cognates: OlP *vin?išti'k* SaP: *win?íštik*. These are just similar derivatives.] NHM: *vin?íšin* '=lentes' MM: Ju *wi:n?íhšṇ* Ja *win?íhšṇ* '=lentes' At *hin?íhšṇ ~ win?íhšṇ* '=lentes' Ct *hin?íhšṇ* 'lentes' LM: Ca *wi:n?íhšt* Gu *wi:n?íhšt* '=lentes'

?I#014 pOM ***?iš-?aht ~ ?iš-?at** *(vt) 'conocer/to know'* NHM: *?iša* (vt) SHM: Tu *<m?iš^y?át^yp^y>* MM: Ju *<?iš^y?ǽt>* Ma *<n?iš̄?áht^yp^yic>* Pu *<n?iš̄^y?áht^yp^yic>* At *<n?iš̄^y?ǽht^yp^yic>* LM: Cn *<ix?aht ~ iš?at>* (vt) Ca *<?iš^y?áht>* Gu *<n?iš^y?áhp^yič>*

?I#015 pOM ***?ihš-n** *(n) 'espejo, vidrio/mirror, glass'* [The *t* in Ca and Gu came about as follows: pOM **-n > -ṇ > -t*.] NHM: *?íšin* '=cristal' SHM: Tl *?eš* MM: Ju,Ja,At,Ct *?ihšṇ* Ma,Pu *?ihšṇ* 'espejo, lentes, anteojos' LM: Cn *<ihš>* Ca *?ihšt* 'espejo' SJ *?ihš* Gu *?ihšt*

?I#016 pM ***?i:š-in** *(n) 'comadreja/weasel'* [pOM **?i:š* with irregular loss of final *n*. There is a LM-Gu form *<?i·?š>* 'pellizcar'; this could be the descendant of a pM verb from which **?i:š-in* would then be a derivative; it would have to be confirmed, however, that a weasel is 'one who pinches (its fur)'.] NHM: *?i:š* 'cacomixtle' SHM: Tu,Tp,Mi *?i:š^y* MM: Ju,Ma,Ja,Pu,At,Ct *?i:š^y* LM: Gu *?i:š^y* OlP: *?i:-šinú'k*

?I#017 pOM ***?išyam** *(adv) 'ahora, hoy/now, today'* NHM: *?išyam* SHM: Tl *?išyom* LM: Cn *ycam* 'ahora' [Hoogshagen 1984] [?]

?I#018 pMZ ***?it** *(vi) 'estar, existir/to be, exist'* NHM: *?iht ~ ?it* 'estar, permanecer' SHM: Tl *?eht* 'permanecer' MM: Ma,Ct *<?ihtp>* '=durar (ropa)' Ja *<?ihtp, ?itá·m̄p>* 'estar' Pu *<?ihtp>* 'durar (ropa)' Ju,At *<?ihtp>* LM: Cn *<iht ~ it>* (vi) 'quedar (en la misma forma o en el mismo lugar); abundar' Gu *<?it, ?ihp, ?idá·m̄p>* Ca *<?ihtp>* SJ *?iht ~ ?it* 'to stay the same; to be in the state of' OlP: *?it* (vi) 'hay; estar; viver; tener' SaP: *?it* (vi) TxZ: *?êč* (vi) estar, vivir SoZ: *?it^y* [Foster and Foster 1948] ChisZ: C *?iht* (vi) 'estar; haber; vivir; existir' (vt) 'tener' N *?iht* (vi) 'estar; haber; viver (tener vida); viver (localidad); produjo' NE *?iht* (vi) 'haber; estar; viver' ChZ: *?a?ŋit* 'tener'

ʔI#019 pOM ***ʔiš-ʔiht ~ ʔiš-ʔit** *(vi) 'vigilar/to watch <u>over</u>'* NHM: *ʔiš ʔiht ~ ʔiš ʔit* '=custodiar' MM: Ma,Ct < *ʔihš ʔī̄t* > 'vigilar', < *ʔis̄ ʔī̄t* > 'cuidar' [sic!] Ja,At < *ʔihš ʔī̄t* >

ʔI#020 pOM ***hot-ʔiht ~ hot-ʔit** *(vi) 'nutrir/to nourish'* NHM: *hot ʔiht ~ hot ʔit* 'nutrir' LM: SJ *hodiht ~ hodit* 'to grow full stature'

ʔI#021 pOM ***mac-ʔiht ~ mac-ʔit** *(vt) 'detener/to detain'* [Cf. OlP: *mači ʔt* (vt) 'soltarlo'; this has the opposite meaning but may nevertheless be related.] NHM: *mac ʔiht ~ mac ʔit* 'detener (p.ej., agarrar a una persona sin soltarla)' MM: Ja < *maẓ ʔī̄t* > At,Ct < *mahc ʔī̄t* > LM: Gu < *maẓ ʔī̄t* >

ʔI#022 pMZ ***ʔit** *(n) 'lugar/place'* [pM, pOM, pZ *ʔit] NHM: *ʔit* SHM: Tl *ʔet* MM: Ju *ʔit* Ma,Ja,Pu,At,Ct *ʔī̄t* LM: Ca,Mz *ʔit* Gu *may ʔī̄t* 'muchos lugares' ChisZ: C *ʔitkuy* 'vivienda, hogar, morada, genio' N *ʔitkuy* 'lugar donde vive uno; las condiciones de la vida' ChZ: *ʔisso* 'lugar' [?]

ʔI#023 pZ ***ʔiyɨ** *(pron) 'quien/who'* [pGZ *ʔiyɨ] TxZ: *ʔe:* (pron interr y rel) 'quién?, quien' ChisZ: C *ʔiwɨ* (pron rel) 'quien; alguien' (pron interr) 'quien?', *tiyɨ ʔiwɨ* (pron indef) 'algo, alguna cosa' N *ʔiyɨ/ i* (pron interr) 'quien?' NE *tiyɨ ʔiyɨ* (pron indef) 'alguna cosa'

ʔE#001 pMZ ***ʔec** *(vi) 'bailar/to dance'* NHM: *ʔehc ~ ʔec* SHM: Tl *ʔac* Tu < *ʔæhck, ʔæc, ʔæhcp, y ʔeč* > Tp < *ʔæc, ʔæhcp, y ʔeč, ʔæhc, ʔæcámp* > Mi < *ʔæc, ʔæhcp, ʔæcp, ʔǽhctïp, ʔæẕwándïp* > MM: Ju < *ʔæc* > Cc < *ʔæc, ʔæhcp, yAhk ʔéhčp^y, ʔæcámp, ʔæhc, y ʔehč, tɨ: y ʔeč* > Ma < *ʔǣc, ʔæhcp* > Ja,Pu,At,Ct < *ʔǣc, ʔæhcp* > LM: Cn < *ehc ~ ec* > Ca < *ʔæc* > SJ *ʔehc ~ ʔec* Gu < *ʔēc, ʔehcp* > OlP: *ʔec* (vi) SoZ: *ʔec* TxZ: *ʔec* (vi) ChisZ: C *ʔehc* (vi) '=girar' N *ʔehc* (vi) NE *ʔehc*

ʔE#002 pMZ ***ʔec-e** *(n) 'baile/dance'* [pM *ʔece > pOM *ʔecy; pZ *ʔece > pGZ **ʔe:ce*] SHM: Tp *ʔeč* MM: Ju,Cc *ʔeč* Ma,Ja,Pu,Ct *ʔēč* At *ʔeč* SaP: *ʔeč* SoZ: *ʔe:ci?* TxZ: *ʔe:c* (=danza) ChisZ: C,N,NE *ʔece*

ʔE#003 pMZ ***ʔec-pa** *(n) 'danzante, bailador/dancer'* [pM *ʔecpa > pOM *ehcpa, pZ *ʔecpa] NHM: *ʔehcpa* '=bailarín' MM: Ju,Ma, Ja,Pu,At,Ct *ʔǽhcpɨ* LM: Ca *ʔǽhcpɨ* SJ *ʔehcpɨ* 'dance; dancer' Gu *ʔéhcpɨ* OlP: *ʔespa?* 'bailador' ChisZ: C *ʔecpawɨ* 'danzante, bailador (en danzas regionales)'

ʔE#004 pOM ***ʔeːʔc** *(vt) 'clavar/to nail'* NHM: *ʔeːʔc ~ ʔeːʔc* 'clavar (p.ej., con fecha o aguja), estacado de rosales' MM: Ja < *ʔæːc, yʔæʔc* > 'clavar (varita)' At < *ʔæːc, yheʔčpʸ* > [sic!] 'clavar (varita)' LM: Cn < *e·c ~ eːc* > (vt) Ca < *ʔæːc* > 'clavar (varita)' Gu < *ʔeːc, yʔe·ʔčp* > 'clavar (varita)' SJ *ʔe·c ~ ʔeːc* 'to pound into the ground'

ʔE#005 pOM ***ʔehk ~ ʔek** *(vi) 'enojarse/to get angry'* NHM: < *ʔehkhup ~ ʔEkhïʸ* > 'enojar' SHM: Tu < *ʔǽhkɨp, kʸeʺ yʔékʸɨ* > 'berrinchudo' _MM: Ma < *ʔǽhkɨp, ʔækánɨp* > _'berrinchudo', < *ʔæhkɨp, ʔækánɨp* > 'enojarse' At < *ʔǽhkɨp, ʔæká·nɨp* > Ct < *ʔǽhkɨp, ʔækánɨp* > 'berrinchudo', < *ʔæhkɨp* > 'enojarse' LM: Cn < *ehk ~ ek* > (vi) 'enojarse' SJ *ʔehk ~ ʔek* 'enojarse' Gu < *ʔegá·nɨp, ʔéhkɨp* > 'berrinchudo'

ʔE#006 pMZ ***ʔeːʔk** *[?] (vt) 'descuartizar/to quarter (an animal)'* NHM: *ʔeːk ~ ʔeːʔk* 'pelar (p.ej., un plátano), desollar' MM: Ma < *ʔæːk, yʔe·kʸpʸ* > '=desollar' Ja < *ʔæːk, yʔe·kpʸ* > 'desollar', < *niʔæːk, yʔe·kʸp͟ʸ, ʔæːk* > 'descuartizar' At < *ʔæːk, yʔe·kʸpʸ* > 'desollar', < *ʔæ·k͟p, ʔæːk, tɨː dʔeːkʸ, yʔe·kʸpʸ* > 'descuartizar', < *ʔæːk, tɨː yʔe·kʸpʸ* > 'pelar, descascarar' Ct < *ʔæːk, yʔe·kʸpʸ* > 'descuartizar', < *ʔæːk, yʔe·kʸpʸ* > 'desollar' LM: Cn < *e·k ~ eʺk* > 'pelar' (vt) Ca < *ʔæʺk* > 'descascarar' SJ *ʔe·k ~ ʔeʺk* 'to skin, peel off' Gu < *ʔeʺk, ʔe·kp, yʔe·kʸpʸ* > '=desollar' ChisZ: C *ʔeʔk*

ʔE#007 pOM ***nɨ-ʔeːʔk** *[?] (vt) 'descascarar/to shell'* NHM: *nɨʔeːk ~ nɨʔeːʔk* 'descargar, pelar (p.ej., un plátano), descascarado' MM: Ma < *nɨʔǽːk, nʸɨʔé·kʸpʸ* > 'descascarar' Pu < *niʔǽːk, nʸiʔé·kʸpʸ* > 'desollar' At < *nɨʔǽːk, nɨʔǽ·kp, nʸɨʔé·kʸpʸ* > 'pelar, descascarar' Ct *nɨʔǽːk, nʸɨʔé·kʸpʸ* 'pelar, descascarar, descuartizar' LM: Gu *nɨʺʔéʺk, nʸɨʺʔé·kʸpʸ* 'descascarar'

ʔE#008 pOM ***ʔeːʔkš** *(vt) 'pellizcar/to pinch'* NHM: *tukʔeːʔkš ~ tukʔeːʔkš* 'pinchar' MM: Ju *ʔaʔš* 'arañar' Ma < *ʔæʔš, yʔeʔšʸpʸ* > 'pinchar', < *ʔæʔš* > 'pellizcar' Ja < *ʔæʔš, yʔæʔš, yʔeʔšʸpʸ* > Pu < *ʔæ!kš, yʔe!kšʸpʸ* > At < *ʔæʔkš, yʔeʔkšʸpʸ* > Ct < *ʔæʔkš, yʔeʔkšʸpʸ* > LM: Cn < *e·kš* > (vt) 'cortar (con los dedos)' SJ *ʔe·kš* 'to pick tender ends of vines'

ʔE#009 pM ***ʔehkšah** *(n) 'chayote/vegetable pear'* [pOM **ʔekšah*] NHM: *ʔehkš* [Sechium edule] SHM: Tl *ʔokšoh* MM: Ju *ʔækšáh* M͟a *ʔæhš* Ja *ʔæhkš ~ ʔæhš* Pu,Ct *ʔæhkš* LM: Ca *ʔakšáh* Gu *ʔakšáh* OlP: *ʔekša* SaP: *ʔékšna* [?]

ʔE#010 pM *ʔe:ʔm (vi) 'endurecerse/to become hardened' LM: Gu
< *ʔe!m̄p, ʔe:má·m̄p* > OlP: *ʔe:m* (vi) 'enconarse, agrandarse (un
grano)'

ʔE#011 pM *ʔe:ʔm-e (n) 'vena, cuerda/vein, cord' [pOM **ʔe:ʔmy*]
NHM: *ʔe:ʔm* SHM: Ay *ʔe:m* 'vena' MM: *ʔe:mʸ* Ju 'vena, cuerda'
Ma 'nervio, vena, tendón' At 'tendón, nervio, vena' Ja 'nervio,
vena, tieso' Pu,Ct 'nervio, vena' LM: Ca *ʔe:mʸ* 'cuerda' Cn
< *e:my* > '=arteria; tendón' Gu *ʔe:mʸ* 'tendón, cuerda, nervio, vena,
tieso' OlP: *ʔe:me* 'vena, cuerda, pellejo de carne; nervio'

ʔE#012 pZ *ʔeme (n) 'tía/aunt' NHM: *ʔɨm* 'tío' [?] ChisZ: C *ʔeme*
N *ʔeme* 'tía—hermana de la madre' S [Tu] *ʔeme?* [Foster 1949]

ʔE#013 pM *ʔe:ʔp 'ver/to see' LM: Cn < *e·p ~ e:p* > (vi) 'divertirse' Gu < *ʔe:p, ʔe·ʔp* > OlP: *ʔe:p* (vi, vt) SaP: *ʔeʔp* (vi, vt)

ʔE#014 pM *ʔepak [?] (n) 'sombra/shadow' [pOM **epk*. In MM
and LM the addition of *áw-* and vowel-leveling in LM. Final *k* lost (?)
in OlP and (independently, as a result of cluster reduction) in NHM.]
NHM: *ʔep* LM: Ca *ʔa·ʔǽpk* 'sombra de persona' Gu *ʔaʔápk* 'sombra de persona' OlP: *ʔepa*

ʔE#015 pMZ *ʔe:si (n) 'cangrejo/crab' [pM **ʔe:ši* > pOM **ʔe:šy*;
pZ **ʔesi* > pGZ **ʔe:ši*] NHM: *ʔE:š* '[fam. Brachyara, p.ej.,
Callinectes sp.]' SHM: Tl,Tu,To,Mi *ʔe:šʸ* MM:
Ju,Cc,Ma,Ja,Pu,At,Ct *ʔe:šʸ* LM: Cn < *e:šy* > 'tipo de cangrejo del
río' Ca,Gu *ʔe:šʸ* OlP: *ʔe:si* '=extranjero' SaP: *ʔe:š* SoZ: *ʔe:ši?*
AyZ: *[e:si]* TxZ: *ʔe:šê?* ChisZ: C,NE *ʔehsi* N *ʔesi* ChZ: *ʔesi?*

ʔE#016 pZ *ʔeʔt (vt) 'hacer uso sexual/to have sexual intercourse'
TxZ: *ʔeʔt* (vt) 'cojer (moviendo las caderas)' ChisZ: C [Te]
< *etpa* > 'fornicar'

ʔE#017 pZ *ʔeya (n) 'otro/other' ChisZ: C *ʔeyapɨ* (adj), *eyane?*
(pron), *eya* (adj) NE *ʔeyabɨ* (adj) ChZ: *ʔeyapɨ? ~ ʔeya*

ʔɨ#001 pMZ *ʔɨ:ci ~ ʔɨc (pron) 'yo/I' [pM **ʔɨ:ci ~ ʔɨc*, pOM **ʔɨ:cy-*
~ ʔɨc (short form reflected NHM and SHM and in LM [Gu], long form
in LM); pZ **ʔɨci ~ ʔɨc*] NHM: *ʔɨc* SHM: Tl *ʔɨc* MM: Ju *ʔɨhc, ʔɨh*
Ma,Ja,Pu,Ct *ʔɨ̄c* At *ʔɨhc* LM: Ca *ʔɨ:č* SJ *ʔɨ: ~ ʔɨ:dzʸ; ʔɨč* '1p clitic'
Cn < *ʔɨ:č* > '=me' Gu *ʔɨ:č* 'yo', *ʔɨhc* 'nosotros (excl)' [reanalysis

of the short alternant] OlP: *ʔiːs* SaP: *ʔiːc ~ ʔiː* AyZ: *[ic]* TxZ: *ʔici ~ ʔic* ChisZ: C *ʔis* (subj of vt; pron pos) 'mi, mis' N *ʔihci ~ ʔic* '=mi' NE *ʔihci ~ ʔiht* ChZ: *ʔic* (dep); *ʔicci?* (indep)

ʔi#002 pM *ʔiːci-at ~ ʔic-at (pron) 'nosotros excl./we excl.' (long form) [pOM **ʔiː-cy-at* (reflex of long form)] MM: Ja *ʔíːdzitʸ* LM: Cn < *ʔiːč ʔaht* > 'nosotros incl.' SJ *ʔiːdzy ʔaht* 'we, us (incl)' Gu *ʔihcáhtim* 'nosotros incl.' [unexplained (analogical?) *im* added with subsequent shift of stress to the suffix.] SaP: *ʔihcat* [reflex of short form]

ʔi#003 pOM *ʔiːc (pron) 'nosotros excl./we excl.' NHM: *ʔiːc* SHM: Tl *ʔiːc* MM: Ma,Ja,Pu,At,Ct *ʔiːc* LM: Cn *ʔiːc ahkšy*

ʔi#004 pMZ *ʔiːʔc (vi) 'vomitar/to vomit' NHM: *ʔiːʔc* '=hervir, oxidar' MM: '=hervir' Ma < *ʔiʔcp, ʔiːc, ʔiːdzámp* > Ju < *ʔiʔcp* > 'hervir' Ja < *ʔiːc, ʔiʔc, ʔiʔcp* > Pu <*tæm y ʔiːč, ʔiʔcp* > 'vomitar', < *ʔiʔcp* > 'burbujear' At < *ʔiʔcp, kʸæh y ʔiːč* > Ct < *ʔiʔcp, ʔiːc* > LM: Cn < *iːc ~ iˑc* > (vi) 'hervir; vomitar; gemir (el viento); chillar (la barriga); zumbar (abejas)' Ca < *ʔiʔcp* > 'hervir' Mz < *ʔic, ʔiːdzáːmp* > 'hervir' Gu < *ʔiːc, ʔiˑʔc, ʔiˑʔcp* > SJ *ʔiˑc ~ ʔiːc* OlP: *ʔiːc* SaP: *ʔiʔc* (vi, vt) SoZ: *ʔic* TxZ: *ʔiʔc* ChisZ: C,N *ʔiʔc* (vi)

ʔi#005 pOM *ni-ʔiːʔc (vi) 'hervir/to boil' NHM: *niʔiːʔcpihk ~ niʔiːʔcpik* 'empezar a hervir' SHM: Tl *niʔiːʔc* MM: At < *niʔíʔcp* >

ʔi#006 pMZ *ʔiːʔc-i (n) 'vómito/vomit' [pM **ʔiːʔci* > pOM **ʔiːʔcy*; pZ **ʔiʔci*] NHM: *ʔiːʔc* '=oxidado' MM: Ju,Ma,Ja,Pu,At,Ct *ʔiːč* LM: Gu *ʔiːč* SoZ: *ʔiːči?* AyZ: *[iʔici]* TxZ: *ʔiːʔč* ChisZ: C [Te] < *hetzi* > 'bómito'

ʔi#007 pM *ʔih (vi) 'pujar/to grunt' NHM: *ʔih* LM: Gu < *ʔahihip* > [Nordell, p.c.] SaP *ʔih*

ʔi#008 pM *ʔik (vi) 'tostar/to toast' NHM: *ʔihk ~ ʔik* MM: Ju < *ʔik* > Ma < *ʔihkp* > Ja < *ʔihk, ʔihkp* > At,Ct < *ʔihkp* > SaP: *ʔik* (vi, vt)

ʔi#009 pM *yak-ʔik (vt) 'tostar/to toast' MM: Ma,At,Ct < *yahk-ʔik* > 'tostar' Ja < *yah ʔik* > 'tostar' SaP: *yak ʔik* 'tostar (pan)' [Clark and Clark 1960]

ʔi#010 pMZ *ʔiks (vi, vt) 'desgranar/to shell (corn)' NHM: *ʔihkš ~ ʔihkš* MM: Ju < *ʔihkš* > Ma < *ʔihš, yʔehsʸpʸ* > Ja < *ʔihš, yʔehsʸpʸ* > Pu,At < *ʔihkš, yʔehksʸpʸ* > Ct < *ʔihkš* > LM: Ca

< *ʔikš* > Cn <*i·kš* > (vt) SJ *ʔi·kš* Gu < *ʔikš, yʔikšʸp* > OIP: *ʔikš* (vi, vt) SaP: *ʔikš* (vi, vt) SoZ: *ʔiks* [Foster and Foster 1948] TxZ: *ʔiks* (vt) ChisZ: C,NE *ʔiks* (vt) ChZ: *ʔiks*

ʔɨ#011 pMZ ***ʔiks-i** *(n) 'maíz desgranado/grains of corn'* [pM **ɨkši* > pOM **ʔikšʸ*; pZ **ʔiksi*] MM: Ma *mo:gʔéhšʸ* Ja *mo:gʔéhšʸ, ʔehšʸ* At,Ct *mo:gʔéhkšʸ* LM: Gu *mo:gʔïkšʸ, ʔïkšʸ* OIP: *ʔikši* SoZ: *ʔikši?* AyZ: *[iksi]* TxZ: *ʔikš* ChisZ: C *ʔiksi* 'maíz desgranado, maíz' N,NE *ʔiksi* S *[iksí?]* 'maíz'

ʔɨ#012 pMZ ***ʔɨ:ʔk** *[?] (vi) 'vender/to sell'* NHM: *ʔɨ:ʔk ~ ʔɨ:ʔk* 'ladear' [has a causative with the derived meaning 'inclinar algo'] ChisZ: C *ʔɨʔk* (vi, vt) N *ʔɨʔkay* (vt)

ʔɨ#013 pMZ ***ʔɨ:kɨ** *(n) 'guácimo/pricklenut tree'* [pOM **ʔɨ:kɨ*, pZ **ʔɨkɨ*] MM: Ma,Ja,Pu,At *ʔɨ:k* LM: Gu *ʔï:k* OIP: *ʔɨ:kikúyɨ* SaP: *ʔɨgɨ:hkuhy* [Clark 1981], *ʔɨgɨ:k* [Clark and Clark 1960] [final *k* unexplained] SoZ: *ʔɨ:kɨ?* TxZ: *ʔɨ:k*

ʔɨ#014 pOM ***ʔɨ:ʔn** *(vt) 'acusar/to accuse'* [Cf. ChisZ: N *ʔɨʔnbɨ?* (vi) 'inclinarse, volcarse; cabecear'. This provides a phonological match but the semantics does not agree] NHM: *ʔɨ:ʔn* MM: Ju <*nɨʔɨ:nɨ* > 'demandar', <*nɨʔɨ:nɨ* > 'acusar' [sic!] Ma <*nɨʔɨ:nɨ, nɨšíʷwɨ, nʸɨšɨʔʔɨpʸ* > 'demandar' At <*nɨʔɨ:nɨ* > 'demandar', <*nɨʔɨ:nɨ, nʸɨʔɨ!nɨp* > 'acusar' [sic!] Ct <*nɨʔɨ:nɨ* > '=demandar' LM: Ca < *ʔɨ:n* > SJ *wiˑnʔɨˑn ~ wiˑnʔɨ:n* 'to fool, deceive'

ʔɨ#015 pMZ ***ʔɨ:ʔp** *(vt) 'amontonar/to pile up'* OIP: *ʔɨ:p* (vt) SaP: *ʔɨʔp* (vi, vt) SoZ: *ʔɨp* 'osar, hocicar' TxZ: *ʔɨʔp* (vt, vi-a) 'hocicar, escarbar tierra con la trompa'

ʔɨ#016 pMZ ***ʔihsɨ** *(n) 'tronco/trunk'* [pM **ʔɨhši* > pOM **ʔihš*; pZ **ʔihsi*] NHM: *ʔihš* 'cadera, parte trasera de los animales' MM: Ma, Ja,Pu,At,Ct *ʔɨhš* 'cabo, mango de machete, tallo' LM: Cn <*ɨhš* > (n) 'descendiente de una persona en particular; p.ej., *Abraham yʔɨhš yʔok* 'los descendientes de Abraham' (adv) 'al pie de (árbol, piedra, cerro); principio (del mes); p.ej., *marzʔɨhš* 'principio de marzo' SJ *ʔɨhš* 'trunk' Gu *ʔïhš* 'cabo, fondo', *nahcʔïhš* 'nuca' [Nordell 1990 and p.c.] OIP: *ʔɨš-* 'verbal prefix' ChisZ: C *ʔɨhsɨ* 'nuca' N *ʔɨhsɨ* 'cuello' *ɨ#017 pM *ʔɨw (vi) 'cantar/to sing'* NHM: *ʔɨːv ~ ʔɨv* '=canturrear' SHM: Tl *ʔɨw* '=leer' Tu < *ʔɨw̄ ~ ʔɨβ, ʔɨːp* > Tp < *ʔɨw, mʔɨːʸpʸ, ʔɨː, ʔɨβámp, ʔɨwámp* > MM: Ju < *ʔɨf* > Cc < *ʔɨw, ʔɨːp* > At < *ʔɨw̄, ʔɨːp, tiː yʔeːpy* > Ma < *ʔɨw̥, ʔɨwΦ, ʔɨf, ʔɨːp, tiː mʔeːpʸ* > Ja < *ʔɨw̄, ʔɨ·w̄, ʔɨ·w̥, ʔɨːp, mʔeːpʸ* > Pu < *ʔɨw̄, ʔɨːp, mʔɨːpʸ* > Ct < *ʔɨw̥, ʔɨΦ, ʔɨːp, mʔeːpʸ* > LM: Ca < *ʔɨw* > Cn < *ɨ·w ~ ɨw* > (vi) '=tocar (radio)' SJ *ʔɨ·w ~ ʔɨw* Gu < *ʔɨw̄* > (fut), < *ʔɨ̈ːp* > (pres), < *mʔɨ̈ːpʸ, ʔɨ̈·w̥* > OlP: *ʔɨv* (vi, vt)

ɨ#018 pM *ʔɨw-i (n) 'canción, canto/song' [pOM **ʔɨwy*] NHM: *ʔɨv* 'himno' SHM: Tu *ʔɨȳ* Tp,Mi *ʔɨy* MM: Ju,Ma *ʔɨy* Cc *ʔɨy yAⁿ§ʸ* Ja,Pu,At,Ct *ʔɨȳ* LM: Cn < *ɨ·y* > Gu *ʔɨȳ* OlP: *ʔɨvi*

ɨ#019 pZ *ʔɨŋ (vi) 'dormir/to sleep' [Both ChisZ-C and -N have causative derivations meaning 'to make go to sleep; if the root is related to pM **ʔɨw*, the meaning of the root could possibly originally have been 'to sing'. The causative meaning in Zoquean would have gone from 'to sing' to 'make sleep' and the root meaning would then have been reanalyzed as 'to sleep'.] TxZ: *ʔɨŋ-de?* (vi-s) 'estar con la cabeza inclinado para abajo' ChisZ: C *ʔɨŋ* (vi) 'dormir, estar dormido; dormirse' N *ʔɨŋ* (vi) 'dormirse, estar dormido'

ʔA#001 pM *ʔaːʔc (vi) 'crecer (bejuco)/to grow (vine)' NHM: *ʔaːʔc* 'enraizar, enredar (p.ej., guias del frijol)' MM: Ma < *ʔaʔcp, ʔaːʒámp* > Ja,Pu,At,Ct < *ʔaːʒá·m̄p, ʔaʔcp* > LM: Cn < *a·dz* > (vi) 'echar guías' Gu < *ʔa·ʔcp (pres), ʔaːʒá·m̄p (fut)* > 'crecer (bejuco)' SaP: < *ʔaʔc* > (vi) 'grow (a vine)'

ʔA#002 pM *ʔaːʔc-a (n) 'bejuco/vine' [pOM **ʔaːʔc*] NHM: *ʔaːʔc* 'raíz' SHM: Tl *ʔoːc* 'raíz' Tu,Tp,Mi *ʔaːc* MM: Ju,Cc,Ma,Ja *ʔaːc* At,Ct *ʔaːc* '=raíz' LM: Ca,Gu *ʔaːc* Cn < *aːdz* > OlP: *ʔaːca*

ʔA#003 pMZ *ʔa(h)ci (n) 'hermano mayor/elder brother' [pM **ʔahci* > pOM **ʔahcy*; pZ **ʔaci*. The pMZ reconstructed meaning is better specified as ***'older brother, uncle'. The importance of the notion 'older (male relative)' is attested to in the ChisZ-N attributive form *ʔač-pɨ*, the form < *atzi* > in ChisZ-C [Te] and the SaP compound *ʔáhči-wáy* 'anciana, vieja'.] NHM: *ʔahč* 'hermano mayor, medio hermano mayor' Hu *ʔahč* [Foster 1949] SHM: Tl *ʔohč* 'hermano del hombre' Ay *ʔač* [Foster 1949] MM: 'hermano mayor de hombre' Ma, Ja,Pu,Ct *ʔahč* At *yʔæhč, nʔahč* [3p possession (the first form) apparently affects the vowel progressively; *n-* marks 1p poss.] LM: Ca

ʔahč SJ *ʔahč* Cn *ʔajč* 'pariente consanguíneo del hombre, de mayor edad; p.ej., hermano, tío, primo' Gu *ʔahč, yʔahč* OlP: *ʔahči* [Foster 1949 adds the meaning 'older sister'] SaP: *ʔahč* '=tío' [Foster 1949 limits the meaning to 'older brother' and gives the term *ʔapwi* for 'uncle, grandfather'] TxZ: *ʔaːč* 'tío, hermano mayor, vocativo de respecto para primos mayores' SoZ: *ʔáːči* '=uncle' [Foster 1949], *ʔaːčI?* 'tío' [Gutiérrez M. 1993] ChisZ: C [Co] *ʔaci* [Te] <*atzi*> 'mayor en edad' N [Ma,FL] *ʔaci* [Ma form in Wonderly 1949, who also notes the form *ʔačɨ ~ ʔačpɨ* 'old man'] NE [Tapalapa, Ocotepec] *ʔanci* [from Wonderly (1949) who rightly thinks that the nasal is a 1p or 2p pronominal infix. He adds the phonetic form [*ʔanzi*]] [Pantepec.] *ʔaci* [Ra] *ʔaci* 'hermano mayor, tío' ChZ: *ʔací?* [Foster 1949 gives the form *ači* for both of the Chimalapas and the meaning 'uncle, older brother']

*ʔA#004 pMZ *ko-ʔa(h)ci (n) 'medio hermano mayor/elder (not the oldest) brother'* [pM *ko?ahci* > pOM *ku?ahcy*; pZ *ko?aci*] NHM: *ku?ahč* 'hermanastro mayor' ChisZ: C *ko?aci* NE *ko?aci* 'medio hermano mayor, primo mayor; sobrino mayor'

*ʔA#005 pMZ *ʔaha (n) 'canoa/canoe'* [pM, pZ *ʔaha*] OlP: *ʔáha* 'canoa, canoa (comedero para animales)' SaP: *ʔah* SoZ: *ʔáːha* [Foster and Foster 1948] AyZ: *[aʔa]* TxZ: *ʔaːʔha?* (n) '=balsa, cayuco, lancha' ChisZ: C *ʔa?* 'canoa grande, hecha de tronco de árbol' N *ʔaha* 'cayuco' NE *ʔaha*

*ʔA#006 pMZ *ʔaha (n) 'cedro/cedar [Cedrela mexicana]'* [pM *ʔaha* > pOM *ʔah*; pZ *ʔaha*] NHM: *ʔah* '[Cedrela sp.]' SHM: Tu *ʔah* Tp *ʔAh* Mi *ʔahképʸ* MM: Ju *ʔáhɨ* Cc *ʔáhɨ* Ja,At,Ct *ʔah* LM: Cn <*ah*> '[Cedrela sp.]' Ca *ʔah* Gu *ʔahk* OlP: *ʔahakuyɨ* 'palo de canoa, remo' SoZ: *ʔaːkuy* TxZ: *ʔaːkuy* 'cedro' ChisZ: C *ʔakuy* N,NE *ʔahkuy*

*ʔA#007 pMZ *capac-ʔaha (n) 'cedro colorado'* [For reconstructions at intermediate levels see pMZ *ʔaha* and pMZ *capac*.] NHM: *capc ah* 'cedro rojo' TxZ: *ca?pa?c?aːkuy*

*ʔA#008 pZ *ʔahu (n) 'chapulín, saltamontes/grasshopper'* AyZ: *[áːu]* ChisZ: C *ʔau* '=langosta' N *koči?ahu* 'chapulín, saltamontes', *ʔahu* 'langosta' ChZ: *ʔahu?*

?A#009 pMZ *__?ak(i)__* *(n)* *'cáscara, piel/bark, skin'* [pM *__?aki__* >
pOM *__?ak__*; pZ, pGZ *__?ak__*] NHM: *?ak* '=cuero fresco, pellejo, piel
de una persona o fruta)' SHM: Tl *?ok* MM: Ju *?æk* 'cáscara', *?ak*
'majahua' [sic!] Ma,Ja *?ak* 'majahua' Pu *?ak* 'concha (pos);
majahua' At *?ak* 'concha (pos); majahua; cáscara' Ct *?ak* 'majahua'
LM: Cn <*ak kipy*> 'jonote, balsa (árbol y corteza) [Heliocarpus sp.],
<*ak*> 'piel; cáscara, corteza, casca' Ca *?ak* 'cáscara; majahua' Gu
?ak 'cáscara, concha (pos); majahua' OIP: *?aki* 'pellejo; mecate'
SaP: *?ak* TxZ: *?ak* 'cáscara'

?A#010 pM *__?aw-?ak__* *(n)* *'labio/lip'* [pOM *__?ahw?ak__*] MM: 'boca'
Ma *?awák* Pu *?awak* Ct *?awák* LM: Cn <*a:wak*> SJ *?awak*
'=boca' SaP: *?au?ák* 'labio'

?A#011 pMZ *__ki?-?ak__* *(n)* *'huarache/sandal'* [pM *ki?ak* > pOM
ki"k; pZ, pGZ *ki?ak*; TxZ forms such as *pak-ki?* 'huella' and *?is-
ki?* 'nuca, cuello, pescuezo' indicate that *ki?* has the wider meaning of
'limb'; this would explain *ki?-?ak* as 'limb leather'.] NHM: *ki"hk*
SHM: Tl *ki"k* Ay *ki?k* MM: Ju *ki"k* Ma *ki!k* '=zapato, calzado'
Ja *ki"k* 'calzado, huaraches' Pu *ki"k* '=calzado' At *ki"k* '=calzado,
zapato' Ct *niwičk'i"k* LM: Cn <*ki"k*> Ca *ki"k* SJ *ki"g* Gu *ki"k*
'=calzado' TaM: *k?ok* [transcription of Wonderly 1949. The form is
followed by (?)] OIP: *ki?a'k* SaP: *ki?ak* [Sa-to-Sp side has *ki-ak*]
SoZ: *ki?ak* 'sandals, Pleiades' [Foster and Foster 1948, Wonderly
1949] AyZ: *[ki?k]* 'chanclas de hilo y cuero' TxZ: *kí?igi?* ChisZ:
C *ki?ak* 'zapato' N [Ma] *ki?ak* [Wonderly 1949] NE *ki?ahk*
'huarache, zapato' S [Tu] *ki?ak* [Wonderly 1949] ChZ: StaMaCh
ki?ak SnMiCh *ki?ak* [Wonderly 1949]

?A#012 pM *__kipi-?ak__* *(n)* *'corteza/bark, crust'* [pOM *kipy?ak*]
NHM: *kip ?ak* SHM: Tl *kipy?ok* Tu *kip'?ák* Tp *kib'?ák* MM: Ma,
Ja,At,Ct *kep'?ák* Pu *kep'y?ák* LM: Gu *kep'?ák* OIP: *kuy?aki* 'cás-
cara de árbol'

?A#013 pM *__mak-?ak__* *(n)* *'caoba/mahogany'* [lit., '10'+'corteza']
[pOM *mahk?ak*] NHM: *mahk ?ak* 'diez cueros, corteza de este árbol
que sirve para amarrar los materiales de un jacal' LM: Cn
<*mahk?ak*> 'corteza (usada para amarrar jacales)' OIP: *mak?aki*
'caoba', *mak?aki* 'palo de caoba'

?A#014 pOM *__ta:ck ?ak__* *(n)* *'oreja (la parte exterior)/exterior part of
ear'* NHM: *ta:ck ?ak* 'especie de hongo comestible que sale en cual-

quier árbol o al pie de los cafetos' MM: Ma,Ja,Pu,At *ta·c̄k?ák* LM: Gu *ta·c̄k?ák*

?A#015 pM *win-?ak* *(n) 'párpado/eyelid'* [pOM *wihn-?ak*] NHM: *vin?akïni?kš* SHM: *wen?ok* MM: Ma *Wi:n?ák* Ja,Pu *wi:n?ák* At *wi:n?ák ~ hïn?ák* Ct *wi·n̄?ák* LM: Cn <*wi:n?ak*> Ca *wi:n?ák* Gu *wi:n?ák* OlP: *vin?akɨ* 'pellejo del ojo', *vinak?akɨ* 'párpado' SaP: *win-ák*

?A#016 pMZ *?a:ka* *(n) 'mejilla; borde/cheek, edge'* [Cf. pMZ *?a:ka-pak* 'cachete, mejilla'] [pM *?a:ka*; pZ *?aka*] LM: Gu *yo??ahk* 'paladar' [?] OlP: *?a:ka* 'cachete, mejilla' SaP: *?a:hk* 'cachete' ChisZ: C *?aka* 'orilla, borde', *?akapoya* 'orilla' N *?aka* 'punta, borde; cara', *?akapoya* (adv) 'por la orilla; orilla'

?A#017 pM *?akáp* *(n) 'larguero/bar'* [pOM *?akap*] NHM: *?akap* 'larguero (p.ej., de un corral)' SaP: *?akápatú?k* 'atravesado', *akapkúhy* 'tirante'

?A#018 pM *?akaš* *(n) 'cal/lime'* [pOM *akš*] NHM: *?akš* OlP: *?aká'š*

?A#019 pOM *tɨk-?aka"w* *(n) 'puerta (la que se abre)/door'* NHM: *tɨk?akɨ"* MM: [MM forms are all later derivations and not properly speaking cognate] Ma *tɨg?ɨgáhɨ* Ja *tɨhk?agáh* At *tɨhk?agáh* Ct *tɨhk?a·gáh* LM: Ca *?a·gɨ"* Gu *tïg?agï"w*

?A#020 pMZ *?akwa?n* *(n) 'fogón/hearth'* [pM *?akwa?n* > pOM *?akwa"n*; pZ *?aka?ŋ* > pGZ *?akaŋ*. There are no other examples of the development of medial *-kw-*, and pZ *n* > pGZ *ŋ/__#* is also unparalleled. The pZ meaning is 'griddle', but this is probably a late specialization, roughly of the same age as pM *wekš-i(n)* (n) 'comal /griddle'.] NHM *?aka"n* 'pichancha, arnero, cedazo' SHM: 'brasero' Tu *?aβá"n* Tp *?Aβá"n* MM: 'brasero' Ju *?æwá"n* Cc *?aWǽ"n* Ma *?aWá"n* Ja,Pu *?awá"n* At *?æwá"n* LM: 'brasero' Ca,Gu *?awá"n* SoZ: *?ágaŋ* 'comal' [Foster and Foster 1948] AyZ: *[a:?ga]* 'comal' TxZ: *?akaŋ* 'comal' ChisZ: 'comal' C [Co] *?aka?ŋ* [Te] <*acang*> N *?akaŋ* NE *?aka?k* ChZ: *?eke?n* [perhaps a loanword from TaM]

?A#021 pMZ *?aksa* *(n) 'pez, pescado/fish'* [pM *?akša* > pOM *?ahkš*; pZ *?aksa*] NHM: *?ahkš* SHM: Tl *?ohkš* MM: Ma *?ahkš* Ja,Pu,Ct *?ahkš* 'pescado salado y aliñado' At *?ahkš* LM: Cn <*akš*> Gu *?akš* '=pescado salado y aliñado' OlP: *?aksa* 'pepesca' SaP:

?akš SoZ: *?áksɨ?* 'especie de pescado (robalo?)' AyZ: *[aksa]* 'pejelagarto' TxZ: *?aksa?* 'robalo (pez)'

?A#022 pOM **?ahktc** *(n) 'totomostle/husk'* NHM: *?ahktic* MM: Ju, Ma,Ja,At,Ct *?ahkc* Pu *?ahks* LM: Cn *<akc>* Ca,SJ *?aks* Gu *?akc*

?A#023 pMZ **?a:?ksyi** *(n) 'zanate/great-tailed grackle [Cassidix mexicanus]'* [pM **?a:?kši* > pOM **?a:?kš*; pZ **?a?ksyi* (loss of *?* in some Zoquean dialects not accounted for)] LM: Gu *?a·?šʸ* OIP: *?a:kši* SaP: *?a?kš* SoZ: *?áksyi* 'pigeon' [Foster and Foster 1948] AyZ: *[a?ksi̲]* TxZ: *?a:?kšê?* ChisZ: C *?aksyih* [?] N *?a?ksyi* NE *?aksyi* [?] S *[?akší?]* ChZ: *?a?ksi?*

?A#024 pM **?ama:?y** *(vi) 'cuidarlo mucho/to look after'* [pOM **?ama:?y*] NHM: *?ama:?y* 'escaso, delicado' MM: 'delicado' Ju *?æmá:y* Ma *?a·ma:y* 'escaso', *?amá:y* 'delicado' [sic!] Ja *?amá:y* '=escaso, débil' At *?æmá:y* '=escaso' Ct *?a·má:y* '=escaso' LM: Gu *?amá:y* 'escaso' Cn *<ama:y>* (adj) 'escaso, delicado, santo (relacionado a las creencias' SaP: *?amá?* 'cuidar de la noche, estar en clueca' [Clark and Clark 1960]

?A#025 pM **?ama:** *(vi) 'clueca/brooding'* [May belong to the preceding set.] NHM: *?ama"* MM: Ct *<?a·má:p>* LM: Gu *<?amá:p>* OIP: *?a:ma:pa* (vi) 'está clueca'

?A#026 pZ **?amay(-hon)** *(n) 'centzontle/mockingbird'* [pGZ **?amay*] SoZ: *?ámay* [Elson 1960] ChisZ: C *?amahyon* 'tipo de centzontle' NE *?amehot* [reanalyzed as 'year-bird']

?A#027 pMZ **?a:me** *(n) 'año/year'* [pM **?a:me* > pOM **?a:my*; pZ **?ame*] MM: 'hace ratos, endenantes' Ma *?æ̃:mʸɨpʸ* 'hace rato, endenantes', *?æ:mʸ*, *?æ̃:mʸ?ɨpʸ* 'hace un rato' [sic!] Ja *?æ̃!m̄ʸpʸ*, *?æ̃!m̄ʸɨp* Ct *?æ̃:mʸɨpʸ*, *?æ:mʸ* At *?æ:mʸd̲ʸíkɨp* 'hace un rato' LM: *<amy>* (adv) 'hace rato' SaP: *?ahmu* [?] TxZ: *?amčê* ChisZ: C *?ame* 'año', *?ame?a* 'año pasado' N *?ame* '=año pasado' NE *?ame* 'año', *?ame?ap* 'año pasado'

?A#028 pMZ **?a:m-in** *(adv) 'hace rato, endenantes/a time ago, meanwhile'* [pM **?a:m-in* > pOM **?a:myn*; pZ **?amin*] MM: Ma *?æ:mʸn̲ʸ* At *?æ̃:mʸin* LM: Gu *?á:mʸin* ChZ: *?amintɨ* 'año'; *?amintɨ?gay* 'el año pasado'

?A#029 pZ *?**a?m** *(vt) 'mirar/to look'* [pGZ *?*a?m*] SoZ: ?*a?m* (vt) TxZ: ?*a?m* (vt) 'mirar, probar' ChisZ: N ?*a?m* (vt) 'mirarlo, verlo; cuidarlo' ChZ: ?*a?m*

?A#030 pOM *?**a:?mwy** *(n) 'bosque medio espeso/half dense forest'* NHM: ?*a:?mu* SHM: Tl ?*o:mʸhv:ht* LM: SJ ?*a·mʸhʸo·t* 'forest'

?A#031 pZ *?**amu** *(n) 'araña/spider'* [pGZ *?*a:mu*] SoZ: ?*a:mu?* 'araña' [Gutiérrez M. 1993], ?*á:mu* 'tarántula' [Foster and Foster 1948] ChisZ: C,NE ?*amu* ChZ ?*amu*

?A#032 pM *?**an** *(vi, vt) 'picar, arder/to sting, burn'* NHM: ?*a:n* ~ ?*a:hn* ~ ?*an* 'picar (p.ej., chile), arder, escaldar' SHM: Tu < ?*am̄p* > 'hace calor' Tp < ?*Amp, yʔanʸ, kʸæh yʔa:nʸ* > 'brillar (sol, luna, etc.)' MM: 'brillar (sol, luna, etc.)' Cc < ?*a:mp, yʔænʸ, ?a:n, ?anǽmp* > Ju < ?*a:mp* > 'hace calor' Ma < ?*a·m̄p, ?anám̄p* > Ja < ?*a·m̄p, ?a·n̄, ?ann̄á·m̄p* > Pu < ?*a·m̄p* > At < ?*a·m̄p* > '=hace calor' Ct < ?*a·m̄p, ?an̄ám̄p* > LM: Cn < *a·n~an* > (vi) 'alumbrar, dar calor' Gu < ?*a·m̄p, ?aná·m̄p* > 'brillar (sol, luna, etc.)', < ?*an̄* > 'hace calor' OlP: ?*an* (vi) 'picar; arder' (vt) 'odiarlo' SaP: ?*an* (vi, vt) 'sting, hate'

?A#033 pOM *?**an** *(adj) 'caliente/hot'* NHM: ?*an* SHM: Tl ?*on* (v-attr) Tu ?*an* MM: Ju ?*æn* Cc ?*an* Ma,Pu,At,Ct ?*an̄* Ja ?*aṇ* LM: Cn < *an* > (adj) SJ,Ca ?*an* Gu ?*an̄*

?A#034 pMZ *?**an-e** *(n) 'tortilla/tortilla'* [pM *?*ane* > pOM *?*any*; pZ *?*ane* > pGZ *?*a:ne*] SHM: Tl *ni?ánʸ* 'atole' [lit., 'water-tortilla'] SoZ: ?*á:ñi* [Foster and Foster 1948], ?*a:ñi?* [Gutiérrez M. 1993] AyZ: *[a:ne]* TxZ: ?*a:n* ChisZ: C,N ?*ane* NE ?*ane* [possessed(?) form *yane* 'mazorca de maíz'] S *[a·né?]* ChZ: ?*ane*

?A#035 pM *?**an-i-way** *(n) 'trueno/thunder'* [pOM *?*ani(:)w*] NHM: ?*anyu* SHM: Tl ?*ana:w* Tm ?*inæ:* MM: Ju ?*ænǽ:* Ma ?*anǽ:w* ~ ?*anǽ:Φ* ~ ?*anǽ:f* Ja,Ca ?*anǽ:* At ?*anǽ:w tú* Ct ?*anǽ:w* LM: Ml < *ane:* > Cn < *ene:* > Gu ?*ané:* SaP: ?*ániway* '=relámpago'

?A#036 pOM *?**a:hn-k** *(n) 'cueva/cave'* NHM: ?*a:hntk* SHM: Tl ?*onk* MM: Ju ?*a·ŋk* At ?*a:ŋk* Ct *ca:?á·ŋk* LM: Gu *pa??á:ŋk*

?A#037 pMZ *?**ápit** *(n) 'espina/thorn'* [pM *?*apit* > pOM *?*apyt*; pZ *?*ápit*] NHM: ?*ápit* 'espina, abrojo' SHM: Tl ?*ahpkʸ* Tp ?*æpʸkʸ* ~ ?*æhpʸtʸ* MM: Ju,Ma,Ja,Pu,At,Ct ?*æpʸṇʸ* LM: Ml < *epy* > Cn

<*apy*> Ca *?epʸťʸ* Gu *?apʸťʸ* OlP: *?apíʼt* SaP: *?ápit* SoZ: *?aːpiťʸ* AyZ: *[aːɓič]* TxZ: *?aː?peˀč* ChisZ: N [Ma,FL] *?apit* [Wonderly 1949] C *?apit* NE *?abiht* [Wonderly 1949. Tapalapa, Pantepec] [Ocotepec, Chapultenango] *?abit* [Wonderly 1949] [Ra] *?abiht* S *[?aˑpít]*

*?A#038 pOM *?apɨk-y (adv) ʻaparte/asideʼ* NHM: *?apɨ̌k* SHM: Tu *?aβík̲ʸ* MM: Ju *?æbékʸɨ*, *?æbékʸ* Ma,Ja,Ct *?abékʸ* Pu *?ɨbékʸ* At *?æbékʸ* LM: Cn <*abɨky*> (adv) Ca *?aˑbťk ʸ*

*?A#039 pOM *?apɨhkɨ(?)ny (n) ʻrecipiente, envase/receptacle, container ʼ* NHM: *?apɨhkin* ʻ=sacoʼ LM: Ml <*abɨgɨ?ñ*>

*?A#040 pZ *?apaH (n) ʻmadre, mamá/mother ʼ* [pGZ *?aːpa] SoZ: *?aːpa?* ʻmadreʼ TxZ: *?aːp* ʻmadreʼ ChisZ: C *?apah* ʻabuelaʼ

*?A#041 pMZ *?apu (n) ʻabuelo/grandfather ʼ* [pM *?apu > pOM *?ap; pZ *?apu] NHM: *?ap* ʻ=nietoʼ SHM: Tl *?op* ʻnietoʼ Tm *?ap* ʻnietoʼ Tp *?ap* ʻantepasadosʼ Tu *y?ap̄* ʻcompadreʼ MM: Cc *?ap* ʻantepasadosʼ Ma *?ap̄máˑŋk* ʻnietoʼ, *?ap̄* ʻantiguos, adivino, insecto palo ʼ, *?ap̄nɨ́ːš* ʻnietaʼ [sic!] Ja,Pu *?ap̄* ʻnieta; nieto; insecto palo; adivino ʼ At *?ap̄*, *?ap̄máˑŋk* ʻnietoʼ Ct *?ap̄máˑŋk* ʻnietoʼ, *?ap̄nɨ́ːš* ʻnietaʼ LM: Cn <*ap*> ʻanciano (palabra de respeto para personas de mayor edad)ʼ Ca *?ap* ʻgrandparentʼ [Wonderly 1949] Gu *y?ap̄* ʻdescendiente, compadreʼ TaM: *?apu* [Wonderly's 1949 transcription] OlP: *?apu* SaP: *?ápuy* [Clark and Clark 1960] *?apwi* ʻuncle, grandfather ʼ [Foster 1949] ChisZ: N [Ma,FL] *?apuhata* ʻmaternal grandfather ʼ ChZ: *?apu* ʻdon, viejoʼ; *?apucɨsi* ʻnietoʼ

*?A#042 pOM *hay-?ap (n pos) ʻcompadre/father-godfather kin ʼ* NHM: *hay?ap* SHM: Tp *hɨyáp* MM: Ma,Ja,At,Ct *hɨyáp̄* LM: Gu *y?ap̄*

*?A#043 pOM *?ašy (adj) ʻenredado/entangled ʼ* NHM: *?ašy ?ašy* ʻcabello desordenadoʼ LM: Cn <*ašy*> (adj) ʻ=desordenadoʼ

*?A#044 pZ *?asa (n) ʻhuipil/native blouse ʼ* [pGZ *?aːsa] SoZ: *?ása* ʻblouseʼ [Foster and Foster 1948] ChisZ: C [Co] *?ahsa* [Te] <*asa*> ʻguaypilʼ N *?asa* ʻblusaʼ NE *?ahsa* ʻvestidoʼ

*?A#045 pZ *?asa (n) ʻmapache/raccoon ʼ* [pGZ *?aːsa] TxZ: *?aːskaːŋ* ʻtlacuache, mapacheʼ ChZ: *?asa* ʻmapacheʼ

*?A#046 pOM *?aš... (part) ʻcomo/like ʼ* NHM: *?aš hvʔn* SHM: Mi *?ɨškɨ̌m* MM: Ju *?ɨštɨm* Ma *?íštɨm* At *?éštɨm*

?A#047 pM ***?á:šik** *(n) 'liendre(s)/nit'* [pOM **?a:šk*] NHM: *?a:šk*
SHM: Tl *?ošk* MM: Ju *?æšk* Ma,Ja,Pu,At,Ct *?a·šk* LM: Cn <*a:š*>
'liendre (larva) [order: Anoplura, Pediculus humanus]' Ca *?a·šk* Gu
?a!šk OlP: *?aši'k* SaP: *?á:šik*

?A#048 pOM ***?a:šk-i-kák** *(n) 'chachalaca/chachalaca'* NHM:
*?a:?šikák_* '[Ortalis vertula]' MM: Ja *?iškák*, *?ažigák* At *?ahkšigák*
Ct *?ižigák* LM: Cn <*ašigak*> 'chachalaca común [Ortalis vetula]'
Ca *?a:ʒigák* Gu *?iškigák*

?A#049 pM ***?a:ti** *'anona/sweet apple'* [pOM **?a:ty*] LM: Gu *?a·?tʸ*
[This cannot be from pOM *?a:y-ti:m* since *?a·tʸp* would then have been
expected; cf. *ku·tʸp* 'avocado' < pOM *ku:y-ti:m*.] SaP: *?a:t /*
?a:tkuhy OlP: *?a:ti / ?a:tikuyi*

?A#050 pM [Veracruz] ***katuc-?a:ti** *(n) 'guanábana/soursop'* OlP:
kacus?a:ti, 'guanábana' *kacus?a:tikuyi* 'palo de guanábana' SaP:
kaduc?á:t

?A#051 pOM ***?atï"cy** *(adv) 'aprisa/quickly'* NHM: *?atï"c* '=pronto,
apurado' LM: Cn <*idi"ch*> (adv)

?A#052 pMZ ***?aw** *(n) 'boca/mouth'* [pM, pOM **?ahw*; pZ **?aw*]
NHM: *?a:h* SHM: Tl *?o:w* Tp,Tu,Ay *?a:* Mi *?a:w~?a:ß* MM: Ju,
Ja *?a:* Cc *?a:w* Pu,At *?a:w* 'abertura' Ct *?a:w* LM: Cn <*?a:w*>
'sufijo; en un sustantivo compuesto indica boca o abertura' Ca *?a:* Gu
?a:w OlP: *?avi* SaP: *?ahw* 'boca' ChisZ: C,N,NE *?aŋnaka*

?A#053 pOM [NHM/SHM] ***wihn-?ahw** *(n) 'cara/face'* NHM: *vi:hn*
a: 'cara, faz, efigie, rostro' SHM: *we:n?o:w*

?A#054 pMZ ***?awin** *(n) 'hermano mayor de mujer/elder brother of*
woman' [pM **?awin* > pOM **?awyn*; pZ **?awin*] SHM: Tl *?ay*
'hermano de la mujer' MM: Ju *?æy* Ma *y?ay*, *n?áyic* Ja *y?aȳ*, *?ay*
Pu *y?æȳ* At *?aȳ*, *y?æȳ* Ct *y?ay*, *m?ay* LM: Cn <*ay*> 'pariente
masculino de la mujer, de mayor edad; p.ej., hermano, tío, primo' Ca
?æy Gu *y?aȳ* ChZ: StaMaCh *?awin* 'hermano', *yomi?awin*
'hermana' SnMiCh *?awinʸ* 'sibling, cousin, nephew, niece' [Foster
1949]

?A#055 pMZ ***?a:wat** *(n) 'piojo/louse'* [pM **?a:wat* > pOM **?a:wt*;
pZ **?awat*; glottal stops in NHM, MM, AyZ, and TxZ not accounted
for] NHM: *?a?vit* MM: Ju,Ma,Ja,Pu,At,Ct *?a?t* 'piojo de la cabeza'
LM: Ca,Gu *?a:t* 'piojo de la cabeza' Cn <*a:d*> 'piojo negro [order:

Anoplura, Pediculus humanus]' OlP: *ʔa:vá't* SaP: *ʔá:wat* SoZ: *ʔà:wat* AyZ: *[áwaʔt]* TxZ: *ʔawaʔt* ChisZ: C,NE *ʔawat* N *ʔawat* 'piojo de la cabeza' ChZ: *ʔawat*

ʔA#056 pMZ *__ʔay__ *(n)* '*hoja/leaf*' [pM, pOM *ʔahy; pZ, pGZ *ʔay] NHM: *ʔa:hy* '=faja, folio' SHM: Tl *ʔo:y* MM: Ju *ʔa:y* Ma *ʔa:y*, y*ʔæ:y* Ja,Pu,Ct,At *ʔa:y* LM: Cn <*a:y*> Ca *ʔa·y* Gu *ʔa:y* SJ *ʔuhc* *ʔa:y* OlP: *ʔayɨ* SaP: *ʔahy* SoZ: *ʔay* AyZ: *[aʔy]* 'tipo de hoja' TxZ: *ʔay* '=hojablanca' ChisZ: N *ʔay* C,NE *ʔay* '=ala de sombrero' ChZ: *ʔay*

ʔA#057 pOM *__hu"ky-ʔahy__ *(n)* '*puro (tabaco)/cigar*' MM: Ma *hi"gʸʔǽ:y* Ja *hi"gʸʔá:y* At *huü"gʸʔǽ:y*, *huü"kʸsʸæ:č* Ct *hi"gʸá:y*, *hi"kʸsʸá:č* LM: Gu *hu"gʸʔá:y*

ʔA#058 pZ *__mok(o)-ʔay__ *(n)* '*hoja de maíz/corn leaf*' SaP: *mo:kʔáhy* [Zo loan] ChisZ: C *mohkoʔay* 'hoja de maíz o milpa' NE *mohkoʔay*

ʔA#059 pM *__wayɨ-ʔay__ *(n)* '*platanillo/canna, arrowroot*' [pOM *wahy-ʔahy] NHM: *vɨ:ʔy a:hy* 'platanillo con tomento' [Canna edulis] OlP: *vayɨʔayɨ*

ʔA#060 pOM *__ʔayohw ~ ʔayow__ *(vi)* '*sufrir/to suffer*' NHM: *ʔayo:v ~ ʔayo:hv ~ ʔayov* 'ser pobre' SHM: Tl *ʔayv:p* MM: Ma <*ʔayó:p, ʔɨyó:p*> 'sufrir', <*ʔayó:p*> 'padecer' Ja <*ʔayó:p*> Pu <*ʔayó:p*> 'padecer' At <*ʔayó:p*> '=padecer' Ct <*ʔayó:p*> '=padecer' LM: Cn <*ayo·w ~ ayow*> (vi) 'empobrecer' Gu <*ʔɨyó:p*>

ʔA#061 pOM *__yak-ʔayohw ~ yak-ʔayow__ *(vt)* '*causar pobreza/cause poverty*' NHM: *yakʔayo:v ~ yakʔayov* 'empobrecer a alguien' LM: Cn <*yahʔayo·w ~ yahʔayow*> (vt) 'desperdiciar; causar pobreza'

ʔA#062 pOM *__ʔayohw-an__ *(n)* '*miseria/misery*' NHM: *ʔayoʔvïn* '=pobreza' LM: Cn <*ayoʔn*> 'catástrofe, desgracia' SJ *ʔayoʔn* 'accident, suffering'

ʔA#063 pOM *__ʔayohw-pa__ *(n)* '*pobre/poor person*' NHM: *ʔayo:va* 'pobre' MM: 'pobreza' Ju *ʔæyó:p* Ma *ʔɨyó:p* Ja,At,Ct *ʔayó:p* LM: SJ *ʔayo·w* 'poor one, suffering one' LM: Gu *ʔɨyó:p* 'pobreza'

ʔA#064 pOM *__ʔayu:hk__ *(n)* '*idioma/language*' NHM: *ʔayv:k* '=dialecto' SHM: Tl *ʔayu:hk* 'voz, palabra' Tm *ʔɨyu:hk* MM: Ju *ʔæyúk* Ma *ʔɨyú·k* 'idioma, palabra' Ja *ʔayú·k* Pu *ʔɨyú·k* At *ʔæyú·k* 'idioma', *ʔayú·k* 'palabra' [sic!] Ct *ʔa·yú·k* LM: Cn <*ayuk*>

'palabra; la lengua _mixe; la raza mixe' SJ *?ayu·k* 'word, Mixe language' Gu *?ayú·k*

*?U#001 pMZ *?uc (vi) 'llenar, pesar/to fill, weigh'* NHM: *?vhc ~ ?vc* 'llenar' MM: 'llenarse' Ja < *?uhc, ?uhcp, ?ucá·m̄p* > Pu,Ma < *?uhcp* > At < *?uhcp, ?ucá·m̄p* > Ct < *?uhcp, ?ucám̄p* > LM: Cn < *uhc ~ uc* > (vi) 'llenarse' Gu < *?uc, ?uhcp, ?udzá·m̄p* > 'llenarse' [Nordell 1990 and p.c.] SJ *?uhc ~ ?uc* 'to be filled' OlP: *?uc* (vi) 'llenarse' [*?uci* (adj) 'lleno'] ChisZ: C *?uhc* (vt) 'compararlo' ChZ: *?uc* 'medir'

*?U#002 pM *yak-?uc (vt) 'llenar/to fill'* NHM: *yak?vhc ~ yak?vc* (vt) SHM: Tl *yik?uc* (vt) MM: Ju < *yæh?úc* > 'rellenar', < *tuk?úc, yæhtuk?úc* > 'rellenar' Ma < *yahk?úc* > '=rellenar' Ja < *yah?úc, yah?účpʸ* > '=rellenar' Pu < *ya?úc* > At < *yahk?úc, yahk?úhčpʸ* > '=rellenar' Ct < *yahk?úc, yahk?úhčpʸ* > '=rellenar' LM: Cn < *yah?uhc ~ yah?uc* > (vt) Ca < *yah?úc* > Gu < *yag?úc, yag?úhčpʸ* > '=rellenar' OlP: *yak?uc* (vt)

*?U#003 pOM *?uc-i (adj) 'lleno/full'* NHM: *?uc* MM: Ju,Ma,Ja,Pu, At,Ct *?uhc* LM: Ca,Gu *?uhc*

*?U#004 pOM *?uhc (n) 'yerba, planta, monte/herb, plant'* NHM: *?vhc* SHM: Tl *?uhc* Ju,Ma,Ja,At,Ct *?uhc* LM: Cn < *uhc* > 'arbusto, hierba, planta' Gu,Ca *?uhc*

*?U#005 pMZ *?u:ci (n) 'hermano, -a menor/younger brother or sister'* [pM *?u:ci* > pOM *?u:cy*; pZ *?uci*] NHM: *?uc* '=medio/a hermano/a menor' MM: Ma,Ja,At,Ct *?uč̄* LM: Cn < *uč* > 'indica un pariente consanguíneo de menor edad que la persona que habla: puede ser hermanito, hermanita, primo, prima, tío o tía; p.ej., *a?uč* 'primo, prima' Ca,Gu *?uč̄* TxZ: *?u:č* 'criatura (humanos, animales)'

*?U#006 pZ *?u?c (vi) 'doblar/to fold'* SaP: *?u?c* (vi) 'be heavy' [Zo loan] ChisZ: C *?u?c* (vi, vi-s) 'doblarse, estar doblado; encorvarse, estar encorvado' (vt) 'doblarlo' N *?u?c* (vi, vt) NE *?u?c* (vi) 'doblarse, pandearse' (vt) 'doblarlo (como las mazorcas de la milpa)'

*?U#007 pGZ *?u:cu? (n) 'chango, mono/monkey'* [A loanword from early Nahua which entered at the pGZ stage; the Classical Nahuatl form is *osomaλi*, where the vowel quantities and presence or absence of glottal stops are unknown.] SoZ: *?u:cu?* AyZ: *u:cu* TxZ: *?u:cu?*

ʔU#008 pGZ *ʔuhuʔ (n) 'piña/pineapple' SoZ: *ʔúhuʔ* AyZ: *uʔu*
TxZ: *ʔuːʔhuʔ*

ʔU#009 pMZ *ʔu(ʔ)k (clitic) 'cuotativo/quotative' [pM **ʔuk* > pOM
*ʔk; pZ **ʔuʔk*] LM: SJ *ʔɨk* TxZ: *ʔuʔk*

ʔU#010 pOM *ʔuk (vi, vt) 'pintar/to paint, color' NHM: *ʔvhk ~ ʔvk*
'pintar (p.ej., un trapo), teñir, colorar' MM: Ju < *ʔuk, ʔikʸ* > 'pintar,
teñir' Ma < *ʔuk, ʔuhkp, nɨʔúkɨ* > 'teñir', < *ʔuhkp* > 'magullarse'
Ja < *ʔuk, yʔihkʸpʸ* > 'teñir', < *ʔuhkp, ʔuká·m̄p* > 'mancharse',
< *ʔuhkp, ʔuká·m̄p* > 'magullarse' [sic!] Pu < *ʔuhkp* > 'magullarse'
At < *ʔuk, yʔühkʸpʸ* > 'teñir', < *ʔuhkp, ʔuká·mp* > 'magullarse' Ct
< *ʔuk, yʔihkʸpʸ* > 'teñir', < *ʔuhkp, ʔukámp* > 'magullarse', < *ʔuhkp,
ʔukámp* > 'mancharse' [sic!] LM: Cn < *uhk ~ uk* > (vi) 'teñirse'
Ca < *ʔuk* > 'teñir' Gu < *ʔugá·mp, tɨ: yʔukʸ, ʔuhp* > 'magullarse',
< *ʔuk, yʔuhpʸ* > 'pintar, teñir'

ʔU#011 pOM *ʔuk-y (adj) 'morado/purple' NHM: *ʔuk* 'ocote cho-
moque, resinoso, pez (substancia negra y pegajosa)' MM: Ma *ʔikʸ*
'azul' Ja *ʔikʸ* '=mancha' Ct *ʔikʸ* 'azul, mancha' LM: Cn < *uky* >
(adj) '=violeta' Ca *ʔukʸ* Gu *ʔukʸ*

ʔU#012 pMZ *ʔuːʔk [?] (vi, vt) 'tomar, beber/to drink' [See Table
4.4. The uncertainty of the reconstruction goes for the derivatives below as well.] NHM: *ʔvːk* 'tomar (p.ej., agua), beber' SHM: Tu
< *ʔuːk, mʔikʸpʸ ~ mʔuikʸpʸ, tʸam̄ nʔuk ʔúi·hkʸɨm* > Tp < *ʔuːk,
mʔukʸpʸ, yʔukʸpʸ, yʔu·hk, yʔuːgám̄pʸ* > MM: Ju < *ʔuːk* > Cc < *ʔuːk,
yʔukʸpʸ, yʔuk, ʔuk, ʔukp, kʸœh yʔukʸ, ʔuːgámp* > Ma < *ʔuːk,
mʔi·kkpʸ* > Ja < *ʔuʔk, ʔuːk, mʔi·kʸpʸ, yʔi·kʸpʸ* > Pu < *ʔuːk,
mʔi·kʸpʸ, ʔu·kp* > At < *ʔuːk, mʔuü·kʸpʸ, yʔü·kʸpʸ* > Ct < *ʔuːk, tɨ:
mʔi·kʸpʸ, yʔi·kʸpʸ* > LM: Cn < *u·k ~ u"k* > _'tomar (p.ej., agua o
licor)' Ca < *ʔuʔk* > Gu < *ʔu"k, ʔu·kp, mʔu·kʸpʸ, yʔu·kʸpʸ* > [Nor-
dell 1990 and p.c.] SJ *ʔu·k ~ ʔu"k* OIP: *ʔuːk* (vi, vt) '=desayunar'
[derivative: *ʔuːki* 'desayuno'] SaP: *ʔuːk ~ ʔuʔk* (vi, vt) '=eat breakfast' SoZ: *ʔuk* TxZ: *ʔuk* (vt, vi-a) '=emborracharse, comer (caldo)'
ChisZ: C *ʔuhk* (vi, vt) '=desayunar' N *ʔuhk* (vi) NE *ʔuhk* (vi, vt)

ʔU#013 pMZ *nɨ:ʔ-u:ʔk (vi) 'tomar agua/to drink water' LM: Gu
< *nɨ:ʔu"k, nɨ:ʔu·kp* > [Nordell, p.c.] OIP: *nɨʔuːk* (vi) 'tomar agua'
SaP: *nɨʔuʔk* 'tomar agua' [Clark and Clark 1960] SoZ: *nɨʔk* 'drink
water' [Foster and Foster 1948]

?U#014 pM ***nac-?u:?k-i** *(vi) 'tragar/to swallow'* [pOM **nac?u:?ky*]
SHM: Tl *nac?u:kɨ* SaP: *nac?í:ki* 'tragar sin masticar' [Clark and
Clark 1960]

?U#015 pOM ***?u:?k-y** *(n) 'bebida/drink'* NHM: *?u:?k* MM: Ju,
Ma,Pu,Ct *?i:kʸ* At *?uü:kʸ* LM: Cn <*u"ky*> Ca *?u?uʸkʸ* Gu *?u"kʸ*

?U#016 pMZ ***?u:?k-kuy** *(n) 'bebida/drink'* OlP: *?u:ku* 'pozole de
maíz' TxZ: *?ukku?* 'bebida' ChisZ: C *?uhkuy* N *?uhkuy* '=pozole'
S *[?uhkúy]* 'pozol'

?U#017 pGZ ***?uk(k)-i?** *(n) 'borracho/drunk person'* [The sequence
k(k) stands for a possible geminate that might explain the TxZ facts.]
SoZ: *?u:ki?* AyZ: *[u:ge]* TxZ: *?u:k:e?* ([k] not voiced, thus analyzed
as a geminate.)

?U#018 pZ ***?uka** *(n) 'espalda/back, shoulders'* ChisZ: N,NE *?uka*
ChZ *?uka?*

?U#019 pMZ ***?uku** *(n) 'cerete/agouti' [Mixean: 'perro/dog']* [pM
*?uku 'dog' > pOM **?uk* 'dog'; pZ **?uku* 'agouti'] [Note also a
late derivation restricted to the Midlands and Lowlands of Oaxaca
meaning 'coyote' (Canis latrans) (lit., 'wild+dog'): MM: Ma,Ct
pa·?úk Ja *pa?uk* Pu *pɨ?úk* At *pæ?úk* LM Cn <*pa?uk*> Ca *pa?úk*
Gu *pa?úk*.] NHM: *?vk* SHM: Ay *?uk* MM: Ju *?uk* Ma,Ja,Pu,At,Ct
?uk LM: Cn,Ca,SJ *?uk* Gu *?uk* OlP *?i:šinú'k* 'comadreja' [analyzed
as *?i:šin-uk* 'weasel-dog'; for the first compound member see ?I#016,
the last compound member unexpectedly loses the final vowel; this
must have happened already in pre-OlP times as a result of the compounding process] TxZ: *?u:k:u?* 'cereque' ChisZ: C *?ukuhyoyah*
'pecarí' N *?uku* 'cereque, agutí [Dasyprocta sp.]'

?U#020 pOM ***nɨ:?-?uk** *(n) 'nutria, perro de agua/river otter' [Lutra
longicaudis annectens]* NHM: *nɨ?vk* LM: Cn <*nɨ:?uk*>

?U#021 pOM ***pa:?-?u:kn** *(n) 'hongo comestible/edible mushroom'*
NHM: *pa:?v:kɨn* 'clase de hongo comestible que brota en el suelo'
SHM: Tl *pa?u:hk* 'hongo'

?U#022 pOM ***?u:?kš** *(vi) 'aguatear, aguatar/to cause prickling'* [The
OlP root *?u:kš* (vt) 'prestarlo' is too far removed semantically to be
an acceptable cognate.] MM: Ju,At,Ct <*?u?kšp*> Ma,Ja <*?u?šp*>
Pu <*?u!kšp*> LM: Cn <*u·kš*> (vi) 'dar comezón (el aguate de

plantas)' SJ *yak?u·kš* (vt) 'to cause prickling' Gu < *?u?šp* > SoZ: *?uksɨ?* AyZ: *[u:?kse]* 'nube' TxZ: *?u?ksu?* 'nube' [?]

?U#023 pOM ***?u:?m** *(vi) 'perder el habla/to be unable to speak'* NHM: *?v:?m* 'perder el habla por poco tiempo por causa de enfermedad' MM: 'enmudecerse' Ma < *?u?m̄p, ?u:mám̄p* > Ja < *yah?ú:m, ?u!m̄, ?u!m̄p, ?u:má·m̄p* > At < *?u?m̄p, ?u:má·m̄p* > Ct < *?u?m̄p, ?u:mám̄p* > LM: Gu < *?u!m̄p, ?u:má·m̄p* > 'enmudecerse' SJ *?u·m ~ ?u:m* 'to be unable to speak'

?U#024 pMZ ***?u:ma** *(n) 'mudo/dumb'* [pM **?u:ma* > pOM **?u:m*; pZ **?uma*] NHM: *?v:m* MM: Ju,Ma,Ja,Pu,At,Ct *?u:m* LM: Cn < *u:m ~ u·m* > (vi) 'estar mudo' Ca,Gu *?u:m* OIP: *?u:ma* SaP: *?u:m* SoZ: *?u:ma?* 'sordomudo' ChisZ: C *?uma* (adj, s) N *?uma* (adj) NE *?umabɨ* (adj, n)

?U#025 pOM ***?umy** *(n) 'moho/mold'* NHM: *?um* MM: Ju *?im^y* 'moreno' LM: Gu *?um̄^y* 'moreno'

?U#026 pMZ ***?unV(k)** *(n) 'niño, niña/child'* [pM **?unak* > pOM **?unk* (glottal stops in SHM and MM not accounted for); pZ **?une*; The use of this form as a diminutive suffix is pM.] NHM: *?vnɨk* 'niño, tierno' SHM: Tl *?u?nk* 'tierno' MM: Ju *?u"ŋk* 'hijo, tierno' Ma *?u?ŋk* 'hijo', *?ɨná?k, miš̃?ɨná?k* 'muchacho' Pu *?ɨná!k* 'muchacho' Ja *?u!ŋk* 'hijo, tierno' At *?u?ŋk* 'tierno, hijo' Ct *?u?ŋk* 'hijo' LM: Cn < *uŋ* > 'hijo o hija (de una persona); cría (de animal); plantita; fruto tierno' SJ *?un* 'criatura' Ca *?uŋk* 'hijo' Gu *?u:ŋk* 'tierno, hijo, hija' [Nordell 1990], *?uŋk* 'child, son' [Foster 1949] OIP: *?una'k* 'niño, niña, hijo; sufijo que indica diminutivo' AyZ: *[u?unI]* 'niño tierno (varón)' TxZ: *?une-ba:* (adj) 'tierno' ChisZ: C *?une* 'hija' [Foster 1949 gives the following meanings communicated by Wonderly: 'son, daughter, child'.] N *?une* 'hijo, hija, cría; cosa chica' NE *?une* 'niño, niña, hijo, hija' S [Tu] *?une* 'son, child' [Foster 1949] ChZ: *?une?* 'criatura'

?U#027 pMZ ***?oko-?unV(k)** *(n) 'nieta, nieto/grandchild'* [For reconstructions at intermediate levels see pMZ **?unV(k)* and pMZ **?oko*.] LM: Gu *?ok?u:ŋk* [Nordell, p.c.] ChisZ: C *?oko?une* N *?oko?une* 'nieto/a—hijo de la hija; primo, prima—hijo o hija de la hermana del padre' NE *?oko?une* S [Tu] *?oko?une* 'woman's grandchild' [Foster 1949]

?U#028 pMZ ***kɨ?-?unV(k)*** *(n) 'dedo meñique de la mano/little finger'*
[For reconstructions at intermediate levels see pMZ **?unV(k)* and pMZ
**kɨ?.*] NHM: *kɨ?únïk* 'dedo' LM: Cn *<kɨ?uŋ>* 'dedo meñique'
ChisZ: C *kɨ?une* 'dedo pequeño de la mano' N *kɨ?aŋune* 'dedo de la
mano' NE *kɨ?une* 'dedo de la mano'

?U#029 pMZ ***ko-?unV(k)*** *(n) 'entenado(a), ahijastro(a)/fosterchild'*
LM: Gu *ku?u:ŋk* [Nordell, p.c.] OIP: *ko?una'k* 'entenado' ChisZ:
C *ko?une* N *ko?une*

?U#030 pMZ ***ma:san-?unV(k)*** *(n) 'ahijado, ahijada/godchild'* [For
reconstructions at intermediate levels see pMZ **?unV(k)* and pMZ
**ma:san.*] NHM: *ma:šïn vnïk* ChisZ: C *masa?nune* N *masan ?une*
'ahijado' NE *masa?une*

?U#031 pOM ***ma:š-?unak*** *(n) 'criatura/baby'* NHM: *ma:š ?vnïk*
'criatura, nene' SHM: Tl *maš?u?nk* LM: Cn *<ma:šuŋ/ma"š?uŋ>*
SJ *ma"žuŋ*

?U#032 pZ ***yawa-?une*** *(n) 'criatura/baby'* SaP: *yawáy* 'criatura,
tierno' [Zo loan] ChisZ: C *yawa?une* 'criatura, nene, nena, bebé'
N *ya ?une* 'niño, tierno' NE *yawa?une* 'bebe, nene, nena'

?U#033 pGZ ****?u:nu?*** *(n) 'atole/corn drink'* SoZ: *?ú:nu?* TxZ:
?u:nu?

?U#034 pOM ****ki:š-?u:nk*** *(n) 'niña/girl'* NHM: *ki:š ?únïk* MM: Ju
kižú"ŋk Ct *ki:šʸ* LM: Gu *kiž̃?ú:ŋk*

?U#035 pOM ****?u:?p*** *(vi) 'salir (savia)/to slobber'* MM: Ja
<yah?u:p, ?u?p, ?u:bá·m̄p> Ma *< ?u?p, ?u:bám̄p>* At *< ?u?pp,
?u:bá·m̄p>* Ct *< ?u?p, ?u:bám̄p>* LM: Cn *<u·p~u:p>* (vi)
'salir trementina (de un árbol)' (vt) '(fig.) hacer mole' SJ *?u·p ~ ?u:p*
'to ooze' Gu *< ?u· ?p, ?u:bá·m̄p>*

?U#036 pM ****?up-i(k)*** *(n) 'resina/resin'* [In pOM **?u:?pyk* length and
glottal stop are not accounted for.] NHM: *?u:?pk* 'resina, trementina,
savia del ocote' MM: Ju *?i?pʸkʸ* 'resina, savia' Ma *?i?pʸkʸ* 'savia,
resina, chomonque' Ja *?i?pʸ* 'chomonque', *?i?pʸkʸ* 'savia' [sic!] At
?uü?pʸkʸ ~ ?ü?pʸkʸ 'resina, savia, chomonque' Ct *?i?pʸkʸ* 'chomonque,
resina, savia' LM: Cn *<u:py>* 'savia; salsa para tamales' OIP: *?upi*
'atole' SaP: *?up* (vi, vt) 'make a sauce (mole, etc.)'

?U#037 pZ ***?up-?ah** *(vi) 'batir mole/to make foam, gravy'* [Cf. OIP: *?u:p* (vt).] ChisZ: C *?upa?* (vi) 'hacer espuma, espumar; burbujear' N *?upu?ah-* (vi) 'hacer espuma' NE *?ubɨy-* 'espumar'

?U#038 pM ***?u:?p-i(k)** *(n) 'mole/gravy'* [pOM **?u:?pyk*] NHM: *nɨ?u:?p* 'atole' MM: Ju,Ma,Ja,Pu,Ct *?i:pʸ* At *?u?pk* [?] LM: Ca *?u:ʸpʸ* Gu *?u:pʸ* OIP: *u:pi'k* 'mole'

?U#039 pMZ ***?us** *(n) 'temblor/tremor'* [pM, pOM **?uhš*] NHM: *?vhš* 'temblor de tierra, terremoto' SHM: Tl,Ay *?uhš* MM: Ju,Ma,Ja,At,Ct *?uhš* LM: Cn <*uhš*> 'terremoto' Gu,Ca *?uhš* OIP: *?ušɨ* SaP: *?uš* ChZ: *?us?us*

?U#040 pOM ***?a?uš-?aht ~ ?a?uš-?at** *(vi) 'cenar/to eat dinner'* NHM: *?a?vša ~ ?a?vši* MM: At <*?æ?uš̄?át*> LM: Ca <*?a?uš?át*>

?U#041 pMZ ***?u:suk** *(n) 'mosquito, zancudo/mosquito'* [pM **?u:šu(k)*, pOM **?u:š(k)*; pZ **?usu(k)*; a final *k* is attested sporadically in all subgroups] NHM: *?v:š* 'jején, mosquita [Accacta furens]' SHM: Tl *?awo:y* *?u:š* Ay *?u:š* MM: 'mosquito' Ma *?u:š* '=cha-quiste' Ja *?u·šk* 'mosquito', *?u:š* 'chaquiste' [sic!] Pu,At *?u:š* Ct *?u:š* '=chaquiste' LM: Cn <*u:š*> 'jején [order: Diptera, fam: Cera-topogonidae, Culicoides furens]' Gu *?u·šk* '=chaquiste' OIP: *?u:šu'k* 'rodador' SaP: *?u:š* 'rodador' [Clark 1981], 'chaquiste' [Clark and Clark 1960] AyZ: *[u:ṣu]* 'jején' TxZ: *?u:s* 'especie de mosquito (sigue al parte del perro)' ChisZ: C *?uhsu* '=jején' N *?usu* 'jején' NE *?uhsuk* 'mosca' ChZ: *?usu?*

?U#042 pM ***?uš(i)** *(n) 'villeja (hormiga)/kind of ant'* [pOM: **?uš*] NHM: *kakyvš* 'hormiga carpintera' OIP: *?uši*

?U#043 pGZ ***?u:su?** *(n) 'especie de insecto/species of insect'* SoZ: *?u:su?* 'rodador' TxZ: *?u:s* 'especie de mosquito (sigue al parte del perro)'

?U#044 pMZ ***?uspin** *(n) 'lagarto/alligator'* [pM **?ušpin* > pOM **?ušpyn*; pZ **?uspin*; final *n* was lost both in ChisZ and ChZ. This could be a shared innovation, but since it is a sporadic change limited to this item it is not a strong argument for setting up a subgroup.] LM: Cn <*ušy*> 'lagarto, caimán [Caiman crocodilus]' Gu *?ušᵛp* [Nordell, p.c.] OIP: *?ušpi'n* SaP: *?úšpin* SoZ: *?úšpiñ* AyZ: *[úspi]* TxZ: *?ušpê?ñ* [Clark, no date], *?ušpe?ŋ* [Wichmann fc.-b] ChisZ: C,NE *?uspi* N *?uspi* 'lagarto, caimán, cocodrilo' ChZ: *?uspi* 'caimán'

?U#045 pMZ **?u:syan* *(adj, adv) 'poco/a little'* LM: Cn <*u:šy u:šy*> (adj) 'poquito' SoZ: *?úsyan* 'a little' [Foster and Foster 1948], *?úšaŋ* [Gutiérrez M. 1993] ChisZ: C *?usya?n* (adj) 'poco'; (adv) 'poco'; (n) 'un poco' N *?usyan ora* (adv) 'un rato'

?U#046 pM **?ut [?] (vi) 'gustar/to like'* [The semantics are contradictory but this may be due to the (unknown) meaning of MM *cɨy*.] MM: 'lastimarse' Ju <*cæyút, cæďút*> Ma <*cɨy?úhtp, tɨ: čɨy?úťʸ*> Ja <*cɨy?út, cɨy?úht, cɨy?úhtp*> Pu,At <*cɨy?úhtp, tɨ: čɨy?úťʸ*> Ct <*cɨy?úhtp*> OlP: *?ut* (vd) 'gostarse'

?U#047 pZ **?uy ~ ?u (part) 'prohibitivo/prohibitive'* TxZ: *?u* (part) 'incompletivo' AyZ: *u* (part) 'no' ChisZ: C *?uy* (v-aux) 'negativo: 'para que no', 'no'; imperativo'; 'no' N *?u ~ ?uy* (v-aux) 'no—negativo del modo imperativo, vetativo' NE *?u ~ ?uy* (v—aux) 'negativo: para que no'

?U#048 pZ **?uya (adj) 'blando/soft'* TxZ: *?uy-kɨ?da:?* (adj) 'flexible (cable, palito), débil (niño)' ChisZ: C *?uya?* 'cartílago' N *?uya* 'blando—como pasta' NE *?uya* 'vainilla—el frijól'

?U#049 pM **?u:?y (vi, vt) 'encorvar/to bend'* NHM: *?v:?y* 'doblar algo, girar una sin aparecer su movimiento' MM: 'doblar (rama)' Ma <*?i"pʸ*> Ja <*?u!y*> Pu <*?i!pʸ, ?u:y*> At <*?u:y, ?uü!pʸ, y?ü!pʸ*> Ct <*?i!pʸ*> LM: Cn <*u·y~u:y*> (vi) 'doblarse (en forma de arco)' SJ *?u·y ~ ?u:y* 'to bend in half-moon shape' Gu <*?u:y, ?u!pʸ, y?u!pʸ*> 'doblar (rama)' OlP: *?u:y* (vt) 'poner trampa' SaP: *?u?y* (vi, vt) 'trap animals'

?U#050 pM **?u:?y-an (n) 'trampa/trap'* NHM: *?v:?y* MM: Ja *ku?ú:y* 'doblado (rama, etc.)' At *?u:y* 'doblado (rama, etc.)' LM: Gu *?u:y* 'doblado (rama, etc.)' OlP: *?u:ya'n* SaP: *?úyan*

?U#051 pM [Veracruz] **?uyuk (adj) 'chueco/crooked, bent'* OlP: *?uyu'k* (adj) 'chueco' SaP: *?úyuk* 'curveado' ChisZ: C,NE *ku?yu?uku* [?] 'tronco'

?O#001 pOM **?ohc ~ ?oc (vi) 'ir u regresar, doblar (cosa larga y delgada)/to leave or return, bend a long object'* NHM: *?ohc ~ ?oc* 'fue' MM: Ma <*ma: tɨ: m?oc̄ʸ*> 'ir u regresar', <*?oc̄, ?ohcp*> 'doblar (papel)' Ja <*?ohc*> 'ir u regresar', <*?oc̄, ?ohc, yah?óc̄*> 'doblar (papel)' Pu <*?ohc, ma: tɨ: m?oc̄ʸ*> 'ir u regresar', <*?oc̄, ?ohcp*> 'doblar (papel)' At <*mo: dɨ: m?oc̄ʸ*> 'ir u regresar', <*?oc̄, ?ohcp, yæhk?óc̄*> 'doblar (papel)' Ct <*ma: dɨ m?oc̄ʸ*> 'ir

u regresar', < *ʔoc̄, ʔohcp* > 'doblar (papel)' LM: Cn < *ohc ~ oc* >
(vi) 'doblar' SJ *ʔohc* ~ *ʔoc* 'to double over long slender objects' Gu
< *ʔoc̄, ʔohcp* > 'doblar (papel)'

ʔO#002 pMZ ***ʔoc-i** *(n) 'doblado (papel etc.)'/folded, curly or rolled
(as paper, hair or cigar)'* [pM *ʔoci > pOM *ʔocy; pZ *ʔoci] MM:
'doblado (papel)' Ma,Ja *ʔoc̄* Ja *ʔoc̄ ʔanéⁿkʸ* LM: Gu *ʔoc̄* 'doblado
(papel)' OIP: *ʔoči* (adj) 'grifo' SaP: *ʔoč* 'grifo' ChisZ: C,N *ʔoci*
'tabaco' NE *ʔoci* 'rollo de hoja—tabaco'

ʔO#003 pMZ ***ʔo:ʔc** *(vi, vt) 'pegar (con cola o pegamento)/to stick'*
MM: Ju < *ʔo:c* > Ja < *ʔo:c, ʔoʔc, yʔoʔčpʸ* > Pu < *ʔo:c, yʔo!čpʸ* >
Ma,At,Ct < *ʔo:c, yʔoʔčpʸ* > LM: Cn < *o·c ~ o:c* > (vt) 'pegar (con
pegamento) (vi) 'ser viscoso' Ca < *ʔo:c* > SJ *ʔo·c ~ ʔo:c* 'to stick,
glue' Gu < *ʔo:c, ʔo·ʔc, yʔo·ʔčp* > TxZ: *ʔoʔc-deʔ* (vi-s) 'sentado'

ʔO#004 pOM ***ʔo:ʔc-y** *(n) 'piojo/louse'* NHM: *ʔɨ:ʔc* SHM: Tl *ʔv:č*
MM: 'piojo blanco' Ju *ʔo:č* Ma,Ja,Pu,At,Ct *ʔo:č* '=coruco' LM: Cn
< *o:č* > 'piojo blanco [order: Anoplura, Pthirus pubis]' Ca,Gu *ʔo:č*
'piojo blanco, coruco'

ʔO#005 pOM ***ʔoh** *[ʔ] (vt) 'regañar/to scold'* [The vowel-quantity in
NHM is wrong; possibly there is some contamination at work.] NHM:
ʔo:h 'regañar, maltratar' Ma < *ʔoh, mʔehpʸ* > Ja < *ʔoh, yʔoh,
yʔehpʸ* > At < *ʔo: yʔö:pʸ, mʔoö:pʸ, yʔo:wǽ·m̄pʸ* > Ct < *ʔo:w,
mʔehpʸ* > LM: Cn < *oh* > (vt) SJ *ʔoh* 'to scold' Gu < *ʔoh, yʔoh,
yʔohpʸ* >

ʔO#006 pM ***ʔoho** *(n) 'tos/cough'* [pOM *ʔoh] NHM: *ʔoh* '=ca-
tarro' SHM: Tl *ʔvh* Tu *ʔoh* 'catarro' MM: Ju *ʔoh* 'catarro, tos' Cc
ʔoh 'catarro' Ma,Ct *ʔoh* 'gripa, resfriado, catarro, tos' Ja *ʔoh*
'gripa, resfriado, tos', *yoʔkʔóh* 'catarro' Pu *ʔoh* 'resfriado' At *ʔoh*
'resfriado, catarro, tos' LM: Cn < *oh* > 'catarro' Ca *ʔoh* 'catarro'
Gu *ʔoh* 'catarro, resfriado, tos, gripa' OIP: *ʔoho* SaP: *ʔoh*

ʔO#007 pM [Veracruz] ***ʔohoʔ** *(vi) 'toser/to cough'* OIP: *ʔohoʔ* (vi)
SaP: *ʔoh* (vi)

ʔO#008 pZ ***ʔoho** *(n) 'maguey/century plant'* SoZ: *ʔo:hoʔ* ChisZ: C
ʔoʔ N *ʔoho* 'henequén' NE *ʔoho*

ʔO#009 pM ***ʔok** *(vt) 'comer caña etc./to eat cane etc.'* SHM: Tu
< *ʔok, ʔohkp, tɨ: dʔoekʸ, yʔekʸpʸ, mʔoehkʸpʸ, tʸa: nʔukʔóehkʸɨm* > Tp
< *ʔo mʔohkʸpʸ* > [sic!] Mi < *wašk?ókp* > MM: Cc < *ʔok,*

m?ohkʸpʸ > Ma < *?ok̄, m?ehkʸpʸ* > At < *?ok̄, m?oöhkʸpʸ* > C̲t̲ < *?ok̄,*
y?ehkʸpʸ > LM: Cn < *ohk~o·k* > (vi) 'pastar' Gu < *?ok, ?ohp,*
y?ohpʸ > SJ *?ohk~?ok* OlP: *?ok* (vt) 'mascar'

?O#010 pMZ ***?ok** *(n) 'muela/molar tooth'* [pOM **tɨ:hc-?ok*; pZ
**?ok*] MM: Ju *tɨ:c?ók* Ma,At,Ct *tɨ:z̲?ó·k* ChisZ: NE *?ohka?kadɨhc*
N *?ohka?ka*

?O#011 pMZ ***?oko** *(n) 'abuela/grandmother'* [pM **?oko* > pOM
**?ok*; pZ **?oko*] NHM: *?o̲k* 'abuela, nieta' SHM: Tm *?ok* MM: Ju
?ok 'nieta, nieto' Ma *?o̲k* 'descendiente' At *?ok* 'nieta' LM: Ca
?ok 'nieta, nieto' Gu *y?ok* 'descendiente' SaP: *?ógoy* 'abuela, tía'
[Borrowed from Zoquean; *y* is added in order to make the word conform to the phonotactics, which prohibits final vowels.] AyZ: *[o:go]*
'viejita' TxZ: *bank-?o:k* 'partera' ChisZ: C *?oko* 'grandfather,
grandmother' [Foster 1949] N *?okomama* 'abuela—por parte de la
madre' NE *?oko* 'abuela' S [Tu] *?oko* 'grandmother' [Foster 1949]
ChZ: *?oko* 'hembra'

?O#012 pOM ***hay-?o̲k** *(n) 'comadre/mother-godmother kin'* NHM:
hay?ok SHM: Tu *y?ok* Tp *hɨyók* MM: Ju *?ɨyók* At,Ct *hɨy?ók*

?O#013 pM ***?o:?k** *[?] (vi) 'morir/to die'* [The uncertainty of the
reconstruction goes for the derivatives below as well.] NHM: *?o:?k*
SHM: Tl *?v:?k* MM: Ju < *?o:k, ?o?kp* > Ma < *?o?kp, ?o:gámp* >
Ja < *?o?k, ?o:gá·m̄p* > Pu < *?o:k, ?o!kp, ?o:gá·m̄p* > At < *?o:k,
?o?kp, ?o:gá·m̄p, tɨ: y?ö:kʸ* > Ct < *?o?kp, ?o:gámp* > LM: Ca
< *?o"k* > SJ *?o?k~?o"k* Cn < *o?k~o"k* > Gu < *?o"k, ?o?k,
?o"gá·m̄p, ?o?p* > OlP: *?o:k* (vi) 'morir' SaP: *?o?k* (vi)

?O#014 pOM ***šɨhw ?o:?k** *(vi) 'haber eclipse del sol/to pass a solar*
eclipse' NHM: *šɨ: y?ɨ:?k~šɨ: y?o:?k* LM: Cn < *šɨ:?o?kp* > (vi)

?O#015 pM ***yak-?o:?k** *(vt) 'matar/to kill'* NHM: *yak?o:k*
~*yak?o:?k* 'matar a alguien' SHM: Tl *yik?v:?k* MM: Ma
< *yahk?ó:k, myahk?é?kʸpʸ, tɨ: dyœhk?é:kʸ* > Ja < *yah?ó:k,
yah?é?kʸpʸ* > Pu < *yah?ó:k, myah?é!kʸpʸ* > At < *yahk?ó:k,
yahk?öö?kʸpʸ, yahk?ö?kʸpʸ* > Ct < *yahk?ó:k, yahkpa·?o:k,
yahkpa·?é?kʸpʸ* > LM: Cn < *yah?o?k ~yah?o"k* > (vt) 'matar' Gu
< *yag?ó"k, yag?ó?pʸ* > OlP: *yak-?o:k* (vt) '=mandar matar' SaP:
?agó?k (vt) ' [Clark and Clark 1960]

?O#016 pM ***yu:h-?o:?k** *(vi) 'tener hambre/to be hungry'* [pOM
*yu:?o:?k]   NHM: <yu?o:?khup~yu?ɨ:?khĭ>   MM: 'hambre'
Ma,Ja,Ct yu:?ó?kɨp   Pu yu?ó!kɨp   At yɨ?ó?kɨp   LM: Gu yɨ?ó?kɨp
'hambre' OlP: yo?o:k (vi) [vowel assimilation]

?O#017 pOM ***yak-hayu-?o:?k-pa** *(n) 'asesino/murderer'* NHM:
yakhayu?o:?kpa   MM: Ju yæhha"y?ó?kpɨ   Ma yahkha"y?ó?kpɨ   Pu
yahha"y?ó?kpɨ   Ct yahkha!y?ó?kpɨ   LM: Ca yahha"y?ó?kpɨ   Gu
hɨya"yyag?ó?pɨ

?O#018 pOM ***?o:?k-y** *(n) 'muerto/dead'*   NHM: *?ɨ:?k* 'muerto'
MM: Ju < ?e:kʸ>   'está muerto, fino'   Ma < ?e:kʸ, tɨ: y?ó?knɨ>
'está muerto, fino'   Ja < ?e:kʸ>   'está muerto'   Pu <tɨ: y?ó!knɨ>
'está muerto'   At < ?oö:kʸ, ?ö:kʸ>   'está muerto, fino'   Ct < ?e:kʸ>
'está muerto, fino' LM: Gu < ?o"kʸ>   'está muerto, fino'

?O#019 pOM ***?o:?k-n** *(n) 'muerte/death'*   NHM: *?o:?kïn* SHM: Tl
?v:?hkɨn MM: Ju *?ó?kɨn*   Pu *?ó!kɨnʸ*   Ja,At,Ct *?ó?k?ɨn*   LM: Cn
<o"kɨn>   Ml <o"khɨñ>   Ca *?ó?kɨnʸ*

?O#020 pOM ***?o:?k-pa** *(n) 'muerto/dead person'*   NHM: *?o:?kpa*
'muerto, cadáver, ánima' MM: 'el muerto'   Ju *?ó?kpɨ*_ Ma *?ó?kpɨ*
'=muerte' Ja,Ct *?ó?kpɨ*   Pu *?ó!kpɨ*   '=muerte' At *?ó?kpɨ*   LM: Cn
<o"kpɨ>   Ca *?ó?kpa* 'el muerto'

?O#021 pMZ ***?o:k** *(n) 'asiento/bottom'*   [Cf. the verbal derivative
prefix ok-; pM, pOM *?o:k, pZ *?ok.] NHM: *?o:k* SHM: Tp *?o·hk*
'anchura' (pos) MM: Ju *?ok* 'anchura; asiento de café' Cc *?ok* 'an-
chura' (pos) Ma *?o·k* 'anchura' (pos), Ja *?o·k* 'asiento de café'; an-
chura' Pu *?o·k* 'anchura' (pos); 'asiento de café' At *?o·k* 'anchura'
(pos) Ct *?o·k* 'anchura' (pos); 'otate' LM: Ca *?o·k* 'asiento de café'
Gu *?o·k* 'anchura' (pos) ChisZ: C *?okpak* 'cadera' N *?okpo?ksa*
'asentaderas, fondo'

?O#022 pMZ ***?o:k?o:?k** *(n) 'pájaro vaquero/squirrel cuckoo'* [pM
*?o:k?o:?k; pZ *?ok?o?k] OlP: *?o:k?o:k* AyZ: [ógo?k]

?O#023 pMZ ***wa:kV-?o:kV** *(n) 'pájaro vaquero/squirrel cuckoo'*
[pOM *wa:k-?o:k; Ju shows the expected MM reflex, other MM and
LM dialects have unexpected loss of final k and sometimes glottalization; pZ *wakV-?okV > pGZ *wa:kV-?o:kV.] MM: Ju wæ:k?ó:k Ma
Wæ:gó" Ja wæ:g?ó: At wæ"g?ó: Ct wæ:gó" LM: Ca wægó" Gu
we:g?ó: TxZ wa:k?o:k

?O#024 pMZ ***?o:kwin** *(n) 'carrizo, otate/reed'* [pM **?o:kwin* >
pOM **?o:kwn* > **?o:kn̥*; pre-pZ **?okwin* > pZ **?ohwin̥*] MM: M̲a
?o·k 'otate', *?o·kn̥* 'carrizo, otate' [sic!] Ja,Pu *?o·k* Ct *?o·kn̥*
SoZ: *?óhwiñ* TxZ: *?ohwê?ñ* (n) 'otate, caña de otate' ChZ: *?ohwit*
'otate' [?-phonology]

?O#025 pZ ***?oks** *(vi) 'enclocarse/to brood'* SoZ: *?oks* 'stretch one's
skin' [Foster and Foster 1948] ChisZ: C *?oks* (vi) 'enclocarse'

?O#026 pMZ ***?om** *(vi) 'sabroso, estar/savory, to be'* OlP: *?om*
(vt-d) 'hacerle daño un deseo de comida frustrado' ChisZ: C *?om* (vi)
'estar sabroso' [derivatives: *oma* 'sabor', *?ombapɨ* (adj) 'sabroso,
agradable', *?omoma* 'aroma, fragrancia, buen olor', *omom* (vi) 'oler,
tener olor'] N *?om* (vi) 'ser sabroso; ser fácil, bonito; sufrirse' NE
?om (vi-s) 'estar sabroso' [derivatives: *?ombabɨ* (adj) 'sabroso',
?omoma 'aroma, olor']

?O#027 pZ ***ko-?omi** *(n) 'dueño, patrón, amo/boss, host'* SoZ:
?ó:mi? TxZ: *?o:m* '=padre, papá' ChisZ: C [Co] *komi* '=imagen'
[Te] <*coymi*> 'a mí señor / dueño y señor' N *komi* '=Jesucristo'
NE *komi* S *[koymí?]* 'dueño'

?O#028 pM ***?o:me** *(n) 'hule/rubber'* [pOM **?o:my*] LM: Cn
<*o:my*> SJ *?o·mʸ* 'rubber, plastic' OlP: *?o:me*

?O#029 pM ***?on** *(vt) 'poner grasoso/to make greasy'* [ChisZ: N *?on*
(vi) 'regañar; hablar' may belong to this set.] NHM: *?o:n ~ ?o:hn
~ ?on* 'poner grasoso' MM: 'untar con aceite' Ma <*?on̄, y?e·mpʸ*>
Ja <*?on̄, y?o·n̄, y?e·mpʸ*> Ct <*?on̄, y?e·mpʸ*> SJ *wi·n?o·n
~wi·n?o:n* 'to make fun of' LM: Gu <*?ón̄, y?o·n̄, y?o·mpʸ*>
'untar con aceite'

?O#030 pM ***?ona** *(n) 'grasa/grease'* [pOM **?on*] NHM: *?on* 'manteca' SHM: Tl *?ʋn* 'graso' MM: Ju *?on* '=manteca' Ma *?on̄*
'=manteca, sebo' Ja *?on̄* '=manteca' Pu *?on̄* 'manteca' At *?on̄*
'=manteca' Ct *?on̄* '=sebo' LM: Cn <*on*> '=gordura' Ca *?on*
'manteca', *?on̄* 'grasa' [sic!] Gu *?on̄* '=sebo, manteca' OlP: *?ona*
'manteca'

?O#031 ***?o?na** *(n) 'nube/cloud' [??]* [This problematic item is by
Campbell and Kaufman (1976) taken to form part of a loanword into
five Mayan languages originating in pZ *nas-?o?na* 'fog'. But, first, this
compound is not, properly speaking, pZ. As far as we know, it is
found only in the C and NE dialects of ChisZ. Second, the head of the

compound (which is more widespread as simplex) behaves irregularly. These irregularities point to the opposite: a loanword into Zoquean.] TxZ: *ʔo:mo?* (n) 'neblina, sereno, rocío' SoZ: *ʔo:ma?* ChisZ: C,N,NE *ʔoʔna* S *[oná?]* ChZ: *ʔiʔni?*

*ʔO#032 pM *ʔo:ʔp (vi) 'espumar/to foam'* [ChZ *ʔopsa?* 'espuma' is the only evidence of the presence of the pM root *ʔo:ʔp* in a Zoquean language.] NHM: *ʔo:ʔp* MM: Ju < *ʔæʔóʔp* > 'espumar de la boca' Ma < *ʔoʔp, ʔo:bámp* > Ja < *yahʔó:p, ʔoʔp, tɨ: yʔe:p^y* > At < *ʔoʔpp, ʔo:bá·m̄p* > LM: Cn < *o·p~o:p* > (vi) 'hacer espuma' SJ *ʔo·p~ʔop* Ca < *ʔoʔp, ʔo:bámp* > Gu < *ʔo·ʔp, ʔo:bá·m̄p* > OlP: *ʔo:p* SaP: *ʔoʔp*

*ʔO#033 pM *ʔo:ʔp-ʔik (n) 'espuma/foam'* [pOM *ʔo:ʔpyk*] NHM: *ʔɨ:ʔpk* SHM: Tl *ʔɨ:ʔpky* MM: Ju,Ma,Ct *ʔeʔp^yk^y* Ja *ʔeʔp^yn^y* [?] At *ʔoöʔp^yk^y* LM: Cn < *o:py* > Ca *ʔo^yp^yk^y* Gu *ʔo·ʔp^yt^y* [?] SJ *ʔo·py* OlP: *ʔo:pi'k* (adj) 'espumoso' SaP: *ʔóʔpak* [?]

*ʔO#034 pOM *ʔo:ʔš (vt) 'arrimar/to bring or place near'* MM: Ma < *mɨhʔó:š, m^yɨhʔóʔš^yp^y* > Ja,Pu,At < *mɨhʔó:š* > LM: SJ *ʔo·š~ʔo:š* 'to carry (clothes, unorganized material)'

*ʔO#035 pMZ [Veracruz] *ʔoso(s) (n) 'sudor/sweat'* SaP: *ʔóhoši, ʔóšoši* 'sudor' [Zo loan?] TxZ: *ʔo:s-a?* (vi) sudar, *ʔo:so?* (s) sudor

*ʔO#036 pZ *ʔote (n) 'voz/voice'* TxZ: *ʔo:t* (n) 'palabra' ChisZ: N *ʔote* 'voz, palabra; notocia' NE *ʔode* '=palabra'

*ʔO#037 pZ *ʔotoŋ (vi) 'hablar/to speak'* TxZ: *ʔo:tɨŋ* (vi) ChisZ: C *ʔotoŋ* (vi) NE *ʔodoŋ* (vi) '=decir', *nɨʔodoŋ* (vt) 'hablarle de algo' ChZ: *ʔotoŋ*

*ʔO#038 pZ *ʔotVʔotV (n) 'especie de pájaro/species of bird'* SaP: *ʔo:t-ot* 'pájaro vaquero' [Clark 1981] [Zo loan] TxZ: *ʔo:tʔo:t* 'especie de pájaro (parecido al picho, pero tiene el pico blanco, plumas negras)'

*ʔO#039 pM *ʔo:ʔy (vt) 'doblar (p.ej., alambre)/to bend wire'* NHM: *ʔo:ʔy* 'doblar (p.ej., el arco para una flecha)' Ma < *ʔo:y, yʔe"p^y* > Ja < *yahʔó:y, ʔolȳy* > Pu < *ʔo:y* > Ct < *yahkʔó:y, yʔelp^y* > LM: Gu < *yagʔó:y, ʔolp^y* > OlP: *ʔo:y* (vt) 'doblarlo (p.ej., alambre, bejuco)'

*ʔO#040 pOM *ʔo:ʔy (n) 'jarro/jar'* NHM: *ʔo:ʔy* '=arqueado (p.ej., una vara)' SHM: Tl *ʔv:y* 'jarra' Mi *ʔo:y* 'asa de canasta u olla' MM: Ju *ʔo:y* 'asa de canasta u olla' Pu *ʔo:y* 'reculón' At *ʔo:y* 'asa de canasta u olla (pos)' LM: Gu *ʔo:y* 'reculón'

?O#041 pMZ *?oy (vi) 'ir (y ya haber regresado)/to go (and have come)' LM: Cn <o·y~oy> SJ ?o·y~?oy Gu <?o·ȳ, tï: y?oȳ> OlP: ?oy (vi) SaP: ?oy (vi) TxZ: ?oy (vi) 'ir (y haber regresado) (v-aux) 'tiempo perfecto' ChisZ: N ?o / oy / oyu (v-aux) 'indica tiempo pretérito' (v-aux) 'ir a (y regresar, pero a veces no tiene sentido de movimiento)' NE ?oy (vi) 'ir (y regresar); venir (y irse)'

?O#042 pMZ *?ohya (n) 'cuñada de mujer/woman's sister-in-law' [pM *?ohya > pOM *?ohy; pZ *?ohya] NHM: To ?ɨh 'nuera' Hu ?ohy [Foster 1949] SHM: Tl ?vhy Ay ?ohih [Foster 1949] MM: Ju ?oh^y Ma ?oh^y 'cuñada (de mujer)' (pos) Ja ?oh^y At,Pu,Ct ?oh^y (pos) LM: Cn <ohy> 'cuñada (mujer hablando de su cuñada; a veces también se usa para referirse a la madre, hermana mayor o tía de la cuñada)' SJ ?ohy 'in-law' Ca ?oh^y Gu ?oh^y [Nordell 1990 and p.c.], ?oyh [Foster 1949] OlP: ?ohya SaP: ?ohy SoZ: ?ohya? [Gutiérrez M. 1993], ?ohyah [Foster 1949] TxZ: ?oh ChisZ: C,NE ?ohya N ?ohyɨ S [Tu] ?ohyatɨwɨ [Foster 1949] ChZ: StaMaCh ?oya SnMiCh ?oyah [Foster 1949]

?O#043 pMZ *?oyV (adj, adv) 'bueno, bien/good, well' [pM *?oya > pOM *?oy; pZ *?oye] NHM: ?oy '=cómodo, correcto, fino'; ?oy ?o:y 'muy bueno' SHM: Tu ?oy 'bueno' Tp ?oy 'bueno' Mi ?oy 'bueno' MM: Ju ?oy 'fino'; ?oy, ?oy 'sí' [sic!] Cc ?oy 'bueno' Ma ?oy 'bien, mejor, sano'; ?oȳ 'bueno' [sic!] Ja ?oȳ '=mejor; sabroso'; ?ŏ^yb^yɨ 'fino' Pu ?oȳ '=mejor; sabroso; correcto' At ?oȳ '=mejor; correcto' Ct ?oȳ '=mejor; correcto; sabroso' LM: Cn <oy> (adj) 'bueno, bonito' (adv) 'muy, mucho' Ca ?oy '=sano; sí' Gu ?oȳ 'bien, mejor; correcto; sabroso; sano'; ?oy 'bueno' OlP: ?oya 'bueno' SaP: ?oy 'bueno, bien'; ChisZ: C ?oye NE ?oye

?O#044 pMZ *ni(yuk)-?oyV (adj, adv) 'mejor/better' [pM *ni(yuk)?oya > pOM *niyuhk?oya; pZ *ni?oye] NHM: niyuhk oy [only in Sp-to-Mixe side; niyuhk means 'bastante, más'] LM: Cn ni"k?oy [Hoogshagen 1984] OlP: ni?oya (adj) 'sano, bueno" ChisZ: C ni?oye (adj) 'un poco bueno, medio bueno'; (adv) 'un poco bien'

?O#045 pM *?oya-?o:?ki (adj, adv) 'muy bien/very good' [pOM *?oya?o:?ky] NHM: ?oy ?ɨ:?k 'muy bueno' SaP: ?oyŏ?k

?O#046 pMZ *?oy-?ah (vi) 'componerse/to settle, improve' NHM: ?o?yi ~ ?oya 'componer, poder' MM: 'mejorarse, componerse' Ma <?ó?ȳ?ip^y> Ja <?ó!ȳɨp> 'mejorarse', <?ó?ȳɨp^y, ?ó?yɨy> 'componerse' [sic!] Pu <?ó!ȳ?ɨp^y> At,Ct <?ó?ȳɨp^y> LM: Gu

< *?oyï:pʸ, ?oyï"w*a·m̄p* > 'componerse, mejorarse' OIP: *?oyatu:t ~ - ?oyahtu?t* (vt) 'colocarlo bien, componerlo' SaP: *?oyák* 'componer' [Clark and Clark 1960] ChisZ: C *?oya?* (vi) '=recuperarse'

?O#047 pOM ***yak-?oy-?ah** *(vt) 'arreglar/to arrange'* NHM: < *yak?o?yi ~ yak?oya* > (vt) 'componer algo, arreglar algo, reparar algo' SHM: Tu < *yahk?óyɨ* > MM: Ju < *yæh?óyyɨ* > Ma < *yahk?óyɨ* > Ja < *yah?óyɨ, yah?ó?yɨp* > Pu < *yah?óyɨ* > At < *yæhk?óyɨ* > LM: Gu < *yag?oyï"w* >

?O#048 pM ***?oya-tun** *(vt) 'componer/to repair'* [pOM **?otyun*] MM: 'construir' Ma < *?oďún* > At < *?ɨďún* > OIP: *?oyahtun* (vt)

?O#049 pM ***?oy-in** *(adj) 'mano derecha/right hand'* NHM: *?aka?yïn* 'derecha' MM: Ma *?a?óy* Ja *?a·?óy* Pu *?a?óȳ* LM: Ca *?a·?óy* Gu *?a?ó:y* SaP: *?oyim* 'derecha', *?óyimay kɨ?* 'mano derecha'

?O#050 pMZ ***?o:yo(?)** *(n) 'camarón/shrimp'* [pM **?o:yo*, pZ **?oyo?*] OIP: *?o:yo* SaP: *?o:y* SoZ: *?óyo?* 'reculador (especie de camarón que se echa para atrás)' TxZ: *?o:ya?* 'reculador (camarón de pantano)' [?-the last vowel]

CI-CO

CI#001 pMZ **ci:?** *(vt) 'dar, pegarse/to give, to yield a crop'* OlP: *ci:~ci?* (vi) 'pegarse una planta' TxZ: *čê?* (vt) 'dar, pegar' ChisZ: C *ci?* (vt) 'darlo' N *ci?* (vt) 'darle; pegarle' NE *ci?* (vt) 'darlo; darse (como una milpa)' ChZ: *ci?* 'dar'

CI#002 pZ **ha?c-ci?** *(vt) 'darle fiado/to give credit'* TxZ: *ha?cčê?* (vt) ChisZ: C *ha?cči?* N *ha?hci?* (vt) NE *ha?cci?* (vt)

CI#003 pZ **cic** *(vi, vt) 'rasgar/to tear, rip'* TxZ: *čêčka?y* (vt, vi-p) 'destapar' ChisZ: C *cihc* (vt) 'romperlo, rasgarlo' N *cihc* (vi) 'rasgarse' (vt) 'rasgarlo' NE *cihc* (vi) 'rasgarse; romperse' (vt) 'romperlo, rasgarlo (como ropa)'

CI#004 pM **ci?c** *(vi) 'mamar/to suck (breast)'* NHM: *ci?c~ci"c* SHM: Tl *ce"c* MM: Ju <*ci?cp*> Ma <*ci"c, ci?cp*> Ja,At,Ct <*ci"c, ci?c, ci?cp, ci"ʒá·m̄p*> Pu <*ci"c, ci!cp*> LM: Ca <*ci"c*> 'mamar' Cn <*ci?t~ci"t*> (vi) SJ *ci·c~ci"c* 'to nurse, suck on the breast' Gu <*ci"c, ci?cp, ci?c, ci"ʒá·m̄p*> OlP: *či?c* (vi)

CI#005 pM **yak-ci?c** *(vt) 'dale de mamar, dar pecho/to suckle'* NHM: *yakci?c~yakci"c* (vt) MM: Ju <*yæhcí"c*> Ma <*yahkcí"c*> Ma <*yahkcí"c, yahkcí?čpʸ*> Ja <*yahcí"c, yahcí?čpʸ, yahcí?c*> 'dar pecho, dale de mamar', <*yahcí"c, yahcí?čpʸ*> 'amamantar' Pu <*yahcí"c*> 'amamantar', <*yahcí"c, yahcí!čpʸ*> 'dale de mamar, dar pecho, amamantar' At <*yahkcí"c, yahkcí?čpʸ*> Ct <*yahkcí"c, yahkcí?čpʸ*> LM: Cn <*yahci?c~yahci"c*> (vt) 'dar de mamar' Ca <*yahcí"c*> Gu <*yahcí"c, yahcí?čp, yahcí?c*> OlP: *yakči?c* (vt) SaP: *?akči?č* (vt) 'rellenar, tapar' [Clark and Clark 1960]

CI#006 pOM **ci?c-k** *(n) 'senos, teta/female breast'* NHM: *ci?ck* SHM: Tl,Ay *ce?ck* MM: Ju,Ma,Ja,At,Ct *ci?ck* Pu *ci!ck* LM: Ca,Gu *ci?ck*

CI#007 pOM ***ci:ʔc** *(vi) 'rellenar/to fill'* NHM: *tukci:ʔcip ~ tukci:ʔca* 'rellenar' MM: 'cargar (rifle)' Ma,Ct <*ci:c*> At <*ci:c, či?č*> LM: Gu <*ci:c, či·ʔčp*> Cn <*ci·c ~ ci:c*> (vt) 'cargar (la escopeta de chispa)' SJ *ci·c ~ ci:c* 'to stuff'

CI#008 pOM ***ʔa-ci:ʔc** *(n) 'tapón/plug'* NHM: *ʔaci:ʔc* MM: Ju *ʔa·ẓíˮt* Ja,At *ʔaẓí:c* Ct *ʔa·ẓí:c*

CI#009 pZ ***cih** *(vt) 'quebrar/to destroy'* [Cf. MM: 'estorbar' Ju <*ʔœẓíhp*> At <*ʔœẓíhpɨp*> Ct <*ʔa·ẓíhp*> ?] ChisZ: N *cih* (vi) 'despostillarse' TxZ: *čêh* (vt, vi) 'golpear, pegar, despulpar' ChZ: *cih* 'tirar'

CI#010 pZ ***cihiʔ** *(n) 'tlacuache/Mexican opossum'* [pGZ **či:hi*] SoZ: *či:hiʔ* 'zorro' AyZ: *[ciʔi]* 'zorro' TxZ: *čê:ʔheʔ* '=zorro' ChisZ: C *ciʔ* '=zarigüeya' N *cihi* '=zorro' NE *cihi* '=zarigüeya' ChZ: *cihiʔ*

CI#011 pMZ ***cik** *(vi, vt) 'pelar/to peal'* NHM: *cihk ~ cik* 'piscar, cosechar' SHM: Tl *cek* 'cosechar' MM: Ju <*nicík*> 'pelar', <*cik, cihk*> 'pizcar, cosechar' Ma <*cihk*>_ 'cosechar', _<*cíhkpɨ*> 'pizcar', <*cik, čihkʸpʸ*> 'pelar' Ja <*niˮẓík, niˮẓíhkp, cik, čihkʸpʸ*> 'pelar', <*cik,_cihkp, čihkʸpʸ*> 'pizcar, cosechar' Pu ≤*cik, čihkʸpʸ*> 'pelar', <*cik, cihkp*> 'pizcar, cosechar' At <*cik, cihk, cihkp, ciká·m̄p*> 'pizcar, cosechar' Ct <*cihk, cik, cihkp*> 'cosechar, pizcar' <*cik, nʸicíhkʸpʸ, nɨˮcík, nʸɨˮcíhkʸpʸ*> 'pelar' LM: Cn <*cihk ~ cik*> (vt) 'pizcar'_ SJ *cihk ~ cik* 'to husk (corn, beans, etc.); to harvest corn' Gu <*nɨˮẓík, nʸɨˮẓíhpʸ*> 'pelar', <*cik, cihk, cihp*> 'pizcar, cosechar' OlP: *čik* (vt) 'pizcar maíz' SaP: *čik* (vi, vt) 'harvest corn' TxZ: *čêk* (vt) 'pizcar' ChisZ: C *cihk* (vt) 'pelarlo, mondarlo; pizcarlo' N *cihk* (vt) 'pelarlo, descascararlo; tapiscarlo' NE *cihk* 'pizcarlo (como maíz); pilarlo (como café); desollarlo; pelarlo, mondarlo (como fruta)' ChZ: *cik*

CI#012 pM ***ci:k ~ ci:kcik** *(n) 'cucaracha; chapulín grande/cockroach; big grasshopper'* [pOM_**či:k ~ či:kčk*] NHM: *ci:k* 'cucaracha' MM: Ju *cikč_* 'grillo' Ma *ci·k máˮdɨ ʔɨ:p* 'grillo', *ci·k* 'chapulín (grande)_' Ja *ci·kč* 'grillo' Pu *ci·k* 'grillo, chapulín (grande)' At *ci·k* 'chapulín (grande), grillo', *yɨkcí·k* 'grillo' Ct *ci·k* 'grillo' LM: Gu *ci·ʔčk, ci·kč* 'grillo' OlP: *či:kɨ* 'cucaracha'

CI#013 pM **ci:ʔk** *(vi, vt) 'pegar, abofetear/to hit, slap'* NHM: *ci:ʔk* 'pegar (p.ej., un manazo), abofetear' MM: 'golpear, pegar (con la mano)' Ma <*ci:k, čiʔkʸpʸ*> Ja <*ci:k, čiʔk, čiʔkʸpʸ*> Pu,At <*ci:k, čiʔkʸpʸ*> Ct <*ci:k, čikʸpʸ*> LM: Cn <*ci·k ~ ci:k*> SJ *ci·k ~ ci:k* 'to fight (chickens)' Gu <*ci:k, ci·ʔp*> 'pelear (aves)' [Nordell, p.c.] SaP: *čiʔk* (vi, vt) 'get stuck'

CI#014 pZ **ciʔki?** *(vi, vt) 'sonar/to sound'* [The last syllable is, as is usual, lost under affixation in TxZ; while there is a phonological match, the fact that this is a onomatopoeic word brings some uncertainty to the reconstruction.] TxZ: *čêʔkčêʔkde?* (vi-s) 'sonar (trineros de ave), chillar (ratón, pollo, trineo de pajarito)' ChisZ: C *ciʔki?* (vt) 'hacerlo sonar' N *ciʔki?* (vi) 'sonar (como marca)'

CI#015 pMZ **cikin** *(adj) 'pinto/spotted'* [pM, pOM, pZ *cikin*] NHM: *cíkïn* 'empedrado, moteado (p.ej., una gallina)' LM: Gu *cikïʸ* 'piña' [Nordell, p.c.] SaP: *čikin* 'tecolote' [Clark 1981] TxZ: *čêkeñ* 'moteado, abado' ChisZ: C *cikin* 'pintojo, moteado' N *cikin* (adj) '=rayado' NE *cikinsïhk* 'frijol pinto' ChZ: *cikin*

CI#016 pMZ **ciku** *(n) 'tejón/coati'* [pM *ciku* > pOM *cik*; pZ *ciku* > pGZ *či:ku?*] NHM: *cik* 'tejón, coatí, pizote [Nasua narica /nasua nasica]' SHM: Tl *cek* 'tejón' MM: '=coatimundi' Ju *cik* Ma,At,Ct *cik* LM: Cn <*cik*> 'tejón, coatí [Nasua nasua narica]' Ca *cik* [Nordell 1990], *ci:k* [Wonderly 1949] '=coatimundi' Gu *cik* '=coatimundi' SaP: *čik* 'tejón' SoZ: *či:ku* [Wonderly 1949], *či:ku?* [Gutiérrez M. 1993] AyZ: *[ci:ku ~ ci:ko]* 'mapache' TxZ: *če:ku?* ~ *če:ko?* ChisZ: C *ciku* '=coatí' N *ciku* NE [Tapalapa, Ocotepec, Chapultenango] *ciku* [Wonderly 1949] [Ra] *ciku* 'mapache' ChZ: StaMaCh *ciku* SnMiCh *ciku* [Wonderly 1949]

CI#017 pZ **ciks...** *(adj) 'chico/little'* [*č* has not been reconstructed for pZ since this would then be the only item in which it occurred.] SaP: *číčik* [?] ChisZ: C *čiks* '=pequeño' N *čiks* 'pequeño'

CI#018 pZ **ciʔks** *(vi) 'comezón, tener/to itch'* [Cf. pGZ: *čiʔkš-i* 'comezón' below.] ChisZ: C *cikskï?* 'comezón' N *ciʔks* (vi) 'darle comezón' ChZ: *ciʔks* 'tener comezón'

CI#019 pGZ **čiʔkš-i** *(n) 'comezón/itch'* SoZ: *čiʔkši?* 'sarna' AyZ: *ciʔksi* 'comezón, sabañón' TxZ: *čêʔkše?* 'comezón (enfermedad), sarna, roncha, rasquiña'

CI#020 pMZ ***cikwiC** *(n) 'piñuela (planta epífita de las Bromelía-ceas)/bromeliad'* [pM **cikwi(n)* > pOM **cikwyn*; pZ **cikwiC*] LM: Cn <*ciky*> 'piña [Ananas comosus]' OlP: *čikwi'n* SaP: *čikiniwihn* [Clark 1981] [?-perhaps this was reanalysed] SoZ: *čikwiñ* [Elson 1960] ChisZ: C *cikuic* 'piña de ocote' N *cihkɨwic* 'piña'

CI#021 pMZ ***cima** *(n) 'jícara/bowl made out of a gourd'* [pM **cima* > pOM **cim*; pZ **cima* > pGZ **či:ma*] NHM: *cim* 'jícara delgada' SHM: Tl,Ay,Tm *cem* MM: Ju *cim* Ma,Ja,At,Ct *cim̄* Pu *cim̦* LM: Ml <*cim*> Ca *cim* Gu *cim̄* OlP: *čima* SaP: *čim* SoZ: *či:ma?* 'plato' TxZ: *ko:kodašče:ma?* 'cajete de barro' ChisZ: C,N *cima* '=taza' NE *cima* S *[ci·má?]* ChZ: *cima?*

CI#022 pM ***cima-kuhy** *(n) 'cuauhtecomate/gourd tree'* [pOM **cimku:hy* is not attested since in NHM the reflex of pM **kuhy* 'tree' was replaced with the reflex of pM **kɨpi* 'wood'.] NHM: *cimɨkɨp* 'cuauhtecomate, cujete, tecomate' [Crescentia cujete] OlP: *čimakuyɨ* 'palo de jícara' SaP: *čimguhy* 'jícaro' [Clark 1981]

CI#023 pM ***ko-cima** *(n) 'calvo, pelón/bald'* [pOM **kucim*] NHM: *kucim* SaP: *kúčim* 'to gourd-head (shave)' [Clark 1969: 42]

CI#024 pOM ***cim(c)y(k)** *(n) 'helecho, ocopetate/fern'* NHM: *cimi* MM: Ma *cim^yk^y* 'helecho', *cim^yk^y* 'ocopetate' [sic!] Ct *cim^yk^y* 'helecho', *cim^yk^y* 'ocopetate' [sic!] Ju *cimč* At *ci·mč* 'helecho', *ci:mč* 'ocopetate' [sic!]

CI#025 pM [Veracruz] ***ci?m-pak** *(n) 'chicle/chicle'* SaP: *čí?mbak* OlP: *či?mpa'k* '=goma de mascar'

CI#026 pGZ ***čimpa?** *(n) 'perro/dog'* SoZ: *čímpa?* TxZ: *čêmpa?*

CI#027 pMZ ***cin** *(n) 'ocote, pino/pitchpine'* [pM, pOM **cihn*; pZ **cin* > pGZ **čiñ*] NHM: *ci:hn* '=candela, vela' [p.ej., Pinus montezumae] SHM: Tl,Ay *ce:n* Tm *cenáy* LM: SJ *ci·n* [*ci·ngɨš* 'up in the pine tree'] MM: Ma *ci:n* 'ocote' Ja *ci:n* 'ocote' Pu *ci:n* 'ocote, antorcha de ocote' At *ci:n* 'ocote' Ct *ci:n* 'antorcha de ocote', *ci·n̄* 'ocote' [sic!] LM: 'ocote' Cn <*ci:n*> Ca *ci:n* Gu *ci:n* '=antorcha de ocote' TaM *čiŋ* [transcription of Wonderly 1949] OlP: *činkuyɨ* SaP: *činkuhy* [Clark 1981] SoZ: *čiŋkuy* TxZ: *čêŋkuy* 'ocote' ChisZ: C *cin* 'ocote, especie de pino'; *wa?cin* 'pino' N *cin* NE *cit* S [Tu] *cin* [Wonderly 1949] ChZ: *cin* 'ocote' [San Miguel] *cin* [Wonderly 1949]

CI#028 pOM *cin?ihtk   (n) 'gavilancillo/American kestrel [Falco sparverius]' NHM: cin?ihtɨk '=gavilán ratonero [F. tinnunculus]' LM: cinihky

CI#029 pOM *ci:?ny   (n) 'aguacate, chinini/avocado [Persea schiedeana]' [The Mixean languages of Veracruz possibly borrowed the Spanish term.] NHM: ci:?n 'aguacate chupón' Ma,Ja,Pu,At ci:nʸ Ct ci·n̄ʸ OIP: čininikuyɨ [?] 'chinini' SaP: čininkúhy 'chinini' [?]

CI#030 pZ ***cinin** (vi) 'bambolearse/to sway, dangle' SaP: činin (vi, vt) 'dangle' [Zo loan?] ChisZ: N cininey (vi) 'estar colgado; balancearse (a veces a punto de caer)'

CI#031 pMZ ***ci:nu** (n) 'miel/honey' [pM *ci:nu > pOM *ci:n; pZ *cinu > pGZ *či:ñu] LM: Gu mɨhci:n 'abeja' [Nordell, p.c.] OIP: či:nu SaP: či:n SoZ: číñu [Foster and Foster 1948], či:ñu? [Gutiérrez M. 1993] AyZ: [ci:ŋu] TxZ: čê:ñ ChisZ: C cinuh N cinu NE cinuh ChZ: cinu 'abeja'; cinuy nɨ? 'miel de colmena'

CI#032 pOM ***cip** (n, adj) 'pleito, difícil/fight, difficult' MM: Ju cip 'pleito', kʸæh čípɨt 'fácil' Ma cip̄ 'pleito, difícil', kæ" čípɨ 'fácil' Ja cip̄ 'pleito, difícil' Pu cip̄ 'difícil' At cip̄ 'pleito, difícil', kʸæh čípɨ 'fácil' Ct cip̄ 'pleito, difícil', kæh čípɨtʸ 'fácil' LM: Cn <cip> (adj) 'difícil, pesado' (n) 'pleito, guerra' Gu cip̄ 'pleito, difícil', kah čípɨ 'fácil'

CI#033 pOM ***cihp~cip** (vi) 'fastidiarse/to become fed up with' SHM: Tp <tɨc ščípnɨ, tɨ: čípʸɨ> 'aburrirse' MM: Cc <tɨ:čípʸɨ> 'aburrirse' Ma <cíhpɨp, ščíhpɨc> 'aburrirse, fastidiar' Ja <cíhpɨp, sʸčíhpɨc, cipá·n̄ɨp> 'enfadarse', <cíhpɨp> 'fastidiar, aburrirse' [sic!] Pu <cíhpɨp, cipá·n̄ɨp, ščíhpɨc> 'aburrirse' At <cíhpɨp, ščíhpɨc> 'aburrirse, enfadarse, fastidiar' Ct <cíhpɨp> 'fastidiar, aburrirse, enfadarse' LM: Ca <cíhpɨp> 'enfadarse' Cn <cihp> 'enfadarse' SJ <cihp~cip> 'to become tired of something' Gu <cíhpɨp, cibá·n̄ɨp> 'aburrirse, fastidiar, enfadarse'

CI#034 pOM ***cipa?an** (n) 'mojón/heap' MM: Ju cibá?æn Ma cɨWá?n̄ Ja cibá!n̄ Pu cɨbá?n̄ At cabá?n̄ Ct cɨbá?n̄ LM: Gu cɨwá!nt

CI#035 pMZ ***cípin** (n) 'verruga/wart' [pM *cipin > pOM *cipn; pZ *cipin > pGZ *či:piñ] NHM: cípɨn 'mezquino (verruga que sale en las manos o en los pies)' MM: Ju cipʸn̥ʸ Ma,Ja cipʸn̥ʸ '=mezquino' Pu cipʸn̥ʸ '=mezquino', cipʸn̥ʸɨ 'verruga' [sic!] At ci·p̄ʸn̥ʸ 'mezquino', *cipʸn̥ʸ* 'verruga' [sic!] Ct *cipʸn̄ʸ* 'verruga', *cipʸn̥ʸ* 'mezquino' [sic!] LM: Ca *cipʸtʸ* 'verruga' Gu *cipʸtʸ* 'mezquino', *ciptʸ* 'verruga' [sic!] OlP: *čipiʼn* 'tomate, viruela' SaP: *čípin* 'tomate, jitomate' SoZ: *číːpiñ* 'tomate'

CI#036 pOM ***cihš ~ ciš** *(vi) ʼtiznarse/to become sooted'* [pOM: **ciš-y* 'negro'] LM: Cn < *cihš ~ ciš* > SJ *cihš ~ ciš* 'to blacken'

CI#037 pOM ***ciš-y** *(adj) ʼmoreno/dark'* NHM: *ciš* '=trigueño' MM: Ma *cišʸ* Ja,Pu *cišʸ* 'prieto, negro' At *cišʸ* LM: Cn < *cišy* > (adj) 'color negro' SJ *ciš* 'black' SaP: *čiʔč* 'negro' [?]

CI#038 pMZ ***ciːsʔ** *(vi) ʼventosear/let out gas'* NHM: *ciːš ~ ciˮš* MM: Ma < *ciˮš, ci·šp, tiː čiˮšʸ, ciˮžámp* > '=peer' Ja < *ci·š, ciˮš, ci·šp, ciˮžá·mp* > '=peer' Pu < *ciˮš, ci·šp, tæm čiˮšʸ* > '=peer' At < *ciˮš, ciˮš, ci·šp, ciˮžá·mp* > 'peer' Ct < *ciˮš, ci·šp, ciˮžámp* > '=peer' LM: Cn < *ci·š ~ ciˮš* > (vi) 'pedorrear' SJ *ci·š ~ ciˮš* Gu < *ciˮš, ci·š, ci·šp, ciˮžá·mp, tiː čiˮšʸ* > '=peer' SaP: *čiːš ~ čiʔš* (vi) 'expel gas, swell from within (tortillas, when heated, balloon)' TxZ: *čêš* (vi) 'echar pedo' ChisZ: C [Te] < *tzis pa* > 'peedar'

CI#039 pGZ ***čiːš-i** *(n) ʼpedo/fart'* SoZ: *čiːši?* AyZ: [*ci?is*] TxZ: *čeːš*

CI#040 pOM ***cíš-tɨk** *(n) ʼtemascal/sweathouse'* NHM: *cišk* SHM: Tl *cešk* MM: Ju,Ma,At *cihtk* Ct *cihtʸkʸ* LM: Cn < *ciːš* > Ca *cišk*

CI#041 pMZ ***cisi(k)** *(n) ʼchinche/bedbug'* [pM **cišik* > pOM **cišk*; pZ **cisi* > pGZ **čiːši*] NHM: *cišk pehkš* 'chinche de jardín, chinche voladora' TxZ: *kekčeːš* 'especie de chinche (apesta, vuela)' ChisZ: C *cisi?* N *čisyi*

CI#042 pOM ***čiːtɨ** *(n) ʼgato/cat'* MM: Ma,Ja,Pu,Ct *čí·tɨ* LM: Gu *čiːt*

CI#043 pM ***ci?t** *(vi, vt) ʼdesalojar/dislodge'* LM: Cn < *ciˮt* > (vt) 'cerrar' OlP: **či?t* [*či?tkot* (vt) 'abotonarlo' (vr) 'atrancarse', *kɨ?mači?t* (vt) 'soltarlo'] SaP: *či?t* (vi, vt) 'dislodge, take away' [?-semantics]

CI#044 pMZ ***ko-ci?t** *(vi, vt) ʼzafar, raspar/to slip away'* NHM: *kuci?t ~ kuciˮt* 'zafar' ChisZ: C *koci?t* (vi) 'dislocarse; escaparse;

zafarse (vt) dislocarselo' N *kɨci?t* (vi) 'resbalarse, zafarse, rasparse (vt) rasparlo, pelarlo' [?]

CI#045 pOM ***?a-ci?t ~ ?a-ci"t** *(vi, vt) 'abotonar, abrochar/to button'* SHM: Tu < *?azí"t* > Tp < *?Azí"t* > MM: Ju < *?ædzi"t* > Cc < *?adzi"t* > Ma < *?azi"t* > < *?azí"t, y?azí?tɨ̄ʸpʸ* > 'embotonar' Ja < *pɨm̄ ?azí"t* > 'embotonar', < *?azi"t, y?adzi?t* > < *y?azí?tʸpʸ* > 'abotonar, abrochar' Pu < *?ɨzi"t, y?ɨdzi!tʸpʸ* > 'abotonar, abrochar', < *?azí"t* > 'embotonar' At < *?azi"t* > 'abotonar, abrochar', < *pɨm̄ ?Fædzí"t* > 'embotonar' Ct < *?a·zí"t, y?a·dzí?tʸpʸ, ?a·zi"t* > LM: Cn < *adzi?t ~ adzi"t* > (vt) 'abotonar, abrochar' Gu < *?azi"t, y?azi?t* > 'abotonar, abrochar', < *?azí"t, y?azí?pʸ* > 'embotonar' [sic!]

CI#046 pOM ***?a-ci"t** *(n) 'botón/button'* NHM: *?aci"t* 'botón o su substituto' SHM: Tu *?azí"t* Tp *?Azí"t* MM: Ju *?a·cí"t* Ma,Ct *?a·zí"t* Ja *?azí"t* Pu *?ɨzí"t* At *?æzí"t* LM: Ca *?a·cí"t*

CI#047 pM ***ci?wa** *(n) 'calabaza/gourd'* [pOM **ci"w*] NHM: *ci"v* 'calabaza, chilacayote' SHM: Ay *ce"* Tu,Tp *ci"* Mi *c"i* MM: Ma *ci"w̥, ci"Φ, ci"f* Ju,Cc,Ja,Pu *ci"* At *ci"w* Ct *ci"w̥, ci"Φ°* LM: Cn < *ci?* > '[Cucurbita sp.]' Ca,SJ,Gu *ci"* OlP: *či?va* 'calabaza', *či?va?a:ca* 'bejuco de calabaza' SaP: *či?kš* [?]

CI#048 pOM ***ka:-ci"w** *(n) 'chilacayote/type of squash'* [Lit., 'feline gourd'; G. Martin (p.c.) suggests that the name may be explained by reference to the stripes on this fruit.] NHM: *ka: ci"v* SHM: Tl *ko:cé?* MM: Ju,Pu *ka:zí"* Ma *ka:zí"f* At *ka:zí"w* LM: Ca *kɨzí"*

CI#049 pOM ***mɨny-ci"w** *(n) 'calabaza castilla/malabar gourd'* [lit., 'sweet potato squash'] NHM: *mɨnci"v* SHM: Tu *monʸzjí"* Mi *menʸzjí?i* MM: At *munʸzjí"w*

CI#050 pMZ ***ci:w?** *(vi) 'bañar/to bathe'* NHM: *ci:v ~ ci"v* SHM: Tl *ce?* Tu < *ci", ci:p, ci?ámp* > 'bañarse' Tp < *ci", či"y, ci:p, ci:, ci"βÁmp* > 'bañarse' MM: 'bañarse' Ju < *ci"* > Cc < *ci", ci:p, ci:, tɨ: či"y, či:y, ci"hÁmp, či:y* > Ma < *ci"w̥, ci"f, ci"Φ, ci:p* > Ja < *ci"w, ci", ci·w̄, ci:p* > Pu < *ci", ci:p* > At < *ci", ci:p* > Ct < *ci"w, ci:p* > Ca < *ci"* > LM: Cn < *ci·w ~ ci· ~ ci"w* > Gu < *ci"w, ci:p, ci·w̄* > SJ *ci·w ~ ci"w* OlP: *čiv ~ či?v* (vi) 'bañarse' SaP: *čiw ~ či?w* SoZ: *čiŋ* [Foster and Foster 1948] TxZ: *čêŋ* (vi) ChisZ: C *ciŋ* (vi) N,NE *ciŋ* (vi, vt) ChZ: *ciŋ*

CI#051 pMZ ***yak-ciw ~ yak-ci?w** *(vt) 'bañar a alguien/to bathe some-one'* NHM: *yakci:v ~ yakci"v* (vt) SHM: Tp *<yæhkcí">* MM: Cc *<yAhkcí", yAhkcí:pʸ>* Ja *<yahcí"w, yahcí:pʸ>* At *<yæhkcí">* LM: Cn *<yahci·w ~ yahci· ~ yahci"w>* (vt) 'bañar' Gu *<yahcí"w>* OlP: *yakčiv ~ yakči?v* (vt) SaP: *?akčiw ~ ?akči?w* (vt) [Clark and Clark 1960] TxZ: *yakčêŋ* (vt-caus) ChisZ: C,N *yakciŋ* (vt) NE *yakciŋ* (vt) '=hacer que se bañara'

CI#052 pOM ***cihw-tahk-n** *(n) 'baño (para bañarse)/bath'* SHM: Tu *ci:δá·hk* Tp *ci:dÁ·hk* MM: Cc *ci:dÁkṇ* Ma,Ja,Pu,At,Ct *ci:dá·kṇ* LM: Gu *ci:dá·kt*

CI#053 pOM ***cihw-y** *(n) 'cántaro/pitcher'* NHM: *civ* '=botija' SHM: Tl,Tu,Mi *ci:y* Tp *ci:y̥* MM: Cc *ci:y̥* At *ci:y*

CI#054 pOM ***ci:?wy** *(n) 'jeme/measure corresponding to the span from the index finger to the thumb'* NHM: *ci:?v* LM: Cn *<ci:y>* 'una medida (usando los dedos para medir)'

CE#001 pZ ***ce?** *(vt) 'lavar/to wash'* SoZ: *ce?* [Foster and Foster 1948] TxZ: *ce?* (vt) ChisZ: C *ce?* (vt) NE *ce?* (vi, vt) ChZ: *ce?*

CE#002 pMZ ***cec** *(vt) 'labrar/to work, trim (a material)'* NHM: *cehc ~ cec* 'labrar (p.ej., madera) LM: Cn *<cehc ~ cec>* (vt) SJ *cehc ~ cec* 'to trim (wood, stone)' Gu *<cec, cehcp>* [Nordell, p.c.] TxZ: *cec* (vt, vi-p) 'labrar, rebajar (carpintería)' ChisZ: C [Te] *<tzetzpa>* 'desbastar madera / dolar / labrar madera o piedras' [Co] *cehc* (vt) 'rozarlo, desmontarlo; machetearlo' N *cehc* (vt) 'cortarlo (con machete)' ChZ: *cec*

CE#003 pOM ***cehc-pa** *(n) 'carpintero/carpenter'* NHM: *cehcpa* SHM: Tp *cǽhcp* MM: Ju,Ma,Ja,Pu,At *cǽhcp* Cc *šǽ"b cǽhcp* LM: Ca *cǽhcp* Gu *céhcp*

CE#004 pOM ***cehč** *(n) 'colorín, tzompantle/coral bean tree [Erythrina spp.]'* NHM: *cEhst* SHM: Mi *cehč* MM: Ju,Ma,Ja,Pu,At,Ct *cehč* LM: Cn *<cehč>* Ca *cehč* Gu *cehčk*

CE#005 pMZ ***cehe** *(n) 'carpintero/carpenter'* [pM *cehe > pOM *ceh (with a regular development in LM only); pZ *cehe > pGZ *ce:he] MM: 'pájaro carpintero' Ma *čiréh* Ja,Ct *čéher* Pu *ciréh̯* LM: [Gu] *?az̧éh* [Nordell, p.c.] SaP: *kuyčéh* SoZ: *ce:he?* 'pájaro carpintero' ChisZ: C *ce?* N,NE *cehe*

CE#006 pZ ***cehV** *(adj) 'delgado/slim'* ChisZ: C *ceya* 'como papel o tela' N *ca?ya* (adj) 'alto y delgado, largo y delgado' ChZ: *cehe* 'muy delgado'

CE#007 pOM ***cek** *(adj) 'insípido/insipid'* NHM: *cek* 'desabrido' MM: Ju *cæk ~ cek* 'simple, sin sal' Ma,Ja,Pu,At,Ct *cæk* 'insípido (le falta sal), simple, sin sal' LM: [*cek* expected; perhaps the forms attested are reanalyses based on the verb root Cn <*cehk ~ cek*> (vi) 'despintarse' SJ *cehk ~ cek* 'to fade'.] Cn <*ceky*> (adj) 'soso, desabrido' [?] Ca *ceksʸ* [?]

CE#008 pZ ***cek** *(n) 'barriga, estómago/stomach'* [pGZ *cek] TxZ: *cek* 'barriga' ChisZ: C,N,S *cek* NE *cehk* '=vientre—de un animal; útero o vientre—de una mujer' ChZ: *cek* '=abdomen'

CE#009 pMZ ***ce:?k** *(vt) 'regañar/to scold'* OIP: *ce:k* (vt) 'regañarlo' SaP: *če?k* (vi, vt) 'scold' SoZ: *ce?k* 'charge' [Foster and Foster 1948] AyZ: *[ce:?gɨ]* 'cóbralo', *[ma ce?k]* 'cobró' TxZ: *ce?k* (vt, vi-p) 'cobrar' ChisZ: C *ce?k* (vt) 'cobrarlo' N *kɨce?k* (vt) 'avergonzarlo' ChZ: *ce?k* 'pedir'

CE#010 pZ ***ceke** *(n) 'tortuga/tortoise'* [pGZ *ce:ke] AyZ: *[ce:ge]* 'pochitoga' TxZ: *ce:k* 'pochitoque' ChisZ: C,N *ceke*

CE#011 pOM ***cehkš** *(vt) 'rasguñar/to scratch'* NHM: *cehkš* 'pellizcar, pellizco' SHM: Tu <*cæhkš, mẓehkšʸpʸ*> 'arañar' MM: 'rasguñar' Ju <*cæhkš*> Ma <*cæhš*> Ja <*cæhš, čehšʸpʸ*> Pu <*cæhkš*> 'arañar' At <*cæhkš, čehkšʸpʸ*> 'rasguñar', <*cæhkš*> 'arañar' Ct <*cæhkš, čehkšʸpʸ*> Ca <*cækš*> '=arañar' LM: Cn <*cekš*> 'rascar; desgarrar; pellizcar' SJ *cekš* 'to scratch, claw' Gu <*cekš, čekšʸp*> 'rasguñar'

CE#012 pOM ***yak-cehkš** *(vt) 'pellizcar a alguien/to pinch somebody'* NHM: *yakcehkš* LM: Cn <*yahcekš*> (vt) 'arañar'

CE#013 pOM ***ce?kš** *(vt) 'rajar leña/to cleave wood'* MM: Ju <*cæ?kš*> LM: Cn <*ce"kš*> (vt) 'rajar en trozos chicos' (p.ej., leña)' SJ *ce?kš* Gu <*ce?š, če?šʸp*> Ca <*cæ?kš*>

CE#014 pZ ***cem** *(n) 'orina/urine'* [pGZ *cem] SoZ: *cem* AyZ: *[cem]* ChisZ: C,N *cem* NE *cep* ChZ: *cem*

CE#015 pZ ***cem** *(vi) 'orinar/to urinate'* TxZ: *cem* ChisZ: C,N,NE *cem*

CE#016 pGZ ***cen** *(vt) 'amarrar/to tie'* SoZ: *cen* (vt) AyZ: *[cen]* TxZ: *cen* (vt, vi-p)

CE#017 pMZ ***ce:?n** *(vt) 'abrazar/to embrace'* NHM: *ce:?n* 'abrazar, abrazo, llevar (p.ej., un niño)' SHM: Tu <*cæ:n, če?mpʸ*> 'abrazar (bebé, persona grande)' Tp <*cæ:n, če?mpʸ, nzǽ?nɨc, čæ:nǽmpʸ*> 'abrazar (bebé)' MM: 'abrazar (bebé)' Ma <*cæ?n?ít, cæ?n?óyɨ*> 'abrazar (persona grande)', <*cæ?n̄?it*> 'abrazar (bebé)' Ja <*cæ:n, čæ!n̄, če?n?íhtʸpʸ*> Pu <*cæ!nɨ"k*> Ju,At,Ct <*cæ:n*> LM: Cn <*ce·n*> (vt) Gu <*ce:n, ce!mp*> 'abrazar (bebé)' [Nordell 1990 and p.c.] LM: SJ *ce·n ~ ce:n* 'to pick up in the arms' OlP: *ce:n* (vi) 'apadrinar un bautiza, ser padrino de un bautismo' (vt) 'bautizarlo' SaP: *če?n* (vi, vt) 'seek, look for' TxZ: *ce?nu?k* (vt, vi-p) 'cerrar de monte, amarrar (casa), atrancar (con amarra)'

CE#018 pOM ***ce?(n)k** *(n) 'musgo/moss'* NHM: *ce"k* '=heno' MM: Ju,At *cæ"ŋk* Ma,Ct *cæ?mk, ce?ŋk* Ja *cæ?mk* Pu *cæ!mk*

CE#019 pMZ ***ce?s** *(n) 'granero para maíz/corn granary'* [pM **ce?š* > pOM **ce?š*; pZ **ce?s* 'bed' > pGZ **ce?s*. SaP reintroduced the item or the meaning of the item by borrowing from Zoquean.] NHM: *ce?š* 'granero para maíz, troje, coscomate' MM: 'coscomate, troje' Ju *cæ?š* Ma *cæ?š, cæ?š̄* [sic!] Ja *cæ!š̄* At *cæ?š̄, cæ?š* [sic!] Ct *cæ?š̄, cæ!š* [sic!] LM: Cn <*ce"š*> 'coscomate' Ca *cæ"š* Gu *ce!š̄* 'troje, coscomate' SaP: *če?š* 'cama' SoZ: *ce?es* 'cama' AyZ: *[ce?s]* 'cama' TxZ: *ce:?s* 'cama' *bok-ĉe:?s* 'coscomate, troje' *ĉap-ĉe:?s* 'tapanco' ChisZ: C [Te] <*tzees*> 'balsa de maderos / pesebre', <*enguitzees*> 'cama, lecho para dormir', <*pacuytsees*> 'presa de rio' N *ce?s* 'cama'

CE#020 pM [Veracruz] ***cet** *(vi) 'ampollarse/to become bruised'* OlP: **cet* [*kɨ?-cet-* (vi) 'ampollarse (la mano)'] SaP: *čet* (vi) 'get bruised (fruit)'

CE#021 pOM ***ce?t ~ ce"t** *(vi) 'reventar (fruta)/to squash, crush'* MM: Ju <*cæ"t, cæ?t*> Ma <*cæ?tp*> Ja <*cæ?tp, cæ"dá·m̄p*> Ct <*cæ?tp, cæ"dám̄p*> Ca <*cæ?tp*> LM: Cn <*ce?t ~ ce"t*> (vi) 'magullarse' SJ *ce?t ~ ce"t* 'to squash, crush (fruit, eye, etc.)' Gu <*ce"t, ce?t, ce?p, ce"dá·m̄p*>

CE#022 pOM ***teky-ce:t** *(n) 'pantorilla/calf of the leg'* MM: Ja *tekʸčæ:t* LM: Cn <*tekyče:t*> '=músculo de la pierna' Gu *tekʸčé:t*

CE#023 pMZ ***ce:wE(kV?)** *'pollo, gallina/chicken, hen'* [pM *ce:wE; pOM *ce:wy 'chicken, hen'; pZ *ceŋ-ke 'one who pricks' [?]. The set is speculative and should perhaps be split into two sets, one headed by pOM *ce:wy and one by pGZ *ceŋ 'to prick'; the ChisZ-NE would then be left out.] NHM: cE:v MM: Ma ce:y 'pollo' Pu ce:y 'gallina' LM: 'gallina' Cn <cey> 'gallina' Ca ce:y 'gallina' SJ ce·y 'chicken' Gu ce:y SoZ: ceŋ 'punzar' TxZ: ceŋ (vt) 'punzar' ChisZ: NE ceŋge 'gallo'

CE#024 pOM ***ná"w-ce:wy** *'gallo/cock'* NHM: na"cE:v MM: Ma ce:nʸá"f ~ ce:nʸá"Φ ~ ce:nʸá"w̥ Ja ce:nʸá" Ct ce:nʸá"f ~ ce:nʸá"Φ ~ ce:nʸá"w̥ LM: Ca ce:nʸi̠?á: Gu ce:nʸi̠?á:

Ci̠#001 pM ***ci̠?** *(n) 'hermana mayor, tía/elder sister, aunt'* NHM: ci̠" 'hermana mayor, media hermana mayor' Hu ci̠"c 'older sister' [Foster 1949] [?] SHM: Tl ci̠? 'hermana del hombre y de la mujer' Ay ci̠? [Wichmann 1990], cu [Foster 1949] MM: 'hermana mayor' Ju,Ma,Ja,At,Ct ci̠" LM: Cn <ci̠?> 'hermana mayor, prima mayor, tía (pariente consanguínea de mayor edad' Ca ci̠" 'hermano mayor' Gu ci̠" 'hermano mayor' OIP: ci̠?i̠ 'mother' [Foster 1949]; ci̠? mamá SaP: ci̠? 'hermana mayor, tía', ci̠?kópak 'la hermana mas mayor'

Ci̠#002 pOM ***ci̠hc** *(n) 'ardilla chica y gris/small and gray squirrel'* NHM: ci̠hc 'ardilla, hurón, moto' SHM: Mi ci̠hc 'ardilla chica y gris (de bosque o montaña)' MM: Ma,Ja,At ci̠hc Pu ci̠hc 'ardilla grande (?) y gris'

Ci̠#003 pZ ***ci̠ci̠** *(n) 'hermana mayor, tía/elder sister, aunt'* [pZ *ci̠:c] SoZ: ci̠:ci̠ 'elder sister, aunt' [Foster 1949], ci̠:ci̠? 'tía' [Gutiérrez M. 1993] AyZ: [ci̠:ci̠] TxZ: ci̠:c 'tía, hermana mayor' ChisZ: C [Te] di̠c 'aunt' [Foster 1949] N,NE ci̠ci̠ ChZ: StaMaCh ci̠ci̠ ['tia' only in Foster 1949] SaMiCh ci̠ci̠

Ci̠#004 pZ ***ci̠k** *(vt) 'agarrar/to grasp'* SaP: ci̠k (vi, vt) 'touch' [Zo loan] SoZ: ci̠k 'grasp, touch' [Foster and Foster 1948] AyZ: [ci̠k] 'curar' TxZ: ci̠k (vt, vi-p) 'tocar, tentar' ChisZ: C ci̠hk (vt) 'hacerlo; construirlo' N: ci̠hk (vt) 'hacerlo; creerlo' ChZ: ci̠k 'hacer'

Ci̠#005 pZ ***ci̠k-i** *(n) 'obra, hecho; dibujo, diseño/work (drawing, handicraft)'* ChisZ: C ci̠ki NE ci̠ki 'diseño' ChZ: ci̠ki 'hecho'

Cɨ#006 pZ ***ko-cɨk** *(n) 'cerro/mountain'* [pZ **kocɨk*] SoZ: *kócɨk* 'mountain' [Foster and Foster 1948], *ko:cɨk* [Wonderly 1949] TxZ: *kocɨk* '=loma, sierra' ChisZ: C *kocɨk* 'cerro, peña' N [Ma] *kocɨk* [Wonderly 1949] [FL] *kocɨk* NE [Tapalapa, Ocotepec, Pantepec] *kocɨhk* [Wonderly 1949] [Ra] *kocɨhk* 'cerro, peña' S [Tu] *kocɨk* [Wonderly 1949]

Cɨ#007 pM ***cɨkɨk** *(n) 'palo mulato/copal tree'* [pM **cɨkɨk* > pOM **cɨkk*; a pGZ reconstruction, **cɨ?k* is possible in itself but does not match phonologically. The tree is confined to a lowland environment —notice the lacking NHM cognate.] MM: Ma *cɨk* '=cocuite, madre-cacao' Ja *cɨk* 'cocuite, madrecacao' Pu *cɨk* '=cocuite, madrecacao' At *cɨk* 'cocuite, madrecacao', *cɨkképʸ* 'palo mulato' Ct *cɨk* LM: Cn <*cɨk kɨpy*> 'nanchicacao, papelillo, árbol de copal [Ximenia americana]' SJ *cɨk* 'a kind of tree' Gu *cɨk* OIP: *cɨkɨ'k*; *cɨkɨkuyɨ* 'palo de mulato' SaP: *cɨgɨ:k* 'mulato' [length unexpected] SoZ: *cɨ?k* [?] AyZ: *[cɨ?kuy]* TxZ: *cɨ?kuy* [?]

Cɨ#008 pM ***cɨ?k-?ɨy** *(vi) 'miedo, tener/to be afraid'* NHM: *cɨ?ki* ~*cɨ"ga* 'temer, asustarse' SHM: Tl *cɨ"kɨ* 'temer' MM: Ma <*cɨ?k?ɨpʸ, kæh mẕɨ"gɨ*> 'temer, tener miedo', <*cɨ?k?ɨpʸ*> 'tiene miedo' Ja <*cɨ"gɨ, cɨ?k?ɨy, cɨ?kɨp*> _'temer, tener miedo', <*cɨ?k?ɨpʸ*> 'tiene miedo' At <*cɨ?kɨp, kʸæh mẕɨ"gɨ*> 'temer, tener miedo', <*cɨ"gɨ, cɨ?k?ɨpʸ*> 'tiene miedo' Pu <*cɨ!k?ɨpʸ*> 'tiene miedo' Ct <*cɨ"gɨ, cɨ?k?ɨpʸ*> 'temer, tener miedo', <*cɨ?k?ɨpʸ*> 'tiene miedo' LM: Gu <*cɨ"gǐ:pʸ*> 'tiene miedo', <*cɨ"gǐ"w, cɨ"gǐ·y, cɨ"gǐ:pʸ*> 'temer, tener miedo' OIP: *yakcɨ?ki:* (vt) 'espantarlo' TxZ: *cɨ:ŋkɨ?y* (vt, vi-p) 'espantar, ahuyentar' [?]

Cɨ#009 pOM ***?a-cɨ?k-?ɨy** *'espantar/to fear'* NHM: *?acɨ?ki* ~ *?acɨ"ga* '=asustar' SHM: Tl *?acɨ"kɨ* Tp <*?Aẕɨ"gɨ*> 'asustar' MM: Ju <*?æẕɨ"gɨ, ?æẕɨ?kɨp*> '=asustar' [sic!] Ma <*?aẕɨ"gɨ*> 'espantar', <*?iẕɨ"gɨ*> 'amenazar, asustar' [sic!] Ja <*?aẕɨ"gɨ, y?aẕɨ?kɨp*> '=amenazar, asustar' Pu <*?iẕɨ"gɨ*> 'asustar', <*y?iẕɨ!k?ɨpʸ*> 'amenazar', <*?aẕɨ"gɨ, m?aẕɨ!kɨpʸ*> 'espantar' [sic!] At <*?æẕɨ"gɨ*> '=asustar' Ct <*?aẕɨ"gɨ, y?aẕɨ?k?ɨpʸ*> 'amenazar, espantar', <*?a·ẕɨ"gɨ*> 'asustar' [sic!] LM: Ca <*?aẕɨgɨ"*> 'asustar', <*?a·ẕig*ɨ"*> 'espantar' [sic!] SJ <*cɨgɨ·y~cɨgɨ"y*> 'to be afraid' Gu <*?aẕɨ"gǐ"w*> '=espantar'

Cɨ#010 pOM ***cɨ?kɨ** *(n) 'susto, espanto/fear'* NHM: *cɨ"ga* 'espanto, miedo, temor, susto' SHM: Tm *cɨ?ka* MM: Ju,Ma,Ja,At,Ct *cɨ"gɨ* LM: Ca *cɨgɨ"wæ* Gu *cɨ"gɨ'''* 'espanto', *cɨ!gɨ'''* 'susto' [sic!]

Cɨ#011 pOM ***ku-cɨ?k-a** *(n) 'peligroso, riesgo/danger'* NHM: *kucɨ"ga* MM: Ma,Pu,Ct *kɨzɨ"gɨ* Ju,Ja,At *kuzɨ"gɨ*

Cɨ#012 pM ***cɨ?kš** *(vi) 'apretar/to become tight'* NHM: *cɨ?kš* LM: SJ *cɨ·kš* 'to break open (egg, head, squash, melon, etc.)' SaP: *cɨ?kš* (vi) 'get tight'

Cɨ#013 pM ***yak-cɨ?kš** *(vt) 'apretar/to tighten'* NHM: *yakcɨ?kš* (vt) 'apretar algo' SaP: *?akcɨ?kš* (vt) 'apretar'

Cɨ#014 pMZ ***cɨm** *(vt) 'cargar en la espalda/to carry on the back'* NHM: *cɨ:hmɨk* 'cargar (p.ej., llevar un bulto en la espalda)' Tu <*cɨm, mẕimpʸ*> 'cargar' SHM: Tp <*cɨm, cɨmɨ"k, čimpʸ, mẕimpʸ, čɨ:m, tAm tcimʸ, čɨmæmpʸ*> 'cargar' MM: 'cargar' Cc <*cɨm*> Ju <*cɨm*> Ja <*cɨm, čɨ·m, nicɨm, nʸicé·mpʸ*> At <*cɨm*> LM: Ca <*cɨm*> 'cargar' SJ *(ni")ẕɨ·m ~ (ni")ẕɨm* 'to haul' Gu <*cɨm, cɨ·mp*> [Nordell 1990 and p.c.] OlP: *cɨm* (vt) 'cargarlo (en la espalda)' SaP: *cɨm* (vi, vt) 'hold down, bear' TxZ: *cɨm* (vt) 'cargar (en la espalda)' ChisZ: C *cɨm* (vt) N *cɨm* (vt) 'cargarlo (en la espalda)' NE *cɨm* (vt) 'cargarlo'

Cɨ#015 pOM ***pa-cɨhm ~ pa-cɨm** *(vt) 'cargar/to carry'* NHM: *pacɨ:m ~ pacɨ:hm ~ pacɨm* 'cargar (p.ej., leña)' MM: Cc <*pAẕɨm, cɨm, pʸAẕɨ:mpʸ, pʸAẕɨ:m, tɨ: tpAẕɨmʸ, kʸæh tpAẕɨ:mʸ*> Ma <*pacɨm*> '=meter (tapos, etc.)' Pu <*pacɨm*> 'meter (tapos, etc.)', *pa·ẕɨm* 'cargar' [sic!] At <*pæcɨm*> Ct <*pa:ẕɨm*>

Cɨ#016 pMZ ***cɨm-i** *(n) 'carga/load'* [pM **cɨmi* > pOM **cɨmy*; pZ **cɨmi* > pGZ **cɨ:mi*] NHM: *cɨm* '=tercio' SHM: Tu,Tp *cɨmʸ* Ay *cɨmʸ* MM: Ju *cemʸ* '=tercio', *cemʸ* 'bulto' [sic!] Cc *cɨmʸ* Ma,Ja,Pu,At,Ct *cemʸ* '=tercio, bulto' LM: Ml <*cemy*> Ca *cɨ́ʸmʸ* 'tercio' SJ *cɨmy* Cn <*cɨmy*> Gu *cɨmʸ* '=bulto, tercio' OlP: *cɨmi* SaP: *cɨm* SoZ: *cɨ:mi* TxZ: *cɨ:m* '=tercio, bulto' ChisZ: C *cɨmi* '=bulto' N,NE *cɨmi* S *[cɨ·mí?]*

Cɨ#017 pOM ***cɨ?m-n** *(n) 'mecapal/tumpline'* NHM: *cɨ?mɨn* SHM: Tl *cɨ:?m* MM: Ju *cɨ"mn̥* Ma,At *cɨ!mn̥* Ja *cɨ!mn̥, cɨ!mk* Pu *cɨ!mt* Ct *cɨ?mn̥* LM: Ca *cɨ"mt* Gu *cɨ!mẕá:y*

Cɨ#018 pZ **cɨmis** *(n) 'mecapal/tumpline'* [pGZ *cɨːmiš*] SaP *cɨmiš* 'mecate' [Zo loan] SoZ: *cɨːmiš* TxZ *cɨːmeš* 'mecapal'

Cɨ#019 pMZ **nam-cɨm(-i)** *(n) 'collar, gargantilla/necklace'* [pM *namcɨ(h)m* > pOM *namcɨm* (with an assimilated nasal in all but NHM); pZ *namcɨmi* (with assimilated nasal)] NHM: *namcɨm* '=rosario' SHM: 'collar' Tl *nancɨm* '=gargantilla' Tu *nanzɨ̄m* Tp *nAnzɨ́m* Mi *nanzɨ̄m* MM: 'collar' Ju *naːnzɨ́m* Cc *nAnzɨ́m* Ma *na·nzɨ̄m, naːnzɨ̄m* Ja,Pu *naːnzɨ̄m* At *nanzɨ́m* Ct *na·nzɨ̄m* LM: Cn <*nandzɨm*> 'collar' Ca *naːncɨ̄m* Gu *namzɨ̄m* 'collar' OlP: *namcɨmɨ* '=soguilla' TxP: *daŋcuŋ* 'collar, cadena, soguilla' [?] ChisZ: C *nanzɨmi* N *nanzɨmi* 'gargantilla'

Cɨ#020 pOM **cɨmahm ~ cɨmam** *(vi) 'brillar (oro, joyas, etc.)/to shine (gold, precious stones, etc)'* SHM: Tp <*cɨmámp*> MM: Cc <*cɨmámp*> Ma <*cɨmá·m̄p, cɨmammámp*> Ja <*cɨmá·m̄p*> At <*cɨmá·m̄p, kʸœh čʸɨmǽm̄ʸ*>

Cɨ#021 pMZ **cɨːnay** *(vi) 'sentarse/to sit down'* [pM *cɨːna(?)* > pOM *cɨːnay* (adopted in different ways to the morphological system); pZ *cɨnay*] NHM: <*cïːnʸi ~ cïːna*> (irreg) 'sentar' Tl *cɨːnɨ* 'sentarse', *cɨnaːpy* 'sentado'; *cɨnaːpy ?ɨc* 'vivo' MM: 'vivir en un lugar' Ma <*cɨnǽːpʸ, maː čɨ́ːnɨ*> Ja <*cɨnǽːpʸ, maː čɨ́ːnɨ*> Pu <*cɨnǽːpʸ, šim̄ čɨ́ːnɨ*> At <*cɨnǽːpʸ, ši: čɨ́ːnɨ*> Ct <*cɨnǽːpʸ, ši: čɨ́ːnɨ*> LM: Gu <*cɨnaꞌꞌw, cɨná·pʸ, cɨná·ȳ, maː čɨnáꞌꞌy*> '=vivir' [Nordell 1990 and p.c.] SaP: *cɨːna* 'sientate!'; *cɨːndá?k* 'sentar a otro' [Clark and Clark 1960] ChZ: *cɨnay* 'sentarse' [cf. also *cɨn* 'sentarse', *cɨnayyɨ* 'sentado']

Cɨ#022 pM **?aw-cɨːnay** *(vi) 'esperar/to wait'* NHM: < *?acïːnyip ~ ?acïːna*> (irreg) 'esperar (cuando se está sentado)' SaP: *?acɨːna* [Clark and Clark 1960]

Cɨ#023 pOM **win-cɨn** *(n) 'patrón/master, boss, host'* NHM: *vincɨn* '=amo, jefe, dueño' MM: Ju *wiːnzɨ́n* Ma *hɨnzɨ́n* '=dueño (pos), maestro, jefe' Ja *winzɨ̄n* '= jefe, dueño, maestro' Pu *winzɨ̄n* '=maestro, dueño', *winzɨ́h* 'jefe' At *hɨnzɨ́n, hɨnzɨ́ːn* '=maestro, dueño, jefe' Ct *hɨnzɨ̄n* '=maestro, dueño (pos), jefe' LM: Gu *wiːnzɨ̄n* '=jefe, dueño (pos)'

Cɨ#024 pOM ***win-cɨʔkɨ-n** *(n) 'respeto/respect'* NHM: *vincɨ"ga* 'tímido' MM: Ju *wincɨʔkɨn* Ma *hɨnzɨʔkʔɨnʸ* Ja *winzɨʔkɨn* At *hɨnzɨʔkɨn* Ct *hɨnzɨʔkʔɨnʸ* LM: Gu *wi:ŋguzɨ"gɨ̃lnʸɨ̃ʸ*

Cɨ#025 pMZ ***cɨpʔV** *(n) 'quelite/edible green'* [pM *cɨʔpi > pOM *cɨ"py; pZ *cɨpɨ > pGZ *cɨ:pɨʔ] NHM: *cɨ̃"p* 'quelite, nombre genérico de hierbas comestibles' SHM: Tl *cɨʔipʸ* LM: Gu *cɨ̃"pʸ* [Nordell, p.c.] OlP: *cɨʔpi* SaP: *cɨʔp* SoZ: *cɨ:pɨʔ* TxP: *bo:ncɨ:pɨʔ* 'palo de quelite' ChisZ: C *cɨpɨ* N *cɨpɨ* 'hierba que se come' NE *cɨbɨ* S *[cɨ·pɨʔ]*

Cɨ#026 pZ ***cɨsi** *(n) 'hijo, hija/son, daughter'* [pGZ *cɨ:ši] SoZ: *cɨ:ši* ChisZ: C [Te] <*tzasi*> 'muchacho', <*yomtzasi*> 'muchacha', <*tzasi acuy*> 'niñez' N *cɨsi* 'mozo; esclavo' ChZ: *cɨsyi*; *yomacɨsyi* 'daughter' [Foster 1949]; *cɨsi* [Knudson 1980]

Cɨ#027 pGZ ***cɨ:wi** *(n) 'tabaco/tobacco'* SoZ: *cɨ:wi* AyZ: [*cɨ:gʷi*] '=cigarro' TxZ: *cɨ:w* tabaco

Cɨ#028 pZ ***cɨy** *(vi) 'cargar en la cabeza/to carry on head'* SaP: *kucɨy* 'carry on head' [Zo loan] SoZ: *cɨy* 'carry (on head in a basket)' [Foster and Foster 1948] TxZ: *cɨy* (vt) 'cargar en la cabeza'

Cɨ#029 pZ ***cɨʔy** *(vi) 'quedarse/to remain'* SoZ: *cɨʔy* 'remain' [Foster and Foster 1948] AyZ: [*cɨʔy*] TxZ: *cɨʔy* (vi) 'quedarse' ChisZ: C *cɨʔy* (vi) 'quedarse; tardarse' N *cɨʔy* (vi) 'quedarse; sobrarse' NE *cɨʔy* (vi) 'quedarse, quedar'

Cɨ#030 pOM ***cɨhy** *(n) 'liquidámbar/sweetgum [Liquidambar styraciflua]'* NHM: *cɨ̃:h* '=yagabito' MM: Ju *cɨhn̥ʸ* [?] Ma *cɨ:y* Pu,At *cɨ:y* LM: Cn <*cɨy*> 'palo volador (la trementina de este palo se usa como copal en ciertas fiestas)' Ca,Mz *cɨ:y* Gu *cɨ̃:nʸ* [?]

CA#001 pMZ ***ca:ʔ** *(n) 'piedra/stone'* [pM, pOM *ca:ʔ; pZ, pGZ *caʔ] NHM: *ca:* '=roca' SHM: Tl *co:* Ay *ca:h* MM: Ma,Ja,Pu,At,Ct *ca:* LM: Cn <*ca:*> Gu *ca:* TaM: *čé* [transcription of Wonderly 1949] OlP: *ca:hɨ* '=roca' SaP: *caʔ* SoZ: *caʔ* AyZ: *caʔ* '=metate' TxZ: *caʔ* '=bala, metate, frente' ChisZ: C,N,NE,S *caʔ* ChZ: *caʔ*

CA#002 pZ ***ʔoko-caʔ** *(n) 'tenamaste/the configuration of three hearthstones for supporting pots over fire'* SoZ: *ʔo:kcaʔ* TxZ: *ʔokcaʔ* ChisZ: C *ʔokocaʔ* N *ʔokča* 'fogón' NE *ʔokcaʔ*

CA#003 pOM ***hɨːn-ca:?** *(n) 'pedernal/flint'* NHM: *hɨnca:* MM: Ju, Ma,Ja,At *hɨːnẓá:* Ct *hɨ·nẓá:* LM: Ca *hɨːnẓá:* Gu *hɨ̈ːnẓá:*

CA#004 pZ ***win-pak-ca?** *(n) 'frente/forehead'* TxZ: *weñpakca?* ChisZ: C,NE *winbakca?* N *winbakca*

CA#005 pM ***ca:hc** *(n) 'maguey/century plant'* [pOM **ca:hc*] [The name 'aloe' found as gloss in the MM and LM lexical collections of N. Nordell is Latin and refers to the well-known medicinal herb which is known in Spanish as 'sábila'. It looks like an agave but was introduced by the Spaniards.] NHM: *ca:c* [Agave atrovirens spp. (G. Martin, p.c.)] SHM: Tl *co:hc* Ay *ca:hc* MM: 'aloe' Ju *cæc* Ja *ca·s̄k* [?] Ma,At *ca·c̄* Ct *ca·cm̦* [?] LM: Cn <*ca:c*> '[Agave spp.]' SJ *cac* Ca *ca:c* 'aloe' Gu *ca·c̄* 'aloe' SaP: *ca:hc* 'ixtle'

CA#006 pZ ***cac** *(vi) 'rajarse/to crack'* TxZ: *cac* (vt) 'rajar' (fruta) (vi) 'partirse' ChisZ: C *cahc* (vi) 'desgajarse; rajarse' [derivative: *caca* 'rajadura'] (vt) 'desgajarlo, rajarlo' N *cahc* (vi) 'rajarse' (vt) 'rajarlo (en la horcadura de un árbol)' NE *cahc* (vi) 'rajarse (como el talón del pie)'

CA#007 pOM ***cušk-cač** *(n) 'moscón/a kind of big fly'* SHM: Ay *ceč* MM: Ju,Ma *cuškcǽč* Ja *cuščæč̄* Pu *cuškcác̄* At *cuškcác̄, cuškcá·c̄* Ct *cuškcǽč̄* LM: Ca *cu·č* Gu *cuščác̄*

CA#008 pOM ***ca:cy** *(n) 'cruel/cruel'* NHM: *ca:čtʊːn ~ ca:čtʊːhn ~ ca:čtʊn* 'castigar, martirizar, escarnecer', *ca:či ~ ca:ča* 'lastimar, herir (p.ej., un golpe contundente), *ca:ča* 'herida, lastimadura' Tp *cečłʔún* 'castigar' Cc *cA:čłʔún* 'castigar' At *ca:čłʔún* 'castigar' Ju *ca:č* 'cruel' LM: Ca *ca:č* 'cruel'

CA#009 pM ***caci** *(n) 'mosca/fly'* [pOM **cacy*] NHM: *cač* [Musca domestica] SHM: Tl,Ay *cač* MM: Ma,Ja,Ct *cæč̄* Pu *cač̄* At *cač̄, ca·č̄* LM: Cn <*cač̄*> 'mosca azúl, moscón [order: Diptera, Phaenicia spp.]' SJ,Gu,Ca *cač̄* OlP: *cači* ChZ: *cuẓasus* [?]

CA#010 pOM ***cahwak** *(adv) 'boca arriba/upwards'* NHM: *cahvák* SHM: Tp *cAhβák* MM: Cc *cAhwák*

CA#011 pZ ***cah** *(vt) 'pegar/to stick'* SoZ: *cah* 'mix, stick together' [Foster and Foster 1948] ChisZ: N *cah* (vi) 'cuajarse' (vt) 'pegarlo; soldarlo' NE *cah* (vt) 'pegarlo (con pegamento); embarrarlo'

CA#012 pZ **cahin** *(n) 'culebra/snake'* [pGZ *ca:ñ*] SoZ: *ca:ñ* 'víbora' AyZ: *[ca:ñu ~ ca:ño]* TxZ: *ca:ñ* '=víbora' ChisZ: C *can* '=gusano' N *can* '=gusano, lombriz' NE *cat* '=serpiente' S *[can]* ChZ: StMaCh *cahin* SnMiCh *cahin* [Wonderly 1949]

CA#013 pZ **mɨʔah-cahin** *(n) 'mazacoate/boa constrictor'* TxZ: *bɨʔ-ca:ñ* 'tatuana, mazacoate' ChisZ: C *mɨʔahcan* 'boa (serpiente)'

CA#014 pZ **nɨʔ-cahin** *(n) 'culebra de agua/garter snake'* TxZ: *dɨ:ca:ñ* 'anguila' ChisZ: C *nɨʔɨcan* '=culebra arroyera' N *nɨcan* 'arroyera—drymarchon sp.' NE *nɨʔɨcat*

CA#015 pMZ **cak** *(vt) 'dejar/to leave'* OIP: *cak* (vt) 'mandarlo; tirarlo' SaP: *cak* (vi, vt) SoZ: *cak* AyZ: *[cak]* (vt) TxZ: *cak* (vt) '=dejar de, poner' ChisZ: C,NE *cahk* (vt) N *cahk* (vt) '=mudar (ropa)' ChZ: *cak*

CA#016 pZ **cam** *(vt) 'decir/to say'* ChisZ: C *cam* (vt) N *cam* (vt) '=contarlo' NE [Ra] *cam* (vt) [Chapultenango] *cam* [Wonderly 1949] ChZ: StaMaCh *cam* 'contar (narrar)' SnMiCh *cam*

CA#017 pZ **cam-cam-nay** *(vi) 'conversar, platicar/to converse, chat'* ChisZ: C *camʐamnay* N *camʐamney* NE *camdʐamnay* ChZ: *camcamnay*

CA#018 pZ **cam-e** *(n) 'palabra, dicho/word, saying'* ChisZ: C *came* N *came* 'cuento, algo que no es cierto' NE *came* ChZ: *came* 'palabra'

CA#019 pMZ **ca:mʔ** *(vi) 'madurar/to ripen, grow'* NHM: *ca:m ~ ca"m* SHM: Tl <*co"mp*> MM: 'madurar(se)' Ma <*ca·m̄p, ca·m̄ʔóʔkp, ca"mámp*> Pu <*ca·m̄p, ca"má·m̄p*> Ct <*ca·m̄p, ca"mámp*> LM: Cn <*ca·m ~ caʔm*> Gu <*ca·m̄, ca·m̄p, ca"má·m̄p*> OIP: *cam* (vi) 'madurarse (una fruta); engordarse (un animal o una persona)' SaP: *cam ~ caʔm* (vi) SoZ: *cam* 'grow' [Wonderly 1949] AyZ: *[cam]* 'crecerse (niño)' TxZ: *cam* (vi) 'crecer (árbol, niño), estar sazón, estar adulto' ChisZ: N *cam* (vi) 'madurarse; endurecerse' NE *cam* (vi-s) 'estar anciano o viejo, es anciano o viejo (como gente o animal)'

CA#020 pM **ca:mʔ** *(adj) 'maduro/ripe'* NHM: *ca"m* '=plátano' MM: Ju,Ma,Ja,Pu,At,Ct *ca"m* '=plátano' LM: Cn <*caʔm*> (adj) 'maduro; gordo' Ca *ca"m* 'plátano' Gu *ca"m* OlP: *ca?a'm* 'gordo' SaP: *cá?mik* 'maduro'

*CA#021 pOM *ku-ca"m (n) 'calvo, pelón/bald'* NHM: *kuca"m* SHM: Tu *kucá"m* Mi *kocá"m* MM: Ma *kɨcá"m* LM: Ca *kucá"m*

*CA#022 pZ *cam-u [?] (adj, n) 'anciano/old person'* [Might be from 'ripen', but may equally be derived from the verb for 'to speak', which in its turn may be identical with 'ripen'.] ChisZ: C *camu* (adj) 'viejo; macizo' *camupɨn* 'anciano', *camuyomo* 'anciana' N *cambɨn* 'anciano, hombre adulto'; *camyomo* 'mujer adulta' NE *camubɨ* (adj, n) 'anciano, viejo—como gente o animal' ChZ: *camɨ?* 'persona viejo'

*CA#023 pOM *ca:m-k (n) 'mojarra/cichlid'* MM: Ma,Ja,Pu,At,Ct *ca·m̄k* LM: Cn <*ca:m*> Gu *cá·m̄k*

*CA#024 pMZ *camam (n) 'quelite blanco/a kind of edible green [probably Chenopodium (G. Martin, p.c.)]'* [pM *camam > pOM *camm; pZ *camam > pGZ *ca:mam] NHM: *cámɨn* 'alache, quelite de espiga, quintonil [Amaranthus hypocondricus]' OlP: *cama'm* 'quelite blanco' SoZ: *cá:mam* 'quelite blanco' [Gutiérrez M. 1993] TxZ: *ca:?ma?* 'quelite blanco' [?]

*CA#025 pMZ *can-can (adj) 'tener olor repugnante de pescado/to have a bad smell of fish'* [pM *cahncan > pOM *ca:ncn; pZ, pGZ *cancan] NHM: *ca:ncɨn* 'olor repugnante que deja el huevo tibio en un recipiente' MM: 'olor de pescado, huevos, etc.' Ma *ca·nc* Ja,Ct *ca·n̄c* Pu,At *ca:nc* LM: Gu *ca:nc* 'olor de pescado, huevos, etc.' OlP: *canca'n* (adj) 'con olor de pescado' SoZ: *cancan* 'choguijoso, tiene mal olor de marisco' AyZ: *[cancan]* 'oler de pescado' TxZ: *cancan* (adj) 'apestar a marisco' ChisZ: N *can* (vi) 'oler (pescado, manteca, agua estancada)' [?-a product of de-reduplication]

*CA#026 pM *ca(:?)nay (n) 'culebra/snake'* [pOM *ca:?ny] NHM: *ca:?n* '=víbora, serpiente; lombriz; tripa' SHM: Tl *co:?nʸ* Ay *ca?y* MM: Ju *ca"nʸ* '=víbora' Ma *ca?n̄ʸ* 'víbora, culebra', *ca?nʸ* 'culebra' [sic!] Ja *ca!n̄ʸ* 'víbora, culebra', *ca!nʸ* 'culebra' [sic!] Pu *ca!n̄ʸ* 'víbora, culebra', *ca!nʸ* 'culebra' [sic!] At *cæ?n̄ʸ* 'víbora, culebra', *cæ?nʸ* 'culebra' [sic!] Ct *ca?n̄ʸ* 'víbora, culebra', *ca!nʸ* 'culebra' [sic!] LM: Cn <*ca?ñ*> '=serpiente (genérico)' SJ *ca"ny* Ca *ca"nʸ* 'víbora, culebra', *cæ"nʸ* 'culebra' [sic!], *ca?añ* [Wonderly 1949] Gu *ca!n̄ʸtʸ* '=víbora' OlP: *cana'y* '=víbora' SaP: *cánay*

CA#027 pM ***ʔa:ʔc-a ca(:ʔ)nay** *(n) 'bejuquilla/vine snake'* [pOM
*ʔa:ʔca ca:ʔny] NHM: *šu:m ʔa:ʔc ca:ʔn* 'bejuquilla parda, bejuquilla
verde [Oxybelis acuminatus, O. fulgidus]' LM: Cn <*šu:mʔa:dz*>
'bejuquillo [probably Oxybelis spp.]' OIP: *ʔa:cacana'y* 'bejuquillo'

CA#028 pM ***haycuʔ-ca(:ʔ)nay** *(n) 'tatuana/boa constrictor'* [pOM
*ha.ycuʔ ca:ʔny] [Mesoamerican semantics] NHM: *ha:č ca:ʔn* 'tatuana, boa, mazacoatl [Constrictor constrictor]' MM: Ju *hæǰu"ʒáʔnʸ*
Ma *hiǰu"ʒáʔnʸ* 'boa', *hiǰu"ʒá!nʸ* 'mazacoate' [sic!] Ja *haǰu"ʒá!nʸ*
'boa', *haǰu"ʒá!nʸ* 'mazacoate' [sic!] Pu *hiǰu"ʒáʔnʸ* 'boa', *hiǰu-
"ʒá!nʸ* 'mazacoate' [sic!] At *hæǰu"ʒǽʔnʸ* 'boa', *haǰu"ʒǽʔnʸ* 'mazacoate' [sic!] Ct *hiǰu"ʒáʔnʸ* 'mazacoate' LM: Cn <*haycuʔcaʔñ*>
'[Boa constrictor]' Gu *haǰú"* OIP: *haycíʔ* 'anciana', *haycuʔcana'y*

CA#029 pM ***nɨ:ʔ-ca(:ʔ)nay** *(n) 'culebra de agua/garter snake'* [pOM
*nɨ:ʔca:ʔny] MM: 'anguila' Ma *nɨ:ʒǽʔnʸ* Ja *nɨ:ʒá!nʸtʸ* Pu, At,Ct
nɨ:ʒáʔnʸ LM: Cn <*nɨ:caʔñ*> 'anguila' Gu *nɨdo:kʸčá!nʸtʸ* 'anguila'
OIP: *nɨ:cana'y* SaP: *nɨʔcanay* [Clark 1981]

CA#030 pM ***pa:wan ... ca(:ʔ)nay** *(n) 'mano de metate
(culebra)/nauyaca'* [pOM *pa:n ma:nk ca:ʔny] NHM: *pa:n mahntc
ca:ʔn* 'mano de piedra (víbora), nauyaca saltadora' Ju *pa:nma·ŋk-
cá"nʸ* 'mano de metate (culebra)' At *pa:nma:ŋkcǽʔnʸ* 'mano de metate (culebra)' OIP: *paʔnkɨʔcana'y* SaP: *pa:wangɨʔcanay* [Clark
1981]

CA#031 pM [Veracruz] ***toʔki-ca(:ʔ)nay** *(n) 'voladora (una culebra)
/Mexican rat snake'* OIP: *toʔkicana'y* 'culebra de petate' SaP: *toʔk-
cánay* 'boladora (una culebra)'

CA#032 pM [Veracruz] ***yɨkɨk-ca(:ʔ)nay** *(n) 'culebra negra/a kind of
black snake'* OIP: *yɨkɨkcana'y* SaP: *yɨgɨkcanay* [Clark 1981]

CA#033 pMZ ***ca:ne** *(n) 'descendientes/descendants'* NHM: *ca:n ko:*
'descendientes, descendencia de una familia' Ma *ča:nʸ* 'consuegro, -a'
Ja *ca:nʸ, ča:nʸ* 'consuegro, -a' LM: Gu *ča:nʸ, ca:nʸ* 'consuegro, -a'
SaP: *ca:n* 'consuegro, consuegra' ⟋TxZ: *ca:neʔ* 'consuegro, consuegra; codo' ChisZ: C [Te] <*tzane*> 'consuegro y consuegra'

CA#034 pMZ ***cap(-hɨ)** *(n) 'cielo/sky'* [pM, pOM *cahp; pZ *cap]
[Probably originated in a verb meaning 'to spread', cf. SaP: *cap* (vi,
vt) 'spread out (clothes)'.] NHM: *capho:tm* [*ho:tm* 'interior, dentro,
en el estómago] SHM: Tl *cohp* Tu,Ay *cahp* Tp *cAhp, cahphítʸpʸ* Mi

capwí:n MM: Cc *cAhp, cAhpót*ʸ Ma,Ja,Ju,Pu,At,Ct *cahp* LM: Cn
<*cahp*> Ca *cahp* Gu *caht* OlP: *capvini* SaP: *cahp* AyZ: *[cap]*
TxZ: *cap* '=paladar' ChisZ: C *cap* N [FL] *cap* [Ma] *cap* [Wonderly
1949] NE [Tapalapa, Ocotepec, Pantepec, Chapultenango] *cahp*
[Wonderly 1949] [Ra] *cahp* S [Tu] *cap* [Wonderly 1949] ChZ:
SnMiCh *caphi* [Wonderly 1949]

CA#035 pMZ ***capac** *(adj) 'rojo/red'* [pM *capac > pOM *capc; pZ,
pGZ *capac] NHM: *capc* 'rojo, colorado' SHM: Tl *cohpc* Ay *capc*
LM: SJ *caps* Cn <*capc*> (adj) Gu *capc* [Nordell 1962] OlP:
capa's SaP: *cábac* SoZ: *cábac* [Foster and Foster 1948] AyZ:
[cába?c] TxZ: *cá?pa?c* '=colorado' ChisZ: C *capas* 'rojo,
colorado' N *capas* NE *cabas* (ve) 'rojo, colorado'; *cabasbi* (adj)
'rojo, colorado' S *[ca·pac]* 'colorado' ChZ: *capac*

CA#036 pMZ ***capac-?ah** *(vi) 'ponerse colorado, enrojecer/to become*
red' NHM: *cápci ~ capca* 'enrojecer, sonrojar' SaP: *kucábaci* 'poner
rojo' [Clark and Clark 1960] ChisZ: C *capasah* (vi) 'ponerse colorado, rojear' NE *cabasah* (vi) 'ponerse colorado, ser rojo o colorado'
ChZ: *capadzah* 'ponerse rojo'

CA#037 pOM ***ca?pš** *'rajar/to cleave (logs)'* NHM: *ca?pš* 'rajar
(p.ej., madera), romper, cuartear (p.ej., leña)', [derivative: *ca?pš*
'rajado (p.ej., madera), rajadura, hendido, agrietado'] At *ca?pš*
'rajada (leña)'

CA#038 pMZ ***cas(i)** *(n) 'mayacate/crayfish'* [pM *caši > pOM
*cašy; pZ, pGZ *cas] MM: 'chacal (langosta del río?)' Ma *caš*ʸ Ju,
Ct *cæš*ʸ At *cašᵛpʸ* LM: Gu *caš*ʸ OlP: *caši* SaP: *čaš* SoZ: *cas* TxZ:
cas '=camarón' ChisZ: C [Te] <*tzas*> 'camarón grande, pescado
pequeño' N *cas* 'langosta (de río)'

CA#039 pMZ ***cat?** *(vi) 'medir por cuartas, medir a palmas/to measure*
by the span of a hand' [The isolated verb root only in MM and LM,
but the nominal derivative **cat?-e* below is evidence for the pMZ
status.] MM: Ma <*ca"t, ca?tp*> Ja <*ca"t, ca?t, ca?tp, ča?tʸpʸ*>
Pu <*ca"t, ca!tp, ča!tʸpʸ*> At <*ca"t, ca?tp*> Ct <*ca"t, ča?tʸpʸ*,
ca?tp> LM: Gu <*ca"t, ca?t, ca?p*>

CA#040 pMZ ***cat?-e** *(n) 'una cuarta/one span of the hand (measure)'*
[pM **ca?te* > pOM **ca"ty*; pZ *cate] MM: Ma,Ja,Pu,Ct *tu?kcá"t*ʸ
At *tukcá"t*ʸ LM: Cn <*cá"t*> 'geómetro (oruga)' Gu *tu?cá"t*ʸ SaP:

ca?t 'cuarta' ChisZ: C [Te] *<tzate>* 'palmo / xeme, medida' N
cate 'cuarta—medida de la mano con los dedos extendidos'

CA#041 pZ **caw** *(vt) 'golpear/to hit'* SaP: *caw* (vi, vt) 'make
tortillas' [Zo loan] ChisZ: C *caŋ* (vt) 'pegarle, darle una palmada'
N *caŋ* (vt) 'golpearlo (con la mano)' NE *caŋ* (vt) 'darle una palmada, pegarlo; golpearlo'

CA#042 pMZ **ca:wi** *(n) 'chango, mono/monkey'* [pM *ca:wi* > pOM
ca:wy; pZ *cawi*] NHM: *ca:?y* '=mono de araña' OlP: *ca:wi*
'chango' ChisZ: C,NE *cawi* N *cawi* 'mono, saraguato' S *[ca·wí?]*
'mono'

CA#043 pZ **cawa** *(n) 'juile/fresh-water fish'* SaP: *ca:u* [Zo loan]
AyZ: *[ca:?gʷa]* TxZ: *ca:wɨ?~ca:wa?* ChisZ: N *cawa* 'bobo liso,
bagre (pez)'

CA#044 pMZ **ca:y?** *'asar/to roast'* NHM: *ca:y~ca"* 'planchar, quemar, sellar, asar' SHM: Tl *co?* Tu *<ca"y, mẓa·ypʸ>* Tp *<ca"y
~cA"y, čA:y, čœ:pʸ, mẓœ:pʸ, čA"yémpʸ>* MM: Ju *<ca"y>* 'asar',
<ca"y> 'sellar, planchar' [sic!] Cc *<cA", čaypʸ~čAyp̄ʸ,
yAhkcáypʸ, čay, tɨ: tca"y, ča"hǽmpʸ, kʸœh tcay>* Ma *<ca"w̥, ca"f,
čœ:pʸ>* 'asar', *<ca:dʸɨw~ca:dʸɨΦ~ca:dʸɨf>* 'planchar', *<ca"w,
čœ:pʸ>* 'herrar, sellar' Ja *<ca"w, ča·ȳ, ca·ȳ, čœ:pʸ>* 'herrar',
<ca"w, čœ:pʸ> 'planchar, asar' Pu *<ca", čœ:pʸ, ča"wǽ·m̄pʸ>*
'planchar, asar, herrar' At *<ca", cœ:pʸ, ča"hǽ·m̄pʸ, cá!hɨm>*
'planchar', *<ca", čœ:pʸ, cá?yɨm>* 'herrar, sellar', *<ca">* 'guisar',
<ca", čœ:pʸ> 'asar' Ct *<ca"w>* 'guisar, herrar', *<ca"w, čœ:pʸ>*
sellar, 'planchar, asar' LM: Ca *<ca">* '=sellar, planchar' Cn
<ca·y~ca"w> (vt) 'asar (carne); planchar; quemar' SJ *ca·y~ca"*
'to iron clothes, brand animals' Gu *<ca"w, ca:pʸ, ča:pʸ>* [Nordell
1990 and p.c.] OlP: *cay~ca?* (vt) 'asarlo' (ejemplo: 'plátano') SaP:
cay~ca? (vi, vt) 'roast meat' TxZ: *cay* (vt, vi-p) ChisZ: C [Te]
<tzaipa> 'tostar maiz en en comal'

CA#045 pOM **?on-ca:y ~ ?on-ca"** *'freir/to fry'* NHM: *?onïca:y
~?onïca"* MM: Ju *?onẓá"* Ma *?onẓá"w* At *?onẓá"* Ct *?onẓá"w*

CA#046 pOM **ca?y-n** *(n) 'sello/mark'* NHM: *ca?yïn* '=fierro caliente' MM: At,Ct *ca"y*

*CA#047 pM [Verazcruz] **cay* (vi) 'rajar/to crack'* OIP: *cay* (vi) 'alumbrar (ejemplo: las estrellas alumbran)' SaP: *cay* (vi, vt) 'crack'

*CA#048 pOM **cay* (adj, n) 'pequeño; arena/small; sand'* NHM: *cay* 'thin, small' [G. Martin, p.c.] SHM: Tp *cay* 'arena' MM: Ju *cæy̨* 'arena' Ma *cay̨* 'pequeño' Ja,Pu,At *caȳ* 'pequeño' LM: Cn <*cay*> 'grava' Gu *caȳ* 'pequeño'

*CA#049 pMZ **cay* (n) 'mecate/rope'* [pM, pOM **cahy*; pZ **cay*] MM: 'hamaca' Ju *ca꞉y* Ma *ca꞉y* '=atarraya' Ja *ca꞉y, ča꞉y* Pu *ca꞉y* 'atarraya' At *ca꞉y* '=atarraya' Ct *ca·ȳ* LM: Cn <*ca꞉y*> Ca *ma"nz̨á꞉y* Gu *ca꞉y* 'hamaca' SaP: *cahy* SoZ: *cay* 'bejuco' AyZ: [*ca?y*] 'bejuco, vena' TxZ: -*cay* 'bejuco' ChisZ: C *cay* '=bejuco; cuerda; lazo, reata; guía; vena' N *cay* '=cuerda, reata; bejuco; vena, tendón' NE *cay* '=reata; lazo; vena - como de una persona' ChZ: *ca?y* '=cuerda'

*CA#050 pM **tihn-cay* (n) 'tripas/intestines'* [pOM **ci꞉ncy*; in pM the last compound member does not carry stress which is why **h* is not reconstructed.] NHM: *ti꞉nc* '=panza, estómago' MM: Ju *ti꞉nʸč* 'tripas', *ti꞉nč* 'intestinos' [sic!] Ma *ti꞉nʸč* 'tripas', *ti·nč* 'intestinas, entrañas' Ja *ti꞉nʸč* '=mondongo, intestinos' At,Ct *ti꞉nʸč* '=intestinos, entrañas' LM: Cn <*ti꞉nč*> 'intestino' SJ *ti·nč* 'intestine' Gu,Ca *ti꞉nʸč* '=entrañas, mondongo, intestinos' OIP: *tinca'y* SaP: *tínčay* '=vientre'

*CU#001 pMZ **cu꞉?* (n) 'noche/night'* [pM, pOM **cu꞉?*; pZ, pGZ **cu?*] NHM: *cv꞉* '=sueño, lunar' SHM: Tl *cu꞉* 'sueño, tarde' MM: Ju *cu꞉* 'tonto' Ma *cu꞉* '=loco, en la tarde, lunar, tonto' Ja *cu꞉* '=lunar, en la tarde' Pu *cu꞉* 'lunar' At *cu꞉* 'noche, necio, en la tarde' Ct *cu꞉* 'tonto, necio, en la tarde, lunar, loco' LM: Ca *cu꞉* 'tonto, en la tarde' Cn <*cu꞉*> (adv) 'tarde' (n) 'lunar' SJ *cu꞉* Gu *cu꞉* 'en la tarde, lunar' OIP: *cu꞉hɨ* 'moreno' [*cuhɨ* 'noche' is another etymon] SaP: *cu?* SoZ: *cu?* [Foster and Foster 1948] TxZ: *cu?* 'noche' ChisZ: C,N,NE *cu?* ChZ: *cu?hi* [derivative]

*CU#002 pMZ **cu꞉?-?ah* (vi) 'anochecer/to grow dark'* NHM: *cv?i* ~*cv?a* 'anochecer' TxZ: *cu꞉-?yɨ?y* (vi) 'anochecerse' [?] ChisZ: NE *cu?ahay* (vt)

*CU#003 pMZ **cu꞉?-hi(t)* (adv) 'anoche/last night'* [pM **cu꞉?hi(t)*; pZ **cu?(y)i*] NHM: *cv?y* SHM: Tu *cu?ú꞉y* Tp *cu?ú꞉y*~*cɨ?ú꞉y* Mi *cɨʔɨ́ːy* MM: Ma *cuʔy* Ja *cuʔy, cu!y* Pu *cu!ȳ* 'ayer en la tarde' At *cuʔy* 'a las ocho de la noche' Ct *cuʔy* SaP: *cuʔhít* 'tarde' [OM derivatives: NHM: *cv:hi ~ cv:ha* 'caer la noche' SHM: Tp < *čú"hɨ* > MM: Ma < *cú:ʔinʸɨp, cú:ʔɨpʸ* > At < *cúʔhɨnɨp* > Ct < *cú:hɨpʸ* > LM: Gu < *cu:hɨ̌:pʸ* > 'atardecer'] TxZ: *cuʔuy* 'noche' ChisZ: N *cuʔi*

CU#004 pM *cu:ʔ-m* *(adv) 'medianoche/midnight'* [pOM *cu:ʔm*] NHM: *cvʔm* 'las once de la noche aproximadamente' [*cu:ʔm* expected] SHM: Tl *cu:ʔm* MM: Ma *cu"m* At *cuʔm, cuʔmʔít* Ct *cuʔm* 'noche' LM: Cn < *cu:m* > (adv) 'noche (completa)' Ca *cu·m* 'noche' Gu *cu!m* [Nordell, p.c.] SaP: *cuʔm* 'en la noche' ChisZ: NE *cuʔmɨhk* [?]

CU#005 pM *cu:ʔ-p* *(adv) 'de noche/at night'* NHM: *cv"p* [*cv:ʔp* expected] MM: Ju *cuʔp* 'medianoche' [*cu:p* expected] OlP: *cu:p* (adv) 'en la noche'

CU#006 pOM *cu:hc* *(n) 'musgo/moss'* NHM: *cu:hst* 'lama' LM: Ca *cuc* Gu *cu·c̄*

CU#007 pOM *cu:čC* *(n) 'tábano/horsefly'* MM: Ma *cu:č* Ja *cu:čmʸ* LM: Ca *cu:č* Cn < *cu:č* > 'tábano [order: Diptera, Tabanus atratus]' Gu *cu·ʔčk*

CU#008 pMZ *cuʔc* *(vi, vt) 'mamar, morder/to suckle, chew'* NHM: *cvʔc ~ cv"c* 'morder, comer carne' SHM: Tu < *cu"c, mʐuʔčpʸ* > 'morder, comer carne' MM: 'morder, comer carne' Ju < *cu"c* > Ma < *cu"c, cuʔcp, čuʔčpʸ* > '=picar, morder (zancudo) (vi); comer (carne) (vt)' Ja < *cu"c, cuʔc, cuʔcp, čuʔčpʸ* > 'morder (vi), comer (carne) (vt)' Pu < *cu"c, cu!cp, ču!čpʸ* > At < *cu"c, cuʔcp, čuʔčpʸ* > 'picar, morder (zancudo) (vi) comer (carne), morder (vi, vt)' Ct < *cu"c, cuʔcp, čuʔčpʸ* > 'picar, morder (zancudo), morder (vi); comer (carne) (vt)' LM: Ca < *cu"c* > 'morder' Cn < *cuʔc ~ cu"c* > (vt) 'comer (carne); morder; morder (culebra)' SJ *cuʔc ~ cu"c* 'to eat meat; to bite' Gu < *cu"c, cuʔcp, čuʔčp* > 'comer (carne) (vt); morder (vi)' OlP: *cuʔc* (vt) 'morderlo' SaP: *cuʔc* (vi) 'nurse, suck' [Zo influence on the semantics] SoZ: *cuʔc* 'mamar' [Gutiérrez M. 1993; Foster and Foster 1948: 'suck (as a baby), kiss'] AyZ: *[cuʔc]* 'mamar' TxZ: *cuʔc* (vt, vi-a) 'chupar, mamar' ChisZ: 'mamar' C *cuʔc* (vi) N *cuʔc* (vi) ChZ: *cuʔc* 'mamar'

CU#009 pZ ***yak-cu?c** *(vt)* *'amamantar/to suckle'* TxZ: *yakcu?c* (vt-caus) 'amamantar' ChisZ: C *yakcu?c* (vt) 'amamantarlo, darle el pecho, darle de mamar; dejarlo mamar' NE *yakcu?c* (vt) 'amamantarlo, darle de mamar, darle el pecho'

CU#010 pMZ ***cu?c-i** *(n)* *'seno, chiche/breast of woman'* [pM **cu?ci* > pOM **cu"cy*; pZ **cu?ci*] NHM: *cu"c* 'carne' SHM: Tl,Tu,Tp *cu"č* 'carne' MM: Ju,Cc,Ma,Ja,Pu,At,Ct *cu"č* 'carne' LM: 'carne' Cn <*cu"č*> Gu *cu"č* OlP: *cu?či* 'carne' ChisZ: C *cu?ci* 'senos, pecho, mama; dentadura del trapiche' N *cu?ci* 'senos, pecho, teta, ubre; leche de pecho' NE *cu?ci* 'mama, pecho de la mujer' S *[cu·cí?]* ChZ: *cu?ci* 'senos'

CU#011 pZ ***cu?c-i nɨ?** *(n)* *'leche/breast milk'* ChisZ: N *cu?ci nɨ?* ChZ: *cu?ci nɨ?*

CU#012 pGZ ***cu?c** *(n)* *'muerto/dead person'* [Cf. SaP: *kuycú?c* 'tronco', lit., 'tree corpse'?] SoZ: *cu?c* AyZ: *cu?c* '=finado' TxZ: *cu?c* '=difunto, cadáver' ChisZ: C *cu?c* 'miserable, mezquino' [?-semantics]

CU#013 pOM ***cuh** *(adj)* *'bonito, hermoso/beautiful'* NHM: *cvh* SHM: Tu *cuh* Tp *cuh* MM: Ju,Cc,Ma,Ja,Pu,At,Ct *cuh* LM: Mz *cuh*

CU#014 pMZ ***cuh** *(vi)* *'escupir/to spit'* NHM: *cvh* MM: Ju <*cuh*> Ma <*cuh*> Ja <*cuh, cuhp*> Pu,At,Ct <*cuh*> LM: Ca <*cuh*> Gu <*cuh, cuhp*> [Nordell 1990 and p.c.] LM: Cn <*cuh*> SJ *cuh* OlP: *cuh* (vi) SaP: *cuh* (vi) SoZ: *cuh* TxZ: *cuh* (vi) ChisZ: N *cuh* (vi) NE *cuh* (vi)

CU#015 pMZ ***cuh-i(C)** *(n)* *'saliva/spit'* [pM* *cuhi(k)* >_pOM **cuhy*; pZ **cuhi(n)*] NHM: *cuh* SHM: Tl *cuh^y* Ju,Ma,At,Ct *cuh^y* Ja *cuh^n^yɨ:* LM: Cn <*cuhyñɨ:*> Ca *cuh^y* Gu *cuh^y* OlP: *cuhi'k* SaP: *cuhnɨ?* AyZ: *[cu:he]* ChisZ: C *cuwin* N *cuhin* ChZ: *cuhi?*

CU#016 pM ***cuk** *(vi, vt)* *'cortar con cuchillo/to cut with a knife'* NHM: *cvhk~cvk* SHM: Tl *cuk* Tu <*cuk, mzuik^yp^y~mdzik^yp^y, n^yaǰik^yɨ, tɨ: n^yaǰuik^yɨ, naǰúkɨ*> Tp <*cuk, mzuk^yp^y, nzúhkɨc, čukœmp^y*> MM: Ju <*cuk*> Cc <*cuk, tɨ: tcuk^y, k^yœh tcuhk^y, čuhk^yp^y, yAhkcúhkp, čuhk, čukœmp^y, cuhkp*> Ma <*cuk, čihk^yp^y*> Ja <*cuk, cuhk, čihk^yp^y*> Pu <*cuk, čuhk, čihk^yp^y*> At <*cuk, čuühk^yp^y*> Ct <*cuk, čihk^yp^y*> LM: Cn <*cuhk~cuk*> (vt) 'cortar (con navaja o cuchillo)' Ca < *cuk* > Gu < *cuk̄, cuhk, čuhpʸ* > SJ *cuhk ~ cuk* OIP: *cuk* (vi, vt) SaP: *cuk* (vi, vt)

CU#017 pOM *cuk-y (adj) 'cortado/cut' NHM: *cuk* MM: Ju *cikʸ* Ma,Ja,Pu,Ct *cikʸ* At *cuükʸ* LM: Ca *cuʸkʸ* Gu *cukʸ*

CU#018 pM *cuk-an (n) 'cuchillo/knife' [pOM **cuhkn*] MM 'cuchillo, navaja' Ju,Ma,Pu,Ct *cuhkn̦* Ja,At *cuhkn̦* '=puñal' LM: Ca *cuhkⱡ* Cn < *cuhk* > '=navaja' SJ *cuhk* Gu *cuht* 'cuchillo, puñal' OIP: *cuka'n* 'machete, cuchillo'

CU#019 pM [Veracruz] *cukin (n) 'pleito/fight' OIP: *cuki'n* SaP: *cúgin* '=guerra'

CU#020 pM *cukut (vi, vt) 'mover (brazo, pierna)/to move (arm, leg)' LM: SJ *cuguht ~ cugut* 'to double up (arm, leg)' SaP: *cugut* (vi, vt) 'move'

CU#021 pMZ *cu:k (n) 'rata, ratón/rat, mouse' [pM, pOM **cu:hk*; pZ **cuk*] MM: Ma,Ct *cu·k* At *cu·k* 'rata' LM: Cn < *cu:k≥* > 'rata [Rattus norvegicus], ratón' [*cu·k* in Hoogshagen 1984] Gu *cu·k* TaM: *cuk* 'mouse' [transcription in Wonderly 1949] OIP: *cu:kⱡ* SaP: *cu:hk* SoZ: *cuk* 'ratón' AyZ: [*cuk*] TxZ: *cuk* ChisZ: C *cuk* 'ratón' [homonym: 'músculo'] N *cuk* NE *cuhk* S [Tu] *cuk* 'mouse' [Wonderly 1949] ChZ: *cuk*

CU#022 pM *cu:?kV (n) 'zapote prieto/black sapote' [pOM **cu:?k(y)*] NHM: *cv:?k* [Diospyros ebenaster] SHM: Tl *cu:kʸ* 'zapote' Ay *cu:ik* LM: Gu *hinʸjú:kʸ* [Nordell, p.c.] MM: Ju,Ma,Ja,Ct *ci:kʸ* At *cuü:kʸ* LM: Ca *cu:ʸkʸ* 'naranja' Gu *cu:kʸ* 'naranja' OIP: *cu:ku*

CU#023 pMZ *cu:ki(-ka:haw) (n) 'anteburro, tapir/tapir' [pM **cu:ki(-ka:haw)* > pOM **cu:ky(-ka:)*; pZ **cuki*] NHM: *cu:?k* '[Tapirella bairdi]' SHM: Tu *cuikʸá:h* 'anteburro' MM: Ju *cikʸkʸá:* Ma *cikʸkʸá:* 'tapir', *cikʸkʸá:* 'anteburro' [sic!] Ja *ci:kʸá:* 'tapir' Pu *ci:kʸ* 'anteburro' At *cuükʸá:* 'anteburro', *cuü:kʸkʸá:* 'tapir' [sic!] Ct *cikʸ:á:* 'anteburro', *cikʸkʸá:* 'tapir' [sic!] LM: Cn < *cu:ky* > 'tapir, danta, anteburro [Tapirus bairdii]' Ca *cu:kʸkʸá:* 'anteburro', *cu:kʸá:* 'tapir' [sic!] Gu *cu:kʸ* ChisZ: [Te] < *tzuqui* > 'elefante'

CU#024 pZ *cu?kin (n) 'gusano/worm' [pGZ **cu?ukiñ*] SoZ: *cu:kiñ* 'gusano' [Gutiérrez M. 1993] *cú?kinʸ* 'hormiga', [Foster and Foster

1948] AyZ: *[cú?ugi ~ cú?uge]* TxZ: *cu:?keñ* ChisZ: S *[cu?gín]* ChZ: *cu?kin*

CU#025 pOM *cukn (n) 'hormiga/ant'* NHM: *cvkïn* '[Monomorium sp.]' LM: Cn <*cuk*> 'hormiga (genérico) [order: Hymenoptera, fam: Formicidae]' SJ *cuk* Ca,Gu *cukt*

CU#026 pM [Veracruz] *cukut(ik) (n) 'hormiga/ant'* OIP: *cukuti'k* SaP: *cúgut* 'gusano'

CU#027 pOM *cuku (n) 'tía/aunt'* NHM: Hu *cugu* [Foster 1949] Ay *cugu* [Foster 1949] *cugúhk* [Wichmann 1990] MM: Ju *cɨgú:* At *cɨk?ú: ~ cɨhk?ú: ~ cuhk?ú:* Ct *cohkkú"*

CU#028 pOM *cukúm (n) 'tío/uncle'* NHM: Hu *cugum* [Foster 1949] SHM: Ay *cugum* [Foster 1949] *cugúm* [Wichmann 1990] Tm *cɨkúm* MM: At *?ɨm̄* Ct *?ɨm̄* LM: Gu *cɨgú!m̄* [Foster 1949 has *cuguum*] ChisZ: N *cu?u* 'tío (esposo de la hermana de la madre)' [?]

CU#029 pMZ *cu:k(-?ɨy) (n) 'calambres/cramp'* NHM: *cv:kma* SHM: Tp *cúkɨp* MM: Ju *cúkɨ* Cc,Pu,Ct *cúk?ipʸ* Ma *cú·k?ipʸ* Ja *cú·kɨp* At *cú·kɨbɨc* LM: Gu *cɨgú·?tɨbɨč* TxZ: *cuk-bɨ:?hah*

CU#030 pMZ *cuks (vt) 'rasguñar/to scratch'* OIP: *cukš* (vt) 'cortarlo (con tijeras)' (v-ap) 'quitárselo' SoZ: *cuks* 'scratch, pinch' [Foster and Foster 1948] TxZ: *cukska?* (vt) 'aruñar' ChisZ: C *cuks* (vt) 'pellizcarlo' N *cuks* (vt) 'rasguñarlo'

CU#031 pM *cu:?kš (vt) 'besar/to kiss'* NHM: *cv:?kš* SHM: Tu,Tp <*cu?kš*> Ay *cu?kšp* MM: Ju,Cc,Ct <*cu?kš*> Ma <*cu?š*> Ja <*cu?š, či?šʸpʸ*> Pu <*cu!kš, či!kšʸpʸ*> At <*cu?kš, čuü?kšʸpʸ*> LM: Cn <*cu"kš*> (vt) Ca,SJ <*cu?kš*> Gu <*cu?š, ču?šʸp*> [?] OIP: *cu:kš* (vt) ChisZ: N *cu?ks* (vi) 'tener mal olor (cedro, ciertas hierbas, comida)'

CU#032 pM *cu:?kš-i (n) 'beso/kiss'* [pOM *cu:?kšy] NHM: *cu:?kš* 'beso, besar' OIP: *cu:kši*

CU#033 pM [Veracruz] *cu?kš (vi) 'tener ajuate/to itch'* OIP: *cu?kš* (vi) 'tener ajuate (aguate, espina pequeña)' [derivative: *cu?kšɨ* 'ajuate'] SaP: *cu?kš* (vi) 'itch'

CU#034 pM *cum (vi, vt) 'amarrar/to tie'* NHM: *cv:m ~ cv:hm ~ cvm* 'amarrar (p.ej., una bestia que lleva un lazo), atar (p.ej., una caja)' MM: Ma <*cum̄*> 'encarcelar' Ja <*cum̄, cu·m̄, či·m̄pʸ*>

'encarcelar' Pu <*cu̅m, tæ̅m tci̅mʸ, yahcú·m̅p*> 'encarcelar' At <*cu̅m*> 'encarcelar' Ct <*cu̅m*> 'encarcelar' LM: Cn <*cum*> (vt) 'atar' Gu <*cu̅m*> 'encarcelar' OlP: *cum* (vr) 'amarrarse, enredarse' (vt) 'amarrarlo' SaP: *cum* (vi, vt) 'tie'

CU#035 pOM ***ku-cuhm~ku-cum** *'amarrar/to tie'* NHM: *kucʋ:m ~kucʋ:hm~kucʋm* 'amarrar la cabeza' MM: Ju *kuẕúm* LM: Ca *ku·cúm*

CU#036 pOM ***?a-cuhm~?a-cum** *(vi) 'empacar/to wrap up'* NHM: *?acʋ:m~?acʋ:hm~?acʋm* 'amarrar (p.ej., un haz de leña)' MM: Cc <*?Aẕúm*> Ju <*n?œẕɨ·mbɨhkɨmɨt*> 'empacar' Ma <*?a·ẕúm*> '=empacar', <*?ɨẕúm*> 'amarrar cosas encimadas (cajas, tamales, etc.)' [sic!] At <*?œẕúm*> Ct <*nɨ·y?a·ẕú·m̅bɨkɨyɨ*> LM: Gu <*?aẕɨ̃mbɨk*>

CU#037 pZ ***cum** *(n) 'maraca/maraca'* TxZ: *cum* 'platanillo' ChisZ: C *cum* 'chinchil—sonaja; cascabel' N *cum* NE *cup* 'sonaja, chinchil; cascabel'

CU#038 pM ***tu?c cumum** *(n) 'cascabel/rattlesnake'* NHM: *tʋ?c cʋmïn* LM: Cn <*cum*> 'víbora de cascabel' Gu *cum* [Nordell, p.c.] OlP: *tu?scumu'm* SaP: *tu?hcúmum*

CU#039 pZ ***cum-i** *(n) 'codo del brazo/elbow'* [pGZ **cu:mi*] TxZ: *cu:mde?* (vi-s) 'trompudo (como uno que está enojado)' ChisZ: C,N,NE *cumi*

CU#040 pOM ***cu"m-k** *(adj) 'color violeta/violet'* NHM: *cʋ"hmk* SHM: Tm *cu?nk* 'color rosa' MM: Ju *cu"ŋk* 'morado' Ct,Ma *cu?ŋk* '=morado' Ja *cu!ŋk* At *cu?ŋk*

CU#041 pMZ ***cun** *(vi) 'gotear/to drip'* NHM: *cʋ:n~cʋ:hn~cʋn* 'gotear (p.ej., una casa)' SHM: Tl *cun* 'gotear' MM: 'gotear (el techo)' MM: Ju <*cu:mp*> Ma <*cu·m̅p, cuná̅mp*> Ma <*kǽh čunʸ*> Ja <*cu·m̅p, cuná·m̅p, cu·n̅*> Pu <*cu·m̅p, cuná·m̅p*> At <*cu·m̅p, cuná·m̅p, tɨ: čunʸ*> Ct <*cu·m̅p, cunam̅p*> LM: Ca <*cump*> Cn <*cu·n~cu:n*> (vi) Gu <*cu·m̅p, cuná·m̅p*> LM: SJ *cu·n~cun* 'gotear el techo' OlP: *cun* (vi) 'pringar, gotear' SaP: *cun* (vi) 'drip (water)'; *kucún* 'gotear' [Clark 1961] ChisZ: C [Te] <*natzunocui*> 'aguamanil', <*tzumba*> 'gotear quando hace hylo' <*natzunba*>, 'chorrear', <*natzunguy*> 'chorro'

CU#042 pZ **cu?ni** *(n) 'grillo/cricket'* SaP: *čú?nčun* [Zo borrowing?] SoZ: *cú?uñi* TxZ: *cu:?ñe?* ChisZ: C *cu?ni* N *cu?ni* 'cucaracha [insecto; fam: Blattidae]'

CU#043 pMZ **cus** *(adj) 'verde, crudo/green (unripe)'* [pOM *cuš-k*; *-k* must be a suffix added after the pOM insertion of /h/ before clusters; pZ *cus*.] NHM: *cvšk* '=fresco' SHM: Ay *cušk* 'verde' Mi *cušk* 'azul' MM: Ma,Ja,Pu,At,Ct *cušk* Ju '=azul' LM: Ca,Gu *cušk* '=azul' Cn <*cuš*> (adj) 'verde (color); verde (no maduro); crudo' SJ *cuš* 'green' ChisZ: N *cus* (adj) 'duro y bonito (maíz)'

CU#044 pOM **cušta** *(n) 'hielo/frost'* NHM: *cvšta* 'helada' SHM: Tl *cušt*

CU#045 pMZ **cus-kuy** *(n) 'chipilcoite/pea'* [pM *cuskuy* > pOM *cuhšky*; pZ *cuskuy*] NHM: *cuhšk* 'belzinic-che, guachipil [Alvaradoa amorphoides]' MM: 'guachipil' Ju *cuš^{y}k^y* Ma,Pu,Ct *cu·š̃^{y}p^y* At *cu·š̃^{y}k^y* TxZ: *cuskuy* 'chipile' ChisZ: C *cuskuy* 'guachipilín' N *cuskuy* ChZ: *?ukicuskuy*

CU#046 pMZ **ki(c)cu(?k)s** *(n) 'uña/fingernail'* [pM *kiccu?š*; pZ *ki(c)cu?(k)s* > pGZ *kicu?ks*; the glottal stop in some Zoquean dialects is contamination from *ki?* 'hand'.] SHM: Tl *kicco"š* 'dedo de la mano' SoZ: *kicis* 'fingernail, claw' [Foster and Foster 1948], *ki:cus* 'finger' [Wonderly 1949] TxZ: *kí?cu?ks* ChisZ: C *ki?čus* 'uña, garra' N *kicus* 'uña, garra' NE *ki?cus* ChZ: StaMaCh *kicus* SnMiCh *kicusy* [Wonderly 1949; he gives the gloss 'finger?'.]

CU#047 pOM **pakuy-cuhš** *(n) 'canilla de la pierna, espinilla/long bone of leg, shin'* NHM: *pakučvhš* MM: Ju *pahkcuhš̩ņ* 'espinilla del pie' Pu *pahkcú"š* 'espinilla del pie' Ma *pahkcú"š* 'canilla de la pierna, espinilla, espinilla del pie' At,Ct *pahkcúš̃* 'espinilla del pie' LM: Gu *pahkcúšk* 'canilla de la pierna, espinilla'

CU#048 pMZ **cu?-si** *(n) 'suegro de mujer/woman's father-in-law'* [pM *cu?(-ši)* > pOM *cu"*; pZ *cu?si*] NHM: *cv"* SHM: Tl *cu?* 'cuñada de hombre' Ay *ču?* MM: Ju *cu"* 'nuera del hombre' Ma *cu"* 'nuera del hombre (pos), suegro de mujer' Ja *cu"* 'nuera del hombre, suegro de mujer (pos)' Pu,Ct *ču"* 'nuera del hombre' At *cu"*, *ču"* 'nuera del hombre, suegro de mujer' LM: Gu *ču"?ap̄* 'suegro de mujer' OIP: *cu?ši ~ cu?iši* SaP: *ču?ná?* SoZ: *cu?u* [Foster 1949] ChisZ: C [Co] *cu?si* 'suegro de mujer, nuera de hombre' [Ocotepec] *cu?si* 'aunt' [Foster 1949]   N *cu?si* 'nuera del hombre; tía del hombre, esposa del hermano de su padre; concuña del hombre, esposa del hermano de su esposa; concuño de la mujer, esposo de la hermana de su esposo'; *cu?u une* 'sobrino, sobrina (del hombre, hijo o hija de la hermana de su esposa)' [The latter form shows that -*si* is a morpheme in Zoquean.]   NE *cu?si* 'suegra de mujer, nuera de hombre' S [Tu] *cusi* 'woman's father-in-law, man's daughter-in-law' [Foster 1949]

CU#049 pMZ **cusu(k)** *(adj) 'verde/green'*   [pM *cušuk* > pOM *cušk*; OlP and SaP respectively have dissimilation and assimilation of the first consonant; pZ *cusu* > pGZ *cu:su*; ChisZ has assimilation of the second consonant.]   NHM: *cvšk* '=crudo, fresco' SHM: Tl *cušk* 'crudo' OlP: *tušu'k* SaP: *šúšuk* '=crudo' SoZ: *cu:s* 'azul' AyZ: *[cu:s]* TxZ: *cu:s* (adj) '=azul' ChisZ: N *cuhci* (adj) '=no maduro' NE *cuhc* (vi-s) 'verde; estar crudo—como fruta' C *cuhcu* '=azul; no maduro' S *[cuhcú?]* ChZ: *cusɨ?* 'crudo'

CU#050 pGZ **cut** *(n) 'tumor/tumor'*   AyZ: *[cut]* '=ampolla' TxZ: *cut* '=nacido, barros (ampollas)'

CU#051 pZ **cut** *(vi) 'brincar para abajo/to jump down'*   SaP: *cut* (vi) 'jump' [Zo loan] SoZ: *cut* (vi) 'caerse' TxZ: *cutde?* (vi-s) 'estar en cuclillas' ChisZ: C [Te] <*tzutnaypa*> 'asentarse en cuchillas / sentarse en cuchillas'

CU#052 pZ **cutu** *(n) 'espiga de maíz/ear of corn'*   [pGZ *cu:tu?*] TxZ: *cu:tu?* ChisZ: N *cutu* 'espiga'

CO#001 pZ **co?c** *(vi) 'empezar/begin'*   ChisZ: C,N,NE *co?c* ChZ: *minco?c* 'venir primero'

CO#002 pZ **coha** *(n) 'algodón/cotton'*   ChisZ: C *cowa* '=moho' N,NE *coha* ChZ: *coha?*

CO#003 pMZ **cok** *(vt) 'desear/to desire'*   NHM: *cohk ~ cok* 'querer, desear' SHM: Tl *cvk* 'gostar' MM: Ju <*cóhkɨp*> 'necesitar', <*cok*> 'amar, gustar', <*čehpʸ*> 'gustar', <*cohkp*> 'querer', <*mẓehkʸpʸ*>_ 'desear' Ma <*cok,_cohkp, čehkʸpʸ*> 'amar, querer, gustar', <*cok*> 'animar' Ja <*cok, čohk, čehkʸpʸ*> 'amar, desear, querer, gustar' Pu <*čehkʸpʸ*> 'gustar', <*cok, čehkʸpʸ*> 'amar' At <*cok, čehkʸpʸ, nẓehkʸpʸɨc*> 'querer, gustar, amar (vi, vt), necesitar (vt)', <*cok*> 'animar' Ct <*cok, čehkʸpʸ*> 'querer, gustar, amar',

< *cóhkɨp, čehkʸpʸ* > 'necesitar' LM: Cn < *cohk ~ cok* > (vt) 'querer, amar' Ca < *cok* > 'gustar, amar, desear' SJ *cohk ~ cok* 'to love, want' Gu < *cok, cohp, čohk, čohpʸ* > 'amar, querer' [Nordell 1990 and p.c.] SoZ: *cok* (vi, vt) 'prender' AyZ: *[cok]* 'prender' TxZ: *kɨʔŋcok* (vt) 'orar, pedir' ChisZ: C [Te] < *tzocpa* > 'lograrse', < *tzocpa naypa* > 'prender planta', < *tzocoy pacuy* > 'placer, deleyte o alegría'

CO#004 pOM ***cohk-ʔɨn(y)** *(n) 'amor/love'* MM: Ju,At *cóhkɨn* '=volundad' Ma *cóhkʔɨn* Ja *cohkʔáhtɨn* Pu *cóhkɨnʸ* Ct *cóhkʔɨn* LM: Ca *cóhkɨnʸ* '=volundad' SJ *cohknɨ* Gu *coht*

CO#005 pOM ***cohk** *(adv) 'pronto/immediately'* NHM: *cohk* MM: Ju *cohk* 'temprano todavía, pronto, al ratito' Ma *cohk* '=rápido, luego' Ja *cohk* At *cohk* 'rápido, luego, urgente, de prisa, pronto' Ct *cohk* 'rápido, urgente, pronto, luego' LM: Cn < *cohk* > (adv) Ca,SJ *cohk*

CO#006 pMZ ***co:kʔ** *(vi) 'sanar/to heal'* NHM: *co:k ~ co"k* 'retoñar (p.ej., una planta), sanar (p.ej., un árbol), salvar, salvación' MM: Ju < *co"k* > '=aliviarse' Ma < *co·kp, co"gámp* > 'pegarse; sanar; salvar, aliviarse' Ja < *co·kp, co"k, co·k, co"gá·mp* > 'pegarse; sanar; salvar, aliviarse' Pu < *co·kp, co"gá·mp* > 'pegarse, aliviarse' At < *co·kp, co"gá·mp* > '=pegarse; salvar' Ct < *co·kpɨhkp* > 'pegarse', < *co·kp, co"gámp* > 'salvar; sanar', < *có·knɨp* > 'aliviarse' LM: Ca < *co"k* > '=aliviarse' Cn < *cok ~ co"k* > (vi) 'sanar (de una enfermedad); salvarse (de una catástrofe); lograrse (planta)' SJ *co·k ~ co"k* _'to heal, save; to take hold after birth, transplanting' Gu < *co·kp, co·k, co"gá·mp* > 'pegarse; salvar; sanar, aliviarse' OlP: *co:k ~ coʔk* (vt) 'pagarlo' SaP: *co:k ~ coʔk* (vi, vt) 'pay' TxZ: *cok* (vi) 'salvarse' ChisZ: C *cohk* (vi) 'criarse, crecer; sanar; pegar; aliviarse' N *cohk* (vi) 'sanar; crecer; criar; arder' NE *cohk* (vi) 'engordarse; estar gordo' ChZ: *cok* 'sanar'

CO#007 pMZ ***yak-co:kʔ** *(vt) 'curar/to cure'* NHM: *yakco:k- ~ yakco"k* (vt) 'sanar a alguien o algo, librar a alguien, salvar a alguien, socorrer a alguien, rescatar a alguien, recate' MM: 'sanar' Ju < *yæhcó"k* > Ma,Ja,At,Ct < *yahkcó"k* > LM: Gu < *yahcó"k* > 'sanar' ChisZ: C *yakcok* (vt) 'sanarlo; criarlo' N *yakcohk* (vt) 'sanarlo, criarlo' NE *yakcohk* (vt) 'sanarlo; criarlo' ChZ: *yakcok* (vt) 'curar'

CO#008 pMZ ***cok?a** *(n) 'brujo/shaman'* [pM **co?ka* > pOM **co"k*; pZ **coka*] NHM: *co"k* 'nagual, tona' MM: Ma,Ja,Pu,At,Ct *co"k* 'nagual' LM: Cn <*co?k*> 'nagual, tona' Gu *co"k* 'nagual' OlP: *co?ka* SaP: *co?k* 'brujo', *co?hkáy* 'embrujar' [Clark and Clark 1960] SoZ: *co:ka?* 'persona que hace llover' TxZ: *ka:ŋco:k* ChisZ: C [Te] <*tzoca*> 'bruxa/hechicero, bruxo' <*tzocatzamba*> 'adivinar' <*cangtzoca*> 'hechicero, bruxo' <*hiyenatzoca*> 'bruxa' <*huyenatzoca*> 'hechicero, bruxo'

CO#009 pZ ***coko** *(adj) 'mojado/soaked, humid'* SaP: *šo?gik* [?] ChisZ: C *coko* (adj) NE *coko* (vi-s) 'estar húmedo, estar mojado', *cokonahs* 'tierra húmada', *cokobɨ* (adj) 'húmedo, mojado' ChZ: *coko?* 'lodo'

CO#010 pMZ ***co:koy** *(n) 'corazón/heart'* [pM **co:koy* > pOM **co:hky*; pZ **cokoy* > pGZ **co:koy*] SHM: Tl *hvtcu:hky* OlP: *hutukotɨ* '=vida' [?] SoZ: *có:koy* 'hígado' [Gutiérrez M. 1993] [Foster and Foster 1948: 'liver, spirit'] *co:goy* 'liver' [Wonderly 1949] AyZ: *[co?go]* 'hígado' TxZ: *[có:go?]* [Clark n.d.] ChisZ: C *cokoy* N *cokoy* '=estómago' NE [Tapalapa, Ocotepec, Pantepec] *cokoy* [Wonderly 1949] [Ra] *coko?* S [Tu] *cokoy* [Wonderly 1949] [Cp] *[co?kóy]* ChZ: *coko?y* 'hígado'

CO#011 pOM ***com** *(n) 'nudo de caña, coyuntura/joint'* NHM: *com* 'cañuto' MM: Ju *com* Ma *com̄t* 'coyuntura', *com̄* 'nudo de caña' [sic!] Ja,Pu,At,Ct *com̄* LM: Cn <*com*> 'coyuntura; nudo' Ca *com* 'coyuntura' Gu *com̄*

CO#012 pMZ ***co:?n** *(vi) 'salir (persona)/to go out (person)'* NHM: *co:?n* 'salir (p.ej., pasear), irse' LM: Cn <*co·n~co:n*> SJ *co·n ~co:n* 'to leave' Gu <*co:n, co!mp*> [Nordell, p.c.] ChisZ: C *co?n* (vi) 'brincar, saltar (como conejo)' N *co?nde?nde?ney* (vi) 'brincar'

CO#013 pOM ***yak-co:?n** *(vt) 'llevar/to take away'* NHM: *yakco:?n* 'llevar algo' LM: Cn <*yahco·n~yahco:n*> (vt) 'traer'

CO#014 pOM ***co:?n-ta?k~co:?n-ta"k** *(vi) 'comenzar, empezar/to begin'* NHM: *co:?ntk~co:?ndɨk* SHM: Tl *cv"nto"k* MM: Ju <*yæhco?ndá"k*> Ma <*yahkco?ndá"k*> Pu <*yahco!ndá"k*> At <*yæhkco?ndá"k*> Ct <*yahkco?ndá"k*> LM: Ca <*yahcondá"k*> Gu <*yahco!n̄dá"k*>

CO#015 pMZ **cot* *(vi) 'salir (objeto)/to come out (object)'* NHM: *coht ~ cot* 'sacar alguna cosa de su cabo (p.ej., una pala, un zapapico)' TxZ: *cotput* (vi-s) 'caer (mierda), salir atravesando' ChisZ: C *coht* (vi) 'ascender el sol, subir el sol'

CO#016 pZ **coʔt* *(vi) 'quitarse/to take off'* SoZ: *coʔt* 'remove, undress' [Foster and Foster 1948] TxZ: *coʔtkaʔy* (vt, vi-p) 'zafar (amarre de animal), mudarse (víbora)' ChisZ: C *coʔt* (vi) 'lastimarse, rasparse; rasparsele' (vt) 'lastimarlo, rasparlo' N *coʔt* (vi) 'quitarse, salirse (ejemplo: si se quita la piel, la carne se pudre)'

CO#017 pMZ **cow* *(vi) 'unir/to unite'* NHM: *coːv ~ cov* 'junto a, entre si' [not listed as a verb, but the usual two variants are there] SaP: *cow* (vi) 'be joined, celebrate birthday' TxZ: *coŋ* (vt, vi-p) 'parchar (ropa), soldar' SoZ: *coŋ* 'answer' [Foster and Foster 1948] ChisZ: C *coŋ* (vi-s) 'estar unido a algo' (vt) 'encontrarlo, toparlo, hallarlo (casualmente)' N *coŋ* (vi) 'colindar, estar junto' (vt) 'toparlo' NE *coŋ* (vt) 'encontrarlo, topar a (como a una persona en la calle)' ChZ: *coŋ* 'unir'

CO#018 pMZ **ʔaw-cow* *(vi, vt) 'contestar/to answer'* NHM: *ʔacoːv ~ ʔacoːhv ~ ʔacov* SHM: Tl *ʔacow* Tu < *ʔazṓw, mʔazóeːpʸ ~mʔazéːpʸ* > Tp < *ʔǽzóː, ʔǽzów, ʔǽzóːp, ʔǽzoβÁmp* > MM: Ju < *ʔǽzóf* > Cc < *ʔA·z̧ów, ʔA·z̧óː, yʔA·z̧óːpʸ, ti: yʔA·z̧óy, kʸǽh yʔA·z̧óːy, ʔA·z̧owÁmp* > Ma < *ʔa·z̧ów, ʔa·z̧óΦ, ʔa·z̧óf* > Ja < *ʔazṓw, yʔazó·w̄, ʔazóːp, yʔaz̧éːpʸ* > Pu < *ʔiz̧ṓw* > At < *ʔǽzṓw* > Ct < *ʔa·z̧ṓw* > LM: Ca < *ʔicṓw* > Cn < *adzo·w ~ adzow* > (vt) SJ *ʔaz̧o·w ~ ʔaz̧ow* Gu < *ʔazṓw, ʔadzoːp* > [Nordell 1990 and p.c.] OlP: *ʔaucov* (vt) TxZ: *ʔaːŋkcoŋ* (vt) ChisZ: C *ʔaŋz̧oŋ* (vi, vt) N *ʔaŋz̧oŋ* (vt) NE *ʔaŋz̧oŋ* (vi, vt) ChZ: *ʔaŋcoŋ*

CO#019 pOM **may-cohw ~ may-cow* *(vt) 'contar (números)/to count'* NHM: *mačoːv ~ mačoːhv ~ mačov* SHM: Tl *maycvw* Tp < *mAǰów, mmAǰóːpʸ* > MM: 'contar (cuento)' Ju < *mǽǰóf* > 'contar (números)' Cc < *miǰów, mmiç̌óːpʸ ~ mmiǰóːpʸ* > Ma < *mʸiǰéːpʸ, miǰów̧, miǰóΦ, miǰóf* > Ja < *miǰów̄, mʸiǰó·w̄, mʸiǰéːpʸ* > Pu,Ct < *miǰów̄, mʸiǰéːpʸ* > At < *mǽǰów̄, mmǽǰóöːpʸ* > LM: Ca < *miǰów* > Cn < *miç̌o·w ~ miç̌ow* > (vt) 'contar' SJ *miǰo·w ~ miǰow* Gu < *miǰów̄, mʸiǰóːpʸ* >

CO#020 pZ *__pɨk-cow__ (vt) 'recibir/to receive' SaP: *pɨkcow* [Zo loan]
ChisZ: NE *pɨkčoŋ* (vt) '=aceptarlo'

CO#021 pOM *__cow__ (n) 'precio/price' NHM: *cow* '=importe, valor'
MM: Cc *cow* 'caro' Ma *coᶭ~coɸ~cof* '=caro' Ja,At *čow̄* Ct *cow̄*
[ᶭ~ɸ~f] '=caro' LM: Cn <*co:w*> '=valor' Gu *čow*

CO#022 pMZ *__cow-ah__ (adj) 'caro/expensive' SHM: Tu *cow̄* Tp,Mi
cow MM: Ja *có·w̥ɨ* Pu *cówɨ* LM: Ca *có·wæ* Gu *co:w* OlP: *cova?ah*
TxZ: *cowa* (adj, n) '=precio'

CO#023 pOM *__co:w-aht ~ co:w-at__ (vi) 'valer/to cost' NHM: *cova*
'costar, valer' MM: At <*co:bá·t̄p*> LM: Gu <*co:bá·t̄p*>

CO#024 pGZ *__co:wi?ñ__ (n) 'mojarra/species of fish [mojarra?]' SoZ:
co:wi? TxZ: *co:?we?ñ*

CO#025 pOM *__cowa?n__ (n) 'lindero/landmark, borderline' NHM:
cova 'límite, lindero, contigüidad' MM: Ju *cibá"n* Ma *cɨWá"m* Ja
cuwá!n Pu,Ct *cɨbá!n* At *cabá!n, cawá!n* LM: Gu *na·š̄cowá!nt*

CO#026 pMZ *__coy__ (n) 'remedio, medicina/remedy, medicine' [pM
cohy > pOM *co:hy*; pZ *coy*] NHM: *co:hy* SHM: Ay *co:y* MM:
Ju,Ma *co:y* Ja,Pu,At *co:y* Ct *co·ȳ* LM: Cn <*co:y*> 'medecina'
Ca, Gu *co:y* OlP: *coyɨ* SoZ: *coy* 'medicina' AyZ: *[coy]* 'bebida que
dan a la mujer después del parto' (hecha de segrón, manzanita y toron-
jil) TxZ: *coy* '=complemento de la guisa' ChisZ: C *coy* '=aguar-
diente, trago' N *coy* NE *coy* '=aguardiente'

CO#027 pMZ *__coy-?ɨy__ (vt) 'curar/to cure' NHM: *co?yi ~ coya* SHM:
Tl *co:yɨp* Ma <*có:yɨ, čo:y?ɨpʸ*> 'curar', <*có:yɨ*> 'curtir' MM:
Ja <*có:yɨ, čo?ʸɨp*> 'curar', <*có:yɨ*> 'curtir' At <*có:yɨ*>
'curtir', <*có:yɨ, čó:yɨp*> 'curar' Ct <*có:yɨ, čó:y?ɨpʸ*> LM: Gu
<*co:yï"w, co:yï̈:pʸ*> 'curtir, curar' TxZ: *co?ɨ?y* (vt) ChisZ: C
co?yɨy (vt) 'curarlo, medicinarlo; abonarlo' N *co?yɨy* (vt) 'curarlo;
rocerlo, aplicarlo (insecticida, fungicida o herbicida)' NE *co?yɨy* (vt)
'curarlo, medecinarlo; abonarlo (como la tierra)'

CO#028 pMZ *__coy-?ɨy-pa__ (n) 'curandero/healer' NHM: *co?yiva*
'=doctor, médico' MM: Ma *có:y?ɨpʸ* Pu *có:y?ɨbʸɨ* At *có:yɨbɨ* Ct
có:y?ɨbʸɨ LM: Ca *co:yɨ:bʸɨ* Gu *co:yï̈:bʸï̈* OlP: *coyi:pa?* ChisZ: C
co?yɨ?opyawɨ '=doctor, médico'

CO#029 pM ***co?y(-tu:n)** *(vi) 'avergonzarse/to be ashamed'* SHM: Tp
<*cɨd'úmp*> MM: Ju <*co'd'ún*> Ma <*co"d'ú?n, co"d'ú·m̄p*> 'le
da pena', <*co"d'ú·m̄p*> '=tener vergüenza', <*co!d'ú·m̄p*>
'apenarse' [sic!] Ja <*co!d'ú·m̄p, co!d'uná·m̄p*> '=apenarse, tener
vergüenza, le da pena' Pu <*co!d'ú!n̄*> 'le da pena', <*co!d'ú·m̄p*>
'=apenarse, tener vergüenza' At <*cɨd'ú·m̄p*> '=le da pena,
apenarse, tener vergüenza' Ct <*co!d'úm̄p*> 'tener vergüenza',
<*co?d'ú·m̄p*> 'le da pena, apenarse', <*co!d'ú·m̄p*> 'avergonzarse'
[sic!] LM: Ca <*co"d'ún*> Gu <*cɨ!d'ú·m̄p, cɨ!d'uná·m̄p*> 'tener
vergüenza, le da pena, apenarse' OlP: *co?y* (vi) 'tener vergüenza'

HI-HO

HI#001 pMZ ***hi:?c** *(vi) 'mudarse (culebras, etc.), plegar (ropa)/to slough, pleat'* MM: Ma <*hi?cp, nɨhí?c?ɨpʸ*> 'retoñar', <*hi?cp, hi:ʒámp*> 'mudarse (culebras, etc.)' Ja <*yahhí:c, hi?cp, hi?c*> 'mudarse (culebras, etc.)', <*hi?cp, hi:ʒá·m̄p*> 'nacer, brotar (plantas)' Pu <*hi!cp, hi:dʒá·m̄p*> 'mudarse (culebras, etc.), nacer, brotar (plantas)' At <*hi?cp, hi:ʒá·m̄p*> 'retoñar, mudarse (pollo)' Ct <*nɨhí?cp, nɨhi:ʒámp*> 'mudarse (culebras, etc.), <*hi?cp, hi:ʒámp*> 'nacer, brotar (plantas)' LM: Cn <*hi·c~hi:c*> (vi) 'despedazarse; mudar' SJ *hi·c~hi:c* 'to break into pieces (stone, head, etc.)' Gu <*hi·?cp, hi:dʒá·m̄p*> 'mudarse (culebras, etc.)' OIP: *hi:c* (vi, vt) 'zafar' TxZ: *hê?č* (vt) refregar ChisZ: C *hi?c* (vt) 'plegarlo' N *hi?c* (vi) 'plegarse, estar plegado' (vt) 'plegarlo, fruncirlo' NE *hi?c* (vt) 'arrugarlo (como ropa)'

HI#002 pMZ ***hi:?c-i** *(n) 'pliegue/fold'* [pM **hi:?ci* > pOM **hi:?cy*; pZ **hi?ci*] NHM: *hi:?c* 'huipil' ChisZ: C *hi?ci* N *hi?ci~hi?cɨ*

HI#003 pOM ***kɨ"-hi:?c** *(n) 'anillo/ring'* NHM: *kɨhi:?c* 'guante' SHM: Tl *kɨhe:c* MM: Ju *kɨhí:c* Ma,Ja,Pu *kɨ"hí:c* At,Ct *kɨ"hí:c* '=guantes' LM: Ca *kɨ"hí:c*

HI#004 pZ ***hik** *(vt) 'desbaratar/to destroy'* [Possibly of pMZ date, cf. OIP: *hik* (vt) 'ensuciarlo', but the semantic development is not clear.] TxZ: *hekeñ-ka?y* (vt, vi-p) ChisZ: N *hihk* (vt) 'quitarlo (de una vez)' [ejemplo: "Vamos a quitar de una vez la fruta del café con la mano, y una parte caerá al suelo"] ChZ: *hik*

HI#005 pZ ***hikɨ** *(pron dem) 'aquel/that'* TxZ: *he?k to:y-e?* 'por eso' [?] ChisZ: N *hikɨ~hik* (adj) 'aquel, ese'; (pron) 'aquél, ése';

(interj) '¡míra!' NE *hikɨ* (pron dem) 'aquél, aquélla'; (adj dem) 'aquel, aquella'

HI#006 pM ***hiʔk** *(vi) 'brillar/shine'* [pOM **hi"k*] MM: Ju *hi"kʸ* 'yema de huevo' Ma *hʸi"kʸ* 'yema de huevo' SaP: *hiʔk* (vi) 'shine'

HI#007 pM ***hiʔkš** *(vi) 'ahogarse/suffocate'* SHM: Tp <*tɨ: nʸɨ:híʔkšʸ*> MM: Ju <*hiʔkš*> Ma <*hiʔšp*> Ja <*hiʔš, hiʔšp*> Pu <*hiʔkšp*> At,Ct <*hiʔkšp*> LM: Cn <*hi"kš*> 'ahogarse; impedir la respiración; inundarse; asfixiarse (con humo)' Ca,SJ *hiʔkš* Gu <*hiʔšp*> OlP: *hiʔkš* (vi)

HI#008 pM ***hin** *(vi) 'refregar/stain'* NHM: *hinɨka:* 'ocelote, tigrillo' OlP: *hi:n* (vt) SaP: *hin* (vi, vt)

HI#009 pMZ ***hinV(k)** *(adj) 'espeso/dense'* [pM **hina(k)* > pOM **hin*; pZ **hini*] MM: Ma *hin̄* 'tierra floja' Ct *hin̄ná·š̃* 'tierra floja' LM: Cn <*hin*> 'polvo o sedimento (que deja la creciente del río)' OlP: *hi:ná'k* ChisZ: C *hinih* 'espeso, turbio' NE *hini* (vi-s) 'estar espeso, turbio'; *hinibɨ* (adj) 'espeso; turbio'

HI#010 pM [Veracruz] ***hipi** *(n) 'catarro/cold (illness)'* OlP: *hipi* SaP: *hip*

HI#011 pM ***hi:ʔpi** *(loc adv) 'allá/there'* [pOM **hi:ʔpy*] LM: Ca,Gu *hi:pʸ* 'allí' Cn *hih:py* 'there—out of sight' [Hoogshagen 1984] OlP: *he:p / hiʔpi* [perhaps syntactically conditioned variants]

HI#012 pZ ***hips** *'quemar comida/to be hot (food)'* SoZ *hips* 'quemar' [Elson 1960] TxZ: *hê:pš* (vi) 'quemarse (milpa)' [?] ChisZ: N *hipsaŋ* 'tizón' ChZ: *hips* 'quemar comida'; *hipsɨʔ* 'calentura'

HI#013 pZ ***hiʔs** *'estrujar/crush'* [pGZ **hiʔš*] TxZ: *baŋ-hêʔš* (vt) matar con el pie, pisar (insecto) ChisZ: N *hiʔspɨʔ* (vt) barrerlo, frotarlo (basura), *kɨhiʔs* (vt) barrerlo, limpiarlo

HI#014 pOM ***yak-hiʔš** *(vt) 'ahogar/to drown'* MM: Ja <*yahhíʔš*> LM: Ca <*yægíʔš*> Gu <*yakhíʔš*> 'ahogar'

HI#015 pZ ***hitiʔ** *(vt) 'jalarlo/to pull'* [pGZ **hi:tʸ*] LM: Cn <*hiht~hit*> (vt) 'destruir' [?] SJ *hiht~hit* 'to tear down a house' [?] TxZ: *hê:č-ɨŋ-tuʔm* (vt, vi-p) 'reunir raspando (basura)' ChisZ: C *hitiʔ* (vt) 'jalarlo' N *hitiʔ* (vt) 'guiarlo (agarrando la mano); jalarlo'

HI#016 pZ ***hi?ya** *(n) 'chicozapote/chewing-gum tree'* [pGZ **hi?iya?*]
AyZ: *[hi:?ya]* TxZ: *hê:?ya?* ChisZ: C *hi?ya* ChZ: *hi?ya?*

HE#001 pMZ ***he ~ he?** *(pron) 'él, ella/he, her'* [pM **he?*, pOM
*he? ~ he, pZ **he? ~ he*] NHM: *he"* 'él, ella', *he* 'el, la' MM:
Ma,Ja, At,Ct *hæ"* LM: SJ *he"* 'he, she, it, him, her—less specific'
Cn *<he?>* (pron) 'él, ella (ausente)', (art) 'él, la' Gu *he"* OlP:
he? 'él, ella, ese, esa' SaP: *he?* TxZ: *he:?pe?* (pron dem) 'ese'
ChisZ: N *he* (adj dem) 'ese, este' NE *he* (art determ) 'él, la'; (adj
dem) 'esa, ese'

HE#002 pMZ ***n-he?** *(pron) 'mio/mine'* [pM **nhe?* > pOM **nhe"*;
pZ, pGZ **ne?*] NHM: *nhe"* 'mío, nuestro (excl)' LM: SJ *?i:zy nhe"*
'mine' TxZ: *ne?* (pron) 'mio' ChisZ: C *?isne?* 'mi, mio, mi, mis',
ne? (pron pos) 'mi/tu/su—de usted' N *ne?* (n) 'lo de uno' NE
?ihne? (pron pos) 'mio' [The root *he?* attested in OlP: *hayhé?* (adj)
'ajeno' where *hay* means 'other'.]

HE#003 pOM ***hec** *(part) 'y/and'* NHM: *hec* '=que' MM: Ct *hæc̄*
LM: Cn *<ec>* 'y' [/h/ lost by an allegro rule specific to this word?]
Ca *hæc*

HE#004 pZ ***hec** *(vt) 'rascar/scrape'* SoZ: *heckuy* 'peine' ChisZ: N
*hec 'rascar' [*hecti?ŋdi?ŋwiy* (vt) 'regarlo por dondequiera rascán-
dolo', *hecwitu?* (vt) 'removerlo rascando']

HE#005 pM ***he?c** *(vi) 'desbrazar, quebrar/to break off (e.g., twig)'*
LM: Cn *<he?c ~ he"c>* (vt) 'limpiar (salpicando con agua)' SJ
he?c ~ he"c 'to splash (wash) water (on pails, pots, gourds, etc.); to
snap corn leaves off the stalk' OlP: **he?c* [*he?ska?pa* (vi) 'se des-
braza (un palo); se quiebra'] SaP: *he?č* 'gajo (de plátano)'

HE#006 pZ ***heh** *(vi) 'descansar/to rest'* TxZ: *heh* (vi) SoZ: *heh*
(vi) ChisZ: C *heh* (vi) N *heh* (vi) '=posar, aterrizar' NE *heh* (vi)
'descansarse' ChZ: *?okheh* 'descansar', *niheh* vivirse

HE#007 pMZ ***he:he** *(n) 'mosquito, zancudo/mosquito'* [pM **he:he*;
pZ **hehe* > pGZ **he:he*] OlP: *he:he* SaP: *he:h* [Clark 1981], *he:*
'zancudo' [Clark and Clark 1960] SoZ: *he:he?* TxZ: *he:h* 'zancudo'
ChisZ: C *he?* 'mosquito—especie de zancudo' N *hehe* NE *hehe?*
ChZ: *hehe*

HE#008 pM *__hek__ *(vi) 'durar/to last'* NHM: *hehk ~ hek* MM: Ja
< *hæhkp, hæká·m̄p* > 'durar (ropa)' LM: Cn < *hehk ~ hek* > (vi)
'=hacer tiempo' SJ *hehk ~ hek* 'to be long lasting' Gu < *hehk* >
'durar (ropa)' SaP: *hek* (vi) 'delay' ChZ: *heke* 'siempre' [a derived
form]

HE#009 pOM *__he?k ~ he"k__ *(vt) 'repasar (masa)/to knead'* NHM:
he?k ~ he"k 'hacer la torta de la masa' LM: < *he?k ~ he"k* > (vt)

HE#010 pOM *__hekém__ *(adv) 'lejos/far'* NHM: *hEkum* 'lejos, distante,
retirado' SHM: Tl *hakam* MM: Ju *hægæm* Ma,At *hægǽm, higǽm*
Ja,Ct *higǽm* Pu *hægǽm* LM: Cn < *higem* > (adv) Ca *hagám*
'lejos', < *hægamgǽ"k* > 'alejarse' SJ *higem* Cn *higem* [Hoogshagen
1984] Gu *higém* TxZ: *hu:?m* 'lejos' [?]

HE#011 pMZ *__he?ks__ *(vi) 'atravezar (p.ej., piernas)/cross (e.g., legs'*
NHM: *he?kš* 'andar sentado en el suelo' SaP: *he?kš* (vi) 'be crossed
(legs, sticks, etc.)' TxZ: *he?ks-kê?(m)* (vi) 'subirse (en un palo de
brazos y piernas)'

HE#012 pOM *__hem__ *(part) 'hay/there is'* NHM: *hem* 'están, hay'
MM: Ja *hæ:, hæp̄* 'hay' [?] Ct *hæm̄* 'hay' SaP: *héme* 'él que, lo
que' [?]

HE#013 pMZ *__hem__ *(loc adv) 'allá/there'* [pM, pOM, pZ, pGZ *hem]
SHM: Tp *hæm* '=allí' MM: Ju *hæm* Ma,Ja,Pu,At *hæm̄* LM: Ca
hæm OlP: *hem* '=allí' SaP: *hem* TxZ: *hem* 'ahí, allí'

HE#014 pMZ *__hem__ *(vi) 'picar, arder sin flama/to burn (as chile)'*
NHM: *he:m ~ he:hm ~ hem* 'arder sin flama' TxZ: *hem-p* (adj) 'estar
picoso'

HE#015 pMZ *__hemec__ *(adj) 'pesado/heavy'* [pM *hemec > pOM
*hemyc (glottalization in some dialects not accounted for; pZ *hemec]
NHM: *hEmïc* SHM: Tl *he?mč* Ay *hʸe?mč* MM: Ju *hemč ~ he"mč*
Ma,Ct *he?mč* Ja,Pu *he!mč* At *hemč, he?mč* LM: Cn < *hemšy* >
(adj) Ca *hemšʸ* SJ *hempʸšʸ* Gu *hemč* ChisZ: C,N *hemec* (adj) ChZ:
hemec

HE#016 pOM *__hen__ *(vt) 'quitar (ropas o zapatos)/to take off (clothes
or shoes)'* NHM: *henmvhk ~ henmuk* 'vestirse con distintas prendas a
un mismo tiempo', *hentikc ~ hentíkïc* 'cambiar de ropa';
pathe:n ~ pathe:hn ~ pathen 'quitar (p.ej., la camiseta y dejarse la

camisa), quitarle las hojas al maizal' MM: Ju <*nihǽn*> 'desnudar'
Ma <*hǽn*> 'desnudar', <*nihǽn*> 'abrigar' Pu <*nihǽn*>
'abrigar' Ja <*nihǽ·ndú"t*> 'desnudar' At <*nɨhǽn*> 'abrigar' Ct
<*nɨhǽn*> 'abrigar', <*hǽn*> 'desnudar' LM: Cn <*he·n~hen*>
(vt) 'quitar' Ca <*nihǽn*> 'desnudar' SJ *he·n~hen* 'to take off
(clothes, shoes)' Gu <*nɨ"hén*> 'abrigar'

HE#017 pOM ***ni:-hen** *(n) 'gabán/poncho'* NHM: *nɨhe:n~nɨhen*
'desvestir' SHM: Tl *nahan* 'camisa' MM: Ma *nɨhǽn* 'abrigo, chamarra, sarape, gabán' Ja *ni"hǽn* 'gabán', *nɨhǽn* 'abrigo, chamarra'
[sic!] Pu *nihǽn* 'abrigo, chamarra', *nɨhǽn* 'sarape' [sic!] At *nɨhǽn*
'abrigo, chamarra' Ct *nɨhǽn* 'abrigo, chamarra', *nɨhǽn* 'sarape'
[sic!] LM: Ca *nihǽn* SJ *ni"he·n* 'shirt'

HE#018 pZ ***he?n** *(vi, vt) 'rascar/to scrape'* SoZ: *he?n* 'dig' [Foster
and Foster 1948] TxZ: *he?n* (vt, vi-a) 'escarbar (con la mano), sacar
(tierra), rascar (tierra)' ChisZ: C *he?n* (vt) 'rascarlo' N *he?n* (vi)
'rascar' (vt) 'escarbarlo, rascarlo' NE *he?n* [*he?ndahs* (vt) 'relle-
narlo (como un hoyo)', *he?ndu?m* (vt) 'recogerlo (como con ras-
trillo)']

HE#019 pOM ***hep** *(loc adv) 'allá/there'* NHM: *hep* 'hay' SHM: Tp
hǽp MM: Cc *hǽp*

HE#020 pMZ ***hep** *(vt) 'raspar/to scrape'* NHM: *hehp~hep* 'trabajar
con coa' MM: Ma <*hǽp, hʸehpʸ, ti: šʸhʸepʸ*> 'raspar, rasurar con
navaja', <*hǽp*> 'afeitar' At <*hǽp, hʸehpʸpʸ*> 'raspar' Ja <*hǽp,
hʸǽhp, hʸǽhpʸ*> 'raspar', <*hǽp, hʸehpʸ*> 'rasurar con navaja' [sic!]
Ma <*hǽp, hʸehpʸ*> 'tallar' Ct <*hǽp, hʸehpʸ*> 'rasurar con navaja,
raspar, afeitar, tallar' LM: Cn <*hehp~hep*> (vi) 'topetear' (vt)
'raspar' SJ *hehp~hep* 'to scrape, clear a field by scraping' OIP: *hep*
(vt) 'rasparlo' [derivative: *ni:hep* (vt) 'pelarlo (un cochino), rasparlo
(un cochino)'] SaP: *hep* (vi, vt) 'butt with horns, root (pigs)' TxZ:
hep 'cepillar (madera)' [Clark, no date].

HE#021 pZ ***hepe?** *(vt) 'raspar/to scrape'* [pGZ **he:p*] SoZ: *he:p*
(vt) TxZ: *he:p* (vt, vi-p) '=afeitar, peinar' ChisZ: C *hepe?* (vt)
'=rayarlo' N *kɨhepe?* (vt) 'rasparlo (para quitar algo)' [derived
forms: SoZ: *hé:pe* 'ixtle' ChisZ: S *[he·bé?]* 'ixtle' ChZ: *hepe* 'maguey']

HE#022 pMZ **hepey** *(n) 'tipo de planta o árbol/species of plant or tree'* [pM, pZ **hepey*] SaP: *hepeykúhy* 'palo de tehuate' TxZ: *hepkuy* 'jomate (como el jícaro, pero son más largas las frutas' ChZ: *hepey sis* 'fibra de maguey'

HE#023 pMZ **he:ʔp** *(vt) 'raspar/to scrape'* NHM: *he:ʔp ~ he:ʔp* 'dar la primera limpieza a los maizales' MM: 'sacar (con cucharón)' Ma,Ct < *hæ:p, hʸeʔpʸ* > Ja < *hæ:p, hʸeʔpʸ, hʸæʔp* > At < *hæ:p, hʸeʔpʸpʸ* > LM: Cn < *he·p ~ he:p* > (vt) 'sacar (con cuchara); limpiar (con sarpala)' SJ *he·p ~ he:p* 'to dip with a spoon, bowl' Gu < *he:p, hʸe·ʔpʸ, hʸe·ʔp* > 'sacar (con cucharón)' OlP: *he:p* (vi) 'pescar' (vt) 'pescarlo; servirlo' SaP: *heʔp* (vi, vt) 'serve, dip' ChisZ: C *heʔp* (vt) 'ixtlearlo, hacerlo fibra' N *heʔp* (vt) 'rasparlo (para sacar la fibra)' [derivatives: ChisZ: C *heʔpe* 'ixtle' N *heʔpe* 'ixtle, fibra—de maguey, de guineo' NE *heʔbe* 'ixtle]

HE#024 pOM **he:ʔp-n** *(n) 'tecomate, bule/gourd'* NHM: *he:ʔpïn* 'cuchara' MM: Ju *hæʔpn̥* 'tecomate, bule; cucharón de madera' Ma,Ct *hæʔpn̥* 'azadón' Ja *hæʔpn̥* 'pala' At *hæʔpn̥* 'cucharón de madera' LM: Ca *hæ·pt* 'tecomate, bule', *hapt* 'cucharón de madera' [sic!] Gu *he·ʔpt* 'cucharón de madera'

HE#025 pZ **heps** *(vt) 'rastrillar/to scrape'* SoZ: *hepskuy* 'jícara para servir café' TxZ: *heps* (vt) 'agarrar (agua con jícara)' ChisZ: C **heps* [*hepsnaʔ* 'una cucharada', *hepsoytyïk* 'cuchara', *hepstïk* 'cuchara', *hepstïktase* 'una cucharada'] N *kïheps* (vt) 'rasparlo (para quitar algo)' NE *heps* (vt)

HE#026 pM **heʔps** *'atascado, estar/to be jammed'* NHM: *heʔpš* 'abrazar repentina y fuertemente' LM: Cn < *he"pš* > (vi) 'atascarse' Ca < *tï: hʸeʔpšʸ* > 'atascarse, atorarse' SJ *heʔpš* 'to be stuck in something' Gu < *heʔš, heʔšp* > 'atascarse, atorarse' [Nordell 1990 and p.c.] OlP: **heʔpš* [*ko:heʔpšpa* (vi) 'se atora'; *tïnko:heʔpšpe* (vt) 'lo estoy colgando'; *yukheʔpš* (vt) 'colgarlo, engancharlo']

HE#027 pZ **heht** *(vt) 'romper/to break'* TxZ: *keʔc-het* (vt) 'romper (costal)' ChisZ: C *heht* (vt) 'romperlo; lastimarlo, herirlo' N *heht* (vi) 'agujerar' (vt) 'agujerarlo (cortánddolo, rompiéndolo)'

HE#028 pM [Veracruz] **heti(ʔ)kš** *(vi) 'estornudar/to sneeze'* OlP: *tïhetiʔkspa* (vi) 'estornudo' SaP: *héteksï* 'estornudar' [Clark and Clark 1960] ChisZ: *heksčih* (vi) 'estornudar' [ʔ]

HE#029 pMZ ***he:?y** *'deshacer/to dissolve'* LM: SJ *he·y ~ he:y* 'to bite hard into something' SoZ: *he?y* (vt) 'batir' TxZ: *he?y* (vt) 'batir (pozole)' ChisZ: C *he?y* (vi) 'disolverse, deshacerse' (vt) 'disolverlo, deshacerlo' NE *he?y* (vi) ChZ: *he?y* 'revolver (pozole)'

Hɨ#001 pMZ ***hɨ:?** *(part) 'sí/yes'* [pM, pOM **hɨ:?*; pZ **hɨ?*; unexplained rearticulation of vowel in ChisZ and nasalization in TxZ] SHM: Tm,Ay *hɨ:* SoZ: *hɨ:h* TxZ: *hɨ̃:* ChisZ: C,N,NE *hɨ?ɨ* ChZ: *hɨ?ɨ*

Hɨ#002 pM ***hɨc** *(vi) 'moler (nixtamal)/to grind (corn)'* NHM: *hɨhc ~ hɨc* 'moler (p.ej., nixtamal)' SHM: Tl *hɨc* 'moler' MM: 'moler (masa de nixtamal)' Ma <*hɨc̄, hɨhcp*> Ja <*hɨhc, hɨhcp*> Pu <*hɨhcp*> Ct <*hɨc̄, hɨhcp*> LM: Cn <*hɨhc ~ hɨc*> (vt) 'moler (nixtamal)' SJ *hɨhc ~ hɨc* 'to make tortillas; to grind (corn, etc.)' Gu <*hɨc̄, hɨ̄hcp*> 'moler (masa de nixtamal)' OIP: *hɨc* (vi, vt) SaP: *hɨc* (vi, vt) 'grind (coffee)' TxZ: *hɨcket* (vi) 'bajarse de rebaladías' [?-semantics]

Hɨ#003 pM ***hɨc-i** *(n) 'masa/dough'* [pOM **hɨcy*] NHM: *hɨ̈c* SHM: Tl *hɨcy* MM: Ju *hɨč* 'atole' Ja,Pu *hɨč̄* 'atole' Ma *hɨč̄* 'pozole' LM: Cn <*hɨč*> SJ *hɨč* 'corn meal' Gu *hɨ̈č* [Nordell, p.c.] OIP: *hɨči*

Hɨ#004 pZ ***hɨhɨ** *(n) 'mosca/fly'* [pGZ **hɨ:hɨ*] SoZ: *hɨ:hɨ?* TxZ: *hɨ:h* '=quereza' ChisZ: C *hɨ?* N *hɨhɨ* ChZ: *hɨhɨ*

Hɨ#005 pOM ***hɨk** *(adj) 'áspero/uneven'* SHM: Tu *hɨhk ~ hɨk* Tp *hɨhk* Mi *hɨ̈k* MM: '=rasposo' Ju,Cc *hɨk* Ma,Ja,Pu,At,Ct *hɨk* LM: Cn <*hɨk*> (adj) Gu *hɨ̈k*

Hɨ#006 pZ ***hɨkɨ?** *(vi) 'jalar/pull'* [pGZ **hɨ:k*] [Cf. LM: Cn <*hɨguhk ~ hɨguk*> (vt) 'arrastrar'.] SoZ: *hɨ:k* TxZ: *hɨ:k* (vt) ChisZ: C *hɨkɨ?* (vi) 'quitarse, desaparecerse' N *hɨkɨ?* (vt) NE *hɨkɨ?* (vi, vt) 'quitar'

Hɨ#007 pOM ***hɨkuš** *(adj) 'jorobado/hunchbacked'* NHM: *hɨkʋš* '=encorvado' SHM: Tl *hɨkušk*

Hɨ#008 pOM ***hɨ?kš** *(vi, vt) 'comer fruta etc./to eat fruit, etc.'* NHM: *hɨ?kš* SHM: Tl *hɨ:?kš* [?] 'comer' Tu <*hɨ?kš, mhɨ?kšᵖpʸ*> Tp <*hɨ?kš, mhɨ?kšᵖpʸ*> Mi <*hɨ̈·?kš*> MM: Ju <*hɨ?kš, hɨ?š*> Cc <*hɨ?kš, mhɨ?kšᵖpʸ*> Ma <*hɨ?kš, hɨ?š, hʸe?šᵖpʸ*> Ja <*hɨ?š, hʸɨ?š, hʸe?šᵖpʸ*> 'comer (fruta, caña, zacate)' Pu <*hɨ!kš*> 'comer (caña,

zacate), *hɨ!kšp* 'comer (panela)' At < *hɨ?kš, hʸe?kšʸpʸ* > Ct < *hɨ?kš* >
LM: Gu < *hɨ·?š, hʸɨ·?šʸp* > Cn < *hɨkš* > (vt) SJ *hɨ·kš*

Hɨ#009 pM [Veracruz] ***hɨ:kš** *(vi) 'rebuznar/to bray'* [By the type of
correspondence this item is likely to have been diffused internally.]
OlP: *hɨ:kš* (vi) 'rebuznar, rugir' SaP: *hɨ:kš* (vi, vt) 'bray'

Hɨ#010 pOM ***hɨ?kš-y** *(n) 'alimentos/food'* NHM: *hɨ?kš* '=fruta',
hɨ?kška 'hipo, hipar' MM: Ju *he?kšʸ, he?šʸ* Ja *he?šʸ* Pu *he!kšʸ* At,Ct
he?kšʸ LM: Ca *hɨ·kšʸ* Gu *hɨ·?šʸ*

Hɨ#011 pM [Veracruz] ***hɨ(?)kš-tuk** *(vi) 'tener hipo/to have the
hiccoughs'* OlP: *tɨhɨ?kštuk* (vi) 'tener hipo' SaP: *hɨkštúk* 'hipo'

Hɨ#012 pM ***hɨm** *(loc adv) 'allá/there'* [pOM **hɨm*] LM: SJ *hɨm*
(specifier, locative) 'there (3p)' Cn *hɨm* (adv) 'allí' Gu *hɨm* SaP:
hɨm '¿donde?'

Hɨ#013 pZ ***hɨ?m** *(vi) 'pender/to hang'* TxZ: *hɨ?m* (vt) 'colgar'
ChisZ: C *hɨ?m* (vi) 'pender' (vi-s) 'estar colgado' (vt) 'colgarlo'
N *hɨ?m* (vi) 'estar amarrado' (vt) 'amarrarlo; colgarlo' NE *hɨ?m*
(vi-s) 'estar colgado' (vt) 'colgarlo'

Hɨ#014 pOM ***hɨmu:m** *(vi) 'picar (chile)/sting (chile)'* MM: M̲a̲
< *hɨmú·m̄p, kœh hʸɨmím̄ʸ* > Ja,Pu < *hɨmú·m̄p* > At < *hɨmú·m̄p, kʸœh
hʸɨmúüm̄ʸ* > Ct < *hɨmú·m̄p* > LM: Gu < *hɨmú·m̄p, kah hʸɨmúmʸ* >

Hɨ#015 pM ***hɨhn** *(n) 'fuego, lumbre/fire, light'* [pM, pOM **hihn*]
NHM: *hɨ:hn* '=fiebre, calentura' SHM: Tl,Ay,Tm *hɨ:n* Tu *hɨ:n*
'tiene calentura' MM: Ju *hɨ:n* '=tiene calentura' Ma *hɨ:n* '=luz' Ja
hɨ:n '=luz, calentura' Pu,At *hɨ:n* Ct *hɨ·n̄* LM: Cn < *hɨ:n* >
'lumbre; calentura' Ca *hɨ:n* SJ *hɨ·n* 'fire' Mz *hɨ:n* 'lumbre' Gu
hɨ:n '=luz' OlP: *hɨnɨ* '=fiebre, calentura' SaP: *hɨhn* 'fuego, fiebre'

Hɨ#016 pMZ ***hɨ:?n** *(vt) 'tragar/to swallow'* NHM: *hɨ:?n* SHM: Tl
hɨ:n MM: Ma < *hɨ:n, hʸe?m̄pʸ* > Ja < *hɨ:n, hʸɨ!n̄, hʸe!m̄pʸ* > At
< *hɨ:n, hʸe?m̄pʸ* > Ct < *hɨ:n, hʸe?m̄pʸ* > LM: Cn < *hɨ·n~hɨ:n* >
'tragar, devorar; atascarse en el lodo' Ca < *hɨ:n* > SJ *hɨ·n~hɨ:n* Gu
< *hɨ:n, hʸɨ!n̄, hɨ!mp, hʸɨ!m̄pʸ* > [Nordell 1990 and p.c.] OlP: *hɨ:n* (vt)
ChisZ: C *hɨ?n* (vt) 'aguantarlo, resistirlo' N *hɨ?n* (vt) 'aguantarlo
(para cargarlo)' NE *hɨ?n* (vt) 'aguantarlo (como una cosa pesada)'

Hɨ#017 pMZ ***hɨp(ɨ)** *(n) 'nariz/nose'* [pM **hɨhp* 'nose' > pOM **hɨhp*
'nose, point'; pZ **hɨp(ɨ)* 'mouth' > pGZ **hɨp*] NHM: *hɨhp* 'nariz,

punta' SHM: Tl *hɨ:hp* Tu *hɨ·hp* 'afilado' Ay *hɨ:hp* Mi *tɨ: yikšón hʸɨ́pa* 'afilado' MM: Ju *hɨhp* 'punta (pos), nariz' Ma *hɨhpáhk* 'nariz', *hɨhp* 'afilado, filoso, tiene filo, punta (pos)', *hɨ·hp* 'cortante' [sic!] Ja *hɨhp* 'cortante, nariz, afilado, filoso, tiene filo, punta (pos)', *yahhɨhpɨ*'afilar' Pu *hɨhp, hɨhpšú!nʸ* 'filoso, tiene filo', *hɨhp* 'afilado, nariz, cortante, afilado' At *hɨhp ní"gɨ* 'cortante', *hɨhp* 'nariz, filoso, tiene filo, punta (pos)' Ct *hɨhp* 'afilado, nariz, cortante, filoso, tiene filo' LM: Cn < *hɨhp*_ > 'punta, filo' Ca *hɨhp* 'nariz, punta (pos)' SJ *hɨhp* 'point' Gu *hɨ́hpút, hɨbút* 'nariz', *hɨ́hp* 'cortante, afilado, filoso, tiene filo, punta (pos)' OIP: *hɨpɨ* SaP: *hɨhp* 'nariz', *hɨpm* 'delante' SoZ: *hɨp* 'mouth' [Foster and Foster 1948, Wonderly 1949] TxZ: *hɨp* 'boca, filo, orilla' ChisZ: C *hɨpɨh* 'mentón' N [FL] *hɨpɨ* 'barbilla' [Ma] *hɨpɨ* 'chin' NE *hɨbɨ* [Wonderly 1949; dialects of Ocotepec, Chapultenango] [Pantepec] *hɨmbɨ* [Wonderly 1949; note 3 in Wonderly's 1949 paper rightly interprets the nasal that occurs in some Pantepec items as 1p or 2p pronominal infixes. This phenomenon occurs in some Mixe dialects too.] S [Tu] *hɨpɨ* 'chin' [Wonderly 1949] ChZ: SnMiCh *hɨp* 'boca' StaMaCh *hɨp* [Wonderly 1949]

Hɨ#018 pM ***kɨ:?-hɨhp** *(n) 'dedo de la mano/finger'* [pOM **kɨ:?hɨhp*] MM: Ma,Ja,Ct *kɨ"hɨhp* OIP: *kɨ?hɨpɨ* SaP: *kɨ?hɨhp*

Hɨ#019 pOM [MM/LM] ***wihn hɨhp** *(n) 'cara/face'* MM: Ju,Ja,Pu *wi:n hɨhp* Ma *Wʸi:n hʸɨhp* At *wʸi:n hʸɨhp* LM: Ca *wi:n hɨhp* Gu *wʸi:n hʸɨhp*

Hɨ#020 pOM ***hɨ:?p** *(vt) 'ensartar/to insert'* NHM: *hɨ:?p* '=enhebrar, amarrar' LM: Cn < *hɨ·p ~ hɨ:p* > (vt) 'ensartar' SJ *hɨ·p ~ hɨ:p* 'to thread' MM: Ma,Ct < *hɨ:p* > At < *hɨ:p, hʸe?pʸpʸ* > LM: Gu < *hɨ̈:p* >

Hɨ#021 pOM ***hɨpa"n** *(n) 'sudadero/cloth used for absorbing sweat from the back of a mount'* MM: Ma,Ct *hɨ:bǽ"n* Ja,At,Ju *hɨbǽ"n* LM: Ca *hɨ:bǽ"n* Gu *hɨ̈bé"n* SaP: *hapan* 'rub' [?]

Hɨ#022 pMZ ***hɨs...** *(n) 'espalda/back'* [pM **hɨhš* > pOM **hɨhš-k* (added suffix); pZ **hɨs* > pGZ **hɨ:s-i* (added suffix)] NHM: *hɨgvhk* 'espalda' [?] SHM: Tl *hɨšk* 'espalda' MM: Ju *hɨšk* Ja,At *hɨ·šk* Ct *hɨ·š̄* LM: Cn < *hɨ:š* > (s) 'espalda' (adv) 'atrás' Ca *hɨ·šk* Gu *hɨ̈·šk* OIP: *hɨ:puši* 'espalda; *hɨ?na* atrás' [?] TxZ: *hɨ:sɨ* (n-pos) 'atrás de, parte abajo' ChisZ: N *hyɨspit* (adv) 'de espalda, para atrás' ChZ: *hɨsho?* 'después'

Hi#023 pM ***hi:?t** *(vi, vt) 'aserrar/to saw'* NHM: *hi:?t* SHM: Tu < *hi:t, mhi?ťpʸ* > Mi < *hï·?tp* > MM: Ju < *hi:t* > Ma < *hi:t, hi?tp, hʸi?ťpʸ* > 'aserrar, cortar (con serrucho)' Ja < *hi:t, hi?tp, hʸi?t, hʸi?ťpʸ* > 'serrar, aserrar, cortar (con serrucho)' Pu < *hi:t, hʸi!ťpʸ* > 'aserrar, cortar (con serrucho)' At < *hi:t, hʸi?ťpʸ* > 'aserrar, cortar (con serrucho), serrar' Ct < *hi:t, hi?tp, hʸi?ťpʸ* > 'aserrar, serrar, cortar (con serrucho)' LM: Cn < *hi·t ~ hi:t* > 'aserrar; rebanar (con navaja)' Ca < *hi:t* > 'aserrar' SJ *hi·t ~ hi:t* 'to saw' Gu < *hï:t, hï·?p, hʸï·?pʸ, hï·?t* > 'serrar, cortar (con serrucho), aserrar' [Nordell 1990 and p.c.] OIP: *hi:t* (vi) 'cortar algo con serrucho' (vt) 'aserrarlo'

Hi#024 pM ***hi:?t-an** *(n) 'serrucho, sierra/saw'* [pOM **hi:?tn*] OIP: *hi:ta'n* 'serrucho' MM: Ju,Ma,Ja,At,Ct *hi?tn̥* LM: Cn < *hi:t* > 'sierra (herramienta)' Ca *hi·t* Gu *hï·?t*

Hi#025 pZ ***hi?t** *(vi) 'correr (líquido)/to run (liquid)'* TxZ: *ce:?hi?t* (vt) 'llevar lavando, limpiar (agua de lluvia)' ChisZ: C *hi?t* (vi) 'correr un líquido' N *hi?t* (vi) 'ser llevado por el río'

Hi#026 pM ***hi:t** *(n) 'palo cuyo cáscara tiene veneno/tree which has a poisonous bark'* [pOM **hi:t*] NHM: *hi:t* 'chancarro, guarumo [Cecropia spp. (G. Martin, p.c.)]' MM: 'chancarro' Ma,Ja,At,Ct *hi:t* LM: Gu *hï:t* 'chancarro, guarumo' OIP: *hi:tuka* 'tortuga de tres lomos, guao'

Hi#027 pMZ ***hitic** *(vt) 'sobar/to rub'* OIP: *hicic* (vt) 'sobarlo; tallarlo' SaP: *hidic* (vi, vt) 'iron (clothes), massage', *hiric* 'sobar, planchar' [Clark and Clark 1960] SoZ: *hi:t* 'barbecharlo' TxZ: *hi:t* (vt) 'rayar, escribir' ChZ: *hiti?* 'sobar'

Hi#028 pZ ***hi?ŋ** *(n) 'plano, llano, valle, llanura/plain, valley'* ChisZ: C *hi?ŋ* N *hi?ŋ* 'llano' NE *hi?ik* [unexplained rearticulation of vowel] ChZ: *hi?ŋ* 'llano'

Hi#029 pMZ ***hi:y?** *(vi) 'derretir, llorar/to melt, cry'* NHM: *hi:y ~ hi"* 'derretir, derretido, fundir' MM: 'derretirse (azúcar, sal, hielo, manteca, cera, vela, etc.)' Ju < *hʸi"y* > 'chillar', < *hi:pʸ* > 'llorar' Ma < *he:pʸ, hi"Wámp* > Ja < *hi·y, hi:ďá·kp* > At < *hiœ:pʸ, hi"há·mp* > Ct < *he:pʸ, hi"wámp* > LM: Cn < *hi·y ~ hi"y* > (vi) 'derretirse; afligirse' Ca *hiy* 'speak' [Wonderly 1949] SJ *hi·y ~ hi"y* 'to melt' Gu < *hï:pʸ, hï"wá·mp* > 'chillar, derretirse (azúcar, sal, hielo, manteca, cera, vela, etc.)', < *hï"w, hï·ȳ,* *hï:pʸ >* 'llorar' OlP: *hɨy ~ hɨ?* (vi) 'llorar' SaP: *hɨy ~ hɨ?* (vi) 'weep' SoZ: *hɨy* 'hablar' [Foster and Foster 1948, Wonderly 1949, Gutiérrez M. 1993] ChisZ: C *hɨy* (vi) 'llorar' N [Ma] *hɨy* 'weep' NE *hɨy* (vi) 'llorar' ChZ: SnMiCh *hɨy* 'weep' [Wonderly 1949]

Hɨ#030 pM ***hɨyi** *(n) 'cuñado de hombre/brother-in-law of man'* [pOM *hɨyy] NHM: *hɨy* SHM: Ay *huy* [Foster 1949] *hɨy* [Wichmann 1990] MM: Ju *hɨy* Ma *huy ~ hɨy* Ja,Pu,At,Ct *hɨȳ* LM: Cn <*hɨy*> 'cuñado, concuño (de hombre)' Ca *hɨy* Gu *hɨȳ* [Nordell 1990], *huy* [Foster 1949] OlP: *hɨyi* SaP: *hɨy*

Hɨ#031 pZ ***hɨyɨ** *(n) 'flor/flower'* ChisZ: C *hɨyɨ* N *hɨyɨ* NE [Tapalapa, Pantepec] *hɨyɨ* [Wonderly 1949] [Ra] *hɨyɨ* S [Tu] *hɨyɨ* [Wonderly 1949] ChZ: StaMaCh *hɨyɨ?* SnMiCh *hɨyɨ* [Wonderly 1949]

Hɨ#032 pOM ***hɨyuk** *'animal, bestia de carga/beast of burden'* SHM: Tp *hɨyúhk* 'animal' MM: Ju,Ja *hɨyúhk* 'animal, caballo' Ma, Pu,At *hɨyúhk* Ct *hɨyúhk* 'animal' LM: Ca *hayúhk* 'animal' Gu *hɨyúhk* 'bestia mular, bestia de carga, mula'

HA#001 pZ ***ha?c** *(vt) 'deber/to owe'* SoZ: *ha?c* (vi) 'fiar' AyZ: *[ha?c]* (vt) 'fiar' TxZ: *ha?c* (vt) 'fiar, pedir fiado' ChisZ: C *ha?c* (vt) '=pedirlo fiado' N *ha?c* (vi, vt) NE *ha?c* (vt) '=comprarlo fiado'

HA#002 pZ ***hahcuku** *(n) 'hormiga/ant'* [/s/ in TxZ and ChisZ-S assimilation to the intial /h/?] OlP: *ha:ša'k* 'pepegua, tepegua (hormiga)' [?] SaP: *háhcuk* [Zo loan] TxZ: *hasuk ~ hassuk ~ ha:suk ~ ha:ssuk* ChisZ: C *huhčuku* N *nahčuku* [unexplained initial nasal] NE *hahčuku* S *[hasčúk]* ChZ: *hahcuku* 'hormiga negrita'

HA#003 pMZ ***hah** *(vi) 'provocar un sensación muy fuerte/to provoke an intense sensation'* NHM: *hah* 'dar luz' MM: Ma <*hahp*> 'arder la boca' Ja <*hah, hahp, hahá·m̄p*> 'arder la boca' At <*hahp*> 'arder la boca' Pu <*hahp*> 'brillar (sol, luna, etc.)' Ct <*hahp*> 'arder la boca, brillar (sol, luna, etc.)' LM: Cn <*hah*> (vi) 'arder' Ca <*hahp*> 'brillar (sol, luna, etc.)' Gu <*hahp, hahá·m̄p*> 'arder la boca, brillar (sol, luna, etc.)' OlP: *hah* (vi) 'estar caliente; hacer calor' (vt-d) 'tener calor' SaP: *hah* (vi) 'emit heat' ChisZ: N *hah* (vi) 'estar muy salado'

HA#004 pOM **?a-hah** *(vi) 'brillar/to shine'* NHM: *?ahah* 'crepúsculo matutino y vespertino' MM: Cc < *?Aháhp* > 'brillar (oro, joyas, etc.) Ma *?ɨháhk* 'reflejo' Ja *?aháhp* 'reflejo', *?aháh* 'luz' [sic!] Pu *?aháhk* 'luz' At *?aháhk* 'luz, reflejo', < *?æháhp* > 'brillar (oro, joyas, etc.) Ct *?a·háhp* 'luz, reflejo, brillar (oro, joyas, etc.)

HA#005 pOM ***hah-tak** *(vi) 'amanecer/to dawn'* NHM: *hahtɨk* MM: Ma < *hahtá·kp* > 'amanecer', < *hahtá·kp* > 'aclararse (el día) [sic!] Pu < *hahtá·kp* > 'aclararse (el día)' At < *hahtá·kp* > 'amanecer' Ct < *hahtá·kp* > 'amanecer, aclararse (el día)'

HA#006 pMZ ***hak** *(vi) 'pasar, atravezar/to pass through'* LM: Cn < *hak, hak-* > (adv, preposición) 'más' (ejemplo: *hak kohy yɨ ka"k kop* 'siembra más matas de plátano') SoZ: *hak* (vi) 'cruzar' TxZ: *hak* (vi) 'pasar' ChisZ: C *hahk* (vi) 'cruzar; cuartearse; reventarse' (vt) 'cortarlo; cruzarlo, atravesarlo' N *hahk* (vi) 'reventarse, cruzar' (vt) 'cortarlo; cruzarlo' NE *hahk* (vi) 'cruzar' (vt) 'cortarlo (como un lazo); atravesarlo, cruzarlo'

HA#007 pZ ***hak(a)** *(adj) 'de olor desagradable/bad smelling* TxZ: *hakhak* (adj) 'oler a masa agria, apestar a frijoles o masa (ya echan espuma)' ChisZ: N *haka* (adj) 'de olor desagradable'

HA#008 pZ ***ham(ɨ)** *(vt) 'acordarse/to remember'* TxZ: *ha:m* (vt) sentir (dolor), saber (qué hacer) [?] ChisZ: C *ham* (vt) 'acordarse de lago' N *hahm* (vt) 'acordarse, recordarlo; echarlo de menos' NE *ham* (vt) 'sentirlo (como un dolor)' ChZ: *hamɨh* 'acordarse'

HA#009 pZ ***ko-ham** *(vt) 'observarlo/to guard (for a day)'* ChisZ: C *koham* (vt) 'guardarlo, observarlo; pertenecerle; tenerlo' N *kohahm* (vt) 'observarlo, guardarlo (dieta); pertenecerle' NE *koham* (vt) 'observarlo, guardarlo (como un día)'

HA#010 pMZ ***ham** *(n) 'cal/lime'* [pM, pOM **hahm*] NHM: *ha:hm* 'ceniza; gris' SHM: Tl *caho:m* Tu,Mi *ha:m* Tp *hA:m* MM: Ju,Pu *ha:m* 'cenizas, cal' Cc *hA:m* Ma *ha:m* Ja,Ct *ha:m* 'gris, cal' At *ha:m* 'gris—color de costoche, cal' LM: Cn < *ha:m* > Ca,Gu *ha:m* TaM: *hem* [transcription of Wonderly 1949] OIP: *hamɨ* 'ceniza' SaP: *hahm* SoZ: *ham* TxZ: *ham* ChisZ: C,N,S *ham* NE [Ocotepec, Pantepec, San Bartolomé, Chapultenango] *hap* [Wonderly 1949] [Ra] *hap* 'ceniza; cal' ChZ *ham*

HA#011 pMZ ***kuy-ham** *(n) 'ceniza/ashes'* [pM, pOM **kuyhahm*; pZ
*kuyham] SHM: Tl *kuyho:m* Tu *kuhʸá:m* Tp *kuhʸá:m* MM: Ju
kuʸhʸá:m Cc,At *kuhʸá:m* Ma *kɨyá:m* Ja *ku·hʸá:m* Ct *kɨhʸá:m* LM:
Cn <*kuyha:m*> Gu *kuhʸá:m* SaP: *kuyháhm* 'cenizas—de palo' SoZ:
kúyam TxZ: *kuyam* ChisZ: C [Co] *kuyham* [Te] <*cuy ham*>
'çeniça de palo' N *kuhyam* ChZ: *kuyham*

HA#012 pZ ***hama** *(n) 'día, sol/day, sun'* [pGZ **ha:ma*] SoZ:
ha:ma? 'sol' TxZ: *ha:m* ChisZ: C *hama* '=nagual' N,NE *hama*
S *[ha·má?]* ChZ: *hama*

HA#013 pM ***ha?m(V)** *'vamos/let's go'* [allegro form with various reflexes that are difficult to explain] NHM: *ha?mï* SHM: *ha?m* MM:
Ju *hó?ɨm* Ma *há?m̄ɨn* Ja *ha!m̄* Pu *ho!m̄*, *hó!mnɨ* At *ha?m̄*, *há?m̄dɨ*,
há?m̄ɨnɨ Ct *ha?mɨ̈* LM: Ca *há?mɨm* Gu *ham̄* [?] OlP: *ha?m* SaP:
hánga [?]

HA#014 pOM ***ha:nc...** *'de veras/truly'* [Cf. OlP: *han* (vi) 'echar
mentiras' and its derivative *hane* 'mentira'.] MM: Ja *ha·nʸč* At *ha:nʸč*
'de veras', *ha:nčpʸɨ* 'verdad', *há:nčpʸɨ* 'verdadera' LM: Ca *há:nǰɨn*
'verdad' Gu *ha:nʸč*

HA#015 pM ***hapóm** *(adv) 'mañana/morning'* [pOM **hapóm*] SHM:
Tl *hapʊm* Ay *habóm̄* MM: Ju *bom̄* Ma *huɨbóm̄* Ja *habóm̄* Pu *hɨgóm̄*
[?] At,Ct *hɨbóm̄* LM: Ca *habóm* SJ *habo·m* Gu *habó:m* Cn
<*habo:m*> SaP: *hóbom*

HA#016 pZ ***ha?p** *(vt) 'moler/to grind'* SaP: *ha?p* (vi, vt) 'grind
cooked corn' [Zo loan] SoZ: *ha?p* (vt) TxZ: *ha?p* (vt) 'moler en
metate' ChZ: *ha?p* 'desquebrar'

HA#017 pZ ***ha?p-e** *(n) 'masa rugosa/rough dough'* SaP: *ha?p*
'áspero' [Zo loan] SoZ: *ha?api?* 'masa' TxZ: *ha:?p* 'masa seca y
granuda' ChisZ: N *ha?pe* 'masa con pedacitos (que no están bien
molidos)'

HA#018 pOM ***hapóm-hapóm** *(adv) 'diario/daily'* NHM: *húvum*
MM: Ja *habóm̄-habóm̄* LM: Gu *habóm̄-habóm̄*

HA#019 pMZ ***ha:s?** *[?] (vi, vt) 'sobar/to rub'* NHM: *ha?š ~ ha:?šy*
[?] SHM: Tl *ho:š* MM: Ju <*ha:š*> 'frotar' (vi) Ma <*ha:š, hʸ?a?š̄*-
pʸ ~ hʸa?š̄pʸ> 'sobar, frotar, tallar (vt), 'frotar' (vi)' Ja <*ha:š,
hʸa?š̄pʸ, hʸa!š̄ ~ hʸa?š̄*> 'sobar, frotar, tallar (vt)' At <*ha:š,*

ʰʸæʔš̄pʸ> 'sobar, frotar, tallar (vt), 'frotar' (vi) Ct <ha:š̌, ʰʸaʔš̄pʸ,
ʰʸaʔš̄pʸ, ʰʸa:žémpʸ> 'sobar, frotar, tallar (vt), 'frotar' (vi)' LM: Cn
<ha·š̌~ha:š̌> (vt) SJ ha·š̌~ha:š̌ 'to rub with the hands' Gu
<ha:š̌, ʰʸalš̄p> 'tallar (vt), 'frotar' (vi)' SaP: haʔš̌ (vi, vt) 'rub
(body)' ChisZ: C *hahs* (vt) 'untarlo, ungirlo' N *has* (vt) 'untarlo,
frotarlo' NE *hahs* (vt) 'ungirlo; sobarlo'

HA#020 pZ ***haʔs** *(vt) 'asar/to roast'* TxZ: *ha:ʔs* (vt, vi-p) 'calentar
comida cerca de la lumbre' ChisZ: C *haʔs* (vt) 'asarlo; hornearlo'
N *haʔs* (vi) 'estar asado, estar horneado, estar tostado' (vt) 'asarlo;
hornearlo; tostarlo' NE *haʔs* (vi-s) 'estar asado' (vt) 'asarlo'

HA#021 pZ ***sis-haʔs-e** *(vt) 'carne asada/roast meat'* [pGZ
*šišhaʔase] TxZ: *šêšha:ʔs* 'carne de res dorada con el vapor de la
lumbre' ChisZ: C *sishaʔse*

HA#022 pOM ***ha:šk** *(adj) 'resbaloso (en lugar donde hay*
grava)/slippery' NHM: *ha:ʔš̌ɨk* 'resbalar' [?] SHM: Ay *hašk* MM:
Ju,At *hæšk* LM: Gu *has̄*

HA#023 pM ***haʔš̌** *(vi) 'leñar/to cut firewood'* NHM: *haʔš̌~ha"š̌*
MM: Ju <ha"š̌> Ma <ha"š̌, haʔšp, háʔšpɨ> 'leñar', <haʔšp,
ha"šč̣ɨ·m̄p> 'acarrear leña' Ja <halšp, ha"žá·m̄p> 'acarrear leña',
<ha"š̌, halš̄, halš̄p> 'leñar' [sic!] Pu <ha"š̌, halš̄p, hálš̄pɨ> At
<ha"š̌, halš̄p, hálš̄pɨ, tɨ: ʰʸǽ"š̌ʸ, nɨhkš mha"š̌ʸ> 'leñar', <haʔšp>
'acarrear leña' Ct <ha"šp> 'acarrear leña', <ha"š̌, haʔšp, tɨ: ʔoh
ʰʸa"š̌ʸ> 'leñar' LM: Ca <ha"š̌> Gu <ha"šhɨžó!p> 'acarrear
leña', <ha"š̌ʸč̣ɨm̄> 'leñar' SaP: haʔš̌ (vi) [Clark and Clark 1960]

HA#024 pM ***haʔš̌-i** *(n) 'leña/firewood'* NHM: *ha"š̌ʸ* MM: Ju,Ma,
Ja,Pu,At,Ct *ha"š̌ʸ* LM: Cn <ha"šy> Ca,Gu *ha"š̌ʸ* SaP: *haʔš̌*

HA#025 pM ***hat** *(vt) 'saber, poder/to know, be able'* NHM: *haht*
~*hat* 'aprender' SHM: Tl *hat [*hyatpy* 'capaz (hábil)'] MM: Ju
<hæt> 'aprender' Ma <hat> 'aprender', <ʰʸahtʸpʸ, ʰʸatémpʸ
~ʰʸatǽm̄pʸ> 'saber hacer', <ʰʸatǽm̄pʸ, ʰʸahtʸpʸ> 'poder' Ja
<ʰʸatǽ·mpʸ, ʰʸaht, ʰʸahtʸpʸ> 'poder', <ʰʸahtʸpʸ, ʰʸatǽ·mpʸ> 'sa-
ber hacer' Pu <hat̄> 'aprender' At <hat> 'aprender',
<ʰʸæhtʸpʸ, ʰʸatǽ·mpʸ, mhahtʸpʸ> 'saber hacer, poder' Ct
<t̬ʸɨkhatǽm̄pʸ, ʰʸahtʸpʸ, t̬ʸɨkháhtʸpʸ> 'poder', <ʰʸahtʸpʸ, ʰʸatémpʸ>
'saber hacer' LM: Cn <haht~hat> (vi) 'poder (saber hacer);
acontecer' Ca <hat> 'saber hacer, aprender' SJ *haht~hat* 'to

happen; to be able, know how, succeed' Gu <*ha͞t, hʸahpʸ, hʸadá·m͞pʸ, hʸaht*> 'saber hacer, poder' OlP: *hat* (vi) 'poder' (vt) 'saber (hacer) algo' SaP: *hat* (vi, vt) 'know how, be able'

HA#026 pOM ***haʔt ~ haʷt** *(vi) 'llegar/to arrive'* [irregular MM forms] SHM: Tl *hoʷt* 'llegar' MM: Ju <*hahtp*> Ma <*hahtp, haǃtám͞p, tǐː hʸaǃtʸ*> Pu <*hahtp, haǃtá·m͞p*> At <*hahtp, haʔtá·m͞p, tǐː hʸæʔtʸ*> Ct <*hahtp, haʔtám͞p, tǐː hʸaʔtʸ*> LM: Cn <*haʔt ~ haʷt*> (vi) Ca <*haʔtp, haʷt*> SJ *haʔt ~ haʷt*

HA#027 pZ ***hatoŋ** *(n) 'padre, papá/father'* [Unexplained reflexes in ChisZ; may be from another item meaning 'man', cf. ChZ *hateʔ* 'man'; the choice of **o* over **u* in the last syllable is motivated by the fact that /uw/, the sequence that would have given rise to a pZ sequence /uŋ/ in the final syllable, is generally not allowed.] SoZ: *háːtun* [Foster and Foster 1948], *haːtuŋ* [Wonderly 1949; Gutiérrez M. 1993] ChisZ: N *hata* 'padre' NE [Chapultenango] *hara* [Wonderly 1949] [Pantepec] *handa* [Wonderly 1949; infixed pronoun] [Ra] *hada* S [Tu] *hata* [Foster 1949] [Cp] *[ʔɨshá·taʔ]* 'mi papá' ChZ: StaMaCh *haton* 'padre' SnMiCh *hatoŋ* [Foster 1949]

HA#028 pM ***hatuʔk** *(n) 'otro/other'* [pOM **hatuʷk* (with /ʔ/ where /ʷ/ is expected in NHM)] NHM: *hadʋʔk* SHM: Tl *hatuʷk* MM: Ju *hætúʷk* Ja *hadúʔk* At *hatúʷk* LM: Ca,Gu *hatúʷk* Cn <*haduʷk*> (adj) SJ *haduʷgpɨ ~ haduʷkpɨ* OlP: *hatuʔk* SaP: *hatúʔk*

HA#029 pOM ***hatuʔn** *(part) 'así/like this'* NHM: *hidïʷm* '=como esto' SHM: Tu *hɨðɨʔn* MM: Ju *dɨʔn* Ma *hɨdúʔn̄* '=sí' Ja *hadúǃn̄* At *hɨdúʔn̄, duʔn̄* 'sí', *doʔn̄, hadúʔn̄* 'así' Ct *duʔn̄* 'sí', *hɨdúʔn̄ tǽʔnɨ* 'así' LM: Cn <*haduʔn*> (adv) Ca *hadúǃn̄* Gu *hadúǃn* '=sí'

HA#030 pOM ***haʔw ~ haʷw** *(vi) 'derrumbarse/to slide'* NHM: *haːv ~ haʷv* 'derrumbar' [The alternant *haːv* listed p. 37 in Schoenhals and Schoenhals (1965), but the verb classified as nonalternating; the expected shape is *haʔw ~ haʷw*.] MM: Ju <*haʷ*> Ja <*haǃp, haʷwá·m͞p*> At <*haǃp, haʷhá·m͞p, haʷwá·m͞p, tǐː hʸæʷy, haǃw̄*> Ct <*haǃp*> LM: Cn <*haʔw ~ haʔ· ~ haʷ*> (vi) Ca <*haʷ*> SJ *haʔw ~ haʷw* 'to slide (landslide)'

HA#031 pM ***haw-ʔɨy** *'saber/to know'* NHM: *nɨhaʔvi ~ nɨhava* (vt) SHM: Tl *nɨhowɨ* MM: Ju <*nʸɨháʷhɨp*> Ma <*nʸɨháʔɨpʸ ~ nʸɨháʔWɨpʸ, nʸɨhaWʔɨæ̃m͞pʸ*> Ja <*nʸɨháǃip, nʸɨháǃɨy,*

nʸihawɨ̄yǽ·m̄pʸ > At <*nʸɨhá?w̄ɨp, nʸɨhawɨ̄yǽ·m̄pʸ*> Ct <*nʸɨhá?w̄ɨpʸ,
nʸɨhawɨ̄yǽmpʸ*> LM: Ca <*niwɨ́"*> Gu <*nahw̥ɨ̈"w, nʸahw̥ɨ̈·ȳ,
nʸahw̥ɨ̈:pʸ*> SaP: *hawi* (vt)

HA#032 pZ ***haw-ay** *(vi) 'arder (la piel)/to burn (skin)'* TxZ:
ha:wo? ~ ha:wɨ? 'calentura' [a nominalized form from a pGZ root
**ha:w*, which would be the expected reflex of pZ *haway*] ChisZ: C
haway (vi) 'arderle' N *haway* (vi) 'arder (la piel)' ChZ: *hawe
pu?ci* 'viruela' ['arena + orilla' is the author's odd suggestion as to
the analytic meaning; I think *hawe* is derived from a lost root *haw
having to do with inflamed skin]

HA#033 pMZ ***ha:y?** *(vi) 'escribir/to write'* NHM: *ha:y ~ ha"* LM:
SJ *ha·y ~ ha:y* MM: Ju <*ha"y, hǽ:pʸ*> Ma <*ha"w, hǽ:pʸ,
hʸa"wémpʸ*> Ja <*ha"w, ha·ȳ, hǽ:pʸ*> Pu <*ha"y, tǣm dha"yá"nʸ*>
At <*ha", hǽ:pʸ, hʸa"hǽ·m̄pʸ*> Ct <*ha"w, hʸǽ:pʸ, hʸa"wémpʸ*>
LM: Cn <*ha·y ~ hay*> (vt) Ca <*ha"*> Gu <*ha:y, ha!pʸ,
ha:yá·m̄p*> OlP: *hay ~ ha?* (vi) 'escribir' (vt) 'escribirlo; engañarlo'
(ejemplo: "no vino; me engañó") SaP: *ha?y* (vi, vt) SoZ: *hay* AyZ:
[hay] (vi) TxZ: *hay* (vt, vi-a) ChisZ: C *hay* (vt) N *hay* (vi, vt)
NE [Chapultenango] *hay* [Wonderly 1949] [Ra] *hay* (vi, vt)
[derivative: *haye* 'escritura'] ChZ: SnMiCh *hay* 'run' [Wonderly
1949] [?-semantics]

HA#034 pMZ **ha:y?-kuy** *(n) 'instrumento para escribir/instrument for
writing'* [pM *haykuy > pOM *hayky; pZ *haykuy; since the data
were elicited on the fly and have not been confirmed by other researchers there may perhaps be reason to doubt their validity.] MM: Ca *haʸkʸ*
[Wonderly 1949] SoZ: *haykuy* [Wonderly 1949] ChisZ: N [Ma]
hakyuy 'act of writing'

HA#035 pOM **hahy-pa** *(n) 'secretario/secretary'* NHM: *ha:yva*
'=escribiente' MM: Ju,Ja,At *hǽ:bʸɨ* 'secretario municipal' LM: Gu
nɨgʸá:bʸɨ 'secretario municipal'

HA#036 pOM ***hayɨhp** *(adv) 'antes/before'* MM: Ju *hǽyɨhp* '=ade-
lante' Ma *hɨyɨhp* 'antes, primero' Pu *hɨyɨhp* At *hǽyɨhp* 'adelante'
Ma *hɨyɨhp tu"yé"pʸ* 'adelante' Ja *hɨyɨhp* 'adelante', *hayɨhp* 'primero'
[sic!] Ct *hɨyɨhp* 'primero' LM: Gu *hayɨ̈hp* 'adelante'

HA#037 pMZ ***hayá(w)** *(n) 'hombre/man'* [Perhaps a composite with
?aw 'mouth': **hay-?aw*. Cf. pMZ **ha:y?* 'to write'? In ChisZ we

find the form *ʔaŋ-kiʔm-ba-pɨ* 'ruler' (-*kiʔm*- means 'to ascend'), which also contains 'mouth'. The /ʔ/ of *ʔaw-* perhaps explains OlP *haʔyu* vs. SaP *háyau*.] NHM: *hayu* 'gente, persona, habitante' SHM: Tl *hoːʔy* Tm *haʔy* MM: Ju *haʔy̨* Ma *ha"y* '=señor' Ja *ha"y* Pu *haĺȳ* At *haʔy* 'gente' Ct *haʔy* 'gente', *haĺy* 'señor' [sic!] LM: SJ *may ha"y* 'mucha gente' Ca *haʔy* Cn *ha"y* '=persona' OlP: *haykaʔk* 'persona, gente', *haʔyu* 'gente de razón, gente rica' SaP: *háyau* 'hombre' SoZ: *haːya?* 'marido' AyZ: [*haːʔya*] TxZ: *haːy* 'macho', *hay-baː* 'hijo' ChisZ: C *hayah* 'esposo, marido' N *haya* 'esposo; hombre de veras, todo un hombre; varón, macho' NE *hayah* 'esposo, marido' S [Tu] *haya* 'husband' [Foster 1949] ChZ: StaMaCh *haya* 'marido' SnMiCh *haya* 'husband' [Foster 1949]

HA#038 pGZ ***pon-haːya?** *(n) 'salamandra/salamander'* SoZ: *ponhaːya?* 'especie de lagartija gordita blandita (a veces se mete en el sexo de la mujer)' TxZ: *pon-haːy* 'salamandra'

HA#039 pOM ***mah haʔy** *(n) 'viejo (persona, animal)/old (man, animal)'* SHM: Tl *mahoːʔy* 'persona viejo, señor' Tu,Tp *mɨhá"y* MM: Ju *mɨhháʔy* Ma *mɨháĺy* Ja *ʔamɨhá"y* Pu *mɨhá!nʸ* At *maháĺy* Ct *mɨhháĺȳ, mɨháĺȳ* Ca *mɨhháʔy* LM: Gu *mahhɨyá"y* [?]

HA#040 pMZ ***(h)a(?)y(aw)** *(n) 'robalo/snook'* OlP: *haykakoʼke* SaP: *hayau-akš* [Clark 1981] ChisZ: N *ʔaʔya*

HA#041 pM ***haycu?** *(n) 'venado/deer'* [pOM **hačyu?*] NHM: *ʔuhc haːč* '=ciervo' [Lit. 'hierba /planta' + 'mula/macho (una bestia)'; the latter must be a product of reanalysis since it is not an expected reflex.] SHM: Tl *ʔuhc hačuʔ* MM: Ju *hœǰú"* Ma,Ja,At *haǰú"* Pu,Ct *hɨǰú"* LM: Ca *hɨz̨ú"* OlP: *haycu?* SaP: *háyču*

HU#001 pMZ ***hu** *(part) 'partícula interrogativa/question marker'* NHM *huːʔ* 'cual' [*hu* expected] LM: SJ *hɨ* 'question marker' [vowel reduction indicative of lack of stress] ChisZ: C *hu* 'question marker'

HU#002 pZ ***huc..** *(part) 'como/how'* TxZ: *hū?c* ChisZ: C *huc* (adv) 'como, cómo' N *hucnɨm* (adv) 'como, cómo' NE *hucɨ* (adv) 'como, cómo'

HU#003 pZ ***huca?ŋ** [?] *(part) 'cuanto/how much, how many'* [Unexpected sporadic loss of final nasal in some ChisZ dialects.] TxZ: *hūːʔca* 'cuánto, cuántos' ChisZ: C *huhče?ŋ* (adj) 'cuanto, cuantos, cuánto, cuántos' N *huhče* (adv) 'cómo, cuanto, cómo, cuánto' NE *huhče* (adv) 'como, cuanto, cómo, cuánto' ChZ *huca?aŋ* 'cuánto'

HU#004 pM ***huk** *(vt)* *'dejar una bulta/to tie together (cargo, etc.)'* NHM: *hʋhk ~ hʋk* SHM: Tl *huk* LM: SJ *huhk ~ huk*

HU#005 pMZ ***huk?** *(vi, vt)* *'fumar/to smoke'* NHM: *hʋ?k ~ hʋ"k* SHM: Tl *hu"k* MM: Ju <*hu"k, hu?kp*> Ma <*hu?kp, hu"k, hʸi?kʸpʸ*> Ja <*hu"k, hʸu?k, hʸu?k*> Pu <*hu"k, hu!kp, hʸi!kʸpʸ*> At <*hu"k, hu?kp,hʸuü?kʸpʸ*> Ct <*hu"k, hu?kp, mhi?kʸpʸ*> LM: Cn <*hu?k ~ hu"k*> (vi) 'fumar (tabaco)' SJ *hu?k ~ hu"k* 'to smoke tobacco' Gu <*hu"k, hu?k, hu?p*> OlP: *hu?k* (vi, vt) SaP: *hu?k* (vi, vt) SoZ: *huk* (vi) ChisZ: C,NE *huhk* (vi, vt) N *huhk* (vt)

HU#006 pMZ ***huk?-i** *(n)* *'cigarro/cigarette'* [The pOM term **hu"ky* must also have referred to the tobacco plant.] NHM: *hu"k* SHM: Tl,Mi *hu"kʸ* Tu *hui"kʸ ~ hi"kʸ* MM: Ju,Ma,Ja,Ct *hi"kʸ* '=tabaco' At *huü"g* Ca *hu"ʸkʸ* 'tabaco' LM: Cn <*hu"ky*> 'tabaco, tabaquillo [Nicotiana tabacum]' Gu *hu"kʸ* '=tabaco' ChisZ: C,NE *huki* N *huki* '=puro' S *[hu·kí?]* ChZ: *huki*

HU#007 pMZ ***huk?-ut** *(n)* *'fuego, lumbre/fire, light'* [pOM **hu?kwt* with metathesis of the two last consonants in pre-NHM; pZ **hukut*; ChisZ and ChZ added the instrumental suffix *tik*.] NHM: *hʋ?ktu* 'fumarón' SoZ: *húkti* [Foster and Foster 1948; Wonderly 1949] TxZ: *hukut* '=llama' ChisZ: C *hukitik* N *huktyik* 'fuego, lumbre, llama' NE [Chapultenango] *huktik* [Wonderly 1949] [Tapalapa, Ocotepec, Pantepec] *huktihk* [Wonderly 1949] [Ra] *huktihk* 'fuego' S [Tu] *hukiti* [Wonderly 1949] ChZ: *hukuti* 'fuego, lumbre'

HU#008 pZ ***hukuk** *(vi)* *'haber tufo/to have a disagreeable odor'* [pGZ **hu:k*] TxZ: *hu:k* (vt) 'apestar, fumar' ChisZ: C *huku?k* (vi) 'haber aroma, haber tufo' N *hukuhk* (vi) 'tener mal olor'

HU#009 pM ***hu?ki** *(n)* *'lechuza, tecolote, buho/owl'* NHM: *hʋ?k* '[Bubo virginianus mayensis, Strix fulvescens]' SHM: Tl *hu"k* 'lechuza' MM: Ma *hu?kn̥* 'tecolote', *hu?k* 'buho' [sic!] Ja *hu?k* 'buho, tecolote' Pu *hu!k* 'tecolote, lechuza' At *hu?k* 'tecolote, buho' Ct *hu?k* LM: Cn <*hu?k*> 'lechuza campanario [Tyto alba]' Ca *hu?k* 'lechuza' Gu *hu?k* 'tecolote, buho' Cn *hu?k* [Hoogshagen 1984] OlP: *hu?ki* 'tecolote'

HU#010 pMZ **hu:?m** *(vt) 'derrumbar/to fling down'* OlP: *hu:m* (vt) 'repellar' ChisZ: C [Te] <*humba*> 'caerse, derrumbarse tierra' N *hu?m* (vi) 'derrumbarse' ChZ: *yakhum* (vt) 'destruir' [?]

HU#011 pM **hu-mV** *(part) 'donde, ¿donde?/where, where?'* NHM: *hʋma* OlP: *humɨ*

HU#012 pGZ **hu:?mɨ?** *(adv) 'lejos/far away'* SoZ: *hú?umɨ?* AyZ: *[hu?m]* TxZ: *hu:?m*

HU#013 pOM **humɨht** *(n) 'año/year'* NHM: *hʋ:hnt* SHM: Tl *humɨht* Tu,Tp *hɨmɨht* MM: Cc,Pu *hɨmɨht* Ju,At '=edad' Ma,Ja,Ct '=edad (pos)' LM: SJ *hɨmɨht* Cn <*hɨmɨht*> Gu *homɨ́ht* '=edad (pos)' Ca *hɨmɨ́ht* '=edad'

HU#014 pMZ **hun** *(vi) 'quemar/to burn (as hot water)'* LM: Gu *hun* 'escaldar' [Nordell, p.c.] TxZ: *hunka?* (vi) 'chamuscarse' ChisZ: C *hun* (vi) 'quemarse con agua caliente' (vt) 'quemarlo con agua caliente; abalandarlo con agua caliente' [derivative: *huni* 'té'] N *hun* (vi) 'ablandarse, podrirse (con agua)' (vt) 'ablandarlo (echándole agua)' [derivative: *hunihuni* 'sucio'] NE *hun* (vt) 'quemarlo con agua caliente'

HU#015 pZ **huhnɨyɨ** *(n) 'tepezcuintle [Cuniculus paca]/paca'* TxZ: *hu:dɨ:y* ChisZ: C *hunhɨyɨ* N *huhnɨyɨ* NE *hunɨyɨ*

HU#016 pMZ **hu:?n** *(vi, vt) 'endurecerse (vi) mecatear (vt)/to become hardened, to rope'* [A similar relationship holds among the semantics of the forms below as with pM *?e:?m 'to become hardened' and pM *?e:?m-e 'vein, cord'.] MM: 'endurecerse' Ju <*yæhhú:nɨ*> Ma <*hu?m̄p, hu:ná̄mp*> Ja <*hu!m̄p, hu:ná·m̄p*> At <*hu?m̄p, tɨ: hʸu:nʸ*> Ct <*hu?m̄p, hu:ná̄mp*> LM: Cn <*hu·n~hu:n*> (vi) 'ponerse duro' Gu <*hu!m̄p, hu:ná·m̄p*> 'endurecerse' AyZ: *[hu?nga?]* (vi) 'ahorcarse' TxZ: *hu?n* (vt) 'lazar' ChisZ: C *hu?n* (vt) 'mecatearlo, enlazarlo, lazarlo' N *hu?n* (vt) 'lazarlo' NE *hu?n* (vt) 'mecatearlo'

HU#017 pMZ **hu:n-i** *(n) 'árbol duro/hard tree'* [pM *hu:ni > pOM *hu:ny; pZ *huni > pGZ *hu:ñi; NHM *hʋ?n* 'corazón del árbol, parte central dura' as well as MM-At *hu?mp* 'tieso' are based on the alternate root. Both alternate roots are used to derive a nominal in At.] MM: [all these forms lack expected palatalization] Ju *hu:n* 'tieso' Ma *hu:n* 'duro (adj.); necio, nudo en madera, macizo, tieso' Ja *hu:n* 'duro (adj.)' Pu *hu:n* 'macizo; necio; duro (adj.)' At *hu:n* 'macizo, tieso, duro (adj.)' Ct *hu:n* 'duro (adj.), tieso' LM: SJ *hu·ny* 'hard' Gu *hu:nʸ* 'duro (adj.), macizo, tieso, nudo en madera' OlP: *hu:ni* 'cocuíte (cochíte, madre de cacao); *hu:nikuyɨ* palo de cocuíto' SoZ: *hu:ñi?* TxZ: *hu:ñ* 'hule'

HU#018 pM *hup (vt) 'voltear/to tip over' LM: SJ *huhp ~ hup* 'to tip over, cover over' Gu < *hup, huhp* > [Nordell, p.c.] OlP: *hup* (vt) 'voltearlo (boca abajo)' [cf. ChisZ: C *kohupu?* (vt) sumergerlo]

HU#019 pOM *?a-húp (vt) 'tapar (olla, etc.)/to cover (pot, etc.)' NHM: *?ahʋp ~ ?ahʋhp* 'tapar (p.ej., con un cajón)' MM: Ju < *?œhúp* > Ma,Ct < *?ahúp* > LM: Cn < *ahuhp ~ ahup* > (vt) 'tapar, cubrir (p.ej., una cubeta de agua)'

HU#020 pOM *ko?-húp (n) 'sombrero/hat' NHM: *kuhʋp* SHM: *kuhúp* MM: Ju *kuhúp, kup* Ma,Ct *kɨhúp* Ja *ku"húp* At *kuhúp* LM: Ca *kuhúp* Gu *ku"húp*

HU#021 pOM *win-hup (n) 'máscara/mask' NHM: *vinhʋp* MM: Ma *hɨnhúp* Pu *winhúp, winúp* At *hɨnhúp* Ct *hɨnúp* LM: SJ *wi·nhup*

HU#022 pGZ *hu:p (vi) 'zumbar/to buzz' SoZ: *hu:p* TxZ: *hu:p* (vi) 'sonar (agua, viento), zumbar (agua, viento)'

HU#023 pMZ *hup? (vt) 'jalar/to pull' NHM: *hʋ?p ~ hʋ"p* LM: SJ *hu?p ~ hu"p* 'to hurt a lot' SaP: *hu?p* (vi, vt) TxZ: *hu:pka?* (vt, vi) 'pegar (alambre) (vt), arrugarse (vi)' [?] ChisZ: C *huhp* (vt) 'apretarlo' N *huhp* (vt) '=afligirlo' ChZ: *hup*

HU#024 pMZ *hu?ps (vt) 'lazar/to rope' NHM: *hʋ?pš* MM: 'pegar con varita' Cc < *hu?pš, hʸu?pšʸpʸ, hʸu?pš, hʸu?pšœmpʸ, tɨ: thu?pšʸ, kʸœh thu?pšʸ* > 'azotar' At < *hu?pš* > 'azotar' Ja < *hu?pš* > 'azotar', < *hu?pš, hʸu?pš, hu?pšpœhtɨ* > Pu < *hu!pš* > At < *hu?pš, hʸü?pšʸpʸ* > Ct < *hu?pš, hu?pšpœhtɨ* > LM: Gu < *hu?š, hʸu?šʸp* > 'pegar (con varita), azotar' OlP: *hu?pš* (vt) 'lazar' TxZ: *hu?ps* (vt) 'agarrar (agua con la mano)' [?-semantics] ChisZ: N *hu?ps* (vt) 'echarlo como sobrecarga'

HU#025 pM *hu?pš-an (n) 'soga/rope' [pOM **hu?pšn*] NHM: *hʋ?pšɨn* OlP: *hu?pša'n* '=reata'

HU#026 pMZ *hu?s (vi) 'rasurar/to shave' LM: Cn < *hu·š ~ hu"š* > (vt) 'alisar' SJ *hu?š ~ hu"š* 'to be smooth, neat' ChisZ: C *hu?s* (vi, vt) '=excluirlo' N *hu?s* (vi, vt) '=cortarle el pelo, rasparlo' NE *hu?s* (vi, vt) '=afeitarlo'

HU#027 pOM *hu"šy (adj) 'liso/smooth' MM: Ma *hu"š* LM: Cn <*hu"šy*> Gu *hu!ṣ̌*

HU#028 pOM *ku-hu:?š (vi) 'cubrir la cabeza/to cover (head)' NHM: *kuhv:?š* 'cubrir la cabeza (p.ej., con un velo), ser padrino de lazo, padrino de paño (padrino de una novia)' MM: 'rebozo' Ju,Ja *kuhú:š* Ma,Ct *kɨhú:š* LM: Ca *kuhú:š* SJ *ko?hu·š ~ ko?hu:š* 'to put on a wedding wreath'

HU#029 pMZ *hut (vt) 'agujerear/to pierce' NHM: *hvht ~ hvt* 'hacer un hoyo, perforar', *yakhvht ~ yakhut* (vt) 'agujerear algo, perforar algo' SHM: Tl *yikhut* (vt) TxZ: *hut-ka?* (vi) 'pasar (hilo por agujero), meterse (iguana), deslizarse (víbora)' ChisZ: N *huht* (vt) 'abrir una zanja'

HU#030 pOM *hut (n) 'hoyo/hole' NHM: *hvt* '=agujero, cajete, agujereado, zanja' SHM: Tl,Ay *hut* 'hoyo' Mi *hut ~ hvt* 'agujero' MM: 'agujero' Ju *hut* Ma *hut* '=cueva, hueco, sepulcro' Ja *hut* '=cueva, hueco' Pu *hut* '=cueva' At *hut* '=hueco' Ct *hut* 'cueva'; *hut* '=sepulcro' [sic!] LM: 'agujero' Cn <*hut*> Ca *hut* SJ *hut* 'cave' Gu *hut* '=cueva, hueco'

HU#031 pM [Veracruz] *hut-hut (n) 'pájaro barranqueño/a kind of bird' OlP: *huthu't* SaP: *huthut* [Clark 1981]

HU#032 pZ *hu-ti (part) 'donde, ¿dónde?/where, where?' [pGZ *hu:t̯ʸi*] TxZ: *hu:če* (adv) 'donde' ChisZ: C *hutɨ* (adv) N *huti ~ hut* (adv)

HU#033 pMZ *hu:?t (vt) 'sacar (cosa delgada)/to pull out (thin object)' NHM: *hv:?t* 'sacar (p.ej., una espada), jalar (p.ej., una raíz), desenvainar (p.ej., una espada)' MM: 'sacar' Ju <*hu:t*> Ja,At <*hu:t, hʸu?t̯ʸpʸ*> LM: Cn <*hu·t ~ hu:t*> (vt) 'desenvainar, sacar; sacar (dinero del banco)' Ca <*hu:t*> Gu <*hu:t, hʸu·?pʸ*> SJ *hu·t ~ hu:t* 'to pull out' OlP: *hu?t* (vd) 'caminar sobre uno un insecto' [?] TxZ: *hu?t* (vt, vi-p) 'batir (con paleta)' ChisZ: C [Co] *hu?t* (vi, vt) 'hilarlo; agitarlo, menearlo' [Te] <*hutpa*> 'hilar' N *hu?t* (vt) 'menearlo, batirlo'

HU#034 pM ***hu:ʔt-yɨk** *(n) 'araña/spider'* NHM: *hʋ"tʸk* '=típula'
OlP: *hu:yɨ'k* SaP: *hútuk* 'insecto'

HU#035 pM ***hutVk** *(adj) 'vivo, despierto/live, awake'* [pOM **huhtyk*
with cluster reduction in non-NHM] NHM: *hʋ:hntyk* [unexplained
nasal] MM: Ju,Pu,Ct *hi:kʸ* 'vivo' Ma,Ja *hi:kʸ* At *huük*ʸ 'despierto',
huü:kʸ 'vivo' [sic!] Ca *hu.ʸkʸ* 'vivo' LM: Cn <*hu:ky*> (adj)
'vivo' (vi) 'vivir' Gu *huhkʸ* 'despierto' OlP: *hutu'k* 'vivo,
despierto', *hutuk* (vi) 'despertarse' SaP: *nihútukna* 'vivo' [Clark
1961], *hutuk* (vi) 'despertarse'

HU#036 pOM ***hu:ʔw** *(n) 'zapote amarillo/yellow sapote'* NHM:
hʋ:ʔv '=zapote blanco' MM: Ju,Ma,At *hu"* LM: Gu,Ca *hu"*

HU#037 pMZ ***huwɨstɨkmɨy** *(adv) 'pasado mañana/the day after tomorrow'* [pM **huwɨštɨhkmɨ* > pOM **hwɨštɨhkm*; pZ **wɨstɨkmɨy*]
NHM: *vɨhškm* SHM: Tl *wɨštɨhkp* MM: Ju *hɨštɨhm̩* Ma *hɨštɨhm̩,*
hɨštɨhkm̩ Ja *hwuštɨhkm̩, huštɨhkm̩, wɨštɨhkm̩* Pu *wɨštɨhkm̩, wɨštɨhm̩* At
wɨštɨhkm̩ ~ hɨštɨhkm̩ Ct *hɨštɨhkm̩* LM: Ca *wɨštɨkp* Gu *huštɨpk*
'=anteayer' OlP: *huštɨkmɨ* SaP: *húštɨkm* TxZ: *wɨ̄s-tɨkɨ* ChisZ: C,N
wɨstɨkmɨy NE *wɨstɨɲmɨ* ChZ: *wɨstɨkhi* [final segments not explained]

HU#038 pMZ ***huʔyi** *(n) 'carbón/coal'* NHM: *hu"* SHM: Tl *huʔy*
Tp *hu"y ~ huʔhy̩* Tu *hu"y* Mi *huʔy* MM: Ju,Cc,Ma,Ct *hu"y* Ja *hu!n̄ʸ*
Pu *hu!ȳ* At *huʔȳ* LM: Ca *hu"nʸ* Gu *hu!n̄ʸtʸ* SaP: *huʔy* AyZ: [*hu:ʔyi*]
'=brasa' TxZ: *hu:ʔy* '=brasa' ChisZ: C *huʔuy* N *huʔyi* '=brasa'
NE *huʔuy* '=brasa' ChZ: *huʔwi*

HU#039 pMZ ***huy** *(vt) 'comprar/to buy'* NHM: *hʋ:y ~ hʋ:hy ~ hʋy*
SHM: Tl *huy* Tu <*huy, mhu·ypʸ, mhu"ypʸ, hú.ʔyɨʔm*> Tp <*huy,*
mhu.ʸpʸ, hʸuȳǽmpʸ> Mi <*huy*> MM: Ju,Ma <*huy*> Cc
<*hu·ypʸ, mhu·ypʸ, huy, hʸu·ypʸ, hʸu·y, tɨ: thuy, hʸuȳǽmpʸ, kʸǽh*
thu·y> Ja <*huȳ, hʸu·ȳ, hi:pʸ*> Pu,Ct <*huȳ*> At <*huȳ, hʸuü:bʸ*>
LM: Cn <*hu·y ~ huy*> (vt) SJ *hu·y ~ huy* Ca <*huy*> Gu <*huȳ,*
hʸu:pʸ, hʸu·ȳ> OlP: *huy* (vi, vt) SaP: *huy* (vi, vt) TxZ: *huy* (vt)
ChisZ: C,N,NE *huy* (vt)

HU#040 pOM ***ku-huhy ~ ku-huy** *(vt) 'pagar/to pay'* NHM: *kuhʋ:y*
~ kuhʋ:hy ~ kuhʋy SHM: Tl *kuhuy* MM: Ju <*kuhúy*> At,Ja
<*kuhúȳ*> Ct,Pu <*kɨhúȳ*> LM: Cn <*kohu·y ~ kohuy*> (vt) Ca
<*kuhúy*> Gu <*kuhúȳ*>

HU#041 pOM *mu-huhy ~ mu-huy* *(vi)* *'pagar/to pay'* NHM:
muhvːy ~ muhvːhy ~ muhvy MM: Ju <*mɨhúy*> Ma <*mɨ·húy*> At
<*mɨhúy*> LM: Ca <*mɨhúy*> Cn <*mɨhu·y ~ mɨhuy*> (vt) 'pagar
sueldo' Gu <*mɨhúy*>

HU#042 pOM *huhy-pa* *(n)* *'comprador/buyer'* [Cf. ChisZ: C
huʔyopyapɨ (adj, n) NE *huʔyobyabɨ* (adj, n)] NHM: *hvːyva* SHM:
Tp *ʔAhúːʸbʸɨ* MM: Cc *ʔAhú·ybʸɨ, hú·ybʸɨ* Ju,Ma,Ja,Pu,Ct *híːbʸɨ* At
húübʸɨ LM: Ca *húːʸbʸɨ* Gu *húːnbʸɨ*

HU#043 pM [Veracruz] *huy-huy* *(n)* *'mosca/fly'* OlP: *huyhuʼy*
'mosquito, mosca menuda' SaP: *húhyuy*

HO#001 pM *hoː* *(part)* *'sí/yes'* [pOM *hoː*] LM: Ca,Gu *hoː* OlP:
hoː SaP: *hoː*

HO#002 pOM *hoʔc ~ hoⁿc* *(vt)* *'borrar/to erase'* NHM: *hoʔc ~ hoⁿc*
'=manchar, tachar (p.ej., lo escrito con tinta)' MM: Ju <*hoⁿc*> Ma
<*hoⁿc, hoʔcʸpʸ*> Ja <*hoⁿc, hʸoʔc, hʸoʔcʸpʸ*> Pu <*hoⁿc, hʸocʸpʸ*>
Ct <*hoⁿc, hʸoʔcʸpʸ*> LM: Gu <*hoⁿc, hʸoʔcʸp*> LM: Cn
<*hoʔc ~ hoⁿc*> (vt) '=despintar' SJ *hoʔc ~ hoⁿc* 'to erase'

HO#003 OM *hoʔc-n* *(n)* *'borrador/eraser'* MM: Ja *hoʔcn̄* Pu *hoꜝcn̪*
Ct,Ma,Ju *hoʔcn̪* LM: Gu *hoʔct*

HO#004 pZ *hoh* *(n)* *'contenido/contents'* TxZ: *hoho* (adv) 'adentro'
ChisZ: C *hoh; hohtaka* (adj) 'vacío, desocupado' ('sin contenido') N
hoh 'contenido, el espacio adentro', *hohɨy* (vi) 'llenarse, estar lleno'
(vt) 'llenarlo; cargarlo (arma de fuego)' NE *hohɨy* (vt) 'llenarlo'
ChZ: *hoh* 'área'; *hoho?* 'adentro'

HO#005 pZ *hoh-mɨ* *(adv)* *'adentro/inside'* SoZ: *hóhmɨ* 'deep' [Fos-
ter and Foster 1948], *hohmɨ?* [Gutiérrez M. 1993] ChisZ: C *hohmo*
N *hohmo* (adj) 'hondo'; (adv) 'adentro' NE *hohmɨ*

HO#006 pZ *hohi(-mɨ)* *(adv)* *'mañana/tomorrow'* [pGZ *hoyi*] SoZ:
hoymɨ [Wonderly 1949], *hoymɨ?* [Gutiérrez M. 1993] TxZ: *hoye*
(adv) ChisZ: C *homih* (adv) N *homi* (adv) NE *homi* [Wonderly
1949, dialects of Tapalapa, Ocotepec] NE *homyɨ* [Wonderly 1949,
dialect of Pantepec] *homye* (adv) [Ra] S [Tu] *hoymɨ* [Wonderly
1949] *hoymi* [Wonderly 1949, Ocotepec] ChZ: SnMiCh *hohi*
[Wonderly 1949] StaMaCh *hohi* (adv)

HO#007 pM ***hok** *(vi) 'humear/to be smoking'* NHM: *hohk ~ hok* SHM: Tu *hokp* 'ahumarse' MM: Ma *< hohkp >* '=ahumarse, ahumar' Ja,At,Ct *< hohkp >* '=ahumar' LM: Cn *< hohk ~ hok >* (vi) 'humear' (vt) 'quemar (incienso)' SJ *hohk ~ hok* 'to be smoking' OlP: *hok* (vi) 'salirle manchas en el cuerpo' SaP: *hok* (vi, vt) 'stain'

HO#008 pOM ***hok-y** *(n) 'tizne/soot'* NHM: *hɨk* '=estar ahumado, ahumado' MM: Ma *hok* 'mancha negra del carbón' Ja *tuhnhók* 'pólvora', *hok* 'tizne' At *hoök^y* '=mancha negra del carbón' Ct *hok* 'pólvora', *hek^y* '=mancha negra del carbón' [sic!] LM: Cn *< hoky >* 'pólvora para escopeta' Gu *hok^y* 'pólvora'

HO#009 pMZ ***hoko** *(n) 'humo/smoke'* [pM *hoko > pOM *hok; pZ *hoko > pGZ *ho:ko] NHM: *hok* SHM: Tl *hUk* Ay *hok* MM: Ju *hok* Ma *hok* 'nubes, nublado' Ja *hok* '=vapor, nubes' Pu *hok* 'nubes', *tæm hok* 'nublado' At *hok* Ct *hok* '=nubes, vapor' LM: Cn *< hok >* 'nube' Ca *hok* 'nubes' Gu *hok* '=nubes' OlP: *hoko* SaP: *hok* 'pólvora, mal de pinta' SoZ: *ho:ko* [Wonderly 1949], *ho:ko?* [Gutiérrez M. 1993] AyZ: *[ho:go]* TxZ: *ho:k* ChisZ: C *hokoh* N, NE *hoko* S *[ho·ko]* ChZ: *?o?ka? ~ ?o?kkɨ* 'húmedo'

HO#010 pOM ***na:hš-hok** *(n) 'polvo de tierra/dust from the ground'* NHM: *našhok* LM: Cn *< na:šhok >*

HO#011 pOM ***ho:ky** *(n) 'cuervo, cacalote/common raven'* NHM: *hɨ:?k* '[Corvus corax xinuatus]' SHM: Tl *hU:ky* 'cuervo' Tp,Mi *ho:k^y* 'cacalote' MM: Ju *he:k^y* Cc *ho:k^y* 'cacalote' At *hoö:k^y* LM: Cn *< ho:ky >* 'cacalote, cuervo' [Corvus corax] Ca *ho:^{y}k^y*

HO#012 pMZ ***ho?k** *(vt) 'esperar/to wait'* LM: Cn *< ho?k ~ ho"k >* (vt) 'enganchar' SJ *ho?k ~ ho"k* 'to pick fruit with a hook, to pull with a hook; to form a tortilla in the hands (the first stage)' TxZ: *ho?k* (vt, vi-p) ChisZ: C,NE *ho?k* (vt) N *ho?k* (vi, vt)

HO#013 pOM ***ho?k-n** *(n) 'gancho/hook'* NHM: *ho?kɨn* MM: Ju, Ma,Ja,At *ho?kn̦* LM: Ca *ho?kt* Gu *?ahó?t, ho?t*

HO#014 pMZ ***hókos** *(adj) 'tibio/tepid'* [pM *hokoš > pOM *hokš; pZ *hokos > pGZ *hokoš, with unexplained palatalization of last consonant.] NHM: *hokš* 'caliente' SHM: 'caliente, pero no mucho' Tu *hokš* Tp *ho?kš* MM: Ju,Cc,Ma,Ja,At,Ct *hokš* LM: Cn *< hokš >* (adj) 'tibio, medio caliente' SJ,Ca,Gu *hokš* OlP: *hoko'š* (adj) 'caliente—la ropa; tibia—el agua' *hokóšni:hi* 'agua tibia' SaP: *hogošni?* 'agua tibia' SoZ: *hókoš* [Gutiérrez M. 1993] TxZ: *hokeš* (adj) 'calientito (persona con sarape; sarape grueso)' [/o/ expected in last syllable]

HO#015 pMZ ***hoks** *(vt)* *'escardar/to weed'* OlP: *ho?kš* (vt) 'engancharlo, jalarlo (con gancho)' [?] SaP: *hokš* (vi, vt) 'hoe' TxZ: *hoks* (vt, vi-a) 'rozar' ChZ: *hoks* 'escardar'

HO#016 pMZ ***ho:?m** *(vi)* *'enmohecer/to mold'* OlP: *ho:m* (vd) 'sudar' ChisZ: C,NE *ho?m* (vi, vt) N *ho?m* (vi)

HO#017 pMZ ***home** *(adj)* *'nuevo/new'* [pM *home > pOM *homy; pZ *home > pGZ *ho:me] SHM: Tl *hem^y* MM: Ju *hem^y* Ma,Ja,Pu, At,Ct *hem̄^y* LM: Gu *hem̄^y* Ca *hem^y* Cn <*hemy*> (adj) SoZ: *ho:mi?* TxZ: *homina?* (adj) ChisZ: C,N *home* ChZ: *home?*

HO#018 pZ ***ho?ma** *(adj)* *'gris/gray'* [pGZ *ho?m- (*ho?oma expected in free form)] TxZ: *ho?mki?da:?* (adj) 'estar cenizo (del cuerpo, p.ej., cuando se queda jabón, tierra o arena en el piel)' ChisZ: C *ho?ma* '=plomo' N *ho?ma*

HO#019 pOM ***homny** *(n)* *'avispa masón/potter wasp'* SHM: Tp *hom^y* Mi *him^yt^y* MM: Cc *hom^y* Ma *he:n^y* Ja *he:m^y* At *hoö:m^y*

HO#020 pMZ ***hon** *(n)* *'pájaro/bird'* [pM, pOM *hohn; pZ *hon] NHM: *ho:hn* 'pájaro—pero pequeño, p.ej., el zanate' SHM: Tl *hU:n* Ay *ho:n* MM: Ju,Ma,Ja,Pu,At,Ct *ho:n* LM: Cn <*ho:n*> Ca *ho:n* SJ *ho·n* Gu *ho:n* 'pajarito silvestre' SaP: *hohn* SoZ: *hon* AyZ: *[hon]* TxZ: *hon* ChisZ: C *hon* [Wonderly (1949), who notes that here the form is taboo 'male genitals'. This explains why the form is missing in Harrison et al. (1981). The Classical Nahuatl word for 'bird', *to:to:tl*, likewise also means 'male genitals'.] N [FL] *poli hon* 'pájaro que no tiene cola' [not attested in isolated form] [Ma] *hon* NE [Tapalapa, Ocotepec, Chapultenango] *hot* [Wonderly 1949] [Ra] *hot* S *hon* ChZ: SnMiCh *hon* [Wonderly 1949]

HO#021 pOM ***mašn-hohn** *(n)* *'codorniz (grande)/large quail'* SHM: Tu *ma:ǯ^yó:n* Mi *maš^yhó:n* MM: Ju *mæš^yn̩hó:n* Ma *maš̄^yn̩yó:n* At *maš̄^yhó:n* Ct *maš^yn̩yó:n* LM: Gu *mazj^yó:n*

HO#022 pGZ ***mo:y-hon** **(< mo:ya?-hon)** *(n)* *'primavera/robin'* SoZ: *mó:yhon* TxZ: *boyhon*

HO#023 pMZ ***yɨk hon** *(n) 'tipo de centzontle/a kind of mockingbird'*
[lit., 'black bird'; pOM *yɨk hohn] NH<u>M</u>: *yɨk ho:hn* 'tipo de
centzontle' MM: Ju *yɨkhó:n* 'tordo' Ma *yɨkhó:n* 'tordo, zanate' At
yɨkhó:nsd 'zanate' ChisZ: NE *yɨkhot* 'cacalote'

HO#024 pMZ ***ho?n** *(vi) 'aflojarse/to be loose'* NHM: *ho?n ~ ho"n*
'flojar' SHM: Tp < *ho?mp, hʸo"nʸ* > OlP: *ho?n* 'robar' (vi, vt) 'ro-
barlo' SaP: *ho?n* (vi, vt) 'be loose' TxZ: *ho?nksa* (vi) 'aflojarse'
ChisZ: C *ho?n* (vi) NE *ho?n* (vi) 'aflojarse (como un tornillo)'
(vi-s) 'estar flojo'

HO#025 pZ ***cɨk-ho?n** *(vt) 'soltar/to untie'* SaP: *cɨkhó?n* 'soltar (persona)' [Zo loan] TxZ: *cɨkho?n* (vt) 'aflojar' ChisZ: NE *cɨkho?n* (vt)
'aflojarlo'

HO#026 pMZ ***yak-ho?n** *(vt) 'aflojar/to loosen'* SHM: Tl *yikhU"n*
(vt) 'aflojar' OlP: *yakho?n* (vt) 'aflojarlo' SaP: *yakho?n* (vt) 'soltar, aflojar' [Clark and Clark 1960] TxZ: *yakho?n* 'aflojar' [Clark
n.d.] ChisZ: C *yakho?n* (vt) 'aflojarlo, desapretarlo' NE *yakho?n*
(vt) 'desapretarlo'

HO#027 pM ***ho?ni(k)** *(adj) 'flojo, suelto/loose, untied'* [pOM
**ho"ny*] NHM: *hɨ"n* 'flojo (p.ej., un vestido), suelto, holgado' MM:
At *he?nʸ* 'flojo (cosas)' Pu *hi"nʸ* 'suelto, flojo' Ct *ho"n* 'flojo (cosas)' OlP: *ho?no'k* [progressive vowel harmony, a sporadic phenome-
non] SaP: *hó?nik* 'suelto' ChisZ: C *ho?nba* 'suelto, no apretado'

HO#028 pOM ***?a-hop** *(n) 'desayuno/breakfast'* NHM: *?ahop* '=al-
muerzo' LM: Cn < *ahop* >

HO#029 pOM ***ho?p ~ ho"p** *(vi) 'enmarañar/to entangle'* NHM:
ho?p ~ ho"p 'enmarañar, enredar (p.ej., hilo enredado)' MM: Ja
< *ho?p, ho"bá·m̄p* > 'enredarse' At < *ho?pp, ho"bá·m̄p* >
'enredarse' Ct < *ho?p, ho"bá m̄ p* > 'enredarse' LM: Cn
< *ho?p ~ ho"p* > (vi) 'enmarañar; enredarse' SJ < *ho?p ~ ho"p* > 'to
entangle' SoZ: *ho:p* 'enrollar' [Elson 1960] [?]

HO#030 pOM ***ho?p-y** *(n) 'maraña/tangle'* NHM: *hɨ"p* MM: Ma
ne·hʸó?pɨp Pu *he"pʸ, ni·hʸó!pɨp* At *hoö!pʸ, hö!pʸ* Ct *nɨ·hʸó?pɨp*

HO#031 pM ***hopoy** *(n) 'mañana/morning'* [pOM *hopy] NHM:
nayhɨp SHM: Tl *hopy* MM: 'por la mañana, en la mañana' Ju *hepʸ*
Ma *hep̄ʸ* Ja *hep̄ʸ* At *hoöpʸ* 'por la mañana, en la mañana', *hepʸm̄ʸón̄ʸ*

'en la madrugada' Ct *hep̄ʸ* LM: Cn <*hopy*> (adv) 'el tiempo de las seis a las ocho de la mañana' Ca *hoypʸ* [Wonderly 1949] Gu *hop̄ʸ* 'por la mañana, en la mañana, en la madrugada' OlP: *hopoy* SaP: *hópoy* 'la mañana', *hopoyít* 'en la mañana'

HO#032 pZ **hos** *(n) 'hoyo/hole'* [pGZ **hos*] SoZ: *hos* 'cueva' AyZ: *[hos]* 'pozo' TxZ: *hos* '=cueva, hueco, abertura, agujero' ChisZ: C *hohs* 'paredón, derrumbe' NE *hos* 'hoyo como para un poste'

HO#033 pMZ **ho:?s** *(vt) 'moler masa/to grind dough'* NHM: *nɨho:?š* 'remoler la masa' ChisZ: C *ho?s* (vt) 'molerlo' N *ho?s* (vt) 'menearlo'

HO#034 pM **hot** *(vi) 'descubrir un hueco/to uncover a hole'* LM: Cn <*hoht~hot*> (vi) 'lastimarse' SJ *hoht~hot* 'to skin (a superficial wound)' Gu <*hot, hohp*> 'lastimarse' [Nordell, p.c.] OlP: *hot* (vi) 'abrirse un hueco, hoyo' SaP: *hot* (vi) 'break open a hole'

HO#035 pM **ho:ht** *(n) 'hígado, corazón/liver, heart'* [pOM **ho:ht*] NHM: *ho:t* 'estómago, entraña' SHM: Tl *hU:ht* 'hígado' Tu,Tp *ho·ht* 'barriga' Mi *ho·ht* 'corazón' Ay *ho:ht* MM: Ju *hot* 'estómago, barriga, hígado' Ma *ho·t̄* 'hígado (pos), vientre, estómago' Ja *ho·t* 'estómago, hígado' Pu *ho·t* 'hígado' At *ho·t* 'estómago, entrañas' Ct *ho·t* '=estómago' LM: Cn *ho·t* 'hígado; centro de las emociones (tristeza, alegría, etc.)' Gu *ho·t̄* 'estómago, hígado' OlP: *hotɨ* [?] 'menudencia' SaP: *ho:ht*

HO#036 pOM **kɨ:?-ho:t** *(n) 'palma de la mano/palm of the hand'* MM: Ju *kɨhót* Ma,Ja,Pu,At,Ct *kɨ"hó·t̄* LM: Gu *kï"hó·t*

HO#037 pM **ho:ht-pi** *(n) 'adentro/inside'* NHM: *hɨ:tp* 'embarazada, encinta, preñada' LM: Gu *ho·t̄ʸp* 'embarazada' OlP: -*hotpi* 'dentro de'

HO#038 pOM **tɨhk-ho:ht** *(n) 'piso de la casa/floor'* MM: Ma *tɨhkhó·t̄* At,Ja,Pu,Ct *tɨgó·t̄* LM: Gu *tïgó·t*

HO#039 pOM **tɨhk-ho:ht-pi** *(adv) 'adentro (de la casa)/inside (the house)'* NHM: *tɨkhɨ:tp* SHM: Tu,Tp *tɨgótʸpʸ* MM: Ju,Cc *tɨgótʸ* Ma, Ja,At,Ct *tɨgó·t̄ʸ* '=dentro' Pu *tɨgó·tʸ* LM: Ca *tɨgó·tʸ* Gu *tïgó·t̄ʸ* 'dentro', *tïgó?tʸ* 'adentro (de la casa)' [sic!]

HO#040 pMZ ***ho?t** *(vi) 'prensar (con pinzas, etc.)/to pinch'* MM:
Ja,Ct *ho·tʸpʸ* LM: Gu *ho·tʸpʸ* SaP: *ho?t* (vi, vt) 'hook something,
pull with hook', *hó?tan* 'gancho' ChisZ: C *ho?tokyuy* 'gancho' NE
ho?di (vi-s) 'estar torcido'

HO#041 pZ ***how** *(vi) 'estar tonto/to be crazy'* ChisZ: C **hoŋ*
[*aŋkɨhoŋpawɨ* (adj, n) 'envidioso', *kɨhoŋbawɨ* (adj, n) 'celoso',
kɨhoŋguy (n) 'celo, envidia', *hoŋtokoy* (vi) 'errar, fallar', *howi* (adj,
n) 'tonto, torpe, zonzo, necio'] N *howi* (adj) 'loco'; (adv) 'de
repente, repentinamente' NE *howi* (vi-s) 'está tonto, está loco'
[derivative: *kɨhuŋbabɨ* (adj, n) 'celoso'] ChZ: *ho?ŋ* 'estar loco' [?]

HO#042 pM ***hoyan** *(n) 'panal de avispa/honeycomb'* NHM: *ho:ydum*
'panal de avispón' OlP: *ho?ya'n* 'bola de avispa'

HO#043 pOM ***hoy** *(n) 'llano/plain'* [cf. pZ **hɨ?ŋ* 'plano, etc.']
NHM: *hoy* '=planicie, llanura' SHM: Tl *hUy* MM: Ju,Ma *hoy* Pu,
At,Ct *hōy* LM: Cn <*hoy*> Ca *hoy* Gu *hōy*

HO#044 pGZ ***ho:y** *(vi) 'andar andando/walk around'* SoZ: *ho:y*
'pasear' TxZ: *ho:yho:yho?y* (vi) 'andar perdido (como cuando se
pierde el camino)'

HO#045 pM ***ho?y** *(vt) 'batir/to whip'* NHM: *ho?y~ho"y* 'batir, en-
turbiar' SHM: Tp <*ho!pʸ*> 'batir (caldo, etc.)' MM: 'disolver' Ju
<*ho"y*> 'batir (caldo, etc.)' Cc <*ho"y, ho!ypʸ*> 'batir (caldo,
etc.)' Ma <*hʸé"pʸ, hʸo"yǽmpʸ*> Ja <*ho"y, hʸo!ȳ*> At <*ho"y,
hoö!pʸ*> Ct <*hʸœ!pyé!pʸ*> LM: Cn <*ho?y~ho"y*> (vt) 'batir'
SJ *ho?y~ho"y* 'to beat liquids, make atole' Gu <*ho"y, ho!pʸ*>
'disolver' OlP: *ho:y* (vt) 'batir (cosa espesa)' [*ho?y* expected] SaP:
ho?y (vi) 'dissolve'

KI-KO

KI#001 pMZ ***kic?** *(vt) 'sofaldar/to roll up, turn up'* LM: Gu <*ki"c, ki?cp*> 'masturbar' [Nordell, p.c.] ChisZ: N *kihc* (vt) 'sofaldarlo'

KI#002 pMZ ***kih** *(vi) 'echar lumbre/to give light'* SaP: *kihan* (vi) 'flash lightning' [A composite verb: *kih* 'brillar' + *?an* 'árder'; Lawrence Clark (p.c.) disagrees and thinks that the second member of the complex is the instrumental suffix *-an*.] TxZ: *kêh* (vt) 'señalar' ChisZ: C *ki?toŋ* (vi) 'brillar, relucir, reflejar, relumbrar' [?] NE **kih* [*kihnem* (vt) 'echarle lumbre'; *kiha?p* (vt) 'echarle lumbre']

KI#003 pZ ***ki?m** *(vi) 'subir/ascend'* SoZ: *ki?m* TxZ: *kê?m* (vi) ChisZ: C,N,NE *ki?m* (vi) ChZ: *ki?m*

KI#004 pZ ***?aŋ-ki?m** *(vi, vt) 'mandar/to order'* TxZ: *?a:ŋkê?(m)* (vt) '=enviar' ChisZ: C *?aŋgi?m* (vi) 'mandar, gobernar, reinar' (vt) 'ordenarlo, mandarlo; gobernarlo' N *?aŋgi?m* (vi) 'tener autoridad' (vt) 'ordenarlo; aconsejarlo' NE *?aŋgi?m* (vi) 'mandar, reinar' (vt) 'ordenarlo, gobernarlo' ChZ: *yak?aŋki?m* (vt) 'aconsejar'

KI#005 pOM ***kin** *(vi) 'sumirse/to sink'* NHM: *ki:n~ki:hn~kin* 'asentar (p.ej., pedazos de limón en un vaso de agua)' MM: Ju <*ki·mp*> Ma <*ki·m̄p, kínámp*> '=hundirse' Ja <*ki·m̄p, kin̄, ki·n̄*> 'hundirse' At <*ki·mp*> Ct <*ki·m̄p, kínámp*> LM: Ca <*kin*> '=hundirse' Cn <*ki·n~kin*> (vi) 'hundirse' SJ *ki·n~kin* 'to sink (in water)' Gu <*kin̄, ki·m̄p, ki·n̄, kiná·m̄p*> '=hundirse'

KI#006 pZ ***kini** *(n) 'nariz; pico/nose'* [pGZ **ki:ñi*] SoZ: *kí:ñi* [Foster and Foster 1948] TxZ: *kêñkuy* 'nariz' ChisZ: C,NE *kini* '=trompa, hocico' N *kini* S *[ki·ni?]* 'nariz' ChZ: *kini*

KI#007 pMZ ***kip** *(vi) 'pelear/to fight'* [The derived MM form attests to the presence of the root in Mixean at some time.] MM: Ja,Ct *kip̄ʸ* 'un puñetazo' ChisZ: C,NE *kihp* (vi) N *kihp* (vt)

KI#008 pOM ***ki:ʔp** *(vt) 'chamuscar/to singe, burn (chile)'* NHM: *ki:ʔp* 'chamuscar (p.ej., el pelo), chamuscado, quemar el pelo' MM: Ju *<ki:p>* Ma,Ja,Ct,At *<ki:p, kʸiʔpʸ>* LM: SJ *ki·p~ki:p* Gu *<ki:p, kʸi·ʔpʸ>*

KI#009 pMZ ***kips** *(vi, vt) 'medir; pensar/to measure; think'* SHM: Tl *kehpš* 'medir' MM: 'medir, pesar' Ja *<kihpš, kʸihpʸšʸpʸ>* Ma,Pu,At,Ct *<kihpš>* LM: 'medir, pesar' LM: Cn *<kipš>* (vt) 'medir' SJ *kipš* Gu *<kipš>* OlP: *kipš* (vi) 'tirar (con flecha)' (vt) 'tirarlo (con flecha); medirlo; pesarlo' SaP: *kipš* (vi, vt) 'measure, weigh' SoZ: *kiʔpš* 'medir' TxZ: *kê?pš* (vt, vi-p) 'medir, pesar' ChisZ: C *kips* (vt) 'pensarlo; creerlo' N *kiʔps* (vt) 'pensarlo' [?] NE *kips* (vi) 'pensar' (vt) 'pensarlo; creerlo, suponerlo'

KI#010 pOM ***kihpš-y** *(adj) 'parejo, raso/equal, level'* NHM: *kihpš* 'iguales, parejo' MM: Ju *kihpšʸ~kihšʸ* Ma,Pu,At,Ct *kihpšʸ* LM: Ca,Gu *kipšʸ*

KI#011 pOM ***kihpš-n** *(n) 'medida/measurement'* NHM: *kihpšïn* '=almud' MM: Ju,Ma,Ja,Pu,At,Ct *kihpšṇ* LM: SJ *kipʸšʸ* 'at the same time' Ca,Gu *kipšt* [OlP: *kipšɨ* 'medida, arroba'; this is another derivative]

KI#012 pM ***tuk-kipš** *(vt) 'medir con/to measure with'* NHM: *tukkihpšïn* 'algo con que se mide' SaP: *tukípš* 'to measure with' [Clark 1961]

KI#013 pZ ***tumɨ-kips** *(vt) 'comparar/to compare'* [The ChisZ-N form is *tum* 'uno' + *kiʔps* 'pensar'. '1' in SaP is *tuʔk*. Thus, the SaP form is a clear Zoquean loan.] SaP: *tumukípš* 'comparar' [Clark and Clark 1960] ChisZ: N *tumgiʔps* (vt) 'resolverlo, pensarlo en serio'

KI#014 pOM ***ki:ʔpš** *(vt) 'raspar/to scrape'* NHM: *ki:ʔpš* 'raspar (p.ej., con una aguja), raspadura, rayado' MM: At *<kiʔpš>* 'prender (cerillo)' Ct *<kiʔpš, kʸiʔpšʸpʸ>* 'prender (cerillo)'

KI#015 pM ***ki:š~kiʔš** *[?] (vi) 'hincharse/swell surface of skin'* NHM: *ki:š~ki"š* MM: Ju *<ki:žɬʔkp>* Ma *<ki·šp̄>* Ja *<ki:žɬʔkp, ki·šp̄>* Pu *<ki·šp̄>* At *<ki·šp̄, ki:žɬʔkp>* Ct *<ki:žɬʔkp, ki·šp̄>*

LM: Cn <*ki·š~ki"š*> Ca <*ki:šł?kp*> Gu <*ki"š, ki"žǐ?p, ki·š̄p*> [Nordell 1990 and p.c.] OIP: *ki:š~ki?š* (vi) SaP: *ki:š~ki?š*

KI#016 pOM ***naš-ki:hš~naš-ki"š** *[?] (vi) 'deshincharse/to stop swelling'* NHM: *naški:š~naški"š* LM: Cn <*naški·š~naški"š*> 'deshinchar, quitar una hinchazón'

KI#017 pOM ***ki"š** *(n) 'hinchazón/swelling'* NHM: *ki"š* '=hinchado' MM: 'hinchazón, bodogue' Ju *ki"š* 'bodogue' Ma,Pu,At,Ct *ki"š* LM: Gu *ki"š*

KI#018 pOM ***ki?šk** *(adj) 'turbio, espeso (liquido)/muddy, thick (liquid)'* NHM: *ki"štk* SHM: Tl *ke?šk* MM: Ju *ki?šk* Ja *ki!š̄k* Ma,At *ki?š̄k* 'espeso (líquido)' Ct *ki?šk* 'espeso (líquido)' LM: Cn <*ki"š*> (adj) Gu *ki!š̄k*

KI#019 pZ ***ki?s** *(vi) 'enojarse/to become angry'* TxZ: *kê:?šku?* (n) 'molesto' ChisZ: C *ki?ška?* (vi) '=incomodarse, embravecerse' N *ki?s* (vi), *ki?ška?* (vt) NE *ki?ška?* (vi)

KI#020 pM ***kišay** *(n) 'niña/girl'* [pOM **kihšy*] NHM: *ki:š* '=muchacha' SHM: Ay *ki:šʸ* MM: 'muchacha' Ma *ki:žʸ?iná?k* Pu *kiš̄ʸ?iná!k* At *kiš̄ʸ* Ja,Ct *ki:šʸ* LM: 'muchacha' Cn <*kišy*> SJ *kišʸ* Gu *kiš̄ʸ* SaP: *kíšay*

KI#021 pMZ ***kit** *(vi) 'tronchar, quebrar/to break'* LM: Gu <*kit, kihp*> [Nordell, p.c.] SoZ: *kity* [Foster and Foster 1948] TxZ: *kêč* (vt) 'cortar (quelite, etc.)' ChisZ: C *kiht* (vi, vt) N *kiht* (vi) ChZ: *kit* 'doblar'; *kidɨm* 'estar quebrado'

KI#022 pMZ ***kitaw** *(vi) 'luchar a brazo partido, chapotear/to wrestle, to wallow'* OM: 'caerse (persona)' NHM: *kitu* SHM: Tu <*kɨdá:p, kɨdáw̥*> Tp <*tɨ: kʸidáy*> MM: Ju <*kɨdá:p*> Cc <*kɨdá:p, tɨ: kʸidáy*> Ma <*kɨdá:p, tɨ: kʸiday̥, kɨdáw̥, kɨdáΦ, kɨdáf*> Ja,Pu <*kɨdá:p, kɨdáw̄*> At <*kɨdá:p, kɨdáw̄*> Ct <*kɨdá:p, kɨdáΦw̥*> LM: Ca <*kɨdá:p*> SJ *kɨda·w~kɨdaw* Gu <*kɨdá:p, kɨdáw̄*> SaP: *kitaw* (vi) TxZ: *kêtɨŋ* (vt) 'hacer cosquillas'

KI#023 pOM ***kiwk** *(n) 'ciempiés/centipede'* NHM: *ki?vɨk* 'milípedo' MM: Ma *kif~kiw̥~kiΦ* Ja *kiw̄* Ct *kiΦk*

KE#001 pM ***ke:c** *(n) 'cerro/mountain'* [pOM **ke:c*] NHM: *ke:c* 'cerro de pura piedra' [only in Sp-to-NHM: side] [?] LM: Cn <*ke:c*>

(adj) 'inclinado'   <*ca:winge:c*>   'peñaso'   OlP: *ke:skot*   (vt)
'juntarlo (p.ej., tierra)'

KE#002 pMZ **ke:ʔc** *(vt) 'crujir/to grate'* NHM: *ke:ʔc* 'rayar (p.ej.,
con un clavo)' MM: Ma <*kæ:c, kʸeʔčpʸ*> 'prender (cerillo)',
<*kæ:c, kʸeʔčpʸ*> 'trazar, crujir los dientes' [sic!] Ja <*kæ:c, kʸæʔc,
kʸeʔčpʸ*> 'prender (cerillo)' Pu <*kæ:c, mgeʔčpʸ*> 'trazar, crujir los
dientes' At <*kæ:c, kʸeʔčpʸ*> 'trazar, crujir los dientes', <*kæ:c,
kʸeʔčpʸ*> 'crujir' [sic!] Ct <*kæ:c*> 'crujir', <*kæ:c, kʸeʔčpʸ*>
'trazar, crujir los dientes', <*kæ:c, kʸeʔčpʸ*> 'prender (cerillo)' [sic!]
TxZ: *keʔc* (vt) 'morder' ChisZ: C *keʔc* (vt) 'morderlo' N *keʔc*
(vt) 'morderlo'

KE#003 pOM **ke:ʔč** *(n) 'pulque/pulque (fermented juice of the ma-*
guey)' NHM: *kE:ʔc* '=raya' SHM: Tl *ke:č* MM: Ju,Ma,Ja,At,Ct
ke:č LM: Cn <*ke:č*> (adj) 'rayado' Ca *ke:č*

KE#004 pM **keh** *(vt) 'desatar/to untie'* NHM: *keh* MM: Ja
<*kæh*> LM: Ca <*kæh*> Cn <*keh*> (vt) SJ *keh* Gu <*keh,*
kehp> [Nordell, p.c.] OlP: *keh* (vt) SaP: *keh* (vi, vt)

KE#005 pM **ku-keh** *'desamarrar/to unfasten'* NHM: *kukeh* 'desamarrar, desatar (p.ej., un buey suelto)' SaP: *kukéh* 'desenredar, des-
hilar, desatarse' [Clark and Clark 1960]

KE#006 pOM **mu-keh-ɨ** *'desatar/to untie'* MM: Ju <*mɨgǽhɨ*> Ja
<*mɨgǽhɨ*> At,Ct <*mɨ·gǽhɨ*> LM: Gu <*mɨgehɨ"w*>

KE#007 pZ **keh** *(vi) 'aparecer/to appear'* SoZ: *keh* TxZ: *keh* (vi)
'=parecer, verse, amanecer' ChisZ: C *keh* (vi) 'aparecer; aclararse'
N *keh* (vi) 'verse; aparecer (lo que se ha perdido)' NE *keh* (vi)
ChZ: *keh* 'verse'

KE#008 pM **kek** *(vt) 'cambiar/to change'* NHM: *tukvinkekva:c*
~*tukvinkekvaʔac* 'llevar por otra parte a alguien' OlP: *kek* (vt)
'cambiarlo'

KE#009 pMZ **ke:kʔ** *(vi) 'volar/to fly'* NHM: *ke:k*~*ke"k* 'correr,
huir, fugarse' SHM: Tu <*kæ"k, kækp*> 'alejarse' MM: Ju <*kæ"k,*
tɨ: kʸe"kʸ> 'fugarse, escapar', <*kugá"k*> 'vuela lejos',
<*kæ·gɨʔkp*> 'volar' Ma <*kæ"k, kæ·kp, tɨ: kʸe"kʸ*> 'escapar,
fugarse, vuela lejos', <*kæ"k, kæ·kp*> 'quitarse', <*kæ·kp, kæ"gámp,*
kæ:gɨʔkp> 'volar' Ja <*kæ"k, kæ·k, kæ·kp*> 'vuela lejos,

escaparse', <kæ·k̄p, kæːgɨʔkp> 'volar', <higǽ"k, higǽ"k̄p>
'alejarse' Pu <kæ"k, kæ·kp> 'vuela lejos' At <kæ"k, kæ·kp, tɨː
kʸe"kʸ> 'escapar, fugarse, vuela lejos', <kæ"k, kæ·kp> 'quitarse',
<kæːgɨʔkp> 'volar' Ct <kæ"k, hɨ·gǽ·kp> 'quitarse', <kæ"k,
kæ·kp, tɨː kʸe"kʸ> 'escapar, vuela lejos, fugarse', <kæːgɨʔkp,
kʸæːgɨdɨ́ʔʸ> 'volar' LM: Cn <ke·k~ke"k> (vi) 'correr, huir;
escapar; hacerse a un lado' SJ ke·k~ke"k 'to run away' OIP:
keːk~keʔk (vi) 'quitarse' SaP: keːk~keʔk SoZ: kek (vi) TxZ: kek
(vi) ChisZ: N kehk (vi) 'caerse' NE kehk (vi) 'caer, caerse; des-
prenderse (como un pedazo de algo)' ChZ: kek 'volar (brincar)'

*KE#010 pOM *nɨ-keʔk~nɨ-ke"k 'abandonar/to leave behind'* SHM:
Tu <nɨkǽ"k, nʸɨkékʸpʸ> MM: Ju,Pu <nikæ"k> Ma,Ja,At,Ct
<nɨkæ"k> LM: Gu <nɨ"ge"k>

*KE#011 pOM *yak-ke"k (vt) 'ahuyentar/to drive away'* SHM: Tu
<yahkǽ"k, mʸakǽ"k> MM: Ma,Pu <yahkǽ"k> At <yæhkkǽ"k>
LM: Ca <yahkǽ"k>

*KE#012 pM *keːk-an (n) 'ala/wing'* [pOM *keːkn] NHM: kéːkɨn
SHM: Tl kank Ay keːhk 'hombro' Tu kæ·hk '=aleta' Tp kæ·hk
(pos) 'ala' Mi kʸæ·hk̩ 'su ala' MM: '=aleta' Ju,Cc kækn̩ Ma,At
kæ·kn̩ Ja,Pu,Ct kʸæ·kn̩ LM: Cn <keːk> 'ala', <akške:k> 'aleta'
Ca kæ·kt 'aleta' Gu ke·kt OIP: keːká'n '=hombro' SaP: kéːgan

*KE#013 pM *keki (n) 'cerete/agouti'* [pOM *keky] [Sources for
SHM, MM, and LM-Gu use 'cereque', sources for OIP and SaP 'se-
rete'—these are synonyms.] SHM: Tp kehkʸ MM: Ju,Ma,Ja,Ct kehkʸ
LM: Cn <kehky> 'cerete, agutí (del tamaño de la liebre) [Dasyprocta
mexicana]' Gu kehkʸ OIP: kéki SaP: kukék

*KE#014 pOM *kehky 'hombro/shoulder'* NHM: kEhk SHM: Tl kenkʸ
MM: Ju,Ma,Ja,Ct,Pu,At kehkʸ LM: Ca kehkʸ TxZ: kehkeʔ 'mentón,
quijada' [?-semantics]

*KE#015 pM *keʔkš 'trenzar/to braid'* NHM: keʔkš 'trenzar' MM:
Cc <kæʔkš, kæʔkámp, kæʔkšp, kʸeʔkšʸpʸ, tɨː tkeʔkšʸ> 'atar las manos
atrás' At <kæʔkš> 'atar las manos atrás' OIP: keʔkš (vt)
'trenzarlo' SaP: keʔkš (vi, vt) 'braid hair'

*KE#016 pOM *kem (vi) 'cercar/to fence'* MM: Pu <kæm̄> LM: Ca
<kæm>

KE#017 pOM ***kem-y** *(n) 'cerca, cerco, corral/fence, corral'* SHM:
Tu *kem^y* MM: Ju *kem^y* Ma,Ja,Pu,At,Ct *kem̄^y* LM: Ca *kem^y*

KE#018 pZ ***kenuk** *'chichicastle/spurge nettle'* [pGZ **ke:nuk*] TxZ:
ke:?nu?k '=chaya, mala mujer' ChisZ: C *kenuk* '=ortiga' N *kenuk*
'chaya, chechén' NE *kenuk*

KE#019 pMZ ***kep** *(vt) 'patear; arrear/to kick; drive animals'* MM:
Ju <*kæp*> 'arrear' LM: Ca <*kæp*> 'arrear' Cn <*kehp*> (vt)
'arrear' SJ *kehp~kep* 'to drive animals' Gu <*kep, kehp*> 'arrear'
[Nordell, p.c.] OlP: *kep* (vt) 'buscarlo' SaP: *kep* (vi, vt) 'hunt
game' TxZ: *kep* (vt, vi-p) 'arrear, acosar' ChZ: *kep* 'patear'

KE#020 pOM ***ke:?p** *(vt) 'cortar con tijeras/to cut with scissors'*
NHM: *ke:?p* SHM: Tp <*kæ:p, mge?p^y*> MM: Ju <*kæ:p*> Cc
<*kæ:p, k^ye?p^yp^y, k^yæ?p, tɨ: tke:p^y, k^yæh tke?p^y, yAhkkǽ?pp,*
k^yæ:bǽmp^y> Ma <*kæ:p, k^ye?p^y*> '=raspar con tijeras', <*kæ:p,*
kæ?p> 'comer (panela)' Ja <*kæ:p, k^yæ?p, k^ye?p^y*> '=raspar con
tijeras' Pu <*kæ:p, mge!p^y*> At <*kæ:p, k^ye?p^yp^y*> Ct <*kæ:p,*
k^ye?p^y> 'cortar papel con tijeras', <*kæ:p*> 'comer (panela)' LM:
Ca <*kæ:p*> 'cortar papel, cabello con tijeras' Cn <*ke·p~ke:p*>
(vt) SJ *ke·p~ke:p* Gu <*ke:p, k^ye·?p^y*> 'cortar papel con tijeras'

KE#021 pM ***ke:?pš** *(vt) 'rasurar/to shave'* NHM: *ke:?pš* '=afeitar'
Tp <*kæ?pš*> 'afeitar' MM: Ju <*kæ?pš*> 'rasurar con navaja' Ma
<*kæ?pš*> 'afeitar' Pu <*kæ!pš*> 'afeitar' At <*kæ!pš, tɨ:*
ŋge?pš^y> 'afeitar' <*kæ?pš, k^ye?p^yš^yp^y*> 'rasurar con navaja' [sic!]
LM: Cn <*kepš*> (vt) SJ *ke·pš* 'to shave' Gu <*ke·?š*> 'afeitar'
OlP: *ke:pš* (vt) 'raspar la barba'

KE#022 pOM ***ke:py** *(n) 'mojarra correntera/a kind of mojarra'* MM:
Ma,Ja,Pu,Ct *ke:p^y* LM: Gu *ke:p^y*

KE#023 pOM ***kehš~keš** *(vt) 'mandar/to send'* NHM: *kehš~keš*
'mandar (p.ej., ordenar un mandado), sembrar (p.ej., un arbolito),
plantar (p.ej., café), enviar, remitir, apreciar' SHM: Tl *keš* 'enviar'
MM: '=enviar' Ju <*kæš*> Ma,Pu <*kæš̄, k^yehš^yp^y*> Ja <*kæš̄,*
k^yehš^yp^y, k^yæš̄ǽ·m̄p^y> At <*kæš̄*> 'enviar' Ct <*kæš̄, k^yehš^yp^y,*
k^yæš̄sémp^y> LM: Cn <*kehš~keš*> SJ *kehš~keš* Ca <*kæš̄*>
'mandar, enviar', <*kæš̄*> 'enviar' [sic!] Gu <*keš, kehšp, k^yehš^yp,*
k^yežá·m̄p^y> 'mandar, enviar', <*keš̄*> 'enviar' [sic!]

KE#024 pM ***keʔš** *(vi) 'nacer, aparecer/to be born, appear'* NHM: *keʔš ~ keˀš* 'nacer (p.ej., un a niño), ver (p.ej., una cosa lejana), descubrir (p.ej., una cosa perdida)' SHM: Tl *kaʔš* 'nacer, parir' MM: Ma <*kæʔš̄p, kæˀžámp, tɨ: kʸeˀš̌ʸ*> 'parir' Ja <*kæ!š̄p, kæˀžá·m̄p*> 'parir', <*tɨ: kʸeˀš̌ʸ, kæʔšp, kǽʔštɨp*> 'nacer (gente, animales), empollar' Pu <*kæ!š̄p, kæˀžá·m̄p*> 'parir' At <*kæʔš̄p, kæˀšá·m̄p, tɨ: kʸeˀš̌ʸ*> 'parir', <*tɨ: kʸeˀš̌ʸ, kæʔšp*> 'nacer (gente, animales), empollar' Ct <*kæʔš̄p, kæˀžámp, tɨ: kʸeˀš̌ʸ*> 'parir' LM: Cn <*keʔš ~ keˀš*> (vi) 'parir' Gu <*ke!š̄p, keˀžá·m̄p, kʸeˀš̌ʸ*> 'parir' OlP: *keʔš* (vi) 'nacer; verse parecerse' SaP: *keʔš* (vi, vt) 'show, appear'

KE#025 pM [Veracruz] ***keʔš-ta:k** *(vi) 'aparecer/to appear'* OlP: *keʔšta:k ~ keʔšta'k* (vi) SaP: *keʔštáʔk* [Clark and Clark 1960]

KE#026 pMZ ***ket** *(vi) 'bajarse/to descend'* NHM: *keht ~ ket* 'cojear (temporalmente), romper (p.ej., un metate)' SoZ: *ket* (vi) TxZ: *ket* (vi) '=caer (lluvia)'

KE#027 pOM ***ke:ʔt** *(vt) 'comer a mordidas (manzanas, totopo, dulce)/to eat in bites'* MM: Ja <*kæ:t, kʸæ ʔt, kʸeʔtʸpʸ*> Pu <*kæ:t, mge!tʸpʸ*> Ct <*kæ:t, kʸeʔtʸpʸ*> LM: Cn <*ke·t ~ ke:t*> (vi) 'rechinar los dientes' SJ *ke·t ~ ke:t* 'to chew (rats, etc.); to grind the teeth; to eat grass (birds)'

KE#028 pMZ ***ke:wʔ** *(vt) 'picar/to sting'* NHM: *ke:v ~ keˀv* 'picar (p.ej., chichicaxtle), arder, ardor (p.ej., el que produce la ortiga o la malamujer)' LM: Cn <*ke·w ~ keˀ*> (vt) 'quemar (con una planta)' SJ *ke·w ~ keˀ* 'to sting' OlP: *kev(~ keʔv)* (vd) 'picarle (el ajuate)' ChisZ: N *keŋ* (vi) 'salir una erupción en la piel' (vt) 'picarlo (una planta o un gusano)' NE *keŋ* (vt) 'quemarlo (como el chichicastle al tocarlo)'

KE#029 pMZ ***keʔw** *(n) 'malamujer (yerba)/spurge nettle'* [pM **keʔw* > **keˀw*; pZ **keʔŋ*] MM: 'malamujer' Ju *kæˀ* 'chichicastle' Ma *kæˀw* '=chichicastle' Ja *kæ!bɨʔúhc* '=chichicaxtle' At *ʔuhckǽ!bɨ, kæ!bǽ!bɨ, tɨkckǽ!bɨ, kæˀw kæˀwʔuhc* '=chichicaxtle' Ct *kæ!bɨ ʔuʔkšpɨ* LM: Ca *kæˀʔúhc* 'chichicaxtle' Gu *ke!bʸɨʔúhc* SaP: *hɨnkéʔw* 'mala mujer' *keʔw* (vi, vt) 'scrape cactus' ChisZ: C *keʔŋ* (vt) 'escocerlo, quemarlo' (example given: "al hombre lo escoció la chaya y le dio calentura")

KE#030 pOM *key* *(vi?)* *'ladearse/to tilt'* NHM: *ke:y ~ ke:hy ~ key* 'ladearse, de lado, chueco, enchuecar (p.ej., una linea)' MM: 'bizco' Ju *wi:ŋgey* Ma *hiŋgéy* Ja *wiŋgéy* Pu *wi:ŋgéy* At,Ct *hiŋgéy* LM: Cn <*key*> (adj) 'chueco, torcido' Gu *wi:ŋgey* 'bizco' Ca *wi:ŋgéy* 'bizco'

KE#031 pM [Veracruz] *ke:?ye* *(n)* *'culpa, pecado/sin'* OlP: *ke:ye* SaP: *ke?y*

Ki#001 pMZ *ki?* *(n)* *'mano, brazo/hand, arm'* [pM *ki?* > pOM *ki"*; pZ *ki?*] [Perhaps a broader meaning 'limb' may be reconstructed, cf. the ChisZ-C [Te] form and pMZ *ki?-?ak* 'sandal' (?A#011)] NHM: *ki"* SHM: Tl *ki?* 'mano' MM: Ju,Ma,Ja,Pu,At,Ct *ki"* LM: Ca,SJ *ki"* 'hand' [According to the Van Haitsmas irregularly derived from *ki·y ~ ki"* 'to carry', an analysis that does not work diachronically.] Cn <*ki?*> 'mano, manazo' Gu *kï"* OlP: *ki?* SaP: *ki?* SoZ: *ki?* 'hand' [Foster and Foster 1948] TxZ: *ki?* 'mano, asa, cabo, rama, brazo (de árbol), mano (medida de cinco)' ChisZ: C [Co] *ki?* '=cabo, mango' [Te] <*cœ*> 'dedo / pié *in comuni*' N,NE *ki?* ChZ: *ki?* 'mano'

Ki#002 pOM *?i:?pš-ki"* *(n)* *'ciempiés/centipede'* NHM: *?i:?pš ki?aš* *i:?pš tEk?aš* Tp *?i?pški"* MM: Ju *?i?pški"* At *?i?pški"w* LM: Ca *?ipški"* Gu *kï"?í·?š*

Ki#003 pZ *?aŋ-ki?* *(n)* *'patio/patio'* TxZ: *?aŋki?* '=potrero' SoZ: *?áŋki?* [Foster and Foster 1948] ChisZ: C,NE *?aŋgi?*

Ki#004 pZ *kic* *(vt)* *'agarrar/to grasp'* TxZ: *kic-meñ* (vi) 'sentarse más acá (junto conmigo)' (vt) 'cambiar un tantito de lugar hacia acá (casa)' ChisZ: C *kokihc* (vt) 'despumarlo; desnatarlo' N *kihc* (vt) 'agarrarlo (con cuchara o jícara)'

Ki#005 pM *ki:?c* *(vt)* *'romper/to break'* NHM: *ki:?c* 'romper (p.ej., ropa), rasgar, roto' SHM: Tl *ki:c* 'romper' LM: Cn <*ki·c ~ki:c*> (vt) 'romper (p.ej., papel, tela)' Gu <*kï:c, kï·?cp*> [Nordell, p.c.] OlP: *ki:c* (vt) 'romperlo'

Ki#006 pMZ *kih* *(n)* *'cueza/peal'* [pM, pOM, pZ, pGZ *kih*] NHM: *kih* 'tejido' [derived from *kih* 'tejer'] SaP: *kih* 'camote' TxZ: *kih* 'camote o yuca de fruta, raíz' ChisZ: C,NE *kih*

Ki#007 pM ***kɨh(k)-** *(pron) 'cada/every'* [pOM **kɨhk*] NHM: *kɨkʋhk* 'por mitad' MM: Cc *kɨhktú"k* 'cada quien' Ma *kɨhktú?k* 'cada uno', *kɨhkhæ'"* 'cada quien' Ja *kɨhtú?k* 'cada uno', *kɨhk, kɨhktú?k* 'cada quien' Pu *kɨhtú!k* 'cada uno', *kɨhhæ'"* 'cada quien' At *kɨhktú"k* 'cada uno', *kɨhkhæ'"* 'cada quien' Ct *kɨhktú?k* 'cada uno', *kɨhkhæ'"* 'cada quien' LM: Gu *kïdú"k* 'cada uno', *kïhhé"* 'cada quien' OlP: *kɨhtu'k* 'cada uno' SaP: *kɨhtú?k* 'uno por uno, alguno'

Ki#008 pOM ***?ahkš-kɨhk** *(n) 'chayocamote/tuber of chayote'* MM: Ma,Ja *?æhškɨhk* Pu,Ct *?æhkškɨhk* LM: Gu *?akšahkɨ̈hk*

Ki#009 pM ***kɨːhk** *(n) 'hondo, pozo, etc./bottom, well'* [pOM **kɨːhk*] NHM: *kɨːk* 'profunda, hondo—p.ej., una fosa' SHM: Tl *kink* 'hondo' MM: Ju̱ *kɨk* Ma,̱Ja,Pu,At,Ct *kɨ·k* LM: Cn <*kɨːky*> (adj) 'hondo' Ca *kɨ·k* Gu *kï·k* OlP: *kɨːkɨ* 'hueco, cueva', *kɨkpi* (adv) 'en el hueco'

Ki#010 pMZ ***kɨ?mɨ** *(adv) 'abajo/down'* [pOM **-kɨ?m*; pZ **kɨ?mɨ*] LM: Gu *pa?kɨ!m̄* 'abajo' TxZ: *kɨ?mɨ* 'abajo', *kɨ?ɨm* 'bajo' ChisZ: C *kɨ?mɨ* (adv) N *-kɨ?mɨ* 'debajo de, al lado de, en' (sufijo preposicional de sustantivo o pronombre) NE: *kɨ?mɨbɨ* (adj, n) 'abajeña'

Ki#011 pZ ***kɨnɨ** *(n) 'cuello/neck'* [pZ **kɨn-*] TxZ: *kɨ́nkɨ?* SoZ: *kɨnkɨ?* [Foster and Foster 1948] ChisZ: C *kɨnɨ* '=garganta, pescuezo' N *kɨnɨ* NE *kɨnɨ* '=garganta' ChZ: *kɨnɨ?* 'voz'

Ki#012 pGZ ***kɨːn** *(adj) 'sabroso/savory'* [May be from pZ **kɨnɨ* 'neck' via 'throat'.] SoZ: *kɨːn* TxZ: *kɨːn* (adj) 'sabroso'

Ki#013 pOM ***kɨːny** *(n) 'cocuyo/lantern click beetle'* MM: Ma,Pu,Ja *kɨːnʸ* LM: Gu *tugï̈ːnʸ*

Ki#014 pMZ ***kɨpi** *(n) 'árbol; leña/tree; wood'* [pM **kɨpi* > pOM **kɨpy*; pZ **kɨpi* > pGZ **kɨːpi*] NHM: *kïp* Tl,Tu,Tp *kipʸ* Tm *kipʸ* 'tronco' Ay *kipʸ* 'tallo' Mi *kepʸ* MM: Ju,Cc *kepʸ* Ma,Ja,Pu,At,Ct *kep̄ʸ* 'árbol, madera, palo' LM: Cn <*kipy*> 'árbol' Ca *kepʸ* OlP: *kɨpi* 'leña' SoZ: *kɨːpi?* 'leña' [Gutiérrez M. 1993], *kɨːpi* 'leña' [Foster and Foster 1948] TxZ: *kɨːp* 'leña' ChisZ: C,N *kɨpi* 'leña' NE *kɨbi* 'leña' S *[kɨ·pí?]* 'leña' ChZ: *kɨpi?ah* (v) 'leñar'

Ki#015 pOM ***poːm kɨpy** *(n) 'árbol de copal/copal tree [Burse sp.]'* NHM: *poːm kïp* 'copal [Bursera jorullensis]' LM: Cn <*poːmgipy*> 'árbol de copal [Bursera sp.]'

Kɨ#016 pMZ ***kɨs** *(n) 'cuerpo/body'* [pM, pOM **kɨhš*; pZ **kɨs*; the item originally meant 'body', but was in MM and LM reanalyzed so as to mean 'over (the body) since the root was mostly used with a locative suffix'.] NHM: *kïš-* 'arriba' [verbal prefix; e.g., *kišpuhš ~ kišpuš* 'cortar algo que está arriba'] SHM: Tl *kɨšp* Tp *kɨhšp* Tu *kɨhšp* 'arriba' LM: Ca *kɨšp* 'alto, arriba (lejos)' SJ *kɨš* 'straight up over-head'; *kɨhš* 'on top of, bed'; *kɨšpɨ* 'higher in the lay of the land' Gu *kïšp* OIP: *kɨšɨ* 'cuerpo'; *na:škɨšɨ* 'él que tiene el cuerpo lleno de tierra' TxZ: *kɨs* 'brazo (de árbol)' ChZ: *ʔaŋkɨs* 'rama'

Kɨ#017 pMZ ***kɨs-mɨ** *(adv) 'arriba, alto/up, high'* [pM **kɨhšmɨ* > pOM **kɨhšm̥*; pZ **kɨsmɨ*] NHM: *kɨhšm* '=altura, elevado' SHM: Mi *kïhšm̥* 'arriba' MM: Ju,Cc,Ma,Ja,Pu,At,Ct *kɨhšm̥* ChisZ: C *kɨsmɨ* '=por encima'

Kɨ#018 pOM ***ni:-kɨš-m** *(adv) 'encima/over'* NHM: *ni?kšm* '=sobre' MM: Ju *nikɨhšm̥* Ma,Ct *nʸigɨhšm̥* Ja *ni"gɨhšm̥* Pu *nigɨhšm̥* LM: Ca *ni·gɨšʸ* Gu *nʸi"gïšp*

Kɨ#019 pMZ ***kɨ:?s** *(vt) 'jalar; morder cosa dura/to pull; bite into something tough'* NHM: *kɨ:?š* 'jalar (p.ej., para sacar pedazos de la pechuga de una gallina), quitar (p.ej., con los dedos liendres del cabello)' LM: Cn <*kɨ·š ~ kɨ:š*> (vt) 'espulgar' SoZ: *kɨ?s* 'eat' [Foster and Foster 1948] TxZ: *kɨ:?s* (vt) 'comer (cualquiera comida que se muerda)' ChisZ: C *kɨ?s* (vt) 'morderlo; comerlo N *kɨ?s* (vt) 'comerlo (cosa dura, como tortillas, pan, etc.), morderlo; picarlo' NE *kɨ?s* (vt) 'comerlo (como carne o tortilla); morderlo' ChZ: *kɨ?soy* 'comer', *kɨ?si* 'comida', *kɨ?sku?y* 'plato'

Kɨ#020 pOM ***kɨ:?šm** *(n) 'camarón del mar/type of shrimp'* NHM: *kɨ:?šm* 'camarón [Penaeus sp.]' SHM: Tu *kɨ·!špɨ* Tp *kɨ?šp ~ kɨ!šp* Mi *kï?šm̥* MM: Ju,Cc *kɨ?šm̥* Ja *kɨ!šm̥* Ma,At,Ct *kɨ?šm* LM: Ca *kɨ"šp* Gu *kï!špákš*

Kɨ#021 pOM ***kɨta:k ~ kɨta"k** *(vi) 'bajar/descend'* NHM: *kɨda:k ~ kɨda"k* 'bajar (p.ej., viene bajando), descender' SHM: Tu <*kɨdákp, kʲidæ̯'"kʲ*> 'caerse de arriba' MM 'llegar (desde arriba)' Ma,Ct <*kɨdá·kp, kɨda"gámp*> Ja,Pu,At <*kɨdá·kp, kɨda"gá·m̄p*> LM: Cn <*kɨda·k ~ kɨda"k*>_ (vi) 'venir bajando (caminando)' SJ *kɨda·k ~ kɨda"k* Gu <*kɨdá·kp, kɨda"gá·m̄p*> 'llegar (desde arriba)' ChisZ: N *kɨht* (vi) 'pasar (ejemplo: algo por la calle); pasar (tiempo)' [?]

Kɨ#022 pM ***hot-kɨta:k ~ hot-kɨta?k** *(vi) 'sanar; contentarse/to heal, be content'* NHM: *hotkɨda:k ~ hotkɨda"k* 'sanar de una enfermedad, aliviar' OlP: *hotkɨ?ta:k* (vi) 'contentarse'

Kɨ#023 pOM ***na:š-kɨta:k ~ na:š-kɨta"k** *(vi) 'aterrizar/to land'* NHM: *naškɨda:k ~ naškɨda"k* 'aterrizar, caer (p.ej., caer un árbol)' LM: Cn <*na:škɨda·k ~ na:škɨda"k*> (vi)

Kɨ#024 pM [Veracruz] ***yak-kɨrɨc** *(vt) 'crujir los dientes/to grate one's teeth'* OlP: *yakɨrɨc* (vt) 'crujir los dientes' SaP: *?ahkɨrɨč* (vt) 'crujir [Clark and Clark 1960]'

Kɨ#025 pM ***kɨš** *(vi) 'acabarse/to finish'* NHM: *kɨhš ~ kɨš* 'terminar (p.ej., una venta de algo), porque, acabar (p.ej., la comida)' SHM: Tu <*kɨhšp*> Tp <*kɨhš, kɨšámp, tɨ:kʸɨšʸ*> Mi <*kɨ̈hšp, tɨ:kʸešʸ*> Tm <*kɨhšp*> 'terminar' MM: Ju <*kɨhjsp*> 'agotarse' Cc <*kɨhšp, kɨhš, tɨ:kʸɨšʸ, kʸæhkʸɨhšʸ, kɨšámp*> Ma <*kɨhšp*> '=agotarse, gastarse (cosas)' Ja <*kɨhš, kɨhšp, tɨ:kʸɨ̄šʸ*> 'acabarse', <*kɨhšp*> 'agotarse' Pu <*kɨhšp, tɨ:kʸɨ̄šʸ*> 'acabarse', <*kɨhšp*> 'agotarse' At *kɨhšp, tɨ:kʸešʸ*> 'acabarse', <*kɨhšp*> 'agotarse, gastarse (cosas)' Ct <*kɨhšp*> '=agotarse, gastarse (cosas)' LM: Cn <*kɨhš ~ kɨ·š*> (vi) 'terminar' Ca <*kɨhšp*> SJ *kɨhš ~ kɨš* 'to be finished, gone' Gu <*kɨ̈hšp*> '=agotarse' OlP: *kɨš* (vi) 'acabar, terminar' SaP: *kɨš* (vi, vt) 'finish'

Kɨ#026 pM ***yak-kɨš** *(vt) 'terminar/to finish'* SHM: 'acabar' Tu <*yahkɨš*>, Tp <*yAhkɨš*> MM: Ju <*yæhkɨš*> '=acabar' At <*yahkɨš̄, yahkéhšʸpʸ*> '=acabar' Ct <*yahkɨhšʸpʸ*> 'terminar' Cc <*yAhkkɨš, yAhkk*hšʸpʸ*> 'acabar' Ma <*yahkɨš̄*> 'acabar' Ja <*yahkɨš̄, yahkɨhšpʸ*> 'acabar' Pu <*yahkɨš̄*> 'acabar' LM: Ca <*yahkɨš*> '=acabar' Gu <*yahkɨš̄*> 'acabar' OlP: *yakɨš* (vt) 'terminarlo, acabarlo'

Kɨ#027 pOM ***ku-kɨš-ah** *(vi) 'finalizar/to come to an end'* NHM: *kukɨhši ~ kukɨša* 'finalizar, terminar (p.ej., una fiesta), concluir' MM: At *kugɨhšip* Ct *kɨgɨhš?ipʸ* LM: Gu *kugɨ̈žɨ̈:pʸ*

Kɨ#028 pMZ ***kɨ:?t** *(vt) 'moler pinole/to grind pinol'* OlP: *kɨ:t* (vt) TxZ: *kɨ?t* (vt, vi-p) 'moler en metate' ChisZ: C *kɨ?t* (vt) 'molerlo; crujirlo' NE *kɨ?t* (vt) 'molerlo; despulparlo' N **kɨ?t* [*kɨ?thahk* (vt) 'cortarlo mordiéndolo'] ChZ: *kɨ?t* 'moler (fino)'

Kɨ#029 pZ ***kɨʔt-i** *(n) 'masa/dough'* [pGZ **kɨʔitʸi*] SaP: *kɨʔt* 'pozo-le, masa' [Zo loan] TxZ: *kɨːʔč* (adj) 'bien molido, fino (masa, café)' N *kɨʔti* 'lo que está molida'

Kɨ#030 pMZ ***kɨːw?** *(vi) 'cocer/to cook'* NHM: *kɨːv~kɨ"v* SHM: 'cocerse' Tu <*kɨːp*> Tp <*kɨːp, kɨː, kɨ"βámp, tɨː kʸɨ"y*> MM: 'cocerse' Cc <*kɨːp, kʸɨ"y, kɨː, kɨ"hámp, kʸœ'h kʸɨ·y*> Ma <*kɨːp, kɨ"wámp*> Ja <*kɨ·w̄, kɨːp*> Pu <*kɨːp, kɨ"wa·m̄p*> At <*kɨːp, kɨ"há·m̄p*> Ct <*kɨːp, kɨ"wámp*> LM: 'cocerse' LM: Cn <*kɨ·w~kɨ·~kɨ"*> (vi) SJ *kɨ·w~kɨ"w* Gu <*kïːp, kï"wá·m̄p, kï·w̄*> OIP: *kɨv~kɨʔv* (vi) 'cocerse' SaP: *kɨw~kɨʔw* (vi, vt) 'cook (beans /tortillas), bake bread' SoZ: *kɨŋ* 'ripen' [Foster and Foster 1948], 'pintar; madurar' [Gutiérrez M. 1993] TxZ: *kɨŋ* (vi) 'cocer' ChisZ: C *kɨʔŋ* (vt) 'pintarlo; teñirlo' [?] N *kɨŋ* (vi) 'madurarse, estar maduro; estar cocido; encanecer' (vt) 'pintarlo' NE *kɨŋ* (vi) 'madurarse'; (vi-s) 'estar maduro' (vi) 'inflamarse' (vi-s) 'estar inflamado' (adj) 'maduro' ChZ: *kɨŋ* 'madurar; quemar'

Kɨ#031 pM ***yak-kɨw~yak-kɨʔw** *(vt) 'cocer, cocinar/to cook'* SHM: Tu <*yakɨ", mʸakɨːpʸ, myakɨʔœ'mpʸ*>' Tp <*yœhkɨʔh, yœhkɨːpʸ*> MM: Ju <*yœhkɨ"*> Cc <*yAhkkɨ", yAhkkɨːpʸ*> Ma <*yahkɨ"w̥, yahkɨ"Φ, yahkɨ"f*> Ma <*yahké·pʸ*> Ja <*yahké·pʸ, yahkɨ"w, kɨ·w̄*> Pu <*yahkɨ", yahkɨːpʸ*> At <*yœhkké·pʸ*> Ct <*yahkɨ"w, yahké·pʸ*> LM: Ca <*yahkɨ"*> Gu <*yahkï"w, yahkï:pʸ, kï·w̄*> OIP: *yakɨv~yakɨʔv* (vt) 'cocerlo (comida); cocerlo (ollas)' SaP: *ʔahkɨʔu* (vt) 'cocer' [Clark and Clark 1960]

Kɨ#032 pM ***kɨʔw** *(adj) 'cocido/cooked'* [pOM **kɨ"*] SHM: Tp *kɨ" yɨʔh* MM: Ma *kɨ"w̥~kɨ"Φ~kɨ"f* Ja,At,Ct *kɨ"w* Pu *kɨ"* LM: SJ *kɨ"* Gu *kï"w* OIP: *kɨʔɨ'u* (adj)

Kɨ#033 pOM ***kɨ"-a:m** *(adv) 'a mano/by hand'* NHM: *kɨʔm* 'en la mano' MM: Ja,Pu,At,Ct *kɨ"ʔám̄* LM: Gu *kï"ʔá:m*

Kɨ#034 pMZ ***kɨːy?** *(vt) 'cargar cosa plana/to carry flat object'* NHM: *kɨːy~kɨːhy~kɨ"* (vt) 'cargar (p.ej., un palo grueso sobre el hombro), llevar (p.ej., una tabla), tomar (p.ej., un cajón)' MM: 'llevar (plato)' Ma <*kɨ"w*> Ja <*kɨ"w, kɨ", kʸɨ·ȳ*> Ct <*pa·gɨ"w*> LM: Cn <*kɨ·y~kɨʔ~kɨ"w*> (vt) 'llevar (cosas planas; p.ej., mesas, libros)' SJ *kɨ·y~kɨ"* 'to carry (tables, boards, flat objects)' OIP: *kɨy~kɨʔ* (vt) 'cargarlo en la cabeza' [the entry form is *ikɨːype*. Is there a misprint?] TxZ: *kɨy* (vt) 'aguantar' ChisZ: C *koʔkɨyɨ* 'sombrero'

Kɨ#035 pMZ ***ʔaw-kɨːy?** *(vt) 'tapar, cerrar/to plug, close'* NHM: yakʔakɨ·y ~ yakʔakɨ?ɨ 'cerrar algo, tapar algo' MM: 'tapar (olla, etc.)' Ju <ægɨ"y> Ma <ʔagɨ"W> Ja <ʔagɨːbʸæ'ɨ> At <ʔagɨ"> Ct <ʔagɨ"w> LM: Ca <ʔagɨ"> 'cerrar' SJ ʔa·gɨ·y ~ ʔa·gɨ"y Gu <ʔagɨ"w, ʔagɨːpʸ> [Nordell 1990 and p.c.] ChisZ: C ʔaŋgɨy (vt) 'cerrarlo'

Kɨ#036 pZ ***ʔaŋ-kɨy** *(n) 'puerta/door'* ChisZ: C ʔaŋgɨyɨ ChZ: ʔaŋkɨy

Kɨ#037 pOM ***ʔa-kɨ"y** *(n) 'tapadera/cover'* NHM: ʔakɨ" MM: Ma ʔagɨ"w̥ ~ ʔagɨ"Φ ~ ʔagɨ"f Ja yʔagɨ" Ct ʔagɨ"ß LM: Gu ʔagɨ"w

Kɨ#038 pOM ***kɨyɨ"k** *(vi) 'alzar/raise'* MM: Ju <kɨyɨ"k> Ma,Ja,At, Ct kɨ·yɨ"k 'recoger (plato)' LM: Ca <kɨyɨ"k> 'recoger plato' Gu kɨyɨ"k 'recoger (plato)'

KA#001 pZ ***kaʔ** *(vi) 'morir/to die'* TxZ: kaʔ (vi) 'morir' ChisZ: C kaʔ (vi) '=perecer, fallecer' (vt) 'sufrirlo, padecerlo' [i.e., the phrase kyaʔ- toya] N kaʔ (vi) 'morirse; secarse; salir bien molido; descolorarse, decolorarse' NE kaʔ (vi) '=fallecer' ChZ: kaʔh

KA#002 pMZ ***yak-kaʔ** *(vt) 'tumbar, matar/to knock down, kill'* OIP: yakaʔ (vt) 'tumbarlo; bajarlo' TxZ: yakaʔ (vt) '=dejar morir, asesinar, cazar' ChisZ: C yahkaʔ (vt) 'matarlo; despacharlo; asesinarlo' N yahkaʔ (vt) 'matarlo NE yahkaʔ (vt) 'matarlo, asesinarlo' ChZ: yahkaʔ (vt) 'matar'

KA#003 pZ ***kaʔ-aŋ** *(n) 'muerte/death'* ChisZ: C kaʔaŋ ChZ: kaʔaŋ

KA#004 pZ ***kaʔ-kuy** *(n) 'enfermedad, muerte/illness, death'* TxZ: ʔeš-kaːʔ-ko 'mal de ojo (enfermedad natural)' ChisZ: C kaʔkuy N kaʔkuy '=muerte' NE kaʔkuʔ 'muerte'

KA#005 pOM ***kač** *(n) 'canasta/basket'* NHM: kač SHM: Tl kač 'canasta sin asa' Tu,Tp kač MM: Ju yeŋʸgʸǽč, winʔoʸgʸǽč Ma kæč̄ '=cesta, chiquihuite, pecho' Ja kæč̄ '=chiquihuite, cesta' Pu kæč̄ '=pecho, cesta' At kač̄ 'pecho, cesta, canasta' Ct kæč̄ '=cesta, chiquihuite' LM: Ca kæč 'chiquihuite' Cn <kaːč̄> 'pecho', <kač> 'chiquihuite grande' Gu kač̄ 'cesta, canasta'

KA#006 pMZ ***kaʔc** *(vi, vt) 'apedrear, moler/to throw at with stone, to grind'* NHM: kaʔc ~ ka"c 'apedrear, rajar leña' SHM: Tp <kA"c, mgaʔčpʸ> 'apedrear' MM: Ju <caːgá"c> 'tirar con piedra' Cc <kA"c, mgAʔčpʸ> 'apedrear' Ma <ka"c, kʸaʔčpʸ> 'tirar con piedra, rajar leña, apedrear' Ja <*ka"c, ka?c, kʸa?čpʸ*> 'tirar con piedra, rajar leña' At <*ka"c, ka?c, kʸæ?čpʸ*> 'tirar con piedra, apedrear, rajar leña' Ct <*ka"c, kʸa?čpʸ*> 'rajar leña, tirar con piedra' LM: Ca <*ka?c*> 'apedrear' Cn <*ka?c~ka"c*> (vt) 'tirar (piedras)' SJ *ka?c~ka"c* 'to throw at with a round object, to fall from above' Gu <*ka"c, ka?c, kʸa?čp*> 'apedrear, tirar con piedra' OIP: *ka?c* (vi) 'cortar (con machete)' (vt) 'cortarlo' SaP: *ka?c* (vi, vt) 'throw solid object' ChisZ: C *ka?c* (vi) 'moler caña' (vt) 'molerlo, moler caña' N *ka?c* (vi) 'rajarse' (vt) 'machacarlo; despulparlo; rajarlo' NE *ka?c* (vt) 'molerlo (como caña)'

KA#007 pOM ***ka:?c** *(vi) 'escarbar (gallinas)/to scratch'* NHM: *ka:?c* 'escarbar la tierra (como hacen las gallinas con las patas)' MM: Ja <*ka:c, ka?c, ka?cp*> Pu <*ka?cp*> At <*ka?cp, kʸæh kʸæ:č*> Ct <*ka?cp*> LM: Gu <*ka:zá·m̄p, ka·?cp*>

KA#008 pGZ ***ka:ca?** *(n) 'cotorro/green parrot, parakeet'* SoZ: *ka:ca?* TxZ: *kactukuba:* 'periquito'

KA#009 pZ ***kacih** *(n) 'tucán/keel-billed toucan [Ramphastos sulfuratus]'* LM: Gu *ká·ta* [?] [Nordell, p.c.] Cn <*ka:t*> 'tucán [Ramphastos sulfuratus]' [?] ChisZ: C *kacih* 'tucán real - pico de hacha' N *kaci* 'tucán, pico de hacha, tucanillo verde' NE *kacih*

KA#010 pMZ ***kacu(c)** *(adj) 'agrio/bitter'* [pM *kacuc; pZ *kacu > pGZ **ka:cu*] OIP: *kacu's* SaP: *káduc* [dissimilation hitting the mid-consonant] SoZ: *ka:cu?* TxZ: *kaco?~ka:co?~kacu?~ka:cu?* ChisZ: C,N *kacu* NE *kacu* (vi-s) ChZ: *kacu?*

KA#011 pMZ ***kacc** *[?] (adj) 'variegado/variegated'* [Presumably the peculiar sequence /cc/ gave rise to the final cluster in NHM and the uncommon consonant /č/ in ChisZ-NE; *kacc is posited for all subgroups; cf. pZ *mecci.] NHM: *kast* 'pinto' SHM: Ay *kahc* 'pinto' MM: Ma,Pu *kac̄* 'variegado' Ja *kac̄* 'moteado, pinto' At,Ct *kac̄* 'moteado, pinto, variegado' LM: Cn *kac* (s) 'color pinto' Gu *kac̄* 'variegado (animal), moteado, pinto' ChisZ: NE *kač* (vi-s) 'amarillo'

KA#012 pOM ***kah** *(part) 'no/no'* MM: Ju *k̠ʸæh* Ma,Ja,Pu,Ct *kæh̄* At *kʸæh* LM: Cn <*ka?p*> Ca *ka?p* Gu *kah, kap*

KA#013 pM ***ka:h** *[?] (part) 'no/no'* [pOM **ka?* (or **ka?h*) possibly a syntactically conditioned variant of **ka:h*] NHM: *ka"* SHM: Tl *ka?*

Ay *ka?t* LM: SJ *ka?* Cn <*ka?*> (adv) Gu *kah, kap-, ka?* [Nordell, p.c.] SaP: *ka:h* [Clark and Clark 1960], *ka* [Clark 1961]

KA#014 pOM *ka?h-nɨm [?] (part) 'todavía no/not yet'* NHM: *ka"num* MM: Ju,At *kʸǽhnɨm* Ma,Ja,Ct *kǽhnɨm* LM: Gu *ká!nɨ, káhnɨ*

KA#015 pM *kah (vi) 'atorar (espina)/to be stuck (thorn)'* NHM: *kah* 'ralo, atorar, atorado' LM: Cn <*kah šap*> (adj) 'ralo' SJ *?eht kah~ ?et kah* 'to squirm, dance (in pain, etc.)' SaP: *kah* (vi, vt) 'extract thorn'

KA#016 pMZ *kahi (adj) 'estrecho, cuadrado/narrow, square'* [pM *kahi* > pOM *kahy*; pZ *kahi* > ChisZ *kayi*] MM: Ma,Ja,At,Ct *kahʸ* 'cuadrado, de cuadros (ropa, cobija, etc.) ChisZ: C *kay* 'angosto, estrecho; delgado' N *kayi* 'estrecho, delgado' NE *kayi* 'anchura, estrecho'

KA#017 pMZ *ká:haw (n) 'tigre (cualquier felino silvestre)/wild feline'* [pM *ka:haw* > pOM *ka:* (or perhaps *ka:h*) with irregular loss of final *w*; pZ *kahaŋ* with loss of medial *h* in all the descendant languages cited.] NHM: *ka:* 'nombre común de los siguientes animales: jaguar, león, tigrillo, puma, gato montes, onza, tigre, pantera, ganado vacuna, toro, etc.' [Schoenhals and Schoenhals 1965], *ka:h* [A. Schoenhals in p.c. to G. Martin] SHM: Tl *ko:* 'león' Ay *ka:h* MM: Ju *ka:* '=león' Ma,Ja,Ct *ka:* '=jaguar, fiera' Pu *ka:* 'jaguar, fiera' At *ka:* '=león, jaguar, fiera, puma' LM: Cn <*ka:*> 'tigre (nombre genérico)' Ca *ka:* SJ *ka·* Gu *ka:* '=jaguar, fiera, león' OlP: *ka:ha'u* SaP: *káhau* [first vowel irregularly shortened] SoZ: *ka:ŋ* TxZ: *ka:ŋ* ChisZ: C,N,S *kaŋ* NE *kak* '=jaguar' ChZ: *kaŋ*

KA#018 pMZ *?apit-ka:haw (n) 'puerco espín/Mexican porcupine' [Coendu mexicanus]* [For reconstructions at levels of subgroups see pMZ *ká:haw* and pMZ *?ápit*.] NHM: *?ápit ka:* MM: Ju,Ma,Ja,At, Ct *?æpʸŋʸgʸá:* LM: Cn <*apyka:*> '[Coendou mexicanus]' Gu *?apɨká:* [Nordell, p.c.] SaP: *?apitkáhau* [Clark and Clark 1960], *?apitka:hau* [Clark 1981] TxZ: *?a:?pe?č-ka:ŋ*

KA#019 pZ *cikin-kahaŋ (n) 'jaguar/jaguar'* TxZ: *čêkeñka:ŋ* 'tigrillo (?)' ChisZ: C *cikiŋgaŋ* ChZ: *cikinkaŋ*

KA#020 pMZ *capac-ka:haw (n) 'león/puma'* [For reconstructions at levels of subgroups see pMZ *capac* and pMZ *?ápit*] LM: Cn <*capcka:*> 'león americano [Felis concolor]' Gu *capcká:* [Nordell, p.c.] OlP: *capaska:ha'u* '=tigre colorado' ChisZ: C [Co] *capaskaŋ* 'león americano, puma' [Te] <*tzapascang*> N *capaskaŋ* 'puma [Felis concolor]' ChZ: *capac kaŋ*

KA#021 pOM ***hahm-ka:** *(n) 'león/mountain lion'* NHM: *hamka:* MM: Ju,Ma,At,Ct *ha:mgá:* Gu *ha:mgá:*

KA#022 pOM ***kɨ"-ka:** *(n) 'dedo pulgar/thumb'* NHM: *kɨka:* MM: Ma,At *kɨ"gá:* Ja *kɨ"tgá:* LM: Cn <*kɨ"ga:*> Gu *kɨ"gá:*

KO#023 pMZ ***ko?-po?** **ka:haw** *(n) 'cabeza de viejo/tayra [Tayra barbara]'* NHM: *kupo"* *ka:* '=cabeza blanca, tayra, vieja del monte [Tayra barbara]' MM: Mi *kupo"ká:* Cc *ku?po"gá:* Ma *kɨpó"* Ja *ku"bo"gá:* Pu *kɨbó"gá:* At *kupó"gá:* Ct *kɨpó"*, *kɨpo"gá:* LM: Cn <*ko"bo?*> 'cabello cano; cabeza de viejo, vieja del monte [Eira barbara]' Gu *ku"bo"gá:* OlP: *po?ka:ha'u* '=tigrillo' ChisZ: C *ko?popo-kaŋ* N *ko?pohkaŋ* '=tayra' NE *kobomgak*

KA#024 pOM ***šɨhk-ka:** *(n) 'gato montés/bobcat, wildcat'* NHM: *šɨka:* '[Felis maculata, Lynx rufus, Felis rufa]' LM: Cn *šɨhkka:* '[Felis rufa]'

KA#025 pOM ***teky-ka:** *(n) 'dedo gordo del pie/big toe'* NHM: *tEk ka:* MM: Ju *tekʸkʸá:* Ma,Ja,At *tekʸkʸá:* Ct *mɨhtékʸ* LM: Ca *tekʸkʸá:* Gu *tekʸ?á:*

KA#026 pZ ***kak** *(vt) 'prestar/to lend'* SoZ: *kak* AyZ: *[kak]* TxZ: *kak* (vt, vi) 'cambiar' ChisZ: C *kahk* (vt) 'cambiarlo, sustituirlo' N *kahk* (vt) 'pedirlo prestado' NE *kahk* (vt) 'cambiarlo'

KA#027 pMZ ***ka?k** *(vt) 'amontonar, cercar/to pile up'* SHM: Tl *yikka"k* (vt) 'amontonar' ChisZ: N *ka?k* (vt) 'cercarlo'

KA#028 pM ***ka?ka** *(n) 'canasta/basket'* [pOM **kak*; ChisZ-S *[ka·ká?]* 'vagina' may be related—this would require that pMZ **kak?a* be posited.] NHM: *kak* 'pecho, costilla' SHM: Tp *kAk* MM: Mi *kak* SaP: *ka?k* OlP: *ka?ka*

KA#029 pMZ ***kakawa** *(n) 'cacao/cacao tree'* [pM **kakawa* (with unexplained loss of final /a/ in OlP) > pOM **kakaw* (with unexplained lengthening of last syllable in non-NHM); pZ **kakawa* > pGZ **ka:kawa* (with a lengthening of the first vowel where lengthening of the second vowel is expected; there are subsequent irregular reductions in individual languages); all these irregularities point to the possibility that a complicated flow of borrowings between MZ languages, which may or may not have involved non-MZ sources, took place.] NHM: *kaku* 'cacao' *kakʋ kɨp* 'cacaotero' [Theobroma cacao] SHM: Tl *kako:w* Mi *kaká:wa* [re-entered by borrowing from Spanish] Ju,Ja,Pu *kɨgá:* Ma *kɨgá:ʷ, kɨgá:Φ°, kɨgá:f* At *kagá:w* LM: Cn <*kɨ"ga:*> 'cacao, cacaotero [Theobroma cacao]' Ca,Gu *kɨgá:* OlP: *kaka'u* SaP: *kágau* SoZ: *ka:kwa?* AyZ: *[ka:gʷa]* TxZ: *ka:k* '=chilate, popo, semilla de cacao' ChisZ: C *kakawa* N *kakwa* ChZ: *kakawa*

KA#030 pMZ ***nas-kakawa*** *(n) 'cacahuate/peanut'* [See pMZ **nas* 'earth'] NHM: *naškakʋ* 'papa' [Solanum tuberosum] OlP: *na:škaka'u* SaP: *na:škágau* ChisZ: C *naskakawa* N *nas kakva*

KA#031 pZ ***kaks*** *(vi) 'partir/to split, separate'* TxZ: *kakskaksde?* (vi-s) 'muñequear, tronar (huesos)' ChisZ: C *kaks* (vi) 'rajarse' N *kaks* (vi) 'partirse, rajarse' NE *kaks* (vt) 'machucarlo (como el cacaté en la boca)'

KA#032 pZ ***kakwE(?n)*** *(n) 'alacrán/scorpion'* SoZ: *kákwi* [Wonderly 1949; Gutiérrez M. 1993] TxZ: *kakwe?ñ* ChisZ: NE [Tapalapa, Ocotepec] *kahkwe* [Wonderly 1949] C,N *kakwe* ChZ: *kakwe*

KA#033 pZ ***ka?m*** *(vt) 'apretar/to press'* SoZ: *ka?m* 'estar colocado' TxZ: *-ka?(m)* (verbo semiderivativo) 'entrando' ChisZ: C *ka?m* (vi-s) 'estar armado' (vt) 'armarlo; apretarlo' N *ka?m* (vi) 'apretarse, estar apretado' (vt) 'apretarlo' NE *ka?m* (vt) 'armarlo (como un mueble)'

KA#034 pZ ***yak-?aŋ-ka?m*** *(vt) 'cerrar/to close'* ChisZ: C *ya?aŋga?m* (vt) '=taparlo' ChZ: *yagaŋka?m* (vt)

KA#035 pZ ***wi?t-ka?m*** *(vi) 'apretar torciendo/to press and twist at the same time'* TxZ: *we?č-ka?(m)* (vt, vi-p) 'atrancar (tornillo)' ChisZ: N *wi?tka?m* (vi) 'apretarse, estar apretado' (vt) 'apretarlo dándole vueltas' ChZ: *wi?tkam* 'apretar torciendo'

KA#036 pMZ ***kama*** *(n) 'milpa/cornfield'* [pM **kama* > pOM **kam*; pZ **kama* > pGZ **ka:ma?*] NHM: *kam* 'campo' SHM: Tu *kam* 'acahual, rastrojo' Tm *kam* 'parcelo' MM: Ja *kam̄* 'campo' LM: Cn <*kam*> 'campo de siembras' Ca *kam* [Wonderly 1949] Gu *kam̄* 'campo' OlP: *kama* SaP: *kam* SoZ: *ka:ma* [Wonderly 1949], *ka:ma?* [Gutiérrez M. 1993] AyZ: *[ka:?ma]* TxZ: *ka:mu? ~ ka:mo?* [a back formation from *ka:mo?o* 'in the cornfield'] ChisZ: C *kama* '=campo sembrado' N *kama* 'la siembra' NE *kama* S [Tu] *kaykama* 'his cornfield' [Wonderly 1949]

KA#037 pM [Veracruz] ***hay-kama** *(n) 'milpa ajena/cornfield belonging to someone else'* SaP: *haykám* 'milpa ajena' OlP: *haykama* 'milpa ajena'

KA#038 pMZ ***mo:k-kama** *(n) 'milpa/cornfield'* [See pMZ **mo:k* 'corn'] NHM: *mokkam* sembrado de maíz)' OlP: *mo:kama* 'milpa de maíz' SHM: Tl *mʋkkom* LM: Cn <*mo:kkam*> ChisZ: N *mohkama* 'milpa'

KA#039 pM ***šɨhk-kama** *(n) 'sembrado de frijoles, frijolar/bean plantation'* NHM: *šɨkam* MM: Ma,Ja,Pu,At,Ct *šɨhkám̄* LM: Cn <*šɨhkkam*> 'frijolar' Gu *šɨ̈hkám̄* SaP: *šɨhkám* 'milpa de frijoles'

KA#040 pOM ***wa:šk kam** *(n) 'cañal/cane field'* NHM: *va:šk kam* 'cañaveral' MM: Ma *Wa·škám̄* Ja,Pu,Ct *wa·škám̄* At *wa·škkám̄* LM: Gu *wa·škám̄*

KA#041 pOM ***kam-ho:ht-y** *(n) 'campo/field'* SHM: Tu *kamótp* 'campesino' Mi *kamhɨ́t'ʸpʸ* 'campesino' MM: Ja *kamhó·t'ʸ* At *kamó·tm̩* Ct *kamó·t'ʸ* LM: Gu Cn <*kamhoty*> (adv) 'en la parcela' *kamó·t'ʸ* TxZ: *ka:mó?o* 'en la milpa' [?-phonology]

KA#042 pMZ ***kam-tɨk** *(n) 'acahual/brush'* NHM: *kam tɨhk* 'rastrojo' MM: '=rastrojo' Ma *kam̄dɨhk* Ja,Pu,At,Ct *kamdɨhk* LM: Cn <*kamdɨhk*> 'rastrojo' Gu *kamdɨhk* 'acahual, rastrojo' OlP: *kamatɨkɨ* SaP: *kamdɨk~kamdɨhk* TxZ: *kamtɨk*

KA#043 pZ ***kamam** *(adj) 'duro/hard'* [pGZ *kamam] SoZ: *kámam* TxZ: *ká:muʔ* [?] ChisZ: N *kamam* NE *kamambɨ* (adj) 'tieso' ChZ: *kamaʔm*

KA#044 pZ ***kan** *(n) 'pene/penis'* [pGZ *kan] SoZ: *kan* 'vagina' AyZ: *kan* TxZ: *kan* ChisZ: C [Te] <*can*> 'miembro del hombre, vere[n]da / natura de hombre / badaxo de campana' [also found under the gloss 'la natura de muger' in Gonzalez's section "Hominis compostio ex partibus yntegrantibus"; cf. meaning in SoZ]

KA#045 pMZ ***ka:na** *(n) 'sal/salt'* [pM **ka:na* > pOM **ka:n*; pZ *kana > pGZ **ka:na*] NHM: *ka:n* SHM: Tl *ko:n* MM: Ju,Ma, Ja,At,Ct *ka:n* LM: Ca,SJ,Gu *ka:n* Cn <*ka:n*> 'sal común' OlP: *ka:na* SaP: *ka:n* SoZ: *ká:na* [Elson 1960], *ká:naʔ* [Gutiérrez M.

1993] AyZ: *[ka:na]* TxZ: *ka:n* ChisZ: C,N,NE *kana* S *[ka·ná?]*
ChZ: *kana*

KA#046 pMZ ***kantVn?i** *(adj) 'perezoso/lazy'* OlP: *kantɨ?ni* '=flojo'
SaP: *kandɨ?n* TxZ: *kañčeñ* (adj) 'flojo'

KA#047 pMZ ***kap** *(vt) 'cargar palo, etc./to carry wood, etc.'* NHM:
kahp~kap (vt) 'llevar (algo largo, p.ej., un palo), tomar (p.ej.,
palos), cargar (p.ej., un palo delgado sobre el hombro)' MM: Ja
<*kap̄, kʸahp*> 'llevar (palo)' LM: Cn <*kahp~kap*> (vt) 'acarrear
(cosas largas como palos, barretas y machetes)' SJ *kahp~kap* 'to
carry long slender objects' OlP: *kap* (vt) 'cargarlo (en el hombro)'
AyZ: *[kap]* 'traer (p.ej., agua)' TxZ: *kap* (vt) 'cargar (en el
hombro)' ChisZ: C *kahp* (vt) 'echarlo al hombro' N *kahp* (vt)
'llevarlo (en el hombro)' ChZ: *yukkap* 'levantar'

KA#048 pM ***?iš-kap** *(vt) 'conocer/to know'* NHM: *?iškahp~ ?iškap*
'reconocer' MM: 'reconocer' Ju <*?iškǽp*> 'conocer' Ma
<*n?iškǽhpʸic, y?iškǽhpʸ*> Ja <*y?ihškǽhpʸ, y?ihškáhp,
y?ihškapǽ·mp̄ʸ*> At <*?ihškáp̄, n?ihškǽhpʸic*> Ct <*y?iškœhpʸ*>
'reconocer', <*?iškáp̄*> 'conocer' LM: Ca <*?ihškáp*> 'conocer'
Cn <*ihškahp*> '=reconocer' Gu <*?iškáhp, y?iškáhpʸ, y?iškáhp,
y?iškabá·m̄pʸ*> 'reconocer', <*n?iškáhpʸič*> 'conocer' OlP: *?iškap*
(vt) 'conocer (una persona); conocer (un lugar)' SaP: *?iškák* 'conocer
(una persona)' [Clark and Clark 1960]

KA#049 pOM ***ka:?p** *(vt) 'menear, etc./to move, etc.'* NHM: *ka:?p*
'cornear, cornada' MM: 'menear' Ju <*ka:p*> Ma <*ka:p, tɨkká:bɨ*>
'batir (caldo, etc.)' Ma,Ja <*ka:p, kʸœ?pʸ*> Pu <*ka!bɨdɨt*> Ct
<*ka:p*> 'batir (caldo, etc.)' <*ka:p, kʸœ?pʸ*> 'menear' At <*ka:p,
kʸœ?pʸpʸ, kʸa:bǽ·mpʸ*> '=remar' LM: SJ *ka·p~ka:p* 'to stir' Cn
<*ka·p~ka:b*> (vt) 'mover, menear (con cuchara o instrumento
parecido)' Gu <*ka:p, ka·?p, kʸa·?pʸ, kʸa:bá·m̄pʸ*> 'remar, menear'
[Nordell 1990 and p.c.]

KA#050 pOM ***kahpVn** *(n) 'pueblo, poblado/village, town'* NHM:
kahpɨn MM: Ju,Ma,Ja,Pu,At,Ct *kahpṇ* LM: SJ *kahp* Cn <*kahp*>
'pueblo' Gu,Ca *kahpt*

KA#051 pOM ***mu-ko-kahpVn** *(n) 'paisano (del mismo pueblo) /fellow
townsman'* NHM: *mukukahpɨn* LM: Cn <*mɨgogajp*> 'vecino del
mismo pueblo'

KA#052 pMZ ***kapay** *(n) 'cuñada de hombre, cuñado de mujer/sister-in-law of man, brother-in-law of woman'* [pM **kapay* > pOM **kapy*; pZ **kapay* > pGZ **ka:pay*] [OM forms from Foster 1949 are all possessed forms containing a 1p pronominal clitic. Nordell recorded a SoZ form rather different from Foster's, suggesting that the latter's data are not quite dependable.] NHM: To *kap* 'cuñada de hombre, cuñado de mujer, cuñada de mujer' Hu *gapic* [Foster 1949] SHM: Tl *kop* 'cuñada de hombre' Ay *kap* [Wichmann 1990] *ʔingopis* [Foster 1949] MM: 'cuñada (de hombre), cuñado (de mujer)' Ju *kæpʸ* Ma,Ja, Pu,At,Ct *kæp̄ʸ* LM: Cn <*kapy*> 'cuñado, cuñada (mujer hablando de su cuñado u hombre hablando de su cuñada' SJ *kapʸ* 'in-law' Ca *kæpʸ* Gu *kap̄ʸ* [Nordell 1990] *gapič* [Foster 1949] OIP: *kapa'y* SaP: *kápay* TxZ: *ka:pe?* SoZ: *kapah* [Foster 1949]; *ka:pay* [Nordell 1962] ChisZ: C,N,S *kapay* NE *kabay* ChZ: StaMaCh *kapay* 'cuñada de hombre' SnMiCh *kapah* [Foster 1949]

KA#053 pMZ ***kape** *(n) 'carrizo/type of bamboo'* [pM **kape* > pOM **kapy*; pZ **kape* > pGZ **ka:pe*] NHM: *kapy* 'carrizo [Arundo donax L. Fam. Gramíneus]' SHM: Tl,Ay *kapy* Tu *kæpʸ* Tp *kæpʸ* MM: Ct *kæp̄ʸ* OIP: *kape* SaP: *kap* TxZ: *ka:p* ChisZ: C,N *kape* NE *kabe* '=cohete' ChZ: *kape* 'carrizo delgado'

KA#054 pM ***kapi(C)** *(n) 'alacrán/scorpion'* [pM **kapi(C)* > pOM **ka(?)pyk*; not impossible that this should be reconstructed as pMZ form **kakwin*; cf. pZ **kakwE(?n)*.] NHM: *ka:ʔpyk* SHM: Tl *kohpy* Tu *kahpʸ* ~ *kæ·hpʸ* Tp *kAhpʸ* Mi,Ay *kahpʸ* MM: Ma *kæʔpʸkʸ* Ja *ka:ʔɨm̥ʸ* Pu *kæ!pʸn̥ʸ* At *kæʔpʸ* ~ *kæʔpʸkʸ* ~ *kæʔpʸn̥ʸ* Ct *kæʔpʸ* LM: Cn <*kaʔky*> '[order: Scorpionida]' Ml <*kaʔip*> Ca *kæʔpʸ* Gu *ka·ʔptʸ*, *ka·ʔtʸ* TaM: *kepéŋ* [transcription of Wonderly 1949] OIP: *kape* SaP: *kápin*

KA#055 pM ***kapš** *(vi) 'hablar/to talk'* SHM: Tl *kohpš* 'hablar', *nukʸkohpš* 'leer' LM: SJ *kapš* [derivative: *kapyšy* 'word'—the form also appears as *kapš*] MM: Ju <*kahš*> 'hablar', <*nekʸkʸáhš*> 'leer' Ma <*kahpš, mgæhpšʸpʸ*> 'leer', <*kahpš*> 'hablar' Ja <*kahpš, kʸæhpšʸpʸ*> 'leer', <*kahpš*> 'hablar' Pu <*kahpš, mgæhpšʸpʸ*> 'leer', <*kahpš*> 'hablar' At <*kahpš, kʸæhpšpʸ*> 'leer'; <*kahpš*> 'hablar' Ct <*kahpš*> '=leer' LM: Cn <*kapš*> (vi) Ca <*kapš*> '=leer' Gu <*kapš, kʸapšʸp*> 'leer', <*kapš*> 'hablar' OIP: *yakapš* (vt) 'hablarle, llamarle; mandarlo hablar' [derivative: *tɨnkapše* 'mi idioma', *kapšpaʔ* 'hablador']

KA#056 pOM ***kahpš-ta:k ~ kahpš-ta"k** *(vi) 'rezar/to recite prayers'*
MM: Ju <*kah$\underline{s}$tá"k*> Ma <*kahštá"k, kahštá·kp*> Ja,Ct <*kahpš-tá"k, kahpštá·kp*> At <*kahpštá"k, kahpštá·kp, kahpšta"gá·$\overline{mp}$*>
LM: Cn <*kapštak*> (vi) Ca <*kapštá"k*> '=estudiar' Gu
<*kapštá"k*> 'estudiar'

KA#057 pMZ ***ka?ps** *(vi) 'completarse/to finish'* MM: Ma <*ka?pšp, tɨ: kʸæ?pšʸ*> Ja <*ka?pš, ka?pšp*> Pu <*ka!pšp, tɨ: kʸæ!pšʸ*> At <*ká?pšp*> Ct <*ka?pšánnɨp*> LM: Cn <*ka?pš*> (vi) SJ *ka?pš*
AyZ: *[ka?ps]* (vi) 'acompletarse' TxZ: *ka?ps* (vt) 'cortar con tijeras' (vi) 'acompletarse'

KA#058 pOM ***ka?pš-y** *(adj) 'completo/finished, complete'* SHM:
Tu,Tp *kæ?pšʸ* MM: Cc,Ja,At,Ct *kæ?pšʸ* LM: Cn <*ka?pš*> (adj) Gu
ka?šʸ

KA#059 pOM ***kaš** *(adj) 'comilón, tragón/glutton'* MM: Ma,Ja,At,Ct
ka$\overline{š}$ 'comilón, tragón' LM: Cn <*kaš*> (adj) Gu,Ca *ka$\overline{š}$* 'comilón, tragón'

KA#060 pM ***ka:?š [?]** *(vt) 'peinar/to comb'* NHM: *ka:?š* 'cepillar (p.ej., la ropa)' MM: Ja <*ka:š, kʸa!$\overline{š}$, kʸa!$\overline{š}$pʸ*> Pu <*ka:š, kʸa!$\overline{š}$pʸ*> At <*ka:š, kʸæ?$\overline{š}$pʸ*> Ct,Ma <*ka:š, kʸa?$\overline{š}$pʸ*> LM: SJ *ka·š~kaš* Cn <*ka·š*> (vi) 'peinarse' Gu <*ka:š, kʸa!$\overline{š}$, kʸa!$\overline{š}$p*> OlP: *ka:š* (vr) 'peinarse' (vt) 'peinarlo' SaP: *ka:š~ka?š* 'comb lice from hair'

KA#061 pM ***ka:?š-an** *(n) 'peine/comb'* [pOM **ka:?šn*] NHM: *ka:?šɨn* 'escopeta, cepillo' MM: '=cepillo' Ma,At,Ct *ka?$\underline{š}$ɳ* Ja *ka?$\underline{š}$n* Pu *ka!$\underline{š}$ɳ* LM: Cn <*ka:š*> Ca *ka·št* Gu *ka!$\underline{š}$t* OlP: *ka:ša'n* SaP: *ká?šan*

KA#062 pOM ***ka:šɨ?k** *(vi) 'aparecerse/to appear'* SHM: Tp
<*kA·žɨ?kp, kʸæšɨ"kʸ*> MM: Ju,Ma,Pu,Ct <*kɨžɨ?kp*> Ja <*n?ihš kʸɨžé"gʸɨc*> At <*nɨgɨžɨ?kp, tɨ: kʸæ"žé"kʸ*> LM: Ca <*kɨžɨ?kp*> Gu
<*kɨ"žɨ?p*>

KA#063 pZ ***kat** *(vt) 'lamer/to lick'* AyZ: *[kat]* TxZ: *kata?y* (vt, vi-p) 'desbocar' ChisZ: C,N *kaht* (vt) ChZ: *?aɳkat*

KA#064 pOM ***ka:ti** *(n) 'tucán/tucan'* MM: Ma,Ja,Ct *ka·$\overline{t}$* At
ka·t~kat LM: Gu *ka·tï*

KA#065 pM ***ka?w** *(vi) 'caer/to fall'* NHM: *ka"* 'caer (p.ej., una hoja)' SHM: Tu <*kʸa"y, ka?ámp*> 'caerse de arriba' MM: 'caerse de arriba' Ju <*ka"p*> Cc <*kA"p, kA"* (imperative), *kA"hámp, kA"* (pas), *tɨ: kʸa"y, kʸæh kʸa"y* (past)> Ma <*ka"p, tɨ: kʸa"y*> Ja <*ka"w, ka!w̄, ka!p*> Pu <*ka!p, tɨ: kʸa"y*> At <*ká!p, ka"há·m̄p*> Ct <*ka!p*> LM: Cn <*ka?w~ka?~ka"*> (vi) 'caer' Ca <*ka"p*> Gu <*ka"w, ka!p, ka!w̄, ka"wá·m̄p, tï: kʸa"y*> OlP: *ka?* (vi) 'caerse; bajarse (persona)' SaP: *ka?w* (vi) 'fall'

KA#066 pM ***yak-ka?w** *(vt) 'hacer caer de arriba/to cause to fall from above'* NHM: *yakka?a* (vt) 'hacer caer algo' SHM: Tu <*yahká"h*> 'hacer caer de arriba' MM: Cc <*yAhkká"pʸ, yAhkká"*> 'hacer caer de arriba' LM: Cn <*yahka?w~yahka"w*> (vt) 'tumbar' SaP: *?aká?u* (vt) 'tumbar' [Clark and Clark 1960]

KA#067 pM ***ka?wak** *(n) 'zapote colorado/marmalade fruit'* [pOM *ka?wk] NHM: *kïpïka?ahk* 'mamey' SHM: Tl *ko:?k* 'mamey' MM: Ju *ka"k* 'mamey (zapote colorado)' Ma *ka!k* 'zapote colorado', *ka!k* 'mamey (zapote colorado)' [sic!] Ja,Pu *ka"k* '=mamey' At,Ct *ka!wk* '=mamey' LM: Cn <*ka"k*> 'plátano (genérico) [Musa]' SJ *ka"k* 'mamey (zapote colorado)' Gu *ka"kpó:t* 'mamey (zapote colorado), zapote colorado' OlP: *kava'k~kava?, kuykava'k* SaP: *ká?wak, kuygá?wak*

KA#068 pOM ***kawVš** *(n) 'guacamaya/macaw'* NHM: *kávuš* 'guacamaya verde, guacamaya roja [Ara militaris, Ara macao]' MM: Ju *ka"š* At *ka?wš* LM: Cn <*ka"š*> '[Ara militaris]' Ca *ka"š*

KA#069 pM ***kay** *(vt) 'comer tortillas, pan/to eat tortillas, bread'* NHM: *ka:y~ka:hy~kay* SHM: Tl *kay* Tu <*kaȳ, mga·ypʸ*> Tp <*ká:yɨc, kayyámp, kay, mgæ:ʸpʸ*> Mi <*ka·ypʸ*> MM: Ju <*kæy*> 'comer (intr., tortillas, pan)' Cc <*kayy, mgA·ypʸ, kʸa·ypʸ, kʸa·ypʸ, kʸa·y, tka·y, tkay, kʸaȳæmpʸ*> Ma <*kæy, kæ:pʸ, mgæ:pʸ*> Ja <*kaȳ, kæ:pʸ*> Pu,At <*kæȳ, kæ:pʸ, mgæ:pʸ*> Ct <*kaȳ*> LM: Cn <*ka·y~kay*> (vt) 'comer (comida con tortillas)' SJ *ka·y~kay* Ca <*kay*> Gu <*kaȳ, ka:pʸ, mga:pʸ*> OlP: *kay* (vt) 'comer' (ejemplo: "estoy comiendo frijoles") SaP: *kay* (vi, vt) 'eat' (generic)

KA#070 pOM ***ko-kahy ~ ko-kay** *(vt) 'comer comida de otro/eat someone else's meal'* NHM: *kuka:y~kuka:hy~kukay* 'comerse lo que a otro le toca' LM: Cn <*koga·y~kogay*> (vt) 'comer (lo de otro)' Cn <*ka·y~kay*> (vt)

KA#071 pOM *mu-kahy ~ mu-kay* *(vt)* *'comer (con alguien)/eat (with someone else)'* NHM: *muka:y ~ muka:hy ~ mukay* 'comer en casa ajena'

KA#072 pOM *yak-kahy ~ yak-kay* *(vt)* *'dar de comer/to give to eat'* NHM: *yahka:y ~ yahkay* 'dar de comer a alguien, comer algo' LM: Cn <*yahka·y ~ yahkay*> (vt) 'dar de comer'

KA#073 pM *kay-an* *(n)* *'comida/meal'* [pOM *kayn] LM: Cn *kayɨn* [Hoogshagen 1984] SJ *ka·yɨn* OlP: *kaya'n* SaP: *káyan*

KA#074 pOM *ka:ky* *(←ka:y-k)* *(n)* *'tortilla/tortilla (also generic for food)'* NHM: *ka:ky* MM: Ju,Ma,Ja,At,Ct *kæ:kʸ* LM: Cn <*ka:gy*> SJ *ka:gy* [<*ka·y* 'to eat'—irregular derivative] Gu *ka:kʸ*

KA#075 pM [Veracruz] *ka:ʔy* *(vt)* *'tostar/to toast'* OlP: *ka:y* (vt) 'tostarlo (p.ej., café o maíz)' SaP: *kaʔy* (vi, vt) 'toast coffee'

KU#001 pMZ *kuh* *(vi)* *'aventar (arena, agua, etc.)/to pitch, throw (sand, water, etc.)'* NHM: *kʋh* 'tirar (p.ej., una piedra chica), aventar, botar (p.ej., un frijol)' LM: Cn <*kuh*> (vi) 'fluir, correr (el agua)' SJ *kuh* 'to run (stream, current)' Gu *kuh* 'echar agua' [Nordell, p.c.] TxZ: *kuh* (vt) 'tapar (con piedras, tierra, arena)' ChisZ: N *kuh* (vt) 'golpearlo; dar culatazo'

KU#002 pMZ *kuk* *(n?)* *'medio/middle'* [pM, pOM *kuhk; pZ *kuk] NHM: *kʋhk* 'vertical, derecho—p.ej., algo en posición vertical' MM: Ma *kúhkɨ* Ju,Ja,At,Ct *kuhk* LM: Cn <*kuhk*> (adv) 'en medio; algo, medio' SJ *kuhk* 'straight' Ca,Gu *kuhk* TxZ: *kyuk-pe* (adv) 'en medio' ChisZ: C *kukwene* (adj) 'medio'; (n) 'mitad' N *kuk ~ kuk we?ne* NE *kuktaŋubɨ* (adj) 'medio' (n) 'mitad'; *kuktawe* 'mitad'; *kuk?ɨdibɨ* (adj) 'medio' (n) 'mitad'

KU#003 pMZ *kuk-mɨ* *(adv)* *'en medio/in the middle'* [pM *kuhk-mɨ > pOM *kuhkm; pZ *kuk-mɨ] NHM: *kʋhkm* 'mitad' MM: Ma,Ct,At *kuhkm̥* 'medio, mitad' Ja,Ju *kuhm̥* 'medio', *kuhm̥n̥* 'medio, mitad' Pu *kuhm̥* 'medio, mitad' LM: Ca *kupk* 'medio' SJ *kuhk ?a·my* 'in the middle' Gu *kuhk* 'medio', *kupk* 'mitad' [?] ChisZ: C *kukmɨ* (adv) 'por en medio, a la mitad, por la mitad; centro' N *kukmɨ* (adv) 'en medio'

KU#004 pOM ***hot-kuhk** *(adj) 'alegre, contento, feliz/glad, content, happy'* SHM: Tp,Mi *hotkúhk* MM: Ju *hotkúhk* Ma,Ja,Pu,At,Ct *ho·tkúhk* LM: Ca *ho·tkúhk* Gu *ho·tkúhk*

KU#005 pM ***ku?ku** *(n) 'familiar, pariente/relative'* [Cf. pOM **mu-ku"k* 'familiar' below] OlP: *ku?ku* 'indio' SaP: *ku?k* 'indigenista' ChisZ: C [Te] <*cuc*> 'comunidad' [?-The source does not show glottal stops.]

KU#006 pOM ***mu-ku"k** *(n) 'familiar/relative'* NHM: *mugʋ"k* 'pariente, familiares' MM: 'familiar, pariente' Ju *mɨgú"k* Ma *mɨ·gú"k* 'pariente', *mɨgú"k* 'familiar, pariente' [sic!] Ja,Pu *mɨ·gú"k* At *mɨgú"k* '=compañero' Ct *mɨ·gú"k* 'familiar, pariente', *mɨ:gú"k* 'compañero' LM: Ca *mugú"k* 'compañero', *mug?ú"k* 'amigo' [sic!] Cn <*mɨgu"k*> Gu *mʸɨgú"k* 'familiar, pariente'

KU#007 pOM ***ku:k** *(n) 'tortola/pigeon'* MM: At *ku:k* LM: Ca,Gu *ku:k*

KU#008 pZ ***ku?ku?** *(n) 'paloma/dove'* [pGZ **ku?uku*] SoZ: *kú?uku?* AyZ: *kú?ugu* TxZ: *-ku:?ku?* [bound] ChisZ: C [Te] <*cucu*> 'corita, paloma'

KU#009 pMZ ***kum** *(vt) 'punzar/to puncture'* NHM: *kʋ:m ~ kʋ:hm ~ kʋm* 'picar (p.ej., con aguja), punzar (p.ej., con aguja)' MM: Ju <*kum*> 'inyectar, apuñalar, vacunar' Ma <*tɨkúmɨ, kum*> 'apuñalar', <*kum, kʸi·mpʸ*> 'punzar (con cuchillo, etc.)' Ja <*kum, ku·m, kʸi·mpʸ*> 'punzar (con cuchillo, etc.), apuñalar' Pu <*kum*> 'apuñalar' At <*kum, kʸü·mpʸ*> 'apuñalar, punzar (con cuchillo, etc.)' Ct <*kum, kʸi·mpʸ*> 'apuñalar, punzar (con cuchillo, etc.)' LM: Cn <*ku·m ~kum*> 'picar (con espina, aguja o cuchillo); inyectar' Ca <*kum*> 'majar (café)' [?] Gu <*kum, ku·m, kʸu·mpʸ*> 'punzar (con cuchillo, etc.), apuñalar' SJ *ku·m~kum* 'to inject, puncture' AyZ: *[kum]* 'esconder, enterrar' TxZ: *kum* (vt) 'sepultar' ChisZ: C *kum* (vi) 'esconderse, ocultarse' (vt) 'rescoldarlo' N *kum* (vi) 'cocerse (envuelto en hojas)' (vt) 'asarlo (envuelto en una hoja)' NE *kum* (vi) 'sudar' (vt) 'hornearlo' ChZ: *kum* 'enterrar'

KU#010 pZ ***kumkuy** *(n) 'pueblo/village'* ChisZ: C *kumguy* '=población, ciudad; pueblo, gente; tierra' N *kumguy* '=, ciudad; la gente del pueblo' NE *kumgu?* ChZ: *kumku?y*

KU#011 pMZ ***kuma** *(n) 'coyole/type of palm'* [pM *kuma > pOM *kum; pZ *kuma > pGZ **ku:ma?*] NHM: *kʊm* 'palma coca, xocoyol, palma de coyol' [Acrocomia mexicana] MM: Ju *kum* Ma,Ja, Pu,At,Ct *kum̄* LM: Cn <*kum*> 'coyol [Acrocomia mexicana]' Ca *kum* Gu *kum̄* OIP: *kuma* SaP: *kum* SoZ: *ku:ma* [Nordell 1962], *ku:ma?* [Gutiérrez M. 1993] TxZ: *ku:ma?* 'fruta de coyole' ChisZ: C *kuma* '=cocoyol'

KU#012 pMZ ***kɨ?-kuma** *(n) 'anillo/ring'* [See pMZ **kɨ?*.] OIP: *kɨ?kuma* SaP: *kɨ?kúm* ChisZ: C,NE *kɨ?kuma* N *kɨkumɨ* ChZ: *kɨ?kuma?*

KU#013 pMZ ***kumu** *(n) 'gusano/worm'* [pM *kumu; pZ *kumu > pGZ **ku:mu*] OIP: *kumu* 'gusano—nombre general'; *hotkumu* 'lombriz' SaP: *kumcugut* 'gusano gallina ciega' TxZ: *ku:m* 'gusano gallina ciega' ChisZ: N *kumu* 'gallina ciega, mayat—larva de unos escarabajos'

KU#014 pM ***nɨ:s-kumu** *(n) 'gusano gallina ciega/a kind of worm'* [NHM has contamination from 'earth'.] NHM: *naškʊm* 'gallina ciega—gusano, larve de mayate o abejorro—coleóptero. Phyllophaga sp.' OIP: *nɨ:škumu* 'gusano gallina ciega'

KU#015 pZ ***kun** *(vi) 'caer/to fall'* TxZ: *kun-pa:č* (s) 'lagartija' [?-semantics] ChisZ: C *kun* (vi) 'caer, caerse' N *kun* (vi) 'caerse' (vt) 'cortarlo (fruta)' NE *kun* (vi) 'caer (como hojas por la lluvia)'

KU#016 pMZ ***kunu** *(n) 'zacua/Montezuma oropendola [Gymnostinops montezuma]'* [pM *kunu > pOM *kun; pZ *kunu] MM: Ma,Ja, Ct *kun̄* LM: Gu *kun̄* OIP: *kunukunu* TxZ: *ku:n* ChisZ: C *ku?munu* [?] N *kunu* NE *ku?muni* [?]

KU#017 pOM ***kup** *(vi) 'clavar (estaca, espeque, etc.)/to nail (stake, etc.)'* MM: Ma <*kup̄*> 'majar (café)' Ja <*kup̄, kʸihpʸ*> 'majar (café)', <*kup̄, kuhp*> 'clavar (estaca, espeque, etc.)' Pu <*kup̄*> 'clavar (estaca, espeque, etc.), majar (café)' At <*kup̄, kʸühpʸpʸ*> 'majar (café)', <*kúpɨ*> 'clavar (estaca, espeque, etc.)' Ct <*kup̄, kʸihpʸ*> 'majar (café)' LM: 'clavar (estaca, espeque, etc.) Cn <*kuhp~kup*> (vt) Ca <*kup*> Gu <*kup̄*> OIP: *kup* (vt) 'punzarlo'

KU#018 pOM ***kup** *(n) 'horcón/house pole'* SHM: 'espina' Tl *kuhp* Ay *kuhp* LM: Cn <*kup*> Ca *kup* LM: Gu *kupk*

KU#019 pM ***ku:?p** *(vt)* *'picar (zancudo)/to bite (mosquito)'* NHM:
kʋ:?p 'inyectar, prender, vacunar' MM: Pu *<ku:p, kʲu?pʲ>* 'vacunar' Pu *<ku:p, kʲi!pʲ>* 'inyectar' Ma *<ku:p, kʲi?pʲ>* 'inyectar,
vacunar', *<ku?p>* 'picar, morder (zancudo)' Ja *<ku:p, kʲi?pʲ>*
'inyectar, vacunar', *<ku:p, kʲu?p, kú?pɨp>* 'picar, morder (zancudo)'
At *<ku:p, kʲi?pʲpʲ>* 'inyectar', *<ku:p, kʲü?pʲpʲ>* 'vacunar',
<ku?pp> 'picar, morder (zancudo)' Ct *<nɨkú:p, nʲɨkí?pʲ>*
'inyectar, vacunar', *<ku?p, kú?pɨp>* 'picar, morder (zancudo)' LM:
Gu *<ku·?p, ku:bá·m̄p, kú·?pɨp>* 'picar, morder (zancudo)' OIP:
ku:p (vt) 'ensartarlo (ejemplo: mecate en aguja de arria / carne en el
asador para asarla)'

KU#020 pMZ ***ku:s?** *(vi)* *'hartar/to fill with food'* NHM: *kʋ:š~kʋ"š*
'hartarse, satisfacer, quedar satisfecho (p.ej., después de comer)'
MM: 'satisfacer' Ma *<ku·šp, kú·šɨp, ku"žán̄ɨp>* Ja *<ku·šp,
kú·šɨp, ku"žá·n̄ɨbɨc>* At *<ku·šp, kú·šɨp, ku"žá·nɨp>* Ct *<ku·šp,
kú·šɨp, ku"žán̄ɨp>* LM: Gu *<ku·šp, kú·šɨp, ku"žá·n̄ɨp>* SJ
ku·š~ku"š 'to be satisfied' SaP: *ku:š* (vi, vt) 'fill with food, be
satisfied' TxZ: *kus* (vi) 'satisfecharse, llenarse (de comida)' SoZ:
kus 'estar satisfecho' [Elson 1960]

KU#021 pOM ***ku"š-y** *(adj)* *'satisfecho/satisfied'* NHM: *ku"š*
'=harto, sin hambre, saciado' LM: Cn *ku"šy* (adj) 'satisfecho (alimento)' SJ *ku"šyi:* 'satisfied'

KU#022 pOM ***ku?š** *(n)* *'camarón del río/type of shrimp'* [May be
indirectly related to the ChisZ-N verb root *ku?s* (vi-s) 'tener una
curva', or directly related to its derivative *ku?sɨ* 'curva'.] SHM: Tp
ku!š MM: Ma *ku"š* Ja,At,Ct *ku!š̄* Pu *kuš̄* LM: Cn *<ku"š>*
'chacal, chacalín, burrita (tipo de camarón de río) [Cambarellus
montezumae]' Gu *ku!š̄* '=chacalín'

KU#023 pZ ***kut** *(vt)* *'arrodillarse/to kneel'* TxZ: *kut* (vt) 'aplastar
(con las manos)' ChisZ: C *kutkɨne?k* (vi) N *kutkɨne?k* (vi) 'hincarse', *kutkehk* (vi) '=hincarse' ChZ: *kutnay*

KU#024 pZ ***ku?t** *(vi, vt)* *'comer cosa blanda/to eat soft foods'* TxZ:
ku?t (vt) 'comer (fruta blanda), tragar' SoZ: *ku?t* [Foster and Foster
1948] ChisZ: C [Co] *ku?t* 'comer' [Te] *<cut pa>* 'comer cosas
blandas como fruta / pacer el ganado' N *ku?t* 'comer cosa blanda' NE
ku?t 'comer'

KU#025 pOM ***ku?t ~ ku"t** *(vt) 'trenzar/to braid'* MM: Ma,Ja,At,Ct
< *ku"t, kʸu?tʸpʸ* > LM: Gu < *ku"t, kʸu?tʸp* >

KU#026 pZ ***kuŋ** *(vt) 'alzar, levantar/to lift, carry'* ChisZ: C,NE *kuŋ*
ChZ: *kuŋ* 'colgar'

KU#027 pMZ ***kuy** *(n) 'árbol, palo/tree, wood'* [pM, pOM **kuhy*;
pZ, pGZ **kuy*] [According to G. Martin (p.c.) in Chinantequilla, north
of Totontepec, the term *kuy* is used in plant names whenever the Totontepec variety has *kɨp*; Chinantequilla may be an extremely interesting
location if it has other such features not shared with the rest of OM.]
MM: 'tipo de árbol que no tiene muchas ramas' [The first morpheme
in the MM forms seems to be *kuy*, carrying the meaning 'branch'.] Ma
ko:dʸú" At *kuʸdʸú"k* Ct *kedʸú"k* LM: Ca *kuyhyam* 'wood ashes'
[Wonderly 1949] TaM: *kuy* [transcription of Wonderly 1949] OlP:
kuyɨ SaP: *kuhy* SoZ: *kuy* AyZ: *[kuy]* TxZ: *kuy* ChisZ: C *kuy*
'=madera, tabla' N *kuy* '=madera' NE *kuy* '=madera; cabo,
mango—como de hacha' S *[kuy]* 'palo' ChZ: StaMaCh *kuy* 'árbol'
SnMiCh *kuy* [Wonderly 1949]

KU#028 pMZ ***capac-kuy** *(n) 'palo colorado/buckthorn'* [See pMZ
*capac.] OlP: *capaskuyɨ* SaP: *cabackuhy* [Clark 1981] TxZ:
ca?pa?c-kuy 'palo nazareno' ChisZ: N *capaskuy* 'palo mulato' [Bur-
sura sp.]

KU#029 pMZ ***ham(ay)-kuy** *(n) 'jobo/hog plum tree'* [pM **hamkuy*;
pZ **hamaykuy*] OlP: *hamkuyɨ / havinkuyɨ* 'jabí' SaP: *hamguhy*
ChisZ: C *hamahkyuy* 'árbol de jobo'; *hamahy* 'fruta de jobo'

KU#030 pM ***maši-kuy** *(n) 'jobo/hog plum tree'* [pOM **mašy* with
development of a parasitic nasal in MM] MM: Ma,Ct *mæ̃šʸn̥ʸ* Ja *mæ̃šʸ*
Pu *pu!cmǽšʸ* At *mæšʸn̥ʸ* LM: Gu *mašʸp* OlP: *maši* SaP: *maškúhy*

KU#031 pM ***nɨ:c-kuy** *(n) 'guayacán/tree of life'* [pOM **nɨ:čky*]
MM: Ma,Ja,Pu,Ct *nɨ·čkʸ* Gu *nɨ·čk* OlP: *nɨ:sku* SaP: *nɨ:ckúhy*

KU#032 pMZ ***puh-kuy** *(n) 'papachote/a species of tree'* [lit., 'seed
tree'] [pM **puhkuy* > pOM **puhky*; pZ, pGZ **puhkuy*] NHM: *puhk*
'jolocín, jonote' [The Sp-to-NHM side has the additional definition
'majagua'.] [Heliocarpus Donnell-Smithii] SaP: *puhkuykúhy* SoZ:
púhki TxZ: *puhkuy*

KU#033 pZ ***kuy-puk-kuy** *(n) 'achiote/annatto'* SaP: *kuypuhkuhy* [Zo loan?] TxZ: *ku:ʔypok*

KU#034 pM [Veracruz] ***kuy-win** *(n) 'tapanco/attic'* OlP: *kuyvinɨ* SaP: *kúywin*

KU#035 pOM ***ku:y** *(n) 'hormiga carpintera/a species of ant'* SHM: Tl *ku:y* 'hormiga' LM: Ml <*ku:y*>

KU#036 pOM ***ku"y** *(n) 'ardilla grande y roja/large, red squirrel'* NHM: *ku"* 'ardilla' [Sciurus aereogaster] SHM: Tl,Ay *kuʔhy* 'ardilla' Tu *ku"y ~ kuʔy* Tp *kuʔy ~ ku"y* Mi *kuʔy* 'ardilla grande y roja de tierra baja' MM: Ju,Ma *ku"y̨* Cc *kuʔy* Pu *ku"y* 'ardilla chica (?) y roja' At *ku!y̨* Ct *ku"y* LM: Cn <*kuʔy*> 'ardilla [Sciurus spp.]' Ca *ku"y* Gu *ku!ȳ* OlP: *kuymu:tu* 'ardilla' [?] SoZ: *kúʔnki* [Foster and Foster 1948] [?] ChZ: *kuru* 'ardilla' [?]

KO#001 pM ***koc** *(vi) 'hablar/to speak'* NHM: *kohc ~ koc* 'hablar, palabra, noticia (p.ej., de palabra)' OlP: *koc* (vt) 'pegarlo con goma (p.ej., papel)' SaP: *koc* (vi, vt) 'speak, read' ChisZ: N *pɨŋgockocney* (vi) 'sonar muchas explosiones' [?]

KO#002 pM ***ʔa-koc** *(v) 'adivinar/to foretell'* NHM: *ʔakohc ~ ʔakoc* 'predecir, anunciar, pronosticar, agüero' SaP: *ʔakoctúk* 'adivinar' [Clark and Clark 1960]

KO#003 pM ***ʔa-koc-ay** *(v) 'aconsejar/to advise'* NHM: *ʔakohcip ~ ʔakoca* SaP: *ʔakóči* [Clark and Clark 1960]

KO#004 pM ***mu-koc** *(v) 'hablar a alguien/to speak to someone'* NHM: *mukohc ~ mukoc* 'hablar a alguien' SaP: *mukóc* 'hablar con' [Clark and Clark 1960]

KO#005 pMZ ***ko:ʔc** *(vt) 'curtir; quebrar/to tan; break'* NHM: *ko:ʔc* 'curtir, roto' LM: Cn <*ko:c ~ ko·c*> (vt) 'curtir' ChisZ: C *koʔc* (vi) 'hundirse, sumirse; quebrarse; suspenderse' (vt) 'quebrarlo; deshacerlo, desbaratarlo' N *koʔc* (vi) 'quebrarse; abollarse, magullarse' (vt) 'quebrarlo, magullarlo' NE *koʔc* (vt) 'quebrarlo (como un huevo)'

KO#006 pM ***ko:ʔco** *(adj) 'obscuro/dark'* [pOM **ko:c*] NHM: *ko:ʔc* '=obscuridad' SHM: Tl *kv:c* '=obscuro' Ay *ko:c* LM: Cn <*ko:dz*> (s) 'noche' (adj) 'ignorante' Gu *ko:c* '=noche' [Nordell, p.c.] OlP: *ko:co*

KO#007 pM ***koh** *(vt) 'tejer/to weave'* NHM: *koh* 'tejer (p.ej., un sarape)' SHM: Tl *kᵥh* 'tejer (una cobija)' LM: Cn <*koh*> (vt) 'construir; plantar' SJ *koh* 'to transplant, to make' Gu <*koh, kohp*> [Nordell, p.c.] OlP: *koh* (vt) 'hacer una faja' SaP: *koh* (vi, vt) 'weave (a sash)'

KO#008 pZ ***koha** *(n) 'culpa, pecado/sin'* TxZ: *kowa* '=delito' [borrowed from other Zoquean?] ChisZ: C *kowa* N,NE *koha* ChZ: *koha*

KO#009 pM ***kohk** *(n) 'espiga/ear of plant'* [pOM **kohk*] SHM: Tl *kᵥhk* Ay *kohk* 'flor de la milpa' OlP: *koki̵* 'flor de maíz' SaP: *kok* 'espiga de maíz' [?] ChisZ: C *tokok* 'joloche; totomostle' [?] NE *tohok* 'joloche; totomostle' [?]

KO#010 pM ***mo:k-kohk** *(n) 'espiga de maíz/ear of corn'* [pOM **mo:kkohk*] NHM: *mokkohk* LM: Cn <*mo:kkohk*> OlP: *mo:koki̵*

KO#011 pOM ***koʔk ~ koⁿk** *(vt) 'acostar/to lie down'* SHM: Tu <*koⁿk, mgoeʔkʸpʸ ~ mgeʔkʸpʸ*> MM: Ju <*koⁿk*> At <*koⁿk, kʸöʔkʸpʸ*> Ct <*koⁿk, kʸeʔkʸpʸ*> LM: Cn <*koⁿk*> (vt) 'agachar' Gu <*koⁿk, kʸoʔpʸ, nahckoⁿgi̵ⁿw*>

KO#012 pOM ***koⁿk** *(n) 'bellota/acorn'* [Cf. also pMZ **šoh-ti̵hm* 'acorn'; this may refer to the fruit of another type of oak; according to G. Martin (p.c.) there are about thirty different species of oak in Oaxaca.] NHM: *koⁿk* SHM: Mi *šohkóⁿk* MM: Ma,At *šohkóⁿk*

KO#013 pMZ ***kokʔe** *(n) 'pez, pescado/fish'* OlP: *koʔke* ChisZ: C *kokeh* N *koke* S *[ko·kéʔ]* ChZ: *koke*

KO#014 pZ ***koks** *(vt) 'tocar, golpear/to knock'* TxZ: *koks* (vt) 'golpear (puerta)' ChisZ: C *koks* (vt) 'tocarlo' N *koks* (vt) 'golpearlo; tocar (a la puerta)' NE *koks* (vt) 'tocarlo (la puerta)'

KO#015 pMZ ***kom** *(vi, vt) 'llenar(se) de un líquido/to fill or be filled with a liquid'* NHM: *kom* 'bastante (p.ej., agua)' LM: Cn <*kom*> (adj) 'bastante (líquido)' Gu <*kom, ko·mp*> 'llenarse con un líquido', *kom* 'crecido (río), lleno' [Nordell, p.c.] OlP: *kom* (vi) 'estar crecido (el río)' (vt) 'sembrarlo; ponerlo en la tierra (p.ej., un poste)' [Perhaps the latter meaning belongs to a different verb—a verbalized form of 'post'.] SaP: *kom* (vi, vt) 'flood, put in' SoZ: *kom* 'llenarse (río, etc.)' AyZ: *[kom]* 'llenarse; derramarse, crecerse (agua)' TxZ: *kom* (vt, vi-p) 'llenar' ChisZ: N *kom* (vt) 'cobrarlo (con canasta o caja)' NE *kom* (vt) 'encarcelarlo, encerrarlo'

*KO#016 pM *komi(k) (n) 'pus/pus'* [pOM *komy] NHM: kɨm SHM: Tl kvmʸ LM: Cn <komy> OlP: komi'k

*KO#017 pMZ *kom(om) (n) 'horcón/house pole'* [pM *komom > pOM *kom; pZ *kom] NHM: kom 'palma coca, palma de coyol' [According to G. Martin *kom* is not a tree but refers to posts or poles.] OlP: komo'm SaP: kómom SoZ: kom AyZ: [kom] '=poste' TxZ: kom ChisZ: C kom '=poste' N kom NE kop '=poste'

*MO#018 pM [Veracruz] *mo?co-komom (n) 'estante/shelf'* OlP: mo?cokomo'm 'estantes, postes de una casa' SaP: mo?ckómom 'estante para embarrar'

*KO#019 pMZ *kon (vi, vt) 'llevar/to carry'* [The ChisZ-C forms are derived and basically mean 'place to sit' just like the LM-Cn form <koñ> 'banco (asiento de madera)', which is derived by the same means; we cannot know whether these derivations in ChisZ and LM were independent or cognate.] NHM: ko:n~ko:hn~kon 'llevar (p.ej., dinero), tomar (p.ej., una cosa pequeña en la mano)' MM: 'llevar (pelota)' At <pakón, pagón> Ct <pa·kón> LM: Cn <ko·n> (vt) 'agarrar (cosa esférica); llevar (a bautizar)' SJ ko·n~kon 'to shrink, wear down in length, shorten; to hold round objects in the hand' SaP: kon (vi, vt) 'carry on shoulder' AyZ: [kon] 'sentarse' TxZ: kon (vi) 'sentarse, cuajarse' ChisZ: N konoc 'trozo de árbol (que se usa para sentarse)' [?-not certain whether in fact the root *kon* is contained herein] C [Co] koni? 'nalga, asentadera' [Te] <coni> 'culo'

*KO#020 pOM *win-kon (adv) 'cerca/close'* SHM: Tu βiŋgónʸɨ Tp βiŋgón Mi wiŋgón MM: Cc hiŋgón Ju,Ja wiŋgón Pu wi:ŋgón Ma,At hiŋgón Ct wiŋgón LM: Ca wi:ŋgón Gu wi:ŋgón

*KO#021 pMZ *kono(k) (adj) 'corto/short'* [pM *kono(k) > pOM *kon (with an unexplained final vowel in NHM); pZ *kono] [The adjectival form derived from a verbal root only attested in OlP yakon (vt) 'acortarlo'.] NHM: kona 'corto—p.ej., cosas; bajo de estatura' SHM: Tl kvn LM: Cn <kon> (adj) OlP: kono'k ChisZ: C,NE kono ChZ: kono?

KO#022 pOM ***koⁿn** *(n) 'tomate/tomato'* NHM: *koⁿn* LM: Cn <*ko?n*> '=jitomate [Lycopersicon esculentum]' SJ *ko?n* SHM: Tl *kⱱⁿn* 'jítomate'

KO#023 pOM ***cap-koⁿn** *(n) 'miltomate/ground cherry [Physalis spp.]'* NHM: *capkoⁿn* 'miltomate' LM: Cn <*cahpko?n*> 'miltomate [Physalis pubescens]'

KO#024 pM ***kopak** *(n) 'cerro/mountain'* [pOM *kopk] NHM: *kopk* '=montaña, sierra, monte, cumbre' LM: Cn <*kop*> 'cerro; origen' OlP: *kopa'k* SaP: *kópak* [homonym: 'cabeza']

KO#025 pOM ***šɨhw-kopk** *(n) 'tiempo de secas/dry season'* NHM: *šɨkopk* '=sequía (abril y mayo)' Ma,Ja,Ct *šɨgópk* At *šɨ:gópk* LM: Gu *šɨgópk*

KO#026 pMZ ***ko?ps** *(vi, vt) 'coger/to catch'* LM: Gu <*ko?š*> 'jugar con bolero' [Nordell, p.c.] SaP: *ko?pš* (vi, vt) 'catch' ChisZ: N *ko?ps* (vi) 'amarrarse, estar amarrado' (vt) 'amarrarlo; cogerlo, agarrarlo' [The composite verb *tɨŋ-go?ps* (vt) 'cogerlo' fits the more specific meaning of the OlP form.] ChZ: *ko?ps* 'gapillar'

KO#027 pMZ ***kos** *(vt) 'golpear con el puño/to hit with the fist'* NHM: *kɨš* SHM: Tl *kⱱš* 'golpear' LM: Cn <*kohš~koš*> (vt) 'pegar (con la mano)' SJ *kohš~koš* 'to hit with the fist' OlP: *koš* (vt) 'golpearlo con el puño' SaP: *koš* (vi, vt) 'cause/desire sickness' TxZ: *cen-kos* (vt) 'amarrar (persona)' (vi) 'azocarse (cuerda)' ChZ: *kos* 'regañar'

KO#028 pOM ***yak-kohš ~ yak-koš** *(vt) 'pegar a alguien/to hit someone'* NHM: *yakkoš* 'pegar a alguien' LM: Cn <*yahkohš~yahkoš*> (vt) 'pegar (con la mano)'

KO#029 pMZ ***koso(k)** *(n) 'rodilla/knee'* [pM **košo(k)* > pOM *koš; pZ *koso > pGZ **ko:so?*] NHM: *koš* SHM: Tl *kⱱš* Ay *koš* 'codo' OlP: *košo* SaP: *košk* SoZ: *ko:so?* TxZ: *ko:so?* ChisZ: N *koso* 'pie, pata, pierna' NE *koso* 'pie, pata'

KO#030 pMZ ***kot** *(vt) 'poner en/to insert'* NHM: *koht~kot* 'dar un golpe con la punta de algo (p.ej., un palo)' LM: Cn <*koht~kot*> (vt) 'poner puntales' SJ *koht~kot* 'to brace' OlP: *cumkot* (vt) 'amarrar un bulto' SaP: *kot* (vi, vt) 'prick, puncture' SoZ: *kot* 'meterlo' TxZ: *kot* (vt) 'poner, echar, meter, ceñir' ChisZ: C *koht* (vt) 'ponerlo, colocarlo; emplearlo' N *koht* (vt) 'echarlo, ponerlo' NE *koht* (vt) 'ponerlo, colocarlo; echarlo; ponerselo (como el sombrero); establecerlo (como un negocio)' ChZ: *kotku?y* 'cosa para guardar' [derived form]

KO#031 pZ **kot-ay** *(vt) 'echarselo/to put on, add'* TxZ: *kota?y* 'agregar, rebajar' [Clark n.d.] ChisZ: N *kohtay* (vt) 'echarselo; darle más (peleando)' NE *kohtay* (v-ditr) 'echarselo, ponerselo'

KO#032 pMZ **kow** *(vi, vt) 'tocar/to play'* [A pMZ status rather than just pM is secured by the age of the derived form **kow-an* below.] NHM: *ko:v ~ ko:hv ~ kov* 'tocar (p.ej., guitarra o órgano)' LM: SJ *ko·w ~ kow* 'to play a stringed instrument' Gu <*kow, ko:p*> 'tocar guitarra' [Nordell, p.c.] OlP: *kov* (vi) 'tocar (un tambor)' (vt) 'tocarlo (el tambor)'

KO#033 pMZ **kowa** *(n) 'tambor/drum'* [pM **kowa* > pOM **kow*; pZ **kowa*] NHM: *kov* 'armonio' LM: Cn <*ko:w*> 'guitarra' OlP: *kova'n* [reanalysis: *kow* 'to play' + *an* 'nominalizing suffix'] SoZ: *kó:wa?* 'jarana' AyZ: *[ko:?wa] ~ [ko:gʷa]* TxZ: *kowa* ChisZ: C *kowah* N,NE *kowa*

KO#034 pZ **koŋ** *(vi) 'gatear/to creep, crawl'* [Possibly pMZ; cf. NHM *kɨ:v* 'banco', OlP *kovo't* 'banco'.] ChisZ: C *koŋ* (vi) 'gatear' N *koŋney* (vi) 'estar asentada (una cosa grande)' NE **koŋ* [*koŋdenay* (vi) 'levantarse, ponerse de pie'; *koŋgehk* (vi) 'agacharse'] ChZ: *koŋnay* 'agacharse'

KO#035 pZ **ko?w** *(vt) 'seguir/to follow'* TxZ: *ko?ŋ* (vt) 'alzar' ChisZ: C *ko?ŋ* (vt) 'seguirlo' N *ko?ŋ* (vt) 'dejar pasar (un día); seguirlo, perseguirlo' NE *ko?ŋ* (vt) 'seguirlo'

KO#036 pMZ **koy** *(vi, vt) 'pintar/to paint'* NHM: *ko:y ~ ko:hy ~ koy* 'pintar (p.ej., una silla)' LM: Cn <*ko·y ~ ko:y*> (vt) SJ *ko·y ~ ko:y* ChisZ: NE *koy* (vi)

KO#037 pMZ **koya** *(n) 'conejo/rabbit'* [pM **koya* > pOM **koy*; pZ **koya* > pGZ **ko:ya?*] NHM: *koy* SHM: Tl *mɨh kʋy* 'liebre' LM: Gu *koy* ['conejo' in the ritual calendar' (Nordell, p.c.)] OlP: *koya* SoZ: *kó:ya* [Foster and Foster 1948], *ko:ya?* [Gutiérrez M. 1993] ChisZ: C *čo?ŋgoya* '=liebre' N *kaŋgoya* NE *čo?ŋgoya* ChZ: *koya?* 'liebre'

KO#038 pZ ***koya** *(n) 'tomate/tomato'*   [pGZ **ko:ya*]   TxZ: *ko:ya?*
ChisZ: C *koya*   '=jitomate'   N,NE *koya*

KO#039 pM [Veracruz] ***ko?y** *(vt) 'chupar/to suck (inside the mouth)'*
OlP: *ko?y* (vt)   SaP: *ko?y* (vi, vt)

LI-LO

LV#001 pOM ***le?k(y) ~ le:?k(y)** *(n) 'nene/baby'* NHM: *lE?k* 'feto'
MM: Ma,Ja *le?kʸ* 'nene, criatura' Pu *le?k* 'criatura', *le!k* 'nene'
[sic!] At *le:kʸ, le?kʸ* 'criatura, nene' Ct *le?kʸ?ú?ŋk, lœ:k* 'criatura,
nene' LM: Gu *le·?k* 'criatura, nene'

LV#002 pMZ ***liklik** *(n) 'gavilancillo/American kestrel'* [pM **liklik*;
pZ, pGZ **liklik*] OlP: *likli'k* SaP: *liklik~i?k?ik* [Clark 1981] TxZ:
lêklêk

MI-MO

MI#001 pOM **mi:c** *(pron) 'ustedes/you (pl)'* [Mixean languages of Veracruz formed the plural of the 2p pronoun by adding a suffix -*at* or -*a:t*; OlP: *mica:tek* SaP: *míhčat*.] NHM: *mi:c* MM: Ma *mi:c, mí:ʒɨtʸ* Ja,At,Ct *mí:ʒɨtʸ* LM: Ca *mí:ɟɨtʸ* Gu *mihc* LM: SJ *mi:ʒy ʔahkyšy* 'you (pl)'

MI#002 pMZ **mici** *(pron) 'usted/you (sg)'* [pM **mi:c* > pOM **mic(y)*; pZ **mic ~ mici*; these correspondences are not regular; syntactically conditioned variation must be involved.] NHM: *mic* SHM: Tl *mec* MM: Ju,At *mihc* Ma,Ja,Ct *mic̄* LM: Cn <*mi:č*> '=tú' SJ *mi:ɟ* 'you (sg)' [short form *mi:*] Gu,Ca *mi:č* OlP: *mi:s* SaP: *mi: / mi:č* SoZ: *mič* TxZ: *bič* AyZ: *[mic]* ChisZ: C *mih* (suj de vi, obj de vt) 'te, le', *mis* (suj de vt, pron pos) 'tú, tu, tus' N *mi / mic / mihci* NE *mih / mihci* (pron pers) 'tú'; (pron pos) 'tu, su—de usted' ChZ: *mic* (dependiente) *micci?* (independiente)

MI#003 pZ **mic-ta?m** *(pron) 'ustedes/you (pl)'* [pGZ **mičta?m*; loss of nasal in TxZ, a process that sporadically affects suffixes.] TxZ: *bič-ta?* ChisZ: C *mista?m* 'ustedes (suj de vt)', *mihta?m* 'ustedes (suj de vi)'

MI#004 pMZ **mici n-he?** *(pron) 'tuyo/your'* [pOM **mi:c m-he"*; the construction + pronoun prefix-*he?* as a whole is pMZ but details concerning the shapes of the pronoun and the prefix are debatable.] LM: SJ *mi:ʒy mhe"* 'yours (sg)' TxZ: *ñe?* ChisZ: C *misne?* (pron pos) 'tuyo, el tuyo, suyo, el suyo (de usted); tu, su (de usted)' NE *mihne?* (pron pos) 'tuyo; suyo (de usted)'

MI#005 pMZ **mi?ks** *(vi) 'temblar/to tremble'* NHM: *mi?kštkp ~ mi?kštïk* 'parpadear' LM: Ml *<mi"kš>* ChisZ: C *mi?ks* (vi) '=moverse' NE *mi?ks* (vi)

MI#006 pMZ **min** *(vi) 'venir/to come'* NHM: *mi:n ~ mi:hn ~ min* '=llegar' SHM: Tl *men* MM: Ju *<min̄>* Ma *<tï: mʸin̄ʸ>* 'nacer (gente, animales)', *<min̄>* 'venir' Ja *<tï: mʸin̄ʸ>* 'nacer (gente, animales)', *<min̄, mi·m̄p>* 'venir' At *<min̄, mi·m̄p, tï: mʸin̄ʸ>* 'venir', *<tï: mʸin̄ʸ, mi·mp>* 'nacer (gente, animales)' Ct *<min̄, mim̄p>* 'venir', *<tï: mʸin̄ʸ>* 'nacer (gente, animales)' LM: Cn *<mi·n ~ min>* (vi) Ca *<min̄>* SJ *mi·n ~ min* Gu *<min̄, mi·m̄p>* 'venir', *<miná·m̄p ka"wá·m̄p>* 'nacer (gente, animales)', *<tï: mʸin̄ʸ tï: kʸa"y>* 'nacer (gente, animales)' OlP: *min ~ mi?n* (vi) SaP: *min ~ mi?n* (vi) SoZ: *miñ* [Foster and Foster 1948; Wonderly 1949] TxZ: *bêñ* (vi) 'venir' (v-aux) 'venitivo-futuro' ChisZ: C *min* (vi) N [FL] *min / minu / minba* (v-aux) 'vino a (moviento); empezó a (incoativo)' (vi) 'venir' [Ma] *min* NE *min* (vi) ChZ: StaMaCh *min* SnMiCh: *min* [Wonderly 1949]

MI#007 pZ **ku-min** *(vt) 'venir a alguien o a algo/to come to somebody or something'* SaP: *kumí?n* 'venirse para acercar' [Clark and Clark 1960] [Zo loan?] ChisZ: C *kɨ?min* (vt) 'venir a alguien o algo, acercarse a alguien o algo' NE *kɨ?min* (vt) 'venir a alguien o a algo'

MI#008 pOM **pa-mihn ~ pa-min** *(vi) 'seguir/to follow'* NHM: *pami:n ~ pami:hn ~ pamin* 'seguir, llegar detrás de alguien' MM: Ju *<pæmín>* LM: Ca *<pamín>* Gu *<pamín̄>*

MI#009 pMZ **yak-min** *(vt) 'traer/to bring'* NHM: *yak-mi:n ~ yakmi:hn ~ yakmin* (vt) MM: Ju *<yæhmín>* Ma *<yahkmín̄>* Pu *<yahkmín̄>* 'arrimar' _ Ja *<yahmín̄, yahmí·mpʸ>* At *<yahkmín̄>* Ct *<yahkmín̄, yak, yahkmí·m̄pʸ>* LM: Gu *<yahmín̄, yahmí·m̄pʸ>* '=arrimar' TxZ: *yakmêñ* (vt-caus) 'hacer venir'

MI#010 pM [Veracruz] **mu-min ~ mu-mi?n** *(vt) 'traer/to bring'* OlP: *mɨ:min ~ mɨ:mi?n* (vt) SaP: *mumí?n* [Clark and Clark 1960]

MI#011 pZ **min-a?** *(vt) 'traer/to bring'* TxZ: *bê:ñ-a?* (vt) [the lengthening is a morphological device] ChZ: *mina?h*

MI#012 pOM **miš** *(pron) 'tú (vocativo masculino), muchacho (voc. addressed to a man)/you (vocative), boy (voc.)'* [A Spanish loan, cognate with the word for 'cat'?] NHM: *mEš* 'muchacho, muchacha'; *miš* 'muchacho'; *miš vnïk* 'chamaco' SHM: Tl *mišy?u?nk* 'niño'; *maš?u?nk* 'criatura' MM: Ma *miš̄ʸ* 'tú 'vocativo masculino)', 'muchacho (vocativo)', *miš̄ʸ?ïná?k* 'muchacho' Ja *mæš̄ʸ, miš̄ʸ* 'tú (vocativo masculino), muchacho (vocativo)', *miš̄ʸ* 'muchacho' Pu *miš̄ʸ, mæš̄ʸ* 'muchacho (vocativo), tú (vocativo masculino)' At *meš̄ʸ* 'muchacho, tú (vocativo masculino), muchacho (vocativo)' Ct *miš̄ʸ, meš̄ʸ* 'muchacho (vocativo), tú (vocativo masculino)', *miš̄ʸ* 'muchacho' LM: SJ *mišʸ* 'boy' Gu *mišʸ* 'niño—lo dicen las mujeres' [Nordell, p.c.]

ME#001 pOM *mehc ~ mec *(vi) 'venir, llegar/to come'* NHM: *mehc ~mec* 'venir, llega' LM: Cn <*mec~me·c*> (vi) 'llegar; alcanzar' SJ *mehc~mec* 'to arrive on the level'

ME#002 pOM *me:?c *(n) 'molleja/grindstone'* NHM: *me:?c* MM: Ju,Ja,Ma,Pu,At,Ct *mæ:c* LM: Ca *mæ:c* Gu *me:c*

ME#003 pMZ *me:?c *(vt) 'robar, buscar/to rob, steal'* NHM: *me:?c* 'robar (p.ej., cosas de valor)' SHM: Tl *ma:c* 'robar' LM: SJ *me·c ~me:c* 'to rob, steal' TxZ: *be?c* (vt) buscar' SoZ: *me?c* 'search' [Foster and Foster 1948] ChisZ: C *me?c* (vt) 'buscarlo' N,NE *me?c* (vt) 'buscarlo'

ME#004 pOM *me:?c-pa *(n) 'bandido/bandit'* NHM: *me:?cpa* '=ladrón, ratero' MM: Ju,Ma,Ja,Pu,At,Ct *mǽ?cpï* LM: Ca *mǽ·cpï* Gu *mǽ·?cpï*

ME#005 pZ *mecci *(n) 'gemelo/twin'* [The sequence /cc/ set up to account for ChisZ /č/, cf. pMZ *kacc] SaP: *me:č* 'cuates' [Zo loan] SoZ: *mé:či* 'gemelos' [Foster and Foster 1948] ChisZ: C *mečiwï* (adj, s) N *meči-* (adj) NE *meč?une / mecabï une*

ME#006 pMZ *me:h? *(vt) 'afilar/to sharpen'* NHM: *me: ~ me"* 'moler (p.ej., masa)' SHM: Tu <*mæ", mme:pʸ*> Tp <*mæ", mme:pʸ, mæ:p, mʸæ:h, mæ"βámp*> Mi <*mæ?h cuhš?ú?ŋk*> MM: Ju <*mæ"*> Cc <*mæ", mme:pʸ*> Ma <*mæ"w̥, mæ"f, mæ"Φ, mʸe:pʸ, mæ:p*> Ja <*mæ"w, mʸæ·w̄, mʸe:pʸ*> Pu,At <*mæ", mʸe:pʸ, mæ:p*> Ct <*mæ"w, mʸe:pʸ*> LM: Cn <*me·w~me·~me"*> (vt) Ca <*mæ"*> SJ *me·w~me"* 'to grind or file back and forth' Gu <*me"w, mʸe:pʸ, me:p, me·w*> OIP: *me:h ~me?h* 'afilarlo; engañarlo' SaP: *me: ~me?* (vi, vt) 'sharpen, file' SoZ: *meh* 'scrape' [Foster and Foster 1948] TxZ:

beh (vt, vi-p) '=planchar' ChisZ: C *meh* (vt) 'afilarlo' N *meh* (vt) 'frotarlo, afilarlo' NE *meh* (vt) 'afilarlo' ChZ: *me?y* 'afilado'

ME#007 pM ***me:?h-an** *(n)* *'lima/file'* [pOM **me:?hn*] MM: Ja *mœ:k* [?] At *mœ!n* OlP: *me?ha'n* SaP: *mé?an*

ME#008 pZ ***mek** *(vt)* *'amarrar; pretender/to bind; court'* SoZ: *mek* 'tie up' [Foster and Foster 1948] ChisZ: C *mehk* (vt) 'pretenderla' N *komehk* (vi) 'echar mentira, mentir', *komeke?ah* (vt) alistarlo, prepararlo

ME#009 pMZ ***me?k** *(vt)* *'atajar/to attach'* MM: At < *hɨnmœ?kp, hɨnmœ"gá·m̄p* > 'parpadear (un ojo)' LM: Gu < *wi:nmé?k, wi:nmé"k* > 'parpadear (un ojo)' ChisZ: C *me?k* (vt) 'atajarlo, prensarlo' N *me?k* (vt) 'atajarlo; atraparlo' NE *me?k* (vt) 'apretarlo, prensarlo (como entre la gente)'

ME#010 pMZ ***me(?)ke** *[?]* *(n)* *'pretil, presa, dique/stone railing'* [pM **meke* > pOM **meky*; pZ **me?ke*] NHM: *mEk* 'pretil' ChisZ: C *me?ke* 'presa, dique'

ME#011 pOM ***me:?kš** *(vi)* *'dispensar/to pardon'* NHM: *me:?kš* (vi, vt) '=perdonar' MM: 'perdonar' Ju < *mœ?kš* > Ma < *nɨmœ?š* > Ja < *nɨmœ?š, nʸimœ?š, nʸimé?šʸpʸ* > Pu < *nimœ!kš* > At < *nɨmœ?kš* > Ct < *nɨmœ?kš, nʸimé?kšʸpʸ* > LM: 'perdonar' Cn < *mekš* > (vt) SJ *me·kš* Ca < *mœ·kš* > Gu < *me·?š* >

ME#012 pGZ ***me:me?** *(n)* *'mariposa/butterfly'* SoZ: *me:me?* TxZ: *be:m*

ME#013 pM ***me:nyu** *(n)* *'dinero/money'* [pOM **me:ny*] [Cf. 'escamas': NHM: *nɨmE:n* MM: Ma *nʸime:nʸ* At *hɨmé:nʸ* Ct *nʸimé:nʸ* LM: Cn < *ni"me:ñ* >; possibly a borrowing from Spanish *medio (real)* or *(di)nero.*] NHM: *mE:n* 'dinero, moneda' SHM: Tl *me:nʸ* MM: Ju,Ma,Ja,Pu,At,Ct *me:nʸ* 'dinero, moneda' LM: Cn < *me:ñ* > Ca,SJ *me:nʸ* '=moneda' Gu *me:nʸ* 'un real' Cn *meh:nʸ* [Hoogshagen 1984] OlP: *me:ñu* SaP: *mé:nyu* 'un real'

ME#014 pMZ ***me?ps** *(vt)* *'tijeretear/to cut with a scissors'* NHM: *me?pš* 'prensar, tijeretazo, tijeretear, cortar' MM: Ct < *mœ?pš, mʸe?pšʸpʸ* > 'cortar cabello, hilo con tijeras (vt), raspar con tijeras (vi)' LM: Cn < *me"pš* > (vt) 'cortar (con tijera)' SJ *me?pš* Gu < *me?š, me?šp, mʸe?šʸp* > 'raspar con tijeras, cortar cabello, hilo con tijeras'

[Nordell 1990 and p.c.] OlP: *me?pš* (vt) 'abrazarlo (ropa)' SoZ: *me?ps* 'tijeretear' TxZ: *be?psde?* (vi-s) 'prensado'

ME#015 pOM ***me?pš-n** *(n)* *'tijeras/scissors'* NHM: *me?pšïn* MM: Ju,Ma,Ja,At,Ct *mæ?pšṇ* Pu *mæ!pšṇ* LM: Cn <*me"pš*> Ca *mæ?pšt* Gu *me?št* SJ *me?pš*

ME#016 pMZ ***me:s?** *(vi, vt)* *'aplicar sobre superficie (p.ej., ropa, trapo, lodo)/ to apply to a surface (e.g., clothes, cloth, mud)'* NHM: *me:š ~ me"š* 'limpiar (p.ej., con hojas o trapo), asear' MM: 'limpiar con trapo' Ma <*hinmǽ"š, hʸinmé·š̄ʸpʸ*> Ja <*winmǽ"š, wʸinmǽ·š̄,* *mʸe·š̄ʸpʸ*> At <*mǽ"š, mʸe·š̄ʸpʸ*> Ct <*hinmǽ"š, hʸinmé·š̄ʸpʸ*> LM: SJ *me·š ~ me"š* 'to dry the hands with a cloth' Gu <*me"š,* *mʸe·š̄ʸp*> 'limpiar con trapo' Cn <*me·š ~ me"š*> (vt) 'limpiar' SaP: *me:š ~ me?š* (vi, vt) 'plaster with mud wattle' TxZ: *be:?s* (vt, vi-p) 'embarrar' [borrowed from Mixean since otherwise *be:s* would be expected] ChisZ: C *mehs* (vt) 'estrenarlo' N *mes* (vi, vt) 'llevarlo puesto' NE *mehs* (vt) 'vestirse, ponerse (como ropa); ciñarlo; emplearlo, ocuparlo (como una máquina)'

ME#017 pM [Veracruz] ***me:?š-i** *(n)* *'pared/wall'* [The age of this item is not certain; may be a SaP innovation.] SaP: *me?š* TxZ: *be:?s* 'pared de embarro' [borrowed from Mixean]

ME#018 pM ***me?t** *(vt)* *'atrancar etc./to press around something with oblong objects'* [Cf. ChisZ: C [Te] <*caa anguetpa*> 'destroçar'.] NHM: *me?t ~ me"t* 'calzar (p.ej., con una piedra pequeña)' SHM: Tp <*mæ"t, mme?tʸpʸ*> 'apretar (con pinzas) MM: 'prensar (con pinzas, etc.)' Cc <*mæ"t, nmé?tʸpʸic*> 'apretar (con pinzas) Ma,At,Ct <*mæ"t, mʸe?tʸpʸ*> Ja <*mæ"t, mʸæ?t, mʸe?tʸpʸ*> 'atrancar, apretar (con pinzas) Pu <*mæ"t, mʸé!tʸpʸ*> 'atrancar' LM: Cn <*me?t ~ me"t*> (vt) 'prensar, agarrar; empollar' SJ *me?t ~ me"t* 'to pinch' Gu <*me"t, mʸe?t, mʸe?pʸ*> 'prensar (con pinzas, etc.)' OlP: *me?t* (vt) 'atrancarlo' SaP: *me?t* (vi, vt) 'carry in the arms'

ME#019 pOM ***me?ty** *(n)* *'tipo de gavilán/type of hawk'* NHM: *mE?t* 'gavilán [Buteo nitidus]' MM: Ju,At *me?tʸ* 'tipo de gavilán' LM: Ca *me?tʸ* 'tipo de gavilán' Ml <*me?ty*> 'gavilán' Cn <*me?ky*> 'gavilán pollero [Buteo albonotatus]' [?] Gu *me?k* 'tipo de gavilán' [?]

ME#020 pMZ ***me(h)ya** *(n)* *'mar/sea'* [pM **mehya* > pOM **mehy*; pZ **meya*] NHM: *mEh* 'hondura' SHM: Tl *mehʸ* MM: Ju *mehṇʸ*

[probably from pOM *mehʸ-nḭ·*] Ma,J̱a,Pu,At,Ct *mehʸ* LM: Cn
<*mehy*> '=lago' Ca,SJ *mehʸ* Gu *mehʸ* AyZ: *[mbe·ʰ]* TxZ: *bey*
'=río grande' ChisZ: C [Co] *meya* 'lago, laguna, pozo' [Te] <*mea*>
'agua sin fondo somo el mar / estanque de agua <*maa*> laguna' N
meya 'pozo—un lugar hondo en el río' NE *meya* 'laguna, lago' ChZ:
meya

Mḭ#001 pZ ***mḭ?ah** *(n) 'venado/deer'* [pGZ **mḭ?a*] SoZ: *mḭ?a* AyZ:
[mbḭ?a] TxZ: *bḭ?* ChisZ: C,NE *mḭ?ah* N *mḭ?a* S *[mḭá?]* ChZ:
mḭ?a

Mḭ#002 pMZ ***mḭ?ut** *(n) 'yerno/son-in-law'* [pM, pOM **mḭ?ut*; pZ
**mḭ?ut* > pGZ **mḭ?ḭt*] NHM: *mḭ?vit* 'yerno, suegra, suegro' SHM:
Tl *mḭ?ht* 'yerno' Ay *miuht* 'man's son-in-law' [Foster 1949] MM:
Ju *mḭ?t* 'yerno', *mu?t* 'suegro, -a de hombre' [sic!] Ja,At,Ma *mḭ?t*
'yerno, suegro, -a de hombre' Pu *mḭ!t* 'yerno' Ct *mḭ?t* 'yerno, suegra de hombre' LM: Cn <*mḭ"t*> 'yerno; suegro, suegra (hombre
hablando de su suegra, suegro o yerno; mujer hablando de su yerno)'
Ca *mḭ"t* 'yerno, suegra de hombre' (Nordell 1990), *mḭ?ḭt* 'father-in-
law or son-in-law' [Wonderly 1949] Gu *mḭ"t* 'yerno' OlP: *mu?u't*
'yerno' SaP: *mḭ?t* 'yerno' SoZ: *mḭ?ḭt* 'man's/woman's son-in-law'
[Foster 1949, Wonderly 1949] TxZ: *bḭ·?t* 'yerno' ChisZ: C *mo?ot*
'yerno, suegro/a de hombre' N [FL] *mo?ot* 'yerno, tío—esposo de la
hermana del padre' [Ma] *mo?ot* 'father-in-law or son-in-law' NE
[Tapalapa, Ocotepec, Pantepec] *mo?oht* 'father-in-law or son-in-law'
[Wonderly 1949] [Ra] *mo?oht* 'yerno, suegro de hombre' S [Tu]
mo?ut 'man's mother-in-law, man's father-in-law, woman's son-inlaw,
man's son-in-law' [Foster 1949] ChZ: StaMaCh *mḭ?ut* [Foster 1949
gives meaning 'man's father-in-law, woman's son-in-law, man's
son-in-law'.] ChZ: SnMiCh *mu?t* 'man's father-in-law, woman's
son-in-law, man's son-in-law' [Foster 1949]

Mḭ#003 pZ ***mḭciy** *(vi) 'jugar/to play'* SoZ: *mḭ·č* TxZ: *bḭčeŋ* (vi)
ChisZ: C *mḭhciy* (vi) N *mḭhciy* (vi, vt) NE *mḭhciy* (vi, vt) '=ri-
farlo' ChZ: *mḭẕiy*

Mḭ#004 pZ ***mḭ?cyḭki** *[?] (adj, adv) 'bastante/a lot'* TxZ: *bḭkske*
[?-phonology] ChisZ: C *mḭ?cyḭki* (adj) 'bastante, mucho, harto' (adv)
'bastante, mucho, algo' (pron) muchos, bastante' N *mḭ?cyḭki* (adv)
'mucho, bastante; quieto' NE *mḭ?cyḭki* (adv) 'bien'

Mɨ#005 pZ **mɨʔ(h)a(h)** *(vi) 'reuma/rheumatism'* [pGZ *mɨʔɨhah]
SoZ *mɨːhpak* 'cintura' [Gutiérrez M. 1993] TxZ: *bɨːʔhah* ChisZ: N
mɨʔa

Mɨ#006 pMZ **mɨha** *(adj) 'mayor, grande/greater, big'* [pM *mɨha >
pOM *mɨh; pZ *mɨha > pGZ *mɨh] NHM: *mɨh* SHM: Tl,Tm,Ay
mɨh 'grande' MM: Ju *mɨh* Ma,Ct *mɨh* '=ancho' Ja,Pu,At *mɨh*
LM: C̲a,SJ *mɨh* 'grande' Cn *mɨh* (adj) 'grande' (adv) 'bastante'
Gu *mïh* SaP: *mɨh* 'grande' SoZ: *mɨh* 'grande' [Foster and Foster
1948] [Since an expected final *a* is missing and the vowel is short this
may be construed as a late borrowing from Sayula Popoluca.] AyZ:
[mbɨːh] 'estar gordo' ChisZ: C *mɨha* 'grande' N *mɨha* (adj)
'grande'; (adv) 'recio' NE *mɨha; mɨhabɨ* (adj, n) 'grande'

Mɨ#007 pOM **ʔa-mɨh** *(adj) 'grande/big'* NHM: *amɨh* 'vieja' ['old
woman'] LM: <*amɨh*> 'grande' [ejemplo: "este avión es muy
grande"]

Mɨ#008 pOM **mɨhɨy** *(vi) 'prenderse lumbre, agrandarse/to light, to
grow bigger'* MM: Ma <*tɨː mʸɨhɨ*> 'prenderse lumbre̲', <*mɨhipʸ*>
'agrandarse' Pu̲ <*mɨhipʸ*> 'agrandarse' At,Ja <*mɨhip*> 'agrandarse', <*tɨː mʸɨhɨ*> 'prenderse lumbre' Ct <*mɨhipʸ*> 'agrandarse',
<*tɨː mʸɨhɨ*> 'prenderse lumbre' LM: Gu <*mïhï·y̲*> 'agrandarse'

Mɨ#009 pOM **yak-mɨhɨy** *(vt) 'agrandar/to grow bigger'* NHM:
yakmɨhi ~ yakmɨha 'ensalzar a alguien, agrandar, engrandecer a alguien' MM: Ju <*yæhmɨhi*> Ma,Ja <*yahmɨhi*> Pu <*yahmɨhi*>
At <*yæhkmɨhi*> Ct <*yahkmɨhi*> LM: Gu <*yahmïhïʺw*>

Mɨ#010 pM **mɨkɨk** *(adj, adv) 'fuerte, macizo/strong, firm'* [pOM
*mɨkk] NHM: *mɨk* '=duro, robusto, recio, potente,̲ lozano, lleno de
salud' SHM: Tl *mɨk* 'fuerte' MM: Ju *mɨk* Ma *mɨk* '=du̲ro (adv),
tiene fuerza, recio'̲ Ja *mɨk* 'recio, duro (adv), fuerte' Pu *mɨk* 'fuerte,
du̲ro (adv)' At *mɨk* 'fuerte, tiene fuerza, duro (adv), recio, sano' Ct
mɨk 'tiene fuerza, recio, duro (adv), fuerte'̲ LM: Cn <*mɨk*> (adj)
'fuerte' (adv̲) 'recio; con dureza' Ca *mɨk* 'macizo', *mɨk* 'fuerte'
[sic!] Gu *mɨk* 'recio, macizo, sano, fuerte, tiene fuerza, duro (adv)'
SaP: *mɨgɨk* 'duro, recio'

Mɨ#011 pOM **hoːht-mɨkk** *(adj) 'valiente/brave'* [Lit., 'heart-strong'.
The reconstructed form is an underlying one; *hoːht* is reduced under
compounding and /kk/ is pronounced as /k/.] NHM: *hotmɨk* 'insen-

sible, necio' MM: Ma,Ja,At *ho·tmɨ́k* Ct *ho·tmɨk* LM: Gu *ho·tmɨ́k, ho·tmɨ́h*

Mɨ#012 pMZ ***mɨ:k?** *(vt) 'amasar/to knead'* MM: 'hacer tamal_es_' Ma *<mɨ"k, mɨ·kp, mɨ"gámp>* Ja,Ct *<mɨ"k, mɨ·kp>* At *<mɨ·kp, mɨ"gá·mp>* LM: 'hacer tamales' _Cn_ *<mɨk~mɨ"k>* (vt) SJ *mɨ·k~mɨ"k* Gu *<mɨ̈"kʸ; mɨ"k, mɨ·kp>* [Nordell 1990 and p.c.] ChisZ: N *mɨhk* (vi) 'quedarse en masa (bola)' (vt) 'amasarlo' C [Te] *<muecpa>* 'fingir cosa de barro / hacer cosa de varro / ordeñar'

Mɨ#013 pZ ***mɨk-i** *(n) 'cosa formada de barro/formed clay object'* ChisZ: C [Co] *mɨki* 'panal' [Te] N *nasmuequi* 'figura de barro' NE *nasmɨki* 'adobe' ChZ: *nas mɨki* 'adobe'

Mɨ#014 pM ***mɨ?k-i** *(n) 'tamal/bread made of steamed cornmeal'* [pOM **mɨ"ky*] NHM: *mɨ"k* Ju,Ma,Ja,At,Ct *me"kʸ* LM: Ml *<me"ky>* Cn *<mɨ"ky>* Ca *mɨ"ʸkʸ* Gu *mɨ̈"kʸ* OIP: *mɨ?ki* SaP: *mɨ?k*

Mɨ#015 pZ ***mɨ?k** *(vt) 'exprimir/to extract'* ChisZ: C,NE *mɨ?k* ChZ: *mɨ?k*

Mɨ#016 pMZ ***mɨk?** *(n) 'rocío/dew'* [pM, pOM **mɨ?k*; pZ **mɨk*] NHM: *mɨ?k* LM: Cn *<mɨ?k>* SoZ: *mɨk* 'sereno' ChisZ: C *mɨk* '=sereno'

Mɨ#017 pMZ ***mɨ:?ks** *(vi) 'exprimir/to squeeze, extract'* NHM: *mɨ:?kš* 'exprimir (p.ej., una naranja), machucar' SHM: Tl *mɨ:kš* MM: Ma *<mɨ?š, hinmɨ?š>* Ja *<mɨ?š, mʸɨ?š, mʸe?šʸpʸ>* Ct *<mɨ?kš>* 'exprimir' LM: Cn *<mɨkš>* (vt) 'ordeñar; exprimir (zumo)' Ca *<mɨ·kš, winmɨ·kš>* SJ *mɨ·kš* 'to milk, squeeze juice out' Gu *<mɨ̈·?š, mɨ̈·?šp>* [Nordell 1990 and p.c.] OIP: *mɨ:kš* (vi) 'ordeñar' (vt) 'ordeñarlo' SaP: *mɨ?kš* (vi, vt) 'squeeze juice out, milk a cow' SoZ: *mɨ?ks* AyZ: *[mbɨ?ks̱]* TxZ: *bɨ?ks* (vt) '=apretar (con la mano), ordeñar'

Mɨ#018 pM ***mɨ:?kš-i(k)** *(n) 'puño/fist'* [pOM **mɨ:?kšy*] SHM: Tl *kɨmmɨ:?kš* OIP: *mɨ:kšiʹk* 'puño de algo'

Mɨ#019 pMZ ***mɨn(i)** *(n) 'camote/sweet potato'* [pM **mɨni* > pOM **mɨny*; pZ **mɨn*] NHM: *mɨn* [Ipomoea batatas] SHM: Tl *po?okmɨnʸ* Ay *mɨnʸ* Tp *munʸ* MM: Ju *munʸ* Ma,Ja,Pu,At *mɨ̄nʸ* Ct *munʸ* LM: Cn

<muñ> 'camote [Ipomoea batatas]' SJ *mun^y* 'edible root' Gu *mïn^yt^y* [Nordell, p.c.] OlP: *mini* SaP: *mɨn* SoZ: *mɨn* AyZ: *[mbɨn]* TxZ: *bɨn* ChisZ: C,N,S *mɨn* NE *mɨt* ChZ: *mɨn*

Mɨ#020 pM ***pa:-mɨni** *(n) 'camotillo/a kind of sweet potato'* [pOM *pa:mɨny] MM: Cc *pA·mún^y* Ma *pa·mïn̄^y* At *pœ·mún^y* LM: Gu *pamïn^yt^y* OlP: *pa:mini* SaP: *pa:mɨn*

Mɨ#021 pOM ***pa"k-mɨny** *(n) 'camote/sweet potato'* NHM: *pa"hk mïn* [G. Martin, p.c.] SHM: Tl *po"kmɨny* Tu *pa"kmón̄^y* MM: Cc *pA"kmún^y* At *pa"kmún^y*

Mɨ#022 pZ ***mɨs** *(vt) 'odiar/to hate'* TxZ: *bɨs* (vt, vi-p) 'tener asco, dar asco' ChisZ: C *mɨhs* (vt) 'darle asco o basca algo, asquearse de algo' N *mɨs* (vt) 'darlo asco' ChZ: *mɨs* 'odiar'

Mɨ#023 pOM ***mɨ?š ~ mɨ"š** *(vi) 'estar parado de espaldas encorvadas en un grupo/to stand shoulder by shoulder forming a group'* NHM: *mɨ:š* 'puño' LM: SJ *mɨ?š ~ mɨ"š* 'to stand around hunched up'

Mɨ#024 pM ***mɨ:t** *(part) 'con/with'* [pOM *mɨ:t] NHM: *mɨ:t* SHM: Tu,Tp *mɨ:t* MM: Ju,Ma,Ja,Pu,At,Ct *mɨ:t* LM: Ca *mɨ:t* Cn <*mɨ:d/mɨ:t*> (prep) Gu *mï:t* OlP: *mɨ:t* '=y' SaP: *mi:t ~ mɨ:t* '=y'

Mɨ#025 pZ ***mɨ?ŋ** *(vi) 'brincar para arriba/to jump up'* SoZ: *mɨ?ŋ* [Foster and Foster 1948] TxZ: *bɨ?ŋ* (vi) 'jugar de chance, andar corriendo jugando' ChisZ: N *mɨ?ŋ* (vi) '=saltar; cojear' NE *mɨ?ŋ* (vi) '=saltar (como conejo)'

Mɨ#026 pM ***mɨhy** *(n) 'zacate/grass'* [pOM *mɨhy] NHM: *mɨ:hy* 'zacate (hojas angostas), zacate de agua' MM: Ju,Ma *mɨ:y* Ja,At *mɨ:y* Ct *mɨ·y* '=pasto' LM: Cn <*mɨ:y/mɨy*> '=pasto' [Festuca sp.] Ca *mɨ:y* Gu *mï:y* '=pasto' OlP: *mɨyɨ* SaP: *mɨhy* TxZ: *bɨ:?y* 'tarquezal (zacate, sale como espina de la tierra)' [?-phonology]

Mɨ#027 pM [Veracruz] ***mɨhy-win** *(n) 'sabana/treeless plain'* OlP: *mɨyvinɨ* SaP: *mɨywin*

Mɨ#028 pZ ***mɨ?y** *(vt) 'sospechar con razón/to suspect'* OlP: *hotmɨ?y* (vt-d) 'tener asco' [?] ChisZ: C *komɨ?y* (vt) 'creerlo, pensarlo, suponerlo' N *kɨmɨ?y* (vt) 'apuntarle (un arma)' NE *mɨ?y* (vt) 'sospecharlo (con razón)'

Mɨ#029 pM ***mɨːhy(n)** *(n) 'concuña/wife of brother-in-law'* [pOM
*mɨːhyn] NHM: *mɨːhyin* 'concuñada, concuño de la esposa' MM: Ju
mɨhn̨ʸ At *mɨːnʸ* Gu *mʸïːy* OIP: *mɨːyɨ* 'concuño, concuña'

MA#001 pOM ***ma:** *(part) 'donde, adonde/where'* SHM: Tl *mo*
'donde, ¿dónde?' MM: Ju,Ma,Ja,Pu,Ct *ma:* At *mo:* LM: SJ *ma·*
'at, where' Cn <*ma*> (prep) 'a, hacia' (adv) ¿adónde?, ¿dónde?;
donde' Ca,Gu *ma:*

MA#002 pMZ ***mac** *(vt) 'agarrar/to grasp'* NHM: *mahc ~ mac* '=co-
ger, tomar (p.ej., un preso)' SHM: Tl *moc* 'coger' Tu <*mac,
mmahčpʸ*> Tp <*mac, mʸAhc, mʸœhčpʸ, mʸAcæmpʸ*> Mi <*mac*>
MM: Ju <*mæc*> Cc <*mAc, mmAhčpʸ, mʸœhčpʸ*> Ma <*mac̄, mʸahčpʸ*> Ja <*mac̄, mʸahc, mʸahčpʸ*> Pu <*mac̄, mʸahčpʸ*> At <*mac̄,
mʸœhč*> Ct <*mac̄, mʸahčpʸ*> LM: Cn <*mahc ~ mac*> (vt)
'agarrar, atrapar' Ca <*mac*> SJ *mahc ~ mac* Gu <*mac̄, mʸahčp*>
OIP: *mac* 'agarrar una cosa; tentarlo, tocarlo' TxZ: *bac* SoZ: *mac*
'grasp' [Foster and Foster 1948] ChisZ: C *mahc* (vt) 'sobarlo;
apretarlo' N *mahc* (vt) 'empujarlo'

MA#003 pOM ***ʔiš-mahc ~ ʔiš-mac** *(vi) 'probar/to try out'* NHM:
ʔišmahc ~ ʔišmac 'probar (p.ej., una bestia si se deja montar o no), ex-
perimentar' MM: Ju <*ʔihšmæc*> Pu <*ʔihšmac̄*> Ma,At
<*ʔihšmac̄*> '=intentar' Ct,Ja <*ʔihšmac̄*> 'intentar' LM: Gu
<*ʔihšmac̄*> '=intentar'

MA#004 pOM ***ton-mahc ~ ton-mac** *(vt) 'palpar, tentar/to feel, grope'*
NHM: *tʋnmahc ~ tʋnmac* 'tocar algo con la mano' LM: Cn
<*tonmahc ~ tonmac*> (vt) 'palpar; escribir (con máquina de escribir)'

MA#005 pGZ ***maʔc** *(n) 'especie de árbol/species of tree'* SoZ: *maʔc*
'palo mulato' TxZ: *baʔc* 'chancarro, guarumo'

MA#006 pMZ ***maʔc** *(vt) 'ordeñar, mezclar/to milk, mix'* MM: Ju
<*ma"c*> 'ordeñar' At <*ma"c, maʔcp, mʸæʔčpʸ*> 'exprimir,
ordeñar' LM: Cn <*maʔc ~ ma"c*> (vt) 'desmenuzar' Ca <*mo"c*>
'exprimir' TxZ: *baʔc* (vt) 'batir (lodo con la mano)' ChisZ: N *maʔc*
(vt) 'mezclarlo, amasarlo; pisarlo' NE *yahmaʔc* (vt) 'punzarlo (como
con machete)'

MA#007 pMZ ***maːcaʔ((a)k)** *(n) 'estrella/star'* [pM **maːcáʔ((a)k)* >
pOM **maːcá"*; pZ *macaʔ > pGZ **maːca?*] NHM: *maːca* 'astro'
SHM: Tl *moːcoʔ* MM: Ju *mɨcá"* Pu *mazá"* At *mæzá"* Ma,Ja,Ct

mɨʐá" LM: Ca *mɨʐa"* [Nordell 1990; Wonderly 1949] Cn
<*madza?*> Gu *maʐá"*, *mɨʐá"* OIP: *ma:ca?a'k* SaP: *ma:hc* SoZ:
ma:ca? AyZ: *[ba:?ca]* 'lucero' TxZ: *ba:ca?* ChisZ: C,N *maca* NE
[Ocotepec] *macah* [Wonderly 1949] [Tapalapa, Pantepec] *maca*
[Wonderly 1949] [Ra] *maca* S [Tu] *maca* [Wonderly 1949] S [Cp]
[ma·ca?] ChZ: *maca?*

MA#008 pZ ***tu?c-maca?** *(n) 'cometa/comet'* [Lit., 'tail-star'. Cf.
pMZ **tu?c(ta)* 'tail'.] TxZ: *tu?č-ba:ca?* ChisZ: C *tu?cmaca*

MA#009 pMZ ***mah** *(vi) 'traer agua/to carry water'* NHM: *mah*
'traer agua' ChisZ: N *mah* (vi) 'acarrarear agua'

MA#010 pM ***mah-an** *(n) 'cántaro/pitcher'* [pOM **mahn*] MM:
Ma,Ja,Pu *mahn̥* Ct *mahkn̥* [?] LM: Cn <*maht*> Ca,Gu *maht* OIP:
maha'n

MA#011 pZ ***mah-kuy** *'cántaro/pitcher'* [SaP replaced pM **mah-an*
with the equivalent Zoquean form *mah-kuy* before truncation set in.]
SaP: *mahk* SoZ: *mahkuy* TxZ: *bahku?~bahko?* ChisZ: C,N *mahkuy*
ChZ: *mahku?y* '=jarra'

MA#012 pMZ ***mah** *(adj) 'fuerza/strength'* [**mah* reconstructed for
all subgroups.] MM: At *mah* 'tiene fuerza, macizo', *po"máh̥* 'luna
llena' Ct *mah* 'fuerte, macizo' Ja *mah* 'macizo', *po"máh* 'luna
llena' LM: Gu *po"máh* 'luna llena' SaP: *mah* 'fuerza' TxZ: *bah-
a?y* (vi) 'cansarse (por el sol), agotarse' [*-a?y* has meaning of
'privative']

MA#013 pM ***maháw** *(n) 'fuerza/strength'* [As in pMZ **hayáw* 'hombre', I propose a composite with 'mouth'; cf. pM **mah* 'fuerza'. The
meaning would literally be 'strong mouth' supposedly connoting '(female?) ruler'. Phonologically everything is in its order.] NHM: *máhu*
'fuerza', *mahu po"* 'luna llena' MM: Ju *mɨhá:* 'fuerza' Ma *mɨhá:w*
'fuerza, valor (pos)' At *mahá:w* 'valor' Ct *mɨhá:w* 'valor (pos),
fuerza' Ja *mɨhá:* 'valor (pos), fuerza' Pu *mɨhá:* 'fuerza' LM: Cn
<*maha:/mɨha:*> (adj) 'fuerte; maduro' Ca,Gu *mɨhá:* 'fuerza' OIP:
maháu 'mujer'

MA#014 pM ***mah-Vt** *(n) 'viejo (persona, animal)/old (living being)'*
[Not certain whether OM lost the second vowel on this compound-like
construction and what the quality of the vowel was.] NHM: *mɨhit hayu*

'los ancianos o padres' SaP: *máhat* 'grandes', *háyau máhatway* 'hombres grandes'

MA#015 pMZ ***ma:h?** *'dormir/to sleep'* NHM: *ma: ~ ma"* SHM: Tl *mo?* MM: Ma < *ma"f ~ ma"Φ ~ ma"w̄* > Ja < *ma"w, ma·w̄, ma:p* > Pu < *ma", ma:p, ma·ẉ* > At < *ma", ma:p, ma:* > Ct < *ma"w, ma:p, tɨ: mʸœ"y* > LM: Cn < *ma· ~ ma"* > (vi) SJ *ma·w ~ ma"* Gu < *ma"w, ma:p, ma·w̄* > OlP: *ma: ~ ma:h ~ ma?h* (vi) SaP: *ma: ~ ma?* TxZ: *ba:weñ* 'sueño, revelación' [← *ba* 'sleep' + *wêñ* 'refl.' ?]

MA#016 pOM ***ku-ma:h ~ ku-ma"h** *(vi) 'soñar/to dream'* NHM: *kuma: ~ kuma"* MM: Ma < *kɨmá:p* > Ja < *kumá:p* > At < *kumá:p, kuma"wá·m̄p* > LM: Gu < *kɨmá:p* > SaP: *kukmá?* [?] [Clark and Clark 1960]

MA#017 pMZ ***ma:k?** *(vt) 'lavar nixtamal, pescar con red/to work with a sieve or net'* NHM: *ma:k ~ ma"k* 'lavar nixtamal, pescar' MM: 'lavar, lavar nixtamal' MM: Ju < *ma"k* ≥ > Ja < *ma"k, ma·k, ma·kp₂, mʸœ·kʸpʸ* > Ma,At < *ma"k, mʸœ·kʸpʸ* > Ct < *ma"k, mʸœ·kkʸpʸ* > 'lavar' Ct < *ma"k* > 'lavar nixtamal' LM: Cn < *ma·k ~ ma"k* > (vt) 'lavar (p.ej.: nixtamal, granos de café)' Gu < *ma"k, ma·kp, mʸa·kkʸpʸ* > 'lavar, lavar nixtamal' SJ *ma·k ~ ma"k* 'to wash (corn, beans, coffee beans, etc.)' SaP: *ma:k ~ ma?k* 'fish with net' SoZ: *mak* 'take out fish with a net' [Foster and Foster 1948] AyZ: [*mba:?gɨ*] 'péscalo', [*ma mbak*] 'se pescó' TxZ: *bak* (vt, vi-a) 'pescar' ChisZ: C *mahk* (vt) 'correrlo, arrearlo' N *mahk* (vt) 'seguirlo, perseguirlo' NE *mahk* (vt) 'correrlo; arrearlo, ahuyentarlo; persiguirlo'

MA#018 pZ ***(ko-)yaw-mak** *(n) 'huérfano/orphan'* SaP: *kuyá:mak* [Zo loan] ChisZ: C,NE *yaŋbak* N *yaŋbak* 'huérfano, viuda, viudo' ChZ: *yaŋmak*

MA#019 pZ ***ma?k** *(vt) 'armar/to load a gun, set a trap'* SaP: *ma?k* (vi, vt) 'load a gun, set a trap' [Zo loan] ChisZ: C **ma?k* [*aŋgoma?kɨ?opyawɨ* (adj, n) 'engañoso'; *aŋgoma?kɨ?okyuy* (n) 'engaño'] N **ma?k* [*aŋgima?kɨy* (vt) 'engañarlo'] ChZ: *ma?k* 'revolver (con un palo)'

MA#020 pZ ***ma?ak** *(n) 'hoy (tiempo pasado)/earlier today'* ChisZ: C [Co] *ma?ak* 'hoy—tiempo pasado' [Te] < *mac, maca* > 'denantes'

'denantes' SoZ: *ma?k* 'a little while ago' [Foster and Foster 1948], 'hace rato' [Gutiérrez M. 1993] TxZ: *ba:?k* 'hace (un) rato', *ma?* (part) 'perfectivo'

MA#021 pMZ ***makoko** *(n) 'cucaracha/cockroach'* [pOM **makok*, with vowel-leveling in LM.] LM: Cn <*muguk*> [order: Dictyoptera, fam: Blattidae] AyZ: [*ko:?go*] ChisZ: C *pombicimakoko* 'cucaracha lisa', *sahmakoko* 'cucaracha grande con alas'

MA#022 pM ***ma:?kš** *(vt) 'estibar/to stack'* NHM: *ma:?kš* 'llevar en la mano una serie de cosas (p.ej., llaves o dinero)' MM: Ma <*ma?š, mʸa?šᵖpʸ*> Ja <*ma?š, mʸa?š, mʸœ?šᵖpʸ*> Pu <*ma?kš*> At,Ct <*ma?kš, mʸœ?kšᵖpʸ*> LM: Cn <*makš*> (vt) 'amontonar en orden' SJ *ma·kš* 'to stack in order, assemble' Gu <*ma·?š, mʸa·?šᵖp*> OlP: *yo?kma?kš* (vi) 'atorar en la garganta' TxZ: *ba:ks* (vt, vi-p) 'batir (con la mano)' [?-semantics] <*macspa-cuy-pit*> 'dar de palos' [?]

MA#023 pZ ***mama** *(n) 'madre, mamá/mother'* [The SJ item may be a Spanish loan and the SaP item a Zoquean loan.] LM: SJ *mama·* 'madre' SaP: *ma:m* 'madre' ChisZ: N,NE *mama* 'madre' ChZ: StaMaCh *mama* 'madre' SnMiCh *mama* 'madre' [Foster 1949]

MA#024 pZ ***ko-mama** *(n) 'madrastra/stepmother'* SaP *ko:má:m* [Zo loan] ChisZ: N,NE *komama*

MA#025 pMZ ***manik** *(n) 'sereno/night humidity'* [pM **maník* > pOM **maník*; pZ **manik* with total assimilation of the onset and peak of the second syllable to the shape of the first syllable.] NHM: *manik* MM: Ju *mæník* Ma *ma·ník* '=neblina' Ja *mɨník* '=neblina' Pu *mɨník* 'neblina' At *ma·ník* 'neblina', *ma:ník* 'sereno' [sic!] Ct *ma·ník* 'neblina', *ma:ník* 'sereno' [sic!] LM: Ml <*manik*> Cn <*ma:ñ*> Ca *mæ·ŋʸkʸ* OlP: *ma:mɨ'k* [?] SaP: *má:nik* AyZ: [*mba:mak*] '=neblina' [?]

MA#026 pMZ ***manɨk** *(n) 'hijo/son'* [pM **manɨk* > pOM **mahnk*; pZ **manɨk* > pGZ **ma:nik*] NHM: *mahntk* SHM: Tl *mohnk* Ay *manguc* [Foster 1949] MM: Ju *ma·ŋk* Ma,Pu *mʸa:ŋk* Ja,At,Ct *ma:ŋk* LM: Cn <*maŋ*> '=plantita' Ca *maŋk* SJ *man* SoZ: *ma:nɨk* TxZ: *ba:n* '=niño, criatura' ChisZ: C [Te] *man* [Foster 1949] ChZ: SnMiCh *manɨk* [Foster 1949]

MA#027 pZ ***?ok-manɨk** *(n) 'nieta, nieto/granddaughter, -son'* [The additional /o/ is TxZ and ChZ-SnMiCh is epenthetic.] SoZ: *?okmanɨk*

[Foster 1949] TxZ: *ʔoŋbanba* [Foster 1949], < *ʔogoBá:n* > 'nieto' [Clark n.d.] ChZ: SnMiCh *ʔokomanɨk* [Foster 1949]

MA#028 pOM ***cohk-mahnk** *(n) 'sobrino/nephew'* NHM: *cokmahntk* MM: Ju *cohmá:ŋk* Ma *cohmá·ŋk* 'sobrino', *cohkmáŋk* 'primo' [sic!] Ja *cohkmá·ŋk* 'sobrino', *cohká:ŋk* 'primo' [sic!] Ct *cohkmá:ŋk* 'sobrino', *cohkmá·ŋk* 'primo mayor de edad' sic!] LM: Ca *cohkmá·ŋk* Gu *cohmáhk* '=primo'

MA#029 pOM ***ku-mahnk** *(n) 'hijastro, entenado/fosterchild'* NHM: *kumahntk* MM: Ju *kumá:ŋk* Ma *kʸɨʔmá·ŋk* 'entenado', *kʸɨmá:ŋk* 'hijastro' [sic!] Ja *kumá:ŋk* 'hijastro (pos), entenado' At *kumá:ŋk* Ct *kʸɨmá:ŋk* 'hijastro' LM: Cn <*komaŋ*> Gu *kumáhk*

MA#030 pOM ***pa:n mahnk** *(n) 'metlapil/metate roller'* [lit. 'metate roller son/daughter'] NHM: *pa:n mahntk* SHM: Tl *po:n mohnk* Ay *po:n mʸoŋk* MM: Ju *pa:nmǽ:ŋk* At *pa:nmá:ŋk* LM: Ca *pa:nmáŋk*

MA#031 pZ ***yom-manɨk** *(n) 'hija/daughter'* [The first morpheme is *yomo 'woman', which lost its last vowel because of the compounding] SoZ: *yo:mmanɨk* [Foster 1949] ChZ: SnMiCh *yommanɨk* [Foster 1949]

MA#032 pZ ***mape** *(adj) 'vacío/empty'* TxZ: *bap* '=sin nada' [*ba:p* expected] ChisZ: C *mape* 'estéril'

MA#033 pM ***mapši(n)** *(adj) 'grueso/thick'* [pOM *mapšyn] NHM: *mahpšyɨn* MM: Ju,Ma,Ja,Pu,At *mæhpšʸ* Ct *mæhpšʸn̥ʸ* LM: Cn <*mapšy*> (adj) Ca,Gu *mapšʸ* SaP: *mapš* TxZ: *bapše?* 'desnudo, en cueros' [?-semantics]

MA#034 pMZ ***ma:san** *(n) 'mana/mana'* [From the descendant meanings it is clear that this could have referred to, among other things, ancient godlike rulers.] [pM **ma:šan*; pZ *masan] OlP: *ma:ša'n* 'espíritu de persona' SaP: *má:šan* 'gente de alta sociedad' AyZ: *[mba:sa]* 'santo' [Final /n/ lost only finally, cf. *[mba:saŋguy]* 'cedro' in MA#037.] ChisZ: C *masan* (adj) 'santo, sagrado' N *masan* (adj) 'sagrado, bendecido' NE *masan-* (adj) 'bendito'

MA#035 pM ***ʔa-ma:šan** *(n) 'idioma sagrado/sacred language'* [pOM **ʔama:šn*] NHM: *ʔama:šɨn* 'español (el idioma)' MM: Ju *ʔæmɨẑǽn* 'castellano, español (idioma)' Ma,Ja,Pu,Ct *ʔa·mɨẑán* 'español (idioma), *ʔamɨẑán* 'castellano' [sic!] At *ʔæmɨẑán* 'español, castellano' LM: Ca *?a·miǯán* 'español (idioma)', *?a·maǯán* 'castellano' [sic!] Cn <*amišan*> 'español (el idioma), persona de raza española' Gu *?amiǯán* 'español, castellano' OlP: *?a:ma:ša'n* 'español' SaP: *?ama:šan* 'doctrina'

MA#036 pZ ***masan-tɨk*** *(n) 'iglesia/church'* TaM: *mehentok* [transcription of Wonderly 1949] Ma *masandɨk* SoZ: *ma:stɨk* TxZ: *ba:stɨk* 'iglesia, templo' ChisZ: C *masandɨk* 'iglesia, templo' N *masandɨk* NE *masandɨhk* 'templo' ChZ: *masantɨk*

MA#037 pMZ ***ma:san-kuy*** *(n) 'cedro/cedar [Cedrela mexicana]'* [pM *ma:šankuhy*; pZ *masankuy* > pGZ *ma:sankuy*] OlP: *ma:ša?nku* SaP: *má:šangúhy* AyZ: [*mba:saŋguy*] TxZ: *ba:sankuy* 'caoba' ChisZ: NE Ox *masankuy*

MA#038 pOM ***ca-ma:šn*** *(n) 'ídolo/stone idol'* [The first member of the compound is *ca:?* 'stone', which is shortened here because it is not stressed.] NHM: *cama:šɨn* SHM: Tl *comašon*

MA#039 pZ ***ma?s*** *(vi) 'espinar/to be stuck by a thorn'* ChisZ: C *ma?s* (vi, vt) N *ma?s* (vi) NE *ma?s* (vi) 'lastimarse' (vt) 'rasparlo (como la carga a una bestia); espinarlo' ChZ: *ma?si?* 'espina'

MA#040 pMZ ***ma:stɨki*** *(n) 'anteayer/the day before yesterday'* [pM *ma:štɨki* > pOM *ma:štɨhky*; pZ *mastɨki*] NHM: *ma:šk* SHM: Tl *maštɨhkʸ* Tu *maštíhkʸ* Tp *mAštíhkʸ* Mi *ma:štíhkʸ* MM: Ju *mæštéhkʸ* Cc *mAštíhkʸ* Ma,Ja,Pu,Ct *mɨštéhkʸ* At *maštéhkʸ* LM: Ca *maštéhkʸ* Gu *maštíhkʸ* OlP: *ma:štɨki* SaP: *má:štɨhk* ChZ: *mastɨkhi?*

MA#041 pM [Veracruz] ***yak-ma:šuy*** *(vt) 'domar, amansar/to tame'* OlP: *yakma:šu?iy* (vt) 'domarlo, amansarlo' [In setting up the underlying form I count on a Vy → V:/p rule] SaP: *?akmá:šui* (vt) 'domar, amansar' [Clark and Clark 1960]

MA#042 pOM ***ma?t~ma"t*** *(vi) 'descomponerse/to go to pieces'* NHM: *ma?t~ma"t* 'descomponer, dislocarse un hueso del cuerpo' MM: Ma <*ma?tp*> Ja <*ma?t, ma?tp, ma"dá·m̄p*> Pu <*ma?tp, tɨ: mʸa"tʸ*> At <*ma?tp, tɨ: mʸæ"tʸ*> Ct <*ma?tp, ma"dámp*> LM: Cn <*ma?t~ma"t*> (vi) 'descomponerse; nacer incapacitado' SJ *ma?t ~ ma"t* 'to make into balls; to be disfigured, a piece broken out of' Gu <*ma?p, ma"dá·m̄p, tɨ: mʸa"tʸ*>

MA#043 pOM ***ho:ht-ma?t ~ ho:ht-ma"t** *(vi) 'enojarse/to become an-gry'* NHM: *hotma?t ~ hotma"t* 'enojar' MM: Ja *< ho·t̄ma?tp, ho·tma"dá·m̄p >* Ct *< ho·tmá?tp >* LM: Cn *< hotma?t ~ hotma"t >* (vi) Gu *< ho·tmá?t >*

MA#044 pOM ***mata:hk ~ mata"k** *(vi) 'triunfar/to win'* NHM: *mɨda:k ~ mɨda"k* 'triunfar, ganar (p.ej., en una carrera), vencer' LM: SJ *mada·k ~ mada"k* 'to endure, tolerate, win, gain'

MA#045 pMZ ***matow** *(vt) 'oír/to hear'* NHM: *motu* (vt) SHM: Tl *matʋw* Tu *< tukmɨδów̄ >* 'contar (cuento)' MM: Ju *< mɨdóf >* Ma *< mɨdów̥ ~ mɨdóΦ ~ mɨdóf, mmɨdé:bʸɨ, ?amɨdo·w̄?ít >* '=obedecer' Ja *< mɨdó:p, kæhpŝʸmʸɨdów̄ >* 'obedecer', *< mɨdów̄, mɨdó·w̄, mʸɨdé:pʸ >* 'oír' Pu *< mɨdów̄, mɨdó:p >* 'obedecer', *< mɨdów̄, ?amɨdo·w̄?ít >* 'oír' At *< mɨdów̄, mɨmɨdów̄ >* 'obedecer', *< mɨdów̄, mʸɨdöö:pʸ >* 'oír' Ct *< mɨdów̥ ~ mɨdóΦ ~ mɨdóf, mʸɨdé:pʸ >* 'oír' LM: Ca *< mɨdów̄ >* 'oír' Cn *< mɨdo·w ~ mɨdow >* (vt) 'escuchar' SJ *mɨdo·w ~ mɨdow* 'escuchar' Gu *< mɨdów̄, mɨdó·w̄, mɨdó:p, mʸɨdó:pʸ >* OIP: *motov* (vt) 'escuchar' SaP: *márau* '=escuchar' SoZ: *matóŋ* TxZ: *batɨŋ* (vt) '=escuchar, entender' ChisZ: C *matoŋ* (vi, vt) N *man* (vt) '=obedecer' [?] NE *madoŋ* (vi, vt) ChZ: *matoŋ*

MA#046 pOM ***win-matow** *(vt) 'entender/to understand'* NHM: *vinmotu* MM: Ma *< hʸinmɨdé:pʸ >* Ja *< winmɨdów̄, wʸinmɨdé:pʸ >* At *< hʸinmɨdóöpʸ >* Ct *< hʸinmɨdé:pʸ >* LM: Gu *< wʸi:nhw̥ɨ́:pʸ >*

MA#047 pM ***matow-an** *(n) 'oído/hearing'* [pOM **matown*] MM: Ju *mʸɨdó"n* Pu *mɨdó!n* At *mɨdó?w̄in* LM: Ca *mɨdó"nt* Gu *mɨdó!nt* OIP: *motova'n* SaP: *márawan*

MA#048 pOM ***?a-matow** *(vi) 'pedir/to ask, court'* NHM: *?amótuvip ~ ?amótuva* '=interrogar' SHM: Tl *?amɨtʋw* 'preguntar' MM: Ju *< ?æmdóf >* Ma *< ?amdów̥ ~ ?amdóΦ ~ ?amdóf >* Ja *< ?amdów̄ >* Pu *< ?amdów̄ >* At *< ?amɨdów̄ ~ ?amdów̄ ~ ?andów̥ >* Ct *< ?andów̥ >* LM: Ca *< ?amɨdów >* Gu *< ?amdów̄, y?amdó:pʸ >* 'pedir a la novia'

MA#049 pOM ***matu:k** *(n) 'trasanteayer/four days ago'* NHM: *madʋ:k?it* 'trasanteayer (hace cuatro días)' MM: Ma,Pu *mɨdú:gɨ* Ja,Ct *mɨdú:k* At *madú:k* LM: Gu *mɨdɨgɨ́:y*

MA#050 pOM ***matc** *(n) 'vara/stick'* NHM: *mádɨc* LM: Cn *< mac >*

MA#051 pZ *ma**ŋ** *(vi) 'ir/to go'* [GZ forms may not be cognate. In ChisZ this verb is also used as an auxiliary verb meaning 'future'; this auxiliary has a shortened form *ma*.] TxZ: *baŋ* (vi, vt) cargar (cría) (vt) batir con los pies SoZ: *maŋ* 'copulate' [Foster and Foster 1948] ChisZ: C *maŋ* (vi) 'ir, irse' (v-aux) 'ir' N *maŋ* (v-aux) 'irse a (y no haber regresado todavía)' (vi) 'irse (y no haber regresado todavía)' NE *maŋ* (vi) 'ir'

MA#052 pZ *ma**ŋ**-kuy *(n) 'pie/foot'* TxZ: *baŋ-k-de?* (vi-s) 'estar parado' (<? *baŋ-ku?-de?*) ChisZ: C *maŋguy* 'act of going' [Wonderly 1949] ChZ: StaMaCh *maŋku?y* SnMiCh *maŋkuy* 'foot: going instrument' [Wonderly 1949]

MA#053 pM *ma:wac *(n) 'placenta/placenta'* [pOM *ma:c] MM: Ju,Ma *ma:c* At *ma:cn̥* LM: Ca,Gu *ma:c* OlP: *ma:va's* SaP: *máwac* 'matriz'

MA#054 pMZ *may *(adj, adv) 'mucho/much'* [*may reconstructed for all subgroups] NHM: *may* 'mucho, bastante—p.ej., ganado, abundante' SHM: Tl *may* 'muchos' Tm *may* 'bastante, varias' MM: Ju *mæy* '=mucho (lluvia), bastante' Ma *may* 'mucho (lluvia)', *maȳ* 'bastante, varios' [sic!] Ma *may* '=manada' Ja *maȳ* '=bastante, manada', *may* 'montón' [sic!] Pu *maȳ* '=mucho (lluvia), montón, bastante', *may?ám* 'manada' At *maȳ, kʸæh mʸǽyɨ* 'bastante', *maȳ, nɨmáy, máyɨtʸ* 'varios', *maȳ* 'mucho (lluvia), montón, manada, mucho' Ct *maȳ* 'bastante, montón, varios, manada', *may* '=mucho (lluvia)' [sic!] LM: Ca *mæȳ* 'mucho', *may* 'bastante' [sic!] SJ *may* '=muchos' Cn <*may*> (adj) '=bastante' Gu *maȳ* 'montón, mucho, mucho (lluvia), varios', *maȳ* 'bastante' SaP: *may* 'bastante'; *mayó?k* 'mucho' ChisZ: C *maya?aŋ* 'abundantemente; maravillosamente; terriblemente' N *maya?aŋbɨ tiyɨ* 'una cosa maravillosa'

MA#055 pOM *ho:ht-may *(n) 'tristeza/sadness'* SHM: Tm *hotmay* MM: Ju *hotmǽy* Ja *ho·tmáȳ* LM: Ca *ho·tmǽȳ* Cn <*hotmay*> Gu *ho·tmáȳ*

MA#056 pOM *win-mahy ~ win-may *(vi) 'pensar/to think'* NHM: *vinma:y ~ vinma:hy ~ vinmay* '=preocupar' MM: Ju <*wimǽy*> Ma <*hɨnmáy, hʸinmǽ:pʸ*> Ja <*winmáȳ, wʸinmá·ȳ, wʸinmæ:pʸ*> Pu <*winmáȳ, winmǽ:pʸ*> At <*hɨnmáȳ, hɨnmǽ:pʸ*> Ct <*hɨnmáy, hɨnmǽ:pʸ*> LM: Ca <*wi:nmǽy*> SJ *wi·nma·y* Gu <*wi:nmáȳ, wi:nmá·ȳ, wi:nmá:pʸ*>

MA#057 pOM *šihw-may-pa* *(n)* *'adivinador/soothsayer'* [Also present in SHM according to my observations.] MM: Ju *ší:mǽ:bʸi, mǽ:bʸi* 'adivinador' At *šǽ:p* 'adivino, mantis' LM: Gu *ša:nʸ* 'adivino, mantis' [?]

MA#058 pOM *win-ma?y-n* *(n)* *'pensamiento/thought'* NHM: *vinma?yïn* '=idea, entendimiento, juicio' MM: Ma *hinma!nʸ* 'pensamiento', *hʸinmá?nʸ* 'costumbre' Ja *winma!nʸ* Pu *wʸi:nmá?nʸ* 'costumbre', *winma!nʸ* 'pensamiento' At *hinmá?nʸ* '=costumbre' Ct *hʸinmá?nʸ* LM: Ca *wi:nmá?inʸ* SJ *wi·nma?ny* Gu *wi:nmá!nʸ*

MA#059 pMZ *ma?ay* *(vt)* *'vender/to sell'* LM: Gu <*ma"w, ma:p*> [Nordell, p.c.] TxZ: *ba?y* (vt, vi-p) SoZ: *ma?y* [Foster and Foster 1948] ChisZ: N *ma?ah ~ ma?ay* (vt) NE *ma?iy* (vt) ChZ: *ma?iy* [synonym: *ma?icik*]

MA#060 pMZ *ma?ah* [?] *(n)* *'venta/sale'* SHM: Tl *mo?y* 'mercado' ChisZ: C *ma?ah* N *ma?a* 'venta, negocio, lo que se vende' NE *ma?ahku?* 'venta, tienda'; *ma?ahpabi* (adj, n) 'vendedor'

MA#061 pMZ *may* *(vt)* *'contar/to count'* NHM: *ma:y ~ ma:hy ~ may* 'adivinar' [homonym: 'mucho, bastante (e.g., ganado), abundante'] SHM: Tl **may* [*mayto?ok* 'contar (narrar); conversar'] LM: Cn <*ma·y ~ may*> (vi) 'terminar' SJ *ma·y ~ may* 'to finish' OlP: *may* (vt-d) 'aguantarse' SaP: *may* (vi, vt) 'count, help' SoZ: *may* 'tell stories' [Foster and Foster 1948] TxZ: *bay* (vt) '=estudiar, leer' ChisZ: C *may* (vt) 'contarlo' N *may* (vt) 'contarlo' ChZ: *may* 'contar (números)'

MA#062 pZ *?aŋ-may* *(vi, vt)* *'aprender, enseñar/to learn, instruct'* ChisZ: C,N,NE *?aŋmay* ChZ: *?aŋmay*

MA#063 pOM *may-?iy* *(vt)* *'multiplicar/to multiply'* NHM: *ma-?yi ~ maya* LM: SJ *mayi·y*

MA#064 pOM *mahy-ta:k ~ mahy-ta"k* *(vi)* *'platicar/to converse'* NHM: *ma:ydik* '=relatar' SHM: Tu <*mid̶ʸá"k*> 'contar (cuento)' MM: Ju <*mæd̶ʸá"k, mæd̶ʸǽkp*> Ma,Ja,Pu <*mid̶ʸá"k, mid̶ʸá·kp*> '=contar (cuento)' At <*mad̶ʸá"k, mad̶ʸá·kp*> 'platicar', <*mæd̶ʸá"k, mæd̶ʸá·kp, mʸæd̶ʸǽ·kʸpʸ*> 'contar (cuento)' [sic!] Ct <*mid̶ʸák, mid̶ʸá·kp*>, <*mid̶ʸá"k, mʸid̶ʸǽ·kʸpʸ*> 'contar (cuento)' [sic!] LM: Gu <*mid̶ʸá"k, mid̶ʸá·kp, mʸid̶ʸá·kʸpʸ*> '=contar (cuento)'

MA#065 pOM ***ma:y-hɨ** *(vi) 'aguantar un peso/to bear a burden'*
NHM: *ma:yhɨ̈ ~ ma:hyhɨ̈ ~ mayhɨ̈* 'aguantar, acabar (p.ej., una comida acabada por una o varias personas)' MM: 'aguantar un peso' MM: Ju,Pu <*má·yɨp*> Ma,Ja,At <*má·ȳɨp*> Ct <*máyɨp*> LM: 'aguantar un peso' Ca <*máyɨp*> Gu <*má·ȳɨp*>

MU#001 pOM ***mu"** *(n) 'chapulín (chico, verde)/grasshopper (little, green)'* SHM: Tl *mu?* Ju,Ma,Pu,At,Ct *mu"* LM: Cn <*mu?*> 'langosta (order: Orthoptera, Melanoplus sp.]' Ca,SJ,Gu *mu"*

MU#002 pMZ ***muc** *(vi) 'poner boca abajo; quebrar; regar/to turn upside down; break; irrigate'* NHM: *mʋhc ~ mʋc* 'poner boca abajo, boca abajo' LM: SJ *muhc ~ muc* 'to tip upside down' OIP: *muc* (vi) 'quebrarse' (vt) 'quebrarlo' SaP: *muc* (vi, vt) 'pour liquids on, water something' TxZ: *bucde?* (vi-s) 'agachado'

MU#003 pMZ ***mu:?c** *(vt) 'tostar, hacer adobes/to toast, make mud bricks'* NHM: *mʋ:?c* (vt) 'agarrar un puño de algo' LM: <*mu:c, mu·?c*> 'hacer adobes, ladrillas, construir casa' [Nordell, p.c.] SoZ: *mu?c* 'tostar (tortilla)' (vi) TxZ: *bu?c* (vt, vi-p) 'tostar' ChisZ: N *mu?c* (vi) 'desmigajarse, desquebrajarse (ejemplo: el muchacho machacó la cáscara de un huevo, y la cáscara se desquebrajó)' NE *mu?c* (vt) 'tostarlo'

MU#004 pOM ***mu:?c-i** *(n) 'adobe/sun-dried mud brick'* NHM: *mu:?c* 'adobe; puñado' SHM: Tl,Tu,Tp,Mi *mu:č* MM: Ju,Cc,Ma,Ja, Pu,At,Ct *mu:č* LM: Cn <*mu:č*> Ca *mu:č* Gu *mu:č* 'ladrillo'

MU#005 pMZ ***mucVC** *(adj) 'pequeño/small'* [pOM **muhck*; pZ **mucV(h)*] MM: Ju *muck* 'chico, angosto, menor' Ma *mu·c̄k* 'menor, angosto, chico' Ja *mu·c̄k* 'chico', *mu·cwí:n* 'angosto', *mú·cpɨ* 'menor' [sic!] Pu *mu·c̄k* 'chico, menor, pequeño' At *mu·c̄k* 'chico, angosto, pequeño', *mu·c̄kpɨ* 'menor' Ct *mu·c̄k* 'menor, pequeño, angosto, chico' LM: SJ *muc* 'little; kitchen' Gu *mu·c̄k* 'chico, pequeño, menor' ChisZ: C *mucih* 'monte chaparro, monte bajo' N *mucu* 'migaja, poso'

MU#006 pMZ ***muh** *(vt) 'mojar/to soak'* NHM: *muh* (vt) 'remojar (p.ej., panela)' MM: Ma <*muhp, muhámp*> 'mojarse (papel)' Ja <*yahmúh, muh, muhp*> 'mojarse (papel)' Pu <*muhp, muhhá·mp*> 'mojarse (papel)' At <*muhp, muhá·mp*> 'se deshace' Ct <*muhp*> 'mojarse (papel)' LM: Cn <*muh*> (vt) 'ensopar' SJ *muh* 'to soak

in liquid (bread, etc.)' Gu <*yahmúh, muh, muhp, muhá·mp*> 'mojarse (papel)' OlP: *muh* (vi) 'madurarse; cambiarse de color (madu-
rando)' SoZ: *muh* (vt) TxZ: *buh* (vt, vi-p) '=bautizar' ChisZ: C
muh (vi) 'mojarse' N *muh* (vi) 'mojarse' NE *muh* (vi)
'humedecerse, mojarse' (vi-s) 'estar húmedo, estar mojado' (adj)
'húmedo' ChZ: *muh* 'mojarse'

MU#007 pMZ ***mu:h?** *(vi) 'bramar/to bellow'* NHM: *mʋ"* 'bramar'
MM: '=mugir' Ju <*mu:p*> 'bramar, mugir' Ma <*mi"pʸ,
mu:yámp*> 'bramar', <*mi"pʸ, mu"yámp*> 'mugir' [sic!] Ja,Pu
<*mu:p, mu"wá·mp*> 'mugir, bramar' At <*mu:p, mu"há·mp, ?oh
mʸu"y*> 'bramar, mugir' Ct <*mu:p, mu"wámp*> 'bramar, mugir'
LM: Cn <*mu:~mu"~mu"w*> (vi) SJ *mu·w~mu"* 'to hum' Gu
<*mu"y, mu!pʸ*> [Nordell, p.c.] ChisZ: C *mu?* (vt) 'tocarlo' NE
mu? (vi) 'bramar' (vt) 'tocarlo' ChZ: *mu?* 'tocar instrumento de
viento'

MU#008 pOM ***?a-mu:h~?a-mu"** *(vi) 'zumbar/to buzz'* NHM: *amʋ"*
MM: Ma <*?a·mí"pʸ*> Ja,At <*?amú:p*> Ct <*?a·mú:p*> LM:
<*amu:~amu"~amu"w*> (vi) Gu <*?amú!pʸ*>

MU#009 pMZ ***muk** *(vt) 'encoger, unir/to shrink, gather'* NHM:
mʋhk~mʋk 'recoger, encoger, unir' SHM: Tp <*?Aßœnmúk
~?Apœnmúk, pœn*> 'apretar con los dedos' MM: Ju <*?œbœ:nmúk*>
'apretar con los dedos' Ma <*muhkp, mukámp*> 'encogerse, juntarse'
Ja <*muk, muhk*> 'encogerse, juntarse' Pu <*muhkp*> 'encogerse,
juntarse' At <*muhkp, muká·mp*> 'encogerse, juntarse' Ct <*muhkp,
mukámp*> 'encogerse, juntarse' LM: Cn <*muhk~muk*> (vt)
'juntar' Gu <*muhp, mugá·mp, muhk, muhkp*> 'encogerse, juntarse'
OlP: *muk* (vi) 'reunirse' SaP: *muk* (vi, vt) 'gather' ChisZ: C *muhk*
(vt) 'pesarlo; medirlo' N *muhk* (vt) 'pesarlo; medirlo' NE *muhk*
(vt) 'pesarlo; medirlo'

MU#010 pOM ***?a-mac-muhk~?a-mac-muk** *(vt) 'agarrar juntos/to
grab many things at once'* NHM: *?amahcmʋhk~?amahcmʋk* 'agarrar
varias cosas a un tiempo' LM: Cn <*amacmuhk~amacmuk*> (vt)

MU#011 pOM ***?a-ma?t-muhk~?a-ma?t-muk** *(v) 'apretar (con pinzas)/to press with the fingers'* SHM: Tu *?amœ?tmúk* MM: Ma
?a·mœ?tmúk Pu *?ɨmœ!tmúk* At *?œmœ?tmúk* Ct *?a·mœ"tmúk* LM:
Gu *?ame?múk*

MU#012 pM ***?a-pɨk-muk** *(vi) 'juntar/to gather'* SHM: Tl *?apɨkmuk* 'mezclar' LM: *?abïhmúk* [Nordell, p.c.] SaP: *?apɨmúk* [Clark and Clark 1960]

MU#013 pM ***yak-muk** *(vt) 'juntar/to gather'* NHM: *yakmʋhk* ~*yakmʋk̲* (vt) 'recaudar algo, cobrar algo, recoger algo'_ MM: Ja,Pu <*yahmúk*> (vt) 'encogerse, juntarse' Ma,Ct <*yah̲múk*> LM: Cn <*yahmuhk~yahmuk*> (vt) 'reunir' Gu <*yahmúk*> OlP: *yakmuk* (vt) 'juntar algo; reunirla (gente)'

MU#014 pOM ***mu:k~mu"k** *(vi) 'emborracharse/to get drunk'* NHM: *mʋ"khï* Ma <*mú·kɨp, tɨ: mʸí"gʸɨ*> MM: Ja <*mu·kɨp, mu"-gá·n̄ɨp*> Pu <*mú·kɨp, tæm mʸu"gá"nʸɨ*> At <*mú·kɨp, kæh mʸ*ü"gʸɨ> Ct <*mú·kɨp, tɨ: mʸí"gʸɨ*> LM: Cn <*mu·k~mu:k*> (vt) 'chupar' (ejemplo: "chúpale a tu cigarro") SJ *mu·k~mu"k* 'to get drunk' Gu <*mú·kïp, tï: mʸu"gyí:, mu"gá·n̄ɨp*>

MU#015 pOM ***ku-mu:k~ku-mu"k** *(vi) 'marearse/to become nauseated'* NHM: *kumʋ:khu~kumu"khï* MM: Ju <*kumí"gʸɨ*> Ma,Pu,Ct <*kɨmú·kɨp*> Ja,At <*kumú·kɨp*> LM: Gu <*ku"mú·kɨp*>

MU#016 pM ***mu:k-(hu)-pa** *(n) 'borracho/drunk'* NHM: *mʋ:khuva* OlP: *mu:kɨpa?*

MU#017 pZ ***mu?k** *(n) 'zacate, pasto/grass, pasture'* SoZ: *mu?k* 'zacate' TxZ: *bu?k* '=hierba, yerba' ChisZ: C *mu?k* N *mu?k* 'pasto' NE *mu?k* 'zacate, paja'

MU#018 pMZ ***mu:?k** *(vt) 'chupar/to suck on something'* NHM: *vinmʋ:?k* 'chupar algo' SHM: Tl *mu:k* MM: Ju <*mu:k*> Ma <*mu:k, mmi?kʸpʸ, mʸi?kʸpʸ*> Ja <*mu:k, mʸu?k, mʸi?kʸpʸ*> Pu <*mu:k, mmi!kʸpʸ, mʸi!kʸpʸ*> At <*mu:k, mmuü?kʸpʸ*> Ct <*mu:k, mʸi?kʸpʸ*> LM: SJ *mu·k~mu:k* Gu <*mu:k, mʸu·?pʸ*> 'chupar' OlP: *mu:k* (vt) 'chuparlo (como mango)' ChisZ: C *mu?k* (vt) 'chuparlo; absorberlo' N,NE *mu?k* (vt) ChZ: *mu?k*

MU#019 pM ***mukuy [?]** *(vt) 'chupar/to suck'* NHM: *mʋ:?y* (vt) 'tomar por buches' LM: SJ *mu·y~mu:y* 'to suck up or off' OlP: *mukuy* (vt) 'chuparlo' SaP: *muguy* (vi, vt) 'masticate'

MU#020 pMZ ***muks** *(vt) 'comer una cosa tostada/to eat toasted foods'* NHM: *mʋhkš* 'comer (p.ej., una cosa tostada)' MM: Ju <*muhš̌*> 'comer (panela)' LM: Cn <*mukš̌*> (vt) 'masticar (cosa dura)' Ca <*mukš*> 'comer (panela)' Gu <*mukš, mukšp*> 'comer (panela)' [Nordell 1990 and p.c.] OlP: *mukšti:pa* (vi) 'está mordiendo (una tuza)' ChisZ: C *muks* (vi) 'estar embrocado' (vt) 'embrocarlo' N *muks* (vt) 'voltearlo, embrocarlo' NE *mukskehk* (vi) 'inclinarse (como para comer)'

MU#021 pMZ ***mumu** *(adj) 'todo/everything'* NHM: *mʋ:m mo:k ~mokmʋ:m* 'mazorca' SHM: Tl *mʋkmu:m* 'mazorca' Tm *mu:m* 'cualquier, por ahí' MM: Ju,At *ʔæmú:m* 'entero' Ma,Ja *ʔamú:m* 'entero' Ja *ʔa·mú:m* 'entero' LM: Cn <*mu:m*> (adv) 'entero' Ca,Gu *ʔamú:m* 'entero' [Nordell, p.c.] TxZ: *-bu:mbe* (adj) 'todo, todos, todas' ChisZ: C *mumu* N *mumu* (adj) 'todo; pron: todos' NE *mumu* 'todo, todos'

MU#022 pGZ ***mu:pi** *(n) 'capulín/Mexican hackberry'* SoZ: *mu:pi?* 'capulín cimarrón' TxZ: *bu:p*

MU#023 pM ***muš** *(vi) 'germinar/to germinate'* NHM: *mʋhš~mʋš* 'germinar (p.ej., maíz o frijol), salir (p.ej., los cuernos de un venado), nacer (p.ej., el maíz)' MM: Ju <*muš*> 'nacer, brotar (plantas)' Ja <*muhšp, mušá·mp*> 'brotar', <*muhšp, mus͞šá·m͞p*> 'nacer, brotar (plantas)' [sic!] At,Pu <*muhšp, mu͞šá·m͞p*> 'nacer, brotar (plantas)' Ma,Ct <*muhšp, mušámp*> 'nacer, brotar (plantas)' LM: Cn <*muhš ~muš*> (vi) '=nacer (agua)' SJ *muhš~muš* 'to germinate' [derivative: *muš* 'spring (of water)'] Gu <*muš, muhšp, mužá·m͞p*> 'nacer, brotar (plantas)' [Nordell 1990 and p.c.] OlP: *muš* 'nacer (una planta)' SaP: *muš* (vi) 'germinate'

MU#024 pZ ***mus** *(vt) 'saber/to know'* TxZ: *bus* (vt) 'aprender, poder, saber', (v-aux) 'poder' ChisZ: C *muhs* (vi) 'saber; poder' (v-aux) 'saber; poder' (vt) 'saberlo' N *mus / musu / muspa* (v modal) 'pudo, podía, puede' (vt) 'saberlo' NE *mus* (vi) 'poder' (vt) 'saberlo' ChZ: *-mus* 'poder' (sufijo), *mus* 'saber'

MU#025 pOM ***muš** *(n) 'hongo, nanacate/mushroom'* NHM: *muš* LM: *mʋš*

MU#026 pM ***mu:ʔši** *(n) 'pájaro/bird'* [pOM **mu:ʔšy*] NHM: *mu:ʔš* 'paloma codorniz [Oreopelia albifacies]' MM: Ju *mu:šʸ* 'paloma' Ma,Ct,Ja *mu:šʸ* 'paloma, tortola' At *mu:šʸ* 'pichón del monte' LM: Cn <*mu:šy*> 'paloma (genérico)' Ca *mu:͞šʸ* 'paloma' Gu *mu:šʸ* 'pájaro' [Nordell, p.c.] OlP: *mu:ši* 'pájaro—nombre general'

MU#027 pM [Veracruz] ***mu:š(ik)** *(n) 'esale/esale'* OIP: *mu:ši'k* 'esale, crema de elote' SaP: *mu:š* 'isale'

MU#028 pMZ ***mu?t** *(vi) 'manar/spring (water)'* NHM: *mʋ?t ~ mʋ"t* MM: Ma,Ct <*mu?tp, mu"dámp*> Ja <*mu?tp, mu?t, mu"dá·m̄p*> Pu <*mu!tp, mu"dá·m̄p*> At <*mu?tp, mu"dá·m̄p*> OIP: *mu?t* (vi) SaP: *mu?t* (vi) TxZ: *bu?t* (vi) '=brotar (agua), salir (orín o "caldito" de mierda)' ChisZ: C *mu?t* (vi) 'rezumarse' N *mu?t* (vi) 'desmigajarse, desmoronarse'

MU#029 pOM ***mu"t** *(n) 'manantial/spring'* NHM: *mʋ"t* 'manantial, nacimiento de agua, ojo de agua, brotar—p.ej., agua)' MM: Ma, Ja,At,Ct *nɨ:mú"t* Pu *nɨ:hút* OIP: *mu?ta:ka'n* [?-phonology]

MU#030 pMZ ***mu:tu** *(n) 'ardilla/squirrel'* [pM **mu:tu*; pZ **mutu* > pGZ **mu:tu?*] OIP: *mu:tu* 'ardilla, persona flaca' SaP: *mú:tu* TxZ: *bu:tu?*

MU#031 pZ ***muŋ** *(n) 'sombra de persona/shadow of person'* TxZ: *buŋkɨ?* ChisZ: C *kɨmɨŋ* N *kɨmɨŋ* 'sombra' NE *kɨmuk* 'sombra'

MU#032 pOM ***muya"y** *(n) 'concuño/husband of sister-in-law'* NHM: *muya:?y* 'concuñado' MM: Ju *mɨ·yǽ"y* Ma *mʸɨ·yǽ"y* Ja *mɨ·yá"y* At *mɨyǽ"y* Ct *mʸɨ:yǽ"y* LM: Gu *mɨyá"y*

MO#001 pM ***kuy-mo?(ak)** *(n) 'abejón, abejorro/drone, bumblebee'* [pOM **kumyo"*] NHM: *kumyo"* SHM: Tu *komʸú"* Tp *kemʸú"* Mi *kumyó?y* MM: Ju *kuʸmʸo"* Cc *kemʸú"* Ma *kɨmyo"m* Pu *kɨmʸo"n* Ct *kɨmʸo"* Ja,At *kumʸo"* LM: Ca,Gu *kumʸo"* Cn <*kuymo?*> 'tipo de abejón silvestre' [order: Hymenoptera, Bombus sp.] OIP: *kuymo?a'k*

MO#002 pMZ ***moc** *(vi) 'revolver/to revolve'* NHM: *mohc ~ moc* 'envolver, envuelto' MM: At <*hɨnmóc*> 'envolver' LM: Cn <*mohc ~ moc*> (vt) 'envolver' Ca <*winmóc*> 'envolver', <*moc*> 'envolver' SJ *mohc ~ moc* 'to diaper' SaP: *moc* (vi, vt) 'bend over (cornstalks, sugarcane stalks)' ChisZ: N *mohc* (vi) 'revolverlo (con otra cosa)'

MO#003 pMZ ***mo?c** *(vt) 'moler (chile)/to grind (chili pepper)'* NHM: *mo?c ~ mo"c* 'rascar LM: SJ *mo?c ~ mo"c* 'to grind in a bowl Gu <*mo"c, mo?cp*> 'moler tomate, chile' [Nordell, p.c.] OIP: *mo?c* (vt) 'molerlo (chile o tomate)' SaP: *mo?c* (vi, vt) 'grind in a bowl (tomatoes, chile)' TxZ: *bo?c* (vt, vi-p) 'moler chile' ChisZ: C *mo?c* (vt) 'rasguñarlo, arañarlo' N *mo?c* (vt) 'machacarlo, molerlo' NE *mo?c* (vt) 'rascarlo (como hace un perro a la tierra); rasguñarlo'

MO#004 pOM *__mo:?c__ *(vt) 'limpiar (cortar plantas)/to cut brush'*
NHM: *kïsmo:?c* 'cortar algo que está arriba', *patmo:?c* 'cortar algo que está debajo' LM: Cn <*mo·c~mo:c*> (vi) 'limpiar (con pala)'

MO#005 pZ *__moc(i)__ *(adj) 'débil/week'* ChisZ: C *moči* N *moči~moci* (adj) 'débil, pequeño' NE *moči* (vi-s) '=débil' ChZ: *moc* 'fine' [Foster and Foster 1948]

MO#006 pM *__mo?(n)co__ *(n) 'lodo/mud'* [pOM *mo"nc] NHM: *mo"c* '=barro, atascadero' MM: Ju *mo"nc* Ma *mo?n̄c* Ja *mo!nc* Pu,At,Ct *mo!n̄c* LM: Cn <*mo?nc*> Ca *mo"nc* SJ *mo?nc* Mz,Gu *mo!n̄c* OlP: *mo?co [*mo?coho:y* (vi) 'batir lodo', *mo?cohï:n* (vt-d) 'atascarse en el lodo'] SaP: *mo?c [*mo?ckómom* 'estante para embarrar']

MO#007 pOM *__nï:?-mo"(n)c__ *(n) 'ciénaga/swamp'* NHM: *nïmo"c* SHM: Tl *nïmo?nchv:ht* 'pántano' MM: Ju *nïmó"nc* Ma *nï:mo"nzó·t* Ja *mo!nzó·t* Pu *nïmo!nzó·t* At *mo?nzó·t* Ct *nï:mó?ndzó·tʸ* LM: Ca *nï:mó"nc* Gu *nï:mo!nzó·t*

MO#008 pM [Veracruz] *__moho__ *(n) 'ojoche/ramon breadnut tree [Brosimum alicastrum]'* [A common Spanish term for this tree is 'moju'. This may have been borrowed from Mixean, or, reversely, Mixean may have the term from Spanish.] OlP: *moho* '=ojite' SaP: *mohkúhy*

MO#009 pMZ *__mo:k__ *(n) 'maíz/corn'* [pM, pOM *mo:hk; pZ *mok] NHM: *mo:k* '=m̲ilpa' SHM: Tl *mv:hk* MM: Ju *mok* '=maíz' Ma, Ja,Pu,At,Ct *mo·k* 'maíz, barro (de la cara)̲, mazorca' LM: Cn <*mo:k*> '[Zea mays]' Ca,SJ *mo·k* Gu *mo·k* '=maíz' TaM: *mak* [transcription of Wonderly 1949] Gu *mo·k* [Nordell 1962] OlP: *mo:kï* SaP: *mo:hk* '=mazorca' SoZ: *mok* [Foster and Foster 1948; Wonderly 1949] AyZ: *[mbok]* TxZ: *bok* '=elote' ChisZ: C *mok* '=mazorca de maíz' N *mok* '=mazorca' NE *mohk* [Wonderly 1949; all dialects] S *mok* ChZ: *mok*

MO#010 pZ *__yaw(a)-mok__ *(n) 'elote/ear of corn'* SaP: *yaumó:hk* [Zo loan?] ChisZ: N *yamok* NE *yawamohk* 'elote tierno'

MO#011 pMZ *__mo:k__ *(n) 'barro/pimple'* [Homonymous with 'corn' at all stages.] NHM *vinmo:k* '=tlacote' ChisZ: C [Te] <*vin moc*>

'barro que nace en la cara' N *mok* '=grano; quiste, sapillo, cisticerco (en la carne de puerco)'

MO#012 pMZ ***mo?ks** *(vt) 'manear/to hobble'* LM: Cn <*mo"kš*> (vt) 'atrapar con la mano' Gu <*mo?š*> 'hacer puño' [Nordell, p.c.] TxZ: *bo?kska?* (vt) 'robar (gallina), pescar (animal chico)' ChisZ: C *mo?ks* (vt) N *mo?ks* (vt) 'abotonarlo, abrocharlo; amarrarlo' NE *mo?ks* (vt)

MO#013 pM ***mon** *(vi) 'callarse/to be silent'* SHM: Tu < *?amúnʸ*> MM: 'callarse' MM: Ju <*?æmón*> Ma < *?imónnʸi̱, ?amón, ?amónʸi̱, ?a·mónʸ?iy*> Ja <*?amón*> Pu <*?imón*> At <*?æmín, ?æmí·m̄p*> Ct <*kimínʸi̱*> LM: Ca <*?amón*> Gu <*?amón, ?amó·m̄p*> 'callarse' OIP: *yakmon* (vt) 'callarlo'

MO#014 pMZ ***mon?** *(vt) 'envolver/to wrap'* LM: Cn <*mo?n*> (vt) SoZ: *mo?n* 'fold' [Foster and Foster 1948] [?] TxZ: *bo?n* (vt, vi-p) [?] ChisZ: C *mon* (vt) N *mon* (vi) 'estar revuelto' (vt) 'envolverlo' NE *mon* (vt)

MO#015 pOM ***mopohp ~ mopop** *(vi) 'aletearse/to flap'* SHM: Tu < *ti: ßʸißóepʸ*> MM: Ma <*mibóhp, ti: mʸibépʸ*> Ja,Pu <*mibóhp*> At <*nænʸiwóhpip*> Ct <*mibohpí?kp*> LM: Ca <*mobóp*> Gu <*mibóhp*>

MO#016 pMZ ***mot** *(vt) 'mezclar/to mix'* OIP: *mot* (vt) 'salarlo' SaP: *mot* (vi, vt) 'mix' TxZ: *bot* (vt) '=revolver' ChisZ: C *moht* (vi) 'mezclarse' (vt) 'mezclarlo, revolverlo' N *moht* (vi) 'revolverse, estar revuelto' NE *moht* (vi) 'mezclarse' (vt) 'mezclarlo' ChZ: *mot*

MO#017 pMZ ***mo:?t** *(vi) 'romper cosas secas/to crush dry things'* LM: SJ *mo·t ~ mo:t* 'to crush dry things' Gu <*mo:t, mo·?p*> 'romper (vidrio)' [Nordell, p.c.] SaP: *mo?t* (vi) 'break (glass)' ChisZ: C *mo?t* (vi) 'picarse'

MO#018 pZ ***moŋ** *(vi) 'empollar; dormir/to hatch; sleep'* SoZ: *moŋ* (vi) 'dormir' AyZ: *[mboŋ]* TxZ: *boŋ* (vi) 'dormir' ChisZ: C *moŋ* (vi) 'empollarse' (vt) 'empollarlo, hacerlo empollar' N *moŋ* (vi) 'ponerse clueca (culeca)' NE *moŋ* (vt) 'protegerlo (como la gallina a sus pollitos)' ChZ: *moŋ* 'dormir'

MO#019 pGZ ***mo:ŋ-i** *() 'sueño/dream'* SoZ: *mo:ŋi?* TxZ: *bo:ŋ* (n)

MO#020 pM(Z) *mo:y? (vi, vt) 'dar/to give' NHM: *mo:y ~ mo:hy ~ mo"* (vi, vt) 'dar (p.ej., de comer)' SHM: Tl *mʋ?* 'dar' MM: 'dar (vditr)' Ju <*mo"y*> Ma <*mo"w̥ ~ mo"Φ ~ mo"f, mʸe:pʸ*> 'dar (vditr)', <*mo"w̥ ~ mo"Φ ~ mo"f*> 'devolver, regalar' Ja <*mo"w, mʸe:pʸ, mʸo·ȳ*> Pu <*mo", mʸo"wǽ·m̄pʸ*> At <*mo", mʸoö:pʸ, nmo"hǽ·m̄pʸ, móö:gʸɨc*> 'dar (vditr)', <*kɨ"mó"*> 'entregar' Ct <*mo"w, mʸe:pʸ*> 'dar (vditr)', <*mo"w*> 'entregar' LM: Cn <*mo·y ~ mo" ~ mo"w*> Ca <*mo"*> SJ *mo·y ~ mo"* 'to give something to someone' Gu <*mo"w, mʸo:pʸ, mmo"wá·m̄pʸ, mó·ȳɨk*> OIP: *moy ~ mo?* (v-ap) 'darselo (p.ej., dinero); darlo (golpe)' SaP: *moy ~ mo?* (vi, vt) 'give, hit' TxZ: *boy ~ mo?y* (v-aux) 'ir a (y regresar de)' [?-semantics] ChZ: *moy* 'estar alegre' [?-semantics]

MO#021 pGZ *mo:ya? (n) 'flor/flower' SoZ: *mo:ya?* AyZ: *[mbo:ya]* TxZ: *bo:ya?*

NI-NO

*NI#001 pM *ni (part) 'negación/negation'* [pM *ni > pOM *ni: (with syntactically conditioned shortening in some dialects); pZ *ni] NHM: *ni heʔe* 'tampoco' LM: Cn <*ni*> (conj) 'ni' SJ *ni:* 'no, not (used with ka?)' TxZ: *ne:* (part) 'también, ni' [*ñe* expected; probably borrowed from Spanish]

*NI#002 pOM *ni:ʔc (vi) 'rugir/to roar'* NHM: *ni:ʔc* 'rezongar, rugir (p.ej., un león), gruñir, descubrir los dientes el perro para morder' MM: 'gruñir' Ja,Pu,At <*niʔcp, ni:ʒá·m̄p*> Ma,Ct <*niʔcp, ni:ʒámp*> LM: Cn <*ni·c~ni:c*> (vt) [sic!] SJ *ni·c~ni:c* 'to growl' Gu <*ni·ʔcp, ni:ʒá·m̄p*> 'gruñir'

*NI#003 pOM *nik (vi) 'humedecer/to be humid, damp, moist'* NHM: *nihk~nik* LM: SJ *nihk~nik*

*NI#004 pOM *nik (adj) 'húmedo/humid'* NHM: *nik* MM: Ju *nik* Ma,At,Ct *nik* '=sombra' Ja *nik* LM: Cn <*nik*> (adj) Ca *nik* '=sombra'

*NI#005 pOM *niʔkš (n) 'cuerpo/body'* NHM: *niʔkš kopk* 'cuerpo' SHM: Tl *neʔkš* Ay *neʔkš* MM: Ju *niʔkš~niʔš* Ma *níʔšɨ* 'gordo', *niʔš* 'cuerpo (vivo)' Ja *niʔkš, niʔš kopk* 'cuerpo (vivo)', *níʔšɨ* 'gordo' Pu *níʔkšɨ* 'gordo', *niʔkš* 'cuerpo (vivo)' At *niʔkš* Ct *níʔkšɨ* LM: Cn <*ni"kš*> (adj) 'gordo' Ca *niʔkš* Gu *niʔš* 'gordo', *niʔš kopk* 'cuerpo (vivo)'

*NI#006 pM *ni:ʔkš (vi) 'marchitarse/to fade, dry (flower)'* NHM: *ni:ʔkš* LM: SJ *ni·kš* Ma <*niʔkšp, niʔšp*> Ja <*niʔšp*> Ju,At,Ct <*niʔkšp*> LM: Cn <*nikš*> (vi) Ca <*nikš*> Gu <*ni·š, ni·ʔšp*> [Nordell 1990 and p.c.] SaP: *niʔkš* (vi) 'deflate'

NI#007 pMZ ***ni:p?** _(vi, vt) 'sembrar/to sow'_ NHM: _ni:p ~ ni"p_
'=plantar (p.ej., maíz), siembra' Ma,Ja _< ni"p, ni·p̄, nʸi·p̄ʸ >_ At
_< ni"p, ni·p̄p >_ Ct _< ni"p, ni·p̄, nʸi·p̄ʸ, nʸi"bém̄pʸ >_ LM: Cn
_< ni·p ~ ni"p >_ (vt) Gu _< ni"p, nʸi·p̄, nʸi·p̄ʸ >_ SJ _ni·p ~ ni"p_ 'to
plant by punching a hole in the ground with a stick' OlP: _ni:p ~ ni?p_
(vt) 'sembrar maíz' SaP: _ni:p ~ ni?p_ (vi, vt) 'plant, bury' SoZ: _ñip_
'sow' [Foster and Foster 1948] TxZ: _dʸêp_ (vt, vi-a) 'sembrar'
ChisZ: C _nihp_ (vt) 'sembrarlo, plantarlo; enterrarlo, sepultarlo' N
nihp (vt) 'sembrarlo; enterrarlo' NE _nihp_ (vt) 'sembrarlo; enterrarlo' ChZ: _nip_ 'plantar (semilla)'

NI#008 pOM ***?a-ni:p-** _(vi) 'resembrar/to sow again'_ NHM:
?ani:vi ~ ?ani:va MM: Ja,At _< ?aní:bɨ, y?ani·pɨp >_ Ct _< ?a·ní:bɨ,_
y?a·ní·p̄ʸɨpʸ > LM: Gu _< ?ani:bɨ"w >_

NI#009 pMZ ***ni:p?-i** _(n) 'siembra/sown field, sowing time'_ [pM
*_ni?pi_ > pOM *_ni"py_; pZ *_nipi_] NHM: _ni"p_ '=primavera (ave:
Turdus assimilis assimilis)' ChisZ: C _nipi_ '=sembrado' N _nipi_ NE
nibi '=huerto'

_NI#010 pM_ ***ni:p-an** _(n) 'estaca para sembrar maíz o frijol/sowing_
stick' [pOM *_ni:hpn_] NHM: _ni:pɨn_ 'estaca para sembrar maíz o
frijol, sembrador de palo' SHM: Tl _ne:hp_ Mi _puhšní·hp_ MM: At
puhšní·pn̥ SaP: _ní:pan_ 'espeque'

NI#011 pMZ ***ni:wi** _(n) 'chile/chili pepper'_ [pM *_ni:wi_ > pOM
*_ni:wy_; pZ *_niwi_ > pGZ *_ni:wi_] NHM: _ni:v_ [Capsicum annuum L.,
C. frutescens L.] SHM: Tl _ni:y_ Ay _ni:h_ MM: Ju,Ma,Pu _ni:y_
Ja,At,Ct _ni:y_ LM: Cn _< ni:y >_ '[Capsicum annuum, C. frutescens]'
Ca,Gu _ni:y_ OlP: _ni:vi_ SaP: _ni:u_ SoZ: _ni:wi_ AyZ: _[nȷ̃i:gʷi]_ TxZ:
dʸê:w ChisZ: C,N,NE _niwi_ ChZ: _niwi_

NI#012 pMZ ***cus(y)(k)-ni:wi** _(n) 'bilis/bile'_ [pM *_cuš(y)(k)ni:wi_ >
pOM *_cuškni:wy_; pZ *_cusniwi_] NHM: _cvšk ni:v_ [only in the Spanish-
to-Mixe side of the dictionary] SHM: Tp _cušní:y_ Mi _cuškní:y_ MM:
Cc,Pu _cuškní:y_ Ju _cuškní:y_ '=hiel' Ma _cuškní:y_ 'hiel', _cušní:y_
'bilis' [sic!] Ja _cusʸnʸí:y, cušní:y_ At _cuškní:y_ '=hiel' Ct _cušní:y_
'bilis', _cuškní·y_ 'hiel' [sic!] LM: Ca,Gu _cusʸnʸí:y_ '=hiel' SaP:
čušní:u SoZ: _čušñi:wi?_ 'hiel' TxZ: _cus-dʸê:w_ 'hiel' ChisZ: C
cusniwi

NI#013 pOM **cušk-ni:wy** *(n) 'chile verde/type of chili pepper'* NHM:
cvšk ni:v MM: At,Ct *cuškní:y* Ma *cušn?i:y* Ja,Pu *cušní:y* LM: Gu
cušní:y

NI#014 pMZ **kuy-ni:wi** *(n) 'cuachile (chile silvestre)/type of chili
pepper'* [See pMZ **kuy* 'tree, wood'.] [According to G. Martin *kuy* as
a first compound member probably refers to the erect habit of the
plant.] NHM: *kuñi:v* 'chile de onza' OIP: *kuyni:vi* SaP: *kuyni:u*
[Clark 1981] SoZ: *kuyñi:wi?* TxZ: *kuyd̯ê:w* 'guachile'

NI#015 pMZ **po:p?o? ni:wi** *(n) 'chile blanco/white chili pepper'* [See
pMZ **po:p?o?* 'white'.] NHM: *po:?p ni:v* ChisZ: N *popo niwi*

NI#016 pOM **niyuk** *(part) 'más/more'* NHM: *niyʋhk* 'más, bastante'
SHM: Tl *ne?ekɨ* Cn *ni"k* [Hoogshagen 1984]

NE#001 pMZ **nek?** *(vt) 'doblar; amontonar/to fold; pile up'* NHM:
ne?k~ne"k 'doblar (p.ej., una carta), doblado, plegar' MM: Pu
<*nǽ"k, nˠe!kˠpˠ*> 'doblar (ropa)' At <*nǽ"k*> 'doblar (ropa)' LM:
Cn <*ne?k~ne"k*> (vt) 'doblar' SJ *ne?k~ne"k* 'to double, bend
(clothes, paper, etc.)' OIP: *ne?k* (vt) 'doblarlo' ChisZ: C *nehk* (vt)
'amontonarlo apilándolo, entongarlo' N *nehk* (vi) 'estar amontonado
(en fila)' (vt) 'amontonarlo' NE *nehk* (vt) 'amontonarlo
(apilándolo)'

NE#002 pOM **?a-ne?k~?a-ne"k** *(vt) 'plegar/to pleat'* MM: Ma
<*?inǽ"k, y?iné?kˠpˠ*> 'plegar (ropa)' Ja,At <*?anǽ"k, y?ané?kˠpˠ*>
'doblar (ropa), plegar (ropa)' Ct <*?a·nǽ"k, y?a·né?kˠpˠ*> 'plegar
(ropa)' LM: Cn <*ane?k~ane"k*> (vt) 'doblar' Gu <*?ané"k,
y?ané?pˠ*> 'doblar (ropa), plegar (ropa)'

NE#003 pOM **yak-ne?k~yak-ne"k** *(vt) 'doblar/to fold'* NHM:
yakne?k~yakne"k 'doblar algo' LM: Cn <*yahne?k~yahne"k*> (vt)
'doblar'

NE#004 pZ **ne?k** *(vt) 'embarrar/to cover with mud'* TxZ: *de?k* (vt)
'esconder, guardar' ChisZ: C *ne?k* (vt) 'embarrarlo' ChZ: *ne?*
'enlodar'

NE#005 pZ **ne?ks** *(vi) 'pegar/to stick'* SoZ: *ne?ks* 'techarlo' TxZ:
de?ks (vt, vi) 'pegar (bloc, tabique, ladrillo)' ChisZ: C *ne?ks* (vi)
'pegarse' (vt) 'encolarlo, pegarlo' N *ne?ks* (vi) 'hay muchos en un

lugar; estar pegado' (vt) 'pegarlo (con pegamento)' NE *ne?ks* (vt) 'pegarlo (con pegamento)'

NE#006 pZ ***ne?ks-cɨ?y** *(vi) 'quedarse pegado/to stick'* TxZ: *de?kscɨ?y* (vt, vi-p) 'dejar pegado, quedar pegado' ChisZ: C *ne?kscɨ?y ~ ne?kscyɨ?y* (vi-a) 'quedarse pegado' N *ne?kscyɨ?y* (vi) 'quedar pegado' NE *ne?kscyɨ?y* (vi) 'quedarse pegado'

NE#007 pZ ***ne?ks** *(adj) 'pegajoso/sticky'* TxZ: *de?ksp* (adj) ChisZ: C *ne?kspapɨ* (adj) NE *ne?kspabɨ nahs* 'barro (como para hacer ollas)'

NE#008 pZ ***nem** *(vi) 'arder (fuego)/to burn (fire)'* [pZ status secured by the age of the derived form *nema] ChisZ: N *nem* (vi) 'arder, flamear, llamear' NE *nem* (vi) 'arder (como el fuego o una herida); encenderse (como una luz); relampaguear'

NE#009 pZ ***nema** *(n) 'llama/flame'* ChisZ: C *nema* NE *nema* '=lumbre; relámpago' ChZ: *nema?*

NE#010 pMZ ***ne?m** *(vi) 'molestar/to bother'* NHM: *ne?m ~ ne"m* 'hacer ruido (p.ej., niños), escandalizar' MM: Ja < *næ!m̄p, næ"-má·m̄p* > 'molestar' Ma,At,Ct < *næ?m̄p* > 'molestar' LM: Cn < *ne?m* > 'hacer ruido; molestar' Gu < *ne!m̄p, ne"má·m̄p* > 'molestar' SJ *ne?m ~ ne"m* 'to bother' SoZ: *ne?m* 'lamer' (vt) [Foster and Foster 1948, Gutiérrez M. 1993] [?] ChisZ: N *ne?m* (vi) 'relampaguear; brillar; verse enojado'

NE#011 pMZ ***nep** *(vt) 'patear/to kick'* NHM: *nehp ~ nep* '=dar un puntapié, poatada' MM: Ju < *næp, næhp* > Ma < *næp, næhp* > Ja < *næp̄, næhp, nʸehpʸ, næpá·m̄p* > Pu < *næp̄, næhp* > At < *næp̄, næhpp, nʸehpʸpʸ* > Ct < *næp̄, næhp, nʸehpʸ* > Ca < *næp* > LM: Cn < *nehp ~ nep* > (vt) SJ *nehp ~ nep* Gu < *nep̄, nehp, nʸehpʸ, nebá·m̄p* > SaP: *nep* (vi, vt) SoZ: *nep* (vt) TxZ: *dep* (vt) ChisZ: C *nehp* (vt) N *nehp* (vi, vt) NE *nehp* (vi)

NE#012 pOM ***nehw ~ new** *(vi) 'enchuecarse/to bend, twist'* NHM: *ne:v ~ ne:hv ~ nev* 'enchuecar (p.ej., un árbol)' MM: Ma < *næ:p, ne:pʸ, næwámp, neyámp* > Ja < *ne:pʸ, neyá·m̄p* > At < *ne!pʸ, neyá·m̄p* > Ct < *ne:pʸ, neyámp* > LM: Gu < *ne·y, neyá·m̄p* >

NE#013 pMZ ***new-e** *(adj) 'chueco, encorvado/bent, twisted'* [pM *newe > pOM *newy; pZ *neŋe] NHM: *nEv* 'chueco' MM: Ma *ney* 'encorvado, chueco, curva' Ja *neȳ* 'chueco' Pu *neȳ* 'chueco, curva'

At *neȳ* 'chueco, chueco, curva' Ct *neȳ* 'encorvado', *ney* 'chueco, curva' [sic!] LM: Cn <*ney*> (adj) 'chueco' Ca *ney* 'chueco' Gu *neȳ* 'chueco, curva' AyZ: *[ndew]* 'nabaguela (tipo de zacate que se corta con machete)' TxZ: *deŋ-ki-deŋ-ki-ho?y* (vi) 'andar para todos lados como un borracho' ChisZ: C *neŋe* 'fila, hilera' N *neŋ* 'raíz ancha y delgada al pie de un árbol, contrafuerte' S *[ne·ŋé?]* 'pie'

NE#014 pMZ ***ne?w** *(vt)* '*colocar piedras en un cerco/to make a stone wall*' NHM: *nE"v* (n) 'pared' ChisZ: C *kine?ŋ* (vt) 'rodearlo, arrodearlo' NE *ne?ŋ* (vt) 'colocarlo (como piedras en un cerco)'

Nɨ#001 pMZ ***nɨ:?** *(n)* '*agua/water*' [pM, pOM **nɨ:?*; pZ, pGZ **nɨ?*] NHM: *nɨ:* 'agua, líquido; aguardiente; aguado' [Schoenhals and Schoenhals 1965] *nɨ:h* [A. Schoenhals in p.c. to G. Martin] SHM: Tl *nɨ:* Tp *nɨ:h* MM: Ju,Cc,Ma,Ja,Pu,At,Ct *nɨ:* LM: Cn <*nɨ:*> Ca,SJ *nɨ:* Gu *nɨ̈:* TaM: *noo* [transcription in Wonderly 1949] OlP: *nɨ:hɨ* SaP: *nɨ?* SoZ: *nɨ?* [Foster and Foster 1948; Wonderly 1949] AyZ: *[ndɨ?]* TxZ: *dɨ?* '=savia, esperma' ChisZ: C *nɨ?* 'agua, río; jugo' N [FL] *nɨ?* '=arroyo, río, jugo' NE,S *nɨ?* ChZ: *nɨ?* 'agua, río' ChZ: SnMiCh *nɨ?* [Wonderly 1949]

Nɨ#002 pMZ ***?aw-nɨ:?** *(n)* '*baba/saliva*' [See pMZ **?aw* 'mouth'.] SHM: Tp *?Anɨ:h* MM: Ju *?anɨ:* Cc *?Anɨ:* Ma,Ja,Ct *?anɨ:* Pu *?a·nɨ:* At *?ænɨ:* LM: <*a:nɨ:*> Ca *?a·nɨ:* Gu *?anɨ̈:* TxZ: *?aŋ-k-dɨ?* ChisZ: C *?aŋnɨ?* N *?aŋñɨ* 'saliva; veneno de una víbora'

Nɨ#003 pOM ***hok-nɨ:?** *(n)* '*mezcal/mescal*' SHM: Tu *hoknɨ:h* 'aguardiente de caña' LM: Ca *hoknɨ:* Gu *hoknɨ̈:* 'mezcal', *hoknɨ̈:* 'aguardiente de caña'

Nɨ#004 pM [Veracruz] ***hokoš-nɨ:?** *(n)* '*agua tibia/tepid water*' OlP: *hokošnɨ:hɨ* SaP: *hogošnɨ?*

Nɨ#005 pMZ ***mɨha nɨ:?** *(n)* '*río/river*' [See pMZ *mɨha 'greater, big'.] NHM: *mɨhɨ nɨ:* SHM: Tl *mɨh nɨ:* LM: Ca *mɨhnɨ:* Cn <*mɨhnɨ:*> Gu *mɨhnɨ̈:* SaP: *mɨhnɨ?* ChisZ: NE *mɨhanɨ?*

Nɨ#006 pMZ ***sɨk-nɨ:?** *(n)* '*caldo de frijoles/bean soup*' [See pMZ *sɨk 'bean'.] OlP: *šɨknɨ:hɨ* SaP: *šɨknɨ?* ChisZ: N *sɨhkɨnɨ?* 'agua de frijoles'

Nɨ#007 pZ ***tuh-nɨ?** *(n) 'agua llovida/rainwater'* [See pMZ **tu:h.*]
SaP: *tu:hnɨ?* [only in Sp.-to-SaP side; Zo loan] AyZ: *[túhndɨ?]* TxZ:
tuh-dɨ? ChisZ: C *tuhkɨñɨ?*

Nɨ#008 pM ***win-nɨ:?** *(n) 'lágrima/tear'* NHM: *vinnɨ:* OlP: *vinanɨhɨ*
SaP: *winnɨ?*

Nɨ#009 pOM ***nɨ:?-wihn-m** *(top) 'Tenochtitlán, Ciudad de*
México/Tenochtitlán, Mexico City' NHM: *nɨvi:nm* 'Ciudad de Mexico'
LM: Cn *<nɨ:wim>*

Nɨ#010 pMZ ***nɨ:c** *(n) 'armadillo/armadillo [Dasypus novemcinctus]'*
[pM, pOM **nɨ:hc*; pZ **nɨc*] NHM: *nɨ:c* SHM: Tl,Tp *nɨc* Tu *nɨ̄c* Mi
nɨ̈c MM: Ju,Cc *nɨc* Ma,Ja,Pu,Ct *nɨ·c̄* At *nɨ·c* LM: Cn *<nɨ:c>* Ca
nɨ·c Gu *nɨ̈:c̄* OlP: *nɨ:cu* [final vowel /ɨ/ expected] SaP: *nɨ:hc* SoZ:
nɨc TxZ: *dɨc* ChisZ: C,N,S *nɨc* NE *nɨhc* ChZ: *nɨc*

Nɨ#011 pOM ***tɨhk nɨ:c** *(n) 'especie de insecto/a kind of insect'* [See
pMZ **tɨk* 'house'.] NHM: *tɨknɨ:c* 'cochinilla de humedad [Oniscus
sp.]' LM: Cn *<tɨhk nɨ:c>* 'tipo de insecto'

Nɨ#012 pM ***nɨ?c** *(vt) 'ajustar/to fit tight'* NHM: *nɨ?c ~ nɨ"c* 'ajustar,
trabarse las mandíbulas un enfermo, juntar la dentadura' LM: Cn
<nɨ?c ~ nɨ"c> (vt) 'machucar' Gu *<nɨ"c, nɨ̈?cp>* 'aplastar'
[Nordell, p.c.] OlP: *nɨ?c* (vt) 'prensarlo'

Nɨ#013 pMZ ***nɨ?pin** *(n) 'sangre/blood'* [pM **nɨ?hpin* > pOM
*nɨ?hpyn; pZ **nɨ?pin* > pGZ **nɨ?ɨpin*] NHM: *nɨ̈:?pɨ̈n* '=sangre del
árbol llorasangre' SHM: Tl *nɨ?hpy* Ay *nɨ?pʸ* MM: Ju,Ma,Ja,At,Ct
ne?pʸn̥ʸ LM: Cn *<nɨ?py>* Ml *<ne?py>* Ca *ne?pʸtʸ* Gu *nɨ̈?tʸ* OlP:
nɨ?pi'n SaP: *nípin* SoZ: *nɨ?ɨpiñ* TxZ: *dɨ:?peñ* ChisZ: C,N *nɨ?pin*
NE *nɨ?bit* S *[nɨ?pín]* ChZ: *nɨ?pin*

Nɨ#014 pGZ ***nɨk** *(vt) 'ir/to go'* TxZ: *dɨk* (vi) 'ir', (v-aux) 'futuro-
andativo' SoZ: *nɨk* 'ir' [Elson 1960]

Nɨ#015 pMZ ***nɨks** *(vi) 'ir/to go'* NHM: *nɨhkš* SHM: Tl *nɨhkš* MM:
Ju *<nɨhš>* Ma,Ja,Pu,Ct *<nɨhkš>* At *<nɨhkš, nɨhkšp, mo:*
mnehkšʸ> LM: Cn *<nɨkš>* (vi) Ca *<nɨkš>* SJ *nɨkš* 'to go'
[derivative: *nɨkʸšʸ* 'going—pertaining to motion in the present or
future'] Gu *<nɨ̈kš, nɨkšp>* [Nordell 1990 and p.c.] OlP: *nɨkš* (vi)
'ir, irse' SaP: *nɨš/nɨkš* (vi) TxZ: *dɨks* (v) 'irse (forma supletiva del
imperativo)' ChZ: *nɨks* 'irse'

Nɨ#016 pOM ***pa-nɨhkš** *(vi) 'seguir/to follow'* NHM: *panïhkš* 'ir detrás de alguien' MM: Ju *pænɨhš* Ma *pa:nɨhš* Ja *panɨhš* At *panɨhkš* Ct *pa:nɨhkš* LM: Ca *panɨkš* Gu *panɨkš*

Nɨ#017 pOM ***yak-nɨhkš** *(vt) 'llevar/to take away'* NHM: *yaknɨhkš* 'llevar algo o a alguien' LM: Cn <*yahnɨkš*> (vt) 'llevar'

Nɨ#018 pMZ ***nɨm** *(vi) 'decir/to say'* SHM: Tl *nɨm* OlP: *nɨm* (vi, vt) SaP: *nɨm* (vi, vt) SoZ: *nɨm* (vi) TxZ: *dɨm* ChisZ: C,N *nɨm* (vi) ChZ: *nɨm*

Nɨ#019 pMZ ***nɨm-hay** *(v ap) 'decirselo/to say something to someone'* NHM: *nɨhmip~nɨhma* (vt), 'decir, decirle' MM: 'decir (tr)' Ma <*nɨ:mi, nʸimǽ:pʸ*> Ja <*nɨ:mi, nʸimá·ȳ, nʸimæ:pʸ*> Pu <*nɨ:mi, nʸimǽ:pʸ, nimá·yɨp*> At <*nɨ:mi, nʸinǽ:pʸ, nimǽ:gʸic*> Ct <*nɨ:mi, nʸimǽ:pʸ, nʸimá:dʸ ip*> LM: Cn <*nima·y~nima"~nima"w*> (vt) 'decir' SJ *nima·y~nima"y* 'to say to someone' Gu <*nimá"w, nʸimá:pʸ, nimá·yɨk*> 'decir (tr)' TxZ: *dɨm-a?* (vt) 'decirle' ChisZ: C *nɨhay* (vditr) N *nɨhay* (vt) 'decirle' NE *nɨhay* (vditr) ChZ: *nɨmhay* 'decirle'

Nɨ#020 pOM ***nɨma"** *(n) 'neblina/fog'* NHM: *nɨma"* 'nubes espesas en el oriente' MM: Pu *hok nɨmá"* 'sereno' At *nɨmá"* LM: Ca,Gu *nɨmá"*

Nɨ#021 pM ***nɨ:nɨ** *(n) 'tortilla/tortilla'* [pM **nɨ:nɨ* > pOM **nɨ:n*; pZ **ninɨ*] [The possibility of associating 'tortilla' with 'atole' testified to in SHM-Tl *nɨ?ány* 'agua + tortilla'.] NHM: *ninnɨha:?šy* 'tortilla enchilada' [?] OlP: *nɨ:nɨ* SaP: *nɨ:n* ChisZ: C *ninɨ* 'atole' ChZ: *ninɨ ?uki* 'atole de maíz nuevo'

Nɨ#022 pOM ***nɨ:š** *(n) 'hija/daughter'* NHM: *nɨ:š* MM: Ju *nɨ:š* Ma,At,Ct *nʸɨ:š* LM: Cn <*nɨ:š*> Ca *nɨ:š* Gu *nɨ:š mahk* 'hijo, -a' SJ *nɨ:ž* Gu *nɨ:š mahk* 'niño, -a'

Nɨ#023 pOM ***cohk-nɨ:š** *(n) 'sobrina/niece'* NHM: *coknɨ:š* MM: Ju *cohnɨ:š* Ma,Ct *cohknɨ:š* '=prima' Ja *cohknɨ:š* '=sobrina' At *cohknɨ:š* LM: Ca *cohknú:š* Gu *cohnɨ:š* '=prima'

Nɨ#024 pOM ***ku-nɨ:š** *(n) 'hijastra/fosterchild (girl)'* NHM: *kunɨ:š* '=entenada' MM: Ju *kunɨ:š* Ma,Ct *kʸɨnɨ:š* Ja,At *kunɨ:š* '=entenada' LM: Gu *kunɨ:š* '=entenada'

Ni#025 pMZ ***nɨʔs** *(vt) 'calzar/to level'* NHM: *kunɨ"š* 'calzas para el comal' MM: Ja <*paʔtnɨ"žɨ, pʸaʔtnɨ"žɨp*> LM: Cn <*nɨʔš~nɨ"š*> (vt) 'poner una cuña' Gu <*paʔnɨ"žɨ"w*> OIP: *nɨʔš* (vt) TxZ: *dɨːʔs* (vt, vi-p) 'calzar' (p.ej., mesa para dejarla al nivel)

Ni#026 pZ ***nɨyi** *(n) 'nombre/name'* SaP: *nɨʔhy* [Zo loan?] TxZ: *dɨy* SoZ: *nɨyi* ChisZ: C *nɨy* N,NE *nɨyi* ChZ: *nɨhi*

Ni#027 pZ ***nɨy-ʔɨy** *(vi, vt) 'bautizar/to baptize'* TxZ: *dɨʔɨʔy* (vt) 'nombrar' ChisZ: C *nɨʔyɨy* (vi) 'ser bautizado' (vt) 'ponerle nombre, nombrarlo' N *nɨʔyɨy* (vi) 'bautizarse' (vt) 'bautizarlo' NE *nɨʔyɨy* (vi) 'ser bautizado' (vt) 'llamarlo, nombrarlo, darle nombre'

NA#001 pM ***nahc-** *(n) 'nuca/neck'* [pOM **nahc-*] NHM: *naspahk* 'pierna de la nuca' MM: Ja *naẓʔɨhš* Pu,Ct *nahcʔɨhš* LM: Cn <*nahcpahk*> 'cerviz' Gu *nahcʔĭhš* OIP: *naskɨʔ* SaP: *nacpáhk*

NA#002 pM ***naʔc** *(vi, vt) 'pintar/to paint'* NHM: *naʔc~na"c* 'pegar (p.ej., un papel con cera negra), soldar' OIP: *naʔc* (vt) 'pintarlo; herrarlo (ganado); echarle (lumbre en la milpa)' (vi) 'pintar' (example: "están pintando las mujeres (con bastidor)")

NA#003 pZ ***nahi** *(n) 'cera/wax'* [pGZ *naːyi] SoZ: *náyi* [Elson 1960], *naːyi* [Gutiérrez M. 1993] TxZ: *day* '=vela, foco, luz, procesión' ChisZ: C *nay* NE *nayi* ChZ: *yɨk nahi* 'cera negra'

NA#004 pZ ***naʔh** *(n) 'hule/gum tree'* SaP: *naʔh* [Zo loan] AyZ: [*ndaʔ*] TxZ: *daʔ* 'chicle'

NA#005 pMZ ***ʔaw-nah-in** *(n) 'izquierda/left'* [pM *ʔawnahin > pOM *ʔanahyn; pZ *ʔaŋnahin with irregularities in descendant languages] NHM: *ʔanah* '=zurdo' MM: '=zurdo' Ju *ʔænáhnʸ,ku·ʔænáhn̥ʸ* Ma,Ja *ʔanáhtʸ* Pu *ʔɨnáhnʸ* At *ʔænáhʸn̥ʸ* Ct *ʔa·náhn̥ʸ* LM: 'izquierdo, zurdo' Ca *ʔænáhtʸ* Gu *ʔanáhtʸ* OIP: *ʔaunahikɨʔ* 'mano izquierda' SaP: *ʔanáhyim* TxZ: *daːyɨm* 'izquierda' [/in/ expected in place of the last two segments] ChisZ: C *ʔaŋña* 'izquierda, zurda', *aŋñakɨʔɨ~ʔaŋñapɨ kɨʔ* 'mano izquierda' N *ʔaŋñay* 'mano izquierda' NE *ʔaŋñak* 'izquierda, zurda', *ʔaŋñakɨʔ* 'mano izquierda'

NA#006 pM ***nak** *(vi) 'poner una jaula/to set a trap'* MM: Ma <*nahkp, nakkamp̄*> 'abollarse' Ja <*nahkp, naká·m̄p*> 'abollarse, aplastarse' Pu <*nahkp, naka·m̄p*> 'abollarse' At <*nahpp,* *nappa·m̄p* > 'abollarse' Ct <*nahkp*> _'abollarse, aplastarse' LM: Gu <*nahp, naga·m̄p*> 'abollarse', <*nakǐ:pʸ*> 'aplastarse' OlP: nak (vi) 'poner una jaula' [derivative: *naka'n* 'jaula'] (vt) 'agarrar con jaula' SaP: *nak* (vi, vt) 'crush'

NA#007 pOM ***nak-y** *(n) 'trampa/trap'* NHM: *na̱ky* 'trampa (de piedra_y troncos de madera)' MM: Ju *nækʸ* At *nækʸ* LM: Ca *nækʸ* Gu *nakʸ*

NA#008 pZ ***na?k** *(vt) 'coser, costurar/to sew'* SoZ: *na?k* (vi-a) 'tejer' ChisZ: C *na?k* (vt) 'coserlo, costurarlo' N *na?k* (vi) 'coser, estar cocido' (vt) 'coserlo' NE *na?k* (vi) 'costurar' (vt) 'clavarlo; costurarlo, coserlo (como ropa)' ChZ: *na?k* 'coser'

NA#009 pMZ ***na:ka** *(n) 'varios/various'* [pM **na:ka* > pOM **na:k*; pZ **naka*] MM: Ma,Ja,Pu *na:k* 'cuántos' Ct *na:k* 'cuántos, algunos' LM: Cn <*na:g*> (adj) '¿cuánto?' Gu *na:k* 'cuántos' SJ *na:g* 'some, how many' ChisZ: C,NE *naka* N *nak*

NA#010 pM ***na?ka** *(n) 'cosa plana/flat object'* [pOM **nak*] LM: Cn <*nak*> 'laja' SJ *nak* OlP: *na?ka* 'tabla'

NA#011 pMZ ***nakak** *(n) 'rana, sapo/frog, toad'* [pM **nakVk* > pOM **tuk-nakk* (The meaning of the morpheme **tuk* is unknown; it may be identical to pO̱M **tuk* 'old'); pZ_**nahak*.] NHM: *tvkïnágïk* 'sapo' MM: Ja,Ct *nak* 'sapo' At *tuknák* 'sapo' LM: Cn <*tuk*> 'rana' SoZ: *nak* TxZ: *dak* ChisZ: C *nak* N *nak* / *ca?nʸak* 'rana' NE *nʸahk* 'rana' ChZ: *nak*

NA#012 pZ ***naka** *(n) 'cáscara, piel/shell, skin'* [pGZ **na:ka*] SoZ: *na:ka?* [Gutiérrez M. 1993], *na:ka* [Wonderly 1949] TxZ: *da:k* '=cuero, pellejo' ChisZ: C *naka* '=cuero; suela; cutis; corteza' N [FL] *naka* '=cuero; envoltura, énvase, caja; corteza' NE [Pantepec] *naŋga* [Wonderly 1949; 1p or 2p pronomial infix] [Ocotepec] *naka* [Wonderly 1949] [Ra] *naka* '=cuero, suela de cuero'; *ku?yiñaka~ku?yunaka* 'corteza del árbol' S [Tu] *naka* [Wonderly 1949] [Cp] *[naká?]* 'pataxete (semilla blanca que se come)' ChZ: StaMaCh *naka* '=casca, corteza' SnMiCh *naka* [Wonderly 1949]

NA#013 pZ ***witïm-naka** *(n) 'párpado/eyelid'* ChisZ: C,N *witïmnaka* NE *widïmnaka* ChZ: *witïm ko?hap*

NA#014 pZ ***naku** *(n) 'barbasco/type of yam'* [pGZ **na:ku*] TxZ: *da:k* ChisZ: C *naku* 'barbasco [planta; Dioscorea composita]'

NA#015 pMZ ***naks** *(vt) 'latir, pegar/to whip, beat'* NHM: *nahkš* 'latir' SoZ: *naks* 'hit, beat' [Foster and Foster 1948] TxZ *daks* (vt) 'pegar (con garrota), varear, aporrear, azotar' ChisZ: C *naks* (vt) 'pegarlo; chicotearlo, echarle cuarta; majarlo; tocarlo' N *naks* (vi) 'pegar' (vt) 'pegarle (con algo como palo o reata); tocar (marimba)' NE *naks* (vt) 'chicotearlo; tocarlo (como un tambor); machucarlo, majarlo (como frijoles)' ChZ: *nakstɨr* 'onda' [derived form]

NA#016 pMZ ***namV** *(adj) 'nuevo/new'* [pM **namɨ* > pOM **nam*; pZ **nama*] NHM: *nam* ' =reciente' LM: Cn < *namnɨ* > (adv) 'hace rato; mientras' (adj) 'nuevo, reciente' OIP: *namɨ ni?ome* 'pequeño —p.ej., un fruto, chaparro—un hombre' [?] SaP: *námay* [possibly borrowed from Zoquean after final vowel were lost in SaP] AyZ: *[mi nama]* 'no más un poquito' TxZ: *na?m-pɨ?* (adv) 'recién' [?] ChisZ: C *nama* 'pequeño'; (n) 'cucuyuche' N *nama* (adj) 'menudito, chiquito', (n) 'piojillo; coruco' NE *nama* 'pequeño, menudo' *namabɨ* (adj) 'pequeño; menudo'

NA#017 pM ***nam-?ɨy** *(v) 'dejarlo nuevo/to make new'* NHM: *námi~nama* 'estrenar una cosa que es igual a otra cosa usada', *yaknámi~yaknama* (vt) 'renovar algo, estrenar algo' OIP: *yaknami* (vt) 'dejarlo nuevo'

NA#018 pGZ ***na:ma?** *(n) 'pepeyoche/bird louse'* SoZ: *ná:ma?* TxZ: *da:ma?*

NA#019 pM ***na?n** *(vi) 'comer cosa blanda/to eat soft foods'* MM: At < *nœ"n, nʸe?m̄pʸ* > 'mordiscar' LM: Gu < *nɨ"n, nɨ!m̄p* > 'mordiscar' Cn *na?n* 'ejote' SaP: *na?n* (vi, vt) 'eat soft foods (bananas, avocado)'

NA#020 pOM ***na"n-y** *(n) 'atole champurrado/drink mixed of choco-late and atole'* SHM: Tu *na"nʸ* Tp *nA"nʸ* MM: Ju,At *na"nʸ* Ma *pa"khɨ=č* Ja *hič̄nʸá"nʸ, na"nʸ, po:pná"nʸ* Pu *pa"kná"nʸ* Ct *pa"kná"nʸ* LM: CN < *na?ñ* > 'atole' Gu,Ca *na"nʸ*

NA#021 pGZ ***na:?na?** *(n) 'encía/gum'* [Cf. ChisZ-C *nanu* 'encía'] SoZ: *ná?na?* TxZ: *da:?na?*

NA#022 pMZ ***nana** *[?] (n) 'madre, mamá/mother'* [This may be a false etymon, cf. missing last syllable deletion in most OM forms.] NHM: To *nana* 'madre' Hu *nana* 'woman's mother-in-law' MM: Ju *næni* 'mamá' Ct *na·n̄* 'mamá' LM: Cn *<nan>* 'mamá (se usa para saludar a la mamá y a las madrinas)' SJ *nan* 'madre' Ca *ná:na* 'mamá' ChisZ: C *nanah* 'mamá, madre'

NA#023 pM [Veracruz] ***nap** *(vt) 'remendar/to mend'* OlP: *nap* (vt) SaP: *nap* (vi, vt)

NA#024 pMZ ***nas** *(vi) 'pasar/to pass by'* NHM: *nahš~naš* 'ir passando, excesivo' SHM: Tl *noš* MM: Ma *<naš̄, nahšp>* Ja *<naš̄, nahš̄, nahšp, našá·m̄p>* Pu,At,Ct *<naš̄, nahšp>* LM: Cn *<nahš~naš>* (vi) SJ *nahš~naš* 'to pass by' Gu *<naš̄, nahš̄, nahšp, nažá·m̄p>* OlP: *naš* (vi, vt) 'pasar' [derivative: *?išnaš* (vi) 'leer'] SaP: *naš* (vi, vt) 'pass by, cross over' SoZ: *nas* (vi) TxZ: *das* (vi) 'aplacarse (lluvia)'

NA#025 pM ***?a-naš** *(vi) 'colar/to strain, filter'* NHM: *?anahš ~ ?anaš* 'pasar por un sitio o sitios' MM: Ma *< ?anáš̄ >* Ja *< ?anáš̄, y?anáhšᵞpᵞ >* 'colar' Pu *< ?ináš̄ >* Ct *< ?a·náš̄, y?a·náhšᵞpᵞ >* LM: Cn *<anahš~anaš>* (vi) 'pasar (reg.), exceder; hacer una acción (demasiado)' (vt) 'colar' Ca *< ?a·náš >* Gu *< ?anáš̄, y?anáhšᵞp, ?anažá·m̄p >* [Nordell 1990 and p.c.] SaP: *?anašhé:k* 'pasar a un lado' [Clark and Clark 1960]

NA#026 pOM ***?a-nahš-a? ~ ?a-naš-a?** *(vt) 'repasar/to rehearse'* NHM: *?anahši ~ ?anaša* '=ensayar; burlarse (en general)' LM: Cn *<anaši·y~anaši"y~anaši?~anaši"y>* (vt)

NA#027 pM ***ko-naš** *'bajar/to descend'* NHM: *kunahš~kunaš* 'bajar (p.ej., ir bajando), sobrar' MM: Ma *<kɨnáhšp>* 'hundirse, ahondarse' Ct *<kɨnáhšp>* 'ahondarse, hundirse' LM: Cn *<konahš~konahš>* (vi) 'sobrar' Gu *<kunaš, kunahšp>* [Nordell, p.c.] SaP: *kunáš* 'pasar por arriba' [Clark and Clark 1960; Clark 1983: 'pass to']

NA#028 pOM ***ma:-naš** *(vi) 'adormecerse/to go to sleep'* [Cf. pMZ **ma:h?* 'dormir/to sleep'.] NHM: *manahš~manaš* 'dormir' MM: Ju *<ma:náš̄>* Ma *<ma:náhšp>* Ja *<mɨnáhšp>* 'adormecerse', *<tɨ: mɨnáhš̄>* 'dormir' Pu,Ct *<ma:náhšp>* At *<manáhšp>* 'adormecerse', *<tɨ: mᵞa:náš̄ᵞ>* 'dormir'

NA#029 pOM *yak-nahš ~ yak-naš *(vt) 'hacer pasar/to make pass'* NHM: *yaknahš ~ yaknaš* 'hacer pasar a algo o alguien' LM: Cn <*ya-hnahš ~ yahnaš*> (vt) 'pasar'

NA#030 pM *na:hš-pi(k) *(adv) 'bajo/down'* SHM: Tp *naš⁹pʸ ~ næš⁹pʸ* 'bajo', *nAškíš⁹* 'bajo, abajo' MM: Ma *na·š̄ʸpʸ* Ja *na·š⁹pʸ* 'chaparro', *na·š̄ʸpʸ* 'bajo', *na·šp̄ʸ* 'abajo' [sic!] At *næ·š̄ʸpʸ* Ju *næš̄ʸpʸ* Cc *naš⁹pʸ* Pu *na·š̄ʸpʸ* 'bajo', *na·šp̄ʸ* 'abajo' [sic!] Ct *na·š̄ʸpʸ* 'bajo', *na·šp̄ʸ* 'abajo' LM: Gu *na·š̄ʸp* 'chaparro, bajo, ?ana·š̄p* 'abajo' OIP: *na:špi'k* (adj)

NA#031 pMZ *na:s *(n) 'tierra, terreno, suelo/earth'* [pM, pOM *na:hš; pZ *nas] NHM: *na:š* SHM: Tl *no:hš* 'tierra' Tm *na:hš* MM: Ju *næš* 'tierra' Ma *na·š̄* 'solar, tierra, terreno, selo' Ja *na·š̄* 'selo, solar, tierra, terreno' At *na·š̄, na·škíhs⁹* 'selo', *na·š̄* 'tierra, terreno' Ct *na·š̄* 'tierra, selo', *na·š̄ kam̄* 'terreno' LM: Cn <*na:š*> 'tierra' Ca *na:š* 'tierra, selo' SJ *na·š* Gu *na·š̄* 'selo, tierra, terreno' Ca *na:s* [Wonderly 1949] OIP: *na:šɨ* 'tierra, suelo' SaP: *na:š* 'tierra' SoZ: *nas* 'earth' [Foster and Foster 1948, Wonderly 1949] AyZ: *[ndas]* 'tierra, pueblo' TxZ: *das* 'tierra, solar, barrio, pueblo' ChisZ: C *nas* N *nas* 'tierra, terreno' NE [Ra] *nahs* [Tapalapa, Ocotepec, Pantepec] *nahs* [Wonderly 1949] S [Tu] *nas* [Wonderly 1949] ChZ: *nas* 'tierra, mundo'

NA#032 pOM *naht ~ nat *(vi) 'ensordecerse/to be deaf'* NHM: *naht ~ nat* MM: Ma,At,Ct <*nahtp, tɨ: nʸæt̄ʸ*> Ja <*nahtp, natá·mp̄*>

NA#033 pOM *nat *(adj) 'sordo/deaf'* NHM: *nat* MM: Ju *næt* Ma, Ja,At,Ct *nat̄* LM: Ca *nat* Gu *ku"nát*

NA#034 pM *na?aw *(n) 'anciano/old man'* [pOM *na"w] NHM: *na"v* '=viejo—p.ej., una persona; palabra de cariño para un joven' OIP: *na?a'u* SaP: *ná?way* 'viejito' [possibly borrowed from some other language after the final vowel loss]

NA#035 pMZ *nawin *(n) 'ixtle/agave fiber'* [pM *nawin (with regular loss of final nasal in OIP); pZ *nawin > pGZ *na:wiñ] OIP: *navi* SaP: *náwin* TxZ: *da:we?ñ* 'ixtle (planta), henequén' SoZ: *náwinʸ* [Foster and Foster 1948]

NA#036 pZ *nay *(vi) 'nacer/to be born'* SoZ: *nay* (vi) TxZ: *nay* (vi) 'nacer (siembra)' ChisZ: C *nay* (vi) 'nacer; germinar' N *nay*

(vi) 'brotar, germinar; brotar (figurado), empezar' NE *nay* (vi) 'nacer o brotar (como semilla)' ChZ: *nay* 'retoñar'

NU#001 pZ ***nuc** *(vi) 'caliente/hot'* AyZ: *[nduc]* 'pabellón' [?semantics] ChisZ: N *nuhc* (vi) 'estar caliente' ChZ: *nuc*

NU#002 pOM ***nuh** *(n) 'arriera/leaf-cutting ant'* NHM: *nʋh* '[Aeccodoma o Atta cephalotes]' SHM: Tl *nuh* MM: Ju *nuh* Ma,Ja,Pu,At,Ct *muh* LM: Cn <*nuh*> '[order: Hymenoptera, Atta sp.]' Gu *nuh*

NU#003 pM ***nuhn** *(n) 'tepejilote/type of palm [Chamaedorea spp.]'* [pOM **nu:hn*] NHM: *nʋ:hn* '[Chemaedorea tepejilote and other species (G. Martin, p.c.)]' MM: Ju,Ma,Ja,Pu,At,Ct *nu:n* LM: Cn <*nu:n*> 'tepejilote (tipo de palmera que produce frutito comestible) [Chamaedorea spp.]; palmera (genérico)' Ca *nu:n* Gu *nun̄* SaP: *nuh* [missing final nasal]

NU#004 pMZ ***nuk** *(vt) 'arrancar/to pull out'* NHM: *nʋhk~nʋk* 'arrancar a tirones con los dedos (p.ej., carne con nervio), arrancar (p.ej., una fruta verde), reventar (p.ej., una flor en botón)' MM: Ma <*nuk*> 'jalonear, jalar' Ja <*nuk, nʸihkʸpʸ*> 'jalonear' At <*nuk, nʸühʸkʸpʸ*> 'jalonear' Ct <*nuhkhɨdít*> 'jalonear' ChisZ: C *nuhk* (vt) 'agarrarlo, capturarlo; cazarlo; prenderlo, aprehenderlo; pegarlo' N *nuhk* (vt) 'cogerlo, agarrarlo' NE *nuhk* (vt) 'agarrarlo, prenderlo, aprehenderlo' ChZ: **nuk* [*malu~toya nukpa* 'enfermo']

NU#005 pZ ***nu?k** *(vt) 'llegar/to arrive'* SoZ: *nuk* [Foster and Foster 1948] [?] AyZ: *[ndu?k]* TxZ: *du?k* (vi) '=arrimar; brillar, alumbrar, arder, prender' ChisZ: C,N *nu?k* (vi)

NU#006 pMZ ***nuku(N(ik))** *(n) 'arriera/leaf-cutting ant'* [pM **nuku(N(ik)*; pZ **nuku?* > pGZ **nu:ku?*] OlP: *nukumi'k* SaP: *núkun* SoZ: *nu:ku?* TxZ: *du:k:u?* ChisZ: C,N *nuku* NE *nuku* '=chicatama —una clase de hormiga' ChZ: *nuku?*

NU#007 pMZ ***nu:?ks** *(vt) 'prestar/to borrow'* NHM: *nʋ:?kš* 'cansar, agonizar' [?-semantics] LM: Cn <*nukš*> (vt) 'fiar' SJ *nu·kš* OlP: *yaknu:kš* (vt) 'fiarlo; pedirle prestado, darle prestado' SoZ: *nuks* [Foster and Foster 1948] [?] TxZ: *du?ks* (vt) ChisZ: C *nu?ks* (vt) 'darlo prestado; pedirlo alquilado' N *nu?ks* (vt) 'pedirlo prestado' NE *nu?ks* (vt) 'alquilarlo, arrendarlo; emplearlo (como empleado)' ChZ: *nu?ks* 'invitar'

NU#008 pOM ***?a-nu?kš** *(vi)* '*pedir prestado/to ask for permission to borrow*' NHM: *?anv:?kš* 'prestar' MM: Ma < *?a·nú?š* > Ja < *?anú?kš ~ ?anú?š* > Pu < *?anúkš* > At < *?anú?kš* > Ct < *?a·nú?kš* > LM: Gu < *?anú·?š* >

NU#009 pOM ***?a-nu?kš-?ɨy** *(vi)* '*cansarse/to be tired*' SHM: Tu < *?anú?kšɨp, ?anu?kšinʸɨ́:* > MM: Ju < *?œnú?šɨ* > Ma < *?ɨnú?šɨpʸ* > Ja < *?anú?šɨp* > At < *?œnú?kšɨp* > Pu < *?ɨnú?kšɨpʸ* > Ct < *?anú?kšɨpʸ* > LM: Gu < *?anu·?šɨ́:pʸ* >

NU#010 pMZ ***ko-nu:ks** *[?] (vi)* '*rezar/to pray*' [Irregularity —*konu?ks* expected in Zoquean—probably due to late derivation under influence of Catholic monks.] NHM: *kunv:?kš* 'bendecir' SHM: Tl *kunu:?kš* Tp < *kʸunú?kšʸpʸ* > 'bendecir' MM: 'bendecir' Ma < *kɨnú?š* > Ja < *kunú?š* > Pu < *kɨnú!kš* > At < *kɨnú?kš, kunú?kš* > Ct < *kɨnú?kš* > LM: Gu < *kunú·?š* > 'bendecir' ChisZ: C *konuks* (vt) 'saludarlo' N *konoks* (vi) 'rezar' NE *konuks* (vi) '=orar', *konuksku?* 'rezo, adoración'.

NU#011 pOM ***ku-nu:?kš** *(adj)* '*bendito/sacred*' NHM: *kunu:?kš* MM: Ma *kɨní?šʸ* Ja *kuní?šʸ* Pu *kɨní!kšʸ* At *kunúü?kšʸ* Ct *kɨni?kšʸ* LM: Gu *kunú·?šʸ*

NU#012 pZ ***nu?m** *(vt)* '*robar/to steal, rob*' SaP: *nu?m* (vi, vt) [Zo loan] SoZ: *nu?m* (vt) TxZ: *du?m* (vi) ChisZ: C *nu?m* (vt) '=hurtarlo' N *nu?m* (vt) NE *nu?m* (vt) '=hurtarlo; arrebatarlo' ChZ: *nu?m*

NU#013 pM [Veracruz] ***nun** *(n)* '*junco/rush*' OIP: *nunɨ, nun?a:ca* SaP: *nun* [Clark 1981]

NU#014 pZ ***nu?n** *(vi)* '*arraigar/to wrinkle*' SoZ: *nu?n* 'sew' [Foster and Foster 1948] TxZ: *du?n* (vt, vi-a) 'costurar, coser' ChisZ: C *nu?n* (vi, vi-s) 'arraigarse, estar arraigado; apretarse, estar apretado; hacerse un bodoque, estar anudado' [der.: *nu?na* 'cicatriz'] N *nu?ni* 'nalga'

NU#015 pGZ ***nu:nu** *(n)* '*seno, chiche/breast of woman*' SoZ: *nu:nu?* TxZ: *du:n*

NU#016 pMZ ***nu?pu** *(n)* '*zopilote/buzzard*' [pM **nu?pu* > pOM **nu"p*; pZ **nu?pu* > pGZ **nu:?pu*] NHM: *nv"p* 'zopilote, águila ratonera, alfaneque [Coragyps atratus]' MM: At *nu"p* 'zopilote rey'

LM: Gu *nu"p* 'zopilote rey' OlP: *nu?pu* SaP: *nu?p* SoZ: *nú?upu?*
TxZ: *du:?p* '=cumbrera de casa'

NU#017 pOM ***nu:?pky** *(n) 'sanguijuela/leech'* NHM: *nu:?pk* MM:
Ju,Ma,Ct *ni?pʸkʸ* Ja *ni?pʸn̥ʸ* At *nuü?pʸkʸ* LM: Ca *nu·ʸpʸkʸ* Gu *nu·?tʸ*

NU#018 pOM ***nu:š** *(n) 'flojo (perezoso)/lazy'* NHM: *nv:š*
'flojo—p.ej., una persona—perzoso, haragán; adivino (insecto),
espectro, mántide, mantis religiosa, predicador, zacatón' MM:
Ju,Ma,Ja,At,Ct *nu:š* LM: Cn <*nu:š*> (adj) SJ *nu:ž* Ca,Gu *nu:š*

NU#019 pMZ ***nu?s** *(vt) 'cobijar/to cover'* OlP: *nu?ša'n* 'cobija,
sarape' SoZ: *nu?s* (vt) 'abrazar' TxZ: *du?s* (vt) 'abrazar' ChisZ:
C *nu?s* (vt) 'taparlo con algo extendido'; *nu?supɨ* (adj) tapado' N
nu?s (vt) 'cobijarlo' NE *nu?s* (vt) 'cobijarlo, taparlo'

NU#020 pZ ***nu?s-kuy** *(n) 'cobija, sarape, chamarra/blanket'* ChisZ:
C,N *nu?skuy* ChZ: *nu?sku?y* 'sarape'

NO#001 pZ ***no?** *(vi) 'encender/to light, set fire to'* SoZ: *no?* (vt)
'quemarlo' TxZ: *do?* (vt, vi-a) 'quemar (milpa), herrar' ChisZ: C
no? (vi) 'encenderse' N *no?* (vt) 'quemarlo' NE *no?* (vi)
'alumbrar' ChZ: *no?* 'quemar desmonte'

NO#002 pM ***no:?c** *(vt) 'comer cosa ancha/to eat something which is
disk-shaped'* [Cf. ChisZ: N *no?c* (vi) 'hacer pared de albañileria'
(vt) 'hacer pared (de albañilería; poner piedras o ladrillos en su lugar
con mezcla)'; perhaps semantic transfer where insertion of a brick is
likened to the act of eating.] NHM: *no:?c* 'comer, morder (p.ej., un
plátano)' MM: 'comer (plátano, taco)' Ju <*no:c*> Ja <*nʸo?čpʸ*,
no:c> Pu <*no:c, nʸo!čpʸ*> Ma,At,Ct <*no:c, nʸo?čpʸ*> LM: Cn
<*no·c*> (vt) 'morder' Ca <*no:c*> Gu <*no:c, no·?cp, nʸo·?čp*>
'comer (plátano, taco)' [Nordell 1990 and p.c.] SJ *no·c~no:c* 'to bite
that which requires the mouth to open wide' SaP: *no?c* (vi, vt) 'eat
tortilla'

NO#003 pM ***nok** *(vi) 'hacer ruido/to make noise'* NHM: *nohk~nok*
'sonar—p.ej., un instrumento, hacer ruido—p.ej., una lata'] MM: Ma
<*nokp*> 'sonar' At <*nohkp*> 'sonar' LM: Cn <*nohk~no·k*>
(vi) 'tronar; disparar' Gu <*yahnók, nohk, nohp*> 'sonar' SJ
nohk~nok 'to make a loud noise, crack joints' ChisZ: N *nohk* (vt)
'burlarse, desprecerlo' [?]

NO#004 pM ***noʔk** *(vt) 'encender/to burn'* NHM: *noʔk ~ noˮk* 'encender, prender fuego' MM: 'quemar (basura, monte, etc.)' Ja <*noˮk, nʸoʔk, nʸeʔkʸpʸ*> At <*noˮk, nʸöʔkʸpʸ*> Ma,Ct <*noˮk, nʸeʔkʸpʸ*> LM: Cn <*noʔk ~ noˮk*> (vt) 'quemar' Gu <*noˮk, nʸoʔk, nʸoʔpʸ*> SaP: *noʔk* (vi, vt)

NO#005 pMZ ***noki** *(n) 'papel/paper'* [pM *noki > pOM *noky; pZ *noki > pGZ **noːki?*] NHM: *nɨk* SHM: Tl *nʋky* Ay *nekʸ* MM: Ju *nekʸ* Ma *nekʸ* '=carta, amate' Ja,Ct *nekʸ* 'carta, papel, recado', *nekʸ* 'amate' [sic!] Pu *nekʸ* At *nekʸ* 'carta, papel, recado', *noökʸ* 'amate' LM: Ix <*naky*> Cn <*neky*> 'amate [Ficus sp.]; papel' Ca *noʸkʸ* Gu *nokʸ* '=carta, amate' OlP: *noki* 'papel'; *nokikuyɨ* 'amate'; *nokinɨp* 'Amapa (arroyo)' SaP: *nok* 'papel'; *nohkúhy* 'amate'; *nokpíhik* 'flor de papel SoZ: *noːki?* 'piste (semilla del zapote mamey)' AyZ: *[ndoːʔgi]* 'pantalón' TxZ: *doːke?* 'casco; semilla del zapote mamey o del palo gusano' ChisZ: NE [Ra] *noki* 'faja que se usa con los calzones' [Ox] *noki* 'calzón'

NO#006 pGZ ***nokkoy** *(n) 'pantalón/trousers'* SoZ: *nókkoy* TxZ: *dohkoy* (n) 'pantalón, calzón'

NO#007 pM ***nokoc** *(adj) 'resbaloso/slippery'* [pOM *nokc] NHM: *nókïc* 'resbaloso, jabonoso' Ma,Ja,At,Ct *nokc* 'resbaloso (en lugar lodoso)' LM: Cn <*nokc*> (adj) SJ *noks* 'slippery' Gu *nokc* 'resbaloso (en lugar lodoso)' SaP: *nógoc* 'liso'

NO#008 pGZ ***noːno?** *(n) 'hongo/fungus'* SoZ: *noːno?* 'hongo' TxZ: *kuydʸoːn* 'oreja de palo'

NO#009 pOM ***noːʔt** *(vi) 'arrugarse/to wrinkle'* [Cf. ChisZ: C [Te] <*notpa*> 'enloquecer / errar / entorpecerse', <*notpa tuyacapa*> 'loco estar, verbo', N,NE *noʔt* 'emborracharse'?] NHM: *noːʔt* 'arrugar' LM: Cn <*noːd*> (adj) 'arrugado'

PI-PO

PI#001 pMZ ***pi?c** _(vi) 'apagarse/to go out (light)'_ NHM: _pi?c ~ pi"c_
SHM: Tu <_pi?cp, tɨ: pʸi"č, tǣm pʸí?cnɨ_> Tp <_pi?cp, pi?hc,_
pi"ʒámp, tɨ: pi"č> MM: Cc <_pi?c, pi?cp, tɨ: pʸi"č, kʸǣh pʸi?č,_
pi"ʒámp> Ja <_pi?c, pi?cp_> Pu <_pi!cp_> At <_pi?cp, pí?cnɨp_>
Ju,Ct,Ma <_pi?cp_> LM: Ca <_pi?cp_> SJ _pi?c ~ pi"c_ Gu <_pi?cp,_
pi"dʒá·mp> OlP: _pi?c_ (vi) SaP: _pi?č_ (vi) AyZ: _[pi?c]_ 'apagar'
TxZ: _suhpê?č_ (vt, vi-p) 'apagar soplando'

PI#002 pMZ ***pi?c-(V)(k)** _(adj) 'obscuro/dark'_ [pM *_pi?c(i)(k)_ >
pOM *_pi"c_; pZ *_pi?cɨ_] NHM: _pi"c_ OlP: _pi?i's_ SaP: _pí?č-ik_ AyZ:
[pí?ici] 'obscuridad' TxZ: _pê:?č_ ChisZ: C,N,NE _pi?cɨ_

PI#003 pOM ***wihn-pi"c** _(vi) 'con los ojos cerrados/with closed eyes'_
NHM: _vimpi?c ~ vimpi"c_ 'cerrar los ojos' MM: Ja _wi:mbí"c_ Pu
wɨ:mbí"c Ma,At,Ct _hɨmbí"c_ LM: Gu _wi:mbí"c_

_PI#004 pM_ ***yak-pi?c** _(vt) 'apagar/to extinguish'_ NHM: _yak-_
pi?c ~ yakpi"c (vt) apagar algo, extinguir (p.ej., un incendio) SHM:
Tu <_yahkpí"c_> Tp <_yǣhkpí"c_> MM: Ju <_yǣhpí"c_> Cc
<_yAhkpí"c, yAhkpí?čpʸ_> Ma <_yahpí"c_> Ja <_yahpí"c, yahpí?čpʸ_>
At <_yǣhkpí"c, yǣhkpí?čpʸ_> Ct <_yahkpí"c_> LM: Cn
<_yahpi?c ~ yahpi"c_> (vt) Ca <_yahpí"c_> Gu <_yahpí"c,_
yahpí?čp> OlP: _yakpi?c_ (vt) apagarlo SaP: _?akpi?č_ (vt) apagar
[Clark and Clark 1960]

PI#005 pMZ ***pic-i** _(n) 'nixtamal/leached cornmeal'_ [pM *_pici_ >
pOM *_picy_; pZ *_pici_ > pGZ *_pi:či_] [Cf. OlP _pic_ (vt) 'bajar maíz',
a descendant of the form from which *_pic-i_ must be a derivative.]
NHM: _pic_ SHM: Tl _pič_ MM: Ju _pič_ Ma,Ja,Pu,Ct _pi͞č_ LM: Ca _pič_
OlP: _piči_ 'maíz bajado, maíz cocido—para nixtamal' AyZ: _[pi:ci]_

'nixtamal molido o en grano' TxZ: *pê:č* '=maíz cocido' ChisZ: C
pici S *[pi·cí?]* 'nixtamal'

PI#006 pMZ ***picɨm** *(vi) 'salir/to go out'* NHM: *pícɨm* 'salir (p.ej.,
el sol), sacar (p.ej., liberar a un preso)' MM: Ju *<picɨm>* Ma
<pɨzɨ́m̄, pɨzɨ́·mp> Ja *<pɨzɨ́m̄, pɨzɨ́·m̄, pɨzɨ́·mp>* Ma,At,Ct
<pɨzɨ́m̄, pɨzɨ́·mp> LM: Cn *<pɨdzɨ·m~pɨdzɨm>* (vi) SJ *pɨzɨ·m-
~pɨzɨm* 'to come out' Ca *<picɨm>* Gu *<pɨzɨ́m̄, pɨzɨ́·m̄,
pɨzɨ́·mp>* OIP: *picɨm* (vi) SaP: *pičin* (vi) TxZ: *pêhpeč* (n)
'sudadera' [*<- pêhE?* 'calor' + bound root] [?-reflex of last syllable]
ChZ: *picɨm*

PI#007 pM ***yak-picɨm** *(vt) 'sacar/to take out'* MM: Ma
<yahkpɨzɨ́m̄, yahkpɨzé·mpʸ> Ja *<yahpɨzɨ́m̄>* At *<yahkpɨzɨ́m̄>*
Ct *<yahkpɨzɨ́m̄, yahkpɨzé·mpʸ>* LM: Cn
<yahpɨdzɨ·m~yahpɨdzɨm> (vt) 'sacar; expulsar' Gu *<yahpɨzɨ́m̄,
yahpɨzɨ́·mpʸ>* OIP: *yakpicɨm* (vt) SaP: *?akpíchin* (vt) [Clark and
Clark 1960]

PI#008 pOM ***huma: šɨ: pyicɨm** *(adv) 'oriente/East'* NHM: *hvma šɨ:
pʸícɨm* MM: Ju *ma: šɨ: pʸicémʸ* Ma *ma: šɨ:w pʸizémʸ* Ja *ma: šɨ:
pʸizémʸ* Pu *ma: šɨ: pʸizémʸin* At *šibɨzémʸ* At *mo: šɨ:w pʸizémʸin*
LM: Gu *ma: šɨ: pʸizɨ́mʸin*

PI#009 **pi:cu** *(n) 'tordo garrapatero/bronzed cowbird [Molothrus
aenus]'* [Probably a Spanish borrowing, thus no specific time depth is
posited.] NHM: *pi:č* 'tordo garrapatero' AyZ: *[pi:cu]* 'guanchín
(pajarito negro)' TxZ: *pê:čo?~pê:ču?* 'picho (pájaro)' ChisZ: C
pičú? N *pičú* 'picho, tordo ojirojo'

PI#010 pMZ ***pih** *(vt) 'calentar/to heat'* NHM: *pih* 'ampollarse'
SaP: *píhan* 'formón' [?] SoZ: *pih* (vt) AyZ: *[pih]* 'hacer calor, estar
caliente' TxZ: *pêh* (vt, vi-p) 'calentar' ChisZ: C *pih* (vi)
'calentarse'

PI#011 pZ ***pih-pa** *(adj) 'caliente/hot'* [pGZ **pihpa*] TxZ: *pêhp*
[Clark n.d.] ChisZ: C *pihpa* (adj) NE *pihpabɨ* (adj)

PI#012 pOM ***pih-n** *(n) 'bolsa/bag'* NHM: *píhɨn* SHM: Tu *pihn̥* Tp
pihn̥, pihny Mi *pihn̥* MM: Ju,Cc,Ja,At *pihn̥* LM: Ca,Gu *pihɨʸ*

PI#013 pOM ***pihky** *(n) 'moyocuil/bot fly'* NHM: *pihk* MM: Pu
pihn̥ʸ Ja,At,Ct *pihkʸ* LM: Gu *pikʸ*

PI#014 pOM ***pi?k** *(adj)* *'chico, pequeño/little'* NHM: *pi?k* MM: Ja
pi?k?iná?k 'niño', *piginá?k* 'criatura' [sic!] At *pi?k* 'chico, niño',
pi?k?ú?ŋk 'niñito', *pi?kyǽ"y* 'niño' LM: Cn <*pi?k/pi?*> (adj)
'chico, chiquito (hablando cariñosamente)' Ca,SJ *pi?k* Gu *pi!giná?k*
'niño', *pi??iná?k* 'criatura' [sic!]

PI#015 pMZ ***pi:?k** *(vt)* *'cosechar, tocar/to harvest, touch'* MM:
Ma,Pu,Ct <*pi:k*> 'cosechar' ChisZ: C,N *pi?k* (vt) 'tocarlo' NE
pi?k (vt) 'tocarlo, tentarlo; tocarlo (como violin o piano)'

PI#016 pMZ ***piks** *(vt)* *'golpear ligeramente con algo punteado/to*
tap, pick at' MM: 'dale un coscorrón' Ju <*pihkš, pihkšp*>
'picotear', <*kupíhkš*> 'dale un coscorrón' Ma <*kipíhš, kipihší"k*>
Ja <*kupihší"k*> Pu <*kiháhpš*> At <*kupihkší"k*> Ct <*kipíhkš*>
LM: Cn <*pikš*> (vt) 'picar' (ejemplo: "los pájaros carpinteros pican
los árboles") SJ *pikš* 'to tap, pick at' Gu <*ku"bíkš*> SaP: *pih/pikš*
(vi, vt) 'chisel' ChisZ: N *piks* (vt) 'tocarlo (ligeramente con el dedo)'

PI#017 pMZ ***pi?ks** *(adj?)* *'punteado/pointed'* [pM, pOM **pi?kš*; pZ
**pi?ks* > pGZ **pi?ks*] NHM: *pi?kš* 'nudo muy apretado (p.ej., de
una reata)' TxZ: *pe?kšpe?kšde?* (vi-s) 'gotear, pingotear' [?-
semantics] ChisZ: NE *pi?kstihk* 'huso' ChZ: *pi?ksku?y* 'flecha'

PI#018 pOM ***pikk** *(adj)* *'redondo/round'* NHM: *pígik* 'bola, redondo, rollizo—p.ej., una pelota, esférico, boludo, circular, círculo'
MM: Ju *pikpi* 'bola' Ma,Ja,Ct *pik* 'redondo, bola' Pu,At *pik* 'bola'
At *pik* 'redondo' LM: Cn <*pik*> (adj) SJ *pik* Gu *pik* 'redondo,
bola'

PI#019 pM ***pikwin** *(n)* *'larva de ditisco, de la mosca Dobson/kind of*
larva' [pOM **pi:n*, with an unique loss of medial material] NHM:
pi:n MM: Pu,Ma,Ja,Ct *pi:nʸ* SaP: *píkuin* 'larva'

PI#020 pMZ ***pimim** *(vi)* *'tronar, brotar/to burst'* OlP: *pimim* (vi)
'tronar' ChisZ: C *pimi?* (vi) 'brotar'

PI#021 pMZ ***pi:?n** *(vt)* *'agarrar, tentar/to grasp, touch'* LM: Cn
<*pi·n~pi:n*> (vt) 'agarrar con las manos (p.ej., lodo o masa)' SJ
pi·n~pi:n 'to carry mud, dough with the hands' SaP: *pi?n* (vi, vt)
'pick leaves from plants' SoZ: *piñ* 'harvest, touch lightly' [Foster and
Foster 1948] [?-missing glottal stop] ChZ: *pi?n* 'tentar'

PI#022 pZ **pini** *(n) 'cuñado de hombre/brother-in-law of man'*
ChisZ: C,N,NE *pini* S [Tu] *pinitɨwɨ* [Foster 1949] ChZ: StaMaCh
pini [Foster 1949] SnMiCh *pini* [Foster 1949]

PI#023 pM **pihš** *(n) 'picho, zanate/grackle'* [pOM *pihš̃*] MM: Pu
piš̄ 'zanate' Ct *pišhó:n* 'zanate' OlP: *piši̧* 'picho (pájaro)' SaP:
píšpiš 'picho' [Clark 1961: 'zanaca (a bird)']

PI#024 pOM **pi:hš ~ pi"š** *(vi) 'soplar con la boca/to blow'* NHM:
pi:štk ~ pi:štɨk MM: Ju <*pi"š*> Ma,Ja,At,Ct <*pi"š, pʸi·s̄ʸpʸ*>

PI#025 pOM **pi"š** *(n) 'cola, rabo/tail'* NHM: *pi"š* SHM: Tl
pi?šytok 'rata' Tu,Tp *pi"šʸ* MM: Ju,Cc,Ma,Ja,Pu,At,Ct,Ca *pi"šʸ*
LM: Cn <*pi"šy*> 'cola'

PI#026 pOM **po:?p pi:?š** *(n) 'flor de Santa María, crisantemo /chry-
santhemum [Chrysanthemum spp.]'* NHM: *po:?p pi:?š* 'Santa María
(planta) [Chrysanthemum parthenium]' LM: Cn <*po:bpi:š*> 'flor de
Santa María [possibly Tagetes sp.]

PI#027 pMZ **pisi** *(n) 'yuca/yucca' [Manihot sp]* [pM *kuhy-piši* (*kuhy*
may refer to the erect nature of the plant [G. Martin, p.c.]) pOM
kuypišy; pZ *pisi* > pGZ *pi:ši*] NHM: *kupiš* 'yuca dulce, guaca-
mote' [Manihot dulce] MM: Ma *kɨbíšʸn̥ʸ* Ja *kɨbíš̄ʸ* At *koʸbʸišn̥ʸ* Ct
kɨbíšʸn̥ʸ Gu *kubíšʸt̪ʸ* OlP: *kuypiši* SaP: *kuypíš* SoZ: *pí:ši?* AyZ:
[pi:si] TxZ: *pê:še?* ChisZ: C,N,NE *pisi*

PI#028 pMZ **pi:?sisi** *(n) 'pichichi/black-bellied tree duck'* [pM
pi:?šiši; pZ *pi?sisi* > pGZ *pi?ši:ší*] OlP: *pi?šiši* SaP: *pi:šiš*
[Clark 1981] AyZ: *[písis]* 'pijiji (ave que vuela como pato' TxZ:
pe:?še:še? 'pichichi (café, parece al pato, es más chico su cuerpo y
más alto de estatura)'

PI#029 pMZ **pistɨk** *(n) 'pulga/flea'* [pM *pištɨk* > pOM *pištk* (with
loss of /t/ everywhere); pZ *pistɨk*] NHM: *pišk* '[Ctenocephalides
sp.]' SHM: Tl,Ay *pešk* MM: Ju,Ma,Ja,At,Ct *pišk* LM: Cn *piš* '[or-
der: Siphonaptera, Ctenocephalides canis, Pulex irritans]' Gu,Ca *pišk*
OlP: *pištɨ'k* SaP: *píštik* SoZ: *písytyɨk* [Foster and Foster 1948] AyZ:
[písčɨk] TxZ: *peššɨk ~ peščɨk* ChisZ: C *pistɨk* '=nigua' N *pistɨk* NE
pistɨhk '=nigua' S *[pištɨk]* ChZ: *pistɨk*

PI#030 pMZ **pistin** *(n) 'ceiba/ceiba, kapok tree'* [pM *pištin* >
pOM *pištn*; pZ *pistin* > pGZ *pištiñ*] NHM: *píštɨn* 'algodón [Gos-

sypium hirsutum]' MM: 'algodón' Ma *pišʸn̩ʸ* Ja *pisʸn̩ʸ*, *pīš* Ju,Cc, Pu,At,Ct *pišʸn̩ʸ* LM: Cn <*pi:šytiñ*> 'ceiba [Ceiba sp.]' Gu *pišʸtʸ* 'algodón' OlP: *pišti'n* 'algodón', *kuypištinkuyɨ* 'ceiba' SaP: *pɨ́štin* 'algodón', *kuypɨ́štin* 'ceiba' SoZ: *pišt̕ʸɨ́ñ* 'tree cotton' (Sp."pochote") [Foster and Foster 1948], 'tipo de palo' [Gutiérrez M. 1993] TxZ: *peše?ŋ* 'ceiba' [unexplained loss of /t/] ChisZ: C *pistiŋ* 'ceiba' N *pistin* 'ceiba' [Ceiba sp.]

PI#031 pOM ***pišy** *(n) 'algodón/tree cotton'* SHM: Tl,Tu,Tp *pišʸ* LM: Cn <*pišy*> ['Gossypium sp.'] SJ,Ca *pišʸ*

PI#032 pOM ***ca-pištn** *(n) 'cobija/blanket'* NHM: *cavíštɨn* '=sarape' SHM: Tu *caβíšʸ* Mi *cabíšʸ* MM: Ju *cæbíšʸn̩ʸ* At,Ct *cɨbíšʸn̩ʸ*

PI#033 pMZ ***pit** *(vt) 'enrollar/to roll'* NHM: **piht~pit* 'envolver' LM: Cn <*piht~pit*> (vt) 'enrollar; enredarse' (vi) 'apretar (un nudo)' SJ *piht~pit* 'to roll (cigars, wrap rope, vine, thread around something)' OlP: *pit* (vt) SaP: *pit* (vi, vt) 'wrap' SoZ: *pitʸ* 'spin' [Foster and Foster 1948] 'amarrar cruzado' [Elson 1960] ChisZ: C *piht* (vt) 'enrollarlo'

PI#034 pOM ***?a-piht~?a-pit** *(vt) 'enrollar/to roll up'* NHM *?apit* 'enrollar (p.ej., alambre)' LM: <*abiht~abit*> (vt)

PI#035 pOM ***nɨ-piht~nɨ-pit** *(vt) 'enrollar/to enroll'* NHM: *nɨpiht ~nɨpit* 'enrollar (p.ej., en un carrete de hilo)' MM: Ma <*nɨbít*> Ct <*nɨpɨ̄t*> LM: Gu <*nɨ"bɨ̄t*>

PI#036 pMZ ***pi:?t** *(vt) 'hilar/to spin thread'* NHM: *pi:?t* '=ronronear' MM: Ju <*pi?tp*> Ma <*pi?tp, pi:t*> LM: Cn <*pi·t~pi:t*> (vt) SJ *pi·t~pi:t* Ca <*pi·tp*> OlP: *pi:t* (vt) 'torcer pabilo (de algodón)' ChisZ: N *pi?t* (vi, vt)

PI#037 pOM ***pi:?t-n** *(n) 'huso, malacate/spindle'* MM: Ju *pi?tn̩* 'huso, malacate', *pi?n* 'malacate' [sic!] Ma,At,Ct *pi?tn̩* Ja *piht* 'malacate', *pihtn̩* 'huso, malacate' [sic!] LM: Ca *pi·tk* 'huso, malacate', *pitk* 'malacate' [sic!] Gu *pi·?t* 'malacate'

PI#038 pMZ ***pi:?t-i** *(n) 'hilo/thread'* [pM **pi:?ti* > pOM **pi:?ty*; pZ **pi?ti* > pGZ **pi?iti*] NHM: *pi:?t* SHM: Mi *pi:t̕ʸt̕ʸá"kʸ* 'cordel para pescar' MM: Ma,At *pi:tʸ* '=cordel para pescar' Ju,Ja,Ct,Pu *pi:tʸ* LM: Cn <*pi:dy*> Ca,Gu *pi:tʸ* OlP: *pi:ti* 'pabilo torcido' SaP: *pí?tpay* 'telaraña' TxZ: *pe:?č* 'hilo para vela, pabilo' ChisZ: N *pi?ti*

PI#039 pMZ **pitit** *(vi, vt) 'rodar/to roll'* MM: Ja <*pɨdít, pʸɨdíht, nipɨdít, nʸipɨdíhtʸpʸ*> 'enrollar' LM: Gu <*pɨdít*> 'enrollar' SaP: *pírat* 'enredar, dar vuelta, enroscar' [Clark and Clark 1960] [?] TxZ: *pê:č* (vt, vi-p) 'remangar' ChisZ: C *piti?* (vi) 'rodar' N *piti?* (vi) 'rodar' (vt) 'rodarlo' NE **piti* [*pidimɨ?n* (vi) 'rodar; caerse de algo', (vt) 'rodarlo (como una piedra)']

PI#040 pMZ **piw** *(vt) 'pepenar/to pick up'* NHM: *pi:v~pi:hv~piv* 'comer (p.ej., las aves), cosechar' SHM: Tu <*piw, mbi:pʸ*> 'cortar (café)' Tp <*piw, pi:p, pʸi:, pʸißǽmpʸ*> 'cortar (café)' MM: 'cortar (café)' Ju <*pif*> Cc <*piw, pʸi:pʸ, tɨ: tpiy, kʸœh tpi:y, pʸiwǽmpʸ, pʸi:, pi:p*> Ma <*piw~piΦ~pif, pʸi:pʸ*> Ja <*piw̥, pi·w̥, pi:p*> Pu <*piw̥, pʸi:pʸ, pʸi·w̥*> At <*piw̄, pʸi:pʸ*> Ct <*piw̄~piΦ, pʸi:pʸ*> LM: Cn <*pi·w~piw*> (vt) 'recoger (con los dedos; p.ej., granos de maíz); comer (aves); cortar (p.ej., café, tomate silvestre)' SJ *pi·w~piw* 'to pick small objects (coffee [beans], etc.)' Gu <*piw̄, pʸi:pʸ, pi·w̄*> 'cortar (café)' OlP: *piv* (vt) 'recogerlo, pepenarlo' SaP: *piw* (vi, vt) 'pick up' SoZ: *piŋ* 'gather' [Foster and Foster 1948], 'levantar' [Gutiérrez M. 1993] AyZ: *[piŋ]* '=recoger' TxZ: *peŋ* (vt, vi-p) '=recoger' ChisZ: C *piŋ* (vt) 'pepenarlo' N *piŋ* (vt) 'recogerlo' NE *piŋ* (vt) 'pepenarlo (como del suelo); cosecharlo (como chayotes)' ChZ: *pi?ŋɨy* 'amontonar'

PI#041 pMZ **piyɨ?k** *(vi) 'correr/to run'* MM: Ju <*piyɨ"k*> Cc <*piyɨ"k, piyɨ?kp, tɨ: pʸiyɨ"kʸ, piyɨ?k, piyɨ"gámp*> Ma <*piyɨ"k, piyɨɨ?kp*> Ja <*piyɨ"k, piyɨ?k, piyɨ?kp*> Pu,At,Ct <*piyɨ"k, piyɨ?kp*> LM: Ca <*piyɨ"k*> SJ *poyɨ?k~poyɨ"k* Gu <*piyɨ"k, piyɨ?p, piyɨ"?k*> OlP: *yakpiyɨ?k* (vt) corretearlo SaP: *puhɨ?k* [?] TxZ: *poykpa?t* (vt) 'encontrar (animal, a persona en el hecho), alcanzar a encontrar'

PE#001 pOM **pe?c** *(vi) 'llenar de un líquido/to fill with a liquid'* NHM: *pe?c~pe"c* 'beber desmedidamente (p.ej., agua), tragar, tomar, p.ej., en grandes bocanadas)' SHM: Tl *yikpe"c* (vt) 'extinguir incendio' LM: Cn <*pe?c~pe"c*> (vi) 'cubrir (con agua)' SJ **pe?c~pe"c* [does not occur alone; carries the idea of filling: *?a·be?cnahš* 'to overflow']

PE#002 pZ **pe?c** *(n) 'pinolillo/tick'* [pGZ **pe?c*] AyZ: *[pe?c]* 'garrapata' TxZ: *pe?c* 'pinolillo' ChisZ: C [Te] <*petz*> 'piojo del cuerpo'

PE#003 pZ ***pecV-pecV** *(n) 'verdolaga/purslane'* [pGZ **pecpe:ce*]
TxZ: *pecpece?* [penultimate vowel expected to be long] ChisZ: C [Te]
<petzu petzu>

PE#004 pM ***pehay** *(adj) 'delgado/thin'* [pOM_**pehy*] NHM: *pEhi*
SHM: Tl *pehy* MM: Ju *peh^y* Ma,Ja,Pu,At,Ct *peh^y* LM: Cn *<pehy>*
(adj) Ca,SJ *peh^y* Gu *peh^y* SaP: *péhay*

PE#005 pZ ***peka** *(adj) 'cosa vieja/old thing'* [pGZ **pe:ka*] SoZ:
péka 'old' [Foster and Foster 1948; first vowel expected to be long]
ChisZ: C,N *peka* NE *peka* (vi-s, adj) ChZ: *peka*

PE#006 pOM ***pehkš** *(n) 'cereza/cherry'* [A competing meaning
throughout OM is 'peach'; I reconstruct *'cherry' since this is a native
fruit, while the peach was brought by Europeans (G. Martin, p.c.).]
NHM: *pehkš* 'durazno' [Prunus persica], *pehkš mu:?k* 'capulín [Mun-
tingia calabura]' SHM: Tu *makpǽkš*, *mik^yp^yǽkš* Mi *cawǽkš* MM: Ja
ca:bǽhš 'durazno' Ct *pǽhkš* '=durazno' Ju,Pu *pǽhkš* Ma *pǽhš*
'=durazno' Ja *pǽhš* At *mut^yp^yǽhkš*

PE#007 pMZ ***pen** *(vt) 'apretar con los dedos/to pinch with the*
fingers' NHM: *pe:n~pe:hn~pen* 'sembrar, p.ej., ajo), apretar'
SHM: Tl *pan* MM: Cc *<pæn, ti: tpen^y>* Ma *<pæn̄>* Ja *<pæn̄,*
p^yæ·n̄, p^ye·mp̄^y> Pu *<pæn̄, p^ye·mp̄^y>* At *<pæn, ?æpæ·n̄múk>*
LM: Cn *<pe·n~pen>* (vt) 'apretar (con los dedos)' Ca *<pæn>*
Gu *<pen̄, pe·m̄p, p^ye·mp̄^y, ?abe·n̄múk>* [Nordell 1990 and p.c.] SJ
pe·n~pen 'to press down with the fingers, plant by pressing, play the
piano' OIP: *pen* (vt) 'sobarlo (una persona que compone los huesos)'
SaP: *pen* (vi, vt) SoZ: *pen* (vt) 'sobar' [Elson 1960] TxZ: *pen* (vt)
'exprimir, apretar (con los dedos), sacar (tripas de pescado)' ChisZ:
C *pen* (vt) 'apretarlo con los dedos o con la mano' N *pen* (vt) 'pre-
sionarlo con el dedo' ChZ: *pen* 'plantar (renuevo)'

PE#008 pMZ ***pe?n** *(vi) 'poner nido/to make a nest'* NHM: *pe?n*
~pe"n 'poner nido' Tp *<pæ?mp>* 'anidar' MM: Cc *<p^ye!mp^y>*
'anidar' Ja *<p^ye"n^y t^yæ·k^yp^y>* 'anidar' LM: SJ *pe?n~pe"n* 'to
make a nest' Gu *<pe"n, pe!mp̄>* [Nordell, p.c.] Cn *<pe?n~pe"n>*
(vt) 'tender' TxZ: *pe?niŋtu?m* (vt) 'abracar'

PE#009 pM ***pe?n-i** *(n) 'nido/nest'* [pOM **pe"ny*] NHM: *pe"n*
[*pE"n* expected] SHM: Tl *pa"n* MM: Ju *pæ"n* Ma *p^ye"n^y* At *pæ"n*

Ja,Pu,Ct *pe"n^y* LM: Cn *<pe?ñ>* '=heno' Ca,Gu *pe"n^y* OlP: *pe?ni'k* SaP: *pe?n*

PE#010 pM ***pepe** *[?] (n) 'especie de pájaro/species of bird'* NHM: *pEpi* 'arrendajo, gayo' [*pEp* expected] SaP: *pe:p* 'pepe (un pájaro)' [*pep* expected]

PE#011 pM ***peš** *(vt) 'menospreciar/to despise'* LM: Cn *<pehš~peš>* (vt) 'despreciar' SJ *pehš~peš* 'to belittle' SaP: *?apeš* 'insult'

PE#012 pM ***pet** *(vi) 'subir/to climb, ascend'* NHM: *peht~pet* SHM: Tl *pat* MM: 'subir (vi)' Ma *<pæt, pæhtp>* Ja *<pæt, pæhtp, p^yet^y>* At *<pæt, pæhtp, ti: p^yet^y>* Ct *<pæt, pæhtp>* LM: *<peht ~pet>* (vi) 'subir; pasar (tiempo)' Gu *<pet, pehp, p^yet^y>* SJ *peht ~pet* 'to climb; to leave, remain where placed' OlP: *pet* (vi) 'subir'

PE#013 pOM ***?a-peht ~ ?a-pet** *(vi) 'cumplir/to fall due'* NHM: *?apeht ~ ?apet* 'cumplirse la fecha de algún acontecimiento' LM: Cn *<abeht~abet>* (vi) 'terminar (año)'

PE#014 pOM ***ku-peht~ku-pet** *(vi) 'encumbrar, subir a la cumbre, pagar/to climb to the top, pay'* NHM: *kupeht ~ kupet* 'trepar, subir en la cabeza' Ma *<kibæt>* 'encumbrar, subir a la cumbre, pagar' Ja *<kubæt>* 'pagar' Pu *<kibæt>* 'pagar' At *<kibæhtp>* 'encumbrar, subir a la cumbre' LM: Gu *<ku"béht>* 'encumbrar, subir a la cumbre'

PE#015 pOM ***ni:?-peht~ni:?-pet** *(vi) 'bautizar(se)/to baptize'* NHM: *nipeht~nipet* SHM: Tu *<yahknißæt, nißætp>* MM: Ju *<nibæt>* Ma,Pu *<ni:bæhtp>* Ja,At *<nibæhtp>* Ct *<ni:bæhtp>* LM: Ca *<ni:bæt>* Gu *<nibéhp>*

PE#016 pM ***wan-pet** *(vt) 'ofrecer/to offer'* NHM: *vampeht ~ vampet* 'ofrecer' LM: Cn *<wambeht~wambet>* (vt) OlP: *vampet* (vt) 'demandarlo'

PE#017 pM ***yak-pet** *(vt) 'subir/to climb, ascend'* MM: Ma *<yahkpæt>* Ja *<yahpæt, yahpéht^yp^y>* At *<yahkpæt, yahpéht^yp^y>* Ct *<yahkpæt, yahpéht^yp^y>* LM: Ca *<yahpæt>* 'montar' Gu *<yahpét, yahpéhp^y>* 'montar' OlP: *yakpet* (vt)

PE#018 pOM ***pet(y)** *(n) 'subida/rise, ascent'* NHM: *pEt* MM: Ma *pæt* '=cuesta' Ja,At,Ct *pæt* Pu *pæt* 'cuesta' LM: Cn <*pet*> Ca *pet^y* Gu *pet*

PE#019 pOM ***peht-n** *(n) 'asador/spit (for roasting)'* MM: Ja *ca:b^yǽhņ* Ma,Ct *tɨ·cpǽhņ* Pu *tɨ·cpǽhņ, ca:b^yǽhņ* At *ca:^yb^yǽhņ* LM: Gu *ca:b^yéht*

PE#020 pOM ***maw-peht-n** *(n) 'cama/bed'* SHM: Tu *ma:ßǽht* Tp *mA:ßǽht* Mi *ma:bǽht* MM: Ju,Ma,At *ma:bǽhņ* Ja *má:bǽhņ* LM: Ca *ma:bǽht* Gu *ma:béht*

PE#021 pOM ***nɨ:?-peht-n** *(n) 'bautismo/baptism'* NHM: *nɨpehtïn* MM: Ju *nibǽtɨn* Ma,At,Ct *nɨ:bǽhtɨn* Pu *nɨ:bǽhtɨn^y* LM: Ca *nibǽhtɨn^y* Gu *nɨbét*

PE#022 pOM ***tun-peht-n** *(n) 'herramienta/tool'* NHM: *tʊmpehtïn* '=instrumentos de trabajo' MM: Ju *tu·mbǽhņ* Ma,At,Ct *tu·mbǽhņ* Ja *tu·nbǽhņ* LM: Gu *tu·mbéht*

PE#023 pMZ ***pe:t?** *(vi, vt) 'barrer/to sweep'* NHM: *pe:t~pe"t* SHM: Tl *pa?at* Tu <*pæ"t, pætp, p^ye"t^y*> Tp <*pæ"t, p^yet^yp^y, pæ·ht*> MM: Ju <*pæ"t*> Cc <*pæ"t, pætp, p^yet^yp^y, tɨ: p^ye"t^y, k^yæh p^yædɨ?k^y, pæ"dámp, p^yæ"dámp^y*> Ma <*pæ"t, pætp*> Ja <*tɨ: yahpædé"k^y*> Ja <*pæ"t, pædɨ"k, pædɨ?kp*> Pu <*pæ"t, pæ·tp, pæ:dɨ"k*> At <*pæ"t, p^yet^yp^y*> Ct <*pæ·tp, pæ"dámp, pæ:dɨ"k*> LM: Cn <*pe·t~pe"t*> (vt) 'limpiar (con machete)' Ca <*pæ"t*> Gu <*pe"t, pe·tp, p^ye·tt^yp, pe"dá·mp*> OlP: *pe:t~pe?t* (vi) SaP: *pe:t~pe?t* (vi, vt) TxZ: *pet* (vt, vi-a) SoZ: *pet* (vi-a) ChisZ: C,NE *peht* (vi, vt) N *peht* (vi, vt) '=limpiarlo con machete' ChZ: *pet*

PE#024 pOM ***pe"t-y** *(n) 'barrido/sweep'* SHM: Tp *pe"t^y* MM: Cc, Ma,Pu,At,Ct *pe"t^y* LM: Gu *pe"t^y*

PE#025 pM ***pe:t-an** *(n) 'escoba/broom'* [pOM *pe:tn] NHM: *pe:tïn* SHM: Tl *pa:ht* MM: Ju *pætņ* Ma *pæ:dɨ?kņ, pæ·tņ* Ja *pædɨ?kņ* Pu *pæ:dɨ!kņ* At *pæ·tņgá?cņ, pæ·tņ* Ct *pæ·dɨ?kņ, pæ·tņ* LM: Cn <*pe:t*> Ca *pæ·tk* Gu *pe·tk* OlP: *pe:ta'n* SaP: *pé:tan*

PE#026 pZ ***pet-kuy** *(n) 'escoba/broom'* [pGZ *petkuy] AyZ: [*petku*] TxZ: *pet-ko?* '=escoba (planta)' ChisZ: C,N,NE *petkuy* ChZ: *petku?y*

PE#027 pZ ***pe?t** *(vt) 'trenzar/to braid'* TxZ: *yak-pe?t* (vt-caus) 'poner en fila' ChisZ: C *pe?t* (vt) '=tejerlo' N,NE *pe?t* (vt)

PE#028 pOM ***pe?typyt** *(adj) 'ágil, liso/agile, smooth'* NHM: *pE?tpit* 'ligero, ágil, presto' MM: Ju *pe?tʸpʸ* Ma *pe?tʸpʸ* '=liviano' Ja *pe?tʸpʸ* 'ágil, de prisa, liso, rápido' Pu *pe!tʸpʸ* 'ágil' At *pe?tʸpʸ* 'ágil, rápido', *pe?tʸpʸ, pe?tʸm̥ʸ* 'liso, liviano' Ct *pe?tʸpʸ* 'ágil, liso, de prisa, rápido, liviano' LM: Ca *pe?tʸpʸ* Mz,Gu *pe?tʸ* 'liviano'

PE#029 pZ ***peye?** *(vt) 'ondear/to wave'* TxZ: *pe:y* (vt) 'mecer' ChisZ: N *peyepeyeney* (vi) 'ondear'; *peyepeyewɨy* (vt) 'hacerlo ondear' NE *peye?* (vt) 'hacerlo ondear'

Pɨ#001 pOM ***pɨ"c** *(n) 'caña de maíz/cornstalk'* MM: Ju,Ma *pɨ?č* At,Ct *pɨ?č* '=rastrojo, acahual' LM: Cn <*mo:kpɨ"c*> 'cañuela de maíz (maíz especial que se cultiva para forraje)' Gu *pɨ"'c*

Pɨ#002 pMZ ***pɨh** *(vi) 'inflar, florear/to swell up, flourish'* NHM: *pɨh* 'reventar, tronar (p.ej., un cohete), florear, agrietar (p.ej., una piedra), detonación' SHM: *pɨh* 'estallar' MM: Ma <*pɨhp, tɨ: pʸɨhʸ*> 'explotarse, florear, reventar (globo, etc.), poncharse, espigar' Ja <*yahpɨh, pɨh, pɨhp, pɨhá·m̄p*> 'poncharse, florear, explotarse, reventar (globo, etc.), espigar' Pu <*pɨhp*> 'florear' At <*pɨhp, pɨhá·m̄p, tɨkpɨhɨp, tɨkpɨhɨyá·m̄p*> 'florear, explotarse, reventar (globo, etc.)' Ct <*pɨhp, tɨ: pʸɨhʸ, pɨhám̄p*> 'florear, explotarse, reventar (globo, etc.), poncharse, espigar' LM: Cn <*pɨh*> (vi) 'florecer; explotar' Ca <*pɨhp*> 'espigar' Gu <*pɨ̈h, pɨ̈hp, pɨ̈há·m̄p, yahpɨ̈h, tɨ̈: pʸɨ̈hʸ*> 'reventar (globo, etc.), explotarse, florear, poncharse, espigar' OlP: *pɨh* (vi) 'abrirse (flor); reventar; empollar' SaP: *pɨh* (vt) 'bloom' TxZ: *-pɨ:h-* (vi) engordarse, (vt) remojar SoZ: *pɨh* 'become fat' [Foster and Foster 1948], *pɨ:* 'engordar' [Elson 1960] ChisZ: C *pɨh* (vi, vi-s) 'esponjarse, estar esponjado; inflarse, estar inflado' (vt) 'inflarlo' N *pɨh* (vi) 'resoplar, estornudar (un animal)'

Pɨ#003 pMZ ***pɨhi** *(adj) 'largo/long'* [pM *pɨhi; pZ *pɨhi > pGZ **pɨ:hi*] OlP: *pɨhicana'y* 'voladora (culebra)' SoZ: *pɨ:hi?* 'gordura' TxZ: *pɨ?y-kɨ?da:?* (adj) 'talludo (monte)' [?] ChisZ: C [Co] *pɨy* [Te] <*puey*> 'largo' N,NE *pɨhi* ChZ: *pɨhi~kɨ?pɨ̈hi* '=largo'

Pɨ#004 pMZ ***pɨhi(k)** *(n) 'flor/flower'* [pMZ **pɨhi(k)* > pOM **pɨhy*]
NHM: *pɨh* SHM: Tl,Tm,Ay *pɨhʸ* MM: Ju,Ma,Ja,Pu,At,Ct *pɨhʸ* LM:
Cn <*pɨhy*> Ca *pɨhʸ* Gu *pïhʸ* OlP: *pɨhi* SaP: *píhik*

Pɨ#005 pOM ***mok-pɨh-y_** *(n) 'flor de maíz/maize flower'* NHM:
mokpïh Ma,Ja,At,Ct *mo·kpɨhʸ* LM: Gu *mo·kpïhʸ*

Pɨ#006 pMZ ***pɨk** *(n) 'pelo, pluma/skin, feather'* [pM, pOM **pɨhk*;
pZ **pɨk*] NHM: *pɨhk* 'pelo de animales, pluma' SHM: Tl,Ay *pɨhk*
'pluma' OlP: *pɨki* SaP: *pɨhk* SoZ: *pɨk* AyZ: *[pɨk]* 'pluma' TxZ: *pɨk*
ChisZ: C *pɨk* '=lana' N *pɨk* NE *pɨhk* '=lana' ChZ: *pɨk* 'pluma'

Pɨ#007 pMZ ***ʔaw-pɨk** *(n) 'barba/beard'* [See pMZ **ʔaw* 'mouth'.]
SaP *ʔau-pɨhk* ChisZ: C *ʔaŋbɨk* 'bigote'

Pɨ#008 pMZ ***kɨʔ-pɨk** *(n) 'vello del brazo/hair of the arms'* [See pMZ
*kɨʔ 'hand'.] OlP: *kɨʔpɨki* SaP: *kɨʔpɨhk* '=vello de los manos' TxZ:
kɨ́:ʔpɨk

Pɨ#009 pM [Veracruz] ***win-kuy-pɨk** *(n) 'cejas/eyebrows'* OlP:
vinkuypɨki SaP: *winguypɨhk*

Pɨ#010 pMZ ***pɨk** *(vt) 'llevar, recoger/to carry, gather'* [Analyses of
Mixe data whereby the meanings 'hurt' (intr) and 'take' (tr) are both
assigned to the same (polysemantic) verb are legitimate; but the meaning 'hurt' is not just idiomatic as, e.g., Eng. "to 'catch' cold", it is
attested everywhere and thus basic. Since this meaning is restricted to
Mixean I set up two etyma.] NHM: *pɨhk ~ pɨk* 'ganar (p.ej., dinero),
llevar (p.ej., ropa), unido en matrimonio, tomar (p.ej., una esposa)'
SHM: Tu <*pɨk, pɨhkpʸ*> 'casarse' Tp <*pɨk, pɨhkp, tɨ: pʸikʸ, pɨhk,
pɨkámpʸ*> 'casarse' MM: Ju <*tɨ: pʸekʸ*> 'casarse' Ma <*pɨk,
pʸehkʸpʸ*> 'llevar (papel)', <*pɨhkpp, pɨhktɨp*> 'casarse' Ja <*pɨk,
pɨhk, pɨka·m̄pʸ*> 'llevar (papel), casarse' Pu <*pɨhkpʸ*> 'casarse' At
<*pɨhkp, pɨhktɨp*> 'casarse' Ct <*pɨk, pa·pɨ́k*> 'llevar (papel)' LM:
Cn <*pɨhk ~ pɨk*> (vt) 'agarrar (para apropiarse de ello); aprender
(fig.)' (vi) 'casar' SJ *pɨhk ~ pɨk* 'to marry; to take away, buy' Ca
<*pɨk*> 'llevar (papel), casarse' Gu <*pïkʸ, pïhp ʔahˢ̌ʸ*> 'casarse'
OlP: *pɨk* (vt) 'tomarlo, agarrarlo' [also: *kɨpi-pɨk* 'traer leña'] SaP: *pɨk*
(vt) 'take, get, marry' SoZ: *pɨk* 'agarrar' TxZ: *pɨk* (vt) 'tomar,
traer, agarrar (para llevar)' ChisZ: C *pɨhk* (v impersonal) 'convener,
deber; ser necesario traceptarlo, tomarlo, cogerlo' N *pɨhk* (vt)

'agarrarlo, tomarlo' NE *pɨhk* (vt) 'cogerlo, tomarlo (como con la mano); agarrarlo' ChZ: *pɨk* 'coger'

Pɨ#011 pMZ ***ʔis-pɨk** *(vi) 'estudiar/to study'* NHM: *ʔišpɨhk* ~ *ʔišpɨk* 'estudiar, persona educada e instruída, civilisado' SHM: Tl *yik?išpɨk* (vt) 'enseñar' MM: 'estudiar' Ju < *ʔišpɨk* > ' =aprend<u>er</u>' At < *ʔišpɨk* > 'aprender', < *ʔišpɨhkp* > 'estudiar' Ma < *ʔišpɨk* > Ja < *ʔašpɨk* > LM: Cn < *išpɨhk* ~ *išpɨk* > (vi) 'aprender' Ca < *ʔišpɨk* > 'estudiar' TxZ: *ʔêš-pɨk* (vt) 'conocer' ChisZ: C,N *ʔispɨhk* (vt) 'conocerlo' NE *ʔispɨhk* (vt) 'conocerlo; reconocerlo' ChZ: *ʔispɨk* 'conocer'

Pɨ#012 pOM ***yak-ʔiš-pɨhk** ~ **yak-ʔiš-pɨk** *(vt) 'enseñar/to show'* NHM: *yak?išpɨhk* ~ *yak?išpɨk* 'instruir a alguien, enseñar a alguien, educar' LM: Cn < *yah?išpɨhk* ~ *yah?išpɨk* > (vt) 'enseñar'

Pɨ#013 pOM ***ʔiš-pɨhk-pa** *(n) 'estudiante/student'* NHM: *ʔišpɨhkpa* MM: Ju *ʔišpɨhkpɨ* Ma *ʔišpɨhkpɨ* 'estudiante', *ʔispɨhkpɨ* 'escuela' Ja *ʔašpɨhkpɨ* At,Ct *ʔišpɨhkpɨ* LM: Ca *ʔišpɨhkpɨ*

Pɨ#014 pOM ***yak-ʔiš-pɨhk-pa** *(n) 'maestro/teacher'* NHM: *yak?išpɨhkpa* ' =profesor' LM: Cn < *yah?išpɨhkpɨ* >

Pɨ#015 pOM ***ʔan-pɨhk** ~ **ʔan-pɨk** **[with n -> m/p]** *(vi) 'hacer calor/to be warm'* NHM *ʔampɨhk* ~ *ʔampɨk* ' =tener calor' LM: Cn < *ambɨhk* ~ *ambɨk* > (vi)

Pɨ#016 pM ***hokos-pɨk** *(vi) 'calentar/to heat'* NHM: *hokšpɨhk* ~ *hokšpɨk* _'entibiar, calentar SHM: Tu *ho?kšpɨk* MM: Ju *hokšpɨk* Ma *hokšpɨk* Pu *hokšpɨhkp* OlP: *hokošpɨk* (vi) 'calentarse'

Pɨ#017 pOM ***ku-pɨhk** ~ **ku-pɨk** *(vi) 'aceptar/to accept'* SHM: Tu < *kupɨk, mgupɨkʸpʸ* > Tp < *kupɨk, ku?pɨk* > MM: Ju < *kupɨk* > _Cc < *ku?pɨk* > Pu _< *kɨpɨk* > Ja < *kupɨk* > 'recibir' At < *kupɨk* > 'recibir', < *kupɨk, kʸupéhkʸpʸ* > 'aceptar' Ct < *kɨpɨk* > LM: Ca < *ku·bɨk* > 'recibir' Gu < *ku"bɨk* > OlP: *pɨkilat* 'deber' [?] SaP: *pɨhki* 'deber' [?]

Pɨ#018 pOM ***mɨk-pɨhk** ~ **mɨk-pɨk** *(vi) 'recobrar la fuerza/recuperate'* NHM: *mɨkpɨhk* ~ *mɨkpɨk* 'poner fuerte, endurecer' LM: Cn < *mɨkpɨhk* ~ *mɨkpɨk* >

Pɨ#019 pMZ ***nɨːʔ-pɨk** *(vi) 'acarrear agua/to carry water'* [See pMZ **nɨːʔ* 'water'.] OIP: *nɨːpɨk* (vi) 'acarrear agua' ChisZ: C *nɨʔpɨhk* (vi) 'traer agua, acarrear agua'

Pɨ#020 pOM ***yak-taʔc-pɨhk ~ yak-taʔc-pɨk** *(vt) 'asegurar, apretar/to secure, squeeze'* SHM: Tu <*yahktaʔcpɨ́k*> MM: Ju <*yæhtaʔcpɨ́k*> Ma,Ja <*yahtaʔcpɨ́k*> At <*yæhktaʔcpɨ́k*> Ct <*yahktaʔcpɨ́k*> LM: Gu <*yahtaʔcpɨ́k*>

Pɨ#021 pM ***pɨk** *(vi) 'doler/to hurt'* SHM: <*pɨk*> MM: Ja <*pɨhkp, pɨká·m̄p*> Ma,Pu,At,Ct <*pɨhkp*> LM: Gu <*pɨ̈hp*> Cn <*pɨhk~pɨ·k*> (vi) SJ <*pɨhk~pɨk*> 'to be sick' OIP: *pɨk* (vi) SaP: *pɨk*

Pɨ#022 pOM ***pɨhk-ʔɨy** *(vi) 'estar enfermo/to be ill'* NHM: *pɨkhɨ* MM: Ma <*pɨ́hkɨp, kæh pʸékʸɨyɨ*> Ja,Ct <*pɨ́hkɨp*> Pu <*pɨ́hkɨp, kæh pʸékʸɨ*> At <*pɨ́hkɨp, kʲæh pʸékʸɨ*> LM: Gu <*pɨ̈́hkɨp, kah pʸɨ̈gʸɨ́ː*> OIP: *pɨkɨpaʔ* (n) 'enfermo'

Pɨ#023 pOM ***pɨhkɨʔk ~ pɨhkɨ"k** *(vi) 'guardar/to keep, guard'* NHM: <*pɨhkɨk*> 'repartir (p.ej., partes iguales de algo), dividir)' MM: Ju <*pɨhkɨ"k*> Ma <*pɨhkɨ"k*> 'guardar, recoger (papel), apartar' Ja <*pɨhkɨ"k*> 'recoger (papel)', <*pɨgɨ"k, pʸɨgéʔkʸpʸ*> 'guardar' [sic!] Pu <*pɨgɨ"k, pʸɨgéʔkʸpʸ*> At <*pɨhkɨ"k, pʸɨhkéʔkʸpʸ*> Ct <*pɨhkɨ"k*> '=apartar' LM: Ca <*pɨgɨ"k*> Gu <*pɨ̈gɨ"k*> 'recoger (papel)'

Pɨ#024 pM ***pɨʔkš** *(vt) 'dar una palmada/to slap'* NHM: *pɨʔkš* 'pegar (p.ej., una bofetada), abofetear, bofetada, manotada), abofetear, bofetada, manotada (p.ej., el león)' OIP: *pɨʔkš* (vt) 'echar tortillas; tortear la masa' SaP: *pɨʔkš* (vi, vt) 'slap, pat (tortillas)'

Pɨ#025 pOM ***pɨhm ~ pɨm** *(vt) 'construir/to construct'* NHM: *pɨːm ~pɨːhm ~pɨm* 'hacer (p.ej., construir algo), poner, construir, crear' MM: Ma <*pɨm̄, tiː mbe·m̄pʸ*> 'plantar plantitas, hacer (to make), poner muchas cosas' Ja <*pɨ·m̄p*> 'plantar plantitas', <*pɨm̄, pʸɨ·m̄, pʸe·m̄pʸ*> 'poner' Pu <*pɨm̄, pʸe·m̄pʸ, pʸɨmǽ·m̄pʸ*> 'hacer (to make)', <*pɨm̄, tiː mbe·m̄pʸ*> 'plantar plantitas' At <*pɨm̄*> 'poner muchas cosas', <*pʸe·m̄pʸ*> 'poner muchas cosas' Ct <*pɨm̄, pʸe·m̄pʸ, pʸɨmǽmpʸ*> 'poner'

Pɨ#026 pZ ***pɨʔm** *(vi) 'gemir/to moan'* SoZ: *pɨʔm* (vi) 'pujar' TxZ: *pɨʔm* (vi) 'pujar' ChisZ: C *pɨʔm* (vi) 'bramar, mugir; quejarse, gemirse; rugir' N *pɨʔm* (vi) NE *pɨʔm* (vi) 'quejarse; rugir (como un león)' ChZ: *pɨʔm* 'sufrir'

Pɨ#027 pZ ***pɨmi** *(adv, adj, n) 'fuerte, recio, fuerza'/strong, strength'* [pGZ **pɨːmi*] SoZ: *pɨːmi* 'fuerza' TxZ: *pɨːm* (n) 'fuerza', (adv) 'recio, fuerte' ChisZ: C *pɨmi* '=aliento' N *pɨmi* NE *pɨmi* '=(vi-s) estar/ser fuerte—como una persona' ChZ: *pɨmi* 'fuerte'

Pɨ#028 pMZ ***pɨn** *(n) 'hombre/man'* [**pɨn* reconstructed for all subgroups; pM meaning is 'who, who?'] NHM: *pɨn* 'cuál, quien' SHM: *pɨn* '¿quien?' MM: Ju *pɨn* '¿quien?, alguien' Ma,Ja,At,Ct *pɨ̄n* 'alguien, ¿quien?' Pu *pɨ̄n* 'alguien' LM: Cn <*pɨn*> (pron interr) '¿quién?' (pron rel) 'que' Ca *pɨn* '¿quien?, alguien' SJ *pɨn* 'who' Gu *pɨ̄n* '¿quien?, alguien' OIP: *pɨn* (pron interr) 'quién?', (adv) 'probablemente' SaP: *pɨn* 'quien' [Clark 1961: 'who, someone'] ChisZ: C *pɨn* N *pɨn* 'hombre, persona, gente' NE *pɨt* S [Tu] *pɨn* [Wonderly 1949] ChZ: *pɨn* 'hombre, gente'

Pɨ#029 pZ ***cinu-pɨn** *(n) 'abeja/bee'* [pGZ **čiːñu-pɨːšin*, with regular reduction of the first morpheme under composition; GZ innovated the shape of the second compound member, but the compound as such must be pZ.] TxZ: *čeñpɨːñ* '=avispa' ChisZ: C *cinuhpɨn* N *cinu pɨnbɨn* NE *cinubɨt*

Pɨ#030 pM ***ni pɨn(a)** *(pron) 'nadie/nobody'* NHM: *nipɨna* MM: Ju *ni pɨn* At *ni pɨ̄n* LM: Ca *ni pɨn* Gu *ni pɨ̄n, ne pɨ̄n, nɨ pɨ̄n* OIP: *nipɨn* 'ninguno'

Pɨ#031 pOM ***pɨnɨ** *(part) 'si/if'* NHM: *pɨn* MM: Ma,Ja,Ct *pɨn* At *pɨnɨ* LM: Gu *pɨ*

Pɨ#032 pZ ***pɨʔn** *(vi) 'flotar/to float'* TxZ: *pɨʔn* (vi) 'nadar' ChisZ: C *pɨʔn* (vi) 'flotar, sobrenadar'

Pɨ#033 pOM ***pɨʔŋyky** *(adj) 'blando (colchón, etc.)/soft (mattress, etc.)'* NHM: *pɨ"hntk* 'suavecito, tibio, sedoso' SHM: Tp *pɨ!ŋʸkʸ* MM: Cc,Pu *pɨ!ŋʸkʸ* Ma,At *peʔŋʸkʸ* Ct *peʔŋʸk*

Pɨ#034 pZ ***pɨs** *(vi) 'sudar/to sweat'* SoZ: *pɨs* 'sanar' [Gutiérrez M. 1993] [?] ChisZ: C *pɨhs* (vi) N *pɨs* (vi) 'sudar' (vt) 'echarle agua'

Pɨ#035 pMZ ***pɨs-V(k)** *(n) 'sudor/sweat'* [pM **pušik* > pOM **pušyk*; pZ **pusA*] NHM: *púšik* 'sudor' ChisZ: C *pɨhsaʔ* N *pɨsɨ* NE *pɨhsɨy* 'sudar'

Pɨ#036 pGZ ***pɨ:šiñ** *(n) 'hombre/man'* [This is most probably the descendant of pMZ **pɨn* suffixed with *-cin*, a honorific borrowed from Classical Nahuatl.] SoZ: *pɨ:šiñ* [Wonderly 1949] AyZ: *[pɨ:si]* TxZ: *pɨ:ñ* '=señor'

Pɨ#037 pZ ***pɨ?t** *(n) 'envolver/wrap'* TxZ: *pɨ?t* (vi) 'pelarse' (vt) 'envolver' ChisZ: N *pɨ?tu* 'musgo', *ku?yupɨ?tu* 'musgo (en un árbol)' [lit., 'wrapper of tree'], *ca?pɨ?tu* 'musgo (en una piedra)' [lit., 'wrapper of stone']

Pɨ#038 pOM ***pita"k** *(vi) 'levantar/to carry'* SHM: *pɨti"k* 'levantar' MM: Ju <*pɨhtá"k*> 'poner muchas cosas' Ma <*pɨhktá"k*> 'poner muchas cosas, meter (en la lumbre)' Pu <*pɨhktá"k*> 'meter (en la lumbre)' Ct <*pɨhktá"k*> 'poner muchas cosas' LM: Ca <*pɨhktá"k*> 'poner' SJ *pɨdɨ?k ~ pɨdɨ"k* 'to get up' Gu <*pɨdá"k*> 'poner'

Pɨ#039 pZ ***pɨŋ** *(vi) 'reventar/to burst'* TxZ: *pɨŋ-ket* (vi) 'caer (persona o cosa con exepción de arena, agua, etc.)' ChisZ: C *pɨŋ* (vi) 'reventarse' (vt) 'reventarlo' N *pɨŋ* (vi) 'reventarse; hacer erupción' NE *pɨŋ* (vi) 'reventarse (como un globo); estallar'

Pɨ#040 pM ***pɨ:yV(n)** *(n) 'caña de otate/wild cane'* [pOM **pɨ:?y*] NHM: *pɨ:?y* 'camelote, zacate camelote' [Oplismenus holciformis] OIP: *pɨ:yi* SaP: *pɨ:yan*

PA#001 pZ ***pa?** *(vt) 'cernir, colar/to strain, filter'* SoZ: *pa?* TxZ: *pa?* (vt) ChisZ: C *pa?* (vt) N,NE *pa?* (vt) 'colarlo'

PA#002 pZ ***pac** *(vt) 'aplastar, golpear/to squash'* SaP: *pac* (vi, vt) 'clap hands', (vt) 'fill up (containers)' [a Zo loan] SoZ: *pac* 'tirar' TxZ: *pac* (vt) 'tender (en el suelo)' ChisZ: C,NE *pahc* (vt) 'aplastarlo' N *pahc* (vt) 'golpearlo; machacarlo' ChZ: *pazɨy* 'tirar'

PA#003 pMZ ***pa:c** *(n) 'zorrillo/skunk'* [pM, pOM **pa:hc*; pZ **pac*] NHM: *pa:c* '[Mephitis macroura and also Spilogale sp. and Conepatus sp.]' SHM: *po:hc* MM: Ju *pæc* Ma,Ja,Pu,At *pa·c̄* Ct *pac̄* LM: Cn <*pa:c*> '[Mephitis spp.]' Ca *pa·c* Gu *pa·c̄* SaP: *pa:hc* ChisZ: C,N *pac* NE *wɨhpacihi* [?] ChZ: *pac*

PA#004 pMZ ***paci** *(n) 'lagartija/lizard'* [pM **paci* > pOM **pacy*; pZ **paci* > pGZ **pa:č̌i*] MM: Ma,Ja,Pu,Ct *pæč̄* 'pasarríos, basilisco' LM: Gu *pač̄* 'pasarríos, basilisco' OIP: *pač̌i* 'cuascorope, basilisco—lagartija que tiene cresta' SaP: *pač* SoZ: *pá:či* 'lizard, large variety' [Foster and Foster 1948], *pa:či?* 'iguana' [Gutiérrez M. 1993] AyZ: *[pa:ci]* TxZ: *pa:č* 'iguana' ChisZ: C *pacih* N *paci* 'iguana' ChZ: *paci* 'camisa' [?]

PA#005 pM ***paciC** *(adj) 'lleno/full'* [pOM **pacn*] NHM: *pácïn tv:* 'aguacero' SaP: *pácik* 'lleno'

PA#006 pMZ ***?aw-wah(-e)** *(n) 'colmillo de los animales/canine tooth of animals'* [pM **?aŋwah* > pOM **?awah*; pZ **?aŋwahe*] NHM: *?avah* '=dientes caninos de animales' ChisZ: NE *?aŋbahe*

PA#007 pGZ ***pah** *(vt) 'recluir/to shut up'* SoZ: *pah* 'encerrar' AyZ: *[pah]* 'encajar (poste, macana)' TxZ: *pah* (vt) 'tapar (olla, vaso), cerrar (ventana, puerta), cobijar'

PA#008 pZ ***pah** *(vi) 'tener diarrea/to have diarrhea'* [The pZ status secured by the derived form **pah-i* reconstructible for pZ.] ChisZ: N *pah* (vi) 'tener diarrea'

PA#009 pZ ***pah-e** *(n) 'diarrea/diarrhea'* [pGZ **pa:he*] SoZ: *pa:hi?* ChisZ: N *pahe*

PA#010 pMZ ***pa:h?** *(vt) 'cincelar, escoplear/to chisel'* NHM: *pa:h~pa"* 'escoplear'_MM: At <*pa"*, *pʸæ!pʸ*> Ct <*pa"w*, *pʸæ!pʸ*> 'escoplear' Ma <*pah*, *pʸæhpʸ*> 'escoplear' Ja <*pah*, *pʸæhpʸ*> LM: SJ *pa?w~pa"w* 'to chisel' Gu <*pa"w*, *pʸa!pʸ*> OlP: *pa:h~- pa?h* (vt) 'clavarlo' TxZ: *pahpahde?* (vi-s) 'sonar (hacha al árbol, machete a la leña)' ChisZ: C [Te] <*papa*> 'hincar palos'

PA#011 pOM ***pa:h-n** *(n) 'formón/wide chisel'* NHM: *pa:hïn* MM: Ju,Ma,Ja *pahṇ* At *pa!n* Ct *pa"n*, *pa:n* 'formón para piedras' LM: Ca *pa"n* Gu *pa!nt*

PA#012 pMZ ***pahak** *(n, adj) 'dulce/sweet'* [pM **pa?ak* > pOM **pa"hk*; pZ **pahak* > pGZ **pa?ak*] NHM: *pa"hk* 'dulce, panela' SHM: Tl *po"k* 'dulce, miel' SHM: Tu *pa"k* 'azúcar' MM: 'azúcar, panela, dulce' Ju,Ma,Ja,Pu,At,Ct *pa"k* 'panela' LM: SJ *pa"g* Cn *pa"k* (n, adj) 'panela; dulce' Ca,Gu *pa"k* 'dulce, panela' OlP: *pa?a'k* SaP: *pa?k* SoZ: *pá?ak* TxZ: *pa:?k* ChisZ: C,N *pa?ak* 'dulce, sabroso con sal o azúcar' NE *pa?ahk* S *[pa?ák]* ChZ: StMaCh *pa?ak* SnMiCh *pahak*

PA#013 pZ ***kana-pahak** *(adj) 'salado/salty'* SaP: *ka:mpá?k* [Zo loan] ChisZ: N *kana pa?ak* NE *kanaba?ak* (adj)

PA#014 pOM ***po:?p pa"hk** *(n) 'azúcar/sugar'* NHM: *po:?p pa"hk* MM: Ju *po:ppá"k* LM: Cn <*po:bpa"k*> Ca,Gu *po:ppá"k*

PA#015 pMZ ***pahak-?ɨy** *(vi, vt) 'endulzar/to sweeten'* NHM: *pa?ahki~pa?ahka* MM: Ma,Ct <*pá"g?ɨpʸ*> Ja,At <*pá"gɨp*> LM: Gu <*pa"gɨ̌:pʸ*> OIP: *pa?ki:pa* 'se está endulzando' ChisZ: C *pa?ahkɨy* (vt) 'endulzarlo' NE *pa?ahkɨy* (vt) 'endulzarlo'

PA#016 pZ ***pak** *(vt) 'mover horizontalmente contra algo/to move horizontally against something'* TxZ: *macpak* 'retener' (Clark n.d.) SoZ: *pak* 'wrestle' [Foster and Foster 1948], 'mover horizontalmente contra algo' [Elson 1960], 'tumbar' [Gutiérrez M. 1993] ChisZ: C *pahk* (vt) 'golpearlo, amontonarlo' N *pahk* (vi) 'cerrarse bien', (vt) 'golpearlo' NE *pahk* (vt) ChZ: *yakpak* (vt) 'apretar (en general)'

PA#017 pOM ***pak** *(n) 'paloma/dove'* NHM: *pak* 'paloma de collar (también: tórtola, huilota, paloma escamosa, paloma piquinegra, paloma con alas blancas, paloma suelero) [Columba fasciata (also: C. speciosa, C. nigrirostris, Zenaida asiatica, Z. macroura, Leptotila verreauxi)]' MM: Ju *pæk* Pu,At *pak* LM: Ca *pak* TxZ: *pakpakde?* (vi-s) 'sonar (ave papaloteando, caballo sacudiéndose sus cascos)' [?]

PA#018 pZ ***pak** *(n) 'arroyo/brook'* [pGZ **pak*] TxZ: *pak-tuŋ* '=manantial' SoZ: *-pak* ChZ: *pak*

PA#019 pMZ ***pakV** *(adj) 'viejo (cosa)/old (thing)'* [pM **pakV* > pOM **pak*; pZ, pGZ **pakV*] NHM: *pak* 'viejo (p.ej., huaraches de medio uso)' MM: Ma,At *pak* SaP: *pak* (vi, vt) 'fade' (vi) 'fade (cloth)' TxZ: *pakde?* (vi-s) 'tirado (trapo)'

PA#020 pMZ ***pak** *(n) 'hueso/bone'* [pM, pOM **pahk*; pZ, pGZ **pak*] NHM: *pahk* SHM: Tl *pohk* MM: Ju,Ma,Ja,Pu,At,Ct *pahk* LM: Cn <*pahk*> 'hueso' <*pahk pahk*> (adj) 'muy flaco' Gu,Ca,SJ *pahk* OIP: *pakɨ* 'hueso, semilla; flaco' SaP: *pahk* SoZ: *pak* 'bone, seed' [Foster and Foster 1948] AyZ: *[pak]* TxZ: *pak* '=espinilla, pie, paso' ChisZ: C,N *pak* NE *pahk* S [Tu] *pak* [Wonderly 1949] ChZ: *pak* [homonym: 'arroyo']

PA#021 pOM *?**ɨš-pahk** *'cadera, nalga/hip, buttocks'* SHM: *?išpahk*
'buttocks' SHM: Tu *?išpáhk* Mi *?iškopkpáhk* [?] MM: Ma,Ja,Pu,At
?išpáhk LM: SJ *?išpahk* 'buttocks' Gu *?išpáhk*

PA#022 pMZ *?**a:ka-pak** *(n)* *'cachete, mejilla/cheek'* [See pMZ
?a:ka 'cheek, edge'.] NHM: *?akopk* 'cachete' MM: 'quijada' Ju
?æbáhk Ma,Ct *?a·báhk* Ja *?a·báhk, ?apáhk* At *?abáhk* OIP:
?a:kapakɨ 'quijada' SaP: *?a:kpɨhk* 'barba' SoZ: *?ákpak* 'mejilla'
TxZ: *?akpak* [homonym: 'palo tres lomos'] ChisZ: C *?akapak* NE
?akpahk ChZ: *?aka pak* 'mejilla'

PA#023 pOM *?**a-pahk** *(n)* *'pico, hocico/beak, snout'* NHM: *?apahk*
LM: SJ *?a·bahkpa?t* 'jaw bone'

PA#024 pMZ *hɨ:pak** *(n)* *'olote/corncob'* [pZ *hɨpak] NHM: *hɨpk*
'=tusa de maíz' SHM: Tl *hɨpk* MM: Ma *hɨp̄k* Ja,Pu *hɨ·p̄k* At,Ct,Ju
hɨpk LM: Cn <*hɨ:p*> Gu *hɨ̈·p̄k* OIP: *hɨ:pa'k* SaP: *hɨ:pak* TxZ:
hɨ:?pak ChisZ: C,N *hɨpak* NE *hɨbak* ChZ: *hɨpak*

PA#025 pOM *hɨhn-pahk** *(n)* *'brasa/red-hot coal'* NHM: *hɨmpahk*
SHM: Ay *hɨmbohk* Tu *hɨ:mbáhk* MM: Ma *hɨmbáhk* Ju,Ja,Pu,At
hɨ:mbáhk Ct *hɨ:nbáhk* LM: Ca *hɨ:mbáhk* Gu *hɨ̈:mbáhk*

PA#026 pM [Veracruz] *hu?-pak** *(n)* *'pierna/thigh'* OIP: *hu?pa'k*
'piernas (rodilla para abajo)' SaP: *hú?pak* 'espinilla de la pierna'

PA#027 pM [Veracruz] *kapap-pahk** *(n)* *'costillas/ribs'* NHM: *kak*
'=pecho' [?] OIP: *kapapakɨ* SaP: *kabahpáhk* 'costillas', *kábap*
'costado'

PA#028 pZ *kuk-pak** *(n)* *'pecho/chest'* AyZ: *[kukpak]* TxZ: *kukpak*
ChisZ: C *kukpak* 'pecho, pechuga' N *kukpak* NE *kukpahk* 'pecho
—como de un hombre'

PA#029 pMZ *ko-pak** *(n)* *'cabeza/head'* [pM *kopák* > pOM
kupáhk; pZ *kopak* > pGZ *ko:pak*] NHM: *kupáhk* 'skull' [Craw-
ford 1963: 69] *kuvahk* '=cráneo' [Schoenhals and Schoenhals 1965]
SHM: Tl *kupohk* Tu,Tp,Ay *kuβáhk* Mi *kuwáhk* MM: Ju,Pu,Ct,-
Cc,Ma *kɨbáhk* Ja *ku"báhk,* [Alotepec] *kobahk* [Wonderly 1949] LM:
Cn <*kowahk*> Ca,SJ *kwahk* Gu *ku"báhk* OIP: *ko?pa'k* SaP: *kópak*
'=cerro' TaM: *?angopik* 'my head' [Wonderly's transcription of
1949] SoZ: *kó:bak* [Foster and Foster 1948] TxZ: *kopɨk* [*ko:pak*

expected] ChisZ: C *kopak* '=copa' NE *kobahk* N *kopak* '=copa del árbol' S *[kopák]* ChZ: StaMaCh *kopak* SnMiCh *kopak*

PA#030 pMZ ***ko-pak-pak** *(n) 'cráneo/skull'* MM: Ju *kubahkpáhk* Ma,At *kɨbáhk* Ja *kubáhk* Pu *kɨbáhkpáhk* Ct *kɨpáhk* LM: Ca *kupáhk* [Nordell 1990; Wonderly 1949] Gu *ku"báhk* TxZ: *kok-pak* 'caballete (cima de una casa), parte superior del cráneo'

PA#031 pM ***košo-pahk** *(n) 'rótula/knee cap'* [See pMZ **koso(k)* 'knee'.] NHM: *koš pahk* OlP: *košopakɨ* SaP: *košpáhk*

PA#032 pOM ***mok-pahk** *(n) 'maíz desgranado/corn grains'* [See pMZ **mo:k* 'corn'.] NHM: *mokpahk* MM: Ju *mokpáhk* Ma,Ja,Pu,At, Ct *mo·kpáhk* LM: Cn *<mo:kpahk>* Gu *mo·kpáhk*

PA#033 pMZ ***win-pak** *(n) 'frente; mecapal/forehead; tumpline'* [See pMZ **win* 'eye'.] OlP: *vimpa'k* 'frente, mecapal' SaP: *wimpáhk* SoZ: *wíñpak* 'frente' TxZ: *wêñpak* 'cara; en frente de' ChisZ: 'mecapal' C,N *winbak* NE [Ra] *winbahk* [Tapalapa, Ocotepec] *witmbak* [Wonderly 1949] [Pantepec, San Bartolomé] *winbahk* [Wonderly 1949] [Chapultenango] *widbak* [Wonderly 1949] S *[winbák]*

PA#034 pOM ***yu?k-pahk** *(n) 'clavícula/collarbone'* SHM: Tu *yu?kpáhk* MM: Ju *yo!kpáhk* Ma,Ja,At,Ct *yo?kpáhk* At *yukpáhk* LM: Gu *yo?páhk*

PA#035 pZ ***paki** *(adj) 'duro/hard'* OlP: *pakpa'k* ChisZ: C *paki* 'duro' (adv) 'fuertemente, recio; firme' N *paki* 'madera dura (del corazón del árbol)' NE *paki* (vi-s, adj) 'macizo; duro; fuerte—como un palo' ChZ: *paki?*

PA#036 pOM ***pahky** *(n) 'tipo de zacate/a kind of grass'* NHM: *pahki* 'tipo de pastura para zacate' LM: Cn *<pahky>* 'tipo de zacate'

PA#037 pMZ ***pakVk** *(n) 'frío/cold'* [pM **pakik* > pOM **pakyk*; pZ, pGZ **pakak*] MM: Ma,Ja,Pu,At,Ct *pækʸ* LM: [LM forms seem to have had the meaning 'ice'.] Mz *pækʸɨ* 'luego, liso' Gu *pákʸɨ* 'luego, liso' OlP: *pakik* (vi) SaP: *páyik* SoZ: *págak* 'cold' [Foster and Foster 1948] AyZ: *[pága?k]* TxZ: *pa:k* (adj) ChisZ: C *pákak* (adj, n) N *pákak* NE *pákak* (n) S *[pakák]* 'frío'

PA#038 pZ ***paks** *(vt) 'doblar/to fold'* TxZ: *paksɨŋtu?m* (vt, vi-p) 'plegar, doblar (lona)' ChisZ: C,N,NE *paks* 'doblarlo'

PA#039 pOM **pa?kš** *(n) 'marchar/to chew'* NHM: *pa?kš* 'marchar'
MM: 'paladar' Ju *pa?kšṇ* Ma *pa?š*, *?a·bá?š* Pu *pa!kšṇ* At *pa?kš*,
?abá?kš, pa?kšwí:n Ct *?a·bá?kš*

PA#040 pMZ **pa?m** *(vi) 'atorarse/to become stuck'* [The pMZ status
suggested by the cognate pOM derivative **pa"m* 'enfermedad'; but
note that the semantic similarity is weak.] ChisZ: N *pa?m* (vi) 'atorarse' NE **pa?m* [*pa?mcyɨ?y* (vi) 'trabarse (como un caballo en el
lodo)'; *cɨ?y* (vi) 'quedarse']

PA#041 pOM **pa"m** *(n) 'enfermedad/illness'* NHM: *pa"m* SHM:
Tl *pa?m* MM: Ju,Ma,Ja,Pu,At,Ct *pa"m* LM: Cn <*pa?m*> Ca,Gu
pa"m

PA#042 pOM **wihn-pa"m** *(n) 'mal de ojo/evil eyes'* NHM: *vimpa"m*
MM: Ma,At *hɨmbá"m* Ju,Ma *wi:mbá"m* At *wi:nmbá"m* Ja *winbá"m*
Pu *wi·mbá"m* Ct *wi·m̄bá"m, hɨmbá"m* LM: Gu *wi:mbá"m*

PA#043 pGZ **pa:n** *(vt) 'hacer en almácigo/to plant in containers*
before moving the plants to a natural environment' SoZ: *pa:n* (vt)
TxZ *pa:n* (vt, vi-p)

PA#044 pMZ **panac** *(adj) 'resbaloso/slippery'* [pM **panac* > pOM
*panc; pZ **panac*] MM: Ma,At,Ct *pa?nc* 'guapetate' OlP: *pana's*
'jonote—un árbol' SaP: *panackúhy* 'jonote—un árbol' AyZ: [*pána?c*]
TxZ: *pa:?na?c* (adj) '=liso' ChisZ: C,N *panac* NE *panac-*

PA#045 pMZ **paps** *(vi) 'rajar/to split'* OlP: **papš* [*papš-ka?* (vi)
'desbrazarse, caerse una rama'] ChisZ: N *paps* (vi) 'rajarse'

PA#046 pM **paš** *(vi) 'golpear a un poste/to pound down a pole'*
SHM: Tp <*pʸahšʸpʸ*> 'armar casa' MM: Cc <*pʸahšʸpʸ*> 'armar
casa' LM: SJ *pahš~paš* 'to put up certain poles in roof construction'
Gu <*paš, pahšp*> 'varillar casa' [Nordell, p.c.] SaP: *paš* (vi, vt)
'pound, beat' ChisZ: C [There is a verb possibly containing a cognate
fossilized root. The entry form is *kyɨpa?sa?ɨyu* (vt) 'echó paral, puso
paral'.]

PA#047 pM **paš-i** *(n) 'vara/stick'* [pOM **pašy*] NHM: *paš* 'larguero (muy delgado); *pašpɨc* pared, cerco de palos relleno de piedra
y barro, jarreado de barra y piedra' MM: Ma *pæš̄ʸṇʸ* Ja,Pu *pæš̄ʸ* At
paš̄ʸṇʸ Ct *pæš̄ʸṇʸ* LM: Gu *paš̄ʸ* OlP: *paša'n* 'vara, vara para enjaular
casa' [reanalysis: suffixation of *-an* 'instrumental'] SaP: *paškúhy* 'chi-

lillo, palo delgado' [Clark and Clark 1960] TxZ: *pašša?* 'carnizuelo' [?]

PA#048 pZ ***pasoŋ** *(n) 'calabaza/squash'* [pGZ **pa:suŋ*] SoZ: *pá:suŋ* AyZ: *[pa:ṣu]* TxZ: *pa:suŋ* 'vagina', *das-pa:suŋ* 'calabaza' ChisZ: C *pahsun* N *pasuŋ* 'calabaza, chayote' NE *pahsok* S *[pasóŋ]* ChZ: *pasoŋ*

PA#049 pZ ***?apit-pasoŋ** *(n) 'chayote/chayote'* ChisZ: C *?apitpahsun* N *?apit pasuŋ* NE *?abitpahsuk* ChZ: *?apit*

PA#050 pGZ ***kuy-pa:suŋ** *(n) 'chayote/chayote'* SoZ: *kuypa:suŋ* TxZ: *kuypa:suŋ*

PA#051 pOM ***pa?t** *'debajo, debajo de algo/down, under something'* NHM: *pa?tkup* MM: Ju *pa?t?išmúk* 'falda' LM: Ca *pa?tk* 'falda' SJ *pa?tkɨ"by* [*pa?t* means 'under'] 'llano'

PA#052 pM ***pa?t-a:m** *(adv) 'abajo/down'* [pOM **pa?ta:m*] NHM: *pa?tm* 'llano grande' LM: SJ *pa"da·m* 'lower in the lay of the land; more or less straight and not too much lower' Ca *pɨda:m* Gu *pa"da:m* SaP: *patám* 'lugar abajo'

PA#053 pOM ***pa?t-kɨ?py** *(adv) 'abajo, debajo/down, underneath'* SHM: Tl *patki?py* 'abajo' Tp *pA?tkɨ?pʸ* 'abajo' MM: Ja *pa?tke?pʸ* 'abajo' Ju *patkɨ?p* 'debajo' Ma,Ja,Ct *pa?tké?pʸ* 'debajo' Pu *pa?tké!pʸ* 'debajo' At *pǽtké?pʸ* LM: Ca *pa?tkɨ?pʸ* 'debajo'

PA#054 pZ ***?aŋ-pa?t-e** *(adj) 'bastante, muy/much'* SoZ: *?ága* 'mucho' [Foster and Foster 1948] [?] ChisZ: C *?aŋba?te* (adj) 'abundante, bastante, mucho, muchos; (adv) bastante, mucho; (pron) bastante, mucho, muchos' N *?aŋba?te* (adv) 'muy' NE *?aŋba?de* (adj) 'bastante, mucho; (pron) bastante, mucho'

PA#055 pMZ ***pa:?t** *[?] (vt) 'encontrar/to find'* NHM: *pa:t~pa:?t* 'hallar, encontrar' SHM: Tl *po:t* 'encontrar' Tu <*pa:t, pʸaɨʸpʸ*> 'alcanzar (algo que está arriba)' MM: Ju <*pa:t*> 'encontrar' Ma <*pa:t, pʸa·ɨʸpʸ*> 'encontrar', <*pa:t*> 'conseguir' Ja <*pa:t, mba·ɨʸpʸ, pʸa·ɨʸpʸ*> 'encontrar' At <*pa:t, pʸæ·ɨʸpʸ*> 'encontrar', <*pa:t*> 'conseguir' Ct <*pa:t, pʸæ·ɨʸpʸ*> 'encontrar' LM: Cn <*pa·t*> (vt) 'encontrar; merecer; adivinar' (vi) 'llegar la hora' Gu <*pa:t, pʸa·ɨʸp*> 'encontrar' LM: SJ *pa·t~pa:t* 'to find' OlP: *pa:t* (vt) 'encontrarlo' SaP: *pa:t~pa?t* 'find' TxZ: *pa?t* (vt) SoZ: *pat* 'meet' [Foster and Foster 1948] ChisZ: C *pa?t* (vt) 'encontrarlo, hallarlo; descubrirlo; conseguirlo; encontrarlo, toparlo' N *pa?t* (vt) 'encontrarlo; darle (con algo tirado)' NE *pa?t* (vt) 'encontrarlo, hallarlo' ChZ: *pa?t* 'encontrar'

*PA#056 pM [Veracruz] *ki?-pa:?t 'casarse/to marry* OlP: *niki?pa:teh* 'boda, casamiento' SaP: *ki?pa?t* 'casarse' TxZ: *ki?pa?t* (vt) 'ayudar' [?-semantics]

*PA#057 pOM *nahc-pa:?t (vi) 'alcanzar (en el camino)/to pass (in the road)'* SHM: Tu <*naspá:di, mnaspá·htip*> Tp <*nAspá:di* ~*næcpá:di, nʸæhcpá·htip, nʸæhcpA:diȳæmpʸ, nʸæhcpá·htiy*> MM: Ju <*næspá:di*> Cc <*nAhcpá:di, nʸAhcpát?ipʸ, nʸAhcpA:diȳæmpʸ, nʸAhcpát?iy, ti: tnAhcpá:di, kʸæh tnAhcpát?iy*> Ma,Ct <*nahcpá:di, nʸahcpá·t?ipʸ*> Ja <*našpá:di, nʸašpá·t?iy*> Pu <*nahcpá:di*> At <*næhcpá:di, nʸæhcpá·tip*> LM: Ca <*nahcpa·tá"k*> Gu <*nahcpa:dï"w, naspa:dï"w*>

*PA#058 pOM *yak-pa:?t (vt) 'encontrar/to find'* NHM: *yakpa:t* ~*yakpa:?t* 'encontrar a alguien o algo' LM: Cn <*yahpa·t*> (vt) 'buscar' (vp) 'encontrarse, hallarse'

*PA#059 pZ *pata (n) 'petate/mat'* [pGZ *pa:ta?] SoZ: *pa:ta?* AyZ: *[pa:?ta]* TxZ: *pa:ta?* ChisZ: C,N *pata* NE [Chapultenango] *para* [Wonderly 1949] [Tapalapa, Ocotepec, Pantepec] *pada* [Wonderly 1949] [Ra] *pada* S [Tu] *pata* [Wonderly 1949] S [Cp] *[pa·?ta?]* ChZ: *pata?*

*PA#060 pM *pa:taš (n) 'langosta/locust'* NHM: *pa:č* '=langosta voladora' SaP: *pa:taš* [Clark 1981]

*PA#061 pZ *paŋ (vt) 'poner algo en posición vertical/to fix something in a vertical position'* TxZ: *paŋ* (vt) 'zurquear, clavar (poste o palo)' ChisZ: C *paŋ* (vt) 'pararlo, ponerlo parado (ejemplo: "el muchacho paró la leña para que se secara")' N *paŋ* (vt) 'picarlo, punzarlo (ejemplo: "la peya pica el maíz cuando está en chapayita")'

*PA#062 pM *paw-an (n) 'metate/grinding stone'* [pOM *pa:n, with a unique loss of a medial consonant.] NHM: *pa:n* SHM: Tl,Ay *po:n* MM: Ju,Ma,Ja,Pu,At,Ct *pa:n* LM: Cn <*pa:n*> Ca,Gu *pa:n* OlP: *pa?a'n* SaP: *pá:wan*

PA#063 pM ***pa?aw** *(n) 'orilla/shore, edge'* [pOM *pa?aw] NHM: pa:?ʋ MM: Ju pa" 'borde, orilla' Ma pya"f, pʸa"Φ, pʸa"w̥ 'borde', pa?á:y 'orilla' Ja,At pa?á:y 'orilla' Ct pa?á:y 'orilla' LM: Ca,Gu pa" 'orilla, borde' OlP: pa?a'u TxZ: pay (vt, vi-a) 'bordar' [?-phonology]

PA#064 pZ ***paya?** *(vt) 'rayar/to streak'* TxZ: ?ɨskpa:yčukuba: (n) 'comadreja (nombre descriptivo que se refiere a su franja blanca)' [?-according to native folk etymology pa:y is from pa:yo? 'paño' and not a native nominalized verb] ChisZ: C paya? (vt) 'arañarlo; rayarlo' N paya? (vi) 'estar rayado' (vt) 'rayarlo'

PA#065 pOM ***payɨm** *(n) 'mataculebra, pepegua/venomous ant'* MM: Ja payɨ̄m 'mataculebra, pepegua, hormiga cazadora' Pu pɨyɨ̄m 'mataculebra, pepegua grande' At payɨ̄m 'mataculebra, pepegua grande', pæyɨ̄m 'hormiga cazadora' [sic!] Ct pa:yɨ̄m 'mataculebra', pa·yɨ̄m 'pepegua grande, hormiga cazadora' [sic!] LM: Gu payɨ̄m 'mataculebra, pepegua, hormiga cazadora'

PU#001 pMZ ***pu:c?** *(vi) 'podrir/to rot'* NHM: pʋ:c ~ pʋ"c ~ pʋ"c SHM: Tl puc MM: Ma <pu·c̄p, pu"z̧ámp> 'podrirse (madera, etc.)' Ja <yahpu"c, pu·c̄, pu·c̄p, pu"z̧á·m̄p> 'podrirse' At <pu·c̄p, pu"z̧á·m̄p> 'podrirse' Ct <pu·c̄p> 'podrirse (madera, etc.)', <pu·c̄p, pu"z̧ámp> 'podrirse' LM: Cn <pu?t ~ pu"t> (vi) 'pudrir; tener mugre' Gu <yahpu"c, pu·c̄, pu·c̄p, pu"z̧á·m̄p> 'podrirse' OlP: pu:c ~ pu?c (vi) SaP: pu:c ~ pu?c (vi) ChisZ: C puhc (vi,vt) N puhc (vi) NE pucpɨ? (vi)

PU#002 pMZ ***pu:c?(-i)** *(n) 'grano de la piel/pimple'* [pM *pu?uc > pOM *pu"hc] NHM: pʋ"hc '=podrido' SHM: Tl,Ay pu"c MM: 'granos (sores)' Ju,Pu pu"c Ma pu"c '=podrido (madera, etc.), podrido (fruta, etc.)' Ja,Ct pu"c '=podrido (fruta, etc.)' At pu"c '=podrido (fruta, etc.), llaga' LM: 'granos (sores)' Ca pu"c Gu pu"c '=podrido (fruta, etc.), llaga' OlP: pu?u's (adj) 'podrido' SaP: pu?c 'grano' SoZ: pu:či? 'basura' ChisZ: C puci N puci '=basura' NE puci 'llaga, nacido' ChZ: puci

PU#003 pMZ ***pu?c(V)** *(adj) 'amarillo/yellow'* [pM, pOM *pu?c; pZ *pu?cV] NHM: pʋ?c SHM: Tl pʋ?c Tu,Tp,Mi pu?c MM: Ju,Cc,Ma,Ja,At,Ct pu?c Pu pu!c LM: Cn <pu?c> (n) Gu,Ca,SJ pu?c OlP: pu?spu's SaP: pú?cpuc SoZ: pú?uč AyZ: [pú?ci] 'amarillo' TxZ: pu:?čê? (adj) 'amarillo, güero (como persona)'

ChisZ: C *pu?cɨ* (adj) '=güero' N *pu?cɨ* NE *pu?cɨ* (vi-s) 'estar/ser amarillo'; (adj) 'amarillo'; (n) 'güero' ChZ: *pu?ci?*

PU#004 pMZ *pu:ci (n) 'basura/waste' [pM **pu:ci*; pZ **puci*] SaP: *pú:cpuc* ChisZ: C *pucih* NE *pucih* '=desperdicio' ChZ: *pucpuc*

PU#005 pM *puc-ta?k (n) 'basura/waste' [pOM **pu?cta"k*] SHM: Tl *pɨsto"k* Tu *pɨstá"k* Tp *pistá"k* MM: Ju *postá"k* Cc *poctá"k* At *pɨštá"k, puhštá"k* LM: Gu *pu!s̆k* OIP: *pu?cɨ'k* [irregular loss of /t/ and vowel change]

PU#006 pM *pu:cɨk (n) 'ombligo/navel' [pOM **pu:ck*] NHM: *pʋ:ck* '=yema' SHM: Tl *puck* MM: Ju *puck* 'ombligo' Ma,Ja,Pu, At,Ct *pu·c̄k* 'ombligo' LM: Cn <*pu:c*> Ca *pu·ck* Gu *pu·c̄k* OIP: *pu:cɨ'k* SaP: *pú:cɨk*

PU#007 pMZ *puh (vt) 'lavar/to wash' NHM: **pʋh* [*pʋhva:c ~pʋhva?ac* 'lavar bien'; *tukpʋh* lavar por dentro'; *vimpʋhnahs̆ ~vimpʋhnás̆* 'lavar ligeramente'‚ 'enjuagar'; *vitïpʋh_* 'lavar ropa'] MM: Ju <*puh*> Ma,Pu,Ct <*puh, mbihpʸ*> Ja <*puh, pʸihpʸ*> At <*pʸühpʸ*> LM: Cn <*puh*> (vt) Ca <*puh*> Gu <*puh, pʸuhpʸ*> OIP: **puh* [*ni:puh* (vt) 'lavarlo (p.ej., las manos, un plato)'; *puhtay* (vi) 'lavar trastes'] TxZ: *puh-a?y* (vt) 'soplar líquido (despues de enjuagarse la boca)'

PU#008 pM *kɨ?-puh (vi) 'lavarse las manos/to wash hands' NHM: *kɨpʋh* OIP: *kɨ?puh* (vr)

PU#009 pM *pu? (n) 'arena/sand' [pOM **pu"*] NHM *pʋ"* '=quebrado' SHM: Tl *pu?* Tu,Tp *pu?h* MM: Ju,Cc,Ma,Pu,At,Ct *pu"* LM: Cn <*pu?*> Ca *pu̧"* Gu *cɨbʸú"* OIP: *pu?ɨ*

PU#010 pMZ *puh (n) 'semilla/seed' [**puh* reconstructed for all subgroups] [In NHM attested in *puhk* (Heliocarpus Donnell-Smithii; a kind of tree) from pMZ **puh-kuy*, lit., 'seed tree' (see this). According to G. Martin (p.c.) the term 'seed tree' makes perfect sense in relation to the Heliocarpus Donnell-Smithii, so there is no doubt that the etymology is right.] LM: Ml *puh* 'grano' SaP: *pu:h* AyZ *[puh]* TxZ: *puh* '=testículos' ChisZ: C *puh* '=pepita' N *puh* NE *puh* 'pepita' ChZ: *puh*

PU#011 pM *pu?hɨk (n) 'cera/wax' [pOM **pu"hk*] NHM: *pʋ"hk* SHM: Tl,Tp *pu"k* 'cera negra' MM: 'cera negra' Ju *pu"k* Cc *pu!ŋk*

Ma,At,Ct *pu?ŋk* LM: Gu *pu"k* 'cera negra' OlP: *pu?hɨ'k* SaP: *pú?hɨk*

PU#012 pMZ ***pu?huyu** *(n) 'correcamino, tapacamino/roadrunner'* [pM **pu?huyu*; pZ **pu?huyu* > pGZ **pu:y*] OlP: *pu?huyu* SaP: *puhuyuy* [Clark 1981] [Possibly borrowed from Zoquean after the general process of loss of final vowels had set in.] AyZ: *[púguyu?]* 'tapacamino' [?phonology] TxZ: *pu:y* 'tapacamino' ChZ: *pu?huyu?* 'tapacamino'

PU#013 pM ***pu:k ~ pu?k** *(vi) 'completar/to finish'* NHM: *pv:k ~ pv"k* OlP: *pu:k ~ pu?k* (vi) 'completarse'

PU#014 pM ***pu?k-(ik)** *(adj) 'completo/complete'* [pOM **pu?k*] NHM: *pv?k* 'tupido' OlP: *pu?ki'k* (adj) 'completo'

PU#015 pGZ ***pu:ki** *(n) 'algodón/cotton'* SoZ: *pú:ki* TxZ: *pu:k*

PU#016 pMZ ***pu?ks** *(vi) 'pintar, madurar/to gain color, ripen'* OlP: *pu?kš* (vi) 'pintar, madurar'; *pu?kši'k* (adj) 'pintón (se dice de la fruta en proceso de maduración)' SaP: *pu?kš* (vi) 'ripen, change color (fruits)' AyZ: *[pu?ks]* 'podrirse' TxZ: *pu?kš-kɨ?da:?* (adj) 'muy pálido, chipujo' N *pu?ksyi* (adj) 'pálido'

PU#017 pM [Veracruz] ***puktun** *(n) 'cocuyo/eyed elater'* OlP: *puktu'n* SaP: *puktun* [Clark 1981]; *pú:ktun* [Clark and Clark 1960]

PU#018 pM [Veracruz] ***pumpum** *(n) 'sulisuchi/frangipani' [Plumeria rubra]* OlP: *pumpu'm* SaP: *pumbumkuhy* 'apompo' [Clark 1981]

PU#019 pZ ***pu?n** *(vi) 'nadar/to swim'* SoZ: *pu?n* (vi) AyZ: *[pu?n]* ChisZ: N *pu?n* (vi)

PU#020 pZ ***pu:nɨ(k)** *(n) 'pus/pus'* [pGZ **pu:nɨk*] SaP: *pú:nɨk* [Zo loan] SoZ: *pú:nɨk* AyZ: *[pu:nu?k]* TxZ: *pu:?nu?k* [vowel-leveling] ChisZ: C,NE *punɨ* N *punɨ* '=savia' ChZ: *pu?ɨ?*

PU#021 pZ ***pup** *(vt) 'sacudir/to shake'* ChisZ: C *puhp* (vt) 'sacudirlo' ChZ: *pup* 'regar semilla'

PU#022 pM ***pu:p** *(n) 'nácara/a kind of fish'* [pOM **pu:p*] MM: Ma,Ja,Pu,At,Ct *pu:p* LM: Gu *pu:p* OlP: *pu:pɨ* SaP: *pu:p* [Clark 1981]

PU#023 pMZ ***pu?pu** *[?] (n) 'intestino/intestines'* [Phonological developments are not under control.] OlP: *pu?pu* 'barriga' SoZ: *pú?u*

[Foster and Foster 1948], *pú?u?* [Gutiérrez M. 1993] TxZ: *pu?*
'=tripas' ChisZ: C,NE *pu?u* N *pu?u* '=tripas' ChZ: StaMaCh
pu?hu? SnMiCh *puhuk*

PU#024 pM ***puš** *(vt) 'cortar con machete/to cut with a machete'*
NHM: *pvhš~pvš* 'trozar, cortar (p.ej., con machete)' SHM: Mi
<*naypʸušïdï*> MM: Ju,Cc <*puš*> Ma <*puš̄, puhšp*> Ja <*puš̄,*
pʸuhš> 'cortar (con machete)', <*pʸuhšʸpʸ*> 'picotear' Pu <*puš̄,*
pʸuhšʸpʸ> At <*puš, pʸuhšʸpʸ*> 'cortar (con machete)', <*puhšp*>
'picotear' Ct <*puhšp, pʸuhšʸpʸ*> 'picotear' LM: Cn <*puhš~puš*>
(vt) 'cortar' SJ *puhš~puš* 'to chop, cut with machete, axe' Ca
<*puš*> Gu <*puš̄, puhšp, pʸuhšʸp*> OlP: *puš* (vt) 'derribarlo (un
árbol)' SaP: *puš* (vi, vt) 'cut with axe, machete'

PU#025 pM ***puš-an** *(n) 'hacha/axe'* [pOM **puhšn*] NHM *pvhšïn*
'hierro, hacha' SHM: *puhš* 'fierro, metal' MM: 'fierro, metal' Ju
puhšn̩ '=campana' Ma *puhšn̩* '=machete, acero, campana' Ja *puhšn̩*
'=campana, acero, machete' Pu *puhšn̩* '=machete' At *puhšn̩* Ct
puhšn̩ '=machete' LM: Cn <*puhš*> 'machete; campana; cualquier
metal' SJ **puhš* [*puhštïhk* 'jail'] Ca,Gu *puhšt* 'machete, metal,
fierro, campana' OlP: *puša'n* 'fierro, campana' SaP: *púšan* 'fierro,
campana'

PU#026 pMZ ***pus?-a?y** *(v) 'botar (semilla, etc., en un recipiente)/to*
throw (seeds, etc., in a container)' NHM: *?apv:?ša* 'echar granos en
un recipiente a fuerza de golpes' LM: Cn <*abu:šï?*> (vt) 'echar
(granos en un recipiente)' TxZ: *pus-a?y* (vt, vi-p) 'botar (tierra,
basura en otro lugar), tirar', *pus-ksa* (vt, vi-p) 'tirar (tierra), regar
(semilla)'

PU#027 pMZ ***pu?si(s)** *(n) 'pedazos/pieces'* [pM **pu?šiš*; pZ **pu?si*]
OlP: *pu?ši'š* 'pedazos' ChisZ: N *pu?ši* 'tortilla tostada con frijoles'

PU#028 pM [Veracruz] ***puša(n)...** *(n) 'paila/straw'* OlP:
pušanyu?u'k SaP: *pušanšúy*

PU#029 pM ***pu?šu(m)** *(n) 'polvo/dust'* [pOM **pu?šm*] NHM: *pv"š*
'basura' MM: Ma *pu?šp* '=basura' Ct *pu?šp* 'basura' *pu!šp*
'polvo' [sic!] Ja *pu!šm̩* '=basura' Pu *pu!šm̩* 'basura' At *pu?šm̩*
LM: Ca *pu"šp* 'basura' Cn <*pu"š*> 'basura' SaP *pu?š* OlP: *pu?šu*
(adj) 'menudo'

PU#030 pOM *?a-pu?šm* *(n) 'migaja, piltrafa/crumb, piece'* NHM:
?apv"š '=miga' LM: Cn <*abu"š*>

PU#031 pOM **pu:šypy** *(n) 'vapor/vapor'* NHM: *pušïš* '=vaporar'
SHM: *pušky* MM: Ma *pu·s̃ᵖpʸ* Ja *pu·s̃ᵖpʸ* 'vapor despues de la lluvia'
At *pu·s̃ʸ*

PU#032 pM [Veracruz] **pu:t-šïhw** *(n) 'mediodía/noon'* OlP: *pu:šïvï*
SaP: *pu:tšïhw*

PU#033 pMZ **put** *(vi) 'saltar/to leap'* SHM: 'correr' Tl *put* Tu
<*put, puhtp, tæm̄ pʸut͂ʸ*> Tp <*put, puhtp, puht, putámp*> MM: Ju
<*put, puhtp*> '=brincar' Cc <*put, puht͟p*> 'brincar' Ma <*put̄,
puhtp*> 'latir (el corazón), brincar', <*put, puhtï"k*> 'saltar' [sic!]
Ja <*puhtp*> 'latir (el corazón)' Pu <*puhtp*> 'latir (el corazón)'
At <*puhtï"k, puhtï?kp*> 'saltar', <*puhtp*> 'latir (el corazón)' Ct
<*puhtp*> 'latir (el corazón)', <*puhtï"k*> 'saltar' LM: Cn
<*puht~pu·t*> 'latir' SJ *puht~put* 'to beat (heart), jump' SoZ: *put*
(vi) 'salir' TxZ: *put* (vi) 'salir' ChisZ: C *puht* (vi) 'salir' N *puht*
(vi) 'salir; resultar' NE *puht* (vi) 'salir (como de la casa); brotar
(como agua)' (vt) 'hacerlo salir, dejarlo salir'

PU#034 pOM **putïhk~putïk** *(vt) 'ayudar/to help'* SHM: Tu
<*puδïkḭ, mbuδïhkïp*> MM: Ju <*pudïkï*> Ma <*pu"díkï*> Ja
<*pu"díkḭ, pʸu"díhk?ïy, pʸu"d̲íhk?ïp*> Pu <*pu"díki, pʸu"díhkïpʸ*>
At <*pudïkú*> Ct <*tïkpu"díkï*> LM: Cn <*pudïgï?*> '=unirse con
otro'

PU#035 pOM **puhtï?k~puhtï"k** *(vi) 'brincar/to hop'* NHM: *pvhtïk*
'levantarse (p.ej., contra de alguien o a servir a alguien)' SHM: Tu
<*puhtï"k*> MM: Ma,At,Ct <*puhtï"k*>

PU#036 pOM **putte:ty** *(n) 'epazote/goosefoot [Chenopodium
ambrosioides]'* NHM: *putEt* SHM: Tl *putte:tʸ* MM: Ju *pundé:č* Ma,
Ja,Ct *pu"dé:tʸ* At *pudé:tʸ* LM: Cn <*pu"de:dy*> 'hierba epazote
[Chenopodium ambrosioides]' Gu *pu"dé:tʸ*

PU#037 pOM **pu"t-y** *(n) 'mugre/dirt, grime'* NHM: *pu"t* MM:
Ma,Pu,Ct *pu"tʸ* Ja,At *pu"tʸ* '=podrido (madera, etc.)' LM: Gu *pu"tʸ*
'=podrido (madera, etc.)'

PU#038 pZ **puŋ** *(vt) 'regar/to sprinkle'* TxZ: *puŋ* (vt) 'desatar'
ChisZ: C *puŋ* (vi, vt) N *puŋ* (vt) '=esparcirlo' NE *puŋ* (vt)

PU#039 pMZ **pu?w** *(vt) 'romper/to break'* NHM: *pʋ"* 'quebrar (p.ej., un cántaro), romper (p.ej., una piedra), hacer almáciga de semillas' MM: 'quebrarse (olla, vidrio, etc.)' Ju *<pu">* Ma *<pu"p, tɨ: pʸu"y>* Ja *<pu!w̄, pu!p, pu"wá·m̄p>* At *<tɨ: pʸu"y>* Ct *<pu!w̄, pu!p, pu"wámp>* LM: Cn *<pu?~pu"~pu"w>* (vt) 'quebrar; deshacer' SJ *pu?w~pu"(w)* 'to chew but not swallow; to break (dishes, comal, etc.)' Gu *<pu!w̄, pu!p, pu"wá·m̄p>* 'quebrarse (olla, vidrio, etc.)' AyZ: *[pu?ŋ]* 'desatarlo' [?-semantics] TxZ: *pu?ŋ* (vt, vi-p) 'desenredar, desatar' [?-semantics] ChisZ: C *pu?ŋ* (vt) 'golpearlo; pilarlo; machucarlo' N *pu?ŋ* (vt) 'pegarle (tirándole algo)' NE *pu?ŋ* (vt) 'pegarlo, golpearlo (como con el puño); machacarlo, machucarlo (como arroz)'

PU#040 pZ **puwa** *(adj) 'pálido/pale'* SaP: *pɨ:u* '=chipujo' [Zo loan?] ChisZ: C *puwa* N *puwa* (adj)

PU#041 pM **pu?y** *(vt) 'mascar/to chew'* NHM: *pʋ?y~pʋ"y* 'mascar, masticar' SHM: *pu"y* MM: 'masticar' Ma *<pu"y, pʸi"pʸ>* Ja,Pu,Ct *<pu"y, pʸi!pʸ>* At *<pu"y, pʸü!pʸ>* LM: Cn *<pu?~pu"y>* (vt) '=masticar' Gu *<pu"y, pʸu!pʸ>* 'masticar' SaP: *pu?y* (vi, vt) 'chew'

PU#042 pOM **?a-pu"y-a?** *(vt) 'rumiar/to ruminate'* NHM: *?apʋ?yi ~ ?apʋ"ya* LM: *<abu"yɨ·y~abu"yɨ"y~abu"yɨ?~abu"yɨ"w>* (vt)

PU#043 pMZ **puy** *(n) 'pierna, muslo/thigh'* [pM, pOM *puhy] NHM: *pʋ:hy* SHM: Tl,Ay *pu:y* 'pierna' MM: Ju,Ma *pu:y* Ja,Pu,At *pu:y* Ct *pu·ȳ* 'pierna, muslo', *pu·y* 'muslo' [sic!] LM: Cn *<pu:y>* Gu *pu:y* OlP: *puyɨ* 'muslo de la pierna' SaP: *puhy* 'muslo de la pierna' TxZ *puy* 'pierna' SoZ: *puy* 'pie' ChZ: *puy* 'muslo de la pierna'

PU#044 pOM **pu"y** *(n) 'tabla, banco, banquito/board, bench'* NHM: *pu"* 'tabla, roto' SHM: *pu?y* MM: Ju,Ma *pu"y* Pu,Ct *pu"y* LM: Cn *<pu"y>* 'tabla' Ca,Gu *pu"y*

PO#001 pM **po:** *(n) 'tlacuache/Mexican opossum'* [pOM *po:] NHM: *po:* 'tlacuache, zarigüeya, zorra mochilera [Didelphis marsupialis]' SHM: Tl *pʋ:* Ay *po:h* MM: Ju,At *po:* LM: Cn *<po:>* 'tlacuachillo de oro [Caluromys derbianus]' Gu *po:* OlP: *po:hɨ* 'tlacuache, zorro'

PO#002 pOM ***po"** *(n) 'cuero/hide'* NHM: *po"* 'cuero; curtido, piel
—p.ej., coyundas, cana, correa' SHM: Tl *pʋ?ok* 'cuero de animal'
MM: Ju,Ma,Ja,Pu,At,Ct *po"* LM: Ca *po"*

PO#003 pZ ***po?** *(vi, vt) 'brotar, nacer/to split, give birth'* SoZ: *po?*
[Foster and Foster 1948] AyZ: *[po?]* 'partir (leña)' TxZ: *po?* (vt,
vi-p) 'partir (leña, papaya, sandía), aserrar, cambiar en sencillas
(moneda), nacer (niño)' ChisZ: C *po?* (vi) 'brotar; nacer; rajarse;
reventarse, abrirse' (vt) 'rajarlo' N *po?* (vi) 'rajarse; abrirse;
espigarse' (vt) 'rajarlo; aserrarlo; abrir callejón' NE *po?* (vi)
'brotar (como pollito); rajarse (como leña)' (vt) 'rajarlo (como leña)'
ChZ: *po?* 'nacer'

PO#004 pM ***po?** *(n) 'canas/white hair, gray hair'* [pOM **po"*]
SHM: Tl *pʋ?* MM: Ju,Ma,Pu,At *po"* Ja *po"w* Ct *kɨpó"* LM: Ca *po"*
OlP: *po?* (vi) 'tiene canas' (adj) 'canoso'

PO#005 pM ***ko-po?** *(adj) 'canoso/white-haired, gray-haired'* [pOM
*kupo"] NHM: *kupo"* SHM: Tp *kupó"h* MM: Cc *ku?pó"* 'canoso',
ku?pó"h 'canas' [sic!] Ma *kɨpó", kɨbó"* Ja *ku"pó"w* Pu,Ct *kɨpó"* At
kupó" LM: Gu *ku"bó"* '=canas' SaP: *kupó?* 'canas'

PO#006 pZ ***po?wah** *(n) 'majagua/majagua bush'* [pGZ **po?owah*]
TxZ: *po:?wa?* 'jonote' ChisZ: C,NE *po?ah* N *po?a*

PO#007 pM ***poc** *(vt) 'embarrar/to muddy'* [Perhaps pMZ **poc* 'to
slap'; cf. ChisZ: N *caŋgɨpocpocwɨy* 'golpear (como pelota)'] NHM:
pohc~poc 'dar una palmada de cariño' MM: 'embarrar' Ma <*pōc,
na·bóc, pʸohčpʸ, nʸa·bóhčpʸ*> Ja <*nipóc, nʸipóhčpʸ*> At
<*nɨbóhcp*> Ct <*pʸohčpʸ, pōc*> LM: Cn <*pohc~poc*> (vt)
'=enlodar (la pared de una casa)' SJ *pohc~poc* 'to mud, cement' Gu
<*pʸohčp, pōc*> 'embarrar' OlP: *poc* (vt) 'embarrar una casa'

PO#008 pM ***poc-e** *(n) 'pared/wall'* [pOM **pocy*] NHM: *pɨc* SHM:
Tm *peč* '=muro' MM: Ju *poč* Ma,Ja,Pu,At,Ct *poč* '=muro, barda'
LM: Cn <*poč*> Ca *poč* '=muro, barda' Gu *pōč* OlP: *poce* (n)
'embarro (mezcla con que se embarra la casa)' [*poca* 'pared' is another
OlP derivative from the same root]

PO#009 pOM ***pohc-pa** *(n) 'albañil/mason'* NHM: *pohcpa* SHM: Tu
póhcpa Tp *póhcpɨ* MM: Ju,Cc,Ma,Ja,Pu,At,Ct *póhcpɨ* LM: Ca
póhcpɨ

PO#010 pZ ***poco?** *(n) 'hermano,-a menor/younger sibling'* TxZ: *po:co?* 'chipe (hijo segundo), compañero' ChisZ: C *poco* S [Tu] *poco?* [Foster 1949] ChZ: *poco?*

PO#011 pZ ***poh** *(n) 'bejuco/vine'* [pGZ *poh] SaP: *poh* '=vena' [Zo loan] TxZ: *poh-?ohwe?ñ* 'caña de hueco (como otate pero más grande y grueso)' [?] ChZ: *poh*

PO#012 pMZ ***poh** *(vi) 'ventear; inflar/to blow (the wind)'* NHM: *poh* 'ventear, hacer viento' LM: Cn <*poh*> (vi) 'soplar (el viento)' SJ *poh* 'to blow (the wind)' OIP: *poh* (vt) 'patearlo (como puerta)' ChisZ: C [Co] *poh* (vi) 'inflarse, esponjarse' [Te] <*pohpa*> 'ampollar' N *poh* (vi) 'salir el color, decolorar'

PO#013 pOM ***poh** *(n) 'viento/wind'* NHM: *poh* 'aire, viento, matlazihuatl' SHM: Tl *pvh* 'aire' MM: Ju *poh* Ma,Ja,Pu,At,Ct *poh* LM: Cn <*poh*> '=aire (poder sobrenatural)' Gu *poh* Ca *poh*

PO#014 pOM ***poh-pa"m** *(n) 'epilepsia/epilepsy'* NHM: *pohïpa"m* MM: Ju *pohpá"m* Ma *poh* LM: Gu *pofpá"m*

PO#015 pMZ ***pok** *(vi, vt) 'hacer brujería/to practice witchcraft'* LM: Cn <*pohk~po·k*> (vi) 'hechizar' SJ *pohk~pok* 'to practice witchcraft' OIP: *pok* (vt) 'ojearle, echarle mal de ojo, hacerle ojo' SaP: *pok* (vi, vt) 'give the evil eye, bewitch' AyZ: *[pok]* 'echar brujería'

PO#016 pOM ***pok-y** *(n) 'brujería/witchcraft'* NHM: *pïk* SHM: Tl *pik^y* 'enfermedad' MM 'culpa, pecado, crimen, etc.' Ju *pek^y* Ma,Ja,Pu,Ct *pek^y* At *poök^y* LM: Cn <*poky*> 'pecado, delito'

PO#017 pM ***pok-pa** *(n) 'brujo/witch'* [pOM *pokpa is presupposed although it is not expected since final vowel would normally become lost.] NHM: *pohkpa* 'hechicero: el que mete objetos en el cuerpo', *pohpa* 'brujo, hechicero' OIP: *pokpa?* 'él que sabe hacer ojo'

PO#018 pMZ ***pok(ok)** *(n) 'tecomate/gourd'* [pM *pokok > pOM *pokk > *pok; pZ, pGZ *pok] NHM: *pok* 'jícara grande y gruesa; jicalpestle—fruto de guaje' SHM: Tu,Tp *pohk* 'bule' Tm *pok* MM: Ju *pok* 'jicalpestle' Ma,Ja,Pu,At,Ct *pok* '=jicalpestle, chical, chical, batea' LM: Cn <*pok*> 'coco, jicalpestle' Ca *pok* 'jicalpestle' LM: SJ *pok* 'bowl made from a gourd' Gu *pok* '=chical, chical, jicalpestle' OIP: *poko·k* SaP: *pógok* SoZ: *pok* TxZ: *pok* 'tecomate (para llevar agua), bule' ChisZ: C *pok* NE *pohk* ChZ: *pok* 'tenate' [?]

PO#019 pOM ***win-pok** *(n) 'frente/forehead'* NHM: *vimpok* 'frente, sien' LM: SJ *wi·mbok* MM: Ca *wimbok* [Wonderly 1949]

PO#020 pMZ ***pok?i** *(n) 'tobillo/heel'* [pM **po?ki*; pZ **poki*] OIP: *po?ki* ChisZ: C *pokipak* [Zo-to-Sp. side has *pokepak*] N,NE *poki*

PO#021 pZ ***poka** *(n) 'huevo/egg'* TxZ: *ka?npuk* [?] ChisZ: C *poka* 'huevo, blanquillo' N *poka* '=testículo' NE *poka* ChZ: *po?ok* [?]

PO#022 pMZ ***pokok** *(n) 'pongolote/cotton tree'* [pM **pokok*, with long-distance assimilation of final consonant in OIP; pZ **pokok* > pGZ **po:k*.] OIP: *cukpoko'p* SaP: *šu:špógo:k* TxZ: *po:k-kê?(m)* (vi) 'subirse (bola por calambre)'

PO#023 pMZ ***poks** *(vt) 'tocar algo extendido/to touch something extended'* LM: Cn <*po"kš*> (vt) 'dar una palmada' [?] SJ *po?kš* 'to slap with the open hand, pat' [?] OIP: *pokš* (vt) 'tocarlo (p.ej., puerta, marimba)' SoZ: *poks* 'doblar (maíz)' TxZ: *poks* (vt, vi-p) 'enrollar' ChisZ: C *poks* (vt) 'montarlo' NE *poks* (vi) 'sentarse' (vi-s) 'estar sentado' (vt) 'montarlo (como al caballo)'

PO#024 pMZ ***po:?ks** *(vi) 'descansar/to rest'* NHM: *po:?kš* SHM: Tl *pv:?kš* MM: Ma <*po?š*> Ja <*po?š, po?šp*> Pu,At,Ct,Ju <*po?kš*> LM: Ca <*po·kš*> Cn <*po·kš*> SJ *po·kš* Gu <*po·?š*> SaP: *po?kš* (vi) TxZ: *po?ks-ket* (vi) 'caer de arriba' [?-semantics] ChisZ: N *po?ks* (vi) 'sentarse; encharcarse' ChisZ: S [*po?kskúy*] 'asiento'

PO#025 pZ ***po?m** *(vt) 'moler/to grind'* TxZ: *po?m* (vt) 'abastecer', (vi) 'rendir' ChisZ: C *po?m* (vt) 'cornearlo, acornearlo' N *po?m* (vt) 'molerlo (que quede en polvo)'

PO#026 pMZ ***po:m(o)** *(n) 'copal, incienso/incense'* [pM, pOM **po:m*; pZ **pomo* > pGZ **po:mo*] NHM: *po:m* SHM: 'copal' Tl *pv:m* Tu,Tp,Mi,Ay *po:m* MM: 'copal' Ma *po·m̄p* Ju,Cc,Ja,Pu,At *po:m* LM: Cn <*po:m*> Ca,Gu *po:m* OIP: *po:mɨ* SaP: *po:m* 'copal' SoZ: *pó:ma?* 'copal' TxZ: *po:m* ChisZ: C *pomoh* N,NE *pomo* 'incienso'

PO#027 pM [Veracruz] ***poni** *(n) 'nudo (de árbol)/knot (of tree)'* OIP: *poni* SaP: *pon*

PO#028 pZ ***ponon** *(adj) 'suave/soft'* [pGZ **pon* (**po:n* expected)] SoZ: *pon* 'blandito' AyZ: [*pon*] 'blando' TxZ: *pon* 'blandito'

ChisZ: C *ponon* [ejemplo: "la carne está suave..."] NE *ponot, pononbɨ* 'blando, suave—como carne cruda' ChZ: *pono?n* 'débil'

PO#029 pZ ***yak-ponon-?ah** *(vt) 'ablandar/to soften'* [Cf. LM-Cn <*po:n*> (vt) 'ablandar'] TxZ: *yak-po:?n* (vt-caus) 'ablandar' ChisZ: C *yahpono?nah* (vt) 'ablandarlo, hacerlo ablandar; dejarlo ablandar' NE *pono?nah* (vi) 'ablandarse' (vt) 'ablandarlo (como una tortilla)'

PO#030 pZ ***ponhi** *(adj, adv) 'despacio/slow'* [ChisZ-N form is fully and the ChZ form partly contaminated with descendant forms of pZ **ponon* 'soft'.] ChisZ: C *ponih* (adv) 'despacio' N *poñi* (adj) 'despacio, suavemente' ChZ: *ponhi* 'suave; lento, despacio'

PO#031 pZ ***po?n** *(vi) 'jadear/to pant'* ChisZ: C *po?n* (vi) 'faltarle aliento, cansarse, fatigarse' N *po?n* (vi) 'jadearse'

PO#032 pMZ ***po:p?o?** *(adj) 'blanco/white'* [pM **po:?po?* > pOM **po:?p*; pZ **popo?* > pGZ **po:po?*] NHM: *po:?p* SHM: Tl *pʉ:p* Tu,Tp,Ay *po:p* MM: Ju,Cc,Ma,Ja,Pu,At,Ct *po:p* LM: Cn <*po:b*> (adj) SJ *po:b* Ca,Gu *po:p* OIP: *po:po?* SaP: *po?p* AyZ: [*pó?oɓo*] TxZ: *popo?* (adj) SoZ: *po:po?* ChisZ: C *popo* '=güero' N *popo* '=claro' [homonym: 'tía—esposa del hermano de la madre'] NE *pobo* (vi-s) ChZ: *popo?*

PO#033 pZ ***ko?-popo?** *(n) 'canas/white hair, gray hair'* TxZ: *ko:?popo?* (n) 'cabeza de viejo (animal)' ChisZ: C *ko?popo* 'canas'

PO#034 pZ ***popo?-?ah** *(vi) 'blanquearse/to become white'* ChisZ: C *popa?* (vi) 'volverse blanco' NE *pobah* (vi) 'destiñarse, blanquearse)' ChZ: *popo?ah* 'ponerse blanco'

PO#035 pOM ***po:?p-?ɨy** *(vi) 'blanquearse/to become white'* NHM: *po:?pip ~ po:?pa* 'blanquear, blanquearse, encalar (p.ej., una pared)' MM: 'emblanquecer(se)' Ja,At <*pó:bɨp*> Ma,Ct <*pó:b?ɨpʸ*> LM: Gu <*po:bĭ:pʸ*> 'emblanquecer(se)'

PO#036 pOM ***yak-po:?p-?ɨy** *(vt) 'blanquear/to make white'* NHM: *yakpo:?pi ~ yakpo:?pa* MM: Ju <*yæhpó:bɨ*> 'emblanquecer(se)' LM: Ca <*yahpo:bɨ"*> 'emblanquecer(se)'

PO#037 pOM ***po:hšy-my** *(n) 'araña/spider'* SHM: Tu,Tp,Mi *po·hšʸ* MM: Ju *pošʸpʸ* Cc *pošʸm̥ʸ* Ma,Ct *po·s̄ʸpʸ* Ja,Pu,At *po·s̄ʸm̥ʸ* LM: Ca *po·šp* Gu *po·s̄ʸp*

PO#038 pM **po:?š** *(vi) 'demorarse/to linger'* MM: Ja <*po"š, po!š̄p*> Pu <*po·š̄p, mbó"ž̇ip*> OIP: *po:š* (vi)

PO#039 pMZ **pos ~ posos ~ pohos** *(n) 'guayaba/guava [Psidium guajava and other species]'* [pM *poš ~ pošoš ~ pohoš* > pOM *poš*; pZ *pohos*] NHM: *poš* '[Psidium guajava]' SHM: Tl *pṽš* MM: Ju *poš* Ma,Ja,Pu,At,Ct *poš̄* LM: Cn <*poš*> '[Psidium guajava]' Ca *poš* Gu *poš̄* OIP: *pošo'š* SaP: *póhoš ~ póšoš* ChisZ: C *po?os* ChZ: *po?s*

PO#040 pOM **cahp-poš** *(n) 'limón/lemon'* [The compound as such is post-Conquest; *cahp* 'sky' is the usual first member in nouns referring to objects associated with the Spanish.] MM: Ma,Ja,Pu,Ct *cahpóš̄* LM: Ca *cahpóš̄* Gu *cibóš̄*

PO#041 pM **pot** *(vi) 'romper una cosa larga y delgado/to break a long, thin object'* NHM: *poht ~ pot* 'romper (p.ej., un mecate)' SHM: Tl *pṽht* 'reventar' MM: Ma <*pohtp*> 'reventar (hilo, etc.)' Ja <*pohtúhkp, pohtuká·m̄p*> 'reventar (hilo, etc.)' At <*pohtp, potá·m̄p*> 'reventar (hilo, etc.)' Ct <*pohtp, potám̄p*> 'reventar (hilo, etc.)' LM: Cn <*poht ~ pot*> (vi) 'reventar', <*poht ~ po·t*> (vt) 'reventar (p.ej.: bejucos y reatas)' [sic!] SJ *poht ~ pot* 'to break (rope, vine, chain, etc.)' Gu <*pot, pohp, podá·m̄p*> 'reventar (hilo, etc.)' OIP: *pot* (vi) 'reventarse'

PO#042 pMZ **po:?t** *(vt) 'cortar con machete/to cut with machete'* SHM: Tl *pṽ:t* Tu <*po:t, mbo?t̸ʸpʸ*> Tp <*po:t, ?ic mbo?t̸ʸpʸ, pʸo:dǽmpʸ, nʸaʸbʸó:dʸi, mbo?t̸ʸpʸ*> Mi <*po:t*> MM: Cc <*po:t, mbo?t̸ʸpʸ, po?ttúk, nʸeybʸó:dʸi*> Ma <*pʸo?t̸ʸpʸ, po:t*> Ja <*po:t, pʸo?t, pʸo?t̸ʸpʸ*> Pu <*po:t, mbo!t̸ʸpʸ*> At,Ct <*po:t, pʸo?t̸ʸpʸ*> LM: SJ *po·t ~ po:t* 'to cut trees into blocks' Gu <*po:t, pʸo?pʸ*> TxZ: *po?t* (vt) 'desbaratar (hacer polvitas con los dedos), (vi) desbaratarse ChisZ: C *po?t* (vt) 'molerlo' N *po?t* (vi) 'moler, estar molido' NE *po?tpi?* (vi) 'picarse (como la madera)' ChZ: *po?t* 'moler (pinol)'

PO#043 pZ **po?te** *(n) 'pinole/flour, something ground'* [pGZ *po?ote*] SaP: *po?t* [Zo loan] SoZ: *pó?otʸi?* AyZ: [*po:?de*] ChisZ: C *po?te* '=harina' N *po?te* '=lo que está molido en forma de polvo' NE *po?de* '=polvillo - expressión regional para pinole de chocolate' ChZ: *po?te*

PO#044 pM ***po:t-an** *(n) 'temporal de agua/spell of rainy weather'*
[pOM **po:tn*] NHM: *po:dïn* 'estación o época lluviosa, maizal de esta
época' MM: Ja *po:tm̥* 'temporal' Ma,At,Ct *po:tn̥* 'temporal' LM:
Cn <*pot*> 'tiempo de lluvias (junio, julio y agosto)' [?] Gu *po:tp*
'temporal' OlP: *po:ta'n* (adv) 'temporal de agua'

PO#045 pMZ ***pot?ot** *[?] (n) 'laja/slab'* [pM **po?tot*; pZ **potot* >
pGZ **po:t*; this scenario is highly hypothetic since there are unexpected
developments in the individual languages.] OlP: *po?to't* SaP: *po:t*
[*po?tot* expected] TxZ: *pot* [*po:t* expected]

PO#046 pM ***ko-po:t(ik)** *(n) 'caspa/dandruff'* [pOM **kupo:tyk*]
NHM: *kupɨ:?tk* SaP: *kupó:t*

PO#047 pOM ***po:ht ~ po?t** *(vt) 'limpiar/to clean'* NHM: *po?t ~ po"t*
'limpiar, borrar (p.ej., con un trapo)' MM: 'limpiar con estropajo,
etc.' Ja <*po"t, pʸo?t, pʸo?t͡ʸpʸ*> At,Ct,Ma <*po"t, pʸo?t͡ʸpʸ*> LM:
Cn <*po?t ~ po"t*> (vt) 'limpiar (frotando con trapo); rascar' SJ
po?t ~ po"t 'to rub, scrub clean with a brush, cloth' Gu <*po"t,
pʸo?t, pʸo?pʸ*> 'limpiar con estropajo, etc.'

PO#048 pMZ ***yak-pot?** *(vt) 'desteñirlo/to discolor'* NHM: *yakpo?t*
~ yakpo"t (vt) 'limpiar algo' LM: Cn <*yahpo?t ~ yahpo"t*> (vt)
'limpiar' ChisZ: C *yahpoht* (vt) 'desteñirlo'

PO#049 pOM ***po?t-n** *(n) 'escobeta/brush'* NHM: *po?tïn* 'borrador,
trapo para limpiar o sacudir' MM: Ma *pa:mbó?tn̥* Ja,Ct *pa:mbó?n*
LM: SJ *po?t* 'brush' [<*po?t* 'to rub, scrub clean with a brush]) Gu
pa:mbó?t 'escobeta'

PO#050 pZ ***pow** *(vi, vt) 'cocer al vapor/to cook over the steam'* SaP:
pow (vi) 'cook in steam' [Zo loan] TxZ: *poŋ* (vt, vi-p) 'asar (pollo
entero en las brasas), hornear' ChisZ: N *poŋ* (vi) 'quemarse' (vt)
'quemarlo' NE *poŋ* (vt) 'quemarlo' ChZ: *poŋ* 'quemar'

PO#051 pZ ***po?yo** *(n) 'arena/sand'* [pGZ **po?oyo*] SaP: *po?y* [Zo
loan] SoZ: *pó?oy* TxZ: *po:?y* '=polvo de la tierra' ChisZ: C,NE
po?yo 'polvo' N *po?yo* '=polvo' S *[po?óy]*

PO#052 pMZ ***po:y?** *(vi) 'correr, huir/to run, escape'* OlP: *poy ~ po?*
(vi) 'huirse' SoZ: *poy* 'correr' AyZ: *[poy]* TxZ: *poy* (vi) ChisZ:
C *poy* (vi) '=escapar; fugarse; circular' NE [Ra] *poy* (vi) '=fu-

garse' NE [Tapalapa, Pantepec, Chapultenango] *poy* [Wonderly 1949] N *poy* (vi) '=soplar (viento)'

PO#053 pOM ***pa-pohy ~ pa-po"y** *(vt) 'corretear/to chase'* MM: Cc <*pAbó", mbAbóyp^y*> Ma <*pa·bó", p^ya·bé:p^y*> 'corretear', <*pa·bó", p^ya·bóö:p^y*> 'cazar' [sic!] Pu <*pɨbó", p^yɨbé:p^y*> At <*pæbó", p^yæbóö:p^y*> 'corretear, cazar', <*pæbó", pæbóö:p^y*> 'acosar' [sic!] Ct <*pa·bó"y*> 'corretear', <*pa·bo"y, p^ya·bé!p^y*> 'acosar' LM: Gu <*pɨbó"w, p^yɨbó:p^y*> 'acosar'

PO#054 pZ ***po:ye?** *(vi) 'correr, huir/to run, escape'* TxZ: *po:y-ke?(m)* (vi) 'subir corriendo' ChisZ: C *poye?* (vi) 'huir, fugarse; correr'

PO#055 pMZ ***poy?a** *(n) 'luna; mes/moon; month'* [pM **po?a* > pOM **po"*; pZ **poya*; the loss of /y/ in Mixean does not have parallels.] NHM: *po"* SHM: Tl *pʋ?* 'luna' Tm *po"* 'mes' MM: Ju *po"* 'luna' Ma,Ja,Pu,At,Ct *po"* LM: Mz *po"* Cn <*po?*> Gu,Ca *po"* 'luna' OlP: *po?a* SaP: *po?* SoZ: *pó:ya?* AyZ: [*po:ya*] TxZ: *po:y* '=perdíz rabón' ChisZ: C [Co] *poyah* [Te] <*poya*> 'costumbre de muger / luna' N,NE *poya*

SI-SO

SI#001 pOM ***ši:** *(loc adv) 'allí/there'* NHM: *ši* SHM: Tu *ši:* MM: Ja,At,Ct *ši:* '=ahí' LM: Gu *ši:* SJ *ši: ya·* 'here, there, and everywhere'

SI#002 pZ ***si?i** *(n) 'ano/anus'* [pGZ **ši?*] TxZ: *šê?* 'fondo (interior y exterior), ano' [*šê:?* expected] ChisZ: C *si?i* 'nalga, asentadera' S [*si?*] 'culo, nalga'

SI#003 pOM ***šihc** *(n) 'aguacatillo/avocado [Persea americana bearing small fruits]'* NHM: *šihc* 'aguacate' [Persea americana] SHM: Tl *šehc* Tu,Tp,Mi *šihc* MM: Cc,Pu,At *šihc* Ja *šihcn?á:y*

SI#004 pOM ***ši?c-n** *(n) 'cascabel, sonaja/rattlesnake, rattle'* NHM: *ši?cïn* 'cascabel' MM: Ma *šihn̦* Ja *šiht* 'cascabel, sonaja', *šihn̦* 'sonaja' [sic!] Pu *šīn* At,Ct *šihn̦* LM: Ca *šikšt* 'sonaja de nene'

SI#005 pZ ***si?c** *(vi) 'encoger/to shrink'* SoZ: *ši?č* (vi) 'marchitarse' TxZ: *šê?č* (vt, vi-a) 'ahorcar' ChisZ: N *si?c* (vi) 'rebajar; marchitar; estar flaco; deshinchar' *si?c* (vi) 'encoger' ChZ: *si?c* 'mascar (caña)'

SI#006 pM ***šico** *(n) 'tacacholota/a kind of insect'* [pOM **šic*] NHM: *šic* 'mosca abeja, eristalo [Sryphidae]' SHM: Tp *šic* 'abeja nativa que no pica, negra' MM: Cc *šic* 'abeja nativa que no pica, negra' Pu *šīc* At *ši·cm̦* Ct *šīc* OlP: *šico*

SI#007 pMZ ***si:k?** *(vi) 'reir/to laugh'* NHM: *ši:k ~ ši"k* '=reirse' SHM: *še?ek* MM: Ju_<*ši:k?æmú:p*> 'sonreír', <*ši"k̲*> 'reir' Ma,At, Ct <*ši"k, ši·kp*> '=sonreír' Ja <*ši"k, ši·k, ši·kp*> '=sonreír' LM: Cn <*ši·k ~ ši"k*> (vi) Ca <*ši"k*> Gu <*ši"k, ši·kp*> '=sonreír' OlP: *ši:k ~ si?k* 'reirse' SaP: *ši:k ~ ši?k* (vi)

'laugh' SoZ: *šik* [Foster and Foster 1948] TxZ: *šek* (vi-e) 'reirse'
ChisZ: C *sihk* (vi) 'reirse' N *sihk* (vi) '=sonreir' NE *sihk* (vi)
'=reirse, sonreir' ChZ: *sik* reirse; *kɨsigɨy* 'reirse de'

SI#008 pMZ ***mu:-si:k?** *(vi) 'reir con alguien/to laugh with somebody'*
NHM: *muši:k ~ muši"k* ChisZ: C *mu?šihk* (vi) 'sonreir' [the glottal
stop possibly explained as contamination from *mu?* (vt) 'tocar /to
play']

SI#009 pMZ ***si:k?-V** *(n) 'sonrisa, risa/smile'* [pM **si?ki* > pOM
*ši"ky; pZ **sikɨ* > pGZ **ši:kɨ*] NHM: *ši"k* OIP: *ši?ki* TxZ: *šê:k*
ChisZ: C *sihkuy* 'risa; lugar donde se juega a los dados' N *sihkɨ* NE
sikɨ?

SI#010 pOM ***šik** *(n) 'sarna/itch'* NHM: *šik* '=roña' MM: Ma *šikn̥*
'=sarnoso' Ja,At *šik* At *šíkɨp* 'sarnoso' Ct *šikn̥* '=sarnoso' LM:
Gu *šikt*

SI#011 pM ***ni:-šik** *(adj) 'sarnoso/itchy'* MM: Ja *nišík̄* LM: Gu
nɨ"žíkt OIP: *nišikɨ*

SI#012 pMZ ***si:kitiw** *(n) 'chicharra/cicada'* [pM **šĩ:kitiw* > pOM
*šikitíw; pZ **sikitiŋ*] NHM: *šikɨtiv* 'chicharra, cicada, cigarra anual
[Tibicen sp.]' MM: Ju *sʸigɨdíf* Ma *šɨgɨdíw̥ ~ šɨgɨdíf ~ šɨgɨdíΦ* Ja,Pu,At
šɨgɨdíw̥ Ct *šɨgɨdíw̥ ~ šɨgɨdíΦ* LM: Cn <*šigɨdiw*> 'cicada, cigarra
anual [order: Homoptera, fam: Cicadidae]' Gu *šigɨdíw̥* SaP: *šĩ:git*
OIP: *ši:škiti* (irregular insertion of an /š/ and loss of final /w/) TxZ:
šêkre:ŋ 'especie de chicharra (sale en abril-junio), especie de cigarra
(azul, sale en agosto-septiembre)' ChisZ: C *sikití?ŋ* N *?isykɨtiŋ*

SI#013 pGZ ***ši?ks** *(vt) 'sacudir/to shake something'* SoZ: *ši?ks* (vt)
TxZ: *šê?kš* (vt)

SI#014 pOM ***šim** *(loc adv) 'allí, allá/there'* SHM: Tu *šim* 'allá' Tp
šim 'allí' Ay *šem* MM: Ma,Ja,Pu,At,Ct *šim̄* '=ahí' Cc *šim* 'allá'
LM: Gu *šim̄*

SI#015 pOM ***ši"m** *(vt) 'estrenar/use for the first time'* NHM: *ši"m*
LM: Cn <*ši?m*>

SI#016 pOM ***šim-pɨt** *(pron) 'aquel/that one'* SHM: Tp *šímbɨt* MM:
Ja,At *ším̄ɨdɨ* LM: Gu *šímbɨ*

SI#017 pOM ***ši:?mha** *(n) 'paludismo/malaria'* NHM: *ši:?mhï* MM:
Ju *ší:myɨ* At *šuü:mʸɨpá"m* LM: Ml <*šimpa?m*> Ca *ší:ma* Gu *ší:mɨ*

SI#018 pMZ ***sin** *(vi) 'mover, hinchar/move, swell'* NHM: *ši:n ~ ši:hn ~ šin* 'mover' TxZ: *šêŋ* (vi) 'hincharse' ChisZ: N *sin* (vi) 'hincharse, estar hinchado (de agua); llenarse, estar lleno'

SI#019 pZ ***si?n** *(vt) 'amarrar/to tie'* SaP: *ši?n* (vi) 'unravel (thread)' [Zo loan] ChisZ: C *si?n* (vt) 'amarrarlo; atarlo; apersogarlo' N *si?n* (vi) 'estar amarrado' (vt) 'amarrarlo' NE *si?n* (vt) 'amarrarlo; ciñarlo'

SI#020 pM ***ši:p ~ ši?p** *(vi) 'comezón, dar/to itch'* MM: Ju < *šipp, šip* > Cc < *šipp* > Ma < *ši·p̄, ši"bámp̄* > Ja < *ši·p, ši"bá·m̄p* > Ct < *ši·p̄, šíˑp̣ip, ši"bán̄ip* > LM: Cn < *ši·p ~ ši"p* > Gu < *ši"bǐ?p cu"zǐ?p, ši·p̄, ši"bá·m̄p* > OIP: *ši:p ~ ši?p* (vi, vt-d) 'tener comezón'

SI#021 pOM ***šipš** *(vi) 'empacharse/to suffer indigestion'* LM: Cn < *šipš* > (vi) 'llenarse de aire' SJ *ši·pš* 'to have a stomachache, gas' MM: 'empacharse' Ma,Ja,At < *šíˑ?pšip* > Ct < *šíˑ·?šip, ši·?š?adúhk* >

SI#022 pZ ***sips** *(vt) 'punzar/to sting'* ChisZ: N *sips* (vt) 'punzarlo, picarlo' ChZ: *sips* 'quitar espina'

SI#023 pMZ ***sis(i)** *(n) 'carne/meat'* [pM **šiši* > pOM **šišy*; pZ **sis* > pGZ **šiš*] NHM: *šiš* 'pechuga, músculo' SHM: Tu,Tp,Mi *šišʸ* 'carne humana' MM: 'carne humana' Cc *šišʸ* Ma,Ja,Pu,At,Ct *šīšʸ* LM: 'carne humana' Ca *šišʸ* Cn < *ši:šy* > '=muslo' Gu *šīšʸ* SaP: *šiš* TxZ: *šêš* '=ganado, buey, res, cuerpo' SoZ: *šiš* 'cattle, bull' [Foster and Foster 1948; Wonderly 1949] ChisZ: C *sis* NE [Tapalapa, Ocotepec, Pantepec] *sis* [Wonderly 1949] [Ra] *sis* N *sis* '=cuerpo' S *sis* ChZ: StaMaCh *sis* SnMiCh *ṣiṣ* [Wonderly 1949]

SI#024 pZ ***?aw-sis** *(n) 'labio/lip'* SaP: *?au-šíš* [Zo loan] ChisZ: C,N,NE *?aŋsis*

SI#025 pOM ***ši:hš** *(n) 'jimba (tipo de carrizo)/type of bamboo'* MM: Ma,Pu *ši·š̄* Ja *ši·š̄* 'jimba (tipo de carrizo), *ši·šk* 'tipo de carrizo' [sic!] LM: Gu *ši·š̄*

SI#026 pM ***ši:šta** *(n) 'gajo/broken branch'* [pOM **ši:št*] NHM: *ši:št* 'gajo, baúl' OIP: *ši:šta*

SI#027 pMZ ***sit** *(vt) 'sacudir/to shake'* NHM: *šiht ~ šit* '=agitar, sacudida' SHM: Tl *wišet* MM: Ju,At < *šihtp* > 'espigar' Ja < *šit,* šⁱiht> LM: Cn <šiht~šit> (vt) 'sacudir (para vaciar)' Gu <šīt, šⁱiht, šⁱihpʸ> OlP: šit (vt) 'regar (como maíz desgranando)'

SI#028 pOM *win-šiht~win-šit *(vt) 'sacudir (trapo)/to shake (cloth)'*
NHM: vinšiht~vinšit 'sacudir (p.ej., un trapo)' LM: Cn <winšiht ~winšit> (vt) 'sacudir' (ejemplo: "sacuda la cobija porque tiene mucha basura") (vi) 'vibrar'

SI#029 pOM *ši:ʔt *(vi) 'sonar la nariz/to blow one's nose'* NHM: ši:t~ši"t 'sonar (p.ej., la nariz)' [?] LM: Ml <ši"t> 'sonar' Cn <ši·t ~ši:t> (vt) 'sonar (las narices)' SJ ši·t~ši:t 'to blow the nose' ChisZ: C si?thay (vt) 'sisearle'

SI#030 pZ *sit *(n) 'moco/mucus'* NHM: ši:ʔc 'moco, sauraucia' [?] ChisZ: C,N sit ChZ: sit

SI#031 pOM *ši"t *(pron dem) 'ése, aquel/that'* NHM: ši:ʔ '=aquello' SHM: Tu ší"δɨ 'aquel' MM: Pu,Ct ší"dɨ 'ése' At ší"dɨtʸ 'esos' Ma,Ct ši"t 'aquel'

SI#032 pM [Veracruz] *ši:tɨ *(n) 'mazate/brocket deer'* OlP: ši:tɨ SaP: ši:t

SI#033 pZ *sitit *(vi) 'temblar (el cuerpo)/tremble (body)'* [Possibly related to SaP: širit 'scatter (seeds, etc.)'?] TxZ: šê:č (vi) 'temblar' ChisZ: N si?ti? (vi) 'sacudir su cuerpo, temblar' [?]

SI#034 pZ *siŋ *(vi) 'hincharse/to swell'* SoZ: šiŋ (vi) AyZ: [siŋ] (vi) TxZ: šêŋtokeñ (vi) ChisZ: C,N siŋ (vi) NE siŋ (vi) 'hincharse (como una herida)' ChZ: siŋ

SI#035 pZ *siŋ-ɨ *(n) 'hinchazón/swelling'* [pGZ *ši:ŋɨ] SoZ: šî:wi 'nacido' TxZ: šê:ŋ ChisZ: NE siwɨ

SI#036 pMZ *si:ʔw *(vt) 'sajar/to cut into (rope)'* NHM: ši:ʔv 'sajar, cortar, hacer un corte a muy poca profundidad, sufrir una escoriación' TxZ: dakšê:ʔŋko? (n) 'honda' ChisZ: N ?aŋsi?ŋ (vt) 'amarrarle la boca o el hocico'

SI#037 pOM *ši:y *(n) 'garrapata/tick'* NHM: ši:hy '[Dermacentor sp.]' MM: Ja ši:y 'pinolillo' LM: Cn <ši:y> '[order: Acarina, Dermacentor sp.]' Ca ši: Gu ši:ȳ 'garrapata', ši:y 'pinolillo' [sic]

SE#001 pM *šeh *(vi) 'respirar/to breathe'* NHM: šeh LM: SJ šeh MM: Ju <šæhp> Ma <šæh, šæhp> Ja <sæh, šæhp, tɨ: šⁱehʸ>

At,Ct <_šǣh, šǣhp, tǐ:_šᵛehᵞ> LM: Cn <šeh> (vi) Ca <šǣh>
Gu <šeh, šehp, tǐ: šᵛehᵞ> OlP: šeh 'salir el aliento, exhalar' SaP:
šeh (vi) ChisZ: C košeh (vi) 'evaporarse' [?]

SE#002 pOM *mɨk-šeh (vi) 'suspirar/to sigh' NHM: mɨhšeh MM:
Ma <mɨkšǽhp> Ja <mɨkšǽh, mɨkšǽhp> At,Ct <mɨkšǽhp> LM:
Gu <mɨkséh, mɨkšéhp>

SE#003 pM *šeh-e (n) 'aliento/breath' [pOM *šehy] SHM: Tu šehᵞ
Tp šehᵞ MM: Ju,Cc šehᵞ Ma,Ja,Pu,At,Ct šehᵞ LM: Cn <šehy> Ca
šehᵞ Gu šehᵞ OlP: šehe

SE#004 pM [Veracruz] *šeket (vt) 'enrollar/to roll up' OlP: šeket
(vr, vt) SaP: šégetik nišégehttɨ 'enrollar (culebra, mono)' [Clark and
Clark 1960]

SE#005 pOM *še:?kš (vi) 'escurrir/to drip' MM: Ju <šǣ?kšp> Ma
<šǣ?kšp> 'gotear (agua de la llave)' Ja <šǣ?kšp> 'gotear (agua
de la llave)', <šǣ?šp, šǣ?šá·m̄p, tɨ: šᵛe?šᵛ> 'escurrir' At,Ct
<šǣ?kšp> '=gotear (agua de la llave)' LM: Cn <šekš> (vi)
'gotear; sangrar' Ca <šǣ·kš> Gu <še·?šp> 'escurrir, gotear
(agua de la llave)'

SE#006 pM *še:?m (vi) 'enfriarse/to become cold' NHM: še:?m
'enfriar, enfriado' MM: Ju <šǣ:m> Ma <šǣ?m̄p, šǣ:m> Ja
<šǣ!m̄, šǣ!m̄p, šǣ:má·m̄p> At <šǽ?m̄p, tɨ: šᵛe:mᵞ, šǣ:má·mp>
LM: Cn <še·m~še:m> (vi) '=calmarse; aminorar (la lumbre)' SJ
še·m~še:m 'to calm, cool off' OlP: se:m (vi) 'enfriarse' ChisZ: N
se?m (vi) 'flotar' [?]

SE#007 pOM *yak-še:?m (vt) 'enfriar/to cool' NHM: yakše:?m
'enfriar algo, refrescar' LM: Cn <yahše·m~yahše:m> (vt)
'calmar; extinguir'

SE#008 pOM *še:?m-y (adj) 'fresco/cool' NHM: šE:?m 'enfriado',
še:?m 'persona de Tlahuitoltepec' SHM: Tp šǣ:m 'brisa' MM: Ma
šǣ:m Ja še:mᵞ Pu,At,Ct šǣ:m Cc šǣ:mbóh 'brisa'

SE#009 pM *še:ne (n) 'cuate, gemelo/twin' [pOM *še:ny] NHM:
šE:n MM: Ju,Ja še:nᵞ Ma še:nᵞ 'gemelo—frutas, etc.' Pu,At,Ct še:nᵞ
'gemelo' LM: Ca še:nᵞ 'gemelo' OlP: še:ne

*SE#010 pM *še:še (n) 'sardina/any small fish'* [pOM *še:šy] MM:
Ma,Ja,Pu,At,Ct šæ·s̄ LM: Cn <še:š> 'sardina del río' Gu še·s̄
OIP: *pakše:še* 'mojarra chiquita' SaP: *pakše:š* 'clase de mojarra'

*SE#011 pGZ *se:t (vi) 'regresar/return'* SoZ: *se:t* TxZ: *se:t*

*SE#012 pZ *se?t (vt) 'tostar/to toast'* SoZ: *se?t* 'fry, cook' [Foster
and Foster 1948] TxZ: *se?t* (vt, vi-p) 'guisar, freir' ChisZ: C *se?t*
(vt) 'tostarlo' N *se?t* (vi) 'estar tostado, estar frito' (vt) 'tostarlo'
NE *se?t* (vi) 'regresar, volver' (vt) 'tostarlo'

*SE#013 pM *še:?w (vt) 'acepillar/to plane'* NHM: *še:?v* 'cepillar
(p.ej., tablas)' SHM: Tu <šæ", mže!pʸ> Tp <šæ", mže"pʸ> Mi
<šæ!p> MM: Cc <šæ", mže"pʸ> Ma <šæ:w ~ šæ:Φ ~ šæ:f,
šʸe"pʸ> 'rebanar, pelar', <šæ:W, šæ"p> 'acepillar' Ja <šæ:w,
šʸæ!w̄, šʸe!pʸ> 'rebanar, pelar' At <šæ", šʸe!pʸ> Ct <šæ:w,
šʸe!pʸ> 'acepillar, rebanar, pelar' LM: Cn <še·wše:w> (vt)
'cepillar, raspar (con machete o cuchillo)' SJ *še·w ~ še:w [only
attested in the causative] 'to plane a board; to sharpen a pencil' Gu
<še:w, šye!w, šʸe!pʸ> 'rebanar, pelar' OIP: *še:v* (vi, vt) SaP: *še?w*
(vi, vt) 'scrape'

*SE#014 pOM *še:?w-n (n) 'cepillo (para acepillar madera)/ carpen-
ter's plane'* NHM: *še:?vïn* '=destroncador' SHM: Tu *šæ!n* MM: Ju
šæ"n '=garlopa' Ma *šæ"n* '=garlopa' At *šæ?n̥* 'cepillo (para acepillar madera)', *šæ?n̥* 'garlopa' [sic!] Ct *šæ!n̥* 'cepillo (para acepillar
madera)', *šæ"n* 'garlopa' [sic!] LM: Ca *šæ"nt* 'garlopa'

*Si#001 pOM *šic (n) 'jabón/soap'* NHM: *šic* 'nudo, jabón'; *tv:t šic*
'una planta cuyo camote se usa para hacer jabón, cabeza de negro'
SHM: Tl *šic* MM: Ju *šic* Ma *šīc̄* (vowel extra short) Ja,Pu,At,Ct *šic*
LM: Cn <šic> 'jaboncillo amole (raíz que sirve como jabón)' Ca *šic*
Gu *šīc̄*

*Si#002 pZ *sih (vi) 'pararse; calmarse/to stop; calm down'* TxZ: *sih-
hak* (vi) 'entrar claridad y ventilación (cuando se corta las ramas),
quedar vacío (cuando sacan cosas de un cuarto para limpiarlo)' ChisZ:
C *sih* (vi) 'pararse' NE *sih* (vi) 'calmarse (como una tempestad)

*Si#003 pMZ *sik (n) 'frijol/bean'* [pM, pOM *šihk; pZ, pGZ *sik]
NHM: *šihk* SHM: Tl *šihk* MM: Ju,Ma,Ja,Pu,At,Ct *šihk* LM: SJ
šihki Gu *šihk* Ca *šihk* Cn <šihk> 'frijol (negro) [Phaseolus
vulgaris]' OIP: *šiki* SaP: *šihk* SoZ: *sik* AyZ: *[sik]* TxZ: *sik* ChisZ:

C,N,S *sɨk* NE [all locations cited in Wonderly 1949 and Ra] *sɨhk*
ChZ: StaMaCh *sɨk* SnMiCh *sɨk* [Wonderly 1949]

Sɨ#004 pM [Veracruz] *kuy-šɨhk *(n) 'ejote/string bean'* OIP: *kuyšɨkɨ*
SaP: *kuyšɨhk* TxZ: *kuysɨk* [borrowing from Mixean?]

Sɨ#005 pMZ *po:pʔoʔ-sɨk *(n) 'frijol blanco/white bean'* [See pMZ
*po:pʔoʔ 'white'.] NHM: *po:ʔp šɨhk* LM: Cn *<po:bšɨhk>* 'Phaseo-
lus vulgaris' AyZ: *[po:psɨk]* TxZ: *po:psɨk* 'frijol bayo' ChisZ: C
poposɨk NE *popsɨhk*

Sɨ#006 pZ *yawa-sɨk *(n) 'ejote/string bean'* ChisZ: C,N *yawasɨk*
NE *yawasɨhk* ChZ: *yawa sɨk*

Sɨ#007 pOM *ʔa-šɨ:ʔk *(n, adj) 'mal, mancha/evil, speck'* NHM:
ʔašɨ:ʔkp 'feo, asqueroso' MM: 'mancha, sucio' Ma *ʔɨžɨ́:k* '=mu-
groso como camisa, mal, malo, grosero' Pu *ʔɨžɨ́:k* 'mugroso como camisa, mal, malo' Ju *ʔažɨ:k* '=mal, malo' Ja *ʔažɨ́:k* 'sucio, asco, mal,
malo, feo' At *ʔažɨ́:k* Ct *ʔa·žɨ́:k* '=mal, malo, feo' LM: 'feo' Ca
ʔɨžɨ́:k Gu *ʔažɨ́:k* '=mal, malo'

Sɨ#008 pM *ʔaw-šɨ:ʔk-ʔɨy *(vi) 'mancharse, ensuciarse/to get dirty'*
MM: Ma *< ʔɨžɨ́:gʔɨpʸ, tɨ: yʔɨžɨ́:gɨ >* Ja *< ʔašɨ́ʔkɨp, ʔašɨ:gɨyá·m̄p >*
'ensuciarse' At *< ʔæžɨ́:gɨp, tɨ: yʔæžɨ́:gɨ >* 'mancharse' *<tɨ:
yʔažɨ́:gɨ >* 'ensuciarse' [sic!] Ct *< ʔažɨ́:gʔɨpʸ >* 'ensuciarse' SaP:
ʔašɨgɨy (vi, vt) 'tener asco'

Sɨ#009 pMZ *sɨm(ɨm) *(vt) 'calar/to pierce'* MM: 'calofríos' Ju
nɨžɨmimʸɨ Ma *nɨšɨmí·m̄ɨp* Pu,Ct *nɨžɨmí:mɨp* At *nɨšɨmí:mʸ* ChisZ: C
sɨʔm (vt) 'penetrarlo (ejemplo: un frío), calarlo' [?-phonology] NE
sɨm (vi) 'calmarse (como un dolor) [?-semantics]

Sɨ#010 pOM *šɨhp~šɨp *(v) 'caminar [?]/to walk [?]'* NHM: *šɨhp*
~*šɨp* 'caminar recto (derecho), alejarse' LM: Cn *<-šɨhp>* (raíz
dep) 'entra en la composición de verbos, con varios significados; p.ej.,
<wa"kšɨhp> 'tardarse', *<hane:kšɨhp>* 'tener el cuerpo encorvado',
<he"cmimb he"cšɨhp> 'hacer olas', *<tenayšɨhp>* 'estar parado'

Sɨ#011 pOM *kuy-šɨpɨhy *(n) 'jaguar, tigre/jaguar' [Felis onca]*
NHM: *kušyɨpɨ̈h* '=tigre real' LM: Cn *<kuyšɨbɨhy>*

Sɨ#012 pMZ *sɨw *(n) 'fiesta, nombre, sol/fiesta, name, sun'* [pM,
pOM *šɨhw; pZ, pGZ *šɨŋ] NHM: *šɨ:* 'día; fiesta; nombre; sol'

SHM: Tl *ší:w* 'fiesta; sol; nombre'; *sɨːnašʸ* 'día' Tm *šɨː* Ay *šɨːh* MM: Ju *šɨː* 'nombre, fiesta, sol' Ma *šɨːw̬ ~ šɨːΦ ~ šɨːf* 'día, fiesta, feria (fiesta), sol, nombre' Ja *šɨː* '=día, feria (fiesta)' Pu *šɨː* 'nombre, día' At *šɨːw* '=feria (fiesta), día' Ct *šɨːw* 'fiesta', *šɨːw̬ ~ šɨːΦ* 'nombre', *šɨːw̬ ~ šɨːΦ ~ šɨːf* 'feria (fiesta)', *šɨːw̬* 'día, sol' LM: Cn <*šɨː*> '=día' Ca *šɨː* SJ *šɨ·* 'day' Gu *šïː* 'nombre (pos), feria (fiesta), día, sol, fiesta' OlP: *šɨvɨ* 'sol, nombre'; *maːšanšɨvɨ* 'día de fiesta' SaP: *sɨhw* 'día, sol'; *maːsɨhw* 'fiesta' [Clark 1961 adds 'fiesta day']); *šɨːm* 'el día' [Clark and Clark 1960] SoZ: *sɨŋ* 'cielo; fiesta' TxZ: *sɨŋ* 'fiesta, tradiciones, sol' ChisZ: 'fiesta, feria' C,N *sɨŋ* NE *sɨk* ChZ: *sɨŋ* 'fiesta'

Sɨ#013 pOM ***kuhk (y-)šɨhw** *(n) 'mediodía/noon'* NHM: *kʋhk šɨː* 'mediodía aproximadamente' MM: Ma *kihkʸšʸɨːw̬ ~ kihkʸšʸɨːΦ ~ kihkʸšʸɨːf* Ja *kihšʸɨ* Pu *kihkʸšʸɨː* At *kuühkʸšʸɨːw* Ct *kihkʸšʸɨːw* LM: Cn *kuhkšɨː* Gu *kuhšʸï:*

Sɨ#014 pM ***ʔV-šɨhw-i** *(adv) 'ayer/yesterday'* [pOM **ʔušɨhwy*] NHM: *ʔuš* SHM: Tl *ʔušɨː* Ay *ʔašɨːy* Tu *ʔažɨ"y* Tp *ʔAžɨ"y* Mi *ʔušɨ̃h* MM: Ju,Ma,Pu,At *ʔɨžɨ"y* Ja *ʔažɨ"y, ʔɨžɨ"y* Ct *ʔažɨ"y* LM: Ca *ʔažɨːy* Gu *ʔɨžïːy* OlP: *ʔušɨvɨ* 'anoche' SaP: *ʔúšu* 'anoche'

Sɨ#015 pOM ***mu-šɨhw** *(n) 'tocayo/namesake'* NHM: *mušɨː* MM: Ju *mɨžɨː* Ja *mʸɨžɨː* At *mɨžɨːw* Ct *mʸɨ·žɨːw* LM: Gu *mɨžï:*

Sɨ#016 pZ ***sɨʔŋaʔ** *(vi) 'festejar/to celebrate'* TxZ: *sɨːʔŋaʔ* '=estar de fiesta' ChisZ: C [Te] <*sengapa*> 'celebrar fiesta'

Sɨ#017 pOM ***šɨhw-n** *(adv) 'de día/at daytime'* NHM: *šïːhɨ̈n* MM: Ma *šɨ·n̄ʸ* Ja,Pu,At *šɨːnʸ* Ct *šɨːnʸ, šɨːwʔám* LM: Cn <*šɨːm*> (adv) Gu *šïːm*

Sɨ#018 pMZ ***sɨʔw** *(vt) 'acusar/to accuse'* NHM: *šɨ"* 'quejarse a las autoridades' MM: Ma <*nɨžɨ"wɨ*> Ja <*nɨ̄šɨ"wɨ, n̄ʸšɨ!w̄ɨp*> Pu <*nišɨ"*> LM: Cn <*šɨʔw ~ šɨʔ ~ šɨ"w*> (vt) 'demandar, acusar' SJ *šɨʔw ~ šɨ"w* 'to accuse to the authorities' Gu <*nɨžï"wï"w*> SoZ: *sɨʔ* 'go along' [Foster and Foster 1948] ChisZ: NE *sɨʔ* (vt) 'sospecharlo (sin razón)'

Sɨ#019 pOM ***šɨwinyky** *(n) 'avispa/wasp'* SHM: Tp *šɨβíŋ̄ʸkʸ* Tu *sɨBíŋʸkʸ* Mi *šubíhkʸ* MM: Ju *šɨbí"ŋʸkʸ* Cc *šɨwíŋʸkʸ* Ma *šɨbíʔŋʸkʸ ~ šɨbí!nʸkʸ* Ja,Pu *šɨmí!ŋʸkʸ* At *šɨ̄bíŋʸkʸ* 'avispa roja' Ct *šɨbí!ŋʸkʸ* LM: Cn <*šubiñ*> 'avispa (tipo solitario)' (pp. 223, 266 in Hoogshagen and

Hoogshagen 1993), <*šibiñ*> 'tipo de avispa [order: Hymeoptera, fam: Sphecidae]' (p. 442) Ca *šimí·ŋʸkʸ* Gu *šibí!ŋʸkʸ*

Si#020 pOM ***šiwat*** *(n) 'veneno de la víbora/snake poison'* NHM: *šivat* MM: Ju *šiwǽt* Ma *šiWát* At *šiwát* LM: Gu *šiwát*

SA#001 pZ ***sa?*** *(vi) 'revivir/revive'* TxZ: *sa?* (vi) 'cicatrizar, sanar' ChisZ: C,N *sa?* (vi) 'despertarse' NE *sa?* (vi) 'despertarse, levantarse'

SA#002 pMZ ***sac*** *(vt) 'batir/to whip liquid'* OM: 'batir (chocolate, etc.)' SHM: Tp <*šAc*> MM: Ju <*šæc*> Cc <*šAc*> Ma,Ct <*šac̄, šʸahčpʸ*> '=restregar' Ja <*šac̄, sʸahc, sʸahčpʸ*> '=restregar' Pu <*šahchidít*> At <*šac̄, sʸæhčpʸ*> LM: Ca <*šac*> Cn <*šahc~šac*> (vt) 'batir' (vi) 'pestañear' Gu <*šac̄, sʸahčp*> '=restregar' SJ *šahc~šac* 'to beat liquid with whip or beater' OlP: *šac* (vi) 'batir (con palito)' (vt) 'batirlo (como chocolate)' SaP: *šač* (vi, vt) 'beat liquid with stick (rubbing between hands)' TxZ: *sac* (vt) 'repellar, batir (chocolate)' ChisZ: C *sahc* (vt) 'batirlo' (ejemplo: batir una bebida con molinillo) N *sahc* (vt) 'batirlo' (ejemplo: "se le pone pinole al agua y se bate, para hacer una bebida") NE *sahc* (vt) 'batirlo' (como una bebida espesa)

SA#003 pM ***ša:c~ša?c*** *(vi) 'enrollar/to roll up'* NHM: *yakša:?c* 'envolver algo (p.ej., un niño con un rebozo)' MM: Ma <*ša:c, sʸa?čpʸ*> 'enrollar' At <*ša:c, ša?cp, ša:ʒá·m̄p*> 'mecatear, hacer mecate' Ct <*ša:c, ša?cp, ša:ʒámp*> 'enrollar, mecatear, hacer mecate' LM: Cn <*ša·c~ša:c*> (vt) 'hilar' Gu <*ša:c, ša·?cp, ša:ʒá·m̄p*> 'mecatear, hacer mecate' LM: SJ *ša·c~ša:c* 'to spin between the hands' OlP: *ša:c* (vt) 'hacerlo (puro)'

SA#004 pM ***ša:?c-e(k)*** *(n) 'rollo de hoja o zacate/roll of leaf or tobacco'* NHM: *ša:?č* 'zacatón, zacate de aparejo, rollo [Muelenbergia disticophylla (?), Spirobolus wrightii (?)]' LM: Cn <*ša:č*> 'zacate de escoba [probably Muhlenbergia macroura]' OlP: *?ay ša:ce'k* 'rollo de hoja de tabaco'

SA#005 pMZ ***sah*** *(vt) 'repartir/to distribute'* NHM: *nišáhi~nišaha* 'extender la mano, tomar una cosa para comerla' TxZ: *sah* (vt) 'regalar, repartir' ChisZ: C *sah* (vt) 'repartirlo; darlo' N *sah* (vt) 'repartirlo' NE *sah* (vt) 'regalarlo, repartirlo'

SA#006 pMZ ***sah** *(n) 'brazada/armful'* [*sah reconstructed for all subgroups] NHM: *šahtïk* 'brazada'; *šahva?kš* 'brazos abiertos)' SHM: Tp *šAhk* MM: Ju *šahk, tukšáhk* Cc *šAhpk* Ma,Ct *šahk* 'sobaco' OlP: *šahku* SaP: *šáhpak* ChisZ: N *sah* 'brazada—medida; linealmente'

SA#007 pZ ***sah(a)** *(n) 'ala/wing'* [pGZ **sah*] TxZ: *sah* SoZ: *šah* ChisZ: C *sah* '=aleta' N *sah* '=brazada' NE *saha* '=aleta' ChZ: *sah*

SA#008 pOM ***ša?k** *(n) 'ixtle/agave fiber'* NHM: *ša?k* SHM: Tl *šo?hk* 'fibra de magey' MM: Ju *ša?k* '=fibra, costal' Ma *ša?k* '=costal' Ja *ša?k?awá:y* 'ixtle', *ša?k* 'costal' Pu *ša!k* 'ixtle' At,Ct *ša?k* LM: Ca *ša?k* Cn <*ša"k*> Gu *ša?k* '=fibra'

SA#009 pMZ ***sak-...** *(n) 'sobaco/armpit'* [Except for the first syllable phonological developments are not under control; in some cases compounding is probably involved, as in Zoquean where *tɨk* 'house' is the second member.] NHM: *šahkïpa?tk* '=axila' [*pa?* or *pa?t* inserted?] SHM: Ay *šɨgát* MM: Ju *šɨgǽt* At *šɨgǽtk* LM: Gu *šɨgétk* OlP: *šahkɨ'k* SaP: *šáhkat* AyZ: *[ṣak]* TxZ: *saktɨk* ChisZ: C *sa?akɨtɨk* '=axila'

SA#010 pMZ ***sake(s)** *(n) 'suegra de mujer, nuera de mujer/mother-, daughter-in-law of woman'* [pM **šakeš* > pOM **šakyš*; pZ **sake* (with raising of /e/ in the Chimalapas) > pGZ **sa:ke?* (with vowel-leveling in TxZ)] NHM: *šákiš* 'suegra de mujer' LM: Cn <*šeky*> 'suegra o nuera (sólo lo usan las mujeres)' Gu *soky* 'man's mother-in-law, woman's daughter-in-law, woman's father-in-law' [Foster 1949] OlP: *šeke'š* 'suegra de mujer' SaP: *šak* 'suegra de mujer' [lacks final /š/ of other Mixean forms; could thus have been borrowed from Zoquean before final vowel loss set in] TxZ: *sa:ka?* 'nuera (de hombre o mujer), suegra (de la mujer), amuche (árbol grande, tiene espinas)' SoZ: *sá:ki* 'suegra de mujer, nuera de mujer, nuera de hombre' [Foster 1949] ChisZ: C *sake* N *sake* 'nuera de la mujer; tía de la mujer, esposa del hermano de su padre' NE *sake* S [Tu] *sake* [Foster 1949] ChZ: StaMaCh *caki* 'suegra de mujer, nuera de muje, nuera de hombre' [Foster 1949] SnMiCh *hasaki* 'woman's daughter-in-law, man's daughter-in-law' [Foster 1949]

SA#011 pMZ ***sa:ka** *(n) 'concha/shell'* [pM **ša:ka*; pZ **saka*] OlP: *ša:ka* SaP: *ša:hk* TxZ: *sakaď'a:k* 'almeja (de arroyo), concha de almeja (se ocupa para rascar jícara)' ChisZ: C [Te] <*saca*> 'concha de pescado'

SA#012 pMZ *sa?ks* *(vi)* *'escurrir, salpicar/to drip, sprinkle'* NHM: *ša?kš* 'escurrir, gotear (p.ej., un trapo mojado)' ChisZ: N *sa?ks* (vi) 'salpicar'

SA#013 pMZ *sam* *(vi)* *'calentarse/to heat'* NHM: *ša:m~ša:hm ~šam* 'calentarse junto a la lumbre' MM: 'calentar' Ju <*šæm*> Cc <*šAm, šA:mp, šam*ʸ> Ma,Ja,Ct <*šam̄, ša·m̄p*> Pu <*ša·m̄p*> At <*ša·m̄p, šam̄*> LM: Cn <*ša·m~šam*> (vi) 'calentar' SJ *ša·m~- šam* 'to warm oneself in the sun or by the fire' Gu <*šam̄, ša·m̄p*> 'calentar' OlP: *šam* (vi) 'calentarse' SaP: *šam* (vi) 'get warm at fire or in the sun' TxZ: *sam* (vi) 'calentar (junto a la lumbre o con el sol)' ChisZ: C *sam* (vi) ChZ: *sam*

SA#014 pMZ *san* *(vi)* *'estar turbio; estar lleno/to be muddy; to be full'* MM: 'turbio' Ma,Ct *šan̄*ʸ Ja *šæn̄*ʸ At *šan̠*ʸ SaP *šan* 'espeso' ChisZ: C [Te] <*sanba*> 'ahitarse' N *san* (vi) 'tener gases en el estómago' ChZ: *san* 'llenarse'

SA#015 pZ *sapane* *(n)* *'mamey/marmelade fruit'* [The meaning changed to 'plantain' when this fruit was introduced by the Spaniards.] AyZ: *[sap]* 'plátano' TxZ: *sapun* 'plátano' [*sapa:n* expected; perhaps influenced analogically by *šapun* 'soap'] ChisZ: C *sapane* 'plátano macho' N *samne* 'plátano macho' NE *sabane* 'plátano macho' S *[saní?]* 'guinéo' ChZ: *sapane* 'mamey'

SA#016 pZ *sas* *(n)* *'cicatriz/scar'* [pGZ *sas*] SoZ: *sas* AyZ: *[sas]* ChisZ: C *sas* [homonym: 'chachalín—especie de camarón'] N,NE *sas*

SA#017 pZ *sawa* *(n)* *'viento/wind'* [pGZ *sa:wa*] SoZ: *sa:wa?* AyZ: *[sa:gʷa]* TxZ: *sa:w* '=aire; loco' ChisZ: C *sawa* 'aire, viento' [homonym: 'buche de ave'] N,NE *sawa* ChZ: *sawa* 'aire'

SU#001 pMZ *su:c* *[?]* *(vi)* *'mecatear; mentir/to rope; lie'* LM: Cn <*šu·c~šu:c*> (vt) 'lazar' SJ *šu·c~šu:c* 'to rope an animal' SaP: *šuc* (vi, vt) 'lasso, rope an animal' TxZ: *suc* (vt) 'tantear, cuidar, vigilar, tener (ganas, culpa)' ChisZ: C *suhc* (vi) 'mentir' N *suhc* (vi) 'mentir, echar mentira; *suckuy* mentira'

SU#002 pOM ***šu:c-n** *(n) 'lazo/cord, lasso'* NHM: *šu:ʔck ʔa:ʔc ca:ʔn* 'cordelilla común, cordelilla manchada' MM: Ja,At,Ct *šuʔcn̦* LM: Gu *šu·ʔct*

SU#003 pOM ***šu:ʔc** *(vt) 'lavar nixtamal/to soak maize in lime water'* MM: Ma,At <*šu:c, mžuʔčpʸ*> Ja <*šu:c, šʸuʔc, šʸuʔčpʸ*> Pu <*šu:c, mžu!čpʸ*> Ct <*šu:c, šʸuʔčpʸ*> Ju <*šu:c*> LM: Ca <*šu:c*> Gu <*šu:c, sʸuʔčpʸ*>

SU#004 pOM ***šu:ʔc** *(adj) 'angosto/narrow'* NHM: *šu:ʔc* 'estrecho' MM: At,Ct,Cc,Pu *šu"c* LM: Cn <*šu"c*> (adj) SJ *šuʔc* Gu *šu"c*

SU#005 pZ ***suʔc** *(n) 'liendre/nit'* [pGZ *suʔt (*suʔc the expected form)] SoZ: *suʔt* TxZ: *suʔt* ChisZ: C,NE *suʔc* ChZ: *suʔc*

SU#006 pMZ ***su:h?** *(vt) 'soplar/to blow'* NHM: *šv:h~šv"* 'rocear, fumigar' SaP: *šuh* (vi) 'blow' SoZ: *suh* (vt) TxZ: *suh* (vt, vi-a) 'soplar' ChisZ: C,NE *suh* (vt) 'soplarlo' N *suh* (vt) 'soplarle'

SU#007 pZ ***suk-ʔɨy** *(vi) 'refrescarse/to cool off'* SoZ: *súksuk* 'cold' [Foster and Foster 1948] ChisZ: C *suhkɨy* (vi) 'refrescarse; enfriarse' N *suhkɨy* (vi) 'enfriarse' NE *suhkɨy* (vi) 'refrescarse'

SU#008 pMZ ***su:ʔk** *(vi) 'oler, besar/to smell, kiss'* NHM: *šv:ʔk* 'oler, heder, apestar' SHM: Tl *šu:kɨ* 'oler' Tu <*ʔažúʔkp*> 'apestar' Tp <*šuʔkp, kæ"p yʔuk šúʔkni, kæ"p šʸu:kʸ*> 'apestar' MM: Ju <*šuʔkp*> 'oler, apestar, está oloroso' Ma <*šuʔkp, kæh šʸi:kʸ, šu:gámp*> 'oler, apestar, está oloroso' Ja <*šu:gá·m̄p, šuʔk, šuʔkp*> 'oler, apestar, está oloroso' Pu <*šu:gá·m̄p, šu!kp, kæh ši:kʸ*> 'oler, apestar, está oloroso' At <*šu:gá·mp, šuʔkp*> 'oler, apestar, está oloroso', <*šuʔkp, šu:gá·m̄p*> 'apestar' [sic!] Ct <*šu:gám̄p, šuʔkp*> 'oler, apestar, está oloroso' LM: Gu <*šu:gá·m̄p, šu·k, šu·ʔp, kah šʸu:kʸ*> 'oler, apestar, está oloroso', <*šu·p, šu:gá·m̄p*> 'apestar' [sic!] LM: Cn <*šu·k~šu:k*> (vi) 'oler' SJ *šu·k~šu:k* 'to smell' OIP: *šu:k* (vi) 'apestar' [derivative: *paʔkšu:kpa* 'huele bonito'; *šu:kɨ'k* 'apeste, mal olor'] SaP: *šuʔk* (vi, vt) 'stink, smell, kiss' [additional meaning 'to kiss' is a result of Zoquean influence] TxZ: *suʔk* (vi) 'apestar, (vt) besar (boca a boca)' SoZ: *suʔk* 'smell' [Foster and Foster 1948] ChisZ: C *suʔk* (vt) 'besarlo' N *suʔk* (vt) 'besarlo; olerlo; chuparlo' NE *suʔk* (vt) 'besarlo' ChZ: *suʔk* 'oler'

SU#009 pOM ***ʔa-šu:ʔk** *(vi) 'oler/to smell'* NHM: *ʔašu:ʔk* 'asquear' LM: Cn <*ašu·k~ašu:k*> (vi)

SU#010 pOM **šu"k* _(adj) 'sabroso/savory'_ NHM: *šv"hk* MM: Ju *šu"k* 'yerba buena' Ma,At,Ct *šu"k*

SU#011 pOM **pa"hk šu:?k* _(vi) 'oler bien/to smell good'_ NHM: *pa"hk šu:?k* 'perfumado' MM: Ju *<pa"kšú?kni>* Ma,Ja,Ct *<pa"kšú?kp>* At *<pa"kšú?kp, šu"k, šʸü:kʸ>* LM: Gu *<pa"kšu:gá·m̄p, pa"kšú·?kp>*

SU#012 pOM **šukuhk~šukuk* _(vi) 'echar tortillas/to make tortillas'_ NHM:_ *švk~šúgik* 'tortear' MM: Ma,At,Ct *<šigúk, šigúhkp>* Ja *<šigúk, šigúhk, šiguhkp>* LM: Gu *<šigúk, šigúhk, šigúhp>*

SU#013 pM [Veracruz] **šuhkut* _(n) 'talzahuate/?'_ OIP: *šuhku's* SaP: *šúhkut*

_SU#014 pZ_ **suks* _(vi) 'ahogarse/to choke'_ SoZ: *suks* 'cough' [Foster and Foster 1948] ChisZ: N *suks* (vi) NE *suks* (vi)

_SU#015 pZ_ **su?ks* _(vi) 'toser/to cough'_ [cf. pZ **suks*] SoZ: *su?ks* (vi) TxZ: *su?ks* (vi) 'toser' ChisZ: C *su?ks* (vi) 'ahogarse' NE *yaksu?kska?* (vt) 'ahogarlo, dejarlo ahogarse' ChZ: *su?ks* 'toser'

_SU#016 pZ_ **su?ks-i* _(n) 'tos/cough'_ SoZ: *su?kši* TxZ: *su?kš* ChZ: *su?ksi?*

SU#017 pMZ **su?ksu(k)* _(n) 'colibrí/hummingbird'_ [pM **šu?kšu(k)* > pOM **šu(:)(?)kš*; pZ **su(?)ksu*] NHM: *šv:kš* '=chuparrosa, chupamirto, chupamiel [Trochilidae familia]' SHM: Tl *šu:?kš* 'chuparrosa' Tu,Tp *šu?kš* Mi *šu·?kš* MM: Cc *šu?kš* Ja,Pu *šu·kš* At,Ct *šukš* LM: Cn *<šu:kš>* (p. 446 in Hoogshagen and Hoogshagen 1993) *<šu?kš>* (p. 224) '=chuparrosa, chupaflor' Gu *šu·?š* OIP: *šu?kšu'k* '=chupamiel' ChisZ: C *suksu* '=chupaflor' N *suksu* 'chupamirto' ChZ: *su?ksu?* 'chupa-rosa'

SU#018 pMZ **sum* _(n) 'juntar/gather'_ SaP: *šum* (vi) 'pile in clusters' TxZ: *sumde?* (v-s-pl) 'juntado, reunido'

SU#019 pOM **šu:m-y* _(n) 'red/net'_ NHM: *šu:m* 'red, tarraya' SHM: Tl *šu:my* MM: Ju *ši:mʸ* 'red para pescar' Ma,Ja *ši:mʸ* 'red grande para cargar' At *šuü:mʸ* 'red grande para cargar' Ct *ši:mʸ* 'red grande para cargar' LM: Cn *<šu:my>* Ca *šu:ʸmʸ* 'red para pescar' Gu *šu:mʸ* 'red grande para cargar'

_SU#020 pZ_ **sun* _(vt) 'querer/to want'_ TxZ: *sun* (vt) 'querer' SoZ: *su:n* 'need, want' [Foster and Foster 1948] ChisZ: C *sun* (vi) 'anto-

jarse' (v-aux) 'querer' (v impersonal) 'requerir, deber, convenir; ser necesario' N *sun / sunu / sunba* (v modal) 'quiso, quería, quiere' (vt) 'quererlo' NE *sun* (v impersonal) 'requerer, deber' (vt) 'amarlo; quererlo, desearlo; enamorarse de alguien'

SU#021 pOM *šuhn ~ šun (vi) 'agriarse/to become sour' NHM: *šv̈nï̈n* 'agriar; ácido' SHM: Tp <*tï: šʸúnnï*> MM: Cc <*tï: šʸunʸ*> Ma <*šu·m̄p, šun̄ám̄p*> Ja,Pu,At <*šu·m̄p, šun̄á·m̄p*> Ct <*šu·m̄p, šun̄ám̄p*> LM: Gu <*šu·m̄p, šun̄á·m̄p*>

SU#022 pOM *šun (adj) 'agrio/sour' SHM: Tl *šun* Tu,Tp,Mi *šun* MM: Ju,Cc *šun* Ma,Ja,Pu,At,Ct *šūn* LM: Cn <*šun*> (adj) Ca *šun* Gu *šūn*

SU#023 pOM *šunïk (vi) 'hacer cosquillas/to tickle' NHM: *šúnïk* 'hacer cosquillas' MM: Ma,At,Ct <*šïnúhkïp*> 'tiene cosquillas' LM: Gu <*šïnúhkïp*> 'tiene cosquillas'

SU#024 pOM *šuʔny (n) 'anzuelo/hook' SHM: Tu *šu!nʸ* Mi *šuʔnʸ* MM: Cc,Ja *šu!nʸ* Ma,At *šuʔnʸ* LM: Cn <*šuʔñ̄*> 'aguja' Gu *šu!nʸď*

SU#025 pZ *sun(uʔ) (n) 'almagre/type of red earth' [pGZ *su:nuʔ] TxZ: *su:nuʔ* ChisZ: C [Te] <*sun*>

SU#026 pOM *šuhpš (vt) 'picotear/to peck' NHM: *šv̈hpš* 'picotear' LM: Cn <*šupš*> (vt) SJ *šupš* 'to peck, fight (chickens)'

SU#027 pM *šu:ʔpš (vt) 'tomar caldo/to eat soup' NHM: *šu:ʔpš* MM: 'chupar' Ma <*šuʔpšp*> Ja <*šuʔpš, šuʔpšp*> Pu <*šu!pš. šʸi!psʸp*> 'chupar' At,Ct <*šuʔpš*> 'chupar' LM: SJ *šu·pš* to suck (up a straw, egg out of shell, etc.) Gu <*šu·ʔš*> 'chupar' OlP: *šu:pš* (vt)

SU#028 pOM *šuhš ~ šuš (vi) 'enfriar/to be cold' NHM: *šv̈hš ~ šv̈š* 'frío, helado, enfriar' SHM: Tl *šuš* 'frío' MM: 'entumecerse, entumirse' Ja <*šuhšp, šušá·m̄p*> Ma,At,Ct <*šuhšp*> LM: Cn <*šuhš ~ šuš*> (vt) 'paralizar; hormiguear; entorpecerse' SJ *šuhš ~ šuš* 'to become numb' Gu <*šužï̈:pʸ*> 'entumecerse, entumirse'

SU#029 pMZ *su:sʔ (vi) 'chiflar, tocar instrumento de viento/to whistle, play a musical instrument' NHM: *šv:š ~ šv"š* 'tocar (p.ej., una trompeta), chiflar (suavemente)' SHM: Tl *šuʔuš* 'tocar (instrumento de viento)' MM: Ju <*šu"š, šušp*> Pu,At,Ct,Ma,Ja <*šu"š, šu·šp*> LM: Ca <*šu"š*> Cn <*šu·š ~ šu"š*> (vi) 'tocar (la música)' SJ <*šu·š~šu"š*> Gu <*šu"š, šu·s̄p, šu·s̄s̄*> OlP: *šu:š~šu?š* (vi) 'tocar (instrumento musical)' SaP: *šu:š~šu?š* (vi) 'whistle, play a wind instrument' SoZ: *sus* 'chiflar' TxZ: *sus* (vi) 'chiflar' ChisZ: C *suhs* (vi) 'silbar, chiflar' N *sus* (vi) 'chiflar; tocar la flauta' NE *suhs* (vi) 'chiflar, silbar'

*SU#030 pM *šu:š-an (n) 'instrumento de musica de viento/flute, horn'* [pOM *šu:šn*] NHM: *šv:šïn* 'instrumento de viento, clarín, silbato' MM: Ju *šušn̥* 'silbato, instrumento musical de viento' Ma *šu·s̄n̥* 'instrumento musical de viento' Ja *šu·s̄n̥* 'silbato', *šu·s̄n̥ wohpn̥* 'instrumento musical de viento' Pu *šu·s̄n̥* At *šu·s̄n̥* 'silbato, instrumento musical de viento' Ct *šu·s̄n̥* 'silbato', *šu·šn̥* 'instrumento musical de viento' [sic!] LM: Ca *šu·št* Cn <*šu:šy*> SJ *šu·š* flute, horn' Gu *šu·s̄t* 'silbato, instrumento musical de viento' OlP: *šu:ša'n* 'instrumento de musica de viento, pito' SaP: *šu:šan*

*SU#031 pMZ *su:s?-hay (v ap) 'chiflarle/to whistle at'* OlP: *šu:šay* (vt-ap) 'chiflar' TxZ: *sus-a?* (vt) 'chiflar a otro' ChisZ: NE *suhsay* (vt) 'silbarle'

*SU#032 pZ *sus-kuy (n) 'flauta, pito/flute'* SoZ: *suskuy* 'tráquea' TxZ: *súsku?* 'silbato' ChisZ: C *suskuy* 'pito—flauta indígena; silbo' N *suskuy* NE *susku?*

*SU#033 pM *šu:š-pa (n) 'músico (instr. de viento)/musician'* [pOM *šu:špa*, although final vowels are generally lost.] NHM: *šv:špa* MM: Ju *šúšpɨ* Ja,Ct *šú·s̄pɨ wóhpɨ* Ma,Pu,At *šú·s̄pɨ* LM: Gu *šú·s̄pɨ* OlP: *šu:špa?*

*SU#034 pMZ *suse:pe (n) 'mariposa/butterfly'* [pM *šuše:pe* > pOM *šupy* by loss of the mid-syllable, a process which does not have parallels (but this is not so strange since tri-syllabics are rare.); pZ *susepe*] LM: Cn <*šupy*> SaP: *šupé:p* [the mid-consonant changed from /š/ to /p/, a kind of sporadic change which is not uncommon in SaP] ChZ: *susepe?*

*SU#035 pMZ *sut (vt) 'perforar/to perforate'* NHM: *tukšvht~tukšvt* (vt) 'ahuecar' LM: Cn <*šuht~šut*> (vt) 'agujerear' SJ *šuht~šut* 'to have a hole through it' SaP: *šut* (vi, vt) 'stab' TxZ: *sut* (vt) 'ensartar' ChisZ: C *suht* (vi, vi-s) 'agujerarse, estar agujerado' (vt) 'agujerarlo, ahoyarlo' N *suht* (vi) 'estar perforado, estar agujerado' (vt) 'perforarlo' NE *suht* (vt) 'agujerarlo, ahoyarlo (como bejiga o llanta)' ChZ: *sut* 'agujerar'

SU#036 pM ***šu:t(Vk)** **[?]** *(n) 'atole/a drink made from cornstarch'*
NHM: *šu:dïk* 'polvo de maíz' SaP: *šu?t* 'atole' [glottal stop not accounted for]

SU#037 pOM ***šuty** *(n) 'calabaza/pumpkin, gourd'* NHM: *šut* SHM: Tp *šuṯʸ* 'bule' MM: 'bule' Ju,Cc *šuṯʸ* Ma,Ja,Pu,At,Ct *šuṯʸ*

SU#038 pOM ***šutyky** *(n) 'chocolín (caracol acuático, comestible)/kind of aquatic snail'* SHM: Tp *šuṯʸkʸ* MM: Ja *šuhṯʸ* Ju,Cc, Ma,Pu,At,Ct *šuhṯʸkʸ* LM: Ca *šuhṯʸ* Gu *šuhṯʸkʸ*

SU#039 pOM ***šutk** *(n) 'arado/plow'* [Contamination from **šutyky* in SHM and MM?] SHM: Tp *šuhṯʸkʸ* MM: Ju,Cc,At *šuhṯʸkʸ* LM: Ca,Gu *šutk*

SU#040 pMZ ***suy** *(vt) 'coser, pescar con anzuelo/to sew, fish with a hook'* NHM: *šv:y ~ šv:hy ~ švy* 'coser' SHM: Tl *šuy* 'coser' MM: Ju <*šuy*> 'coser, costurar' Ma <*šuy, ši:pʸ*> 'pescar con anzuelo', <*šuȳ, šʸi:pʸ*> 'coser, costurar', <*šuȳ, ?ɨžúyyɨ*> 'remendar' [sic!] Ja <*šuȳ, šu·ȳ, ši:pʸ, šʸi:pʸ*> 'pescar con anzuelo, coser, costurar' Pu <*šuȳ, ši:pʸ*> 'pescar con anzuelo', <*šuȳ, šʸi:pʸ, šʸu·ȳ*> 'coser, costurar' At <*šuȳ, šʸuü:pʸ*> 'coser, costurar' Ct <*šuy, šʸi:pʸ*> 'coser, costurar', <*šuȳ, ši:pʸ*> 'pescar con anzuelo', <*šuȳ*> 'remendar' LM: Ca <*šuy*> 'coser, costurar' Cn <*šu·y ~ šuy*> 'coser (con aguja); pescar' SJ *šu·y ~ šuy* 'to sew, to fish with hook and line' Gu <*šuȳ, šu·ȳ, šu:pʸ*> 'pescar con anzuelo', <*šuȳ, šu·ȳ, šʸu:pʸ*> 'coser, costurar' OlP: *šuy* (vt) 'costurarlo' SaP: *šuy* (vi, vt) 'fish with hook and line' SoZ: *suy* 'lasso, fish with a line' [Foster and Foster 1948]' AyZ: *[ṣutak]* 'aguja' TxZ: *suy* (vt, vi-p) 'pescar con anzuelo' ChisZ: C *suy* (vi) 'pescar' (vt) 'pescarlo' N *suy* (vi) 'pescar (con anzuelo)'

SU#041 pMZ ***suy-i** *(n) 'camisa/shirt'* [pM **šuyi* > pOM **ni:-šuy* (the prefix has to do with 'corporeal matter' of 'surface'); pZ **suyi* > pGZ **su:yi*] NHM: *nɨšvya* SHM: Tu *nɨšúyɨ* Tp *nɨšúy* MM: Ju *nɨšúy* Ma *nɨžúy* Ja *ni"žúȳ* Pu,At,Ct *nɨšúȳ* LM: 'blusa, camisa de mujer' Cn <*ni"šuy*> Ml <*nišuy*> Ca *nɨžúy* 'camisa' AyZ: *[su?uyi]* TxZ: *su:y* 'pellejo de tumor'

SU#042 pOM ***?a-šuy-?ay** *(vi) 'remendar/to mend'* NHM: *?ašv?yi ~ ?ašvya* '=coser' MM: Ju <*?æžúyɨ*> Ja,At <*?ažúyɨ*> LM: Gu <*?ažuyɨ"w*>

SU#043 pZ ***suyu*** *[?] (n) 'olla/pot'* SaP: *šuy* [Zo loan] SoZ *sú?uŋ* [?] AyZ: *[sū?ū]* 'olla de barro' [?] TxZ: *su:?ŋ* 'olla' [?-phonology] ChZ: *suyu?*

SO#001 pMZ ***soc*** *(vt) 'amarrar/to tie'* NHM: *šohc ~ šoc* LM: SJ *šohc ~ šoc* 'to tie with rope, vine' MM: Ju <*šoc*> Ma <*šōc*> Ja <*šōc, šohc, šʸohčpʸ*> LM: Cn <*šohc ~ šoc*> (vt) Ca <*šoc*> Gu <*šōc*> ChZ: *soc* 'amarrar puerta'

SO#002 pOM ***šoc-y*** *(n) 'nudo en mecate/knot (of rope)'* NHM: *šɨc* MM: Ma,At,Ct *šōč* Pu *šočáhtinʸ* LM: Gu *šōč*

SO#003 pMZ ***so:?c*** *(vi) 'arrugarse/to wrinkle'* LM: Cn <*šo·c ~ šo:c*> (vi) 'aplastar, arrugar (p.ej., latas)' SJ *šo·c ~ šo:c* 'to wrinkle up, shrink up' ChisZ: C *so?c* (vi) 'arrugarse' (vt) 'ajarlo, arrugarlo' N *so?c* (vt) 'doblarse; abollarse'

SO#004 pMZ ***soho*** *(n) 'encino/oak'* [pM **šoho* > pOM **šoh*; pZ, pGZ **soho* (pGZ fails to lengthen the first syllable as would have been expected.)] NHM: *šoh* '=roble' MM: Ju *šoh* Ma,Ja,Pu,At,Ct *šoh* LM: Cn <*šoh*> 'encino, roble [Quercus spp.]' Ca *šoh* Gu *šoh* OlP: *šoho* 'encina' SaP: *šoh* 'encina' SoZ: *soh* [*so:ho* expected] TxZ: *sohkuy*

SO#005 pOM ***po:?p šoh*** *(n) 'encino blanco/type of oak [Quercus spp.]'* NHM: *po:?p šoh* 'tipo de roble [Quercus prinus]' LM: Cn <*po:bšoh*> 'especie de encino, encino blanco, roble [Quercus spp.]'

SO#006 pZ ***so?k*** *(n) 'zacate/grass'* [pGZ **so?k*] TxZ: *so?k* '=pasto' SoZ: *so?k* 'fodder' [Foster and Foster 1948] ChisZ: C *so?k* '=paja' N *so?k* 'zacate alto, pajón' NE *so?k* 'zacate verde'

SO#007 pM ***šo:?k*** *(vi) 'mojarse/to become wet'* NHM: *šo:?k* 'mojar, empapar' MM: Ma,Ct <*šo?kp, šo:gámp*> Pu <*šo!kp, šo:gá·m̄p*> At <*šo?kp, šo:gá·m̄p*> Ja <*šo:k, šo?kp, šo?k, šo:gá·m̄p*> LM: Cn <*šo·k ~ šo:k*> (vi) 'mojar' SJ *šo·k ~ šo:k* Gu <*šo:k, šo·?k, šo·?p, šo:gá·m̄p*> OlP: *šo:k* (vi) SaP: *šo?k* (vi)

SO#008 pM ***šo?ok*** *(adj) 'mojado/wet'* [pOM **šo"hk*] NHM: *šo"hk* MM: Ju *šo:k* Ma,Ja,Pu,At,Ct *šo"k* LM: Gu *šo:k* OlP: *šo?o'k* (adj) SaP: *šo?g-ik*

SO#009 pOM ***šohk ~ šok*** *(vt) 'vigilar, acechar/to keep guard, lurk'* NHM: *šohk ~ šok* 'vigilar, vigilancia, acechar, espiar (p.ej., estar en espera de alguien)' MM: 'acechar' Ma <*šok, šʸehkʸpʸ*> At <*šok,*

šʸöhkʸpʸ > Ct < *šok̄, šʸehkʸpʸ* > LM: Gu < *šok̄, šʸohpʸ* > 'acechar'
OlP: *šok* (vi) 'estar acostado' [?]

SO#010 pZ ***soki** *(n) 'caracol/snail'* [NHM *šɨk* 'panal de avispa' is
a perfect phonological match; a pMZ form **soki* 'structure like snail
shell or honeycomb' may probably be reconstructed; a further, more
speculative hypothesis is that pMZ **soki* could be a derivative of an
antecedent of pOM **šohk ~ šok* 'to keep guard, lurk'.] SoZ: *šó:ki*
'snail, large variety' [Foster and Foster 1948, Wonderly 1949, who
notes that the presence of *š* is problematic], *so:ki ~ šo:ki* 'caracol'
[Gutiérrez M. 1993 and p.c., in which he says that *s* and *š* are in free
variation.] AyZ: [*sọ:?gi*] TxZ: *so:k:e?* 'caracol acuático' C,N,NE
soki

SO#011 pM ***šo:ki** *(n) 'uña/nail'* [pOM **šo:ky*] NHM: *šɨ:?k* '=pez-
uña, casco' SHM: Tl *šʋ:ky* MM: 'garra (de ave, etc.)' Ju,Pu *še:kʸ*
'=uña de la mano, pezuña' Ma,Ct,Ja *še:kʸ* At *šoö:kʸ* LM: Cn
< *šo:ky* > '=casco; pezuña' Ca *šo:ʸkʸ* 'uña de la mano' Gu *šo:kʸ*
'garra (de ave, etc.)' OlP: *šo:ki* SaP: *šo:hk*

SO#012 pM ***kɨ?-šo:ki** *(n) 'uña de mano/nail'* [See pMZ **kɨ?* 'hand,
arm'.] MM: Ma,Ja,Ct *kɨ"žé:kʸ* At *kɨ"žöö:kʸ* LM: Gu *kï"žó:kʸ* OlP:
kɨ?šo:ki SaP: *kɨ?šó:hk*

SO#013 pMZ ***sokeCV** *(interj) 'saludo/greeting'* [An unsyncopated,
Zoquean form was probably the origin of the language designation
'Zoque'.] [pM **sokena* > pOM **šoken*] LM: SJ *skeht...* greetings
[alternate form used by some speakers: *sɨgeh...* ChisZ: NE [Ra] *šekta*
(interj) 'una salutación' [Ox] *sokena* [e.g., *sokena mama* 'hello,
mother']

SO#014 pM ***šokot** *(n) 'zacate/grass'* [pOM **šokót*] LM: Gu *šɨgótʸ*
'camelote' [final palatalization unexplained] [Nordell, p.c.] OlP: *šoko't*
SaP: *šógot*

SO#015 pOM ***šokšy** *(n) 'nuera de la mujer, suegra de mujer /mother-
in-law of woman, daughter-in-law of woman'* SHM: Ay *šʸe?kš* 'suegra
de mujer' MM: 'nuera de la mujer, suegra de mujer' Ju *šækšʸ*
Ma,Ja,Pu,At,Ct *šækʸšʸ* (pos) LM: Gu *šokʸ* 'suegra de mujer'

SO#016 pMZ ***so?m** *(vt) 'empapar/to soak'* NHM: *nišo?m ~ nišo"m*
'enramar, enramado' ChisZ: C *so?m* (vt) 'empaparlo, meterlo'

SO#017 pOM ***šohn~šon** *(vi)* *'alegrarse/to be happy'* NHM: *šo:n* ~*šo:hn~šon* 'estar feliz, feliz', *šo:ndïk* 'estar contento, alegrar, sentir gozo' SHM: Tu <*šondá"k, šondákp*> Tp <*šondákp*> MM: Ju <*šo·ndǽ"k, šondákp*> '=gozar' Cc <*šo·ndákp*> Ma <*šo·n̄dá·kp, šo·n̄dá"k*> '=gozar' Ja <*šo·n̄dá"k*> 'alegrarse', <*šo·šo·n̄dá·kp*> 'alegre', <*šo·mb̄?íhtp*> 'divertirse, gozar' Pu <*šo·n̄dá·kp*> 'divertirse, alegre, alegrarse, gozar' At <*šo·n̄dá·kp, šo·n̄dá"k*> Ct <*šo·n̄dá·kp, šo·n̄dá"k*> 'gozar, divertirse' LM: Cn <*šo·n~šon*> (vi) Ca <*šo·ndá"k*> Gu <*šo·n̄dá·Fp*> 'alegre', <*šo·n̄dá"k, šo·n̄dá·kp*> 'alegrarse', <*šo·n̄dá·kp*> 'gozar', <*šo·ndá·kp*> 'divertirse' [sic!]

SO#018 pOM ***yakšon** *(adj)* *'bonito/beautiful'* NHM: *yakšon* 'simpático, guapo' MM: Ju *yæhšón* 'lindo' Ma,Ct *yahkšón* 'con cuidado' LM: Ca *yahšón* Gu *yahšón̄* 'bonito, lindo' Cn <*yahšon*> (adv) 'muy bien, correcto' SJ *yahšon* 'good'

SO#019 pOM ***šohn-tak** *(n)* *'gozo/pleasure'* NHM: *šo:ndïk* '=contento, alegre' SHM: Tl *švnto"k* 'alegre' MM: Ju *šondǽkɨn* Ma *šo·n̄dá·kɨn* Ja *šo·n̄k* Ct *šo·n̄dá·kp* LM: Gu *šo·n̄dá"kʸ*

SO#020 pOM ***šoš** *(vi)* *'vestir/to dress'* NHM: *šohš~šoš* MM: 'vestirse' Ma <*ne·ẑʸóšïyɨ, ne·ẑʸóhšïp*> Ja <*nižóšï, nižʸóhšïp*> At <*nažʸóhšïp*> Ct <*nɨ·ẑʸóhšïp, nɨ·ẑʸóšïyɨ*> LM: Cn <*šohš~šoš*> (vt) 'hacer ofrenda; dar'

SO#021 pMZ ***so:s?** *(vt)* *'cocer/to cook in water'* MM: 'cocer (tr), cocinar' At <*šo"š*> Ct <*šo"š, sʸo!šʸpʸ*> LM: Ca <*šo"š*> 'cocer (tr), cocinar' Gu <*šo"š, sʸo·šʸp*> 'cocer (tr), cocinar' OIP: *šo:š~šo?š* (vt) SaP: *šo:š~šo?š* (vi, vt) 'cook in water (potatoes, yams, etc.)' TxZ: *sos* (vt, vi-p) ChisZ: C *sohs* (vi) 'cocer' (vt) 'cocerlo, cocinarlo' N *sos* (vt) NE *sohs* (vt) 'cocerlo, cocinarlo' ChZ: *sos* 'cocinar'

SO#022 pMZ ***sow?** *(vt)* *'picotear, golpear con el puño/to peck, punch'* [pM **šo?w*; pZ *soŋ] SaP *šo?w* (vi, vt) 'peck (fowls)' [cannot be a borrowing since it presupposes ancient sound laws] SoZ *soŋ* 'golpear algo con el puño' TxZ: *soŋ* (vt) 'picotear'

TI-TO

TI#001 pMZ ***ti** *(part) '¿qué?/what?'* [pM **ti* > pOM **ti:*; pZ **ti* > pGZ **tʸi*] NHM: *ti* '=¿cual?' SHM: Tl *ti* Tm *te:* MM: Ju,Ma,Ja,At, Ct *ti:* LM: Cn <*ti*> (pron interr) '¿qué cosa?, ¿qué?' (pron rel) 'que' Ca,SJ,Gu *ti:* OlP: *ti* SaP: *ti* [only in the Sp.-to-SaP side] TxZ: *če?* (part interr) 'qué' ChisZ: C *tiyɨ* (adj) 'qué' (pron rel) 'qué'; 'lo que'; (pron indef) 'algo' (pron interr) ¿que?) N *ti ~ tiyɨ* (adj) 'qué' (pron indef) 'algo' (pron rel) 'qué, lo que' (n) 'cosa' NE *tiyɨ* (adj) 'qué' (pron indef) 'algo' (pron rel) 'qué, lo que' (n) 'cosa' ChZ: *ti* '¿que?', *ti?e* '¿porque?'

TI#002 pM ***ka ti** *(part) 'nada/nothing'* [Details of phonology uncertain because of syntactically conditioned variation.] MM: Ju *nikætí:* Ma,Ja,Pu,Ct *kæh ti:* At *katí:, kʸæh ti:* LM: Ca *ka?p ti:, kanití:* OlP: *ka:ti / ka?ti* SaP: *katí* [Clark 1961]

TI#003 pMZ ***ni ti** *(part) 'nada/nothing'* [pM **ni ti* > pOM **ni ti:*; pZ **ni ti-yɨ*] NHM: *nitiya* [a borrowing from Zoquean?] MM: Ju *nití:* LM: Ca *nití:* SJ *ka? ni: ti·* 'none, nothing' SaP: *netí* ChisZ: C *nitiyɨ* N *ni tiyɨ ~ ni ti* NE *nitiyɨ* 'pron indef: nada, ninguna cosa'

TI#004 pM ***tih** *(vt) 'apretar/to tighten'* NHM: *tih* 'apretar, apretado, cosas apretadas dentro de un recipiente' SHM: Tl *teh* 'apretar' MM: At <*tih*> 'sobar, frotar, tallar' LM: Ca <*tih*> 'empollar' _Cn <*tih*> (vt) 'empujar' SJ *tih* 'to hurt as a knot in cargo' Gu <*tih*> 'empollar, empujar' [Nordell 1990 and p.c.] OlP: *tih* (vi) 'quedar, quedarse'

TI#005 pM ***?aw-tih** *(vi) 'atorarse/to jam'* NHM: *?atiha* 'encajar, meter' OlP: *?autih* (vi) 'atorarse'

TI#006 pOM*tih *(vi) 'decir/say'* NHM: *tih* 'querer decir' LM: Cn <*tih*> (vi) 'decir; llamar' SJ *tih* 'to have a mistaken impression; to name, call'

TI#007 pM *tik *(n) 'lagartija/lizard'* [pOM *tik] NHM: *tik* SHM: Tl,Ay *tek* MM: Ju *tik* 'chintete (clase de lagartija)' LM: Cn <*tik*> 'lagartija chiquita' Ca *tik* 'chintete (clase de lagartija)'

TI#008 pM *tikac *(vi) 'mudar/to change'* NHM: *tikc ~ tíkïc* 'mudar, cambiar (p.ej., una cosa repuesta)' SHM: Tu <*tigáhcp*> 'cambiarse' MM: Ju <*tigǽč*> 'alterarse' Ma <*tigáhcp, tï: tʸigǽč̄*> 'alterarse, mudarse, cambiarse' Ja <*tigáhc, tigáhcp*> 'alterarse, cambiarse' Pu <*tigáhcp,tï: tʸigǽč̄*> 'alterarse, cambiarse, mudarse' At <*tigáhcp*> 'alterarse, cambiarse' Ct <*tigáhcp*> 'cambiarse, alterarse' LM: SJ *tïgahc ~ tïgac* Gu *tigáhc ~ tigác* 'alterarse, cambiarse' SaP: *tigac* (vi, vt)

TI#009 pOM *yak-tikahc ~ yak-tikac *(vt) 'cambiar/to change'* NHM: *yaktíkïc ~ yaktikc* 'cambiar algo' SHM: Tu <*yahktïgác, yahktïgáčpʸ*> 'cambiar' MM: Ju <*yǽhtïgǽc*> Ma <*yahktïgác̄*> Ja <*yahtïgác̄, yahtïgáhčpʸ*> Pu <*yahtïgác̄*> At <*yǽhktïgác̄, yǽhktïgáhčpʸ*> LM: Gu <*yahtïgác̄, yahtïgáhčpʸ*>

TI#010 pZ *tikin *(vi) 'tocar/to touch'* SaP: *tikin* (vi, vt) 'tickle someone' [Zo loan] ChisZ: C *tikniki?m* (vi) 'sobresalir, superarse; tiknikïtïhk* (vt) tocarlo al pasar'

TI#011 pM *tikcik *(n) 'raíz/root'* [pOM *tikcyk] MM: Ma,Ja,Ct *tikc* LM: Cn <*tikc*> Ca,Gu *tikc* SaP: *tíkčik* TxZ: *čéčïk* [? *čêkčêk* expected]

TI#012 pM *ti?kš *(vi) 'pellizcar/to pinch between the fingernails'* LM: SJ *ti?kš* Gu <*ti?š̄, ti?šp*> [Nordell, p.c.] OlP: *ti?kš* (vi) 'quebrarse (ejemplo: palo)' TxZ: *če?kš-ka?* (vt) 'matar con las uñas (insecto)'

TI#013 pMZ *timam *(vi) 'hinchar/to swell'* NHM: *timm* 'hinchar (p.ej., madera)' SaP: *timam* 'swell (action of yeast in bread)'

TI#014 pMZ *tin *(n) 'excremento/excrement'* [pM *tihn, attested as a bound form in pM *tihn-cahy 'intestines'; pZ *tin > pGZ *tʸiñ] TxZ: *čêñ* '=mierda, diarrea' SoZ: *tʸiñ* ChisZ: C *tin* 'abono; orín; estiércol, excremento' N *tin* '=herrumbre' ChZ: *tin*

TI#015 pMZ ***tinin** *(vi) 'crepitar/to crackle'* NHM: *tinn ~ tínïn* 'hacer ruido (p.ej., un motor o un temblor de tierra)' SaP: *tinin* (vi) 'burn (fire)' SoZ: *tiñ* 'make noise' [Foster and Foster 1948] [?] TxZ: *če:ñ* (vi) 'zumbar, sonar (hojas del árbol, p.ej., cuando están secas), tronar'

TI#016 pOM ***tip** *(n) 'friolento/chilly'* NHM: *tip* 'escalofrío, frío' MM: Ma *tip̄* At *tip̄, tïbó?kp* LM: Cn <*tippa?m*> 'paludismo' Gu *wi:ndíp̄*

TE#001 pZ ***te?-** *(pron dem) 'ese/that'* [pM **te?* > pOM **te"*; pZ **te?*] MM: Ja,Pu,At,Ct *tǽ"dɨ* 'ése' Ja,At *tǽ"dɨ* 'aquel' ChisZ: C *te?* (artículo determinativo) 'el, la' (indica oración sin verbo); (adj dem) 'ese, esa' ChZ: *te?p* 'ese'; *te?k* 'así'

TE#002 pZ ***tek** *(vt) 'verter/to pour'* TxZ: *tek* (vt) 'tirar (líquido)', (vi) rebosar SoZ: *tek* 'serve' [Foster and Foster 1948] ChisZ: C *tehk* (vt) 'verterlo, derramarlo; molderlo virtiéndolo; derramarlo, desparramarlo' N *tehk* (vt) 'servirlo; derramarlo' NE *tekse?t* (vt) 'verterlo (como de un vaso a otro)'

TE#003 pOM ***teky** *(n) 'pie/foot'* NHM: *tEk* 'pie, pata; viaje' SHM: Tl *teky* 'pie' MM: Ju *teky* 'cabo, pie, pierna, pata, huella (pos)' Ma *teky* 'pata, huella (pos), cabo (pos), mango de hacha (pos), pie, pierna', *tyeky* 'rastro, huella' Ja *teky* 'mango (de hacha), pata, pie, pierna' Pu *tyeky* 'cabo (pos), mango de hacha (pos), pata, pie, pierna' At *tyeky* 'rastro, huella', *teky* 'cabo, huella (pos), pata, pie, pierna' Ct *teky* 'cabo', huella (pos), pata, pie, pierna, rastro (pos), huella (pos)' LM: Ca *teky* 'pie, pierna' Cn <*teky*> 'pie, pierna de persona; pata de pájaro; pata trasera de animales; pata de la mesa; mango (p.ej., de hacha)' SJ *teky* 'lower leg, foot' Gu *teky* 'pie, pierna, pata, huella (pos)', *teky* 'cabo' [sic!]

TE#004 pZ ***te?ksi** *(n) 'enagua, falda/skirt'* [pGZ **te?kši*] TxZ: *te?ks* 'falda tradicional, refajo' [*te?kš* expected] SoZ: *té?kši* 'vestido' [Gutiérrez M. 1993], *téksi* 'skirt' [Foster and Foster 1948] C,NE *teksi* [*te?ksi* expected] N *te?ksi*

TE#005 pMZ ***tem** *(vt) 'derramar/to spill'* NHM: *te:m ~ te:hm ~ tem* 'echar agua, tirar (p.ej., agua para beber)' LM: <*te·m ~ tem*> (vt) 'vaciar, echar (líquido)' SJ *te·m ~ tem* 'to pour a liquid' Gu <*tem̄, te·mp̄*> [Nordell, p.c.] SaP: *tem* (vi, vt) 'pour liquid' ChisZ: N *te ?m* [*te ?mbuht* (vi) 'salpicar (para afuera)'; *te ?mde ?mney* (vi) 'on-dear (agua)'] [?]

TE#006 pOM ***?iš-tehm ~ ?iš-tem** *(vt) 'tirar (líquido)/to throw (liquid)'*
NHM: *?ište:m ~ ?ište:hm ~ ?ištem* LM: Cn <*ište·m ~ ištem*>

TE#007 pOM ***?a-tehm** *(n) 'labio/lip'* NHM: *?ate:m* SHM: Tl
?ata:m Gu *?adé:m̄t* [Nordell, p.c.]

TE#008 pMZ ***tenay** *(vi) 'pararse/to stand up'* NHM: *tÉna* 'pararse'
SHM: Tl *tyanɨ* 'parado' MM: Ma <*tǽn̄ɨ, tinǽ:pʸ*> 'estar parado,
estar de pie, ponerse de pie (pararse)' Ja <*tǽn̄ɨ, tiná·ȳ, tinǽ:pʸ*>
'estar parado, estar de pie' Pu <*tǽn̄ɨ, tinǽ:pʸ*> 'estar parado, estar
de pie', <*tǽn̄ɨ, tina:yɨ"k*> 'ponerse de pie (pararse)' At <*tǽn̄ɨ,*
tænɨyá·m̄p> 'ponerse de pie (pararse)', <*tǽn̄ɨ, tinǽ:pʸ*> 'estar parado, estar de pie' Ct <*tinǽ:pʸ*> 'estar de pie, estar parado', <*tǽn̄ɨ,*
tæn̄ɨyámp> 'ponerse de pie (pararse)' LM: SJ *tina·y ~ tina"y* 'to
stand up' Gu <*tɨná:pʸ, tɨná"w, tɨná·ȳ*> 'estar parado, estar de pie'
OIP: *teniy* (vi) 'pararse' SaP: *tentan* 'stop'; *tendá?k* 'parar a otro'
[Clark and Clark 1960] SoZ: *te:n* 'pararse' TxZ: -*te:ñe?* 'sufijo cla-
sificador numeral (humanos)', *te:n-te:n-ho?y* (vi) 'andar paseando (por
el patio)' ChisZ: C *tenay* (vi, vi-s) 'pararse, estar parado, ponerse de
pie, estar puesto de pie' [derivative: *tenayupɨ* (adj) 'parado'] NE
tenay (vi) 'pararse, ponerse de pie' (vi-s) 'estar parado, estar puesto
de pie' ChZ: *tenay [*?istenay* 'cuidar']

TE#009 pMZ ***yak-tenay** *(vt) 'pararlo/to make stand up'* OIP:
yakteniy (vt) 'pararlo' ChisZ: C *yahtenay* (vt) 'hacerlo pararse, hacerlo ponerse de pie; edificarlo, construirlo, levantarlo' NE *yaktenay*
(vt) 'leventarlo (como una casa); hacer que se pare, hacer que se pare
de pie; pararlo'

TE#010 pM ***košo-tenay** *(vi) 'hincarse/to kneel down'* [See pMZ
**koso(k)*.] NHM: *koštEñip ~ koštEna* 'arrodillarse, estar hincado,
arrodillado, postrarse' SHM: Tp <*koštǽnɨ*> 'arrodillarse' MM: Ju
<*koštǽnɨ*> Ma,Ja,Pu,At,Ct <*koštǽn̄ɨ, koštɨnǽ:pʸ*> '=arrodillarse'
LM: Ca <*koštɨná"*> Gu <*koštɨná"w*> 'arrodillarse' SaP: *košaténa*
[Clark and Clark 1960]

TE#011 pMZ ***te:?n** *(vi) 'pisar, pararse/to step, stand up'* NHM:
te:?n 'pisar (p.ej., batir barro)' MM: 'pisar' Ju <*tuktǽ:n,*
nǽškutǽ:nɨ> Ja <*tuktǽ:n, tʸuktǽ!n̄, tʸukté!mpʸ*> Pu

<*na·šmatǽ:nɨ*> At <*tuktǽ:n, tʸukté?m̄pʸ*> Ct <*tɨktǽ:n, tʸɨkté!m̄pʸ*> LM: Ca <*tǽ:n*> 'pisar' SJ *te·n* ~*te:n* 'to step on hard; to copulate (birds, fowl)' Gu <*te:n, te!mp, yahté:n, yahté!n̄, yahté!m̄pʸ*> 'pisar' [Nordell 1990 and p.c.] SaP: *te?n* (vi, vt) 'copulate (birds, fowls)' SoZ *te:nʸ* 'stop' [Foster and Foster 1948, probably bad translation of 'parar(se)'] TxZ: *te?n-te?n-ho?y* (vi-s) 'andar parándose en las puntas de los pies' ChisZ: C *te?n* (vi) 'empinarse, ponerse de puntillas' NE *te?n* (vi) 'pararse, estar de pie' N *te?n* (vi) 'pararse, estar de pie'

TE#012 pM ***te:?n-i(k)** *(n) 'escalera de un solo palo/ladder made of one piece of wood'* [pOM **te:?ny*] NHM: *tE:?n* 'escalera' MM: Ju, Ma,Ja,Pu,At,Ct *te:nʸ* LM: Cn <*te:ñ*> Gu,Ca *te:nʸ* OlP: *te:ní'k* 'escalera de palo' SaP: *te?nk* 'escalera'

TE#013 pMZ ***te?ps** *(vi) 'salpicar/to sprinkle'* NHM: *tE?pš* 'golpe que se da con la punta del pie al bailar' [?] ChisZ: N *te?ps* (vi) 'salpicar' (vt) 'sacarlo, hacerlo salpicar (agua)'

TE#014 pOM ***tehš~teš** *(vi) 'topetear/to butt'* MM: At <*teš̄ʸ*> 'trasladar' LM: Cn <*tehš~teš*> 'prender (p.ej., con lanza)' SJ *tehš~teš* 'to butt, shoot at with a stick (pool, carroms, etc.)' Gu <*teš̄ʸ*> 'trasladar' TxZ: *tes* (vt) 'rascar' [?-semantics]

TE#015 pOM ***tešy** *(n) 'plato/plate'* NHM: *tEš* MM: Ju *tešʸ* Ma *teskʸ* Ja,Pu,At,Ct *tešʸ* LM: Cn <*tešy*> Ca *tešʸ* Gu *teš̄ʸ*

TE#016 pZ ***tet** *(vt) 'rajar/to split, tear'* SaP: *tet* (vi, vt) 'tear (paper, cloth)' [Zo loan] SoZ: *tet* 'reventar' (vi) TxZ: *tet* (vt, vi-p) 'reventar (tomate, uva)' ChisZ: C *teht* (vt) 'rajarlo' N *teht* (vi) 'rajarse (quedarle un canal)' (vt) 'rajarlo, abrirlo'

TE#017 pM ***te:tE** *(n) 'padre, papá/father'* ["E" stands for either /i/ or /e/; pOM **te:ty*.] NHM: *tE:?* 'padre, cura, sacerdote' [*tE:?t* expected] SHM: Tl *te:tʸ* 'padre, cura, sacerdote' Tm *te:tʸ* Hu *dedy* [Foster 1949] MM: Ju *te:tʸ* 'papá, cura' Pu *te:tʸ* 'papá' At,Ma,Ja,Ct *te:tʸ* 'papá, cura, sacerdote' LM: SJ *de:dʸɨč* Cn <*uŋde:dy*> 'papá, padre', <*te:dy*> 'padre de familia (con pronombre posesivo); cura (sin pronombre posesivo)' Gu *te:tʸ* 'papá, cura, sacerdote' TaM: *?até* [?; transcription of Wonderly 1949] SaP: *te:t*

TE#018 pOM ***ʔap-te:ty** *(n) 'abuelo/uncle'* [See pMZ *ʔapu 'grandfather'] SHM: Tu ʔapté:tʸ MM: Ju ʔœpté:tʸ LM: Ca ʔapté:tʸ Gu te:d̯ʸʔáp

TE#019 pM ***ko-te:tE** *(n) 'padrastro/stepfather'* [pOM *kute:ty] NHM: kutE:ʔ SHM: Tm kɨtɛ:tʸ MM: Ju,Ma,Ja,At kudé:tʸ Pu kɨdé:tʸ Ct kʸɨdé:tʸ LM: Gu kudé:tʸ SaP ko:té:t

Tɨ#001 pOM ***tɨ:** *(part) 'ya/already'* NHM: tɨ MM: Ju,Ma,Ja,At,Ct tɨ: LM: Cn <tɨ> (adv) 'ya (rige la forma adverbial del verbo, con la cual forma el tiempo pretérito perfecto) Ca tɨ: Gu tɨ̈:

Tɨ#002 pMZ ***tɨ:c?** *(vi) 'secarse, enflaquecerse/to dry out, become thin'* NHM: tɨ:c~tɨ"c 'secar, recibir o dar una topetada (como hace el carnero), topar, poner flaco' MM: Ma <tɨ·c̄p, tɨ"ʒámp> '=enflaquecerse, adelgazarse' Ja <tɨ·c̄p, tɨ·c̄, tɨ"ʒá·m̄p> At <tɨ·c̄p, tɨ"ʒá·m̄p> '=adelgazarse, enflaquecerse' Ct <tɨ·c̄p, tɨ"ʒámp> 'secarse' LM: Cn <tɨ·c~tɨ"c> (vi) Ca <tɨ·ckɨdá"k> 'enflaquecerse' SJ tɨ·c~tɨ"c 'to dry; to die (plants)' Gu <tɨ̈·c̄p, tɨ̈·c̄, tɨ̈"ʒá·m̄p> '=adelgazarse, enflaquecerse' SaP: tɨ:c~tɨ?c (vi) 'secarse' TxZ: tɨc (vi) 'secar' SoZ: tɨc 'dry' [Foster and Foster 1948] ChisZ: C tɨhc (vi) 'secarse, agotarse un líquido' N tɨhc (vi) 'secarse; enflaquecer' NE tɨhc (vi) 'secarse; agotarse (como agua)' ChZ: tɨc 'secar'

Tɨ#003 pMZ ***yak-tɨ:c?** *(vt) 'secar/to dry'* NHM: yaktɨ:c~yaktɨ"c SHM: Tl yɨktɨ?ɨc MM: Ju <yœhtɨ"c> Ma <yahtɨ"c> 'asolear', <yahktɨ"c, yahktɨ·c̄pʸ> 'secar' [sic!] Ja <yahtɨ"c> At <yahktɨ"c> Ct <yahktɨ"c, yahktɨ·c̄pʸ> '=asolear' LM: Ca <yahtɨ"c> Gu <yahtɨ̈"c, yahtɨ̈·c̄p> OlP: yaktɨ:c~yaktɨ?c SaP: ʔaktɨ:c~ʔaktɨ?c [Clark and Clark 1960] TxZ: yak-tɨc (vt-caus) 'secar (granos, ropas)' ChisZ: C yahtɨhc NE yaktɨhc

Tɨ#004 pM ***tɨ:c-tu** *(n) 'granizo/hail'* [Probably from a pre-pM form *tɨ:c tu:h 'dry rain'; pOM *tɨ:ct.] NHM: tɨ:št SHM: Tl,Ay tɨct MM: Ju tɨcn̥ Ma tɨ·c̄ Ct tɨ·c̄ OlP: tɨ:stu

Tɨ#005 pMZ ***tɨ?ɨc** *(adj) 'seco, flaco/dry, thin'* [pM *tɨ?ɨc > pOM *tɨ"hc; pZ *tɨ?ɨc > pGZ *tɨc with expected loss of the glottal] NHM: tɨ"hc MM: Ju,At tɨ"c Ma tɨ"c '=delgado' Ja,Ct tɨ"c 'seco' Pu tɨ"c 'delgado, flaco' LM: Ca tɨ"c 'seco' Gu tɨ̈"c OlP: tɨ?ɨ's (adj) 'seco'

SaP: *kuytɨ?c* 'flaco, palo seco' AyZ: *[tɨckɨna]* TxZ: *tɨcka?* ChisZ: C *tɨ?c* NE *tɨcɨ* (adj)

Tɨ#006 pMZ *tiːc-?ɨy (n) 'tener sed/to be thirsty' NHM: *tiːca ~ tiːcɨ* MM: Ju <*tɨ́ːʐ̣ɨ*> Ma,Ct <*tɨ́·c̄ɨp?ɨpʸ*> Ja <*tɨ́·cɨp, tɨːʐ̣ɨyá·n̄ɨp*> At <*tɨ́·cɨp, tɨːʐ̣ɨyá·m̄p*> LM: Gu <*tïʐ̣ïˮwïː, tïʐ̣ɨ́·yɨp, tïʐ̣ɨ́ˮwá·n̄ɨpF*> Cn <*tɨdzɨ·y ~ tɨdzɨˮy*> (vi) SJ *tɨʐ̣ɨ·y ~ tɨʐ̣ɨˮy* ChisZ: C *yoktɨcɨ* 'sed' N *yo?ktɨhc* (vi) NE *kɨndɨcɨ* 'sed'

Tɨ#007 pOM *pa-tɨˮhc (adj) 'flaco/skinny' NHM: *patɨˮhc* 'fisis, flamenco, tuberculoso' SHM: Tl *patɨ́ˮc* 'delgado' MM: Ja *padɨ́ˮc* Ct *paːdɨ́ˮc*

Tɨ#008 pMZ *tiːc (n) 'diente/tooth' [pM, pOM **tɨːhc*; pZ, pGZ **tɨc*] NHM: *tɨːc* SHM: Tl *tɨːhc* Ay *tɨhc* MM: Ma,Ja,Pu,At,Ct *tɨ·c̄* LM: Cn <*tɨːc*> Ca *tɨc* [Wonderly 1948] Gu *tï·c̄* OlP: *tɨːcɨ; tɨskɨ?* 'todos los dientes' SaP: *tɨːhc* SoZ: *tɨc* AyZ: *[tɨc]* TxZ: *tɨc* ChisZ: C *tɨc* '=muela' N *tɨc* NE *tɨhc* S [Tu] *tɨc* [Wonderly 1948] ChZ: *tɨc* ChZ: SnMiCh *tɨc*

Tɨ#009 pMZ *tiːcɨC (n) 'iguana/iguana' [pM **tɨːcɨh* > pOM **tɨcɨh*; pZ **tɨcɨ?(ŋ)*] LM: Cn <*tɨdzɨh*> '[Iguana sp.]' Gu *tïʐ̣ɨh* [Nordell, p.c.] TaM: *dóco* [transcription of Wonderly 1949] SaP *tɨːcɨ* 'chiquipila—iguana' ChisZ: C *tɨcɨ?ŋ* NE *tɨcɨ?ŋ* [Wonderly 1949. Dialects of Tapalapa, Ocotepec] ChZ: StaMaCh *yɨk tɨcɨ?* SnMiCh *tɨcɨ?* [Wonderly 1949]

Tɨ#010 pM *tɨh (vi) 'quebrarse (palo, etc.)/to break (long, thin object)' NHM: *tɨh* 'romper, quebrar (p.ej., una rama), fracturar (p.ej., un hueso)' MM: Ju <*tɨh*> Ma <*tɨh*> Ja <*tɨh, tɨhtúk*> At <*tɨh, tɨː tʸɨhʸ, tʸehpʸ*> Ct <*tɨh*> LM: Ca <*tɨh*> Cn <*tɨh*> (vi) 'quebrar (doblando (p.ej., diente del peine))' (vt) 'doblar (p.ej., tela)' SJ *tɨh* 'to break long slender objects' Gu <*tïh*> OlP: *tɨh* (vi) 'zafarse' (vt) 'doblerlo' (ejemplo: 'mecate')

Tɨ#011 pMZ *tɨhɨk(ay) (adv) 'ayer/yesterday' OlP: *tɨ?ɨy* SaP: *tɨ?hy* ChisZ: C,N *tɨ?ɨk* NE *tɨ?ɨhk* ChZ: *tɨhɨgay, tɨhɨk*

Tɨ#012 pMZ *tɨk (n) 'casa/house' [pM, pOM **tɨhk*; pZ, pGZ **tɨk*] NHM: *tɨhk* '=hogar' SHM: Tl,Tu,Tp,Tm *tɨhk* MM: Ju,Cc,Ma,Ja,Pu, At,Ct *tɨhk* LM: Ca *tɨhk* Cn <*tɨhk*> '=vaina, cubierta' Gu *tïhk* '=techo' TaM: *tok* [transcription of Wonderly 1949] OlP: *tɨkɨ* SaP: *tɨhk* SoZ: *tɨk* [Foster and Foster 1948] AyZ:

[tɨk] TxZ: *tɨk* [Gutiérrez M. 1993] ChisZ: C,N,S *tɨk* NE [All dialects cited in Wonderly 1949] *tɨhk* [Ra] *tɨhk* '=hogar, morada' ChZ: *tɨk*

Tɨ#013 pZ **ca-tɨk** *(n) 'cueva/cave'* ChisZ: C *catɨk* '=caverna; sima, fosa' N *catɨk* '=hoyo, pozo' NE *cadɨhk* '=caverna' ChZ: *catɨk* 'hoyo; agujero'

Tɨ#014 pOM **cahp-tɨhk** *(n) 'iglesia/church'* [a post-Conquest composite] NHM: *captɨhk* 'iglesia, templo' SHM: Tl *captɨhk* MM: Ma *cahtɨ́hk* Ju,Ja,Pu,At,Ct *cahptɨhk* LM: Cn <*cahptɨhk*> Ca *cahptɨ́hk* Gu *cahtɨ́hk*

Tɨ#015 pOM **kahy-tɨhk** *(n) 'buche del ave/crop (of a bird)'* [lit., 'eat-house'] NHM: *katyɨhk* MM: Ju *kæˑʸdʸɨhk* Ma *kaʸdʸɨhk* Ja *kʸæːdʸɨhk* At,Ct *kaːdʸɨhk* LM: Gu *kaːdʸɨ́hk*

Tɨ#016 pOM **ku-tɨhk** *(n) 'casero/owner of the house'* NHM: *kutɨhk* '=jefe de la casa, dueño de la casa' MM: Ju *kudɨ́hk* Ma *kɨdɨ́hk* '=dueño' Ja *kudɨ́hk* 'casero', *kuˑdɨ́hk* 'dueño' [sic!] Pu *kɨdɨ́hk* At *kudɨ́hk* '=dueño' LM: Gu *kudɨ́hk* '=dueño'

Tɨ#017 pOM **puš-n-tɨhk** *(n) 'cárcel/jail'* NHM: *pvšɨ́ntɨhk* SHM: Tu,Tp *puhštɨ́hk* Mi *puhštɨ́hk* MM: Ju,Ma,At,Ct *puhšndɨ́hk* Cc,Ja,Pu *puhštɨ́hk* LM: Cn <*puhštɨhk*> Ca *puhštɨ́hk* Gu *puhštɨ́hk*

Tɨ#018 pM [Veracruz] **puːš-tɨk** *(n) 'iglesia/church'* OlP: *puːštɨki* SaP: *puːštɨhk~puːš*

Tɨ#019 pMZ **tɨk-ʔɨy** *(vi) 'entrar/to enter'* NHM: *tɨhki~tɨka* 'entrar, penetrar' SHM: Tu <*tɨ́hkɨp*> 'caber' MM: Ju <*tɨ́kɨ*>_ Ma <*tɨ́kɨ, tɨ́hkʔɨpʸ*> 'caber' Ja <*tɨ́kɨ, tɨ́hkʔɨy, tɨ́hkɨp*> Pu <*tɨkɨ, tɨ́hkɨpʸ*> At <*tɨ́kɨ, tɨ́hkɨp*> 'caber' Ct <*tɨ́kɨ, tɨ́hkʔɨpʸ*> '=caber' LM: Ca <*tɨgɨ́"*> SJ *tɨgɨˑy~tɨgɨ"y* '=to put on clothes; to begin' Gu <*tɨgɨ́"w, tɨgɨ́ːpʸ*> 'caber' OlP: *tɨkiy* (vt) 'meterlo' SaP: *tɨgɨy* 'entrar' [Clark and Clark 1960] TxZ: *tɨkeñ* (vi) '=caber' ChisZ: C *tɨhkɨy* (vi) '=caber; meterse; subir' N *tɨhkɨy* (vi) '=caber' NE *tɨhkɨy* (vi) '=meterse; caber' (vt) 'penetrarlo' ChZ: *tɨgɨh* 'vestirse'

Tɨ#020 pMZ **yak-tɨk-ʔɨy** *(vt) 'meter/to put'* NHM: *yaktɨhki ~yaktɨka* (vt) 'meter a alguien, introducir a alguien' SHM: Tl *yiktɨkɨ* 'meter' ChisZ: C *yahtɨhkɨy* (vt) 'meterlo; dejarlo entrar' NE *yaktɨhkɨy* (vt) 'meterlo (de uso general)'

Ti#021 pM ***tik-ʔahw-kVʔ** *(n) 'puerta/door'* [OM **tik-ʔa-ki″*] NHM: *tik?aki″* 'puerta de la casa' OlP: *tik?auku* [/i?/ expected in place of final /u/] SaP: *tik?áhw*

Ti#022 pZ ***tik-hoh** *(n) 'interior de la casa/inside (of a house)'* LM: SJ *tigoty* 'inside (a building, etc.)' [?] TxZ: *tik-o:?* (adv) 'adentro de la casa, en la casa' ChisZ: C *tihkihoh* 'el espacio dentro de la casa; el contenido de la casa' N *tihkihoh* 'interior de la casa'

Ti#023 pM ***tiʔkš** *(vi) 'aclararse (agua)/to become clear (water)'* NHM: *tiʔkš* 'liso, aguado, dar luz' SHM: Tp <*tiʔkšp, ti: tⁱiʔkšʸ*> MM: Ma <*téʔšʸʔipʸ*> At <*tiʔkšp*> Ct <*tiʔkš*> LM: Ca <*tiʔkšámp*> Cn <*ti″kš*> (vi) 'aclararse; gastar (bienes)' SJ *tiʔkš* 'to settle out' (coffee grounds, mud, etc.), to be clean (life, thoughts, etc.)' Gu <*tïʔšp*> 'aclararse (agua)', <*ti·ʔšp*> 'brillar, alumbrar' [Nordell, p.c.] OlP: *tiʔkš* (vi) 'amanecer, velar, brillar' SaP: *tiʔkš* (vi)

Ti#024 pOM ***tiʔkš-y** *(adj) 'claro (agua, etc.)/clear (water, etc.)'* SHM: Tp *tiʔkšʸ* MM: Cc *tiʔkšʸ* Ma *teʔšʸ* Ja *teʔšʸ* '=puro (agua)' Pu *te!kšʸ* At *teʔkšʸ* '=puro (agua)' Ct *teʔkšʸ* LM: Gu *tïʔšʸ* '=puro (agua)'

Ti#025 pM ***tiʔkš-pa** *(n) 'velador/candle'* [pOM **tiʔkšpa*] NHM: *tiʔkšpa* 'candil, luz artificial, lámpara' OlP: *tiʔkšpa?*

Ti#026 pOM ***tiʔkš** *(adj) 'liso/smooth'* [pOM **tiʔkš*] NHM: *tïʔkš* '=aguado' MM: Ju *tiʔšk* '=pulido' Ma *tiʔš* '=resbaloso (en lugar donde hay grava), liso' Ja *tiʔš* '=resbaloso (en lugar donde hay grava), liso' Pu *tiʔkš* At *tiʔkš* '=pulido' Ct *tiʔkš* '=resbaloso (en lugar donde hay grava), pulido' LM: Ca,Mz *tikš* 'liso' Gu *tï·ʔš*

Ti#027 pZ ***tiʔks** *(vt) 'trozar/to break or cut'* SoZ: *tiʔks* 'tocar (jarana)' TxZ: *tiʔks* (vi) 'reventarse' (vt) 'picotear' ChisZ: C *tiʔks* (vi, vt) 'unirse, estar unido' (vt) 'repicarlo, tocarlo; trozarlo' N *tiʔks* (vt) 'cortarlo, trozarlo; machucarlo' NE *tiʔks* (vt) 'machetearlo; trozarlo'

Ti#028 pMZ ***tim** *(n) 'fruta/fruit'* [pM, pOM **tihm*; pZ, pGZ **tim*] MM: Ma,Ct *ti:m* (pos)' Ja *ti·m* LM: Cn <*ti:m*> '=semilla' Ca *ti·m* Gu *tï:m* OlP: *timi* SaP: *tihm* SoZ: *tim* AyZ: *[tim]* TxZ: *tim* ChisZ: C,N *tim* NE *tip* ChZ: *tim*

Tɨ#029 pOM *ʔahy-tm (n) 'anona/sweet apple' [Cf. pM *ʔa:ti and pZ *yati. These are all different etyma.] NHM: ʔa:ydum '=chirimoya [Anona cherimolia, A. squamosa]' SHM: Tl ʔatpy Tu ʔatʸpʸ Tp ʔæpʸkʸ ~ ʔæpʸtʸ [metathesis; variant with /k/ unexplained] Mi ʔætʸpʸ ~ ʔætʸm̥ʸ MM: Ju ʔætʸm̥ʸ Ja ʔatʸm̄ʸ Ma,Pu,At,Ct ʔa·tʸm̥ʸ LM: Ca ʔa·tʸpʸ

Tɨ#030 pM *cahy-tɨm (n) 'agrás (uva silvestre)/a kind of grape' [pOM *cahytm] NHM: ca:ydum 'uva' [Vitis sp.] MM: Ju cætʸm̥ʸ Ma ca·tʸm̥ʸ Ja ca·tʸm̄ʸ Ct ca·tʸm̄ʸ ~ catʸm̥ʸ LM: Ca ca·tʸpʸ Gu ca·tʸp OIP: mu:šicaytɨ'm [mu:ši 'pájaro'] SaP: cáytɨm

Tɨ#031 pMZ *kúy-tɨm (n) 'aguacate/avocado' [Persea americana bearing large fruit] [pM *kuhytɨhm > pOM *kuhytm; pZ *kuytɨm > pGZ *kutʸɨm] NHM: kv:ydum '[Persea americana (G. Martin, p.c.)]' SHM: Tl kutpy Tu,Tp,Ay,Tm kutʸpʸ Mi kutʸm̄ʸ MM: Ju,Cc kutʸm̥ʸ Ma,Ja,At ku·tʸm̥ʸ Pu kü·tʸm̥ʸ Ct ku·tʸm̥ʸ LM: Cn <ku:ty> '[Persea sp.]' Gu ku·tʸp OIP: kuytɨ'm; kuytɨmkuyɨ 'palo de aguacate' SaP: kúytɨm TxZ: kučɨm ChisZ: C kuytyɨm 'aguacate de tierra caliente' N kutyɨm ~ ku?yutɨm S [kuydɨm] ChZ: kuytɨm

Tɨ#032 pMZ *šoh-tɨm (n) 'bellota/acorn' [pM, pOM *šohtɨhm] [Cf. also pOM *ko"k 'acorn'; this must be the fruit of another type of oak] SHM: Tu šohtɨ:m MM: Ju šohtɨ:mp Ma,Pu,Ct šohtɨ:m LM: Gu šohtɨ:m SoZ: sohtɨm TxZ: sohtɨm

Tɨ#033 pOM *ta:t tɨhm (n) 'tuna/prickly pear' NHM: ta:t tɨ:hm '=pitahaya' SHM: Tl tv:t tɨ:m 'pitaya' MM: Ja,At,Ct ta:ttɨ:m LM: Gu ta:ttɨ:m

Tɨ#034 pOM *tɨhm-t (n) 'semilla/seed' NHM: tɨ:mt SHM: Tl tɨmt MM: Ju tɨ:mp Ma,Ja,Ct tɨ·mk At tɨ:mt LM: Ca tɨ:mt Gu tɨ:mt

Tɨ#035 pZ *tɨm-ʔɨy (vi) 'dar fruta/to yield fruit' ChisZ: N tɨʔmɨy (vi) 'dar fruta' ChZ: tɨʔmɨy 'tener fruta'

Tɨ#036 pZ *tɨm-ʔah (vi) 'dar fruta/to yield fruit' NHM: tɨʔmi ~ tɨʔma 'dar la cosecha' [?] ChisZ: C tɨʔmah (vi) 'dar fruta, produjar, rendir (como cosecha)' N tɨʔmah (vi) 'dar fruto'

Tɨ#037 pMZ *tɨ:n? (vi) 'defecar/to defecate' MM: Ja <tɨ"n, tɨ·n̄, tɨ·m̄p> Ma,Pu,At,Ct <tɨ"n, tɨ·m̄p> LM: Gu <tɨ"n, tɨ·m̄p> SJ *tɨ·n ~ tɨ"n* SaP: *tɨn~tɨʔn* TxZ: *tɨn* (vi) '=cagar' ChisZ: C,N *tɨn* NE *tɨnbɨʔ* (vi) 'oxidarse' (vt) 'oxidarlo'

Tɨ#038 pM [Veracruz] *nɨ:ʔ-tɨn ~ nɨ:ʔ-tɨʔn (vi) 'tener diarrea/to have diarrhea' OIP: *nɨ:tɨn* (vi) 'tener diarrea' SaP: *nɨʔtɨʔn* 'diarrea'

Tɨ#039 pM *tɨʔn-i (n) 'excremento/excrement' [pOM **tɨ"ny*] NHM: *tɨ"n* SHM: Tl *tɨ"nʸ* MM: Ma,Ja,Pu,At,Ct *tɨ"nʸ* LM: Cn <*tɨʔñ*> Gu *tɨ"nʸ* OIP: *tɨʔni* SaP: *tɨʔn*

Tɨ#040 pM *hɨhp-tɨʔni (n) 'moco/snot' [pOM **hɨhptɨ"ny*] NHM: *tʋ:tk hɨptɨ"n* 'moco de pavo' SHM: Tl *hɨptɨʔiny* MM: Ja,At *hɨhptɨ"nʸ* 'moco, moco de guajolote (pos)' Ju,Ma,Pu,Ct,Ca *hɨhptɨ"nʸ* 'moco' LM: Gu *hɨhptɨ"nʸ* 'moco de guajolote' SaP: *hɨptɨʔn*

Tɨ#041 pOM *tack tɨ"n-y (n) 'cerilla/match' NHM: *ta:ck tɨ"n* MM: Ma,Ja,Pu,At,Ct *ta·c̄tɨ"nʸ* LM: Gu *ta·c̄tɨ"nʸ*

Tɨ#042 pM [Veracruz] *tɨʔnik (n) 'gusano/worm' OIP: *tɨʔniʔkukuyɨ* SaP: *tɨʔnik* [Clark 1981]

Tɨ#043 pOM *tɨni?k (n) 'gusano/worm' NHM: *tɨnɨ̈k* 'animal mamífero; insecto, bicho' SHM: Tl *tɨnɨ?ɨk* MM: Ju,Ma,Ja,Ct *tɨnɨ?k* Pu *tɨnɨ̈!k* At *tɨnɨ?k* 'lombriz' Ca *tɨ:ŋk* 'gusano' LM: Gu *tɨ:ŋk*

Tɨ#044 pMZ *tɨp (vt) 'picar, flechar/to sting, shoot with bow and arrow' NHM: *tɨhp ~ tɨp* 'picar (p.ej., una abeja)' MM: 'picar (abeja, avispa, etc.)' Ju,Ma,Pu,Ca <*tɨhp*> Ja <*tɨp, tɨhp, tɨ́hpɨp, tɨ́hpɨ, tɨ: tʸépFʸɨ*> At <*tɨhpp, tɨpFá·m̄p*> Ct <*tɨhp, tɨpá·n̄ɨp, tɨ: tʸépFʸɨyɨ*> LM: Cn <*tɨhp ~ tɨp*> (vt) 'picar (insecto)' SJ *tɨhp ~ tɨp* 'to be bitten by insect, snake' LM: Gu <*tɨhp, tɨ́hpɨp, tɨbá·m̄p, tɨ: tʸɨbʸí:*> 'picar (abeja, avispa, etc.)' OIP: *tɨp* (vi) 'picar' SaP: *tɨp* (vi, vt) 'shoot with sling, bow; to be bitten by insect' SoZ: *tɨp* 'shoot with bow and arrow' [Foster and Foster 1948] AyZ: *[tɨp]* 'tirarlo (mezcla, pelota, etc.)' TxZ: *tɨp* (vt) 'jarponear' ChisZ: C *tɨhp* (vi) 'brincar' (vt) 'picarlo; ensartarlo; clavarlo, flecharlo' N *tɨhp* (vt) 'ensartarlo, pasarlo por un agujero' NE *tɨhp* (vi) 'brincar' (vt) 'ensartarlo (como el hilo en la aguja)'

Tɨ#045 pMZ *tɨ:?p (vi) 'tirar; ponerse el sol/to shoot with sling; set (sun)' [Mythological] NHM: *tɨ:?p* 'tirar de punta (p.ej., una jabalina), botar (p.ej., un palo)' LM: Cn <*tɨ·p ~ tɨ:p*> (vt) 'tirar con flecha' SJ *tɨ·p ~ tɨ:p* 'to shoot something in a slingshot, rubber band'

Gu <*tïːp, tïˑ ʔp*> 'extender tela con palo' [Nordell, p.c.] SoZ: *tiʔp* 'invitar a alguien' [Elson 1960], 'flechar' [Gutiérrez M. 1993] ChisZ: C,NE *tiʔp* (vi) 'ponerse el sol' N *tiʔp* (vi) 'ocultarse (el sol, la luna)'

Tɨ#046 pMZ ***tɨ(ʔm)pic** *(n) 'tuza/gopher' [Geomys sp.]* [pM **tɨpic* > pOM **tɨpyc*; pZ **tɨʔ(m)pic* > pGZ **tɨʔɨpic*] NHM: *tïpïc* 'tuza, gemís [Geomys sp.]' MM: Ju,Ja,Ct *tepč* Ma,At *tepʸč* LM: Cn <*tɨpšy*> '[Orthogeomys spp.]' Gu *tïpč* OIP: *tɨpiʼs* SaP: *típič* TxZ: *tɨˑʔpêʔč* SoZ: *tɨʔɨpič* ChisZ: C *tɨʔmbic* '=topo' N *tɨʔmbic* NE *tɨʔmbic* 'topo'

Tɨ#047 pM ***tɨpš** *(vt) 'torcer reata/to twist a rope'* NHM: *tɨhpš* 'torcer (p.ej., un mecate delgado), mecate, lazo, reata' MM: Ma <*tɨhpšp*> 'mecatear, hacer mecate' Ja *tɨhpš* 'mecatear, hacer mecate' LM: SJ *tɨpš* 'does not occur alone; carries the idea of jumping: *tɨpšɨʔk* 'to hop' OIP: *tɨpš* (vt) 'hacerlo (reata)'

Tɨ#048 pM ***tɨpš-i** *(n) 'reata/rope'* [pM **tɨpši* > pOM **tɨpšy*] NHM: *tïhpš* SHM: Tl *tehpsʸ* Ay *tepsʸ* MM: 'mecate, cuerda, reata' Ju *tehsʸn̥ʸ* 'mecate' [different derivation with **-an*] Ma *tehpsʸ* '=soga, lazo' Ja *tehpsʸ* '=soga' Pu *tehpsʸ* '=lazo' At *tehpsʸ* 'cuerda, reata', *tehpsʸn̥ʸ* 'mecate, soga de cuero' [sic!] Ct *tehpsʸn̥ʸ* 'reata, soga, lazo, mecate', *tehpsʸ* 'cuerda' [sic!] OIP: *tɨpši* SaP: *tɨpš*

Tɨ#049 pZ ***tɨʔps** *(vt) 'torcer reata/to twist a rope'* AyZ: [*tɨʔps*] (vt) 'entorchar (lia)' TxZ: *tɨʔps* (vt, vi-p) 'torcer (pita)' ChisZ: C *tɨʔps* (vi-s) 'estar torcido' (vt) 'torcerlo' N *tɨʔps* (vi) 'hilarse, estar hilado' (vt) 'enrollarlo, hilarlo' NE *tɨʔps* (vi) 'hilar' (vt) 'hilarlo'

Tɨ#050 pZ ***tɨʔps-i** *(n) 'cuerda/cord'* SoZ: *tɨpši* [*tɨʔpši* expected] AyZ [*tɨʔpsi*] TxZ: *tɨʔpš* '=reata' ChisZ: N *tɨʔpsi* 'hilo, cuerda' NE *tɨʔpsi* 'cuerda que se usa en la construcción; hilo'

Tɨ#051 pM ***hɨn-tɨpš** *(n) 'gusano de mariposa/caterpillar'* [pOM **hɨntɨhpš*] NHM: *hɨntïhpš* 'larva de mariposa IO' SaP: *hɨntɨpš* 'clase de gusano'

Tɨ#052 pMZ ***tɨːsi** *(n) 'murciélago/bat'* [pM **tɨːši* > pOM **tɨːšy*; pZ **tɨsi* > pGZ **tɨːši*] NHM: *tïːš* '[Tadarida bsasiliensis]' SHM: Tl *tɨːsʸ* MM: Ju,Ma,Pu *tɨːsʸ* Ja,Ct *tɨːsʸ* '=vampiro' LM: Cn <*tɨːšyʔak*> 'vampiro, murciélago [Desmondus rotundus or Diphylla ecaudata]' Gu *tïːsʸ* '=vampiro' OIP: *tɨːši* SaP: *tɨːš* SoZ: *tɨːši* [Foster and Foster

1948] AyZ: *[tɨ:si]* ChisZ: C *tɨhsi* '=vampiro' N *tɨsi* NE *tɨhsi* ChZ: *tɨsi*

Tɨ#053 pOM *tɨ:šy(š) *(n) 'tipo de palmera/type of palm'* NHM: *tɨ:šɨš* 'palma' SHM: Tl *tɨ:šy* 'palma' MM: Ju *tɨ:šʸ* 'palma, capisaya' At *tɨ:šʸ* 'palma' LM: Cn *<tɨ:šy>* 'tipo de palmera'

Tɨ#054 pMZ *tɨw *(vi) 'recto, estar; tumbar/to be straight, upright; to fall'* NHM: *tɨ:v~tɨ:hv~tɨv* 'estar recto, enderezar (p.ej., una aradura), directo, recto, derecho (p.ej., una calle)' MM: 'enderezarse' Ma *<tɨ:p, tɨwámp, tɨwɨ́:p>* Ja *<tɨ·w̄, tɨ:p, tɨw̄á·m̄p>* At *<tɨ:p, tɨw̄á·m̄p>* Ct *<tɨwɨ́:p>* Gu *<tɨ̈:p, tɨ̈·w̄, tɨ̈wá·m̄p>* 'enderezarse' LM: SJ *tɨ·w~tɨw* 'to act steadily, continually; to straighten' OlP: *tɨv* (vi) 'estirarse' (vt) 'estirarlo, apretarlo' SaP: *tɨw* (vi) 'be straight' SoZ: *tɨŋ* 'cut down' [Foster and Foster 1948] AyZ: *[tɨŋ]* 'tumbarlo' TxZ: *tɨŋ* (vi) 'caer en mano de la justicia, caer (muerto), calmarse (enfermedad)' (vt) 'trozar (con machete), cortar (árboles), tumbar (árboles)', *kas-k-tɨŋ* (vt) 'acostar, poner en posición vertical' (vi) 'acostarse boca arriba' ChisZ: C *tɨŋ* (vt) 'tumbarlo; echarlo abajo' N *tɨŋ* (vi) 'caerse; llegar, alcanzar (a ver)' (vt) 'tumbarlo' NE *tɨŋ* (vt) 'tumbarlo (como un árbol)' ChZ: *tɨŋ* 'cortar (árbol)'

Tɨ#055 pOM *ye?p-tɨhw~ye?p-tɨw *(vi) 'extender(se)/to stretch'* MM: Ju *<yœ?ptɨ́f>* Ma *<yœ?ptɨ́w̥~yœ?ptɨ́Φ~yœ?ptɨ́f>* Ja *<yœ?ptɨ́w̥>* At *<yœ?ptɨ́w̄, yœ?ptɨ́:pʸ>* Ct *<yœ?ptɨ́w̄>* LM: Gu *<ye?ptɨ́w̄>*

Tɨ#056 pOM *yak-tɨhw~yak-tɨw *(vt) 'enderezar/to straighten'* NHM: *yaktɨ:v~yaktɨ:hv~yaktɨv* MM: Ju *<yœhtɨw>* Ma *<yahktɨ́w̥ ~yahktɨ́Φ~yahktɨ́f, yahktɨ́:pʸ>* '=preguntar' Ja *<yahnɨdɨ́wɨ, yahtɨ́w̄, yahtɨ́·w̄, yahtɨ́:pʸ~yahtɨ́:pʸ>* 'preguntar', *<yahtɨ́w̄, yahtɨ́:pʸ>* 'enderezar' Pu *<yahtɨ́w̄, yahtɨ́:pʸ>* '=preguntar' At *<yœhktɨ́w̄, yœhktɨ́:pʸ>* 'enderezar', *<yahktɨ́w̄, yahktɨ́:pʸ>* 'preguntar' [sic!] Ct *<yahktéyɨ>* 'enderezar', *<yahktɨ́w̥, yahktɨ́:pʸ>* 'preguntar' Ca *<yahtɨ́w>* 'extender(se)' LM: Gu *<yahtɨ́w̄, yahtɨ́:pʸ, yahtɨ́·w̄>* '=enderezar'

Tɨ#057 pZ *tɨwɨ *(n) 'hermano/sibling'* [pGZ **tɨ:wɨ*] SoZ: *tɨ:wɨ* 'sibling, cousin' [Foster 1949], *tɨ:wɨ?* 'hermano, primo; compañero' [Gutiérrez M. 1993] TxZ: *tɨ:w* 'hermano menor (de mujer o hombre), sobrino/a', *haytɨ:w* 'hermano (mayor o adulto), amigo', *saktɨ:w* 'concuña', *yomtɨ:w* 'hermana (mayor o adulta)' ChisZ: C *tɨwɨ* 'amigo, compañero; familiar; prójimo' [has a vocative *tiwiy* 'hablándole con cariño'] N *tiwi* 'hermano, pariente, compañero; lo que es similar, lo que es igual; a mí' NE *tiwi* 'amigo, compañero; hijo—hablándole con cariño' S [Tu] *tiwi* 'sibling' [Foster 1949]

Ti#058 pOM ***tiwy** *(adj) 'cierto/certain'* NHM: *tiv* 'directo, recto, derecho (p.ej., un calle)' MM: Ma *tiy* 'cierto, de veras' At *tiȳ* 'de veras' Pu *tiȳ* 'cierto' LM: Gu *tiȳ* 'cierto'

Ti#059 pZ ***ti?ŋ-kuy** *(n) 'fierro, metal/iron, metal'* TxZ: *ti?ŋ-ko?* ~ *ti?ŋ-ku?*) 'campana, hierro' ChisZ: C,NE *ti?ŋguy* N *ti?ŋguy* 'metal, campana' ChZ: *ti?ŋku?y*

Ti#060 pMZ ***tiy** *(vt) 'tender/to hang'* NHM: *ti:y* ~ *ti:hy* ~ *tiy* 'pesar, colgar' MM: 'pesar' Ju <*tiy*> At,Ct <*tiȳ*> OIP: *tiy* (vt) 'tenderlo' SaP: *tiy* (vi, vt) 'hang' ChisZ: C *tiyi?* 'hebra'

Ti#061 pOM ***ku-tiy** *'colgar/to hang'* SHM: Tu <*mguδí·yp^y* ~ *mgudí:p^y, kudíy*> Tp <*kudíy*> MM: Ju <*kudíy*> Cc <*kudíy*> At <*kudíy*>

Ti#062 pM ***ta:cik-tiy** *(n) 'arete/earring'* NHM: *ta:ck tiy* SHM: Tu *tactíy* Tp *tAcktíy* Mi *tacktíȳ* MM: Ju *tæcktíy* Cc *tAcktíy* Ma,Ja,Pu *ta·ctíy* At *ta·cktíy* Ct *ta·cktíy* LM: Gu *ta·ctíȳ* SaP: *tá:ciktiy*

Ti#063 pOM ***tiy-i** *(adj) 'derecho/straight'* SHM: Tl *tiy* MM: Ju *tíyi* Ma *tíȳi* '=directo' Ja *tíȳi* '=directo' At *tiȳ* 'derecho', *midíyi* 'directo' Ct *téyi* '=directo' Ca *tiy* LM: Cn <*tiy*> (adj) 'derecho, directo; fijo; cierto' Gu *tíȳi* '=directo'

Ti#064 pM ***ti:?y** *(vt) 'mecer/to rock'* MM: Ma <*ti:y, t^ye"p^y*> Ja,Pu, Ct <*ti:y, t^yi!p^y*> At <*tiȳ, t^ye:p^y, t^yi·ȳ*> LM: Gu <*tiyi"w, t^yiyi:p^y, t^yiyí·ȳ*> OIP: *ti:y* (vi, vt) SaP: *ti?y* (vi, vt) 'swing someone in a hammock, swing'

TA#001 pM ***ta:c ~ ta?c** *(vi) 'orinar/to urinate'* NHM: *ta"c* MM: Ju <*ta"c*> Ja <*ta"c, ta·c̄, ta·c̄p*> Ma,Pu,At,Ct <*ta"c, ta·c̄p*> LM: Cn <*ta·c ~ ta"c*> (vi) Ca <*ta"c*> SJ *ta·c ~ ta"c* Gu <*ta"c, ta·c̄, ta·c̄p, ta"ʒá·m̄p*> OIP: *ta:c ~ ta?c* (vi) SaP: *ta:c ~ ta?c* (vi)

TA#002 pM ***ta?c-i** *(n) 'orina/urine'* [pOM **ta"cy*] NHM: *ta"č* SHM: Tl *to"č* MM: Ma *ta"čn^yi:* Ja *ta"čn^yi:* Ct *ta"č, ta"čn^yi:* Ju,Pu, At *ta"č* LM: Ca,Gu *ta"č* OIP: *ta?či's* [last consonant not accounted for] SaP: *ta?č*

TA#003 pMZ ***ta?c** *(vt) 'estibar/to pack'* LM: SJ *cu·mda?c* ~ *cu·mda"c* SoZ: *ta?c* (vt) TxZ: *ta?c* (vt, vi-p) 'estibar (costales, leñas, tamales de siete vueltas), poner (palos tupidos)' ChisZ: C *ti?ksta?c* (vt) 'emparejarlo' NE *ta?ctu?m* (vt) 'plegarlo (como tela)' N *ta?c* (vi) 'estar parejo; estar lleno'

TA#004 pMZ ***ta:cɨk** *(n) 'oreja/ear'* [pM **ta:cɨk* > pOM **ta:ck*; pZ **tacɨk* > pGZ **ta:cɨk*] NHM: *ta:ck* 'oreja', *ta:ck ak* 'especie de hongo comestible que sale en cualquier árbol o al pie de los cafetos' SHM: Tl *tock* Ay *tack* MM: Ju *tæck* Ma,Ct *ta·c̄k* '=oído' Ja,Pu,At *ta·c̄k* LM: Ca *tack* [Wonderly 1949] [Ixcuintepec] *tacak* [Wonderly 1949] Gu *tá·cɨk* OlP: *ta:cɨ'k* 'oreja', *kuyta:cɨ'k* 'orejita de palo; hongo' SaP: *tá:cɨk* TaM: *técɨk* [Wonderly's transcription of 1949] SoZ: *ta:cɨk* TxZ: *ta:cɨk* ChisZ: C *tacɨk* '=asa' N *tacɨk* NE *tacɨhk* '=asa—como de una vasija' S [Tu] *tacɨk* [Wonderly 1949] ChZ: StaMaCh *tacɨk* SnMiCh *tacɨk* [Wonderly 1949]

TA#005 pMZ ***ta?c(k)V(k)** *(n) 'cuajinicuil; machetón/jinicuil; inga'* [pM **ta?ckV(k)* > pOM **ta?cky*; pZ **ta?cɨk* > pGZ **ta?acɨk*] NHM: *ta?tyki* 'jinicuil, cuajinicuil' [Inga paterna, Inga jinicuil (G. Martin, p.c.] MM: 'guasamando, vaina, guajinicuil, cuajinicuil' Ma *ta?čkʸ* 'cuajinicuil, guasamando' Ju,Ja,At,Ct, *ta?čkʸ* Pu *ta!čkʸ* LM: 'guasamando, vaina, guajinicuil, cuajinicuil' Cn <*ta?č*> 'cuajinicuil, jinicuil (árbol) [Inga sp.]' Ca *ta?čkʸ* Gu *ta?čk* OlP: *ta?skɨ'k* 'vaina' [?] SaP: *tá?cɨk* 'vaina' [Zo loan?] SoZ: *tá?acɨk* 'vaina' TxZ: *ta:?cɨk* 'vaina' ChisZ: C *ta?cɨk* 'machetón—fruta de un árbol regional' N *ta?cɨ* 'machetón, cuajinicuil—fruta de un árbol' [Inga radians]

TA#006 pMZ ***tah** *(vt) 'escarbar/to dig'* NHM: *tah* 'cavar, tajar, escarbar (p.ej., con un palo)' MM: Ju <*tah*> Ma <*tah, mdæhpʸ*> Ja <*tah, t'æhpʸ*> Pu,Ct <*tah*> At <*tah, tahp*> '=entristecerse' LM: Ca <*tah*> Cn <*tah*> (vt) 'excavar' SJ *tah* 'to dig a fairly deep hole' Gu <*tah, mdahpʸ*> 'escarbar' <*tahp ma:pʸ*> 'entristecerse' OlP: *tah* (vt) 'tarpalearlo; escarbarlo' SaP: *tah* (vi, vt) 'dig' SoZ: *tah* (vt) TxZ: *tah* (vt, vi-p) '=cavar' ChisZ: C *tah* (vt) 'cavarlo, escarbarlo, excavarlo' N *tah* (vt) 'escarbarlo; punzarlo' NE *tah* (vt) 'picarlo, punzarlo (como con espina)' ChZ: *tah*

TA#007 pOM ***yak-tah** *(vt) 'escarbar algo/to dig up something'* NHM: *yaktah* 'escarbar algo' LM: Cn <*yahtah*> (vt) 'escarbar'

TA#008 pOM ***tahe?py** *(adv) 'afuera/outside'* SHM: Tu *tahǽ?p^y*
MM: Ju *tɨhǽ?p* Cc,Ja *tɨhǽ?p^y* Pu *tɨhœ!p^y* At *tœhǽ?p^y* LM: Ca
tɨwǽ?p

TA#009 pM ***taha?w** *(n) 'patio/patio'* [pOM **taha"w*] NHM: *tagʋhk*
[?] MM: Ju *tɨhhá"* At,Ct *tahá"w* LM: Ca *tɨwá"* Gu *tïbá"* OlP:
ta?a'u

TA#010 pM ***ko?tak** *(adj) 'calvo, pelón/bald'* [pOM **kutak*] NHM:
kutak MM: Ju *kutǽk* Ma *kɨták* Ja *ku"ták* At *kuták* Ct *kɨ"ták* LM:
Ca *tæk* Gu *ku"dák* OlP: *ko?takɨ*

TA#011 pOM ***ta:k** *(n) 'madre, mamá/mother'* [Cf. OlP *ta:k~ta?k*
(vi) 'dar a luz'.] NHM: *ta:k* SHM: Tl *to:k* Tm *kɨta:k* MM: Ju,Ma,
Ja,Pu,At,Ct *ta:k* 'madre' LM: Ca *ta:k* SJ *tah* Gu *tah*

TA#012 pOM ***ku-ta:k** *(n) 'madrastra/stepmother'* NHM: *kuta:k*
MM: Ma *k^yɨdá:k* Ju,Ja,At *kudá:k* Pu,Ct *kɨdá:k* LM: Ca *kudá:k* SJ
ko·dah

TA#013 pOM ***ma:h-ta:hk-n** *(n) 'paraje (para pasar la noche) /dwel-
ling place'* MM: Ju *ma:dǽkn̥* Ma,Ja,Pu,At,Ct *ma:dá·kn̥* LM: Ca
ma:dá·kt Gu *tu"ma:dá·kt*

TA#014 pMZ ***ta:k?** *(vi, vt) 'tejer/to weave'* NHM: *ta:k~ta"k* 'tejer
(p.ej., una bata)' SHM: *to"k* 'tejer (una gorra)' MM: Ju <*ta"k*>
Ja <*ta"k, ta·k, t^yæ·k^yp^y*> Ma,At,Ct <*ta"k, t^yæ·k^yp^y*> LM: Ca
<*ta"k*> Cn <*ta·k~ta"k*> (vt) SJ *ta·k~ta"k* 'to weave; to do
over and over' Gu <*ta"k, ta·k, t^ya·k^yp^y*> SoZ: *tak* 'weave; lack'
[Foster and Foster 1948] TxZ: *tak* (vt, vi-a) ChisZ: C,N *tahk* (vi,
vt) ChZ: *tak*

TA#015 pMZ ***ta:k?-e** *(n) 'telaraña/cobweb'* [pM **ta?ke* > pOM
*ta"ky; pZ **take*] MM: Ju *po·š^yp^yt^yǽ"k^y* Ma *po·š^yp^yt^yǽ"k^y* Ja
po·š^yt^yé"k^y At *po·š^ym^yd^yǽ"k^y* Ct *po·š^yp^yt^yǽ"k^y* Gu *po·š^yt^yá"k^y* TxZ:
tak-ta:k ChisZ: C *taketake* N *take* '=tela' NE *?amutake*

TA#016 pOM ***?oy-ta"ky** *(adv) 'suavemente, con cuidado/slowly,
gently'* NHM: *?otya"ky* 'con mucho cuidado, muy despacio, muy
lento, muy suave' SHM: *?utya"kyɨ* 'suave, lento, despacio'; *utya"ky*
'lento' MM: 'lento' Ju *?ǽd^yǽ"g^yɨ* Ja,Pu,At *?ɨd^yǽ"k^y* Ct *?a·d^yǽ"g^yɨ*
LM: 'lento' Gu *?od^yɨgá:mp^y*

TA#017 pMZ ***taka** *(n) 'perro/dog'* [Presumably pM **taka*; pZ **taka* > pGZ **ta:ka*, but restricted to the Gulf area.] SaP: *tak* AyZ: [*ta:?ga*]

TA#018 pMZ ***tak(us)** *(n) 'bastón, bordón/walking stick'* [pM, pOM **tahk*; pZ **takus*] NHM: *tahk* SHM: Tp *tAhk* 'bastón' Tu,Mi *tahk* 'bastón' MM: Ju *tahk* 'topil' Cc *tAhk* 'bastón' Ja *tahkṇ* 'bastón', *tahk* '̥topil' [sic!] Pu,Ma *tahkṇ* 'bastón' At *tahk* 'bastón', *tahk* *mayú·t* 'topil' Ct *tahkṇ* 'bastón', *tahk* 'topil' [sic!] LM: Ca *tahk* 'bastón' Cn <*tahk*> 'bastón; topil, alguacil' SJ *tahk* 'walking stick' Gu *tahk* 'topil' OIP: *kuytahkɨ* ChisZ: C *kuytyakus* N *takus* NE *takus* 'bastón'

TA#019 pM ***ta?kš** *'gotear/to drip'* NHM: *ta?kš* 'gotear muy lentamente' MM: 'regar con agua' MM: Ju <*ta?kš*> Ja <*ta?š*, *ťœ?šᵖpʸ*> At <*ta?kš, ťœ?kʸšᵖpʸ*> LM: Cn <*ta"kš*> (vi) 'gotear' Gu <*ta?š, ťašᵖp*> 'regar con agua'

TA#020 pOM ***ta"kš-y** *(n) 'gota/drop'* NHM: *ta?kš* LM: Cn <*ta"kšy*>

TA#021 pZ ***ta?ks** *'alumbrar/to give light'* SaP: *ta?kš* (vi, vt) 'give light, light candles for religious events' [Zo loan or product of contamination by the route 'to drip' > 'to drip (candle)' > 'to give light (candle)'; cf. pM **ta?kš* 'to drip'.] TxZ: *ta?ks* (vt, vi-p) 'lamer' [?] ChisZ: C [Te] <*tacspa*> 'lucir / solar, echar suelo a la casa' ChZ: *ta?ks* 'alumbrar'

TA#022 pOM ***tam** *(adv) 'ahora/now'* SHM: Tp *ťʸAm* MM: Ju *ťʸœm* 'ahora, hoy', *tim ťʸœm* 'ahorita' Cc *ťʸAm, ti!mďʸám* 'ahorita' Ma *ťʸam̄* 'ahorita, ahora, hoy' Ja *ťʸam* 'ahora, ahorita, hoy' Pu *ťʸám̄?ɨy* 'ahorita', *ťʸam̄* 'ahora' At *ťʸam̄* '=hoy' Ct *ťʸam̄* 'ahora, ahorita, hoy' LM: Ca *ťʸam*

TA#023 pMZ ***tam?** *(adj) 'amargo/bitter'* [pM **ta?m* > pOM **ta"m*; pZ, pGZ **tam*] NHM: *ta"m* SHM: Tl *to"m* Tu *ta?m* Tp *tA"m* MM: Cc *tA"m* Ju,Ma,Ja,Pu,At,Ct *ta"m* LM: Cn <*ta?m*> (adj) Ca,Gu *ta"m, ta!m̄* SoZ: *tam* AyZ: [*tam*] TxZ: *tam* (adj) ChZ: *tam*

TA#024 pM ***ta:mac** *(adj) 'salado/salty'* [pOM **ta"m*] NHM: *ta?mïc* MM: Ju *ta"mc?é:kʸ* Ma *ta?mc* Ja *ta!mc* At *ta?mẕ?öö:kʸ* Ct *ta?mc* LM: Cn <*tamc*> (adj) SJ *ta·ms* Gu *ta·m̄c* OIP: *ta:ma's* SaP: *tá:mac*

TA#025 pM **tan** *(vi) 'quedar/to stay'* NHM: *ta:n ~ ta:hn ~ tan* 'quedar, dejar (p.ej., una cosa olvidada)' SHM: *yikton* (vt) 'dejar una cosa' Ja <*tan̄, ta·n̄, ta·m̄p*> 'quedarse, atrasarse' Pu <*ta·m̄p*> 'atrasarse' At <*tan̄, ta·m̄p, tá?n̄im*> 'quedarse' Ct,Ma <*tan̄, ta·m̄p*> 'quedarse, atrasarse' SaP: *tan* (vi) 'stay'

TA#026 pOM ***?iš-ta?n** *(n) 'seña/sign'* Ma *?ihštán̄ʸ* 'seña' Ja *?ihštán̄ʸ* 'marca', *?ihštá!n̄* 'seña, señal' At *?ihštá?nin* 'marca', *?ihštá?n̄* 'muestra', *?ihštá!n̄in, ?ihštá!n̄* 'seña' [sic!] Ct *?ihštán̄ʸ* 'seña, marca' [sic!] LM: Ca *?ihštá"nim* 'señal' Gu *?ihštá!nt* 'señal', *?ihštá!nt* 'marca, muestra, seña' [sic!]

TA#027 pMZ ***ta?n** *(vi) 'atascarse/to become stuck'* [pOM **ta?n-?iy*] NHM: *ta?ni ~ tana* 'tardar, demorar' Ma <*ta·m̄p*> 'tardar', <*ta·m̄p, tá?n̄?ipʸ*> 'demorar' Ma <*tá?n̄?ipʸ, ta?cpihkp, ta·m̄p, tan̄ámp*> 'atascarse, atorarse' Ja <*tá?niyi*> 'atascarse, atorarse' Pu <*tá!n̄ipʸ, ti: ti: tʸáni*> 'atascarse, atorarse' At <*tá?n̄ip, ti: tʸáni*> 'atascarse, atorarse', <*táni, tá?n̥ip*> 'tardar', <*tá?n̄ip*> 'demorar' Ct <*tá?n̄?ipʸ, taniyámp*> 'demorar', <*ta·m̄p, tá?n̄ip*> 'tardar', <*ta·m̄p, tán?ipʸ*> 'atascarse, atorarse' OlP: *ta?na* (adj) 'mucho(s), bastante'; *ta?nik* (adj) 'grande' SoZ: *ta?n* (vt) 'cercar' TxZ: *ta?n* (vt, via) 'cercar, tapar' ChisZ: C *ta?n* (vi) 'completarse' N *ta?n* (vi) 'completarse, estar completo; cumplir' NE *yakta?n* (vt) 'completarlo; cumplirlo; ajustarlo' ChZ: *ta?n* 'completar'

TA#028 pZ ***tahpi** *(n) 'gavilán/hawk'* [pGZ **tahpi*] SaP: *tahp* [Zo loan] SoZ: *táhpi* [Foster and Foster 1948, Gutiérrez M. 1993] AyZ: *[táhpi]* TxZ: *tahpe?ñ* [*tahpe* expected] ChisZ: C,NE *tahpi* '=águila' N *tahpi*

TA#029 pZ ***tapu** *(n) 'verruga/wart'* [pGZ **ta:pu*] SoZ: *tá:pu* AyZ: *[ta:?bo]* TxZ: *tá:pu?* [Clark n.d.], *ta:pi?* [Wichmann fc.-b] ChisZ: C,N *tapu*

TA#030 pMZ ***ta?ps** *(vi) 'castañetear/to rattle'* NHM: *ta?pš* 'castañetear' ChisZ: N *ta?ps* (vi) 'ondear (haciendo ruido)'

TA#031 pMZ ***tas** *(vi) 'llenarse/to become full'* NHM: *tahš ~ taš* 'sangrar, desangrar' MM: 'sangrar' Ju,Ma <*tahšp*> Ja,At <*tahšp, tašá·m̄p*> Ct <*tahšp, tašámp*> LM: Cn <*tahš ~ taš*> (vi) 'tener hemorragia' ChisZ: C *tahs* (vi) 'llenarse; hartarse' N *tas* (vi) 'llenarse, estar lleno' (vt) 'llenarlo' NE *tahs* (vi) 'llenarse; crecer (como un río)'

TA#032 pOM ***taš** *(n) 'cascada/cascade'* NHM: *taš* 'canal, chorro de agua' SHM: Tp *tÁš* Mi *taš* MM: Ju *tæš* Cc *nɨːdáš* Ma,Ja,Pu *taš̄* At *taš̄* '=chorro de agua' Ct *táš̤ɨ* 'chorro de agua', *taš̄* 'cascada' [sic!] LM: Cn <*taš*> Ca *taš* Gu *taš̄* '=chorro de agua'

TA#033 pMZ ***tata** *(n) 'padre, papá/father'* [pM *tata > pOM *tat with an unexpected final vowel in all but LM; pZ *tata > pGZ *taːta] [except ChisZ-C and TxZ all from Foster 1949] NHM: *tata* SHM: Ay *data* Hu *tata* 'woman's father-in-law' MM: Ju *tǽtɨ* 'papá' Ct *tá·tɨ* 'papá' LM: Cn <*tat*> 'papá (se usa para saludar al papá y al suegro)' Ca *tá·ta* 'papá' OIP: *tata* 'grandmother, grandson, granddaughter' TxZ: *taːta?* 'bisabuelo' ChisZ: C *tatah*

TA#034 pOM ***taːt** *(n) 'nopal/prickly pear cactus'* NHM: *taːt* [Opuntia lasiacantha] SHM: *toːt* Ju,Ja,At,Ct *taːt* LM: Cn <*taːd*> 'nopal (genérico) [Opuntia spp.]' SJ *taːd* Ca,Gu *taːt* OIP: *ta?t* 'pitahaya' [?]

TA#035 pMZ ***taŋ** *(vi) 'abrir; rajar/to open; split'* SHM: *yiktawwo?oc* (vt) vaciar ChisZ: NE *taŋ* (vi) 'abrirse (como una puerta); rajarse (como un árbol)' (vi-s) 'estar abierto; estar rajado' (vt) 'abrirlo (como una puerta); rajarlo (como un árbol)' ChZ: *taŋ* 'rajar'

TA#036 pMZ ***tay** *(vi) 'cicatrizarse/to close (a wound)'* NHM: *taːy* ~ *taːhy* ~ *tay* 'secar o sanar una herida, cicatrizar' SHM: Tu <*táy̤ɨ*> Tp <*tAy*> Mi <*tïː t̮á·yn̮ʸï*> MM: Cc <*tA·ypʸ*, *tïː t̮á·yn̮ʸï*> Ma,Ct <*tǽy?ipʸ*> Ja <*táy̤ip*> Pu <*tǽy̤ipʸ*> At <*tá·y̤ip, tæːpʸ*, *tïː t̮ǽy*> OIP: *tay* (vi) 'cicatrizar' TxZ: *tay [*še?-taːye?* 'ano (interior)'] ChisZ: C *tay [in the noun *nɨ?-tay* 'canal, zanha']

TA#037 pM ***tay-a** *(n) 'cicatriz/scar'* [pOM *tay] NHM: *tay* '=cicatrizado' SHM: Tu *taȳ* Tp *tAy* MM: Cc *tAy* Ma *tæy* Ja,At *taȳ* Pu,Ct *tæȳ* LM: Cn <*tay*> OIP: *taya*

TA#038 pOM ***matuːk tay** *(n) 'tipo de planta/a kind of plant'* NHM: *madʋːk tay* 'coralillo, cacahuapastle [Hamelia erecta]' LM: Cn <*maduːktay*> 'cielitos [Ageratum corymbosum]'

TA#039 pOM ***?iš-ta?y** *(vt) 'buscar/to search for'* SHM: Tu <*?ištá"y, m?ištá·ypʸ*> Mi <*?ištá?h*> MM: '=conseguir' Ju <*?ištá"*> 'buscar' Ma <*?ištá"w̤, ?ištá"Φ, ?ištá"f*> Ja <*?aštá"w,*

m?aštǽ:pʸ> Pu,At *< ?ištá">* Ct *< ?ištá"w>* LM: Ca *<ištá">*
'buscar' Gu *< ?ištá"w, m?ištá:pʸ>*

TU#001 pMZ ***tu:c-kuy** *(n) 'palma/palm tree'* [pM **tu:ckuhy*; pZ,
pGZ **tuckuy*] OlP: *tu:skuyɨ* 'palo de palma' AyZ: *[tuckuy]* 'palma
de guano (largo)' TxZ: *tuckuy* 'mata de la palma'

TU#002 pOM ***tu?c** *(n) 'olla/pot'* NHM: *tv?c* SHM: Tl,Ay *tu?hc*
MM: '=jarro' At,Ju,Ma,Ja *tu?c* Pu *tu!c* 'olla, jarro', *tu?c* 'botello,
vidrio' [sic!] Ct *tu?c* '=botella' LM: Cn *<tu"c>* 'olla (de barro)'
Ca,Gu *tu?c*

TU#003 pMZ ***tu?c(ta)** *(n) 'cola/tail'* [pM, pOM **tu?cta* (uncommon
retention of final vowel in pOM); pZ, pGZ **tu?c*] NHM: *tv?šta*
'=rabo' SHM: Tl *tu?ct* OlP: *tu?sta* SaP: *tu?hc* SoZ: *tu?c* AyZ:
[ču?c] 'su cola' TxZ: *tu?c* '=rabo' ChisZ: C,NE *tu?c* N *tu?c*
'=parte de atrás, extremo—de una canoa, del campo de aviación'
ChZ: *tu?c*

TU#004 pMZ ***tuh** *(vt) 'cazar/to hunt'* NHM: *tvh* 'tirar (con arma de
fuego)' MM: 'tirar (con arma de fuego)' Ju̱ *<tuh>* Ma *<tuẖ,*
mdihpʸ> Ja *<tuẖ, tʸihpʸ>* '=cazar' Pu *<tuh>* 'cazar' At *<tuh,*
tʸühpʸ> Ct *<tuh, tʸihpʸ>* LM: 'tirar (con arma de fuego)' Cn
<tuh> (vt) SJ *tuh* Gu *<tuh, tʸuhpʸ>* OlP: *tuh* (vt) 'tirar (con
arma de fuego)' SaP: *tuh* (vi, vt) 'tirar (con arma de fuego)' SoZ:
tuh (vt) 'tirar, disparar' AyZ: *[tuh]* 'tirar' TxZ: *tuh* (vt, vi-a)
'tirar (con rifle)' ChisZ: 'tirar (con arma de fuego)' C *tuh* (vi,vt) N
tuh (vt) NE *tuh* (vi,vt) 'cazarlo a tiros'

TU#005 pOM ***tuh-pa** *(n) 'cazador/hunter'* NHM: *tvhpa* 'soldado'
MM: Ju,Pu *túhpɨ* LM: Ca *túhpɨ* Gu *túhpɨ tí?s*

TU#006 pM ***tuh-an** *(n) 'instrumento para tirar/instrument for*
shooting' [pOM **tuhn*] NHM: *tvhïn* 'arma de fuego' SHM: Tp *tuhn̥*
'arma de fuego' MM: Ju,Cc *tuhn̥* 'arma de fuego' Ma,Ja,Pu *tuhn̥*
'rifle, arma de fuego, escopeta' At *tuhn̥* '.22 de una bala, arma de
fuego' Ct *tuhn̥* 'rifle, arma de fuego', *mɨhtúhn̥* 'escopeta' LM: Ca
tuht 'arma de fuego, escopeta' Cn *<tuht>* 'rifle' SJ *tuht* Gu *tuht*
'arma de fuego, rifle' OlP: *tuha'n* 'escopeta, rifle' SaP: *túhan* 'escopeta'

TU#007 pZ ***ca?-tuh** *(n) 'granizo/hail'* SaP: *ca?tú:* [Zo loan] ChisZ:
C *ca?tuh* N *catuh* NE *caduh*

TU#008 pOM ***tu:h ~ tu"h** *(vi) 'llover/to rain'* NHM: *tʋ: ~ tʋ"* MM: Ma *< tu:p, tu·w̥, tɨ: ťu"y >* Ja *< tu:p, tu"wá·m̄p, tu·w̄ >* Pu *< tu:p, tu"wá·m̄p >* At *< tu:p, tu"há·m̄p, tu: >* Ct *< tu:p, tu"wám̄p, tu·w̥ >* LM: Cn *< tuy ~ tu· ~ tu"w >* Gu *< tu:p, tu"wá·m̄p, tu·w̄ >*

TU#009 pMZ ***tu:h** *(n) 'lluvia/rain'* [pM, pOM **tu:h*; pZ **tuh*] NHM: *tʋ:* [Schoenhals and Schoenhals 1965] *tʋ:h* [A. Schoenhals in p.c. to G. Martin] SHM: Tl *tu:h* MM: Ju,Ma,Ja,At,Ct *tu:* LM: Cn *< tu: >* Gu *tu:* OIP: *tu:h* SaP: *tu:* SoZ: *tuh* AyZ: *[tuh]* TxZ: *tuh* ChisZ: C,N,NE *tuh* ChZ: *tuh*

TU#010 pMZ ***tuk** *(vi) 'gastarse/to wear out (things)'* NHM: *tʋhk ~ tʋk* 'poner(se) viejo' MM: Ja *< tuhkp, tuká·m̄p >* Pu *< tuhkp, tɨ: ťúhknɨ, tuká·m̄p >* At,Ma,Ct *< tuhkp >* LM: Gu *< tuhp, tugá·m̄p >* ChisZ: C *tuhk* (vi,vt) 'rematarlo, terminarlo' N *tuhk* (vi) 'suceder; terminarse; hacerse, ser hecho' NE *tuhk* (vi) 'acontecer, suceder'

TU#011 pZ ***kɨ-tuk** *(vi) 'cruzar/to cross'* ChisZ: C *kɨtɨhk* (vi) 'cruzar; pasar; acontecer, suceder' (vt) 'cruzarlo' NE *kɨdɨhk* (vi) 'pasar, cruzar' (vt) 'cruzarlo, atravesarlo; pasarlo, rebasarlo' ChZ: *kɨtuk* 'pasar'

TU#012 pOM ***win-tuk** *(n) 'mezquino (tacaño)/stingy'* NHM: *vintʋk* 'mezquino (persona miserable o avaro)' MM: Ja,Pu,At *windúk* MM: Ju *wi:ndúk* Ma,At,Ct *hɨndúk* LM: Ca *wi:ndúk* Gu *wi:ndúk*

TU#013 pOM ***win-tuk-y** *(adj) 'nublado/cloudy'* NHM: *vintuk* MM: Ju *windík^y* Ma,Ct *hɨndík^y* Ja *wimbék^y* At *hɨndúük^y* LM: Gu *wi:mbík^y*

TU#014 pMZ ***tuku** *(adj) 'viejo (cosa)/old (thing)'* [pM **tuku >* pOM **tuk*; pZ **tuku*] NHM: *tʋk* 'viejo, p.ej., huaraches muy usados' SHM: Tl *tuk* 'vagina' MM: 'gastado, viejo (cosa)' Ju *tuk* Ma,Ja,Pu, At,Ct *tuk* 'viejo (cosa)' LM: Ca *tuk* 'viejo (cosa)' Cn *< tuk >* (adj) 'viejo, usado; sobrante' SJ *tuk* 'old' Gu *tuk* 'viejo (cosa), gastado, viejo' OIP: *tuku* 'viejo' SaP: *nigutuhkɨ* 'cover oneself' AyZ: *tuk-* (prefijo de sustantivos) 'viejo' TxZ: *-tuku?* (sufijo de sustantivos) 'viejo' ChisZ: C *pamdyuku* 'ropa usada, trapo' N *tuku* 'viejo'

TU#015 pMZ ***kɨ?-tuku** *(n) 'manco/one-armed, one-handed'* [See pMZ **kɨ?* 'hand, arm'.] MM: Ju *kɨ·túk* Ma,Ja,Pu,At,Ct *kɨ"dúk* LM: Cn *< kɨ"duk >* 'trunco, mocho' Ca *kɨ"dúk* Gu *kɨ"dúk* OIP: *kɨ?tuku* SaP: *kɨ?túk* ChisZ: C *kɨ?tuku ~ kɨ?tyuku* 'manco, trunco'

TU#016 pMZ **tu?c-tuku** *(n) 'sin cola/tailless'* [See pMZ *tu?c(ta)* 'tail'.] OIP: *tu?stuku* 'sin cola' ChisZ: C *tu?ctyuku* 'sin cola'

TU#017 pMZ **tuk** *(vt) 'cortar fruta/to sever fruits, etc., from the plant'* NHM: *tʋhk ~ tʋk* 'cortar (p.ej., con los dedos), cosechar (p.ej., frijoles)' SHM: Tu < *tuk, mduikʸpʸ ~ mdikʸpʸ* > 'cortar (fruta)' Tp < *tuk, mduhkʸpʸ, tʸuhk, tʸukǽmpʸ* > 'cortar (fruta)' MM: Cc < *tuk, tɨ:ttukʸ, kʸæh ttuhkʸ, tʸuhkʸpʸ, tʸukǽmpʸ, mduhkʸpʸ, hʸindúhkʸpʸ* > 'cortar (fruta)' Ma < *tuk, tʸihkʸpʸ* > 'cortar (fruta)', < *tʸi·hkʸpʸ* > 'cortar (café)' [sic!] Ja,Pu < *tuk, tʸihkʸpʸ, tʸuhk* > 'cortar (fruta)'_At < *tuk* > 'cortar (café)', < *tuk, tʸuühkʸpʸ* > 'cortar (fruta)' Ct < *tuk, tʸihkʸpʸ* > 'cortar (fruta)' LM: Cn < *tuhk ~ tuk* > (vt) 'cortar' SJ *tuhk ~ tuk* 'to pick, sever from the plant (fruit, beans, flowers, pineapple, etc.)' Gu < *tuk, tʸuhpʸ, tʸuhk* > 'cortar (fruta)' OIP: *tuk* (vt) 'cortar fruta; cruzar (p.ej., un río)' SaP: *tuk* (vi, vt) 'pick (coffee, oranges, etc.), break, snap' SoZ: *tuk* 'pluck (fruit) [Foster and Foster 1948]' AyZ: *[tuk]* 'cortarlo (con la mano)' TxZ: *tuk* (vt) 'cortar (fruta con mano)' ChisZ: C *tuhk* (vt) 'cosechar fruta, cortarlo' N *tuhk* (vt) 'cortarlo (fruta)' NE *tuhk* (vt) 'cosecharlo (como café); cortarlo (como fruta de un árbol)' ChZ: *tuk* 'cortar (fruta)'

TU#018 pMZ **?aw-tuk** *(vi) 'cerrar/to close'* NHM: *?atʋhk ~ ?atʋk* 'cerrar (p.ej., una puerta), tapar (p.ej., con un petate), tapado' SHM: Tp < *y?Adúkʸ* > MM: Cc < *y?Adúkʸ* > At < *?ædúhkp* > Ma < *?adúk, ?ɨdúk* > 'atajar' Ja < *?adúk* > 'atajar'_ Pu < *?ɨdúk* > 'atajar' Ct < *?a·dúk* > 'atajar' LM: Gu < *?adúk (imp), ?adúhp (pres)* > 'atajar' SaP: < *?atúk* >

TU#019 pOM **yak-?a-tuhk ~ yak-?a-tuk** *(vt) 'cerrar/to close'* NHM: *yak?atʋhk ~ yak?atʋk* (vt) 'cerrar algo, impedir un pleito, tapar algo' SHM: Tl *yik?atuk* Tu < *yak?adúk, myák?adúikʸpʸ* > MM: Ma < *yahk?ɨdúk, ?ɨdúhkp* > Ja < *yah?adúk, yah?adíhkʸpʸ, ?adúhkp* > Pu < *yah?ɨdúk, ?ɨdúhkp* > At < *yæhk?ædúk* > Ct < *yahk?adúk* > LM: Gu < *yag?adúk* >

TU#020 pOM **?a-hutyuk** (← *?a-huy-tuk*) *(vi) 'alquilar/to rent'* NHM: *ahʋtyuk* '=arrendar' MM: Ma < *?a·hu:dʸúk* > Ju < *?ahu:ʸdʸúk* > Ja < *?ahu:dʸúk* > Pu < *?ɨhu:dʸúk* > At < *?æhu:dʸúk* > Ct < *?a·hu:dʸúk* > LM: < *?ahu:ʸdʸúk* > Gu < *?aho:dʸúk* >

TU#021 pOM ***me"pš-tuhk ~ me"pš-tuk** *(vt) 'cortar en dos/to cut in two'* NHM: *me"pštʋhk ~ me"pštʋk* LM: Cn < *me"pštuhk ~ me"pštuk* > (vt) 'trozar (con tijera)'

TU#022 pZ ***ʔa-šohc-tuhk ~ ʔa-šohc-tuk** *(vt) 'anudar/to knot'* NHM: *ʔašohctʋhk ~ ʔašohctʋk* ' = amarrar (p.ej., asegurar una puerta)' LM: Cn < *ʔašohctuhk ~ ʔašohctuk* > (vt) 'anudar'

TU#023 pOM ***puhš-tuhk ~ puhš-tuk** *(vt) 'cortar con machete/to cut with machete'* NHM: *pʋhštʋhk ~ pʋhštʋk* 'cortar en dos, trozar en dos' LM: Cn < *puhštuhk ~ puhštuk* >

TU#024 pOM ***ʔa-tɨtyuk (← ʔa-tɨy-tuk)** *(n) 'cortina/curtain'* NHM: *ʔatɨtyʋk* ̲MM: Ma,Pu *ʔɨdɨ:ɟʸúk* Ja *ʔadɨ:ɟʸúk* At *ʔædɨ:ɟʸúk* Ct *ʔa·dɨ:ɟʸúk* LM: Gu *ʔadɨ:ɟʸúk*

TU#025 pMZ ***tuka** *(n) 'tortuga/tortoise'* [pM *tuka > pOM *tuk; pZ *tuka > pGZ *tu:ka]̲ MM: Ma,Ja,Ct *tuk* LM: Ml < *pɨhytuk* > 'tipo de tortuga' Gu *tuk* OlP: *tuka* SoZ: *tyú:ki* 'tortoise, turtle' [Foster and Foster 1948] TxZ: *tu:k*

TU#026 pOM ***tuʔk- [?]** *(adj) 'quieto/quiet'* NHM: *tu"hk* MM: Ju *tɨmíhtkɨ* Ja *tuʔkítʸɨ* At *tɨgwíñʸɨ* Ct *tuʔgwíñʸɨ* LM: Gu *tu!m̄ʔít*

TU#027 pM [Veracruz] ***tukši** *(n) 'calzón/white cotton trousers'* OlP: *tukši* 'calzoncillo' SaP: *tukš*

TU#028 pM [Veracruz] ***tuktukpanik** *(n) 'poposquela, tutpana /gray-necked woodrail'* OlP: *tuktukpani'k* SaP: *tuhtupalik* [Clark 1981]

TU#029 pZ ***tuʔm** *(vi) 'juntar/to gather'* TxZ: *ɨŋ-tuʔm* (suffix on verbs) 'juntando' SoZ: *tuʔm* 'keep' [Foster and Foster 1948] ChisZ: N *tuʔm* (vi) 'juntar' (vt) 'juntarlo; guardarlo' NE *tuʔm* (vi) 'unirse' (vt) 'amontonarlo, almacenarlo (como maíz); juntarlo'

TU#030 pMZ ***na:y-tum** *(n) 'solo/alone'* [In pre-MM an innovative form *nay-tuʔk 'alone, bachelor' exists alongside *nay-tuʔm*] NHM: *na:ydum* 'soltero, solo' MM: Ma *ne·ɟʸuʔm̥* Ja *niɟʸu!myǽ"y* 'soltero' LM: Gu *niɟʸú!m̄* 'soltero, solo' TxZ: *ntu:ʔmo:ʔmče* (adv) 'en un solo lugar' ChisZ: C *naytyumɨ*

TU#031 pOM ***tunn** *(n) 'loma/hill'* NHM: *túnïn* SHM: Tm *tunk* 'cerro' MM: Ju *tun* Ma,Ja,Pu,At *tun̄* Ct *tun̄* 'sierra, montaña, cerro, loma' LM: Cn,Mz < *tun* > Ca *tu·n* LM: Gu *tun̄* 'cerro, loma, sierra, montaña'

TU#032 pOM ***kuy-tuhn ~ kuy-tun** *(vi)* *'cumplir/to fulfill'* NHM: *kutyv꞉n ~ kutyv꞉hn ~ kutyvn* MM: Ju <*kuʸdʼún*> Pu <*kɨdʼún*> At <*koʸdʼún*> LM: Gu <*kudʼún*>

TU#033 pOM ***yak-tuhn ~ yak-tun** *(vt)* *'ocupar/to use'* NHM: *yaktv꞉n ~ yaktvn* 'dar trabajo a alguien, usar algo (p.ej., un machete), emplear algo, hacer algo, ocupar' LM: Cn <*yahtu·n ~ yahtun*> (vt) 'usar'

TU#034 pOM ***ku-tun-k** *(n)* *'presidente municipal/mayor'* SHM: Tu *kuδúŋk* 'autoridades municipales' MM: Ma *kɨdú·ŋk* 'presidente municipal' Pu *kɨdú·ŋk* 'autoridades municipales' Ja,At *kudú·ŋk* 'autoridades municipales, presidente municipal' Ct *kɨdú·ŋk* 'presidente municipal, autoridades municipales' LM: 'presidente' Ml <*kuduŋ*> Cn <*koduŋ*> Gu *kudú·ŋk* 'autoridades municipales, presidente municipal'

TU#035 pOM ***kam-tuhn-pa** *(n)* *'campesino/peasant'* SHM: Tu *kamdúmba* Mi *kamdúmba kampo* MM: Ju *kamdú·mbɨ* Ma,Ja,At,Ct *kamdú·mbɨ*

TU#036 pZ ***tuʔn** *(vt)* *'espiar/to spy on'* SaP: *tuʔn* (vi, vt) 'hurt (emotions)' [Zo loan?—semantic bond is weak] ChisZ: C *tuʔn* (vi) 'espiar' (vt) 'leerlo, estudiarlo' N *tuʔn* (vt) 'leerlo; visitarlo; revisarlo'

TU#037 pMZ ***tu꞉ni** *(n)* *'tipo de fruta parecida a la ciruela/type of fruit resembling the plum'* [pM **tu꞉ni* > pOM **tu꞉ny*; pZ **tuni*] NHM: *tu꞉ʔn* 'a kind of tree with edible fruit [Pseudolmedia]' [G. Martin, p.c.] SHM: Tu,Mi *tu꞉nʸ* 'ciruela nativa' MM: Ju,Ma,Ja, Pu,Ct *tu꞉nʸ* 'ciruela nativa' LM: 'ciruela' Cn <*tu꞉ñ*> 'ciruela colorada' SJ *tu·nʸ* Ca,Gu *tu꞉nʸ* ChZ: *tuni?* 'ciruela'

TU#038 pZ ***tunu** *(n)* *'ombligo/navel'* [pGZ **tu꞉nuʔ*] TxZ: *tu꞉nu?* SoZ: *tú꞉nu* ChisZ: C,N,NE *tunu* S *[tu·nú?]* ChZ: *tunu?*

TU#039 pMZ ***tup** *(vi)* *'brincotear/to make small hops'* NHM: *nahktup pohctup ~ naky pɨc* 'chapalear con las manos y los pies en el agua (p.ej., los niños)' [?] SaP: *tutéʔn* 'pisar' [Clark and Clark 1960] ChisZ: N *tupteʔndeʔney* (vi) 'andar brincando, brincotear'

TU#040 pZ ***tuʔnuk** *(n)* *'guajolote, pavo/turkey'* [pGZ **tuʔunuk*] SaP: *túʔnuk* 'guajolote' [Zo loan] TxZ: *tu꞉ʔn* 'guajolote (macho), totole (macho)' SoZ: *tú ?unuk* 'totole' ChisZ: C *tu ?kune* 'guajolotillo' [*tu ?nuk-?une* contracted?] *tu ?kmama* 'guajolote, pava' N *tu ?nuk* 'pava' S *[tunúk]* 'guajolote (hembra); "tamale" de mujer' ChZ: *tunuk* 'guajolote—hembra'

TU#041 pM ***tun** *(vi, vt) 'hacer/to do'* NHM: *tʋːn ~ tʋːhn ~ tʋn* 'hacer (p.ej., un trabajo), trabajar, obrar' MM: Ju < *tun, tu·mp* > 'trabajar', < *tun* > 'hacer (to do)' Ma < *tun̄, tu·m̄p* > 'trabajar', < *tun̄, mdi·mpʸ* > 'hacer (to do)' Ja < *tun̄, tu·n̄, tu·m̄p* > 'trabajar', < *tun̄, tʸu·n̄, tʸi·m̄pʸ* > 'hacer (to do)' Pu < *tun̄, ti: mdi·m̄pʸ* > 'hacer (to do)' At < *tun̄, tu·m̄p* > 'trabajar', < *tun̄, mduü·m̄pʸ* > 'hacer (to do)' Ct < *tun̄, tu·m̄p* > 'trabajar', < *tun̄, mdim̄pʸ* > 'hacer (to do)' LM: Cn < *tu·n ~ tun* > (vi) 'trabajar' Ca < *tun̄* > 'trabajar', < *tun* > 'hacer (to do)' < *tu·mp, tʸu·m̄pʸ* > 'hacer (to do)' SJ *tu·n ~ tun* 'to work' Gu < *tun̄, tu·n̄, tu·m̄p* > 'trabajar' OlP: *tun* (vt) SaP: *tun* (vi) 'lay eggs, sit on eggs (hen)'

TU#042 pOM ***yak-tuhn ~ yak-tun** *(vt) 'usar/to utilize, employ'* NHM: *yaktʋːn ~ yaktʋːhn ~ yaktʋn* (vt) 'dar trabajo a alguien, usar algo (p.ej., un machete), emplear algo, hacer algo, ocupar' MM: Ju < *yæhtún* > Ma < *yahktún̄* > '=emplear' Ja < *yahtún̄, yahtú·m̄pʸ* > '=emplear' At < *yahktún̄, yahktúü·m̄pʸ* > 'usar', < *yæhktún̄* > 'emplear' [sic!] Ct < *yahktún̄, yahktí·m̄pʸ* > '=emplear' LM: Ca < *yahtún̄* > Gu < *yahtún̄, yahtú·m̄pʸ* > '=emplear'

TU#043 pOM ***tuhn-k** *(n) 'trabajo/work'* NHM: *tʋːnk* 'trabajo, ocupación, obra' SHM: Tl *tunk* MM: Ju *tuːŋk* Ma,Ja,At,Ct *tu·ŋ̄k* LM: Ca *tu·ŋk* Cn < *tuŋ* > '=oficio' SJ *tu·n* Gu *tu·ŋ̄k*

TU#044 pOM ***tuhn-pɨ** *(n) 'trabajador/worker'* SHM: Tm *tumb* MM: Ju *túːmbɨ* Ma,Ja,Pu,At,Ct *tú·mbɨ* 'peón, trabajador' LM: Ca *tú:mbɨ* Gu *tú·m̄bɨ*

TU#045 pZ ***tunun** *(vi) 'poner encima/to put on top of'* TxZ: *tuːn-de?* (vi-s) 'sentado (arriba), sentado (jarro, olla, etc.)' ChisZ: C *tunun* (vi) 'amontonarse' (vt) 'amontonarlo' N *tunun* (vi) 'amontonarse; chorrear' (vt) 'amontonarlo'

TU#046 pMZ ***tus** *(vi) 'entumirse/to become numb'* OlP: *tuš* (vi) 'hacer frío' SaP: *tuš* (vi) 'entumecer' SoZ: *tusaka?* TxZ: *tus-kom-kɨ?daː?* (adj) 'entumido'

TU#047 pM ***tuš** *(n) 'nanche/pickle tree'* [pOM **tuš̄*] MM: Ma,Ja,
Pu,At,Ct *tuš̄* LM: Cn <*tuš*> Gu *tuš̄* OlP: *tuš*

TU#048 pOM ***tu:t** *(n) 'bejuco arbóreo (genérico)/woody vine (generic)'* [Cf. ChisZ-C [Te] <*tutu*> 'nervio'. This is a perfect phonetic
match; initial *t* is faint in the original as noted by Ruz fc: 186, n. 11.]
NHM: *tʋːt* 'woody (not herbaceous) vine (generic)' [G. Martin, p.c.]
MM: 'tipo de bejuco' Ma,Ja,At,Ct *tuːt*

TU#049 pOM ***tuta"ky** *(adv) 'despacio/slowly'* NHM: *tʋtaʔky* 'con
cuidado, despacio, lento, suave' SHM: Tl *tutoʔoky* 'despacio' MM:
'serio' MM: Ju *tudǽ"kʸ* Ma,Ja,Ct *tu"dǽ"kʸ*

TU#050 pM ***tu:t~tuʔt** *(vi) 'poner huevos/to lay eggs'* NHM: *tʋːt*
~*tʋ"t* MM: Ju <*tutp*> Ma <*tu·tp, tu"dámp*> Ja <*tu"t, tu·t,
tu·t̄p, tu"dá·m̄p*> At <*tu·t̄p, tu"dá·m̄p*> Ct <*tu·tp, tu"dámp*>
LM: Ca <*tu·tp*> Cn <*tu·t~tu"t*> (vi) SJ *tu·t~tu"t* '=to free'
Gu <*tu"t, tu·t, tu·tp, tu"dá·m̄p*> OlP: *tu:t~tuʔt* (vi) 'poner (una
gallina)' (vt) 'poner (ropa); poner (una cosa)' ChisZ: NE *koduʔt* (vi)
retoñar [?]

TU#051 pM ***tuʔt-i(k)** *(n) 'huevo/egg'* [pOM **tu"ty*] NHM: *tu"t*
'huevo' SHM: Tl *tuttu"tʸ* LM: SJ *tu"dy* [derived from *tu·t* 'to lay
eggs'] Cn <*tu"ty*> OlP: *tuʔti'k* [derived from *tu:t~tuʔt* 'poner
huevos']

TU#052 pM ***tu:tuk** *(n) 'guajolote, pavo/turkey'* [pOM **tu:tk*] NHM:
tʋːtk SHM: Tl,Ay *tutk* 'gallina, pollo', *kupohktut* 'lechuza' MM: Pu
tu·tk 'guajolote hembra' LM: Cn <*tu:t*> 'guajolote' Ca *tu·tk*
'guajolote hembra' SJ *tu·t* OlP: *tu:tu'k*

TU#053 pOM ***tu:htk-na"w** *(n) 'guajolote macho/turkey cock'* NHM:
na"tʋːtk MM: Ja,Pu *tu·tná"* Ma,Ct *tu·tkná"w* LM: Ca *tu·tknaʔá:*
Gu *tu·tnɨʔá:*

TU#054 pMZ ***tu:ʔ-ʔaw** *(n) 'camino/road'* [pM, pOM **tu:ʔ-ʔahw*;
pre-pZ **tu:w* (a contraction) > pZ **tuŋ*] NHM: *tʋːʔ* 'camino, calle,
hilera, senda' SHM: Tl *tu:ʔ* Tp *tuʔu* Mi *tu·ʔu* MM: Ju,Cc,Ma,Ja,
Pu,At,Ct *tu"* LM: Ca,Gu *tu"* Cn <*tuʔ, tu"ʔa:*> OlP: *tuʔa'u* [?]
SaP: *to:u* [could be a pre-pZ borrowing or an independent contraction]
SoZ: *tuŋ* AyZ: *[tuŋ]* TxZ: *tuŋ* '=rastro, jalón (de bebida)' ChisZ:
C *tuŋ* '=sendero, vía' N *tuŋ* '=huella' NE *tuk* '=calle' S *[tuŋ]*
ChZ: StaMaCh *tuŋ* '=vereda' SnMiCh *tuŋ* [Wonderly 1949]

TU#055 pOM ***tu:?-?am** *(adv) 'en el camino, por el camino/in the road'* NHM: *tʋ:?ám* 'en fila, en carrera, en camino' SHM: Tp *tu"?ám ~ tu?ám* MM: Ja *tu"?á:y* At *tu??ám* Ma *tu??ám̄* LM: Gu *tu??á:m*

TU#056 pOM ***ku-tu:?** *(n) 'guía, práctico/guide'* NHM: *kutʋ:?* 'guía en un camino' MM: Ju,Ja,At *kudú"* Pu,Ct,Ma *kɨdú"* LM: Gu *kudú"*

TU#057 pZ ***tuŋ-?ah** *(vi) 'caminar, avanzar (p.ej., trabajo)/to walk, advance (a work)'* ChisZ: C,N,NE *tu?ŋah* (vi) ChZ: *tu?ŋah* 'caminar'

TU#058 pZ ***tu?y** *'estirarse/to stretch out'* SaP: *tu?y* (vi, vt) 'pat out tortillas' [Zo loan] SoZ: *[tu?y]* 'estirarlo' TxZ: *tu?y-dʸe?* (vi-s) 'estirado derecho' ChisZ: C *tu?y* (vi) 'apagarse, extinguirse' N *tu?y* (vi) 'apagarse; desmayarse, tener un ataque' NE *tu?y* (vi) 'apagarse (como una luz); cansarse; desmayarse' (vt) 'extinguirlo, apagarlo; fatigarlo' ChZ: *tu?y* (vi) 'estirarse'

TO#001 pOM ***to"** *(n) 'tenate/basket woven of palm'* NHM: *to"* SHM: Tl *tuh* [?] MM: Ju *tuh* [?] Ma,Ja,Pu,At,Ct *to"*

TO#002 pZ ***toc** *(vi) 'apalancar/to quench with forked stick'* SaP: *toc* (vi) 'break (hard things)' [Zo loan] TxZ: *toc* (vt) 'cortar (fruta con palanca)' ChisZ: C *tohc* (vt) 'punzarlo' N **toc [tocpiti?* (vt) 'rodarlo (cosa grande, con palanca)'; *tocte?n* (vt) 'apalancarlo' ChZ: *toc* 'clavar'

TO#003 pMZ ***to:c** *(n) 'lengua/tongue'* [pM, pOM **to:hc*; pZ, pGZ **toc*] NHM: *to:c* '=lenguaje' SHM: Tl *tʋ:hc* MM: Ma,Ja,Pu,At,Ct *to·c̄* LM: Cn *<to:c>* Ca *to·c* Gu *to·c̄* OlP: *to:cɨ* SaP: *to:hc* SoZ: *toc* AyZ: *[toc]* ChisZ: C,N,S *toc* NE *tohc*

TO#004 pZ ***toh** *(vi) 'ampollarse/to blister'* SoZ: *toh* (vi, vt) 'reventar, cachetear' TxZ: *toh* (vt) 'echar (tortilla), tortear, (vi) florecer' ChisZ: C *toh* (vi) 'ampollarse, salirle una ampolla' N *toh* (vi) 'ampollarse, esponjarse' NE *toh* (vi) 'ampollarse'

TO#005 pZ ***tok** *(vi) 'hervir; pintar/to boil; paint'* [Cf. LM-Cn *<tohk ~ tok>* 'apestar'?] SoZ: *tok* 'paint' [Foster and Foster 1948] ChisZ: NE *tohk* (vi) 'hervir' (vt) 'hervirlo

TO#006 pM ***to:?k** *(vt) 'vender/to sell'* NHM: *to:?k* SHM: Tl *tʋ:k* MM: Ju *<to:k>* Ma *<to:k, mde?kʸpʸ>* Ja *<to:k, to?k, tʸe?kʸpʸ>*

Pu <*to:k, mde!kʸpʸ*> At <*to:k, mdoö?kʸpʸ*> Ct <*to:k, tʸe?kʸpʸ*> LM: Ca <*to:k*> Cn <*to·k~to:k*> (vt) SJ *to·k~to:k* Gu <*to:k, to·?k, tʸo·?pʸ*> OlP: *to:k* (vi) SaP: *to?k* (vi, vt)

TO#007 pOM ***to:?k-y** *(n) 'mercancía/goods'* NHM: *tɨ:?k* 'mercancía, venta' MM: Ma,Ja,Pu,Ct *te:kʸ* At *toö:kʸ, tö:kʸ, te:kʸ* LM: Gu *to:kʸ*

TO#008 pOM ***to:?k-pa** *(n) 'vendedor/seller'* NHM: *to:?kpa* MM: Ju,Ma,Ja,At,Ct *tó?kpɨ* Pu *tó!kpɨ* LM: Gu *tó·?pɨ*

TO#009 pMZ ***to?k** *(vt) 'tender en el suelo/to spread out on the ground'* [These Zoquean forms can either descend from pMZ **to:?k* or pMZ **to?k*. The derivative pM **to?k-i* 'mat', however, presupposes pMZ **to?k* 'spread out on the ground'; pM **to:?k*, then, is restricted to Mixean.] SoZ: *to?k* 'spread out' [Foster and Foster 1948] AyZ: *[to?k]* 'tenderlo' TxZ: *to?k* (vt) 'tender' ChisZ: C *to?k* (vt) 'tenderlo (p.ej., un petate); tenderlo (p.ej., ropa)' N *to?k* (vi) 'estar tendido' (vt) 'tenderlo' NE *to?k* (vt) 'tenderlo, extenderlo (como ropa)'; *to?kɨy* (vt) 'tenderlo, extenderlo (como un petate)'

TO#010 pM ***to?k-i** *(n) 'petate/mat'* [pOM **to"ky*] NHM: *tɨ"k* SHM: Tl *tʋ"ky* MM: Ju,Ma,Ja,Pu,Ct *te"kʸ* At *toö"kʸ* Ca *to"ʸkʸ* LM: Cn <*to"ky*> Gu *to"kʸ* OlP: *to?ki* SaP: *to?k*

TO#011 pMZ ***to:ki** *(n) 'iguana/iguana'* [pM **to:ki* > pOM **to:ky*; pZ *toki] MM: Ma *nɨ:dékʸ* Ja *nɨ:dékkʸ* Pu *nɨdékʸ* Ct *nɨ:dékʸ* LM: Gu *nɨdó:kʸ* Cn <*nɨdo:gy*> 'iguana verde' [Iguana sp.] OlP: *to:ki* SaP: *to:hk* ChisZ: C *toki* 'iguana macho' N *toki* 'estrella fugaz'

TO#012 pMZ ***tokoy** *(vi) 'perder/to lose'* NHM: *yaktʋki* 'perder algo' MM: Ju <*tɨgé:pʸ, tɨ: tʸɨgóy*> 'fallar', <*tɨgóy*> 'perder' Ma <*tɨgé:pʸ, tɨ: tʸɨgóy*> 'perder, extraviarse', <*tɨgé:pʸ*> 'fallar' Ja <*tɨ: tʸɨgóy, tɨgó·y, tɨgé:pʸ*> 'extraviarse', <*yahtɨgóy, tɨgó·y, tɨgé:pʸ*> 'perder' Pu <*tɨgóy, tɨgé:pʸ*> At <*tɨ: tʸɨgóy*> 'extraviarse', <*tɨgóöpʸ*> 'fallar', <*tɨgóö:pʸ, tɨgoyá·mp*> 'perder, equivocarse' [sic!] Ct <*tɨ: tʸɨgóy*> 'extraviarse', <*tɨgé:pʸ*> 'fallar, equivocarse', <*yahktɨgóy, tɨgé:pʸ, tɨgoyámp*> 'perder' LM: Ca <*tɨgóy*> Gu <*tɨgó:pʸ, tɨ: tʸɨgóy*> 'fallar', <*tɨ: tʸɨgóy*> 'extraviarse', <*yahtɨgóy, tɨgó·y, tɨgó:pʸ, tɨgoyámp*> 'perder' [sic!] SJ *tɨgo·y~tɨgoy* SaP: *togoy* (vi) 'get lost'; *ha?ydógoy* 'borrar' [Clark and Clark 1960] SoZ: *tokoy* (vi) 'perderse' TxZ: *tokeñ* (vi) faltar, (vt) perder ChisZ: C *tokoy* (vi) perderse, extraviarse; echarse a perder, descomponerse; desaperecer N *tokoy* (vi) perderse NE *tokoy* (vi) perderse, extraviarse; desaparecer; descomponer (como carne); fracasar (como en un negocio)

TO#013 pZ ***cɨk-tokoy** *(vt) 'echar a perder/to spoil'* TxZ: *cɨk-tokeñ* (vt) 'perder' ChisZ: C *cɨktokoy* (vt) 'descomponerlo; deshonrarlo, violarlo; perjudicarlo, echarlo a perder' N *cɨktokoy* (vt) 'hacerle perder' NE *cɨktokoy* (vt) 'echarlo a perder; descomponerlo'

TO#014 pMZ ***yak-tokoy** *(vt) 'perder/to lose'* SaP: *ʔaktógoy* (vt) 'perder' [Clark and Clark 1960] [Zo loan] ChisZ: C *yahtokoy* (vt) 'perderlo' NE *yaktokoy* (vt) 'perderlo; desperdecerlo'

TO#015 pMZ ***toks** *(vt) 'hervir/to boil'* NHM: *tohkš* 'comer (p.ej., comida aguada)' SHM: Tp <*tohkš*> 'comer (caldo)' MM: Cc <*tohkš*> 'comer (caldo)' LM: <*tokš*> 'mojar (p.ej., tortillas en salsa)' ChisZ: C *toks* (vi,vt) N *toks* (vt) NE *toks* (vi) 'ampollarse'

TO#016 pOM ***tohkš** *(n) 'comida/food'* NHM: *tohkš* '=guiso' SHM: Tu *tokš* Tp *tohkš* Mi *tohkš* 'caldo' MM: Ju *tohš* Cc,At,Ct *tohkš* Ma,Ja *tohkš, tohš* 'caldo' LM: Ca *tokšk* 'comida', *tokš* 'caldo'

TO#017 pOM ***to:ʔkš** *(vi) 'roncar/to snore'* NHM: *to:ʔkš* LM: SJ *to·kš*

TO#018 pZ ***to?ks** *(vt) 'pelar/to peel, shell'* SaP: *to?kš* (vi) 'hatch (eggs)' [Zo loan] TxZ: *to?ks* (vt, vi-p) 'tirar (mezcla), agarrar y aventar (lodo a la pared)' ChisZ: C *to?ks* (vt) 'descostrarlo, pelarlo' N *to?ks* (vt) 'palmearlo'

TO#019 pMZ ***tome(k)** *(adv) 'cerca/close'* [pM **tome(k)*; pZ *tome > pGZ **to:me*] OlP: *tome'k* SaP: *tom* SoZ: *tó:mi* 'near' [Foster and Foster 1948] ChisZ: C *tome* '=cercano (adj)' N,NE *tome* ChZ: *tome?*

TO#020 pMZ ***tom-?ɨy** *(vi, vt) 'acercarse/to draw near'* NHM: *tɨmip* ~*tɨma* SaP: *kutomi* 'come near to someone', *nigutómihyɨ* 'draw near, come near' ChisZ: C *to?mɨy* (vi) N *to?mɨy* (vi) 'acercarse' (vt) 'acercarlo' NE *to?mɨy* (vi)

TO#021 pMZ ***ton** *(vt) 'tentar; empujar/to touch; push'* NHM: *to:n* ~*to:hn*~*ton* 'tentar, tocar con la mano' SHM: Tl *tʋn* 'tentar' MM: 'tocar, tentar' Ju <*ton*> Ma <*ton̄, mde·mpʸ*>, <*kæh šʲt̓ónit̓ʲ*>

Ja <*toōn̄, t̓o·n̄, t̓e·m̄p̓, kæh š̓t̓óńit̓*> 'tentar, tocar', _<*toōn̄, t̓o·n̄*>
'pegar (con la mano)' _At <*to·n̄díw̄, toōn̄, t̓ö·m̄p̓, k̓æh š̄tóńit̓*> _Ct
<*toōn̄, ti: mdé·m̄p̓, kæh š̓t̓on̄ʸ, kæh š̓t̓óńit̓*> 'tentar, tocar', <*toōn̄*>
'pegar (con la mano)' Ma <*toōn̄*> 'castigar' LM: 'tocar, tentar' Ca
<*toōn̄*> Gu <*nɨ"dón̄, n̓ɨ"dó·n̄, n̓ɨ"dó·m̄p̓, ka" mnɨ"dón̄ʸ, kah
mnɨ"dóńit̓*> OIP: *ton* (vt) 'empujarlo' ChisZ: C *tonʒɨʔy* (vt)
'detenerlo; atrancarlo' N *tonbɨʔ* (vt) 'empujarlo'

TO#022 pZ ***toʔn** *(vi) 'levantarse (como polvo)/to be lifted into the air
(as dust)'* ChisZ: C *toʔn* (vi) 'brincar; levantarse' N *toʔn* (vi) 'volar en el aire (polvo)' NE *toʔn [*toʔnmahk* (vt) 'correrlo rápida-
mente'; *caktoʔnbɨʔ* (vt) 'dejar todo'; *toʔnboy* (vi) 'ir corriendo']

TO#023 pMZ ***top** *(vt) 'tirar algo de un envase/to throw something
from a container'* OIP: *top* (vt) 'tirar con honda' SaP: *tom* (vi, vt)
'take out with bucket' [?] SoZ: *top* (vt) 'sacar'

TO#024 pGZ ***toʔp** *(vt) 'empatar/to hamper'* SoZ: *toʔp* (vt) TxZ:
toʔp (vt, vi-p) ChisZ: C *toʔpcɨʔy* (vi) 'atascarse'

TO#025 pMZ ***tops** *(vi) 'reventar/to burst'* LM: Cn <*topš̌*> (vi) SJ
topš̌ ChisZ: N *tops* (vi) 'estar cortado alrededor' (vt) 'cortarlo alrededor'

TO#026 pZ ***toʔs** *(vt) 'mojar/to soak'* TxZ: *to:ʔs* (vt) 'mojar (tortilla
en los frijoles, pan en un caldo)' ChisZ: C *toʔs* (vt) 'remojarlo,
sopetearlo' N *toʔs* (vt) 'tomarlo (con cuchara)' NE *toʔs* (vt) 'mo-
jarlo, remojarlo (como pan en el café)'

TO#027 pM ***toʔš-hay** *(n) 'hembra/female'* [pOM **to"š̌y*] NHM: *tɨ"š̌*
SHM: Tl *tʋʔʋš̌y* MM: Ju *to"š̌ʸ* Ju,Ma,Ja,Ct *to"š̌ʸ* Pu *to"š̌ʸp̓ɨ* At *to"š̌ʸ*
'=esposa (pos)' LM: SJ *to"š̌yhya"y* 'wife, woman' Cn <*to"š̌y*>
'hembra' Ca,Gu *to"š̌ʸ* SaP: *tóʔš̌ay* 'mujer'; *toʔš̌ray* 'wife' [Foster
1949]

TO#028 pOM ***to"š̌y-tɨhk** *(n) 'mujer/woman'* NHM: *tɨ"š̌tɨhk* SHM:
Tl *tʋʔʋš̌ytɨhk* Hu *dooyic* 'wife' [Foster 1949] [?] MM: *to"š̌ʸt̓ɨhk,
tosk̓ʸt̓ɨhk* Ma *to"š̌ʸt̓ɨhk* 'mujer, esposa (pos), señorita' Ja *to"š̌ʸt̓ɨhk*
'esposa (pos), mujer' Pu *to"š̌ʸt̓ɨhk* At *to"š̌ʸt̓ɨhk, tošʸt̓ɨhk* Ct *to"š̌ʸt̓ɨhk*
'=esposa (pos), señorita' LM: Ca *to"ǯʸɨhk* Gu *todyɨk* 'wife' [Foster
1949] *to"ǯɨ̄hk* 'esposa (pos), mujer', *to"ǯɨ̄hk* 'señora' [sic!] [Nordell
1990]

TO#029 pZ ***to?t** *(n) 'lombriz de la tierra/earthworm'* [pGZ **to?t*]
SoZ: *to?t* 'sabañón' AyZ: *[to?t]* 'anguila de agua' TxZ: *to?t* 'lombriz de tierra' ChisZ: C [Te] <*tot, thot*> 'lombriz'

TO#030 pZ ***toto** *(n) 'papel/paper'* [pGZ **to:to?*] SoZ: *to:to?* [Gutiérrez M. 1993], *to:to* [Wonderly 1949] AyZ: *[to:?do]* TxZ: *to:to?* 'lectura, libro, amate (material, palo)' ChisZ: C *toto* N *toto* '=;amate —ficus Sp.' NE [Chapultenango] *toto* [Wonderly 1949] [Tapalapa, Ocotepec, Pantepec] *todo* [Wonderly 1949] [Ra] *todo* S [Tu] *toto* [Wonderly 1949] [Cp] *[totó?]* ChZ: StaMaCh *toto?* SnMiCh *toto* [Wonderly 1949]

TO#031 pM ***totok** *(n) 'mariposa/butterfly'* [pOM *totk] NHM: *tótïk* '=polilla' SHM: Tl *tʋtk* Ma,Ja,Pu,At,Ct *to·tk* OlP: *toto'k* ChisZ: C *to?titandan* 'mariposa nocturna' [?]

TO#032 pMZ ***toy** *(vi) 'quemar, doler/to burn, hurt'* NHM: *to:y* ~*to:hy*~*toy* 'quemar' SHM: Tl <*tʋ:py*> 'se está quemando' Tp <*to:pʸ, tʸoy, to:y, toӯámp*> 'arder' Mi <*to·ypʸ*> 'arder' MM: 'arder' Ju <*te:pʸ*> Cc <*to:ypʸ, tï: tʸoy, to:y, toӯámp, kʸœh tʸo:y*> Ma,Ct <*te:pʸ, toӯámp*> '=quemar (lumbre)' Ja <*te:pʸ, toӯá·m̄p*> Pu <*te:py*> 'arder' At <*toö:pʸ, toӯá·m̄p*> '=quemar (lumbre)' LM: Ca <*tooʸpʸ*> 'arder' Cn <*to:y*~*to·y*> (vi) 'arder' (vt) 'quemar' SJ *to·y*~*toy* 'to burn' Gu <*to·ӯ, to:pʸ, toyá·m̄p*> 'arder' OlP: *toy* (vi) 'estar caliente; quemarse (una persona)' (vt) 'quemarlo' SaP: *toy* (vi) 'be hot, get burned' AyZ: *[toy]* 'sentirlo (sabor, tocadura)' TxZ: *toy* (vi) 'doler' (vt) 'tener lástima' SoZ: *toy* (vi) 'doler' ChisZ: C,NE *toy* (vi) 'dolerle' N *toy* (vi) 'dolerle' (vt) 'negarlo' ChZ: *toy* 'doler'

TO#033 pMZ ***nɨ-toy** *(vt) 'sufrir una herida, quemadura/to be wounded or burnt'* NHM: *nɨto:y*~ *nɨto:hy*~*nɨtoy* 'quemar por encima (p.ej., un palo), quemarse superficialmente' ChisZ: NE *nɨdoy* (vt) 'sufrirlo (como una herida)'

TO#034 pMZ ***yak-toy** *(vt) 'quemar (lumbre)/to light'* NHM: *yakto:y* ~*yakto:hy*~*yaktoy* 'quemar algo' SHM: Tl *yiktʋy* 'quemar algo' MM: Ju <*yœhtóy*> Ma <*yahktoy*> At,Ct <*yahktóy*> LM: Cn <*yahto:y*~*yahto·y*> (vt) 'quemar' Ca <*yahtóy*> Gu <*yahtóӯ, yahtó:pʸ*> SaP: *?aktoy* (vt) 'hacer quemar' [Clark and Clark 1960] ChisZ: C *yahtoy* (vt) 'dolerle' N *yaktoy* (vt) 'le hacer doler; no quererlo' NE *yaktoy* (vt) 'dolerle algo'

TO#035 pMZ ***toy-a** *[?] (n) 'dolor/pain'* [pM **toya* > pOM **to:y*; pZ **toya* > pGZ **to:ya?*] NHM: *to:?y* 'quemadura' SaP: *ho:htó?* 'dolor del estómago, dolor cólico' [/y/ expected in place of final /?/] SoZ: *to:ya?* TxZ: *to:ye?* 'enfermedad' [*to:ya?* expected] ChisZ: C *toya* 'dolor, sufrimiento; angustia, desgracia' NE *toya* 'sufrimiento; angustia, desgracia' N *toya* 'dolor, sufrimiento; desgracia' ChZ: *toya?* 'herida'

WI-WO

WI#001 pOM ***wihc~wic** *(vt) 'llevar/to carry away'* NHM: *vihc~vic* 'llevar, cargar (p.ej., agua), tomar (p.ej., una persona del brazo), manojo (p.ej., de tasajo)' MM: Ma <*Wic̄, Wihcnłhš*> 'llevar (caballo)' Ja <*wic̄, wʸihc, wihcnłhkš*> 'llevar (caballo)' LM: Cn <*wihc~wic*> (vt) 'llevar (p.ej., cubetas, reatas, sillas, cobijas)'

WI#002 pOM ***wicɨ:hk~wicɨ"k** *'recoger (trapo, mecate, etc.)/to gather'* NHM: *vihcɨk* 'alzar (p.ej., una silla de montar), guardar (p.ej., cosas colgando)' MM: Ma <*Wihcɨ"k*> Ja,At,Ct <*wihcɨ"k*> LM: Gu <*wiz̦ɨ"k*>

WI#003 pOM ***wicuk** *(vi) 'relampaguear/to flash lightning'* NHM: *vick~vícɨk* MM: Ma *hɨz̦úhkp* Ja,Ct *wɨz̦úhkp* At *hɨz̦úhkp, wɨz̦úhkp* LM: Gu *wɨz̦uká·m̄p*

WI#004 pOM ***wicuk** *(n) 'rayo, relámpago/lightning'* NHM: *vícɨk* MM: Ju *hɨz̦úk* Ma *hɨz̦úk* Ja,At,Ct *wɨz̦úk* LM: Ca *wɨz̦úk* Gu *wɨz̦úk*

WI#005 pMZ ***wih** *(vi) 'ser listo/to be ready'* NHM: *vih* LM: SJ *wih* 'to be sober, awake' SaP: *wih* (vi) 'be sober' SoZ: *wih* (vi) 'desatarse' ChisZ: N *wih* (vi) 'bucear' ChZ: *pwisyu pɨn* 'vivo' [the /p/ unexplained] [?]

WI#006 pM ***wih-i(k)** *(adj) 'inteligente/intelligent'* _[pOM *wihy] NHM *vih* 'listo, vivo' MM: Ju *wihʸ* 'áspero' Ma *Wih͟ʸ* 'inteligente, despierto; áspero, li͟so', *nɨWíhʸ* 'despierto' Pu *wih͟ʸ* 'liso', *wihʸ* 'áspero' [sic!] At *wihʸ* 'sabio, despierto; áspero', *kuwíhʸ* 'inteligente' Ct *wihʸ* 'despierto, sabio', *kɨwíhʸ* 'áspero, inteligente' LM: Cn <*wihy*> (adj) 'li͟sto, abusado' SJ *wihy* 'smart, sober' Gu *ma"wyíhʸ* 'despierto', *ku"wíh* 'inteligente' SaP: *wíhik* 'estar en juicio'

WI#007 pZ **wik** *(vt) 'batir; regar/to beat, spread out'* SaP: *wik* (vi, vt) 'beat (eggs, syrup)' [Zo loan] ChisZ: N *wihk* (vt) 'regarlo, echarlo (polvo, arena, semilla, agua)'

WI#008 pZ **wi?k** *(vi, vt) 'comer comida caliente/to eat hot food'* TxZ: *wê?k* (vi) 'comer (todo tipo de comida: caldo, carne, etc.), cenar' (vt) 'repartir, compartir' SoZ: *wi?k* 'eat (dine)' [Foster and Foster 1948] ChisZ: C *wi?k* (vi) 'comer (comida caldosa de pollo, tortilla, pan)' (vt) 'comerlo (comida caldosa)' N *wi?k* (vi) 'comer' (vt) 'comerlo (carne, frijoles, arroz)'

WI#009 pZ **wi?k-kuy** *(n) 'comida/food'* SoZ: *wi?kkuy* TxZ: *wê?k-ko? ~ wê?k-ku?* (n) 'comida' ChisZ: C *wi?kuy* 'comida caldosa' N *wi?hkuy* 'comida' NE *wi?ku?* 'alimento'

WI#010 pM **wi:k ~ wi?k** *(vi) 'silbar/to whistle'* NHM: *vi:k ~ vi"k* 'silbar, chiflar (fuertemente)' MM: 'silbar, chiflar (con la lengua media sacada)' Ju < *wi"k* > Ma < *Wi"k, Wi?kp* > 'silbar, chiflar (con la lengua media sacada)', < *wi·kp, wi"gámp* > 'gritar' Ja < *wi·kp hohp* > 'gritar' Pu,At,Ct < *wi"k, wi·kp* > LM: Cn < *wik ~ wi"k* > (vi) 'gritar' Ca < *wi"k* > 'silbar' Gu < *wi"k, wi·kp* > 'silbar, chiflar (con la lengua media sacada)' OlP: *vi:k* (vi) 'chiflar'

WI#011 pM **wi(:k)cɨn** *(n) 'gavilán/hawk'* [pOM *wihcn*] NHM: *vihcɨn* 'gavilán, águila, águila real' MM: Ct *wicn̥* LM: Gu *wí·stɨ* OlP: *vi:kcɨ'n*

WI#012 pMZ **wi?ks** *(vt) 'sacar o ensartar/to pull out or through'* OlP: *vi?kš* (vt) 'sacarla (espina)' ChisZ: C [Te] < *vicspa* > 'desencaxar los güesos / desconcertarse güeso o miembro' N *wi?ks* (vi) 'golpearse' (vt) 'golpearlo (según una creencia regional, el cargar objetos pesados provocó que se enfermara—"nos golpea")'

WI#013 pM **wimpit** *(vi) 'regresar/to return'* NHM: *vimpiht ~ vimpit* 'regresar, volver, devolver, envolver' MM: Ju < *hɨmbít, hɨmbíhtp* > 'volver, voltearse, regresar, dar vuelta' Ja < *wimbít, wimbíht, wimbíhtp* > 'regresar, volver' At < *hɨmbít, hɨmbíhtp* > 'regresar, dar vuelta, volver' Ma,Ct < *hɨmbít, hɨmbíhtp* > 'regresar, volver' LM: Cn < *wimpiht ~ wimpit* > (vi) Ca < *wi·mbít* > 'volver, voltearse' Gu < *wi:mbít, wi:mbíht, wi:mbíhp* > 'regresar, volver, volver' OlP: *vimpit* (vi) 'regresar, voltearse, volcarse'

WI#014 pOM **wimpit** *(adj?)* '*contrario al, al revés/opposite, back-wards*' NHM: *vimpit* 'contrario, volteado, revés (p.ej., un vestido)' MM: Ju *hɨmbít* Ma *hɨ:wimbít, hɨ:mbit* Ja *hɨwimbít* Pu *hɨwi:mbit* At *hɨmbit* Ct *hɨ:wɨmbít* LM: Ca *hɨwɨmbít* Gu *hɨwi:mbít*

WI#015 pOM **kon-wimpit** *(vt)* '*voltear/to turn around*' NHM: *konumpiht ~ konumpit* 'devolver, dar vuelto, voltear al lado contrario' MM: At,Ct <*ko:nɨmbít*> LM: Gu <*ko·n̄wi:mbít*>

WI#016 pOM **wa?k-wimpit** *(vi)* '*voltearse/to turn over*' NHM: *va?kumpiht ~ va?kumpít* 'voltear, dar media vuelta' MM: Ma <*Wa"gɨmbít*> At <*wa?kɨmbít*> 'voltearse', <*tɨ: wʸakhɨmbítʸ*> 'volcarse' Ct <*wa!gɨmbít*> 'voltearse', <*tɨ: wʸa?khɨmbítʸ*> 'volcarse' LM: Gu <*wa?wi:mbít*>

WI#017 pM **yak-wimpit** *(vt)* '*devolver/to return*' NHM: *yakvimpiht- ~ yakvimpit* 'devolver algo a alguien' MM: Ma <*yahkhɨmbít*> 'de-volver', <*yahkwɨmbít*> 'voltear' [sic!] Ja <*yahwimbít*> At <*yæhkhɨmbít*> Ct <*yahkhɨmbít*> 'devolver', <*yahkhɨmbít*> 'voltear' LM: Cn <*yahwimbiht ~ yahwimbit*> (vt) 'restituir; devol-ver; corresponder; hacer regresar' Gu <*yahwi:mbít*> OlP: *yakvimpit* (vt) 'voltearlo; devolverlo'

WI#018 pMZ **win** *(n)* '*ojo/eye*' [pM, pOM *wihn; pZ, pGZ *wiñ] NHM: *vi:hn* 'ojo'; *vi:nm* 'mismo, personalmente' SHM: Tl,Ay *we:n* MM: Ju,Ma,Ja,Pu,At *wi:n* Ct *wi·n̄* LM: Cn <*wi:n*> Ca,Gu *wi:n* SJ *wi·n* 'self, face, eye, surface' OlP: *vinɨ* SaP: *wihn* 'ojo'; *kúkuin* 'pechuga' TxZ: *wêñ* 'reflexivo, primero' ChisZ: C [Co] *win* 'ojo, uno mismo, persona; punta' [Te] <*vin*> 'haz, nuez / punta de alguna cosa / semblante de cara' N *win* 'punta, filo; superficie; boca de un costal; uno mismo—forma reflexiva del pronombre personal' NE *wit* 'cuerpo, persona' ChZ: *win* 'cuerpo'

WI#019 pOM **mɨh-wihn** *(adj)* '*ancho/wide*' NHM: *mɨhɨ vi:hn* '=amplio, anchura' SHM: Tl *mɨwe:n* Tu,Tp *mɨhßí:n* MM: Ju *mɨhwí:n* Ma *mɨhwíŋk* Ja *mɨhwí·n* Pu *mɨhwí:n* At *mʸihwíŋk* 'an-chura', *mɨhwí:n* 'ancho' Ct *mɨhwíŋk* LM: Gu *mɨhwí:n* ChZ: *win wɨti?* [?]

WI#020 pOM **na:hš-wihn** *(n)* '*mundo*' NHM: *?it našvi:hn* SHM: Tm *našwi?nt* MM: Ju *næšwínʸɨdɨ* Ma *na:ží:nʸɨdɨ* Ja *na:žwí:m* Pu *na:žwí:n* At *na:žwínʸɨdɨ* Ct *na:žwí?nʸ?ɨt, na:žwínʸ* LM: Ca *na:šwí:nʸɨdɨ* Gu *na·šwí:n*

<u>*WI#021 pM* *wihn-c *(adj)* 'ciego/blind'</u> [pOM *wi:n-c] NHM: *vi:nc* SHM: Tp *βin̄c* MM: Cc *winc* Ma *Wi·nc* Ju,Ja,Pu,At,Ct *wi:nc* LM: SJ *wi·nc* Ca,Gu *wi:nc* SaP: *winč*

<u>*WI#022 pOM* *wihn-c-?ɨy *(vi)* 'cegarse/to become blind'</u> NHM: *vi:nca~ vi:nci* 'cegar, ponerse ciego' MM: Ju <*wí:nzɨp*> Ma <*Wí·nz̨?ɨpʸ, tɨ: Wʸí·nzɨ*> Ja <*wí:nzɨp*> Pu <*wí:nzɨpʸ*> Ct <*wí:nz̨?ɨpʸ*> LM: Gu <*wi:nzĭ:pʸ*>

<u>*WI#023 pM* *wihn-kuhk *(adv)* 'enfrente de/in front of'</u> NHM: *vinkuhk* 'resencia, delante' LM: Cn *windu:* [?] [Hoogshagen 1984] OlP: *vinkukmɨ*

<u>*WI#024 pOM* *win-tak *(vi)* 'agacharse/to stoop'</u> NHM: *vi:hntk ~ vi:ndïk* SHM: Tu <*βindá"k*> Tp <*βindá"k*> MM: Ju,Pu <*wi:ndá"k*> Ma,At,Ct <*hɨndá"k*> LM: Ca <*wi:ndá"k*>

<u>*WI#025 pOM* *wihnt *(n)* 'correa de huarache/leather strap of sandal'</u> SHM: Tu *βʸint* Tp *kɨ"kβin̄t* MM: Ju *kɨ"kwí:nt* Ma *kɨ!gwí·n̄t* Ja *kɨ"kwí:n* Pu *kɨ??ɨgwí·nt* At *kɨ"kwí·nt* LM: Ca *kɨ"gwí:nt* Gu *kï"kwí:nt*

<u>*WI#026 pOM* *wip *(n)* 'guía de chayote'/chayote vine</u> NHM: *vip* 'guía del chayote cuando empieza a crecer' MM: Ja *?æhšhɨhp* At *?æhkšwíp, ?æhkšíp̄* Ct *?æhkšwípk* Ju *hɨhp* LM: Cn <*wip/wɨpy*> 'guía' Gu *wip̄*

<u>*WI#027 pMZ* *wipip *(vt)* 'pegar con algo/to beat with something'</u> OlP: *vipip* (vt) 'garrotearlo' TxZ: *wê:p* (vt) 'tirar (con honda)'

<u>*WI#028 pM* *wipš *(vt)* 'hozar, levantar/to turn up the earth, to raise'</u> NHM: *vihpš* 'levantar una cosa por medio de un gato o una palanca, palanca para alzar un objeto' OlP: *vipš* (vt) 'hozarlo'

<u>*WI#029 pMZ* *wis *(vt)* 'arrancar/to uproot'</u> NHM: *viš* 'arrancar con las manos, desenraizar, cosechar' SHM: Tu <*βihšɨ"k*> 'arrancar hierbas' MM: Ju <*wiš, wihšɨ"k*> Cc <*βiš, mwihšʸpʸ*> Ma <*wiš̄, wʸihšʸpʸ*> Ja <*wiš, wʸihš, wihšɨ"k, wʸihšʸpʸ, wʸihšé?kʸpʸ*> Pu <*wiš̄, wʸihšʸpʸ*> At <*wihšɨ"k*> Ct <*wihšɨ"k*> LM: Cn <*wihš~ wiš*> (vt) 'arrancar (p.ej., plantas)' Ca <*wiš, wihšɨ"k*> Gu <*wiš̄, wihšɨ"k*> OlP: *viš* (vt) SaP: *wiš* (vi, vt) TxZ: *weš* (vt, vi-p)

'arrancar' ChisZ: C *wihs* (vt) '=cosecharlo' N *wis* (vt) NE *wihs* (vt) 'arrancarlo (como frijoles)'

WI#030 pOM ***ni:-wihš ~ ni:-wiš** *'desplumar/to pluck (a fowl)'* NHM: *nɨviš* 'desplumar, hacer una reprensión' MM: Ju <*niwíš*> At <*nɨw̄ɨ̄š*> LM: Gu <*nɨ"wɨ̄š*>

WI#031 pM ***wi:?š** *(vi) 'humear/to smoke'* NHM: *vi:?š* 'salir un pequeño penacho de humo' SHM: Tu <*βi?šp, tɨ: βʸi:šʸ*> 'ahumarse' Tp <*βi?šp, βʸi:šʸ*> 'ahumarse' MM: Ju <*?æwí?šp*> 'ahumarse' Cc <*wi?š, wʸi:šʸ*> 'ahumarse' Ma <*Wi?šp*> 'ahumar con humo negro' Ja <*?awí!š̄, ?awi:žá·m̄p*> 'humear, ahumar' Pu <*hɨ:nwíʃšp*> 'humear, ahumar' At <*wi?šp*> 'ahumar con humo negro' Ct <*wi?šp*> 'humear, ahumar, ahumarse' LM: Cn <*wi·š~wi:š*> (vi) '=hacer humo' Ca <*?awí·šp*> 'ahumarse', *hɨ·nwíšk* 'humo' Gu <*wi!šp, wi:žá·m̄p*> 'humear, ahumar' OlP: *vi:š* (vi) 'ahumar' SaP: *wi?š* (vi) 'smoke' (fire)

WI#032 pOM ***wi:?š-y** *(n) 'tizne/soot'* NHM: *vi:?š* 'ahumado, humo que despide la llama del petróleo o del ocote, pequeño penacho de humo' MM: Ma *hɨ:nWí?šʸ* 'tizne' Ja *wi!šk* 'hollín' At *wi?šʸkʸ* 'tizne' LM: Gu *wi!šk* 'hollín'

WI#033 pGZ ***wi:ši** *(n) 'barba/beard'* SoZ *wí:ši* 'barba corrrida' AyZ: *[gʷi:se]* TxZ: *wê:še?*

WI#034 pMZ ***wi:?t** *(vi) 'torcer/to wring, twist'* NHM: *vi:?t* 'torcer (p.ej., una reata de jonote)' MM: Ma <*Wi:t*> 'manejar', <*Wi:t, wʸi?tʸpʸ*> 'torcer' Ja <*wi:t, wʸi?t*> At <*wi:t*> 'torcer', *wʸi?tʸpʸ*> 'manejar' Ct <*wi:t*> 'torcer', <*wi:t, wʸi?tʸpʸ*> 'manejar' LM: Cn <*wi·t~wi:t*> (vt) '=exprimir; moler (caña)' Gu <*wi:t, wʸi·?t, wʸi·?pʸ*> 'torcer, manejar' OlP: *vi:t* (vi, vt) SaP: *wi?t* (vi, vt) TxZ: *we?č* (vt) 'exprimir, torcer' SoZ: *wi?tʸ* 'twist' [Foster and Foster 1948] ChisZ: C *wi?t* (vi) 'torcerse' (vi-s) 'estar cerrado con llave; estar torcido' (vt) 'cerrarlo con llave, le echar llave; torcerlo' N *wi?t* (vi) 'torcerse, enredarse' (vt) 'torcerlo, enroscarlo' NE *wi?t* (vi-s) 'estar cerrado con llave' (vt) 'echarle llave; torcerlo'

WI#035 pMZ ***wi:?t-i** *(adj) 'torcido/twisted'* [pM *wi:?ti > pOM *wi:?ty; pZ *wi?ti] MM: Ja,At *wi:tʸ* Ct *wi?cp* [?] LM: Gu <*wi:ty*> (adj) *wi:tʸ* ChisZ: C *wi?ti* 'yagual' N *wi?ti*

WI#036 pOM ***ʔa-wi:ʔt** *(vt) 'torcer/to wring, twist'* NHM: *avi:ʔt* 'retorcer (p.ej., un trapo mojado)' MM: Ma < *ʔa·Wí:t* > At < *ʔawí:t, yʔawíʔtʸpʸ* > Ja < *ʔawí:t* > Ct < *ʔa·wí:t* > LM: Gu < *ʔawí:t* >

WI#037 pOM ***ʔa-wi:ʔt-y** *(adj) 'torcido/twisted'* NHM: *avi:ʔt* 'retorcido' MM: Ma *ʔaWí:tʸ* At *ʔawí:tʸ* Ct *ʔa·wí:tʸ* LM: Gu *ʔawí:tʸ*

WI#038 pOM ***wi:ʔt-n** *(n) 'trapiche/small mill'* NHM: *vi:ʔtïn* '=molino de caña de azúcar' MM: Ma Wi*ʔtn̥* Ja *wiʔn̥* 'trapiche', *wiʔtn̥* 'torno, taladro' [sic!] At *wiʔttá·kn̄* 'trapiche', *wiʔtn̥* 'torno, taladro, trapiche' Ct *wiʔtn̥* '=torno, taladro' LM: Gu *wi·ʔt* 'torno, taladro'

WI#039 pMZ ***wit** *(vi) 'andar/to walk'* OIP: *vit* (vi) '=pasear' TxZ: *wêč* (vi) 'andar caminando' SoZ: *witʸ* [Foster and Foster 1948] ChisZ: C *wiht* (vi) '=caminar; pasear; itajar' N *wiht* (vi) NE *wiht* (vi) '=viajar'

WI#040 pM ***witit** *(vi) 'pasear/to stroll'* NHM: *vit ~ vídït* 'pasear, andar vagando' SHM: Tp < *βɨδíhtp, tæp ʔitʸ βʸɨδítʸ* > 'andar' MM: Ma < *hɨdít, hɨdíhtp* > 'andar, viajar, pasear' Ja < *wɨdít, wɨdíht, wɨdíhtp* > 'andar, viajar, pasear' Pu < *wɨdíhtp* > 'andar, pasear' At < *hɨdíhtp* > 'andar, viajar, pasear', < *nawɨdíhtp* > 'viajar' Ct < *hɨdít, hɨdíhtp* > 'andar, viajar, pasear' LM: Ca < *wɨdít, wɨdíhp* > 'andar, pasear' Cn < *wɨdiht ~ wɨdit* > (vi) '=confundir' SJ *widiht ~ widit* 'to walk around, go on' Gu < *wɨdít, wɨdíht, wɨdíhp, wɨditá·mp* > 'andar, viajar, pasear' OIP: *vitit* (vi) 'dar vuelta'

WI#041 pOM ***pa-witiht ~ pa-witit** *(vi) 'seguir/to follow'* NHM: *pavídït ~ pavit* '=andar detrás de alguien' MM: Ju < *pæhɨdít* > LM: Ca < *pawɨdít* > Gu < *pawɨdít* >

WI#042 pM ***witiʔ** *(n) 'ropa, tela/clothes, cloth'* [pOM **wit*] NHM: *vit* 'ropa, tela, trapo, género' SHM: Tl,Ay *wet* MM: Ju *wit* Ma *Wī̄t* 'tela, trapo' Ja *wit* 'tela' At *wit̄* 'tela, vestido' Ct *wit̄* 'tela, trapo, vestido' LM: Cn < *wit* > Ca *wit* 'trapo' Gu *wit̄* 'tela' OIP: *vitɨʔ* 'faja de la mujer'

WI#043 pZ ***witɨm** *(n) 'ojo/eye'* [May be from *win* 'eye' + *tɨm* 'fruit'.] ChisZ: C *witɨm* N *witɨm* [homonym: 'guaya—palmera'] NE [Tapalapa, Ocotepec] *widɨm* [Wonderly 1949] [Pantepec] *widɨp* [Wonderly 1949] [Ra] *widɨp* [Chapultenango] *wirɨŋ* [Wonderly 1949] S *[witɨm]* 'ojo' ChZ: StaMaCh *witɨm* SnMiCh *witɨm* [Wonderly 1949]

WI#044 pZ ***witu?** *(vi) 'regresar/to return'* ChisZ: C *witu?* (vi) 'regresar, volver' N *witu?* (vi) 'regresar; dar vueltas' ChZ: *witu?* 'regresar'

WI#045 pMZ ***wi(?)yuk(s)** *(n) 'mico de noche/kinkajou [Potos flavus]'* [pM **wiyuk(š)*; pZ **wi(?)yuk*] OIP: *viyu'k* SaP: *wíyukš* ChisZ: C *wiloh* NE *wi?yuk*

WE#001 pM ***we:?c** *(vi) 'arrastrarse/to crawl'* MM: 'gatear (en las nalgas) Ma <*wæ:c, wæ?cp*> Ja <*wæ?cp, wæ:ʒá·m̥p*> At <*wæ?cp, wæ:ʒá·m̥p*> Ct <*wæ?cp*> LM: Cn <*we·c*> (vi) 'arrastrarse; bullir; rascarse' Gu <*we:c, we·?cp*> 'gatear (en las nalgas)' OIP: *ve:c* (vi) 'arrastrarse'

WE#002 pM [Veracruz] ***wec** *(vt) 'meter la comida en la salsa/to dip food in sauce'* OIP: *vec* (vt) 'lamerlo' SaP: *weč* (vi, vt) 'dip food in sauce'

WE#003 pMZ ***wece(w)** *(n) 'comején/termite'* [pM **wece* > pOM **wecy*; pZ **wece(ŋ)* > pGZ **we:ce*] NHM: *vec* '=termita' [*wEc* expected] SHM: Tp *βeč* MM: Ju *weč* Ma *Wec̄* LM: Cn <*weč*> 'tipo de comején [order: Isoptera]' Gu *wec̄* OIP: *vece* SaP: *na:šwéč* SoZ: *we:či* TxZ: *we:ce?* ChisZ: N *weceŋ* [order: Isoptera] NE [Ra,Ox] *wecek*

WE#004 pZ ***weh** *(vi) 'gritar, llorar/to shout, cry'* [Cf. NHM *veh* 'germinar (p.ej., rábano o col), partir una fruta, brotar'.] TxZ: *weh* (vi) '=llorar, cantar (ciertos pájaros)' SoZ: *weh* 'llorar' ChisZ: C *weh* (vi) 'gritar, dar gritos; maullar; cantar' (vt) 'llamarle' N *weh* (vi) 'llorar; gritar; cantar (gallo)' NE *weh* (vi) 'gritar; cantar (como el gallo)' (vt) 'llamarlo; clamarlo' ChZ: *weh*

WE#005 pZ ***we?k** *(vt) 'rajar leña/to split (logs)'* SaP: *we?k* 'split (logs)' [Zo loan] TxZ: *we?k* (vt) 'apartar' SoZ: *we?k* 'split' [Foster and Foster 1948]

WE#006 pZ ***weki?** *(vt) 'hombro/shoulder'* [pGZ **we:ki?*] ChZ: *weki?* TxZ: *we:ke?*

WE#007 pM [Veracruz] ***weka** *(n) 'rana, sapo/frog, toad'* OIP: *veka* SaP: *wek*

WE#008 pM ***wekš-i** *(n) 'comal/griddle'* [pOM **wekšy*] NHM: *vEhkšïn* 'comal de barro' [-*n* is in analogy to nouns derived by the in-

strumental suffix pM *-an* > pOM *-n*] SHM: Tl *wekšy* Tu,Tp *βehkšy*
Mi *wehkšy* MM: Ju *wehšy* Ma *Wehšy* Cc,Ja,Pu,At,Ct *wehkšy* LM: Cn
< *wekšy* > Ca,Gu *wekšy* OlP: *vɨkši* [?-first vowel wrong] SaP: *wekš*

WE#009 *pOM* ***mak-wehkš-n** *(n) 'aura (tipo de buitre)/turkey vulture'*
NHM: *mokvEhkšɨn* SHM: Tp *mAkβékšy* Mi *makwékšy* MM: At
mahkwéhkšy

WE#010 *pZ* ***we?ks** *(vt) 'abrazar de la cintura/to embrace around the
waist'* TxZ: *we?ks* (vt, vi-p) 'trenzar, agarrar una persona entre las
piernas' ChisZ: C *we?ks* (vt) 'abrazarlo de la cintura' N *we?ks* (vt)
'abrazarlo (al costado)'

WE#011 *pMZ* ***wen** *(vi, vt) 'quebrar/to break'* LM: SJ *mo·kwe·n*
~ *mo·kwen* 'to strip ears of corn off the stalk' TxZ: *we?na?y* (vi)
'quebrarse' (vt) 'partir, quitar' ChisZ: C *wen* (vi) 'quebrarse, romperse' (vt) 'quebrarlo, romperlo' N *wen* (vi) 'romperse' (vt) 'romperlo, quebrarlo' NE *wen* (vi) 'quebrarse, romperse (como un plato);
partirse (como un melón)'

WE#012 *pZ* ***wen-e** *(n) 'pedazo/piece'* TxZ: *we:ñe?* (n) '=astilla;
los demás' [*we:ne* expected] ChisZ: C *wene* '=parte' N *wene* 'una
parte'

WE#013 *pZ* ***we?n** *(vi, vt) 'apartar/to remove'* ChisZ: C *we?n* (vi)
partirse, dividirse; apartarse (vt) dividirlo, partirlo N *we?n* (vi) se-
pararse (vt) repartirlo NE *we?n* (vi) dividirse (como un camino)
(vt) partirlo

WE#014 *pMZ* ***we:?n-V** *(n) 'parte, pedazo/part, piece'* [pOM
we:?ny [?]; pZ *we?ne*] NHM: *ve:?n ~ ve:?nhi* 'poco' SHM: Tl
wa:nɨ 'poco' MM: Ju *wæ:ndí?knɨ* 'poquito' Ma *Wǽ:nɨ* 'poquito,
poco', *wǽ:nɨ* 'otro poco' [sic!] Ja *wǽ:nɨ* 'poco' At *wǽ:nɨ* 'poco,
poquito', *wæ:n* 'otro poco' Ct *wǽ:nɨ* 'poquito, poco' LM: SJ *we·ny*
'few' Cn < *we:n* > (adj) 'poco' ChisZ: NE [Ox] *we?ne* 'alguno'

WE#015 *pMZ* ***we:?nV(k)** *(n) 'avispa/wasp'* [pM *we:?nik*; pZ
we?ni(k) > pGZ *we?enVk*] OlP: *vɨ:ni'k* [/e/ expected as the first
vowel] SoZ: *wé?nik* TxZ: *wê:?ñu?k* (n) 'avispa campanera, avispa
lengua de vaca' ChisZ: C,N,NE *we?ni* S *[we·ní?]*

WE#016 *pOM* ***ku-wet** *(vt) 'pagar una deuda/to pay a debt'* NHM:
kuveht ~ kuvet 'pagar (p.ej., una deuda o impuesto)' LM: Cn < *kueht*

~*kue·t>* (vt) 'reponer; pagar' (vi) 'escalar, subir (a la cumbre)'
SJ *kweht~kwet* 'to pay debts'

WE#017 pOM **we:ʔy** *(vt) 'lamer/to lick'* NHM: *ve:ʔy* SHM: Tl
<*we:ʔpy*> LM: Cn <*we·y~wey*> (vt) ChZ: **weʔy* [in the
phrase *mɨyɨ weʔypa* 'relampaguear'] [?]

Wɨ#001 pZ ***wɨ-ʔah** *(vi) 'salir bien, sanar/to turn out well, heal'* SoZ:
wɨʔá: 'be able' [Foster and Foster 1948] TxZ: *wɨ:ʔha?* (vi) 'sanar,
componerse' ChisZ: C *wɨʔah* (vi) 'salirle bien, darse bien' N *wɨʔah*
(vi) 'salir bien, componerse, estar compuesto, estar arreg lado' NE
wɨʔah (vi) 'componerse; salir bien; recuperarse'

Wɨ#002 pMZ ***wɨc** *(vt) 'peinar; gotear/to comb; drip'* LM: Gu *wɨ̈hc*
~*wɨ̈c* 'picar, morder (culebra), picotear (gallina)' [Nordell, p.c.] SaP:
wɨc (vi, vt) 'whip' SoZ: *wɨc* 'drip' [Foster and Foster 1948] ChisZ:
C *wɨhc* (vi) 'peinarse; gotear' (vt) 'peinarlo; cepillarlo' N *wɨhc*
(vt) 'peinarlo' NE *wɨhc* (vi) 'gotear, caerse gotas' (vt) 'peinarlo;
cepillarlo (como a un caballo)' ChZ: *wɨc* 'gotear'

Wɨ#003 pOM ***wɨcɨ"** *(n) 'huipil/native blouse'* NHM: *hi:ʔc* MM: Ju
hɨcɨ" Ma,Ct *hɨzɨ"* Ja *hɨzɨ"* Pu *wɨzɨ"* LM: Ca *wɨcɨ"* Gu *hɨzɨ"*

Wɨ#004 pOM ***wɨcuk** *(n) 'rayo/ray'* NHM: *vícɨk* 'rayo, relampaguear; relámpago' SHM: *wɨcuk*

Wɨ#005 pMZ ***wɨh** *(vt) 'arrojar; desatar/to throw; loosen'* NHM: *vɨh*
'echar o arrojar (p.ej., maíz a las gallinas), plantar o sembrar (p.ej.,
semilla de chile), tirar (p.ej., flores)' MM: _'tirar (arenas, granos),
regar (granos)' MM: Ju_<*wɨh*> Ma <*Wɨh, Wʸehpʸ*>_ Ja <*wɨh,
wʸɨh, wʸehpʸ*> At <*wɨh, wʸehpʸ*> Ct <*wɨh, wɨhhɨdít, wʸehpʸ*>
LM: Cn *wɨh* (vt) 'esparcir; adivinar (con granos de maíz)' SJ *wɨh*
'to broadcast seed' Gu <*wɨh, wʸɨh, wʸɨhpʸ*> 'tirar (arenas, granos),
regar (granos)' OIP: *vɨh* (vi) 'desatarse' (vt) 'desatarlo' ChisZ:
C,NE *wɨh* (vi) 'apestar' N *wɨh* (vt) 'apestarse, heder'

Wɨ#006 pZ ***wɨhɨ** *(adj, adv) 'bueno, bien/good, well'* [pGZ **wɨhɨ*]
TxZ: *wɨ:* (adj) '=bonito, amable, correcto', *wɨ:-* (prefijo de verbos)
'bien' SoZ: *wɨ:* ChisZ: C *wɨpɨpɨʔnahkuy* 'honor, buen genio' N
wɨhɨ (adj) 'bueno; sano'; (adv) 'bien'; *wɨhpɨ* (adj) 'bueno, sano' NE
wɨbɨ 'bueno, honrado'

Wɨ#007 pZ ***wɨk** *(vt) 'rebanar/to slice'* SoZ: *wɨk* (vt, vi) 'cortar con cuchillo' (p.ej., carne en bisteces) TxZ: *wɨ:k* (vt) 'cortar (carne)' ChisZ: C *wɨhk* (vt) 'rebanarlo; repicarlo' N *wɨhk* (vt) 'cortarlo (con algo como cuchillo)' ChZ: *wɨktuk* 'cortar'

Wɨ#008 pOM ***ʔa-wɨʔk ~ ʔa-wɨ"k** *(v) 'abrir la boca/to open the mouth'* MM: Ma < *ʔawɨ"k, ʔawɨʔkp* > Ja < *ʔawɨ"k* > Pu < *ʔɨwɨ"k* > LM: Gu < *ʔawɨ"k* > SJ *ʔa·wɨʔk ~ ʔa·wɨ"k* OIP: *vɨ:k* (vt) 'moverlo'

Wɨ#009 pM ***wɨ:ki** *(n) 'cojolite/crested guan'* [pOM **wɨ:ky*; OIP and SaP have a reduplicated form that must have diffused in the Veracruz area.] NHM: *vɨ̈:k* 'pavo silvestre, cojolite [Penelope purpurascens pur- purascens]' MM: 'pavo montés, cojolite o guan' Ju *wɨ:kʸ* Ma,Ja, Pu *we:kʸ* Ct *we:ky* 'pavo montés' At *woö:kʸ* LM: Cn < *wɨ:ky* > 'pavo, guajolote silvestre' [probably Penelope purpurascens] Ca *wɨ:kʸ* Gu *wɨ̈:kʸ* 'cojolite o guan, pavo montés' OIP: *vɨ:kvɨ'k* 'faisán' SaP: *wɨ:kwɨk* 'faisán' [Clark 1981]

Wɨ#010 pM ***wiki** *(n) 'avispa concha de armadilla/a type of wasp'* NHM: *vɨk* 'avispa' OIP: *vɨki*

Wɨ#011 pZ ***wɨ:ku** *(n) 'faisán/great curassow'* ChisZ: C *wɨku* 'fai- sán, pavo real' N *wɨku* 'cojolite—Penelope purpurascens' NE [Ox] *wɨku?* 'cojolite—ave de la montaña'

Wɨ#012 pZ ***wɨʔks** *(vt) 'enganchar/to hook'* SaP: *wɨʔkš* (vi) 'limp' [Zo loan] ChisZ: C *wɨʔks* (vt) 'abotonarlo, abrocharlo; engancharlo' N *wɨʔks* (vt) 'engancharlo, colgarlo; abrazarlo'

Wɨ#013 pOM ***wɨʔm ~ wɨ"m** *(vi) 'quedarse/to remain'* MM: Ju < *wɨ"m* > LM: Cn < *wɨʔm* > (vi) 'quedar' Ca < *wɨ"m* > SJ *wɨʔm ~ wɨ"m* Gu < *wɨ̈"m, wɨ̈!m̄p, mɨ̈"mɨ̈"w, mɨ̈"mɨ̈·ȳ, mɨ̈"mɨ̈:pʸ* >

Wɨ#014 pMZ ***wɨʔm-ʔiy** *(v) 'cabecear/to nod'* NHM: *ʔakuvɨʔmip ~ ʔakuvɨʔima* 'dar con la cabeza un golpe en la boca cuando se está durmiendo sentado' ChisZ: N *wɨʔmɨy* (vt) 'convenir, estar de acuerdo'

Wɨ#015 pM ***wɨ:ʔn** *(vt) 'jalar, etc./to pull, etc.'* NHM: *vɨ:ʔn* 'jalar (p.ej., una bestia), estirar (p.ej., una viga)' MM: Ju < *wɨ:n* > 'ceñir' Ma < *Wɨ:n, Wᵉeʔm̄pʸ* > 'ceñir', < *wɨ:n* > 'cinchar', < *Wɨ:n* > 'uncir' [sic!] Ja < *wɨ:n* > 'cinchar, uncir', < *wɨ:n, wʸɨ!n̄, wʸe!m̄pʸ* >

'ceñir' Pu <*wɨːn*> 'ceñir, cinchar' At <*wɨːn*> 'cinchar, uncir', <*wɨːn, wɨ?n̄dá"c*> 'ceñir' Ct <*wɨːn, wʸe?m̄pʸ*> 'ceñir', <*wɨːn*> 'cinchar, uncir' LM: Cn <*wɨ·n~wɨːn*> (vt) 'ceñir; ensillar' Gu <*wïːn, wʸï!m̄pʸ*> 'cinchar, ceñir' OlP: *vɨːn* (vt) 'jalarlo'

Wɨ#016 pOM *?a-wɨːʔn (v) 'amarrar bulto/to tie a bundle' NHM: *ʔavɨːʔn* 'cerrar (p.ej., una red o costal)' SHM: Tu <*ʔaβɨːn*> 'amarrar bulto' Tp <*ʔAβáːy, ʔAβɨːn*> 'amarrar' MM: At <*ʔæwɨːn*> 'amarrar'

Wɨ#017 pOM *ku-wɨːʔn (vt) 'amarrar/to tie' NHM: *kuvɨːʔn* 'amarrar (p.ej., una bestia en un lugar)' SHM: Tu <*kuβɨːn*> 'amarrar animal' Tp <*kuβɨːn, kuβɨʔŋgɨ*> MM: Ju <*kuwɨːn*> Pu <*kɨwɨːn*> 'uncir' Ct <*kɨwɨːn*> LM: Gu <*ku"wïːnɨ"w*> 'uncir'

Wɨ#018 pZ *wɨʔn (vt) 'hacer algo a escondidas/to do something secretly' TxZ: *wɨʔn* (vi) 'mentir, hablar chisme' ChisZ: NE *wɨʔn* (vt) 'guardarlo (como en una caja)' N **kɨ-wɨʔn* [*wɨʔhkɨwɨʔn* (vi) 'comer a escondidas'; *ʔaŋgɨwɨʔn* (vi) 'esconderse' (vt) 'esconderlo'; *nipkɨwɨʔn* (vt) 'sembrarlo a escondidas; esconderlo enterrándolo'

Wɨ#018 pOM *wɨːʔpš (v) 'palanquear/to pry with a pole' NHM: *vɨːʔpš* 'arrancar (p.ej., con palanca), palanquear' LM: Cn <*wɨ·pš*> (vt) SJ *wɨ·pš*

Wɨ#019 pMZ *(hu)wɨs-tɨk-(p)i (adv) 'anteayer/the day before yesterday' [pOM **hwɨštɨkpy*; pZ **wɨstɨki*] LM: Gu *huštɨpk* TxZ: *wɨ̄š-kya* (adv) ChisZ: C *wɨstɨkyaʔa* N,NE *wɨstɨhki*

Wɨ#020 pZ *wɨt (vt) 'romper/to break' SoZ: *wɨːt* 'chop down' [Foster and Foster 1948] ChZ: *wɨt* 'romper'; *wɨdɨm* 'romperse'

Wɨ#021 pM *wɨːʔt (vt) 'liar (postes, carrizo)/to tie together (poles, cane)' NHM: *vɨːʔt* 'cercar' MM: Ja,Ct <*kepʸwʸɨːtʸ*> Ma <*kepʸwyɨːt*> LM: Cn <*wɨ·t~wɨːt*> (vt) 'amarrar (carrizo o palma)' SJ *wɨ·t~wɨːt* OlP: *vɨːt* (vt) 'juntarlo' SaP: *wɨʔt* (vi, vt) 'thatch a roof, line up in rows' TxZ: *wɨʔt* (vt) 'azocar, apretar (amarra)' ChisZ: C *wɨʔt* (vt) 'batirlo' N *wɨʔt* (vt) 'lastimarse la piel'

Wɨ#022 pOM *wɨːʔt-y (n) 'tapanco/attic' NHM: *vïːʔt* 'cercado, cerco' Ma,Ja,Pu,At,Ct *wɨːtʸ* 'cama' LM: Cn <*wɨːty*> SJ *wɨːdʸ* 'platform of poles tied together' Gu *wïːtʸ*

Wɨ#023 pMZ ***wɨ:yi** *(n) 'sarna/mange'* [pM *wɨ:yi; pZ *wɨyi > pGZ *wɨ:y (only attested in a reduplicated form where the vowel is shortened against expectations)] OIP: *vɨ:yi* 'jiote; un grano que sigue agrandando' SaP: *wɨ:y* TxZ: *wɨywɨy* (adj) 'apestar a sarna'

WA#001 pM ***wa:c~wa?c** *(vi) 'limpiarse/to clean oneself'* NHM: *va:c~va"c* 'limpiar (p.ej., barrer un sitio), aclarar (el tiempo), despejar' MM: At *wa·c̄p*, tɨ: *wʸæ"č* Ct *wa·c̄p*, tɨ: *wʸa"č* LM: SJ *wa·c~wa"c* 'to clean, free, save' Gu *wa·c̄p* OIP: *va:c~va?c* (vi) SaP: *wa:c ~wa?c* (vi, vt) 'open up, strip off, clean out (a well)' TxZ: *wačwač* (n) 'llovizna' [?-A nominalized and reduplicated form of a hypothetical verb meaning 'to sprinkle' or the like would take the shape *wačwa:č*.]

WA#002 pM ***win-wa:c~win-wa?c** *(vi) 'limpiar (superficie)/to clean (surface)'* NHM: *vinva:c~vinva?ac* 'aclararse el tiempo, barbechar, quitarse de la presencia de alguien, desteñir, descolorar, limpiar la superficia de algo' OIP: *vinva:c~vinva?c* (vi) 'limpiar'

WA#003 pOM ***yak-wa:hc~yak-wa"c** *(vt) 'limpiar/to clean'* NHM: *yakva:c~yakva"c* 'limpiar algo' SHM: Tu <*yahkßá"c*> 'asear' MM: Ju <*yæhwá"c*> 'asear' Ma <*yahkwá"c, myahkwá·čpʸ*> '=asear' Ja <*yahwá"c, yahwá·čpʸ*> '=asear' Pu <*yahwá"c, myahwá·čpʸ*> At <*yahkwá"c, yahkwá·čpʸ*> Ct <*yahkwá"c, yahkwá·čpʸ*> LM: Cn <*yahwa?c~yahwa"c*> (vt) '=vaciar' Ca <*yahwá"c*> 'asear' Gu <*yahwá"c, yahwá·čp*> '=asear'

WA#004 pM ***wa?ac** *(adj) 'limpio/clean'* [pOM *wa"hc] NHM: *va"hc* '=claro' SHM: Tl *wo"c* Tp *ßA"c* 'claro (tiempo)' Ay *wa?ac* 'güero' MM: Ju *wa"c* 'claro (tiempo), limpio, puro' Cc *wA"c* 'claro (tiempo)' Ma *Wa"c* '=puro' Ja *wa"c* '=claro (tiempo), puro, santo' Pu *wa"c* At *wa"c* '=santo, puro' Ct *wa"c* '=puro' LM: Ca *wa"c* Cn <*wa?c/wa"c*> (adj) SJ *wa"ẕ/wa"c* Gu *wa"c* '=claro (tiempo), puro' OIP: *va?a's* (adj)

WA#005 pOM ***ni:-wa"c** *(adj) 'desnudo/naked'* NHM: *nɨva"c* MM: Ju *niwá"c* Ma *niwá"c kɨwá"c* 'desnudo', *nɨWá"c* 'encuerado' Ja *niwá"c* 'encuerado', *niwá"c ?ɨšwá"c* 'desnudo' Pu *niwa"c* 'encuerado' At *nɨẉá"c* 'encuerado', *nɨwá"c* 'desnudo' Ct *nɨwá"c* 'desnudo', *nɨwá"c ?ɨšwá"c* 'encuerado' LM: Gu *nɨ"wá"c ?ɨšwá"c* '=encuerado'

WA#006 pM ***tuk-wa?ac** *(adj) 'vacío/empty'* [pOM **tukwa"c*] NHM:
tukva"hc 'vacio, hueco' OlP: *tohwa?a's*

WA#007 pM ***?aw-wa:c ~ ?aw-wa?c** *(vi) 'abrirse/to open'* NHM:
?ava:c ~ ?ava"cy 'abrir' SHM: Tp < *?Aßácp, y?Aßá"č* > Mi
< *?awácp* > MM: Cc < *?Awácp, y?Awá"č* > LM: Gu < *?awá"c,*
?awá·c̄p > 'abrir' [Nordell, p.c.] OlP: *?ava:c ~ ?ava?c* (vi, vt) SaP:
?awá?c 'abrir' [Clark and Clark 1960]

WA#008 pOM ***yak-?a-wa:hc ~ yak-?a-wa"c** *(vt) 'abrir/to open'*
NHM: *yak?ava:c ~ yak?ava"c* 'abrir algo, destapar (p.ej., una botella)'
SHM: Tl *yik?awo"c* 'abrir' Tu < *yak?aßa"c, yak?aßácp* > Tp
< *yæhk?Aßá"c* > Mi < *yïk?awá"c* > MM: Ju < *yæh?œwá"c* > Ma
< *yahk?awá"c* > 'destapar' Ja < *yah?awá"c, yah?awá·c̄p* >
'=destapar' At < *yæhk?awá"c, yæhk?œwá·c̄* > 'abrir',
< *yæhk?œwá"c* > 'destapar' [sic!] Ct < *yahk?awá"c* > 'destapar'
LM: Cn < *yah?awa?c ~ yah?awa"c* > (vt) Ca < *yah?ïwá"c* > Gu
< *yag?awá"c* > 'abrir, destapar'

WA#009 pM ***?aw-wa?c** *(adj) 'abierto/open'* [*?awa"c*] NHM:
?ava"hc '=abertura' SHM: Tu *?aßá"c* Tp *?Aßá"c* Mi *?awá"c* MM:
Ju *?œwa"c* Cc *?Awá"c* Ma *?aWa"c* Ja *?awa"c* Pu *?awá"c* At
?awa"c Ct *?awa"c* LM: Ca *?awa"c* Gu *?awa"ctïgï"* 'abertura en
algo, *?awá"c* 'abierto' OlP: *?ava?a's* (adj) SaP: *?awá?c* 'ancho'

WA#010 pM ***ku-wa:c ~ ku-wa?c** *(vt) 'desprender/to unfasten'* NHM:
kuva:c ~ kuva"c 'desprender (p.ej., una reata de un clavo), quitar
(p.ej., un lazo con qué está amarrada una bestia)' SaP: *kuwa:c
~ kuwá?c* 'strip' [Clark 1983]; 'descubrir' [Clark and Clark 1960]

WA#011 pOM ***?a-wa:hc-n** *(n) 'llave/key'* NHM: *?ava:cïn* MM: Ju
?œwæcn̄ Ma *?a·Wá·cn̠* Ja,At *?awá·cn̠* Pu *?ïwá·cn̠* Ct *?a·wá·cn̠*
LM: SJ *?awa·st* [Acc. to the Van Haitsmas (1976: 8) a loan word
"from another dialect of Mixe.") This appears to be wrong. With *n̠*
> *t* as in all of LM and *c* > *s/__t* (a synchronic rule) the cluster -st-
turns out to be normal (albeit rare).] Gu *?awá·ct*

WA#012 pZ ***waci** *(n) 'raíz/root'* ChisZ: C,N,NE *waci* ChZ: *wa?c*
[?]

WA#013 pMZ ***waha(w)** *(n) 'cuerno/horn'* [pM **waha* > pOM
*waha; pZ **waha(ŋ)* > pGZ **wa:ŋ*, with unexpected final /a/ in AyZ
and TxZ] NHM: *vah* '=cacho' MM: Ju,Ja *wah* Ma *wah* 'guaje',

Wah̄ 'cuerno' [sic!] Pu,At,Ct *wah̄* '=guaje' LM: Cn *wah* 'ganado vacuno' Ca *wah* 'ganado' SJ *wah* 'ox' Gu *wah* 'ganado' OlP: *vaha* SaP: *wah* SoZ: *wa:ŋ* AyZ: *[wlaŋa]* 'su cuerno' TxZ: *wa:ŋa?* [?] ChisZ: C *wa?* N,NE *waha*

*WA#014 pZ *?aŋ-wak (vi) 'abrir/to open'* ChisZ: C *?aŋwah* (vi-s) 'abrirse, estar abierto' N *?aŋwahk* (vi,vt) ChZ: *?aŋwak*

*WA#015 pZ **wa?k~wa? (part) 'para que, para/conditional* TxZ: *wa?* 'imperativo negativo' ChisZ: C *wa?y* N *wa?~wa?k~wa:k* (conj aux) 'para que—proposito; si—condición; para que, a, para—introduce una oración que funciona como sustantivo, como complemento directo o sujeto de un verbo o de un predicado descriptivo)' NE *wa?* ~ *wa?ko*

*WA#016 pM **wa?k (vi) 'pisar/to step'* NHM: **va?k~va"k* [*kïsva?k* ~ *kïsva"k* 'bajar un escalón'; *našva?k~našva"ky* 'pisada, pisar (p.ej., de costumbre)'] LM: Cn <*wa"k-*> 'prefijo; se refiere a la posición de los pies al pararse' (ejemplo: *wa"kpet* 'pisar') OlP: *va?k* (vi) 'ir rápido' [derivative: *va?ke* 'un paso'] SaP: *wa?k* (vi) 'step, take steps'

*WA#017 pOM **mih-wa?k~mih-wa"k (vi) 'acercarse/to draw near, approach'* [Antonym in MM-Ct <*hi·wá"k, hi·wá?kp*> 'quitarse'.] SHM: Tu,Tp <*mihßá"k*>   MM: '=arrimarse' Ju,Ma,Pu,At,Ct <*mihwá"k*>   Ja <*mihwá?k*>   LM: Ca <*mihwá"k*>   Gu <*mïhwá"k*> 'acercarse', <*mïywá"k*> 'arrimarse' [sic!]

*WA#018 pOM **na:hš-wa?k~na:hš-wa"k (vi) 'caer (al suelo)/to fall (to the ground)'* NHM: *našva?k~našva"k* 'pisar (p.ej., de costumbre)' LM: Cn <*na:šwa?k~na:šwa"k*> (vi) 'bajar (a la tierra); caer (la lluvia)'

*WA#019 pM **yuk-wa?k (vi) 'pisar/to step'* NHM: *yukva?k ~ yukva"k* 'ascender (p.ej., una escalera)' OlP: *yukva?k* (vi) 'dar un paso, pisar'

*WA#020 pZ **wa?k (vt) 'pedir/to ask'* TxZ: *wa?k* (vt, vi-p) 'pedir, solicitar' SoZ: *wa?k* ChisZ: C *wa?k* (vt) 'pedirlo' (v ap) 'regalarselo; hacer que lo pidiera' N *wa?k* (vt) 'pedirlo' NE *wa?k* (vt) 'pedirlo; pretenderla, pedir la mano'

*WA#021 pZ **wa?ka (n) 'abertura en forma de horqueta o zanja /opening of the shape of a trench or fork'* [pGZ **wa?aka*] AyZ: *[wá?kuy]* 'palo que tiene gancho, horqueta' TxZ: *wa:ʔka?* 'horqueta (del árbol)' ChisZ: N *waʔka* 'zanjón'

WA#022 pZ **waka** *(n) 'canasta/basket'* ChisZ: C,N *waka* NE *waka* '=cesta' S *[wa·ká]* 'canasto'

WA#023 pMZ **waʔks** *(vi) 'partirse/to be divided, parted'* NHM: *vaʔkš* 'repartir, seperar' SHM: Tl *yikwoʔkš* 'distribuir' MM: Ju <*waʔšp*> Ma <*waʔšp, waʔšámp*> Ja <*tuhwáʔšp*> Pu <*kuhm̥ wʸǽ!kšʸ*> Pu <*walkšp*> At <*waʔkšp, yahwǽʔkʸšʸpʸ*> Ct <*waʔkšp*> LM: Cn <*wa"kš*> (vi) 'partirse; salir (de una reunión)' SJ *waʔkš* 'to be divided, parted; to be changed (money)' Gu <*waʔšp*> ChisZ: N *waʔks* (vt) 'echarlo (con la mano)'

WA#024 pM **wan~waʔn** *(vt) 'querer/to want'* [This was also lexicalized in pre-pM as a verbal suffix meaning 'future'.] NHM: *va:n ~va"n* 'decir' LM: SJ *wa·n~wa"n* 'to want for a certain purpose' OIP: *van~vaʔn* (vt) 'quererlo' SaP: *wan~waʔn* (vi, vt) 'want, love'

WA#025 pOM **ku-wahn~ku-wa"n** *(vt) 'defender/to defend'* NHM: *kuva:n~cuva"n* 'defender' LM: Cn <*kowa·n~kowan*> (vt) '=salvar'

WA#026 pZ **wan** *(vi) 'cantar/to sing'* SoZ: *wan* (vi) [Gutiérrez M. 1993; Foster and Foster 1948 has the additional meaning 'succeed'] AyZ: *[wángu]* 'canción' TxZ: *wan* (vt, vi-a) ChisZ: C,NE *wan* (vi) 'cantar' (vt) 'cantarlo' N *wan* (vi) S *[wa·nú?]* 'estoy cantando' ChZ: *wan* 'cantar (leer)' [with 'paper' incorporated: *toto-wan-*]

WA#027 pZ **wan-e** *(n) 'canción, himno, canto/song'* [pGZ **wa:ne*] TxZ: *wa:n* ChisZ: C,N,NE *wane*

WA#028 pMZ **(k)wanak** *[?] (vi) 'bajarse/to descend'* NHM *vahntk ~váñik* 'bajar (acción general), desprender (p.ej., un sombrero de la percha)' SHM: Tl *winok* 'bajar' Tp <*βihák, βinákp, βináhk, βinAkámp*> MM: Ju <*hinǽk*> Cc <*hinák, hináhkp*> Ma <*hinák*> Ja <*winák, wináhkp*> Pu <*winák, wináhkp*> At <*hinák*> Ct <*hinák, hináhkp*> 'bajarse' LM: Ml <*hanahk*> Cn <*minahk~minak*> (vi) 'bajar; bajar (precio)' SaP: *manak* (vi) 'go down'; *ʔakmának* 'bajar' [Clark and Clark 1960] [?] ChisZ: C *wanahk* (vi) 'bajar, descender' ChZ: *wanak*

WA#029 pMZ *yak-(k)wanak [?] (vt) 'bajar/to make descend' NHM: yakwáñĭk 'bajar algo' SHM: Tp <yæhkβinák> MM: Cc <yAhkhinák> Ja <yahwinák> At <yæhkhinák> LM: Gu <yahminák> ChisZ: C yakwanahk (vt) 'bajarlo, hacerlo bajar; rebajarlo, redujarlo; desmontarlo; dejarlo bajar' (vt-caus) 'hacer que lo bajara'

WA#030 pMZ *(k)wanak-ɨ [?] (n) 'bajada/descent' MM: Ju hinǽk Ma Wɨnák Ma Wɨnakkɨhš^y Ja winwɨnák Pu kɨwɨnák At hɨnák, hinɨnák Ct hininákkɨhš^y LM: Gu minák ChisZ: C,NE wanakɨ

WA#031 pOM *wanahn~wana"n (vi) 'decir/to say' MM: Ma <hiná"n, hiná·m̄p> 'decir (intr), sonarse' Ja <wɨná"n, wɨná·n̄, wɨná·m̄p> 'decir (intr), sonarse' Pu <wɨná"n, wɨná·m̄p> 'decir (intr)' At <hiná"n, hiná"m̄p> 'decir (intr)', <hiná·m̄p> 'sonarse' Ct <hiná"n, hiná·m̄p> 'decir (intr), sonarse'

WA#032 pZ *was (vt) 'masticar/to chew' SoZ: was (vt) AyZ: [was] 'morder, doler' TxZ: was (vi) 'masticar, mascar' ChisZ: C wahs (vt) '=rocerlo' N was (vi, vt) NE wahs (vt) 'mascarlo' ChZ: was 'mascar; morder'

WA#033 pOM *wa:hš (n) 'zorra/skunk' NHM: va:š '[Urocyon cinereoargentus]' MM: Ju wæš Ma Wa·šká: Ja,At,Ct wa·š̄ LM: Cn <wa:š> 'zorra gris [Vulpes cinereoargentus]' Ca,SJ wa·š

WA#034 pM *wa:šuk (n) 'caña de azúcar/sugarcane [Saccharum officinarum]' [pOM *wa:šk] NHM: va:šk [Saccharum officinarum] SHM: Tl wošk 'caña' Tu cahβášk Tp βAšk Mi po:bwášk 'caña blanca', wašk 'caña de azúcar', cahpswášk 'caña colorada' MM: Ju wæšk Cc wAšk Ma Wa·šk Ja,Pu,At,Ct wa·šk LM: Cn <wa:š> Ca wa·šk Gu wa·šk OIP: va:šu'k SaP: wá:šuk

WA#035 pM [Veracruz] *pa:-wa:šuk (n) 'caña cimarrón/wild sugarcane' OIP: pa:va:šu'k SaP: pa:wa:šuk [Clark 1981]

WA#036 pMZ *wat (vt) 'amarrar cosas encimadas/to bind together things that are placed on top of each other' NHM: vaht~vat 'cuartear (p.ej., una piedra), rajar (p.ej., una piedra)' MM: 'amarrar cosas encimadas (cajas, tamales, etc.)' Ja <wat, w^yaht, w^yaht^yp^y> At <wat> Gu <wat> 'amarrar cosas encimadas (cajas, tamales, etc.)' SaP: wat (vt) 'do, make' [semantics influenced by Gulf Zoquean; also used to assimilate Spanish loans, again just as in Gulf

Zoquean] AyZ: *[ma gʷéa]* 'lo hizo' SoZ: *wat* (vt) 'hacerlo' TxZ: *wat* (vt) 'hacer' [The nominalization *wa:t* 'brujería' must be a Mayan calque.] ChisZ: C *waht* (vi-s) 'estar amarrado' (vt) 'cincharlo, fajarlo; amarrarlo, atarlo' N *waht* (vi) 'estar amarrado' (vt) 'amarrarlo' NE *waht* (vt) 'cincharlo, fajarlo'

WA#037 pM ***wa:w** *(n) 'acuyo, yerba santa/edible piper'* [pOM *wo:w by a unique kind of vowel assimilation; OIP affixed -uk (an element whose meaning is unknown) and /v/ went to /h/ before /u/; already in pM times *?ahy 'herb' occurred with *wa:w.] NHM: *vo:?v a:hy* 'yerba santa, hoja santa' [Piper auritum, P. sanctum Schl.]' MM: Ju,Pu *wo:* Ma *Wo:w̥ ~ Wo:Φ ~ Wo:f* Ja *wo:w* At *wow̄ ~ wow̥* Ct *wo:* 'yerba santa, acuyo', *wo·w̄, wo·β, wo·Φ* 'acuyo, yerba santa' [sic!] LM: Cn <*wo?a:y*> 'hierba santa' [Piper sp.] Gu,Ca *wo:* OIP: *va:hu'k* 'hierba santa, acuyo' SaP: *wa:wáhy* 'hierba santa, acuyo' [Clark 1981]

WA#038 pMZ ***wa(?)y** *(n) 'cabello/hair'* [pM, pOM *wahy; pZ, pGZ *wa(?)y] NHM: *va:hy* 'cabello, pelo de una persona' SHM: Tl *wo:y* Tu *βa:y* Tp *βA:y* Mi *wa:y* MM: Ju *wa:y* 'pelo (humano), cabello' Ma *Wa:y* 'pelo (humano)', *wa:y̥* 'cabello, peludo' [sic!] Ja *wa:y* 'pelo (humano)' Pu *wa:y* 'cabello, peludo, pelo (humano)' At *wa:y* 'pelo (humano), cabello' Ct *wa·ȳ* 'cabello, pelo (humano)' LM: Cn <*wa:y*> Ca *wa:y* 'pelo (humano)' Gu *wa:y* 'pelo (humano), pubic hair' OIP: *vayɨ* SaP: *kuahy* SoZ: *way* [Foster and Foster 1948] [final -y can be strongly aspirated] AyZ: *[wa?y]* '=pelo, trenza' TxZ: *wa?y* '=pelo, trenza' ChisZ: C *way* 'cabello, pelo' N *way* 'cabello, pelo' NE *way* 'cabello, pelo' S *[way]* ChZ: *wa?y*

WA#039 pMZ ***?aw-wa(?)y** *(n) 'barba/beard'* [See pMZ *?aw 'mouth'.] NHM: *?ava:hy* 'bigote' SHM: Tl *?awo:y* Tu *?aβá:y* Mi,Ay *y?awá:y* MM: Ju *?æwá:y* 'bigotón', *?awá:y* 'barba' [sic!] Ma *?aWá:y* 'bigotón, bagre, barba' Ja *?awá:y* 'bagre', *?a·wá:y* 'barba' [sic!] Pu *?awá:y* '=bagre' At *?æwá:y* '=bagre, bigotón' Ct *?a·wá·ȳ* 'bagre, barba', *?a·wá:y* 'bigotón' [sic!] LM: Cn <*a:wa:y*> '=barbo, bagre (pez)' Ca *?a·wá:y* 'bigotón, barba' Gu *?awá:y* 'bagre, bigotón, barba' OIP: *?a:vayɨ* 'bigote' ChisZ: C *?aŋway* N *?aŋway* 'barba, bigote' NE *?aŋway* 'bigote' ChZ: *?aŋwa?y*

WA#040 pOM **mehc-wahy** *(n) 'espinilla (enfermedad)/blackhead'*
NHM: *mehcva:hy* 'enfermedad que causa el crecimiento de vello fino,
como peluza en la piel, ocasionado por nutrición deficiente. Conocida
como guimiche' MM: Ju,At *mæhcwá:y* Ma *mæhcWá:y* Ct *mæcwá·ȳ*
LM: Gu *mecwá:y*

WA#041 pOM **ni:-wahy** *(adj) 'peludo/hairy'* NHM: *nɨva:hy* '=ve-
lludo (p.ej., un animal)' MM: Ja *nɨ"wá:yž̦*? At *nɨwá:y* Ct *nɨ"wá·yž̦ɨ*,
nɨwá·ȳ LM: Gu *nɨ"wá:y*

WA#042 pMZ **way** *(vi, vt) 'moler/to grind'* NHM: *va:y ~ va:hy ~ vay*
'moler (p.ej., café)' MM: 'moler (café)' Ja <*waȳ, wʸa·ȳ, wʸæ:pʸ*>
Pu,At <*waȳ, wʸæ:pʸ*> Ct, Ma <*way, wʸæ:pʸ*> LM: Cn <*way*>
(vt) Gu <*waȳ, wʸa:pʸ, wʸa·ȳ*> 'moler (café)' SoZ: *way* (vt) AyZ:
[gʷay] (vt) TxZ: *way* (vt, vi-a) 'moler (en el metate)' ChisZ: C *way*
(vi,vt) 'moler nixtamal' N,NE *way* (vi, vt) ChZ: *way* 'moler'

WA#043 pOM **mo:hk-way** *(n) 'pinole/something ground'* NHM:
mokvay SHM: Tl *mʋkway* MM: Ju *mo:gwǽy̦* Ma *mo:gWáy̦* Ja,Pu,
Ct *mo:gwáȳ* LM: Ca *mo:gwǽy*

WA#044 pMZ **way-e** *(n) 'molido/ground'* [pM *waye* > pOM
wayy; pZ *waye* > pGZ *wa:ye*] MM: 'molido' Ju *wæy* Ma *way*
Ja,Pu *waȳ* At *waȳ* '=pinole' Ct *waȳ* 'polvo', *way* 'molido' [sic!]
LM: Cn <*way*> 'polvo' Gu *waȳ* 'molido, polvo, pinole' OlP: *váye*
'pinole' TxZ: *wa:y* 'masa, pozole, atole agrio' SoZ: *wa:yi?* 'pozole'
ChisZ: C *waye* 'masa de nixtamal; pozol' N *waye* 'masa, pozol' NE
waye 'masa de nixtamal; pozol' ChZ: *waye* 'masa'

WA#045 pM [Veracruz] **(?apit)-waya-kuy** *(n) 'tepezontle/silk tree'*
OlP: *?apitvayakuyɨ* SaP: *waykuhy* [Clark 1981]

WA#046 pM [Veracruz] **wa:yan** *(n) 'guaya, palmera/a type of palm'*
OlP: *vaya'n* SaP: *wá:yan*

WA#047 pGZ **wayay** *(adj) 'delgado/thin, slender'* SoZ: *wayay* TxZ:
wa:ye? (adj) '=angosto'

WO#001 pMZ **woc?** *(vt) 'punzar/to puncture'* SaP: *wo?c* (vi, vt)
'scratch, play a guitar' ChisZ: C *wohc* (vt) 'estacarlo' N *wohc* (vt)
'punzarlo, picarlo'

WO#002 pOM **wo:?c** *(vi) 'extender/to extend'* NHM: *vo:?c* 'extender (p.ej., cuando una persona está acostado)' MM: Ja < *yawwó:c*,

wo?c, wo?cp > 'estirar' Ja < *?ihšwó:c* > 'asomarse, estirar' Pu < *?ihšwó:c* > 'asomarse' LM: Cn < *wo·c ~ wo:c* > (vi) 'estirar' Gu < *?išwó:c* > 'asomarse', < *yahwó:c, wo·?cp* >

WO#003 pMZ **woh** *(vi) 'ladrar/to bark'* NHM: *voh* SHM: *wʋh* MM: Ju,Pu,At < *wohmú:p* > 'aullar' LM: Ca < *wohmú:p* > 'aullar' ChisZ: C *wo?ah* (vi) '=ladrar' [back formation] N,NE *woh* (vi) ChZ: *woh*

WO#004 pOM **wok** *(vi) 'picado/to have a hole in'* NHM: *vok* 'picado' LM: Cn < *wohk ~ wo·k* > (vi) 'picar' SJ *wohk ~ wok* 'to have a hole in (not through) (corn, beans, tooth, etc.)'

WO#005 pGZ **wok** *(vi) 'gruñir/to grunt'* SoZ: *wok* 'ladrar' [Gutiérrez M. 1993] TxZ: *wok* (vi) 'bravearse, enojarse, gruñir, pararse (pene)'

WO#006 pZ **wok** *(vt) 'recogerlo/to pick from a hole'* SoZ: *wok* 'to pick from a hole' [Foster and Foster 1948] ChisZ: C *wohk* (vt) 'recogerlo' N *wohk* (vt) 'recogerlo (empujando con la mano)'

WO#007 pOM **wok** *[?] (n) 'arroyo/brook'* Ma *Wok̄* Ja,Pu,At *wok̄* MM: Ju *wok* 'barranca'_ Ct *wok* '=barranca' LM: Cn < *wok* > Ca *wok* 'barranca' Gu *wok*

WO#008 pM **wok(ak)** *(n) 'gorgojo/weevil'* [pOM *wok*; probably belongs with the preceding set] OlP: *voka'k* SaP: _*wok* MM: Ju *wok* 'carcomido' Ma,At *wok* _'gorgojo de frijol' Ct *wok* 'comido por gorgojo, zanja' LM: Gu *wok* '=gorgojo de frijol'

WO#009 pMZ **wo:?k** *(vt) 'agarrar un puño de algo/to grasp a fistful of something'* NHM: *vo:?k* 'peinar' MM: 'rascar, arañar' Ma < *Wo:k, Wʸe?kʸpʸ* > Ja < *wo:k, wʸe?kʸpʸ* > Pu < *wo:k* > 'arañar' At < *wo:k, nwóö?kʸpʸic, nꜣwʸó?kɨp* > 'arañar', < *wo:k, wʸö?kʸpʸ* > 'rascar' Ct < *wo:k, wʸe?kʸpʸ* > LM: Cn < *wo·k ~ wo:k* > (vt) 'escarbar tierra' Gu < *wo:k, wʸo·?pʸ* > 'rascar, arañar' OlP: *vo:k* (vt) 'tocarla (guitarra)' SaP: *wo?k* (vi, vt) 'scoop' TxZ: *wo?k* (vt) juntar (basura al cesto)' ChisZ: C *wo?k* (vt) agarrar un puño de algo NE *wo?ktu?m* (vt) 'recogerlo, reunirlo (con las manos)'

WO#010 pMZ **wo?m** *(vi) 'aflojar la tierra/to loosen earth'* NHM: *vo?m* 'aflojar la tierra con garabato o zapapico' LM: Cn < *wo?m* > (vt) 'dar un trompón, hocicar' SJ *wo?m ~ wo"m* 'to fight (pigs)'

OIP: *vo?mtay* (vi) 'andar pepenando' TxZ: *wo?m* (vi) 'salir (botones)' ChisZ: C *wo?m* (vi) 'crecer; retoñar' N *wo?m* (vi) 'retoñar' NE *yakwo?m* (vt) 'hacerlo brotar (como una planta de la tierra)'

WO#011 pMZ ***won** *(vi) 'jalar, llevar/to pull, carry'* NHM: *vo:n ~ vo:hn ~ von* 'jalar (p.ej., con enojo), dar un tirón fuerte' ChisZ: N *wonʒim* (vi) 'llevar mucha carga'

WO#012 pM ***won-i** *(n) 'caracol/snail'* [pOM **wony*] LM: Cn < *won* > 'tipo de caracol' OIP: *voni* SaP: *won*

WO#013 pM ***wo:?n** *(vt) 'jalar/to pull'* NHM: *vo:?n* estirar (p.ej., una liga), larguero (muy grueso) MM: Ju < *wo:n* > Ma < *Wo:n, Wʸe?mpʸ* > Ja < *wo:n, wʸe!m̄pʸ* > Ja < *wo:n* > 'jalonear' Pu < *wo:n, wʸe!m̄pʸ* > At < *wo:n, wʸö?mpʸ* > Ct < *wo:n, wʸe?mpʸ* > LM: Cn < *wo·n ~ wo:n* > (vt) 'estirar' Gu < *mĭk wo:n* > 'jalonear', < *wo:n, wʸo!m̄pʸ* > OIP: *vo:n* (vr) estirarse

WO#014 pMZ ***wonon** *[?] (n) 'perdiz/partridge'* [Phonological developments not well understood.] SaP: *šuwónon* SoZ: *wóhno* 'heron' [Foster and Foster 1948] ChisZ: C *wo?ŋsoh*

WO#015 pM ***wop** *(vt) 'pegar, azotar/to beat, whip'* NHM: *vohp ~ vop* 'pegar (p.ej., un cuartazo), azotar' SHM: Tu < *βop* > 'azotar' Tp < *βohp, βʸopǽmpʸ* > 'azotar' MM: Ju < *wop* > 'azotar, pegar (con cuerda)' Ma < *Wop̄, Wʸehpʸ* > 'pegar (con cuerda), azotar, golpear con palo, pegar (con mecate), pegar (con varita)', < *wop̄* > 'castigar' [sic!] Ja < *wop* > 'azotar', < *wop̄, wʸohp, wʸehpʸ* > 'pegar (con cuerda), golpear con palo' [sic!] Pu < *wop̄, wʸehpʸ* > 'pegar (con cuerda), azotar' At < *wop̄, wʸehpʸpʸ* > 'golpear con palo', < *wop̄, wʸoöhpʸpʸ* > 'azotar, pegar (con cuerda)' [sic!] Ct < *wop̄, wʸehpʸ* > 'pegar (con cuerda), golpear con palo, castigar, azotar' LM: Cn < *wohp ~ wop* > (vt) 'golpear (con vara o mecate)' Ca < *wop* > 'azotar, pegar (con cuerda)' Gu < *wop̄, wʸohp, wʸohpʸ* > 'pegar (con cuerda), golpear con palo, pegar (con mecate), azotar' SJ *wohp ~ wop* 'to hit with a long slender object' OIP: *vop* (vt) 'pegarle; golpearle' SaP: *wop* (vi, vt) 'pound, beat'

WO#016 pOM ***pa-wohp-pa-wop** *(vt) 'llevar (caballo)/to carry (horse)'* NHM: *pavohp ~ pavop* 'pegar a alguien por detrás, arrear, correr de la casa hacia alguien con enojo' SHM: Tp < *pАβóp* >

'arrear' MM: Ju <*pæwóp*> 'arrear' Cc <*pA·wóp*> 'arrear' Ma <*pa·Wóp̄*> 'arrear, llevar (caballo)' Ja <*pawóp̄, pʸawopǽ·m̄pʸ*> 'arrear' Pu <*pɨwóp̄*> 'arrear' At <*pæwóp̄*> 'arrear, llevar (caballo)' Ct <*pa·wóp̄*> 'llevar (caballo), arrear' LM: Cn <*pawohp~pawop*> (vt) 'arrear (golpeando)'

WO#017 pMZ ***wo:?s** *(vt) 'raspar/to scrape'* NHM: *vo:?š* 'rayar (p.ej., con un lápiz)' MM: Ma < *Wo:š, Wʸo?s̄ʸpʸ*> 'trazar', < *Wo:š, Wʸo?s̄ʸpʸ*> 'rayar' [sic!] Ja <*wo:š, wʸo!s̄, wʸo!s̄ʸpʸ*> 'acepillar' Pu < *wo:š, wʸo!s̄ʸpʸ*> 'acepillar' At <*wo:š, wʸo?s̄ʸ*> 'trazar' Ct <*wo:š, wʸo?s̄ʸpʸ*> 'rayar' LM: Cn <*wo·š~wo:š*> (vt) Gu < *wo:š, wʸo!s̄ʸp*> 'acepillar' ChisZ: C *wo?s* (vt) rasparlo; acepillarlo, cepillarlo; afeitarlo' N *wo?s* (vt) rasparlo, cepillarlo' NE *wo?s* (vt) rasparlo (como carrizo); afeitarlo, rasurarlo'

WO#018 pZ ***wo?t** *(vi) 'torcer/to twist'* TxZ: *wo?t* (vt, vi-p) 'enrollar (papel, cigarro)' ChisZ: C *wo?t* (vi) 'enroscarse' (vt) 'torcerlo, doblarlo' N *wo?t* (vi) estar torcido ChZ: *wo?t* 'caminar, andar'

WO#019 pOM ***wohw~wow** *(vi) 'mandar, invitar/to call, summon'* NHM: *vo:v~vo:hv~vov* 'invitar, llamar (con palabras), mandar a una persona por alguien, llevar (p.ej., una persona)' MM: Ja <*wow̄*> 'llevar (pelota)' LM: Cn <*wo·w~wow*> (vt) 'llamar' SJ *wo·w~wow* Gu <*wow̄*> 'llevar (pelota)'

WO#020 pGZ ***wo?ŋ** *(n) 'pez, pescado'* AyZ: *[wo?ŋ]* TxZ: *wo?ŋ*

WO#021 pZ ***woy** *(vi) 'enrollar/to roll up'* SaP: *woy* (vi) 'go in a circle, revolve' [Zo loan] TxZ: *woy* (vi) 'desfilar' (vt) 'enrollar (hilo en bola)' ChisZ: C *woy* (vi) 'enrollarse; enroscarse' (vt) 'enrollarlo; enroscarlo' N *woy* (vi) 'enrollarse, estar enrollado' (vt) 'enrollarlo; poner algo enrededor (como hilo o alambra)' NE *woy* (vt) 'enrollarlo'

YE-YO

YE#001 pOM ***ha:?m-yehc ~ ha:?m-yec** *(vt) 'acordarse/to remember'*
[Cf. MM: 'zafarse' Ja <*yǽhcp*> Ca <*yǽc*>] NHM: *ha:?myéc ~ ha:?myehc* '=recordar' SHM: Tu <*ham^yǽhc, mham^yéčp^y*> Tp <*tɨ:dœ:m^yœhcɨ"k^y, tɨ:dA:m^yéč, nhA·m^yœhcɨm*> MM: Ma <*ha"m^yǽc̄*> '=recordar, adorar' Ja <*ha"m^yǽc̄, h^ya"m^yéhčp^y*> 'acordarse', <*ha!m^yǽc̄, h^ya!m^yehčp^y*> 'recordar' [sic!] Pu <*ha"m^yǽc̄*>_ At <*hœ"m^yǽc̄, h^yœ"m^yéhčp^y*> 'acordarse', <*hœm^yœhcpɨk, h^yœm^yéhčp^y*> 'recordar' [sic!] Ct <*ha!m^yǽc̄, h^ya!m^yéhčp^y*> '=recordar' LM: Ca <*hœ?^ym^yǽc*> 'recordar', <*ha·m^yác*> 'acordarse' [sic!] Gu <*ha!m^yéc̄, h^ya!m^yéhčp*> '=recordar'

YE#002 pMZ ***yeh** *(vt) 'saciar/to satiate'* NHM: *yeh* 'saciar (p.ej., tomar agua hasta mitigar la sed)' ChisZ: N *yehmay* (vt) llamarlo (con la mano)

YE#003 pM ***ye:?k** *(vi) 'crecer/to grow'* NHM: *ye:?k* 'engordar, crecer' SHM: Tl *ya:?k* MM: Ju,Ma,Pu,Ct <*yœ?kp*> Ja <*yœ?k, yœ?kp, yœ:gá·m̄p*> At <*yœ?kp, yœ:gá·m̄p, tɨ: yǽ?knɨ*> LM: Cn <*ye·k~ye:k*> (vi) SJ *ye·k~ye:k* Gu <*ye:gá·m̄p, ye·?p*> OlP: *ye:k* (vi) 'crecer (una persona); crecer (la hierba)' SaP: *ye?k* (vi)

YE#004 pM ***yak-ye:?k** *(vt) 'criar/to breed'* NHM: *yakye:?k* (vt) 'engordar a alguien, criar, hacer crecer algo' MM: Ju <*yahyǽ:k*> Ma <*yahkyǽ:k, yahkyé?k^yp^y*> Ja,Pu <*yahyǽ:k, yahyé?k^yp^y*> At <*yœhkyǽ:k, yœhyé?k^yp^y*> Ct <*yahkyǽ:k, yahkyé?k^yp^y*> LM: Cn <*yahye·k~yahye:k*> (vt) '=hacer crecer' Gu <*yahyé:k, yahyé·?p^y*>, <*ye·?p, ye:gá·m̄p*> 'crecer (milpa)' SaP: *?akye?k* (vt) 'crecer' [Clark and Clark 1960]

YE#005 pOM ***ye:?k-y** *(adj) 'gordo/fat'* NHM: *yE:?k* '=gordura'
SHM: Tl *ye:ky* MM: Ma,Pu,At *ye:kʸ* 'crecido (gente o animal)' LM:
'crecido (gente o animal)' Ca *ye:kʸ* Gu *tï: ye:kʸ*

YE#006 pMZ ***yem** *(vi) 'soplar, abanicar/to fan'* NHM: *ye:m ~ ye:hm
~ yem* 'soplar (p.ej., con soplador), llamar (p.ej., con algún
movimiento)' SHM: Tl *yam* 'soplar con soplador' Tp <*yæm, yempʸ,
yæ:m, yæmǽmpʸ*> 'abanicar' Mi <*yæm*> 'abanicar' MM: Ju
<*yæm*> 'soplar (con abanico)' Cc <*yæm*> 'abanicar' Ma <*yæm,
ye·mpʸ*> 'soplar (con abanico)' Ja <*yæm, yæ·m, ye·mpʸ*> 'soplar
(con abanico)' At <*yæm, ye·mpʸ, hïnyǽ·mp*> 'soplar (con abanico)'
Ct <*yæm, ye·mpʸ*> 'soplar (con abanico)' LM: Cn <*ye·m ~ ye:m*>
(vt) 'soplar; abanicar; llamar con señas' SJ *ye·m ~ ye:m* 'to fan' Gu
<*yem, ye·m, ye·mpʸ*> 'soplar (con abanico)' OIP: *yem* (vt) 'soplar
la lumbre (con abanico)' TxZ: *yem* (vt) 'soplar (con abanico),
abanicar' SaP: *yem* (vi, vt) 'fan a fire' SoZ: *yem* 'soplar, abanicar'
ChisZ: C *yem* (vi) 'tremolar' N *yem* (vi) 'abanicar, moverse (como
abanicándose)' (vt) 'abanicarlo'

YE#007 pOM ***win-yehm ~ win-yem** *(vt) 'abanicar/to fan'* NHM:
vinye:m ~ vinye:hm ~ vinyem LM: Cn <*winye·m ~ winye:m*>

YE#008 pM ***yem-?an** *(n) 'abanico, soplador/fan'* [pOM **ye?mn*]
NHM: *ye?mïn* SHM: Tp *yemʸ* Mi *yæ?m* MM: Cc,At *yæ?mn̥* Ma
yæ?mt Pu *yæ!mn̥* Ct *yæ·mn̥* LM: Gu *ye·mt* OIP: *yema'n ~ yeme*
SaP: *yéman*

YE#009 pGZ ***yem-kuy** *(n) 'abanico/fan'* [Cf. LM-Ml *yemk* 'flama']
SoZ: *yémkuy* TxZ: *yem-ku? ~ yemko?*

YE#010 pOM ***ye:?n** *[?] (vi) 'flamear/to to flame'* [Other OM only
attested to by the forms (selected): MM: Ju *hï:nyǽ"ŋk* LM: Ca *yæ"ŋk*
Gu *hï:nye:n* all meaning 'flama, llama de lumbre'.] NHM: *ye:?n*
'flamear, arder, llamear' LM: SJ *ye?n ~ ye"n* 'to flame'

YE#011 pMZ ***ye?p** *(vt) 'extender/to lay out'* NHM: *ye?p* 'extender,
tender' LM: Cn <*ye?p ~ ye"p*> (vt) SJ *ye?p ~ ye"p* 'to unfold, lay
out (clothes, petates, etc.)' OIP: *ye?p* (vt) 'tender ropa' [derivative:
ye?pe (adj) 'tendido'] SaP: *ye?p* (vi, vt) 'spread out (clothes, mat)'
TxZ: *ye?p* (vt, vi-p) 'tender (ropa)'

YE#012 pMZ ***ye(?)y** *(vi) 'regar café, marchitarse/to lay out (coffee
beans), dry'* MM: 'tender' Ma,Ct <*yæ"p, ye?pʸ*> Ja <*yæ"p, yæ?p,*

ye?pʸ > At <*yæ"p, ye?pʸpʸ*> LM: Gu <*ye"p, ye?p, ye?pʸ*> OIP: *yey* (vt) 'regar café' SoZ: *yey* (vt) 'asolear (p.ej., frijoles)' ChisZ: C *ye?~ye?y* (vi, vi-s) 'marchitarse, estar marchito'

Yɨ#001 pMZ ***yɨ?** *(pron dem) 'este/this'* [pM *yɨ? > pOM *yɨ"; pZ, pGZ *yɨ?] NHM: *yɨ"* SHM: Tl *yɨ?* 'ese' Tp *yɨ"* 'aquel' MM: 'él, ella' Ma *yɨ"* '=aquel' Ja,Ct *yɨ"* '=ése' Pu *yɨ"* 'aquel, ése' At *yɨ"* '=aquel, ése' LM: Gu *yɨ̈"* 'ése, aquel, él, ella' Cn <*yɨ?*> 'él, ella (a la vista)' SJ *yɨ"* 'he, she, it, him, her—specific' SoZ: *yɨ?ɨm* 'aquí' TxZ: *yɨ:?* '=aquí, acá, por aquí, por acá' ChisZ: C *yɨ?* (adj dem) '=esta; indica oración sin verbo' *yɨ?wɨ* (pron dem) '=ésta, ésto' ChZ: *yɨ?pɨ?*

Yɨ#002 pZ ***yɨhi** *(loc adv) 'aquí/here'* ChisZ: C *yɨy* '=acá' S *[yɨy]* 'este' ChZ: *yɨhi*

Yɨ#003 pZ ***yɨ?k** *(vi) 'sacudir/to shake'* OIP: *yɨ?k* (vi) 'salir; nacer el maíz' [?] SoZ: *yɨ?k* 'hit' [Foster and Foster 1948] ChisZ: C *yɨ?k* (vt) 'sacudirlo' N *yɨ?k [*yɨ?kɨka?m* (vt) 'sacudirlo (para acomodarse)'; *yɨ?kte?n* (vt) 'levantarla (la mano)']

Yɨ#004 pMZ ***yɨk(ɨk)** *(adj) 'negro/black'* [pM *yɨkɨk > pOM *yɨk; pZ *yɨk(ɨk)] NHM: *yɨk_* '=prieto' SHM: Ay *yɨk* MM: Ju *yɨk̲* 'prieto, negro' Ma,Ct *yɨk̲* 'moreno, negro̲, prieto, trigueño' Ja *yɨk* 'trigueño, moreno' Pu *yɨk* 'moreno' At *yɨk* 'prieto, negro' LM: Ca *yɨk* 'negro' OIP: *yɨkɨ'k* SaP: *yɨgɨk* SoZ: *yɨk* AyZ: *[yɨk]* TxZ: *yɨk* ChisZ: C,N,S *yɨk* NE *yɨhkɨhk* (adj) *yɨkpɨ* (adj) 'negro' ChZ: *yɨk* '=moreno; gris', *yɨkɨk* 'oscura'

Yɨ#005 pM [Veracruz] ***yɨmɨm** *(vi) 'lloviznar/to drizzle'* OIP: *yɨmɨm* (vi) 'lloviznar' [derivative: *yɨmɨmɨ'k* 'llovizna'] SaP: *yɨmɨm* (vi) 'drizzle (rain)' [derivative: *yɨmɨm tu:* 'llovizna']

Yɨ#006 pM ***yɨmA** *(n) 'cocoyuche, pepeyochi/bird louse'* [pOM *yɨm] NHM: *yɨm* 'cocoyuche (parásitos que producen algunas gallinas cuando están empollando. Son parecidos a la larva de una garrapata del género Ixodes con nombre vulgar de pinolillo)' MM: Ju,Cc *yɨm* 'cocoyuche' Ma,Ja,Pu,At,Ct *yɨ̄m* LM: Cn <*yɨm*> 'gorupo, coruco [order: Anoplura, Haematopinus sp.]' Gu *yɨ̄m* SaP: *yɨm* 'pepeyochi'

YA#001 pOM ***ya:** *(loc adv) 'aquí/here'* NHM: *ya* SHM: Tl *yo* Tu *ya:* Tp *yA:* MM: Ju *ya:* '=acá' Cc *yA:* Ma,Ja,Pu,At,Ct *ya:* 'aquí, acá' LM: SJ *ya·* 'here—non-specific, closer to speaker' Ca,Gu *ya:* 'aquí, acá' Cn <*ya*> (adv) 'aquí'

YA#002 pM ***ya-m** *(loc adv) 'aquí/here'* MM: At *yam̄* 'allá' LM: Cn <*yam*> (adv) SJ *yam* [< *ya·*] Gu *yam̄* 'allá' OlP: *yam~ya:p* SaP: *yam*

YA#003 pOM ***yac** *(v) 'mover/to move'* NHM: *mavyahc~mavyac* 'confesar' MM: 'confesar' Ju <*mæyǽc*> Ma,Pu <*mi̇́:yác*> Ja,At <*mayác̄*> LM: Ca <*mi̇́:yác*> SJ *yahc~yac* 'to work out of position'

YA#004 pM ***yah...** *(loc adv) 'aquí/here'* NHM: *yaha* OlP: *yahi'k*

YA#005 pZ ***yah** *(vi) 'acabar/to finish'* TxZ: *yah* (vt, vi-p) '=terminar' SoZ: *yah* (vt) ChisZ: C *yah* (vi) 'acabarse, agotarse' (vt) 'acabarlo, agotarlo; destruirlo' N *yah* (vi) 'acabarse; lastimarse' [derivative: *yahe* 'herida']

YA#006 pZ ***ya?hi** *(adv) 'lejos/far away'* SaP: *yágac* '=largo' [?] ChisZ: C *ya?ay* '=lejano, distante' N *ya?i* NE *ya?yi* ChZ: *ya?hi*

YA#007 pMZ ***yak** *(vt) 'dar/to give'* NHM: *yahk~yak* 'dar (p.ej., dinero)'_ MM: Ju <*yæk*> Ja <*yak, yæhkʸpʸ, yahk*> Ma,Pu,At,Ct <*yak, yæhkʸpʸ*> LM: Ca <*yæk*> Gu <*yek, yehpʸ*> OlP: *yak* (vt) 'darlo (voluntariamente); dejarlo' SaP: *yak* (vi, vt) 'give freely, donate; place, put' SoZ: *yak* 'push' [Foster and Foster 1948] TxZ: *yak-ka?y* (vt-caus, vi-p) 'quitar (mesa, persona, cerillo, etc.)'

YA#008 pM ***ko-yak-i** *(vt) 'dar por otro/to give away'* NHM: *kuyahk~kuyak* (vt) 'dar por otro' SaP: *kuyági* 'abandonar' [Clark and Clark 1960]

YA#009 pZ ***ya?k** *(vt) 'empujar, quebrar/to push, break'* SoZ: *ya?k* (vt) 'empujarlo' AyZ: [*ya?k*] 'rempujarlo' TxZ: *ya?k* (vt) 'empujar, acarraer' ChisZ: NE *ya?k* (vt) 'troncharlo; quebrarlo (como un palo)'

YA#010 pOM ***ya:?kwet** *(n) 'verdolaga/purslane'* [The quality of the two vowels of the protoform is not secure; at the different locations there have been various attempts at reanalysis perhaps based on descendants of pOM **ye:?k* 'to grow' (NHM, MM-Ja, LM-Ca), pOM **waht~wat* 'to cinch' (MM-Ct, LM-Ca), and pOM **yo?kt* 'neck, throat, voice' (MM-Ju,Ja,Ct); if reanalysis is involved it is reasonable to posit an unanalyzable protoform, which is why pOM *ya:ʔkwet was chosen] NHM: *ye:ʔkvét* MM: Ju *yoʔkwǽt* Ja *yǽ:gwǽt, yoʔkwǽt* At *ya"gwǽt* Ct *yoʔgwát* LM: Ca *yǽ"kwát* Gu *ya:kwét*

YA#011 pM ***yakš** *(vi) 'estar recto/to be straight'* [Cf. ChisZ-C *yaksnucɨhk* (vt) 'maltratarlo', N *yaksnucɨhk* (vt) 'castigarlo'?.] NHM: *yahkš* 'estar recto, enderezar (p.ej., una regla)' SaP: *yakš* (vi)

YA#012 pZ ***yam** *(vt) 'esconderse/to hide oneself'* SoZ: *yam* 'esconderse' (vi) ChisZ: C *yam* (vt) 'ponerselo, calzarselo'

YA#013 pM ***ya:š ~ ya?š** *(vi) 'llorar, gritar/to cry'* NHM: *ya:š ~ ya"š* 'llorar, balar, maullar, rebuznar, tocar (p.ej., una campana)' SHM: Tl *yo"š* 'llorar' MM: Ju <*yǽšp, ʔǽyǽšp*> Ma <*ya·š̄p, ya"š*> 'llorar, chillar, mugir, maullar' Ja <*ya·š̄p, ya·š̄, ya"š, ya"žá·m̄p*> 'llorar, chillar, maullar, rechinar' Pu <*ya·š̄p, ya"š*> 'llorar, maullar' At <*ya·š̄p, ya"žá·m̄p, tɨ: yǽ"šᵛ*> 'llorar, chillar, rechinar, maullar, maullar' Ct <*ya"š, ya·š̄p, tɨ: ya"šᵛ*> 'llorar, chillar, maullar, cacarear' LM: Cn <*ya·š ~ ya"š*> (vt) [sic!] 'llorar; tocar' SJ *ya·š ~ ya"š* 'to cry' Gu <*ya·š̄p*> 'chillar, mugir, maullar, cacarear' OlP: *ya:š ~ ya?š* (vi) 'gritar; ladrar (un perro); cantar (el gallo)' SaP: *ya:š ~ ya?š* (vi, vt) 'ring, sound; yell, scream, shout'

YA#014 pM ***ya:š-hay** *(vt) 'llamar/to call'* NHM: *ya:ši ~ ya:šha* 'llamar (con palabras)' MM: Ju <*yǽšɨ*> 'llamar' Ma,Ja,Pu,At,Ct <*yá·š̄ɨ*> OlP: *ya:šay* (v-ap) 'gritarle'

YA#015 pOM ***ʔa-ya"šy** *(adj) 'llorón/like a crybaby'* NHM: *ʔaya"šy* LM: Cn <*aya"xy*> (adj)

YA#016 pZ ***yati** *(n) 'anona/sweet apple'* [pGZ *ya:tʸi*] SoZ: *ya:tʸi* ChisZ: C *yati* '=chirimoya'; *yatitɨk* 'anonal' N *yati* NE [Chapultenango] *yari* [Wonderly 1949] [Ocotepec, Pantepec] *yadi* [Wonderly 1949] S [Tu] *yati* [Wonderly 1949] ChZ: *yati?* '=candón'

YA#017 pMZ ***ya(:)wa** *(adj) 'tierno/tender'* [pM *ya(:)wa* 'tender' > pOM *ya:w* 'corn on the cob'; pZ *yawa* 'tender'] OM: 'elote' NHM: *ya:v* SHM: Tl *yow* MM: Ju *yo:* Ma *ya:w̥ ~ ya:Φ ~ ya:f* Ja,Pu, At *ya:w* Ct *ya·w̄* LM: Ca,SJ *yow* Gu *ya:w* OlP: *yova* SaP: *yau* ChisZ: C,N,NE *yawa* ChZ: *yawa?*

YA#018 pOM ***ya"wy** *(n) 'macho/male'* NHM: *ya:ʔy* MM: Ju,Ma, Ja,Pu,At,Ct *yǽ"y* LM: Cn <*ya"y*> Ca *ye"y* Gu *ya"y*

YA#019 pM ***ya?we-tɨk** *(n) 'hombre/man'* [pOM **ya"wtyɨhk*; as-similation of /a/ before /w/ in OIP] NHM: *ya:?tyɨhk* SHM: Tl *yo:?ytɨhk* MM: Ju *ye:ʸdʸɨhk* Ma *ye"dʸɨhk* Ja,Pu *yæ"dʸɨhk* At *yɨdʸɨhk* At *hɨdʸɨhk* Ct *ya"dʸɨhk* LM: Ca,SJ *ye"dʸɨhk, ye:dʸɨhk* Gu *ya"dʸɨhk* OIP: *yo?ve* 'esposo'; *yo?ohwa* '=varón'

YA#020 pM ***nɨ-ya?we** *(n) 'marido/husband'* NHM: *nɨya:?y* SHM: Hu *ñayek* [Foster 1949] Ay *neyekwic* Tl *nɨyo:?y* MM: Ma *nʸɨye"dʸɨhk* Ja *nʸɨyæ"dʸɨhk* Pu *nʸɨyæ"dʸɨhk* At *nʸɨyæ"y* At *nʸɨyɨdʸɨhk* Ct *nʸi"dʸɨhk* LM: Gu *ñaay* [Foster 1949] SaP: *na?u*

YU#001 pZ ***yu?** *(vi) 'tener hambre/to be hungry'* ChisZ: C,NE *yu?* (vi) ChZ: *yukka?h*

YU#002 pMZ ***yu:?** *(n) 'hambre/hunger'* [pM, pOM **yu:?*; pZ, pGZ **yu?*] NHM: *yʋ:* SHM: Tl *yu:* MM: Ma,Ja,Pu,At,Ct *yu:* LM: Cn <*yu:*> SJ,Gu *yu:* OIP: *yu:hɨ* 'hambre' SaP: *yu?* TxZ: *yu?* 'hambre' SoZ: *yú?u?* ChisZ: C,NE *yu?* N *yu?* 'escasez de víveres'

YU#003 pOM ***yu?c** *(vi) 'esconder/to hide'* NHM: *yʋ?c~yʋ"c* '=ocultar' SHM: Tl *yu"č* 'escondido' At <*yu"c, yu?čpʸ*> LM: Ca <*yu"c*> Cn <*yu?c~yu"c*> (vt) SJ *yu?c~yu"c* Gu <*yu"c, yu?čp*> ChisZ: C *yu?c* (vt) 'arrugarlo, fruncirlo' [?]

YU#004 pGZ ***yu:či?** *(n) 'tepegua/army ant'* SoZ: *yú:či* TxZ: *yu:?če?* '=pepegua, hormiga cazadora, yuche'

YU#005 pMZ ***yuh** *(vi) 'acostumbrar/to accustom, feel at home'* NHM: *yʋh* 'acostumbrar (p.ej., la querencia de un animal) LM: Cn <*yuh*> (vi) 'acostumbrarse' SJ *yuh* OIP: *yuh* (vi) 'hallarse' SaP: *yuh* (vi) 'feel at home, at ease' SoZ: *yuhó?y* (vi) 'acostumbrarse' TxZ: *yuh* (vt) 'aclimarse, acostumbrarse, hallarse'

YU#006 pM ***mu-yuh** *(vi) 'acostumbrarse con/to become accustomed to'* NHM: *muyʋh* 'acostumbrarse' LM: Cn <*mɨyuh*> (vi) Gu <*mɨyuh, mɨyúhp*> [Nordell, p.c.] SaP: *muyúh* 'acostumbrarse con' [Clark and Clark 1960]

YU#007 pOM ***yak-yuh** *(vt) 'amansar/to tame'* NHM: *yakyʋh* 'aman-sar un animal' LM: Cn <*yahyuh*> (vt) 'acostumbrar'

YU#008 pMZ ***yu:h?** *(vi, vt) 'rozar/to clear underbrush'* NHM: *yʋ:v ~yʋ"* 'arar, rozar, labrar (p.ej., la tierra) MM: 'desmontar' Ma <*yu:p, yu"w̥~yu"Φ~yu"f*> Ja,Ct <*yu"w, yu:p*> At <*yu:p*>

LM: Cn <*yu: ~yu"w*> (vt) 'desmontar, talar el monte' SJ *yu·w~yu"* 'to cut off brush, surface growth' Gu <*yu:p, yu"w, yu·w̥*> 'desmontar' OlP: *yu: ~yu:h~yu?h* (vi, vt) SaP: *yu:~yu?* (vi, vt) 'clear land, cut off brush' ChisZ: N *yuh* (vi) NE *yuh* (vt)

YU#009 pMZ ***yu:h?-i** *(n) 'rozadura/field cleared for underbrush'* [pM **yu?h* > pOM **yu"h*; pZ *yuhi] NHM: *yu"* 'roza' ChisZ: N *yuhi* 'roza—lugar donde se rozó' NE *yuhi* ChZ: *yuhi*

YU#010 pZ ***yuh-kuy** *(n) 'roza/the action of clearing underbrush'* ChisZ: N *yuhkuy* 'roza—la acción de rozar' ChZ: *yuhuku?y* 'milpa' [Knudson (1980: 154); possibly this has epenthesis], *yuhku?y* [elsewhere]

YU#011 pMZ ***yuk-** *'hacia arriba (prefijo locacional)/upwards (locational prefix)'* NHM: *yuk-* [*yukvohp~yukvop* 'arrear animales hacia arriba'] SHM: *yuk-* [*yukpan* 'apretar la garganta'] OlP: *yuk-* [*yuktɨy* (vt) 'colgarlo arriba'] SaP: *yuk-* [*yukpɨk* 'alzar' (Clark and Clark 1960)] TxZ: *yuku* (adv) 'arriba de' ChZ: *yuk-* [*yukkap* 'levantar', *yukhɨ?* 'arriba']

YU#012 pM ***yuk-mɨ** *(adv, adj) 'arriba, alto/upward, tall'* [pOM *yuhkm] LM: SJ *yuhk* 'upward' OlP: *yukmɨ* SaP: *yukm* 'arriba' TxZ: *yukum* (adj) 'alto' [?]

YU#013 pMZ ***yu:?k** *(vt) 'meter, esconder/to put, hide'* MM: Ma <*yu:k, mʸi?kʸpʸ*> 'esconder' Pu <*yu:k, myi!kʸpʸ*> 'esconder' At <*yu:k, yü?kʸpʸ*> 'meter (en la lumbre)' LM: Cn <*yu·k~yu:k*> (vt) 'echar bajo algo' SJ *yu·k~yu:k* 'to slip something underneath (corn, bananas in coals, etc.)' Gu <*yu:k, yu·?pʸ*> 'meter (en la lumbre)' OlP: *yu:k* (vt) 'esconderlo' [derivative: *yu:ki* (adj) 'escondido'] ChisZ: C *yu?k* (vi) 'mancharse' N *yu?k* (vi) 'mancharse; oscurecer; enfermarse' NE *yu?k* (vt) 'penetrarlo (como agua a la tierra)'

YU#014 pM ***yu:hk** *(n) 'bosque/woods'* [pOM **yu:hk*] NHM *yuk-* [*yukhɨ:tp* 'dentro del bosque', *yukho:tm* 'en el bosque'] MM: Ju *yuk* Ma,Pu,At,Ct *yu·k* LM: Ca *yu·k* Gu *yu·k* TaM: <*yuc*> 'tierra'

YU#015 pOM ***yu:kcin** *(n) 'faisán/great curassow' [Crax rubra]* NHM: *yu:kcin* 'faisán, hoco faisán [Crax rubra rubra]' LM: Cn <*yu:kšy*> '[Crax rubra]'

YU#016 pM ***yukho?** *(n) 'tepezcuintle [Cuniculus paca]/paca'* [pOM *yukho"] NHM: *yukho"* LM: Cn <*yɨ:go?*> OIP: *yukho? ~ yu:ko?* SaP: *yúhku*

YU#017 pOM ***yu?kš** *(vi) 'moverse/to move'* MM: Ju <*yu?kš, yu?š*> Ma <*yu?kšp, yu?šp*> At <*yu?kšp*> At <*yahkyúü?kʸšʸpʸ*> Ct <*yu?kšp*> LM: Ca <*yu?kš*> SJ *yu?kš* Gu <*yu?š, yu?šp*>

YU#018 pM ***yum** *(vi) 'escarbar/to scrape'* NHM: *yʋ:m ~ yʋ:hm ~ yʋm* 'escarbar (p.ej., el cerdo, la tuza, o la hormiga)' OIP: *yum* (vi) 'dar comezón' (ejemplo: "yumpa tɨnkɨ?šta 'me come el sabañon'")

YU#019 pZ ***yum** *(vi) 'hervir/to boil'* SoZ: *yum* (vi) TxZ: *yum* (vi) 'hervir, burbujear' ChisZ: C *yum* (vi) 'hervir; alborotar' N *yum* (vi) 'hervir, burbujear' NE *yum* (vi, vt) ChZ: *yum*

YU#020 pMZ ***yu:?m** *(vt) 'amontonar/to come together (many)'* LM: Cn <*yu·m ~ yu:m*> (vi) 'salir' (vt) 'sacar (por montones)' SJ *yu·m ~ yu:m* 'to come together (many)' SaP: *yu?m* (vi, vt) 'molest (by insects)' ChisZ: C *yu?mči?ŋnay* (vi-s) 'estar amontonado' N *yu?m* (vi) 'subirse, amontonarse; aumentarse, hincharse' (vt) 'subirlo'

YU#021 pMZ ***yun** *(vi) 'nadar/to swim'* SHM: *yum [nɨ:yum 'nadar'] [?] OIP: *yun* (vi) SaP: *yun* (vi) ChZ: *yun*

YU#022 pOM ***yu:nk** *(adj) 'blando (tierra, colchón, etc.)/soft (earth, mattress, etc.)'* NHM: *yúnɨk* 'blando, suave' SHM: Tp *yu?ŋk* 'blando (tierra, etc.)', <*tɨ: yú?ŋgɨ*> 'aflojarse' MM: 'blando (tierra, etc.), suave' Ju *yuŋk* 'blando (tierra, colchón, etc.), *yu·ŋk* 'suave' [sic!] Ma *yu?ŋk* Ja *yu?ŋk* 'blando (tierra, colchón, etc.), *yu!ŋk* 'suave, flojo (cosas), esponjoso' [sic!] Pu *yu!ŋk* 'blando (tierra, etc.)' At *yu:ŋk* Ct *yu?ŋk* '=flojo (cosas), esponjoso' LM: 'blando (tierra, colchón, etc.)' Ca *yuŋk* Gu *yu:ŋk* '=suave', *yu!ŋk* 'esponjoso' (sic!)

YU#023 pMZ ***yus** *(vt) 'despertar/to wake up'* NHM: *yʋhš ~ yʋš* 'despertar (p.ej., hablar o mover a alguien para que se despierte)' SHM: Tl *yuš* 'despertar a' SoZ: *yus* 'despertar'

YU#024 pZ ***yus-** *[?] 'saludo/greeting'* [borrowed from Sp. *Dios*?] SaP: *ni?ktíyu:š* 'gracias' [borrowed from Zo?] ChisZ: N *yusči?* (vi) 'saludar' NE *yusči?* (vt) 'saludarlo'

YO#001 pGZ***yo?** *(vt)* '*aliñar/to skin*' SoZ: *yo?* (vt) 'aliñarlo' TxZ: *yo?* (vt, vi) 'mudarse (víbora)' (vi), 'quitar (piel a víbora)' (vt)

YO#002 pOM ***yo?c ~ yo"c** *(v)* '*picar, punzar/to pierce*' NHM: *yo?c ~ yo"c* 'picar (p.ej., una espina), punzar (p.ej., una espina)' MM: 'lloviznar' Ma < *tu.yó?cp* > Ja < *tu.yó?c, tu.yo"ʐá·m̄p* > Pu < *tu.yó!cp* > Ct < *tu.yó?cp, tu.yo:ʐám̄p* >

YO#003 pMZ ***yoh** *(vi, vt)* '*deber (vi); pagar (vt) /to owe, pay*' NHM: *yohi ~ yoha* 'deber' S̲HM: Tl *yʋh* 'deber' MM: 'deber' Ma < *mʸi̲.yóh* >_ Ja < *mʸi̲yoh?áht̲ʸpʸ* > At < *mʸi̲yoh?áht̲ʸpʸ, yoh?áht̲ʸpʸ* > Ct < *mʸi̲.yoh?áht̲ʸpʸ* > TxZ: *yoh* (vi) 'poner (huevo)', (vt) 'pagar' SoZ: *yoh* 'pay' [Foster and Foster 1948] ChisZ: N *yoh* (vi) 'caerse (hoja o fruta de un árbol)' [?] NE *yoh* (vt) 'pagarlo' ChZ: *yoh* 'cobrar'

YO#004 pOM ***yoh** *(n)* '*fiado/debt*' NHM: *yoh* 'fiado, adeudo, deuda' MM: Ma,Pu,At,Ja,Ct *yoh* 'deuda'

YO#005 pMZ ***yo?k(-tu)** *(n)* '*cuello/neck*' [pM **yo?ktu* > pOM **yo?kt*; pZ **yo?k*] NHM: *yo?kt* 'cuello, garganta, pescuezo', *?a:h yo?kt* 'voz' SHM: Tl *yʋ?kt* MM: [Some locations have an unexplained presence of /n̲/ in final position.] Ju *yo?kn̲* 'voz' Ma *yo?kn̲* 'voz, pescuezo' Ja *yo?kn̲* 'cuello, voz', *yo?k* 'pescuezo' [sic!] Pu *yo?kn̲* 'cuello', *yo!kn̲* 'pescuezo' [sic!] At *yo?kpáhk, yukpahk* 'pescuezo', *yo?kt* 'cuello', *yo?tk* 'voz' [sic!] Ct *yo?kn̲* 'pescuezo, cuello, voz' LM: Gu *yo?t* 'pescuezo, cuello, voz' Cn < *yo"k* > 'faringe, garganta, voz' SJ *yo"kpahk* 'neck, throat' OlP: *yo?ktu* 'garganta' SaP: *yo?k* 'pescuezo' ChZ: *yo?k*

YO#006 pM ***ki̲?-yo?k(-tu)** *(n)* '*muñeca de la mano/wrist*' [pOM **ki̲"yo?kt*] MM: Ju *ki̲·yó?kn̲* Ma,Ct *ki̲"yó?kn̲* Ja *ki̲"yó?k* Pu *ki̲"yó!kn̲* At *ki̲"yó?tk* LM: Ca *ki̲"yó?kt* Gu *ki̲"yó?t* OlP: *ki̲?yo?ktu* SaP: *ki̲?yó?k*

YO#007 pOM ***teky-yo?k̲-t** *(n)* '*tobillo/ankle*' NHM̲: *tEki̲yo?kt* MM: Ju *tekʸyó?kn̲* M̲a,Ct *tekʸyó?kn̲* Ja *tekʸyó?k* At *tekʸyó?tk* LM: Ca *tekʸyó?kt* Gu *tekʸyó?t*

YO#008 pZ ***yomo** *(n)* '*mujer, esposa/woman, wife*' [pGZ **yo:mo?*] SoZ: *yó:mo?* AyZ: [*yo:?mo?*] 'mujer' TxZ: *yo:ma? ~ yo:mi̲?* 'mujer, señora' ChisZ: C,NE *yomo* N *yomo* '=señora, hembra' S [Tu] *yomo* [Foster 1949] ChZ: StaMaCh *yomi̲?* 'mujer' SnMiCh *yoma?* 'wife'

YO#009 pZ *cu-yomo (n) 'mapache/raccoon' NHM: yɨmïcik 'tejón pizote (más obscuro)' [?] OIP: cuːyoʔve [?] ChisZ: C,N cuyomo

YO#010 pMZ *yon (vi) 'alargarse/to grow' NHM: yoːn ~ yoːhn ~ yon 'alargar' MM: Cc <yoːmp, tɨ: yonʸ> 'alargarse' Ju <yo·mp> 'alargarse, crecer (milpa)' Ma,Ct <yo·n̄, yo·m̄p, yonámp> 'alargarse, crecer (milpa)' Ja,Pu,At <yo·n̄, yo·m̄p, yonn̄á·m̄p> 'alargarse, crecer (milpa)' LM: SJ yo·n ~ yon 'to lengthen; to grow (plants)' Gu <yo·m̄p, yoná·m̄p, yonʸɨ̄ɨ̃pʸ> 'alargarse' OIP: yon (vi) 'alargar' (vt) 'alargarlo' SaP: yon (vi) 'spread (a sore)' SoZ: yoʔn 'grow' [Foster and Foster 1948] [?] TxZ: yontɨŋkaʔy (vi-pl) 'moverse (montón de gusanos)' [?] ChisZ: C <yon-ba> 'brotar las arboles' ChZ: yon 'caerse' [?]

YO#011 pOM *yak-yohn ~ yak-yon (vt) 'alargar/to grow' NHM: yakyoːn ~ yakyoːhn ~ yakyon (vt) 'hacer crecer algo' MM: Ju <yæhyón> Ma <yahkyón̄> Ja,Pu <yahyón̄, yahyé·m̄pʸ> At <yæhkyón̄> 'alargar', <yahkyón̄> 'estirar' Ct <yahkyón̄> '=estirar' LM: Gu <yahyonʸɨ̄ʺw>

YO#012 pOM *yon-y (adj) 'alto, crecido/tall, grown' NHM: yɨn 'largo, alto' SHM: Tl yvnʸ 'largo' Tu yon̄ʸ 'alto' MM: 'crecido (milpa)' Ma yon̄ʸ '=crecido (gente o animal)' Pu yon̄ʸ At yon̄ʸ '=alto' Ct yon̄ʸ '=crecido (gente o animal)' LM: Ca yonʸ 'crecido (milpa)' Gu yon̄ʸ 'alto'

YO#013 pMZ *yos (vt, vi) 'ofrendar, trabajar/to offer, work' NHM: yohš ~ yoš 'ofrendar, ofrenda' MM: 'ofrendar' Ma,Pu <yoš̄> Ja,At,Ct <yoš̄, yohšʸpʸ> LM: Cn <yohš ~ yoš> (vt) 'ofrendar' SJ yohš ~ yoš 'to offer something to a saint, spirit' SoZ: yoːsyáː 'work' [Foster and Foster 1948] ChisZ: C yohs (vi) 'trabajar; funcionar; servir' N yos (vi) 'trabajar' NE yohs (vi) 'trabajar' (vt) 'trabajarlo; cultivarlo'

YO#014 pMZ *yos-e (n) 'trabajo, ofrenda/work, offering' [pM *yoše > pOM *yošy; pZ *yose > pGZ *yoːse] MM: Ma,Ja,Pu,At,Ct yoš̄ʸ 'ofrenda' OIP: yoše [incorp.: yošetun (vi) 'trabajar'] SaP: yoš [incorp.: yošwát 'trabajar' (Clark and Clark 1960)] TxZ: yoːs 'trabajo, chamba' ChisZ: C [Te] <yose> 'tributo'

YO#015 pZ *yos-kuy (n) 'trabajo/work' ChisZ: C,N yoskuy NE yosku? ChZ: yoskuʔy

YO#016 pMZ ***yo:?t** *(vt) 'amasar/to knead'* [The pMZ status attested to by pZ **yo?t-e*.] MM: Ma <*pič̄yó?tp, yo:t*> 'lavar nixtamal' Pu <*yo:t, yo?tʸpʸ*> 'lavar nixtamal' Pu <*yo:t, yo?tp*> 'lavar' Ct <*yo:t, yo?tʸpʸ*> 'lavar' <*yo:t*> 'lavar nixtamal' LM: Cn <*yo·t~yo:t*> (vt) 'amasar (la masa de pan); estregar (cuando lava la ropa)' SJ *yo·t ~yo:t* 'to knead (bread, clothes, etc.)' SaP: *yo?t* (vi, vt) 'ask, beg'

YO#017 pZ ***yo?t-e** *'camisa/shirt'* [pGZ **yo?ote*] SoZ: *yo:tʸi?* TxZ: *yo:?t* ChisZ: NE *yo?de* ChZ: *yo?te* 'ropa, trapo'

YO#018 pZ ***yoya(h)** *(n) 'cerdo, marrano/pig, hog'* [pGZ **yo:ya*] SoZ: *yó:ya?* 'cochino' AyZ: *[yo:ya]* 'puerco' TxZ: *yo:y* 'cochino, puerco, cerdo' ChisZ: C,NE *yoyah* '=puerco' N *yoya* S *[yoyá?]* 'coche' ChZ: *yoya* 'cerdo'

YO#019 pGZ ***mok-yo:ya** *(n) 'jabalí/wild pig'* SoZ: *mokyo:ya?* TxZ: *bokyo:y*

YO#020 pMZ ***yo?y** *(vi) 'caminar/to walk'* NHM: *yo?y~yo"y* 'andar, caminar' SHM: Tl *yʋ?ʋy* Tu <*yo"y, yo?ypʸ*> Tp <*yoꞓpʸ*> Mi <*yo"y, yó?ydʰïp*> MM: Ju <*yo"y*> Cc <*yo"y, yo!pʸ, yo!y, yo"yámp, tɨ: yo"y, kʸæh yo!y, yAhkyó!ypʸ*> Ma <*yo"y, ye"pʸ*> Ja <*yo"y, yo!ȳ, ye!pʸ*> At <*yo"y, yoö!pʸ*> Pu,Ct <*yo"y, ye!pʸ*> LM: Ca <*yo"y*> Cn <*yo?y~yo"y*> (vi) 'andar' SJ *yo?y~yo"y* Gu <*yo"y, yo!pʸ, yo!ȳ*> OIP: *yo?y* (vi) 'gatear' SaP: *yo?y* SoZ: *yo?y* (vi) 'brincar' TxZ: *yo?y* (vi) 'brincar, saltar'

YO#021 pOM ***pa-yo?y ~ pa-yo"y** *(vt) 'seguir/to follow'* NHM: *payo?y ~payo"y* 'perseguir, ir o andar atrás de alguien, seguir, pensar' LM: Cn <*payo?y~payo"y*> (vt) 'seguir'

YO#022 pM ***yak-yo?y** *(vt) 'manejar/to drive'* NHM: *yakyo?y ~yakyo"y* (vt) 'hacer caminar, manejar algo' MM: Ma <*yahkuó"y*> Ja <*yahyó"y*> Pu <*yahye!pʸ, yahyó"y*> At <*yahkyó"y, yahkyöö!pʸ*> Ct <*yahkyó"y, yahkyé!pʸ*> LM: Cn <*yahyo?y~yahyo"y*> (vt) 'hacer andar, hacer caminar' Gu <*yahyó"y, yahyó!pʸ*> SaP: *?akyo?y* (vt) hacer caminar [Clark and Clark 1960]

Numerals

All SaP and most TxZ forms are from Clark (1982). Forms in angled brackets of Clark (1982) are cited from E. Calderón (1908). Forms in square brackets are Clark's phonemic interpretations and unbracketed forms are those actually heard by Clark. When Clark "reconstructs" forms on the basis of conjectures, they are parenthesized. Note Clark's comment on the SaP form for '7': "For some reason, Calderón used the letter g to write the phoneme h at the beginning of this word. He uses j (Spanish jota) elsewhere. Perhaps he heard it as lenis and without friction."

The SHM [Ay,Tm] data were collected by me (1990). Sometimes the data collected by Beals (1945) from Ayutla are provided for comparison if they are indicative of some change between 1945 and 1990.

Concerning the numeral suffixes (classifiers?) in SoZ, Elson (1960: 44) writes: "La diferencia entre los dos sufijos numerales -te:n y -na: no es muy clara. El primero se emplea generalmente al contar y cuando el numeral es un sujeto o un objeto; el último cuando el numeral está en la posición de atributivo, aunque ambas formas se han observado en todas las posiciones." Later Elson declares that "[t]he suffix -te:n is obligatory with numbers two through five and with the word for 'how many'" (1967: 282).

NS#001 pMZ ***tu?-~tum-~tu-~tuh-** *'1'* NHM: *tv?k* SHM: Tl,Ay,
Tm *tu"k* MM: Ju,At *tu"k* Ma,Ja,Ct *tu?k* LM: Ca,Gu *tu"k* Cn
<*tu"k*> SJ *tu"g~tu"k* OIP: *tu?k* SaP: <*tuc*> [*tuk*] *tu?k* SoZ: *tum*
[Foster and Foster 1948] AyZ: *[tum~tu]* TxZ: <*tum*> [*tum*] *tum*
[Clark 1982] ChisZ: C *tum* '=pron: uno, una' N *tumɨ~tum* 'adj:
uno; adj: todo —duración de tiempo o espacio' NE *tumɨ* '=art
indeterm, único, pron indef' ChZ: *tumɨ*

NS#002 pZ ***tum-tum-** *'uno por uno/one by one'* TxZ: *tumtum*
'=cada uno' [Wichmann fc.-b] ChisZ: C *tumdúmɨ* (adj) 'cada'; (adv)
'uno por uno'; (pron) 'cada uno' N *tumdúmɨ* (adj) 'cada; uno por uno'
NE *tumdúmɨ* (adj) 'cada'; (pron) 'cada uno'

NS#003 pMZ ***mec-** *'2'* NHM: *mehck* SHM: Tl *mahck* Ay *mack*
Tm *mæhck* MM: Ja,At,Ct *mæhck* LM: Gu *meck* SJ *mec~meck* Cn
<*mehc/mec*> OIP: *mesko* SaP: <*mechki*> [*mecki*] *meck* TxZ: *be:c*
(palabra arcáica) [Wichmann fc.-b] ChisZ: C,NE *meca* N *meckuy*
ChZ: *meca?aŋ* (in Knudson 1980, p.149 + elsewhere); *meca?ŋ* (p.31)

NS#004 pOM ***mu-mehc-** *'segundo/second'* NHM: *mumehck* SHM:
Tm *mʸɨmahck* MM: Ju *mɨ·mæhck* Ma *mʸɨ·mæhckpɨ* Ja *mimæhcpɨ* At
mimæhck Ct *mɨ·mæhckpɨ* LM: SJ *mɨ·mec* Cn <*mɨmecpɨ*> Ca
mɨ·mǽck

NS#005 pGZ ***wɨs-** *'2'* SoZ: *wɨs-tén* [Foster and Foster 1948] TxZ:
<*huisna*> [*wisna*] *wɨsna?* [Clark 1982]; *wɨsna?, wɨste:ñe?*
[Wichmann fc.-b]

NS#006 pMZ ***tuk-** *'3'* NHM: *tv:hk* '=tercer' SHM: Tl *tɨkɨ:k* Tm,
Ay *tɨgɨ:k* MM: Ju,Ma,Ja,At,Ct *tɨgɨ:k* LM: Cn <*tugɨ:g*> Gu *tɨgɨ:k*
OIP: *tuvɨ'k* SaP: <*tugup*> [*tugup*] *tú:gup* SoZ: *tuku-tén* [Foster and
Foster 1948] AyZ: *[tuguna?]* 'tres, son tres gente' TxZ: <*tuguná*>
[*tuguná*] *túguna?* [Clark 1982]; *tukna?, tukte:ñe?* (personas), *-tukpe*
'entre (nos, ustedes, etc.) tres' [Wichmann fc.-b] ChisZ: C *tuka?y* N
tu?kay NE *tuka?* ChZ: *tuga?aŋ*

NS#007 pOM ***mɨ-tɨkɨ:k** *'tercero/third'* SHM: Tm *mʸitɨgɨ:k* MM: Ju
mɨ:tɨgɨ:k Ma *mɨ·dɨgɨ:k* Ja *mɨdugɨ:k* At *mɨdigɨ:k* Ct *mɨ·dɨgɨ:kpɨ*
LM: Cn <*mɨdugɨ:kpɨ*> Ca *mɨdigɨ"k* Gu *mʸidigɨ̆:kpɨ*

NS#008 pOM ***tɨkɨ́m** *'en tres días/in three days'* MM: Ma,Ja,Pu,At,
Ct *tɨgɨ̄m* LM: Cn <*tugɨ:m*> (adj) 'el día después de pasado mañana'
Gu *tugɨ̆:m*

NS#009 pMZ ***makta:s-** '4' NHM: *makta:šk* SHM: Tl *maktošk* Ay *maktá:šk* Tm *mɨktášk* MM: Ma,Ct *mahktá·s̄k* Ja *mahktá·s̄k, ta·s̄k* LM: Cn <*mɨda:š*> OlP: *maktasko* SaP: <*mactax*> [*maktaš*] *máktašp* SoZ: *maktas-tén* [Foster and Foster 1948] AyZ: [*baksna?*] TxZ: <*bacsná*> [*baksná*] *báksna?* [Clark 1982]; *baksna?, bakste:ñe?* (personas), -*bakspe* (entre), *bakske* (veces), *kêñbaktas* 'culebra cuatronarices' [Wichmann fc.-b] ChisZ: C *maksku?y* [entry p.71 in Harrison et al. (1981)], *maksyku?y* [Appendice B, p.473] N *maksykuy* NE *maksyku?* ChZ: *maktasaŋ*

NS#010 pOM ***mɨ-makta:hš-k** '*cuarto/fourth*' SHM: Tm *mʸimɨktašk* MM: Ma,Ct *mɨ:mahktá·šk* Ja,At *mɨmahktá·s̄k* LM: Gu *mʸimɨdá·špɨ*

NS#011 pMZ ***m(ok)os-** '5' NHM: *mugo:šk* SHM: Tl *makʋšk* Ay *mugó:šk* [Wichmann 1990] <*magóshk*> [Beals 1945] Tm *mɨkóšk* Tu *mɨgóšk* Mi *muwóšk* MM: Ju,Cc *mɨgóšk* Ma,Ja *mɨgó·šk* Pu,At,Ct *mɨgó·s̄k* LM: Ca *mogó·šk* Cn <*mɨgo:š*> SJ *mɨgo·š* Gu *mɨgó·s̄k* OlP: *mokoško* SaP: <*mogoxp*> [*mogošp*] *mógošp* SoZ: *mos-tén* [Foster and Foster 1948] AyZ: [*bo:sa*]~[*bosna?*] TxZ: <*bosná*> [*bosná*] *bósna?* [Clark 1982]; *bosna?, boste:ñe?* (personas), *bosnakɨ?* (manos—una medida), *boske* (veces) [Wichmann fc.-b] ChisZ: C *mohsa?y* N *mosay* NE *mosa?* ChZ: *mosaŋ*

NS#012 pMZ ***tuhtu-** '6' NHM: *tʋhtɨk* SHM: Tl *tutuhk* Ay *tudúk* Tm *tɨdúhk* MM: Ju,Ma,Ja,At,Ct *tɨdúhk* LM: Cn <*tuduhk*> Ca *tɨdúhk* Gu *tɨdúhk* OlP: *tuhtuhko* SaP: <*tujtup*> [*tuhtup*] *túhtup* SoZ: *tuhtu-tén* [Foster and Foster 1948] TxZ: <*tujná*> [*tuhná*] *túhna?* [Clark 1982]; *tuhna?*, -*tuhpe* (entre), *tuhte:ñe?* (personas) [Wichmann fc.-b] ChisZ: C *tuhta?y* N *tuhtay* NE *tuhta?* ChZ: *tuhta?aŋ*

NS#013 pMZ ***huwɨs-tuhtu-** '7' NHM: *vɨštʋhtɨk* [Mixe-to-Sp. side]; *vuštʋhtɨk* [Sp.-to-Mixe side] SHM: Tl *wɨšuhk* Ay *?uštúhk* MM: Ju,Ma,Ct *hɨštúhk* Ja *hwuštúhk* At *hɨštúhk*~*wɨštúhk* LM: Cn <*wɨštuhk*> Ca *wɨštúhk* Gu *huštúhk* OlP: *huštukuhtuhko* SaP: <*guxtujtup*> [*huštuhtup*] TxZ: <*huestujná*> [*westuhná*] *wɨstúhna?* [Clark 1982] ChZ: *wɨstuhta?aŋ*

NS#014 ChisZ **kuy-** '7' ChisZ: C *ku?ya?y* N *ku?yay* NE *ku?ya?* [According to Nordell, p.c., related to *koy* 'conejo' of the Guichicovi Mixe ritual calendar.]

NS#015 pMZ ***tuku-tuhtu-** '*8*' NHM: *tʋdʋhtïk* SHM: Tl *tuktuhk* Tm *tu?ktúhk* MM: Ju,Ja,Pu,At *tuktúhk* Ma,Ct *tïktúhk* LM: Cn <*tuktuhk*> Ca *tuktúhk* Gu *tuktúhk* OlP: *tukutuhko* SaP: <*tugutujtup*> [*tugutuhtup*] TxZ: <*tugtujná*> [*tuhtuhná*] *tuktúhna?* [Clark 1982] ChisZ: C *tukutuhta?y* N *tukutuhtay* NE *tukuduhta?* ChZ: *tuguruhta?aŋ*

NS#016 pM ***taš-tuku-tuhtu** '*9*' NHM: *taštʋhtïk* SHM: Tl *toštuhk* Tm *taštúhk* Ay *ta:štúhk* MM: Ju *tæštúhk* Ma,Ja,Pu,At,Ct *ta·štúhk* LM: Cn <*taštuhk*> Ca *ta·štúhk* Gu *ta·štúhk* OlP: *ta:stutuhko* SaP: <*taxtujtup*> [*taštuhtup*]

NS#017 pZ ***mak(ta)s-tuht-** '*9*' TxZ: <*bacstujná*> [*bakstuhná*] *bakstúhna?* ChisZ: C *makstuhta?y* N *makstuhtay* NE *maksytuhta?* ChZ: *makstuhta?aŋ*

NS#018 pMZ ***mak-** '*10*' NHM: *mahk* SHM: Tl *mohk* Tm *mahk* MM: Ma,Ja,Pu,At,Ct *mahk* LM: Cn <*mahk*> SJ *mahk* Gu *mahk* OlP: *maku* SaP: <*macp*> [*makp*] *mak* TxZ: <*bacná*> [*bakná*] *bákna?* [Clark 1982]; *bakna?* [Wichmann fc.-b] ChisZ: C *mahka?y* N *mahkay* NE *mahka?* ChZ: *magaŋ*

NS#019 pM ***mak-tu?k** '*11*' NHM: *maktʋ?k* SHM: Ay *maktú"k* Tm *mahktú"k* MM: Ju,At *mahktú"k* Ma,Pu,Ct *mahktu?k* Ja *mahtú?k* LM: Cn <*mahtu"k*> Ca *mahktú"k* Gu *mahtú"k* SaP: <*macpimujtup*> [*makpimuhtup*]

NS#020 pZ ***mak-tum-** '*11*' TxZ: <*bactumná*> [*baktumná*] *baktúmna?* [Clark 1982], *Baktúmna?* [Clark n.d.] ChisZ: C *maktuma?y* NE *maktumɨ* ChZ: *maktumɨ*

NS#021 pM ***mak-mec-** '*12*' NHM: *makmæhck* SHM: Ay *makmæhck* Tm *mahkmahck* MM: Ma,At,Ct *mahkmæhck* Ja,Pu *mahmæhck* LM: Cn <*mahmec*> Gu *mahméck* SaP: <*macpimujmechki*> [*makpimuhmečki*]

NS#022 pZ ***mak-wɨs-** '*12*' TxZ: <*bac'huisná*> [*bakwɨsná*] *bakwɨsna?* [Clark 1982]; *bakwɨsna?* [Wichmann fc.-b] ChisZ: C *makwɨstɨhka?y* NE *makwɨstɨhka?*

NS#023 pMZ ***mak-tuku-** '*13*' NHM: *maktʋ:hk* SHM: Ay *maktɨgɨ́:k* Tm *mahktɨgɨ́:k* MM: Ju,Ma,At,Ct *mahktɨgɨ́:k* Ja *mahtɨgɨ́:k* LM: Cn <*mahktugɨ:g*> Gu *mahtɨgɨ́:k* SaP: <*macpimujtugup*>

[*makpimuhtugup*] TxZ: <*bactuguná*> [*baktuguná*] *baktúguna?* [Clark 1982]; *baktukna?* [Wichmann fc.-b] ChisZ: C *maktuka?y* NE *maktuka?*

NS#024 pMZ *mak-makta:s- *'14'* NHM: *makmahkc* SHM: Ay *makmahck* Tm *mahkmahck* Tu *makmákc* Tp *mAkmákc* Mi *makmáhks* MM: Ju,Pu *mahkmáhkc* Ma,Ja,Ct *mahkmáhkc* At *mahmáhkc* LM: Cn <*mahmakc*> Gu *mahmákc* SaP: <*macpimujmactax*> [*makpimuhmaktaš*] (*makpimuhmaktašp*) TxZ: <*bacbacsná*> [*bakbaksná*] *bakbáksna?* [Clark 1982]; *bakbaksna?* [Wichmann fc.-b] ChisZ: C *makmaktasku?y* NE *mahkmaktasku?*

NS#025 pMZ *mak-m(ok)os- *'15'* NHM: *makmokš* SHM: Tl *makmʊkš* Ay *makmokš* Tm *mahkmohkš* MM: Ma,Ja,At,Ct *mahkmókš* LM: Cn <*mahmokš*> Gu *mahmókš* SaP: <*macpimujmogosp*> [*makpimuhmogošp*] TxZ: <*bacbosná*> [*bakbosná*] (*bakbósna?*) [Clark 1982] ChZ: *mak (ko) mosaŋ*

NS#026 ChisZ yɨt- *'15'* ChisZ: C *yɨhta?y* NE *yɨhta?*

NS#027 pMZ *mak-tu? ~ mak-tuh *'16'* NHM: *maktʊht* SHM: Ay *maktúhk* Tm *mahktúht* MM: Ma,Ja *mahmokštú?k* Pu *mahmokštú!k* At *mahkmokštú"k* Ct *mahkmokštu?k* LM: Cn <*mahmokštu"k*> Gu *mahmokštú"k* SaP: <*macpimujtujtup*> [*makpimuhtuhtup*] TxZ: <*bactujná*> [*baktuhná*] *baktúhna?* [Clark 1982]

NS#028 ChisZ yɨt-ko-tumɨ *'16'* ChisZ: C *yɨt-ko-tumɨ* NE *yɨt-ko-tumɨ*

NS#029 pMZ *mak-huwɨs-tu? ~ mak-huwɨs-tuh *'17'* NHM: *makvɨštʋht* SHM: Ay <*makushtúk*> [Beals 1945], *makstúhk* [Wichmann 1990] Tm *mahk hɨštúhk* MM: Ma,Ja,Pu *mahmokšmǽhck* At,Ct *mahkmokšmǽhck* LM: Cn <*mahmokšmec*> Gu *mahmokšméck* SaP: <*macpimujguxtujtup*> [*makpimuhhuštuhtup*] TxZ: <*bac'huestujná*> [*bakwestuhná*] (*bakwɨstúhna?*) [Clark 1982]

NS#030 ChisZ yɨt-ko-meca *'17'* ChisZ: C *yɨt-ko-meca* NE *yɨtkomeca*

NS#031 pMZ *mak-tuku-tuhtu- *'18'* NHM: *maktʊdʋht* SHM: Ay *maktuktúk* Tm *mahktu?ktúhk* LM: Cn <*mahmokštugɨ:g*> SaP: <*macpimujtugutujtup*> [*makpimuhtugutuhtup*] TxZ: <*bactujtujná*> [*baktuhtuhná*] (*baktuhtúhna?*) [Clark 1982]

NS#032 ChisZ yɨt-ko-tuk- *'18'* ChisZ: C *yɨt-ko-tuka?y* NE *yɨt-kotuka?*

NS#033 pMZ ***makta:s-tuku-tuhtu-** *[?]* '19' [Double obliques separate what would be separate sets.] NHM: *maktaštʋht* SHM: Ay *maktaštúk* Tm *mahktaštúhk* At *mahkta·štúhk* // MM: Ma *mahmokšmahktá·š̄k* Ja *mahmokšmahktá·šk* Pu *mahmokšmahtá·š̄k* Ct *mahkmokšmahktá·š̄k* LM: Cn <*mahmokšmɨda:š*> Gu *mahkmokšmɨdá·š̄k* // SaP: <*macpimujtagaxtujtup*> [*makpimuhtagaštuhtup*] // TxZ: <*bacbacstujná*> [*bakbakstuhná*] (*bakbakstúhna?*) [Clark 1982]

NS#034 ChisZ **yɨt-ko-mak(ta)s-** '19' ChisZ: C *yɨt-ko-makšku?y* NE *yɨt-ko-makšku?*

NS#035 pMZ ***?i:?ps** '20' NHM: *?i:?pš* SHM: Tl *?e:?pš* Ay *?e?pš* Tm *?e?pš* MM: Ju,Ma,Ja,At,Ct *?i?pš* Pu *?i!pš* LM: Ca *?ipš* Gu *?i·?š* Cn <*i:pš*> OlP: *i:pšɨ* SaP: <*ipx*> [*ipš*] *i?pš* TxZ: <*ipxñá*> [*ipšñá*] *é?pšña?* [Clark 1982]; *?é?pšña?* [Clark n.d.] ChisZ: C,NE *?ips* ChZ: *?ipsaŋ*

NS#036 pM ***?i:?ps-tu?** '21' NHM: *?i:?pštʋ?k* SHM: Ay <*epshtúk*> Tm *?e?pštú?uk* MM: Ma,Ja,Ct *?i?pštú?k* At *?i?pštú"k* LM: Gu *?i·?štú"k* SaP: <*ipxtuc*> [*ipštuk*] (*i?pštu?k*)

NS#037 pZ ***?ips-(ko)-tum-** '21' TxZ: <*ipxtumná*> [*ipštumná*] (*e?pštúmna?*) ChisZ: C *?ips-ko-tumɨ*

NS#038 pMZ ***?i:?ps-(ko)-mec-** '22' SHM: Ay <*epshmátsk*> Tm *?e?pšmáhck* ChisZ: C *?ips-ko-meca*

NS#039 pMZ ***?i:?ps-tuku-** '23' SHM: Ay <*epshtugúg*> Tm *?e?pštɨgɨ:k* ChisZ: C *?ips-ko-tuka?y*

NS#040 pMZ ***?i:?ps-(ko)-makta:s-** '24' SHM: Ay <*epshmatáshk*> ChisZ: C *?ips-ko-makšku?y* NE *ips-ko-makšku?*

NS#041 pMZ ***?i:?ps-(ko)-m(ok)os** '25' SHM: Ay <*epshmagóshk*> ChisZ: C *?ips-ko-mos*

NS#042 pMZ ***?i:?ps-(ko)-tuhtu-** '26' SHM: Ay <*epstudúk*> ChisZ: C *?ips-ko-tuhta?y*

NS#043 pMZ ***tuku-tuhtu-** '28' SHM: Ay <*epstuktúk*> ChisZ: C *?ips-ko-tukutuhta?y*

NS#044 pMZ ***?i:?ps-mak-** '30' NHM: *?i:?pšmahk* SHM: Ay *?e?pšmók* Tm *?e?pšmáhk* MM: Ju,Ma,Ja,At,Ct *?i?pšmáhk* LM: Cn

<i:pšmahk> Gu *ʔi·ʔšmáhk* SaP: <ipximucmap> [ipšimukmap] (ipšimukmakp) TxZ: <ipxcomoc> [ipškomok] (eʔpškomak) [Clark 1982] ChisZ: C *ʔips-ko-mak* NE *ips-ko-mahka?*

NS#045 pMZ **ʔi:ʔps-(ko)-mak-tu? ~ ʔi:ʔps-(ko)-mak-tum* '31'
SHM: Ay <epsmaktúk> Tm *ʔeʔpšmahktúʔuk* TxZ: <ipxcomoctumná> [ipškomoktumná] (eʔpškomaktúmna?) [Clark 1982] ChisZ: C *ʔips-ko-maktuma?y*

NS#046 pMZ **wɨs-tɨk-ʔi:ʔps* '40'* NHM: *vïhštkupš* SHM: Tl *wištɨhkš^y* Tm *štikš^y* Ay *ʔištíkš^y* MM: Ju,Ma,Ct *hɨš^yt^yíkš^y* Ja *huš^yikš* Pu,At *wɨš^yt^yíkš^y* LM: Ca *wɨš^yt^yíkš^y* Ml <wišyčikšy> Cn <wišyčigi"pš> Gu *huš^yčɨgíʔš* SaP: <machipx> [mečipš] TxZ: <vuuskipx> [vuuskipš] (wɨskeʔpš) [Clark 1982] ChisZ: C *wɨstɨhkiʔs* NE *wɨstɨhkips*

NS#047 pMZ **wɨs-tɨk-ʔi:ps-mak-* '50'* NHM: *vïhštkupšɨkmahk* SHM: Ay <hustikshmák> [Beals 1945], *ʔištikš^ym^yɨhk* [Wichmann 1990] Tm *štikš^ym^yahk* Tu,Tp *βɨštikš^ym^yáhk* Mi *wišteks^ym^yáhk* MM: Ju,Ct *hɨš^yt^yikš^ym^yáhk* Ma,Pu *š^yt^yikš^ym^yáhk* Ja *huš^yčikš^ym^yáhk* At *wɨš^yt^yikš^ym^yáhk* LM: Ml <wišyčikšymahk> Cn <wišyčigi"pš mahk> Ca *wɨš^yt^yikš^ym^yáhk* Gu *huš^yčɨgiʔšmáhk* SaP: <mogoxmac> [mogošmak] TxZ: <vuuskipx comöc> [vuuskipškomɨk] (wɨskeʔpškomak) [Clark 1982] ChisZ: C *wɨstɨhkiʔs-ko-mak* NE *wɨstɨhkips-ko-mahk*

NS#048 pMZ **tuku-ʔi:ps-* '60'* NHM: *tv:gupš* SHM: Tl *tuki?pš^y* Ay <tigúbsh> [Beals 1945] Tm *tɨgi?pš^y* MM: Ju,Ma,Ja,At,Ct *tɨgíʔpš* LM: Cn <tugɨ"pš> Gu *tɨgïːgʔí·ʔš* SaP: <tujtujmac> [tuhtuhmak] TxZ: <tuguipx> [tugu ipš] (tugukeʔpš) ChisZ: C *tuki?s* NE *tukips* ChZ: *tugaʔn ipsaŋ*

NS#049 pMZ **tuku-ʔi:ps-mak-* '70'* NHM: *tv:gupšɨkmahk* SHM: Tm *tɨgi?pšm^yáhk* Ay *ʔigi?pšmɨɨhk* MM: Ma *tɨgi?pšmáhk* Ja *tɨgɨ?pšmáhk* At *tɨgi?pšmáhk* Ct *tɨgɨ?pšmáhk* LM: Cn <tugɨ"pš mahk> Gu *tɨgïːgʔí·ʔškumáhk* SaP: <guxtujtujmac> [huštuhtuhmak] TxZ: <tuguipx comöc> [tugu ipš komɨk] (tugukeʔpškomak) [Clark 1982] ChisZ: C *tuki?s-ko-mak* NE *tukips-ko-mahk*

NS#050 pMZ **makta:s-ʔi:ʔps-* '80'* NHM: *mahktupš* SHM: Ay *makta?pš* Tm *maktæ?pš^y* MM: Ju,Ma,Ja,At,Ct *mahktá?pš* Pu *mahktá!pš* LM: Cn <mɨda"pš> SaP: <tugutujtujmac>

[*tugutuhtuhmak*] TxZ: <*bac chipx*> [*bak čipš*] (*bakské?pš*) [Clark 1982]; *bak?ê?pš* '400 = 80 "manos" (medida de a 5)' [Wichmann fc.-c] ChisZ: C *maktahsi?s*

NS#051 pMZ *makta:s-?i:?ps-mak '90' NHM: *mahktupšĭkmahk* SHM: Tm *maktœ?pš^ym^yáhk* Ay *makta?pšm^yĭhk* MM: Ju,Ma,Ja,At,Ct *mahkta?pšmáhk* Pu *mahkta!pšmáhk* LM: Cn <*mĭda"pšmahk*> Gu *mĭda·šk?i·?škumáhk* SaP: <*taxtujtujmac*> [*taštuhtuhmak*] TxZ: <*bac chipx comöc*> [*bak čipš komĭk*] (*bakske?pšbákna?*) [Clark 1982] ChisZ: C *maktahsi?s-ko-mak*

NS#052 pMZ *m(ok)os-?i:?ps '100' NHM: *mókupš* SHM: Tl *makʋ?pš^y* Ay *tukmuge?pš* Tm *tu?kmigé?pš^y* Tu *mĭgœ?pš^y* Tp *mĭgó?pš^y* MM: Ju,Ma,Ja,At,Ct *mĭgó?pš* Pu *mĭgó!pš* LM: Cn <*mĭgo"pš*> Ca *mogó?pš* Gu *mĭgó?š* OIP: *aukuptuki* SaP: <*tucmun*> [*tuk mun*] *tu?k mun* TxZ: <*box*> [*boš*] *boské?pš* [Clark 1982] ChisZ: C *mohsi?s* NE *mohsips* ChZ: *mosaŋ ipsaŋ*

NS#053 pMZ *m(ok)os-?i:?ps-ko-?i:?ps '120' SHM: Ay <*tukmugépsh kaépsh*> Tm *mĭge?pš ?e?pš* ChisZ: C *mohsi?s-ko-ips*

NS#054 pMZ *m(ok)os-?i:?ps-wĭs-tĭk-?i:?ps '140' SHM: Ay <*tukmugépsh haushtĭksh*> ChisZ: C *mohsi?s-ko-wĭstĭhki?s*

NS#055 pMZ *m(ok)os-?i:?ps-wĭs-tĭk-i:?ps-mak '150' SHM: Ay <*tukmugépsh haushtĭksh mak*> ChisZ: C *mohsi?s-ko-wĭstĭhki?s-ko-mak*

NS#056 pM *mec-mok(os)-?i:?pš '200' NHM: *mehck mókupš* SHM: Ay *macmĭge?pš* Tm *mahck mĭge?pš* LM: Cn <*mehc mĭgo"pš*>

NS#057 '200' ChisZ: C *mahki?s* ChZ: *magaŋ ipsaŋ*

NS#058 '300' ChisZ: C *yĭhti?s*

NS#059 '320' ChisZ: C *yĭhti?s-ko-ips*

NS#060 pMZ *mon?i '*zontle (medida de 400)/zontle (measure of 400)*' OIP: *mo?ni* SaP: *mo?n* TxZ: *bo:n* '=80 "manos"' [Wichmann fc.-b] ChisZ: C,NE *tumĭ mone?* S [*tum moné?*] 'un zontle'

NS#061 pMZ *makta:s-m(ok)os-?i:?ps '400' NHM: *makta:šk mókupš* SHM: Ay *maktašmĭge?pš* MM: Ma *mahkta·šmĭgó?pš* Ja *mahkta·šmĭgó?pš* Pu *ta·škmĭgó?pš* At *ta·šmĭgó?pš* Ct

mahkta·šmɨgó?pš   LM: Gu *mɨda·šmɨgó?š*   TxZ: <*bacsnabox*>
[*baksnaboš*] (*baksnaboš*) [Clark 1982]; *Ba?kške?pšBós* [Clark n.d.]

NS#062 pOM *mokoš-mokoš-?i:?pš   '500'   NHM: *mugo:šk mókupš*
SHM: Ay *mogošmɨge?pš* MM: Ju *mɨgoškmɨgó?pš* Ma *mɨgo·šmɨgó?pš*
Ja *mɨgo·šmɨgó?pš* At *mɨgo·škmɨgó?pš* Ct *mɨgo·šmɨgó?pš* LM: Gu
mɨgo·šmɨgó?š

NS#063 '1000' TxZ <*bacnabox*>   [*baknaboš*]   *baknaboš* [Clark
1982]

Derivational Morphology

Default sources for this section are LM-SJ: Van Haitsma and Van Haitsma (1976), MM: Nordell (1990), NHM: Schoenhals and Schoenhals (1965), TaM: Lehmann (1920), OlP: Clark (1981), SaP: Clark (1961), SoZ: (Elson 1960), ChZ: Knudson (1980), ChisZ-N: Engel and Engel (1987), -NE: Harrison and Harrison (1984), -C: Wonderly (1951-52).

Abbreviations and conventions used in the information about the position of a morpheme in the word, the parts of speech with which it combines, and whatever derivational properties it may have are

"→"	'affixation causes shift in wordclass or transitivity'
"n"	'noun'
"a"	'attributive' (=adjective or adverb)
"v"	'verb'
"i"	'intransitive'
"t"	'transitive'
"aux"	'auxiliary'
"dem"	'demonstrative'
"part"	'particle'
"pron"	'pronoun'
"{}"	'position (to the right or the left) of the stem'
"^"	'word-clitic boundary'

Other conventions: When the source has a system for numbering the affixes, the number will occur within the curly brackets. So, for instance, "n → v{241}" means: "the morpheme, which is numbered #241 in the default source for the given language, is affixed to the left of a noun stem, thereby causing it to change into a verb stem." The grammatical information may not always be complete since I include only the information the source is explicit about and reserve interpretive efforts for the protoforms. In the end of some of the cognate sets I quote selected reconstructed stems that contain the grammatical morpheme in question from elsewhere in Part Two. These quotations will be introduced by the symbol □.

For inflectional morphology and the morphology of numerals see 3.5-.6.

I am implicit about the positions of the morphemes in the stem organization of the individual languages. Kaufman (1963), who was more explicit about this, referred to positions in the (inner) derivational and (outer) inflectional layer by means of two sets of numbers (negative for prefixes, positive for suffixes), one for each layer. In 3.6 I presented my view of the position of each proto-morpheme in the overall morphological layout.

Verb Morphology

DM#001 pMZ ***yak-** *'causative'* [Recognized by Kaufman (1963: 70, 3122) as a position -3 verbal derivational prefix.] LM-SJ *yah-* {}v 'causative (always transitive), instrumental, locative, passive (intransitivizing), direct object (when preceded by the prefix *mɨ·-*)'. OIP *yak-* {}v 'causative' (raises transitivity but may also occur on intransitive stems and have passive meaning). SaP *ʔak-* v → {}vt 'causative' [The reanalysis whereby *y* is taken to be identical with the 3p prefix such that *y* → Ø is likely to have been borrowed from Gulf Zoquean.] ChisZ-C *yah-* {21}v 'causative-permissive'. SoZ *ʔak-* {21}v,{53}n 'causativo'. ChZ *yak-* {}v 'causative'. □ The prefix is attested in numerous reconstructed stems, e.g., pMZ *yak-toy 'to light' ← *toy 'to burn, hurt'.

DM#002 pMZ ***nay-** *'reciprocal/reflexive'* [Recognized by Kaufman as a position -3 verbal derivational affix. He notes that "[i]n the Zoque group this suffix seems always to co-occur with the suffix *tah* of the +3 position. *tah* also occurs without *nay-*" (1963: 71, 3123).] LM-SJ *na·y-* {}v 'reflexive/reciprocal' (intransitivizing). OIP *ni-* {}v 'reflexive'. SaP *ni-* {}v 'personal/reciprocal' [also a reflex of *ni:* 'associative'—the two prefixes fell together in SaP as Kaufman already observed.] SoZ *nah-* {31}v 'reflexivo-recíproco'. ChisZ-C *nay-* {111}v 'reciprocal'. ChZ *-ney* 'mismo' [in *yɨhi-ney* 'aquí mismo'; may not be cognate].

DM#003 pM(Z) **mu:-** *'associative (with)'* [Not productive in Zoquean but has survived in a single lexical item in ChisZ-C. Not recognized by Kaufman who thinks (1963: 71, 3123) that SaP *mu-* and OM *mɨ(t)-* (he invents the parenthesis, i.e., conflates two different forms) are identical with the pM conjunction **mɨ:t*. Against this are the poor phonological correspondence and the fact that LM-SJ has another prefix *mɨ:d-*, which is definitely from **mɨ:t*]. LM-SJ *mɨ·-* {}v,{}n 'associative (with)' (on verbs it is transitivizing *or* intransitivizing), {}a 'relative order' (the suffix takes the function of deriving ordinal numerals in Oaxaca Mixean at large, e.g., NHM *mu-*) OIP *mɨ:-* {}v 'associative (with)' (valency-augmenting)'. SaP *mu-* {}n,{}v 'associative (with)' (e.g., *mu-cúgin* 'enemy', *mu-nɨš* 'to go with, carry', *mu-mín* 'to bring'). ChisZ-C *mu?-šihk* vi 'sonreir' (this has NHM cognate *mu-ši:k ~ mu-ši?ik* 'reir con alguien'; the glottal of the ChisZ form is probably a contamination from *mu?* vt 'to play'; a simple compound of 'to play' + 'to laugh' is a possibility, but a weak one). □ pOM **mu-huhy ~ mu-huy* 'to pay' ← **huhy ~ huy* 'buy'; pOM **mu-šɨhw* 'namesake' ← **šɨhw* 'fiesta, name, sun'; pM **mu-yuh* 'to become accostumed to' ← *yuh* 'to accustom, feel at home'.

DM#004 pMZ **ko:-** *'benefactive'* [Kaufman (1963: 70, 3122) bases a reconstruction of a position -1 verbal prefix **ko-* on SaP *ku-*, SoZ *ku-*, and ChisZ-C *ko- ~ ko?-*. The last two are indeed cognate, but SaP *ku-* belongs to a different set.] OIP *ko:-* {}v 'benefactive?' (e.g., *i-ko-?o:k-tu:t-pe* '1. lo deja viudo, 2. se muere y deja su trabajo', *i-ko:-puh-pe i-tuku* 'está lavando su ropa', *tɨ-naš-ko-?e:p-ta:k-pa* vi 'miro para abajo', *tɨn-ko:-ka?-ta:k-pe* vt 'caigo sobre algo'; *ko:-* is reduced to *ko-* before a glottal by way of regular morphophonemic rules). SaP *ko:-* {}v,{}n 'benefactive' [in Clark (1983: 6), e.g., *ko:-wan* 'to defend someone, *ko:-koc* 'to speak in behalf of someone'; in Clark and Clark 1960 these examples are cited with a short *o*.] SoZ *ku-* {11}v 'diferencia'. ChisZ-C *ko ~ ko?-* {11}v 'associative, etc.' (also contained in *kotoya-* pron{},n{} 'benefactive). ChZ *kɨ ~ ko* 'acción dirigida a/con otro'.

DM#005 pMZ **nɨ-** *'associative'* [Attestations for Veracruz Mixean are absent. Recognized by Kaufman 1963, but only for pZ, as a position -2 verbal derivative prefix. His protoform is **na-*.] NHM *nɨ-* v → {}vt 'associative'. LM-SJ *ni·-* v → {}v 'purposive (for, about)'. ChisZ-C *ni-* {13}v 'causative-associative'. SoZ *na-* {22}v 'causativo-associativo', {54}n 'associativo'. □ pMZ *ni-toy* 'to be wounded, or burnt' ← **toy* 'to burn, hurt'; pOM **ni-ke?k~ni-ke?ek* 'to leave behind' ← **ke?k~ke?ek* 'to fly'.

DM#006 pMZ *hɨ(s)- 'back' LM: SJ *hɨ·-* {}v 'out of the way, pertaining to the back'. ChZ *hɨs-* {}v 'acción dirigida atrás o aparte'.

DM#007 pMZ *?aw- 'pertaining to the mouth or other opening' [Kaufman (1963) recognizes a position -1 verbal prefix of this shape. To this he assigns the meaning 'endocentricity', which would mirror the other prefix he reconstructs for this class: **ko-* (my **ko:-* 'benefactive'), meaning 'extensive' or 'exocentricity'.] Kaufman admits (1963: 70, 3122) that he does not offer a clear understanding of the meaning and function of these morphemes. In OM the prefix seems to have become productive with an iterative meaning. Cf. also my work (1993c, secs. 1.2.3, 1.4.6). LM-SJ *?a·-* {}v 'iterative, pertaining to an opening'. OIP *?aw-* {}v (e.g., *?a:-pa:t-pa* 'besa a un santo', *?a:-ma:-pa* vi 'está clueca'). SaP *?a-* {}v 'simultaneity'. SoZ *?aŋ-* {12}v 'simultaneidad'. ChZ *?aŋ-* {}v 'perceptional' ChisZ-C *?a~-* {15}v 'perceptional, etc.'. □ pMZ **?aw-cow* 'to answer' ← **cow* 'to unite'; pMZ **?aw-kɨ:y?* 'to plug, close' ← **kɨ:y?* 'to carry flat object'; pMZ **?aw-tuk* 'to close' ← **tuk* 'to sever fruits, etc., from the plant'; pM **?aw-tih* 'to jam' ← **tih* 'to tighten'; pM **?aw-?iš* 'to wait' ← **?iš* 'to see'; pM **?aw-cɨ:nay* 'to wait' ← **cɨ:nay* 'to sit down'; pOM **?a-nu?kš* 'to ask for permission to borrow' ← **nu?kš* 'to borrow'; pOM **?a-cuhm~?a-cum* 'to wrap up' ← **cuhm-cum* 'to tie'; pZ **aŋ-ki?m* 'to order' ← **ki?m* 'to ascend'; pZ **yak-?aŋ-ka?m* 'to close' ← pZ *ka?m* 'to press'.

DM#008 pMZ *ni:- {}v,{}n,{}a 'to surface, corporeal' [Not even traces of this morpheme are found in SaP, whereas it is very productive in both LM and OIP. It has varying reflexes in Oaxaca, sometimes even within a single dialect, and no rules have been found that can describe the phonological alternations. Not in Kaufman, who claims that ChisZ-C *ni-* {61}n has no cognates in other languages (1963: 115, 3320.4). NHM *ni-*. MM: Ma *ni-* Ja *ni-~ni"-* Ju *ni-* Pu *ni-~ni-*. LM: SJ *ni"-* {}v,{}n,{}a 'pertaining to the body, skin, surface (on, over; literally and figuratively)' Cn *ni·-~ni-* Gu *ni"-*. OIP *ni:-* n → {}a,{}v 'surface, etc.'. ChisZ-C *ni-* {61}n 'surface' (only example in Wonderly

1951-52: *ni-yam* 'outer clothes'; cf. *yam* (vt) 'ponerselo, calzarselo', *yamwitu?* (vt) 'mudarse de ropa' in Harrison et al. 1981). ChZ *ni-~ni?-* {}v 'corpóreo'. □ pOM *ni:-hen* 'poncho' ← *hehn~hen* 'to take off clothes or shoes'; pOM *ni:-kiš-m* 'over' ← *kiš-m* 'up, high'; pOM *ni-wa"c* 'naked' ← *wa"c* 'clean'; pM *ni:-šik* 'itchy' ← *šik* 'itch'.

DM#009 pMZ ***ku-** *'from surface'* [As yet no parallels to Mixean **u* = Zoquean **i* have been found. So phonologically the reconstruction is still weakly supported.] SaP *ku-* {}v 'surface/specifier' (e.g., *ku-wiš-* 'pluck feathers from ← *wiš* 'uproot') indicates a related but more specific action that differs from the normal routine action suggested in the root form (e.g., *ku-wi?t* 'to rewring' ← *wi?t* 'to wring', *ku-pik* 'to believe' ← *pik* 'to take—as in marriage. It occurs with motion verbs to indicate specialized action with reference to someone or something (e.g., *ku-po?k* 'to flee from' ← *po?k* 'to flee', *ku-niš* 'to go to' ← *niš* 'to go', *ku-yo?y* 'to investigate' ← *yo?y* 'to walk'); frequently combines with *-i* 'activizer' to form verb stems of 'accidental action'—a meaning very close to that of Zoquean **ki-* (which, at least in SoZ, combines with the suffix *-i*; cf. Elson [1960: 55]; SaP may have borrowed this affix combination from Gulf Zoquean). ChisZ-N *ki-* {}v "El prefijo *ki-* indica que una cosa se quita de otra de la que formaba parte o que se reduce o se pierde completamente. . . . Los verbos transitivos con el prefijo *ki-* implican que el sujeto le quita parcialmente algo al complemento indirecto. . . . El prefijo *ki-* en unos cuantos vocablos parece señalar algo diferente al sentido de quitar" (Engel and Engel 1987: 371-372). ChisZ-C *ki-~ki?-* {12}v ". . . denota generalmente acción ejecutada con otra persona o con una cosa" (Harrison et al. 1981: 423); "chance-associative" (Wonderly 1951-52: 138).

DM#010 pMZ ***nah-** *'circumvention'* [The etymon is weakly supported. The "reflexes" may be individual lexicalizations of some former free motion verb. But which?] LM-SJ *na·-* {}v 'to circumvent (around)'. ChZ *nah-* 'va a ir a' (tema que require que lo preceda la forma gerundiva pero tiene otros sufijos).

Derivational Verb Suffixes

DM#011 pMZ *-ʔoy 'antipassive' [The suffix is well attested in Zoquean. The available sources for Oaxaca Mixean points to the possibility that the suffix may have merged with another suffix of the shape **-ay* in what in LM appears as *-ɨ·y* 'iterative/directional' and in NHM as the 'root extension' *-i/a* (see 7.1). The only available evidence for this, however, is the possible cognate status of NHM *maʔyi ~ maya* 'to multiply', LM *mayɨ·y* 'to multiply', and ChisZ-C *maʔyoy* (vi) 'to count'.] SaP *-i* v{} 'extension/verbalizer'. SoZ *-oʔy* v{213} 'intransitivizer'. ChisZ-C *-ʔoy-* v{212} 'generalizing' ChZ *-ʔoy* v{} 'intransitivizer'.

DM#012 pMZ *-hay 'valency-augmenting' The etymon pMZ **su:sʔ-hay* 'to whistle at' ← **su:s* 'to whistle' shows that a suffix *-hay* is present in OlP and ChisZ-NE.

DM#013 pMZ *-ʔɨy v,n,a → v{} '*inchoative, etc.'* NHM *-i/a* (pre-NHM **-ʔɨy* as in Midland Mixe verb stems cited in Nordell 1990). SaP *-i* v{} 'extension/verbalizer'. TxZ *-ɨʔy*. SoZ *-ɨʔy* n → v{241} 'posesivo'. ChisZ: C *-ʔɨy* v,n,a → v{241} "marks a wide range of specialized meanings" (Wonderly 1951: 152); "tiene significado variado" (Harrison et al. 1981: 424); n *-ɨy* v,n → v{} "la raíz intransitiva con *-ɨy* indica que el sujeto tiene lo que la raíz significa. . . . Con algunos raíces verbales intransitivas el sufijo *-ʔɨy* indica que la ubicación de la acción o la vía del movimiento es importante. No resulta en verbo transitivo. . . . La raíz transitiva con *-ʔɨy* señala que el sujeto puso en algo que la raíz simple significa." NE *-ʔɨy* v,n → {}v. ChZ *-ʔɨy* v,n → v{} "generalizador o verbalizador; el verbalizador hace de un tema verbal un verbo y se traduce como 'se hace...' o 'tiene...'," n{} 'possesive' (e.g., *nas-ɨy* 'tierra de', *kopag-ʔɨy* 'cabeza-de', *pɨʔnɨy* 'hombre de'); *-ʔɨh* v{} 'personalizador de una calidad' (e.g., *tob-ɨh-pa* 'tiene calor' ← *toppa* 'hace calor', *nuzɨhpa* 'suda' ← *nucpa* 'está caliente', *wayaʔyɨhpa* 'tiene frío' ← *wayaʔy* 'está frío'; notice that in these attestations the phonological environment is everywhere the same, i.e., *-pa*; there could possibly be other allomorphs). □ pMZ **pahak-ʔɨy* 'to sweeten' ← **pahak* 'sweet'; pMZ **tɨk-ʔɨy* 'to enter' ← **tɨk* 'house'; pOM **pɨhk-ʔɨy* 'to be ill' ← **pɨhk ~ pɨk* 'to hurt'; pZ **nɨy-ʔɨy* 'to baptize' ← **nɨyi* 'name'.

DM#014 p(M)Z *-**nay** *'aimless, corporeal, reduplication'* SaP -*na* v{}
'positional'—also occurs with reduplicated verb stems indicating
'repetitive'; -*na* v^{},n^{},a^{} 'durative' [Zoquean borrowing?]. SoZ
-*ne?* 'persistente' (indicates that the result of past actions still continues
or that an action is still is progress; has an optional allomorph -*ni* in
unaccented positions before a consonant). ChisZ-C -*nay-* ~ -*ñay-*
v{215} 'aimless or corporeal'. aChZ -*nay* v{} 'corpóreo, acción sin
intención' (also used automatically in reduplicated stems).

DM#015 pMZ *-**i:y?** *'directional'* LM: SJ -*i·y* ~ *i"y* v{} 'iterative/-
directional' SoZ: -*i?yi?y* v{211} 'dirección'.

DM#016 p(M)Z *-**pi?** v,a → v{} *'all, distributive'* [Recognized by
Kaufman (1963: 72, 3124) as a position 2 verbal suffix]. SaP -*pi?n*
'action inclusive, all' (e.g., *nišpingap* 'they all go' [Zoquean
borrowing?]. SoZ -*piy* 'medida, dimensión' (e.g., *te:ñ-piy* 'la altura
de un hombre' ← *te:n* 'pararse', *y-iks-piy* 'como este, como este
tanto' ← *y-iks* 'como este'. ChisZ-C -*pi?-* v → v{211} 'completive,
reversive, etc.' (e.g., *pik-pi?* 'to take all' ← *pik* 'to take', *cik-pi?* 'to
do completely' ← *cihk* 'do', *pahčihk-pi?* 'walk all around' ← *pahčihk*
'take a walk'.

DM#017 p(M)Z *-**itah** *'reciprocal'.* [Recognized by Kaufman (1963:
73, 3126) as a pZ position 3 verbal derivative suffix. He comments that
"this morpheme is of obligatory occurrence whenever the prefix **nay-*
'reciprocal' of -3 position is present. It may also derive passive (intransitive) verbs from transitive verb stems."] LM-SJ -*ta·y* ~ -*ta"* v{}
'all' (e.g., *yahtina·yi?kta"* 'put them all up!') [?]. SoZ -*ta:* v{521}
'asociado indefinido'. ChisZ-C -*Xa/i tih* v{521} 'mandatory or reciprocal, non-3p plural recipient' (*X* is a morphophoneme causing the
change to *w* of a preceding *ŋ*), *yatih* v{522} 'mandatory or reciprocal,
3p plural recipient'. ChZ -*itah-* 'reciprocal' (e.g., *ney yutihpa* 'se
golpean—uno a otro'—as against *yutpa* 'golpea').

Noun Morphology: Prefixes

DM#018 pM(Z) *-**ko-:** *'ownership, step-, half-'* [Recognized by
Kaufman (1963: 76, 3132) for pM as a position -1 nominal derivative
prefix meaning 'for someone else'.] LM-SJ *ko·-* 'ownership, step-,
half-'. OlP *ko:-* {}n 'augmentative (?); step-' (e.g., *ko:-pu?pu* 'panzón'

← *pu?pu* 'barriga', *ko:-te:ku* 'dueño' ← *te:ku* 'dueño'— *te:ku* may be a Uto-Aztecan borrowing—*ko:-vayɨ* 'peludo' ← *vayɨ* 'cabello', *ko:-kapa?p* 'frijolillo [hierba]' ← *kapa?p* 'pecho', *ko:-ma?hi* 'sueño' ← *ma?hi* 'sueño'; *ko:-takaw* 'padrastro' ← *takaw* 'padre', *ko:-cɨ?* 'madrastra', *ko?una'k* 'entenado', *hay-ko-?o:ke* 'viudo' [unspecified sex]. SaP *ko(:)-* {}n 'benefactive' [vowel long in Clark and Clark (1960: 11,12,117,123), but short in Clark (1961: 182)]. ChisZ-C *ko-* {}n 'step-'. □ pMZ **ko-?a(h)ci* 'elder (not oldest) brother' ← **?a(h)ci* 'elder brother'; pM **ko:-te:tE* 'stepfather' ← **te:tE* 'father'; pOM **ku-ta:k* 'stepmother' ← **ta:k* 'mother'; pZ **ko-mama* 'stepmother' ← **mama* 'stepmother'.

DM#019 pMZ *?aw- 'perception, pertaining to the mouth' < pMZ *?aw 'mouth' [Recognized by Kaufman (1963: 76, 3132) for pZ as a position -1 nominal derivative prefix.] LM-SJ *?a-* {}n 'iterative; pertaining to the mouth'. OIP *?aw-* {}n 'mouth' (e.g., *?au-?e:ši* 'idioma de los estranjeros', *?au-kehku* 'mentón', *?au-tɨ?tɨ* 'tartamudo', *?avɨ* 'boca'). SoZ *?aŋ-* {51}n 'punta' (also contained in *-aŋho:m* {623}n 'entre' and *aŋ-ku?k* n{627} 'en medio de'. ChisZ-C *?aŋ-* {51}n,a 'mouth, etc.' (also contained in *-?aŋi* n{615} 'locative' and *-?aŋɨ* n{616} 'locative'). ChZ *-?aŋ* v → n{} 'perceptivo o que pertenece a la cara o superficie' (e.g., *ma?ŋaŋ* 'pasos' ← *maŋ* 'walk', *maktuma?aŋ* 'once' ← *maktumɨ* 'once'). □ pMZ **?aw-?ak* 'lip' ← **?ak* 'bark, skin'; pOM **?a-pahk* 'beak, snout' ← **pahk* 'bone'; pZ **?aŋ-kɨ?* 'patio' ← **kɨ?* 'hand, arm'; pMZ **aw-nɨ:?* 'spit' ← **nɨ:?* 'water'; pZ **aŋ-sis* ← **sis* 'meat'; pZ **aŋ-siŋ* 'season of the year' ← **siŋ* 'fiesta'; pOM **?a-yu:hk* 'Mixe language' ← **yu:hk* 'woods' (perhaps formerly 'land, territory'; cf. the meaning 'tierra' in Tapachulteco).

DM#020 pMZ *ko-~ko?- 'head, reach' [The development **o > u* which is found both in SaP and SoZ may be an areal phenomenon which, according to our theory of a Gulf Zoquean substratum must have originated in Zoquean. Recognized by Kaufman 1963 for pMZ as a position -1 nominal derivative prefix. He reconstructs **ko-*]. LM-SJ **ko?-* v → {}v, {}n,a 'pertaining to the head, top'. OIP *ko?-* {}n 'pertaining to the head' (e.g., *ko?-pa'k* 'cabeza', *ko?-pa'n* 'sombrero', *ko?-ši?k* 'sesos', *ko?-takɨ* 'calvo', *ko?-vita'n* 'caballete, la cima de una casa'). SaP *ku-* {}n,{}v 'extremative' (e.g., *ku-mo?n* 'sombrero'). SoZ *ku-* {52}n 'alcance' ChisZ-C *ko·-~ko?-* {52}n,a 'head, etc.'.

DM#021 pMZ ***ma-** *'days hence'* LM: SJ *ma·-* {}a 'ago in relationship to time' SoZ *ma-* {56}n 'días pasados'.

Ligature

DM#022 pMZ ***-ko-** *n{}n 'ligature in nominal compounds'* [The status of this reconstruction is not secured. Certainly it is rare: only found in a dubious pM reconstruction **mo?co-ko-mo?n* 'shelf' (based on only OlP and SaP) and in pChisZ **mok-ko-tɨk* n 'corn granary'.]

Noun Morphology: Suffixes

DM#023 pMZ ***-Ø** v → n{} *'deverbalizer'* [Van Haitsma and Van Haitsma 1976 analyze the reflex of this as -*?*, although, in my view, Ø- would be a possible synchronic analysis; consider *kɨ·y ~ kɨ"* 'to carry' → *kɨ"* 'hand', *mu·w ~ mu"* 'to hum' → *mu"* 'grasshopper', *ke·w ~ ke"* 'to sting' → *ke"* 'stinging insect, worm'. These all have cognates. The morpheme is not listed in the grammars of other MZ languages, but is nevertheless present (though productively only in Oaxaca Mixean) and everywhere has the shape -Ø.] □ pMZ **?it* 'place' ← pMZ **?it* 'to be, exist'; pZ **cem* 'urine' ← pZ **cem* 'to urinate'.

DM#024 pMZ ***-ɨ/a** v → n{},a{} *'deverbalizer (result)'* [The alternation is governed by the height of the preceding vowel; whether a preceding *a* governs a high or low harmonic vowel is not determined. Recognized by Kaufman (1963: 77, 3133) as a position 1 nominal suffix with the meaning 'result of an action'.] LM-SJ *-ɨ:* v → n{} 'specific'. OlP: *-ɨ ~ -a* v → n{} (e.g., *poc-a* 'pared'; cf. *poc-e* 'embarro'; *kipš-ɨ* 'medida, una arroba', cf. *kipš-ɨ* 'medido'; *tay-a* 'cicatriz'). SaP *-a* {}n 'attributivizer' (may not be related since it is functionally different: *mo?c-a* 'muddy' ← *mo?c* 'mud', *na:š-a* 'dirty' ← *na:š* 'dirt'). ChisZ-C *-Xɨ/a* v → n,a{315} 'result' (e.g., *nem-a* 'flame', *no?-a* 'candle', *ko-yow-a* 'price', *cac-a* 'crack', *ki?m-ɨ* 'ascent', *wanak-ɨ* 'descent'). SoZ *-ɨ/a* v → n{315} *pú?·k-ɨ* 'úlcera tropical', *tɨŋpú?·k-ɨ* 'la milpa no quemada se preparó y sembró durante la época de lluvias', *mó·y-a* 'flor', *kuyšá?·m-ɨ* 'astilla', *aŋnáks-ɨ* 'viga longitudinal de la casa'. ChZ *-ɨ* v → n{}. □ pM **?a:?c-a* 'vine' ← **?a:?c* 'to grow (vine)'; pOM **tɨy-ɨ* 'straight' cf. pMZ **tɨy* 'to hang'; pChisZ **no?-a* 'candle' ← *no?* 'to light, set fire to'; pChisZ *sok-a* 'bachelor'; cf. pOM *šohk ~ šok* 'to keep guard, lurk'.

DM#025 pMZ *-i/e v → n{},a{} 'deverbalizer (product)' [Recognized by Kaufman (1963: 77, 3133) for pZ as a nominal derivative position 1 suffix meaning 'result of an action'.] LM-SJ ⁻ʸ v → n,a{} 'produces a derived noun, attribute, or adverb stem' (e.g., in the Van Haitsmas 1976 work, p.40: *cim-ʸ* 'cargo', *tu"d-ʸ* 'egg', *wi:d-ʸ* 'platform of poles tied together', *wih-ʸ* 'smart, sober'. OIP *-i/e* v → n{} 'nominalizer' (high-low harmony, e.g., *kapš-e* ← *kapš*, *?ikš-i* ← *?ikš*, *pih-i* ← *pih*, *koš-e* ← *koš*, *yoš-e* ← *yoš*, *han-e* [bound], *poc* ← *poc-e*, *ti?n-i* [bound]; to these should perhaps be added an example of a derived adjective, i.e., *hitityeye* adj. 'bien regado' containing *hiti't* 'delgado (persona/cosa)' and *-yey-* 'regar'). ChisZ-C *-Xi/e* v → n,a{314} 'result'. SoZ *-i* v → n{314} 'resultado'. ChZ *-i/e* v → n{} (e.g., *way-e* 'masa', *cik-i* 'hecho', *cak-e* 'dejado'). □ pMZ **?ec-e* 'dance' ← **?ec* 'to dance'; pMZ **?i:?c-i* 'vomit' ← *?i:?c* 'to vomit'; pMZ **?iks-i* 'grains of corn' ← **ikš* 'to shell (corn)'; pMZ **?an-e* 'tortilla' ← **?an* 'to sting, burn'; pMZ **?oc-i* 'folded, curly or rolled (as paper, hair or cigar); cf. pOM **?ohc ~ ?oc* 'to leave or return; to bend a long object'; pMZ **cim-i* 'load' ← **cim* 'to carry'; pMZ **cat?-e* 'one span of the hand (measure)' ← **cat?* 'to measure by the span of a hand'; pMZ **cu?c-i* 'meat' ← **cu?c* 'to suckle, chew'; pZ **cum-i* 'elbow'; cf. pM **cum* 'to tie'; pMZ **ni:p?-i* 'sown field, sowing time' ← **ni:p?* 'to sow'; pMZ **ni:wi* 'chili pepper'; cf. pChisZ **ni?ŋ* 'to emit heat'; pMZ **new-e* 'bent, twisted' cf. pOM **nehw ~ new* 'to bend, twist'; pMZ **pic-i* 'leached corn meal'; pMZ **pi:?t-i* 'thread' ← **pi:?t* 'to spin thread'; pMZ **pu:c?(-i)* 'pimple' ← **pu:c?* 'rot'; pMZ **ta:k?-e* 'cobweb' ← **ta:k?* 'to weave'; pMZ **wi:?t-i* 'twisted' ← **wi:?t* 'to wring, twist'; pMZ **way-e* 'ground, something ground' ← **way* 'to grind'; pMZ **yu:h?-i* 'field cleared for underbrush' ← **yu:h?* 'to clear underbrush'; pMZ **yos-e* 'work' ← **yos* 'to offer, work'.

DM#026 pMZ *-ik v → n{},a{} 'deverbalizer (inanimate participial)' OIP *-i'k* v → a,n (e.g., *te:n-i'k* 'escalera [de palo]', *toy-i'k* 'quemado', *ti:kš-i'k* 'está clara [el agua], *cuk-i'k* 'una cortada', *cuh-i'k* n 'saliva'). SaP *-ik* a,v → a{} 'participle' (e.g., *nú?m-ik* 'stolen' ← *nu?m* 'to steal', *há?y-ik* 'written' ← *ha?y* 'to write'). ChisZ-C *-Xihk(-)* v → n,a{316} (e.g., *mic-ihk(-)* 'toy' ← *mihc-* 'dependent root' cf. *mihciy* 'play'). □ pMZ **pih-i(k)* n 'flower' ← **pih* 'to swell up, flourish'.

DM#027 pMZ *-pɨʔ v,a → n{} 'participial (human participial)' LM-SJ
-pɨ/-b v,a → n{} 'one (a specific person or object)' (*-b* follows *y* or
replaces *w*, *-pɨ* occurs in all other positions. Some speakers drop the
final *ɨ*). SoZ *-pɨk* n{421} 'participial'. ChisZ-C *pɨ ~ -wɨ*
v,n,a,Dem,Num → Participle{441} 'suffix that appears in participle
stems' (the alternant in *p* most often follows consonants, the one in *w*
most often vowels, but the alternation is rather free according to
Wonderly [1952: 45]). ChZ *-pɨʔ ~ -p* n{} 'especificador: él que../el
uno que...' (e.g., *yos-pa* 'trabaja', *yos-pa-pɨʔ* 'él que trabaja', *yos-pa-p
pɨn* 'el hombre trabajador'). □ pChisZ **ʔaŋ-kiʔm-pa-pɨ* 'ruler' ←
*aŋ-kiʔm 'to order'; pChisZ **nuʔm-pa-pɨ* 'thief' ← **nuʔm* 'to steal,
rob'.

DM#028 pMZ *-kuy v → n{} 'deverbalizer (instrument)' [Attested in
a few reconstructed stems, not as a productive morpheme as such, in
Mixean. The sound laws that would account for its Mixean reflexes
have not yet been worked out. Recognized by Kaufman (1963: 76,
3133) as a position 1 nominal derivational suffix. The Tapachultec
Mixe form is quoted from Kaufman.] TaM *<ku>*. SoZ *-kuy* v →
{311}n 'instrumento, objeto'. ChisZ-C *-kuy* v → n,a{311} 'action,
instrument, etc.'. ChZ *-kuʔy* v → n{}. □ pMZ **haːyʔ-kuy* 'instrument
for writing' ← **haːyʔ* 'to write'; pMZ **ʔuːʔk-kuy* n 'drink' ← **ʔuːʔk*
'to drink'; pZ **mah-kuy* 'pitcher' ← **mah* 'to carry water'; pZ
*nuʔs-kuy 'blanket' ← **nuʔs* 'to cover'; pZ **pet-kuy* 'broom' ← **pet*
'to sweep'; pZ **sus-kuy* 'flute' ← **sus* 'to whistle, play a musical
instrument'; pZ **wiʔk-kuy* 'food' ← **wiʔk* 'to eat hot food'; pZ
*yos-kuy n 'work' ← **yos* 'to work.

DM#029 pMZ *-tɨk v → n{} 'deverbalizer (instrument)' [pMZ **-tɨk*
'place' and pMZ **tɨk* 'instrument' fell together in ChisZ-C. They originally differed as to stress. The latter has an irregular reflex in ChZ.]
LM-SJ *-t* v → n{} 'instrument' (only example: *tuht* 'gun' ← *tuh* 'to
hunt, to shoot a gun'). OIP *-tiʔk* v → n{} 'instrument' (e.g., *ʔiš-tiʔk*
'espejo; vidrio', *maː-tiʔk* 'cama'). ChisZ-C *-tɨhk(-)* n,v → n{321}
'habitat or instrument'. ChZ *-tɨ* v → n{} (e.g., *huku-tɨ* 'fuego').

DM#030 pMZ *-tɨk v,n → n{} 'place' LM-SJ *-ta·k* v → n{} 'place'
[*-tɨ·k* expected]. OIP: *-tɨkɨ* n{} 'lugar'. ChisZ-C *-tɨhk(-)* n,v → n{321}
'habitat or instrument'. □ pMZ **kam-tɨk* 'brush (acahual)'.

DM#031 pMZ ***-tɨk(ay)** *'plural'* LM-SJ *-tɨhk* n{} 'all, a group collectively'.   OIP *-tɨk* n{} 'plural' (e.g., *mi?niya?te-tɨk* 'fueranos', *tɨnhayma?apu-tɨk* 'mis abuelitos', *camnɨpak tɨn?i:cimɨ-tɨk* 'ya están engordando mis cochinos'). ChZ *-tɨgay* n{} 'plural' (e.g., *kapne-tɨgay* 'café-PL', *yomɨ-tɨgay* 'mujer-PL').

DM#032 pMZ ***-taka** *'without'* OIP *-taka* 'sin' (e.g., *ni:taka* adj. 'pelón'; *ni:-* has to do with hair. It doesn't occur in free form; the form *ko?takɨ* 'pelón' appears to contain an allomorph. Oaxaca Mixean cognates for **taka* show the expected reflexes, but cannot show the quality of the final vowel). SoZ *-ťa:ka* n → n{332} 'sin'.

DM#033 pMZ ***-kuk** *'in the middle of'* SoZ *-kukɨ?:m* n{626} 'debajo', *-aŋ kū?k* n{627} 'en medio de'. ChisZ-C *-kuhk-* pron,n{628} 'in the middle of', *-kuhk-oyh* pron,n{627} 'in the middle of', *-kuk-mɨ* pron,n{626} 'in the middle of', *-kuhk-i* pron,n{625} 'in the middle of'. □ pZ **kuk-pak* n 'chest'. Not productive in Mixean, but attested in pM **win-kuk* a 'in front of'.

DM#034 pMZ ***-kɨš-i** *'on, at'* LM-SJ *-kɨš* n{} 'at, on, by the top of'. ChisZ-C *-kɨsi* pron,n{621} 'on'.

DM#035 pMZ ***-i** *'locative'* LM-SJ *-ʸ* n{} 'locational: in, to'. ChisZ-C *-i ~ -y* pron,n{619} 'locative' (also contained in *-?a ~ -i* pron,n{615} 'locative', *-kuhk-i* pron,n{625} 'in the middle of'). StaMaCh *-i ~ -hi* v,n → n{} 'lugar' (e.g., *yuh-i* 'rozar-lugar', *nip-i* 'sembrar-lugar', *kape-hi* 'carrizo-lugar'). □ pOM **kam-ho:ht-y* n 'field' (field-stomach-loc.).

DM#036 pMZ ***-kɨs-mɨ** *'position with respect to the ground'* OIP *-kɨš-mɨ* 'en el suelo'. ChisZ-C *-kɨs-mɨ* pron,n{622} 'above'. □ pMZ **kɨs-mɨ* 'up, high'.

DM#037 pMZ ***-mɨ** *'locative'* [Recognized by Kaufman (1963: 77, 3133) for pMZ as a position 1 nominal derivative suffix. He notes that it "derives place names from noun stems formed by compounding". This is partly wrong since the noun stems need not necessarily be compounds.] OIP *-mɨ* 'position' (e.g., *tɨn-tɨk-mɨ* 'en mi casa'), *-vin-mɨ* n{} 'sobre, encima de' (e.g., *me:ša-vin-mɨ* 'sobre la mesa', *tɨpetu kopak-mɨ* 'subí en la loma', *yuk-mɨ* 'arriba'), *-hɨp-mɨ* n{} 'en la punta'. SaP *-m ~ -Vm* n,v → n{} 'location'. SoZ *-mɨ* n{621} 'instrumental, locative'. ChisZ-C *-mɨ* n → n{331} 'place-name marker or locative' (also contained in *-kɨs-mɨ* pron,n{622} 'above' and *-kuk-mɨ* pron,n{625} 'in the middle of'). □ pM **cu:?-m* 'midnight' (night-loc.); pZ **hoh-mɨ* 'inside' (contents-loc., see Wichmann 1993c, 1.4.6); pMZ **kɨs-mɨ* 'up, high' (body-loc.); pOM **ni:-kɨš-m* 'corporeal-body-loc.'; pMZ **kuk-mɨ* 'in the middle' (middle-loc.); pM **ya-m* (here-loc.) 'here' [reduced form], pM **yuk-mɨ* (up-loc.) 'upwards'.

Attributive Morphology: Prefixes

DM#038 pMZ *ni(?)- 'like, very [?]' LM-SJ *ni?-* {}a '-ish as to colors'. ChisZ: C *ni-* {}a 'very [?]' (e.g., *ni-?oy-e* 'very good').

Attributive Morphology: Suffixes

DM#039 pMZ *-in 'position (time or space)' Only attested in reconstructed stems: □ pMZ **?a:m-in* 'ago, meanwhile' ← **?a:me* 'year'; pMZ **?aw-nah-in* 'left' (mouth-bound form-*in*); pM **?oy-in* 'right hand' ← **?oy* 'good'.

DM#040 pMZ *-hi n → a{} 'before (time or space)' [Has a limited distribution and only barely compatible meanings across the attestations. On closer inspection it will probably turn up recognizably as a morpheme in one of the individual languages.] □ pMZ **cu:?-hi(t)* 'last night' ← **cu:?* 'night'.

Derivational Prefix on Particles

DM#041 pMZ *hu- 'question marker' Frequently occurs in question words, for example, □ pZ **hu-c* [?] 'how?'; pZ **hu-ca?ŋ* [?] 'how much?, how many?'; pChisZ **hu-če?k* [?] 'when?'; pChisZ **hu-ti-pɨ* 'which?' (question-thing-participial); pZ **huc...* 'how?'. Although none of these reconstructed items are pMZ, the pMZ status seems secured by NHM *hv-ma* 'where'.

Omnipresent Suffixes/Enclitics

DM#042 pMZ *^nam 'still' LM-Gu *ka!nɨ, kahnɨ* 'todavía no' MM: Ju,At *kʸæhnɨm* 'todavía no' Ma,Ja,Co *kæhnɨm* 'todavía no' (LM and MM forms from Nordell 1990). SoZ *-nam* omnipresent^{} 'todavía'. StaMaCh *-naʔm* 'todavía'

DM#043 pMZ *^ʔamV? 'just now, already' OIP *-ame?* n^{} 'ya' (e.g., *porke tɨ-ka:-ha-ʔit-ip tɨn-u:k-ame?* 'porque ya no tengo para tomar'). SaP *-ama?* v^{} 'definite' (e.g., *nɨš-p-ama?* 'he definitely is going'). SoZ *-am* {722} 'ahora mismo, ahora'. ChisZ-C *-a?~-a?a ~-a?M* v,aux,n,a,dem,part{721} 'perfective'. ChZ *-ma?* 'pues' (e.g., *nɨks-pa* 'se va' → *nɨks-pa-ma?* 'se va pues', *nɨks-ɨ-ma?* 'se fue pues'); *-?am~ ?m* {omnipresent} 'ya' (e.g., *sta-?am* 'sólo-ya', *tukk-a?m* 'terminar-compl-ya', *cɨkk-a?m* 'hacer-compl-ya', *nipp-ɨ* 'sembró', *nipp-a?am* 'ya sembró').

DM#044 pMZ *^ay 'perfective' SaP ^*ay* v^{} 'perfective'. StaMaCh *-ay* '?' (Cf. *tɨhɨg-ay* 'ayer' vs. *neksa?h-wɨ-tɨhɨk* 'empapar-compl -ayer'.)

DM#045 pMZ *^ti 'emphatic' LM-SJ att{} *-ti"gʸ* 'very' (may be composed of *-ti + -?o"gʸ*). SaP *-ti* n,v{} 'quantity'. SoZ *-tʸi* n{641} 'sólo' (also contained in *-tʸim* omnipresent 'también, sólo' ← *tʸi + -am* 'ahora, ahora mismo' [cf. Elson (1960: 28, note 2)]. ChZ v{} *-ne?te?* 'también' may contain this; could the first element be identical with *nay* 'corpóreo, etc.' < p(M)Z *-nay* (see DM#014)? The full meaning would then be 'just going on and on', or the like; is contained (attested) in *min-pa-ne?te?* 'viene también' and *min-nɨ-ne?te?* 'vino también.

Spanish-MZ Index

~ *ha:?m-yec* (vt) YE#001

acostar pOM **ko?k ~ ko"k* (vt)
KO#011

acostumbrar pMZ **yuh* (vi)
YU#005

acostumbrarse con pM **mu-yuh* (vi)
YU#006

acusar pMZ **si?w* (vt) Si#018

acusar pOM **?i:?n* (vt) ?i#014

acuyo, yerba santa pM **wa:w*
(n) WA#037

adentro pM **ho:ht-pi* (n) HO#037

adentro pZ **hoh-mi* (adv) HO#005

adentro (de la casa) pOM
*tihk-ho:ht-pi (adv) HO#039

adivinador pOM **sihw-may-pa* (n)
MA#057

adivinar pM **?a-koc* (v) KO#002

adobe pOM **mu:?c-i* (n) MU#004

adobes, hacer → tostar

adonde → donde

adormecerse pOM **ma:-nas* (vi)
NA#028

afilar pMZ **me:h?* (vt) ME#006

aflojar pMZ **yak-ho?n* (vt)
HO#026

aflojar la tierra pMZ **wo?m* (vi)
WO#010

aflojarse pMZ **ho?n* (vi) HO#024

afuera pOM **tahe?py* (adv)
TA#008

agacharse pOM **win-tak* (vi)
WI#024

agarrar pMZ **mac* (vt) MA#002

agarrar pZ **cik* (vt) Ci#004

agarrar pZ **kic* (vt) Ki#004

agarrar juntos pOM
*?a-mac-muhk ~ ?a-mac-muk (vt)
MU#010

agarrar un puño de algo pMZ
*wo:?k (vt) WO#009

agarrar; tentar pMZ **pi:?n* (vt)
PI#021

ágil, liso pOM **pe?typyt* (adj)
PE#028

agran___ ___M **yak-mihiy* (vt)
Mi#009

agrandarse → prenderse lumbre

agrás (uva silvestre) pM **cay-tim*
(n) Ti#030

agriarse pOM **suhn ~ sun* (vi)
SU#021

agrio pMZ **kacu(c)* (adj) KA#010

agrio pOM **sun* (adj) SU#022

agua pMZ **ni:?* (n) Ni#001

agua llovida pZ **tuh-ni?* (n)
Ni#007

agua tibia pM [Veracruz]
*hokos-ni:? (n) Ni#004

aguacate pMZ **kúy-tim* (n) Ti#031

aguacate, chinini pOM **ci:?ny* (n)
CI#029

aguacatillo pOM **sihc* (n) SI#003

aguantar un peso pOM **ma:y-hi*
(vi) MA#065

aguatar → aguatear

aguatear, aguatar pOM **?u:?ks* (vi)
?U#022

agujerear pMZ **hut* (vt) HU#029

ahijado(a) pMZ **ma:san-?unV(k)*
(n) ?U#030

ahijastro(a) → entenado(a)

ahogar pOM **yak-hi?s* (vt) HI#014

ahogarse pM **hi?ks* (vi) HI#007

ahogarse pZ **suks* (vi) SU#014

ahora pOM **tam* (adv) TA#022

ahora, hoy pOM **?isyam* (adv)
?I#017

ahuyentar pOM **yak-ke"k* (vt)
KE#011

ajuate, tener pM [Veracruz] **cu?ks*
(vi) CU#033

ajustar pM **ni?c* (vt) Ni#012

ala pM **ke:k-an* (n) KE#012

ala pZ **sah(a)* (n) SA#007

alacrán pM **kapin* (n) KA#054

alacrán pZ **kakw(E?n)* (n)
KA#032

alargar pOM **yak-yohn ~ yak-yon*
(vt) YO#011

albañil pOM *pohc-pa* (n) PO#009

alcanzar (en el camino) pOM
nahc-pa:?t (vi) PA#057

alargarse pMZ *yon* (vi) YO#010

alegrarse pOM *šohn ~ šon* (vi)
SO#017

alegre, contento, feliz pOM
hot-kuhk (adj) KU#004

aletearse pOM *mopohp ~ mopop*
(vi) MO#015

algodón pOM *pišy* (n) PI#031

algodón pZ *coha* (n) CO#002

algodón pGZ *pu:ki* (n) PU#015

aliento pM *šeh-e* (n) SE#003

alimentos pOM *hɨ?kš-y* (n)
Hɨ#010

aliñar pGZ *yo?* (vt) YO#001

almácigo, hacer en pGZ *pa:n* (vt)
PA#043

almagre pZ *sun(u?)* (n) SU#025

alquilar pOM *?a-hu:y-tuk* (vi)
TU#020

alto → arriba

alto, crecido pOM *yon-y* (adj)
YO#012

alumbrar pZ *ta?ks* TA#021

alzar pOM *kɨyɨ"k* (vi) Kɨ#038

alzar, levantar pZ *kuŋ* (vt)
KU#026

allá pMZ *hem* (loc adv) HE#013

allá pM *hi:?pi* (loc adv) HI#011

allá pM *hɨm* (loc adv) Hɨ#012

allá pOM *hep* (loc adv) HE#019

allá → allí

allí, allá pOM *šim* (loc adv)
SI#014

allí pOM *ši:* (n) SI#001

amamantar pZ *yak-cu?c* (vt)
CU#009

amanecer pOM *hah-tak* (vi)
HA#005

amansar → domar

amansar pOM *yak-yuh* (vt)
YU#007

amargo pMZ *tam?* (adj) TA#023

amarillo pMZ *pu?c(V)* (adj)
PU#003

amarrar pMZ *soc* (vt) SO#001

amarrar pM *cum* (vi, vt) CU#034

amarrar pOM *ku-cuhm ~ ku-cum*
CU#035

amarrar pOM *ku-wɨ:?n* (vt)
Wɨ#017

amarrar pZ *si?n* (vt) SI#019

amarrar pGZ *cen* (vt) CE#016

amarrar bulto pOM *?a-wɨ:?n* (v)
Wɨ#016

amarrar cosas encimadas pMZ *wat*
WA#036

amarrar; pretender pZ *mek* (vt)
ME#008

amasar pMZ *mɨ:k?* (vt) Mɨ#012

amasar pMZ *yo:?t* (vt) YO#016

amo → dueño

amontonar pMZ *?ɨ:?p* (vt) ?ɨ#015

amontonar pMZ *yu:?m* (vt)
YU#020

amontonar → doblar

amontonar, cercar pMZ *ka?k* (vt)
KA#027

amor pOM *cohk-?ɨn(y)* (n)
CO#004

ampollarse pM [Veracruz] *cet* (vi)
CE#020

ampollarse pZ *toh* (vi) TO#004

ancho pOM *mɨh-wihn* (adj)
WI#019

anciano pM *na?aw* (n) NA#034

anciano pZ *cam-u* [?] (adj, n)
CA#022

andar pMZ *wit* (vi) WI#039

andar andando pGZ *ho:y* (vi)
HO#044

angosto pOM *šu:?c* (adj) SU#004

anillo pMZ *kɨ?-kuma* (n) KU#012

anillo pOM *kɨ"-hi:?c* (n) HI#003

animal, bestia de carga pOM *hɨyuk*
Hɨ#032

ano pZ *si?i* (n) SI#002

anoche pMZ *cu:?-hi(t)* (adv)

CU#003
anochecer pMZ *cu:?-?ah* (vi)
CU#002
anona pM *?a:ti* ?A#049
anona pOM *?ahy-tm* (n) Ti#029
anona pZ *yati* (n) YA#016
anteayer pMZ *ma:stiki* (n)
MA#040
anteayer pMZ *(hu)wis-tik-(p)i*
(adv) Wi#019
anteburro, tapir pMZ
cu:ki(-ka:haw) (n) CU#023
anteojos pOM *win-?ihš-n* (n)
?I#013
antes pOM *hayihp* (adv) HA#036
anudar pZ *?a-šohc-tuhk*
~ *?a-šohc-tuk* (vt) TU#022
anzuelo pOM *šu?ny* (n) SU#024
año pMZ *?a:me* (n) ?A#027
año pOM *humiht* (n) HU#013
apagar pM *yak-pi?c* (vt) PI#004
apagarse pMZ *pi?c* (vi) PI#001
apalancar pZ *toc* (vi) TO#002
aparecer pZ *keh* (vi) KE#007
aparecer → nacer
aparecerse pOM *ka:ši?k* (vi)
KA#062
apartar pZ *we?n* (vi, vt) WE#013
aparte pOM *?apik-y* (adv)
?A#038
apedrear, moler pMZ *ka?c* (vi, vt)
KA#006
aperecer pM [Veracruz] *ke?š-ta:k*
(vi) KE#025
aplastar, golpear pZ *pac* (vt)
PA#002
aplicar sobre superficie (p.ej., ropa,
trapo, lodo) pMZ *me:s?* (vi, vt)
ME#016
aprender, enseñar pZ *?aŋ-may* (vi,
vt) MA#062
apretar pM *ci?kš* (vi) Ci#012
apretar pM *yak-ci?kš* (vt)
Ci#013
apretar pM *tih* (vt) TI#004

apretar pZ *ka?m* (vt) KA#033
apretar → asegurar
apretar con los dedos pMZ *pen*
(vt) PE#007
apretar torciendo pZ *wi?t-kam* (vi)
KA#035
apretar (con pinzas) pOM
?a-ma?t-muhk ~ ?a-ma?t-muk
(v)
MU#011
aprisa pOM *?ati"cy* (adv) ?A#051
aquel pOM *šim-pit* (pron) SI#016
aquel pZ *hiki* (pron dem) HI#005
aquel → ése
aquí pM *ya-m* (loc adv) YA#002
aquí pM *yah...* (loc adv) YA#004
aquí pOM *ya:* (loc adv) YA#001
aquí pZ *yihi* (loc adv) Yi#002
arado pOM *šutk* (n) SU#039
araña pM *hu:?t-yik* (n) HU#034
araña pOM *po:hšy-my* (n)
PO#037
araña pZ *?amu* (n) ?A#031
árbol, palo pMZ *kuy* (n) KU#027
árbol de copal pOM *po:m kipy* (n)
Ki#015
árbol duro pMZ *hu:n-i* (n)
HU#017
árbol, especie de pGZ *ma?c* (n)
MA#005
árbol; leña pMZ *kipi* (n) Ki#014
arco iris pM *?i(:?)nciC...* (n)
?I#005
arder → picar
arder sin flama → picar
arder (fuego) pZ *nem* (vi)
NE#008
arder (piel) pZ *haw-ay* (vi)
HA#032
ardilla pMZ *mu:tu* (n) MU#030
ardilla chica y gris pOM *cihc* (n)
Ci#002
ardilla (grande y roja) pOM *ku"y*
(n) KU#036
arena pM *pu?* (n) PU#009

arena pZ *po?yo* (n) PO#051

arena → pequeño

arete pM *ta:cɨk-tɨy* (n) Tɨ#062

armadillo pMZ *nɨ:c* (n) Nɨ#010

armar pZ *ma?k* (vt) MA#019

arraigar pZ *nu?n* (vi) NU#014

arrancar pMZ *nuk* (vt) NU#004

arrancar pMZ *wis* (vt) WI#029

arrastrarse pM *we:?c* (vi)
WE#001

arrear → patear

arreglar pOM *yak-?oy-?ah* (vt)
?O#047

arriba, alto pMZ *kɨs-mɨ* (adv)
Kɨ#017

arriba, alto pM *yuk-mɨ* (adv, adj)
YU#012

arriba, hacia pMZ *yuk-* YU#011

arriera pMZ *nuku(N(ɨk))* (n)
NU#006

arriera pOM *nuh* (n) NU#002

arrimar pOM *?o:?š* (vt) ?O#034

arrodillarse pZ *kut* (vt) KU#023

arrojar; desatar pMZ *wɨh* (vt)
Wɨ#006

arroyo pOM [?] *wok* (n) WO#007

arroyo pZ *pak* (n) PA#018

arrugarse pMZ *so:?c* (vi) SO#003

arrugarse pOM *no:?t* (vi)
NO#009

asador pOM *peht-n* (n) PE#019

asar pMZ *ca:y?* CA#044

asar pZ *ha?s* (vt) HA#020

asegurar, apretar pOM
yak-ta?c-pɨhk ~ yak-ta?c-pɨk (vt)
Pɨ#020

aserrar pM *hɨ:?t* (vi, vt) Hɨ#023

asesino pOM *yak-hayu-?o:?k-pa*
(n) ?O#017

así pOM *hatu?n* (part) HA#029

asiento pMZ *?o:k* (n) ?O#021

áspero pOM *hɨk* (adj) Hɨ#005

atajar pMZ *me?k* (vt) ME#009

atascado, estar pM *he?ps* HE#026

atascarse pMZ *ta?n* (vi) TA#027

aterrizar pOM *na:š-kɨta:k*
~ na:š-kɨta"k (vi) Kɨ#023

atole pM *šu:t(Vk) [?]* (n) SU#036

atole pGZ *?u:nu?* (n) ?U#033

atole champurrado pOM *na"n-y*
(n) NA#020

atorar (espina) pM *kah* (vi)
KA#015

atorarse pMZ *pa?m* (vi) PA#040

atorarse pM *?aw-tih* (vi) TI#005

atrancar etc. pM *me?t* (vt)
ME#018

atravezar (p.ej., piernas)
pMZ *he?ks* (vi) HE#011

atravezar → pasar

aura (tipo de buitre) pOM
mak-wehkš-n (n) WE#009

avanzar (p.ej., trabajo) → caminar

aventar (arena, agua, etc.) pMZ *kuh*
(vi) KU#001

avergonzarse pM *co?y(-tu:n)* (vi)
CO#029

avispa pMZ *we:?nV(k)* (n)
WE#015

avispa pOM *šiwinyky* (n) Sɨ#019

avispa concha de armadilla pM
wɨki (n) Wɨ#010

avispa masón pOM *homny* (n)
HO#019

ayer pMZ *tɨhɨk(ay)* (adv) Tɨ#011

ayer pM *?V-šihw-i* (adv) Sɨ#014

ayudar pOM *putɨhk ~ putɨk* (vt)
PU#034

azotar → pegar

azúcar pOM *po:?p pa"hk* (n)
PA#014

baba pMZ *?aw-nɨ:?* (n) Nɨ#002

bailador → danzante

bailar pMZ *?ec* (vi) ?E#001

baile pMZ *?ec-e* (n) ?E#002

bajada pMZ *(k)wanak-ɨ [?]* (n)
WA#030

bajar pMZ *yak-(k)wanak [?]* (vt)
WA#029

bajar pM *ko-naš* NA#027

bajar pOM *kɨta:k ~ kɨta"k (vi)
Kɨ#021

bajarse pMZ *ket (vi) KE#026

bajarse pMZ *(k)wanak [?] (vi)
WA#028

bajo pM *na:hš-pi(k) (adv)
NA#030

bambolearse pZ *cinin (vi)
CI#030

banco → tabla

bandido pOM *me:?c-pa (n)
ME#004

banquito → tabla

bañar pMZ *ci:w? (vi) CI#050

bañar a alguien pMZ
*yak-ciw ~ yak-ci?w (vt) CI#051

baño (para bañarse) pOM
*cihw-tahk-n (n) CI#052

barba pMZ *?aw-pɨk (n) Pɨ#007

barba pMZ *?aw-wa(?)y (n)
WA#039

barba pGZ *wi:ši (n) WI#033

barbasco pZ *naku (n) NA#014

barrer pMZ *pe:t? (vi, vt) PE#023

barrido pOM *pe"t-y (n) PE#024

barriga, estómago pZ *cek (n)
CE#008

barro pMZ *mo:k (n) MO#011

bastante pZ *mɨ?cyɨki [?] (adj, adv)
Mɨ#004

bastante, muy pZ *?aŋ-pa?t-e (adj)
PA#054

bastón, bordón pMZ *tak(us) (n)
TA#018

basura pMZ *pu:ci (n) PU#004

basura pM *puc-ta?k (n) PU#005

batir pMZ *sac (vt) SA#002

batir pM *ho?y (vt) HO#045

batir mole pZ *?up-?ah (vi)
?U#037

batir; regar pZ *wik (vt) WI#007

bautismo pOM *nɨ:?-peht-n (n)
PE#021

bautizar pZ *nɨy-?ɨy (vi, vt)
Nɨ#027

bautizar(se) pOM *nɨ:?-peht
~ nɨ:?-pet (vi) PE#015

beber → tomar

bebida pMZ *?u:?k-kuy (n)
?U#016

bebida pOM *?u:?k-y (n) ?U#015

bejuco pM *?a:?c-a (n) ?A#002

bejuco pZ *poh (n) PO#011

bejuco arbóreo (genérico) pOM *tu:t
(n) TU#048

bejuquilla pM *?a:?c-a ca(:?)nay
(n) CA#027

bellota pMZ *šoh-tɨm (n) Tɨ#032

bellota pOM *ko"k (n) KO#012

bendito pOM *ku-nu:?kš (adj)
NU#011

besar pM *cu:?kš (vt) CU#031

besar → oler

beso pM *cu:?kš-i (n) CU#032

bestia de carga → animal

bien → bueno

bien, muy pM *?oya-?o:?ki (adj,
adv) ?O#045

bilis pMZ *cus(y)(k)-ni:wi (n)
NI#012

blanco pMZ *po:p?o? (adj)
PO#032

blando pZ *?uya (adj) ?U#048

blando (colchón, etc.) pOM
*pɨ?ŋyky (adj) Pɨ#033

blando (tierra, colchón, etc.) pOM
*yu:nk (adj) YU#022

blanquear pOM *yak-po:?p-?ɨy
(vt) PO#036

blanquearse pOM *po:?p-?ɨy (vi)
PO#035

blanquearse pZ *popo?-?ah (v)
PO#034

boca pMZ *?aw (n) ?A#052

boca arriba pOM *cahwak (adv)
CA#010

bolsa pOM *pih-n (n) PI#012

bonito pOM *yakšon (adj) SO#018

bonito, hermoso pOM *cuh (adj)
CU#013

borde → mejilla
bordón → bastón
borracho pM *mu:k-(hu)-pa (n) MU#016
borracho pGZ *ʔuk(k)-i? (n) ʔU#017
borrador pOM ho?c-n (n) HO#003
borrar OM *ho?c~ho"c (vt) HO#002
bosque pM *yu:hk (n) YU#014
bosque medio espeso pOM *ʔa:ʔmwy (n) ʔA#030
botar (semilla, etc., en un recipiente) pMZ *pusʔ-aʔy (v) PU#026
botón pOM *ʔa-ci"t (n) CI#046
bramar pMZ *mu:hʔ (vi) MU#007
brasa pOM *hɨhn-pahk (n) PA#025
brazada pMZ *sah (n) SA#006
brazo → mano
brillar pM *hiʔk (vi) HI#006
brillar pOM *ʔa-hah (vi) HA#004
brillar (oro, joyas, etc.) pOM *cɨmahm~cɨmam (vi) Cɨ#020
brincar pOM *puhtɨʔk~puhtɨ"k (vi) PU#035
brincar para abajo pZ *cut (vi) CU#051
brincar para arriba pZ *mɨʔŋ (vi) Mɨ#025
brincotear pMZ *tup (vi) TU#039
brotar → tronar
brotar, nacer pZ *poʔ (vi, vt) PO#003
brujería pOM *pok-y (n) PO#016
brujería, hacer pMZ *pok (vi,vt) PO#015
brujo pMZ *cokʔa (n) CO#008
brujo pM *pok-pa (n) PO#017
buche del ave pOM *kahy-tɨhk (n) Tɨ#015
bueno, bien pMZ *ʔoyV (adj, adv) ʔO#043
bueno, bien pZ *wɨ- (adj, adv) Wɨ#007

buho → lechuza
bule → tecomate
buscar pOM *ʔiš-taʔy (vt) TA#039
buscar → robar
cabecear pMZ *wɨʔm-ʔɨy (v) Wɨ#014
cabello pMZ *wa(ʔ)y (n) WA#038
cabeza pMZ *ko-pak (n) PA#029
cabeza de viejo pMZ *koʔ-poʔ-ka:haw (n) KO#022
cacahuate pMZ *nas-kakawa (n) KA#030
cacao pMZ *kakawa (n) KA#029
cachete, mejilla pMZ *ʔa:ka-pak (n) PA#022
cada pM *kɨh(k)- (pron) Kɨ#007
cadera, nalga pOM *ʔiš-pahk PA#021
caer pM *kaʔw (vi) KA#065
caer pZ *kun (vi) KU#015
caer de arriba, hacer pM *yak-kaʔw (vt) KA#066
caer (al suelo) pOM *na:hš-waʔk ~na:hš-wa"k (vi) WA#018
cal pMZ *ham (n) HA#010
cal pM *ʔakaš (n) ʔA#018
calabaza pM *ciʔwa (n) CI#047
calabaza pOM *šuty (n) SU#037
calabaza pZ *pasoŋ (n) PA#048
calabaza castilla pOM *mɨny-ci"w (n) CI#049
calambres pMZ *cu:k(-ʔɨy) (n) CU#029
calar pMZ *sɨm(ɨm) (vt) Sɨ#009
caldo de frijoles pMZ *sɨk-nɨ:ʔ (n) Nɨ#006
calentar pMZ *pih (vt) PI#010
calentar pM *hokos-pɨk (vi) Pɨ#016
calentarse pMZ *sam (vi) SA#013
caliente pOM *ʔan (adj) ʔA#033
caliente pZ *nuc (vi) NU#001
caliente pZ *pih-pa (adj) PI#011
callarse pM *mon (vi) MO#013
calmarse → pararse

calor, hacer pOM *_?an-pɨhk_
~ _?an-pɨk_ (vi) Pɨ#015

calvo, pelón pM *_ko-cima_ (n)
CI#023

calvo, pelón pM *_ko?tak_ (adj)
TA#010

calvo, pelón pOM *_ku-ca"m_ (n)
CA#021

calzar pMZ *_nɨ?s_ (vt) Nɨ#025

calzón pM [Veracruz] *_tukšɨ_ (n)
TU#027

cama pOM *_maw-peht-n_ (n)
PE#020

camarón pMZ *_?o:yo(?)_ (n)
?O#050

camarón del mar pOM *_kɨ:?šm_ (n)
Kɨ#020

camarón del río pOM *_ku?š_ (n)
KU#022

cambiar pM *_kek_ (vt) KE#008

cambiar pOM *_yak-tikahc_ ~ _yak-tikac_
(vt) TI#009

caminar pMZ *_yo?y_ (vi) YO#020

caminar [?] pOM *_šɨhp_ ~ _šɨp_ (v)
Sɨ#010

caminar, avanzar (p.ej., trabajo) pZ
*_tuŋ-?ah_ (vi) TU#057

camino pMZ *_tu:?-?aw_ (n)
TU#054

camino, en el; por el camino pOM
*_tu:?-?am_ (adv) TU#055

camino, por el → camino, en el

camisa pMZ *_suy-i_ (n) SU#041

camisa pZ *_yo?t-e_ YO#017

camote pMZ *_mɨn(i)_ (n) Mɨ#019

camote pOM *_pa"k-mɨny_ (n)
Mɨ#021

camotillo pM *_pa:-mɨni_ (n)
Mɨ#020

campesino pOM *_kam-tuhn-pa_ (n)
TU#035

campo pOM *_kam-ho:ht-y_ (n)
KA#041

canas pZ *_ko?-popo?_ (n) PO#033

canasta pM *_ka?ka_ (n) KA#028

canasta pOM *_kač_ (n) KA#005

canasta pZ *_waka_ (n) WA#022

canción, canto pM *_?ɨw-i_ (n)
?ɨ#018

canción, himno, canto pZ *_wan-e_
(n) WA#027

cangrejo pMZ *_?e:si_ (n) ?E#015

canilla de la pierna, espinilla pOM
*_pakuy-cuhš_ (n) CU#047

canoa pMZ *_?aha_ (n) ?A#005

canoso pM *_ko-po?_ (adj) PO#005

cansarse pOM *_?a-nu?kš-?ɨy_ (vi)
NU#009

cantar pM *_?ɨw_ (vi) ?ɨ#017

cantar pZ *_wan_ (vi) WA#026

cántaro pM *_mah-an_ (n) MA#010

cántaro pOM *_cihw-y_ (n) CI#053

cántaro pZ *_mah-kuy_ MA#011

canto → canción

caña cimarrón pM [Veracruz]
*_pa:-wa:šuk_ (n) WA#035

caña de maíz pOM *_pɨ"c_ (n)
Pɨ#001

caña de otate pM *_pɨ:yV(n)_ (n)
Pɨ#040

caña de azúcar pM *_wa:šuk_ (n)
WA#034

cañal pOM *_wa:šk kam_ (n)
KA#040

caoba pM *_mak-?ak_ (n) ?A#013

capulín pGZ *_mu:pi_ (n) MU#022

cara pOM [NHM/SHM] *_wihn-?ahw_
(n) ?A#053

cara pOM [MM/LM] *_wi:n hɨhp_
(n) Hɨ#019

caracol pM *_won-i_ (n) WO#012

caracol pZ *_soki_ (n) SO#010

carbón pMZ *_hu?yi_ (n) HU#038

cárcel pOM *_puš-n-tɨhk_ (n) Tɨ#017

carga pMZ *_cɨm-i_ (n) Cɨ#016

cargar pOM *_pa-cɨhm_ ~ _pa-cɨm_ (vt)
Cɨ#015

cargar cosa plana pMZ *_kɨ:y?_ (vt)
Kɨ#034

cargar en la cabeza pZ *_cɨy_ (vi)

Ci#028

cargar en la espalda pMZ *cim (vt)
Ci#014

cargar palo, etc. pMZ *kap (vt)
KA#047

carne pMZ *sis(i) (n) SI#023

carne asada pZ *sis-ha?s-e (vt)
HA#021

caro pMZ *cow-ah (adj) CO#022

carpintero pMZ *cehe (n) CE#005

carpintero pOM *cehc-pa (n)
CE#003

carrizo, otate pMZ *?o:kwin (n)
?O#024

carrizo pMZ *kape (n) KA#053

casa pMZ *tik (n) Ti#012

casarse pM [Veracruz] *ki?-pa:?t
PA#056

cascabel pM *tu?c cumum (n)
CU#038

cascábel, sonaja pOM *ši?c-n (n)
SI#004

cascada pOM *taš (n) TA#032

cáscara, piel pMZ *?ak(i) (n)
?A#009

cáscara, piel pZ *naka (n) NA#012

casero pOM *ku-tihk (n) Ti#016

caspa pM *ko-po:t(ik) (n)
PO#046

castañetear pMZ *ta?ps (vi)
TA#030

catarro pM [Veracruz] *hipi (n)
HI#010

cazador pOM *tuh-pa (n) TU#005

cazar pMZ *tuh (vt) TU#004

cedro pMZ *?aha (n) ?A#006

cedro pMZ *ma:san-kuy (n)
MA#037

cedro colorado pZ *?ahu (n)
?A#008

cegarse pOM *wihn-c-?ay (vi)
WI#022

ceiba pMZ *pistin (n) PI#030

cejas pM [Veracruz] *win-kuy-pik
(n) Pi#009

cenar pOM *?a?uš-?aht ~ ?a?uš-?at
(vi) ?U#040

ceniza pMZ *kuy-ham (n) HA#011

centzontle pZ *?amay(-hon) (n)
?A#026

centzontle, tipo de pMZ *yik hon
(n) HO#023

cepillo (para acepillar madera) pOM
*še:?w-n (n) SE#014

cera pM *pu?hik (n) PU#011

cera pZ *nahi (n) NA#003

cerca pMZ *tome(k) (adv) TO#019

cerca pOM *win-kon (adv)
KO#020

cerca, cerco, corral pOM *kem-y
(n) KE#017

cercar pOM *kem (vi) KE#016

cercar → amontonar

cerco → cerca

cerdo, marrano pZ *yoya(h) (n)
YO#018

cerete pMZ *?uku (n) ?U#019

cerete pM *keki (n) KE#013

cereza pOM *pehkš (n) PE#006

cerilla pOM *tack ti"n-y (n)
Ti#041

cernir, colar pZ *pa? (vt) PA#001

cerrar pMZ *?aw-tuk (vi) TU#018

cerrar pOM *yak-?a-tuhk ~ yak-?a-
tuk
(vt) TU#019

cerrar pZ *yak-?aŋ-ka?m (vt)
KA#034

cerrar → tapar

cerro pM *ke:c (n) KE#001

cerro pM *kopak (n) KO#024

cerro pZ *ko-cik (n) Ci#006

cicatriz pM *tay-a (n) TA#037

cicatriz pZ *sas (n) SA#016

cicatrizarse pMZ *tay (vi) TA#036

ciego pM *wihn-c (adj) WI#021

cielo pMZ *cap(-hi) (n) A#033

ciempiés pOM *kiwk (n) KI#023

ciempiés pOM *?i:?pš-ki" (n)
Ki#002

ciénaga pOM *nɨːʔ-moʷ(n)c (n)
  MO#007
cierto pOM *tɨwy (adj) Tɨ#058
cigarro pMZ *hukʔ-i (n) HU#006
cincelar, escoplear pMZ *paːhʔ (vt)
  PA#010
cinchar pMZ *wat (vt) WA#036
Ciudad de México → Tenochtitlán
claro (agua, etc.) pOM *tɨʔkš-y
  (adj) Tɨ#024
clavar pOM *ʔeːʔc (vt) ʔE#004
clavar (estaca, espeque, etc.) pOM
  *kup (vi) KU#017
clavícula pOM *yuʔk-pahk (n)
  PA#034
clueca pM *ʔamaː (vi) ʔA#025
cobija pOM *ca-pištn (n) PI#032
cobija, sarape, chamarra pZ
  *nuʔs-kuy (n) NU#020
cobijar pMZ *nuʔs (vt) NU#019
cocer pMZ *kɨːwʔ (vi) Kɨ#030
cocer pMZ *soːsʔ (vt) SO#021
cocer, cocinar pM *yak-kɨw
  ~yak-kɨʔw (vt) Kɨ#031
cocer al vapor pZ *pow (vi, vt)
  PO#050
cocido pM *kɨʔw (adj) Kɨ#032
cocinar → cocer
cocoyuche, pepeyochi pM *yɨmA
  (n) Yɨ#006
cocuyo pM [Veracruz] *puktun (n)
  PU#017
cocuyo pOM *kɨːny (n) Kɨ#013
codo del brazo pZ *cum-i (n)
  CU#039
codorniz (grande) pOM *mašn-hohn
  (n) HO#021
coger pMZ *koʔps (vi, vt) KO#026
cojolite pM *wɨːki (n) Wɨ#009
cola pMZ *tuʔc(ta) (n) TU#003
cola, rabo pOM *piʷš (n) PI#025
cola, sin pMZ *tuʔc-tuku (n)
  TU#016
colar pM *ʔa-naš (vi)   NA#025
colar → cernir

colgar pOM *ku-tɨy Tɨ#061
colibrí pMZ *suʔksu(k) (n)
  SU#017
collar, gargantilla pMZ *nam-cɨm(-i)
  (n) Cɨ#019
colmillo de los animales pMZ
  *ʔaw-wah(-e) (n) PA#006
colocar piedras en un cerco pMZ
  *neʔw (vt) NE#014
colorado, ponerse; enrojecer pMZ
  *capac-ʔah (vi) CA#036
colorín, tzompantle pOM *cehč (n)
  CE#004
comadre pOM *hay-ʔok (n)
  ʔO#012
comadreja pM *ʔiːš-in (n) ʔI#016
comal pM *wekš-i (n) WE#008
comején pMZ *wece(w) (n)
  WE#003
comenzar, empezar pOM
  *coːʔn-taʔk~coːʔn-taʷk (vi)
  CO#014
comer a mordidas (manzanas, totopo,
  dulce) pOM *keːʔt (vt)
  KE#027
comer caña, etc. pM *ʔok (vt)
  ʔO#009
comer comida caliente pZ *wiʔk
  (vi, vt) WI#008
comer comida de otro pOM
  *ko-kahy~ko-kay (vt) KA#070
comer cosa ancha pM *noːʔc (vt)
  NO#002
comer cosa blanda pM *naʔn (vi)
  NA#019
comer cosa blanda pZ *kuʔt (vi, vt)
  KU#024
comer fruta, etc. pOM *hɨʔks (vi,
  vt) Hɨ#008
comer tortillas, pan pM *kay (vt)
  KA#069
comer una cosa tostada pMZ *muks
  (vt) MU#020
comer (con alguien) pOM
  *mu-kahy~mu-kay (vt) KA#071

me"pš-tuhk ~ me"pš-tuk (vt)
TU#021

cortar fruta pMZ *tuk* (vt) TU#017

corteza pM *kipi-?ak* (n) ?A#012

cortina pOM *?a-tiy-tuk* (n)
TU#024

corto pMZ *kono(k)* (adj) KO#021

cosa formada de barro pZ *mik-i*
(n) Mi#013

cosa plana pM *na?ka* (n)
NA#010

cosa vieja pZ *peka* (adj) PE#005

cosechar; tocar pMZ *pi:?k* (vt)
PI#015

coser, costurar pZ *na?k* (vt)
NA#008

coser, pescar con anzuelo pMZ *suy*
(vt) SU#040

cosquillas, hacer pOM *šunik* (vi)
SU#023

costillas pM [Veracruz] *kapap-pahk*
(n) PA#027

cotorro pGZ *ka:ca?* (n) KA#008

coyole pMZ *kuma* (n) KU#011

coyuntura → nudo de caña

cráneo pMZ *ko-pak-pak* (n)
PA#030

crecer pM *ye:?k* (vi) YE#003

crecer (bejuco) pM *?a:?c* (vi)
?A#001

crecido → alto

crepitar pMZ *tinin* (vi) TI#015

criar pM *yak-ye:?k* (vt) YE#004

criatura pOM *ma:š-?unak* (n)
?U#031

criatura pZ *yawa-?une* (n)
?U#032

crisantemo → flor de Santa María

crudo → verde

cruel pOM *ca:cy* (n) CA#008

crujir pMZ *ke:?c* (vt) KE#002

crujir los dientes pM [Veracruz]
yak-kiric (vt) Ki#024

cruzar pZ *ki-tuk* (vi) TU#011

cuachile (chile silvestre) pMZ

kuy-ni:wi (n) NI#014

cuadrado → estrecho

cuajinicuil pMZ *?i:?(n)ki* (n)
?I#006

cuajinicuil; machetón pMZ
ta?c(k)V(k) (n) TA#005

cuanto pZ *huca?ŋ* [?] (part)
HU#003

cuarta, una pMZ *cat?-e* (n)
CA#040

cuate, gemelo pM *še:ne* (n)
SE#009

cuauhtecomate pM *cima-kuhy* (n)
CI#022

cubrir la cabeza pOM *ku-hu:?š*
(vi) HU#028

cucaracha pMZ *makoko* (n)
MA#021

cucaracha; chapulín grande pM
ci:k ~ ci:kcik (n) CI#012

cuchillo pM *cuk-an* (n) CU#018

cuello pMZ *yo?k(-tu)* (n) YO#005

cuello pZ *kini* (n) Ki#011

cuerda pZ *ti?ps-i* (n) Ti#050

cuerda → vena

cuerno pMZ *waha(w)* (n)
WA#013

cuero pOM *po"* (n) PO#002

cuerpo pMZ *kis* (n) Ki#016

cuerpo pOM *ni?ks* (n) NI#005

cuervo, cacalote pOM *ho:ky* (n)
HO#011

cueva pOM *?a:hn-k* (n) ?A#036

cueva pZ *ca-tik* (n) Ti#013

cueza pMZ *kih* (n) Ki#006

cuidado, con → suavemente

cuidarlo mucho pM *?ama:?y* (vi)
?A#024

culebra pM *ca(:?)nay* (n)
CA#026

culebra pZ *cahin* (n) CA#012

culebra de agua pM *ni:?-ca(:?)nay*
(n) CA#029

culebra de agua pZ *ni?-cahin* (n)
CA#014

culebra negra pM [Veracruz]
*yɨkɨk-ca(:?)nay (n) CA#032
culpa, pecado pM [Veracruz]
*ke:?ye (n) KE#031
culpa, pecado pZ *koha (n)
KO#008
cumplir pOM *?a-peht ~ ?a-pet (vi)
PE#013
cumplir pOM *kuy-tuhn ~ kuy-tun
(vi) TU#032
cuñada de hombre, cuñado de mujer
pMZ *kapay (n) KA#052
cuñada de mujer pMZ *?ohya (n)
?O#042
cuñado de hombre pM *hɨyi (n)
Hɨ#030
cuñado de hombre pZ *pini (n)
PI#022
cuñado de mujer → cuñada de
hombre
cuotativo pMZ *?u(?)k (clitic)
?U#009
curandero pMZ *coy-?ɨy-pa (n)
CO#028
curar pMZ *yak-co:k? (vt)
CO#007
curar pMZ *coy-?ɨy (vt) CO#027
curtir; quebrar pMZ *ko:?c (vt)
KO#005
chachalaca pOM *?a:šk-ɨ-kák (n)
?A#048
chamarra → cobija
chamuscar pOM *ki:?p (vt)
KI#008
chango, mono pMZ *ca:wi (n)
CA#042
chango, mono pGZ *?u:cu? (n)
?U#007
chapotear → luchar a brazo partido
chapulín grande → cucaracha
chapulín, saltamontes pZ *?ahu (n)
?A#008
chapulín (chico, verde) pOM *mu"
(n) MU#001
chayocamote pOM *?ahkš-kɨhk (n)

Kɨ#008
chayote pM *?ehkšah (n) ?E#009
chayote pZ *?apit-pasoŋ (n)
PA#049
chayote pGZ *kuy-pa:suŋ (n)
PA#050
chicharra pMZ *si:kitiw (n) SI#012
chiche → seno
chichicastle pZ *kenuk KE#018
chicle pM [Veracruz] *ci?m-pak (n)
CI#025
chico pZ *ciks... (adj) CI#017
chico, pequeño pOM *pi?k (adj)
PI#014
chicozapote pZ *hi?ya (n) HI#016
chiflar, tocar instrumento de viento
pMZ *su:s? (vi) SU#029
chiflarle pMZ *su:s?-hay (vt)
SU#031
chilacayote pOM *ka:-ci"w (n)
CI#048
chile pMZ *ni:wi (n) NI#011
chile blanco pMZ *po:p?o? ni:wi
(n) NI#015
chile verde pOM *cušk-ni:wy (n)
NI#013
chinche pMZ *cisi(k) (n) CI#041
chinini → aguacate
chipilcoite pMZ *cus-kuy (n)
CU#045
chocolín pOM *šutyky (n) SU#038
chueco pM [Veracruz] *?uyuk (adj)
?U#051
chueco, encorvado pMZ *new-e
(adj) NE#013
chupar pMZ *mu:?k (vt) MU#018
chupar pM *mukuy [?] (vt)
MU#019
chupar pM [Veracruz] *ko?y (vt)
KO#039
danzante, bailador pMZ *?ec-pa (n)
?E#003
dar pMZ *yak (vt) YA#007
dar pM(Z) *mo:y? (vi, vt)
MO#020

dar de comer pOM
*yak-kahy ~ yak-kay (vt)
KA#072

dar, pegarse pMZ **ci:?* (vt)
CI#001

dar por otro pM **ko-yak-i* (vt)
YA#008

dar una palmada pM **pɨ?kš* (vt)
Pɨ#024

debajo → abajo

debajo, debajo de algo pOM **pa?t*
PA#051

debajo de algo → debajo

deber pZ **ha?c* (vt) HA#001

deber (vi); pagar (vt) pMZ **yoh* (vi,
vt) YO#003

débil pZ **moc(i)* (adj) MO#005

decir pMZ **nɨm* (vi) Nɨ#018

decir pOM**tih* (vi) TI#006

decir pOM **wanahn ~ wana"n* (vi)
WA#031

decir pZ **cam* (vt) CA#016

decirselo pMZ **nɨm-hay* (v ap)
Nɨ#019

dedo de la mano pM **kɨ:?-hɨhp* (n)
Hɨ#018

dedo gordo del pie pOM **teky-ka:*
(n) KA#025

dedo meñique de la mano pMZ
*kɨ?-?unV(k) (n) ?U#028

dedo pulgar pOM **kɨ"-ka:* (n)
KA#022

defecar pMZ **tɨ:n?* (vi) Tɨ#037

defender pOM **ku-wahn ~ ku-wa"n*
(vt) WA#025

dejar pMZ **cak* (vt) CA#015

dejar una bulta pM **huk* (vt)
HU#004

delgado pM **pehay* (adj) PE#004

delgado pZ **cehV* (adj) CE#006

delgado pGZ **wayay* (adj)
WA#047

delicado → escaso

demorarse pM **po:?š* (vi) PO#038

derecho pOM **tɨy-i* (adj) Tɨ#063

derramar pMZ **tem* (vt) TE#005

derretir, llorar pMZ **hɨ:y?* (vi)
Hɨ#029

derrumbar pMZ **hu:?m* (vt)
HU#010

derrumbarse pOM **ha?w ~ ha"w*
(vi)
HA#030

desalojar pM **ci?t* (vi, vt) CI#043

desamarrar pM **ku-keh* KE#005

desatar pM **keh* (vt) KE#004

desatar pOM **mu-keh-i* KE#006

desatar → arrojar

desayuno pOM **?a-hop* (n)
HO#028

desbaratar pZ **hik* (vt) HI#004

desbrazar, quebrar pM **he?c* (vi)
HE#005

descansar pMZ **po:?ks* (vi)
PO#024

descansar pZ **heh* (vi) HE#006

descascarar pOM **nɨ-?e:?k* [?] (vt)
?E#007

descendientes pMZ **ca:ne* (n)
CA#033

descomponerse pOM **ma?t ~ ma"t*
(vi) MA#042

descuartizar pMZ **?e:?k* [?] (vt)
?E#006

descubrir un hueco pM **hot* (vi)
HO#034

desear pMZ **cok* (vt) CO#003

desgranar pMZ **?iks* (vi, vt)
?ɨ#010

deshacer pMZ **he:?y* HE#029

deshincharse pOM
*naš-ki:hš ~ naš-ki"š [?] (vi)
KI#016

desnudo pOM **ni:-wa"c* (adj)
WA#005

despacio pOM **tuta"ky* (adv)
TU#049

despacio pZ **ponhi* (adj, adv)
PO#030

despertar pMZ **yus* (vt) YU#023

despierto → vivo

desplumar pOM *ni:-wihš ~ ni:-wiš WI#030

desprender pM *ku-wa:c ~ ku-wa?c (vt) WA#010

desteñirlo pMZ *yak-pot? (vt) PO#048

detener pOM *mac-?it ~ mac-?it (vt) ?I#021

devolver pM *yak-wimpit (vt) WI#017

día, de pOM *šihw-n (adv) Si#017

día, sol pZ *hama (n) HA#012

diario pOM *hapóm-hapóm (adv) HA#018

diarrea pZ *pah-e (n) PA#009

diarrea, tener pM [Veracruz] *ni:?-tin ~ ni:?-ti?n (vi) Ti#038

diarrea, tener pZ *pah (vi) PA#008

dibujo → obra

diente pMZ *ti:c (n) Ti#008

difícil → pleito

dinero pM *me:nyu (n) ME#013

dique → pretil

diseño → obra

dispensar pOM *me:?kš (vi) ME#011

divisar pOM *ni-?ihš ~ ni-?iš (vt) ?I#010

doblado (papel, etc.) pMZ *?oc-i (n) ?O#002

doblar pOM *yak-ne?k ~ yak-ne"k (vt) NE#003

doblar pZ *?u?c (vi) ?U#006

doblar pZ *paks (vt) PA#038

doblar → ir u regresar

doblar; amontonar pMZ *nek? (vt) NE#001

doblar (p.ej., alambre) pM *?o:?y (vt) ?O#039

doler pM *pik (vi) Pi#021

doler → quemar

dolor pMZ *to:?y-a [?] (n) TO#035

domar, amansar pM [Veracruz]

*yak-ma:šuy (vt) MA#041

donde, ¿donde? pM *hu-mV (part) HU#011

donde, ¿dónde? pZ *hu-ti (part) HU#032

donde, adonde pOM *ma: (part) MA#001

dormir pMZ *ma:h? MA#015

dormir pZ *?iŋ (vi) ?i#019

dormir → empollar

dueño, patrón, amo pZ *ko-?omi (n) ?O#027

dulce pMZ *pahak (n, adj) PA#012

durar pM *hek (vi) HE#008

duro pZ *kamam (adj) KA#043

duro pZ *paki (adj) PA#035

echar a perder pZ *cik-tokoy (vt) TO#013

echar tortillas pOM *šukuhk ~ šukuk (vi) SU#012

echarselo pZ *kot-ay (vt) KO#031

eclipse del sol, haber pOM *šihw ?o:?k (vi) ?O#014

ejote pM [Veracruz] *kuy-šihk (n) Si#004

ejote pZ *yawa-sik (n) Si#006

él, ella pMZ *he ~ he? (pron) HE#001

ella → él

elote pZ *yaw(a)-mok (n) MO#010

embarrar pM *poc (vt) PO#007

embarrar pZ *ne?k (vt) NE#004

emborracharse pOM *mu:k ~ mu"k (vi) MU#014

empacar pOM *?a-cuhm ~ ?a-cum (vi) CU#036

empacharse pOM *šipš (vi) SI#021

empapar pMZ *so?m (vt) SO#016

empatar pGZ *to?p (vt) TO#024

empezar pZ *co?c (vi) CO#001

empezar → comenzar

empollar; dormir pZ *moŋ (vi) MO#018

empujar → tentar

empujar, quebrar pZ *ya?k* (vt)
YA#009

enagua, falda pZ *te?ksi* (n)
TE#004

encender pM *no?k* (vt) NO#004

encender pZ *no?* (vi) NO#001

enchuecarse pOM *nehw ~ new* (vi)
NE#012

encía pGZ *na:?na?* (n) NA#021

encima pOM *ni:-kiš-m* (adv)
Ki#018

encino pMZ *soho* (n) SO#004

encino blanco pOM *po:?p šoh* (n)
SO#005

enclocarse pZ *?oks* (vi) ?O#025

encoger pZ *si?c* (vi) SI#005

encoger, unir pMZ *muk* (vt)
MU#009

encontrar pMZ *pa:?t* [?] (vt)
PA#055

encontrar pOM *yak-pa:?t* (vt)
PA#058

encorvar pM *?u:?y* (vi, vt)
?U#049

encumbrar, subir a la cumbre, pagar
pOM *ku-peht ~ ku-pet* (vi)
PE#014

encurvado → chueco

endenantes → hace rato

enderezar pOM *yak-tihw ~ yak-tiw*
(vt) Ti#056

endulzar pMZ *pahak-?iy* (vi, vt)
PA#015

endurecerse pM *?e:?m* (vi)
?E#010

endurecerse (vi), mecatear (vt) pMZ
hu:?n (vi, vt) HU#016

enfermedad pOM *pa"m* (n)
PA#041

enfermedad, muerte pZ *ka?-kuy*
(n) KA#004

enfermo, estar pOM *pihk-?iy* (vi)
Pi#022

enflaquecerse → secarse

enfrente de pM *wihn-kuhk* (adv)

WI#023

enfriar pOM *yak-še:?m* (vt)
SE#007

enfriar pOM *šuhš ~ šuš* (vi)
SU#028

enfriarse pM *še:?m* (vi) SE#006

enganchar pZ *wi?ks* (vt) Wi#012

enmarañar pOM *ho?p ~ ho"p* (vi)
HO#029

enmohecer pMZ *ho:?m* (vi)
HO#016

enojarse pOM *?ehk ~ ?ek* (vi)
?E#005

enojarse pOM *ho:ht-ma?t*
~ *ho:ht-ma"t* (vi) MA#043

enojarse pZ *ki?s* (vi) KI#019

enredado pOM *?ašy* (adj) ?A#043

enrojecer → colorado, ponerse

enrollar pMZ *pit* (vt) PI#033

enrollar pOM *?a-piht ~ ?a-pit* (vt)
PI#034

enrollar pOM *ni-piht ~ ni-pit* (vt)
PI#035

enrollar pM [Veracruz] *šeket* (vt)
SE#004

enrollar pM *ša:c ~ ša?c* (vi)
SA#003

enrollar pZ *woy* (vi) WO#021

ensartar pOM *hi:?p* (vt) Hi#020

ensartar → sacar

enseñar pOM *yak-?iš-pihk*
~ *yak-?iš-pik* (vt) Pi#012

enseñar → aprender

enseñar, mostrar pOM *tuk-?ihš*
~ *tuk-?iš* (vt) ?I#011

ensordecerse pOM *naht ~ nat* (vi)
NA#032

ensuciarse → mancharse

entenado → hijastro

entenado(a), ahijastro(a) pMZ
ko-?unV(k) (n) ?U#029

entender pOM *win-matow* (vt)
MA#046

entrar pMZ *tik-?iy* (vi) Ti#019

entumirse pMZ *tus* (vi) TU#046

envase → recipiente
envolver pMZ *mon?* (vt)
MO#014
envolver pZ *pɨ?t* (n) Pɨ#037
epazote pOM *putte:ty* (n) PU#036
epilepsia pOM *poh-pa"m* (n)
PO#014
esale pM [Veracruz] *mu:š(ik)* (n)
MU#027
escalera de un solo palo pM
te:?n-i(k) (n) TE#012
escarbar pMZ *tah* (vt) TA#006
escarbar pM *yum* (vi) YU#018
escarbar algo pOM *yak-tah* (vt)
TA#007
escarbar (gallinas) pOM *ka:?c* (vi)
KA#007
escardar pMZ *hoks* (vt) HO#015
escoba pZ *pet-kuy* (n) PE#026
escoba pM *pe:ht-an* (n) PE#025
escobeta pOM *po?t-n* (n) PO#049
escoger pOM *win-?ihš ~ win-?iš*
(vt) ?I#012
esconder pOM *yu?c* (vi) YU#003
esconder → meter
esconderse pZ *yam* (vt) YA#012
escondidas, hacer algo a pZ *wɨ?n*
(vt) Wɨ#018
escoplear → cincelar
escribir pMZ *ha:y?* (vi) HA#033
escupir pMZ *cuh* (vi) CU#014
escurrir pOM *še:?kš* (vi) SE#005
escurrir, salpicar pMZ *sa?ks* (vi)
SA#012
ese pZ *te?-* (pron dem) TE#001
ése, aquel pOM *ši"t* (pron dem)
SI#031
espalda pMZ *his...* (n) Hɨ#022
espalda pZ *?uka* (n) ?U#018
espantar pOM *?a-cɨ?k-?ɨy* Cɨ#009
espanto → susto
espejo, vidrio pOM *?ihš-n* (n)
?I#015
esperar pMZ *ho?k* (vt) HO#012
esperar pM *?aw-?iš* (vi) ?I#008

esperar pM *?aw-cɨ:nay* (vi)
Cɨ#022
espeso pMZ *hinV(k)* (adj) HI#009
espeso → turbio
espiar pZ *tu?n* (vt) TU#036
espiga pM *kohk* (n) KO#009
espiga de maíz pM *mo:k-kohk* (n)
KO#010
espiga de maíz pZ *cutu* (n)
CU#052
espina pMZ *?ápit* (n) ?A#037
espinar pZ *ma?s* (vi) MA#039
espinilla → canilla de la pierna
espinilla (enfermedad) pOM
mehc-wahy (n) WA#040
esposa → mujer
espuma pM *?o:?p-?ik* (n) ?O#033
espumar pM *?o:?p* (vi) ?O#032
estaca para sembrar maíz o frijol pM
ni:p-an (n) NI#010
estante pM [Veracruz]
mo?co-komom (n) MO#018
estar, existir pMZ *?it* (vi) ?I#018
estar tonto pZ *how* (vi) HO#041
este pMZ *yɨ?* (pron dem) Yɨ#001
estibar pMZ *ta?c* (vt) TA#003
estibar pM *ma:?kš* (vt) MA#022
estirarse pZ *tu?y* TU#058
estómago → barriga
estornudar pM [Veracruz]
heti(?)ks (vi) HE#028
estrecho, cuadrado pMZ *kahi* (adj)
KA#016
estrella pMZ *ma:ca?((a)k)* (n)
MA#007
estrenar pOM *ši"m* (vt) SI#015
estrujar pZ *hi?s* HI#013
estudiante pOM *?iš-pɨhk-pa* (n)
Pɨ#013
estudiar pMZ *?is-pɨk* (vi) Pɨ#011
excremento pMZ *tin* (n) TI#014
excremento pM *tɨ?n-i* (n) Tɨ#039
existir → estar
exprimir pMZ *mɨ:?ks* (vi)
Mɨ#017

exprimir pZ *mɨ?k (vt) Mɨ#015

extender pMZ *ye?p (vt) YE#011

extender pOM *wo:?c (vi) WO#002

extender(se) pOM *ye?p-tɨhw ~ ye?p-tɨw (vi) Tɨ#055

faisán pOM *yu:kcin (n) YU#015

faisán pZ *wɨ:ku (n) Wɨ#011

falda → enagua

familiar pOM *mu-ku"k (n) KU#006

familiar, pariente pM *ku?ku (n) KU#005

fastidiarse pOM *cihp ~ cip (vi) CI#033

feliz → alegre

festejar pZ *sɨ?ŋa? (vi) Sɨ#016

fiado pOM *yoh (n) YO#004

fiado, darle pZ *ha?c-ci? (vt) CI#002

fierro, metal pZ *tɨ?ŋ-kuy (n) Tɨ#059

fiesta, nombre, sol pMZ *sɨw (n) Sɨ#012

finalizar pOM *ku-kɨš-ah (vi) Kɨ#027

flaco pOM *pa-tɨ"hc (adj) Tɨ#007

flaco → seco

flamear pOM *ye:?n [?] (vi) YE#010

flauta, pito pZ *sus-kuy (n) SU#032

flechar → picar

flojo, suelto pM *ho?ni(k) (adj) HO#027

flojo (perezoso) pOM *nu:š (n) NU#018

flor pMZ *pɨhi(k) (n) Pɨ#004

flor pZ *hɨyɨ (n) Hɨ#031

flor pGZ *mo:ya? (n) MO#021

flor de maíz pOM *mok-pɨh-y (n) Pɨ#005

flor de Santa María, crisantemo pOM *po:?p pi:?š (n) PI#026

florear → inflar

flotar pZ *pɨ?n (vi) Pɨ#032

fogón pMZ *?akwa?n (n) ?A#020

formón pOM *pa:h-n (n) PA#011

freir pOM *?on-ca:y ~ ?on-ca" CA#045

frente pOM *win-pok (n) PO#019

frente pZ *win-pak-ca? (n) CA#004

frente; mecapal pMZ *win-pak (n) PA#033

fresco pOM *še:?m-y (adj) SE#008

frijol pMZ *sɨk (n) Sɨ#003

frijol blanco pMZ *po:p?o?-sɨk (n) Sɨ#005

frijolar → sembrado de frijoles

frío pMZ *pakVk (n) PA#037

friolento pOM *tip (n) TI#016

fruta pMZ *tɨm (n) Tɨ#028

fruta, dar pZ *tɨm-?ɨy (vi) Tɨ#035

fruta, dar pZ *tɨm-?ah (vi) Tɨ#036

fruta parecida a la ciruela, tipo de pMZ *tu:ni (n) TU#037

fuego, lumbre pMZ *huk?-ut (n) HU#007

fuego, lumbre pM *hɨhn (n) Hɨ#015

fuerte, macizo pM *mɨkɨk (adj, adv) Mɨ#010

fuerte, recio, fuerza' pZ *pɨmi (adv, adj, n) Pɨ#027

fuerza pMZ *mah (adj) MA#012

fuerza pM *maháw (n) MA#013

fuerza → fuerte

fumar pMZ *huk? (vi, vt) HU#005

gabán pOM *ni:-hen (n) HE#017

gajo pM *ši:šta (n) SI#026

gallina → pollo

gallo pOM *ná"w-ce:wy CE#024

gancho pOM *ho?k-n (n) HO#013

gargantilla → collar

garrapata pOM *ši:y (n) SI#037

gastarse pMZ *tuk (vi) TU#010

gatear pZ *koŋ (vi) KO#034

gato pOM *či:tɨ (n) CI#042

gato montés pOM *šihk-ka: (n)
    KA#024
gavilán pM *wi(:k)cin (n) WI#011
gavilán pZ *tahpi (n) TA#028
gavilán, especie de pZ * ?i?k?i?k
    (n) ?I#002
gavilán, especie de pOM *me?ty (n)
    ME#019
gavilancillo pMZ *liklik (n)
    LV#002
gavilancillo pOM *cin?ihtk (n)
    CI#028
gemelo pZ *mecci (n) ME#005
gemelo → cuate
gemir pZ *pɨ?m (vi) Pɨ#026
germinar pM *muš (vi) MU#023
golpear pZ *caw (vt) CA#041
golpear → aplastar
golpear → tocar
golpear a un poste pM *paš (vi)
    PA#046
golpear con el puño pMZ *kos (vt)
    KO#027
golpear con el puño → picotear
golpear ligeramente con algo pun-
    teado pMZ *piks (vt) PI#016
gordo pOM *ye:?k-y (adj) YE#005
gorgojo pM *wok(ak) (n) WO#008
gota pOM *ta"kš-y (n) TA#020
gotear pMZ *cun (vi) CU#041
gotear pM *ta?kš TA#019
gotear → peinar
gozo pOM *šohn-tak (n) SO#019
grande pOM * ?a-mɨh (adj)
    Mɨ#007
grande → mayor
granero para maíz pMZ *ce?s (n)
    CE#019
granizo pM *tɨ:c-tu (n) Tɨ#004
granizo pZ *ca?-tuh (n) TU#007
grano de la piel pMZ *pu:c?(-i) (n)
    PU#002
grasa pM * ?ona (n) ?O#030
grillo pZ *cu?ni (n) CU#042
gris pZ *ho?ma (adj) HO#018

gritar → llorar
gritar, llorar pZ *weh (vi) WE#004
grueso pM *mapši(n) (adj)
    MA#033
gruñir pGZ *wok (vi) WO#005
guacamaya pOM *kawVš (n)
    KA#068
guácimo pMZ * ?i:k (n) ?ɨ#013
guajolote macho pOM *tu:htk-na"w
    (n) TU#053
guajolote, pavo pM *tu:tuk (n)
    TU#052
guajolote, pavo pZ *ka?ncyi (n)
    KA#046
guajolote, pavo pZ *tu?nuk (n)
    TU#040
guanábana pM [Veracruz]
    *katuc-?a:ti (n) ?A#050
guardar pOM *pɨhkɨ?k ~ pɨhkɨ"k (vi)
    Pɨ#023
guaya, palmera pM [Veracruz]
    *wa:yan (n) WA#046
guayaba pMZ *pos ~ posos ~ pohos
    (n) PO#039
guayacán pM *nɨ:c-kuy (n)
    KU#031
guía de chayote pOM *wip (n)
    WI#026
guía, práctico pOM *ku-tu:? (n)
    TU#056
gusano pMZ *kumu (n) KU#013
gusano pM [Veracruz] *tɨ?nik (n)
    Tɨ#042
gusano pOM *tini?k (n) Tɨ#043
gusano pZ *cu?kin (n) CU#024
gusano de mariposa pM *hin-tɨpš
    (n) Tɨ#051
gusano gallina ciega pM *nɨ:s-kumu
    (n) KU#014
gustar pM *?ut [?] (vi) ?U#046
hablar pM *kapš (vi) KA#055
hablar pM *koc (vi) KO#001
hablar pZ *?otoŋ (vi) ?O#037
hablar a alguien pM *mu-koc (v)
    KO#004

hace rato, endenantes pMZ *?a:m-in
(adv) ?A#028

hacer pM *tun (vi, vt) TU#041

hacha pM *puš-an (n) PU#025

hambre pMZ *yu:h (n) YU#002

hambre, tener pM *yu:h-?o:?k (vi)
?O#016

hambre, tener pZ *yu? (vi)
YU#001

hartar pMZ *ku:s? (vi) KU#020

hay pOM *hem (part) HE#012

hecho → obra

helecho, ocopetate pOM *cim(c)y(k)
(n) CI#024

hembra pM *to?š-hay (n) TO#027

hermana mayor, tía pM *ci? (n)
Ci#001

hermana mayor, tía pZ *cici (n)
Ci#003

hermano pZ *tiwi (n) Ti#057

hermano mayor pMZ *?a(h)ci (n)
?A#003

hermano mayor de mujer pMZ
*?awin (n) ?A#054

hermano,-a menor pMZ *?u:ci (n)
?U#005

hermano,-a menor pZ *poco? (n)
PO#010

hermoso → bonito

herramienta pOM *tun-peht-n (n)
PE#022

hervir pMZ *toks (vt) TO#015

hervir pOM *ni-?i:?c (vi) ?i#005

hervir pZ *yum (vi) YU#019

hervir; pintar pZ *tok (vi) TO#005

hielo pOM *cušta (n) CU#044

hígado, corazón pM *ho:ht (n)
HO#035

hija pOM *ni:š (n) Ni#022

hija pZ *yom-manik (n) MA#031

hija → hijo

hijastra pOM *ku-ni:š (n) Ni#024

hijastro, entenado pOM *ku-mahnk
(n) MA#029

hijo pMZ *manik (n) MA#026

hijo, hija pZ *cisi (n) Ci#026

hilar pMZ *pi:?t (vt) PI#036

hilo pMZ *pi:?t-i (n) PI#038

himno → canción

hincarse pM *košo-tenay (vi)
TE#010

hinchar pM *timam (vi) TI#013

hinchar → mover

hincharse pM *ki:š ~ ki?š [?] (vi)
KI#015

hincharse pZ *siŋ (vi) SI#034

hinchazón pOM *ki"š (n) KI#017

hinchazón pZ *siŋ-i (n) SI#035

hipo, tener pM [Veracruz]
*hi(?)kš-tuk (vi) Hi#011

hocico → pico

hoja pMZ *?ay (n) ?A#056

hoja de maíz pZ *mok(o)-?ay (n)
?A#058

hombre pMZ *hayá(w) (n)
HA#037

hombre pMZ *pin (n) Pi#028

hombre pM *ya?we-tik (n)
YA#019

hombre pGZ *pi:šiñ (n) Pi#036

hombro pOM *kehky KE#014

hombro pZ *weki? (vt) WE#006

hondo, pozo, etc. pM *ki:hk (n)
Ki#009

hongo pGZ *no:no? (n) NO#008

hongo comestible pOM *pa:?-?u:kn
(n) ?U#021

hongo, nanacate pOM *muš (n)
MU#025

horcón pMZ *kom(om) (n)
KO#017

horcón pOM *kup (n) KU#018

hormiga pM [Veracruz] *cukut(ik)
(n) CU#026

hormiga pOM *cukn (n) CU#025

hormiga pZ *hahcuku (n) HA#002

hormiga carpintera pOM *ku:y (n)
KU#035

hoy → ahora

hoy (tiempo pasado) pZ *ma?ak (n)

MA#020

hoyo pOM *hut* (n) HU#030

hoyo pZ *hos* (n) HO#032

hozar, levantar pM *wipš* (vt) WI#028

huarache pMZ *kɨʔ-ʔak* (n) ʔA#011

huérfano pZ *(ko-)yaw-mak* (n) MA#018

hueso pMZ *pak* (n) PA#020

huevo pM *tuʔt-i(k)* (n) TU#051

huevo pZ *poka* (n) PO#021

huevos, poner pM *tu:t ~ tuʔt* (vi) TU#050

huipil pOM *wɨcɨ"* (n) Wɨ#003

huipil pZ *ʔasa* (n) ʔA#044

huir → correr

huir → corretear

hule pM *ʔo:me* (n) ʔO#028

hule pZ *naʔh* (n) NA#004

humear pM *hok* (vi) HO#007

humear pM *wi:ʔš* (vi) WI#032

humedecer pOM *nik* (vi) NI#003

húmedo pOM *nik* (adj) NI#004

humo pMZ *hoko* (n) HO#009

huso, malacate pOM *pi:ʔt-n* (n) PI#037

idioma pOM *ʔayu:hk* (n) ʔA#064

idioma sagrado pM *ʔa-ma:san* (n) MA#035

ídolo pOM *ca-ma:šn* (n) MA#038

iglesia pM [Veracruz] *pu:š-tɨk* (n) Tɨ#018

iglesia pOM *cahp-tɨhk* (n) Tɨ#014

iglesia pZ *masan-tɨk* (n) MA#036

iguana pMZ *tɨ:cɨC* (n) Tɨ#009

iguana pMZ *to:ki* (n) TO#011

incienso → copal

inflar → ventear

inflar, florear pMZ *pɨh* (vi) Pɨ#002

insecto, especie de pOM *tɨhk nɨ:c* (n) Nɨ#011

insecto, especie de pGZ *ʔu:su?* (n) ʔU#043

insípido pOM *cek* (adj) CE#007

instrumento de musica de viento pM *šu:š-an* (n) SU#030

instrumento para escribir pMZ *ha:yʔ-kuy* (n) HA#034

instrumento para tirar pM *tuh-an* (n) TU#006

inteligente pM *wih-i(k)* (adj) WI#006

interior de la casa pZ *tɨk-hoh* (n) Tɨ#022

interrogativa, partícula pMZ *hu* (part) HU#001

intestino pMZ *puʔpu* [?] (n) PU#023

invitar → mandar

ir pMZ *nɨks* (vi) Nɨ#015

ir pZ *maŋ* (vi) MA#051

ir pGZ *nɨk* (vt) Nɨ#014

ir u regresar, doblar (cosa larga y delgada) pOM *ʔohc ~ ʔoc* (vi) ʔO#001

ir (y ya haber regresado) pMZ *ʔoy* (vi) ʔO#041

ixtle pMZ *nawin* (n) NA#035

ixtle pOM *šaʔk* (n) SA#008

izquierda pMZ *ʔaw-nah-in* (n) NA#005

jabalí pM *ʔi:cɨmɨ* (n) ʔI#001

jabalí pGZ *mok-yo:ya* (n) YO#019

jabón pOM *šic* (n) Sɨ#001

jadear pZ *poʔn* (vi) PO#031

jaguar pZ *cikin-kahaŋ* (n) KA#019

jaguar, tigre pOM *kuy-šipɨhy* (n) Sɨ#011

jalar pMZ *hupʔ* (vt) HU#023

jalar pM *wo:ʔn* (vt) WO#013

jalar pZ *hikiʔ* (vi) Hɨ#006

jalar, etc. pM *wɨ:ʔn* (vt) Wɨ#015

jalar, llevar pMZ *won* (vi) WO#011

jalar; morder cosa dura pMZ *kɨ:ʔs*

(vt) Kɨ#019
jalarlo pZ *hiti? (vt) HI#015
jarro pOM *?o:?y (n) ?O#040
jeme pOM *ci:?wy (n) CI#054
jícara pMZ *cima (n) CI#021
jimba (tipo de carrizo) pOM *ši:hš
   (n) SI#025
jobo pMZ *ham(ay)-kuy (n)
   KU#029
jobo pM *maši-kuy (n) KU#030
jorobado pOM *hɨkuš (adj)
   Hɨ#007
jugar pZ *miciy (vi) Mɨ#003
juguete pM *?i:k-an (n) ?I#003
juile pZ *cawa (n) CA#043
junco pM [Veracruz] *nun (n)
   NU#013
juntar pMZ *sum (n) SU#018
juntar pM *?a-pɨk-muk (vi)
   MU#012
juntar pM *yak-muk (vt)
   MU#013
juntar pZ *tu?m (vi) TU#029
labio pM *?aw-?ak (n) ?A#010
labio pZ *?aw-sis (n) SI#024
labio pOM *?a-tehm (n) TE#007
labrar pMZ *cec (vt) CE#002
ladearse pOM *key (vi?) KE#030
ladrar pMZ *woh (vi) WO#003
lagartija pMZ *paci (n) PA#004
lagartija pM *tik (n) TI#007
lagarto pMZ *?uspin (n) ?U#044
lágrima pM *win-nɨ:? (n) Nɨ#008
laja pMZ *pot?ot [?] (n) PO#045
lamer pZ *kat (vt) KA#063
lamer pOM *we:?y (vt) WE#017
langosta pM *pa:taš (n) PA#060
largo pMZ *pɨhi (adj) Pɨ#003
larguero pM *?akáp (n) ?A#017
larva de ditisco, de la mosca Dobson
   pM *pikwin (n) PI#019
latir, pegar pMZ *naks (vt)
   NA#015
lavar pMZ *puh (vt) PU#007
lavar pZ *ce? (vt) CE#001

lavar nixtamal pOM *šu:?c (vt)
   SU#003
lavar nixtamal, pescar con red pMZ
   *ma:k? (vt) MA#017
lavarse las manos pM *kɨ?-puh (vi)
   PU#008
lazar pMZ *hu?ps (vt) HU#024
lazo pOM *šu:c-n (n) SU#002
leche pZ *cu?c-i nɨ? (n) CU#011
lechuza, tecolote, buho pM *hu?kɨ
   (n) HU#009
lejos pOM *hekém (adv) HE#010
lejos pZ *ya?hi (adv) YA#006
lejos pGZ *hu:?mɨ? (adv) HU#012
lengua pMZ *to:c (n) TO#003
leña pM *ha?š-i (n) HA#024
leña → árbol
leñar pM *ha?š (vi) HA#023
león pMZ *capac-ka:haw (n)
   KA#020
león pOM *hahm-ka: (n) KA#021
levantar pOM *pɨta"k (vi) Pɨ#038
levantar → alzar
levantar → hozar
levantarse (como polvo) pZ *to?n
   (vi) TO#022
liar (postes, carrizo) pM *wɨ:?t (vt)
   Wɨ#021
liendre pZ *su?c (n) SU#005
liendre(s) pM *?á:šik (n) ?A#047
lima pM *me:?h-an (n) ME#007
limón pOM *cahp-poš (n) PO#040
limpiar pOM *po:ht~po?t (vt)
   PO#047
limpiar pOM *yak-wa:hc~yak-wa"c
   (vt) WA#003
limpiar (cortar plantas) pOM *mo:?c
   (vt) MO#004
limpiar (superficie) pM
   *win-wa:c~win-wa?c (vi)
   WA#002
limpiarse pM *wa:c~wa?c (vi)
   WA#001
limpio pM *wa?ac (adj) WA#004
lindero pOM *cowa?n (n) CO#025

liquidámbar pOM *cɨhy* (n) Cɨ#030

liso pOM *hu"š^y* (adj) HU#027

liso pOM *tɨʔkš* (adj) Tɨ#026

liso → ágil

lodo pM *moʔ(n)co* (n) MO#006

loma pOM *tunn* (n) TU#031

lombriz de la tierra pZ *toʔt* (n)
TO#029

lorrar → derretir

luchar a brazo partido, chapotear
pMZ *kitaw* (vi) KI#022

lugar pMZ *ʔit* (n) ʔI#022

lumbre → fuego

lumbre, echar pMZ *kih* (vi)
KI#002

luna; mes pMZ *poyʔa* (n)
PO#055

llama pZ *nema* (n) NE#009

llamar pM *ya:š-hay* (vt) YA#014

llano pOM *hoy* (n) HO#043

llano → plano

llanura → plano

llave pOM *ʔa-wa:hc-n* (n)
WA#011

llegar pOM *haʔt~ha"t* (vi)
HA#026

llegar pZ *nuʔk* (vt) NU#005

llegar → venir

llenar pM *yak-ʔuc* (vt) ʔU#002

llenar(se) de un líquido pOM *peʔc*
(vi, vt) PE#001

llenar, pesar pMZ *ʔuc* (vi)
ʔU#001

llenarse pMZ *tas* (vi) TA#031

llenarse con un líquido pMZ *kom*
(vt) KO#015

lleno pM *paciC* (adj) PA#005

lleno pOM *ʔuc-i* (adj) ʔU#003

lleno, estar → turbio, estar

llevar pMZ *kon* (vi, vt) KO#019

llevar pOM *yak-co:ʔn* (vt)
CO#013

llevar pOM *yak-nɨhkš* (vt)
Nɨ#017

llevar pOM *wihc~wic* (vt)
WI#001

llevar → jalar

llevar, recoger pMZ *pɨk* (vt)
Pɨ#010

llevar (caballo) pOM
pa-wohp-pa-wop (vt) WO#016

llorar → gritar

llorar, gritar pM *ya:š~yaʔš* (vi)
YA#013

llorón pOM *ʔa-ya"šy* (adj)
YA#015

llover pOM *tu:h~tu"h* (vi)
TU#008

lloviznar pM [Veracruz] *yɨmɨm*
(vi) Yɨ#005

lluvia pMZ *tu:h* (n) TU#009

machetón → cuajinicuil

macho pOM *ya"wy* (n) YA#018

macizo → fuerte

madrastra pOM *ku-ta:k* (n)
TA#012

madrastra pZ *ko-mama* (n)
MA#024

madre, mamá pMZ *nana* [?] (n)
NA#022

madre, mamá pOM *ta:k* (n)
TA#011

madre, mamá pZ *ʔapaH* (n)
ʔA#040

madre, mamá pZ *mama* (n)
MA#023

madurar pMZ *ca:mʔ* (vi) CA#019

madurar → pintar

maduro pM *ca:mʔ* (adj) CA#020

maestro pOM *yak-ʔiš-pɨhk-pa* (n)
Pɨ#014

maguey pM *ca:hc* (n) CA#005

maguey pZ *ʔoho* (n) ʔO#008

maíz pMZ *mo:k* (n) MO#009

maíz desgranado pMZ *ʔiks-i* (n)
ʔɨ#011

maíz desgranado pOM *mok-pahk*
(n) PA#032

majagua pZ *poʔwah* (n) PO#006

mal de ojo pOM *wihn-pa"m* (n)

PA#042

mal, mancha pOM *ʔa-ší:ʔk (n, adj) Sɨ#007

malacate → huso

malamujer (yerba) pMZ *keʔw (n) KE#029

mamar pM *ciʔc (vi) CI#004

mamar, darle de; dar pecho pM *yak-ciʔc (vt) CI#005

mamar, morder pMZ *cuʔc (vi, vt) CU#008

mamey pZ *sapane (n) SA#015

mana pMZ *ma:san (n) MA#034

manantial pOM *mu"t (n) MU#029

manar pMZ *muʔt (vi) MU#028

mancha → mal

mancharse, ensuciarse pM *ʔaw-ší:ʔk-ʔɨy (vi) Sɨ#008

manco pMZ *kɨʔ-tuku (n) TU#015

mandar pOM *kehš ~ keš (vt) KE#023

mandar pZ *ʔaŋ-kiʔm (vi, vt) KI#004

mandar, invitar pOM *wohw ~ wow (vi) WO#019

manear pMZ *moʔks (vt) MO#012

manejar pM *yak-yoʔy (vt) YO#022

mano, a pOM *kɨ"-am (adv) Kɨ#033

mano, brazo pMZ *kɨʔ (n) Kɨ#001

mano de metate (culebra) pM *pa:wan … ca(:ʔ)nay (n) CA#030

mano derecha pM *ʔoy-in (adj) ʔO#049

mañana pM *hapóm (adv) HA#015

mañana pM *hopoy (n) HO#031

mañana pZ *hohi(-mɨ) (adv) HO#006

mapache pZ *ʔasa (n) ʔA#045

mapache pZ *cu-yomo (n) YO#009

mar pMZ *me(h)ya (n) ME#020

maraca pZ *cum (n) CU#037

maraña pOM *hoʔp-y (n) HO#030

marchar pOM *paʔkš (n) PA#039

marchitarse pM *ni:ʔkš (vi) NI#006

marchitarse → regar café

marearse pOM *ku-mu:k ~ ku-mu"k (vi) MU#015

marido pM *nɨ-yaʔwe (n) YA#020

mariposa pMZ *suse:pe (n) SU#034

mariposa pM *totok (n) TO#031

mariposa pGZ *me:meʔ (n) ME#012

marrano → cerdo

más pOM *niyuk (part) NI#016

masa pM *hɨc-i (n) Hɨ#003

masa pZ *kɨʔt-i (n) Kɨ#029

masa rugosa pZ *haʔp-e (n) HA#017

mascar pM *puʔy (vt) PU#041

máscara pOM *win-hup (n) HU#021

masticar pZ *was (vt) WA#032

mataculebra, pepegua pOM *payɨm (n) PA#063

matar pM *yak-ʔo:ʔk (vt) ʔO#015

matar → tumbar

mayacate pMZ *cas(i) (n) CA#038

mayor, grande pMZ *mɨha (adj) Mɨ#006

mazacoate pZ *mɨʔah-cahin (n) CA#013

mazate pM [Veracruz] *ší:tɨ (n) SI#032

mecapal pOM *cɨʔm-n (n) Cɨ#017

mecapal pZ *cɨmis (n) Cɨ#018

mecapal → frente

mecate pMZ *cay (n) CA#049

mecatear → endurecerse

mecatear; mentir pMZ *su:c [?] (vi) SU#001

mecer pM *tɨ:ʔy (vt) Tɨ#064

medianoche pM *cu:ʔ-m (adv) CU#004

medicina → remedio

medida pOM *kihpš-n (n) KI#011

medio pMZ *kuk (n?) KU#002

medio, en pMZ *kuk-mɨ (adv) KU#003

medio hermano mayor pMZ *ko ?aci (n) ?A#004

mediodía pM [Veracruz] *pu:t-šɨhw (n) PU#032

mediodía pOM *kuhk (y-)šɨhw (n) Sɨ#013

medir a palmas → medir por cuartas

medir con pM *tuk-kipš (vt) KI#012

medir; pensar pMZ *kips (vi, vt) KI#009

medir por cuartas, medir a palmas pMZ *cat? (vi) CA#039

mejilla → cachete

mejilla; borde pMZ *?a:ka (n) ?A#016

mejor pMZ *ni(yuk)-?oyV (adj, adv) ?O#044

menear, etc. pOM *ka:?p (vt) KA#049

menospreciar pM *peš (vt) PE#011

mentir → mecatear

mercancía pOM *to:?k-y (n) TO#007

mes → luna

metal → fierro

metate pM *pa:w-an (n) PA#062

meter pMZ *yak-tɨk-?ɨy (vt) Tɨ#020

meter, esconder pMZ *yu:?k (vt) YU#013

meter la comida en la salsa pM [Veracruz] *wec (vt) WE#002

metlapil pOM *pa:n mahnk (n) MA#030

mezcal pOM *hok-nɨ:? (n) Nɨ#003

mezclar pMZ *mot (vt) MO#016

mezclar → ordeñar

mezquino (tacaño) pOM *win-tuk (n) TU#012

mico de noche pMZ *wi(?)yuk(s)

(n) WI#045

miedo, tener pM *cɨ?k-?ɨy (vi) Cɨ#008

miel pMZ *ci:nu (n) CI#031

migaja, piltrafa pOM *?a-pu?šm (n) PU#030

milpa pMZ *kama (n) KA#036

milpa pMZ *mo:k-kama (n) KA#038

milpa ajena pM [Veracruz] *hay-kama (n) KA#037

miltomate pOM *cap-ko"n (n) KO#023

mio pMZ *n-he? (pron) HE#002

mirar pZ *?a?m (vt) ?A#029

miseria pOM *?ayohw-an (n) ?A#062

moco pM *hɨhp-tɨ?ni (n) Tɨ#040

moco pZ *sit (n) SI#030

moho pOM *?umy (n) ?U#025

mojado pM *šo?ok (adj) SO#008

mojado pZ *coko (adj) CO#009

mojar pMZ *muh (vt) MU#006

mojar pZ *to?s (vt) TO#026

mojarra pOM *ca:m-k (n) CA#023

mojarra pGZ *co:wi?n (n) CO#024

mojarra correntera pOM *ke:py (n) KE#022

mojarse pM *šo:?k (vi) SO#007

mojón pOM *cipa?an (n) CI#034

mole pM *?u:?p-i(k) ?U#038

moler pMZ *way (vi, vt) WA#042

moler pZ *ha?p (vt) HA#016

moler pZ *po?m (vt) PO#025

moler → apedrear

moler masa pMZ *ho:?s (vt) HO#033

moler pinole pMZ *kɨ:?t (vt) Kɨ#028

moler (chile) pMZ *mo?c (vt) MO#003

moler (nixtamal) pM *hɨc (vi) Hɨ#002

molestar pMZ *ne?m (vi) NE#010

molido pMZ *way-e (n) WA#044

molleja pOM **me:?c* (n) ME#002

mono → chango

morado pOM **?uk-y* (adj) ?U#011

morder cosa dura → jalar

moreno pOM *ciš-y (adj) CI#037

morir pM **?o:?k [?]* (vi) ?O#013

morir pZ **ka?* (vi) KA#001

mosca pM *caci (n) CA#009

mosca pZ *hɨhɨ (n) Hɨ#004

mosca pM [Veracruz] *huy-huy (n)
HU#043

moscón pOM *cušk-cač (n)
CA#007

mosquito, zancudo pMZ **?u:su(k)*
(n) ?U#041

mosquito, zancudo pMZ **he:he* (n)
HE#007

mostrar → enseñar

mover pOM *yac (v) YA#003

mover, hinchar pMZ *sin (vi)
SI#018

mover horizontalmente contra algo
pZ *pak (vt) PA#016

mover (brazo, pierna) pM *cukut
(vi, vt) CU#020

moverse pOM **yu?kš* (vi) YU#017

moyocuil pOM *pihky (n) PI#013

muchacho (vocativo) → tú (vocativo
masculino)

mucho pMZ *may (adj, adv)
MA#054

mudar pM *tikac (vi) TI#008

mudarse (culebras, etc.), pMZ **hi:?c*
(vi) HI#001

mudo pMZ **?u:ma* (n) ?U#024

muela pMZ **?ok* (n) ?O#010

muerte pOM **?o:?k-n* (n) ?O#019

muerte pZ **ka?-aŋ* (n) KA#003

muerte → enfermedad

muerto pOM **?o:?k-pa* (n)
?O#020

muerto pOM **?o:?k-y* (n) ?O#018

muerto pGZ **cu?c* (n) CU#012

mugre pOM **pu"t-y* (n) PU#037

mujer pOM **to"šy-tɨhk* (n)
TO#028

mujer, esposa pZ *yomo (n)
YO#008

multiplicar pOM **may-?ɨy* (vt)
MA#063

mundo pOM **na:hš-wihn* (n)
WI#020

muñeca de la mano pM
**kɨ?-yo?k(-tu)* (n) YO#006

murciélago pMZ **tɨ:si* (n) Tɨ#052

musgo pOM **ce?(n)k* (n) CE#018

musgo pOM **cu:hc* (n) CU#006

músico (instr. de viento) pM
**šu:š-pa* (n) SU#033

nácara pM **pu:p* (n) PU#022

nacer pZ *nay (vi) NA#036

nacer → brotar

nacer, aparecer pM **ke?š* (vi)
KE#024

nada pMZ *ni ti (part) TI#003

nada pM *ka ti (part) TI#002

nadar pMZ *yun (vi) YU#021

nadar pZ **pu?n* (vi) PU#019

nadie pM **ni pɨn(a)* (pron) Pɨ#030

nalga → cadera

nanacate → hongo

nanche pM *tuš (n) TU#047

nariz pMZ **hɨp(ɨ)* (n) Hɨ#017

nariz; pico pZ *kinɨ (n) KI#006

neblina pOM **nɨma"* (n) Nɨ#020

negación pM *ni (part) NI#001

negro pMZ **yɨk(ɨk)* (adj) Yɨ#004

nene pOM **le?k(y) ~ le:?k(y)* (n)
LV#001

nido pM **pe?n-i* (n) PE#009

nieta, nieto pMZ **?oko-?unV(k)* (n)
?U#027

nieta, nieto pZ **?ok-manɨk* (n)
MA#027

nieto → nieta

niña pM *kišay (n) KI#020

niña pOM **ki:š-?u:nk* (n) ?U#034

niña → niño

niño, niña pMZ **?unV(k)* (n)
?U#026

nixtamal pMZ *pic-i (n) PI#005

no pM *ka:h [?] (part) KA#013

no pOM *kah (part) KA#012

noche pMZ *cu:? (n) CU#001

noche, de pM *cu:?-p (adv) CU#005

nombre pZ *nɨyi (n) Nɨ#026

nombre → fiesta

nopal pOM *ta:t (n) TA#034

nosotros (excl) pM *?ɨ:ci-at ~ ?ɨc-at ?I#002

nosotros (excl) pOM *?ɨ:c (pron) ?ɨ#003

nube ?O#031

nublado pOM *win-tuk-y (adj) TU#013

nuca pM *nahc- (n) NA#001

nudo de caña, coyuntura pOM *com (n) CO#011

nudo en mecate pOM *šoc-y (n) SO#002

nudo (de árbol) pM [Veracruz] *poni (n) PO#027

nuera de la mujer, suegra mujer pOM *šokšy (n) SO#015

nuevo pMZ *home (adj) HO#017

nuevo pMZ *namV (adj) NA#016

nuevo, dejarlo pM *nam-?ɨy (v) NA#017

nutria, perro de agua pOM *nɨ:?-?uk (n) ?U#020

nutrir pOM *hot-?iht ~ hot-?it (vi) ?I#020

obra, hecho; dibujo, diseño pZ *cɨk-i (n) Cɨ#005

obscuro pMZ *pi?c-(V)(k) (adj) PI#002

obscuro pM *ko:?co (adj) KO#006

observarlo pZ *ko-ham (vt) HA#009

ocopetate → helecho

ocote, pino pMZ *cin (n) CI#027

ocupar pOM *yak-tuhn ~ yak-tun (vt) TU#033

odiar pZ *mɨs (vt) Mɨ#022

ofrecer pM *wan-pet (vt) PE#016

ofrenda → trabajo

ofrendar, trabajar pMZ *yos (vt, vi) YO#013

oído pM *matow-an (n) MA#047

oír pMZ *matow (vt) MA#045

ojo pMZ *win (n) WI#018

ojo pZ *witɨm (n) WI#043

ojoche pM [Veracruz] *moho (n) MO#008

ojos cerrados, con los pOM *wihn-pi"c (vi) PI#003

oler pOM *?a-šu:?k (vi) SU#009

oler, besar pMZ *su:?k (vi) SU#008

oler bien pOM *pa"hk šu:?k (vi) SU#011

olor desagradable, de pZ *hak(a) (adj) HA#007

olor repugnante de pescado, tener pMZ *can-can (adj) CA#025

olote pMZ *hɨ:pak (n) PA#024

olla pOM *tu?c (n) TU#002

olla pZ *suyu [?] (n) SU#043

ombligo pM *pu:cɨk (n) PU#006

ombligo pZ *tunu (n) TU#038

ondear pZ *peye? (vt) PE#029

ordeñar, mezclar pMZ *ma?c (vt) MA#006

oreja pMZ *ta:cɨk (n) TA#004

oreja (la parte exterior) pOM *ta:ck ?ak (n) ?A#014

oriente pOM *huma: ši: pyicɨm (adv) PI#008

orilla pM *pa?aw (n) PA#063

orina pM *ta?c-i (n) TA#002

orina pZ *cem (n) CE#014

orinar pM *ta:c ~ ta?c (vi) TA#001

orinar pZ *cem (vi) CE#015

otate → carrizo

otro pM *hatu?k (n) HA#028

otro pZ *?eya (n) ?E#017

padrastro pM *ko-te:tE (n) TE#019

padre, papá pMZ *tata (n) TA#033

padre, papá pM *te:tE (n) TE#017

padre, papá pZ *hatoŋ (n) HA#027

pagar pOM *ku-huhy ~ ku-huy (vt) HU#040

pagar pOM *mu-huy (vi) HU#041

pagar → deber

pagar → encumbrar

pagar una deuda pOM *ku-wet (vt) WE#016

paila pM [Veracruz] *puša(n).. (n) PU#028

paisano (del mismo pueblo) pOM *mu-ko-kahpVn (n) KA#051

pájaro pMZ *hon (n) HO#020

pájaro pM *mu:?ši (n) MU#026

pájaro barranqueño pM [Veracruz] *hut-hut (n) HU#031

pájaro, especie de pM *pepe [?] (n) PE#010

pájaro, especie de pZ *?otV?otV (n) ?O#038

pájaro vaquero pMZ *?o:k-?o:?k (n) ?O#022

pájaro vaquero pMZ *wa:kV-?o:kV (n) ?O#023

palabra, dicho pZ *cam-e (n) CA#018

palanquear pOM *wɨ:?pš (v) Wɨ#018

pálido pZ *puwa (adj) PU#040

palma pMZ *tu:c-kuy (n) TU#001

palma de la mano pOM *kɨ:?-ho:ht (n) HO#036

palmera → guaya

palmera, tipo de pOM *tɨ:šy(š) (n) Tɨ#053

palo → árbol

palo colorado pMZ *capac-kuy (n) KU#028

palo cuyo cáscara tiene veneno pM *hɨ:t (n) Hɨ#026

palo mulato pMZ *cɨkɨk (n) Cɨ#007

paloma pOM *pak (n) PA#017

paloma pZ *ku?ku? (n) KU#008

palpar, tentar pOM *ton-mahc

~ ton-mac (vt) MA#004

paludismo pOM *ši:?mha (n) SI#017

panal de avispa pM *hoyan (n) HO#042

pantalón pGZ *nokkoy (n) NO#006

pantorilla pOM *teky-ce:t (n) CE#022

papá → padre

papachote pMZ *puh-kuy (n) KU#032

papel pMZ *noki (n) NO#005

papel pZ *toto (n) TO#030

para → para que

para que, para pZ *wa?k ~ wa? (part) WA#015

parado de espaldas encorvadas en un grupo, estar pOM *mɨ?š ~ mɨ"š (vi) Mɨ#023

paraje (para pasar la noche) pOM *ma:h-ta:hk-n (n) TA#013

pararlo pMZ *yak-tenay (vt) TE#009

pararse pMZ *tenay (vi) TE#008

pararse → pisar

pararse; calmarse pZ *sɨh (vi) Sɨ#002

pared pM [Veracruz] *me:?š-i (n) ME#017

pared pM *poc-e (n) PO#008

parejo, raso pOM *kihpš-y (adj) KI#010

pariente → familiar

párpado pM *win-?ak (n) ?A#015

párpado pZ *witɨm-naka (n) NA#013

parte, pedazo pMZ *we:?n-V (n) WE#014

partir pZ *kaks (vi) KA#031

partirse pMZ *wa?ks (vi) WA#023

pasado mañana pMZ *huwɨstɨkmɨy (adv) HU#037

pasar pMZ *nas (vi) NA#024

pasar, atravezar pMZ *hak (vi)

HA#006

pasar, hacer pOM
*yak-nahš ~ yak-naš   (vt)
NA#029

pasear pM **witit* (vi) WI#040

pasto → zacate

patear pMZ **nep* (vt) NE#011

patear; arrear pMZ **kep* (vt)
KE#019

patio pM **taha?w* (n) TA#009

patio pZ **?aŋ-kɨ?* (n) Kɨ#003

patrón pOM **win-cɨn* (n) Cɨ#023

patrón → dueño

pavo → guajolote

pecado → culpa

pecho pZ **kuk-pak* (n) PA#028

pecho, dar → mamar, darle de

pedazo pZ **wen-e* (n) WE#012

pedazo → parte

pedazos pMZ **pu?si(s)* (n)
PU#027

pedernal pOM **hɨ:n-ca:?* (n)
CA#002

pedir pOM **?a-matow* (vi)
MA#048

pedir pZ **wa?k* (vt) WA#020

pedir prestado pOM **?a-nu?kš* (vi)
NU#008

pedo pGZ **či:š-i* (n) CI#039

pegado, quedarse pZ **ne?ks-cɨ?y*
(vi) NE#006

pegajoso pZ **ne?ks* (adj) NE#007

pegar pZ **cah* (vt) CA#011

pegar pZ **ne?ks* (vi) NE#005

pegar → latir

pegar a alguien pOM
*yak-kohš ~ yak-koš (vt) KO#028

pegar, abofetear pM **ci:?k* (vi, vt)
CI#013

pegar, azotar pM **wop* (vt)
WO#015

pegar con algo pMZ **wipip* (vt)
WI#027

pegar (con cola o pegamento) pMZ
*?o:?c (vi, vt) ?O#003

pegarse → dar

peinar pM **ka:?š [?]* (vt) KA#060

peinar; gotear pMZ **wɨc* (vt)
Wɨ#002

peine pM **ka:?š-an* (n) KA#061

pelar pMZ **cik* (vi, vt) CI#011

pelar pZ **to?ks* (vt) TO#018

pelear pMZ **kip* (vi) KI#007

peligroso, riesgo pOM **ku-cɨ?k-a*
(n) Cɨ#011

pellizcar pM **ti?kš* (vi) TI#012

pellizcar pOM **?e:?kš* (vt) ?E#008

pellizcar a alguien pOM **yak-cehkš*
(vt) CE#012

pelo, pluma pMZ **pɨk* (n) Pɨ#006

pelón → calvo

peludo pOM **ni:-wahy* (adj)
WA#041

pender pZ **hɨ?m* (vi) Hɨ#013

pene pZ **kan* (n) KA#044

pensamiento pOM **win-ma?y-n* (n)
MA#058

pensar pOM **win-mahy ~ win-may*
(vi) MA#056

pensar → medir

pepegua → mataculebra

pepenar pMZ **piw* (vt) PI#040

pepeyoche pGZ **na:ma?* (n)
NA#018

pepeyoche → cocoyuche

pequeño pMZ **mucVC* (adj)
MU#005

pequeño → chico

pequeño; arena pOM **cay* (adj, n)
CA#048

perder pMZ **tokoy* (vi) TO#012

perder pMZ **yak-tokoy* (vt)
TO#014

perder el habla pOM **?u:?m* (vi)
?U#023

perdiz pMZ **wonon [?]* (n)
WO#014

perezoso pMZ **kantVn?i* (adj)
KA#046

perforar pMZ **sut* (vt) SU#035

perro pMZ *taka* (n) TA#017
perro pGZ *čimpa?* (n) CI#026
perro de agua → nutria
pesado pMZ *hemec* (adj) HE#015
pescado → pez
pescar con red → lavar nixtamal
petate pM *to?k-i* (n) TO#010
petate pZ *pata* (n) PA#059
pez, pescado pMZ *?aksa* (n)
   ?A#021
pez, pescado pMZ *kok?e* (n)
   KO#013
pez, pescado pGZ *wo?ŋ* (n)
   WO#020
picado pOM *wok* (vi) WO#004
picar pMZ *ke:w?* (vt) KE#028
picar, arder pM *?an* (vi, vt)
   ?A#032
picar, arder sin flama pMZ *hem*
   (vi) HE#014
picar (chile) pOM *himu:m* (vi)
   Hɨ#014
picar, flechar pMZ *tip* (vt) Tɨ#044
picar, punzar pOM *yo?c ~ yo"c* (v)
   YO#002
picar (zancudo) pM *ku:?p* (vt)
   KU#019
pichichi pMZ *pi:?sisi* (n) PI#028
picho; zanate pM *pihš* (n) PI#023
pico → nariz
pico, hocico pOM *?a-pahk* (n)
   PA#023
picotear pOM *šuhpš* (vt) SU#026
picotear, golpear con el puño pMZ
   sow? (vt) SO#022
pie pOM *teky* (n) TE#003
pie pZ *maŋ-kuy* (n) MA#052
piedra pMZ *ca:?* (n) CA#001
piel → cáscara
pierna pM [Veracruz] *hu?-pak* (n)
   PA#026
pierna, muslo pMZ *puy* (n)
   PU#043
piltrafa → migaja
pino → ocote

pinole pOM *mo:hk-way* (n)
   WA#043
pinole pZ *po?te* (n) PO#043
pinolillo pZ *pe?c* (n) PE#002
pintar pMZ *koy* (vi, vt) KO#036
pintar pM *na?c* (vi, vt) NA#002
pintar pOM *?uk* (vi, vt) ?U#010
pintar → hervir
pintar, madurar pMZ *pu?ks* (vi)
   PU#016
pinto pMZ *cikin* (adj) CI#015
piña pGZ *?uhu?* (n) ?U#008
piñuela pMZ *cikwiC* (n) CI#020
piojo pMZ *?a:wat* (n) ?A#055
piojo pOM *?o:?c-y* (n) ?O#004
pisar pM *wa?k* (vi) WA#016
pisar pM *yuk-wa?k* (vi) WA#019
pisar, pararse pMZ *te:?n* (vi)
   TE#011
piso de la casa pOM *tihk-ho:ht* (n)
   HO#038
pito → flauta
placenta pM *ma:wac* (n) MA#053
plano, llano, valle, llanura pZ *hɨ?ŋ*
   (n) Hɨ#028
planta o árbol, tipo de pMZ *hepey*
   (n) HE#022
planta, tipo de pOM *matu:k tay*
   (n) TA#038
platanillo pM *wayɨ-?ay* (n)
   ?A#059
platicar pOM *mahy-ta:k ~ mahy-ta"k*
   (vi) MA#064
platicar → conversar
plato pOM *tešy* (n) TE#015
plegar pOM *?a-ne?k ~ ?a-ne"k* (vt)
   NE#002
pleito pM [Veracruz] *cukin* (n)
   CU#019
pleito, difícil pOM *cip* (n, adj)
   CI#032
pliegue pMZ *hi:?c-i* (n) HI#002
pluma → pelo
poblado → pueblo
pobre pOM *?ayohw-pa* (n)

?A#063

pobreza, causar pOM
yak-?ayohw ~ yak-?ayow (vt)
?A#061

poco pMZ *?u:syan* (adj, adv)
?U#045

poder → saber

podrir pMZ *pu:c?* (vi) PU#001

pollo, gallina pMZ *ce:wE(kV?)*
CE#023

polvo pM *pu?šu(m)* (n) PU#029

polvo de tierra pOM *na:hš-hok* (n)
HO#010

poner algo en posición vertical pZ
paŋ (vt) PA#061

poner boca abajo; quebrar; regar
pMZ *muc* (vi) MU#002

poner en pMZ *kot* (vt) KO#030

poner encima pZ *tunun* (vi)
TU#045

poner grasoso pM *?on* (vt)
?O#029

poner nido pMZ *pe?n* (vi)
PE#008

poner una jaula pM *nak* (vi)
NA#006

ponerse el sol → tirar

pongolote pMZ *pokok* (n)
PO#022

poposquela, tutpana pM [Veracruz]
tuktukpanik (n) TU#028

pozo → hondo

práctico → guía

precio pOM *cow* (n) CO#021

prenderse lumbre, agrandarse pOM
mihiy (vi) Mi#008

prensar (con pinzas, etc.) pMZ *ho?t*
(vi) HO#040

presa → pretil

presidente municipal pOM *ku-tun-k*
(n) TU#034

prestar pMZ *nu:?ks* (vt) NU#007

prestar pZ *kak* (vt) KA#026

pretender → amarrar

pretil, presa, dique pMZ *me(?)ke*

[?] (n) ME#010

primavera pGZ *mo:y-hon*
(< mo:ya-hon) (n) HO#022

probar pOM *?iš-mahc ~ ?iš-mac*
(vi) MA#003

prohibitivo pZ *?uy ~ ?u* (part)
?U#047

pronto pOM *cohk* (adv) CO#005

provocar un sensación muy fuerte
pMZ *hah* (vi) HA#003

pueblo pZ *kumkuy* (n) KU#010

pueblo, poblado pOM *kahpVn* (n)
KA#050

puerco espín pMZ *?apit-ka:haw*
(n) KA#018

puerta pM *tik-?ahw-kV?* (n)
Ti#021

puerta pOM *tik-?aka"w* (n)
?A#019

puerta pZ *?aŋ-kiy* (n) Ki#036

pujar pM *?ih* (vi) ?i#007

pulga pMZ *pistik* (n) PI#029

pulque pOM *ke:?č* (n) KE#003

punteado pMZ *pi?ks* (adj?)
PI#017

punzar pMZ *kum* (vt) KU#009

punzar pMZ *woc?* (vt) WO#001

punzar pZ *sips* (vt) SI#022

punzar → picar

puño pM *mi:?kš-i(k)* (n) Mi#018

puro (tabaco) pOM *hu"ky-?ahy* (n)
?A#057

pus pM *komi(k)* (n) KO#016

pus pZ *pu:ni(k)* (n) PU#020

¿qué? pMZ *ti* (part) TI#001

quebrar pMZ *wen* (vi, vt)
WE#011

quebrar pZ *cih* (vt) CI#009

quebrar → curtir

quebrar → desbrazar

quebrar → empujar

quebrar → poner boca abajo

quebrar → tronchar

quebrarse (palo, etc.) pM *tih* (vi)
Ti#010

quedar pM *tan (vi) TA#025
quedarse pOM *wɨʔm ~ wɨ"m (vi)
  Wɨ#013
quedarse pZ *cɨʔy (vi) Cɨ#029
quelite pMZ *cɨpʔV (n) Cɨ#025
quelite blanco pMZ *camam (n)
  CA#024
quemar pMZ *hun (vi) HU#014
quemar comida pZ *hips HI#012
quemar, doler pMZ *toy (vi)
  TO#032
quemar (lumbre) pMZ *yak-toy (vt)
  TO#034
querer pM *wan ~ waʔn (vt)
  WA#024
querer pZ *sun (vt) SU#020
quien pZ *ʔiyɨ (pron) ʔI#023
quieto pOM *tuʔk- [?] (adj)
  TU#026
quitar (ropas o zapatos) pOM *hen
  (vt) HE#016
quitarse pZ *coʔt (vi) CO#016
rabia, tener pMZ *ʔin (vi) ʔI#004
rabo → cola
raíz pM *tikcik (n) TI#011
raíz pZ *waci (n) WA#012
rajar pMZ *paps (vi) PA#045
rajar pM [Veracruz] *cay (vi)
  CA#047
rajar pOM *caʔpš CA#037
rajar pZ *tet (vt) TE#016
rajar → abrir
rajar leña pOM *ceʔkš (vt)
  CE#013
rajar leña pZ *weʔk (vt) WE#005
rajarse pZ *cac (vi) CA#006
rana, sapo pMZ *nakak (n)
  NA#011
rana, sapo pM [Veracruz] *weka (n)
  WE#007
rascar pZ *hec (vt) HE#004
rascar pZ *heʔn (vi, vt) HE#018
rasgar pZ *cic (vi, vt) CI#003
rasguñar pMZ *cuks (vt) CU#030
rasguñar pOM *cehkš (vt) CE#011

raso → parejo
raspar → zafar
raspar pMZ *hep (vt) HE#020
raspar pMZ *he:ʔp (vt) HE#023
raspar pMZ *wo:ʔs (vt) WO#017
raspar pOM *ki:ʔpš (vt) KI#014
raspar pZ *hepeʔ (vt) HE#021
rastrillar pZ *heps (vt) HE#025
rasurar pMZ *huʔs (vi) HU#026
rasurar pM *ke:ʔpš (vt) KE#021
rata, ratón pMZ *cu:k (n) CU#021
ratón → rata
rayar pZ *payaʔ (vt) PA#064
rayo pOM *wɨcuk (n) Wɨ#004
rayo, relámpago pOM *wicuk (n)
  WI#004
reata pM *tɨpš-i (n) Tɨ#048
rebanar pZ *wɨk (vt) Wɨ#007
rebuznar pM [Veracruz] *hɨ:kš (vi)
  Hɨ#009
recibir pZ *pɨk-cow (vt) CO#020
recio → fuerte
recipiente, envase pOM
  *ʔapɨhkɨ(ʔ)ny (n) ʔA#039
recluir pGZ *pah (vt) PA#007
recobrar la fuerza pOM
  *mɨk-pɨhk ~ mɨk-pɨk (vi) Pɨ#018
recoger (trapo, mecate, etc.) pOM
  *wici:hk ~ wici"k WI#002
recogerlo pZ *wok (vt) WO#006
recto, estar pM *yakš (vi) YA#011
recto, estar; tumbar pMZ *tɨw (vi)
  Tɨ#054
red pOM *šu:m-y (n) SU#019
redondo pOM *pikk (adj) PI#018
refregar pM *hin (vi) HI#008
refrescarse pZ *suk-ʔɨy (vi)
  SU#007
regañar pOM *ʔoh [?] (vt) ʔO#005
regañar pMZ *ce:ʔk (vt) CE#009
regar pZ *puŋ (vt) PU#038
regar → batir
regar → poner boca abajo
regar café, marchitarse pMZ *ye(ʔ)y
  (vi) YE#012

regresar pM **wimpit* (vi) WI#013
regresar pZ **witu?* (vi) WI#044
regresar pGZ **se:t* (vi) SE#011
reir pMZ **si:k?* (vi) SI#007
reir con alguien pMZ **mu:-si:k?* (vi) SI#008
relámpago → rayo
relampaguear pOM **wicuk* (vi) WI#003
rellenar pOM **ci:?c* (vi) CI#007
remedio, medicina pMZ **coy* (n) CO#026
remendar pM [Veracruz] **nap* (vt) NA#023
remendar pOM **?a-šuy-?ay* (vi) SU#042
repartir pMZ **sah* (vt) SA#005
repasar pOM **?a-nahš-a?* ~ *?a-naš-a?* (vt) NA#026
repasar (masa) pOM **he?k ~ he"k* (vt) HE#009
resbaloso pMZ **panac* (adj) PA#044
resbaloso pM **nokoc* (adj) NO#007
resbaloso (en lugar donde hay grava) pOM **ha:šk* (adj) HA#022
resembrar pOM **?a-ni:p* (vi) NI#008
resina pM **?up-i(k)* (n) ?U#036
respeto pOM **win-cí?kɨ-n* (n) CI#024
respirar pM **šeh* (vi) SE#001
reuma pZ **mɨ?(h)a(h)* (vi) Mɨ#005
reventar pMZ **tops* (vi) TO#025
reventar pZ **piŋ* (vi) Pɨ#039
reventar (fruta) pOM **ce?t ~ ce"t* (vi) CE#021
revés, al → contrario al
revivir pZ **sa?* (vi) SA#001
revolver pMZ **moc* (vi) MO#002
rezar pMZ **ko-nu:ks* [?] (vi) NU#010
rezar pOM **kahpš-ta:k ~ kahpš-ta"k* (vi) KA#056

riesgo → peligroso
río pMZ **mɨha nɨ:?* (n) Nɨ#005
risa → sonrisa
robalo pMZ **(h)a(?)y(aw)* (n) HA#040
robar pZ **nu?m* (vt) NU#012
robar, buscar pMZ **me:?c* (vt) ME#003
rocío pMZ **mɨk?* (n) Mɨ#016
rodar pMZ **pitit* (vi, vt) PI#039
rodilla pMZ **koso(k)* (n) KO#029
rojo pMZ **capac* (adj) CA#035
rollo de hoja o zacate pM **ša:?c-e(k)* (n) SA#004
romper pMZ **pu?w* (vt) PU#039
romper pM **kɨ:?c* (vt) Kɨ#005
romper pZ **heht* (vt) HE#027
romper pZ **wɨt* (vt) Wɨ#020
romper cosas secas pMZ **mo:?t* (vi) MO#017
romper una cosa larga y delgado pM **pot* (vi) PO#041
roncar pOM **to:?kš* (vi) TO#017
ropa, tela pM **witɨ?* (n) WI#042
rótula pM **košo-pahk* (n) PA#031
roza pZ **yuh-kuy* (n) YU#010
rozadura pMZ **yu:h?-i* (n) YU#009
rozar pMZ **yu:h?* (vi, vt) YU#008
rugir pOM **ni:?c* (vi) NI#002
ruido, hacer pM **nok* (vi) NO#003
rumiar pOM **?a-pu"y-a?* (vt) PU#042
sabana pM [Veracruz] **mɨhy-win* (n) Mɨ#027
saber pM **haw-?ɨy* HA#031
saber pZ **mus* (vt) MU#024
saber, poder pM **hat* (vt) HA#025
sabroso pOM **šu"k* (adj) SU#010
sabroso pGZ **kɨ:n* (adj) Kɨ#012
sabroso, estar pMZ **?om* (vi) ?O#026
sacar pM **yak-picɨm* (vt) PI#007
sacar o ensartar pMZ **wi?ks* (vt)

WI#012

sacar (cosa delgada) pMZ *hu:?t
(vt)   HU#033

saciar pMZ *yeh (vt) YE#002

sacudir pMZ *sit (vt) SI#027

sacudir pZ *pup (vt) PU#021

sacudir pZ *yɨ?k (vi) Yɨ#003

sacudir pGZ *ši?ks (vt) SI#013

sacudir (trapo) pOM *win-šiht
~ win-šit (vt) SI#028

sajar pMZ *si:?w (vt) SI#036

sal pMZ *ka:na (n) KA#045

salado pM *ta:mac (adj) TA#024

salado pZ *kana-pahak (adj)
PA#013

salamandra pGZ *pon-ha:ya? (n)
HA#038

salir pMZ *picɨm (vi) PI#006

salir bien, sanar pZ *wɨ-?ah (vi)
Wɨ#001

salir (objeto) pMZ *cot (vi)
CO#015

salir (persona) pMZ *co:?n (vi)
CO#012

salir (savia) pOM *?u:?p (vi)
?U#035

saliva pMZ *cuh-i(C) (n) CU#015

salpicar pMZ *te?ps (vi) TE#013

salpicar → escurrir

saltamontes → chapulín

saltar pMZ *put (vi) PU#033

saludo pMZ *sokeCV (interj)
SO#013

saludo pZ *yus- [?] YU#024

sanar pMZ *co:k? (vi) CO#006

sanar → salir bien

sanar; contentarse pM *hot-kɨta:k
~ hot-kɨta?k (vi) Kɨ#022

sangre pMZ *nɨ?pin (n) Nɨ#013

sanguijuela pOM *nu:?pky (n)
NU#017

sapo → rana

sarape → cobija

sardina pM *še:še (n) SE#010

sarna pMZ *wɨ:yi (n) Wɨ#023

sarna pOM *šik (n) SI#010

sarnoso pM *ni:-šik (adj) SI#011

satisfecho pOM *ku"š-y (adj)
KU#021

secar pMZ *yak-tɨ:c? (vt) Tɨ#003

secarse, enflaquecerse pMZ *tɨ:c?
(vi) Tɨ#002

seco, flaco pMZ *tɨ?ɨc (adj)
Tɨ#005

secretario pOM hahy-pa (n)
HA#035

sed, tener pMZ *tɨ:c-?ɨy (n)
Tɨ#006

seguir pOM *pa-mihn ~ pa-min (vi)
MI#008

seguir pOM *pa-nɨhkš (vi) Nɨ#016

seguir pOM *pa-witiht ~ pa-witit (vi)
WI#041

seguir pOM *pa-yo?y ~ pa-yo"y (vt)
YO#021

seguir pZ *ko?w (vt) KO#035

sello pOM *ca?y-n (n) CA#046

sembrado de frijoles, frijolar pM
*šɨhk-kama (n) KA#039

sembrar pMZ *ni:p? (vi, vt)
NI#007

semilla pMZ *puh (n) PU#010

semilla pOM *tɨhm-t (n) Tɨ#034

seno, chiche pMZ *cu?c-i (n)
CU#010

seno, chiche pGZ *nu:nu (n)
NU#015

senos, teta pOM *ci?c-k (n)
CI#006

sentarse pMZ *cɨ:nay (vi) Cɨ#021

seña pOM *?iš-ta?n (n) TA#026

ser listo pMZ *wih (vi) WI#005

sereno pM *manik (n) MA#025

serrucho, sierra pM *hɨ:?t-an (n)
Hɨ#024

si pOM *pɨnɨ (part) Pɨ#031

sí pMZ *hɨ:? (part) Hɨ#001

sí pM *ho: (part) HO#001

siembra pMZ *ni:p?-i (n) NI#009

sierra → serrucho

silbar pM *wi:k~wi?k (vi) WI#010
sobaco pMZ *sak-... (n) SA#009
sobar pMZ *ha:s? [?] (vi, vt)
  HA#019
sobar pMZ *hɨtɨc (vt) Hɨ#027
sobrina pOM *cohk-nɨ:š (n)
  Nɨ#023
sobrino pOM *cohk-mahnk (n)
  MA#028
sofaldar pMZ *kic? (vt) KI#001
soga pM *hu?ps-an (n) HU#025
sol → fiesta
solo pMZ *na:y-tum (n) TU#030
soltar pZ *cɨk-ho?n (vt) HO#025
soltar → detener
sombra pM *?epak [?] (n) ?E#014
sombra de persona pZ *muŋ (n)
  MU#031
sombrero pOM *ko?-húp (n)
  HU#020
sonaja → cascábel
sonar pZ *ci?ki? (vi, vt) CI#014
sonar la nariz pOM *ši:?t (vi)
  SI#029
sonrisa, risa pMZ *si:k?-V (n)
  SI#009
soñar pOM *ku-ma:h~ku-ma"h (vi)
  MA#016
soplador → abanico
soplar pMZ *su:h? (vt) SU#006
soplar, abanicar pMZ *yem (vi)
  YE#006
soplar con la boca pOM *pi:hš~pi"š
  (vi) PI#024
sordo pOM *nat (adj) NA#033
sospechar con razón pZ *mɨ?y (vt)
  Mɨ#028
suave pZ *ponon (adj) PO#028
suavemente, con cuidado pOM
  *?oy-ta"ky (adv) TA#016
subida pOM *pet(y) (n) PE#018
subir pM *pet (vi) PE#012
subir pM *yak-pet (vt) PE#017
subir pZ *ki?m (vi) KI#003
subir a la cumbre → encumbrar

sudadero pOM *hɨpa"n (n) Hɨ#021
sudar pZ *pɨs (vi) Pɨ#034
sudor pMZ *?oso(s) (n) ?O#035
sudor pMZ *pɨs-V(k) (n) Pɨ#035
suegro de mujer pMZ *cu?-si (n)
  CU#048
suegra de mujer → nuera de mujer
suegra de mujer, nuera de mujer
  pMZ *sake(s) (n) SA#010
suelo → tierra
suelto → flojo
sueño pGZ *mo:ŋ-i () MO#019
sufrir pOM *?ayohw~?ayow (vi)
  ?A#060
sufrir una herida, quemadura pMZ
  *nɨ-toy (vt) TO#033
sulisuchi pM [Veracruz] *pumpum
  (n) PU#018
sumirse pOM *kin (vi) KI#005
suspirar pOM *mɨk-šeh (vi)
  SE#002
susto, espanto pOM *ci?kɨ (n)
  Cɨ#010
tabaco pGZ *cɨ:wi Cɨ#027
tábano pOM *cu:čC (n) CU#007
tabla, banco, banquito pOM *pu"y
  (n) PU#044
tacacholota pM *šico (n) SI#006
talzahuate pM [Veracruz] *šuhkut
  (n) SU#013
tamal pM *mɨ?k-i (n) Mɨ#014
tambor pMZ *kowa (n) KO#033
tapacamino → correcamino
tapadera pOM *?a-kɨ"y (n) Kɨ#037
tapanco pM [Veracruz] *kuy-win
  (n) KU#034
tapanco pOM *wɨ:?t-y (n) Wɨ#022
tapar, cerrar pMZ *?aw-kɨ:y? (vt)
  Kɨ#035
tapar (olla, etc.) pOM *?a-húp (vt)
  HU#019
tapir → anteburro
tapón pOM *?a-ci:?c (n) CI#008
tatuana pM *haycu?-ca(:?)nay (n)
  CA#028

tecolote → lechuza

tecomate pMZ *pok(ok)* (n) PO#018

tecomate, bule pOM *he:?p-n* (n) HE#024

tejer pMZ *ta:k?* (vi, vt) TA#014

tejer pM *koh* (vt) KO#007

tejón pMZ *ciku* (n) CI#016

tela → ropa

telaraña pMZ *ta:k?-e* (n) TA#015

temascal pOM *cíš-tɨk* (n) CI#040

temblar pMZ *mɨ?ks* (vi) MI#005

temblar (el cuerpo) pZ *sitit* (vi) SI#033

temblor pMZ *?us* (n) ?U#039

temporal de agua pM *po:t-an* (n) PO#044

tenamaste pZ *?oko-ca?* (n) ?O#025

tenate pOM *to"* (n) TO#001

tender pMZ *tɨy* (vt) Tɨ#060

tender en el suelo pMZ *to?k* (vt) TO#009

Tenochtitlán, Ciudad de México pOM *nɨ:?-wihn-m* (top) Nɨ#009

tentar → agarrar

tentar → palpar

tentar; empujar pMZ *ton* (vt) TO#021

tepegua pGZ *yu:či?* (n) YU#004

tepejilote pM *nuhn* (n) NU#003

tepezcuintle pM *yukho?* (n) YU#016

tepezcuintle pZ *huhnɨyɨ* (n) HU#015

tepezontle pM [Veracruz] *(?apit)-waya-kuy* (n) WA#045

terminar pM *yak-kɨš* (vt) Kɨ#026

terreno → tierra

teta → senos

tía pOM *cuku* (n) CU#027

tía pZ *?eme* (n) ?E#012

tía → hermana mayor

tibio pMZ *hókos* (adj) HO#014

tiempo de secas pOM *šɨhw-kopk* (n) KO#025

tierno pMZ *ya(:)wa* (adj) YA#017

tierra, terreno, suelo pMZ *na:s* (n) NA#031

tigre → jaguar

tigre (cualquier felino silvestre) pMZ *ká:haw* (n) KA#017

tijeretear pMZ *me?ps* (vt) ME#014

tijeras pOM *me?pš-n* (n) ME#015

tío pOM *cukúm* (n) CU#028

tirar (líquido) pOM *?iš-tehm ~ ?iš-tem* (vt) TE#006

tirar algo de un envase pMZ *top* (vt) TO#023

tirar; ponerse el sol pMZ *tɨ:?p* (vi) Tɨ#045

tiznarse pOM *cihš ~ ciš* (vi) CI#036

tizne pOM *hok-y* (n) HO#008

tizne pOM *wi:?š-y* (n) WI#032

tlacuache pM *po:* (n) PO#001

tlacuache pZ *cihi* (n) CI#010

tobillo pMZ *pok?i* (n) PO#020

tobillo pOM *teky-yo?k-t* (n) YO#007

tocar pMZ *kow* (vi, vt) KO#032

tocar pZ *tikin* (vi) TI#010

tocar → cosechar

tocar algo extendido pMZ *poks* (vt) PO#023

tocar, golpear pZ *koks* (vt) KO#014

tocar instrumento de viento → chiflar

tocayo pOM *mu-šɨhw* (n) Sɨ#015

todavía no pOM *ka?h-nɨm* [?] (part) KA#014

todo pMZ *mumu* (adj) MU#021

tomar agua pMZ *nɨ:?-u:?k* (vi) ?U#013

tomar, beber pMZ *?u:?k* [?] (vi, vt) ?U#012

tomar caldo pM *šu:?pš* (vt) SU#027

tomate pOM *ko"n (n) KO#022
tomate pZ *koya (n) KO#038
topetear pOM *tehš~teš (vi)
TE#014
torcer pMZ *wi:?t (vi) WI#034
torcer pOM *?a-wi:?t (vt) WI#036
torcer pZ *wo?t (vi) WO#018
torcer reata pM *tipš (vt) Ti#047
torcer reata pZ *ti?ps (vt) Ti#049
torcido pMZ *wi:?t-i (adj) WI#035
torcido pOM *?a-wi:?t-y (adj)
WI#037
tordo garrapatero pi:cu (n) PI#009
tortilla pMZ *?an-e (n) ?A#034
tortilla pM *ni:ni (n) Ni#021
tortilla pOM *ka:ky (←ka:y-k) (n)
KA#074
tortola pOM *ku:k (n) KU#007
tortuga pMZ *tuka (n) TU#025
tortuga pZ *ceke (n) CE#010
tos pM *?oho (n) ?O#006
tos pZ *su?ks-i (n) SU#016
toser pM [Veracruz] *?oho? (vi)
?O#007
toser pZ *su?ks (vi) SU#015
tostar pM *?ik (vi) ?i#008
tostar pM *yak-?ik (vt) ?i#009
tostar pZ *se?t (vt) SE#012
tostar; hacer adobes pMZ *mu:?c
(vt) MU#003
tostarlo pM [Veracruz] *ka:?y (vt)
KA#075
totomostle pOM *?ahktc (n)
?A#022
trabajador pOM *tuhn-pi (n)
TU#044
trabajar → ofrendar
trabajo pOM *tuhn-k (n) TU#043
trabajo pZ *yos-kuy (n) YO#015
trabajo, ofrenda pMZ *yos-e (n)
YO#014
traer pMZ *yak-min (vt) MI#009
traer pM [Veracruz]
*mu-min~mu-mi?n (vt) MI#010
traer pZ *min-a? (vt) MI#011

traer agua pMZ *mah (vi)
MA#009
tragar pMZ *hi:?n (vt) Hi#016
tragar pM *nac-?u:?k-i (vi)
?U#014
tragón → comilón
trampa pM *?u:?y-an (n) ?U#050
trampa pOM *nak-y (n) NA#007
trapiche pOM *wi:?t-n (n) WI#038
trasanteayer pOM *matu:k (n)
MA#049
trenzar pM *ke?kš KE#015
trenzar pOM *ku?t~ku"t (vt)
KU#025
trenzar pZ *pe?t (vt) PE#027
tripas pM *tihn-cay (n) CA#050
tristeza pOM *ho:ht-may (n)
MA#055
triunfar pOM *mata:hk~mata"k
(vi)
MA#044
tronar, brotar pMZ *pimim (vi)
PI#020
tronchar, quebrar pMZ *kit (vi)
KI#021
tronco pMZ *?ihsi (n) ?i#016
trozar pZ *ti?ks (vt) Ti#027
trueno pM *?an-i-way (n) ?A#035
tú (vocativo masculino), muchacho
(voc.) pOM *miš (pron)
MI#012
tucán pOM *ka:ti (n) KA#064
tucán pZ *kacih (n) KA#009
tufo, haber pZ *hukuk (vi)
HU#008
tumbar, matar pMZ *yak-ka? (vt)
KA#002
tumbra → recto, estar
tumor pGZ *cut (n) CU#050
tuna pOM *ta:t tihm (n) Ti#033
turbio, espeso (liquido) pOM *ki?šk
(adj) KI#018
turbio, estar; estar lleno pMZ *san
(vi) SA#014
tutpana → poposquela

tuyo pMZ *mici n-he?* (pron)
MI#004

tuza pMZ *tɨ(?m)pic* (n) Tɨ#046

tzompantle → colorín

unir pMZ *cow* (vi) CO#017

unir → encoger

uña pMZ *kɨ(c)cu(?k)s* (n)
CU#046

uña pM *šo:ki* (n) SO#011

uña de mano pM *kɨ?-šo:ki* (n)
SO#012

usar pOM *yak-tuhn ~ yak-tun* (vt)
TU#042

uso sexual, hacer pZ *?e?t* (vt)
?E#016

usted pMZ *mici* (pron) MI#002

ustedes pZ *mic-ta?m* (pron)
MI#003

ustedes pOM *mi:c* (pron) MI#001

vacío pM *tuk-wa?ac* (adj)
WA#006

vacío pZ *mape* (adj) MA#032

valer pOM *co:w-aht ~ co:w-at* (vi)
CO#023

valiente pOM *ho:ht-mɨkk* (adj)
Mɨ#011

valle → plano

vamos pM *ha?m(V)* HA#013

vapor pOM *pu:šypy* (n) PU#031

vara pM *paš-i* (n) PA#047

vara pOM *matc* (n) MA#050

variegado pMZ *kacc* [?] (adj)
KA#011

varios pMZ *na:ka* (n) NA#009

velador pM *tɨ?kš-pa* (n) Tɨ#025

vello del brazo pMZ *kɨ?-pɨk* (n)
Pɨ#008

vena, cuerda pM *?e:?m-e* (n)
?E#011

venado pM *haycu?* (n) HA#041

venado pZ *mɨ?ah* (n) Mɨ#001

vendedor pOM *to:?k-pa* (n)
TO#008

vender pMZ *?ɨ:?k* [?] (vi) ?ɨ#012

vender pMZ *ma?ay* (vt) MA#059

vender pM *to:?k* (vt) TO#006

veneno de la víbora pOM *šiwat*
(n) Sɨ#020

venir a alguien o a algo pZ *ku-min*
(vt) MI#007

venir pMZ *min* (vi) MI#006

venir, llegar pOM *mehc ~ mec* (vi)
ME#001

venta pMZ *ma?ah* [?] (n)
MA#060

ventear; inflar pMZ *poh* (vi)
PO#012

ventosear pMZ *ci:s?* (vi) CI#038

ver pMZ *?is* (vi, vt) ?I#007

ver pM *?e:?p* ?E#013

veras, de pOM *ha:nc..* HA#014

verde pMZ *cusu(k)* (adj) CU#049

verde, crudo pMZ *cus* (adj)
CU#043

verdolaga pOM *ya:?kwet* (n)
YA#010

verdolaga pZ *pecV-pecV* (n)
PE#003

verruga pMZ *cípin* (n) CI#035

verruga pZ *tapu* (n) TA#029

verter pZ *tek* (vt) TE#002

vestir pOM *šoš* (vi) SO#020

vidrio → espejo

viejo (cosa) pMZ *pakV* (adj)
PA#019

viejo (cosa) pMZ *tuku* (adj)
TU#014

viejo (persona, animal) pM
mah-Vt (n) MA#014

viejo (persona, animal) pOM *mah
ha?y* (n) HA#039

viento pOM *poh* (n) PO#013

viento pZ *sawa* (n) SA#017

vigilar pOM *?iš-?iht ~ ?iš-?it* (vi)
?I#019

vigilar, acechar pOM *šohk ~ šok*
(vt) SO#009

villeja (hormiga) pM *?uš(i)* (n)
?U#042

violeta, color pOM *cu"m-k* (adj)

CU#040

visitar pOM *ku-?ihš ~ ku-?iš* (vt)
?I#009

vivo, despierto pM *hutVk* (adj)
HU#035

voladora (una culebra) pM
[Veracruz] *to?ki-ca(:?)nay* (n)
CA#031

volar pMZ *ke:k?* (vi) KE#009

voltear pM *hup* (vt) HU#018

voltear pOM *kon-wimpit* (vt)
WI#015

voltearse pOM *wa?k-wimpit* (vi)
WI#016

vomitar pMZ *?i:?c* (vi) ?i#004

vómito pMZ *?i:?c-i* (n) ?i#006

voz pZ *?ote* (n) ?O#036

y pOM *hec* (part) HE#003

ya pOM *ti:* (part) Ti#001

yerba, planta, monte pOM *?uhc*
(n) ?U#004

yerba santa → acuyo

yerno pMZ *mi?ut* (n) Mi#002

yo pOM *?ihc* (pron) ?i#003

yo pMZ *?i:ci ~ ?ic* (pron) ?i#001

yuca pMZ *pisi* (n) PI#027

zacate pM *mihy* (n) Mi#026

zacate pM *šokot* (n) SO#014

zacate pZ *so?k* (n) SO#006

zacate, pasto pZ *mu?k* (n)
MU#017

zacate, tipo de pOM *pahky* (n)
PA#036

zacua pMZ *kunu* (n) KU#016

zafar, raspar pMZ *ko-ci?t* (vi, vt)
CI#044

zanate pMZ *?a:?ksyi* (n) ?A#023

zanate → picho

zancudo → mosquito

zapote amarillo pOM *hu:?w* (n)
HU#036

zapote colorado pM *ka?wak* (n)
KA#067

zapote prieto pM *cu:?kV* (n)
CU#022

zopilote pMZ *nu?pu* (n) NU#016

zorra pOM *wa:hš* (n) WA#033

zorrillo pMZ *pa:c* (n) PA#003

zumbar pOM *?a-mu:h ~ ?a-mu"*
(vi) MU#008

zumbar pGZ *hu:p* (vi) HU#022

zurdo → izquierdo

English-Spanish Index

able, be → saber, poder
accept → aceptar
accuse → acusar
accustom → acostumbrar
accustomed to, become
    → acostumbrarse con
acorn → bellota
advance (a work) → caminar, avan-
    zar (p.ej., trabajo)
advise → aconsejar
afraid, be → miedo, tener
agave fiber → ixtle
agile → ágil, liso
agouti → cerete
alligator → lagarto
alone → solo
already → ya
American kestrel → gavilancillo
and → y
angry, become → enojarse
ankle → tobillo
annatto → achiote
answer → contestar
ant → hormiga
ant, a species of → hormiga car-
    pintera
ant, kind of → villeja (hormiga)
anus → ano
appear → aparecer
appear → aparecerse
appear → nacer, aparecer
apply to a surface (e.g., clothes,

cloth,
    mud) → aplicar sobre superficie
    (p.ej., ropa, trapo, lodo)
aquatic snail, kind of → chocolín
    (caracol acuático, comestible)
arm → mano, brazo
armadillo → armadillo
armful → brazada
armpit → sobaco
army ant → tepegua
arrange → arreglar
arrowwood → canna
arrive → llegar
ascend → subir
ascent → subida
ashamed, be → avergonzarse
ashes → ceniza
aside → aparte
ask → pedir
ask for permission to borrow →
    pedir prestado
attach → atajar
attic → tapanco
aunt → hermana mayor, tía
aunt → tía
avocado → aguacate
avocado → aguacate, chinini
avocado → aguacatillo
awake → vivo, despierto
axe → hacha
baby → criatura
baby → nene

back → espalda
back, shoulders → espalda
backwards → contrario al, al revés
bad smelling → olor desagradable, de
bad smell of fish, have a → olor
    repugnante de pescado, tener
bag → bolsa
bald → calvo, pelón
bamboo, type of → carrizo
bamboo, type of → jimba (tipo de
    carrizo)
bandit → bandido
baptism → bautismo
baptize → bautizar
baptize → bautizar(se)
bar → larguero
bark → cáscara, piel
bark → ladrar
bark, crust → corteza
basket woven of palm → tenate
basket → canasta
bat → murciélago
bath → baño (para bañarse)
bathe → bañar
bathe someone → bañar a alguien
be → estar, existir
beak → pico, hocico
bean → frijol
bean plantation → sembrado de
    frijoles, frijolar
bean soup → caldo de frijoles
bear a burden → aguantar un peso
beard → barba
beast of burden → animal, bestia de
    carga
beat → batir; regar
beat → latir, pegar
beat → pegar, azotar
beat with something → pegar con
    algo
beautiful → bonito
beautiful → bonito, hermoso
bed → cama
bedbug → chinche
bee → abeja

before → antes
begin → empezar
begin → comenzar, empezar
bellow → bramar
bench → tabla, banco, banquito
bend → encorvar
bend → enchuecarse
bend → ir u regresar, doblar (cosa
    larga y delgada)
bend wire → doblar (p.ej., alambre)
bent → chueco, encorvado
better → mejor
big → grande
big grasshopper → cucaracha;
    chapulín grande
bile → bilis
bind → amarrar; pretender
bind together things that are placed
    on top of each other → amarrar
    cosas encimadas
bird, a kind of → pájaro barranqueño
bird, species of → pájaro, especie de
bird → pájaro
bird louse → cocoyuche, pepeyochi
bird louse → pepeyoche
birth, give → brotar, nacer
bite (mosquito) → picar (zancudo)
bite into something tough → jalar;
    morder cosa dura
bitter → agrio
bitter → amargo
black → negro
black sapote → zapote prieto
black snake, a kind of → culebra
    negra
black-bellied tree duck → pichichi
blackhead → espinilla (enfermedad)
blanket → cobija
blanket → cobija, sarape, chamarra
blind → ciego
blind, become → cegarse
blister → ampollarse
blood → sangre
blow → soplar
blow → soplar con la boca

blow one's nose → sonar la nariz
blow (the wind) → ventear; inflar
boa constrictor → mazacoate
boa constrictor → tatuana
board → tabla, banco, banquito
bobcat → gato montés
body → cuerpo
boil → hervir
boil → hervir; pintar
bone → hueso
borderline → lindero
born, be → nacer
born, be → nacer, aparecer
borrow → prestar
boss → dueño, patrón, amo
boss → patrón
bot fly → moyocuil
bother → molestar
bottom → asiento
bottom → hondo, pozo, etc.
bowl made out of a gourd → jícara
boy (voc.) → tú (vocativo masculino), muchacho (voc. addressed to a man)
braid → trenzar
brave → valiente
bray → rebuznar
bread made of steamed cornmeal → tamal
break → boca abajo, poner; quebrar; regar
break → curtir; quebrar
break → quebrar
break → romper
break → tronchar, quebrar
break a long, thin object → romper una cosa larga y delgado
break or cut → trozar
break (long, thin object) → quebrarse (palo, etc.)
break off (e.g., twig) → desbrazar, quebrar
breakfast → desayuno
breast of woman → seno, chiche
breast milk → leche

breath → aliento
breathe → respirar
breed → criar
bring → traer
bring or place near → arrimar
brocket deer → mazate
broken branch → gajo
brook → arroyo
bromeliad → piñuela
bronzed cowbird → tordo garrapatero
brood → enclocarse
brooding → clueca
brook → arroyo
broom → escoba
brother-in-law of man → cuñado de hombre
brother-in-law of woman → cuñada de hombre, cuñado de mujer
bruised, become → ampollarse
brush → acahual
brush → escobeta
buckthorn → palo colorado
bumblebee → abejón, abejorro
burn → encender
burn → quemar, doler
burn (as chile) → picar, arder sin flama
burn (as hot water) → quemar
burn (chile) → chamuscar
burn (fire) → arder (fuego)
burn (skin) → arder (piel)
burst → reventar
burst → tronar, brotar
butt → topetear
butterfly → mariposa
buttocks → cadera, nalga
button → abotonar, abrochar
button → botón
buy → comprar
buyer → comprador
buzz → zumbar
buzzard → zopilote
cacao tree → cacao
calf of the leg → pantorilla
call → llamar

call → mandar, invitar
calm down → pararse; calmarse
candle → velador
cane field → cañal
canine tooth of animals → colmillo
    de los animales
canna → platanillo
canoe → canoa
carne asada → roast meat
carpenter → carpintero
carpenter's plane → cepillo (para
    acepillar madera)
carry → alzar, levantar
carry → cargar
carry → jalar, llevar
carry → levantar
carry → llevar
carry → llevar, recoger
carry away → llevar
carry flat object → cargar cosa plana
carry on the back → cargar en la
    espalda
carry on the head → cargar en la
    cabeza
carry water → acarrear agua
carry water → traer agua
carry wood, etc. → cargar palo, etc.
carry (horse) → llevar (caballo)
cascade → cascada
cat → gato
caterpillar → gusano de mariposa
catch → coger
cause to fall from above → caer
    de arriba, hacer
cause prickling → aguatear, aguatar
cave → cueva
cedar → cedro
ceiba → ceiba
celebrate → festejar
centipede → ciempiés
century plant → maguey
certain → cierto
chachalaca → chachalaca
change → cambiar
change → mudar

chase → corretear
chat → conversar, platicar
chayote → chayote
chayote vine → guía de chayote
cheek → cachete, mejilla
cheek → mejilla; borde
cherry → cereza
chest → pecho
chew → mamar, morder
chew → marchar
chew → mascar
chew → masticar
chewing-gum tree → chicozapote
chicken → pollo, gallina
chicle → chicle
child → niño, niña
chili pepper → chile
chili pepper, type of → cuachile
    (chile silvestre)
chili pepper, type of → chile verde
chilly → friolento
chisel → cincelar, escoplear
choke → ahogarse
choose → escoger
chrysanthemum → flor de Santa
    María, crisantemo
church → iglesia
cicada → chicharra
cichlid → mojarra
cigar → puro (tabaco)
cigarette → cigarro
clean → limpiar
clean → limpio
clean oneself → limpiarse
clear underbrush → rozar
clean (surface) → limpiar (superficie)
clear (water, etc.) → claro (agua,
    etc.)
clear (water), become → aclararse
    (agua)
clearing underbrush, the action of →
    roza
cleave (logs) → rajar
cleave wood → rajar leña
climb → subir

climb to the top → encumbrar, subir
a la cumbre, pagar
close → cerca
close → cerrar
close → tapar, cerrar
close (a wound) → cicatrizarse
closed eyes, with → ojos cerrados,
con los
cloth → ropa, tela
cloth used for absorbing sweat from
the back of a mount → sudadero
clothes → ropa, tela
cloud → nube
cloudy → nublado
coal → carbón
coati → tejón
cobweb → telaraña
cock → gallo
cockroach → cucaracha
cockroach → cucaracha; chapulín
grande
cold → frío
cold, be → enfriar
cold, become → enfriarse
cold (illness) → catarro
collarbone → clavícula
comb → peinar
comb → peinar; gotear
comb → peine
come → venir
come → venir, llegar
come out (object) → salir (objeto)
come to an end → finalizar
come to somebody or something →
venir a alguien o a algo
come together (many) → amontonar
comet → cometa
common raven → cuervo, cacalote
compare → comparar
complete → completo
conditional → para que, para
construct → construir
container → recipiente, envase
content → alegre, contento, feliz
content, be → sanar; contentarse

contents → contenido
converse → conversar, platicar
converse → platicar
cook → cocer
cook → cocer, cocinar
cook in water → cocer
cook over the steam → cocer al
vapor
cooked → cocido
cool → fresco
cool → enfriar
cool off → refrescarse
copal tree → árbol de copal
copal tree → palo mulato
coral bean tree → colorín, tzompantle
cord → cuerda
cord → lazo
cord → vena, cuerda
corn → maíz
corn drink → atole
corn grains → maíz desgranado
corn granary → granero para maíz
corn leaf → hoja de maíz
corn stalk → caña de maíz
corncob → olote
cornfield → milpa
cornfield belonging to someone else
→ milpa ajena
corral → cerca, cerco, corral
cost → valer
cotton → algodón
cotton tree → pongolote
cough → tos
cough → toser
count → contar
count → contar (números)
court → amarrar; pretender
court → pedir
cover → cobijar
cover → tapadera
cover with mud → embarrar
cover (head) → cubrir la cabeza
cover (pot, etc.) → tapar (olla, etc.)
crab → cangrejo
crack → rajar

crack → rajarse
crackle → crepitar
cramp → calambres
crawl → arrastrarse
crayfish → mayacate
crazy, be → tonto. estar
creep, crawl → gatear
crested guan → cojolite
cricket → grillo
crooked, bent → chueco
crop (of a bird) → buche del ave
cross → cruzar
cross (e.g., legs) → atravezar (p.ej.,
 piernas)
cruel → cruel
crumb → migaja, piltrafa
crush → estrujar
crush dry things → romper cosas
 secas
cry → derretir, llorar
cry → gritar, llorar
cry → llorar, gritar
crybaby, like a → llorón
cure → curar
curtain → cortina
cut → cortado
cut brush → limpiar (cortar plantas)
cut firewood → leñar
cut in two → cortar en dos
cut into (rope) → sajar
cut with a knife → cortar con cuchillo
cut with a scissors → tijeretear
cut with machete → cortar con
 machete
cut with scissors → cortar con tijeras
daily → diario
damp, be → humedecer
dance → bailar
dance → baile
dancer → danzante, bailador
dandruff → caspa
danger → peligroso, riesgo
dangle → bambolearse
dark → moreno

dark → obscuro
daughter → hija
daughter → hijo, hija
dawn → amanecer
day → día, sol
day after tomorrow, the → pasado
 mañana
day before yesterday, the → anteayer
daytime, at → día, de
dead → muerto
dead person → muerto
deaf → sordo
deaf, be → ensordecerse
death → enfermedad, muerte
death → muerte
debt → fiado
deer → venado
defecate → defecar
defend → defender
delicate → escaso, delicado
dense → espeso
descend → bajar
descend → bajarse
descend, make → bajar
descendants → descendientes
descent → bajada
desire → desear
despise → menospreciar
destroy → desbaratar
destroy → quebrar
detain → detener, soltar
dew → rocío
diarrhea → diarrea
diarrhea, have → diarrea, tener
die → morir
difficult → pleito, difícil
dig → escarbar
dig up something → escarbar algo
dip food in sauce → meter la comida
 en la salsa
dirt → mugre
dirty, get → mancharse, ensuciarse
discolor → desteñirlo
dislodge → desalojar
dissolve → deshacer

elbow → codo del brazo
elder brother → hermano mayor
elder brother of woman → hermano
    mayor de mujer
elder sister → hermana mayor, tia
elder (not the oldest) brother →
    medio hermano mayor
embrace → abrazar
embrace around the waist → abrazar
    de la cintura
employ → usar
empty → vacío
enroll → enrollar
entangle → enmarañar
entangled → enredado
enter → entrar
epilepsy → epilepsia
equal → parejo, raso
erase → borrar
eraser → borrador
esale → esale
escape → correr, huir
every → cada
everything → todo
evil → mal, mancha
evil eyes → mal de ojo
excrement → excremento
exist → estar, existir
expensive → caro
extend → extender
extinguish → apagar
extract → exprimir
eye → ojo
eyebrows → cejas
eyed elater → cocuyo
eyelid → párpado
face → cara
fade → marchitarses
fall → caer
fall → recto, estar; tumbar
fall due → cumplir
fall (to the ground) → caer (al
    suelo)
fan → abanicar
fan → abanico

fan → abanico, soplador
fan → soplar, abanicar
far → lejos
far away → lejos
fart → pedo
fat → gordo
father → padre, papá
father-godfather kin → compadre
fear → espantar
fear → susto, espanto
feather → pelo, pluma
fed up with, become → fastidiarse
feel → palpar, tentar
feel at home → acostumbrar
fellow-townsman → paisano (del
    mismo pueblo)
female → hembra
female breast → senos, teta
fence → cerca, cerco, corral
fence → cercar
fern → helecho, ocopetate
field → campo
field cleared for underbush →
    rozadura
fiesta → fiesta, nombre, sol
fight → pelear
fight → pleito
fight → pleito, difícil
file → lima
fill → llenar
fill → llenar, pesar
fill → rellenar
fill or be filled with a liquid
    → llenar(se) de un líquido
fill with food → hartar
find → encontrar
finger → dedo de la mano
fingernail → uña
finish → acabar
finish → acabarse
finish → completar
finish → completarse
finish → terminar
finished → completo
fire → fuego, lumbre

firewood → leña
firm → fuerte, macizo
fish → pez, pescado
fist → puño
fish, a kind of → nácara
fish, any small → sardina
fish with a hook → coser, pescar con
   anzuelo
fish [mojarra?], species of → mojarra
fit tight → ajustar
fix something in a vertical position
   → poner algo en posición vertical
flame → flamear
flame → llama
flap → aletearse
flash lightning → relampaguear
flat object → cosa plana
flea → pulga
fling down → derrumbar
flint → pedernal
float → flotar
floor → piso de la casa
flour, something ground → pinole
flourish → inflar, florear
flower → flor
flute → instrumento de musica de
   viento
flute → flauta, pito
fly → mosca
fly → volar
fly, a kind of big → moscón
foam → espuma
foam → espumar
foam, make → batir mole
fog → neblina
fold → doblar
fold → doblar; amontonar
fold → pliegue
folded, curly or rolled (as paper, hair
   or tobacco) → doblado (papel,
   etc.)
follow → seguir
food → alimento
food → comida
foot → pie

forehead → frente
forehead → frente; mecapal
forest, half dense → bosque medio
   espeso
foretell → adivinar
formed clay object → cosa formada
   de barro
fosterchild → entenado(a),
   ahijastro(a)
fosterchild → hijastro, entenado
fosterchild (girl) → hijastra
four days ago → trasanteayer
frangipani → sulisuchi
fresh-water fish → juile
frog → rana, sapo
frost → hielo
fruit resembling the plum, type of →
   fruta parecida a la ciruela, tipo de
fruit → fruta
fry → freir
fulfill → cumplir
full → lleno
full, be → turbio, estar; estar lleno
full, become → llenarse
fungus → hongo
gain color → pintar, madurar
garter snake → culebra de agua
gather → encoger, juntar
gather → juntar
gather → llevar, recoger
gather → recoger (trapo, mecate,
   etc.)
gently → suavemente, con cuidado
germinate → germinar
girl → niña
give → dar
give → dar, pegarse
give away → dar por otro
give credit → darle fiado
give light → alumbrar
give light → echar lumbre
give to eat → dar de comer
glad → alegre, contento, feliz
glass → espejo, vidrio
glasses → anteojos

glutton → comilón, tragón
go → ir
go out → salir
go (and have come) → ir (y ya haber regresado)
go out (light) → apagarse
go out (person) → salir (persona)
godchild → ahijado, ahijada
good → bueno, bien
good, very → muy bien
goods → mercancía
goosefoot → epazote
gopher → tuza
gourd → calabaza
gourd → tecomate
gourd → tecomate, bule
gourd tree → cuauhtecomate
grab many things at once → agarrar juntos
grackle → picho; zanate
grains of corn → maíz desgranado
grandchild → nieta, nieto
granddaughter, -son → nieta, nieto
grandfather → abuelo
grandmother → abuela
grape, a kind of → agrás (uva silvestre)
grasp → agarrar
grasp → agarrar; tentar
grasp a fistful of something → agarrar un puño de algo
grass → zacate
grass → zacate, pasto
grass, a kind of → tipo zacate
grasshopper → chapulín, saltamontes
grasshopper (little, green) → chapulín (chico, verde)
grate → crujir
grate one's teeth → crujir los dientes
gravy → mole
gravy, make → batir mole
gray → gris
gray hair → canas
gray-haired → canoso
gray-necked woodrail → poposquela, tutpana
grease → grasa
greasy, make → grasoso, poner
great curassow → faisán
great-tailed grackle → zanate
greater, big → mayor, grande
green → verde
green parrot → cotorro
green (unripe) → verde, crudo
greeting → saludo
griddle → comal
grind → apedrear, moler
grind → moler
grind (corn) → moler (nixtamal)
grind (chili pepper) → moler (chile)
grime → mugre
grind dough → moler masa
grind pinol → moler pinole
grindstone → molleja
grope → palpar, tentar
ground → molido
ground cherry → miltomate
ground, something → pinole
grow → alargar
grow → alargarse
grow → crecer
grow → madurar
grow bigger → agrandar
grow bigger → prenderse lumbre, agrandarse
grow dark → anochecer
grow (vine) → crecer (bejuco)
grown → alto, crecido
grunt → gruñir
grunt → pujar
guard → guardar
guava → guayaba
guide → guía, práctico
gum → encía
gum tree → hule
hail → granizo
hair → cabello
hair of the arms → vello del brazo
hairy → peludo
hamper → empatar

hand → mano, brazo
hand, by → a mano
hang → colgar
hang → pender
hang → tender
happy → alegre, contento, feliz
happy, be → alegrarse
hard → duro
hard tree → árbol duro
hardened, become → endurecerse
hardened, become → endurecerse
   (vi), mecatear (vt)
harvest → cosechar; tocar
hat → sombrero
hatch → empollar; dormir
hate → odiar
have a disagreeable odor → tufo,
haber
have a hole in → picado
hawk → gavilán
hawk, type of → gavilán, tipo de
he → él, ella
head → cabeza
heal → salir bien, sanar
heal → sanar
heal → sanar; contentarse
healer → curandero
heap → mojón
hear → oír
hearing → oído
heart → corazón
heart → hígado, corazón
hearth → fogón
hearthstones for supporting pot over
   fire, configuration of three →
   tenamaste
heat → calentar
heat → calentarse
heavy → pesado
heel → tobillo
help → ayudar
hen → pollo, gallina
her → él, ella
herb → yerba, planta, monte
here → aquí

hiccoughs, to have the → hipo, tener
hide → cuero
hide → esconder
hide → meter, esconder
hide oneself → esconderse
high → arriba, alto
hill → loma
hip → cadera, nalga
hit → golpear
hit → pegar, abofetear
hit someone → pegar a alguien
hit with the fist → golpear con el
   puño
hobble → manear
hog → cerdo, marrano
hog plum tree → jobo
hole → hoyo
honey → miel
honeycomb → panal de avispa
hook → anzuelo
hook → enganchar
hook → gancho
hop → brincar
hops, make small → brincotear
horn → cuerno
horn → instrumento de musica de
   viento
horsefly → tábano
host → dueño, patrón, amo
host → patrón
hot → caliente
hot (food), be → quemar comida
house → casa
house pole → horcón
how → como
how many → cuanto
how much → cuanto
humid → húmedo
humid → mojado
humid, be → humedecer
hummingbird → colibrí
hunchbacked → jorobado
hunger → hambre
hungry, be → hambre, tener
hunt → cazar

hunter → cazador
hurt → doler
hurt → quemar, doler
husband → marido
husband of sister-in-law → concuño
husk → totomostle
I → yo
if → si
iguana → iguana
ill, be → estar enfermo
illness → enfermedad
illness → enfermedad, muerte
immediately → pronto
improve → componerse
in front of → enfrente de
incense → copal, incienso
inch → cinchar
indigestion, suffer → empacharses
inga → cuajinicuil; machetón
insect, a kind of → insecto, especie de
insect, a kind of → tacacholota
insert → ensartar
insert → poner en
inside → adentro
inside (of a house) → interior de la casa
inside (the house) → adentro (de la casa)
insipid → insípido
instruct → aprender, enseñar
instrument for shooting → instrumento para tirar
instrument for writing → instrumento para escribir
intelligent → inteligente
intestines → intestino
intestines → tripas
iron → fierro, metal
irrigate → boca abajo, poner; quebrar; regar
itch → ajuate, tener
itch → comezón
itch → comezón, dar
itch → comezón, tener

itch → sarna
itchy → sarnoso
jaguar → jaguar
jaguar → jaguar, tigre
jail → cárcel
jam → atorarse
jammed, be → atascado, estar
jar → jarro
jinicuil → cuajinicuil
jinicuil → cuajinicuil; machetón
joint → nudo de caña, coyuntura
jump down → brincar para abajo
jump up → brincar para arriba
kapok tree → ceiba
keel-billed toucan → tucán
keep → guardar
keep guard → vigilar, acechar
key → llave
kick → patear
kick → patear; arrear
kill → matar
kill → tumbar, matar
kinkajou → mico de noche
kiss → besar
kiss → beso
kiss → oler, besar
knead → amasar
knead → repasar (masa)
knee → rodilla
knee cap → rótula
kneel → arrodillarse
kneel down → hincarse
knife → cuchillo
knock → tocar, golpear
knock down → tumbar, matar
knot → anudar
knot (of rope) → nudo en mecate
knot (of tree) → nudo (de árbol)
know → conocer
know → saber
know → saber, poder
ladder made of one piece of wood → escalera de un solo palo
land → aterrizar
landmark → lindero

language → idioma
lantern click beetle → cocuyo
large quail → codorniz (grande)
larva, kind of → larva de ditisco, de la mosca Dobson
lasso → lazo
last → durar
last night → anoche
laugh → reir
laugh with somebody → reir con alguien
lay out → extender
lay out (coffee beans), dry → regar café, marchitarse
lazy → flojo (perezoso)
lazy → perezoso
leached cornmeal → nixtamal
leaf → hoja
leaf-cutting ant → arriera
leap → saltar
learn → aprender, enseñar
leather strap of sandal → correa de huarache
leave → dejar
leave behind → abandonar
leave or return → ir u regresar, doblar (cosa larga y delgada)
leech → sanguijuela
left → izquierda
lemon → limón
lend → prestar
let out gas → ventosear
let's go → vamos
level → calzar
level → parejo, raso
lick → lamer
lie → mecatear; mentir
lie down → acostar
lift → alzar, levantar
lifted into the air (as dust), be → levantarse (como polvo)
light → encender
light → fuego, lumbre
light → prenderse lumbre, agrandarse
light → quemar (lumbre)

lightning → rayo, relámpago
like → como
like → gustar
like this → así
lime → cal
linger → demorarse
lip → labio
little → chico
little → chico, pequeño
little, a → poco
little finger → dedo meñique de la mano
live → vivo, despierto
liver → hígado, corazón
lizard → lagartija
load → carga
load a gun → armar
locust → langosta
long → largo
long bone of leg, shin → canilla de la pierna, espinilla
look → mirar
look after → cuidarlo mucho
loose, untied → flojo, suelto
lose → perder
loose, be → aflojarse
loosen → arrojar; desatar
loosen → aflojar
loosen earth → aflojar la tierra
lot, a → bastante
louse → piojo
love → amor
lurk → vigilar, acechar
macaw → guacamaya
mahogany → caoba
maize flower → flor de maíz
majagua bush → majagua
malabar gourd → calabaza castilla
malaria → paludismo
male → macho
man → hombre
mana → mana
mange → sarna
maraca → maraca
mark → sello

marmalade fruit → zapote colorado
marry → casarse
mask → máscara
mason → albañil
master → patrón
mat → petate
match → cerilla
mayor → presidente municipal
meal → comida
meanwhile → hace rato, endenantes
measure → medir; pensar
measure by the span of a hand → medir por cuartas
measure corresponding to the span from the index finger to the thumb → jeme
measure with → medir con
measurement → medida
meat → carne
medicine → remedio, medicina
melt → derretir, llorar
mend → remendar
mescal → mezcal
metal → fierro, metal
metate → grinding stone
metate roller → metlapil
Mexican hackberry → capulín
Mexican opossum → tlacuache
Mexican porcupine → puerco espín
Mexican rat snake → voladora (una culebra)
Mexico City → Tenochtitlán, Ciudad de Mexico
middle → medio
middle, in the → medio, en
midnight → medianoche
milk → ordeñar, mezclar
mine → mio
mirror → espejo, vidrio
misery → miseria
mix → mezclar
mix → ordeñar, mezclar
moan → gemir
mockingbird → centzontle
mockingbird, a kind of → centzontle,

tipo de
moist, be → humedecer
mojarra, a kind of → mojarra correntera
molar tooth → muela
mold → enmohecer
mold → moho
money → dinero
monkey → chango, mono
Montezuma oropendola → zacua
month → luna; mes
moon → luna; mes
more → más
morning → mañana
mosquito → mosquito, zancudo
moss → musgo
mother → madre, mamá
mother-, daughter-in-law of woman → suegra de mujer, nuera de mujer
mother-godmother kin → comadre
mother-in-law of woman, daughter-in-law of woman → nuera de la mujer, suegra de mujer-in-law
mountain → cerro
mountain lion → león
mouse → rata, ratón
mouth → boca
move → mover
move → mover, hinchar
move, etc. → menear, etc.
move horizontally against something → mover horizontalmente contra algo
move (arm, leg) → mover (brazo, pierna)
much → bastante, muy
much → mucho
mucus → moco
mud → lodo
mud bricks, make → tostar, hacer adobes
muddy → embarrar
muddy → turbio, espeso (liquido)
muddy, be → turbio, estar; estar

lleno

multiply → multiplicar

murderer → asesino

mushroom → hongo, nanacate

musician → músico (instr. de viento)

nail → clavar

nail → uña

nail → uña de mano

nail (stake, etc.) → clavar (estaca, espeque, etc.)

naked → desnudo

name → fiesta, nombre, sol

name → nombre

namesake → tocayo

narrow → angosto

narrow → estrecho, cuadrado

native blouse → huipil

nauseated, become → marearse

nauyaca → mano de metate (culebra)

navel → ombligo

neck → cuello

neck → nuca

necklace → collar, gargantilla

negation → negación

nephew → sobrino

nest → nido

nest, make a → nido, poner

net → red

new → nuevo

new, make → dejarlo nuevo

niece → sobrina

night → noche

night, at → noche, de

night humidity → sereno

nit → liendre(s)

no → no

nobody → nadie

nod → cabecear

noise, make → hacer ruido

noon → mediodía

nose → nariz

nose → nariz; pico

not yet → todavía no

nothing → nada

nourish → nutrir

now → ahora

now → ahora, hoy

numb, become → entumirse

oak → encino

oak, type of → encino blanco

offer → ofrecer

offer → ofrendar, trabajar

offering → trabajo, ofrenda

often → ablandar

old man → anciano

old person → anciano

old thing → cosa vieja

old (living being) → viejo (persona, animal)

old (man, animal) → viejo (persona, animal)

old (thing) → viejo (cosa)

one-armed, one-handed → manco

open → abierto

open → abrir

open → abrir; rajar

open → abrirse

open the mouth → abrir la boca

opening of the shape of a trench or fork → abertura en forma de horqueta o zanja

opposite → contrario al, al revés

order → mandar

orphan → huérfano

other → otro

outside → afuera

over → encima

owe → deber

owe → deber (vi); pagar (vt)

owl → lechuza, tecolote, buho

owner of the house → casero

paca → tepezcuintle

pack → estibar

pain → dolor

paint → hervir; pintar

paint → pintar

paint, color → pintar

pale → pálido

palm of the hand → palma de la mano

palm tree → palma
palm, type of → coyole
palm, type of → guaya, palmera
palm, type of → palmera, tipo de
palm, type of → tepejilote
pant → jadear
paper → papel
parakeet → cotorro
pardon → dispensar
part → parte, pedazo
parted → partirse
partridge → perdiz
pass by → pasar
pass, make → pasar, hacer
pass through → pasar, atravezar
pass (in the road) → alcanzar (en el
    camino)
pasture → zacate, pasto
patio → patio
pay → deber (vi); pagar (vt)
pay → encumbrar, subir a la cumbre,
    pagar
pay → pagar
pay a debt → pagar una deuda
pea → chipilcoite
peal → cueza
peal → pelar
peanut → cacahuate
peasant → campesino
peck → picotear
peck → picotear, golpear con el puño
penis → pene
perforate → perforar
pick at → golpear ligeramente con
    algo punteado
pick from a hole → recogerlo
pick up → pepenar
pickle tree → nanche
piece → migaja, piltrafa
piece → parte, pedazo
piece → pedazo
pieces → pedazos
pieces, go to → descomponerse
pierce → agujerear
pierce → calar

pierce → picar, punzar
pig → cerdo, marrano
pigeon → tortola
pile up → amontonar
pile up → amontonar, cercar
pile up → doblar; amontonar
pimple → barro
pimple → grano de la piel
pinch → pellizcar
pinch → prensar (con pinzas, etc.)
pinch between the fingernails →
    pellizcar
pinch somebody → pellizcar a al-
    guien
pinch with the fingers → apretar con
    los dedos
pineapple → piña
pitch (sand, water, etc.) → aventar
    (arena, agua, etc.)
pitcher → cántaro
pitchpine → ocote, pino
place → lugar
placenta → placenta
plain → plano, llano, valle, llanura
plane → acepillar
plant → yerba, planta, monte
plant, a kind of → planta, tipo de
plant in containers before moving the
    plants to a natural environment
    → almácigo, hacer en
plant or tree, species of → planta o
    árbol, tipo de
plate → plato
play → jugar
play → tocar
play a musical instrument → chiflar,
    tocar instrumento de viento
pleasure → gozo
pleat → mudarse (culebras, etc.), ple-
    gar (ropa)
pleat → plegar
plow → arado
pluck (a fowl) → desplumar
plug → tapar, cerrar
plug → tapón

pointed → punteado
poncho → gabán
poor person → pobre
pot → olla
potter wasp → avispa masón
pound down a pole → golpear a un
   poste
pour → verter
poverty, cause → causar pobreza
practice witchcraft → hacer brujería
pray → rezar
press → apretar
press and twist at the same time →
   apretar torciendo
press around something with oblong
   objects → atrancar, etc.
press with the fingers → apretar (con
   pinzas)
price → precio
pricklenut tree → guácimo
prickly pear → tuna
prickly pear cactus → nopal
prohibitive → prohibitivo
provoke an intense sensation →
   provocar un sensación muy fuerte
pull → jalar, llevar
pull → jalar; morder cosa dura
pull → jalarlo
pull, etc. → jalar, etc.
pull out (thin object) → sacar (cosa
   delgada)
pull out or through → sacar o en
   sartar
pulque (fermented juice of the
   maguey) → pulque
puma → león
pumpkin → calabaza
punch → picotear, golpear con el
   puño
puncture → punzar
purple → morado
purslane → verdolaga
pus → pus
push → tentar; empujar
push, break → empujar, quebrar

put → meter
put → meter, esconder
put on, add → echarselo
put on top of → poner encima
quarter (an animal) → descuartizar
quench with forked stick
   → apalancar
question marker → partícula
   interrogativa
quickly → aprisa
quiet → quieto
quotative → cuotativo
rabbit → conejo
raccoon → mapache
rage → rabia, tener
rain → llover
rain → lluvia
rainwater → agua llovida
rainbow → arco iris
raise → alzar
ramon breadnut tree → ojoche
rare → escaso, delicado
rat → rata, ratón
rattle → castañetear
rattlesnake → cascabel
rattlesnake, rattle → cascábel, sonaja
ray → rayo
ready, be → listo, ser
receive → recibir
receptacle → recipiente, envase
recite prayers → rezar
recuperate → recobrar la fuerza
red → rojo
red, become → colorado, ponerse;
   enrojecer
red-hot coal → brasa
reed → carrizo, otate
rehearse → repasar
relative → familiar
relative → familiar, pariente
remain → quedarse
remedy → remedio, medicina
remember → acordarse
remove → apartar
rent → alquilar

repair → componer
resin → resina
respect → respeto
rest → descansar
return → devolver
return → regresar
revive → revivir
revolve → revolver
rheumatism → reuma
ribs → costillas
right hand → mano derecha
ring → anillo
ripe → maduro
ripen → madurar
ripen → pintar, madurar
rise → subida
river → río
river otter → nutria, perro de agua
road → camino
road, in the → camino, en el; por el
    camino
roadrunner → correcamino,
    tapacamino
roar → rugir
roast → asar
rob → robar, buscar
robin → primavera
rock → mecer
roll → enrollar
roll → rodar
roll of leaf or tobacco → rollo de
    hoja o zacate
roll up → enrollar
roll up → sofaldar
root → raíz
rope → endurecerse (vi), mecatear
    (vt)
rope → lazar
rope → mecate
rope → mecatear; mentir
rope → reata
rope → soga
rot → podrir
rough dough → masa rugoso
round → redondo

rub → sobar
rubber → hule
ruminate → rumiar
run → correr
run → correr, huir
run (liquid) → correr (líquido)
rush → junco
sacred → bendito
sacred language → idioma sagrado
sadness → tristeza
salamander → salamandra
sale → venta
saliva → baba
salt → sal
salty → salado
sand → arena
sand → pequeño; arena
sandal → huarache
satiate → saciar
satisfied → satisfecho
savory → sabroso
savory, be → sabroso, estar
saw → aserrar
saw → serrucho, sierra
say → decir
say something to someone
    → decirselo
saying → palabra, dicho
scar → cicatriz
scissors → tijeras
scold → regañar
scorpion → alacrán
scrape → escarbar
scrape → rascar
scrape → raspar
scrape → rastrillar
scratch → escarbar (gallinas)
scratch → rasguñar
sea → mar
search for → buscar
secretly, do something → escon-
    didas, hacer algo a
secretary → secretario
secure → asegurar, apretar
see → ver

seed → semilla
sell → vender
seller → vendedor
send → mandar
separate → partir
set a trap → armar
set (sun) → tirar; ponerse el sol
set fire to → encender
settle → componerse
sever fruits, etc., from the plant →
    cortar fruta
sew → coser, costurar
sew → coser, pescar con anzuelo
sexual intercourse, have → uso
    sexual, hacer
shadow → sombra
shadow of person → sombra de
    persona
shake something → sacudir
shake (cloth) → sacudir (trapo)
shake → sacudir
shaman → brujo
sharpen → afilar
shave → rasurar
shelf → estante
shell → cáscara, piel
shell → concha
shell → descascarar
shell → pelar
shell (corn) → desgranar
shine → brillar
shine (gold, precious stones, etc.) →
    brillar (oro, joyas, etc.)
shirt → camisa
shoot with bow and arrow → picar,
    flechar
shoot with sling → tirar; ponerse el
    sol
shore → orilla
short → corto
shoulder → hombro
shout → gritar, llorar
show → enseñar
show → enseñar, mostrar
shrimp → camarón

shrimp, type of → camarón del mar
shrimp, type of → camarón del río
shrink → encoger
shrink → encoger, unir
shut up → recluir
sibling → hermano
sigh → suspirar
sign → seña
silent, be → callarse
silk tree → tepezontle
sin → culpa, pecado
sing → cantar
singe → chamuscar
sink → sumirse
sister-in-law of man → cuñada de
    hombre, cuñado de mujer
sit down → sentarse
skin → aliñar
skin → cáscara, piel
skin → pelo, pluma
skinny → flaco
skirt → enagua, falda
skull → cráneo
skunk → zorra
skunk → zorrillo
sky → cielo
slab → laja
slap → dar una palmada
slap → pegar, abofetear
sleep → dormir
sleep → empollar; dormir
sleep, go to → adormecerse
slender → delgado
slice → rebanar
slide → derrumbarse
slim → delgado
slip away → zafar, raspar
slippery → resbaloso
slippery → resbaloso (en lugar donde
    hay grava)
slobber → salir (savia)
slough → mudarse (culebras, etc.),
    plegar (ropa)
slow → despacio
slowly → despaciolay eggs → poner

huevos
slowly → suavemente, con cuidado
small → pequeño
small → pequeño; arena
small mill → trapiche
smell → oler
smell → oler, besar
smell good → oler bien
smile → sonrisa, risa
smoke → fumar
smoke → humear
smoke → humo
smoking, be → humear
smooth → ágil, liso
smooth → liso
snail → caracol
snake → culebra
snake poison → veneno de la víbora
sneeze → estornudar
snook → robalo
snore → roncar
snot → moco
snout → pico, hocico
soak → empapar
soak → mojar
soak maize in lime water → lavar
    nixtamal
soaked → mojado
soap → jabón
soft → blando
soft → suave
soft (earth, mattress, etc.) → blando
    (tierra, colchón, etc.)
soft (mattress, etc.) → blando (col-
    chón, etc.)
solar aclipse, pass a → eclipse del sol,
haber
son → hijo
son → hijo, hija
son-in-law → yerno
song → canción, canto
song → canción, himno, canto
soot → tizne
sooted, become → tiznarse
soothsayer → adivinador

sound → sonar
sour → agrio
sour, become → agriarse
soursop → guanábana
sow → sembrar
sow again → resembrar
sowing stick → estaca para sembrar
    maíz o frijol
sowing time → siembra
sown field → siembra
span of the hand (measure), one →
    cuarta, una
speak → hablar
speak to someone → hablar a alguien
species of hawk → gavilán, especie
    de
species of insect → insecto, especie
    de
species of tree → especie de árbol
speck → mal, mancha
spell of rainy weather → temporal de
    agua
spider → araña
spill → derramar
spin thread → hilar
spindle → huso, malacate
spit → escupir
spit → saliva
spit (for roasting) → asador
split → abrir; rajar
split → brotar, nacer
split → partir
split → rajar
split, tear → rajar
split (logs) → rajar leña
spoil → perder, echar a
spotted → pinto
spread out → batir; regar
spread out on the ground → tender
    en el suelo
spring → manantial
spring (water) → manar
sprinkle → regar
sprinkle → salpicar
sprinkle → salpicar, escurrir

spry with a pole → palanquear
spurge nettle → chichicastle
spurge nettle → malamujer (yerba)
spy on → espiar
square → estrecho, cuadrado
squash → aplastar, golpear
squash → calabaza
squash, crush → reventar (fruta)
squash, type of → chilacayote
squeeze → asegurar, apretar
squeeze → exprimir
squirrel → ardilla
squirrel, large and red → ardilla
    grande y roja
squirrel, small and gray → ardilla
    chica y gris
squirrel cuckoo → pájaro vaquero
stack → estibar
stain → refregar
stand shoulder by shoulder forming a
    group → parado de espaldas en-
    corvadas en un grupo, estar
stand up → pararse
stand up → pisar, pararse
stand up, make → pararlo
star → estrella
stay → quedar
steal → robar, buscar
steal, rob → robar
step → pisar
step → pisar, pararse
stepfather → padrastro
stepmother → madrastra
stick → pegar
stick → pegar (con cola o
    pegamento)
stick → quedarse pegado
stick → vara
sticky → pegajoso
sting → picar
sting → picar, flechar
sting → punzar
sting, burn → picar, arder
sting (chile) → picar (chile)
stingy → mezquino (tacaño)

stomach → barriga, estómago
stone → piedra
stone idol → ídolo
stone railing → pretil, presa, dique
stone wall, make a → colocar piedras
    en un cerco
stoop → agacharse
stop → pararse; calmarse
stop swelling → deshincharse
straight → derecho
straight, be → recto, estar
straight, be → recto, estar; tumbar
straighten → enderezar
strain, filter → cernir, colar
strain, filter → colar
straw → paila
streak → rayar
strength → fuerte, recio, fuerza
strength → fuerza
stretch → extender(se)
stretch out → estirarse
string bean → ejote
stroll → pasear
strong → fuerte, macizo
strong → fuerte, recio, fuerza
stuck by a thorn, be → espinar
stuck, get → atascarse
stuck, get → atorarse
stuck (thorn), be → atorar (espina)
student → estudiante
study → estudiar
suck → chupar
suck on something → chupar
suck (breast) → mamar
suck (inside the mouth) → chupar
suckle → amamantar
suckle → dale de mamar, dar pecho
suckle → mamar, morder
suffer → sufrir
suffocate → ahogarse
sugar → azúcar
sugarcane → caña de azúcar
summon → mandar, invitar
sun → día, sol
sun → fiesta, nombre, sol

sun-dried mud brick → adobe
suspect → sospechar con razón
swallow → tragar
swamp → ciénaga
sway → bambolearse
sweat → sudar
sweat → sudor
sweathouse → temascal
sweep → barrer
sweep → barrido
sweet → dulce
sweet apple → anona
sweet potato → camote
sweet potato, a kind of → camotillo
sweeten → endulzar
sweetgum → liquidámbar
swell → hinchar
swell → hincharse
swell → mover, hinchar
swell up → inflar, florear
swell surface of skin → hincharse
swelling → hinchazón
swim → nadar
tail → cola
tail → cola, rabo
tailless → cola, sin
take off → quitarse
take off (clothes or shoes) → quitar
  (ropas o zapatos)
take out → sacar
take away → llevar
talk → hablar
tall → alto, crecido
tall → arriba, alto
tame → amansar
tame → domar, amansar
tan → curtir; quebrar
tangle → maraña
tap → punteado
tapir → anteburro, tapir
tayra → cabeza de viejo
teacher → maestro
tear → lágrima
tear, rip → rasgar
tender → tierno

Tenochtitlán → Tenochtitlán, Ciudad
  de Mexico
tepid → tibio
tepid water → agua tibia
termite → comején
that → aquél
that → ese
that → ése, aquel
that one → aquel
there → allá
there → allí
there → allí, allá
there is → hay
thick → grueso
thick (liquid) → turbio, espeso
  (liquido)
thigh → pierna
thigh → pierna, muslo
thin → delgado
thin → seco, flaco
thin, become → secarse,
  enflaquecerse
think → medir; pensar
think → pensar
thirsty, be → sed, tener
this → este
thorn → espina
thought → pensamiento
thread → hilo
throw (seeds, etc., in a container) →
  botar (semilla, etc., en un
  recipiente)
throw → arrojar; desatar
throw at with stone → apedrear,
  moler
throw something from a container →
  tirar algo de un envase
throw (liquid) → tirar (líquido)
throw (sand, water, etc.) → aventar
  (arena, agua, etc.)
thumb → dedo pulgar
thunder → trueno
tick → garrapata
tick → pinolillo
tickle → hacer cosquillas

tie → amarrar

tie a bundle → amarrar bulto

tie together (cargo, etc.) → dejar una bulta

tie together (poles, cane) → liar (postes, carrizo)

tight, become → apretar

tighten → apretar

tilt → ladearse

time ago → hace rato, endenantes

tip over → voltear

tired, be → cansarse

toad → rana, sapo

toast → tostar

toast → tostar, hacer adobes

tobacco → tabaco

today → ahora, hoy

toe, big → dedo gordo del pie

tomato → tomate

tomorrow → mañana

tongue → lengua

tool → herramienta

tooth → diente

tortilla → tortilla

tortilla (also generic for food) → tortilla

tortillas, make → tortillas, echar

tortoise → tortuga

touch → agarrar; tentar

touch → cosechar; tocar

touch → tentar; empujar

touch → tocar

touch something extended → tocar algo extendido

town → pueblo, poblado

toy → juguete

trap → trampa

trap, set a → jaula, poner una

tree → árbol; leña

tree → árbol, palo

tree, a species of → papachote

tree cotton → algodón

tree of life → guayacán

tree which has a poisonous bark → palo cuyo cáscara tiene veneno

treeless plain → sabana

tremble → temblar

tremble (body) → temblar (el cuerpo)

tremor → temblor

trim (a material) → labrar

trousers → pantalón

truly → veras, de

trunk → tronco

try out → probar

tuber of chayote → chayocamote

tucan → tucán

tumor → tumor

tumpline → frente; mecapal

tumpline → mecapal

turkey → guajolote, pavo

turkey cock → guajolote macho

turkey vulture → aura (tipo de buitre)

turn around → voltear

turn over → voltearse

turn up → sofaldar

turn up the earth, to raise → hozar, levantar

turn upside down → boca abajo, poner; quebrar; regar

twin → cuate, gemelo

twin → gemelo

twist → enchuecarse

twist → torcer

twist a rope → torcer reata

twisted → chueco, encurvado

twisted → torcido

unable to speak, be → perder el habla

uncle → abuelo

uncle → tío

uncover a hole → descubrir un hueco

under something → debajo, debajo de algo

underneath → abajo, debajo

understand → entender

uneven → áspero

unfasten → desamarrar

unfasten → desprender

unfasten → detener, soltar

unite → unir
untie → desatar
untie → soltar
up → arriba, alto
upright → recto, estar; tumbar
uproot → arrancar
upward → arriba, alto
upwards → boca arriba
urinate → orinar
urine → orina
use → ocupar
use for the first time → estrenar
utilize → usar
valley → plano, llano, valle, llanura
vapor → vapor
variegated → variegado
various → varios
vegetable pear → chayote
vein → vena, cuerda
venomous ant → mataculebra,
    pepegua
village → pueblo
village → pueblo, poblado
vine → bejuco
vine snake → bejuquilla
violet → color violeta
visit → visitar
voice → voz
vomit → vomitar
vomit → vómito
wait → esperar
wake up → despertar
walk → andar
walk → caminar
walk → caminar, avanzar (p.ej.,
    trabajo)
walk around → andar andando
walking stick → bastón, bordón
wall → pared
wallow → luchar a brazo partido,
    chapotear
want → querer
warm, be → hacer calor
wart → verruga
wash → lavar

wash hands → lavarse las manos
wasp → avispa
wasp, a type of → avispa concha de
    armadilla
waste → basura
watch over → vigilar
water → agua
wave → ondear
wax → cera
we excl. → nosotros excl.
wear out (things) → gastarse
weasel → comadreja
weave → tejer
weed → escardar
week → débil
weevil → gorgojo
weigh → encogerse, pesar
weigh → llenar, pesar
well → bueno, bien
well → hondo, pozo, etc.
well, turn out → salir bien, sanar
wet → mojado
wet, become → mojarse
what? → ¿qué?
where → donde, ¿dónde?
where → donde, adonde
where? → donde, ¿dónde?
whip → batir
whip → latir, pegar
whip → pegar, azotar
whip liquid → batir
whistle → chiflar, tocar instrumento
    de viento
whistle at → chiflarle
whistle → silbar
white → blanco
white bean → frijol blanco
white, become → blanquearse
white chili pepper → chile blanco
white cotton trousers → calzón
white hair → canas
white, make → blanquear
white-haired → canoso
who → quien
wide → ancho

wide chisel → formón
wife → mujer, esposa
wife of brother-in-law → concuña
wild cane → caña de otate
wild feline → tigre (cualquier felino silvestre)
wild pig → jabalí
wild sugarcane → caña cimarrónc
wildcat → gato montés
win → triunfar
wind → viento
wing → ala
witch → brujo
witchcraft → brujería
with → con
woman → mujer
woman → mujer, esposa
woman's father-in-law → suegro de mujer
woman's sister-in-law → cuñada de mujer
wood → árbol; leña
wood → árbol, palo
woods → bosque
woody vine (generic) → bejuco arbóreo (genérico)
word → palabra, dicho
work → labrar
work → ofrendar, trabajar
work → trabajo
work → trabajo, ofrenda
work (drawing, handicraft) → obra, hecho; dibujo, diseño
work with a sieve or net → lavar nixtamal, pescar con red
worker → trabajador
world → mundo
worm → gusano
worm, a kind of → gusano gallina ciega
wounded or burnt, be → sufrir una herida, quemadura
wrap → envolver
wrap up → empacar
wrestle → luchar a brazo partido, chapotear
wring → torcer
wrinkle → arraigar
wrinkle → arrugarse
wrist → muñeca de la mano
write → escribir
yam, type of → barbasco
year → año
yellow → amarillo
yellow sapote → zapote amarillo
yes → sí
yesterday → ayer
yield a crop → dar, pegarse
yield fruit → fruta, dar
you (sg) → usted
you (pl) → ustedes
you (vocative) → tú (vocativo masculino), muchacho (voc. addressed to a man)
younger brother or sister → hermano, -a menor
younger sibling → hermano, -a menor
your → tuyo
yucca → yuca

References

Adams, Karen L., and Nancy F. Conklin
    1973   Toward a Theory of Natural Classification. In *Papers from the Ninth Regional Meeting of the Chicago Linguistics Society*, ed. Claudia Corum et al., 1-11. Chicago: Chicago Linguistic Society.

Árnason, Kristján
    1980   *Quantity in Historical Phonology: Icelandic and Related Cases.* Cambridge: Cambridge University Press.

Beals, Ralph L.
    1945   *Ethnology of the Western Mixe.* Berkeley, California: University of California Press.

Belmar, Francisco
    1902   *Lenguas indígenas del Estado de Oaxaca: Estudio del idioma ayook, Oaxaca.* México, D.F.: Imprenta del Comercio.

Bickford, J. Albert
    1985   Fortis/Lenis Consonants in Guichicovi Mixe: A Preliminary Acoustic Study. *Work Papers of the Summer Institute of Linguistics, University of North Dakota Session* 39: 195-207.

Boas, Franz
    1917   El dialecto mexicano de Pochutla, Oaxaca. *International Journal of American Linguistics* 1: 9-44.

Calderón, Eustorgio
    1908   *Estudios lingüisticos*, vol 2: *Las lenguas de Oluta, Sayula, Texistepec, en el Istmo de Tehuantepec en México.* Guatemala.

Campbell, Lyle, and Terrence S. Kaufman
    1976   A Linguistic Look at the Olmecs. *American Antiquity* 41: 80-89.

Campbell, Lyle, Terrence S. Kaufman, and Thomas Smith-Stark
    1986   Meso-America as a Linguistic Area. *Language* 62: 530-570.

Canger, Una
    1980   *Five Studies Inspired by Nahuatl Verbs in -oa.* Copenhagen: Akademisk Forlag.

Chomsky, Noam, and Morris Halle
    1968   *The Sound Pattern of English.* New York: Harper & Row.

Clark, Lawrence E.
1961   *Sayula Popoluca Texts with Grammatical Outline*. Ed. Benjamin Elson. Summer Institute of Linguistics. Norman: University of Oklahoma.
1969   Initiation at School: A Sayula Popoluca Text. *Tlalocan* 6: 38-45.
1981   *Diccionario popoluca de Oluta*. México, D.F.: Summer Institute of Linguistics.
1982   An Obsolete Numbering System Uncovered. *International Journal of American Linguistics* 48: 22-25.
1983   *Sayula Popoluca Verb Derivation*. Dallas, Texas: Summer Institute of Linguistics.
No date   [*Texistepec Popoluca Vocabulary*] [Untitled ms., 94 pp. It is referenced by Elson 1992: 591 as having been coauthored by Norman Nordell and written in 1980].

Clark, Lawrence E., and Nancy Davis Clark
1960   *Vocabulario popoluca de Sayula*. México, D.F.: Summer Institute of Linguistics.

Clements, George N., and Samuel Jay Keyser
1983   *CV Phonology. A Generative Theory of the Syllable*. Cambridge, Mass.: The M.I.T. Press.

Cordry, Donald B., and Dorothy M. Cordry
1941   Costumes and Weaving of the Zoque Indians of Chiapas, Mexico. *Southwest Museum Papers*, no. 15. Los Angeles, Calif.

Crawford, John Chapman
1963   *Totontepec Mixe Phonotagmemics*. Norman: Summer Institute of Linguistics, University of Oklahoma.

Cruz Lorenzo, Enrique
1987   Gramática de la lengua zoque del Municipio de San Miguel Chimalapa, Oaxaca. Tesis para optar el grado de Licenciatura en etnolingüística. Apetitlán, Tlaxcala: Secretaría de Educación Pública /Instituto Nacional Indigenista.

Elert, Claes-Christian
1964   *Phonologic Studies of Quantity in Swedish, Based on Material from Stockholm Speakers*. Uppsala: Monografier utgivna av Stockholms Kommunalförvaltning.

Elson, Benjamin F.
1947   Sierra Popoluca Syllable Structure. *International Journal of American Linguistics* 13: 13-17.
1951   Review of Foster and Foster's Sierra Popoluca Speech. *International Journal of American Linguistics* 17: 57-61.
1954   Sierra Popoluca Intonation. MA thesis, Cornell University.
1960   *Gramática Popoluca de la Sierra del Municipio Soteapan, Veracruz*. Xalapa: Universidad Veracruzana.

1965   Sierra Popoluca Intonation. In *Homenaje a Juan Comas en su 65 aniversario*, vol. 1, 177-189. México, D.F. [Shortened version of Elson 1954.]

1967   Sierra Popoluca. In *Handbook of Middle American Indians*, vol 5: *Linguistics*, ed. Norman A. McQuown. Austin: University of Texas Press.

1992   Reconstructing Mixe-Zoque. In *Language in Context: Essays for Robert E. Longacre*, ed. Shin Ja J. Hwang and William R. Merrifield, 572-592. Publications in Linguistics, 107. Arlington: Summer Institute of Linguistics and University of Texas at Arlington.

Engel, Ralph, and Mary Allhiser Engel
1987   *Diccionario zoque de Francisco León*. México, D.F.: Summer Institute of Linguistics.

Foster, George M.
1949   Sierra Popoluca Kinship Terminology and Its Wider Relationships. *Southwestern Journal of Anthropology* 5: 330-344.

1969   The Mixe, Zoque, Popoluca. In *Handbook of Middle American Indians*, vol. 7: *Ethnology*, ed. Evon Z. Vogt, 448-477. Austin: University of Texas Press.

Foster, Mary L., and George M. Foster
1948   *Sierra Popoluca Speech*. Institute of Social Anthropology, Publication 8. Washington, D.C.

Garnes, Sara
1974   Quantity in Icelandic: Production and Perception. Ph.D. diss., Ohio State University. Published 1976 as *Hamburger Phonetische Beiträge* 18. Hamburg: Buske Verlag.

Garvin, Paul L.
1974   Distinctive Features in Zoque Phonemic Acculturation. *Studies in Linguistics* 5: 13-20.

González, Fray Luis
1672   *Arte breve y vocabulario de la lengua tzoque, conforme se habla en el pueblo de Tecpatlán*. Ms., 330 pp. [In the Bibliothèque Nationale, Paris. Published in printed form by de la Grasserie (1898) and Ruz (fc.); I cite from the latter, more careful, edition; original date possibly 1652.]

Grasserie, Raoul de la
1898   *Langue zoque et langue mixe; grammaire, dictionaire, textes traduits et analysés*. Paris.

Gutiérrez Morales, Salomé
1993   [Sierra Popoluca word files from Amamaloya]. No title. [Salomé Gutiérrez Morales collected the files from his own speech and read them aloud to Søren Wichmann.]

Halle, Morris, and George N. Clements
1983   *Problem Book in Phonology*. Cambridge, Mass.: The M.I.T. Press.

Harrison, W. Roy, and Margaret B. Harrison
1984   *Vocabulario zoque de Rayon.* México, D.F.: Summer Institute of Linguistics.

Harrison, W. Roy, Margaret Harrison, and Cástulo García H.
1981   *Diccionario zoque de Copainalá.* México, D.F.: Summer Institute of Linguistics.

Hockett, Charles F.
1947   Componential Analysis of Sierra Popoluca. *International Journal of American Linguistics* 13: 258-267.

Hoogshagen, Searle
1959   Three Contrastive Vowel Lengths in Mixe. *Zeitschrift für Phonetik* 12: 111-115. [Coatlán]
1984   Coatlán Mixe. *Supplement to the Handbook of Middle American Indians,* vol. 2: *Linguistics,* ed. Munro S. Edmonson, 3-19. Austin: University of Texas Press.

Hoogshagen Noordsy, Searle, and Hilda Halloran de Hoogshagen
1993   *Diccionario mixe de Coatlán, Oaxaca.* Mexico, D.F.: Instituto Lingüístico de Verano.

Ja oibyu tui'yɑjtun mudu Hesukristu kujxm kungu'umbu kyajxy
1980   *El nuevo testamento de Nuestro Señor Jesucristo en mixe de Juquila.* Mexico, D.F.: La Biblioteca Mexicana del Hogar, A.C.

Justeson, John S., and Terrence Kaufman
1993   A Decipherment of Epi-Olmec Writing. *Science* 259: 1703-1711.

Kaufman, Terrence S.
1963   *Mixe-Zoque Diachronic Studies.* Ms. 150 pp.
1964   Mixe-Zoque Subgroups and the Position of Tapachulteco. In *Actas y memorias del XXXV Congreso Internacional de Americanistas, 1962,* vol. 2, 403-411. México, D.F.

Knudson, Lyle M., Jr.
1975   A Natural Phonology and Morphophonemics of Chimalapa Zoque. *Papers in Linguistics* 8: 283-346.
1980   *Zoque de Chimalapa, Oaxaca.* México, D.F.: Centro de Investigación para la Integración Social.
No date   [Santa María Chimalapa vocabulary]. [Unpublished ms. Two thirds xeroxed from a handwritten interpretive copy by Nordell.]

Lass, Roger
1983   Quantity Resolution and Syllable Geometry. *Stellenbosch Papers in Linguistics* 10: 33-66.

Lee, Michael
1987   The Cognitive Basis of Classifier Systems. In *Berkeley Linguistics Society, Proceedings of the Thirteenth Annual Meeting,* 395-407. Berkeley, Calif.

Lehiste, Ilse
1970   *Suprasegmentals.* Cambridge, Mass.: The M.I.T. Press.

Lehmann, Walter
1920   *Zentral-Amerika I-II*. Berlin.

Longacre, Robert E.
1967   Systematic Comparison and Reconstruction. In *Handbook of Middle American Indians*, vol 5: *Linguistics*, ed. Norman A. McQuown, 117-160. Austin: University of Texas Press.

Lyon, Don D.
1980   *Mixe. Tlahuitoltepec, Oaxaca*. México, D.F.: Centro de Investigación para la Integración Social.

Nahmad, Salomón
1965   *Los mixes. Estudio social y cultural de la región del Zempoaltépetl y del Istmo de Tehuantepec*. Memorias del Instituto Nacional Indigenista, 6. México, D.F.: Instituto Nacional Indigenista.

Navarrete, Carlos
1970   Fuentes para la historia cultural de los zoques. *Anales de Antropología* 7: 207-246. México, D.F.: Universidad Nacional Autónoma de México.

Nordell, Norman
1962   On the Status of Popoluca in Zoque-Mixe. *International Journal of American Linguistics* 28: 146-149.
1967/69/70   No title. [Texistepec Popoluca field notes. Unpublished ms.]
1990   No title. [A computerized manuscript of a collective vocabulary of Oaxaca Mixean dialects. Contains ca. 19,739 items gathered under headings of Spanish glosses.]
No date   No title. [Field notes from Ayapa. Unpublished ms.]

Pétursson, Magnús
1974   *Les articulations de l'islandais à la lumière de la radiocinématographie*. Paris: Libraire C. Klincksieck.

Ruz, Mario Humberto
fc.   *Las lenguas del Chiapas Colonial*, vol 2: *Lengua zoque*. México, D.F.: Seminario de Lenguas Indígenas, Instituto de Investigaciones Filológicas, Universidad Nacional Autónoma de México.

Schoenhals, Alvin
1962   A Grammatical Classification of Totontepec Mixe Verbs. MA thesis, University of Texas, Austin.

Schoenhals, Louise C.
1988   *A Spanish-English Glossary of Mexican Flora and Fauna*. México, D.F.: Instituto Lingüístico del Verano.

Schoenhals, Alvin, and Louise C. Schoenhals
1965   *Vocabulario mixe de Totontepec*. Mexico, D.F.: Summer Institute of Linguistics.

Thomas, Norman D.
1974   The Linguistic, Geographic and Demographic Position of the Zoque of Southern Mexico. *Papers of the New World Archeological Foundation*, 36. Provo: Brigham Young University.

Thomason, Sarah G., and Terrence S. Kaufman
  1988   *Language Contact, Creolization, and Genetic Linguistics.* Berkeley,
            Los Angeles, London: University of California Press.

Trager, George L.
  1950   Review of Foster and Foster's Sierra Popoluca Speech. *International Journal of American Linguistics* 16: 46-50.

Van Haitsma, Willard, and Julia Dieterman Van Haitsma
  1976   *A Hierarchical Sketch of Mixe as Spoken in San Juan el Paraíso.*
            Norman: University of Oklahoma/Summer Institute of Linguistics.

Villa Rojas, Alfonso et al.
  1975   *Los zoques de Chiapas.* Serie de Antropología Social, 39. México,
            D.F.: Instituto Nacional Indigenista/Secretaría de Educación Pública.

Voegelin, Charles F.
  1950   Review of Foster and Foster's Sierra Popoluca Speech. *International Journal of American Linguistics* 16: 46.

Voegelin, Charles F., Florence M. Voegelin, and Kenneth L. Hale
  1962   *Typological and Comparative Grammar of Uto-Aztecan*, vol. 1:
            (Phonology). Memoir 17, *International Journal of American Linguistics*.

Whistler, Kenneth W.
  1981   Ablaut in Hill Patwin. In *Survey Reports 1981*, ed. Alica Schlichter,
            Wallace L. Chafe, and Leanne Hinton, 42-94. *Reports from the
            Survey of California and Other Indian Languages*, no. 1. Berkeley,
            Calif.

Whorf, Benjamin L.
  1935   The Comparative Linguistics of Uto-Aztecan. *American Anthropologist* 37: 600-608.

Wichmann, Søren
  1988   Chiapas Zoque Field Notes from Oxolotán, Tabasco. [Northeastern
            dialect. 1,600 items lexicon, texts.]
  1990   South Highland Mixe Field Notes. [Short word lists from Tamazulapan and Ayutla; Tamazulapan paradigms.]
  1991   Review of Thomason and Kaufman (1988). *Acta Linguistica Hafniensia* 23: 217-221.
  1993a   Ayapa Zoque Field Notes. 131 Pp. [Corpus, mostly lexical items.]
  1993b   Chiapas Zoque Field Notes from Copoya, Chiapas. [Short vocabulary.]
  1993c   Grammaticalization in Mixe-Zoquean languages. *Sprachtypologie
            und Universalienforschung* 46: 45-60.
  1993d   Proto-Mixe-Zoquean Morphology. Ms., 42 pp.
  1994   Underspecification in Texistepec Popoluca Phonology. *Acta Linguistica Hafniensia* 27: 455-473.
  fc.-a   "Empathy" and "Grounding" in Sayula Popoluca. [16 pp. Written
            1990, now under publication by the English Department, University
            of Copenhagen.]

fc.-b   *Diccionario analítico del popoluca de Texistepec*. México, D.F.: Seminario de Lenguas Indígenas, Instituto de Investigaciones Filológicas, Universidad Nacional Autónoma de México.

fc.-c   Mixe-Zoquean Linguistics: A Status Report. [70 pp. Written for a volume on the studies of the languages of Mexico, ed. Yolanda Lastra.]

fc.-d   On the Relationship between MixeZoquean and UtoAztecan (Conceived of as a Study in MacroPenutian). [10 pp. Paper presented at the 13th International Congress of Anthropological Sciences, Mexico City, July 29-August 3, 1993; forthcoming in *Copenhagen Working Papers in Linguistics*.]

in prep.   *Cuentos y colorados en popoluca de Texistepec*. Ms., 420 pp.

Witkowski, Stanley, and Cecil H. Brown

1978   Mesoamerican: A Proposed Language Phylum. *American Anthropologist* 80: 942-943.

Wonderly, William L.

1946   Phonemic Acculturation in Zoque. *International Journal of American Linguistics* 12: 92-95.

1949   Some Zoquean Phonemic and Morphophonemic Correspondences. *International Journal of American Linguistics* 15: 1-11.

1951-52   Zoque: Phonemics and Morphology. Reprinted from *International Journal of American Linguistics* 17, nos. 1,2,3,4, 1951; 18, nos. 1,4, 1952.